HALSBURY'S
Laws of England

FIFTH EDITION
2013

Volume 37

This is volume 37 of the Fifth Edition of Halsbury's Laws of England, containing the first part of the title ELECTIONS AND REFERENDUMS.

The title ELECTIONS AND REFERENDUMS replaces the Fourth Edition title ELECTIONS AND REFERENDUMS, contained in vol 15(3) (2007 Reissue) and vol 15(4) (2007 Reissue). Both of those Fourth Edition volumes have been completely replaced and may now be archived.

For a full list of volumes comprised in a current set of Halsbury's Laws of England please see overleaf.

Fifth Edition volumes:

1 (2008), 2 (2008), 3 (2011), 4 (2011), 5 (2013), 6 (2011), 7 (2008), 8 (2010), 9 (2012), 10 (2012), 11 (2009), 12 (2009), 13 (2009), 14 (2009), 15 (2009), 16 (2011), 17 (2011), 18 (2009), 19 (2011), 21 (2011), 22 (2012), 23 (2013), 24 (2010), 25 (2010), 26 (2010), 27 (2010), 28 (2010), 30 (2012), 31 (2012), 32 (2012), 33 (2013), 34 (2011), 35 (2011), 36 (2011), 37 (2013), 38 (2013), 38A (2013), 39 (2009), 40 (2009), 41 (2009), 42 (2011), 43 (2011), 44 (2011), 45 (2010), 46 (2010), 48 (2008), 49 (2008), 50 (2008), 51 (2013), 52 (2009), 53 (2009), 54 (2008), 55 (2012), 56 (2011), 57 (2012), 60 (2011), 61 (2010), 62 (2012), 63 (2012), 64 (2012), 65 (2008), 66 (2009), 67 (2008), 68 (2008), 69 (2009), 70 (2012), 71 (2013), 72 (2009), 73 (2009), 74 (2011), 75 (2013), 76 (2013), 77 (2010), 78 (2010), 79 (2008), 80 (2013), 81 (2010), 82 (2010), 83 (2010), 84 (2013), 84A (2013), 85 (2012), 86 (2013), 87 (2012), 88 (2012), 88A (2013), 89 (2011), 90 (2011), 91 (2012), 92 (2010), 93 (2008), 94 (2008), 95 (2013), 96 (2012), 97 (2010), 98 (2013), 99 (2012), 100 (2009), 101 (2009), 102 (2010), 103 (2010)

Fourth Edition volumes (bold figures represent reissues):

1(1) (2001 Reissue), **8(1)** (2003 Reissue), **8(2)**, **12(1)**, **16(2)**, **17(2)**, **23(1)**, **23(2)**, **24**, **39(1B)**, **48** (2007 Reissue), *51*, *52*

Additional Materials:

Housing (*Housing Benefit*) containing vol **22** (2006 Reissue) paras 140–186; *Sentencing and Disposition of Offenders* (*Release and Recall of Prisoners*) containing vol **92** (2010) paras 761–820; *Tort* (*Conversion and Wrongful Interference with Goods*) containing vol **45(2)** (Reissue) paras 542–686

Fourth and Fifth Edition volumes:

2013 Consolidated Index (A–E), 2013 Consolidated Index (F–O), 2013 Consolidated Index (P–Z), 2014 Consolidated Table of Statutes, 2014 Consolidated Table of Statutory Instruments, etc, 2014 Consolidated Table of Cases (A–G), 2014 Consolidated Table of Cases (H–Q), 2014 Consolidated Table of Cases (R–Z, ECJ Cases)

Updating and ancillary materials:

2013 Annual Cumulative Supplement; Monthly Current Service; Annual Abridgments 1974–2012

December 2013

HALSBURY'S
Laws of England

FIFTH EDITION

LORD MACKAY OF CLASHFERN
Lord High Chancellor of Great Britain
1987–97

Volume 37

2013

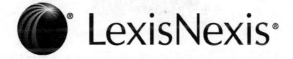 LexisNexis®

Members of the LexisNexis Group worldwide

United Kingdom	LexisNexis, a Division of Reed Elsevier (UK) Ltd, Lexis House, 30 Farringdon Street, LONDON, EC4A 4HH, and London House, 20–22 East London Street, EDINBURGH, EH7 4BQ
Australia	LexisNexis Butterworths, Chatswood, New South Wales
Austria	LexisNexis Verlag ARD Orac GmbH & Co KG, Vienna
Benelux	LexisNexis Benelux, Amsterdam
Canada	LexisNexis Canada, Markham, Ontario
China	LexisNexis China, Beijing and Shanghai
France	LexisNexis SA, Paris
Germany	LexisNexis GmbH, Dusseldorf
Hong Kong	LexisNexis Hong Kong, Hong Kong
India	LexisNexis India, New Delhi
Italy	Giuffrè Editore, Milan
Japan	LexisNexis Japan, Tokyo
Malaysia	Malayan Law Journal Sdn Bhd, Kuala Lumpur
New Zealand	LexisNexis NZ Ltd, Wellington
Poland	Wydawnictwo Prawnicze LexisNexis Sp, Warsaw
Singapore	LexisNexis Singapore, Singapore
South Africa	LexisNexis Butterworths, Durban
USA	LexisNexis, Dayton, Ohio

FIRST EDITION	*Published in 31 volumes between 1907 and 1917*
SECOND EDITION	*Published in 37 volumes between 1931 and 1942*
THIRD EDITION	*Published in 43 volumes between 1952 and 1964*
FOURTH EDITION	*Published in 56 volumes between 1973 and 1987, with reissues between 1988 and 2008*
FIFTH EDITION	*Commenced in 2008*

A CIP Catalogue record for this book is available from the British Library.

ISBN 13 (complete set, standard binding): 9781405734394

ISBN 13: 9781405763660

ISBN 978-1-4057-6366-0

9 781405 763660

Typeset by Letterpart Limited, Caterham on the Hill, Surrey CR3 5XL
Printed and bound by CPI Group (UK) Ltd, Croydon, CR0 4YY
Visit LexisNexis at www.lexisnexis.co.uk

Editor in Chief

THE RIGHT HONOURABLE

LORD MACKAY OF CLASHFERN
LORD HIGH CHANCELLOR OF GREAT BRITAIN

1987–97

ELECTIONS AND REFERENDUMS

Consultant Editor

RICHARD PRICE, LLB, OBE, QC,

Bencher of the Honourable Society of Gray's Inn

The law stated in this volume is in general that in force on 1 November 2013, although subsequent changes have been included wherever possible.

Any future updating material will be found in the Current Service and annual Cumulative Supplement to Halsbury's Laws of England.

TABLE OF CONTENTS

HOW TO USE HALSBURY'S LAWS OF ENGLAND ·

Volumes

Each text volume of Halsbury's Laws of England contains the law on the titles contained in it as at a date stated at the front of the volume (the operative date).

Information contained in Halsbury's Laws of England may be accessed in several ways.

First, by using the tables of contents.

Each volume contains both a general Table of Contents, and a specific Table of Contents for each title contained in it. From these tables you will be directed to the relevant part of the work.

Readers should note that the current arrangement of titles can be found in the Current Service.

Secondly, by using tables of statutes, statutory instruments, cases or other materials.

If you know the name of the Act, statutory instrument or case with which your research is concerned, you should consult the Consolidated Tables of statutes, cases and so on (published as separate volumes) which will direct you to the relevant volume and paragraph. The Consolidated Tables will indicate if the volume referred to is a Fifth Edition volume.

(Each individual text volume also includes tables of those materials used as authority in that volume.)

Thirdly, by using the indexes.

If you are uncertain of the general subject area of your research, you should go to the Consolidated Index (published as separate volumes) for reference to the relevant volume(s) and paragraph(s). The Consolidated Index will indicate if the volume referred to is a Fifth Edition volume.

(Each individual text volume also includes an index to the material contained therein.)

Additional Materials

The reorganisation of the title scheme of Halsbury's Laws for the Fifth Edition means that from time to time Fourth Edition volumes will be *partially* replaced by Fifth Edition volumes.

In certain instances an Additional Materials softbound book will be issued, in which will be reproduced material which has not yet been replaced by a Fifth Edition title. This will enable users to remove specific Fourth Edition volumes from the shelf and save valuable space pending the replacement of that material in the Fifth Edition. These softbound books are supplied to volumes subscribers free of charge. They continue to form part of the set of Halsbury's Laws Fourth Edition Reissue, and will be updated by the annual Cumulative Supplement and monthly Noter-Up in the usual way.

Updating publications

The text volumes of Halsbury's Laws should be used in conjunction with the annual Cumulative Supplement and the monthly Noter-Up.

The annual Cumulative Supplement

The Supplement gives details of all changes between the operative date of the text volume and the operative date of the Supplement. It is arranged in the same volume, title and paragraph order as the text volumes. Developments affecting particular points of law are noted to the relevant paragraph(s) of the text volumes. As from the commencement of the Fifth Edition, the Supplement will clearly distinguish between Fourth and Fifth Edition titles.

For narrative treatment of material noted in the Cumulative Supplement, go to the Annual Abridgment volume for the relevant year.

Destination Tables

In certain titles in the annual *Cumulative Supplement*, reference is made to Destination Tables showing the destination of consolidated legislation. Those Destination Tables are to be found either at the end of the titles within the annual *Cumulative Supplement*, or in a separate *Destination Tables* booklet provided from time to time with the *Cumulative Supplement*.

The Noter-Up

The Noter-Up is contained in the Current Service Noter-Up booklet, issued monthly and noting changes since the publication of the annual Cumulative Supplement. Also arranged in the same volume, title and paragraph order as the text volumes, the Noter-Up follows the style of the Cumulative Supplement. As from the commencement of the Fifth Edition, the Noter-Up will clearly distinguish between Fourth and Fifth Edition titles.

For narrative treatment of material noted in the Noter-Up, go to the relevant Monthly Review.

REFERENCES AND ABBREVIATIONS

ACT	Australian Capital Territory
A-G	Attorney General
Admin	Administrative Court
Admlty	Admiralty Court
Adv-Gen	Advocate General
affd	affirmed
affg	affirming
Alta	Alberta
App	Appendix
art	article
Aust	Australia
B	Baron
BC	British Columbia
C	Command Paper (of a series published before 1900)
c	chapter number of an Act
CA	Court of Appeal
CAC	Central Arbitration Committee
CA in Ch	Court of Appeal in Chancery
CB	Chief Baron
CCA	Court of Criminal Appeal
CCR	County Court Rules 1981 (SI 1981/1687) as subsequently amended
CCR	Court for Crown Cases Reserved
C-MAC	Courts-Martial Appeal Court
CO	Crown Office
COD	Crown Office Digest
CPR	Civil Procedure Rules 1998 (SI 1998/3132) as subsequently amended (see the Civil Court Practice)
Can	Canada
Cd	Command Paper (of the series published 1900–18)
Cf	compare
Ch	Chancery Division
ch	chapter
cl	clause

Cm	Command Paper (of the series published 1986 to date)
Cmd	Command Paper (of the series published 1919–56)
Cmnd	Command Paper (of the series published 1956–86)
Comm	Commercial Court
Comr	Commissioner
Court Forms (2nd Edn)	Atkin's Encyclopaedia of Court Forms in Civil Proceedings, 2nd Edn. See note 2 post.
Court Funds Rules 1987	Court Funds Rules 1987 (SI 1987/821) as subsequently amended
CrimPR	Criminal Procedure Rules 2010 (SI 2010/60) as subsequently amended
DC	Divisional Court
DPP	Director of Public Prosecutions
EAT	Employment Appeal Tribunal
EC	European Community
ECJ	Court of Justice of the European Community
EComHR	European Commission of Human Rights
ECSC	European Coal and Steel Community
ECtHR Rules of Court	Rules of Court of the European Court of Human Rights
EEC	European Economic Community
EFTA	European Free Trade Association
EWCA Civ	Official neutral citation for judgments of the Court of Appeal (Civil Division)
EWCA Crim	Official neutral citation for judgments of the Court of Appeal (Criminal Division)
EWHC	Official neutral citation for judgments of the High Court
Edn	Edition
Euratom	European Atomic Energy Community
Ex Ch	Court of Exchequer Chamber
ex p	ex parte
Fam	Family Division
Fed	Federal
Forms & Precedents (5th Edn)	Encyclopaedia of Forms and Precedents other than Court Forms, 5th Edn. See note 2 post.
GLC	Greater London Council
HC	High Court
HC	House of Commons
HK	Hong Kong
HL	House of Lords

IAT	Immigration Appeal Tribunal
ILM	International Legal Materials
INLR	Immigration and Nationality Law Reports
IRC	Inland Revenue Commissioners
Ind	India
Int Rels	International Relations
Ir	Ireland
J	Justice
JA	Judge of Appeal
Kan	Kansas
LA	Lord Advocate
LC	Lord Chancellor
LCC	London County Council
LCJ	Lord Chief Justice
LJ	Lord Justice of Appeal
LoN	League of Nations
MR	Master of the Rolls
Man	Manitoba
n	note
NB	New Brunswick
NI	Northern Ireland
NS	Nova Scotia
NSW	New South Wales
NY	New York
NZ	New Zealand
OHIM	Office for Harmonisation in the Internal Market
OJ	The Official Journal of the European Community published by the Office for Official Publications of the European Community
Ont	Ontario
P	President
PC	Judicial Committee of the Privy Council
PEI	Prince Edward Island
Pat	Patents Court
q	question
QB	Queen's Bench Division
QBD	Queen's Bench Division of the High Court
Qld	Queensland
Que	Quebec
r	rule
RDC	Rural District Council
RPC	Restrictive Practices Court

RSC	Rules of the Supreme Court 1965 (SI 1965/1776) as subsequently amended
reg	regulation
Res	Resolution
revsd	reversed
Rly	Railway
s	section
SA	South Africa
S Aust	South Australia
SC	Supreme Court
SI	Statutory Instruments published by authority
SR & O	Statutory Rules and Orders published by authority
SR & O Rev 1904	Revised Edition comprising all Public and General Statutory Rules and Orders in force on 31 December 1903
SR & O Rev 1948	Revised Edition comprising all Public and General Statutory Rules and Orders and Statutory Instruments in force on 31 December 1948
SRNI	Statutory Rules of Northern Ireland
STI	Simon's Tax Intelligence (1973–1995); Simon's Weekly Tax Intelligence (1996-current)
Sask	Saskatchewan
Sch	Schedule
Sess	Session
Sing	Singapore
TCC	Technology and Construction Court
TS	Treaty Series
Tanz	Tanzania
Tas	Tasmania
UDC	Urban District Council
UKHL	Official neutral citation for judgments of the House of Lords
UKPC	Official neutral citation for judgments of the Privy Council
UN	United Nations
V-C	Vice-Chancellor
Vict	Victoria
W Aust	Western Australia
Zimb	Zimbabwe

NOTE 1. A general list of the abbreviations of law reports and other sources used in this work can be found at the beginning of the Consolidated Table of Cases.

NOTE 2. Where references are made to other publications, the volume number precedes and the page number follows the name of the publication; eg the reference '12 Forms & Precedents (5th Edn) 44' refers to volume 12 of the Encyclopaedia of Forms and Precedents, page 44.

NOTE 3. An English statute is cited by short title or, where there is no short title, by regnal year and chapter number together with the name by which it is commonly known or a description of its subject matter and date. In the case of a foreign statute, the mode of citation generally follows the style of citation in use in the country concerned with the addition, where necessary, of the name of the country in parentheses.

NOTE 4. A statutory instrument is cited by short title, if any, followed by the year and number, or, if unnumbered, the date.

TABLE OF STATUTES

TABLE OF STATUTORY INSTRUMENTS

TABLE OF CIVIL PROCEDURE

Practice Directions supplementing Civil Procedure Rules 1998, SI 1998/3132 (CPR)

TABLE OF EUROPEAN UNION LEGISLATION

TABLE OF CONVENTIONS ETC

TABLE OF CASES

PARA

Y

Decisions of the European Court of Justice are listed below numerically. These decisions
are also included in the preceding alphabetical list.

ELECTIONS AND REFERENDUMS

VOLUME 37

1. INTRODUCTION AND GENERAL FRAMEWORK

(1) INTRODUCTION

1. Scope of title. This title sets out the law relating to the electoral procedures which govern the administration, conduct and questioning of parliamentary[1] and local government elections[2], of Welsh Assembly elections[3] and of elections to the European Parliament[4]. Because many of the statutory provisions that govern the different elections set out the same basic processes, especially with regard to polling, this title considers the law relating to the various elections together wherever possible[5].

This title also sets out the law relating to the administration, conduct and questioning of referendums or other polls held in pursuance of any provision made by or under an Act of Parliament[6]. There is coverage of the standing statutory arrangements which provide a framework for national or regional referendums[7] and of the statutory provisions relating to local authority referendums, and polls held on a question consequent on a parish or community meeting[8].

Extensive provision is made in statute for the combination of polls for elections and referendums with other relevant elections or referendums, and this is achieved mostly by applying the usual statutory rules with modifications to accommodate the various combinations that are catered for[9]. These modifications are noted in this title but, in order to avoid repetition, the rules as they have been modified for these purposes are not set out in full.

In addition to the material that relates specifically to the administration, conduct and questioning of elections and referendums, this title includes the following ancillary material:

(1)   the establishment, constitution and functions of the Electoral Commission[10] and the Boundary Commissions[11];

(2)   the establishment and review of electoral boundaries[12];

(3)   the procedure for initiating the various elections and for the filling of vacancies[13], the various voting systems employed in them[14], and the qualifications for candidacy[15]; and

(4)   the procedure for initiating the various referendums[16].

The following matters are dealt with elsewhere in this work:

(a)   the oversight of political parties in the ordinary conduct of their political work (that is, in contradistinction to the extraordinary activities undertaken by parties (and by candidates, whether affiliated to a political party or not) during an election period, when particular restrictions apply, which are set out in this title)[17];

(b)   the terms attached to offices to which candidates are elected[18]; and

(c)   the establishment and constitution of the assemblies to which candidates are elected[19].

Election to a professional or trade body also falls outside the scope of this title[20], as does the election of Police and Crime Commissioners[21].

1   As to the different types of election see PARA 9 et seq. In this title, the term 'parliamentary election' (without anything further) is used to denote an election to the United Kingdom Parliament: see PARA 9.

In any Act, unless the contrary intention appears, 'United Kingdom' means Great Britain and Northern Ireland: Interpretation Act 1978 s 5, Sch 1. 'Great Britain' means England, Scotland and Wales: Union with Scotland Act 1706 preamble art I; Interpretation Act 1978 s 22(1), Sch 2 para 5(a). Neither the Channel Islands nor the Isle of Man are within the United Kingdom.

'England' means, subject to any alteration of the boundaries of local government areas, the areas consisting of the counties established by the Local Government Act 1972 s 1 (see LOCAL GOVERNMENT vol 69 (2009) PARAS 5, 22), and Greater London and the Isles of Scilly: see the Interpretation Act 1978 s 5, Sch 1. As to local government areas in England see LOCAL GOVERNMENT vol 69 (2009) PARA 22 et seq; and as to boundary changes see LOCAL GOVERNMENT vol 69 (2009) PARA 54 et seq. As to Greater London as an administrative area see LONDON GOVERNMENT vol 71 (2013) PARA 14. 'Wales' means the combined areas of the counties created by the Local Government Act 1972 s 20 (as originally enacted) (see LOCAL GOVERNMENT vol 69 (2009) PARAS 5, 37), but subject to any alteration made under s 73 (consequential alteration of boundary following alteration of watercourse: see LOCAL GOVERNMENT vol 69 (2009) PARA 90): see the Interpretation Act 1978 Sch 1 (definition substituted by the Local Government (Wales) Act 1994 s 1(3), Sch 2 para 9). As to Scotland see further CONSTITUTIONAL LAW AND HUMAN RIGHTS vol 8(2) (Reissue) PARA 51 et seq; and as to Northern Ireland see further CONSTITUTIONAL LAW AND HUMAN RIGHTS vol 8(2) (Reissue) PARA 3.

2 The treatment of local government elections includes mayoral and London mayoral and London Assembly elections. As to local government statutes covering the election of councillors and mayors see PARA 10; and as to the provision for local government elections that is made under the Representation of the People Acts see PARA 11. As to City of London elections see PARA 33.

3 In this title, the term 'Welsh Assembly election' is used to denote a Welsh Assembly election and to distinguish such an election from a 'London Assembly election'. Notwithstanding the inclusion of Welsh Assembly elections (see PARA 12), this title does not deal in any detail with (but may note): (1) Scotland and/or Scottish Parliament Elections and Referendums; or (2) Northern Ireland and/or Northern Ireland Assembly Elections. As to the general application of the Representation of the People Act 1983 to Scotland and Northern Ireland see PARA 3 note 2.

4 In this title, the term 'European parliamentary election' is used to denote an election to the European Parliament. As to European parliamentary elections see PARA 13.

5 Accordingly, many paragraphs that deal with low-level procedure will contain a general statement of the relevant law, based upon a conflation of provisions from various sources to produce a concordant text, where this is appropriate. Any variations to that general statement are accommodated in the footnotes (or, less commonly, in the text of the paragraph itself). Occasionally, where differences in the way that the various elections are administered are substantial enough to warrant it, matters may be set out in separate paragraphs or under separate headings.

6 As to the different types of referendum and poll see PARAS 14, 15. As to polling held eg for election to a trade or professional bodies see the text and note 20.

7 Ie under the Political Parties, Elections and Referendums Act 2000 Pt VII (ss 101–129): see PARA 527 et seq. Discussion in this title of the various provisions that have been made for specific referendums to be held within this framework is limited, however, because their significance and relevance tend to fade very quickly and lose currency: see PARAS 4, 14, 15. The general framework does not apply to polls which are held with regard to the exercise of functions by the Welsh Ministers; such polls are deal with separately: see PARAS 662–664.

8 As to the conduct of local authority referendums see PARA 555 et seq; and as to polls held on a question consequent on a parish or community meeting see PARA 556 et seq. Provision has been made also for local referendums to be held under local government finance or local planning legislation, eg to approve Council Tax Increases or neighbourhood development plans: see PARA 15.

9 As to the provision made for the combination of polls see PARA 16 et seq.

10 As to the Electoral Commission see PARA 34 et seq.

11 As to the Boundary Commissions see PARA 68 et seq. See also LOCAL GOVERNMENT vol 69 (2009) PARA 54 et seq; PARLIAMENT vol 78 (2010) PARA 896.

12 As to the establishment and review of electoral boundaries see PARA 73 et seq. As to structural and boundary changes which are required for the purposes of local administration (rather than for electoral purposes) see LOCAL GOVERNMENT vol 69 (2009) PARA 54 et seq.

13 See PARA 189 et seq. As to parliamentary elections see also PARLIAMENT vol 78 (2010) PARAS 998–1000, 1094–1095; as to local government and mayoral elections see also LOCAL GOVERNMENT vol 69 (2009) PARAS 126 et seq, 320 et seq; as to elections for the Mayor of London and the London Assembly see also LONDON GOVERNMENT vol 71 (2013) PARA 76 et seq; and as to Welsh Assembly elections see also CONSTITUTIONAL LAW AND HUMAN RIGHTS. As to European parliamentary elections see, in particular, PARA 217 et seq.

14 See PARA 339 et seq.

15 See PARA 224 et seq. As to parliamentary elections see also PARLIAMENT vol 78 (2010) PARA 897 et seq; as to local government and mayoral elections see also LOCAL GOVERNMENT vol 69

(2009) PARAS 126 et seq, 320 et seq; as to London mayoral or London Assembly elections see also LONDON GOVERNMENT vol 71 (2013) PARAS 73–75; and as to Welsh Assembly elections see also CONSTITUTIONAL LAW AND HUMAN RIGHTS. As to European parliamentary elections see, in particular, PARAS 228–229.

16 As to initiating a national or regional referendum see PARA 527 et seq. As to polls regarding the functions of the Welsh Ministers see PARAS 662–664. As to the forms of executive for which a local authority referendum is required see PARA 558 et seq; and LOCAL GOVERNMENT vol 69 (2009) PARA 312 et seq. As to how polls consequent on a parish or community meeting come about see PARA 581 et seq; and LOCAL GOVERNMENT vol 69 (2009) PARA 638.

17 As to the continuing activity of political parties see CONSTITUTIONAL LAW AND HUMAN RIGHTS. The registration of political parties is a condition precedent to candidacy at certain elections (see PARA 253), but the subject of registration generally (together with the accounting and financial responsibilities that attend registration) is dealt with in CONSTITUTIONAL LAW AND HUMAN RIGHTS. Matters that relate more specifically to elections, such as the control of donations to candidates at an election, the limitation of candidates' election expenses, the control of expenditure by registered parties in a national parliamentary election campaign and the control of donations to, and the control of expenditure by, recognised third parties in national parliamentary election campaigns (along with the particular accounting and financial responsibilities that apply during election periods) are dealt with in this title: see PARA 253 et seq. However, the wider subject of the law relating to political donations is dealt with otherwise in CONSTITUTIONAL LAW AND HUMAN RIGHTS.

18 See CONSTITUTIONAL LAW AND HUMAN RIGHTS; LOCAL GOVERNMENT vol 69 (2009) PARA 117 et seq; LONDON GOVERNMENT vol 71 (2013) PARAS 69–72; PARLIAMENT vol 78 (2010) PARA 892 et seq, 1069 et seq.

19 See CONSTITUTIONAL LAW AND HUMAN RIGHTS; LOCAL GOVERNMENT vol 69 (2009) PARA 1 et seq; LONDON GOVERNMENT vol 71 (2013) PARAS 67, 68; PARLIAMENT vol 78 (2010) PARAS 801 et seq, 892 et seq.

20 As to trades union elections for office and ballots on industrial action see EMPLOYMENT vol 40 (2009) PARA 908 et seq; as to elections to professional or vocational organisations see e g MEDICAL PROFESSIONS; and as to the church electoral roll (which constitutes representation of the laity in the parochial church councils and the synods of the Church of England) see ECCLESIASTICAL LAW vol 34 (2011) PARA 324 et seq.

21 See the Police Reform and Social Responsibility Act 2011 Pt 1 Ch 6 (ss 50–76, Schs 9, 10) (Police and Crime Commissioners: elections and vacancies); the Police and Crime Commissioner Elections Order 2012, SI 2012/1917; and POLICE AND INVESTIGATORY POWERS vol 84 (2013) PARA 62 et seq.

2.   Functions of the Secretary of State.   At the date at which this volume states the law, various functions of the Secretary of State[1] in relation to elections, political parties and related matters are exercisable concurrently with the Lord President of the Council[2], including some functions that have been exercisable concurrently by the Secretary of State and the Lord Chancellor[3].

The power to make provision about Welsh Assembly elections is exercisable by the Secretary of State for Wales[4].

1 In any enactment, 'Secretary of State' means one of Her Majesty's principal Secretaries of State: see the Interpretation Act 1978 s 5, Sch 1. As to the office of Secretary of State generally see CONSTITUTIONAL LAW AND HUMAN RIGHTS vol 8(2) (Reissue) PARA 355.

2 As to the Lord President of the Council see CONSTITUTIONAL LAW AND HUMAN RIGHTS vol 8(2) (Reissue) PARA 526. At the date at which this volume states the law, the Lord President of the Council, who is customarily Leader of the House of Commons, is a post held by the Deputy Prime Minister. Following the formation of the coalition Government, the Lord President of the Council was given special responsibility for political and constitutional reform and acquired policy responsibility for the Electoral Commission, the Boundary Commission and the Independent Parliamentary Standards Authority: see 510 HC Official Report (6th series), 2 June 2010, Prime Minister's Written Ministerial Statement col 23WS. The Cabinet Office takes the lead in promulgating policy and enforcing the reforms accordingly. Prior to these developments, the Secretary of State for Justice took the lead in political and constitutional reform, some functions being exercisable concurrently with the Lord Chancellor. As to the Lord Chancellor see CONSTITUTIONAL LAW AND HUMAN RIGHTS vol 8(2) (Reissue) PARA 477 et seq.

3   Specifically, the Secretary of State's functions under the following enactments, and any
     instrument having effect under any of those enactments, are to be exercisable concurrently with
     the Lord President of the Council:
     (1)   the Representation of the People Act 1983, excluding s 10ZA (Northern Ireland: timing
            of canvass), s 54 (payment of expenses of registration: functions relating to Northern
            Ireland), s 161 (justice of the peace reported to have been guilty of corrupt practice: see
            PARA 902) and Sch 1 r 3(3) (order specifying the manner in which writs are to be
            conveyed: see PARA 192), Sch 1 r 51(6) (writ returned to the Clerk of the Crown for
            Northern Ireland: attestation) (s 199ZA (added by SI 2010/1837); Lord President of the
            Council Order 2010, SI 2010/1837, art 3(1)(a));
     (2)   the Representation of the People Act 1985, excluding ss 6–10 (absent and proxy voting:
            Northern Ireland) (s 27(2ZA) (added by SI 2010/1837); Lord President of the Council
            Order 2010, SI 2010/1837, art 3(1)(b));
     (3)   the Parliamentary Constituencies Act 1986 (as it has been amended by the
            Parliamentary Voting System and Constituencies Act 2011 s 10) (Parliamentary
            Constituencies Act 1986 s 6B (added by SI 2010/1837); Parliamentary Voting System
            and Constituencies Act 2011 s 10(11); Lord President of the Council Order 2010,
            SI 2010/1837, art 3(1)(c));
     (4)   the Greater London Authority Act 1999 s 17A (amended by SI 2010/1837) (right to
            send election address post free: see PARA 330); Lord President of the Council
            Order 2010, SI 2010/1837, art 3(1)(d));
     (5)   the Representation of the People Act 2000 (s 16A (added by SI 2010/1837);
            Lord President of the Council Order 2010, SI 2010/1837, art 3(1)(e));
     (6)   the Local Government Act 2000 s 44 (power to make provision about elections (Wales
            only): see LOCAL GOVERNMENT vol 69 (2009) PARA 320) (s 48A (added by
            SI 2010/1837; and amended by the Localism Act 2011 s 22, Sch 3 paras 8, 69);
            Lord President of the Council Order 2010, SI 2010/1837, art 3(1)(f));
     (7)   the European Parliamentary Elections Act 2002 (s 16B (added by SI 2010/1837);
            Lord President of the Council Order 2010, SI 2010/1837, art 3(1)(g));
     (8)   the European Parliament (Representation) Act 2003 (s 26A (added by SI 2010/1837);
            Lord President of the Council Order 2010, SI 2010/1837, art 3(1)(h));
     (9)   the Electoral Administration Act 2006, excluding s 63 (regulation of loans: Northern
            Ireland) (s 74A (added by SI 2010/1837); Lord President of the Council Order 2010,
            SI 2010/1837, art 3(1)(i));
     (10)   the Political Parties and Elections Act 2009, excluding s 9(9)–(11) (provision to make
            order relating to Northern Ireland) and s 19(5)–(7) (provision to make order relating to
            Northern Ireland) (s 38A (added by SI 2010/1837); Lord President of the Council
            Order 2010, SI 2010/1837, art 3(1)(j));
     (11)   the Town and Country Planning Act 1990 Sch 4B para 16 (regulations about
            referendums relating to neighbourhood development orders) by virtue of s 333(1)(b)
            (see PLANNING vol 81 (2010) PARA 3) (Transfer of Functions (Elections and
            Referendums) Order 2013, SI 2013/2597, art 2(a));
     (12)   the Local Government Finance Act 1992 s 52ZQ (regulations about referendums
            relating to council tax increases: see LOCAL GOVERNMENT FINANCE vol 70 (2012) PARA
            356) (Transfer of Functions (Elections and Referendums) Order 2013, SI 2013/2597,
            art 2(b));
     (13)   the Local Government Act 2000 s 9HE (regulations about elections for elected mayors
            in England: see PARA 383), s 9MG (regulations about referendums relating to local
            authority governance arrangements in England: see PARA 558) (Transfer of Functions
            (Elections and Referendums) Order 2013, SI 2013/2597, art 2(c)).
     For the purposes of heads (1) to (10) above, 'instrument' includes, in particular, Royal Charters,
     Royal Warrants, Orders in Council, Letters Patent, judgments, decrees, orders, rules,
     regulations, schemes, bye-laws, awards, licences, authorisations, consents, approvals, contracts
     and other agreements, memoranda and articles of association, certificates, deeds and other
     documents: Lord President of the Council Order 2010, SI 2010/1837, art 2(1). The
     Lord President of the Council Order 2010, SI 2010/1837, does not affect the validity of
     anything done (or having effect as if done) by or in relation to a Minister of the Crown, or the
     department or an officer of a Minister of the Crown, before 18 August 2010 (ie before the
     coming into force of the Order: see art 1(2)): art 2(2). The functions covered by heads (1) to (10)
     above include any functions under any provision not yet in force on 21 July 2010 (ie at the time
     the Order was made); and, in heads (1) to (10) above, a reference to an enactment includes a
     reference to the enactment as amended by any provision of an enactment or instrument passed
     or made before that time even though the amending provision is not yet in force at that time:

art 3(2). As to the transfer of functions to the Lord President from the Secretary of State for Justice see further art 3(3)–(9). As to the transfer of functions to the Lord President from the Lord Chancellor and Secretary of State see further art 4(1)–(9); and the Transfer of Functions (Elections and Referendums) Order 2013, SI 2013/2597, art 3.

Further, in the Political Parties, Elections and Referendums Act 2000, except s 9 (Electoral Commission's involvement in changes to electoral procedures: see PARA 55), Pt IV Ch VI (control of donations to registered parties and their members etc; Northern Ireland), Pt IVA Ch 2 (regulation of loans and related transactions; Northern Ireland), and Sch 9 para 7 (general limits on campaign expenditure: general elections to Northern Ireland Assembly), the 'Secretary of State' means the Secretary of State or the Lord President of the Council: see s 159A (added by SI 2002/2626; amended by SI 2008/1319; SI 2010/1837). Similar provision is made in relation to the Electoral Registration and Administration Act 2013 (see s 25(1)); and, in the Lord President of the Council Order 2010, SI 2010/1837, art 3(1), a reference to an enactment that is amended by the Electoral Registration and Administration Act 2013 is to that enactment as amended (see the Electoral Registration and Administration Act 2013 s 25(2)).

The Secretary of State and the Lord President of the Council are designated for the purposes of the European Communities Act 1972 s 2(2) in relation to the European Parliament, and in relation to local government elections in England, Wales and Scotland and local elections in Northern Ireland: see the European Communities (Designation) Order 2013, SI 2013/1445, arts 2, 3.

4 See the Government of Wales Act 2006 s 13; and PARA 12. As to the Secretary of State for Wales see CONSTITUTIONAL LAW AND HUMAN RIGHTS vol 8(2) (Reissue) PARA 520. It is within the Assembly's legislative competence to make provision by way of an Act of the Assembly in relation to electoral arrangements for local authorities (but not including police and crime commissioners, and not with respect to the local government franchise or electoral registration and administration): see the Government of Wales Act 2006 s 108, Sch 7; and CONSTITUTIONAL LAW AND HUMAN RIGHTS. Assembly Measures may be made in relation to electoral arrangements for elected local government institutions for communities (but these arrangements do not include the local government franchise, electoral registration and administration, or the voting system for the return of members in an election): see s 94, Sch 5 Matter 12.9; and CONSTITUTIONAL LAW AND HUMAN RIGHTS. As to the National Assembly for Wales see CONSTITUTIONAL LAW AND HUMAN RIGHTS.

(2) LEGAL FRAMEWORK

(i) The Legislative Basis

3. Outline of legislation relating to elections. Statute law and subordinate legislation describe the procedures which govern the conduct and administration of parliamentary and local government elections[1], Welsh Assembly elections[2] and elections to the European Parliament[3]. These statutes and related legislation set out in full the procedural rules that are required to conduct polling[4]. Provision is made, however, also with regard to: (1) the franchise and its exercise[5]; (2) the conduct of election campaigns, especially in relation to how such campaigns are organised, funded and conducted by candidates and their supporters[6]; and (3) the questioning of elections on the basis of electoral irregularity[7].

Any of the elections mentioned above may be combined with any other relevant election or referendum by applying the statutory provisions and rules in a modified form that is set out in secondary legislation for the particular purpose[8].

1 The main statutory provisions governing parliamentary and local government elections are contained in the Representation of the People Acts, and secondary legislation made thereunder. The Acts which may be cited as 'the Representation of the People Acts' include the Representation of the People Act 1981, the Representation of the People Act 1983, the Representation of the People Act 1985, the Parliamentary Constituencies Act 1986, the Representation of the People Act 1989, the Boundary Commissions Act 1992 and the Representation of the People Act 2000: see the Representation of the People Act 1981 s 4; the Representation of the People Act 1983 s 207(1); the Representation of the People Act 1985

s 29(1); the Parliamentary Constituencies Act 1986 s 9(1); the Representation of the People Act 1989 s 8(1); the Boundary Commissions Act 1992 s 5(1), (2); and the Representation of the People Act 2000 s 17(1). The Representation of the People Act 1981 provides for the disqualification of certain offenders for election to the House of Commons (see PARA 263 note 11), but the basic framework for the current system of conduct and administration of elections is contained in the Representation of the People Act 1983. For these purposes, 'election' means a parliamentary election, an Authority election or an election under the local government Act: Representation of the People Act 1983 s 202(1) (definition amended by the Greater London Authority Act 1999 s 17, Sch 3 paras 1, 38(1), (2)(a)). As to the meaning of 'parliamentary election' see PARA 9; and as to the meanings of 'Authority election' and 'election under the local government Act' see PARA 11. As to basic terminology see further note 4.

The Representation of the People Act 1983 consolidated the Representation of the People Acts 1949, 1969, 1977, 1978 and 1980, the Electoral Registers Acts 1949 and 1953, the Elections (Welsh Forms) Act 1964, the Local Government Act 1972 Pt III (ss 39–45), the Representation of the People (Armed Forces) Act 1976, the Representation of the People Act 1981 s 3, the Mental Health (Amendment) Act 1982 s 62, Sch 2, and it repealed the obsolete Representation of the People Act 1979. However, the Acts that preceded the Representation of the People Act 1983 often consolidated or incorporated legislation dating back to the nineteenth century. Accordingly, much of the detail that is contained in the current legislation bears the recognisable mark of that era, and many of the cases that provide much of the gloss to the current legislation were decided under enactments that have been re-enacted subsequently as part of the 1983 Act.

The Representation of the People Act 1983 has been supplemented and amended by other Acts since it came into force: the Representation of the People Act 1985 extended the franchise for United Kingdom parliamentary and European parliamentary elections to British citizens overseas and provided for the combination of polls taken on the same date; the Representation of the People Act 1989 increased the maximum amount of candidates' election expenses at parliamentary by-elections and made further provision relating to the entitlement of British citizens resident outside the United Kingdom to vote at parliamentary elections and elections to the European Parliament; the Representation of the People Act 1991 (prospectively repealed) made provision by amendment for moneys given to returning officers for services rendered during United Kingdom parliamentary elections; the Representation of the People Act 1993 amended the Representation of the People Act 1983 in relation to the armed forces franchise; the Representation of the People Act 2000 introduced a system of 'rolling' registration of voters for the purposes of parliamentary and local government elections (see PARA 117 note 3), allowed for pilot schemes to introduce new electoral procedures for local elections in England and Wales and re-enacted the provisions allowing for absent and proxy voting at parliamentary or local government elections, which were first introduced in the Representation of the People Act 1985 ss 5–9 (repealed in relation to England, Wales and Scotland), and modified slightly by the Representation of the People Act 1990 (repealed); the Electoral Administration Act 2006 introduced measures aimed at increasing access to voting and securing the highest possible turnout whilst guarding against electoral fraud. The Representation of the People Act 1983, the Representation of the People Act 1985, the Representation of the People Act 1989, the Representation of the People Act 1993, the Representation of the People Act 2000, the Electoral Administration Act 2006, and any enactment referring to any such enactment ('enactments relating to the representation of the people') may by order have such amendments made to them by the Secretary of State as in his opinion facilitate or are otherwise desirable in connection with the consolidation of some or all of those enactments: see the Electoral Administration Act 2006 s 72(1), (2). Such an order must be made by statutory instrument, but no such order may be made unless a draft of the statutory instrument containing the order has been laid before, and approved by a resolution of, each House of Parliament (s 72(8)); and such an order is not to come into force until immediately before an Act has been passed, and comes into force, that consolidates the enactments amended by the order (with or without other enactments relating to the representation of the people) (see s 72(3), (4)). If the provisions of that Act come into force at different times, so much of an order as amends an enactment repealed and re-enacted by a provision of that Act comes into force immediately before that provision: see s 72(5), (6). An order under s 72 must not be made unless the Secretary of State first consults the Electoral Commission: s 72(7). As to the meaning of 'United Kingdom' see PARA 1 note 1. As to the Secretary of State see PARA 2. As to the Electoral Commission see PARA 34 et seq.

The Political Parties and Elections Act 2009 made further changes to the conduct and administration of elections, including the regulation of political party finance and expenditure (affecting candidate spending and donations to political parties and other entities), and it has strengthened the regulatory role of the Electoral Commission; the Parliamentary Voting System and Constituencies Act 2011 has amended the Parliamentary Constituencies Act 1986, providing for a system of review that affects both the number and size of parliamentary constituencies (see PARA 78 et seq); and the Electoral Registration and Administration Act 2013 has provided for the implementation of compulsory individual electoral registration in Great Britain (overtaking the phased implementation provided for in the Political Parties and Elections Act 2009: see PARA 152), as well as introducing further reforms aimed at improving the integrity and security of the vote while producing an electoral system that is more convenient and accessible to the electorate. As to the meaning of 'Great Britain' see PARA 1 note 1. As to the Political Parties, Elections and Referendums Act 2000 see note 6.

2 The main statutory provisions governing Welsh Assembly elections are contained in the Government of Wales Act 2006 ss 1–19, and the National Assembly for Wales (Representation of the People) Order 2007, SI 2007/236: see PARA 12 et seq. For the purposes of the National Assembly for Wales (Representation of the People) Order 2007, SI 2007/236, 'Assembly election' means either a 'constituency election' (ie an election to return an Assembly member for an Assembly constituency) or a 'regional election' (ie an election to return Assembly members for an Assembly electoral region): see art 2(1). 'Assembly constituency' is to be construed in accordance with the Government of Wales Act 2006 s 2(1) (see PARA 76), and 'Assembly electoral region' is to be construed in accordance with s 2(3), Sch 1 (Sch 1 now repealed): see the National Assembly for Wales (Representation of the People) Order 2007, SI 2007/236, art 2(1) (both definitions substituted by SI 2010/2931). For these purposes, in relation to elections and returns under the Government of Wales Act 2006 Pt 1 (ss 1–43) (National Assembly for Wales: see PARA 12 et seq), the 'Assembly' means the National Assembly for Wales constituted by the 2006 Act, and all related expressions are to be construed accordingly: see the National Assembly for Wales (Representation of the People) Order 2007, SI 2007/236, art 2(1). As to the National Assembly for Wales see CONSTITUTIONAL LAW AND HUMAN RIGHTS.

Notwithstanding the discussion of Welsh Assembly elections, this title does not deal in detail with either Scotland and/or Scottish Parliament Elections or Northern Ireland and/or Northern Ireland Assembly Elections. As to the application of the Representation of the People Act 1983 to Scotland generally see s 204 (amended by the Local Governance (Scotland) Act 2004 s 5(1)(e); and the Local Government etc (Scotland) Act 1994 s 180, Sch 13 para 130(8), Sch 14). As to the application of the Representation of the People Act 1983 to Northern Ireland generally see s 205 (amended by the Representation of the People Act 1985 s 24, Sch 4 para 72). As to the application of the Representation of the People Act 1985 to Northern Ireland see s 29(4), (5) (s 29(5) amended by the Electoral Registration and Administration Act 2013 s 15(2)). As to the application of the Political Parties, Elections and Referendums Act 2000 to the United Kingdom and Gibraltar see s 163(8)–(11) (s 163(11) added by SI 2004/366; and amended by SI 2009/185). As to the application of the Representation of the People Act 2000 to the United Kingdom see s 17(5)–(9). As to the application of the Electoral Administration Act 2006 to the United Kingdom see s 78. As to the application of the Political Parties and Elections Act 2009 to the United Kingdom and Gibraltar see s 42. As to the special position of Gibraltar in relation to European parliamentary elections see note 3.

3 The main statutory provisions governing elections to the European Parliament are contained in the European Parliamentary Elections Act 2002, and the European Parliamentary Elections Regulations 2004, SI 2004/293 made thereunder: see PARA 13 et seq. The European Parliamentary Elections Act 2002 consolidated the European Parliamentary Elections Acts of 1978, 1993 and 1999, but has been amended by the European Parliament (Representation) Act 2003 to provide for the accession of new member states to the European Union and for the Electoral Commission to advise on the revision of electoral regions. The European Parliament (Representation) Act 2003 also provided for free elections to the European Parliament to be held in Gibraltar, consequent on the decision in Application 24833/94 *Matthews v United Kingdom* (1999) 28 EHRR 361, ECtHR: see further PARA 13. For the purposes of the European Parliamentary Elections Regulations 2004, SI 2004/293, 'election' means a European parliamentary election: see reg 2(1) (substituted by SI 2009/186). As to basic terminology see further note 4.

4 The main rules in accordance with which proceedings at the various elections must be conducted appear in the following statute law and subordinate legislation:
  (1) the Representation of the People Act 1983 s 23(1), Sch 1 (the 'parliamentary elections rules': see PARA 383 note 2) and the Representation of the People (England and Wales) Regulations 2001, SI 2001/341;
  (2) the European Parliamentary Elections Regulations 2004, SI 2004/293, reg 9(1), Sch 1 (the 'European parliamentary elections rules': see PARA 383 note 16); and
  (3) the National Assembly for Wales (Representation of the People) Order 2007, SI 2007/236, art 17(1), Sch 5 (the 'Assembly election rules': see PARA 383 note 20).

Local elections must be conducted in accordance with rules made under the Representation of the People Act 1983 s 36, *viz.* the Local Elections (Principal Areas) (England and Wales) Rules 2006, SI 2006/3304, r 3, Sch 2, and the Local Elections (Parishes and Communities) (England and Wales) Rules 2006, SI 2006/3305, r 3, Sch 2: see PARA 383 note 6. The latter rules are also applied, by virtue of the Interpretation Act 1978 s 17(2), to the conduct of a poll consequent on a parish or community meeting: see the Parish and Community Meetings (Polls) Rules 1987, SI 1987/1; and PARA 383 note 6. The Local Authorities (Mayoral Elections) (England and Wales) Regulations 2007, SI 2007/1024, reg 3(1), Sch 1 (see PARA 383 note 14) provide for polling in local authority mayoral elections where executive arrangements are in place under the Local Government Act 2000 (as to which see PARA 558 et seq; and LOCAL GOVERNMENT vol 69 (2009) PARA 320 et seq). The Greater London Authority Elections Rules 2007, SI 2007/3541, provide rules of the conduct of polling for the various London Authority elections as follows: r 3(2), Sch 1 (Constituency Members elections rules); r 3(3), Sch 2 (London Members elections rules); and r 3(4), Sch 3 (Mayoral election rules) (see PARA 383 note 10). The texts of these procedural provisions are often very similar and are considered together in this title wherever possible: see PARA 1 note 5.

Although the word 'election' is often defined in the various pieces of election legislation to refer specifically to their subject (e g in the Representation of the People Act 1983 (see note 1), and in the European Parliamentary Elections Regulations 2004, SI 2004/293 (see note 3)), the term is used more generally in the Representation of the People Acts to describe the entire process that begins with the issue of the notice of election (or writ, in the case of a parliamentary election) and ends with the return of the successful candidate (or candidates). In order to avoid confusion, it should be noted that the words 'poll' or 'polling' are used in this title to refer to the more narrow process of an electorate registering its votes; and 'polling day' is used to refer to the actual day on which 'voting' takes place in designated polling districts and polling places. (This is so notwithstanding the fact that it is possible for a candidate to be elected without the need for a poll, and for an eligible member of the electorate to make a postal vote in advance of polling day itself). The term 'ballot' refers even more narrowly to the method by which polling is carried out and there is an implication of secrecy in this use of the term: before the Ballot Act 1872 (repealed) introduced the secret ballot, a poll was achieved by the open counting of heads. (Indeed, the Parliamentary Elections Act 1695 (repealed) was enacted in order to ensure that a parliamentary election was conducted in public). The term 'poll' is applied also to the process by which parish and community council elections and elections to the chair of such a council or of a parish meeting are conducted, which are provided for by applying the Representation of the People Act 1983 subject to modifications effected by rules made under s 36: see s 187; and PARA 383 note 6. (The same rules are applied to conduct a poll on a question arising from a parish or community meeting, which is more in the nature of a referendum: see PARA 556).

5   See the Representation of the People Act 1983 Pt I (ss 1–66B); the National Assembly for Wales (Representation of the People) Order 2007, SI 2007/236, Pt 2 (arts 3–36); the European Parliamentary Elections Regulations 2004, SI 2004/293, regs 6–30; and PARA 95 et seq. A uniform franchise which included a qualification based upon residence (rather than qualification based exclusively on the ownership or occupation of property) was first established by the Representation of the People Act 1918 (repealed), which also for the first time introduced votes for women (who qualified upon attaining the age of 30 years). The franchise and its exercise continues to be affected by statute: the Representation of the People Act 2000 allows patients in mental hospitals who are not detained offenders or on remand, persons who are remanded in custody, and persons who are homeless to be registered as parliamentary and local government electors on the basis of declarations of local connection: see PARA 117 et seq. The implementation of compulsory individual electoral registration in Great Britain will overtake the current system of electoral registration that is based on an annual canvass of households: see PARA 152.

6   See the Representation of the People Act 1983 Pt II (ss 67–119); the National Assembly for Wales (Representation of the People) Order 2007, SI 2007/236, Pt 3 (arts 37–85); and the European Parliamentary Elections Regulations 2004, SI 2004/293, Pt 2 (regs 31–81); and PARA 230 et seq.

The Representation of the People Act 1983 (as originally enacted) did not recognise the role of political parties in elections and its focus on restricting candidates' expenses at a constituency level had no effect on what political parties as a whole spent on fighting elections at a national level. In 1997, the Committee on Standards in Public Life was given extended terms of reference to consider the whole area of the funding of political parties: see 300 HC Official Report (6th series), 12 November 1997, col 899. The government responded to the publication of the Committee's report (*Standards in Public Life (Fifth Report): The Funding of Political Parties in the United Kingdom* (Cm 4057) (October 1998) (the 'Neill Report')) by enacting the Political Parties, Elections and Referendums Act 2000. This Act made provision (*inter alia*) for the registration and financial accountability of political parties and for controls on donations and expenditure for political purposes, including during election campaigns, but it proved inadequate to the challenge and subsequent reforms to the system were made by both the Electoral Administration Act 2006 and the Political Parties and Elections Act 2009: see PARA 269 et seq. The Political Parties, Elections and Referendums Act 2000 sought to underpin its reforms by establishing an independent Electoral Commission with widespread executive and investigative powers, to which the Political Parties and Elections Act 2009 has since added supervisory powers in order to strengthen the Commission's capabilities as a regulator: see PARA 34 et seq. As to the Neill Report's consideration of referendum campaigns, to ensure that they were conducted by properly-funded participants and with the minimum of interference from the executive, see PARA 4.

7   See the Representation of the People Act 1983 Pt III (ss 120–186); the National Assembly for Wales (Representation of the People) Order 2007, SI 2007/236, Pt 4 (arts 86–138); the European Parliamentary Elections Regulations 2004, SI 2004/293, Pt 4 (regs 86–122); and PARA 682 et seq. See also, in relation to a United Kingdom parliamentary or local government election, the Election Petition Rules 1960, SI 1960/543 (which also have effect subject to modifications in relation to a Welsh Assembly election petition by virtue of the National Assembly for Wales (Representation of the People) Order 2007, SI 2007/236, art 134, Sch 9); and, in relation to a European parliamentary election, the European Parliamentary Election Petition Rules 1979, SI 1979/521. Certain principles and rules that were developed and applied to election petitions by committees of the House of Commons are still to be observed by the High Court and the election court: see PARA 767. In particular, the principles and rules with regard to agency (see PARA 244 et seq), evidence (see PARA 831 et seq) and scrutiny (see PARA 839 et seq) must be observed.
8   See further PARA 16 et seq.

4.   Outline of legislation relating to referendums.

4.   Outline of legislation relating to referendums.   Historically, referendums have been called only rarely in the United Kingdom[1]. When called, they have taken place under specially enacted provisions which invited the eligible electorate to consider such questions as the future of Northern Ireland following the introduction of direct rule in that province[2]; whether the United Kingdom should withdraw from membership of the European Economic Community (as it was then)[3]; whether certain proposals to devolve power to Scotland and to Wales should be approved[4]; whether a Scottish Parliament should be established and should have tax-varying powers[5]; whether a Welsh Assembly should be established[6]; whether a Greater London Authority should be established with a directly-elected Mayor and Assembly[7]; and whether the Good Friday Agreement relating to Northern Ireland should be accepted[8].

The Fifth Report on the Funding of Political Parties in the United Kingdom published in October 1998[9], in considering how political parties and election campaigns should be funded, recommended that referendum campaigns also should be conducted by properly-funded participants and with the minimum of interference from the executive[10]. In response to that report, the Political Parties, Elections and Referendums Act 2000 was enacted, which (amongst other things) sets out a legal framework within which national and regional referendums within the United Kingdom are to be held[11].

However, the legislative framework provided by the Political Parties, Elections and Referendums Act 2000 does not apply to polls held to ascertain the views of the public in Wales or in any part of Wales with regard to how relevant functions of the Welsh Ministers should be exercised[12]. Nor does it apply to referendums held at a local level such as referendums held to consider proposals for the adoption of executive arrangements under the Local Government Act 2000[13], to local polls held under the Local Government Act 2003[14], or to polls held on a question consequent on a parish or community meeting[15].

In England, any referendum that is to be held may be combined with any other relevant election or referendum by applying the statutory provisions and rules in a modified form that is set out in secondary legislation for the particular purpose[16].

1 As to the meaning of 'United Kingdom' see PARA 1 note 1.

2 See the Northern Ireland (Border Poll) Act 1972 (repealed).

3 See the Referendum Act 1975 (repealed).

4 See the Scotland Act 1978 s 85, Sch 17 (repealed); and the Wales Act 1978 s 80, Sch 12 (repealed).

5 See the Referendums (Scotland and Wales) Act 1997.

6 See note 5.

7 See the Greater London Authority (Referendum) Act 1998; and the Greater London Authority (Referendum Arrangements) Order 1998, SI 1998/746.

8 See the Northern Ireland Negotiations (Referendum) Order 1998, SI 1998/1126, which has now lapsed on the repeal of the Northern Ireland (Entry to Negotiations, etc) Act 1996.

9 Ie *Standards in Public Life (Fifth Report): The Funding of Political Parties in the United Kingdom* (Cm 4057) (October 1998) (the 'Neill Report').

10 See *Standards in Public Life (Fifth Report): The Funding of Political Parties in the United Kingdom* (Cm 4057) (October 1998) Ch 12. The main recommendations of the Neill Report that bore upon referendums were directed principally at ensuring that each side in a referendum campaign (which would not necessarily divide along party lines) had a fair opportunity to put its views to the public (particularly with regard to access to funding) and that referendum campaigns were not skewed by the intervention of the government of the day: see Recommendations R83–R93. As to the Neill Report's conclusions regarding the wider subject of the funding of political parties, their financial accountability, and controls on donations and expenditure for political purposes, see PARA 3 note 6.

11 See the Political Parties, Elections and Referendums Act 2000 Pt VII (ss 101–129); and PARA 527 et seq. Although these provisions introduced standing arrangements for the conduct of referendums, further legislation is required to provide for the holding of any particular referendum within this framework: see eg the Regional Assemblies (Preparations) Act 2003 (repealed); the Parliamentary Voting System and Constituencies Act 2011 Pt 1 (ss 1–9, Schs 1–10, 12 Pt 1) (s 9, Schs 10, 12 Pt 1 repealed).

12 See the Government of Wales Act 2006 s 64; and PARA 105.

13 See the Local Government Act 2000 Pt 1A (ss 9B–9R) (arrangements with respect to local governance in England), Pt II (ss 10–48A) (Local authorities in Wales: arrangements with respect to executives etc); and **LOCAL GOVERNMENT** vol 69 (2009) PARA 303 et seq. Provision for the conduct for such referendums is made by the Local Authorities (Conduct of Referendums) (Wales) Regulations 2008, SI 2008/1848, and the Local Authorities (Conduct of Referendums) (England) Regulations 2012, SI 2012/323, which contain bespoke referendum rules as well as applying and modifying electoral Acts and subordinate legislation for the purpose: see PARA 555 et seq. A similar approach is adopted where provision has been made for local referendums to be held under local government finance or local planning legislation, eg to approve Council Tax increases or neighbourhood development plans: see PARA 15.

14 Ie polls conducted by a local authority to ascertain the views of those polled about matters relating to services provided by the authority, the authority's expenditure on such services, or any other matter relating to the authority's power to promote the well-being of its area: see PARA 557 et seq.

15 In the application of those provisions referred to in the Representation of the People Act 1983 s 187(1) to a poll consequent on a parish or community meeting, the adaptations, alterations and exceptions have effect as specified in the Parish and Community Meetings (Polls) Rules 1987, SI 1987/1, r 6: see PARA 556 et seq.

16 Provision is made for combining local authority referendums in England with any other relevant election or referendum by applying the statutory provisions and rules in a modified form: see the Local Authorities (Conduct of Referendums) (England) Regulations 2012, SI 2012/323, regs 10–13, Schs 4, 5; and PARA 31. The Local Authorities (Conduct of Referendums) (Wales) Regulations 2008, SI 2008/1848, make no provision for polls at local authority referendums in Wales to be taken together with polls at another election or referendum. As to the meanings of 'England' and 'Wales' see PARA 1 note 1.

(ii) Rights and Freedoms

5.   The integrity of parliamentary elections. The Bill of Rights contains the declaration: 'election of Members of Parliament ought to be free'[1].

1   See the Bill of Rights (1688) s 1. The Preamble to the Bill of Rights (1688) recites that James II, 'by the assistance of divers evil counsellors, judges and ministers employed by him, did endeavour to subvert and extirpate the Protestant religion and the laws and liberties of this Kingdom', *inter alia*, 'by violating the freedom of election of members to serve in Parliament'. See also 3 Edw 1 (Statute of Westminster the First) (1275) c 5 ('And because Elections ought to be free, the King commandeth upon great Forfeiture that no Man nor other by Force of Arms, nor by Malice, or menacing shall disturb any to make free Election'). As to the history of the right to participate in free elections under domestic law see RIGHTS AND FREEDOMS vol 88A (2013) PARA 573.

6.   European Treaty articles governing elections to the European Parliament. The Treaty on European Union[1] provides that members of the European Parliament must be elected for a term of five years by direct universal suffrage in a free and secret ballot[2].

The Treaty on the Functioning of the European Union requires the European Parliament to draw up a proposal to lay down the provisions necessary for the election of its members by direct universal suffrage in accordance with a uniform procedure in all member states, or in accordance with principles common to all member states, with the Council, acting unanimously in accordance with a special legislative procedure and after obtaining the consent of the European Parliament (acting by a majority of its component members) laying down the necessary provisions, which are to enter into force following their approval by the Member States in accordance with their respective constitutional requirements[3]. On 20 September 1976, the Council adopted an Act concerning the election of the representatives of the European Parliament by direct universal suffrage[4]. The 1976 Act established that, subject to the other provisions of the Act[5], and pending the entry into force of a uniform electoral procedure, the electoral procedure is to be governed in each member state by its national provisions[6].

The Treaty on the Functioning of the European Union also provides that every citizen of the European Union residing in a member state of which he is not a national has the right to vote and to stand as a candidate in elections to the European Parliament[7] and at municipal elections in the member state in which he resides, under the same conditions as nationals of that state[8].

Nevertheless, neither the EU Charter[9] nor the Treaties define expressly and precisely who might be entitled to the rights to vote or to stand as a candidate for the European Parliament[10]: this falls within the competence of each member state[11], and it is therefore open to member states to set eligibility conditions by reference to the criterion of residence in the territory in which the elections are held[12] and to grant the right to vote and stand as a candidate to non-nationals who have close links with them[13] However, the principle of equal treatment will prohibit criteria that results in different treatment of nationals who are in comparable situations, unless that difference in treatment is capable of objective justification[14].

1   Ie the Treaty on European Union signed at Maastricht on 7 February 1992 ('TEU') (Cm 1934); and taking effect on 1 November 1993 (OJ L293, 27.11.1993, p 61). The European Union is founded on this treaty together with the Treaty establishing the European Atomic Energy Community (Rome, 25 March 1957; TS 1 (1973) Cmnd 5179) ('Euratom Treaty': see ENERGY AND CLIMATE CHANGE vol 44 (2011) PARAS 761–763) and the Treaty on the Functioning of the

European Union (Rome, 25 March 1957; TS 1 (1973); Cmnd 5179) ('TFEU'). TFEU was formerly cited as the Treaty Establishing the European Community (Rome, 25 March 1957; TS 1 (1973); Cmnd 5179) ('TEC'), to which the United Kingdom acceded by virtue of the Act of Accession 1972. The Treaty has been renamed since and its provisions renumbered: (1) by the Treaty of Amsterdam (ie the Treaty of Amsterdam Amending the Treaty on European Union, the Treaties Establishing the European Communities and Related Acts (Amsterdam, 2 October 1997, ECS 14 (1997); Cm 3780)): see *Treaty Citation (No 2) (Note)* [1999] All ER (EC) 646, ECJ; and (2) by the Treaty of Lisbon (ie the Treaty of Lisbon Amending the Treaty Establishing the European Union and the Treaty Establishing the European Community (Lisbon, 13 December 2007, ECS 13 (2007); Cm 7294)). As to the meaning of 'United Kingdom' see PARA 1 note 1.

2   See TEU art 14(3) (formerly art 190(1), (3) TEC: see note 1). The total number of representatives elected to the European Parliament, and the minimum and maximum numbers of seats that can be allocated to an individual member state, on the principle of degressively proportional representation, are all specified in the TEU, and provision is made for the European Council to adopt by unanimity, on the initiative of the European Parliament and with its consent, a decision establishing the composition of the European Parliament that respects these principles: see TEU art 14(2) (formerly art 190(2) TEC). See also note 5.

3   TFEU art 223(1) (formerly art 190(4) TEC: see note 1). A uniform electoral procedure has not yet been introduced: see the text and notes 9–14. A challenge to the failure of the Community institutions to provide for such a procedure was defeated as serving no further purpose in Case C-41/92 *Liberal Democrats v European Parliament* [1993] ECR I-3153, ECJ, on the basis that the European Parliament had adopted Resolution A3–0381/92 (OJ C115, 26.04.93, p 121) on a draft uniform electoral procedure for the election of members of the European Parliament.

4   See the 1976 Act concerning the election of the representatives of the Assembly by direct universal suffrage (OJ L278, 08.10.76, p 5) (the '1976 Act') (amended and renumbered by Council Decision (EC and Euratom) 2002/772 (OJ L283, 21.10.2002, p 1)), annexed to Decision (ECSC, EEC and Euratom) 76/787 (OJ L278, 08.10.76, p 1)).

5   The 1976 Act confirms, for example, that representatives in the Assembly must be elected by direct universal suffrage for a term of five years (see arts 1, 3 (as amended and renumbered: see note 4)); and provides that no one may vote more than once in any election of representatives to the Assembly (see art 8 (as so amended and renumbered)); that elections to the Assembly are to be held on a date fixed by each member state that falls within the same period for all member states, starting on a Thursday morning and ending on the following Sunday, with the counting of votes postponed until after the close of polling in the member state whose electors are the last to vote within this period (see arts 9, 10 (as so amended and renumbered)); that the office of representative in the Assembly is compatible with membership of the Parliament of a member state (see art 5 (as so amended and renumbered)), but that it is incompatible with membership of the Government of a member state and with certain offices in or connected with European Union institutions (see art 6 (as so amended and renumbered)); and that, pending the entry into force of the uniform electoral procedure (see the text and note 3), the Assembly is to verify the credentials of representatives (see art 11 (as so amended and renumbered)). The 1976 Act also provides for when a seat falls vacant: see art 13; and PARA 218.

6   See the 1976 Act art 7 (as amended and renumbered: see note 4). As to the national provisions which govern European parliamentary elections in the United Kingdom see PARA 13 et seq.

7   In the case of elections to the European Parliament, this right is expressed to be without prejudice to TFEU art 223(1) (formerly art 190(4) TEC: see note 1) (see the text and note 3) and to the provisions adopted for its implementation (see the text and notes 4–6): see TFEU art 22 (formerly art 19 TEC).

8   See TFEU art 22 (formerly art 19 TEC: see note 1). This right is to be exercised subject to detailed arrangements adopted by the Council, acting unanimously in accordance with a special legislative procedure and after consulting the European Parliament, which may provide for derogations where warranted by problems specific to a member state: see art 22. See further Council Directive (EC) 93/109 of 6 December 1993 (OJ L329, 30.12.1993, p 34) laying down detailed arrangements for the exercise of the right to vote and to stand as a candidate in elections to the European Parliament for citizens of the Union residing in a member state of which they are not nationals (amended by Council Directive (EU) 2013/1 (OJ L26, 26.01.2013, p 27)). Nothing in Council Directive (EC) 93/109 of 6 December 1993 affects each member state's provisions concerning the right to vote or to stand as a candidate of its nationals who reside outside its electoral territory: see art 1. See further the text and notes 9–14. The European Parliamentary Elections (Franchise of Relevant Citizens of the Union) Regulations 2001, SI 2001/1184, were enacted to implement Council Directive (EC) 93/109 of 6 December 1993 (OJ L329, 30.12.1993, p 34): see PARA 100 note 20.

9   Ie the Charter of Fundamental Rights of the European Union (OJ C364, 18.12.2000, p 1), the applicable provisions of which for these purposes are arts 39, 40 (see RIGHTS AND FREEDOMS vol 88A (2013) PARA 574).

10 See Case C-300/04 *Eman v College van burgemeester en wethouders van Den Haag* [2007] All ER (EC) 486 at [40], [2006] ECR I-8055 at [40], ECJ (Grand Chamber); Case C-145/04 *Spain v United Kingdom* [2007] All ER (EC) 486 at [50], [2006] ECR I-7917 at [50], ECJ (Grand Chamber).

11 See Case C-145/04 *Spain v United Kingdom* [2007] All ER (EC) 486 at [45], [2006] ECR I-7917 at [45], ECJ (Grand Chamber); and see also R *(on the application of Preston) v Lord President of the Council* [2012] EWCA Civ 1378, [2013] QB 687, [2013] 1 All ER 869 (although the right to vote was created and conferred by domestic law, it did not follow that member states could lay down in their electoral law the conditions of the parliamentary franchise without regard to the impact that the conditions might have on the exercise of the fundamental rights that existed by virtue of the TFEU). Note however that European law does not incorporate any right to vote paralleling that recognised by the European Court of Human Rights in its case law: see R *(on the application of Chester) v Secretary of State for Justice, McGeoch v The Lord President of the Council* [2013] UKSC 63, [2013] All ER (D) 174 (Oct), (2013) Times, 22 October (cited in PARA 7 note 6).

12 See Case C-300/04 *Eman v College van burgemeester en wethouders van Den Haag* [2007] All ER (EC) 486 at [60], [2006] ECR I-8055 at [60], ECJ (Grand Chamber) (a case brought by Dutch nationals residing in Aruba who were excluded from the right to register to vote in both domestic and European elections because Dutch law required residence within the Netherlands as a pre-condition); and see R *(on the application of Preston) v Lord President of the Council* [2012] EWCA Civ 1378, [2013] QB 687, [2013] 1 All ER 869, [2013] 2 WLR 733 (suspension of a person's entitlement to register to vote in parliamentary elections of those British citizens who voluntarily chose to reside in another member state for more than 15 years does not create a restriction on free movement that has to be objectively justified under EU law because it is both qualitatively and quantitatively different from those more direct, certain and immediate obstacles and barriers to basic day-to-day living that were set up by certain social benefits rules which had been held to amount to restrictions on free movement).

13 See Case C-145/04 *Spain v United Kingdom* [2007] All ER (EC) 486, [2006] ECR I-7917, ECJ (Grand Chamber). See also Council Directive (EC) 94/80 of 19 December 1994 (OJ L368, 31.12.1994, p 38) laying down detailed arrangements for the exercise of the right to vote and to stand as a candidate in municipal elections by citizens of the Union residing in a member state of which they are not nationals.

14 See Case C-300/04 *Eman v College van burgemeester en wethouders van Den Haag* [2007] All ER (EC) 486 at [60], [2006] ECR I-8055 at [60], ECJ (Grand Chamber).

7.   Rights guaranteed under the Convention for the Protection of Human Rights and Fundamental Freedoms.   The right of free elections to the legislature is guaranteed in the scheme provided by the Convention for the Protection of Human Rights and Fundamental Freedoms (1950)[1], whereby contracting states[2] undertake to hold free elections at reasonable intervals by secret ballot, under conditions which will ensure the free expression of the opinion of the people in the choice of the legislature[3]. This is a 'Convention right' for the purposes of the Human Rights Act 1998[4]. The contracting states have a wide margin of appreciation in this sphere[5], but it is for the European Court of Human Rights to determine in the last resort whether the requirements have been complied with[6].

The right to freedom of expression, which includes the freedom to hold opinions and to receive and impart information and ideas without interference by public authority and regardless of frontiers[7], has been applied to political discourse generally and to election campaign communications in particular[8].

1   Ie the scheme arising from the Convention for the Protection of Human Rights and Fundamental Freedoms (Rome, 4 November 1950; TS 71 (1953); Cmd 8969; Council of Europe, ETS no 5) and the First Protocol (Paris, 20 March 1952; TS 46; Cmnd 9221; Council of Europe, ETS no 9) (see RIGHTS AND FREEDOMS vol 88A (2013) PARAS 572–593). The main provisions of the Convention for the Protection of Human Rights and Fundamental Freedoms (1950) and its Protocols have been incorporated into English law by the Human Rights

Act 1998: see RIGHTS AND FREEDOMS vol 88A (2013) PARAS 14–30. As to the Convention and its Protocols generally see RIGHTS AND FREEDOMS vol 88A (2013) PARA 88 et seq.

2   Ie the contracting states to the Convention for the Protection of Human Rights and Fundamental Freedoms (1950), First Protocol (1952).

3   Convention for the Protection of Human Rights and Fundamental Freedoms, First Protocol art 3. The leading decision on the First Protocol art 3 is Application 9267/81 *Mathieu-Mohin and Clerfayt v Belgium* (1987) 10 EHRR 1, ECtHR (see the text and notes 5–6).

4   See the Human Rights Act 1998 ss 1(1)(b), (3), 2, 6, Sch 1; and RIGHTS AND FREEDOMS vol 88A (2013) PARAS 14, 21, 23. The right of free elections to the legislature that is guaranteed under the Convention for the Protection of Human Rights and Fundamental Freedoms, First Protocol art 3 is not included in the 'absolute' rights and freedoms from which derogation is disallowed (see the Convention for the Protection of Human Rights and Fundamental Freedoms art 15(2)) although art 15(1) has the effect of preventing a state party from entering a derogation that is 'inconsistent with its other obligations under international law': see RIGHTS AND FREEDOMS vol 88A (2013) PARAS 649, 650.

5   The rights in question are recognised but not set forth in express terms so they may be subject to conditions by the contracting states: *Mathieu-Mohin and Clerfayt v Belgium* (1987) 10 EHRR 1, ECtHR. See also Application 19840/09 *Shindler v United Kingdom* [2013] ECHR 19840/09, [2013] All ER (D) 239 (May), ECtHR (imposition of residence restriction pursued the legitimate aim of confining the parliamentary franchise to those citizens with a close connection with the United Kingdom and who would therefore be most directly affected by its laws; the measure was proportionate given that 15 years is not an unsubstantial period of time, that the general measure in this case serves to promote legal certainty, and that Parliament itself has sought to weigh the competing interests and to assess the proportionality of the 15-year rule).

6   *Mathieu-Mohin and Clerfayt v Belgium* (1987) 10 EHRR 1, ECtHR. It is for the European Court of Human Rights to satisfy itself that any conditions imposed do not curtail the rights to such an extent as to impair their essence or remove their effectiveness, that they pursue a legitimate aim and that the means employed are proportionate to that aim: *Mathieu-Mohin and Clerfayt v Belgium* at [52]. See also Application 24833/94 *Matthews v United Kingdom* (1999) 28 EHRR 361 at [62], 5 BHRC 686 at [62], ECtHR; and see RIGHTS AND FREEDOMS vol 88A (2013) PARAS 579, 581, 582, 589, 591.

In domestic law, the Representation of the People Act 1983 s 3(1) disqualifies all convicted persons detained in a penal institution from voting at parliamentary or local government elections, and this general prohibition has been subjected to scrutiny by the European Court of Human Rights which has held that its role is confined to determining whether any restriction affecting all convicted prisoners in custody exceeded any acceptable margin of appreciation, leaving it to the legislature to decide on the choice of means for securing the rights guaranteed by the Convention for the Protection of Human Rights and Fundamental Freedoms, First Protocol art 3: see Application 74025/01 *Hirst v United Kingdom (No 2)* (2005) 42 EHRR 849, 19 BHRC 546, (2005) Times, 10 October, ECtHR (Grand Chamber) (affg (2004) 38 EHRR 825, 16 BHRC 409, (2004) Times, 8 April, ECtHR); Application 60041/08 *Greens v United Kingdom* (2010) 53 EHRR 710, (2010) Times, 24 November, ECtHR; Application 126/05 *Scoppola v Italy (No 3)* (2012) 33 BHRC 126, [2012] ECHR 126/05, ECtHR; and PARA 107. See also *R (on the application of Chester) v Secretary of State for Justice* [2010] EWCA Civ 1439, [2011] 1 WLR 1436, [2010] All ER (D) 219 (Dec) (an advisory opinion as to what legislation, as yet undrafted, might properly contain or omit would have been quite beyond the pale; the nature and scope of measures amending or replacing the Representation of the People Act 1983 s 3 were likely to be acutely controversial concerning aspects not of the law but of social policy which is a political responsibility, and that was where it should remain); and *R (on the application of Chester) v Secretary of State for Justice, McGeoch v The Lord President of the Council* [2013] UKSC 63, [2013] All ER (D) 174 (Oct), (2013) Times, 22 October (prohibition on prisoners voting in the UK had previously been the subject of a declaration of incompatibility with the ECHR and was, at the instant time, under active consideration by Parliament; in those circumstances, there was no point in making a further declaration of incompatibility and any legislative amendment would not in any case be likely to remedy the prisoner's particular grievance). There are no reasonable grounds in domestic law for bringing a claim for damages or a declaration for being disenfranchised whilst a prisoner: *Tovey v Ministry of Justice* [2011] EWHC 271 (QB), [2011] NLJR 290, [2011] All ER (D) 202 (Feb). As to current law and policy relating to prisoners' voting eligibility and registration see PRISONS AND PRISONERS vol 85 (2012) PARA 551.

To the extent that English and Welsh domestic law made the right to vote conditional on acquiescence in the sale of copies of the electoral register to commercial interests with no right of objection, it operated in a way which contravened the Convention for the Protection of Human

Rights and Fundamental Freedoms, First Protocol art 3: *R (on the application of Robertson) v Wakefield Metropolitan District Council* [2001] EWHC 915 (Admin), [2002] QB 1052, [2002] LGR 286. The practice of selling the electoral register for direct marketing purposes without affording an individual elector a right of objection was also found to be a disproportionate interference with the individual's right to respect for his private and family life, home and correspondence under the Convention for the Protection of Human Rights and Fundamental Freedoms art 8 (see RIGHTS AND FREEDOMS vol 88A (2013) PARA 317 et seq) when the electors had provided their details under legal compulsion and for public purposes: *R (on the application of Robertson) v Wakefield Metropolitan District Council*. The Representation of the People (England and Wales) Regulations 2001, SI 2001/341, reg 114 (see PARA 188) was amended as a consequence of this decision.

7   See the Convention for the Protection of Human Rights and Fundamental Freedoms art 10(1); and RIGHTS AND FREEDOMS vol 88A (2013) PARA 398. The exercise of the right to freedom of expression may be subject to such formalities, conditions, restrictions or penalties as are prescribed by law and are necessary in a democratic society for preventing the disclosure of information received in confidence: see art 10(2); and RIGHTS AND FREEDOMS vol 88A (2013) PARA 398.

8   See eg Application 24744/94 *Huggett v United Kingdom* (1995) 82-A DR 98 (BBC policy of allocating broadcasting time only to political parties presenting candidates in at least 12.5% of seats in an election, being intended to facilitate the public expression of political opinions which are likely to be of general interest, did not disclose arbitrariness or discrimination). As to consideration before the domestic courts of the right to free expression see also *R (on the application of ProLife Alliance) v BBC* [2002] EWCA Civ 297, [2004] 1 AC 185, [2002] 2 All ER 756 (freedom of political speech enjoyed by accredited political parties at general election time must be interfered with only on exceptional grounds which would seldom be found in appeals to taste and decency); revsd on different grounds without argument on this point [2003] UKHL 23, [2004] 1 AC 185, [2003] 2 All ER 977.
   The low statutory limit set on expenses incurred by outsiders in publicising a candidate or in promoting political debate at an election (see PARA 272 et seq) was found to violate the Convention for the Protection of Human Rights and Fundamental Freedoms art 10 because it operated effectively as a total bar on the provision of information by third parties, while the press was not restricted in like fashion. The limit was found to be disproportionate to the aim pursued of ensuring that political debate in any individual constituency was not dominated by third party issues: Application 24839/94 *Bowman v United Kingdom* (1998) 26 EHRR 1, 4 BHRC 25, ECtHR (interference with applicant's freedom of expression, employed in seeking to influence voters in favour of anti-abortion candidates, was not necessary in a democratic society). The Representation of the People Act 1983 s 75 was amended accordingly (see PARA 272 note 15).

8. Rights guaranteed under international conventions.

The Universal Declaration of Human Rights[1] guarantees that: (1) everyone has the right to take part in the government of his country, directly or through freely chosen representatives[2]; (2) everyone has the right to equal access to public service in his country[3]; and (3) the will of the people must be the basis of the authority of government, and this will must be expressed in periodic and genuine elections by universal and equal suffrage and must be held by secret vote or by equivalent free voting procedures[4].

Under the International Covenant on Civil and Political Rights[5], every citizen has the right and the opportunity, without discrimination[6] and without unreasonable restrictions: (a) to take part in the conduct of public affairs, directly or through freely chosen representatives[7]; (b) to vote and to be elected at genuine periodic elections by universal and equal suffrage and by secret ballot, guaranteeing the free expression of the will of the electors[8]; and (c) to have access, on general terms of equality, to public service in his country[9].

The right to vote and to participate in free elections is recognised also under the International Convention on the Elimination of All Forms of Racial Discrimination[10], the Convention on the Elimination of All Forms of

Discrimination against Women[11], the International Convention on the Protection of the Rights of Migrant Workers[12], and the UN Convention on the Rights of Persons with Disabilities[13].

1 Ie the Universal Declaration of Human Rights (Paris, 10 December 1948; UN 2 (1949); Cmd 7662): see RIGHTS AND FREEDOMS vol 88A (2013) PARAS 100, 574.
2 Universal Declaration of Human Rights art 21(1).
3 Universal Declaration of Human Rights art 21(2).
4 Universal Declaration of Human Rights art 21(3).
5 Ie the International Covenant on Civil and Political Rights (New York, 16 December 1966; ratified by the United Kingdom 20 May 1976; UN TS 6 (1977); Cmnd 6702): see RIGHTS AND FREEDOMS vol 88A (2013) PARAS 104, 574.
6 Ie without any of the distinctions mentioned in the International Covenant on Civil and Political Rights art 2.
7 See the International Covenant on Civil and Political Rights art 25(a).
8 See the International Covenant on Civil and Political Rights art 25(b).
9 See the International Covenant on Civil and Political Rights art 25(c).
10 See the International Convention on the Elimination of All Forms of Racial Discrimination (New York, 7 March 1966; TS (1969) 77; Cmnd 4108) art 5(c); and RIGHTS AND FREEDOMS vol 88A (2013) PARAS 108, 574.
11 See the International Convention for the Elimination of All Forms of Discrimination Against Women (New York, 18 December 1979; 1249 UNTS 13) art 7; and RIGHTS AND FREEDOMS vol 88A (2013) PARAS 109, 574.
12 See the International Convention on the Protection of the Rights of All Migrant Workers and Members of Their Families (New York, 18 December 1990; UN General Assembly Resolution 158) art 41; and RIGHTS AND FREEDOMS vol 88A (2013) PARAS 111, 574.
13 See the Convention on the Rights of Persons with Disabilities (New York, 13 December 2006; TS 10 (2010); Cm 7905) art 29; and RIGHTS AND FREEDOMS vol 88A (2013) PARAS 110, 574.

(3) THE DIFFERENT TYPES OF ELECTION

9. **Parliamentary elections.** In any Act, 'parliamentary election' means the election of a member to serve in Parliament for a constituency[1]; and 'constituency' means[2] an area having separate representation in the House of Commons[3]. For the purpose of parliamentary elections, county and borough constituencies are established, each returning a single member[4].

The franchise for, the conduct of, and the questioning of parliamentary elections are governed by the Representation of the People Acts and associated legislation[5]. Provision is made for the combination of polls for parliamentary elections with any other relevant election or referendum[6].

1 Interpretation Act 1978 s 5, Sch 1. Whilst it is customary to speak of a parliamentary general election in the singular (see eg the Fixed-term Parliaments Act 2011; and PARA 189 et seq), the Representation of the People Act 1983 in fact provides for a separate election in each parliamentary constituency and it is more accurate to regard a 'general election', for the purposes of the law, as a series of separate elections taking place simultaneously in all the constituencies in the United Kingdom: see *R v Tronoh Mines Ltd* [1952] 1 All ER 697, [1952] 1 TLR 461, CCA (the term 'parliamentary election' is defined in the Interpretation Act 1978 in terms which make it plain that it means an election for a particular constituency and not a panoply of elections commonly known as a general election).
    In this title, the term 'parliamentary election' (without anything further) is used to denote an election to the United Kingdom Parliament. As to the meaning of 'United Kingdom' see PARA 1 note 1. As to the usage of 'election' and related terms in this title see PARA 3 note 4.
2 Ie in the Parliamentary Constituencies Act 1986 and, except where the context otherwise requires, in any Act passed after 30 July 1948 (ie in any Act passed after the date on which the Representation of the People Act 1948 (repealed) received Royal Assent): see the Parliamentary Constituencies Act 1986 s 1(2).
3 Parliamentary Constituencies Act 1986 s 1(2). See further PARA 73.
4 See the Parliamentary Constituencies Act 1986 s 1(1); and PARA 73. Constituencies are designated as either county or borough constituencies in Orders in Council made under the

Parliamentary Constituencies Act 1986: see s 1(1); and PARA 73. As to members and constituencies of the House of Commons generally see PARLIAMENT vol 78 (2010) PARA 892 et seq.
5 See PARA 3.
6 See PARA 16 et seq.

10. Local government statutes requiring the election of councillors and mayors. The following are elections under the Local Government Act 1972[1]: (1) the election of the chairman of a principal council[2] and councillors for a principal area[3]; (2) the election of the mayor[4] and councillors[5] of a London borough; and (3) the election of the chairman[6] and councillors[7] of a parish or community council[8].

Under the Local Government Act 2000, local authorities in England may change their form of governance[9], or vary their executive arrangements, in order to take on the form of a directly elected mayor together with two or more councillors of the authority appointed to the executive by the mayor (a 'mayor and cabinet executive')[10], subject to any such change being passed by a resolution of the local authority (and approved in a referendum, where this is required by order of the Secretary of State)[11]. A council for a principal area in Wales also may operate executive arrangements which involve a mayor and cabinet executive, where the mayor is elected[12].

1 The Representation of the People Act 1983 uses the expression 'election under the local government Act' where 'local government Act' is defined to mean the Local Government Act 1972: see the Representation of the People Act 1983 s 203(1); and PARA 11 note 2.
2 See the Local Government Act 1972 s 3(1); and LOCAL GOVERNMENT vol 69 (2009) PARA 144. Filling the office of vice-chairman of a principal council is not an election for this purpose, as the vice-chairman is appointed: see s 5(1). The election of the chairman of a principal council, although an election under the Local Government Act 1972, is not a local government election as defined in the Representation of the People Act 1983 (as to which see PARA 11). As to the meaning of 'principal council' see LOCAL GOVERNMENT vol 69 (2009) PARA 23.
3 See the Local Government Act 1972 ss 6, 7 (England), ss 25, 26 (Wales); and LOCAL GOVERNMENT vol 69 (2009) PARA 126 et seq. As to the meaning of 'principal area' see LOCAL GOVERNMENT vol 69 (2009) PARA 23. As to ordinary elections for the election of councillors of a principal council, as specified in an order made by the Secretary of State, under the Local Government Act 2000 see Pt IV (84–89); and LOCAL GOVERNMENT vol 69 (2009) PARA 134. See also the power conferred by ss 87, 105(2) and 106(1)(b), (c), and now exercisable by the National Assembly for Wales by virtue of the Government of Wales Act 2006 s 162, Sch 11 para 30, to make provision by order which changes the years in which the ordinary elections of councillors of any specified local authority are to be held but which does not change the scheme which prevails for the ordinary elections of those councillors (cited in LOCAL GOVERNMENT vol 69 (2009) PARA 134). As to ordinary elections for the election of councillors under the Local Government and Public Involvement in Health Act 2007 (metropolitan and non-metropolitan district councils in England having resolved to be subject to a scheme for whole-council elections) see Pt 2 Ch 1 (ss 31–54); and LOCAL GOVERNMENT vol 69 (2009) PARA 135 et seq.
4 See the Local Government Act 1972 s 8, Sch 2 para 2(1); and LONDON GOVERNMENT vol 71 (2013) PARA 21. Where a London borough council is operating executive arrangements which involve a mayor and cabinet executive or a mayor and council manager executive, Sch 2 para 2(1) has effect with the modifications specified in Sch 2 para 5D: see Sch 2 para 5B; and LONDON GOVERNMENT vol 71 (2013) PARA 21. As to councils operating executive arrangements see LOCAL GOVERNMENT vol 69 (2009) PARA 320.
5 See the Local Government Act 1972 Sch 2 para 6(1); and LONDON GOVERNMENT vol 71 (2013) PARA 21.
6 See the Local Government Act 1972 ss 15(1), 34(1); and LOCAL GOVERNMENT vol 69 (2009) PARAS 145, 147. Filling the office of vice-chairman is not to be treated as an election for this purpose as the vice-chairman is appointed: see ss 15(6), 34(6).
7 See the Local Government Act 1972 s 16(2), s 35(1); and LOCAL GOVERNMENT vol 69 (2009) PARAS 132–133.
8 In a parish not having a separate parish council, the chairman of a parish meeting is elected at its annual assembly: see the Local Government Act 1972 s 15(10); and LOCAL GOVERNMENT

vol 69 (2009) PARA 146. Certain provisions of the Representation of the People Act 1983 have effect in relation to such an election subject to specified adaptations, modifications and exceptions: see PARA 383 note 6. As to the conduct of a poll consequent on a parish or community meeting on a question other than one involving appointment to an office see PARA 556 et seq.

9　A local authority in England can operate: (1) executive arrangements (see the Local Government Act 2000 ss 9D–9GC; and LOCAL GOVERNMENT); (2) a committee system (ie arrangements made for or in connection with the discharge of its functions in accordance with the Local Government Act 1972 Pt 6 (ss 101–110) (see LOCAL GOVERNMENT vol 69 (2009) PARA 369 et seq), and the Local Government Act 2000 Pt 1A (ss 9B–9R) (see LOCAL GOVERNMENT)); or (3) prescribed arrangements (ie according to regulations made under s 9BA: see LOCAL GOVERNMENT): see s 9B; and LOCAL GOVERNMENT. At the date at which this volume states the law, no regulations have been made yet under s 9BA.

10　See the Local Government Act 2000 s 9C; and LOCAL GOVERNMENT. A reference in any enactment (whenever passed or made) to a member of a local authority, or a councillor of a local authority, does not include a reference to an elected mayor of the authority (meaning an individual elected as mayor of the authority by the local government electors for the authority's area in accordance with the provisions made by or under Pt 1A): see s 9H(1)–(5); and LOCAL GOVERNMENT.

The other form of executive allowed in England under the Local Government Act 2000 is a 'leader and cabinet executive' (ie an executive leader, elected by full council from among the councillors, together with two or more councillors of the authority appointed to the executive by the leader): see further ss 9C, 9I–9ID; and LOCAL GOVERNMENT.

11　See the Local Government Act 2000 ss 9K–9KC; and LOCAL GOVERNMENT.

12　See the Local Government Act 2000 Pt 2 (ss 10–48A) (Local authorities in Wales: arrangements with respect to executives etc), which has been amended by the Localism Act 2011 s 22, Sch 3 so that it applies only to local authorities in Wales: see LOCAL GOVERNMENT vol 69 (2009) PARA 303 et seq.

11.　Provision for local government elections made under the Representation of the People Acts.　In the Representation of the People Act 1983, 'local government election' means either the election of councillors for any electoral area, or any Authority election[1]. 'Electoral area' means:

(1)　any electoral division or ward (or, in the case of a parish or community in which there are no wards, the parish or community) for which the election of councillors is held under the local government Act[2];

(2)　Greater London[3], in the case of any election of the Mayor of London[4], or the election of the London members of the London Assembly at an ordinary election[5];

(3)　any Assembly constituency for which the election of a constituency member of the London Assembly is held[6].

The procedure by which electoral areas are established and reviewed is described elsewhere in this work[7]. 'Authority election' means: (a) any election of the Mayor of London[8]; (b) any election of a constituency member of the London Assembly[9]; or (c) the election of the London members of the London Assembly at an ordinary election[10].

The franchise for, the conduct of, and the questioning of local government elections are governed by the Representation of the People Act 1983 and associated legislation[11]. The Representation of the People Acts[12] are applied with modifications[13] for the purpose of electing a local authority mayor where executive arrangements are in place under the Local Government Act 2000[14]. Certain provisions of the Representation of the People Act 1983[15] apply in relation to the City of London as if the City were a London borough and the Common Council of the City were a London borough council[16]. The Representation of the People Act 1983 applies in relation to the Isles of Scilly as if those isles were a county and as if the council of those isles were a county council[17].

Provision is made for the combination of polls for local government elections with any other relevant election (or, in England, any other relevant election or referendum)[18].

1   See the Representation of the People Act 1983 s 203(1) (definition amended by the Greater London Authority Act 1999 s 17, Sch 3 paras 1, 39(1), (4)(c)). In the application of the Representation of the People Act 1983 in relation to England and Wales, unless the context otherwise requires, any reference to a local government election must be taken to include a reference to an Authority election: see s 203(1A)(a) (s 203(1A) added by the Greater London Authority Act 1999 Sch 3 paras 39(1), (5)). See note 15. As to the meaning of 'Authority election' see the text and notes 8–10. As to the meanings of 'England' and 'Wales' see PARA 1 note 1.

    For most of the purposes of the Representation of the People Act 1983, 'local government election' includes a municipal election in the City of London (ie an election to the office of mayor, alderman, common councilman or sheriff and also the election of any officer elected by the mayor, aldermen and liverymen in common hall): see s 191(1); and PARA 33.

2   See the Representation of the People Act 1983 s 203(1) (definition of 'electoral area' substituted by the Representation of the People Act 1985 s 24, Sch 4 para 71; and amended by the Greater London Authority Act 1999 Sch 3 paras 1, 39(1), (3)). For these purposes, the 'local government Act' means the Local Government Act 1972: see the Representation of the People Act 1983 s 203(1) (definition amended by the Local Government Act 1985 ss 18(1), 19, Sch 9 Pt I; and the Education Reform Act 1988 s 237, Sch 13 Pt I). For the purposes of the election of councillors, every non-metropolitan county in England and every principal area in Wales is required to be divided into electoral divisions and every metropolitan or non-metropolitan district in England is required to be divided into wards: see the Local Government Act 1972 ss 6(2), 25(2); and PARA 74. For the same purposes, every London borough is required to be divided into wards: see s 8(1), Sch 2 para 7(1)(b); and PARA 74. For each electoral division or ward, there must be a separate election: see s 6(2), s 25(2), Sch 2 para 7(1); and PARA 74. Where a parish (in England) is divided into parish wards, there must be a separate election of parish councillors for each ward, and where it is not, there must be one election of parish councillors for the whole parish: see s 16(4), (5); and PARA 74. Where a community (in Wales) is divided into community wards, there must be a separate election of community councillors for each ward, and where it is not, there must be one election of community councillors for the whole community: see s 35(3), (4); and PARA 74. The Representation of the People Act 1983 s 60 (personation: see PARA 730), s 62A (offences associated with postal or proxy voting: see PARA 731), s 66 (requirement of secrecy: see PARA 739), Pt II (ss 67–119) (the election campaign: see PARA 230 et seq), Pt III (ss 120–186) (legal proceedings: see PARA 682 et seq) and s 189 (voting offences at certain local elections: see PARA 700) are applied to an election in England and Wales of parish or community councillors, and of the chairman of a parish or community council or a parish meeting: see s 187(1); and PARAS 383 note 6, 556. As to the election of councillors under local government legislation see PARA 10.

    In the application of the Representation of the People Act 1983 in relation to England and Wales, unless the context otherwise requires, any reference to an election under the local government Act must be taken to include a reference to an Authority election: see s 203(1A)(b) (s 203(1A) as added: see note 1). See note 15. For most of the purposes of the Representation of the People Act 1983, 'election under the local government Act' includes a municipal election in the City of London (ie an election to the office of mayor, alderman, common councilman or sheriff and also the election of any officer elected by the mayor, aldermen and liverymen in common hall); and 'electoral area' means, in relation to a ward election, the ward, and in relation to any other municipal election in the City of London, the City: see s 191(1); and PARA 33. For the purposes of the Political Parties, Elections and Referendums Act 2000, 'local government election' means a local government election within the meaning of the Representation of the People Act 1983 s 191 (ie municipal elections in the City of London: see PARA 33), s 203, or s 204 (Scotland: see PARA 3 note 2) or an election under the Local Government Act 2000 Pt 1A (ss 9B–9R) (arrangements with respect to local governance in England: see LOCAL GOVERNMENT), Pt II (ss 10–48A) (Local authorities in Wales: arrangements with respect to executives etc: see LOCAL GOVERNMENT vol 69 (2009) PARA 303 et seq) for the return of an elected mayor (see PARA 198 et seq): see the Political Parties, Elections and Referendums Act 2000 s 160(1); Interpretation Act 1978 s 17(2)(b).

3   As to Greater London as an administrative area see LONDON GOVERNMENT vol 71 (2013) PARA 14.

4   For these purposes, 'election of the Mayor of London' means either any such election at an ordinary election or an election under the Greater London Authority Act 1999 s 16 (election to

fill a vacancy in the office of Mayor of London: see PARA 204; and LONDON GOVERNMENT vol 71 (2013) PARA 88 et seq): see the Representation of the People Act 1983 s 203(1) (definition added by the Greater London Authority Act 1999 Sch 3 paras 1, 39(1), (2)). As to London Mayoral ordinary elections see PARA 199; and LONDON GOVERNMENT vol 71 (2013) PARA 76 et seq.

5   See the Representation of the People Act 1983 s 203(1) (definition as substituted and amended: see note 2). In relation to the London Assembly, 'London member' has the same meaning as in the Greater London Authority Act 1999 (see ss 2(2)(b), 424(1); and LONDON GOVERNMENT vol 71 (2013) PARA 70): see the Representation of the People Act 1983 s 203(1) (definition added by the Greater London Authority Act 1999 Sch 3 paras 1, 39(1), (2)). As to London Assembly ordinary elections see PARA 199; and LONDON GOVERNMENT vol 71 (2013) PARA 76 et seq.

6   See the Representation of the People Act 1983 s 203(1) (definition as substituted and amended: see note 2). For these purposes, 'Assembly constituency' has the same meaning as in the Greater London Authority Act 1999 (see s 2(4), (5); and LONDON GOVERNMENT vol 71 (2013) PARA 80): see the Representation of the People Act 1983 s 203(1) (definition added by the Greater London Authority Act 1999 Sch 3 paras 1, 39(1), (2)). 'Election of a constituency member of the London Assembly' means either any such election at an ordinary election or an election under the Greater London Authority Act 1999 s 10 (election to fill a vacancy in an Assembly constituency: see PARA 204; and LONDON GOVERNMENT vol 71 (2013) PARA 111): see the Representation of the People Act 1983 s 203(1) (definition added by the Greater London Authority Act 1999 Sch 3 paras 1, 39(1), (2)). In relation to the London Assembly, 'constituency member' has the same meaning as in the Greater London Authority Act 1999 (see ss 2(2)(a), 424(1); and LONDON GOVERNMENT vol 71 (2013) PARA 70): see the Representation of the People Act 1983 s 203(1) (definition added by the Greater London Authority Act 1999 Sch 3 paras 1, 39(1), (2)).

7   As to the establishment of electoral areas for the purpose of local government elections see PARA 74 et seq; LOCAL GOVERNMENT vol 69 (2009) PARA 54 et seq; and LONDON GOVERNMENT vol 71 (2013) PARA 14 et seq.

8   See the Representation of the People Act 1983 s 203(1) (definition added by the Greater London Authority Act 1999 Sch 3 paras 1, 39(1), (2)).

9   See the Representation of the People Act 1983 s 203(1) (definition as added: see note 8).

10 See the Representation of the People Act 1983 s 203(1) (definition as added: see note 8).

11 See PARA 3.

12 As to the meaning of 'the Representation of the People Acts' see PARA 3 note 1.

13 Ie by regulations made, in relation to England, under the Local Government Act 2000 s 9HE, and, in relation to Wales, under ss 44, 105: see PARA 383; and LOCAL GOVERNMENT vol 69 (2009) PARA 303 et seq. At the date at which this volume states the law, no such regulations had been made under s 9HE, and the Local Authorities (Mayoral Elections) (England and Wales) Regulations 2007, SI 2007/1024, continue to apply to England as well as to Wales: see PARA 383.

14 See PARA 198; and LOCAL GOVERNMENT vol 69 (2009) PARA 320. The provisions in the Representation of the People Act 1983, the Representation of the People Act 1985, the Representation of the People Act 2000, the Electoral Administration Act 2006, and the Representation of the People (England and Wales) Regulations 2001, SI 2001/341, which have effect in relation to the conduct of the election of councillors for any county electoral division or district or London borough ward (in England) or any county electoral division or county borough ward (in Wales) have effect, in relation to the conduct of a mayoral election in England, as they have effect in relation to the conduct of an election of councillors for any county electoral division or district or London borough ward, and, in relation to the conduct of a mayoral election in Wales, as they have effect in relation to the conduct of an election of councillors for any county electoral division or county borough ward: see the Local Authorities (Mayoral Elections) (England and Wales) Regulations 2007, SI 2007/1024, reg 3(2), (3), (5). Those provisions have effect, however, subject to (see reg 3(2), (4)):

(1)   general references to 'local government elections' being taken to include mayoral elections (reg 3(4)(a));

(2)   general references to a 'candidate' being taken to include a candidate at a mayoral election (reg 3(4)(b)); and

(3)   modifications to specified provisions as they are set out in reg 3(2), (4), Sch 2 (reg 3(4)(c) (amended by virtue of SI 2012/2059), as follows:

(a)   various specified provisions of the Representation of the People Act 1983 have effect, in relation to such an election, subject to the modifications specified in the

Local Authorities (Mayoral Elections) (England and Wales) Regulations 2007, SI 2007/1024, Sch 2 Table 1 (Representation of the People Act 1983);

(b) the Representation of the People Act 1985 s 15 (combination of polls at parliamentary, European and local elections: see PARA 17 et seq) has effect, in relation to such an election, subject to the modifications specified in the Local Authorities (Mayoral Elections) (England and Wales) Regulations 2007, SI 2007/1024, Sch 2 Table 2 (Representation of the People Act 1985);

(c) the Representation of the People Act 2000 s 12 (changes relating to absent voting at elections in Great Britain: see PARA 363 et seq), Sch 4 (absent voting at elections in Great Britain: see PARA 363 et seq) have effect, in relation to such an election, subject to the modifications specified in the Local Authorities (Mayoral Elections) (England and Wales) Regulations 2007, SI 2007/1024, Sch 2 Table 3 (Representation of the People Act 2000);

(d) various interpretative provisions of the Representation of the People (England and Wales) Regulations 2001, SI 2001/341, have effect, in relation to such an election, subject to the modifications specified in the Local Authorities (Mayoral Elections) (England and Wales) Regulations 2007, SI 2007/1024, Sch 2 Table 4 (Representation of the People (England and Wales) Regulations 2001); and

(e) the Electoral Administration Act 2006 s 32 (pilot orders relating to schemes for modifying ballot papers used at local government elections: see PARA 524), s 44 (access to election documents: see PARA 505), and s 69 (encouraging electoral participation: see PARAS 141 144, 350 et seq) have effect, in relation to such an election, subject to the modifications specified in the Local Authorities (Mayoral Elections) (England and Wales) Regulations 2007, SI 2007/1024, Sch 2 Table 5 (Electoral Administration Act 2006).

Accordingly, the definition of 'local government election' given in the Representation of the People Act 1983 s 203(1) (see the text and note 1) includes 'any mayoral election', where 'mayoral election' means the election of an elected mayor under the Local Government Act 2000 Pt 1A (ss 9B–9R) (arrangements with respect to local governance in England: see LOCAL GOVERNMENT), Pt II (ss 10–48A) (local authorities in Wales: arrangements with respect to executives etc: see LOCAL GOVERNMENT vol 69 (2009) PARA 303 et seq): see the Local Authorities (Mayoral Elections) (England and Wales) Regulations 2007, SI 2007/1024, Sch 2 Table 1; Interpretation Act 1978 s 17(2)(b).

In the application of the Representation of the People Act 1983 in relation to England and Wales, unless the context otherwise requires, any reference to a local government election, or an election under the local government Act (see note 2), is taken to include a reference to a mayoral election: see s 203(1A) (as added (see note 1); as so applied and modified). See also notes 1, 2.

15 Ie the Representation of the People Act 1983 Pt I (ss 1–66B) (parliamentary and local government franchise and its exercise: see PARA 95 et seq), so far as it has effect for the purposes of parliamentary elections, and Pts I–III (ss 1–186), so far as they have effect for the purposes of Authority elections, and subject to any express provision contained in the Part or Parts in question: see s 203(2) (substituted by the Greater London Authority Act 1999 Sch 3 paras 39(1), (6)). As to the conduct of parliamentary and Authority elections see PARA 383 et seq.

In relation to the conduct of a mayoral election in England or Wales (see note 14), the Representation of the People Act 1983 s 203(2) is modified so that it reads: 'Pts I–III (ss 1–186), so far as they have effect for the purposes of Authority elections or mayoral elections': see s 203(2) (as so substituted; as applied and modified (see note 14)).

16 Representation of the People Act 1983 s 203(2) (as substituted: see note 15). For these purposes, the Inner Temple and the Middle Temple are treated as forming part of the City of London: see s 203(2) (as so substituted). The modifications made by s 203(2) do not affect s 52(4) (duty of a district council or London borough council to assign officers to assist the registration officer: see PARA 140): s 203(3). As to the Court of Common Council see LONDON GOVERNMENT vol 71 (2013) PARA 34 et seq; and as to the Temples see LONDON GOVERNMENT vol 71 (2013) PARA 17.

The Representation of the People Act 1983 is further modified in its application to City of London elections (ward and municipal) by ss 191–198 (s 192 repealed), which also modify the various City of London Acts governing ward elections: see PARA 33. However, the law applying to elections in the City of London is unique in many respects and the detail, accordingly, is not dealt with in this title: see further LONDON GOVERNMENT vol 71 (2013) PARA 24 et seq.

17 Representation of the People Act 1983 s 203(4). However, the council is required to appoint an officer of the council to be registration officer for the isles and s 53, Sch 2 para 1(1) (power to prescribe arrangements for carrying out of registration duties by a registration officer: see PARA 112 note 1) applies as if the isles were a district and the council were a district council:

s 203(4)(a) (amended by the Representation of the People Act 1985 ss 24, 28, Sch 4 para 71(b), Sch 5). This function normally falls on the council for the principal area: see PARA 139. The provisions of the Representation of the People Act 1983 Pt I (parliamentary and local government franchise and its exercise: see PARA 95 et seq) relating to the conduct of local government elections have effect in relation to those isles subject to such adaptations as the Secretary of State may by regulations prescribe: s 203(4)(b). For the purposes of the Local Government Act 1972 s 265 (application to Isles of Scilly: see LOCAL GOVERNMENT vol 69 (2009) PARA 36) the provisions of the Representation of the People Act 1983 as to rules made by the Secretary of State under s 36 (ie rules for the conduct of local government elections: see PARA 383) are deemed to be contained in a public general Act relating to local government: s 203(5). As to the making of regulations under the Representation of the People Act 1983 see PARA 28 note 16. At the date at which this volume states the law, no such regulations had been made under s 203. As to the Secretary of State see PARA 2. As to counties and county councils see LOCAL GOVERNMENT vol 69 (2009) PARA 24 et seq. As to the Council of the Isles of Scilly see LOCAL GOVERNMENT vol 69 (2009) PARA 36. As to the Secretary of State responsible for functions relating to local government see LOCAL GOVERNMENT vol 69 (2009) PARA 96.

18 See PARA 16 et seq.

12.   Welsh Assembly elections.   The National Assembly for Wales[1] consists of:
(1)   one member for each Assembly constituency ('Assembly constituency members')[2]; and
(2)   members for each Assembly electoral region ('Assembly regional members')[3].

Members of the National Assembly for Wales ('Assembly members') are returned in accordance with the provision made for: (a) the holding of ordinary general elections of Assembly members[4]; and (b) the filling of vacancies in Assembly seats[5]. An 'ordinary general election' involves the holding of elections for the return of the entire Assembly[6]. Where the seat of an Assembly member returned for an Assembly constituency is vacant, an election is held in the Assembly constituency to fill the vacancy[7]. Where the seat of an Assembly member returned for an Assembly electoral region is vacant, then, if the Assembly member was returned from the list of a registered political party[8], the regional returning officer[9] must notify to the presiding officer the name of the person who is to fill the vacancy[10] and, subject to certain conditions regarding such notification[11], that person is treated as declared to be returned as an Assembly member for the Assembly electoral region on the day on which notification of his name is received by the presiding officer[12]. However, the seat remains vacant until the next ordinary general election if the Assembly regional member was returned as an individual candidate[13], or if that Assembly regional member was returned from the list of a registered political party but there is no-one who satisfies the necessary conditions[14].

The Secretary of State[15] may by order[16] make provision as to:
(i)   the conduct of elections for the return of Assembly members[17];
(ii)   the questioning of an election for the return of Assembly members and the consequences of irregularities[18]; and
(iii)   the return of an Assembly member otherwise than at an election[19].

Provision is made under head (i) above for the combination of polls at elections for the return of Assembly members and other elections[20].

1   As to the National Assembly for Wales generally, including the terms of office of Assembly members etc, see CONSTITUTIONAL LAW AND HUMAN RIGHTS. In this title, the term 'Welsh Assembly election' is used to denote a Welsh Assembly election and to distinguish such an election from a 'London Assembly election'.

2   Government of Wales Act 2006 s 1(2)(a). As to the establishment of constituencies for the purpose of Welsh Assembly elections see PARA 76 et seq.

3   Government of Wales Act 2006 s 1(2)(b).

4   See the Government of Wales Act 2006 s 1(3)(a).

5   Government of Wales Act 2006 s 1(3)(b).

6   See the Government of Wales Act 2006 s 1(3)(a). As to the holding of ordinary general elections and extraordinary general elections and as to the power of the Secretary of State to vary the date of an ordinary general election see PARA 213. As to the entitlement to vote in such elections generally see PARA 99; and as to the manner of voting at such an election see PARA 364.

7   See PARA 214.

8   As to the voting system used to return Assembly members from the list of a registered political party see PARA 340 et seq.

9   In the Government of Wales Act 2006, 'regional returning officer', in relation to any Assembly electoral region, means the person designated as the regional returning officer for the Assembly electoral region in accordance with an order under s 13 (see the text and notes 15–19): s 7(7).

10 See PARA 215.

11 As to the conditions referred to in the text see PARA 215.

12 See PARA 215.

13 As to Assembly regional members returned having stood as individual candidates see PARA 340 et seq.

14 See PARA 215.

15 As to the Secretary of State see PARA 2.

16 Such an order may:

    (1)   apply or incorporate, with or without modifications or exceptions, any provision of, or made under, the Representation of the People Acts, the Political Parties, Elections and Referendums Act 2000, the European Parliamentary Elections Act 2002 or any other enactment relating to parliamentary elections, European parliamentary elections or local government elections (Government of Wales Act 2006 s 13(4)(a), (5));

    (2)   modify any form contained in, or in regulations or rules made under, the Representation of the People Acts so far as may be necessary to enable it to be used both for the original purpose and in relation to elections for the return of Assembly members (s 13(4)(b)); and

    (3)   so far as may be necessary in consequence of any provision made by the Government of Wales Act 2006 or an order under s 13, amend any provision made by or under any enactment relating to the registration of parliamentary electors or local government electors (s 13(4)(c)).

No order is to be made under s 13 unless a draft of the statutory instrument containing it has been laid before, and approved by a resolution of, each House of Parliament: s 13(7). As to the meaning of 'the Representation of the People Acts' see PARA 3 note 1; as to the meaning of 'parliamentary election' see PARA 9; and as to the meaning of 'local government election' see PARA 11. As to European parliamentary elections see PARA 13. As to the power of a Minister of the Crown or the Welsh Ministers under the Government of Wales Act 2006 generally to make an order see s 157; and CONSTITUTIONAL LAW AND HUMAN RIGHTS.

17 Government of Wales Act 2006 s 13(1)(a). The provision which may be made under s 13(1)(a) includes, in particular, provision:

    (1)   about the registration of electors (s 13(2)(a));

    (2)   for disregarding alterations in a register of electors (s 13(2)(b));

    (3)   about the limitation of the election expenses of candidates, and the creation of criminal offences in connection with the limitation of such expenses (s 13(2)(c));

    (4)   for the combination of polls at elections for the return of Assembly members and other elections (s 13(2)(d)); and

    (5)   for modifying the operation of ss 6, 8(2) (voting at ordinary elections: see PARA 340) in a case where the poll at an election for the return of the Assembly member for an Assembly constituency is abandoned, or notice of it is countermanded (s 13(2)(e)).

In so far as orders made by the Secretary of State under s 13 relate to the matters mentioned in head (3) above, see further the Political Parties, Elections and Referendums Act 2000 s 8 (powers with respect to elections exercisable only on recommendation of Electoral Commission); and PARA 56.

    As to provision made under the Government of Wales Act 2006 s 13(1)(a) see, by virtue of the Interpretation Act 1978 s 17(2)(b), the National Assembly for Wales (Representation of the People) Order 2007, SI 2007/236, Pt 2 (arts 3–36) (assembly franchise and its exercise: see generally PARAS 17 et seq, 139 et seq, 392 et seq), Pt 3 (arts 37–85) (the election campaign: see PARA 230 et seq). As to the rules of conduct for Welsh Assembly elections generally see PARA 383. As to the Welsh Language Act 1993 s 26 (power to prescribe Welsh forms) see CONSTITUTIONAL LAW AND HUMAN RIGHTS vol 8(2) (Reissue) PARA 44; and as to relevant orders made thereunder see the National Assembly for Wales (Elections: Nomination Papers)

(Welsh Form) Order 2001, SI 2001/2914; the Local Elections (Declaration of Acceptance of Office) (Wales) Order 2004, SI 2004/1508; the Local Elections (Communities) (Welsh Forms) Order 2007, SI 2007/1013; the Parliamentary Elections (Welsh Forms) Order 2007, SI 2007/1014; the Local Elections (Principal Areas) (Welsh Forms) Order 2007, SI 2007/1015; the Local Authorities (Conduct of Referendums) (Wales) Regulations 2008, SI 2008/1848; and the European Parliamentary Elections (Welsh Forms) Order 2009, SI 2009/781.

18 Government of Wales Act 2006 s 13(1)(b). No return of an Assembly member at an election is to be questioned except by an election petition under the provisions of the Representation of the People Act 1983 Pt III (ss 120–186) (see PARA 761 et seq) as applied by or incorporated in an order under the Government of Wales Act 2006 s 13: s 13(6). As to the order that has been made see the National Assembly for Wales (Representation of the People) Order 2007, SI 2007/236, Pt 4 (arts 86–138) (legal proceedings: see PARA 764 et seq).

19 Government of Wales Act 2006 s 13(1)(c). The provision that may be made under s 13(1)(c) includes, in particular, provision making modifications to s 11(3)–(5) (vacancies in electoral region seats in the National Assembly for Wales: see PARA 215): s 13(3). Provision is made by the National Assembly for Wales (Representation of the People) Order 2007, SI 2007/236, for the filling of vacancies: see, in particular, art 17(1), Sch 5 paras 77–79; and PARAS 214–215.

20 See PARA 16 et seq.

13. European parliamentary elections. There are 73 members of the European Parliament ('MEPs') elected for the United Kingdom[1]. For the purposes of electing MEPs, the area of England and Gibraltar[2] is divided into nine electoral regions[3], and Wales forms a single electoral region[4]. The procedure by which European parliamentary electoral regions are established and reviewed is described elsewhere in this title[5]. The system of election of MEPs in an electoral region is a regional list system, whereby a vote may be cast for a registered party or an individual candidate, with seats being allocated according to calculations based on the totals of votes cast for each party or candidate[6]. When a seat is or becomes vacant, a by-election may be held in specified circumstances[7] or a seat last filled from a party's list of candidates[8] may be filled, in specified circumstances, from such a list (without a by-election)[9].

The Secretary of State[10] may[11] by regulations[12] make provision as to: (1) the conduct of elections to the European Parliament[13]; and (2) the questioning of such an election and the consequences of irregularities[14].

Provision is made also for the combination of polls for European parliamentary elections with any other relevant election or referendum[15].

1   See the European Parliamentary Elections Act 2002 s 1(1); and PARA 77. As to the meaning of 'United Kingdom' see PARA 1 note 1. As to the basis of European parliamentary elections in EU law see PARA 6. In this title, the term 'European parliamentary election' is used to denote an election to the European Parliament.

2   In Application 24833/94 *Matthews v United Kingdom* (1999) 28 EHRR 361, ECtHR, it was held that the United Kingdom was responsible for securing for the citizens of Gibraltar the right to free elections to the European Parliament, as that body forms part of Gibraltar's legislature. See note 3.

3   See the European Parliamentary Elections Act 2002 s 1(2)(a); and PARA 77. The electoral regions for these purposes are those specified in s 1, Sch 1 and the number of MEPs to be elected for each electoral region is specified in s 1(3): see PARA 77 note 5. Gibraltar forms part of a 'combined region' in the United Kingdom for the purpose of elections to the European Parliament: see the European Parliament (Representation) Act 2003 Pt 2 (ss 9–24), which apply rules governing the franchise (see PARA 100 note 3) and eligibility to stand as a candidate for election (see PARA 228), laid down both for national elections in the United Kingdom and for elections to the Gibraltar House of Assembly, to the European Parliament elections in Gibraltar: see note 12; and PARA 77 note 4. The terms of the European Parliament (Representation) Act 2003 are not contrary to Community law: Case C-145/04 *Spain v United Kingdom* [2007] All ER (EC) 486, [2006] ECR I-7917, ECJ (definition of persons entitled to vote and to stand as a candidate in elections to the European Parliament fell within the competence of each member state in compliance with Community law; qualifying Commonwealth citizens resident in Gibraltar who were not Community nationals had the right to vote and to stand as candidates

in elections). See also Case C-300/04 *Eman v College van burgemeester en wethouders van Den Haag* [2007] All ER (EC) 486, [2006] ECR I-8055, ECJ (Grand Chamber); and PARA 6. Gibraltar is discussed in this title only within the context of general arrangements. As to the constitution of Gibraltar see COMMONWEALTH vol 13 (2009) PARA 859.

4　See the European Parliamentary Elections Act 2002 s 1(2)(b); and PARA 77. Scotland and Northern Ireland also each form a single electoral region for these purposes: see s 1(2)(b); and PARA 77.

5　See PARAS 77, 91 et seq.

6　See the European Parliamentary Elections Act 2002 s 2; and PARA 340. The first seat is allocated to the party or individual candidate with the greatest number of votes, and the second and subsequent seats are allocated in the same way, except that the number of votes given to a party to which one or more seats have already been allocated is adjusted: see s 2; and PARA 340. An elector who votes more than once at an election to the European Parliament commits an offence: see PARA 700.

7　See the European Parliamentary Elections Act 2002 s 5(2)(a); and PARA 218 et seq. The circumstances mentioned in the text are specified in regulations: see s 5(2)(a); the European Parliamentary Elections Regulations 2004, SI 2004/293; and PARA 218 et seq.

8　As to MEPs returned from the list of a registered political party see PARA 340.

9　See the European Parliamentary Elections Act 2002 s 5(2)(b); and PARA 218 et seq. The circumstances mentioned in the text are specified in regulations: see s 5(2)(b); the European Parliamentary Elections Regulations 2004, SI 2004/293; and PARA 218 et seq.

10　As to the Secretary of State see PARA 2.

11　Ie subject to the provisions of the European Parliamentary Elections Act 2002: see s 7(1).

12　Regulations under the European Parliamentary Elections Act 2002 may apply, with such modifications or exceptions as may be specified in the regulations:

(1)　any provision of the Representation of the People Acts or of any other enactment relating to parliamentary elections or local government elections (European Parliamentary Elections Act 2002 s 7(3)(a)); and

(2)　any provision made under any enactment (s 7(3)(b)).

Such regulations may amend any form contained in regulations made under the Representation of the People Acts so far as may be necessary to enable it to be used both for the purpose indicated in regulations so made and for the corresponding purpose in relation to elections to the European Parliament: European Parliamentary Elections Act 2002 s 7(4). Without prejudice to the generality of the power under which they are made, regulations under the European Parliamentary Elections Act 2002 may make different provision for different electoral regions and, in particular, for the part of the combined region which is in England and Wales, and for Gibraltar: s 7(4A) (added by the European Parliament (Representation) Act 2003 s 22). In the European Parliamentary Elections Act 2002, 'combined region' means the electoral region which includes Gibraltar: s 17 (definition added by the European Parliament (Representation) Act 2003 s 20(1), (5)). The Welsh Language Act 1993 s 26 (power to prescribe Welsh version: see CONSTITUTIONAL LAW AND HUMAN RIGHTS vol 8(2) (Reissue) PARA 44) applies in relation to regulations under the European Parliamentary Elections Act 2002 as it applies in relation to Acts of Parliament: s 7(5). As to the regulations made under the European Parliamentary Elections Act 2002 s 7 see notes 13–14; and as to relevant orders made under the Welsh Language Act 1993 s 26 see PARA 12 note 17. As to the meaning of 'the Representation of the People Acts' see PARA 3 note 1. As to the combined region and Gibraltar see PARA 77.

　　Regulations and orders made under the European Parliamentary Elections Act 2002 must be made by statutory instrument: s 13(1). However, no such regulations may be made unless a draft of the regulations has been laid before Parliament and approved by a resolution of each House of Parliament: s 13(2). A statutory instrument containing an order under either s 10(2)(d) or s 11(5) (entitlement to be an MEP: see PARA 228) is subject to annulment in pursuance of a resolution of either House of Parliament (s 13(3) (amended by the European Parliament (Representation) Act 2003 s 8(1), (2))); and an order under the European Parliamentary Elections Act 2002 s 10(4A) (disqualification from the office of MEP of persons connected to Gibraltar: see PARA 228) may not be made unless a draft of the order has been laid before, and approved by a resolution of, each House of Parliament (s 13(3A) (s 13(3A)–(3C) added by the European Parliament (Representation) Act 2003 s 21(3))). However, the European Parliamentary Elections Act 2002 s 13(3A) does not apply if it appears to the Secretary of State that by reason of urgency the order should be made without being approved in draft (s 13(3B) (as so added; and amended by SI 2003/1887)). Where an order is made without being approved in draft, by virtue of the European Parliamentary Elections Act 2002 s 13(3A), it must be laid before Parliament after being made and, if it is not approved by a resolution of each House of Parliament within the period of 40 days after the date on which it is made, the order ceases to have effect at the end of that period: s 13(3C) (as so added). A statutory instrument containing an order under s 4 (date of elections: see PARA 222) or s 5(3) (regulations providing for a by-election: see PARA 218) is to be laid before Parliament after being made: s 13(4).

13　European Parliamentary Elections Act 2002 s 7(1)(a). Such regulations may make provision (including the creation of criminal offences):
　　(1)　about the limitation of election expenses of candidates (s 7(2)(a));
　　(2)　for the allocation of seats in the case of an equality of votes (s 7(2)(b)); and
　　(3)　for securing that no person stands for election more than once at a general election, whether by being nominated as a candidate or by being included in a party's list of candidates (s 7(2)(c)).
　　As to the regulations so made see the European Parliamentary Elections Regulations 2004, SI 2004/293, Pts 1–3 (regs 1–85); and PARA 383 note 16.
14　European Parliamentary Elections Act 2002 s 7(1)(b). As to the regulations so made see the European Parliamentary Elections Regulations 2004, SI 2004/293, Pt 4 (regs 86–122) (legal proceedings); and PARA 765 et seq. As to the questioning of elections to the European Parliament see also the European Parliamentary Election Petition Rules 1979, SI 1979/521, which, by virtue of the Interpretation Act 1978 s 17(2)(b), have effect under the European Parliamentary Elections Regulations 2004, SI 2004/293, reg 120 (rules of procedure); and PARA 767 et seq.
15　See PARA 16 et seq.

(4)　THE DIFFERENT TYPES OF REFERENDUM

14.　National and regional referendums.　Part VII of the Political Parties, Elections and Referendums Act 2000[1] provides standing arrangements for the conduct of any referendum[2] held throughout: (1) the United Kingdom[3]; (2) one or more of England[4], Scotland, Wales[5] and Northern Ireland[6]. Within the framework of these arrangements, further legislation is required to provide for the holding of any particular referendum[7].

A poll held in an area consisting of Wales or any part (or parts) of Wales for the purpose of ascertaining the views of those polled about whether or how any of the functions of the Welsh Ministers should be exercised[8] is not a referendum to which the Political Parties, Elections and Referendums Act 2000[9] applies[10]. Nor do the provisions of that Act apply to referendums or polls which are not included in heads (1) and (2) above, most notably referendums held by local authorities or polls held consequent on parish or community meetings[11].

1　Ie the Political Parties, Elections and Referendums Act 2000 Pt VII (ss 101–129) (see PARA 527 et seq), subject to s 101(2)–(5): see s 101(1); and PARA 527.
2　As to the meaning of 'referendum' for these purposes see PARA 527.
3　See the Political Parties, Elections and Referendums Act 2000 s 101(1)(a); and PARA 527. As to the meaning of 'United Kingdom' see PARA 1 note 1.
4　As to the meaning of 'England' see PARA 1 note 1.
5　As to the meaning of 'Wales' see PARA 1 note 1. See also the text and notes 8–10.
6　See the Political Parties, Elections and Referendums Act 2000 s 101(1)(b); and PARA 527. A further head, relating to any region in England specified in the Regional Development Agencies Act 1998 s 1, Sch 1, is set out in the Political Parties, Elections and Referendums Act 2000 s 101(c), but the Regional Development Agencies Act 1998 s 1, Sch 1 has been repealed by the Public Bodies Act 2011 s 30(3), Sch 6, with effect from 1 July 2012 (see the Public Bodies Act 2011 (Commencement No 2) Order 2012, SI 2012/1662, art 2(2)(b)).
7　See eg the Regional Assemblies (Preparations) Act 2003 (repealed by the Local Democracy, Economic Development and Construction Act 2009 Sch 7 Pt 4, with effect from 1 April 2010); and the Parliamentary Voting System and Constituencies Act 2011 Pt 1 (ss 1–9, Schs 1–10, 12 Pt 1) (s 9, Schs 10, 12 Pt 1 repealed). See also the European Union Act 2011 Pt 1 (ss 1–14); and CONSTITUTIONAL LAW AND HUMAN RIGHTS.
8　Ie a poll held under the Government of Wales Act 2006 s 64 (see PARA 105): see the Political Parties, Elections and Referendums Act 2000 s 101(3); and PARA 527.
9　Ie the Political Parties, Elections and Referendums Act 2000 Pt VII: see s 101(3); and PARA 527.
10　See the Political Parties, Elections and Referendums Act 2000 s 101(3); and PARA 527.
11　See PARA 15.

15. Local referendums and polls. A local authority[1] must, in certain circumstances, hold a referendum under the Local Government Act 2000 on proposals for changes to arrangements for local governance before taking any steps to implement them[2]. Such a referendum also may be held at a more local level under local government finance or local planning legislation (for example, to approve Council Tax increases or neighbourhood development plans)[3].

A local authority may conduct a poll to ascertain the views of those polled about: (1) any matter relating to services provided in pursuance of the authority's functions or the authority's expenditure on such services; or (2) any other matter if it is one relating to the authority's power to promote the economic, social or environmental well-being of its area[4].

A poll may be demanded before the conclusion of a parish or community meeting[5] on any question arising at the meeting[6].

1   As to the meaning of 'local authority' for these purposes see LOCAL GOVERNMENT vol 69 (2009) PARA 23.

2   See the Local Government Act 2000 Pt 1A (ss 9B–9R) (arrangements with respect to local governance in England), Pt II (ss 10–48A) (Local authorities in Wales: arrangements with respect to executives etc); and LOCAL GOVERNMENT vol 69 (2009) PARA 303 et seq. Provision for the conduct for such referendums is made by the Local Authorities (Conduct of Referendums) (Wales) Regulations 2008, SI 2008/1848, and the Local Authorities (Conduct of Referendums) (England) Regulations 2012, SI 2012/323, which contain bespoke Local Government Act referendums rules (see the Local Authorities (Conduct of Referendums) (Wales) Regulations 2008, SI 2008/1848, reg 8, Sch 3; the Local Authorities (Conduct of Referendums) (England) Regulations 2012, SI 2012/323, reg 8, Sch 3; and PARA 555 et seq) as well as provision made for applying and modifying electoral Acts and subordinate legislation for the purpose, as follows:
   (1)   various specified provisions of the Representation of the People Act 1983 have effect, in relation to such a referendum, subject to the modifications specified in the Local Authorities (Conduct of Referendums) (Wales) Regulations 2008, SI 2008/1848, reg 8, Sch 4 Table 1 (Representation of the People Act 1983), and the Local Authorities (Conduct of Referendums) (England) Regulations 2012, SI 2012/323, reg 8, Sch 4 Table 1 (Representation of the People Act 1983);
   (2)   the Representation of the People Act 1985 s 15 (combination of polls at parliamentary, European and local elections: see PARA 17 et seq) has effect, in relation to such a referendum held in England, subject to the modifications specified in the Local Authorities (Conduct of Referendums) (England) Regulations 2012, SI 2012/323, Sch 4 Table 2 (Representation of the People Act 1985);
   (3)   the Representation of the People Act 2000 s 10 (pilot schemes for local elections in England and Wales: see PARAS 521, 522), s 12 (changes relating to absent voting at elections in Great Britain: see PARA 363 et seq), Sch 4 (absent voting at elections in Great Britain: see PARA 363 et seq) have effect, in relation to such a referendum, subject to the modifications specified in the Local Authorities (Conduct of Referendums) (Wales) Regulations 2008, SI 2008/1848, Sch 4 Table 2 (Representation of the People Act 2000), and the Local Authorities (Conduct of Referendums) (England) Regulations 2012, SI 2012/323, Sch 4 Table 3 (Representation of the People Act 2000);
   (4)   the Political Parties, Elections and Referendums Act 2000 ss 6A–6F (Commission representatives and accredited observers to attend electoral proceedings and observe working practices: see PARA 53) have effect, in relation to such a referendum, subject to the modifications specified in the Local Authorities (Conduct of Referendums) (Wales) Regulations 2008, SI 2008/1848, Sch 4 Table 3 (Political Parties, Elections and Referendums Act 2000), and the Local Authorities (Conduct of Referendums) (England) Regulations 2012, SI 2012/323, Sch 4 Table 4 (Political Parties, Elections and Referendums Act 2000);
   (5)   the Electoral Administration Act 2006 ss 42–44 (election documents: see PARA 505 et seq), s 46 (returning officers: correction of procedural errors: see PARAS 530 note 26, 354 note 25) and s 69 (encouraging electoral participation: see PARAS 141 144, 350 et seq) have effect, in relation to such a referendum, subject to the modifications specified in the Local Authorities (Conduct of Referendums) (Wales) Regulations 2008, SI 2008/1848, Sch 4 Table 4 (Electoral Administration Act 2006), and the Local

Authorities (Conduct of Referendums) (England) Regulations 2012, SI 2012/323, Sch 4 Table 5 (Electoral Administration Act 2006); and

(6)   various specified provisions of the Representation of the People (England and Wales) Regulations 2001, SI 2001/341, have effect, in relation to such a referendum, subject to the modifications specified in the Local Authorities (Conduct of Referendums) (Wales) Regulations 2008, SI 2008/1848, Sch 4 Table 5 (Representation of the People (England and Wales) Regulations 2001), and the Local Authorities (Conduct of Referendums) (England) Regulations 2012, SI 2012/323, Sch 4 Table 6 (Representation of the People (England and Wales) Regulations 2001).

At the date at which this volume states the law, the Local Authorities (Conduct of Referendums) (Wales) Regulations 2008, SI 2008/1848, make no provision for polls at local authority referendums in Wales to be taken together with polls at another election or referendum (see head (2) above). As to the meanings of 'England' and 'Wales' see PARA 1 note 1.

3   The approach of combining bespoke rules with applied and modified provisions (ie the approach used to regulate the conduct of local authority referendums: see note 2) is adopted to conduct polls where provision has been made for local referendums to be held under local government finance or local planning legislation, but these referendums are not otherwise discussed in this title.

4   See the Local Government Act 2003 s 116; and PARA 557 et seq.

5   As to parish and community meetings see LOCAL GOVERNMENT vol 69 (2009) PARA 635 et seq.

6   See the Local Government Act 1972 s 99, Sch 12 Pt III para 18(4)–(6), Pt V para 34(4)–(6); and LOCAL GOVERNMENT vol 69 (2009) PARA 638. As to the conduct of such a poll see PARA 556. Such a poll may be taken also on a question relating to an appointment to office, and this form is discussed in this title in the context of elections: see PARA 383 et seq.

(5) COMBINED POLLS

(i) In general

16.   General provision for the combination of polls.   Provision is made in statute and in related legislation for polls that are to be taken on the same date to be taken together in the following combinations[1]:

(1)   a parliamentary general election and a European Parliamentary general election[2];

(2)   an ordinary local government election and a parliamentary general election[3];

(3)   an ordinary local government election and a European Parliamentary general election[4];

(4)   an election for the return of an elected mayor and any other election[5] specified in regulations[6];

(5)   an ordinary Welsh Assembly election and an ordinary local government election[7];

(6)   elections taken on the same day for related areas[8], being:

(a)   the ordinary election of district councillors for any district ward or an election to fill a casual vacancy occurring in the office of such a councillor and the ordinary election of parish councillors for any parish or an election to fill a casual vacancy occurring in the office of such a councillor[9];

(b)   the ordinary election of councillors for any electoral division of a county in England in which there are no district councils or an election to fill a casual vacancy occurring in the office of such a councillor, and the ordinary election of parish councillors for any parish or an election to fill a casual vacancy occurring in the office of such a councillor[10];

(c)   the ordinary election of councillors for any electoral division of a

Welsh county or county borough or an election to fill a casual vacancy occurring in the office of such a councillor, and the ordinary election of community councillors for any community or an election to fill a casual vacancy occurring in the office of such a councillor[11];

(d) a local authority mayoral election and an election falling within any of heads (a) to (c) above[12];

(7) elections (or the polls at elections and a local authority referendum) which are not otherwise required to be taken together, but may nevertheless be so taken if the returning officer for each election thinks fit[13];

(8) the polls at referendums held in England under the Local Government Act 2000 and the poll at any other election specified in regulations[14];

(9) the polls at referendums held in England under the Local Government Act 2000 taken on the same day, at the district and/or county level[15].

The rules of conduct that relate to each type of election or referendum mentioned in heads (1) to (8) above are applied and modified for the purposes of accommodating each combination of poll specified in heads (1) to (8) above[16].

Provision has been made also in relation to the discharge of the functions of the respective returning officers (and counting officers, as the case may be)[17], the polling stations to be used[18], and proceedings on the issue and receipt of postal ballot papers[19], in connection with the combining of polls at such elections (or, in England, at such elections and/or referendums, as the case may be).

1 As to the combination of polls generally see PARAS 1, 3 et seq.
2 See PARA 21.
3 See PARA 22. This category includes a parliamentary general election taken together with a London Authority election (included in the definition of 'local government election' for the purposes of the Representation of the People Act 1983): see PARA 22. Until 2 April 2013, the poll at parish or community council elections was not to be combined with the poll at a parliamentary or European parliamentary election: see PARA 25.
4 See PARA 24. This category includes a European parliamentary general election taken together with a London Authority election: see PARA 24. See note 3.
5 This category also includes a local authority mayoral election (other than a Greater London Authority election) taken together with a London Authority election: see PARA 26.
6 See PARA 26. The regulations referred to in the text are those made under the Local Government Act 2000 ss 9HE(2)(d), 44(2)(d), 105, which may make provision for the combination of polls at elections for the return of elected mayors and other elections: see PARA 26.
7 Particular provision is made for Assembly elections taken together with a local authority mayoral election, an election of county or county borough councillors, or an election of community councillors: see PARA 23.
8 As to the meaning of 'related areas' see PARAS 28–30. See note 3.
9 See PARA 28.
10 See PARA 28.
11 See PARA 28.
12 See PARA 29.
13 See PARAS 30, 31. This category includes a local government election (other than a Greater London Authority election) taken together with a London Authority election: see PARA 30.
14 See PARA 27. The regulations referred to in the text are those made under the Local Government Act 2000 s 9MG (ie, the Local Authorities (Conduct of Referendums) (England) Regulations 2012, SI 2012/323: see PARA 558): see PARA 27. At the date at which this volume states the law, the Local Authorities (Conduct of Referendums) (Wales) Regulations 2008, SI 2008/1848, make no provision for polls at local authority referendums in Wales to be taken together with polls at another election or referendum. As to the meanings of 'England' and 'Wales' see PARA 1 note 1.
15 See PARA 32.
16 See PARAS 21–32.

17 As to the transferred functions of returning officers and counting officers where polls are combined see PARA 18.
18 As to the polling stations to be used where polls are combined see PARA 19.
19 As to proceedings on the issue and receipt of postal ballot papers where polls are combined see PARA 20.

17. Expenses at combined polls. Where the polls at certain local government and general elections in England and Wales[1] are combined[2], the cost of taking the combined polls (excluding any cost solely attributable to one election) and any cost attributable to their combination must be apportioned equally among the elections[3].

Where the polls at a Welsh Assembly general election[4] and an ordinary local government election[5] are combined[6], the cost of taking the combined polls (excluding any cost solely attributable to one election) and any cost attributable to their combination must be apportioned among the elections in such proportions as the Assembly may by order specify[7]. However, where the polls at an Assembly election[8] and local government election for related areas[9] are to be taken on the same date[10], the cost of taking the combined polls (excluding any cost solely attributable to one election) and any cost attributable to their combination must be apportioned equally among the elections[11].

Where the polls at any elections and a local authority referendum in England[12] are combined[13], the cost of taking the combined polls (excluding any cost solely attributable to one election or the referendum) and any cost attributable to their combination must be apportioned equally among the elections and the referendum[14].

1 As to the meanings of 'England' and 'Wales' see PARA 1 note 1.
2 Ie where the polls at any elections are combined under the Representation of the People Act 1983 s 36 or under the Representation of the People Act 1985 s 15 (see PARA 21 et seq): see the Representation of the People Act 1983 s 36(3B) (substituted by the Representation of the People Act 1985 s 17); and the Representation of the People Act 1985 s 15(4). As to polls at different referendums which are taken at the same time see PARA 32.
    The Representation of the People Act 1983 s 36 and the Representation of the People Act 1985 s 15 are applied and modified for the purpose of mayoral elections in England and Wales by the Local Authorities (Mayoral Elections) (England and Wales) Regulations 2007, SI 2007/1024, reg 3(2)–(5), Sch 2 Tables 1, 2: see PARA 11 note 14. As to elections for the return of an elected local authority mayor see PARA 198.
3 Representation of the People Act 1983 s 36(3B) (as substituted: see note 2); Representation of the People Act 1985 s 15(4) (as originally enacted; and as applied and modified (see note 2)). As to the discharge of a returning officer's functions including payments made consequently see PARA 350 et seq.
4 For these purposes, 'Assembly general election' means the holding of constituency and regional elections for the return of all Assembly members: see the National Assembly for Wales (Representation of the People) Order 2007, SI 2007/236, art 2(1). As to the meanings of 'constituency election' and 'regional election' for these purposes see PARA 3 note 2.
5 For these purposes, 'local government election' includes a mayoral election; and 'mayoral election' means an election for the return of an elected mayor of a local authority in Wales: see the National Assembly for Wales (Representation of the People) Order 2007, SI 2007/236, art 2(1).
6 Ie under the National Assembly for Wales (Representation of the People) Order 2007, SI 2007/236, art 16(1) (see PARA 23): see art 16(4).
7 National Assembly for Wales (Representation of the People) Order 2007, SI 2007/236, art 16(4). The power to make orders under art 16(4) must be exercised by statutory instrument and for the purposes of the Statutory Instruments Act 1946 s 1 (definition of 'statutory instrument': see STATUTES AND LEGISLATIVE PROCESS vol 96 (2012) PARA 1045), the National Assembly for Wales (Representation of the People) Order 2007, SI 2007/236, art 16(6) has effect as if contained in an Act of Parliament: art 16(6). An order under art 16(4) may specify different proportions in relation to different functions: see art 16(4). The National Assembly for Wales (Combination of Polls) (Apportionment of Cost) Order 1999, SI 1999/943, art 3, has effect as if

made under the National Assembly for Wales (Representation of the People) Order 2007, SI 2007/236, art 16(4), by virtue of the Interpretation Act 1978 s 17(2)(b).

8   As to the meaning of 'Assembly election' see PARA 3 note 2.

9   Ie where one area is coterminous with or situated wholly or partly within the other: see the National Assembly for Wales (Representation of the People) Order 2007, SI 2007/236, art 16(3); and PARA 30.

10 Ie under the National Assembly for Wales (Representation of the People) Order 2007, SI 2007/236, art 16(2) (see PARA 30): see art 16(5).

11 National Assembly for Wales (Representation of the People) Order 2007, SI 2007/236, art 16(5).

12 The Representation of the People Act 1983 s 36 and the Representation of the People Act 1985 s 15 are applied and modified for the purpose of a local authority referendum in England by the Local Authorities (Conduct of Referendums) (England) Regulations 2012, SI 2012/323, reg 11(3), Sch 4 Tables 1, 2: see PARA 27 note 7. There is no provision made for the combination of polls in the Local Authorities (Conduct of Referendums) (Wales) Regulations 2008, SI 2008/1848.

13 Ie under the Representation of the People Act 1985 s 15 (as applied and modified: see note 12): see s 15(4) (as so applied and modified).

14 Representation of the People Act 1985 s 15(4) (as applied and modified: see note 12).

18.   Transferred functions of returning officer where polls are combined. Where polls are combined, the following functions of the returning officer at one election or referendum[1] must be discharged by the returning officer at the other election or referendum[2]:

(1)   preparing the corresponding number list[3];

(2)   giving notice of the situation of polling stations[4];

(3)   the provision of polling stations[5];

(4)   the appointment of presiding officers and clerks to assist them[6];

(5)   the equipment of polling stations[7];

(6)   notification of the requirement of secrecy at polling stations[8];

(7)   signing a certificate as to employment for a person employed by a returning officer[9];

(8)   authorisation to order removal of persons from polling stations[10];

(9)   functions in connection with the verification of the ballot paper accounts and the separation of the ballot papers[11]; and

(10)   where the proceedings on the issue and receipt of postal ballot papers at more than one election or referendum in England, or at two or more elections in Wales, are taken together[12], the issue, receipt and return of postal ballot papers[13], as well as the general functions conferred for those purposes[14].

Where those functions of a returning officer at an election or referendum which are specified in heads (1) to (10) above are discharged by the returning officer at another election or referendum in England[15], the provisions about expenses in the Representation of the People Act 1983[16] are modified[17]; and, where those functions of a returning officer at an election which are specified in heads (1) to (10) above are discharged by the returning officer at another election in Wales[18], the provisions about expenses in both the Representation of the People Act 1983 and the National Assembly for Wales (Representation of the People) Order 2007[19] are modified[20].

1   For these purposes, 'referendum' means a referendum conducted under the Local Authorities (Conduct of Referendums) (England) Regulations 2012, SI 2012/323 (see PARA 555 et seq): see the Representation of the People (Combination of Polls) (England and Wales) Regulations 2004, SI 2004/294, reg 2(1); Interpretation Act 1978 s 17(2)(b). In the case of a referendum, a reference to a returning officer must be construed as a reference to a counting officer, within the meaning of the Local Authorities (Conduct of Referendums) (England) Regulations 2012,

SI 2012/323, reg 2(1) (see PARA 576 note 1): see the Representation of the People (Combination of Polls) (England and Wales) Regulations 2004, SI 2004/294, reg 2(2); Interpretation Act 1978 s 17(2)(b). There is no provision made for the combination of polls in the Local Authorities (Conduct of Referendums) (Wales) Regulations 2008, SI 2008/1848. As to the meanings of 'England' and 'Wales' see PARA 1 note 1. As to returning officers generally see PARA 350 et seq. As to polls at different referendums which are taken at the same time see PARA 32.

The functions of the returning officer mentioned in the text are those conferred, at a parliamentary election, by rules contained in the Representation of the People Act 1983 s 23(1), Sch 1 (see PARA 383 note 2) that are specified in the Representation of the People (Combination of Polls) (England and Wales) Regulations 2004, SI 2004/294, reg 5(2) (see heads (1)–(10) in the text); and: (1) at a European parliamentary election, by corresponding rules that are contained in the regulations made under the European Parliamentary Elections Act 2002 s 7 (see PARA 13); (2) at a local government election, by corresponding rules that are contained in rules made under the Representation of the People Act 1983 s 36 (see PARA 383); (3) at a mayoral election, by corresponding rules that are contained in the regulations made under the Local Government Act 2000 ss 9HE, 105 (conduct of elections for the return of elected mayors in England: see PARA 383), ss 44, 105 (conduct of elections for the return of elected mayors in Wales: see PARA 383); (4) at a local authority referendum, by corresponding rules that are contained in the regulations made under the Local Government Act 2000 ss 9MG, 105 (conduct of local authority referendums in England: see PARA 558), ss 45, 105 (conduct of local authority referendums in Wales: see PARA 558); and (5) at the election of a police and crime commissioner in accordance with the Police Reform and Social Responsibility Act 2011 Pt 1 Ch 6 (ss 50–76, Schs 9, 10) (Police and Crime Commissioners: elections and vacancies: see POLICE AND INVESTIGATORY POWERS vol 84 (2013) PARA 62 et seq) (a 'PCC election'), by corresponding rules that are contained in an order made under ss 58, 154 (conduct of Police and Crime Commissioner Elections): see the Representation of the People (Combination of Polls) (England and Wales) Regulations 2004, SI 2004/294, reg 5(1)(a)–(f) (reg 5(1)(f) added by SI 2012/1917); Interpretation Act 1978 s 17(2)(b). 'Mayoral election' means an election conducted under the Local Authorities (Mayoral Elections) (England and Wales) Regulations 2007, SI 2007/1024: see the Representation of the People (Combination of Polls) (England and Wales) Regulations 2004, SI 2004/294, reg 2(1); Interpretation Act 1978 s 17(2)(b).

The functions of the returning officer mentioned in the text are those conferred, in the case of a Welsh Assembly election, by rules contained in the National Assembly for Wales (Representation of the People) Order 2007, SI 2007/236, art 17(1), Sch 5 (see PARA 383) that are specified in art 16(7), Sch 4 para 2(2) (see heads (1)–(10) in the text); and: (a) in the case of a local government election which is not a mayoral election, by corresponding rules that are contained in rules made under the Representation of the People Act 1983 s 36; and (b) in the case of a local government election which is a mayoral election, by corresponding rules that are contained in the regulations made under the Local Government Act 2000 ss 44, 105: see the National Assembly for Wales (Representation of the People) Order 2007, SI 2007/236, Sch 4 para 2(1)(a)–(c). As to the meaning of 'Assembly election' for these purposes see PARA 3 note 2; and as to the meaning of 'local government election' for these purposes see PARA 17 note 5.

2 See the Representation of the People (Combination of Polls) (England and Wales) Regulations 2004, SI 2004/294, reg 4; and the National Assembly for Wales (Representation of the People) Order 2007, SI 2007/236, Sch 4 para 1.

Where the poll at a parliamentary general election is taken together with the poll at another election or referendum in England, or at another election in Wales, under a relevant enactment, those functions of the returning officer at the poll at the other election or referendum which are specified in heads (1)–(10) in the text must be discharged by the returning officer at the parliamentary election for such part of the electoral region, local government area, voting area or police area (as the case may be) as is situated in the parliamentary constituency: Representation of the People (Combination of Polls) (England and Wales) Regulations 2004, SI 2004/294, reg 4(1)(a) (amended by SI 2012/1917). For these purposes, 'relevant enactment' means any of the Representation of the People Act 1985 s 15(1) (see PARA 21 et seq), or the Representation of the People Act 1983 s 36(3), s 36(3AB) or s 36(3AC) (see PARAS 28, 29), and includes a reference to each of those provisions as applied in orders or regulations made under any of the 'listed provisions' (ie under the Local Government Finance Act 1992 ss 52ZQ, 113 (referendums relating to council tax increases: see LOCAL GOVERNMENT FINANCE vol 70 (2012) PARA 356), the Local Government Act 2000 ss 9HE, 105 (conduct of elections for the return of elected mayors in England: see PARA 383), ss 9MG, 105 (conduct of local authority referendums in England: see PARA 558), ss 44, 105 conduct of elections for the return of elected mayors in Wales: see PARA 383), or ss 45, 105 (conduct of local authority referendums in Wales: see PARA 558), and the Police Reform and Social Responsibility Act 2011 ss 58, 154 (conduct of Police and Crime Commissioner Elections: see POLICE AND INVESTIGATORY POWERS vol 84 (2013) PARA 62 et seq)): see the Representation of the People (Combination of Polls) (England and Wales) Regulations 2004, SI 2004/294, reg 4(10) (definition of 'relevant enactment' amended, definition of 'listed provisions' added, by SI 2012/1917). 'Police area' means a police area listed in the Police Act 1996 Sch 1 (police areas outside London: see POLICE AND INVESTIGATORY POWERS vol 84 (2013) PARA 52): see the Representation of the People (Combination of Polls) (England and Wales) Regulations 2004, SI 2004/294, reg 4(10) (definition added by SI 2012/1917).

Where the Representation of the People (Combination of Polls) (England and Wales) Regulations 2004, SI 2004/294, reg 4(1) does not apply, and where the poll at an ordinary Authority election is taken together with the poll at another election or referendum under a relevant enactment, those functions of the returning officer at the poll at the other election or referendum which are specified in heads (1)–(10) in the text must be discharged by the returning officer at the Authority election for such part of the electoral region, local government area, voting area or police area (as the case may be) as is situated in the area for which he acts: reg 4(2)(a) (amended by SI 2012/1917). For the purposes of the Representation of the People (Combination of Polls) (England and Wales) Regulations 2004, SI 2004/294, reg 4, except the first reference in reg 4(8)(a), any reference to a returning officer which applies to the returning officer at a European parliamentary election must be construed as including a reference to the local returning officer, any reference to a returning officer which applies to the returning officer at an Authority election must be construed as a reference to the constituency returning officer for the Assembly constituency in which the functions specified in heads (1)–(10) in the text are to be discharged, and any reference to a returning officer which applies to the returning officer at a PCC election must be construed as including a reference to the police area returning officer: see reg 4(11) (amended by SI 2012/1917).

Where neither the Representation of the People (Combination of Polls) (England and Wales) Regulations 2004, SI 2004/294, reg 4(1) nor reg 4(2) applies, and where the poll at an ordinary county council election is taken together with the poll at another election or referendum in England, or at another election in Wales, under a relevant enactment, those functions of the returning officer at the poll at the other election (or referendum, as the case may be) which are specified in heads (1)–(10) in the text must be discharged by the returning officer at the county council election for such part of the electoral region, local government area, voting area or police area (as the case may be) as is situated in the county or county borough: reg 4(3)(a) (amended by SI 2012/1917). For these purposes, 'county council election' means an election of councillors of a county or county borough (see PARA 10): see the Representation of the People (Combination of Polls) (England and Wales) Regulations 2004, SI 2004/294, reg 4(10).

Where none of reg 4(1)–(3) applies, and where the poll at an ordinary principal area council election (other than a county council election) is taken together with the poll at another election or referendum in England, or at another election in Wales, under a relevant enactment, those functions of the returning officer at the poll at the other election (or referendum, as the case may be) which are specified in heads (1)–(10) in the text must be discharged by the returning officer at the principal area council election for such part of the electoral region, local government area, voting area or police area (as the case may be) as is situated in the principal area: reg 4(4)(a) (amended by SI 2012/1917). For these purposes, 'principal area' means a county, district or London borough in England, or a county or county borough in Wales; and 'principal area council election' means an election of councillors of London borough councillors (as the case may be) of a principal area: see the Representation of the People (Combination of Polls) (England and Wales) Regulations 2004, SI 2004/294, reg 4(10). As to local government areas in England and Wales see LOCAL GOVERNMENT vol 69 (2009) PARA 22 et seq. As to Greater London as an administrative area see LONDON GOVERNMENT vol 71 (2013) PARA 14.

Where none of the Representation of the People (Combination of Polls) (England and Wales) Regulations 2004, SI 2004/294, reg 4(1)–(4) applies, and where the poll at a mayoral election is taken together with the poll at an election under a relevant enactment, those functions of the returning officer at the poll at the other election which are specified in heads (1)–(10) in the text must be discharged by the returning officer at the mayoral election for such part of the electoral region, local government area or police area (as the case may be) as is situated in the local government area as respects which the mayoral election is held: reg 4(5)(a) (amended by SI 2012/1917).

Where none of the Representation of the People (Combination of Polls) (England and Wales) Regulations 2004, SI 2004/294, reg 4(1)–(5) applies, and where, in England, the poll at a referendum is taken together with the poll at an election under a relevant enactment, those functions of the returning officer at the poll at the election which are specified in heads (1)–(10) in the text must be discharged by the returning officer at the referendum for such part of the electoral region, local government area or police area (as the case may be) as is situated in the voting area: reg 4(6)(a) (amended by SI 2012/1917).

Where none of the Representation of the People (Combination of Polls) (England and Wales) Regulations 2004, SI 2004/294, reg 4(1)–(6) applies, and where the poll at an ordinary parish or community council election is taken together with the poll at another election under a relevant enactment, those functions of the returning officer at the other election which are specified in heads (1)–(10) in the text must be discharged by the returning officer at the parish or community council election for such part of the electoral region or police area as is situated in the area of the parish or community council: reg 4(7)(a) (reg 4(7) substituted, reg 4(7A) added, by SI 2012/1917).

Where none of the Representation of the People (Combination of Polls) (England and Wales) Regulations 2004, SI 2004/294, reg 4(1)–(7) applies, and where the poll at a PCC election is taken together with the poll at a European parliamentary election under a relevant enactment, those functions of the returning officer at the European parliamentary election which are specified in heads (1)–(10) in the text must be discharged by the returning officer at the PCC election for such part of the electoral region as is situated in the police area: reg 4(7A)(a) (as so added).

Where the polls for related areas (within the meaning of the Representation of the People Act 1985 s 15(3): see PARA 30) are taken together under s 15(2) (including by virtue of s 15(2) and s 15(3) as applied by orders or regulations made under any of the 'listed provisions') (see PARA 30) (see the Representation of the People (Combination of Polls) (England and Wales) Regulations 2004, SI 2004/294, reg 4(8) (reg 4(8), (9) amended by SI 2012/1917)), the returning officers for each election (or referendum, as the case may be) must decide which returning officer is to discharge in the related area those functions of the other (or others) which are specified in heads (1)–(10) in the text (except that the returning officer at a European parliamentary election must not discharge those functions) (Representation of the People (Combination of Polls) (England and Wales) Regulations 2004, SI 2004/294, reg 4(8)(a)). However, where the polls at two or more elections (or, in England, at more than one election or referendum) are taken together other than under a relevant enactment, but one or more such polls are also taken together with the poll at another election (or a referendum, as the case may be) under a relevant enactment, the provisions of reg 4(1)–(7A) apply as if each election (other than a mayoral election) were an ordinary election, and as if the polls at each election (or referendum) were taken together under a relevant enactment: see reg 4(9) (as so amended).

Where the polls at a Welsh Assembly general election and an ordinary local government election are taken together under the National Assembly for Wales (Representation of the People) Order 2007, SI 2007/236, art 16(1) (see PARA 23), those functions of the returning officer at the local government election which are specified in heads (1)–(10) in the text must be discharged by the constituency returning officer for an Assembly constituency for such part of the local government area as is situated in the constituency: Sch 4 para 1(1)(a). For these purposes, 'constituency returning officer' means the person who is the returning officer for a constituency election: see art 2(1). As to the meaning of 'constituency election' for these purposes see PARA 3 note 2. As to Welsh Assembly general elections see PARA 12; and as to returning officers for Welsh Assembly elections see PARA 357 et seq.

Where the polls at a Welsh Assembly election and a local government election for related areas (ie within the meaning of art 16(3)) are taken together under art 16(2) (see PARA 30), the returning officers for those elections must decide which returning officer is to discharge in the area in which the polls are combined (the 'combined area') those functions of the other which are specified in heads (1)–(10) in the text: Sch 4 para 1(2)(a). Where the polls at a Welsh Assembly general election and a local government election for related areas are taken together under art 16(2), however, then Sch 4 para 1(1)(a) also applies: Sch 4 para 1(4). Where, by virtue of Sch 4 para 1(2)(a), functions in respect of another election fall to be discharged by a regional returning officer, he in turn must delegate the discharge of those functions to the constituency returning officer for an Assembly constituency that is wholly or partly situated in the combined area in relation to such part of the combined area as is situated in the Assembly constituency; and, where functions are so delegated, subsequent references in Sch 4 Pt I paras 1–3 (see also the text and notes 1, 3–20) to the returning officer who discharges the functions specified in heads (1)–(10) in the text are to be treated as references to such a constituency returning officer: Sch 4 para 1(3). For these purposes, 'regional returning officer' means the person who is the returning officer for a regional election: see art 2(1). As to the meaning of 'regional election' for these purposes see PARA 3 note 2.

Accordingly, for the purposes of the National Assembly for Wales (Representation of the People) Order 2007, SI 2007/236, 'appropriate returning officer' means a constituency returning officer in relation to a constituency election and a regional returning officer in relation to a regional election: see art 2(1).

3   Ie under the Representation of the People Act 1983 Sch 1 r 19A or the National Assembly for Wales (Representation of the People) Order 2007, SI 2007/236, Sch 5 para 27 (see PARA 387): see the Representation of the People (Combination of Polls) (England and Wales) Regulations 2004, SI 2004/294, reg 5(2)(za), (zb) (reg 5(2)(za), (zb) added by SI 2006/3278); and the National Assembly for Wales (Representation of the People) Order 2007, SI 2007/236, Sch 4 para 2(2)(a). Head (1) in the text applies to the Representation of the People Act 1983 Sch 1 r 19A:

(1)   to the extent that it relates to ballot papers to be provided in pursuance of Sch 1 r 29 (see PARA 391) (see the Representation of the People (Combination of Polls) (England and Wales) Regulations 2004, SI 2004/294, reg 5(2)(za) (as so added)); and

(2)   where proceedings on the issue and receipt of postal ballot papers at more than one election or referendum are taken together under the Representation of the People (England and Wales) Regulations 2001, SI 2001/341, reg 65 (see PARA 20) (see the Representation of the People (Combination of Polls) (England and Wales) Regulations 2004, SI 2004/294, reg 5(2)(zb) (as so added)).

For these purposes, references to the Representation of the People (England and Wales) Regulations 2001, SI 2001/341, reg 65, include references to: (a) the provisions in regulations made under the European Parliamentary Elections Act 2002 s 7 which correspond to that regulation; (b) that regulation as applied by regulations made under the Local Government Act 2000 ss 44, 105 or ss 45, 105; and (c) the provisions in an order made under the Police Reform and Social Responsibility Act 2011 ss 58, 154, which correspond to the Representation of the People (England and Wales) Regulations 2001, SI 2001/341, reg 65: see the Representation of the People (Combination of Polls) (England and Wales) Regulations 2004, SI 2004/294, reg 5(3) (amended by SI 2012/1917).

4   Ie under the Representation of the People Act 1983 Sch 1 r 23(2) or the National Assembly for Wales (Representation of the People) Order 2007, SI 2007/236, Sch 5 para 32(2), (3) (see PARA 388): see the Representation of the People (Combination of Polls) (England and Wales) Regulations 2004, SI 2004/294, reg 5(2)(a); and the National Assembly for Wales (Representation of the People) Order 2007, SI 2007/236, Sch 4 para 2(2)(b).

5   Ie under the Representation of the People Act 1983 Sch 1 r 25 or under the National Assembly for Wales (Representation of the People) Order 2007, SI 2007/236, Sch 5 para 34 (see PARA 390): see the Representation of the People (Combination of Polls) (England and Wales) Regulations 2004, SI 2004/294, reg 5(2)(c); and the National Assembly for Wales (Representation of the People) Order 2007, SI 2007/236, Sch 4 para 2(2)(d).

6   Ie to the extent that the rule under the Representation of the People Act 1983 Sch 1 r 26(1), (2) or under the National Assembly for Wales (Representation of the People) Order 2007, SI 2007/236, Sch 5 para 35(1), (3) (see PARA 393) concerns such appointments: see the Representation of the People (Combination of Polls) (England and Wales) Regulations 2004, SI 2004/294, reg 5(2)(d); and the National Assembly for Wales (Representation of the People) Order 2007, SI 2007/236, Sch 4 para 2(2)(e).

7   Ie under the Representation of the People Act 1983 Sch 1 r 29 or under the National Assembly for Wales (Representation of the People) Order 2007, SI 2007/236, Sch 5 para 37 (see PARA 391): see the Representation of the People (Combination of Polls) (England and Wales) Regulations 2004, SI 2004/294, reg 5(2)(e); and the National Assembly for Wales (Representation of the People) Order 2007, SI 2007/236, Sch 4 para 2(2)(f).

8   Ie under the Representation of the People Act 1983 Sch 1 r 31(a) or under the National Assembly for Wales (Representation of the People) Order 2007, SI 2007/236, Sch 5 para 39(a) (see PARA 385): see the Representation of the People (Combination of Polls) (England and Wales) Regulations 2004, SI 2004/294, reg 5(2)(f); and the National Assembly for Wales (Representation of the People) Order 2007, SI 2007/236, Sch 4 para 2(2)(g).

9   Ie under the Representation of the People Act 1983 Sch 1 r 32(3) or under the National Assembly for Wales (Representation of the People) Order 2007, SI 2007/236, Sch 5 para 41(5) (see PARA 395): see the Representation of the People (Combination of Polls) (England and Wales) Regulations 2004, SI 2004/294, reg 5(2)(g); and the National Assembly for Wales (Representation of the People) Order 2007, SI 2007/236, Sch 4 para 2(2)(i).

10   Ie under the Representation of the People Act 1983 Sch 1 r 33(2)(b) or under the National Assembly for Wales (Representation of the People) Order 2007, SI 2007/236, Sch 5 para 42(2)(b) (see PARA 396): see the Representation of the People (Combination of Polls)

(England and Wales) Regulations 2004, SI 2004/294, reg 5(2)(h); and the National Assembly for Wales (Representation of the People) Order 2007, SI 2007/236, Sch 4 para 2(2)(j).

11 Ie under the Representation of the People Act 1983 Sch 1 r 45(1), (5) (r 45(1) as substituted, applied and modified by the Representation of the People (Combination of Polls) (England and Wales) Regulations 2004, SI 2004/294, reg 8, Sch 2 para 22) or the National Assembly for Wales (Representation of the People) Order 2007, SI 2007/236, Sch 5 para 55(1), (8) (Sch 5 para 55(1) as substituted, applied and modified by Sch 4 para 20) (see PARAS 21 et seq, 424 et seq): see the Representation of the People (Combination of Polls) (England and Wales) Regulations 2004, SI 2004/294, reg 5(2)(i); and the National Assembly for Wales (Representation of the People) Order 2007, SI 2007/236, Sch 4 para 2(2)(k).

12 Ie under the Representation of the People (England and Wales) Regulations 2001, SI 2001/341, reg 65 (see note 3) or the National Assembly for Wales (Representation of the People) Order 2007, SI 2007/236, Sch 3 para 2 (see PARA 20).

13 Ie, where the proceedings on the issue and receipt of postal ballot papers at more than one election or referendum are taken together under the Representation of the People (England and Wales) Regulations 2001, SI 2001/341, reg 65 (see note 3), the functions conferred by the Representation of the People Act 1983 Sch 1 r 24 (issue and receipt of postal ballot papers: see PARA 406), Sch 1 r 31A (return of postal ballot papers: see PARA 418), and Sch 1 r 45(1B)(d) (verifying date of birth and signature of elector or proxy where this is required: see PARA 425) (see the Representation of the People (Combination of Polls) (England and Wales) Regulations 2004, SI 2004/294, reg 5(2)(b), (fa), (j) (reg 5(2)(fa), (j) added by SI 2006/3278)); or, where the proceedings on the issue and receipt of postal ballot papers at two or more elections are taken together under the National Assembly for Wales (Representation of the People) Order 2007, SI 2007/236, Sch 3 para 2, the functions conferred by Sch 5 para 33 (issue and receipt of postal ballot papers: see PARA 406), Sch 5 para 40 (return of postal ballot papers: see PARA 418), and Sch 5 para 55 (count: see PARA 459) (see Sch 4 para 2(2)(c), (h)).

14 Representation of the People (Combination of Polls) (England and Wales) Regulations 2004, SI 2004/294, reg 5(1); National Assembly for Wales (Representation of the People) Order 2007, SI 2007/236, Sch 4 para 2(1). The functions referred to in the text are those conferred by the Representation of the People (England and Wales) Regulations 2001, SI 2001/341, Pt V (regs 64–91) (issue and receipt of postal ballot papers) or the National Assembly for Wales (Representation of the People) Order 2007, SI 2007/236, Sch 3 (issue and receipt of postal ballot papers) (see PARA 20). For these purposes, references to the Representation of the People (England and Wales) Regulations 2001, SI 2001/341, Pt V include references to: (1) the provisions in regulations made under the European Parliamentary Elections Act 2002 s 7 which correspond to that Part; (2) that Part as applied by regulations made under the Local Government Act 2000 ss 44, 105 or ss 45, 105; and (3) the provisions in an Order made under the Police Reform and Social Responsibility Act 2011 ss 58, 154, which correspond to the Representation of the People (England and Wales) Regulations 2001, SI 2001/341, Pt V: see the Representation of the People (Combination of Polls) (England and Wales) Regulations 2004, SI 2004/294, reg 5(3) (as amended: see note 3).

15 Ie under the Representation of the People (Combination of Polls) (England and Wales) Regulations 2004, SI 2004/294, reg 4 (see note 2): see reg 6(1).

16 Ie the Representation of the People Act 1983 s 29(3), (4), (5), (7), (8) (payments by and to returning officer: see PARA 352), s 30 (detailed assessment and examination of returning officer's account: see PARA 353), s 36(4), (4B), (5), (5A) (expenses at local elections: see PARA 355), s 36(6), (6A) (advance of expenses by council: see PARA 355): see the Representation of the People (Combination of Polls) (England and Wales) Regulations 2004, SI 2004/294, reg 6(1)–(4). For these purposes, references to any provision of an enactment include references to any provision in regulations made under the European Parliamentary Elections Act 2002 s 7 which corresponds to that provision; any provision in the Police Reform and Social Responsibility Act 2011 Pt 1 Ch 6 which corresponds to that provision; and that provision as applied by orders or regulations made under any of the 'listed provisions' (see note 2): see the Representation of the People (Combination of Polls) (England and Wales) Regulations 2004, SI 2004/294, reg 6(5) (amended by SI 2012/1917).

17 See the Representation of the People (Combination of Polls) (England and Wales) Regulations 2004, SI 2004/294, reg 6(1)–(4).

18 Ie under the National Assembly for Wales (Representation of the People) Order 2007, SI 2007/236, Sch 4 para 1 (see note 2): see Sch 4 para 3(1).

19 Ie the Representation of the People Act 1983 s 36(4), (5A) (expenses at local elections: see PARA 355), s 36(6) (advance of expenses by council: see PARA 355) and the National Assembly for Wales (Representation of the People) Order 2007, SI 2007/236, art 23(1)–(4), (7), (9), (10)

    (payments by and to returning officer: see PARA 358), art 24 (detailed assessment of returning officer's account: see PARA 359): see Sch 4 para 3(1)–(4).

20 See the National Assembly for Wales (Representation of the People) Order 2007, SI 2007/236, Sch 4 para 3(1)–(4).

19.   Polling stations to be used where polls are combined. Where polls are combined, provision is made as to which polling stations are to be used, as follows:

(1)   where the poll at a parliamentary general election is taken together with the poll at another election or referendum in England, or at two or more elections in Wales, under a relevant enactment[1], only polling stations used for the parliamentary election are to be used for the other election or referendum[2];

(2)   where head (1) above does not apply, and where the poll at an ordinary Authority election is taken together with the poll at another election or referendum under a relevant enactment, only polling stations used for the Authority election are to be used for the poll at the other election or referendum[3];

(3)   where neither head (1) nor head (2) above applies, and where the poll at an ordinary county council election[4] is taken together with the poll at another election or referendum in England, or at two or more elections in Wales, under a relevant enactment, only polling stations used for the county council election are to be used for the poll at the other election or referendum[5];

(4)   where none of heads (1) to (3) above applies, and where the poll at an ordinary principal area council election[6] (other than a county council election) is taken together with the poll at another election or referendum in England, or at two or more elections in Wales, under a relevant enactment, only polling stations used for the principal area council election are to be used for the poll at the other election or referendum[7];

(5)   where none of heads (1) to (4) above applies, and where the poll at a mayoral election is taken together with the poll at an election under a relevant enactment, only polling stations used for the mayoral election are to be used for the poll at the other election[8];

(6)   where none of heads (1) to (5) above applies, and where the poll at a referendum in England is taken together with the poll at an election under a relevant enactment, only polling stations used for the referendum are to be used for the poll at the election[9];

(7)   where none of heads (1) to (6) above applies, and where the poll at an ordinary parish or community council election is taken together with the poll at another election under a relevant enactment, only polling stations used for the parish or community council election are to be used at the other election[10];

(8)   where none of heads (1) to (7) above applies, and where the poll at a PCC election[11] is taken together with the poll at a European parliamentary election under a relevant enactment, only polling stations used for the PCC election are to be used for the European parliamentary election[12];

(9)   where the polls for related areas[13] are taken together[14], the only polling stations which are to be used at each election (or referendum, as the case

may be) are the polling stations used at the election (or referendum) for which the returning officer who discharges the conferred functions[15] acts as returning officer[16];

(10)   where the polls at a Welsh Assembly general election and an ordinary local government election are taken together[17], only polling stations used for the Assembly general election are to be used for the local government election[18]; and

(11)   where the polls at a Welsh Assembly election and a local government election for related areas[19] are taken together[20], the only polling stations which are to be used in the combined area[21] at such elections are the polling stations used at the election for which the returning officer who discharges the conferred functions[22] acts as returning officer[23].

1   Where the polls at two or more elections (or, in England, at more than one election or referendum) are taken together other than under a relevant enactment, but one or more such polls are also taken together with the poll at another election (or a referendum, as the case may be) under a relevant enactment, the Representation of the People (Combination of Polls) (England and Wales) Regulations 2004, SI 2004/294, reg 4(1)–(7A) (see heads (1) to (8) in the text) applies as if each election (other than a mayoral election) were an ordinary election, and as if the polls at each election (or referendum) were taken together under a relevant enactment: see reg 4(9) (amended by SI 2012/1917). There is no provision made for the combination of polls in the Local Authorities (Conduct of Referendums) (Wales) Regulations 2008, SI 2008/1848. As to the meanings of 'England' and 'Wales' see PARA 1 note 1. As to the meanings of 'mayoral election' and 'referendum' for these purposes see PARA 18 note 1. As to the meaning of 'relevant enactment' for these purposes see PARA 18 note 2.

2   Representation of the People (Combination of Polls) (England and Wales) Regulations 2004, SI 2004/294, reg 4(1)(b). See note 1.

3   Representation of the People (Combination of Polls) (England and Wales) Regulations 2004, SI 2004/294, reg 4(2)(b). See note 1. As to the meaning of 'Authority election' see PARA 11.

4   As to the meaning of 'county council election' for these purposes see PARA 18 note 2.

5   Representation of the People (Combination of Polls) (England and Wales) Regulations 2004, SI 2004/294, reg 4(3)(b). See note 1.

6   As to the meanings of 'principal area' and 'principal area council election' for these purposes see PARA 18 note 2.

7   Representation of the People (Combination of Polls) (England and Wales) Regulations 2004, SI 2004/294, reg 4(4)(b). See note 1.

8   Representation of the People (Combination of Polls) (England and Wales) Regulations 2004, SI 2004/294, reg 4(5)(b). See note 1.

9   Representation of the People (Combination of Polls) (England and Wales) Regulations 2004, SI 2004/294, reg 4(6)(b). See note 1.

10   Representation of the People (Combination of Polls) (England and Wales) Regulations 2004, SI 2004/294, reg 4(7)(b) (reg 4(7) substituted, reg 4(7A) added, by SI 2012/1917). See note 1.

11   As to the meaning of 'PCC election' for these purposes see PARA 18 note 1.

12   Representation of the People (Combination of Polls) (England and Wales) Regulations 2004, SI 2004/294, reg 4(7A)(b) (reg 4(7A) as added: see note 10). See note 1.

13   Ie within the meaning of the Representation of the People Act 1985 s 15(3) (see PARA 30): see the Representation of the People (Combination of Polls) (England and Wales) Regulations 2004, SI 2004/294, reg 4(8) (reg 4(8), (9) amended by SI 2012/1917).

14   Ie under the Representation of the People Act 1985 s 15(2), including by virtue of s 15(2) and s 15(3) as applied by orders or regulations made under any of the 'listed provisions' (as to the meaning of which see PARA 18 note 2) (see PARA 30): see the Representation of the People (Combination of Polls) (England and Wales) Regulations 2004, SI 2004/294, reg 4(8) (as amended: see note 13). The text refers to a combination of polls at an election: (1) in England, with another election or referendum; or (2) in Wales, with another election.

15   Ie the functions which are specified in the Representation of the People (Combination of Polls) (England and Wales) Regulations 2004, SI 2004/294, reg 5 (see PARA 18): see reg 4(8)(a), (b). As to the meaning of references to a returning officer in the case of a referendum see PARA 18 note 1. As to returning officers generally see PARA 350 et seq.

16   Representation of the People (Combination of Polls) (England and Wales) Regulations 2004, SI 2004/294, reg 4(8)(b).

17 Ie under the National Assembly for Wales (Representation of the People) Order 2007, SI 2007/236, art 16(1) (see PARA 23): see art 16(7), Sch 4 para 1(1). As to the meaning of 'local government election' for these purposes see PARA 17 note 5. As to Welsh Assembly general elections see PARA 12.
18 National Assembly for Wales (Representation of the People) Order 2007, SI 2007/236, Sch 4 para 1(1)(b).
19 Ie within the meaning of the National Assembly for Wales (Representation of the People) Order 2007, SI 2007/236, art 16(3) (see PARA 30): see Sch 4 para 1(2). As to the meaning of 'Assembly election' for these purposes see PARA 3 note 2.
20 Ie under the National Assembly for Wales (Representation of the People) Order 2007, SI 2007/236, art 16(2) (see PARA 30): see Sch 4 para 1(2).
21 Ie the area where the polls at a Welsh Assembly and a local government election for related areas are taken together: see the National Assembly for Wales (Representation of the People) Order 2007, SI 2007/236, Sch 4 para 1(2)(a); and PARA 18 note 2.
22 Ie the functions which are specified in the National Assembly for Wales (Representation of the People) Order 2007, SI 2007/236, Sch 4 para 2 (see PARA 18): see Sch 4 para 1(2)(a), (b).
23 National Assembly for Wales (Representation of the People) Order 2007, SI 2007/236, Sch 4 para 1(2)(b). Where the polls at a Welsh Assembly general election and a local government election for related areas are taken together under art 16(2) (see PARA 30), however, then Sch 4 para 1(1)(b) (see the text and notes 17–18) applies: see Sch 4 para 1(4). As to returning officers for Welsh Assembly elections see PARA 357 et seq.

20.   Proceedings on issue and receipt of postal ballot papers where polls are combined. Where the polls at parliamentary, European parliamentary and local government elections are taken together[1], the proceedings on the issue and receipt of postal ballot papers[2] in respect of each election[3] may, if the returning officers[4] concerned agree, be taken together[5]. Where the poll at the European parliamentary election is to be taken together either with the poll at a parliamentary or local government election[6] or with the poll at a mayoral election (or, in England, the poll at a mayoral election or a referendum)[7], or together with two or more such polls, the proceedings on the issue and receipt of postal ballot papers in respect of each election (or referendum, as the case may be) may, if all the returning officers concerned[8] agree, be taken together[9].

Where the polls at a Welsh Assembly general election[10] and an ordinary local government election[11] (or, if the returning officer[12] for each election thinks fit, the polls at an Assembly election[13] and local government election for related areas[14]) are taken together[15], the proceedings on the issue and receipt of postal ballot papers in respect of each election may, if the returning officers agree, be taken together[16].

1 Ie under the Representation of the People Act 1985 s 15(1), (2) (combination of polls at parliamentary, European parliamentary and local government elections: see PARA 21 et seq) or under the Representation of the People Act 1983 s 36(3), (3AB) (combination of polls at local elections: see PARA 28): see the Representation of the People (England and Wales) Regulations 2001, SI 2001/341, reg 65. As to the meanings of 'parliamentary election' and 'European parliamentary election' see PARAS 9, 13. As to the meaning of 'local government election' see PARA 11.
    The Representation of the People (England and Wales) Regulations 2001, SI 2001/341, reg 65, is applied and modified:
    (1)   for the purposes of a mayoral election, by the Local Authorities (Mayoral Elections) (England and Wales) Regulations 2007, SI 2007/1024, reg 3(2)–(5), Sch 2 Table 4, so that the Representation of the People (England and Wales) Regulations 2001, SI 2001/341, reg 65 applies where the polls at elections are taken together under the Representation of the People Act 1985 s 15(1), (2), under the Representation of the People Act 1983 s 36(3), (3AB), or under the Representation of the People Act 1983 s 36(3), (3AB), (3AC), as modified by the Local Authorities (Mayoral Elections) (England and Wales) Regulations 2007, SI 2007/1024, Sch 2 Table 1 (see Sch 2 Table 4); and
    (2)   in relation to England, by the Local Authorities (Conduct of Referendums) (England)

Regulations 2012, SI 2012/323, regs 8(2), 11–13, Sch 4 Table 6 (see PARA 15 note 2), so that the Representation of the People (England and Wales) Regulations 2001, SI 2001/341, reg 65 applies where the polls at elections are taken together under the Representation of the People Act 1985 s 15(1), (2), under the Representation of the People Act 1983 s 36(3), (3AB), or under the Local Authorities (Conduct of Referendums) (England) Regulations 2012, SI 2012/323 (see Sch 4 Table 6).
There is no provision made for the combination of polls in the Local Authorities (Conduct of Referendums) (Wales) Regulations 2008, SI 2008/1848. As to the meanings of 'England' and 'Wales' see PARA 1 note 1.

2   As to the issue and receipt of postal ballot papers see PARA 406 et seq.
3   Ie, in England, in respect of each election or referendum: see note 1.
4   As to returning officers generally see PARA 350 et seq.
5   Representation of the People (England and Wales) Regulations 2001, SI 2001/341, reg 65 (as originally enacted; and as applied and modified (see note 1)).
6   Ie under the Representation of the People Act 1985 s 15(1), (2) (combination of polls at parliamentary, European parliamentary and local government elections: see PARA 21 et seq): see the European Parliamentary Elections Regulations 2004, SI 2004/293, reg 10, Sch 2 para 41 (Sch 2 substituted by SI 2009/186).
7   Ie the poll at a mayoral election, in accordance with regulations made under the Local Government Act 2000 ss 9HE, 105 (conduct of elections for the return of elected mayors in England: see PARA 383), ss 44, 105 (conduct of elections for the return of elected mayors in Wales: see PARA 383), or the poll at a local authority referendum in accordance with regulations made under ss 9MG, 105 (conduct of local authority referendums in England: see PARA 558), ss 45, 105 (conduct of local authority referendums in Wales: see PARA 558): see the European Parliamentary Elections Regulations 2004, SI 2004/293, Sch 2 para 41 (Sch 2 as substituted: see note 6); Interpretation Act 1978 s 17(2)(b).
8   In the case of a referendum, a reference to a returning officer must be construed as a reference to a counting officer, within the meaning of the Local Authorities (Conduct of Referendums) (England) Regulations 2012, SI 2012/323, reg 2(1) (see PARA 576 note 1): see the European Parliamentary Elections Regulations 2004, SI 2004/293, Sch 2 para 40(2) (Sch 2 as substituted: see note 6); Interpretation Act 1978 s 17(2)(b).
9   See the European Parliamentary Elections Regulations 2004, SI 2004/293, Sch 2 para 41 (Sch 2 as substituted: see note 6); Interpretation Act 1978 s 17(2)(b).
10 As to Welsh Assembly general elections see PARA 12.
11 As to the meaning of 'local government election' for these purposes see PARA 17 note 5.
12 As to returning officers for Welsh Assembly elections see PARA 357 et seq.
13 As to the meaning of 'Assembly election' for these purposes see PARA 3 note 2.
14 Ie within the meaning of the National Assembly for Wales (Representation of the People) Order 2007, SI 2007/236, art 16(3) (see PARA 30).
15 Ie under the National Assembly for Wales (Representation of the People) Order 2007, SI 2007/236, art 16(1) (combined Assembly general election and ordinary local government election: see PARA 23) or under art 16(2) (Assembly election and local government election for related areas: see PARA 30): see art 15(4), Sch 3 para 2.
16 National Assembly for Wales (Representation of the People) Order 2007, SI 2007/236, Sch 3 para 2.

(ii) The Different Combinations of Polls

21. Combined polls at parliamentary general election and European parliamentary general election. Where the polls at a parliamentary general election[1] and a European parliamentary general election[2] are to be taken on the same date, they must be taken together[3]. The Secretary of State[4] may by regulations[5] make such provision as he thinks fit in connection with the combining of polls at such elections including provision modifying the Representation of the People Acts[6] in relation to them[7]. Accordingly, provision has been made in relation to the discharge of the functions of the respective returning officers[8], the polling stations to be used[9], and proceedings on the issue and receipt of postal ballot papers[10]; and where the polls at such elections are taken together, the elections rules which apply at each election have effect subject to certain modifications[11].

1   As to the meaning of 'parliamentary election' and as to use of the expression 'parliamentary general election' see PARA 9.
2   For these purposes, 'European parliamentary election' means an election of a representative to the European Parliament; and 'European parliamentary general election' means a general election of such representatives: see the Representation of the People Act 1985 s 27(1) (definition amended by virtue of the European Communities (Amendment) Act 1986 s 3). As to European parliamentary elections see PARA 13 et seq.
3   See the Representation of the People Act 1985 s 15(1)(a) (amended by virtue of the European Communities (Amendment) Act 1986 s 3).
4   As to the Secretary of State see PARA 2.
5   As to the making of regulations under the Representation of the People Act 1985 generally see PARA 28 note 16.
6   As to the meaning of 'the Representation of the People Acts' see PARA 3 note 1.
7   Representation of the People Act 1985 s 15(5). As to the regulations made under s 15(5) see (*inter alia*) the Representation of the People (Combination of Polls) (England and Wales) Regulations 2004, SI 2004/294; and the text and notes 8–11.
8   As to the transferred functions of returning officers where polls are combined see PARA 18.
9   As to the polling stations to be used where polls are combined see PARA 19.
10 As to proceedings on the issue and receipt of postal ballot papers where polls are combined see PARA 20.
11 Where the poll at a parliamentary election is to be taken with the poll at a European parliamentary general election under the Representation of the People Act 1985 s 15(1)(a), or two or more such polls:
    (1)   the parliamentary elections rules contained in the Representation of the People Act 1983 s 23(1), Sch 1 (see PARA 383 note 2) have effect subject to the modifications contained in the Representation of the People (Combination of Polls) (England and Wales) Regulations 2004, SI 2004/294, Sch 2 (amended by SI 2006/3278; SI 2007/1025; SI 2012/1917) (see the Representation of the People (Combination of Polls) (England and Wales) Regulations 2004, SI 2004/294, reg 8(1)(a) (amended by SI 2012/1917)); and
    (2)   the European parliamentary elections rules contained in the European Parliamentary Elections Regulations 2004, SI 2004/293, reg 9(1), Sch 1 (see PARA 383 note 16) have effect in England and Wales subject to the modifications contained in reg 11, Sch 3 Pt 1 (rr 1–29) (Sch 3 substituted by SI 2009/186; the European Parliamentary Elections Regulations 2004, SI 2004/293, Sch 3 Pt 1 amended by SI 2012/1917) (see the European Parliamentary Elections Regulations 2004, SI 2004/293, reg 11(a), (i)).
    As to polls at elections for related areas that may be taken together under the Representation of the People Act 1985 s 15(2) see PARA 30.

22. Combined polls at parliamentary general election and ordinary local government election.

Where the polls at an ordinary local government election[1] and a parliamentary general election[2] are to be taken on the same date, they must be taken together[3]. The Secretary of State[4] may by regulations[5] make such provision as he thinks fit in connection with the combining of polls at such elections including provision modifying the Representation of the People Acts[6] in relation to them[7]. Accordingly, provision has been made in relation to the discharge of the functions of the respective returning officers[8], the polling stations to be used[9], and proceedings on the issue and receipt of postal ballot papers[10]; and, where the polls at such elections are taken together, the elections rules which apply at each election have effect subject to certain modifications[11].

1   The Representation of the People Act 1985 s 15 has effect as if contained in the Representation of the People Act 1983 Pt I (ss 1–66B): see the Representation of the People Act 1985 s 27(2). Accordingly, as to the meaning of 'local government election' see PARA 11. As to ordinary local government elections see PARA 197 et seq.
2   As to the meaning of 'parliamentary election', and as to use of the expression 'parliamentary general election', see PARA 9.
3   See the Representation of the People Act 1985 s 15(1)(b).
4   As to the Secretary of State see PARA 2.
5   As to the making of regulations under the Representation of the People Act 1985 generally see PARA 28 note 16.

6   As to the meaning of 'the Representation of the People Acts' see PARA 3 note 1.
7   Representation of the People Act 1985 s 15(5). As to the regulations made under s 15(5) see (*inter alia*) the Representation of the People (Combination of Polls) (England and Wales) Regulations 2004, SI 2004/294; and the text and notes 8–11.
8   As to the transferred functions of returning officers where polls are combined see PARA 18.
9   As to the polling stations to be used where polls are combined see PARA 19.
10   As to proceedings on the issue and receipt of postal ballot papers where polls are combined see PARA 20.
11   Where the poll at a parliamentary election is to be taken with the poll at an ordinary local government election (election of councillors to the council of a principal area) under the Representation of the People Act 1985 s 15(1)(b), or two or more such polls:
     (1)   the parliamentary elections rules contained in the Representation of the People Act 1983 s 23(1), Sch 1 (see PARA 383 note 2) have effect subject to the modifications contained in the Representation of the People (Combination of Polls) (England and Wales) Regulations 2004, SI 2004/294, Sch 2 (amended by SI 2006/3278; SI 2007/1025; SI 2012/1917) (see the Representation of the People (Combination of Polls) (England and Wales) Regulations 2004, SI 2004/294, reg 8(1)(a) (amended by SI 2012/1917)); and
     (2)   the rules set out in the Local Elections (Principal Areas) (England and Wales) Rules 2006, SI 2006/3304, r 3, Sch 2 (see PARA 383 note 6) apply to the principal area election subject to modifications as set out in r 4, Sch 3 (Sch 3 amended by SI 2010/1172; SI 2011/563; SI 2011/1043) (see the Local Elections (Principal Areas) (England and Wales) Rules 2006, SI 2006/3304, rr 2(2)(a), 4);
     (3)   the rules set out in the Local Elections (Parishes and Communities) (England and Wales) Rules 2006, SI 2006/3305, r 3, Sch 2 (as to which see PARA 383 note 6) apply to the parish or community election subject to modifications as set out in r 4, Sch 3 (Sch 3 amended by SI 2010/1172; SI 2011/562; SI 2011/1043) (see the Local Elections (Parishes and Communities) (England and Wales) Rules 2006, SI 2006/3305, rr 2(2)(a), 4).
     In relation to a London Authority election (included in the definition of 'local government election' for the purposes of the Representation of the People Act 1983: see PARA 11) that is taken together with the poll at a parliamentary election under the Representation of the People Act 1985 s 15(1)(b), the Greater London Authority Elections Rules 2007, SI 2007/3541, rr 3, 4, (see PARA 383 note 10) do not apply and the election must be conducted in accordance with the rules specified as follows (see r 5(1)(a), (2)):
     (a)   the constituency members election rules in r 5(3), Sch 5 have effect for the purposes of any election of constituency members of the London Assembly whether at an ordinary election or in the circumstances mentioned in the Greater London Authority Act 1999 s 10 (filling a vacancy in an Assembly constituency: see PARA 204) (Greater London Authority Elections Rules 2007, SI 2007/3541, r 5(3));
     (b)   the London members election rules in r 5(4), Sch 6, with the exception of Sch 6 Pt 7 (rr 63–67) (list candidates and the filling of vacancies), have effect for the purposes of any election of London members; and Sch 6 Pt 7 has effect for the purposes of the Greater London Authority Act 1999 s 11 (filling a vacancy among the London members: see PARA 204) (Greater London Authority Elections Rules 2007, SI 2007/3541, r 5(4)); and
     (c)   the Mayoral Election Rules in r 5(5), Sch 7 have effect for the purposes of any election of the Mayor of London at an ordinary election, and any election under the Greater London Authority Act 1999 s 16(2) (filling a vacancy in the office of Mayor: see PARA 204) (Greater London Authority Elections Rules 2007, SI 2007/3541, r 5(5)).
     As to the modification of the combined poll rules contained in Schs 5–7 (see heads (a) to (c) above) where votes are counted without the use of an electronic counting system see r 6, Sch 8 (the 'combined manual count rules': see r 2(1)) (r 6 amended by SI 2012/198). As to polls at elections for related areas that may be taken together under the Representation of the People Act 1985 s 15(2) see PARA 30.

23.   Combined polls at Welsh Assembly general election and local government election. Where the polls at a Welsh Assembly general election[1] and an ordinary local government election[2] are to be taken on the same date, they must be taken together[3]. Where those polls are taken together, provision has been made in relation to the discharge of the functions of the respective returning officers[4], the polling stations to be used[5], and proceedings on the issue and receipt of postal ballot papers[6].

Provision is made also for the conduct of polls at Assembly elections when they are taken together with polls at local government elections[7].

1 As to the meaning of 'Assembly general election' see PARA 17 note 4.
2 As to the meaning of 'local government election' for these purposes see PARA 17 note 5.
3 National Assembly for Wales (Representation of the People) Order 2007, SI 2007/236, art 16(1).
4 As to the transferred functions of returning officers where polls are combined see PARA 18.
5 As to the polling stations to be used where polls are combined see PARA 19.
6 As to proceedings on the issue and receipt of postal ballot papers where polls are combined see PARA 20.
7 See the National Assembly for Wales (Representation of the People) Order 2007, SI 2007/236, art 16(7). The provision referred to in the text is made by art 16(7), Sch 4, although where the poll at an Assembly election is combined with a mayoral election, only Sch 4 Pt 1 (paras 1–3) (general: see PARAS 18, 19) and Pt 2 (paras 4–26) (modifications to art 17(1), Sch 5 (Assembly Election Rules: see PARA 383 note 20) to apply where the poll at an Assembly election is taken with the poll at a local government election under art 16(1), (2)) apply: see art 16(7).
    Where the poll at an Assembly election is taken with the poll at a local government election under art 16(1), then Sch 5 has effect subject to the modifications set out in Sch 4 Pt 2 paras 5–26: Sch 4 Pt 2 para 4.
    Where the poll at an election of county or county borough councillors is taken together with the poll at an Assembly election under art 16(1), the Local Elections (Principal Areas) (England and Wales) Rules 2006, SI 2006/3304, r 4, Sch 3 (rules for conduct of an election of councillors of a principal area where the poll is taken together with the poll at a relevant election or referendum) ('the principal area election rules': see PARA 383 note 6) have effect subject to the modifications set out in the National Assembly for Wales (Representation of the People) Order 2007, SI 2007/236, Sch 4 Pt 3 paras 28–45: Sch 4 Pt 3 para 27.
    Where the poll at an election of community councillors is taken together with the poll at an Assembly election under art 16(1), the Local Elections (Parishes and Communities) (England and Wales) Rules 2006, SI 2006/3305, r 4, Sch 3 (rules for conduct of an election of councillors of a parish or community where the poll is taken together with the poll at a relevant election or referendum) ('the community election rules': see PARA 383 note 6) have effect subject to the modifications set out in the National Assembly for Wales (Representation of the People) Order 2007, SI 2007/236, Sch 4 Pt 3 paras 47–63: Sch 4 Pt 4 para 46.

24. Combined polls at ordinary local government election and European parliamentary general election. Where the polls at an ordinary local government election[1] and a European parliamentary general election[2] are to be taken on the same date, they must be taken together[3]. The Secretary of State[4] may by regulations[5] make such provision as he thinks fit in connection with the combining of polls at such elections including provision modifying the Representation of the People Acts[6] in relation to them[7]. Accordingly, provision has been made in relation to the discharge of the functions of the respective returning officers[8], the polling stations to be used[9], and proceedings on the issue and receipt of postal ballot papers[10]; and, where the polls at such elections are taken together, the elections rules which apply at each election have effect subject to certain modifications[11].

1 The Representation of the People Act 1985 s 15 has effect as if contained in the Representation of the People Act 1983 Pt I (ss 1–66B): see the Representation of the People Act 1985 s 27(2). Accordingly, as to the meaning of 'local government election' see PARA 11. As to ordinary local government elections see PARA 197 et seq.
2 As to the meaning of 'European parliamentary general election' for these purposes see PARA 21 note 2.
3 See the Representation of the People Act 1985 s 15(1)(c) (amended by the European Communities (Amendment) Act 1986 s 3).

4   As to the Secretary of State see PARA 2.
5   As to the making of regulations under the Representation of the People Act 1985 generally see PARA 28 note 16.
6   As to the meaning of 'the Representation of the People Acts' see PARA 3 note 1.
7   Representation of the People Act 1985 s 15(5). As to the regulations made under s 15(5) see (*inter alia*) the Representation of the People (Combination of Polls) (England and Wales) Regulations 2004, SI 2004/294; and the text and notes 8–10.
8   As to the transferred functions of returning officers where polls are combined see PARA 18.
9   As to the polling stations to be used where polls are combined see PARA 19.
10   As to proceedings on the issue and receipt of postal ballot papers where polls are combined see PARA 20.
11   Where the poll at an ordinary local government election is to be taken with the poll at a European parliamentary election under the Representation of the People Act 1985 s 15(1)(c):
    (1)   the European parliamentary elections rules contained in the European Parliamentary Elections Regulations 2004, SI 2004/293, reg 9(1), Sch 1 (see PARA 383 note 16) have effect in England and Wales subject to the modifications contained in reg 11, Sch 3 Pt 1 (rr 1–29) (Sch 3 substituted by SI 2009/186; the European Parliamentary Elections Regulations 2004, SI 2004/293, Sch 3 Pt 1 amended by SI 2012/1917) (see the European Parliamentary Elections Regulations 2004, SI 2004/293, reg 11(a), (i));
    (2)   the rules set out in the Local Elections (Principal Areas) (England and Wales) Rules 2006, SI 2006/3304, r 3, Sch 2 (see PARA 383 note 6) apply to the principal area election subject to modifications as set out in r 4, Sch 3 (Sch 3 amended by SI 2010/1172; SI 2011/563; SI 2011/1043) (see the Local Elections (Principal Areas) (England and Wales) Rules 2006, SI 2006/3304, rr 2(2)(b), 4);
    (3)   the rules set out in the Local Elections (Parishes and Communities) (England and Wales) Rules 2006, SI 2006/3305, r 3, Sch 2 (as to which see PARA 383 note 6) apply to the parish or community election subject to modifications as set out in r 4, Sch 3 (Sch 3 amended by SI 2010/1172; SI 2011/562; SI 2011/1043) (see the Local Elections (Parishes and Communities) (England and Wales) Rules 2006, SI 2006/3305, rr 2(2)(b), 4).
  In relation to a London Authority election (included in the definition of 'local government election' for the purposes of the Representation of the People Act 1983: see PARA 11) that is taken together with the poll at a European parliamentary election under the Representation of the People Act 1985 s 15(1)(c), the Greater London Authority Elections Rules 2007, SI 2007/3541, rr 3, 4, (see PARA 383 note 10) do not apply and the election must be conducted in accordance with the rules specified as follows (see r 5(1)(a), (2)):
    (a)   the constituency members election rules in r 5(3), Sch 5 have effect for the purposes of any election of constituency members of the London Assembly whether at an ordinary election or in the circumstances mentioned in the Greater London Authority Act 1999 s 10 (filling a vacancy in an Assembly constituency: see PARA 204) (Greater London Authority Elections Rules 2007, SI 2007/3541, r 5(3));
    (b)   the London members election rules in r 5(4), Sch 6, with the exception of Sch 6 Pt 7 (rr 63–67) (list candidates and the filling of vacancies), have effect for the purposes of any election of London members; and Sch 6 Pt 7 has effect for the purposes of the Greater London Authority Act 1999 s 11 (filling a vacancy among the London members: see PARA 204) (Greater London Authority Elections Rules 2007, SI 2007/3541, r 5(4)); and
    (c)   the Mayoral Election Rules in r 5(5), Sch 7 have effect for the purposes of any election of the Mayor of London at an ordinary election, and any election under the Greater London Authority Act 1999 s 16(2) (filling a vacancy in the office of Mayor: see PARA 204) (Greater London Authority Elections Rules 2007, SI 2007/3541, r 5(5)).
  As to the modification of the combined poll rules contained in Schs 5–7 (see heads (a) to (c) above) where votes are counted without the use of an electronic counting system see r 6, Sch 8 (the 'combined manual count rules': see r 2(1)) (r 6 amended by SI 2012/198). As to polls at elections for related areas that may be taken together under the Representation of the People Act 1985 s 15(2) see PARA 30.

25. Poll at parish or community council elections not to be combined with a parliamentary or European parliamentary election. Until 2 April 2013, the following provisions had effect[1].

Where the date of the poll at a parliamentary general election[2] or at a European parliamentary general election[3] is the same as the ordinary day of election[4] of councillors for local government areas[5], any poll at an election of parish or community councillors to be held on that date[6] must be postponed for three weeks[7]. The date to which any such poll is so postponed is to be taken to be the ordinary day of election for the purposes of the provisions concerning the election, term of office and retirement of parish or community[8] councillors and the day of election for the purposes of any rules concerning the conduct of elections of such councillors made by the Secretary of State[9].

Any expenses of any returning officer for an election at which the poll is postponed under this provision which are attributable to the postponement must be charged on and paid out of the Consolidated Fund[10].

1   The Representation of the People Act 1985 s 16 was repealed by the Electoral Registration and Administration Act 2013 s 15(1), as from 2 April 2013 (see the Electoral Registration and Administration Act 2013 (Commencement No 2) Order 2013, SI 2013/702, art 3(b)), thereby allowing polls at parish and community council elections more often to be run in combined form with polls at other elections. See also PARAS 22–24, 28.
2   As to the meaning of 'parliamentary election' and as to use of the expression 'parliamentary general election' see PARA 9.
3   As to the meaning of 'European parliamentary general election' for these purposes see PARA 21 note 2. As to the polls at European parliamentary general elections see PARA 217 et seq.
4   As to the ordinary day of election of councillors for local government areas see PARA 197 et seq.
5   See the Representation of the People Act 1985 s 16(1) (amended by the European Communities (Amendment) Act 1986 s 3) (Representation of the People Act 1985 s 16 repealed: see note 1). As to the meaning of 'local government area' see PARA 33 note 7. As to the date of the poll at a parliamentary general election or by-election see PARA 195; as to the date of the poll at local government elections (including elections to fill vacancies) see PARAS 206–209; and as to the date of the poll at a European parliamentary election see PARA 222.
6   As to the election of councillors of the council of a parish or community see PARA 200 et seq.
7   Representation of the People Act 1985 s 16(1)(a) (repealed: see note 1).
8   The provisions referred to in the text are the Local Government Act 1972 s 16(3), s 35(2) (see PARA 200; and LOCAL GOVERNMENT vol 69 (2009) PARAS 132–133): see the Representation of the People Act 1985 s 16(1)(b) (repealed: see note 1).
9   Representation of the People Act 1985 s 16(1)(b) (repealed: see note 1). The rules referred to in the text are those made under the Representation of the People Act 1983 s 36 (see the Local Elections (Parishes and Communities) (England and Wales) Rules 2006, SI 2006/3305; and PARA 383 note 6): see the Representation of the People Act 1985 s 16(1)(b) (now repealed). As to the Secretary of State see PARA 2.
10 Representation of the People Act 1985 s 16(1)(c) (repealed: see note 1). As to the expenses of returning officers generally see PARA 352 et seq. As to the Consolidated Fund generally see CONSTITUTIONAL LAW AND HUMAN RIGHTS vol 8(2) (Reissue) PARA 711 et seq; PARLIAMENT vol 78 (2010) PARAS 1028–1031.

26.   Combined polls at a local authority mayoral election and at parliamentary or European parliamentary election or ordinary local government election. Where the polls at a local authority mayoral election[1] and a parliamentary election[2], a European parliamentary election[3], or an ordinary local government election[4] are to be taken on the same date, they must be taken together[5].

Where the polls at any such elections are taken together, provision has been made in relation to the discharge of the functions of the respective returning officers[6], the polling stations to be used[7], and proceedings on the issue and receipt of postal ballot papers[8]. The rules which apply to the poll at a local authority mayoral election are modified when such a poll is taken together with the poll at a relevant election (or referendum, as the case may be)[9], as are the rules that apply at each election (or referendum) in turn, specifically where the poll at a local authority mayoral election is taken together with: (a) the poll at a parliamentary election[10]; (b) the poll at a European parliamentary election[11]; (c) the poll at a local government election[12]; or (d) the poll at a local authority referendum held in England[13].

1   As to the meaning of 'mayoral election' for these purposes, and as to the application of provisions in the Representation of the People Act 1985 in relation to the conduct of such an election, see PARA 11 note 14.

2   As to the meaning of 'parliamentary election', and as to use of the expression 'parliamentary general election', see PARA 9.

3   As to the meaning of 'European parliamentary general election' for these purposes see PARA 21 note 2. As to the polls at European parliamentary general elections see PARA 217 et seq.

4   The Representation of the People Act 1985 s 15 has effect as if contained in the Representation of the People Act 1983 Pt I (ss 1–66B): see the Representation of the People Act 1985 s 27(2). Accordingly, as to the meaning of 'local government election' see PARA 11. As to the polls at ordinary local government elections see PARA 197 et seq.

5   See the Representation of the People Act 1985 s 15(1)(d) (s 15 applied and modified by the Local Authorities (Mayoral Elections) (England and Wales) Regulations 2007, SI 2007/1024, Sch 2 Table 2). See note 1. As to combined polls in related electoral areas see PARA 28.

6   As to the transferred functions of returning officers where polls are combined see PARA 18.

7   As to the polling stations to be used where polls are combined see PARA 19.

8   As to proceedings on the issue and receipt of postal ballot papers where polls are combined see PARA 20.

9   Where the poll at a local authority mayoral election is taken together with the poll at a relevant election or referendum, the mayoral elections rules (ie the rules contained in the Local Authorities (Mayoral Elections) (England and Wales) Regulations 2007, SI 2007/1024, reg 3(1), Sch 1: see reg 2; and PARA 383) are modified so as to have effect as set out in reg 4(1), Sch 3 (Sch 3 amended by SI 2010/1172; SI 2011/926; SI 2012/1917; SI 2012/2059): see the Local Authorities (Mayoral Elections) (England and Wales) Regulations 2007, SI 2007/1024, reg 4(1) (reg 4(1) renumbered, reg 4(2), Sch 3A added, by SI 2012/2059). Where the poll at a mayoral election is taken together with a poll at a police and crime commissioner election and is not also taken together with a poll at any other relevant election or referendum, the Local Authorities (Mayoral Elections) (England and Wales) Regulations 2007, SI 2007/1024, Sch 3 has effect subject to the modifications set out in Sch 3A (as so added): see reg 4(2) (as so added). For these purposes, 'relevant election or referendum' means one or more of: a parliamentary election; a European parliamentary election; a local government election; another mayoral election; and a local authority referendum or a police and crime commissioner election, the poll at which is taken together with the poll at the mayoral election: see reg 2 (definition amended by SI 2012/1917). 'Election' or 'mayoral election' means an election for the return of an elected mayor; 'European parliamentary election' has the same meaning as in the Representation of the People Act 1985 s 27(1) (see PARA 21 note 2); 'local government election' has the same meaning as in the Representation of the People Act 1983 s 203(1) (see PARA 11); and 'referendum' means a referendum conducted under the Local Authorities (Conduct of Referendums) (England) Regulations 2012, SI 2012/323 (see PARA 555 et seq): see the Local Authorities (Mayoral Elections) (England and Wales) Regulations 2007, SI 2007/1024, reg 2; Interpretation Act 1978 s 17(2)(b). 'Police and crime commissioner election' means an election of a police and crime commissioner in accordance with the Police Reform and Social Responsibility Act 2011 Pt 1 Ch 6 (ss 50–76, Schs 9, 10) (Police and Crime Commissioners: elections and vacancies: see POLICE AND INVESTIGATORY POWERS vol 84 (2013) PARA 62 et seq): see the Local Authorities (Mayoral Elections) (England and Wales) Regulations 2007, SI 2007/1024, reg 2 (definition added by SI 2012/1917).

10 Where the poll at a parliamentary election is to be taken with the poll at a local authority mayoral election in accordance with regulations made under the Local Government Act 2000 ss 9HE, 105 (conduct of elections for the return of elected mayors in England: see PARA 383), ss 44, 105 (conduct of elections for the return of elected mayors in Wales: see PARA 383), or two or more such polls, the parliamentary elections rules contained in the Representation of the People Act 1983 s 23(1), Sch 1 (see PARA 383 note 2) have effect subject to the modifications contained in the Representation of the People (Combination of Polls) (England and Wales) Regulations 2004, SI 2004/294, Sch 2 (amended by SI 2006/3278; SI 2007/1025; SI 2012/1917): see the Representation of the People (Combination of Polls) (England and Wales) Regulations 2004, SI 2004/294, reg 8(1)(b) (amended by SI 2012/1917); Interpretation Act 1978 s 17(2)(b).

11 Where the poll at a local authority mayoral election is taken together with the poll at a European parliamentary election, the European parliamentary elections rules contained in the European Parliamentary Elections Regulations 2004, SI 2004/293, reg 9(1), Sch 1 (see PARA 383 note 16) have effect in England and Wales subject to the modifications contained in reg 11, Sch 3 Pt 1 (rr 1–29) (Sch 3 substituted by SI 2009/186; the European Parliamentary Elections

Regulations 2004, SI 2004/293, Sch 3 Pt 1 amended by SI 2012/1917): see the European Parliamentary Elections Regulations 2004, SI 2004/293, reg 11(b), (i).

12 Where the poll at a local authority mayoral election is taken together with the poll at a local government election:

(1) the rules set out in the Local Elections (Principal Areas) (England and Wales) Rules 2006, SI 2006/3304, r 3, Sch 2 (see PARA 383 note 6) apply to the principal area election subject to modifications as set out in r 4, Sch 3 (Sch 3 amended by SI 2010/1172; SI 2011/563; SI 2011/1043) (see the Local Elections (Principal Areas) (England and Wales) Rules 2006, SI 2006/3304, rr 2(2)(d), 4);

(2) the rules set out in the Local Elections (Parishes and Communities) (England and Wales) Rules 2006, SI 2006/3305, r 3, Sch 2 (as to which see PARA 383 note 6) apply to the parish or community election subject to modifications as set out in r 4, Sch 3 (Sch 3 amended by SI 2010/1172; SI 2011/562; SI 2011/1043) (see the Local Elections (Parishes and Communities) (England and Wales) Rules 2006, SI 2006/3305, rr 2(2)(d), 4).

In relation to a London Authority election (included in the definition of 'local government election' for the purposes of the Representation of the People Act 1983: see PARA 11) that is taken together with the poll at a mayoral election, held in accordance with rules that are contained in regulations made under the Local Government Act 2000 ss 9HE, 105 (conduct of elections for the return of elected mayors in England: see PARA 383), ss 44, 105 (conduct of elections for the return of elected mayors in Wales: see PARA 383), the Greater London Authority Elections Rules 2007, SI 2007/3541, rr 3, 4, (see PARA 383 note 10) do not apply and the election must be conducted in accordance with the rules specified as follows (see r 5(1)(b), (2); Interpretation Act 1978 s 17(2)(b)):

(a) the constituency members election rules in the Greater London Authority Elections Rules 2007, SI 2007/3541, r 5(3), Sch 5 have effect for the purposes of any election of constituency members of the London Assembly whether at an ordinary election or in the circumstances mentioned in the Greater London Authority Act 1999 s 10 (filling a vacancy in an Assembly constituency: see PARA 204) (Greater London Authority Elections Rules 2007, SI 2007/3541, r 5(3));

(b) the London members election rules in r 5(4), Sch 6, with the exception of Sch 6 Pt 7 (rr 63–67) (list candidates and the filling of vacancies), have effect for the purposes of any election of London members; and Sch 6 Pt 7 has effect for the purposes of the Greater London Authority Act 1999 s 11 (filling a vacancy among the London members: see PARA 204) (Greater London Authority Elections Rules 2007, SI 2007/3541, r 5(4)); and

(c) the Mayoral Election Rules in r 5(5), Sch 7 have effect for the purposes of any election of the Mayor of London at an ordinary election, and any election under the Greater London Authority Act 1999 s 16(2) (filling a vacancy in the office of Mayor: see PARA 204) (Greater London Authority Elections Rules 2007, SI 2007/3541, r 5(5)).

As to the modification of the combined poll rules contained in Schs 5–7 (see heads (a) to (c) above) where votes are counted without the use of an electronic counting system see r 6, Sch 8 (the 'combined manual count rules': see r 2(1)) (r 6 amended by SI 2012/198). As to polls at elections for related areas that may be taken together under the Representation of the People Act 1985 s 15(2) see PARA 30.

13 Where the poll at a local authority mayoral election is taken together with the poll at a referendum conducted under the Local Authorities (Conduct of Referendums) (England) Regulations 2012, SI 2012/323, the referendum must be conducted under the rules given in regs 11, 13, Sch 4, Sch 5 (the local government act referendums (combination of polls) rules): see regs 10(1), (2)(k), 11(1)–(3); and PARA 27 note 7.

27. Combined polls at local authority referendum and election in England.

When the poll at a local authority referendum held in England[1], and the poll (or polls) at a parliamentary election, a European parliamentary election or an ordinary local government election[2], are to be taken on the same date, they must be taken together[3]. Where any polls are taken together in this way, provision has been made in relation to the discharge of the functions of the respective returning officers (or counting officers, as the case may be)[4], the polling stations to be used[5], and proceedings on the issue and receipt of postal ballot papers[6]. The rules which apply to the poll at a local authority referendum held in England are modified when such a poll is taken together with the poll at a relevant election[7], as are the rules that apply at each election in turn, specifically where the poll at a local authority referendum is taken together with: (1) the poll at a parliamentary election[8]; (2) the poll at a European parliamentary election[9]; (3) the poll at a local government election[10]; or (4) the poll at a local authority mayoral election[11].

1   As to the meaning of 'referendum' for these purposes see PARA 574 note 2. The Local Authorities (Conduct of Referendums) (Wales) Regulations 2008, SI 2008/1848, continue to make no provision for polls at local authority referendums in Wales to be taken together with polls at another election or referendum: see PARA 15 note 2. As to the meanings of 'England' and 'Wales' see PARA 1 note 1.

Where the poll at a referendum would be taken on a day that falls within the period beginning 28 days before the day on which the poll is to be taken at an election, and ending 28 days after the day on which the poll is to be taken at any such election, the poll at the referendum must be taken on the day on which the poll is to be taken at the election; and the polls must be taken together: see the Local Authorities (Conduct of Referendums) (England) Regulations 2012, SI 2012/323, reg 10(1). The descriptions of elections to which reg 10(1) applies are:

(1)   an ordinary election of councillors for a county electoral division or a district or London borough ward (as the case may be) of the local authority by which or as regards which the referendum is to be held (reg 10(2)(a));

(2)   an ordinary election of councillors for a county electoral division or a district or London borough ward (as the case may be) of any other local authority, where that division or ward is wholly or partly within the area of the local authority by which or as regards which the referendum is to be held (reg 10(2)(b));

(3)   a parliamentary general election (reg 10(2)(c));

(4)   an election to fill a vacancy in a parliamentary constituency that is wholly or partly within the area of the local authority by which or as regards which the referendum is to be held (reg 10(2)(d));

(5)   a European Parliamentary general election (reg 10(2)(e));

(6)   a European parliamentary election in respect of an electoral region within the meaning of the European Parliamentary Elections Act 2002 s 1 (see PARA 77) in which the area of the local authority by which or as regards which the referendum is to be held falls (Local Authorities (Conduct of Referendums) (England) Regulations 2012, SI 2012/323, reg 10(2)(f));

(7)   an ordinary election within the meaning of the Greater London Authority Act 1999 Pt I (ss 1–29) (the Greater London Authority: see LONDON GOVERNMENT vol 71 (2013) PARA 14 et seq), where the local authority by which or as regards which the referendum is to be held is a London borough (Local Authorities (Conduct of Referendums) (England) Regulations 2012, SI 2012/323, reg 10(2)(g));

(8)   an election (other than an ordinary election) of the Mayor of London under the Greater London Authority Act 1999 s 16(2) (filling a vacancy in the office of Mayor: see PARA 204), where the local authority by which or as regards which the referendum is to be held is a London borough (Local Authorities (Conduct of Referendums) (England) Regulations 2012, SI 2012/323, reg 10(2)(h));

(9)   an ordinary election of police and crime commissioners under the Police Reform and Social Responsibility Act 2011 s 50 (see POLICE AND INVESTIGATORY POWERS vol 84 (2013) PARA 62) (Local Authorities (Conduct of Referendums) (England) Regulations 2012, SI 2012/323, reg 10(2)(i));

(10) an election to fill a vacancy in the office of a police and crime commissioner under the Police Reform and Social Responsibility Act 2011 s 51 (see POLICE AND INVESTIGATORY POWERS vol 84 (2013) PARA 69) for a police area in which the area of the local authority by which or as regards which the referendum is to be held falls (Local Authorities (Conduct of Referendums) (England) Regulations 2012, SI 2012/323, reg 10(2)(j));

(11) an election of an elected mayor (reg 10(2)(k)).

Where the poll at a referendum would be taken together with the poll at an election of a description mentioned in heads (3), (4), (6), (8), or (10) above, reg 10(1) does not apply where notice of the date of the referendum is given under reg 4 (see PARA 574) before the date on which notice is given of the date of election, and the date of the referendum is not the same as that of the election: reg 10(3). In a case to which reg 10(3) applies, the poll at a referendum is to be taken on the day of which the notice has been given under reg 4: reg 10(4). The poll at a referendum may be taken together with the poll at an election under the Local Government Act 1972 s 89 (filling of casual vacancies in the case of councillors: see PARA 202; and LOCAL GOVERNMENT vol 69 (2009) PARA 140), or under the Greater London Authority Act 1999 s 10 (filling a vacancy in an Assembly constituency: see PARA 204), where the referendum is to be held in compliance with a direction of the Secretary of State (if he or she so determines); and, in any other case, if the authority by which the referendum is to be held so determines: see the Local Authorities (Conduct of Referendums) (England) Regulations 2012, SI 2012/323, reg 10(5). Notice of such a determination must be given in writing (where the determination is made by the Secretary of State) to the authority (or authorities, as the case may be) by which the election and the referendum concerned is (or are) to be held or (where the determination is made by an authority), to the authority (other than itself) by which the election concerned is to be held: see reg 10(6). As to the meaning of 'parliamentary election' and as to use of the expression 'parliamentary general election' see PARA 9. As to local government statutes covering the election of councillors and mayors see PARA 10; and as to the provision for local government elections that is made under the Representation of the People Acts see PARA 11. As to the meaning of 'European parliamentary general election' for these purposes see PARA 21 note 2. As to the polls at European parliamentary general elections see PARA 217 et seq.

2   The Representation of the People Act 1985 s 15 has effect as if contained in the Representation of the People Act 1983 Pt I (ss 1–66B): see the Representation of the People Act 1985 s 27(2). Accordingly, as to the meaning of 'local government election' see PARA 11. As to the polls at ordinary local government elections see PARA 197 et seq.

3   See the Representation of the People Act 1985 s 15(1)(d) (s 15 applied and modified by the Local Authorities (Conduct of Referendums) (England) Regulations 2012, SI 2012/323, Sch 4 Table 2). See note 7. As to combined polls at elections and a local authority referendum in England where the Representation of the People Act 1985 s 15(1) does not require them to be taken together see PARA 31.

4   As to the transferred functions of returning officers (and counting officers, as the case may be) where polls are combined see PARA 18.

5   As to the polling stations to be used where polls are combined see PARA 19.

6   As to proceedings on the issue and receipt of postal ballot papers where polls are combined see PARA 20.

7   Where polls are taken together in accordance with the Local Authorities (Conduct of Referendums) (England) Regulations 2012, SI 2012/323, reg 10(1), (5) (see note 1), the referendum is to be conducted in accordance with the rules contained in reg 11, Sch 5 ('the Local Government Act referendums (combination of polls) rules': see reg 2(1)): see reg 11(1), (2). The Representation of the People Act 1983, the Representation of the People Act 1985, the Representation of the People Act 2000, the Political Parties, Elections and Referendums Act 2000, the Electoral Administration Act 2006 and the Representation of the People (England and Wales) Regulations 2001, SI 2001/341, have effect in relation to such a referendum, subject to the modifications specified in the Local Authorities (Conduct of Referendums) (England) Regulations 2012, SI 2012/323, Sch 4 Table 1 (Representation of the People Act 1983), Sch 4 Table 2 (Representation of the People Act 1985), Sch 4 Table 3 (Representation of the People Act 2000), Sch 4 Table 4 (Political Parties, Elections and Referendums Act 2000), Sch 4 Table 5 (Electoral Administration Act 2006) and Sch 4 Table 6 (Representation of the People (England and Wales) Regulations 2001, SI 2001/341), and subject to any contrary provision of the Local Authorities (Conduct of Referendums) (England) Regulations 2012, SI 2012/323: reg 11(3). Where a person applies under the Representation of the People Act 2000 s 12, Sch 4 (see PARA 363 et seq) to vote by post, or to vote by proxy, at the election, that person is to be treated as applying also to vote by post, or to vote by proxy, at the referendum: Local Authorities (Conduct of Referendums) (England) Regulations 2012, SI 2012/323, reg 11(4).

In relation to an election (or elections, as the case may be), where polls are taken together in accordance with the Local Authorities (Conduct of Referendums) (England) Regulations 2012, SI 2012/323, reg 10(1), (5), the Representation of the People Act 1985, the Representation of the People Act 2000, and the Representation of the People (England and Wales) Regulations 2001, SI 2001/341, have effect, subject to the modifications specified in Sch 4 Table 2 (Representation of the People Act 1985), Sch 4 Table 3 (Representation of the People Act 2000), and Sch 4 Table 6 (Representation of the People (England and Wales) Regulations 2001, SI 2001/341), and subject to any contrary provision of the Local Authorities (Conduct of Referendums) (England) Regulations 2012, SI 2012/323: see reg 12(1), (2). Where a person applies under the Representation of the People Act 2000 Sch 4 to vote by post, or to vote by proxy, at the referendum, that person is to be treated as applying also to vote at the election by post or by proxy: Local Authorities (Conduct of Referendums) (England) Regulations 2012, SI 2012/323, reg 12(3).

8   Where the poll at a local authority referendum, conducted in accordance with rules that are contained in the regulations made under the Local Government Act 2000 ss 9MG, 105 (conduct of local authority referendums in England: see PARA 558) (ie in accordance with rules that are contained in the Local Authorities (Conduct of Referendums) (England) Regulations 2012, SI 2012/323), is taken together with the poll at a parliamentary election, the parliamentary elections rules contained in the Representation of the People Act 1983 s 23(1), Sch 1 (see PARA 383 note 2) have effect subject to the modifications contained in the Representation of the People (Combination of Polls) (England and Wales) Regulations 2004, SI 2004/294, Sch 2 (amended by SI 2006/3278; SI 2007/1025; SI 2012/1917): see the Representation of the People (Combination of Polls) (England and Wales) Regulations 2004, SI 2004/294, reg 8(1)(b) (amended by SI 2012/1917); Interpretation Act 1978 s 17(2)(b).

9   Where the poll at a local authority referendum, conducted in accordance with rules that are contained in the regulations made under the Local Government Act 2000 ss 9MG, 105 (conduct of local authority referendums in England: see PARA 558) (ie in accordance with rules that are contained in the Local Authorities (Conduct of Referendums) (England) Regulations 2012, SI 2012/323), is taken together with the poll at a European parliamentary election, the European parliamentary elections rules contained in the European Parliamentary Elections Regulations 2004, SI 2004/293, reg 9(1), Sch 1 (see PARA 383 note 16) have effect in England and Wales subject to the modifications contained in reg 11, Sch 3 Pt 1 (rr 1–29) (Sch 3 substituted by SI 2009/186; the European Parliamentary Elections Regulations 2004, SI 2004/293, Sch 3 Pt 1 amended by SI 2012/1917): see the European Parliamentary Elections Regulations 2004, SI 2004/293, reg 11(b), (1); Interpretation Act 1978 s 17(2)(b).

10   Where the poll at a local authority referendum is taken together with the poll at a local government election:

    (1)   the rules set out in the Local Elections (Principal Areas) (England and Wales) Rules 2006, SI 2006/3304, r 3, Sch 2 (see PARA 383 note 6) apply to the principal area election subject to modifications as set out in r 4, Sch 3 (Sch 3 amended by SI 2010/1172; SI 2011/563; SI 2011/1043) (see the Local Elections (Principal Areas) (England and Wales) Rules 2006, SI 2006/3304, rr 2(2)(e), 4);

    (2)   the rules set out in the Local Elections (Parishes and Communities) (England and Wales) Rules 2006, SI 2006/3305, r 3, Sch 2 (as to which see PARA 383 note 6) apply to the parish or community election subject to modifications as set out in r 4, Sch 3 (Sch 3 amended by SI 2010/1172; SI 2011/562; SI 2011/1043) (see the Local Elections (Parishes and Communities) (England and Wales) Rules 2006, SI 2006/3305, rr 2(2)(e), 4).

For these purposes, 'referendum' means a referendum conducted under the Local Authorities (Conduct of Referendums) (England) Regulations 2012, SI 2012/323 (see PARA 555 et seq): see the Local Elections (Principal Areas) (England and Wales) Rules 2006, SI 2006/3304, r 2(1); Local Elections (Parishes and Communities) (England and Wales) Rules 2006, SI 2006/3305, r 2(1); Interpretation Act 1978 s 17(2)(b). In relation to a London Authority election (included in the definition of 'local government election' for the purposes of the Representation of the People Act 1983: see PARA 11) that is taken together with the poll at a local authority referendum, held in accordance with rules that are contained in regulations made under the Local Government Act 2000 ss 9MG, 105 (conduct of local authority referendums in England: see PARA 555) (ie in accordance with rules that are contained in the Local Authorities (Conduct of Referendums) (England) Regulations 2012, SI 2012/323), the Greater London Authority Elections Rules 2007, SI 2007/3541, rr 3, 4, (see PARA 383 note 10) do not apply and the election must be conducted in accordance with the rules specified as follows (see r 5(1)(b), (2); Interpretation Act 1978 s 17(2)(b)):

    (a)   the constituency members election rules in the Greater London Authority Elections Rules 2007, SI 2007/3541, r 5(3), Sch 5 have effect for the purposes of any election of constituency members of the London Assembly whether at an ordinary election or in the circumstances mentioned in the Greater London Authority Act 1999 s 10 (filling a vacancy in an Assembly constituency: see PARA 204) (Greater London Authority Elections Rules 2007, SI 2007/3541, r 5(3));

    (b)   the London members election rules in r 5(4), Sch 6, with the exception of Sch 6 Pt 7 (rr 63–67) (list candidates and the filling of vacancies), have effect for the purposes of any election of London members; and Sch 6 Pt 7 has effect for the purposes of the

Greater London Authority Act 1999 s 11 (filling a vacancy among the London members: see PARA 204) (Greater London Authority Elections Rules 2007, SI 2007/3541, r 5(4)); and

(c) the Mayoral Election Rules in r 5(5), Sch 7 have effect for the purposes of any election of the Mayor of London at an ordinary election, and any election under the Greater London Authority Act 1999 s 16(2) (filling a vacancy in the office of Mayor: see PARA 204) (Greater London Authority Elections Rules 2007, SI 2007/3541, r 5(5)).

As to the modification of the combined poll rules contained in Schs 5–7 (see heads (a) to (c) above) where votes are counted without the use of an electronic counting system see r 6, Sch 8 (the 'combined manual count rules': see r 2(1)) (r 6 amended by SI 2012/198). As to polls at elections for related areas that may be taken together under the Representation of the People Act 1985 s 15(2) see PARA 30.

11 Where the poll at a mayoral election conducted under the Local Authorities (Mayoral Elections) (England and Wales) Regulations 2007, SI 2007/1024, is taken together with the poll at a local authority referendum, the mayoral elections rules contained in reg 3(1), Sch 1 (see PARA 383) are modified so as to have effect as set out in reg 4(1), Sch 3 (Sch 3 amended by SI 2010/1172; SI 2011/926; SI 2012/1917; SI 2012/2059): see the Local Authorities (Mayoral Elections) (England and Wales) Regulations 2007, SI 2007/1024, reg 4(1) (reg 4(1) renumbered by SI 2012/2059). As to the meaning of 'referendum' for these purposes see PARA 26 note 9.

28. Combined polls at local government elections for related electoral areas.
Where certain combinations of polls for local government elections[1] are to be taken on the same day and the elections are for related electoral areas[2], the polls at those elections are taken together[3], namely:

(1) the ordinary election of district councillors for any district ward[4] or an election to fill a casual vacancy occurring in the office of such a councillor[5] and the ordinary election of parish councillors for any parish[6] or an election to fill a casual vacancy occurring in the office of such a councillor[7];

(2) the ordinary election of councillors for any electoral division of a county in England in which there are no district councils[8] or an election to fill a casual vacancy occurring in the office of such a councillor[9], and the ordinary election of parish councillors for any parish or an election to fill a casual vacancy occurring in the office of such a councillor[10]; or

(3) the ordinary election of councillors for any electoral division of a Welsh county or county borough[11] or an election to fill a casual vacancy occurring in the office of such a councillor[12], and the ordinary election of community councillors for any community[13] or an election to fill a casual vacancy occurring in the office of such a councillor[14].

The Secretary of State[15] may by regulations[16] make such provision as he thinks fit in connection with the combining of polls at any elections under head (1), head (2) or head (3) above, including provision modifying the Representation of the People Acts[17] in relation to such elections[18]. Accordingly, provision has been made in relation to the discharge of the functions of the respective returning officers[19], the polling stations to be used[20], and proceedings on the issue and receipt of postal ballot papers[21]; and, where the polls at such elections are taken together, the elections rules which apply at each election have effect subject to certain modifications[22].

1 As to the meaning of 'local government election' see PARA 11.
2 For these purposes, electoral areas are 'related' if they are coterminous or if one is situated within the other: Representation of the People Act 1983 s 36(3A) (s 36(3) substituted, s 36(3A)–(3C) added, by the Representation of the People Act 1985 s 17). As to the meaning of 'electoral area' see PARA 11.

3   See the Representation of the People Act 1983 s 36(3) (as substituted: see note 2); s 36(3AB) (added by the Local Government (Wales) Act 1994 s 66(6), Sch 16 para 68(8)); and the Representation of the People Act 1983 s 36(3AC) (added by the Local Government and Rating Act 1997 s 33(1), Sch 3 para 17).
4   As to the establishment of district wards for the purpose of local government elections see PARA 74; and as to the ordinary election of district councillors see PARA 197.
5   Representation of the People Act 1983 s 36(3)(a) (as substituted: see note 2). As to elections to fill a casual vacancy occurring in the office of district councillor see PARA 202.
6   As to parishes see LOCAL GOVERNMENT vol 69 (2009) PARA 27 et seq. As to the ordinary elections of parish councillors for any parish see PARA 200.
7   Representation of the People Act 1983 s 36(3)(b) (s 36(3) as substituted (see note 2); s 36(3)(b) amended by the Local Government (Wales) Act 1994 s 66(8), Sch 16 para 68(8), Sch 18). As to elections to fill a casual vacancy occurring in the office of parish councillor see PARA 205.
8   As to electoral divisions of a county in England in which there are no district councils see PARA 74; and as to the ordinary election of councillors for such an area see PARA 197. As to the meanings of 'England' and 'Wales' see PARA 1 note 1.
9   Representation of the People Act 1983 s 36(3AC)(a) (as added: see note 3). As to elections to fill a casual vacancy occurring in the office of councillor for a county in England in which there are no district councils see PARA 202.
10 Representation of the People Act 1983 s 36(3AC)(b) (as added: see note 3).
11 As to the establishment of electoral divisions of a Welsh county or county borough for the purpose of local government elections see PARA 74; and as to the ordinary election of county or county borough councillors see PARA 197.
12 Representation of the People Act 1983 s 36(3AB)(a) (as added: see note 3). As to elections to fill a casual vacancy occurring in the office of county or county borough councillor see PARA 202.
13 As to communities see LOCAL GOVERNMENT vol 69 (2009) PARA 41 et seq. As to the ordinary elections of community councillors for any community see PARA 200.
14 Representation of the People Act 1983 s 36(3AB)(b) (as added: see note 3). As to elections to fill a casual vacancy occurring in the office of community councillor see PARA 205.
15 As to the Secretary of State see PARA 2.
16 Any power conferred by the Representation of the People Act 1983 to make regulations is, except where the Act otherwise provides, a power exercisable by the Secretary of State by statutory instrument: s 201(1) (amended by the Political Parties, Elections and Referendums Act 2000 s 158(1), (2), Sch 21 para 6(1), (7)(a), Sch 22). No regulations are to be so made, however, otherwise than under the Representation of the People Act 1983 s 110(7) (provision regarding details to appear on election publications: see PARA 748) or s 203(4) (application in relation to the Isles of Scilly: see PARA 11), unless a draft of the regulations has been laid before and approved by a resolution of each House of Parliament: s 201(2) (substituted by the Representation of the People Act 1985 s 24, Sch 4 para 69; and amended by the Political Parties, Elections and Referendums Act 2000 Sch 21 para 6(1), (7)(b); and SI 1991/1728). Any regulations under the Representation of the People Act 1983 may make different provision for different cases, circumstances or areas and may contain such incidental, supplemental, saving or transitional provisions as the Secretary of State or the Electoral Commission (in the case of any regulations made by the Commission) thinks fit: s 201(3) (added by the Representation of the People Act 2000 s 8, Sch 1 paras 1, 21; and amended by the Political Parties, Elections and Referendums Act 2000 Sch 21 para 6(1), (7)(d)). Any regulations under the Representation of the People Act 1983 s 110(7) are subject to annulment in pursuance of a resolution of either House of Parliament: s 201(2A) (added by the Political Parties, Elections and Referendums Act 2000 Sch 21 para 6(1), (7)(c)). As to the Electoral Commission see PARA 34 et seq. The Representation of the People Act 1983 s 201 applies to the Representation of the People Act 1985 by virtue of s 27(2), which provides that the Representation of the People Act 1983 and the Representation of the People Act 1985 ss 1–12 (see PARAS 96, 101, 114, 132, 136, 170, 735), ss 15–18 (see PARAS 17–21, 30, 31), s 21 (see PARAS 200–201) and Sch 1 (special polling stations in Northern Ireland) have effect as if the latter provisions were contained in the Representation of the People Act 1983 Pt I (ss 1–66B).

As from a day to be appointed under the Political Parties and Elections Act 2009 s 43(1), in carrying out the consultation required by the Political Parties, Elections and Referendums Act 2000 s 7 (Electoral Commission to be consulted on certain instruments relating to electoral law: see PARA 54), in the case of regulations under the Representation of the People Act 1983 s 10(4C) (prospectively amended so that it refers to Northern Ireland only) (form to be used in annual canvass: see PARA 151 note 17), s 10A(1C) (prospectively amended so that it refers to Northern Ireland only) (regulations made regarding persons without a national insurance number: see PARA 157 note 6) or s 13A(2C) (prospectively added) (regulations made regarding persons without a national insurance number: see PARA 168), the Secretary of State must seek the views of the Electoral Commission as to whether the provision to be made by the regulations would help or hinder the achievement of the registration objectives within the meaning given by s 10ZB (prospectively extended to England Wales, Scotland) (relevant registration objectives (Northern Ireland): see PARA 141): s 201(2B) (prospectively added by the Political Parties and Elections Act 2009 s 33(2), (9)). At the date at which this volume states the law, no such day had been appointed.

As from a day to be appointed under the Electoral Registration and Administration Act 2013 s 27(1), regulations made for the purposes only of omitting a particular kind of evidence from the kinds of evidence that a person is or may be required to provide by virtue of regulations under the Representation of the People Act 1983 s 52, Sch 2 paras 1(2A), 3ZA(3) (see PARA 112) are subject to annulment in pursuance of a resolution of either House of Parliament (and s 201(2) does not apply to regulations made for those purposes only): see s 201(2C) (prospectively added by the Electoral Registration and Administration Act 2013 s 2(1), (5)). At the date at which this volume states the law, no such day had been appointed.

17   As to the meaning of 'the Representation of the People Acts' see PARA 3 note 1.
18   Representation of the People Act 1983 s 36(3C) (as added: see note 2). As to the regulations made under the Representation of the People Act 1983 s 36(3C) see the Representation of the People (England and Wales) Regulations 2001, SI 2001/341; the Representation of the People (Combination of Polls) (England and Wales) Regulations 2004, SI 2004/294; and the text and notes 19–21.
19   As to the transferred functions of returning officers where polls are combined see PARA 18.
20   As to the polling stations to be used where polls are combined see PARA 19.
21   As to proceedings on the issue and receipt of postal ballot papers where polls are combined see PARA 20.
22   Where the poll at an election of councillors to the council of either a principal area or a parish or community is to be taken together with the poll at another local government election:
   (1)   the rules set out in the Local Elections (Principal Areas) (England and Wales) Rules 2006, SI 2006/3304, r 3, Sch 2 (see PARA 383 note 6) apply to the principal area election subject to modifications as set out in r 4, Sch 3 (Sch 3 amended by SI 2010/1172; SI 2011/563; SI 2011/1043) (see the Local Elections (Principal Areas) (England and Wales) Rules 2006, SI 2006/3304, rr 2(2)(c), 4);
   (2)   the rules set out in the Local Elections (Parishes and Communities) (England and Wales) Rules 2006, SI 2006/3305, r 3, Sch 2 (see PARA 383 note 6) apply to the parish or community election subject to modifications as set out in r 4, Sch 3 (Sch 3 amended by SI 2010/1172; SI 2011/562; SI 2011/1043) (see the Local Elections (Parishes and Communities) (England and Wales) Rules 2006, SI 2006/3305, rr 2(2)(c), 4).

29.   Combined polls at a local authority mayoral election and at local government elections for related electoral areas.   Where the polls at a local authority mayoral election[1] and at certain local government elections[2] are to be taken on the same day and the elections are for related electoral areas[3], the polls at those elections are taken together, as follows:
   (1)   the election of an elected mayor of a district council and the ordinary election of parish councillors for any parish[4] or an election to fill a casual vacancy occurring in the office of such a councillor[5];
   (2)   the election of an elected mayor of the council of a county in England in which there are no district councils[6], and the ordinary election of parish councillors for any parish or an election to fill a casual vacancy occurring in the office of such a councillor[7]; or
   (3)   the election of an elected mayor of a Welsh county or county borough council[8], and the ordinary election of community councillors for any community[9] or an election to fill a casual vacancy occurring in the office of such a councillor[10].

Where the polls at any such elections are taken together, provision has been made in relation to the discharge of the functions of the respective returning officers[11], the polling stations to be used[12], and proceedings on the issue and receipt of postal ballot papers[13]. The rules which apply to the poll at a local authority mayoral election are modified when such a poll is taken together with the poll at a relevant election (or referendum, as the case may be)[14].

1   As to the meaning of 'mayoral election' for these purposes, and as to the application of provisions in the Representation of the People Act 1983 in relation to the conduct of such an election, see PARA 11 note 14.
2   The Representation of the People Act 1985 s 15 has effect as if contained in the Representation of the People Act 1983 Pt I (ss 1–66B): see the Representation of the People Act 1985 s 27(2). Accordingly, as to the meaning of 'local government election' see PARA 11. As to the polls at ordinary local government elections see PARA 197 et seq.
3   For these purposes, electoral areas are 'related' if they are coterminous or if one is situated within the other: Representation of the People Act 1983 s 36(3A) (s 36(3) substituted, s 36(3A)–(3C) added, by the Representation of the People Act 1985 s 17; the Representation of the People Act 1983 s 36 applied and modified by the Local Authorities (Mayoral Elections) (England and Wales) Regulations 2007, SI 2007/1024, Sch 2 Table 1). See note 1. As to the meaning of 'electoral area' see PARA 11.
4   As to parishes see LOCAL GOVERNMENT vol 69 (2009) PARA 27 et seq. As to the ordinary elections of parish councillors for any parish see PARA 200.
5   Representation of the People Act 1983 s 36(3) (s 36(3) as substituted (see note 3); s 36 as applied and modified (see note 3)). As to elections to fill a casual vacancy occurring in the office of parish councillor see PARA 205.
6   As to electoral divisions of a county in England in which there are no district councils see PARA 74; and as to the ordinary election of councillors for such an area see PARA 197.
7   Representation of the People Act 1983 s 36(3AC) (added by the Local Government and Rating Act 1997 s 33(1), Sch 3 para 17; the Representation of the People Act 1983 s 36 as applied and modified (see note 3)). As to elections to fill a casual vacancy occurring in the office of councillor for a county in England in which there are no district councils see PARA 202.
8   As to the establishment of electoral divisions of a Welsh county or county borough for the purpose of local government elections see PARA 74.
9   As to communities see LOCAL GOVERNMENT vol 69 (2009) PARA 41 et seq. As to the ordinary elections of community councillors for any community see PARA 200.
10 Representation of the People Act 1983 s 36(3AB)(b) (s 36(3AB) added by the Local Government (Wales) Act 1994 s 66(6), Sch 16 para 68(8); the Representation of the People Act 1983 s 36 as applied and modified (see note 3)). As to elections to fill a casual vacancy occurring in the office of community councillor see PARA 205.
11 As to the transferred functions of returning officers where polls are combined see PARA 18.
12 As to the polling stations to be used where polls are combined see PARA 19.
13 As to proceedings on the issue and receipt of postal ballot papers where polls are combined see PARA 20.
14 See PARAS 26, 27.

30.   Combined polls at elections for related areas.   Where the polls at elections[1] for related areas are to be taken on the same date but are not required to be taken together[2], they may nevertheless be so taken if the returning officer for each election thinks fit[3]. For these purposes, two areas are related if one is coterminous with or situated wholly or partly within the other[4]. The Secretary of State[5] may by regulations[6] make such provision as he thinks fit in connection with the combining of polls at such elections (or at such elections and a referendum) including provision modifying the Representation of the People Acts[7] in relation to them[8]. Provision has been made accordingly in relation to the discharge of the functions of the respective returning officers (and counting officers, as the case may be)[9], the polling stations to be used[10], and proceedings on the issue and receipt of postal ballot papers[11]. Where elections are taken together in this way[12], the rules which apply to the conduct of polls at each election are modified[13].

Where the polls at an Assembly election[14] and a local government election for related areas are to be taken on the same date, but are not required to be taken together[15], they may nevertheless be so taken if the returning officer for each election thinks fit[16]. For these purposes, two areas are related if one is coterminous with or situated wholly or partly within the other[17]. Provision has been made in relation to the discharge of the functions of the respective returning officers[18], the polling stations to be used[19], and proceedings on the issue and receipt of postal ballot papers[20]. Provision is made also for the conduct of polls at Assembly elections when they are taken together with polls at local government elections[21].

1 For these purposes, the reference to 'elections' includes European parliamentary elections but does not include elections under the local government Act which are not local government elections: see the Representation of the People Act 1985 s 15(3) (amended by the European Communities (Amendment) Act 1986 s 3). The Representation of the People Act 1983 and the Representation of the People Act 1985 ss 15–17 have effect as if those provisions were contained in the Representation of the People Act 1983 Pt I (ss 1–66): see the Representation of the People Act 1985 s 27(2). Accordingly, as to the meanings of 'election under the local government Act' and 'local government election' see PARA 11. As to combined polls for local government elections for related electoral areas see PARA 28. As to the polls at ordinary local government elections see PARA 197 et seq.

The Representation of the People Act 1985 s 15 has effect in relation to the conduct of a mayoral election in England or Wales, subject to modifications that are set out in the Local Authorities (Mayoral Elections) (England and Wales) Regulations 2007, SI 2007/1024, reg 3(2), (4), Sch 2: see reg 3(2), (3), (5); and PARAS 11 note 14, 26 note 12.

2 Ie are not required to be taken together by either the Representation of the People Act 1985 s 15(1) (see PARAS 21–22, 24, 26–27) or the Representation of the People Act 1983 s 36 (see PARAS 28, 29): see the Representation of the People Act 1985 s 15(2) (as originally enacted; and as applied and modified (see note 1)).

3 See the Representation of the People Act 1985 s 15(2) (as originally enacted; and as applied and modified (see note 1)). As to returning officers see PARA 350 et seq.

4 See the Representation of the People Act 1985 s 15(3) (as originally enacted; and as applied and modified (see note 1)).

5 As to the Secretary of State see PARA 2.

6 As to the making of regulations under the Representation of the People Act 1985 generally see PARA 28 note 16.

7 As to the meaning of 'the Representation of the People Acts' see PARA 3 note 1.

8 Representation of the People Act 1985 s 15(5) (as originally enacted; and as applied and modified (see note 1)). As to the regulations made under s 15(5) see (*inter alia*) the Representation of the People (Combination of Polls) (England and Wales) Regulations 2004, SI 2004/294; and the text and notes 9–11.

9 As to the transferred functions of returning officers (and counting officers, as the case may be) where polls are combined see PARA 18.

10 As to the polling stations to be used where polls are combined see PARA 19.

11 As to proceedings on the issue and receipt of postal ballot papers where polls are combined see PARA 20.

12 Ie under the Representation of the People Act 1985 s 15(2) (see the text and notes 1–3).

13 The same modifications apply to polls that are combined under the Representation of the People Act 1985 s 15(2) as to polls that are combined under s 15(1). Accordingly:
   (1) as to combined polls at a parliamentary general election and a European parliamentary general election see PARA 21;
   (2) as to combined polls at a parliamentary general election and an ordinary local government election see PARA 22;
   (3) as to combined polls at an ordinary local government election and a European parliamentary general election see PARA 24;
   (4) as to combined polls at a local authority mayoral election and at a parliamentary or European parliamentary election or ordinary local government election see PARA 26;
   (5) as combined polls at a local authority referendum and an election in England see PARA 27.

As to the modifications that apply to polls that are combined under the Representation of the People Act 1983 s 36 see PARAS 28, 29.

In relation to a London Authority election (included in the definition of 'local government election' for the purposes of the Representation of the People Act 1983: see PARA 11) that is taken together with the poll at an ordinary local government election (other than an Authority election) under the Representation of the People Act 1985 s 15(2), the Greater London

Authority Elections Rules 2007, SI 2007/3541, rr 3, 4, (see PARA 383 note 10) do not apply and the election must be conducted in accordance with the rules specified as follows (see r 5(1)(a), (2)):

    (a)   the constituency members election rules in r 5(3), Sch 5 have effect for the purposes of any election of constituency members of the London Assembly whether at an ordinary election or in the circumstances mentioned in the Greater London Authority Act 1999 s 10 (filling a vacancy in an Assembly constituency: see PARA 204) (Greater London Authority Elections Rules 2007, SI 2007/3541, r 5(3));

    (b)   the London members election rules in r 5(4), Sch 6, with the exception of Sch 6 Pt 7 (rr 63–67) (list candidates and the filling of vacancies), have effect for the purposes of any election of London members; and Sch 6 Pt 7 has effect for the purposes of the Greater London Authority Act 1999 s 11 (filling a vacancy among the London members: see PARA 204) (Greater London Authority Elections Rules 2007, SI 2007/3541, r 5(4)); and

    (c)   the Mayoral Election Rules in r 5(5), Sch 7 have effect for the purposes of any election of the Mayor of London at an ordinary election, and any election under the Greater London Authority Act 1999 s 16(2) (filling a vacancy in the office of Mayor: see PARA 204) (Greater London Authority Elections Rules 2007, SI 2007/3541, r 5(5)).

As to the modification of the combined poll rules contained in Schs 5–7 (see heads (a) to (c) above) where votes are counted without the use of an electronic counting system see r 6, Sch 8 (the 'combined manual count rules': see r 2(1)) (r 6 amended by SI 2012/198).

14 As to the meaning of 'Assembly election' see PARA 3 note 2.

15 Ie are not required to be taken together by the National Assembly for Wales (Representation of the People) Order 2007, SI 2007/236, art 16(1) (see PARA 23): see art 16(2).

16 National Assembly for Wales (Representation of the People) Order 2007, SI 2007/236, art 16(2). As to returning officers for Welsh Assembly elections see PARA 357 et seq.

17 National Assembly for Wales (Representation of the People) Order 2007, SI 2007/236, art 16(3).

18 As to the transferred functions of returning officers where polls are combined see PARA 18.

19 As to the polling stations to be used where polls are combined see PARA 19.

20 As to proceedings on the issue and receipt of postal ballot papers where polls are combined see PARA 20.

21 See the National Assembly for Wales (Representation of the People) Order 2007, SI 2007/236, art 16(7). The provision referred to in the text is made by art 16(7), Sch 4, although where the poll at an Assembly election is combined with a mayoral election, only Sch 4 Pt 1 (paras 1–3) (general: see PARAS 18, 19) and Pt 2 (paras 4–26) (modifications to art 17(1), Sch 5 (Assembly Election Rules: see PARA 383 note 20) to apply where the poll at an Assembly election is taken with the poll at a local government election under art 16(1), (2)) apply: see art 16(7).

Where the poll at an Assembly election is taken with the poll at a local government election under art 16(2), then Sch 5 has effect subject to the modifications set out in Sch 4 Pt 2 paras 5–26: Sch 4 Pt 2 para 4.

Where the poll at an election of county or county borough councillors is taken together with the poll at an Assembly election under art 16(2), the Local Elections (Principal Areas) (England and Wales) Rules 2006, SI 2006/3304, r 4, Sch 3 (rules for conduct of an election of councillors of a principal area where the poll is taken together with the poll at a relevant election or referendum) ('the principal area election rules': see PARA 383 note 6) have effect subject to the modifications set out in the National Assembly for Wales (Representation of the People) Order 2007, SI 2007/236, Sch 4 Pt 3 paras 28–45: Sch 4 Pt 3 para 27.

Where the poll at an election of community councillors is taken together with the poll at an Assembly election under art 16(2), the Local Elections (Parishes and Communities) (England and Wales) Rules 2006, SI 2006/3305, r 4, Sch 3 (rules for conduct of an election of councillors of a parish or community where the poll is taken together with the poll at a relevant election or referendum) ('the community election rules': see PARA 383 note 6) have effect subject to the modifications set out in the National Assembly for Wales (Representation of the People) Order 2007, SI 2007/236, Sch 4 Pt 3 paras 47–63: Sch 4 Pt 4 para 46.

31. Combined polls at elections and a local authority referendum in England. Where the polls at elections and a local authority referendum in England[1] are to be taken on the same date but are not required to be taken together[2], they may nevertheless be so taken if the returning officer for each election thinks fit[3]. The Secretary of State[4] may by regulations[5] make such provision as he thinks fit in connection with the combining of polls at such elections and a referendum, including provision modifying the Representation of the People Acts[6] in relation to them[7]. Provision has been made accordingly in relation to the discharge of the functions of the respective returning (or counting) officers[8], the polling stations to be used[9], and proceedings on the issue and receipt of postal ballot papers[10]. The rules which apply to the poll at a local authority referendum held in England are modified when such a poll is taken together with the poll at a relevant election, as are the rules that apply at each election in turn[11].

1   The Representation of the People Act 1985 s 15 has effect in relation to an election (or elections, as the case may be), where polls are taken together in accordance with the Local Authorities (Conduct of Referendums) (England) Regulations 2012, SI 2012/323, reg 10(1), (5) (see PARA 27 note 1), subject to the modifications specified in Sch 4 Table 2 (Representation of the People Act 1985), and subject to any contrary provision of the Local Authorities (Conduct of Referendums) (England) Regulations 2012, SI 2012/323: see reg 12(1), (2); and PARA 27 note 7. As to the meaning of 'referendum' for these purposes see PARA 574 note 2. The Local Authorities (Conduct of Referendums) (Wales) Regulations 2008, SI 2008/1848, continue to make no provision for polls at local authority referendums in Wales to be taken together with polls at another election or referendum. As to the meanings of 'England' and 'Wales' see PARA 1 note 1.
2   Ie are not required to be taken together by the Representation of the People Act 1985 s 15(1) (as applied and modified: see PARA 27): see s 15(2) (as applied and modified: see note 1).
3   See the Representation of the People Act 1985 s 15(2) (as applied and modified: see note 1).
4   As to the Secretary of State see PARA 2.
5   As to the making of regulations under the Representation of the People Act 1985 generally see PARA 28 note 16.
6   As to the meaning of 'the Representation of the People Acts' see PARA 3 note 1.
7   Representation of the People Act 1985 s 15(5) (as applied and modified: see note 1). As to the regulations made under s 15(5) see (*inter alia*) the Representation of the People (Combination of Polls) (England and Wales) Regulations 2004, SI 2004/294; and the text and notes 8–11.
8   As to the transferred functions of returning officers (and counting officers, as the case may be) where polls are combined see PARA 18.
9   As to the polling stations to be used where polls are combined see PARA 19.
10 As to proceedings on the issue and receipt of postal ballot papers where polls are combined see PARA 20.
11 See PARA 27.

32.   Combined polls at local authority referendums in England.   Where an authority ('the first authority') has given notice[1] of the date on which a referendum[2] is to be held in its area, no other authority whose area includes that of the first authority, or whose area is part of that of the council of the same county as that of the first authority, may hold a referendum in its area within the period beginning 28 days before the date of the first authority's referendum and ending 28 days after that date unless the polls at the referendums are combined[3]. Where the date on which a referendum is to be held in a county is the same as that on which a referendum is to be held in any district within that county, the polls must be taken together[4].

Where polls at referendums are taken together in either of these ways[5]:

(1)   specified functions[6] are all to be discharged by one counting officer, and the counting officers are to agree as to which of them that should be[7];

(2)   the referendums must be conducted in accordance with the special combined polls rules[8], with other provisions applied and modified as set out for the purpose[9];

(3)   the cost of taking the combined poll (excluding any cost solely attributable to one referendum) and any cost attributable to the combination is to be apportioned equally among the referendums[10].

1 Ie under the Local Authorities (Conduct of Referendums) (England) Regulations 2012, SI 2012/323, reg 4(1) (see PARA 574): see reg 10(7).
2 As to the meaning of 'referendum' for these purposes see PARA 574 note 2. The Local Authorities (Conduct of Referendums) (Wales) Regulations 2008, SI 2008/1848, continue to make no provision for polls at local authority referendums in Wales to be taken together with polls at another election or referendum. As to the meanings of 'England' and 'Wales' see PARA 1 note 1.
3 Local Authorities (Conduct of Referendums) (England) Regulations 2012, SI 2012/323, reg 10(7).
4 Local Authorities (Conduct of Referendums) (England) Regulations 2012, SI 2012/323, reg 10(8).
5 Ie in accordance with either the Local Authorities (Conduct of Referendums) (England) Regulations 2012, SI 2012/323, reg 10(7) (see the text and notes 1–3) or reg 10(8) (see the text and note 4): see reg 13(1).
6 Ie the functions specified in the Local Authorities (Conduct of Referendums) (England) Regulations 2012, SI 2012/323, reg 13(3), as follows (see reg 13(2), (3)):
   (1) those under the following rules contained in reg 13(4), Sch 5 (ie the 'Local Government Act Referendums (Combination of Polls) Rules': see reg 2(1)) (see note 8) (see reg 13(3)):
       (a) unless head (b) below applies, Sch 5 r 8 (the corresponding number list) to the extent that it relates to ballot papers to be provided in pursuance of Sch 5 r 17(1) (reg 13(3)(a)(i));
       (b) where the proceedings on the issue and receipt of postal ballot papers at the referendums are taken together under the Representation of the People (England and Wales) Regulations 2001, SI 2001/341, reg 65 as applied by the Local Authorities (Conduct of Referendums) (England) Regulations 2012, SI 2012/323, reg 13(5): see note 9), Sch 5 r 8 (the corresponding number list) (reg 13(3)(a)(ii));
       (c) Sch 5 r 12(3) (notice of situation of polling stations, etc) (reg 13(3)(a)(iii));
       (d) where the proceedings on the issue and receipt of postal ballot papers at the referendums are taken together under the Representation of the People (England and Wales) Regulations 2001, SI 2001/341, reg 65 (as so applied), the Local Authorities (Conduct of Referendums) (England) Regulations 2012, SI 2012/323, Sch 5 r 13 (postal ballot papers) (reg 13(3)(a)(iv));
       (e) Sch 5 r 14 (provision of polling stations) (reg 13(3)(a)(v));
       (f) Sch 5 r 15(1), (2) (appointment of presiding officers and clerks) to the extent that that rule concerns the appointment of presiding officers and clerks to assist them (reg 13(3)(a)(vi));
       (g) Sch 5 r 17 (equipment of polling stations) (reg 13(3)(a)(vii));
       (h) Sch 5 r 20 (notification of requirement of secrecy in relation to polling stations) (reg 13(3)(a)(viii));
       (i) where the proceedings on the issue and receipt of postal ballot papers at the referendums are taken together under the Representation of the People (England and Wales) Regulations 2001, SI 2001/341, reg 65 (as so applied), the Local Authorities (Conduct of Referendums) (England) Regulations 2012, SI 2012/323, Sch 5 r 22 (return of postal ballot papers) (reg 13(3)(a)(ix));
       (j) Sch 5 r 23(3) (signature as to certificate of employment) (reg 13(3)(a)(x));
       (k) Sch 5 r 24(2)(b) (keeping of order in station) (reg 13(3)(a)(xi));
       (l) Sch 5 r 38(1) (the count) (reg 13(3)(a)(xii)); and
   (2) where the proceedings on the issue and receipt of postal ballot papers at more than one referendum are taken together under the Representation of the People (England and Wales) Regulations 2001, SI 2001/341, reg 65 (as so applied), the functions conferred by Pt V (regs 64–91) (as so applied) (issue and receipt of postal ballot papers) (Local Authorities (Conduct of Referendums) (England) Regulations 2012, SI 2012/323, reg 13(3)(b)).
7 See the Local Authorities (Conduct of Referendums) (England) Regulations 2012, SI 2012/323, reg 13(2). As to the meaning of 'counting officer' see PARA 576 note 1.
8 Ie the referendums must be conducted in accordance with the rules contained in the Local Authorities (Conduct of Referendums) (England) Regulations 2012, SI 2012/323, reg 13(4), Sch 5 (the 'Local Government Act Referendums (Combination of Polls) Rules': see note 6): see reg 13(4).
9 Ie the Representation of the People Act 1983, the Representation of the People Act 1985, the Representation of the People Act 2000, the Political Parties, Elections and Referendums Act 2000, the Electoral Administration Act 2006 and the Representation of the People (England

and Wales) Regulations 2001, SI 2001/341, have effect in relation to the referendums, subject to the modifications specified in the Local Authorities (Conduct of Referendums) (England) Regulations 2012, SI 2012/323, reg 13(5), Sch 4 Table 1 (Representation of the People Act 1983), Sch 4 Table 2 (Representation of the People Act 1985), Sch 4 Table 3 (Representation of the People Act 2000), Sch 4 Table 4 (Political Parties, Elections and Referendums Act 2000), Sch 4 Table 5 (Electoral Administration Act 2006) and Sch 4 Table 6 (Representation of the People (England and Wales) Regulations 2001, SI 2001/341), and subject to any contrary provision of the Local Authorities (Conduct of Referendums) (England) Regulations 2012, SI 2012/323: see reg 13(5).

10 Local Authorities (Conduct of Referendums) (England) Regulations 2012, SI 2012/323, reg 13(6).

(6) ELECTIONS IN THE CITY OF LONDON

33. City elections. Certain provisions of the Representation of the People Act 1983[1] apply in relation to the City of London as if the City were a London borough and the Common Council of the City were a London borough council[2]; and expressions used for certain purposes in the Representation of the People Act 1983[3] are modified so that: (1) 'local government election'[4] and 'election under the local government Act'[5] include a municipal election in the City of London[6]; (2) 'local government area'[7] includes the City; and (3) 'electoral area'[8] means, in relation to a ward election[9], the ward and, in relation to any other municipal election in the City, the City[10].

Further provision is made in relation to municipal elections in the City[11], subject to modifications affecting personation and other voting offences[12], broadcasting during the period of elections[13], disturbances at election meetings[14] and the payment of certain costs and expenses[15]. The Representation of the People Act 1983 also applies with modifications to ward elections in the City of London[16]. Special provision is made regarding the expenses of candidates at ward, and liverymen in common hall, elections[17].

In most of its other respects, the law that applies to elections in the City of London is unique, being governed by custom, by certain local Acts and by various Acts of the Common Council, and is discussed elsewhere in this work[18].

1 Ie the Representation of the People Act 1983 Pt I (ss 1–66B) (parliamentary and local government franchise and its exercise: see PARA 95 et seq), so far as it has effect for the purposes of parliamentary elections, and Pts I–III (ss 1–186), so far as they have effect for the purposes of Authority elections, and subject to any express provision contained in the Part or Parts in question: see s 203(2); and PARA 11. As to the meaning of 'parliamentary election' see PARA 9; and as to the meaning of 'Authority election' see PARA 11.
2 See the Representation of the People Act 1983 s 203(2); and PARA 11. For these purposes, the Inner Temple and the Middle Temple are treated as forming part of the City: s 203(2); and PARA 11. The modifications made by s 203(2) do not affect s 52(4) (duty of a district council or London borough council to assign officers to assist the registration officer: see PARA 140): s 203(3); and PARA 11. As to London boroughs and London borough councils generally see LONDON GOVERNMENT vol 71 (2013) PARA 20 et seq. As to the Court of Common Council see LONDON GOVERNMENT vol 71 (2013) PARA 34 et seq; and as to the Temples see LONDON GOVERNMENT vol 71 (2013) PARA 17.
3 Ie for the purposes of the Representation of the People Act 1983 Pt I s 60 (personation: see PARA 730), s 61 (other voting offences: see PARA 700) and s 62A (offences associated with postal or proxy voting: see PARA 731) (s 191(1)(a) (amended by the Representation of the People Act 1985 s 28, Sch 5; and the Electoral Administration Act 2006 s 74(1), Sch 1 Pt 7 paras 104, 125)); the Representation of the People Act 1983 Pt II (ss 67–119) (the election campaign: see PARA 230 et seq) except s 96 (schools and rooms for local election meetings: see PARA 337) and s 99 (prohibition on officials acting as candidates' agents: see PARA 746) (s 191(1)(b)); Pt III (ss 120–186) (legal proceedings: see PARA 761 et seq) (s 191(1)(c)); s 189 (voting offences at certain local elections: see PARA 700), s 193–198 (City elections) (s 191(1)(d) (amended by the

Representation of the People Act 1985 s 24, Sch 4 para 66)); and the Representation of the People Act 1983 Pt V (ss 200–207) (general and supplemental) (s 191(1)(e)).

4   As to the meaning of 'local government election' generally see PARA 11.

5   As to the expression 'election under the local government Act' generally see PARA 11.

6   For these purposes, 'municipal election in the City of London' means an election to the office of Mayor, Alderman, Common Councilman or sheriff and also the election of any officer elected by the Mayor, Aldermen and Liverymen in Common Hall; and 'corporate office' includes each of those offices: see the Representation of the People Act 1983 s 191(1). As to the election of the Lord Mayor of London see LONDON GOVERNMENT vol 71 (2013) PARA 27; as to the election of Aldermen see LONDON GOVERNMENT vol 71 (2013) PARA 32; as to the election of Common Councilmen see LONDON GOVERNMENT vol 71 (2013) PARA 35; and as to elections in Common Hall see LONDON GOVERNMENT vol 71 (2013) PARA 39.

Where a candidate who has been elected to a corporate office is, either by a certificate of an election court, or by a decision of the High Court, declared not to have been duly elected, acts done by him in execution of the office before the time when the certificate or decision is certified to the clerk of the authority for which the election was held are not to be invalidated by reason of that declaration: s 198. For these purposes, 'clerk of the authority' means, in relation to the City, the town clerk of the City: see s 191(1). As to the avoidance of elections generally see PARA 894 et seq.

7   For the purposes of the Representation of the People Act 1983, 'local government area' means Greater London, a county, county borough, London borough district, parish or community, and includes the City of London: see ss 191(1), 203(1) (definition of 'local government area' in s 203(1) amended by the Local Government Act 1985 ss 18(1), 19, Sch 9 Pt I; the Education Reform Act 1988 s 237, Sch 13 Pt I; the Local Government (Wales) Act 1994 s 66(6), Sch 16 para 68(16); and the Greater London Authority Act 1999 s 17, Sch 3 paras 1, 39(1), (4)(b)). As to local government areas in England and Wales see LOCAL GOVERNMENT vol 69 (2009) PARA 22 et seq. As to Greater London as an administrative area see LONDON GOVERNMENT vol 71 (2013) PARA 14.

8   As to the meaning of 'electoral area' generally see PARA 11.

9   As to ward elections in the City of London see the text and note 16.

10   See the Representation of the People Act 1983 s 191(1).

11   Ie the provisions of the Representation of the People Act 1983 listed at note 3 have effect.

12   See the Representation of the People Act 1983 s 191(1) (amended by the Representation of the People Act 1985 s 24, Sch 4 para 66), s 193 (amended by the Electoral Administration Act 2006 Sch 1 Pt 7 paras 104, 126). As to personation and other voting offences generally see PARAS 700, 730, 731 et seq.

13   See the Representation of the People Act 1983 s 191(1) (as amended: see note 12), s 194. As to broadcasting offences generally see PARAS 331–332.

14   See the Representation of the People Act 1983 s 191(1) (as amended: see note 12), s 195. As to disturbances at election meetings generally see PARA 338.

15   See the Representation of the People Act 1983 s 191(1) (as amended: see note 12), s 196 (amended by the Representation of the People Act 1985 Sch 5). The text refers to any costs or expenses directed to be paid under the Representation of the People Act 1983 s 132 (remuneration and allowances to be paid to the election commissioner: see PARA 778).

16   Without prejudice to the provisions applied by virtue of the Representation of the People Act 1983 ss 191–196 (see the text and notes 3–15), Sch 6 (amended by the City of London (Ward Elections) Act 2002 s 9(1), (2), Sch 1 Pt II, Sch 2) (ward elections in the City) also has effect as regards the operation of the City of London (Various Powers) Act 1957 Pt II (ss 4–11) (ward elections) and the City of London (Ward Elections) Act 2002: see the Representation of the People Act 1983 s 191(2) (amended by the City of London (Ward Elections) Act 2002 s 9(1), Sch 1 Pt 2 para 4). Specified provisions of the Representation of the People Act 1983, in addition to the provisions which apply by virtue of ss 191–196, are applied to and in respect of ward elections by the City of London (Various Powers) Act 1957 s 8 (amended by the City of London (Various Powers) Act 1958 s 16; the Representation of the People Act 1983 s 206, Sch 8; the Representation of the People Act 1985 ss 11, 28, Sch 2 Pt III, Sch 5; the Representation of the People Act 2000 s 15(1), Sch 6 para 1; and by virtue of the City of London (Various Powers) Act 1968 s 3(2), (3)). The City of London (Various Powers) Act 1957 Pt II governs the qualification of voters at ward elections in the City of London; and the City of London (Ward Elections) Act 2002 ss 1–10 extend the categories of persons entitled to vote at such elections better to reflect the present nature of commercial occupation of premises in the City: see further LONDON GOVERNMENT vol 71 (2013) PARA 24 et seq.

17   See the Representation of the People Act 1983 s 197 (amended by the Representation of the People Act 1985 Sch 4 para 67; the Electoral Administration Act 2006 Sch 1 paras 104, 127;

and by SI 2005/153). Functions of the Secretary of State under the Representation of the People Act 1983 s 197 (ie in respect of varying maximum amounts specified), and any instrument having effect under it, are to be exercised concurrently with the Lord President of the Council: see the Lord President of the Council Order 2010, SI 2010/1837, art 3(1)(a), (2)–(9); and PARA 2 note 3.

As to candidates' expenses generally see PARA 269 et seq. See also *Finch v Richardson* [2008] EWHC 3067 (QB), [2009] 1 WLR 1338, [2009] PTSR 841, [2009] All ER (D) 01 (Jan) (Aldermanic Election in the City of London); and PARAS 269 note 18, 690 note 10, 691 note 1, 693 note 9.

18 See further LONDON GOVERNMENT vol 71 (2013) PARA 23 et seq.

2. THE ELECTORAL COMMISSION ETC

(1) THE ELECTORAL COMMISSION

(i) The Commission and Bodies with Related Functions

A. CONSTITUTION, ADMINISTRATION AND PROCEEDINGS OF THE ELECTORAL COMMISSION

34. Establishment and constitution of the Electoral Commission. The Political Parties, Elections and Referendums Act 2000[1] established a body corporate known as the Electoral Commission ('the Commission')[2]. The Commission consists of nine or ten members, known as Electoral Commissioners[3] and appointed by Her Majesty[4], who also appoints one of the Commissioners to be the chairman of the Commission[5].

The Commission is not to be regarded as the servant or agent of the Crown[6] or as enjoying any status, immunity or privilege of the Crown[7], and the Commission's property is not to be regarded as property of the Crown or as property held on its behalf[8].

1 Ie the Political Parties, Elections and Referendums Act 2000 Pt I (ss 1–21): see also PARA 35 et seq. These provisions were enacted following the publication of *Standards in Public Life (Fifth Report): The Funding of Political Parties in the United Kingdom* (Cm 4057) (October 1998) (the 'Neill Report'). In the opinion of the authors of the report, a new body with widespread executive and investigative powers was required to oversee compliance with the serious and continuing duties they had proposed for political parties with regard to their funding, to institute action where necessary, and to make proposals to HM Government as to any necessary reforms in the working of the machinery: see para 2.32; Ch 11; and Recommendations R70–R82. However, the controls contained in the Political Parties, Elections and Referendums Act 2000 (as originally enacted) were widely considered not to be strong enough, leading to further remedy of the more glaring problems by means of the Electoral Administration Act 2006, and the establishment of a further review of the funding of political parties ('Sir Hayden Phillips's review'), which concluded with a published report: *Strengthening Democracy: Fair and Sustainable Funding of Political Parties (The Review of the Funding of Political Parties)* (March 2007) (ISBN 9780108507113). The Phillips review, which had failed to secure a consensus among the major political parties about proposed changes to the system, was followed by *Party finance and expenditure in the United Kingdom: the Government's proposals* (Cm 7329) (June 2008), and the Political Parties and Elections Act 2009 (which, inter alia, strengthened the regulatory role of the Electoral Commission, distinguishing this from its supervisory role, by assigning a wider range of investigatory powers and sanctions, clarifying its advisory role and reforming its governance arrangements so that, for example, four Commissioners must be nominated by the leaders of qualifying political parties, but nominated Commissioners will always be a minority of Commissioners: see PARA 35).

2 Political Parties, Elections and Referendums Act 2000 s 1(1). In Welsh, the Commission is known as 'Comisiwn Etholiadol': see s 1(1).

Further provision in relation to the Electoral Commission is made by Sch 1, which has effect: s 1(6). The Commission may do anything (except borrow money) which is calculated to facilitate, or is incidental or conducive to, the carrying out of any of its functions: Sch 1 para 2. For these purposes, 'functions' includes powers and duties: see s 160(1). As to the Commission's functions generally see PARA 51 et seq. The Electoral Commission is subject to investigation by the Parliamentary Commissioner for Administration: see the Parliamentary Commissioner Act 1967 s 4, Sch 2; and ADMINISTRATIVE LAW vol 1(1) (2001 Reissue) PARA 41 et seq.

The Secretary of State may by order provide for the transfer to the Commission of such property, rights and liabilities to which he is entitled or subject, and which are specified in the order, as he considers appropriate in connection with the establishment of the Commission: see the Political Parties, Elections and Referendums Act 2000 Sch 1 para 14(7). Such an order may in particular provide for the order to have effect despite any provision (of whatever nature) which would prevent or restrict the transfer of any such property, rights or liabilities otherwise than by the order: Sch 1 para 14(8). At the date at which this volume states the law, no such order had been made. As to the Secretary of State see PARA 2.

Any power of the Secretary of State to make any order or regulations under the Political Parties, Elections and Referendums Act 2000 must be exercised by statutory instrument: s 156(1). Subject to s 156(3), (4), (4A), a statutory instrument containing any order or regulations so made by the Secretary of State is subject to annulment in pursuance of a resolution of either House of Parliament (s 156(2) (amended by the Political Parties and Elections Act 2009 s 39, Sch 6 para 25)); but this provision does not apply to:

(1) any order under the Political Parties, Elections and Referendums Act 2000 s 163(2) (commencement) or Sch 1 para 14(7) (s 156(3)(a) (amended by the Local Democracy, Economic Development and Construction Act 2009 s 146(1), Sch 7 Pt 3)); or

(2) any order made in pursuance of the Political Parties, Elections and Referendums Act 2000 s 155(2)(a) (power to vary sums: see PARA 299 note 36) (s 156(3)(b)); and

(3) any order under s 51(4) (see CONSTITUTIONAL LAW AND HUMAN RIGHTS), s 67(1) (see PARA 311), any provision of Pt IV Ch VI (ss 71A–71C) (control of donations to registered parties and their members etc: special provision in connection with Northern Ireland), s 71F(13) (see CONSTITUTIONAL LAW AND HUMAN RIGHTS), s 71H(4) (see CONSTITUTIONAL LAW AND HUMAN RIGHTS), s 71U(1) (see PARA 312), any provision of Pt IVA Ch 2 (ss 71Z–71Z2) (regulation of loans and related transactions: special provision in connection with Northern Ireland), s 101(4) (see PARA 527), s 108(3) (see PARA 530), s 109(6) (see PARA 530), s 129 (see PARA 554), s 71Q(5), Sch 6A para 9 (see PARA 312 note 15), s 71Y, Sch 7A paras 2(9), 4(4) (see CONSTITUTIONAL LAW AND HUMAN RIGHTS), s 72, Sch 8 para 4 (see PARA 299), s 95, Sch 11 para 3(4) (see PARA 325), s 111, Sch 13 para 4 (see PARA 535), s 118, Sch 14 para 2 (see PARA 541) or s 119, Sch 15 para 3(4) (see PARA 546 note 25) (s 156(4) (amended by the Electoral Administration Act 2006 s 61(4), (7), Sch 1 Pt 6 paras 97, 100; the Northern Ireland (Miscellaneous Provisions) Act 2006 ss 11(8)(a)(iii), 13(1), 30(2), Sch 5; the Local Democracy, Economic Development and Construction Act 2009 Sch 7 Pt 3; and by SI 2008/1319)).

No such order is to be made under the Political Parties, Elections and Referendums Act 2000 s 156(4) (see head (3) above), whether alone or with other provisions, unless a draft of the statutory instrument containing the order has been laid before, and approved by a resolution of, each House of Parliament: see s 156(4).

An order under s 147, Sch 19C Pt 5 para 16 (civil sanctions: supplementary orders: see PARA 757 note 2) that contains provision made by virtue of Sch 19C Pt 1 para 1(1)–(5) (fixed money penalties: see PARA 757), Sch 19C Pt 2 para 5(1)–(4) (discretionary requirements: see PARA 758), Sch 19C Pt 3 para 10(2)(b), (3)(b) (stop notices: see PARA 759), or Sch 19C Pt 4 para 15(1)(a) (enforcement undertakings: see PARA 760), or that contains provision amending an Act, may not be made unless a draft of the statutory instrument containing the order has been laid before, and approved by a resolution of, each House of Parliament: s 156(4A) (added by the Political Parties and Elections Act 2009 s 3(4)). The Political Parties, Elections and Referendums Act 2000 s 156(2) does not apply to such an order: see s 156(4A) (as so added).

Any order or regulations made by the Secretary of State under the Political Parties, Elections and Referendums Act 2000 may contain such consequential, incidental, supplementary or transitional provisions or savings (including provisions amending, repealing or revoking enactments) as the Secretary of State considers appropriate, and may make different provision for different cases (s 156(5)); and nothing in the Political Parties, Elections and Referendums Act 2000 is to be read as affecting the generality of s 156(5), including s 156(5) as applied by s 19(9) (repealed) (s 156(6)). Provisions relating to regulations made by the Electoral Commission are contained in Sch 1 paras 21–23 (see PARAS 47–48): see s 156(7).

3   See the Political Parties, Elections and Referendums Act 2000 s 1(2), (3) (s 1(3) amended by the Political Parties and Elections Act 2009 s 6). All members of the Electoral Commission are disqualified for membership of the House of Commons: see the House of Commons Disqualification Act 1975 s 1(1), Sch 1 Pt II; and PARLIAMENT vol 78 (2010) PARAS 905, 908.

4   See the Political Parties, Elections and Referendums Act 2000 s 1(4). The Commissioners are appointed by Her Majesty in accordance with s 3 (see PARA 35): see s 1(4). As to the appointment of Assistant Electoral Commissioners see PARA 40.

5   Political Parties, Elections and Referendums Act 2000 s 1(5) (amended by the Political Parties and Elections Act 2009 Sch 6 para 9). The chairman of the Commission is appointed by Her Majesty in accordance with the Political Parties, Elections and Referendums Act 2000 s 3 (see PARA 35), but subject to s 3A(6) (nominated Commissioner may not be appointed as the chairman of the Commission: see PARA 35): see s 1(5) (as so amended).

6   Political Parties, Elections and Referendums Act 2000 Sch 1 para 1(1)(a). As to the position of the staff of the Commission see PARA 38 et seq.

7	Political Parties, Elections and Referendums Act 2000 Sch 1 para 1(1)(b).
8	Political Parties, Elections and Referendums Act 2000 Sch 1 para 1(2). For these purposes, 'property' includes any description of property: see s 160(1).
	The administrative and departmental records of the Electoral Commission are public records as defined for the purposes of the Public Records Act 1958: see s 10, Sch 1 para 3, Table Pt II; and CONSTITUTIONAL LAW AND HUMAN RIGHTS vol 8(2) (Reissue) PARA 835.

35. Appointment of Electoral Commissioners and Commission chairman.
The powers of Her Majesty to appoint Electoral Commissioners[1], and to appoint the chairman of the Commission[2], are exercisable on an address from the House of Commons[3]. Such an address must specify the period, not exceeding ten years, for which each proposed Electoral Commissioner to whom the address relates is to hold office as such Commissioner or (as the case may be) the period for which the proposed chairman of the Commission is to hold office as such chairman[4]. A person may not be appointed as an Electoral Commissioner if the person[5]:

(1)	is a member of a registered party[6];
(2)	is an officer or employee of a registered party or of any accounting unit of such a party[7];
(3)	holds a relevant elective office[8]; or
(4)	at any time within the last five years[9]: (a) has been such an officer or employee as is mentioned in head (2) above[10]; or (b) has held such an office as is mentioned in head (3) above[11]; or (c) has been named as a donor in the register of donations[12]; or (d) has been named as a participant in the register of recordable transactions[13].

Four of the Electoral Commissioners must each be a person whom the registered leader of a qualifying party[14] put forward to be considered for appointment as an Electoral Commissioner (a 'nominated Commissioner')[15]. Three of the nominated Commissioners must each be a person put forward by the registered leader of one of the three largest nominating parties[16] at the time of the person's appointment[17], but no appointment may be made that would result in two or more nominated Commissioners being persons put forward by the leader of the same party[18]. A nominated Commissioner may not be appointed as the chairman of the Electoral Commission[19].

An Electoral Commissioner, or the chairman of the Commission, may be re-appointed, or further re-appointed[20].

1	Ie under the Political Parties, Elections and Referendums Act 2000 s 1(4) (see PARA 34): see s 3(1).
2	Ie under the Political Parties, Elections and Referendums Act 2000 s 1(5) (see PARA 34): see s 3(1).
3	Political Parties, Elections and Referendums Act 2000 s 3(1). A motion for such an address may be made only if:
	(1)	the Speaker of the House of Commons agrees that the motion may be made (s 3(2)(a) (s 3(2) substituted by the Political Parties and Elections Act 2009 s 4(1), (2)));
	(2)	the motion has been the subject of consultation with the registered leader of each registered party to which two or more members of the House of Commons then belong (Political Parties, Elections and Referendums Act 2000 s 3(2)(b) (as so substituted)); and
	(3)	each person whose appointment is proposed in the motion has been selected in accordance with a procedure put in place and overseen by the Speaker's Committee (s 3(2)(c) (as so substituted)).
	For the purposes of head (2) above, the reference to members of the House of Commons does not include any member of that House who at the time in question: (a) has not made and subscribed the oath required by the Parliamentary Oaths Act 1866 (or the corresponding affirmation) (Political Parties, Elections and Referendums Act 2000 s 3(6)(a)); or (b) is disqualified from sitting and voting in that House (s 3(6)(b)). For these purposes, 'registered party' means a party registered under Pt II (ss 22–40) (see PARA 253): see s 160(1). In the case of

a re-appointment, or further re-appointment, of an Electoral Commissioner (see the text and note 20), the reference in head (3) above to being selected in accordance with a procedure put in place and overseen by the Speaker's Committee is to be read as including a reference to being recommended for re-appointment, or further re-appointment, by that Committee: s 3(5A) (added by the Political Parties and Elections Act 2009 s 4(1), (3)). As to the Speaker's Committee see PARA 49; and as to the Speaker of the House of Commons see PARLIAMENT vol 78 (2010) PARA 931 et seq. As to the disqualification of members of the House of Commons see PARLIAMENT vol 78 (2010) PARA 897 et seq; and as to the oath or affirmation required by the Parliamentary Oaths Act 1866 see PARLIAMENT vol 78 (2010) PARA 1001.

4 Political Parties, Elections and Referendums Act 2000 s 3(3).

5 See the Political Parties, Elections and Referendums Act 2000 s 3(4) (amended by the Political Parties and Elections Act 2009 s 39, Sch 6 para 10). The provision made by the Political Parties, Elections and Referendums Act 2000 s 3(4) is subject to s 3(4A) (see notes 6, 9): see s 3(4) (as so amended).

6 Political Parties, Elections and Referendums Act 2000 s 3(4)(a). Head (1) in the text does not apply to the appointment of a person as a nominated Commissioner (within the meaning of s 3A: see the text and notes 14–15): see s 3(4A) (added by the Political Parties and Elections Act 2009 s 5(1)).

7 Political Parties, Elections and Referendums Act 2000 s 3(4)(b). As to the meaning of 'accounting unit' for these purposes see PARA 253 note 15.

For the purposes of head (2) in the text, 'registered party' includes, in relation to times before 1 April 1999, any political party: see s 3(7)(b). Otherwise, in relation to times before 16 February 2001, 'registered party' includes a party registered under the Registration of Political Parties Act 1998: see the Political Parties, Elections and Referendums Act 2000 s 3(7)(a). There was no registration of political parties before the enactment of the Registration of Political Parties Act 1998 (largely repealed).

8 Political Parties, Elections and Referendums Act 2000 s 3(4)(c). Head (3) in the text refers to a relevant elective office within the meaning of s 71, Sch 7 (see CONSTITUTIONAL LAW AND HUMAN RIGHTS): see s 3(4)(c).

9 See the Political Parties, Elections and Referendums Act 2000 s 3(4)(d) (amended by the Political Parties and Elections Act 2009 s 7(1)). Head (4) in the text does not apply to the appointment of a person as a nominated Commissioner (within the meaning of the Political Parties, Elections and Referendums Act 2000 s 3A: see the text and notes 14–15): see s 3(4A) (as added: see note 6).

10 Political Parties, Elections and Referendums Act 2000 s 3(4)(d)(i). See note 9.

11 Political Parties, Elections and Referendums Act 2000 s 3(4)(d)(ii). See note 9.

12 Political Parties, Elections and Referendums Act 2000 s 3(4)(d)(iii). Head (4)(c) in the text refers to a donor reported under Pt IV Ch III (ss 62–69) (reporting of donations to registered parties) or Pt IV Ch V (s 71) (control of donations to individuals and members associations) (see CONSTITUTIONAL LAW AND HUMAN RIGHTS): see s 3(4)(d)(iii). See note 9.

13 Political Parties, Elections and Referendums Act 2000 s 3(4)(d)(iv) (added by the Electoral Administration Act 2006 s 74(1), Sch 1 Pt 7 paras 138, 139). Head (4)(d) in the text refers to a participant reported under the Political Parties, Elections and Referendums Act 2000 Pt IVA (ss 71F–71Y) (see PARA 312; and CONSTITUTIONAL LAW AND HUMAN RIGHTS): see s 3(4)(d)(iv) (as so added). See note 9.

14 For these purposes, 'qualifying party' means a registered party with two or more members of the House of Commons at the time of the person's appointment: Political Parties, Elections and Referendums Act 2000 s 3A(2) (s 3A added by the Political Parties and Elections Act 2009 s 5(2)). Any reference to a member of the House of Commons does not include any member of that House who at the time in question has not made and subscribed the oath required by the Parliamentary Oaths Act 1866 (or the corresponding affirmation) (see PARLIAMENT vol 78 (2010) PARA 1001) or is disqualified from sitting and voting in that House: see the Political Parties, Elections and Referendums Act 2000 s 3A(8) (as so added).

15 Political Parties, Elections and Referendums Act 2000 s 3A(1) (as added: see note 14).

16 For these purposes, 'nominating party' means a party whose registered leader either has put forward three persons to be considered for appointment as a nominated Commissioner, or has previously put forward persons one of whom was appointed as a nominated Commissioner and is expected to continue to hold office: see the Political Parties, Elections and Referendums Act 2000 s 3A(4) (as added: see note 14). The relative size of any two or more registered parties is to be determined according to the number of members of the House of Commons belonging to each party at the time in question (or, in the case of two parties with the same number of

members, according to the total number of votes cast for persons standing for election in the name of each of those parties at the most recent parliamentary general election): s 3A(7) (as so added).

17 Political Parties, Elections and Referendums Act 2000 s 3A(3) (as added: see note 14).

18 See the Political Parties, Elections and Referendums Act 2000 s 3A(5) (as added: see note 14). Nothing in s 3A has effect so as to require the result mentioned in the text: see s 3A(5) (as so added).

19 Political Parties, Elections and Referendums Act 2000 s 3A(6) (as added: see note 14).

20 Political Parties, Elections and Referendums Act 2000 s 3(5). See note 3.

36. Tenure of Electoral Commissioners and Commission chairman. An Electoral Commissioner[1] holds office[2] as such Commissioner for the period for which he is appointed[3], and otherwise in accordance with the terms of his appointment[4]. An Electoral Commissioner ceases to hold office on the occurrence of any of the following events[5]:

(1) he consents to being nominated as a candidate at a relevant election[6] or to being included in a registered party's list of candidates at such an election[7];

(2) he takes up any office or employment in or with: (a) a registered party or any accounting unit of such a party[8]; (b) a recognised third party[9]; or (c) a permitted participant[10];

(3) he is named as a donor in the register of donations[11] or in any statement of donations included in a return delivered to the Commission[12];

(4) he is named as a participant in the register of recordable transactions[13];

(5) he becomes a member of a registered party[14].

An Electoral Commissioner may be removed from office by Her Majesty in pursuance of an address from the House of Commons[15], or he may be relieved of his office by Her Majesty at his own request[16].

The chairman of the Commission[17] holds office[18] as such chairman for the period for which he is appointed[19], and otherwise in accordance with the terms of his appointment[20]. The chairman of the Commission may be relieved of his office of chairman by Her Majesty at his own request[21]. If the chairman of the Commission ceases to be an Electoral Commissioner, he also ceases to be chairman[22].

1 As to the appointment of Electoral Commissioners see PARA 35.

2 Ie subject to the provisions of the Political Parties, Elections and Referendums Act 2000 s 1(6), Sch 1 para 3 (see also the text and notes 3–16): see Sch 1 para 3(1).

3 Political Parties, Elections and Referendums Act 2000 Sch 1 para 3(1)(a). The period for which an Electoral Commissioner is appointed is the period specified in relation to him in the address pursuant to which he is appointed (see PARA 35): Sch 1 para 3(2).

4 Political Parties, Elections and Referendums Act 2000 Sch 1 para 3(1)(b).

5 See the Political Parties, Elections and Referendums Act 2000 Sch 1 para 3(3) (Sch 1 para 3(3) amended, Sch 1 para 3(3A) added, by the Political Parties and Elections Act 2009 s 39, Sch 6 para 27(1), (2)). Similar restrictions are placed on the chief executive and members of the staff of the Commission: see PARA 39.

6 Ie within the meaning of the Political Parties, Elections and Referendums Act 2000 Pt II (ss 22–40) (see PARA 253): see Sch 1 para 3(3)(a).

7 Political Parties, Elections and Referendums Act 2000 Sch 1 para 3(3)(a). For these purposes, in relation to times before 16 February 2001, 'registered party' includes a party registered under the Registration of Political Parties Act 1998: see the Political Parties, Elections and Referendums Act 2000 Sch 1 para 3(8). There was no registration of political parties before the enactment of the Registration of Political Parties Act 1998 (largely repealed). As to a registered party's list of candidates see PARA 253 et seq.

8 Political Parties, Elections and Referendums Act 2000 Sch 1 para 3(3)(b)(i). As to the meaning of 'accounting unit' for these purposes see PARA 253 note 15.

9   Political Parties, Elections and Referendums Act 2000 Sch 1 para 3(3)(b)(ii). Head (2)(b) in the text refers to a recognised third party within the meaning of Pt VI (ss 85–100) (controls relating to third party national election campaigns: see PARA 313 note 15): see Sch 1 para 3(3)(b)(ii).

10 Political Parties, Elections and Referendums Act 2000 Sch 1 para 3(3)(b)(iii). Head (2)(c) in the text to a permitted participant within the meaning of Pt VII (ss 101–129) (referendums: see PARA 529): see Sch 1 para 3(3)(b)(iii).

11 Ie the register of donations reported under the Political Parties, Elections and Referendums Act 2000 Pt IV Ch III (ss 62–69) (reporting of donations to registered parties: see CONSTITUTIONAL LAW AND HUMAN RIGHTS) or Pt IV Ch V (s 71) (control of donations to individuals and members associations: see CONSTITUTIONAL LAW AND HUMAN RIGHTS): see Sch 1 para 3(3)(c).

12 Political Parties, Elections and Referendums Act 2000 Sch 1 para 3(3)(c). Head (3) in the text refers to a return delivered to the Commission under s 98 (delivery of returns (recognised third parties): see PARA 322) or s 122 (return delivered to the Commission (permitted participants): see PARA 543): see Sch 1 para 3(3)(c).

13 Political Parties, Elections and Referendums Act 2000 Sch 1 para 3(3)(ca) (added by the Electoral Administration Act 2006 s 74(1), Sch 1 paras 138, 152). Head (4) in the text refers to a participant reported under the Political Parties, Elections and Referendums Act 2000 Pt IVA (ss 71F–71Y) (see PARA 312; and CONSTITUTIONAL LAW AND HUMAN RIGHTS): see Sch 1 para 3(3)(ca) (as so added).

14 Political Parties, Elections and Referendums Act 2000 Sch 1 para 3(3)(d). Head (5) in the text does not apply to the appointment of a person as a nominated Commissioner (within the meaning of s 3A: see PARA 35): Sch 1 para 3(3A) (as added: see note 5).

15 Political Parties, Elections and Referendums Act 2000 Sch 1 para 3(4). No motion is to be made for such an address, however, unless the Speaker's Committee has presented a report to the House of Commons stating that the Committee is satisfied that one or more of the following grounds is made out in the case of the Electoral Commissioner in question (see Sch 1 para 3(5)):

(1)   he has failed to discharge the functions of his office for a continuous period of at least three months (Sch 1 para 3(5)(a));

(2)   he has failed to comply with the terms of his appointment (Sch 1 para 3(5)(b));

(3)   he has been convicted of a criminal offence (Sch 1 para 3(5)(c));

(4)   he is an undischarged bankrupt or his estate has been sequestrated in Scotland and he has not been discharged (Sch 1 para 3(5)(d));

(5)   a moratorium period under a debt relief order applies in relation to him (ie under the Insolvency Act 1986 Pt VIIA (ss 251A–251X) (debt relief orders: see BANKRUPTCY AND INDIVIDUAL INSOLVENCY)) (Political Parties, Elections and Referendums Act 2000 Sch 1 para 3(5)(da) (Sch 1 para 3(5)(da), (9) added by SI 2012/2404));

(6)   he has made an arrangement or composition contract with, or has granted a trust deed for, his creditors (Political Parties, Elections and Referendums Act 2000 Sch 1 para 3(5)(e));

(7)   he is otherwise unfit to hold his office or unable to carry out its functions (Sch 1 para 3(5)(f)).

A motion for such an address is not to be made on the ground mentioned in head (1) above if more than three months have elapsed since the end of the period in question: Sch 1 para 3(6). For these purposes, head (5) above does not extend to Gibraltar: Sch 1 para 3(9) (as so added). As to the meaning of 'functions' see PARA 34 note 2. As to the Speaker's Committee see PARA 49. As to discharge from bankruptcy see BANKRUPTCY AND INDIVIDUAL INSOLVENCY vol 5 (2013) PARA 638 et seq; and as to compositions and arrangements with creditors see BANKRUPTCY AND INDIVIDUAL INSOLVENCY vol 5 (2013) PARA 852 et seq.

16 Political Parties, Elections and Referendums Act 2000 Sch 1 para 3(7).

17 As to the appointment of the chairman of the Electoral Commission see PARA 35.

18 Ie subject to the provisions of the Political Parties, Elections and Referendums Act 2000 Sch 1 para 4 (see also the text and notes 19–22): see Sch 1 para 4(1)(a).

19 Political Parties, Elections and Referendums Act 2000 Sch 1 para 4(1)(a). The period for which a person is appointed as chairman of the Commission is the period specified in relation to him in the address pursuant to which he is appointed (see PARA 35): Sch 1 para 4(2).

20 Political Parties, Elections and Referendums Act 2000 Sch 1 para 4(1)(b).

21 Political Parties, Elections and Referendums Act 2000 Sch 1 para 4(3).

22 Political Parties, Elections and Referendums Act 2000 Sch 1 para 4(4).

37.   Salaries, pensions etc of Electoral Commissioners.   An Electoral Commissioner[1] is paid such remuneration, and any such allowances or expenses,

as may be specified in a resolution of the House of Commons[2]. If a resolution of the House of Commons so provides in the case of any person who is an Electoral Commissioner or former Electoral Commissioner, such amounts are to be paid towards the provision of superannuation benefits for or in respect of him as may be specified in the resolution[3] and, in the case of a former Electoral Commissioner, such pension[4] is to be paid to or in respect of him as may be so specified[5].

Any amount so payable (other than by way of expenses) must be charged on and issued out of the Consolidated Fund[6]; and any amount so payable by way of expenses must be paid by the Commission[7].

1 As to the appointment and tenure of Electoral Commissioners see PARAS 35–36.
2 Political Parties, Elections and Referendums Act 2000 s 1(6), Sch 1 para 5(1). A resolution for these purposes may:
   (1) specify the amounts to be paid (Sch 1 para 5(3)(a));
   (2) provide that the amounts to be paid are the same as, or calculated on the same basis as, those payable to or in respect of a person employed in a specified office under, or in a specified capacity in the service of, the Crown (Sch 1 para 5(3)(b));
   (3) specify the amounts to be paid and provide for them to be increased by reference to such variables as may be specified in the resolution (Sch 1 para 5(3)(c));
   (4) have the effect of making different provision for different Electoral Commissioners or former Electoral Commissioners (Sch 1 para 5(3)(d)).
   A resolution for these purposes may take effect from the date on which it is passed or from any earlier or later date specified in the resolution: Sch 1 para 5(4).
3 Political Parties, Elections and Referendums Act 2000 Sch 1 para 5(2)(a).
4 For these purposes, 'pension' includes allowance and gratuity: see the Political Parties, Elections and Referendums Act 2000 Sch 1 para 5(7).
5 Political Parties, Elections and Referendums Act 2000 Sch 1 para 5(2)(b).
6 Political Parties, Elections and Referendums Act 2000 Sch 1 para 5(5). As to the Consolidated Fund see CONSTITUTIONAL LAW AND HUMAN RIGHTS vol 8(2) (Reissue) PARA 711 et seq; PARLIAMENT vol 78 (2010) PARAS 1028–1031.
7 Political Parties, Elections and Referendums Act 2000 Sch 1 para 5(6).

38. The chief executive and staff of the Electoral Commission. The Electoral Commission[1] must appoint a chief executive[2], and may appoint such other staff as it considers necessary to assist the Commission and its committees[3] in the performance of its functions[4].

The staff of the Commission are appointed on such terms and conditions as the Commission may determine; and the Commission must pay its staff such remuneration as may be provided for by or under their terms of appointment[5]. However, the appointment of a member of the staff of the Commission is barred, and any existing appointment terminated, if the person in question acts against the political restrictions that are specified as applying to such staff[6].

Service as an officer or employee of the Commission is included in the kinds of employment to which a scheme under the Superannuation Act 1972[7] can apply[8]. The Commission must pay to the Minister for the Civil Service[9], at such times as he may direct, such sums as he may determine in respect of any increase[10] in the sums payable out of money provided by Parliament under the Superannuation Act 1972[11].

No member of the staff of the Commission is to be regarded either as the servant or agent of the Crown[12], or as enjoying any status, immunity or privilege of the Crown[13].

1 As to the establishment and constitution of the Electoral Commission see PARA 34 et seq.
2 Political Parties, Elections and Referendums Act 2000 s 1(6), Sch 1 para 11(1)(a). As to political restrictions on the appointment of a chief executive see PARA 39. As to the power that was

available to the Secretary of State to make arrangements until such time as the first person to be appointed by the Commission as its chief executive took up office see Sch 1 para 11(9)–(11).

3 As to committees of the Electoral Commission see PARA 41.

4 Political Parties, Elections and Referendums Act 2000 Sch 1 para 11(1)(b). As to political restrictions on the appointment of a member of the staff of the Electoral Commission see PARA 39. As to the power that was available to the Secretary of State to make arrangements until such time as the Commission appointed its own staff see Sch 1 para 11(9)–(11). As to the meaning of 'functions' see PARA 34 note 2. As to the functions of the Electoral Commission see PARA 51 et seq.

Any person who for the time being is a member of the staff of the Electoral Commission is disqualified for membership of the House of Commons: see the House of Commons Disqualification Act 1975 s 1(1), Sch 1 Pt III; and PARLIAMENT vol 78 (2010) PARAS 905, 908.

5 Political Parties, Elections and Referendums Act 2000 Sch 1 para 11(3) (amended by the Political Parties and Elections Act 2009 s 39, Sch 6 para 27(1), (4)). See note 6. In determining the terms and conditions of staff under the Political Parties, Elections and Referendums Act 2000 Sch 1 para 11(3), the Commission must have regard to the desirability of keeping the remuneration and other terms and conditions of employment of its staff broadly in line with those applying to persons employed in the civil service of the state: Sch 1 para 11(5).

6 Ie the provision made by the Political Parties, Elections and Referendums Act 2000 Sch 1 para 11(3) (see also the text and note 5) is subject to Sch 1 para 11A(4) (termination of appointment of staff members of the Commission: see PARA 39): see Sch 1 para 11(3) (as amended: see note 5).

7 Ie under the Superannuation Act 1972 s 1 (see CONSTITUTIONAL LAW AND HUMAN RIGHTS vol 8(2) (Reissue) PARA 567): see the Political Parties, Elections and Referendums Act 2000 Sch 1 para 11(6).

8 Political Parties, Elections and Referendums Act 2000 Sch 1 para 11(6); and see the Superannuation Act 1972 s 1, Sch 1 (amended by the Political Parties, Elections and Referendums Act 2000 Sch 1 para 11(6)).

The Superannuation Act 1972 s 1(2) (delegation of functions relating to civil service superannuation schemes by the Minister for the Civil Service to another officer of the Crown etc: see CONSTITUTIONAL LAW AND HUMAN RIGHTS vol 8(2) (Reissue) PARA 567) has effect as if the reference to an officer of the Crown other than a minister included the Commission's chief executive: Political Parties, Elections and Referendums Act 2000 Sch 1 para 13(1). Any administration function so conferred on the Commission's chief executive, as it has effect in accordance with Sch 1 para 13(1), may be exercised by (or by employees of) such person as may be authorised in that behalf by the Commission's chief executive: Sch 1 para 13(2). For these purposes, an 'administration function' is a function of administering schemes made under the Superannuation Act 1972 s 1 and from time to time in force: see the Political Parties, Elections and Referendums Act 2000 Sch 1 para 13(3). An authorisation given by virtue of Sch 1 para 13(2) may authorise the exercise of an administration function: (1) either wholly or to such extent as may be specified in the authorisation (Sch 1 para 13(4)(a)); (2) either generally or in such cases as may be so specified (Sch 1 para 13(4)(b)); and (3) either unconditionally or subject to the fulfilment of such conditions as may be so specified (Sch 1 para 13(4)(c)). Such an authorisation is to be treated for all purposes as if it were given by virtue of an order under the Deregulation and Contracting Out Act 1994 s 69 (contracting out of functions of ministers and office-holders: see CONSTITUTIONAL LAW AND HUMAN RIGHTS vol 8(2) (Reissue) PARA 364) and may be revoked at any time by the Commission (as well as by the chief executive): see the Political Parties, Elections and Referendums Act 2000 Sch 1 para 13(5).

9 As to the Minister for the Civil Service see CONSTITUTIONAL LAW AND HUMAN RIGHTS vol 8(2) (Reissue) PARA 427.

10 Ie attributable to the Political Parties, Elections and Referendums Act 2000 Sch 1 para 11(6) (see the text and notes 7–8): see Sch 1 para 11(7).

11 Political Parties, Elections and Referendums Act 2000 Sch 1 para 11(7).

12 Political Parties, Elections and Referendums Act 2000 Sch 1 para 11(8)(a). As to the position of the Commission itself see PARA 34.

13 Political Parties, Elections and Referendums Act 2000 Sch 1 para 11(8)(b).

39. Political restrictions on chief executive and staff of the Electoral Commission. A member of a registered party[1] may not be appointed as chief executive of the Electoral Commission[2]. The appointment of the chief executive terminates on the occurrence of any of the following events[3]:

(1)　　he consents to being nominated as a candidate at a relevant election[4] or to being included in a registered party's list of candidates at such an election[5];

(2)　　he takes up any office or employment in or with: (a) a registered party or any accounting unit of such a party[6]; (b) a recognised third party[7]; or (c) a permitted participant[8];

(3)　　he is named as a donor in the register of donations[9] or in any statement of donations included in a return delivered to the Commission[10];

(4)　　he is named as a participant in the register of recordable transactions[11];

(5)　　he becomes a member of a registered party[12].

A person may not be appointed as a member of the staff of the Electoral Commission if the person[13]:

(i)　　is an officer or employee of a registered party or of any accounting unit of such a party[14];

(ii)　　holds a relevant elective office[15];

(iii)　　at any time within the relevant period[16]: (A) has been such an officer or employee as is mentioned in head (i) above[17]; or (B) has held such an office as is mentioned in head (ii) above[18]; or (C) has been named as a donor in the register of donations[19]; or (D) has been named as a participant in the register of recordable transactions[20].

The appointment of any member of the staff of the Commission (that is, apart from the chief executive) terminates, on the occurrence of such an event as is mentioned in any of heads (1) to (4) above[21].

1　　As to the meaning of 'registered party' for these purposes see PARA 35 note 3.

2　　Political Parties, Elections and Referendums Act 2000 s 1(6), Sch 1 para 11A(3) (Sch 1 paras 11A, 11B added by the Political Parties and Elections Act 2009 s 7(2)). As to the appointment of a chief executive of the Electoral Commission see PARA 38.

　　The amendment made to the Political Parties, Elections and Referendums Act 2000 Sch 1 para 11A(1) by the Political Parties and Elections Act 2009 s 7(2) does not apply to the appointment of a person to assist the Boundary Committee for England in the performance of its functions, to assist the Commission in carrying out functions transferred to them by an order under the Political Parties, Elections and Referendums Act 2000 s 18(1) (repealed) (transfer of functions of Local Government Commission for England: see PARA 71 note 1), or to perform duties including either or both of those: see the Political Parties and Elections Act 2009 s 7(3).

3　　See the Political Parties, Elections and Referendums Act 2000 Sch 1 para 11A(4)(a) (as added: see note 2). Heads (1) to (5) in the text refer to the occurrence of such an event as is mentioned in Sch 1 para 3(3)(a)–(d) (see PARA 36): see Sch 1 para 11A(4)(a) (as so added).

4　　Ie within the meaning of the Political Parties, Elections and Referendums Act 2000 Pt II (ss 22–40) (see PARA 253): see Sch 1 para 3(3)(a) (as applied: see note 3).

5　　See the Political Parties, Elections and Referendums Act 2000 Sch 1 para 3(3)(a) (as applied: see note 3). As to the meaning of 'registered party' for the purposes of Sch 1 para 3 see PARA 36 note 7. As to a registered party's list of candidates see PARA 253 et seq.

6　　See the Political Parties, Elections and Referendums Act 2000 Sch 1 para 3(3)(b)(i) (as applied: see note 3). As to the meaning of 'accounting unit' for these purposes see PARA 253 note 15.

7　　See the Political Parties, Elections and Referendums Act 2000 Sch 1 para 3(3)(b)(ii) (as applied: see note 3). Head (2)(b) in the text refers to a recognised third party within the meaning of Pt VI (ss 85–100) (controls relating to third party national election campaigns: see PARA 313 note 15): see Sch 1 para 3(3)(b)(ii) (as so applied).

8　　See the Political Parties, Elections and Referendums Act 2000 Sch 1 para 3(3)(b)(iii) (as applied: see note 3). Head (2)(c) in the text refers to a permitted participant within the meaning of Pt VII (ss 101–129) (referendums: see PARA 529): see Sch 1 para 3(3)(b)(iii) (as so applied).

9　　Ie under the Political Parties, Elections and Referendums Act 2000 Pt IV Ch III (ss 62–69) (reporting of donations to registered parties) or Pt IV Ch V (s 71) (control of donations to individuals and members associations) (see CONSTITUTIONAL LAW AND HUMAN RIGHTS): see Sch 1 para 3(3)(c) (as applied: see note 3).

10 See the Political Parties, Elections and Referendums Act 2000 Sch 1 para 3(3)(c) (as applied: see note 3). Head (3) in the text refers to a return delivered to the Commission under s 98 (see PARA 322) or s 122 (see PARA 543): see Sch 1 para 3(3)(c) (as so applied).

11 See the Political Parties, Elections and Referendums Act 2000 Sch 1 para 3(3)(ca) (added by the Electoral Administration Act 2006 s 74(1), Sch 1 paras 138, 152; the Political Parties, Elections and Referendums Act 2000 Sch 1 para 3(3)(ca) as applied (see note 3)). Head (4) in the text refers to a participant reported under the Political Parties, Elections and Referendums Act 2000 Pt IVA (ss 71F–71Y) (see PARA 312; and CONSTITUTIONAL LAW AND HUMAN RIGHTS): see Sch 1 para 3(3)(ca) (as so added and applied).

12 See the Political Parties, Elections and Referendums Act 2000 Sch 1 para 3(3)(d) (as applied: see note 3).

13 See the Political Parties, Elections and Referendums Act 2000 Sch 1 para 11A(1) (as added: see note 2). As to the appointment of staff of the Electoral Commission see PARA 38.

14 Political Parties, Elections and Referendums Act 2000 Sch 1 para 11A(1)(a) (as added: see note 2).

15 Political Parties, Elections and Referendums Act 2000 Sch 1 para 11A(1)(b) (as added: see note 2). Head (ii) in the text refers to a relevant elective office within the meaning of s 71, Sch 7 (control of donations to individuals and members associations: see CONSTITUTIONAL LAW AND HUMAN RIGHTS): see Sch 1 para 11A(1)(b) (as so added).

16 See the Political Parties, Elections and Referendums Act 2000 Sch 1 para 11A(1)(c) (as added: see note 2). For these purposes, the relevant period is:
    (1)   in relation to appointment as chief executive of the Electoral Commission, the last five years (Sch 1 para 11A(2)(a) (as so added));
    (2)   in relation to appointment to a post on the staff of the Electoral Commission that is designated by a notice in force under Sch 1 para 11B, the period, immediately preceding the appointment, specified by the notice (Sch 1 para 11A(2)(b) (as so added));
    (3)   in relation to appointment as any other member of the staff of the Electoral Commission, the last 12 months (Sch 1 para 11A(2)(c) (as so added)).
    The chief executive of the Commission may, by giving notice to the Speaker's Committee, designate a particular post on the staff of the Commission, and specify as the relevant period for that post, for the purposes of Sch 1 para 11A(2)(b) (see head (2) above), a period of two years or more, if the chief executive reasonably believes that it is necessary to do so in order to maintain public confidence in the effectiveness of the Commission in carrying out any of its functions: see Sch 1 para 11B(1) (as added: see note 2). Such a notice must be in writing: see s 157(1). The period so specified may not be more than five years (Sch 1 para 11B(2) (as so added)); but, in deciding what that period should be, the chief executive of the Commission must take into account the level of seniority of the post, and how likely it is that any holder of the post will be required to deal with politically sensitive matters (see Sch 1 para 11B(3) (as so added)). Each notice under Sch 1 para 11B(1) must relate to only one post (Sch 1 para 11B(4) (as so added)), and has effect from the day on which it is received by the Speaker's Committee, expiring at the end of the period of three years beginning with that day (see Sch 1 para 11B(5) (as so added)). Such an expiration does not prevent a further notice being given under Sch 1 para 11B(1) in relation to the post in question, either before the previous notice would have expired, or at any time after the expiry of the previous notice; and a further notice received by the Speaker's Committee before the previous notice would have expired supersedes the previous notice, however: see Sch 1 para 11B(6) (as so added). If the chief executive of the Commission gives notice (a 'cancellation notice') to the Speaker's Committee cancelling a notice under Sch 1 para 11B(1), the notice under Sch 1 para 11B(1) ceases to have effect on the day on which the cancellation notice is received by the Speaker's Committee, or (if later) on such date as may be specified in the cancellation notice: see Sch 1 para 11B(7) (as so added). Before giving a notice under Sch 1 para 11B, the chief executive of the Commission must consult the Speaker's Committee: Sch 1 para 11B(8) (as so added). The Commission must publish, in such manner as it considers appropriate, information setting out the effect of all notices under Sch 1 para 11B(1) that are in force at any particular time: Sch 1 para 11B(9) (as so added). As to the Speaker's Committee see PARA 49.

17 Political Parties, Elections and Referendums Act 2000 Sch 1 para 11A(1)(c)(i) (as added: see note 2).

18 Political Parties, Elections and Referendums Act 2000 Sch 1 para 11A(1)(c)(ii) (as added: see note 2).

19 Political Parties, Elections and Referendums Act 2000 Sch 1 para 11A(1)(c)(iii) (as added: see note 2). Head (iii)(C) in the text refers to the register of donations reported under Pt IV (ss 62–69, 71) (see CONSTITUTIONAL LAW AND HUMAN RIGHTS): see Sch 1 para 11A(1)(c)(iii) (as so added).

20　Political Parties, Elections and Referendums Act 2000 Sch 1 para 11A(1)(c)(iv) (as added: see note 2). Head (iii)(D) in the text refers to the register of recordable transactions reported under Pt IVA (ss 71F–71Z2: see PARA 312 and CONSTITUTIONAL LAW AND HUMAN RIGHTS): see Sch 1 para 11A(1)(c)(iv) (as so added).

21　See the Political Parties, Elections and Referendums Act 2000 Sch 1 para 11A(4)(b) (as added: see note 2).

40.　Assistant Electoral Commissioners.　The Electoral Commission[1] may appoint one or more Assistant Electoral Commissioners to inquire into, and report to the Commission on, such matters as the Commission or a Boundary Committee thinks fit[2]. However, a person is not to be appointed as an Assistant Electoral Commissioner if he is a person who may not be appointed as an Electoral Commissioner[3].

An Assistant Electoral Commissioner is appointed either for a fixed term or for the purposes of a particular inquiry[4]. He holds and vacates office in accordance with the terms of his appointment[5] but his appointment terminates on the occurrence of any of the following events[6]:

(1)　he consents to being nominated as a candidate at a relevant election[7] or to being included in a registered party's list of candidates at such an election[8];

(2)　he takes up any office or employment in or with: (a) a registered party or any accounting unit of such a party[9]; (b) a recognised third party[10]; or (c) a permitted participant[11];

(3)　he is named as a donor in the register of donations[12] or in any statement of donations included in a return delivered to the Commission[13];

(4)　he is named as a participant in the register of recordable transactions[14];

(5)　he becomes a member of a registered party[15].

1　As to the establishment and constitution of the Electoral Commission see PARA 34 et seq.

2　Political Parties, Elections and Referendums Act 2000 s 1(6), Sch 1 para 7(1) (amended by the Local Democracy, Economic Development and Construction Act 2009 s 146(1), Sch 7 Pt 3). As to the Boundary Committees see PARA 67.

3　Political Parties, Elections and Referendums Act 2000 Sch 1 para 7(2) (amended by the Political Parties and Elections Act 2009 s 39, Sch 6 para 27(1), (3)). The text refers to a person who is prevented by the Political Parties, Elections and Referendums Act 2000 s 3(4) (see PARA 35), read without regard to s 3(4A) (which disapplies certain provisions to the appointment of a person as a nominated Commissioner: see PARA 35), from being appointed as an Electoral Commissioner: see Sch 1 para 7(2) (as so amended).

4　Political Parties, Elections and Referendums Act 2000 Sch 1 para 7(3)(a).

5　Political Parties, Elections and Referendums Act 2000 Sch 1 para 7(3)(b). The Commission must pay an Assistant Electoral Commissioner such remuneration, and any such allowances or expenses, as may be provided for by or under the terms of his appointment: Sch 1 para 7(5).

6　See the Political Parties, Elections and Referendums Act 2000 Sch 1 para 7(4). Heads (1) to (5) in the text refer to the occurrence of such an event as is mentioned in Sch 1 para 3(3)(a)–(d) (see PARA 36): see Sch 1 para 7(4).

7　Ie within the meaning of the Political Parties, Elections and Referendums Act 2000 Pt II (ss 22–40) (see PARA 253): see Sch 1 para 3(3)(a) (as applied: see note 6).

8　See the Political Parties, Elections and Referendums Act 2000 Sch 1 para 3(3)(a) (as applied: see note 6). As to the meaning of 'registered party' for the purposes of Sch 1 para 3 see PARA 36 note 7. As to a registered party's list of candidates see PARA 253 et seq.

9　See the Political Parties, Elections and Referendums Act 2000 Sch 1 para 3(3)(b)(i) (as applied: see note 6). As to the meaning of 'accounting unit' for these purposes see PARA 253 note 15.

10　See the Political Parties, Elections and Referendums Act 2000 Sch 1 para 3(3)(b)(ii) (as applied: see note 6). Head (2)(b) in the text refers to a recognised third party within the meaning of Pt VI (ss 85–100) (controls relating to third party national election campaigns: see PARA 313 note 15): see Sch 1 para 3(3)(b)(ii) (as so applied).

11 See the Political Parties, Elections and Referendums Act 2000 Sch 1 para 3(3)(b)(iii) (as applied: see note 6). Head (2)(c) in the text refers to a permitted participant within the meaning of Pt VII (ss 101–129) (referendums: see PARA 529): see Sch 1 para 3(3)(b)(iii) (as so applied).

12 Ie under the Political Parties, Elections and Referendums Act 2000 Pt IV Ch III (ss 62–69) (reporting of donations to registered parties) or Pt IV Ch V (s 71) (control of donations to individuals and members associations) (see CONSTITUTIONAL LAW AND HUMAN RIGHTS): see Sch 1 para 3(3)(c) (as applied: see note 6).

13 See the Political Parties, Elections and Referendums Act 2000 Sch 1 para 3(3)(c) (as applied: see note 6). Head (3) in the text refers to a return delivered to the Commission under s 98 (see PARA 322) or s 122 (see PARA 543): see Sch 1 para 3(3)(c) (as so applied).

14 See the Political Parties, Elections and Referendums Act 2000 Sch 1 para 3(3)(ca) (added by the Electoral Administration Act 2006 s 74(1), Sch 1 paras 138, 152; the Political Parties, Elections and Referendums Act 2000 Sch 1 para 3(3)(ca) as applied (see note 6)). Head (4) in the text refers to a participant reported under the Political Parties, Elections and Referendums Act 2000 Pt IVA (ss 71F–71Y) (see PARA 312; and CONSTITUTIONAL LAW AND HUMAN RIGHTS): see Sch 1 para 3(3)(ca) (as so added and applied).

15 See the Political Parties, Elections and Referendums Act 2000 Sch 1 para 3(3)(d) (as applied: see note 6).

41.   Committees of the Electoral Commission.   The Electoral Commission[1] may establish any committees which it considers to be appropriate[2]; and any committee so established may establish one or more sub-committees[3]. A person is not to be a member of a committee or sub-committee so established unless he is an Electoral Commissioner[4].

1   As to the establishment and constitution of the Electoral Commission see PARA 34 et seq.
2   Political Parties, Elections and Referendums Act 2000 s 1(6), Sch 1 para 8(1) (amended by the Local Democracy, Economic Development and Construction Act 2009 s 146(1), Sch 7 Pt 3).
3   Political Parties, Elections and Referendums Act 2000 Sch 1 para 8(2).
4   Political Parties, Elections and Referendums Act 2000 Sch 1 para 8(3). As to the appointment and tenure of Electoral Commissioners see PARAS 35–36.

42.   Delegation to committees and to staff.   The Electoral Commission[1] may delegate[2] its functions[3], to such extent as it may determine, to any committee[4] of the Commission[5]; and such a committee may delegate its functions, to such extent as it may determine, to any sub-committee of the committee[6].

Each of: (1) the Commission[7]; (2) any committee of the Commission[8]; (3) any sub-committee of such a committee[9]; and (4) the Commission's chief executive[10], may delegate functions of theirs or his, to such extent as they or he may determine, to the Commission's staff[11], either generally or otherwise[12].

1   As to the establishment and constitution of the Electoral Commission see PARA 34 et seq.
2   For these purposes, 'delegate' includes further delegate: Political Parties, Elections and Referendums Act 2000 s 1(6), Sch 1 para 25.
3   As to the meaning of 'functions' see PARA 34 note 2.
4   Ie any committee established under the Political Parties, Elections and Referendums Act 2000 Sch 1 para 8(1) (see PARA 41): see Sch 1 para 9(1).
5   Political Parties, Elections and Referendums Act 2000 Sch 1 para 9(1).
6   Political Parties, Elections and Referendums Act 2000 Sch 1 para 9(3).
7   Political Parties, Elections and Referendums Act 2000 Sch 1 para 12(a).
8   Political Parties, Elections and Referendums Act 2000 Sch 1 para 12(b) (amended by the Local Democracy, Economic Development and Construction Act 2009 s 146(1), Sch 7 Pt 3).
9   Political Parties, Elections and Referendums Act 2000 Sch 1 para 12(c).
10 Political Parties, Elections and Referendums Act 2000 Sch 1 para 12(d). As to the appointment of the Commission's chief executive, and as to the delegation of functions relating to civil service superannuation schemes by the Minister for the Civil Service to the Commission's chief executive, see PARA 38.
11 As to the appointment of staff of the Commission see PARA 38.
12 See the Political Parties, Elections and Referendums Act 2000 Sch 1 para 12.

43.   Proceedings of the Electoral Commission.   The Electoral Commission[1] must regulate its own procedure, and the procedure of its committees and sub-committees, including the quorum for meetings[2]. The validity of any proceedings of the Commission, or of any of its committees or sub-committees, is not affected either by any vacancy among the members of the Commission, or of the committee or sub-committee[3], or by any defect in the appointments of any such member[4].

1   As to the establishment and constitution of the Electoral Commission see PARA 34 et seq.
2   Political Parties, Elections and Referendums Act 2000 s 1(6), Sch 1 para 10(1) (amended by the Local Democracy, Economic Development and Construction Act 2009 s 146(1), Sch 7 Pt 3).
3   See the Political Parties, Elections and Referendums Act 2000 Sch 1 para 10(2)(a).
4   See the Political Parties, Elections and Referendums Act 2000 Sch 1 para 10(2)(b).

44.   Finances, financial estimates and the five-year plan.   The expenditure of the Electoral Commission[1], so far as it cannot be met out of income received by the Commission, must be met[2] out of money provided by Parliament[3].

For each financial year[4], the Commission must prepare, and submit to the Speaker's Committee[5], an estimate of the Commission's income and expenditure[6]; and the Speaker's Committee must:

(1)   examine each such estimate submitted to it[7]; and

(2)   decide whether it is satisfied that the estimated level of income and expenditure is consistent with the economical, efficient and effective discharge by the Commission of its functions[8]; and

(3)   if it is not so satisfied, make such modifications[9] to the estimate as it considers appropriate for the purpose of achieving such consistency[10].

Before deciding whether it is so satisfied, or making any such modifications, the Speaker's Committee must have regard to the most recent report made to it by the Comptroller and Auditor General[11] and to any recommendations contained in that report[12], and the Committee must consult the Treasury[13] and have regard to any advice which the Treasury may give[14]. The Speaker's Committee must, after concluding its examination and making its modifications (if any) to the estimate, lay the estimate before the House of Commons[15]. If the Speaker's Committee, in the discharge of these functions[16], does not follow any recommendation contained in the report of the Comptroller and Auditor General[17], does not follow any advice given to it by the Treasury[18], or makes any modification to the estimate[19], it must include in the next statutory report which it makes to the House of Commons[20] a statement of its reasons for so doing[21].

When the Commission submits to the Speaker's Committee such an estimate, the Commission must also submit to the Committee a plan prepared by the Commission setting out the Commission's aims and objectives for the period of five years beginning with the financial year to which the estimate relates[22], and setting out estimated requirements for resources during that five-year period[23]. The Speaker's Committee must:

(a)   examine each plan submitted to it[24];

(b)   decide whether it is satisfied that the plan is consistent with the economical, efficient and effective discharge by the Commission of its functions[25]; and

(c)   if it is not so satisfied, make such modifications to the plan as it considers appropriate for the purpose of achieving such consistency[26].

Before deciding whether it is so satisfied, or making any such modifications, the Speaker's Committee must have regard to the most recent report made to it by the Comptroller and Auditor General[27] and to any recommendations contained in that report[28], and must consult the Treasury and have regard to any advice which the Treasury may give[29]. The Speaker's Committee must, after concluding its examination and making its modifications (if any) to the plan, lay the plan before the House of Commons[30]. If the Speaker's Committee, in the discharge of these functions[31], does not follow any recommendation contained in the report of the Comptroller and Auditor General[32], does not follow any advice given to them by the Treasury[33], or makes any modification to the plan[34], it must include in the next statutory report which it makes to the House of Commons[35] a statement of its reasons for so doing[36].

For the purpose of assisting the Speaker's Committee to discharge its functions in relation to the Commission's financial estimates[37] and in relation to the Commission's five-year plan[38], the Comptroller and Auditor General must in each year: (i) carry out an examination into the economy, efficiency or effectiveness (or, if he so determines, any combination thereof) with which the Commission has used its resources in discharging its functions (or, if he so determines, any particular functions)[39]; (ii) report to the Speaker's Committee the results of the examination[40]; and (iii) include in his report such recommendations as he considers appropriate in the light of the examination[41].

1   As to the establishment and constitution of the Electoral Commission see PARA 34 et seq.

2   Ie in accordance with the Political Parties, Elections and Referendums Act 2000 s 1(6), Sch 1 para 14 (see also the text and notes 3–21), except so far as it is (see Sch 1 para 14(1)):

    (1)   reimbursed by the Secretary of State under s 18(9) (repealed) (provision of advice to the Secretary of State relating to the transfer of functions of the Local Government Commission for England) or the Scottish Ministers in pursuance of s 13A (reimbursement of costs by Scottish Ministers), s 19(11) (provision of advice relating to the transfer of functions of the Local Government Boundary Commission for Scotland) or s 145(6) (monitoring compliance with controls in relation to local government elections in Scotland) (Sch 1 para 14(1)(a) (amended by the Local Electoral Administration (Scotland) Act 2011 s 16(1), (4); and by SI 2007/1388));

    (2)   met by the Welsh Ministers in pursuance of the Political Parties, Elections and Referendums Act 2000 s 5(3) (report on the administration of a poll regarding the functions of the Welsh Ministers: see PARA 51) or s 20(12) (repealed) (transfer of functions of the Local Government Boundary Commission for Wales: see PARA 71 note 1) (Sch 1 para 14(1)(b) (Sch 1 para 14(1)(b) substituted, Sch 1 para 14(1)(c) added, by SI 2007/1388)); or

    (3)   met by the National Assembly for Wales Commission under the Government of Wales Act 2006 s 27, Sch 2 para 6 (ie financial assistance to the Electoral Commission for the purpose of enabling it to carry out its functions so far as relating to the promotion of public awareness of the current or any pending system for the election of Assembly members, and the current or any pending system of devolved government in Wales: see CONSTITUTIONAL LAW AND HUMAN RIGHTS) (Political Parties, Elections and Referendums Act 2000 Sch 1 para 14(1)(c) (as so added)).

As to the Secretary of State and the Welsh Ministers see PARA 2. The Local Government Boundary Commission for Wales continues in existence but it is renamed, and is to be known as, the Local Democracy and Boundary Commission for Wales: see the Local Government (Democracy) (Wales) Act 2013 s 2; and PARA 72.

3   See the Political Parties, Elections and Referendums Act 2000 Sch 1 para 14(1).

4   Ie other than the Commission's first financial year: see the Political Parties, Elections and Referendums Act 2000 Sch 1 para 14(2). The Commission's first financial year was the period beginning with the date of the establishment of the Commission and ending with the next 31 March: see s 21. For the purposes of Pt I (ss 1–21), 'financial year', in relation to the Commission, means a period of 12 months ending with 31 March: see s 21.

5   As to the Speaker's Committee see PARA 49.

6   Political Parties, Elections and Referendums Act 2000 Sch 1 para 14(2).

7   Political Parties, Elections and Referendums Act 2000 Sch 1 para 14(3)(a).

8   Political Parties, Elections and Referendums Act 2000 Sch 1 para 14(3)(b). As to the meaning of 'functions' see PARA 34 note 2.

9   For these purposes, 'modifications' includes additions, omissions and amendments; and 'modify' must be construed accordingly: see the Political Parties, Elections and Referendums Act 2000 s 160(1).

10   Political Parties, Elections and Referendums Act 2000 Sch 1 para 14(3)(c).

11   Ie under the Political Parties, Elections and Referendums Act 2000 Sch 1 para 16 (see the text and notes 37–41): see Sch 1 para 14(4)(a). As to the Comptroller and Auditor General see CONSTITUTIONAL LAW AND HUMAN RIGHTS vol 8(2) (Reissue) PARAS 724–726.

12   Political Parties, Elections and Referendums Act 2000 Sch 1 para 14(4)(a).

13   As to the Treasury see CONSTITUTIONAL LAW AND HUMAN RIGHTS vol 8(2) (Reissue) PARAS 512–517.

14   Political Parties, Elections and Referendums Act 2000 Sch 1 para 14(4)(b).

15   Political Parties, Elections and Referendums Act 2000 Sch 1 para 14(5).

16   Ie its functions under the Political Parties, Elections and Referendums Act 2000 Sch 1 para 14 (see the text and notes 4–15): see Sch 1 para 14(6)(a).

17   Political Parties, Elections and Referendums Act 2000 Sch 1 para 14(6)(a).

18   Political Parties, Elections and Referendums Act 2000 Sch 1 para 14(6)(b).

19   Political Parties, Elections and Referendums Act 2000 Sch 1 para 14(6)(c).

20   Ie under the Political Parties, Elections and Referendums Act 2000 Sch 2 para 1 (see PARA 49): see Sch 1 para 14(6).

21   Political Parties, Elections and Referendums Act 2000 Sch 1 para 14(6).

22   Political Parties, Elections and Referendums Act 2000 Sch 1 para 15(1)(a).

23   Political Parties, Elections and Referendums Act 2000 Sch 1 para 15(1)(b).

24   Political Parties, Elections and Referendums Act 2000 Sch 1 para 15(2)(a).

25   Political Parties, Elections and Referendums Act 2000 Sch 1 para 15(2)(b).

26   Political Parties, Elections and Referendums Act 2000 Sch 1 para 15(2)(c).

27   Ie under the Political Parties, Elections and Referendums Act 2000 Sch 1 para 16 (see the text and notes 37–41): see Sch 1 para 15(3)(a).

28   Political Parties, Elections and Referendums Act 2000 Sch 1 para 15(3)(a).

29   Political Parties, Elections and Referendums Act 2000 Sch 1 para 15(3)(b).

30   Political Parties, Elections and Referendums Act 2000 Sch 1 para 15(4).

31   Ie its functions under the Political Parties, Elections and Referendums Act 2000 Sch 1 para 15 (see the text and notes 22–30): see Sch 1 para 15(5)(a).

32   Political Parties, Elections and Referendums Act 2000 Sch 1 para 15(5)(a).

33   Political Parties, Elections and Referendums Act 2000 Sch 1 para 15(5)(b).

34   Political Parties, Elections and Referendums Act 2000 Sch 1 para 15(5)(c).

35   Ie under the Political Parties, Elections and Referendums Act 2000 Sch 2 para 1 (see PARA 49): see Sch 1 para 15(5).

36   Political Parties, Elections and Referendums Act 2000 Sch 1 para 15(5).

37   Ie under the Political Parties, Elections and Referendums Act 2000 Sch 1 para 14 (see the text and notes 4–21): see Sch 1 para 16(1)(a).

38   Ie under the Political Parties, Elections and Referendums Act 2000 Sch 1 para 15 (see the text and notes 22–36): see Sch 1 para 16(1)(a).

39   Political Parties, Elections and Referendums Act 2000 Sch 1 para 16(1)(a). The National Audit Act 1983 s 8 (right to obtain documents and information) applies in relation to any examination under the Political Parties, Elections and Referendums Act 2000 Sch 1 para 16 as it applies in relation to an examination under the National Audit Act 1983 s 6: Political Parties, Elections and Referendums Act 2000 Sch 1 para 16(2). As to economy, efficiency and effectiveness examinations of public departments conducted under the National Audit Act 1983 see CONSTITUTIONAL LAW AND HUMAN RIGHTS vol 8(2) (Reissue) PARA 717.

40   Political Parties, Elections and Referendums Act 2000 Sch 1 para 16(1)(b).

41   Political Parties, Elections and Referendums Act 2000 Sch 1 para 16(1)(c).

45. Accounts of the Electoral Commission. The Electoral Commission[1] must keep proper accounting records[2] and must, for each financial year[3], prepare accounts in accordance with directions given to the Commission by the Treasury[4]. Such directions may include, in particular, directions as to:

(1)   the information to be contained in the accounts and the manner in which it is to be presented[5];

(2)   the methods and principles in accordance with which the accounts are to be prepared[6]; and

(3)   the additional information, if any, that is to accompany the accounts[7].

The accounts prepared by the Commission for any financial year must be submitted by the Commission to the Comptroller and Auditor General[8], and to the Speaker's Committee[9], as soon after the end of the financial year as may be practicable[10]. The Comptroller and Auditor General must examine and certify any accounts submitted to him in this way[11] and lay before each House of Parliament a copy of the accounts as certified by him together with his report on them[12].

The Speaker's Committee must designate a member of the Commission's staff to be the Commission's accounting officer[13], who has, in relation to the Commission's accounts and finances, the responsibilities[14] that are from time to time specified by the Speaker's Committee[15].

1   As to the establishment and constitution of the Electoral Commission see PARA 34 et seq.
2   Political Parties, Elections and Referendums Act 2000 s 1(6), Sch 1 para 17(1). For these purposes, 'record' means a record in whatever form it is kept: see s 160(1).
3   As to the meaning of 'financial year' for these purposes see PARA 44 note 4.
4   Political Parties, Elections and Referendums Act 2000 Sch 1 para 17(2). As to the Treasury see CONSTITUTIONAL LAW AND HUMAN RIGHTS vol 8(2) (Reissue) PARAS 512–517.
5   Political Parties, Elections and Referendums Act 2000 Sch 1 para 17(3)(a).
6   Political Parties, Elections and Referendums Act 2000 Sch 1 para 17(3)(b).
7   Political Parties, Elections and Referendums Act 2000 Sch 1 para 17(3)(c).
8   Political Parties, Elections and Referendums Act 2000 Sch 1 para 18(1)(a). As to the Comptroller and Auditor General see CONSTITUTIONAL LAW AND HUMAN RIGHTS vol 8(2) (Reissue) PARAS 724–726.
9   Political Parties, Elections and Referendums Act 2000 Sch 1 para 18(1)(b). As to the Speaker's Committee see PARA 49.
10   See the Political Parties, Elections and Referendums Act 2000 Sch 1 para 18(1).
11   Political Parties, Elections and Referendums Act 2000 Sch 1 para 18(2)(a).
12   Political Parties, Elections and Referendums Act 2000 Sch 1 para 18(2)(b).
13   Political Parties, Elections and Referendums Act 2000 Sch 1 para 19(1). As to the Secretary of State's power to designate any member of the Commission's staff or other person to be the Commission's accounting officer until such time as the first designation took effect see Sch 1 para 19(6). As to the Secretary of State see PARA 2.
14   For these purposes, references to responsibilities include in particular: (1) responsibilities in relation to the signing of accounts (Political Parties, Elections and Referendums Act 2000 Sch 1 para 19(3)(a)); (2) responsibilities for the propriety and regularity of the Commission's finances (Sch 1 para 19(3)(b)); and (3) responsibilities for the economy, efficiency and effectiveness with which the Commission's resources are used (Sch 1 para 19(3)(c)).
15   Political Parties, Elections and Referendums Act 2000 Sch 1 para 19(2). The responsibilities which may be specified under Sch 1 para 19 include responsibilities owed to the Commission, the Speaker's Committee or the House of Commons or its Committee of Public Accounts: Sch 1 para 19(4). Any reference to the Public Accounts Committee of the House of Commons for these purposes must, if the name of the Committee is changed, be taken to be references to the Committee by its new name: see Sch 1 para 19(5).

46. Annual report of the Electoral Commission. The Electoral Commission[1] must: (1) as soon after the end of each financial year[2] as may be practicable, prepare and lay before each House of Parliament a report about the performance of the Commission's functions[3] during that financial year[4]; and (2) on so laying such a report, publish the report in such manner as it determines[5].

1   As to the establishment and constitution of the Electoral Commission see PARA 34 et seq.
2   As to the meaning of 'financial year' for these purposes see PARA 44 note 4.
3   As to the meaning of 'functions' see PARA 34 note 2.
4   See the Political Parties, Elections and Referendums Act 2000 s 1(6), Sch 1 para 20(1). Each report by the Commission under Sch 1 para 20 must contain information about the use made by the Commission of its investigatory powers under s 146, Sch 19B (see PARAS 63–66, 753) and its enforcement powers under Sch 19C (see PARAS 757–760) during the year in question: see Sch 19B para 15, Sch 19C para 27; and PARAS 63, 760 note 18.

The functions referred to in Sch 1 para 20(1) do not include, however, the Commission's functions under Pt I (ss 1–21) in relation to local government elections in Scotland: see Sch 1 para 20(3) (Sch 1 paras 20(3), 20A added by the Local Electoral Administration (Scotland) Act 2011 s 17(1)–(3)). As to annual reports to be laid by the Electoral Commission before the Scottish Parliament see the Political Parties, Elections and Referendums Act 2000 Sch 1 para 20A (as so added).

5 See the Political Parties, Elections and Referendums Act 2000 Sch 1 para 20(2).

47.   Regulations made by the Electoral Commission. If the Electoral Commission[1] makes any regulations, it must give a copy to the Secretary of State[2] without delay[3]; and, if the Commission alters or revokes any regulations, it must give notice to the Secretary of State without delay[4].

Any power conferred on the Commission to make regulations[5] is exercisable in writing[6]. An instrument by which regulations are made by the Commission (a 'regulation-making instrument') must specify the provision under which the regulations are made[7] and, to the extent to which any regulation-making instrument does not comply with this requirement, it is void[8]. Immediately after a regulation-making instrument is made, it must be printed and made available to the public[9]. The Commission may charge a reasonable fee for providing a person with a copy of a regulation-making instrument[10].

Regulations made by the Commission are not statutory instruments and are not recorded in this work[11].

1 As to the establishment and constitution of the Electoral Commission see PARA 34 et seq.
2 As to the Secretary of State see PARA 2.
3 Political Parties, Elections and Referendums Act 2000 s 1(6), Sch 1 para 21(1).
4 Political Parties, Elections and Referendums Act 2000 Sch 1 para 21(2). Such a notice must be in writing (see s 157(1)); and notice of an alteration must include details of the alteration (Sch 1 para 21(3)).
5 Any power of the Commission to make regulations includes power to make different provision for different cases: Political Parties, Elections and Referendums Act 2000 Sch 1 para 22(7).
6 Political Parties, Elections and Referendums Act 2000 Sch 1 para 22(1).
7 Political Parties, Elections and Referendums Act 2000 Sch 1 para 22(2).
8 Political Parties, Elections and Referendums Act 2000 Sch 1 para 22(3). As to the proof of regulation-making instruments see PARA 48.
9 Political Parties, Elections and Referendums Act 2000 Sch 1 para 22(4). A person is not to be taken to have contravened any regulation made by the Commission if he shows that at the time of the alleged contravention the regulation-making instrument concerned had not been made available in accordance with Sch 1 para 22: Sch 1 para 22(6).
10 Political Parties, Elections and Referendums Act 2000 Sch 1 para 22(5).
11 However, the regulations so made may be ascertained by reference to the Electoral Commission website (which, at the date at which this volume states the law, is to be found at *www.electoralcommission.org.uk*).

48.   Proof of instruments. A document[1] purporting to be duly executed under the seal of the Electoral Commission[2], or signed on behalf of the Commission[3], must be received in evidence and, unless the contrary is proved, be taken to be so executed or signed[4].

The production of a printed copy of a regulation-making instrument[5] purporting to be made by the Commission on which is endorsed a certificate signed by a member of the Commission's staff authorised by the Commission for that purpose[6], and which contains the required statements[7], is evidence of the facts stated in the certificate[8].

1 For these purposes, 'document' means a document in whatever form it is kept: see the Political Parties, Elections and Referendums Act 2000 s 160(1).
2 Political Parties, Elections and Referendums Act 2000 s 1(6), Sch 1 para 24(a). As to the establishment and constitution of the Electoral Commission see PARA 34 et seq.

3　Political Parties, Elections and Referendums Act 2000 Sch 1 para 24(b) (amended by the Local Democracy, Economic Development and Construction Act 2009 s 146(1), Sch 7 Pt 3).

4　See the Political Parties, Elections and Referendums Act 2000 Sch 1 para 24.

5　As to the meaning of 'regulation-making instrument' see PARA 47.

6　Political Parties, Elections and Referendums Act 2000 Sch 1 para 23(1)(a). A certificate purporting to be signed as mentioned in Sch 1 para 23(1) is to be taken to have been properly signed unless the contrary is shown: Sch 1 para 23(3).

7　Political Parties, Elections and Referendums Act 2000 Sch 1 para 23(1)(b). The required statements are:

(1)　that the instrument was made by the Commission (Sch 1 para 23(2)(a));

(2)　that the copy is a true copy of the instrument (Sch 1 para 23(2)(b)); and

(3)　that on a specified date the instrument was made available to the public in accordance with Sch 1 para 22(4) (see PARA 47) (Sch 1 para 23(2)(c)).

8　Political Parties, Elections and Referendums Act 2000 Sch 1 para 23(1). A person who wishes in any legal proceedings to rely on a regulation-making instrument may require the Commission to endorse a copy of the instrument with a certificate of the kind mentioned in Sch 1 para 23(1): Sch 1 para 23(4).

B. ESTABLISHMENT AND CONSTITUTION OF RELATED BODIES

49. Speaker's Committee. A Committee known as the 'Speaker's Committee' performs the functions conferred on it by the Political Parties, Elections and Referendums Act 2000[1]. The Committee consists of the Speaker of the House of Commons[2], who is the chairman of the Committee, and the following other members[3], namely:

(1)　the member of the House of Commons who is for the time being the Chairman of the Home Affairs Select Committee of the House of Commons[4];

(2)　the Lord President of the Council[5];

(3)　a member of the House of Commons who is a Minister of the Crown with responsibilities in relation to local government[6]; and

(4)　five members of the House of Commons who are not Ministers of the Crown[7].

An appointed member of the Speaker's Committee[8] ceases to be a member of the Speaker's Committee if he ceases to be a Member of the House of Commons[9] or if another person is appointed to be a member of the Committee in his place[10]. An appointed member may resign from the Committee at any time by giving notice to the Speaker[11] but is otherwise[12] a member of the Committee for the duration of the Parliament in which he is appointed[13]. An appointed member may be re-appointed, or further re-appointed, to membership of the Committee[14].

The validity of any proceedings of the Committee is not affected by any vacancy among[15], or by any defect in the appointment of any of[16], the members of the Committee[17]. The Committee may determine its own procedure[18], and may appoint a member of the Committee to act as chairman at any meeting of the Committee in the absence of the Speaker[19].

The Committee must, at least once in each year, make to the House of Commons a report on the exercise by the Committee of its functions[20].

1　Political Parties, Elections and Referendums Act 2000 s 2(1). As to the meaning of 'functions' see PARA 34 note 2. As to the functions so conferred see s 1(6), Sch 1 para 3 (report on Electoral Commissioner's removal from office: see PARA 36), Sch 1 para 11B (special designation of relevant period for post on staff of Electoral Commission: see PARA 39 note 16), Sch 1 para 14 (submission of Electoral Commission's estimate of income and expenditure: see PARA 44), Sch 1 para 15 (submission of Electoral Commission's five-year plan: see PARA 44), Sch 1 para 18 (submission of accounts prepared by Electoral Commission: see PARA 45), Sch 1 para 19 (appointment of Electoral Commission's accounting officer: see PARA 45); and see the text and notes 2–20.

2   As to the Speaker of the House of Commons see PARLIAMENT vol 78 (2010) PARA 931 et seq.

3   See the Political Parties, Elections and Referendums Act 2000 s 2(2).

4   Political Parties, Elections and Referendums Act 2000 s 2(2)(a). For these purposes, references to the Home Affairs Select Committee must, if the name of that Committee is changed, be taken to be references to the Committee by its new name: see s 2(6)(a). As to select committees of the House of Commons generally see PARLIAMENT vol 78 (2010) PARA 979 et seq; and as to the Home Affairs Select Committee of the House of Commons see PARLIAMENT vol 78 (2010) PARA 987.

5   Political Parties, Elections and Referendums Act 2000 s 2(2)(b) (substituted by SI 2002/2626; and amended by SI 2010/1837). As to the Lord President of the Council see the Lord President of the Council Order 2010, SI 2010/1837; and PARA 2.

6   Political Parties, Elections and Referendums Act 2000 s 2(2)(c). The member of the Committee mentioned in s 2(2)(c) must be appointed to membership of the Committee by the Prime Minister: s 2(3). As to the departments of central government concerned with local government see LOCAL GOVERNMENT vol 69 (2009) PARA 95 et seq.

7   Political Parties, Elections and Referendums Act 2000 s 2(2)(d). The members of the Committee mentioned in s 2(2)(d) must be appointed to membership of the Committee by the Speaker of the House of Commons: s 2(4).

8   For these purposes, 'appointed member' means a member of the Speaker's Committee other than the Speaker of the House of Commons, the member who is the Chairman of the Home Affairs Committee of the House of Commons or the member who is the Lord President of the Council: see the Political Parties, Elections and Referendums Act 2000 s 2(5), Sch 2 para 2(1) (amended by SI 2010/1837).

9   Political Parties, Elections and Referendums Act 2000 Sch 2 para 2(2)(a).

10   Political Parties, Elections and Referendums Act 2000 Sch 2 para 2(2)(b).

11   Political Parties, Elections and Referendums Act 2000 Sch 2 para 2(3).

12   Ie subject to the Political Parties, Elections and Referendums Act 2000 Sch 2 para 2(2), (3) (see the text and notes 3–11): see Sch 2 para 2(4).

13   Political Parties, Elections and Referendums Act 2000 Sch 2 para 2(4).

14   Political Parties, Elections and Referendums Act 2000 Sch 2 para 2(5).

15   See the Political Parties, Elections and Referendums Act 2000 Sch 2 para 3(2)(a).

16   See the Political Parties, Elections and Referendums Act 2000 Sch 2 para 3(2)(b).

17   See the Political Parties, Elections and Referendums Act 2000 Sch 2 para 3(2).

18   Political Parties, Elections and Referendums Act 2000 Sch 2 para 3(1).

19   Political Parties, Elections and Referendums Act 2000 Sch 2 para 3(3).

20   Political Parties, Elections and Referendums Act 2000 Sch 2 para 1(1). For the purposes of the law of defamation, the publication of any matter by the Speaker's Committee in making such a report is absolutely privileged: Sch 2 para 1(2). As to absolute privilege in the law of defamation see DEFAMATION vol 32 (2012) PARA 594 et seq.

50.   Parliamentary Parties Panel.   A panel known as the 'Parliamentary Parties Panel' consists of representatives of qualifying parties[1] and its function[2] is to submit representations or information to the Electoral Commission[3] about such matters affecting political parties as the panel thinks fit[4]. Where the panel submits any such representations or information to the Commission, the Commission must consider the representations or information[5] and decide whether, and (if so) to what extent, it should act on the representations or information[6].

Each qualifying party is entitled to be represented on the panel by a person appointed to the panel by the treasurer of the party[7]. A person so appointed is a member of the panel for such period as the treasurer of the party may determine when making the appointment[8] but a person so appointed ceases to be a member of the panel if at any time his appointment is terminated for any reason by the treasurer of the party[9], or if at any time the party ceases to be a qualifying party[10]. The validity of any proceedings of the panel is not affected by any failure by the treasurer of a qualifying party to make any appointment in accordance with these provisions[11].

The panel may determine its own procedure[12].

1   See the Political Parties, Elections and Referendums Act 2000 s 4(1). For these purposes, 'qualifying party' means a registered party:
    (1)   to which two or more members of the House of Commons for the time being belong, who have made and subscribed to the oath required by the Parliamentary Oaths Act 1866 (or the corresponding affirmation) and are not disqualified from sitting or voting in the House (Political Parties, Elections and Referendums Act 2000 s 4(9)(a)); or
    (2)   to which two or more such members belonged immediately after the most recent parliamentary general election (s 4(9)(b)).
    The representatives of qualifying parties are appointed to the panel in accordance with s 4: see s 4(1). As to the meaning of 'registered party' for these purposes see PARA 35 note 3. As to the disqualification of members of the House of Commons see PARLIAMENT vol 78 (2010) PARA 897 et seq; and as to the oath or affirmation required by the Parliamentary Oaths Act 1866 see PARLIAMENT vol 78 (2010) PARA 1001.
2   As to the meaning of 'function' see PARA 34 note 2.
3   As to the establishment and constitution of the Electoral Commission see PARA 34 et seq.
4   Political Parties, Elections and Referendums Act 2000 s 4(2).
5   Political Parties, Elections and Referendums Act 2000 s 4(3)(a).
6   Political Parties, Elections and Referendums Act 2000 s 4(3)(b).
7   Political Parties, Elections and Referendums Act 2000 s 4(4). In the Political Parties, Elections and Referendums Act 2000, 'treasurer', in relation to a registered party, means registered treasurer: see s 160(1). As to the requirement for treasurers of a registered party to be registered see PARA 253.
8   Political Parties, Elections and Referendums Act 2000 s 4(5).
9   Political Parties, Elections and Referendums Act 2000 s 4(6)(a).
10   Political Parties, Elections and Referendums Act 2000 s 4(6)(b).
11   Political Parties, Elections and Referendums Act 2000 s 4(8).
12   Political Parties, Elections and Referendums Act 2000 s 4(7).

(ii) The Commission's General Functions

51.   Reports on elections and referendums.   The Electoral Commission[1] must, after each relevant election[2] and each relevant referendum[3], prepare and publish, in such manner as the Commission may determine, a report on the administration of the election or referendum (as the case may be)[4].

After a poll held with regard to the exercise of functions by the Welsh Ministers[5], the Commission must, if requested to do so by the Welsh Ministers, at their expense prepare and publish, in such manner as the Commission may determine, a report on the administration of the poll[6].

1   As to the establishment and constitution of the Electoral Commission see PARA 34 et seq.
2   Political Parties, Elections and Referendums Act 2000 s 5(1)(a). The provision made by s 5 applies to the following elections (see s 5(2)), namely:
    (1)   a parliamentary general election (s 5(2)(a));
    (2)   a European parliamentary general election (s 5(2)(b));
    (3)   a Scottish parliamentary general election (s 5(2)(c));
    (4)   a National Assembly for Wales general election (s 5(2)(d) (s 5(2)(d) substituted, s 5(2A)(c), (3) amended by SI 2007/1388));
    (5)   a Northern Ireland Assembly general election (Political Parties, Elections and Referendums Act 2000 s 5(2)(e));
    (6)   an ordinary election of police and crime commissioners (s 5(2)(f) (s 5(2)(f), (2A)(d) added, s 5(2A)(b) amended, by the Police Reform and Social Responsibility Act 2011 s 74, Sch 10 paras 8, 9)).

The Commission has discretion also to prepare and publish, in such manner as the Commission may determine, a report on the administration of the following elections (see the Political Parties, Elections and Referendums Act 2000 s 5(2A) (added by the Electoral Administration Act 2006 s 28)), namely:

(a) a parliamentary by-election (Political Parties, Elections and Referendums Act 2000 s 5(2A)(a) (as so added));

(b) an election held under the Scotland Act 1998 s 9 (election for the Scottish Parliament in the case of a constituency vacancy) (Political Parties, Elections and Referendums Act 2000 s 5(2A)(b) (as so added and amended)); or

(c) an election held under the Government of Wales Act 2006 s 10 (election for the National Assembly for Wales in the case of a constituency vacancy: see PARA 214) (Political Parties, Elections and Referendums Act 2000 s 5(2A)(c) (as so added and amended));

(d) an election held under the Police Reform and Social Responsibility Act 2011 s 51 (election to fill vacancy in office of police and crime commissioner: see POLICE AND INVESTIGATORY POWERS vol 84 (2013) PARA 69) (Political Parties, Elections and Referendums Act 2000 s 5(2A)(d) (as so added)).

As to parliamentary general elections see PARA 9 et seq; as to Welsh Assembly general elections see PARA 12 et seq; and as to European parliamentary general elections see PARA 13 et seq. As to parliamentary by-elections see PARA 191. As to the election of police and crime commissioners see POLICE AND INVESTIGATORY POWERS vol 84 (2013) PARA 62 et seq.

3 Political Parties, Elections and Referendums Act 2000 s 5(1)(b). The provision made by s 5 applies to referendums to which Pt VII (ss 101–129) applies (see PARA 527 et seq): see s 5(1)(b).
4 See the Political Parties, Elections and Referendums Act 2000 s 5(1).
5 Ie after a poll held under the Government of Wales Act 2006 s 64 (see PARA 105): see the Political Parties, Elections and Referendums Act 2000 s 5(3) (as amended: see note 2). As to the Welsh Ministers see PARA 2.
6 Political Parties, Elections and Referendums Act 2000 s 5(3) (as amended: see note 2).

52. Reviews of electoral and political matters. The Electoral Commission[1] must keep under review, and from time to time submit reports to the Secretary of State[2] on, the following matters[3], namely:

(1) such matters relating to relevant elections[4] as the Commission may determine from time to time[5];

(2) such matters relating to relevant referendums[6] as the Commission may so determine[7];

(3) the redistribution of seats at parliamentary elections[8];

(4) if any functions of the Local Government Commission for England or of the Local Government Boundary Commission for Scotland or of the Local Government Boundary Commission for Wales are transferred[9], the matters in relation to which those functions are exercisable[10];

(5) the registration of political parties and the regulation of their income and expenditure[11];

(6) political advertising in the broadcast and other electronic media[12];

(7) the law relating to the matters mentioned in each of heads (1) to (6) above[13].

At the request of the Secretary of State, and within such time as the Secretary of State may specify, the Commission must review, and submit a report to the Secretary of State on such matter or matters, whether or not falling within heads (1) to (7) above, as the Secretary of State may specify[14]. Each report so made by the Commission must be published by it in such manner as it may determine[15].

1 As to the establishment and constitution of the Electoral Commission see PARA 34 et seq.
2 As to the Secretary of State see PARA 2.
3 See the Political Parties, Elections and Referendums Act 2000 s 6(1).
4 Ie elections to which the Political Parties, Elections and Referendums Act 2000 s 6 applies (see s 6(1)(a), (6)), namely:
(1) a parliamentary general election (ss 5(2)(a), 6(6)(a)(i));

(2)   a European parliamentary general election (ss 5(2)(b), 6(6)(a)(i));

(3)   a Scottish parliamentary general election (ss 5(2)(c), 6(6)(a)(i));

(4)   a National Assembly for Wales general election (s 5(2)(d) (substituted by SI 2007/1388), Political Parties, Elections and Referendums Act 2000 s 6(6)(a)(i));

(5)   a Northern Ireland Assembly general election (ss 5(2)(e), 6(6)(a)(i));

(6)   an ordinary election of police and crime commissioners (s 5(2)(f) (added by the Police Reform and Social Responsibility Act 2011 s 74, Sch 10 paras 8, 9), Political Parties, Elections and Referendums Act 2000 s 6(6)(a)(i)).

(7)   local government elections in England or Wales (s 6(6)(a)(ii)); and

(8)   local elections in Northern Ireland (s 6(6)(a)(iii)).

Where any review carried out under s 6 relates to elections in Northern Ireland, the Commission must consult the Chief Electoral Officer for Northern Ireland with respect to such elections: s 6(4). Where a statement is delivered to the Electoral Commission under the Representation of the People Act 1983 Sch 1 r 53ZA(1)(b), by a returning officer who has failed to comply with his duty to begin the counting of the votes given on ballot papers within the period specified in Sch 1 r 45(3A), the Commission must specify in any election report they produce that a statement has been delivered to them under Sch 1 r 53ZA(1)(b) in respect of the constituency to which the statement relates: see Sch 1 r 53ZA(3); and PARA 425 note 15. As to the meaning of 'local government election' see PARA 11. As to parliamentary general elections see PARA 9 et seq; as to ordinary elections to the National Assembly for Wales see PARA 12 et seq; and as to European parliamentary general elections see PARA 13 et seq. As to the meanings of 'England' and 'Wales' see PARA 1 note 1. As to the election of police and crime commissioners see POLICE AND INVESTIGATORY POWERS vol 84 (2013) PARA 62 et seq.

5   Political Parties, Elections and Referendums Act 2000 s 6(1)(a).

6   Ie referendums to which the Political Parties, Elections and Referendums Act 2000 s 6 applies, namely referendums to which Pt VII (ss 101–129) applies (see PARA 527 et seq) and those under the Local Government Act 2000 Pt 1A (ss 9B–9R) (arrangements with respect to local governance in England: see LOCAL GOVERNMENT), Pt II (ss 10–48A) (Local authorities in Wales: arrangements with respect to executives etc: see LOCAL GOVERNMENT vol 69 (2009) PARA 303 et seq) (see PARA 558 et seq): see the Political Parties, Elections and Referendums Act 2000 s 6(1)(b), (6)(b); Interpretation Act 1978 s 17(2)(b).

7   Political Parties, Elections and Referendums Act 2000 s 6(1)(b). The Commission must not, however, carry out any review or make any report under the Political Parties, Elections and Referendums Act 2000 s 6 with respect to:

(1)   the conduct of referendums held in pursuance of any provision made by or under an Act of the Scottish Parliament or the Northern Ireland Assembly or the conduct of any poll under the Government of Wales Act 2006 s 64 (poll held to ascertain views about whether or how any of the functions of the Welsh Ministers should be exercised: see PARA 105) (Political Parties, Elections and Referendums Act 2000 s 6(3)(b) (s 6(3)(a), (b) amended by SI 2007/1388)); or

(2)   the law relating to such matters as are mentioned in head (1) above (Political Parties, Elections and Referendums Act 2000 s 6(3)(c)).

8   Political Parties, Elections and Referendums Act 2000 s 6(1)(c). As to the meaning of 'parliamentary election' see PARA 9. As to the redistribution of seats at parliamentary elections see PARA 78 et seq.

9   Ie by an order under the Political Parties, Elections and Referendums Act 2000 s 18(1) (repealed) (transfer of functions of the Local Government Commission for England: see PARA 71 note 1), s 19(1) (repealed) (transfer of functions of the Local Government Boundary Commission for Scotland) or s 20(1) (repealed) (transfer of functions of the Local Government Boundary Commission for Wales: see PARA 71 note 1): see s 6(1)(d). As to the meaning of 'functions' see PARA 34 note 2. The Local Government Boundary Commission for Wales continues in existence but it is renamed, and is to be known as, the Local Democracy and Boundary Commission for Wales: see the Local Government (Democracy) (Wales) Act 2013 s 2; and PARA 72.

10   Political Parties, Elections and Referendums Act 2000 s 6(1)(d).

11   Political Parties, Elections and Referendums Act 2000 s 6(1)(e). The Commission must not, however, carry out any review or make any report under s 6 with respect to:

(1)   the funding of political parties under the Scotland Act 1998 s 97 (assistance for opposition parties), or for the purpose of assisting members of the Northern Ireland Assembly connected with such parties to perform their Assembly duties, or the funding of political groups under the Government of Wales Act 2006 s 24 (assistance to groups of Assembly members: see CONSTITUTIONAL LAW AND HUMAN RIGHTS) (Political Parties, Elections and Referendums Act 2000 s 6(3)(a) (as amended: see note 7); or

(2)   the law relating to the matters mentioned in head (1) above (s 6(3)(c)).

As to the registration of political parties and the regulation of their income and expenditure see PARA 253.

12 Political Parties, Elections and Referendums Act 2000 s 6(1)(f).
13 Political Parties, Elections and Referendums Act 2000 s 6(1)(g).
14 See the Political Parties, Elections and Referendums Act 2000 s 6(2).
15 Political Parties, Elections and Referendums Act 2000 s 6(5).

53.   Commission representatives and accredited observers to attend electoral proceedings and observe working practices.   A representative of the Electoral Commission[1] may[2] attend:

(1)   proceedings relating to a specified election[3] which are the responsibility of the returning officer for the election[4]; or

(2)   proceedings relating to a referendum under the Political Parties, Elections and Referendums Act 2000[5] which are the responsibility of the relevant counting officer[6]; or

(3)   proceedings relating to a local authority referendum[7] which are the responsibility of the counting officer[8].

A representative of the Commission may observe the working practices of any of the following[9]:

(a)   an electoral registration officer[10];

(b)   a returning officer[11];

(c)   a relevant counting officer[12]; or

(d)   any person acting under the direction of a person mentioned in heads (a) to (c) above[13].

A representative of the Commission may also observe the working practices of a counting officer at a local authority referendum[14], and any person acting under the counting officer's direction[15].

A person who is aged 16 or over may apply to the Commission to be an 'accredited observer'[16] at any of the following proceedings relating to a specified election[17], to a referendum held under the Political Parties, Elections and Referendums Act 2000[18], or to a referendum[19] which is a local authority referendum[20], namely:

(i)   proceedings at the issue or receipt of postal ballot papers[21];

(ii)   proceedings at the poll[22]; or

(iii) proceedings at the counting of votes[23].

If the Commission grants the application, the accredited observer may[24] attend the proceedings in question[25]. An organisation[26] may apply to the Commission to be accredited for the purpose of nominating observers[27] at any of the proceedings listed in heads (i) to (iii) above relating to a specified election[28], to a referendum under the Political Parties, Elections and Referendums Act 2000[29], or to a referendum[30] which is a local authority referendum[31]. If the Commission grants such an application, the organisation may[32] nominate members who may attend the proceedings in question[33], although the Commission, in so granting an application, may specify a limit on the number of observers nominated by the organisation who may attend[34], at the same time, the specified proceedings[35]. A relevant officer[36] may also limit the number of accredited persons who may be present at any proceedings[37] at the same time[38]. If a person who is entitled to attend any proceedings as an accredited observer[39] misconducts himself while attending the proceedings, the relevant officer may cancel the person's entitlement[40].

The Commission must prepare a code of practice on the attendance of representatives of the Commission[41], accredited observers[42], and nominated members of accredited organisations[43], at specified elections[44] or at referendums under the Political Parties, Elections and Referendums Act 2000[45]. The code must in particular:

(A) specify the manner in which applications for accreditation[46] are to be made to the Commission[47];

(B) specify the criteria to be taken into account by the Commission in determining such applications[48];

(C) give guidance to relevant officers[49] as to the exercise of the power conferred[50] in relation to limiting the number of persons who may be present at any proceedings at the same time[51];

(D) give guidance to such officers as to the exercise of the power[52] to cancel the entitlement to attend proceedings of a person who misconducts himself[53];

(E) give guidance to such officers as to the exercise of any power under any enactment to control the number of persons present at any proceedings relating to an election or referendum as it relates to a person having such permission[54];

(F) give guidance to representatives of the Commission, accredited observers and nominated members of accredited organisations on the exercise of the rights conferred[55] on them[56].

The code may make different provision for different purposes[57]. Before preparing the code, the Commission must consult the Secretary of State[58] and it must lay the code before each House of Parliament[59]. The Commission must publish the code, in such manner as the Commission may determine[60], and the Commission may at any time revise the code[61]. In exercising any function conferred in relation to the attendance of representatives of the Commission at elections[62], the observation of working practices by representatives of Commission[63], the accreditation of observers[64] or the attendance and conduct of observers[65], the Commission[66], representatives of the Commission[67], relevant officers[68], and relevant counting officers[69] must each have regard to the code[70].

1 For these purposes, 'representative of the Electoral Commission' means any of the following (see the Political Parties, Elections and Referendums Act 2000 s 6A(3) (ss 6A–6G added by the Electoral Administration Act 2006 s 29)):
 (1) a member of the Commission (Political Parties, Elections and Referendums Act 2000 s 6A(3)(a) (as so added));
 (2) a member of staff of the Commission (s 6A(3)(b) (as so added));
 (3) a person appointed by the Commission for the purposes of s 6A (s 6A(3)(c) (as so added)).
 As to the establishment and constitution of the Electoral Commission see PARA 34 ct seq; and as to the staff of the Commission see PARA 38 et seq.

2 Ie subject to any enactment which regulates attendance at the proceedings in question: see the Political Parties, Elections and Referendums Act 2000 s 6A(2) (as added: see note 1). For these purposes, 'enactment' includes any provision of an Act (including the Political Parties, Elections and Referendums Act 2000) and any provision of subordinate legislation (within the meaning of the Interpretation Act 1978: see STATUTES AND LEGISLATIVE PROCESS vol 96 (2012) PARA 609): see the Political Parties, Elections and Referendums Act 2000 s 160(1).

3 Ie an election specified in the Political Parties, Elections and Referendums Act 2000 s 6A(5) (see s 6A(1)(a) (as added: see note 1)), namely:
 (1) a parliamentary general election (ss 5(2)(a), 6A(5)(a) (s 6A as so added));
 (2) a European parliamentary general election (ss 5(2)(b), 6A(5)(a) (s 6A as so added));
 (3) a Scottish parliamentary general election (ss 5(2)(c), 6A(5)(a) (s 6A as so added));
 (4) a National Assembly for Wales general election (s 5(2)(d) (s 5(2)(d) substituted, s 6A(5)(d) amended, by SI 2007/1388), Political Parties, Elections and Referendums Act 2000 s 6A(5)(a) (s 6A as so added));
 (5) a Northern Ireland Assembly general election (ss 5(2)(e), 6A(5)(a) (s 6A as so added));

(6) an ordinary election of police and crime commissioners (s 5(2)(f) (s 5(2)(f), s 6A(5)(da) added by the Police Reform and Social Responsibility Act 2011 s 74, Sch 10 paras 8–10), Political Parties, Elections and Referendums Act 2000 s 6A(5)(a) (s 6A as so added)).

(7) a parliamentary by-election (s 6A(5)(b) (s 6A as so added));

(8) an election held under the Scotland Act 1998 s 9 (election for the Scottish Parliament in the case of a constituency vacancy) (Political Parties, Elections and Referendums Act 2000 s 6A(5)(c) (s 6A as so added));

(9) an election held under the Government of Wales Act 2006 s 10 (constituency vacancy: see PARA 214) (Political Parties, Elections and Referendums Act 2000 s 6A(5)(d) (s 6A as so added, s 6A(5)(d) as so amended));

(10) an election held under the Police Reform and Social Responsibility Act 2011 s 51 (election to fill vacancy in office of police and crime commissioner: see POLICE AND INVESTIGATORY POWERS vol 84 (2013) PARA 69) (Political Parties, Elections and Referendums Act 2000 s 6A(5)(da) (s 6A, s 6A(5)(da) as so added)).

(11) a local government election in England or Wales (s 6A(5)(e) (s 6A as so added)); or

(12) a local government election in Scotland (s 6A(5)(ea) (s 6A as so added, s 6A(5)(ea) added by the Local Electoral Administration (Scotland) Act 2011 s 11(1))); or

(13) a local election in Northern Ireland (Political Parties, Elections and Referendums Act 2000 s 6A(5)(f) (s 6A as so added)).

As to the meanings of 'England' and 'Wales' see PARA 1 note 1. As to the meaning of 'local government election' see PARA 11. As to parliamentary general elections see PARA 9 et seq; as to Welsh Assembly general elections see PARA 12 et seq; and as to European parliamentary general elections see PARA 13 et seq. As to parliamentary by-elections see PARA 191. As to the election of police and crime commissioners see POLICE AND INVESTIGATORY POWERS vol 84 (2013) PARA 62 et seq.

4 Political Parties, Elections and Referendums Act 2000 s 6A(1)(a) (as added: see note 1). As to returning officers for the various elections see PARA 350 et seq.

5 Ie referendums to which the Political Parties, Elections and Referendums Act 2000 Pt VII (ss 101–129) applies (see PARA 527 et seq): see s 6A(1)(b) (as added: see note 1).

6 Political Parties, Elections and Referendums Act 2000 s 6A(1)(b) (as added: see note 1). A reference to the relevant counting officer must be construed: (1) if the area to which the proceedings relates is in Great Britain, in accordance with s 128(3) (Chief Counting Officer to appoint a counting officer for each relevant area in Great Britain: see PARA 553); (2) if the area to which the proceedings relates is Northern Ireland, as a reference to the Chief Electoral Officer for Northern Ireland: see s 6A(4) (as so added). As to the meaning of 'Great Britain' see PARA 1 note 1.

7 Ie a referendum, in relation to Wales, under the Local Authorities (Conduct of Referendums) (Wales) Regulations 2008, SI 2008/1848, or, in relation to England, under the Local Authorities (Conduct of Referendums) (England) Regulations 2012, SI 2012/323 (see PARA 555 et seq): see the Political Parties, Elections and Referendums Act 2000 s 6A(1)(c) (s 6A as added (see note 1); s 6A(1)(c) added, in relation to Wales, by the Local Authorities (Conduct of Referendums) (Wales) Regulations 2008, SI 2008/1848, reg 8(2), Sch 4 Table 3; and, in relation to England, by the Local Authorities (Conduct of Referendums) (England) Regulations 2012, SI 2012/323, reg 8(2), Sch 4 Table 4. As to the meaning of 'counting officer' for these purposes see PARA 576 note 1. As to the Political Parties, Elections and Referendums Act 2000 ss 6A–6E, as they are applied and modified, in relation to Wales, by the Local Authorities (Conduct of Referendums) (Wales) Regulations 2008, SI 2008/1848, Sch 4 Table 3, and, in relation to England, by the Local Authorities (Conduct of Referendums) (England) Regulations 2012, SI 2012/323, Sch 4 Table 4, see PARA 15 note 2.

8 Political Parties, Elections and Referendums Act 2000 s 6A(1)(c) (s 6A as added (see note 1); s 6A(1)(c) as added (see note 7)).

9 See the Political Parties, Elections and Referendums Act 2000 s 6B(1) (as added: see note 1). For these purposes, 'representative of the Commission' must be construed in accordance with s 6A (see note 1): see s 6B(2)(b) (as so added).

10 Political Parties, Elections and Referendums Act 2000 s 6B(1)(a) (as added: see note 1). As to electoral registration officers see PARA 139 et seq.

11 Political Parties, Elections and Referendums Act 2000 s 6B(1)(b) (as added: see note 1).

12 Political Parties, Elections and Referendums Act 2000 s 6B(1)(c) (as added: see note 1). For these purposes, 'relevant counting officer' must be construed in accordance with s 6A (see note 6): see s 6B(2)(a) (as added: see note 1).

13 Political Parties, Elections and Referendums Act 2000 s 6B(1)(d) (as added: see note 1).

14 Ie a referendum, in relation to Wales, under the Local Authorities (Conduct of Referendums) (Wales) Regulations 2008, SI 2008/1848, or, in relation to England, under the Local Authorities (Conduct of Referendums) (England) Regulations 2012, SI 2012/323 (see PARA 555 et seq): see the Political Parties, Elections and Referendums Act 2000 s 6B(2A) (s 6B as added (see note 1); s 6B(2A) added, in relation to Wales, by the Local Authorities (Conduct of Referendums) (Wales) Regulations 2008, SI 2008/1848, Sch 4 Table 3; and, in relation to England, by the Local Authorities (Conduct of Referendums) (England) Regulations 2012, SI 2012/323, Sch 4 Table 4). See note 7.

15 Political Parties, Elections and Referendums Act 2000 s 6B(2A) (s 6B as added (see note 1); s 6B(2A) as added (see note 14)).

16 An application under the Political Parties, Elections and Referendums Act 2000 s 6C(1) must be made in the manner specified in the code of practice issued under s 6F (see head (A) in the text): see s 6C(3) (as added: see note 1).

17 Ie an election specified in the Political Parties, Elections and Referendums Act 2000 s 6A(5) (see note 3): see s 6C(1) (as added: see note 1).

18 Ie a referendum to which the Political Parties, Elections and Referendums Act 2000 Pt VII applies (see PARA 527 et seq): see s 6C(1) (as added: see note 1).

19 Ie a referendum which is held, in relation to Wales, under the Local Authorities (Conduct of Referendums) (Wales) Regulations 2008, SI 2008/1848, or, in relation to England, under the Local Authorities (Conduct of Referendums) (England) Regulations 2012, SI 2012/323 (see PARA 555 et seq): see the Political Parties, Elections and Referendums Act 2000 s 6C(1) (as added (see note 1); as originally enacted and as applied and modified, in relation to Wales, by the Local Authorities (Conduct of Referendums) (Wales) Regulations 2008, SI 2008/1848, Sch 4 Table 3; and, in relation to England, by the Local Authorities (Conduct of Referendums) (England) Regulations 2012, SI 2012/323, Sch 4 Table 4). See note 7.

20 See the Political Parties, Elections and Referendums Act 2000 s 6C(1) (as added (see note 1); as originally enacted and as applied and modified (see note 19)).

21 Political Parties, Elections and Referendums Act 2000 s 6C(1)(a) (as added: see note 1). As to proceedings at the issue or receipt of postal ballot papers see PARA 406 et seq.

22 Political Parties, Elections and Referendums Act 2000 s 6C(1)(b) (as added: see note 1). As to proceedings at the poll see PARA 363 et seq.

23 Political Parties, Elections and Referendums Act 2000 s 6C(1)(c) (as added: see note 1). As to proceedings at the counting of votes see PARA 424 et seq.

24 Ie subject to any enactment which regulates attendance at the proceedings in question: see the Political Parties, Elections and Referendums Act 2000 s 6C(6) (as added: see note 1).

25 Political Parties, Elections and Referendums Act 2000 s 6C(2) (as added: see note 1). The Commission may at any time revoke the grant of an application under s 6C(1): s 6C(4) (as so added). However, if the Commission either refuses such an application or revokes the grant of any such application, it must give its decision in writing and must at the same time give reasons in writing for the refusal or revocation: see s 6C(5) (as so added).

26 For these purposes, 'organisation' includes any body corporate and any combination of persons or other unincorporated association: see the Political Parties, Elections and Referendums Act 2000 s 160(1).

27 An application under the Political Parties, Elections and Referendums Act 2000 s 6D(1) must be made in the manner specified in the code of practice issued under s 6F (see the text and notes 41–70): s 6D(4) (as added: see note 1).

28 Ie an election specified in the Political Parties, Elections and Referendums Act 2000 s 6A(5) (see note 3): see s 6D(1) (as added: see note 1).

29 Ie a referendum to which the Political Parties, Elections and Referendums Act 2000 Pt VII applies (see PARA 527 et seq): see s 6D(1) (as added: see note 1).

30 Ie a referendum which is held, in relation to Wales, under the Local Authorities (Conduct of Referendums) (Wales) Regulations 2008, SI 2008/1848, or, in relation to England, under the Local Authorities (Conduct of Referendums) (England) Regulations 2012, SI 2012/323 (see PARA 555 et seq): see the Political Parties, Elections and Referendums Act 2000 s 6D(1) (as added (see note 1); as originally enacted and as applied and modified, in relation to Wales, by the Local Authorities (Conduct of Referendums) (Wales) Regulations 2008, SI 2008/1848, Sch 4 Table 3; and, in relation to England, by the Local Authorities (Conduct of Referendums) (England) Regulations 2012, SI 2012/323, Sch 4 Table 4). See note 7.

31 See the Political Parties, Elections and Referendums Act 2000 s 6D(1) (as added (see note 1); as originally enacted and as applied and modified (see note 30)).

32 Ie subject to any enactment which regulates attendance at the proceedings in question: see the Political Parties, Elections and Referendums Act 2000 s 6D(7) (as added: see note 1).

33 Political Parties, Elections and Referendums Act 2000 s 6D(2) (as added: see note 1). The Commission may at any time revoke the grant of an application under s 6D(1): s 6D(5) (as so added). However, if the Commission either refuses such an application or revokes the grant of any such application, it must give its decision in writing and must at the same time give reasons in writing for the refusal or revocation: s 6D(6) (as so added).

34 Ie by virtue of the Political Parties, Elections and Referendums Act 2000 s 6D: see s 6D(3) (as added: see note 1).

35 Political Parties, Elections and Referendums Act 2000 s 6D(3) (as added: see note 1).

36 For these purposes, a relevant officer is:
   (1)   in the case of proceedings at a polling station, the presiding officer (Political Parties, Elections and Referendums Act 2000 s 6E(4)(a) (as added: see note 1));
   (2)   in the case of any other proceedings at an election, the returning officer (s 6E(4)(b) (as so added));
   (3)   in the case of any other proceedings at a referendum to which Pt VII applies (see PARA 527 et seq), the relevant counting officer within the meaning of s 6A (see note 6) (s 6E(4)(c) (s 6E as so added; s 6E(4)(c) as originally enacted and as substituted, in relation to Wales, by the Local Authorities (Conduct of Referendums) (Wales) Regulations 2008, SI 2008/1848, Sch 4 Table 3; and, in relation to England, by the Local Authorities (Conduct of Referendums) (England) Regulations 2012, SI 2012/323, Sch 4 Table 4));
   (4)   in the case of any other proceedings at a referendum held, in relation to Wales, under the Local Authorities (Conduct of Referendums) (Wales) Regulations 2008, SI 2008/1848, or, in relation to England, under the Local Authorities (Conduct of Referendums) (England) Regulations 2012, SI 2012/323 (see PARA 555 et seq), the counting officer (Political Parties, Elections and Referendums Act 2000 s 6E(4)(ca) (s 6E as so added; s 6E(4)(ca) as added, in relation to Wales, by the Local Authorities (Conduct of Referendums) (Wales) Regulations 2008, SI 2008/1848, Sch 4 Table 3; and, in relation to England, by the Local Authorities (Conduct of Referendums) (England) Regulations 2012, SI 2012/323, Sch 4 Table 4));
   (5)   such other person as a person mentioned in head (1), (2), (3), or (4) above authorises for the purposes of the proceedings mentioned in the relevant head (Political Parties, Elections and Referendums Act 2000 s 6E(4)(d) (s 6E as so added; s 6E(4)(d) as originally enacted and as amended, in relation to Wales, by the Local Authorities (Conduct of Referendums) (Wales) Regulations 2008, SI 2008/1848, Sch 4 Table 3; and, in relation to England, by the Local Authorities (Conduct of Referendums) (England) Regulations 2012, SI 2012/323, Sch 4 Table 4)).
As to presiding officers at an election see PARA 393; and as to presiding officers at a referendum or poll see PARA 613.

37 Ie in pursuance of the Political Parties, Elections and Referendums Act 2000 s 6C (see the text and notes 16–25) or s 6D (see the text and notes 26–35): see s 6E(1) (as added: see note 1).

38 Political Parties, Elections and Referendums Act 2000 s 6E(1) (as added: see note 1).

39 Ie by virtue of the Political Parties, Elections and Referendums Act 2000 s 6C (see the text and notes 16–25) or s 6D (see the text and notes 26–35): see s 6E(2) (as added: see note 1).

40 Political Parties, Elections and Referendums Act 2000 s 6E(2) (as added: see note 1). This provision does not affect any power a relevant officer has by virtue of any enactment or rule of law to remove a person from any place: s 6E(3) (as so added).

41 Political Parties, Elections and Referendums Act 2000 s 6F(1)(a) (as added: see note 1). For these purposes, 'representative of the Commission' has the same meaning as in s 6A (see note 1): s 6F(10)(d) (as so added).

42 Political Parties, Elections and Referendums Act 2000 s 6F(1)(b) (as added: see note 1). For these purposes, 'accredited observer' must be construed in accordance with s 6C (see the text and notes 16–25): s 6F(10)(a) (as so added).

43 Political Parties, Elections and Referendums Act 2000 s 6F(1)(c) (as added: see note 1). For these purposes, 'accredited organisation' must be construed in accordance with s 6D (see the text and notes 26–35); and 'nominated member' must be construed accordingly: see s 6F(10)(b) (as so added).

44 Ie at elections specified in the Political Parties, Elections and Referendums Act 2000 s 6A(5) (see note 3), other than a local government election in Scotland: see s 6F(1) (s 6F as added (see note 1); s 6F(1) amended, s 6G added, in relation to Scotland, by the Local Electoral Administration (Scotland) Act 2011 s 11(5)(a), (6)). As to the code of practice relating to the attendance of observers at local government elections in Scotland see the Political Parties, Elections and Referendums Act 2000 s 6G (as so added).

45 See the Political Parties, Elections and Referendums Act 2000 s 6F(1) (s 6F as added (see note 1); s 6F(1) as amended (see note 44)). The text refers to referendums to which Pt VII applies (see PARA 527 et seq): see s 6F(1) (as so added and amended).
46 Ie applications under the Political Parties, Elections and Referendums Act 2000 s 6C(1) (see the text and notes 16–23) or s 6D(1) (see the text and notes 26–31): see s 6F(2)(a) (as added: see note 1).
47 Political Parties, Elections and Referendums Act 2000 s 6F(2)(a) (as added: see note 1).
48 Political Parties, Elections and Referendums Act 2000 s 6F(2)(b) (as added: see note 1).
49 Ie within the meaning of the Political Parties, Elections and Referendums Act 2000 s 6E (see the text and note 36): see s 6F(2)(c) (as added: see note 1).
50 Ie the power conferred by the Political Parties, Elections and Referendums Act 2000 s 6E(1) (see the text and notes 36–38): see s 6F(2)(c) (as added: see note 1).
51 Political Parties, Elections and Referendums Act 2000 s 6F(2)(c) (as added: see note 1).
52 Ie the power mentioned in the Political Parties, Elections and Referendums Act 2000 s 6E(2) (see the text and notes 39–40) as it relates to a person having the permission mentioned in s 6E(1) (see the text and notes 36–38): see s 6F(2)(d) (as added: see note 1).
53 Political Parties, Elections and Referendums Act 2000 s 6F(2)(d) (as added: see note 1).
54 Political Parties, Elections and Referendums Act 2000 s 6F(2)(e) (as added: see note 1).
55 Ie the rights conferred by the Political Parties, Elections and Referendums Act 2000 s 6A (see the text and notes 1–8), s 6B (see the text and notes 9–15), s 6C (see the text and notes 16–25) and s 6D (see the text and notes 26–35): see s 6F(2)(f) (as added: see note 1).
56 Political Parties, Elections and Referendums Act 2000 s 6F(2)(f) (as added: see note 1).
57 Political Parties, Elections and Referendums Act 2000 s 6F(3) (as added: see note 1).
58 Political Parties, Elections and Referendums Act 2000 s 6F(4) (as added: see note 1). As to the Secretary of State see PARA 2.
59 Political Parties, Elections and Referendums Act 2000 s 6F(5) (as added: see note 1).
60 Political Parties, Elections and Referendums Act 2000 s 6F(6) (as added: see note 1).
61 Political Parties, Elections and Referendums Act 2000 s 6F(8) (as added: see note 1). The provisions of s 6F(4)–(7) (see the text and notes 58–60, 62–70) apply in relation to a revision of the code as they apply in relation to the code: s 6F(9) (as so added).
62 Ie the function conferred by the Political Parties, Elections and Referendums Act 2000 s 6A (see the text and notes 1–8): see s 6F(7) (as added: see note 1).
63 Ie the function conferred by the Political Parties, Elections and Referendums Act 2000 s 6B (see the text and notes 9–15): see s 6F(7) (as added: see note 1).
64 Ie the function conferred by the Political Parties, Elections and Referendums Act 2000 s 6C (see the text and notes 16–25) or s 6D (see the text and notes 26–35): see s 6F(7) (as added: see note 1).
65 Ie the function conferred by the Political Parties, Elections and Referendums Act 2000 s 6E (see note 36): see s 6F(7) (as added: see note 1).
66 Political Parties, Elections and Referendums Act 2000 s 6F(7)(a) (as added: see note 1).
67 Political Parties, Elections and Referendums Act 2000 s 6F(7)(b) (as added: see note 1).
68 Political Parties, Elections and Referendums Act 2000 s 6F(7)(c) (as added: see note 1). The text refers to relevant officers within the meaning of s 6E (see note 36): see s 6F(7)(c) (as so added).
69 Political Parties, Elections and Referendums Act 2000 s 6F(7)(d) (as added: see note 1). For these purposes, 'relevant counting officer' must be construed in accordance with s 6A (see note 6); see s 6F(10)(c) (as so added).
70 See the Political Parties, Elections and Referendums Act 2000 s 6F(7) (as added: see note 1).

54. Commission to be consulted on certain instruments relating to electoral law. Before making any of the following instruments[1], namely any instrument containing:

(1)   regulations under the European Parliamentary Elections Act 2002[2];

(2)   an order[3] designating regional returning officers[4];

(3)   an order[5] designating returning officers and acting returning officers[6];

(4)   rules[7] making provision for local government elections in England and Wales[8];

(5)   regulations under the Representation of the People Act 1983 or under the Representation of the People Act 1985 which may not be made unless a draft of them has been laid before and approved by a resolution of each House of Parliament[9];

(6)   an order making provision for the conduct of elections to the National Assembly for Wales[10] and for the conduct of polls held by Welsh Ministers[11];

(7)   an order making provision for the conduct of elections of persons as police and crime commissioners in England and Wales[12] or orders or regulations made in relation to returning officers and local returning officers[13] for such elections[14];

(8)   an order making provision for the free delivery of election addresses at elections to the Greater London Authority[15],

the authority making the instrument must consult the Electoral Commission[16].

1   See the Political Parties, Elections and Referendums Act 2000 s 7(1).
2   Political Parties, Elections and Referendums Act 2000 s 7(2)(a) (s 7(2)(a), (b) amended by the European Parliamentary Elections Act 2002 s 15, Sch 3 para 8(1), (2)). As to the making of regulations under the European Parliamentary Elections Act 2002 see PARA 13 note 12.
3   Ie an order under the European Parliamentary Elections Act 2002 s 6(2)(b) (designation of returning officers for regions in England and Wales including the combined region: see PARA 360): see the Political Parties, Elections and Referendums Act 2000 s 7(2)(b) (as amended: see note 2).
4   Political Parties, Elections and Referendums Act 2000 s 7(2)(b) (as amended: see note 2).
5   Ie an order under the Representation of the People Act 1983 s 24(1)(c), s 24(1)(cc), s 24(1)(e) (see PARA 350), s 28(1)(b) (see PARA 351) or s 35(2B) (see PARA 354): see the Political Parties, Elections and Referendums Act 2000 s 7(2)(c).
6   Political Parties, Elections and Referendums Act 2000 s 7(2)(c).
7   Ie rules made under the Representation of the People Act 1983 s 36 (see PARA 383): see the Political Parties, Elections and Referendums Act 2000 s 7(2)(d).
8   Political Parties, Elections and Referendums Act 2000 s 7(2)(d). As to the meaning of 'local government election' see PARA 11.
9   Political Parties, Elections and Referendums Act 2000 s 7(2)(e). The text refers to regulations in relation to which the Representation of the People Act 1983 s 201(2) (see PARA 28 note 16) has effect: see the Political Parties, Elections and Referendums Act 2000 s 7(2)(e).
10 As to the conduct of Welsh Assembly elections see PARA 383 et seq.
11 Political Parties, Elections and Referendums Act 2000 s 7(2)(f) (substituted by SI 2007/1388). The text refers to provision made under the Government of Wales Act 2006 s 13 (power to make provision about the conduct of Welsh Assembly elections: see PARA 12), s 64(3) (provision as to the conduct of polls (or any poll), or for the combination of polls (or any poll): see PARA 664): see the Political Parties, Elections and Referendums Act 2000 s 7(2)(f) (as so substituted).
12 Ie an order under the Police Reform and Social Responsibility Act 2011 s 58 (conduct of elections of persons as police and crime commissioners in England and Wales: see POLICE AND INVESTIGATORY POWERS vol 84 (2013) PARA 64): see the Political Parties, Elections and Referendums Act 2000 s 7(2)(hc) (s 7(2)(ha)–(hc) added by the Police Reform and Social Responsibility Act 2011 s 74, Sch 10 paras 8, 11).
13 Ie an order under the Police Reform and Social Responsibility Act 2011 s 54(1)(b) (designations of returning officers for elections of persons as police and crime commissioners in England and Wales: see POLICE AND INVESTIGATORY POWERS vol 84 (2013) PARA 64) (see the Political Parties, Elections and Referendums Act 2000 s 7(2)(ha) (as added: see note 12), or regulations under the Police Reform and Social Responsibility Act 2011 s 54(2) (functions of returning officers and local returning officers for such elections: see POLICE AND INVESTIGATORY POWERS vol 84 (2013) PARA 64) (see the Political Parties, Elections and Referendums Act 2000 s 7(2)(hb) (as so added)).
14 See the Political Parties, Elections and Referendums Act 2000 s 7(2)(ha)–(hc) (as added: see note 12).
15 Political Parties, Elections and Referendums Act 2000 s 7(2)(i). The text refers to provision made under the Greater London Authority Act 1999 s 17A (see PARA 330): see s 7(2)(i).
16 See the Political Parties, Elections and Referendums Act 2000 s 7(1). As to the establishment and constitution of the Electoral Commission see PARA 34 et seq.

55.   Involvement of Commission in changes in electoral procedures for local elections in England and Wales. The Electoral Commission[1]:

(1)   may participate with any relevant local authority[2] in the joint submission of proposals relating to pilot schemes for local elections in England and Wales[3]; and

(2)   has such other functions[4] in relation to orders and schemes relating to such proposals[5], and orders relating to the revision of procedures in the light of such schemes[6],

as are conferred on the Commission[7]. Where any pilot scheme for local elections in England and Wales[8] falls to be implemented following the approval by the Secretary of State[9] of proposals jointly submitted by the Commission and a relevant local authority as mentioned in head (1) above[10], the Commission may, in connection with the implementation of the scheme, provide that authority with such assistance (except financial assistance) as the Commission thinks fit[11].

1   As to the establishment and constitution of the Electoral Commission see PARA 34 et seq.
2   For these purposes, 'relevant local authority' has the same meaning as in the Representation of the People Act 2000 s 10 (pilot schemes for local elections in England and Wales: see PARA 521 note 1): Political Parties, Elections and Referendums Act 2000 s 9(3).
3   Political Parties, Elections and Referendums Act 2000 s 9(1)(a). The text refers to the joint submission of proposals falling within the Representation of the People Act 2000 s 10(1) (see PARA 521): see the Political Parties, Elections and Referendums Act 2000 s 9(1)(a). As to the meanings of 'England' and 'Wales' see PARA 1 note 1.
4   As to the meaning of 'functions' see PARA 34 note 2.
5   Political Parties, Elections and Referendums Act 2000 s 9(1)(b)(i). The text refers to orders and schemes under the Representation of the People Act 2000 s 10 (see PARA 521): see the Political Parties, Elections and Referendums Act 2000 s 9(1)(b)(i).
6   Political Parties, Elections and Referendums Act 2000 s 9(1)(b)(ii). The text refers to orders under the Representation of the People Act 2000 s 11 (revision of procedures in the light of pilot schemes: see PARA 523): see the Political Parties, Elections and Referendums Act 2000 s 9(1)(b)(ii).
7   See the Political Parties, Elections and Referendums Act 2000 s 9(1). The text refers to such other functions as are conferred on the Commission by the Representation of the People Act 2000 ss 10–11 (see PARAS 521–523): see the Political Parties, Elections and Referendums Act 2000 s 9(1).
8   Ie any scheme under the Representation of the People Act 2000 s 10 (see PARA 521): see the Political Parties, Elections and Referendums Act 2000 s 9(2).
9   As to the Secretary of State see PARA 2.
10 As to the approval of proposals by the Secretary of State as mentioned in the text see PARA 521.
11 Political Parties, Elections and Referendums Act 2000 s 9(2).

56.   Powers with respect to elections exercisable only on Commission recommendation.   The function of giving directions as to the discharge of registration duties[1] is exercisable only on, and in accordance with, a recommendation of the Electoral Commission[2].

The functions[3] listed under heads (1) to (3) below are exercisable only on, and in accordance with, a recommendation of the Commission, unless the Secretary of State[4] considers that the exercise of the function is expedient in consequence of changes in the value of money[5]:

(1)   the making of orders limiting expenses in connection with elections: (a) to the Greater London Authority[6]; or (b) to the National Assembly for Wales[7];

(2)   the making of regulations limiting expenses in connection with elections to the European Parliament[8]; and

(3)   as from a day to be appointed[9], the making of orders[10] so far as relating to the funding and expenditure of candidates, political parties and other persons in connection with elections of persons as police and crime commissioners in England and Wales[11].

1   Ie directions under the Representation of the People Act 1983 s 52(1) (see PARA 141): see the
    Political Parties, Elections and Referendums Act 2000 s 8(1).
2   Political Parties, Elections and Referendums Act 2000 s 8(1). As to the establishment and
    constitution of the Electoral Commission see PARA 34 et seq.
3   As to the meaning of 'functions' see PARA 34 note 2.
4   As to the Secretary of State see PARA 2.
5   See the Political Parties, Elections and Referendums Act 2000 s 8(2).
6   Political Parties, Elections and Referendums Act 2000 s 8(3)(a). Head (1)(a) in the text refers to
    an order made under the Representation of the People Act 1983 s 76(2A) (see PARA 273): see the
    Political Parties, Elections and Referendums Act 2000 s 8(3)(a).
7   Political Parties, Elections and Referendums Act 2000 s 8(3)(b) (amended by the Government of
    Wales Act 2006 s 160(1), Sch 10 paras 58, 59). Head (1)(b) in the text refers to an order made
    under the Government of Wales Act 2006 s 13 (see PARA 12 note 17): see the Political Parties,
    Elections and Referendums Act 2000 s 8(3)(b) (as so amended).
8   Political Parties, Elections and Referendums Act 2000 s 8(3)(c) (amended by the European
    Parliamentary Elections Act 2002 s 15, Sch 3 para 8(1), (3)). Head (2) in the text refers to
    regulations made under the European Parliamentary Elections Act 2002 s 7(2)(a) (see PARA 13
    note 13): see the Political Parties, Elections and Referendums Act 2000 s 8(3)(c) (as so
    amended).
9   As from a day to be appointed under the Police Reform and Social Responsibility Act 2011
    s 157(1), the Political Parties, Elections and Referendums Act 2000 s 8(3)(d) is added by the
    Police Reform and Social Responsibility Act 2011 s 74, Sch 10 paras 8, 12. However, at the date
    at which this volume states the law, no such day had been appointed.
10 Ie orders under the Police Reform and Social Responsibility Act 2011 s 58 (conduct of elections
    of persons as police and crime commissioners in England and Wales: see POLICE AND
    INVESTIGATORY POWERS vol 84 (2013) PARA 64): see the Political Parties, Elections and
    Referendums Act 2000 s 8(3)(d) (prospectively added: see note 9).
11 Political Parties, Elections and Referendums Act 2000 s 8(3)(d) (prospectively added: see
    note 9). Head (3) in the text refers to the making of orders under the Police Reform and Social
    Responsibility Act 2011 s 58 relating to the matters mentioned in s 58(2)(d) (see POLICE AND
    INVESTIGATORY POWERS vol 84 (2013) PARA 64): see the Political Parties, Elections and
    Referendums Act 2000 s 8(3)(d) (prospectively added).

57. Setting of performance standards for electoral officers. The Electoral
Commission[1] may from time to time determine standards of performance for
relevant officers[2], and publish, in such form and in such manner as it considers
appropriate, the standards so determined[3]. Before so determining standards, the
Commission must consult the Secretary of State[4], and any other person it thinks
appropriate[5]. When the Commission publishes standards in this way, it must
send a copy of the published standards to the Secretary of State who must lay a
copy of the published standards before each House of Parliament[6].

The Commission may from time to time issue directions to relevant officers to
provide the Commission with such reports regarding their level of performance
against the standards so determined[7] as may be specified in the direction[8]. Such a
direction:

(1)   must specify the relevant officer or officers to whom it is issued (and
        may specify a description or descriptions of relevant officers)[9];
(2)   may require the report or reports to relate to such elections or
        referendums (or both) as may be specified in the direction[10]; and
(3)   may require the report or reports to be provided in a form specified in
        the direction[11].

A report so provided to the Commission[12] may be published by the relevant
officer to whom it relates[13]. The Commission must from time to time prepare
and publish, in such manner as the Commission may determine, assessments of
the level of performance by relevant officers against the determined[14]
standards[15]. Such an assessment:

(a)   must specify the relevant officer or officers to whom it relates[16];

(b)	must specify the period to which it relates[17]; and

(c)	may specify the elections or referendums (or both) to which it relates[18]. However, the Commission must not prepare such an assessment unless it has received reports[19] from the relevant officer or officers for the matters to which the assessment relates[20]. Before publishing such an assessment, the Commission must provide to each relevant officer a copy of those parts of the assessment which relate to him[21], and have regard to any comments made by him regarding the factual accuracy of the assessment[22].

The Commission may by notice in writing also direct a relevant officer to provide the Commission with such expenditure information[23] as may be specified in the direction[24]. Such a direction may: (i) require the information to relate to such elections or (as the case may be) referendums as may be specified in the direction[25]; (ii) require the information to be provided in a form specified in the direction[26]; (iii) specify the time within which the information must be provided[27].

1	As to the establishment and constitution of the Electoral Commission see PARA 34 et seq.

2	See the Political Parties, Elections and Referendums Act 2000 s 9A(1)(a) (ss 9A–9C added by the Electoral Administration Act 2006 s 67). For these purposes, the relevant officers are (see the Political Parties, Elections and Referendums Act 2000 s 9A(8) (as so added)):
	(1)	electoral registration officers (s 9A(8)(a) (as so added));
	(2)	in relation to elections within s 9A(6), returning officers (s 9A(8)(b) (as so added));
	(3)	in relation to referendums within s 9A(7), counting officers (s 9A(8)(c) (as so added)).

	The standards of performance are such standards as the Commission thinks ought to be achieved by (see s 9A(2) (as so added)):
	(a)	electoral registration officers in the performance of their functions (s 9A(2)(a) (as so added));
	(b)	returning officers in the administration of the elections specified in s 9A(6) (s 9A(2)(b) (as so added));
	(c)	counting officers in the administration of the referendums specified in s 9A(7) (s 9A(2)(c) (as so added)).

The Commission may determine different standards for different descriptions of relevant officers: s 9A(4) (as so added).

	The elections specified in s 9A(6) are:
	(i)	a parliamentary general election (ss 5(2)(a), 9A(6)(a) (s 9A as so added));
	(ii)	a European parliamentary general election (ss 5(2)(b), 9A(6)(a) (s 9A as so added));
	(iii)	a Scottish parliamentary general election (ss 5(2)(c), 9A(6)(a) (s 9A as so added));
	(iv)	a National Assembly for Wales general election (s 5(2)(d) (s 5(2)(d) substituted, s 9A(6)(d) amended, by SI 2007/1388), Political Parties, Elections and Referendums Act 2000 s 9A(6)(a) (s 9A as so added));
	(v)	a Northern Ireland Assembly general election (ss 5(2)(e), 9A(6)(a) (s 9A as so added));
	(vi)	an ordinary election of police and crime commissioners (s 5(2)(f) (s 5(2)(f), s 9A(6)(da) added by the Police Reform and Social Responsibility Act 2011 s 74, Sch 10 paras 8, 9, 13), Political Parties, Elections and Referendums Act 2000 s 9A(6)(a) (s 9A as so added)).
	(vii)	a parliamentary by-election (s 9A(6)(b) (s 9A as so added));
	(viii)	an election held under the Scotland Act 1998 s 9 (election for the Scottish Parliament in the case of a constituency vacancy) (Political Parties, Elections and Referendums Act 2000 s 9A(6)(c) (s 9A as so added));
	(ix)	an election held under the Government of Wales Act 2006 s 10 (constituency vacancy: see PARA 214) (Political Parties, Elections and Referendums Act 2000 s 9A(6)(d) (s 9A as so added, s 9A(6)(d) as so amended));
	(x)	an election held under the Police Reform and Social Responsibility Act 2011 s 51 (election to fill vacancy in office of police and crime commissioner: see POLICE AND INVESTIGATORY POWERS vol 84 (2013) PARA 69) (Political Parties, Elections and Referendums Act 2000 s 9A(6)(da) (s 9A, s 9A(6)(da) as so added)).
	(xi)	a local government election in England or Wales (s 9A(6)(e) (s 9A as so added)); or
	(xii)	a local government election in Scotland (s 9A(6)(f) (s 9A as so added, s 9A(6)(f) added by the Local Electoral Administration (Scotland) Act 2011 s 11(1))).

The referendums specified in the Political Parties, Elections and Referendums Act 2000 s 9A(7) are a referendum to which Pt VII (ss 101–129) applies (see PARA 527 et seq) (s 9A(7)(a) (as so added)) and those under the Local Government Act 2000 Pt 1A (ss 9B–9R) (arrangements with respect to local governance in England: see LOCAL GOVERNMENT), Pt II (ss 10–48A) (Local authorities in Wales: arrangements with respect to executives etc: see LOCAL GOVERNMENT vol 69 (2009) PARA 303 et seq) (see PARA 558 et seq) (see the Political Parties, Elections and Referendums Act 2000 s 9A(7)(b) (as so added); Interpretation Act 1978 s 17(2)(b)).

As to the meanings of 'England' and 'Wales' see PARA 1 note 1. As to the meaning of 'local government election' see PARA 11. As to the meaning of 'functions' see PARA 34 note 2. As to electoral registration officers see PARA 139 et seq; as to returning officers see PARA 350 et seq; and as to counting officers see PARA 553 et seq. As to parliamentary general elections see PARA 9 et seq; as to Welsh Assembly general elections see PARA 12 et seq; and as to European parliamentary general elections see PARA 13 et seq. As to parliamentary by-elections see PARA 191. As to the election of police and crime commissioners see POLICE AND INVESTIGATORY POWERS vol 84 (2013) PARA 62 et seq.

3 See the Political Parties, Elections and Referendums Act 2000 s 9A(1)(b) (as added: see note 2).

4 See the Political Parties, Elections and Referendums Act 2000 s 9A(3)(a) (as added: see note 2). As to the Secretary of State see PARA 2.

5 See the Political Parties, Elections and Referendums Act 2000 s 9A(3)(b) (as added: see note 2).

6 Political Parties, Elections and Referendums Act 2000 s 9A(5) (as added: see note 2).

7 Ie determined under the Political Parties, Elections and Referendums Act 2000 s 9A(1) (see the text and notes 1–3): see s 9B(1) (as added: see note 2).

8 Political Parties, Elections and Referendums Act 2000 s 9B(1) (as added: see note 2).

9 Political Parties, Elections and Referendums Act 2000 s 9B(2)(a) (as added: see note 2).

10 Political Parties, Elections and Referendums Act 2000 s 9B(2)(b) (as added: see note 2).

11 Political Parties, Elections and Referendums Act 2000 s 9B(2)(c) (as added: see note 2).

12 Ie in pursuance of the Political Parties, Elections and Referendums Act 2000 s 9B(1) (see the text and notes 7–8): see s 9B(3) (as added: see note 2).

13 Political Parties, Elections and Referendums Act 2000 s 9B(3) (as added: see note 2).

14 Ie determined under the Political Parties, Elections and Referendums Act 2000 s 9A(1) (see the text and notes 1–3): see s 9B(4) (as added: see note 2).

15 Political Parties, Elections and Referendums Act 2000 s 9B(4) (as added: see note 2).

16 Political Parties, Elections and Referendums Act 2000 s 9B(5)(a) (as added: see note 2).

17 Political Parties, Elections and Referendums Act 2000 s 9B(5)(b) (as added: see note 2).

18 Political Parties, Elections and Referendums Act 2000 s 9B(5)(c) (as added: see note 2).

19 Ie in pursuance of the Political Parties, Elections and Referendums Act 2000 s 9B(1) (see the text and notes 7–8): see s 9B(6) (as added: see note 2).

20 Political Parties, Elections and Referendums Act 2000 s 9B(6) (as added: see note 2).

21 See the Political Parties, Elections and Referendums Act 2000 s 9B(7)(a) (as added: see note 2).

22 See the Political Parties, Elections and Referendums Act 2000 s 9B(7)(b) (as added: see note 2).

23 For these purposes, expenditure information is information relating to: (1) in the case of an electoral registration officer, expenditure in connection with the performance of his functions (Political Parties, Elections and Referendums Act 2000 s 9C(2)(a) (as added: see note 2)); (2) in the case of a returning officer, expenditure in connection with the election or elections specified in s 9A(6) (see note 2) for which he is appointed or otherwise holds office (s 9C(2)(b) (as so added)); (3) in the case of a counting officer, expenditure in connection with the referendum or referendums specified in s 9A(7) (see note 2) for which he is appointed (s 9C(2)(c) (as so added)).

24 Political Parties, Elections and Referendums Act 2000 s 9C(1) (as added: see note 2). Section 9C does not affect any other power of the Commission to request information: s 9C(4) (as so added).

25 Political Parties, Elections and Referendums Act 2000 s 9C(3)(a) (as added: see note 2).

26 Political Parties, Elections and Referendums Act 2000 s 9C(3)(b) (as added: see note 2).

27 Political Parties, Elections and Referendums Act 2000 s 9C(3)(c) (as added: see note 2).

58. Giving of advice and assistance. The Electoral Commission[1] may, at the request of any relevant body[2], provide the body with advice and assistance[3] as respects any matter in which the Commission has skill and experience[4]. The Commission may also:

(1)   provide advice and assistance to registration officers[5], returning officers at relevant elections[6], registered parties[7], recognised third parties[8] and permitted participants[9]; and

(2)   provide advice and assistance to other persons which is incidental to, or otherwise connected with, the discharge by the Commission of its functions[10].

The Commission may make charges for advice or assistance provided by it at the request of any relevant body[11] but may not make charges for the advice and assistance provided under heads (1) and (2) above[12].

1   As to the establishment and constitution of the Electoral Commission see PARA 34 et seq.
2   For these purposes, 'relevant body' means:
     (1)   the Scottish Parliament (Political Parties, Elections and Referendums Act 2000 s 10(6)(a));
     (2)   the Scottish Executive (s 10(6)(b));
     (3)   the National Assembly for Wales (s 10(6)(c));
     (4)   the National Assembly for Wales Commission (s 10(6)(ca) (added by the Government of Wales Act 2006 s 160(1), Sch 10 paras 58, 60));
     (5)   the Welsh Ministers (Political Parties, Elections and Referendums Act 2000 s 10(6)(caa) (added by SI 2007/1388));
     (6)   the Northern Ireland Assembly (Political Parties, Elections and Referendums Act 2000 s 10(6)(d));
     (7)   the Executive Committee of the Northern Ireland Assembly (s 10(6)(e));
     (8)   any of the following local authorities: (a) in England, the council of a county, district or London borough (s 10(6)(f)(i)); (b) in Wales, the council of a county or county borough (s 10(6)(f)(ii)); and (c) in Scotland, a council constituted under the Local Government etc (Scotland) Act 1994 s 2 (Political Parties, Elections and Referendums Act 2000 s 10(6)(f)(iii));
     (9)   a national or regional parliament or government in a country other than the United Kingdom (s 10(6)(g));
     (10)   a body in any such other country having functions corresponding to any of the functions of the Commission (s 10(6)(h));
     (11)   an organisation of which two or more countries (or their governments) are members or a subordinate body of such an organisation (s 10(6)(i)).
   For these purposes, 'body', without more, means a body corporate or any combination of persons or other unincorporated association: see s 160(1). As to the meanings of 'United Kingdom', 'England' and 'Wales' see PARA 1 note 1. As to the meaning of 'functions' see PARA 34 note 2. As to the Welsh Ministers see PARA 2. As to the National Assembly for Wales and the National Assembly for Wales Commission see CONSTITUTIONAL LAW AND HUMAN RIGHTS. As to the council of a county, district or London borough in England and the council of a county or county borough in Wales see LOCAL GOVERNMENT vol 69 (2009) PARA 23. The Political Parties, Elections and Referendums Act 2000 s 10 is applied with modifications by the National Assembly for Wales Referendum (Assembly Act Provisions) (Referendum Question, Date of Referendum Etc) Order 2010, SI 2010/2837, art 27, Sch 5: see STATUTES AND LEGISLATIVE PROCESS vol 96 (2012) PARA 602.
3   The assistance which may be so provided includes (in particular) the secondment of members of the Commission's staff: Political Parties, Elections and Referendums Act 2000 s 10(2). However, nothing in s 10 authorises the Commission to provide any form of financial assistance: s 10(5). As to the staff of the Electoral Commission see PARA 38.
4   Political Parties, Elections and Referendums Act 2000 s 10(1).
5   Political Parties, Elections and Referendums Act 2000 s 10(3)(a)(i). As to electoral registration officers see PARA 139 et seq.
6   Political Parties, Elections and Referendums Act 2000 s 10(3)(a)(ii). For these purposes, 'relevant election' means any election falling within s 22(1), (5) (see PARA 253): s 10(7). As to returning officers see PARA 350 et seq.
7   Political Parties, Elections and Referendums Act 2000 s 10(3)(a)(iii). As to the meaning of 'registered party' for these purposes see PARA 35 note 3.
8   Political Parties, Elections and Referendums Act 2000 s 10(3)(a)(iv). The text refers to recognised third parties within the meaning of Pt VI (ss 85–100) (controls relating to third party national election campaigns: see PARA 313 et seq): see s 10(3)(a)(iv).

9   Political Parties, Elections and Referendums Act 2000 s 10(3)(a)(v). The text refers to permitted
    participants within the meaning of Pt VII (ss 101–129) (referendums: see PARA 527 et seq): see
    s 10(3)(a)(v).
10 Political Parties, Elections and Referendums Act 2000 s 10(3)(b).
11 Political Parties, Elections and Referendums Act 2000 s 10(4)(a). The text refers to the advice or
    assistance provided by the Commission under s 10(1) (see the text and notes 1–4): see s 10(4)(a).
12 Political Parties, Elections and Referendums Act 2000 s 10(4)(b).

**59.   Views expressed by Commission on political, election and referendum
campaign broadcasts.**   The following bodies must have regard to any views
expressed by the Electoral Commission[1] in the following circumstances relating
to political, election and referendum campaign broadcasting[2]:

(1)   the British Broadcasting Corporation ('the BBC')[3], in determining its
      policy with respect to party political broadcasts[4];

(2)   the Office of Communications ('OFCOM')[5], before making any rules
      with respect to party political broadcasts and referendum campaign
      broadcasts[6]; and

(3)   a broadcasting authority[7], before drawing up a code of practice with
      respect to the participation of candidates at a parliamentary or local
      government election in items about the constituency or electoral area in
      question[8].

1   As to the establishment and constitution of the Electoral Commission see PARA 34 et seq.
2   As to party political and campaign broadcasting generally see BROADCASTING vol 4 (2011) PARA
    890 et seq; CONSTITUTIONAL LAW AND HUMAN RIGHTS vol 8(2) (Reissue) PARA 221 et seq. A
    broadcaster may not include in its broadcasting services any party political broadcast made on
    behalf of a party which is not a registered party: see the Political Parties, Elections and
    Referendums Act 2000 s 37; and CONSTITUTIONAL LAW AND HUMAN RIGHTS. As to the
    registration of parties see PARA 253. Similar restrictions apply in relation to referendum
    campaign broadcasts which may be made only on behalf of a designated person or body: see
    s 127; and PARA 552.
3   As to the BBC see BROADCASTING vol 4 (2011) PARA 603 et seq.
4   Political Parties, Elections and Referendums Act 2000 s 11(3) (amended by the Communications
    Act 2003 s 406(1), Sch 17 para 167(1), (2)). See also BROADCASTING vol 4 (2011) PARAS 893,
    896; CONSTITUTIONAL LAW AND HUMAN RIGHTS vol 8(2) (Reissue) PARAS 222–223.
5   As to OFCOM see TELECOMMUNICATIONS vol 97 (2010) PARA 2 et seq.
6   See the Communications Act 2003 s 333; and BROADCASTING vol 4 (2011) PARA 890.
7   As to the meaning of 'broadcasting authority' see PARA 332 note 1.
8   See the Representation of the People Act 1983 s 93; and PARA 332.

60.   Policy development grants.   The Electoral Commission[1] must submit
recommendations to the Secretary of State[2] for the terms of a scheme for the
making by the Commission of policy development grants[3]. Where the Secretary
of State receives such recommendations, he must make an order[4] setting out such
a scheme in terms which, with any modifications[5] he considers appropriate, give
effect to the recommendations[6]. The scheme must, in particular, specify or
provide for the determination of:

(1)   the parties eligible for policy development grants[7]; and

(2)   how any money provided to the Commission for the making of policy
      development grants is to be allocated between the parties eligible for
      such grants[8].

The Commission must keep under review the terms of any such scheme and
must make recommendations to the Secretary of State for any variations to the
scheme which it considers appropriate[9]. Where the Secretary of State receives
such recommendations for variation, he must make an order giving effect, with
any modifications he considers appropriate, to the recommendations[10]. However,

where any modifications that are made following recommendations of the Commission in respect of either the terms of a scheme[11] or any variations to the scheme[12] would result in an order giving effect with modifications to any recommendations of the Commission in respect of either of the matters mentioned in heads (1) and (2) above, the order must not be made without the agreement of the Commission to the modifications so far as relating to those matters[13].

The Commission must make such grants as are provided for under any scheme for the making of policy development grants[14], and any such grants may be made subject to such conditions[15] as (consistently with the terms of the scheme) the Commission considers appropriate[16].

1 As to the establishment and constitution of the Electoral Commission see PARA 34 et seq.
2 As to the Secretary of State see PARA 2.
3 Political Parties, Elections and Referendums Act 2000 s 12(2). For these purposes, a 'policy development grant' is a grant to a represented registered party to assist the party with the development of policies for inclusion in any manifesto on the basis of which candidates authorised to stand by the party will seek to be elected at an election which is a relevant election for the purposes of Pt II (ss 22–40) (see PARA 253), or the party itself will seek to be so elected (in the case of such an election for which the party itself may be nominated) (s 12(1)(a)); and a registered party is 'represented' if there are at least two members of the House of Commons belonging to the party who have made and subscribed the oath required by the Parliamentary Oaths Act 1866 (or the corresponding affirmation), and are not disqualified from sitting or voting in that House (Political Parties, Elections and Referendums Act 2000 s 12(1)(b)). For these purposes, a person stands for election in the name of a registered party if his nomination paper includes a description authorised by a certificate issued by or on behalf of the registered nominating officer of the party: see s 22(6); and PARA 253 note 8. As to the meaning of 'registered party' for these purposes see PARA 35 note 3. As to the disqualification of members of the House of Commons see PARLIAMENT vol 78 (2010) PARA 897 et seq; and as to the oath or affirmation required by the Parliamentary Oaths Act 1866 see PARLIAMENT vol 78 (2010) PARA 1001. As to payments made to registered political parties see also CONSTITUTIONAL LAW AND HUMAN RIGHTS.
4 As to the making of orders under the Political Parties, Elections and Referendums Act 2000 generally see PARA 34 note 2.
5 As to the meaning of 'modifications' see PARA 44 note 9.
6 Political Parties, Elections and Referendums Act 2000 s 12(3). As to the scheme so made which has effect in relation to the year ending on 31 March 2007 and subsequent years see the Elections (Policy Development Grants Scheme) Order 2006, SI 2006/602.
7 Political Parties, Elections and Referendums Act 2000 s 12(4)(a).
8 Political Parties, Elections and Referendums Act 2000 s 12(4)(b).
9 Political Parties, Elections and Referendums Act 2000 s 12(5).
10 Political Parties, Elections and Referendums Act 2000 s 12(6). The scheme contained in the Elections (Policy Development Grants Scheme) Order 2006, SI 2006/602 (see note 6) incorporates variations which give effect to the recommendations of the Electoral Commission.
11 Ie under the Political Parties, Elections and Referendums Act 2000 s 12(3) (see the text and notes 4–6): see s 12(7).
12 Ie under the Political Parties, Elections and Referendums Act 2000 s 12(5) (see the text and note 9): see s 12(7).
13 Political Parties, Elections and Referendums Act 2000 s 12(7).
14 Ie under any scheme under the Political Parties, Elections and Referendums Act 2000 s 12: see s 12(8).
15 References in the Political Parties, Elections and Referendums Act 2000 to conditions, in the context of grants being made subject to conditions, include conditions requiring repayment of the grants in specified circumstances: s 160(5).
16 Political Parties, Elections and Referendums Act 2000 s 12(8). However, nothing in a scheme under s 12 has effect to authorise the Commission to make in any financial year more than £2 million in policy development grants: see s 12(8). As to the meaning of 'financial year' for these purposes see PARA 44 note 4. The sum for the time being specified in s 12(8) may be varied by the Secretary of State by order made with the consent of the Treasury: s 12(9). At the date at which this volume states the law, no order had been made under s 12(9) and, accordingly, the

amount available for allocation by the Commission in each year for which the Scheme under the Elections (Policy Development Grants Scheme) Order 2006, SI 2006/602 has effect is £2 million: see art 2, Schedule para 4. As to the making of orders under the Political Parties, Elections and Referendums Act 2000 generally see PARA 34 note 2. As to the Treasury see CONSTITUTIONAL LAW AND HUMAN RIGHTS vol 8(2) (Reissue) PARAS 512–517.

61.   Education about electoral and democratic systems.   The Electoral Commission[1] must promote public awareness of current electoral systems in the United Kingdom[2] and any pending[3] such systems, together with such matters connected with any such existing or pending systems as the Commission may determine[4]. The Commission must perform these functions[5] in such manner as it thinks fit but may, in particular, do so[6]:

(1)   by carrying out programmes of education or information to promote public awareness of current electoral systems in the United Kingdom and any pending such systems[7]; or

(2)   by making grants to other persons or bodies for the purpose of enabling them to carry out such programmes[8].

However, the total expenditure incurred in any financial year[9] by the Commission in performing its functions in promoting public awareness[10] (whether by making grants or otherwise) must not exceed such sum as is for the time being specified for these purposes by an order made by the Secretary of State[11] with the consent of the Treasury[12].

1   As to the establishment and constitution of the Electoral Commission see PARA 34 et seq.

2   The Political Parties, Elections and Referendums Act 2000 s 13(1) applies with modifications to the promotion of public awareness in Gibraltar of current electoral systems for elections to the European Parliament in the United Kingdom and Gibraltar: see s 13(1A) (added by SI 2004/366; amended by the Political Parties and Elections Act 2009 s 39, Sch 7). As to the meaning of 'United Kingdom' see PARA 1 note 1. As to the meaning of 'modifications' see PARA 44 note 9. As to Gibraltar see PARA 77.

3   For these purposes, any system such as is mentioned in the Political Parties, Elections and Referendums Act 2000 s 13(1)(a) is pending at a time when arrangements for giving effect to it have been made by any enactment but the arrangements are not yet in force: s 13(2) (s 13(1), (2) amended by the Political Parties and Elections Act 2009 s 8, Sch 7). As to the meaning of 'enactment' see PARA 53 note 2.

4   See the Political Parties, Elections and Referendums Act 2000 s 13(1)(a). The Commission is not prevented by s 13 from continuing to provide information about systems of government and EU institutions (see s 13(1)(b), (c) (repealed)) insofar as it is needed to help promote understanding of electoral systems in the United Kingdom.

5   Ie its functions under the Political Parties, Elections and Referendums Act 2000 s 13(1) (see the text and notes 1–4): see s 13(4). As to the meaning of 'functions' see PARA 34 note 2.

6   See the Political Parties, Elections and Referendums Act 2000 s 13(4).

7   Political Parties, Elections and Referendums Act 2000 s 13(4)(a). Head (1) in the text refers to carrying out programmes of education or information to promote public awareness of any of the matters mentioned in s 13(1) (see the text and notes 1–4): see s 13(4)(a).

8   Political Parties, Elections and Referendums Act 2000 s 13(4)(b). Any grant under s 13(4)(b) may be made subject to such conditions as the Commission considers appropriate: s 13(5). As to the meaning of references in the Political Parties, Elections and Referendums Act 2000 to 'conditions', in the context of grants being made subject to conditions, see PARA 60 note 15.

9   As to the meaning of 'financial year' for these purposes see PARA 44 note 4.

10   Ie in performing its functions under the Political Parties, Elections and Referendums Act 2000 s 13(1) (see the text and notes 1–4): see s 13(6).

11   As to the Secretary of State see PARA 2. As to the making of orders under the Political Parties, Elections and Referendums Act 2000 generally see PARA 34 note 2.

12   Political Parties, Elections and Referendums Act 2000 s 13(6). As to the Treasury see CONSTITUTIONAL LAW AND HUMAN RIGHTS vol 8(2) (Reissue) PARAS 512–517. The provision made by s 13(6) does not apply, however, to the expenditure incurred by the Commission:

(1) in performing its functions exercisable in relation to local government elections in Scotland (see s 13(8) (amended by the Local Electoral Administration (Scotland) Act 2011 ss 15(1), (3), 16(1), (2)(a))); or

(2) to the extent that the expenditure is, or is to be, met under the Government of Wales Act 2006 s 27, Sch 2 para 6 (ie financial assistance to the Electoral Commission for the purpose of enabling it to carry out its functions so far as relating to the promotion of public awareness of the current or any pending system for the election of Assembly members, and the current or any pending system of devolved government in Wales: see CONSTITUTIONAL LAW AND HUMAN RIGHTS) (see the Political Parties, Elections and Referendums Act 2000 s 13(12) (added by the Government of Wales Act 2006 s 160(1), Sch 10 paras 58, 61)).

As to the order made under the Political Parties, Elections and Referendums Act 2000 s 13(6) see the Electoral Commission (Limit on Public Awareness Expenditure) Order 2002, SI 2002/505 (which specifies the sum of £7,500,000 for these purposes: see art 2). This Order extends to Gibraltar: see the European Parliamentary Elections (Combined Region and Campaign Expenditure) (United Kingdom and Gibraltar) Order 2004, SI 2004/366, art 5(1)(f); and PARA 77 note 4. As to reimbursement by the Scottish Ministers for any expenditure incurred by the Commission which is attributable to the exercise of the Commission's functions in relation to local government elections in Scotland (see head (1) above) see the Political Parties, Elections and Referendums Act 2000 s 13A (added by the Local Electoral Administration (Scotland) Act 2011 s 16(1), (3)).

(iii) Commission's Regulatory Functions in respect of Controls imposed on Party Funding and Expenditure etc

62. Monitoring and regulating compliance with controls. The Electoral Commission[1] has the function of monitoring, and taking such steps as it considers appropriate with a view to securing, compliance with[2]:

(1) the restrictions and other requirements imposed by or by virtue of the provisions relating to the accounting requirements for registered parties[3], the control of donations to registered parties, individuals and members associations[4], the regulation of loans and related transactions[5], the control of campaign expenditure[6] and the controls relating to third party national election campaigns[7] and referendums[8]; and

(2) the restrictions and other requirements imposed by other enactments in relation to[9]: (a) election expenses incurred by or on behalf of candidates at elections[10]; or (b) donations to such candidates or their election agents[11].

The Electoral Commission may prepare and publish guidance setting out, in relation to any requirement referred to in heads (1) and (2) above, its opinion on any of the following matters[12]: (i) what it is necessary, or is sufficient, to do (or avoid doing) in order to comply with the requirement[13]; (ii) what it is desirable to do (or avoid doing) in view of the purpose of the requirement[14].

1 As to the establishment and constitution of the Electoral Commission see PARA 34 et seq.
2 See the Political Parties, Elections and Referendums Act 2000 s 145(1) (s 145(1) amended, s 145(6A) added, by the Political Parties and Elections Act 2009 s 1(1)–(3)).
3 Ie the Political Parties, Elections and Referendums Act 2000 Pt III (ss 41–49) (see PARA 253): see s 145(1)(a). As to the meaning of 'registered party' for these purposes see PARA 35 note 3.
4 Ie the Political Parties, Elections and Referendums Act 2000 Pt IV (ss 50–71C) (see CONSTITUTIONAL LAW AND HUMAN RIGHTS): see s 145(1)(a).
5 Ie the Political Parties, Elections and Referendums Act 2000 Pt IVA (ss 71F–71Z2) (see PARA 312; and CONSTITUTIONAL LAW AND HUMAN RIGHTS): see s 145(1)(a).
6 Ie the Political Parties, Elections and Referendums Act 2000 Pt V (ss 72–84) (see PARA 299 et seq): see s 145(1)(a).
7 Ie the Political Parties, Elections and Referendums Act 2000 Pt VI (ss 85–100) (see PARA 313 et seq): see s 145(1)(a).

8　Political Parties, Elections and Referendums Act 2000 s 145(1)(a). The text refers to the provisions relating to referendums contained in Pt VII (ss 101–129) (see PARA 527 et seq): see s 145(1)(a).

9　See the Political Parties, Elections and Referendums Act 2000 s 145(1)(b). As to the meaning of 'enactment' see PARA 53 note 2.

10　Political Parties, Elections and Referendums Act 2000 s 145(1)(b)(i). For these purposes, 'election' means a relevant election for the purposes of Pt II (ss 22–40) (see PARA 253): see s 145(7) (amended by the Political Parties and Elections Act 2009 s 39, Sch 6 para 22). The Political Parties, Elections and Referendums Act 2000 145(1)(b) does not apply in relation to local government elections in Scotland unless and to the extent that the Scottish Ministers by order so provide: see s 145(2)–(6). As to election expenses incurred by or on behalf of candidates at elections see PARA 269 et seq.

11　Political Parties, Elections and Referendums Act 2000 s 145(1)(b)(ii). See note 10. For these purposes, 'election agent' includes a sub-agent: see s 145(7) (as amended: see note 10). As to the nomination of sub-agents at certain parliamentary and local government elections see PARA 233. As to the control of donations to individual candidates or their election agents during election periods see PARA 286 et seq.

12　See the Political Parties, Elections and Referendums Act 2000 s 145(6A) (as added: see note 2).

13　Political Parties, Elections and Referendums Act 2000 s 145(6A)(a) (as added: see note 2).

14　Political Parties, Elections and Referendums Act 2000 s 145(6A)(b) (as added: see note 2).

63.　Investigatory powers of the Commission.　The Electoral Commission[1] has the following main investigatory powers:

(1)　the power to require disclosure by giving a disclosure notice[2];

(2)　the power, on application to a justice of the peace, to have an inspection warrant issued in relation to premises[3];

(3)　powers requiring a person by notice to produce documents for inspection, or to provide the Commission with any information or explanation, in relation to suspected offences or contraventions[4].

The Commission must prepare and publish guidance as to[5]:

(a)　the circumstances in which the Commission is likely to give either a disclosure notice under head (1) above[6] or a notice under head (3) above[7];

(b)　the consequences (including criminal sanctions) that may result from a failure to comply with such a notice[8];

(c)　the circumstances in which the Commission is likely to apply for a warrant under head (2) above[9];

(d)　the procedures to be followed in connection with questioning under head (3) above[10];

(e)　the circumstances in which the Commission is likely to apply for either a document-disclosure order[11] or an information-disclosure order[12];

(f)　the principles and practices to be applied in connection with the exercise of powers governing the retention of documents[13], or the making of copies and records[14] of information or explanations that have been provided or the making of copies and records of information contained in documents that have been provided[15];

(g)　any other matters concerning the exercise of its investigatory powers[16] about which the Commission considers that guidance would be useful[17].

Where appropriate, the Commission must revise guidance that has been published in this way[18], and it must publish the revised guidance[19]. The Commission must consult such persons as it considers appropriate before publishing such guidance (or revised guidance)[20]; and the Commission must have regard to the guidance (or revised guidance) so published[21] in exercising its functions[22].

Each annual report of the Electoral Commission[23] must contain information about the use made by the Commission of its investigatory powers[24] during the year in question[25]; and the report must, in particular, specify[26]:

(i) the cases in which a disclosure notice was given under head (1) above[27] or a notice was given under head (3) above[28];

(ii) the cases in which premises were entered under a warrant issued under head (2) above[29];

(iii) the cases in which a requirement was imposed under head (3) above[30] for a person to attend before the investigator at a specified time and place and answer any questions that the investigator reasonably considers to be relevant[31];

(iv) the cases in which either a document-disclosure order[32] or an information-disclosure order[33] was applied for and/or was made[34].

However, the Commission is not so required[35] to include in a report any information that, in its opinion, it would be inappropriate to include on the ground that to do so would or might be unlawful, or might adversely affect any current investigation or proceedings[36].

1 As to the establishment and constitution of the Electoral Commission see PARA 34 et seq.
2 See the Political Parties, Elections and Referendums Act 2000 s 146, Sch 19B para 1; and PARA 64.
3 See the Political Parties, Elections and Referendums Act 2000 Sch 19B para 2; and PARA 64.
4 See the Political Parties, Elections and Referendums Act 2000 Sch 19B para 3; and PARA 65. The Commission has further powers to apply to the High Court to make either a document-disclosure order (see Sch 19B para 4; and PARA 65) or an information-disclosure order (see Sch 19B para 5; and PARA 65) against a person ('the respondent') suspected of failing to make full disclosure under Sch 19B para 3 and the Commission may retain documents delivered under Sch 19B para 4 for three months (or longer if the statutory conditions are satisfied) (see Sch 19B para 6; and PARA 65).
5 See the Political Parties, Elections and Referendums Act 2000 Sch 19B para 14(1) (Sch 19B added by the Political Parties and Elections Act 2009 s 2(1), (2), Sch 1).
6 Ie a notice under the Political Parties, Elections and Referendums Act 2000 Sch 19B para 1 (see PARA 64): see Sch 19B para 14(1)(a) (as added: see note 5).
7 Political Parties, Elections and Referendums Act 2000 Sch 19B para 14(1)(a) (as added: see note 5). The text refers to a notice given under Sch 19B para 3(2) (see PARA 65): see Sch 19B para 14(1)(a) (as so added).
8 Political Parties, Elections and Referendums Act 2000 Sch 19B para 14(1)(b) (as added: see note 5). As to the Commission's powers to apply civil sanctions to offences and contraventions under the Political Parties, Elections and Referendums Act 2000 see PARAS 757–760.
9 Political Parties, Elections and Referendums Act 2000 Sch 19B para 14(1)(c) (as added: see note 5). The text refers to an application for an inspection warrant under Sch 19B para 2 (see PARA 64): see Sch 19B para 14(1)(c) (as so added).
10 Political Parties, Elections and Referendums Act 2000 Sch 19B para 14(1)(d) (as added: see note 5). The text refers to questioning under Sch 19B para 3(4) (see PARA 65): see Sch 19B para 14(1)(d) (as so added).
11 Ie a document-disclosure order under the Political Parties, Elections and Referendums Act 2000 Sch 19B para 4 (see PARA 65): see Sch 19B para 14(1)(e) (as added: see note 5).
12 Political Parties, Elections and Referendums Act 2000 Sch 19B para 14(1)(e) (as added: see note 5). The text refers to an information-disclosure order under Sch 19B para 5 (see PARA 65): see Sch 19B para 14(1)(e) (as so added).
13 Ie the exercise of powers under the Political Parties, Elections and Referendums Act 2000 Sch 19B para 6 (see PARA 65): see Sch 19B para 14(1)(f) (as added: see note 5).
14 Ie the exercise of powers under the Political Parties, Elections and Referendums Act 2000 Sch 19B para 7 (see PARAS 64 note 10, 65 note 7): see Sch 19B para 14(1)(f) (as added: see note 5).
15 Political Parties, Elections and Referendums Act 2000 Sch 19B para 14(1)(f) (as added: see note 5).
16 Ie the exercise of powers under the Political Parties, Elections and Referendums Act 2000 Sch 19B (see PARAS 64–66): see Sch 19B para 14(1)(g) (as added: see note 5).

17 Political Parties, Elections and Referendums Act 2000 Sch 19B para 14(1)(g) (as added: see note 5).

18 Ie published under the Political Parties, Elections and Referendums Act 2000 Sch 19B para 14: see Sch 19B para 14(2) (as added: see note 5).

19 Political Parties, Elections and Referendums Act 2000 Sch 19B para 14(2) (as added: see note 5).

20 Political Parties, Elections and Referendums Act 2000 Sch 19B para 14(3) (as added: see note 5).

21 Ie published under the Political Parties, Elections and Referendums Act 2000 Sch 19B para 14: see Sch 19B para 14(4) (as added: see note 5).

22 Political Parties, Elections and Referendums Act 2000 Sch 19B para 14(4) (as added: see note 5).

23 Ie each report by the Commission under the Political Parties, Elections and Referendums Act 2000 s 1(6), Sch 1 para 20 (see PARA 46): see Sch 19B para 15(1) (as added: see note 5).

24 Ie the use made by the Commission of its powers under the Political Parties, Elections and Referendums Act 2000 Sch 19B (see PARAS 64–66): see Sch 19B para 15(1) (as added: see note 5).

25 Political Parties, Elections and Referendums Act 2000 Sch 19B para 15(1) (as added: see note 5).

26 See the Political Parties, Elections and Referendums Act 2000 Sch 19B para 15(2) (as added: see note 5).

27 Ie a notice under the Political Parties, Elections and Referendums Act 2000 Sch 19B para 1 (see PARA 64): see Sch 19B para 15(2)(a) (as added: see note 5).

28 Political Parties, Elections and Referendums Act 2000 Sch 19B para 15(2)(a) (as added: see note 5). The text refers to the cases in which a notice was given under Sch 19B para 3(2) (see PARA 65): see Sch 19B para 15(2)(a) (as so added).

29 Political Parties, Elections and Referendums Act 2000 Sch 19B para 15(2)(b) (as added: see note 5). The text refers to the cases in which premises were entered under an inspection warrant issued under Sch 19B para 2 (see PARA 64): see Sch 19B para 15(2)(b) (as so added).

30 Ie under the Political Parties, Elections and Referendums Act 2000 Sch 19B para 3(4) (see PARA 65): see Sch 19B para 15(2)(c) (as added: see note 5).

31 Political Parties, Elections and Referendums Act 2000 Sch 19B para 15(2)(c) (as added: see note 5).

32 Ie an order under the Political Parties, Elections and Referendums Act 2000 Sch 19B para 4 (see PARA 65): see Sch 19B para 15(2)(d) (as added: see note 5).

33 Ie an order under the Political Parties, Elections and Referendums Act 2000 Sch 19B para 5 (see PARA 65): see Sch 19B para 15(2)(d) (as added: see note 5).

34 See the Political Parties, Elections and Referendums Act 2000 Sch 19B para 15(2)(d) (as added: see note 5).

35 Ie the Political Parties, Elections and Referendums Act 2000 Sch 19B para 15 does not require: see Sch 19B para 15(3) (as added: see note 5).

36 See the Political Parties, Elections and Referendums Act 2000 Sch 19B para 15(3) (as added: see note 5).

64. Investigatory powers of the Commission: disclosure notices and inspection warrants. The Electoral Commission[1] may give a disclosure notice to a person who is either a relevant individual[2] or the treasurer or another officer of a relevant organisation[3] (or who has been the treasurer or another officer of such an organisation at any time in the period of five years ending with the day on which the notice is given)[4]; and that person must comply with such a notice within such reasonable time as is specified therein[5]. For these purposes, a 'disclosure notice' is a notice requiring the person to whom it is given[6]:

(1) to produce, for inspection by the Commission or a person authorised by the Commission[7], any documents[8] which relate to the income and expenditure of the organisation or individual in question[9], and which are reasonably required by the Commission for the purposes of carrying out its functions[10]; or

(2) to provide the Commission, or a person authorised by the Commission, with any information or explanation which relates to that income and expenditure and is reasonably required by the Commission for those purposes[11].

A justice of the peace[12] may issue an inspection warrant in relation to premises occupied by any relevant organisation or individual[13] if satisfied, on information on oath given by or on behalf of the Commission, that[14]:

(a) there are reasonable grounds for believing that on those premises there are documents relating to the income and expenditure of the organisation or individual[15];

(b) the Commission needs to inspect the documents for the purposes of carrying out functions of the Commission other than investigatory functions[16]; and

(c) permission to inspect the documents on the premises has been requested by the Commission and has been unreasonably refused[17].

For these purposes, an 'inspection warrant' is a warrant authorising a member of the Commission's staff, at any reasonable time, to enter the premises specified in the warrant[18], and, having entered the premises, to inspect any documents within head (a) above[19]. An inspection warrant also authorises the person who executes the warrant to be accompanied by any other persons whom the Commission considers are needed to assist in executing it[20]. The person executing an inspection warrant must, if required to do so, produce the warrant, and documentary evidence that the person is a member of the Commission's staff, for inspection by the occupier of the premises that are specified in the warrant or by anyone acting on the occupier's behalf[21]. An inspection warrant continues in force until the end of the period of one month beginning with the day on which it is issued[22].

1   As to the establishment and constitution of the Electoral Commission see PARA 34 et seq.
2   Ie an individual to whom the Political Parties, Elections and Referendums Act 2000 s 146, Sch 19B para 1 applies: see Sch 19B para 1(2)(b) (s 146 substituted, Sch 19B added, by the Political Parties and Elections Act 2009 s 2(1), (2), Sch 1). The Political Parties, Elections and Referendums Act 2000 Sch 19B para 1 applies to the following organisations and individuals (see Sch 19B para 1(1) (as so added)):
    (1)   a registered party (or, in the case of a registered party with accounting units, the central organisation of the party and an accounting unit of the party) (see Sch 19B para 1(1)(a) (as so added));
    (2)   a recognised third party, within the meaning of Pt VI (ss 85–100) (controls relating to third party national election campaigns: see PARA 313 et seq) (Sch 19B para 1(1)(b) (as so added));
    (3)   a permitted participant, within the meaning of Pt VII (ss 101–129) (referendums: see PARA 527 et seq) (Sch 19B para 1(1)(c) (as so added));
    (4)   a regulated donee, within the meaning of s 71, Sch 7 (control of donations to individuals and members associations: see CONSTITUTIONAL LAW AND HUMAN RIGHTS) (Sch 19B para 1(1)(d) (as so added));
    (5)   a regulated participant, within the meaning of s 71Y, Sch 7A (control of loans and certain other transactions to individuals and members associations: see CONSTITUTIONAL LAW AND HUMAN RIGHTS) (Sch 19B para 1(1)(e) (as so added));
    (6)   a candidate at an election (other than a local government election in Scotland) (Sch 19B para 1(1)(f) (as so added));
    (7)   the election agent for such a candidate (Sch 19B para 1(1)(g) (as so added));
    (8)   an organisation or individual formerly falling within any of heads (1) to (7) above (Sch 19B para 1(1)(h) (as so added)).
    As to the meaning of 'election' see PARA 62 note 10; and as to the meaning of 'election agent' see PARA 62 note 11. As to the meaning of 'registered party' for these purposes see PARA 35 note 3; as to the meaning of 'treasurer' see PARA 50 note 7; and as to the meanings of 'accounting unit' and 'central organisation', in relation to a registered party, see PARA 253 note 15. As to election agents and candidates see PARA 230 et seq.
3   Ie an organisation to which the Political Parties, Elections and Referendums Act 2000 Sch 19B para 1 applies (see note 2): see Sch 19B para 1(2)(a) (as added: see note 2).
4   See the Political Parties, Elections and Referendums Act 2000 Sch 19B para 1(2)(a) (as added: see note 2).

5 See the Political Parties, Elections and Referendums Act 2000 Sch 19B para 1(4) (as added: see note 2).

6 See the Political Parties, Elections and Referendums Act 2000 Sch 19B para 1(3) (as added: see note 2).

7 An authorisation of a person by the Commission under the Political Parties, Elections and Referendums Act 2000 Sch 19B must be in writing: Sch 19B para 8 (as added: see note 2).

8 See the Political Parties, Elections and Referendums Act 2000 Sch 19B para 1(3)(a) (as added: see note 2). For this purpose, 'documents' includes any books or records: see Sch 19B para 9 (as so added). In the case of documents kept in electronic form, a power of the Commission under Sch 19B to require documents to be produced for inspection includes power to require a copy of the documents to be made available for inspection in legible form: see Sch 19B para 10(1)(a) (as so added). The Commission, or a person authorised by the Commission, may make copies of, or make records of any information contained in any copy made available as mentioned in Sch 19B para 10(1)(a): see Sch 19B paras 7, 10(2) (as so added). As to the meaning of 'record' see PARA 45 note 2. As to the meaning of 'document' see PARA 48 note 1.

9 Political Parties, Elections and Referendums Act 2000 Sch 19B para 1(3)(a)(i) (as added: see note 2).

10 Political Parties, Elections and Referendums Act 2000 Sch 19B para 1(3)(a)(ii) (as added: see note 2). The Commission, or a person authorised by the Commission, may make copies of, or make records of any information contained in any documents produced or inspected under Sch 19B, and may make copies or records of any information or explanation provided under Sch 19B: see Sch 19B para 7 (as so added). However, nothing in Sch 19B requires a person to produce or provide, or authorises a person to inspect or take possession of, anything in respect of which a claim to legal professional privilege could be maintained in legal proceedings: Sch 19B para 11 (as so added). As to legal professional privilege see CIVIL PROCEDURE vol 11 (2009) PARA 558 et seq; and CRIMINAL PROCEDURE vol 28 (2010) PARA 506.

11 Political Parties, Elections and Referendums Act 2000 Sch 19B para 1(3)(b) (as added: see note 2). See note 10. A statement made by a person ('P') in compliance with a requirement imposed under Sch 19B is admissible in evidence in any proceedings, as long as it also complies with any requirements governing the admissibility of evidence in the circumstances in question: Sch 19B para 12(1) (as so added). However, in criminal proceedings in which P is charged with an offence other than an offence under Sch 19B para 13(3) (knowingly or recklessly providing false information in purported compliance with a requirement: see PARA 753), or under the Perjury Act 1911 s 5 (false statutory declarations and other false statements without oath: see CRIMINAL LAW vol 26 (2010) PARA 673), or in proceedings (to which both the Commission and P are parties) that arise out of the exercise by the Commission of any of its powers under s 147, Sch 19C (see PARAS 757–760), other than powers in relation to offence under Sch 19B para 13(3) (see PARA 753) (see Sch 19B para 12(2)–(4) (as so added)):
    (1)   no evidence relating to the statement is admissible against P (Sch 19B para 12(2)(a) (as so added)); and
    (2)   no question relating to the statement may be asked on behalf of the prosecution or (as the case may be) the Commission in cross-examination of P (Sch 19B para 12(2)(b) (as so added)),
unless evidence relating to it is adduced, or a question relating to it is asked, in the proceedings by or on behalf of P (see Sch 19B para 12(2) (as so added)).

12 As to justices of the peace see MAGISTRATES vol 71 (2013) PARA 401 et seq.

13 Ie an individual to whom the Political Parties, Elections and Referendums Act 2000 Sch 19B para 2 applies: see Sch 19B para 2(1), (2) (as added: see note 2). The Political Parties, Elections and Referendums Act 2000 Sch 19B para 2 applies to the following organisations and individuals (see Sch 19B para 2(1) (as so added)):
    (1)   a registered party (or, in the case of a registered party with accounting units, the central organisation of the party and an accounting unit of the party) (see Sch 19B para 2(1)(a) (as so added));
    (2)   a recognised third party, within the meaning of Pt VI (controls relating to third party national election campaigns: see PARA 313 et seq) (Sch 19B para 2(1)(b) (as so added));
    (3)   a permitted participant, within the meaning of Pt VII (referendums: see PARA 527 et seq) (Sch 19B para 2(1)(c) (as so added));
    (4)   a members association, within the meaning of s 71, Sch 7 (control of donations to individuals and members associations: see CONSTITUTIONAL LAW AND HUMAN RIGHTS) (Sch 19B para 2(1)(d) (as so added)).

14 See the Political Parties, Elections and Referendums Act 2000 Sch 19B para 2(2) (as added: see note 2).

15 Political Parties, Elections and Referendums Act 2000 Sch 19B para 2(2)(a) (as added: see note 2).

16 Political Parties, Elections and Referendums Act 2000 Sch 19B para 2(2)(b) (as added: see note 2). An inspection warrant may not be used for the purposes of carrying out investigatory functions: Sch 19B para 2(7) (as so added). For these purposes, 'investigatory functions' means functions of investigating suspected offences under the Political Parties, Elections and Referendums Act 2000 or suspected contraventions of restrictions or requirements imposed by or by virtue of the Political Parties, Elections and Referendums Act 2000: see Sch 19B para 2(8) (as so added).

17 Political Parties, Elections and Referendums Act 2000 Sch 19B para 2(2)(c) (as added: see note 2).

18 See the Political Parties, Elections and Referendums Act 2000 Sch 19B para 2(3)(a) (as added: see note 2).

19 See the Political Parties, Elections and Referendums Act 2000 Sch 19B para 2(3)(b) (as added: see note 2). See note 10. In the case of documents kept in electronic form, a power of a person ('the inspector') under Sch 19B to inspect documents includes power to require any person on the premises in question to give any assistance that the inspector reasonably requires to enable the inspector either to inspect and make copies of the documents in legible form or to make records of information contained in them, or to inspect and check the operation of any computer, and any associated apparatus or material, that is or has been in use in connection with the keeping of the documents: see Sch 19B para 10(1)(b) (as so added).

20 Political Parties, Elections and Referendums Act 2000 Sch 19B para 2(4) (as added: see note 2).

21 See the Political Parties, Elections and Referendums Act 2000 Sch 19B para 2(5) (as added: see note 2).

22 Political Parties, Elections and Referendums Act 2000 Sch 19B para 2(6) (as added: see note 2).

65. Investigatory powers of the Commission in relation to suspected offences or contraventions under the Political Parties, Elections and Referendums Act 2000. Where the Electoral Commission[1] has reasonable grounds to suspect that[2]:

(1)　a person has committed an offence under the Political Parties, Elections and Referendums Act 2000[3]; or

(2)　a person has contravened (otherwise than by committing an offence) any restriction or other requirement imposed by or by virtue of the Political Parties, Elections and Referendums Act 2000[4],

the Commission may by notice require any person[5]:

(a)　to produce, for inspection by the Commission or a person authorised by the Commission[6], any documents that they reasonably require for the purposes of investigating the suspected offence or contravention[7]; and

(b)　to provide the Commission, or a person authorised by the Commission, with any information or explanation that they reasonably require for those purposes[8].

A person to whom such a notice is given must comply with it within such reasonable time as is specified in the notice[9]; and a person authorised by the Commission ('the investigator') may require the person mentioned in head (1) or head (2) above (if that person is an individual)[10], or an individual whom the investigator reasonably believes to have relevant information[11], to attend before the investigator at a specified time and place and answer any questions that the investigator reasonably considers to be relevant[12].

Where the Commission has given such a notice[13] requiring documents to be produced[14], the High Court may make a document-disclosure order against a person ('the respondent') if satisfied on an application by the Commission that[15]:

(i)　there are reasonable grounds to suspect that a person (whether or not the respondent) has committed an offence under the Political Parties, Elections and Referendums Act 2000 or has contravened (otherwise than by committing an offence) any restriction or other requirement imposed by or by virtue of the Political Parties, Elections and Referendums Act 2000[16]; and

(ii) there are documents referred to in the notice[17] which have not been produced as required by the notice (either within the time specified in the notice for compliance or subsequently)[18], which are reasonably required by the Commission for the purposes of investigating the offence or contravention referred to in head (i) above[19], and which are in the custody or under the control of the respondent[20].

For these purposes, a 'document-disclosure order' is an order requiring the respondent to deliver to the Commission, within such time as is specified in the order, such documents falling within head (ii) above as are identified in the order (either specifically or by reference to any category or description of document)[21]. A person who fails to comply with a document-disclosure order may not, in respect of that failure, be both punished for contempt of court and convicted of an offence[22]. The Commission may retain any documents delivered to it in compliance with a document-disclosure order[23] for a period of three months (or for longer if any of the statutory conditions are satisfied)[24].

Where the Commission has given such a notice[25] requiring any information or explanation to be provided[26], the High Court may make an information-disclosure order against a person ('the respondent') if satisfied on an application by the Commission that[27]:

(A) there are reasonable grounds to suspect that a person (whether or not the respondent) has committed an offence under the Political Parties, Elections and Referendums Act 2000 or has contravened (otherwise than by committing an offence) any restriction or other requirement imposed by or by virtue of the Political Parties, Elections and Referendums Act 2000[28]; and

(B) there is any information or explanation referred to in the notice[29] which has not been provided as required by the notice (either within the time specified in the notice for compliance or subsequently)[30], which is reasonably required by the Commission for the purposes of investigating the offence or contravention referred to in head (A) above[31], and which the respondent is able to provide[32].

For these purposes, an 'information-disclosure order' is an order requiring the respondent to provide to the Commission, within such time as is specified in the order, such information or explanation falling within head (B) above as is identified in the order[33]. A person who fails to comply with an information-disclosure order may not, in respect of that failure, be both punished for contempt of court and convicted of an offence[34].

1   As to the establishment and constitution of the Electoral Commission see PARA 34 et seq.

2   See the Political Parties, Elections and Referendums Act 2000 s 146, Sch 19B para 3(1) (s 146 substituted, Sch 19B added, by the Political Parties and Elections Act 2009 s 2(1), (2), Sch 1).

3   Political Parties, Elections and Referendums Act 2000 Sch 19B para 3(1)(a) (as added: see note 2).

4   Political Parties, Elections and Referendums Act 2000 Sch 19B para 3(1)(b) (as added: see note 2).

5   Ie including an organisation to which, or an individual to whom, the Political Parties, Elections and Referendums Act 2000 Sch 19B para 1 applies (see PARA 64): see Sch 19B para 3(2) (as added: see note 2),

6   An authorisation of a person by the Commission under the Political Parties, Elections and Referendums Act 2000 Sch 19B must be in writing: Sch 19B para 8 (as added: see note 2).

7   Political Parties, Elections and Referendums Act 2000 Sch 19B para 3(2)(a) (as added: see note 2). For these purposes, the 'suspected offence or contravention' means the offence or contravention referred to in Sch 19B para 3(1) (see the text and notes 1–4): see Sch 19B para 3(1) (as so added). The Commission, or a person authorised by the Commission, may make copies of, or make records of any information contained in any documents produced or inspected under Sch 19B, and may make copies or records of any information or explanation provided under Sch 19B: see Sch 19B para 7 (as so added). For this purpose, 'documents' includes any books or records: see Sch 19B para 9 (as so added). In the case of documents kept in electronic form, a power of the Commission under Sch 19B to require documents to be produced for inspection includes power to require a copy of the documents to be made available for inspection in legible form: see Sch 19B para 10(1)(a) (as so added). The Commission, or a person authorised by the Commission, may make copies of, or make records of any information contained in any copy made available as mentioned in Sch 19B para 10(1)(a): see Sch 19B paras 7, 10(2) (as so added). However, nothing in Sch 19B requires a person to produce or provide, or authorises a person to inspect or take possession of, anything in respect of which a claim to legal professional privilege could be maintained in legal proceedings: Sch 19B para 11 (as so added). As to legal professional privilege see CIVIL PROCEDURE vol 11 (2009) PARA 558 et seq; and CRIMINAL PROCEDURE vol 28 (2010) PARA 506.

8   Political Parties, Elections and Referendums Act 2000 Sch 19B para 3(2)(b) (as added: see note 2). See note 7. A statement made by a person in compliance with a requirement imposed under Sch 19B is admissible in evidence in any proceedings, as long as it also complies with any requirements governing the admissibility of evidence in the circumstances in question: see Sch 19B para 12; and PARA 64 note 11.

9   Political Parties, Elections and Referendums Act 2000 Sch 19B para 3(3) (as added: see note 2).

10 See the Political Parties, Elections and Referendums Act 2000 Sch 19B para 3(4)(a) (as added: see note 2).

11 See the Political Parties, Elections and Referendums Act 2000 Sch 19B para 3(4)(b) (as added: see note 2). For this purpose, 'relevant' means relevant to an investigation by the Commission of the suspected offence or contravention: see Sch 19B para 3(5) (as so added).

12 See the Political Parties, Elections and Referendums Act 2000 Sch 19B para 3(4) (as added: see note 2).

13 Ie a notice under the Political Parties, Elections and Referendums Act 2000 Sch 19B para 3 (see the text and notes 1–12): see Sch 19B para 4(1) (as added: see note 2).

14 See the Political Parties, Elections and Referendums Act 2000 Sch 19B para 4(1) (as added: see note 2).

15 See the Political Parties, Elections and Referendums Act 2000 Sch 19B para 4(2) (as added: see note 2).

16 Political Parties, Elections and Referendums Act 2000 Sch 19B para 4(2)(a) (as added: see note 2).

17 Ie the notice under the Political Parties, Elections and Referendums Act 2000 Sch 19B para 3 (see the text and notes 1–12): see Sch 19B para 4(2)(b) (as added: see note 2).

18 Political Parties, Elections and Referendums Act 2000 Sch 19B para 4(2)(b)(i) (as added: see note 2).

19 Political Parties, Elections and Referendums Act 2000 Sch 19B para 4(2)(b)(ii) (as added: see note 2).

20 Political Parties, Elections and Referendums Act 2000 Sch 19B para 4(2)(b)(iii) (as added: see note 2). For this purpose, a document is under a person's control if it is in the person's possession or if the person has a right to possession of it: see Sch 19B para 4(4) (as so added).

21 Political Parties, Elections and Referendums Act 2000 Sch 19B para 4(3) (as added: see note 2). The Commission, or a person authorised by the Commission, may make copies of, or make records of any information contained in any documents delivered to them in compliance with an order under Sch 19B para 4: see Sch 19B para 7 (as so added).

22 Political Parties, Elections and Referendums Act 2000 Sch 19B para 4(5) (as added: see note 2). The text refers to an offence under Sch 19B para 13(1) (see PARA 753): see Sch 19B para 4(5) (as so added).

23 Ie an order under the Political Parties, Elections and Referendums Act 2000 Sch 19B para 4 (see the text and notes 13–22): see Sch 19B para 6(1) (as added: see note 2).

24 Political Parties, Elections and Referendums Act 2000 Sch 19B para 6(1) (as added: see note 2). For this purpose, the 'documents' and the 'three-month period' mean the documents and the period mentioned in Sch 19B para 6(1): see Sch 19B para 6(1) (as so added). The text refers to retention for a period longer than three months if any of Sch 19B para 6(2)–(7) applies: see Sch 19B para 6(1) (as so added). Accordingly, if, within the three-month period:

    (1)   proceedings to which the documents are relevant are commenced against any person for

any criminal offence, the documents may be retained until the conclusion of those proceedings (Sch 19B para 6(2) (as so added));

(2) the Commission serves a notice under s 147, Sch 19C para 2(1) of a proposal to impose a fixed monetary penalty on any person (see PARA 757), and the documents are relevant to the decision to serve the notice, the documents may be retained (see Sch 19B para 6(3) (as so added)): (a) until liability for the penalty is discharged as mentioned in Sch 19C para 2(2) (see PARA 757) (if it is) (Sch 19B para 6(3)(a) (as so added)); (b) until the Commission decides not to impose a fixed monetary penalty (if that is what it decides) (Sch 19B para 6(3)(b) (as so added)); (c) until the end of the period given by Sch 19B para 6(5) (see head (4) below) (if the Commission does impose a fixed monetary penalty) (Sch 19B para 6(3)(c) (as so added));

(3) the Commission serves a notice under Sch 19C para 6(1) of a proposal to impose a discretionary requirement on any person (see PARA 758), and the documents are relevant to the decision to serve the notice, the documents may be retained (see Sch 19B para 6(4) (as so added)): (a) until the Commission decides not to impose a discretionary requirement (if that is what it decides) (Sch 19B para 6(4)(a) (as so added)); (b) until the end of the period given by Sch 19B para 6(5) (see head (4) below) (if the Commission does impose a discretionary requirement) (Sch 19B para 6(4)(b) (as so added));

(4) either: (a) a notice is served imposing a fixed monetary penalty on any person under Sch 19C para 2(4) (see PARA 757), and the documents are relevant to the decision to impose the penalty (see Sch 19B para 6(5)(a) (as so added)); or (b) a notice is served imposing a discretionary requirement on any person under Sch 19C para 6(5) (see PARA 758), and the documents are relevant to the decision to impose the requirement (see Sch 19B para 6(5)(b) (as so added)), the documents may be retained until the end of the period allowed for bringing an appeal against that decision (or, if an appeal is brought, until the conclusion of proceedings on the appeal) (see Sch 19B para 6(5) (as so added));

(5) a stop notice is served on any person under Sch 19C para 10 (see PARA 759) (see Sch 19B para 6(6)(a) (as so added)), and the documents are relevant to the decision to serve the notice (see Sch 19B para 6(6)(b) (as so added)), the documents may be retained until the end of the period allowed for bringing an appeal against that decision (or, if an appeal is brought, until the conclusion of proceedings on the appeal) (see Sch 19B para 6(6) (as so added)).

If, within the three-month period, or the period given by Sch 19B para 6(6) (see head (5) above) (or, if applicable, by Sch 19B para 6(4) (see head (3) above) or by Sch 19B para 6(5)(b) (see head (4)(b) above)) (see Sch 19B para 6(7) (as so added)): (i) the Commission, having served a stop notice on any person under Sch 19C para 10, decides not to issue a completion certificate under Sch 19C para 12 (see PARA 759) in relation to the stop notice (see Sch 19B para 6(7)(a) (as so added)); and (ii) the documents are relevant to the decision not to issue the certificate (see Sch 19B para 6(7)(b) (as so added)), the documents may be retained until the end of the period allowed for bringing an appeal against that decision (or, if an appeal is brought, until the conclusion of proceedings on the appeal) (see Sch 19B para 6(7) (as so added)).

25 Ie a notice under the Political Parties, Elections and Referendums Act 2000 Sch 19B para 3 (see the text and notes 1–12): see Sch 19B para 5(1) (as added: see note 2).

26 See the Political Parties, Elections and Referendums Act 2000 Sch 19B para 5(1) (as added: see note 2).

27 See the Political Parties, Elections and Referendums Act 2000 Sch 19B para 5(2) (as added: see note 2).

28 Political Parties, Elections and Referendums Act 2000 Sch 19B para 5(2)(a) (as added: see note 2).

29 Ie the notice under the Political Parties, Elections and Referendums Act 2000 Sch 19B para 3 (see the text and notes 1–12): see Sch 19B para 5(2)(b) (as added: see note 2).

30 Political Parties, Elections and Referendums Act 2000 Sch 19B para 5(2)(b)(i) (as added: see note 2).

31 Political Parties, Elections and Referendums Act 2000 Sch 19B para 5(2)(b)(ii) (as added: see note 2).

32 Political Parties, Elections and Referendums Act 2000 Sch 19B para 5(2)(b)(iii) (as added: see note 2).

33 Political Parties, Elections and Referendums Act 2000 Sch 19B para 5(3) (as added: see note 2). See note 7.

34 Political Parties, Elections and Referendums Act 2000 Sch 19B para 5(4) (as added: see note 2). The text refers to an offence under Sch 19B para 13(1) (see PARA 753): see Sch 19B para 5(4) (as so added).

66. Investigatory powers of the Commission: offences. A person commits an offence if he:

(1) fails, without reasonable excuse, to comply with any requirement imposed under or by virtue of the provisions[1] that govern the Electoral Commission's investigatory powers[2];

(2) intentionally obstructs a person authorised by or by virtue of those provisions[3] in the carrying out of that person's functions under the authorisation[4];

(3) knowingly or recklessly provides false information in purported compliance with a requirement imposed under or by virtue of those provisions[5].

An offence under head (1) or head (2) above is punishable on summary conviction with a fine not exceeding level 5 on the standard scale[6]; an offence under head (3) above is punishable (on summary conviction) with a fine not exceeding the statutory maximum[7] or with one year's imprisonment or (on conviction on indictment) with a fine or with up to one year's imprisonment[8].

1 Ie imposed under or by virtue of the Political Parties, Elections and Referendums Act 2000 s 146, Sch 19B (see PARAS 64, 65): see Sch 19B para 13(1) (s 146 substituted, Sch 19B added, by the Political Parties and Elections Act 2009 s 2(1), (2), Sch 1); and PARA 753.
2 See the Political Parties, Elections and Referendums Act 2000 Sch 19B para 13(1) (as added: see note 1); and PARA 753. As to the establishment and constitution of the Electoral Commission see PARA 34 et seq; and as to the Electoral Commission's investigatory powers see PARAS 64, 65.
3 Ie authorised by or by virtue of the Political Parties, Elections and Referendums Act 2000 Sch 19B (see PARAS 64, 65): see Sch 19B para 13(2) (as added: see note 1); and PARA 753.
4 See the Political Parties, Elections and Referendums Act 2000 Sch 19B para 13(2) (as added: see note 1); and PARA 753.
5 See the Political Parties, Elections and Referendums Act 2000 Sch 19B para 13(3) (as added: see note 1); and PARA 753. Head (3) in the text refers to purported compliance with a requirement imposed under or by virtue of Sch 19B (see PARAS 64, 65): see Sch 19B para 13(3) (as so added); and PARA 753.
6 See the Political Parties, Elections and Referendums Act 2000 s 150, Sch 20 (Sch 20 amended by the Political Parties and Elections Act 2009 s 2(3)); and PARA 753. As to the standard scale see SENTENCING AND DISPOSITION OF OFFENDERS vol 92 (2010) PARA 142. As to the Commission's powers to apply civil sanctions to offences and contraventions under the Political Parties, Elections and Referendums Act 2000 see PARAS 757–760.
7 As to the statutory maximum see SENTENCING AND DISPOSITION OF OFFENDERS vol 92 (2010) PARA 140.
8 See the Political Parties, Elections and Referendums Act 2000 Sch 20 (as amended: see note 6); and PARA 753.

(iv) **The Transfer of Property, Rights and Liabilities from the Electoral Commission to the Local Government Boundary Commission for England**

67. Duty to make schemes for the transfer of property, etc to the Local Government Boundary Commission for England. For the purpose of the exercise of functions relating to local government boundary and electoral change that are conferred on the Local Government Boundary Commission for England[1] by or under Part 3 of the Local Democracy, Economic Development and Construction Act 2009[2], the Electoral Commission[3] was under a duty to make one or more schemes for the transfer of property, rights and liabilities from the Electoral Commission to the Local Government Boundary Commission for England[4]. The Electoral Commission was not empowered to make such a scheme, however, without consulting the Secretary of State[5] or without the consent of the Electoral Commission's Boundary Committee[6]; and, if the Electoral Commission and the Electoral Commission's Boundary Committee failed to agree on the provision to be included in such a scheme, the Secretary of State had the power by order to specify the provision to be included in the scheme[7].

A transfer under such a scheme has effect in accordance with the terms of the scheme[8]; and may have effect whether or not the property, rights and liabilities would otherwise be capable of being transferred, and without any instrument or other formality being required[9].

Where such a scheme has been made, the Electoral Commission and the Local Government Boundary Commission for England may[10] agree in writing to modify the scheme[11]; and any such modification is to have effect as from the date the original scheme came into effect[12].

1   As to the Local Government Boundary Commission for England see PARA 71.

2   Ie the Local Democracy, Economic Development and Construction Act 2009 Pt 3 (ss 55–68) (local government boundary and electoral change: see also PARA 71 et seq): see s 62(1).

3   As to the establishment and constitution of the Electoral Commission see PARA 34 et seq.

4   Local Democracy, Economic Development and Construction Act 2009 s 62(1). A scheme under s 62 had to be made on or before 31 December 2009, or on or before such later date as the Secretary of State may by order specify: see s 62(4). An order under s 62 is made by statutory instrument, subject to annulment in pursuance of a resolution of either House of Parliament: see s 62(12), (13). As to the Secretary of State see PARA 2. No such order had been made under s 62(4), however, and the Local Government Boundary Commission for England was duly established on 1 April 2010.

A scheme under s 62 may define the property, rights and liabilities to be transferred by specifying or describing them (s 62(9)); and such a scheme may include supplementary, incidental, transitional and consequential provision, and may in particular (s 62(10)):

(1)   make provision for the continuing effect of things done by the Electoral Commission in relation to anything transferred by the scheme (s 62(10)(a));

(2)   make provision for the continuation of things (including legal proceedings) in the process of being done, by or on behalf of or in relation to the Electoral Commission in relation to anything transferred by the scheme (s 62(10)(b));

(3)   make provision for references to the Electoral Commission in an agreement (whether written or not), instrument or other document in relation to anything transferred by the scheme to be treated (so far as necessary for the purposes of or in consequence of the transfer) as references to the Local Government Boundary Commission for England (s 62(10)(c));

(4)   make provision for the shared ownership or use of any property or facilities (s 62(10)(d)).

The rights and liabilities which may be transferred by a scheme under s 62 include rights and liabilities in relation to a contract of employment: s 62(7). The Transfer of Undertakings (Protection of Employment) Regulations 2006, SI 2006/246 (see EMPLOYMENT vol 39 (2009) PARA 111 et seq) apply to the transfer under a scheme under the Local Democracy, Economic Development and Construction Act 2009 s 62, whether or not the transfer is a relevant transfer for the purposes of those regulations: s 62(8). As to the meaning of 'relevant transfer' for the purposes of the Transfer of Undertakings (Protection of Employment) Regulations 2006, SI 2006/246 see EMPLOYMENT vol 39 (2009) PARA 111.

5   Local Democracy, Economic Development and Construction Act 2009 s 62(2)(a).

6   Local Democracy, Economic Development and Construction Act 2009 s 62(2)(b). As to the Electoral Commission's Boundary Committee see PARA 71 note 1.

7   See the Local Democracy, Economic Development and Construction Act 2009 s 62(3). At the date at which this volume states the law, no such order had been made.

8   See the Local Democracy, Economic Development and Construction Act 2009 s 62(5).

9   See the Local Democracy, Economic Development and Construction Act 2009 s 62(6).

10 Ie subject to any order made under the Local Democracy, Economic Development and Construction Act 2009 s 62 (see the text and notes 4, 7): see s 62(11).

11 See the Local Democracy, Economic Development and Construction Act 2009 s 62(11).

12 See the Local Democracy, Economic Development and Construction Act 2009 s 62(11).

(2) THE BOUNDARY COMMISSIONS

(i) Parliamentary Boundaries

68.   The permanent parliamentary Boundary Commissions. For the purpose of the continuous review of the distribution of seats at parliamentary elections[1], there are four permanent Boundary Commissions[2], namely a Boundary Commission for England[3], a Boundary Commission for Scotland, a Boundary Commission for Wales[4] and a Boundary Commission for Northern Ireland[5].

1   As to the meaning of 'parliamentary election' see PARA 9. As to the review of the distribution of seats at parliamentary elections see the Parliamentary Constituencies Act 1986 ss 3, 5, Sch 2; and PARAS 78–82.

2   As to the constitution of, and other matters relating to, the Boundary Commissions see the Parliamentary Constituencies Act 1986 s 2(2), Sch 1; and PARAS 69–70.

3   As to the meaning of 'England' see PARA 1 note 1.

4   As to the meaning of 'Wales' see PARA 1 note 1.

5   Parliamentary Constituencies Act 1986 s 2(1). See PARA 71 note 1. See also PARLIAMENT vol 78 (2010) PARA 896.

69.   Constitution of the Boundary Commissions. Each of the four Boundary Commissions[1] consists of:

(1)   the chairman (who, for each of the four Commissions, is the Speaker of the House of Commons)[2];

(2)   a deputy chairman (who must be a judge)[3]; and

(3)   two other members appointed by the Secretary of State[4].

The deputy chairmen and the two remaining members hold their appointments on terms and conditions determined by the person appointing them in each case[5]. Assistant commissioners may be appointed by the Secretary of State at the request of any Commission to assist the Commission in the discharge of its functions[6]. Provision is made as to their appointment, duties and remuneration[7]. The officers of each Commission include a secretary[8] and assessors[9]. The expenses of each Commission (including the remuneration and travelling and other expenses of the members, assistant commissioners, secretary and other officers) are paid out of money provided by Parliament[10].

1   As to the provision made for the permanent parliamentary Boundary Commissions see PARA 68. See also PARLIAMENT vol 78 (2010) PARA 896.

2   See the Parliamentary Constituencies Act 1986 s 2(2), Sch 1 paras 1, 2. See PARA 71 note 1. As to the Speaker of the House of Commons see PARLIAMENT vol 78 (2010) PARA 931 et seq.

3   See the Parliamentary Constituencies Act 1986 Sch 1 paras 2, 3. The deputy chairmen of the commissions for England and for Wales are judges of the High Court appointed by the Lord Chancellor (see Sch 1 para 3(a), (c)); the deputy chairman of the commission for Scotland is a judge of the Court of Session appointed by the Lord President of the Court of Session (see Sch 1 para 3(b)); and the deputy chairman of the commission for Northern Ireland is a judge of the High Court in Northern Ireland appointed by the Lord Chief Justice of Northern Ireland (see Sch 1 para 3(d)). As to the meanings of 'England' and 'Wales' see PARA 1 note 1. As to the Lord Chancellor see PARA 2; and CONSTITUTIONAL LAW AND HUMAN RIGHTS vol 8(2) (Reissue) PARA 477 et seq.

4   See the Parliamentary Constituencies Act 1986 Sch 1 para 2. As to the Secretary of State see PARA 2. Boundary Commissioners appointed under Sch 1 are disqualified for membership of the House of Commons: see the House of Commons Disqualification Act 1975 s 1(1), Sch 1 Pt III; and PARLIAMENT vol 78 (2010) PARAS 905, 908.

5   See the Parliamentary Constituencies Act 1986 Sch 1 para 4. In the case of members other than the chairman or deputy chairman, the conditions referred to in Sch 1 para 4 may include such provisions with respect to remuneration as the Secretary of State may determine with the

approval of the Treasury: Sch 1 para 4A (added by the Boundary Commissions Act 1992 s 1(1), (2)). As to the Treasury see CONSTITUTIONAL LAW AND HUMAN RIGHTS vol 8(2) (Reissue) PARAS 512–517.

6	Parliamentary Constituencies Act 1986 Sch 1 para 6(1) (amended by the Parliamentary Voting System and Constituencies Act 2011 s 10(1), (10)(a)). Assistant commissioners appointed under the Parliamentary Constituencies Act 1986 Sch 1 are disqualified for membership of the House of Commons: see the House of Commons Disqualification Act 1975 Sch 1 Pt III; and PARLIAMENT vol 78 (2010) PARAS 905, 908.

7	Accordingly, any such assistant commissioner is appointed either for a certain term or for the purposes of a particular matter, and on such conditions as to remuneration and otherwise as may be determined before his appointment by the Secretary of State with the approval of the Treasury: Parliamentary Constituencies Act 1986 Sch 1 para 6(2) (amended by the Parliamentary Voting System and Constituencies Act 2011 s 10(1), (10)(b)).

8	See the Parliamentary Constituencies Act 1986 Sch 1 para 7. Accordingly, the Secretary of State must appoint a secretary to each of the Commissions, and may appoint such other officers of any Commission as he may determine with the approval of the Treasury: see Sch 1 para 7. The terms and conditions of any such appointment are to be such as may be so determined: see Sch 1 para 7.

9	See the Parliamentary Constituencies Act 1986 Sch 1 para 5. In the case of the Boundary Commission for England and the Boundary Commission for Wales, the Statistics Board and the Director General of Ordnance Survey are the appointed assessors: see Sch 1 para 5(a), (c) (Sch 1 para 5(a), (c) amended by the Statistics and Registration Service Act 2007 s 25(3), Sch 1 para 10). As to the appointments made in the case of the Boundary Commission for Scotland and the Boundary Commission for Northern Ireland see Sch 1 para 5(b), (d) (Sch 1 para 5(d) amended by the Parliamentary Voting System and Constituencies Act 2011 s 10(1), (9)). As to the Ordnance Survey see NATIONAL CULTURAL HERITAGE vol 77 (2010) PARA 1110 et seq; and as to the Statistics Board see REGISTRATION CONCERNING THE INDIVIDUAL vol 88 (2012) PARA 353.

10	Parliamentary Constituencies Act 1986 Sch 1 para 8 (amended by the Boundary Commissions Act 1992 s 1(1), (4)).

70. Procedure of the Boundary Commissions. A Boundary Commission[1] has power to act notwithstanding any vacancy in its members[2]. Provision is made as to quorum[3], joint meetings of the Commissions[4] and the reception in evidence of documents purporting to be issued by a Commission[5]. Subject to the other provisions of the Parliamentary Constituencies Act 1986, each of the Commissions has power to regulate its own procedure[6].

1	As to the provision made for the permanent parliamentary Boundary Commissions see PARA 68. See also PARLIAMENT vol 78 (2010) PARA 896.

2	See the Parliamentary Constituencies Act 1986 s 2(2), Sch 1 para 9. See PARA 71 note 1.

3	Ie at any meeting of a Commission two, or such greater number as the Commission determines, is to be the quorum: see the Parliamentary Constituencies Act 1986 Sch 1 para 9.

4	Accordingly, all the Commissions, or any two or three of them, may hold joint meetings for the purpose of considering any matter of common concern: see the Parliamentary Constituencies Act 1986 Sch 1 para 10.

5	Accordingly, every document purporting to be an instrument made or issued by a Commission and to be signed by the secretary or any person authorised to act in that behalf is to be received in evidence and is, until the contrary is proved, deemed to be an instrument made or issued by the Commission: see the Parliamentary Constituencies Act 1986 Sch 1 para 12.

6	Parliamentary Constituencies Act 1986 Sch 1 para 11.

(ii) Local Government Boundaries

71. The Local Government Boundary Commission for England. The Local Government Boundary Commission for England is established as a body corporate[1]; and may do anything (except borrow money) which is calculated to facilitate, or is incidental or conducive to, the exercise of its functions[2].

The Local Government Boundary Commission for England ('the Commission') consists of[3]:

(1)　the chair of the Commission[4]; and

(2)　at least four and no more than eleven other members ('ordinary members')[5].

The Commission must pay to or in respect of the members (including the chair and deputy chair) such sums by way of or in respect of remuneration, allowances, expenses, pensions or gratuities as the Speaker of the House of Commons, after consulting the Speaker's Committee, may determine[6]. The Commission must appoint a chief executive, and may appoint other employees[7].

The Commission may establish any committees which it considers appropriate[8]; and a committee of the Commission may establish one or more sub-committees[9]. The Commission may[10] regulate its own proceedings and the proceedings of any of its committees or sub-committees (including quorum)[11]; and the validity of proceedings of the Commission, or of any of its committees or sub-committees, is not affected by a vacancy, or by a defective appointment[12]. The Commission may delegate any of its functions to any of its members, employees, committees or sub-committees[13]; the chief executive of the Commission may delegate any of the chief executive's functions to any other employee of the Commission[14]; a committee of the Commission may delegate any of its functions to any of its sub-committees[15]; and a committee or sub-committee of the Commission may delegate any of its functions to any employee of the Commission[16].

The Commission must, as soon after the end of each financial year[17] as may be practicable, prepare and lay before Parliament a report about the performance of the Commission's functions during that financial year[18]; and the Commission must, on so laying such a report, publish it in such manner as it may determine[19].

The fixing of the seal of the Commission is to be authenticated by the signature of the chair or of another person authorised by the Commission to act for that purpose[20]. A document purporting to be duly executed under the seal of the Commission, or to be signed on its behalf, is to be received in evidence and, unless the contrary is proved, is to be treated as having been so executed or signed[21].

1　Local Democracy, Economic Development and Construction Act 2009 s 55(1). The Local Government Boundary Commission for England is not to be regarded as a servant or agent of the Crown or as enjoying any status, immunity or privilege of the Crown: s 55(2). Accordingly, the property of the Local Government Boundary Commission for England is not to be regarded as the property of the Crown or as property held on behalf of the Crown: s 55(3).

　　A body previously known as the Local Government Boundary Commission for England was established under the Local Government Act 1972, and was the body responsible for reviewing the boundaries of the local government areas in England and their electoral arrangements: see s 46 (repealed with savings by the Local Government Act 1992 s 29(2), (3), Sch 4 Pt II). In 1992, this body was replaced by the Local Government Commission for England, established under the Local Government Act 1992 s 12, Sch 2, but, on 1 April 2002, the functions of the Local Government Commission for England were transferred to the Electoral Commission by virtue of the Political Parties, Elections and Referendums Act 2000 s 18 and the Local Government Commission for England (Transfer of Functions) Order 2001, SI 2001/3962. On the same day, the Boundary Committee for England was established under the Political Parties, Elections and Referendums Act 2000 s 14, as a statutory committee of the Electoral Commission; and the Local Government Commission for England ceased to exist at the start of the day on 1 August 2002 (see the Local Government Commission for England (Winding-up) Order 2002, SI 2002/1723). As to the historical context see further LOCAL GOVERNMENT vol 69 (2009) PARAS 55, 56. As to the establishment and constitution of the Electoral Commission see PARA 34 et seq.

　　With effect from 1 April 2010, the Electoral Commission's duty under the Political Parties, Elections and Referendums Act 2000 s 14 to establish Boundary Committees was abolished so far as relating to England (Local Democracy, Economic Development and Construction

Act 2009 s 61(1); Local Democracy, Economic Development and Construction Act 2009 (Commencement No 2) Order 2009, SI 2009/3318, art 4); and the functions of the 'Electoral Commission's Boundary Committee' (ie the Boundary Committee for England constituted by the Electoral Commission under the Political Parties, Elections and Referendums Act 2000 s 14) relating to structural and boundary change were transferred to the Local Government Boundary Commission for England (see the Local Democracy, Economic Development and Construction Act 2009 ss 60(1), (4), 68; and the Local Democracy, Economic Development and Construction Act 2009 (Commencement No 2) Order 2009, SI 2009/3318, art 4). The functions relating to structural and boundary change referred to are those that are currently governed by the Local Government and Public Involvement in Health Act 2007 Pt 1 Ch 1 (ss 1–23) (see LOCAL GOVERNMENT vol 69 (2009) PARA 56 et seq): see the Local Democracy, Economic Development and Construction Act 2009 s 60(1). Also transferred to the Local Government Boundary Commission for England, subject to ss 61–68 (see PARA 83 et seq), are the functions of the Electoral Commission under the Greater London Authority Act 1999 s 2(4) (constituencies for the Greater London Assembly: see PARA 75; and LONDON GOVERNMENT vol 71 (2013) PARA 80), under the Local Government and Public Involvement in Health Act 2007 Pt 2 Ch 1 (ss 31–54) (power of District Councils in England to change electoral scheme: see LOCAL GOVERNMENT vol 69 (2009) PARA 134 et seq), under s 59 (change of name of electoral area: see LOCAL GOVERNMENT vol 69 (2009) PARA 126) and under Pt 4 Ch 3 (ss 79–102) (Parishes: Reorganisation) (see PARA 85; and LOCAL GOVERNMENT vol 69 (2009) PARAS 68–76): see the Local Democracy, Economic Development and Construction Act 2009 s 60(2), (3). The following provisions of the Political Parties, Elections and Referendums Act 2000 are repealed, accordingly:

(1) s 14 (Boundary Committees), so far as relating to England (Local Democracy, Economic Development and Construction Act 2009 s 61(2)(a));

(2) the Political Parties, Elections and Referendums Act 2000 s 15 (Deputy Electoral Commissioners) (Local Democracy, Economic Development and Construction Act 2009 s 61(2)(b)).

In the Political Parties, Elections and Referendums Act 2000, the following provisions (which provide for the transfer of functions etc to the Electoral Commission and which are not in force or in force only to a limited extent) are repealed also:

(a) s 14 (Boundary Committees) so far as relating to Scotland, Wales and Northern Ireland (Local Democracy, Economic Development and Construction Act 2009 s 61(3)(a));

(b) the Political Parties, Elections and Referendums Act 2000 ss 16, 17 (transfer of functions and property etc of Boundary Commissions to the Electoral Commission) (Local Democracy, Economic Development and Construction Act 2009 s 61(3)(b));

(c) the Political Parties, Elections and Referendums Act 2000 ss 19, 20 (transfer of functions of Local Government Boundary Commissions for Scotland and Wales to Electoral Commission) (Local Democracy, Economic Development and Construction Act 2009 s 61(3)(c));

(d) the Political Parties, Elections and Referendums Act 2000 Sch 3 Pt 1 (amendments relating to the transfer of functions of Boundary Commissions) (Local Democracy, Economic Development and Construction Act 2009 s 61(3)(d));

(e) in the Political Parties, Elections and Referendums Act 2000 s 158(2), Sch 22 (repeals), the entries relating to the Parliamentary Constituencies Act 1986 and the Boundary Commissions Act 1992 (Local Democracy, Economic Development and Construction Act 2009 s 61(3)(e)).

Further to head (e) above, the Political Parties, Elections and Referendums Act 2000 had provided that, as from a day to be appointed under s 163(2): (i) the Parliamentary Constituencies Act 1986 s 2, Sch 1 were to be repealed by the Political Parties, Elections and Referendums Act 2000 s 158(2), Sch 22; and (ii) the functions of each of the Boundary Commissions with respect to keeping under review, and reporting on, representation in the House of Commons of the part of the United Kingdom with which it is concerned were to be transferred to the Electoral Commission under s 16. The Local Government Act 1992 s 12 (rendered redundant from 1 April 2002) was repealed by the Local Democracy, Economic Development and Construction Act 2009 s 66(a), 146(1), Sch 7 Pt 3, also with effect from 1 April 2010: see the Local Democracy, Economic Development and Construction Act 2009 (Commencement No 2) Order 2009, SI 2009/3318, art 4. As to the meanings of 'England' and 'Wales' see PARA 1 note 1.

2   See the Local Democracy, Economic Development and Construction Act 2009 s 55(4). As to the functions of the Local Government Boundary Commission for England see Pt 3 (ss 55–68) (local government boundary and electoral change); and PARA 83 et seq.

3   See the Local Democracy, Economic Development and Construction Act 2009 s 55(5), Sch 1 para 1(1). A person who holds any office of the Local Government Boundary Commission for England is disqualified for membership of the House of Commons: see the House of Commons Disqualification Act 1975 s 1(1), Sch 1 Pt II; and PARLIAMENT vol 78 (2010) PARAS 905, 908.

4   Local Democracy, Economic Development and Construction Act 2009 Sch 1 para 1(1)(a). The chair of the Commission is to be appointed by Her Majesty on an Address from the House of Commons: Sch 1 para 2(1). A motion for such an Address may be made only if the Speaker of the House of Commons agrees that the motion may be made, and if the person whose appointment is proposed in the motion has been selected in accordance with a procedure put in place and overseen by the Speaker's Committee (see the Political Parties, Elections and Referendums Act 2000 s 2; and PARA 49) (see the Local Democracy, Economic Development and Construction Act 2009 Sch 1 para 2(2)), although, in the case of a re-appointment, the reference to being selected in accordance with a procedure put in place and overseen by the Speaker's Committee is to be read as including a reference to being recommended for re-appointment by the Speaker's Committee (see Sch 1 para 2(11)). Such an Address must specify the period, not exceeding five years, for which the proposed chair is to be appointed: Sch 1 para 2(3). No-one may serve as chair for more than ten years (continuously or otherwise): Sch 1 para 2(10). One of the ordinary members of the Commission may be designated to be the deputy chair: see note 5. As to the Speaker's Committee see PARA 49. As to the Speaker of the House of Commons see PARLIAMENT vol 78 (2010) PARA 931 et seq.

A person may not be appointed as chair under Sch 1 para 2(1), however, if by virtue of Sch 1 para 1(3)(a)–(d) (see note 5) that person may not be appointed as an ordinary member: Sch 1 para 2(4). Subject to the provisions of Sch 1 para 2, the chair holds office for the period of their appointment (which is to be that specified under Sch 1 para 2(3)), and otherwise in accordance with the terms of their appointment: see Sch 1 para 2(5). The chair ceases to hold office on the occurrence of such an event as is mentioned in any of Sch 1 para 1(6)(a)–(e) (see note 5): Sch 1 para 2(6). The chair may, on the chair's request, be relieved of office as chair by Her Majesty (Sch 1 para 2(7)); and the chair may be removed from office by Her Majesty on an Address from the House of Commons (Sch 1 para 2(8)). However, no motion may be made for such an Address unless the Speaker's Committee has presented a report to the House of Commons stating that the Speaker's Committee is satisfied that one or more of the following grounds is made out in relation to the chair (Sch 1 para 2(9)):

(1)   failure to discharge the functions of their office for a continuous period of at least three months (Sch 1 para 2(9)(a));

(2)   failure to comply with the terms of appointment as chair (Sch 1 para 2(9)(b));

(3)   conviction of a criminal offence (Sch 1 para 2(9)(c));

(4)   being an undischarged bankrupt or having their estate sequestrated in Scotland and not being discharged (Sch 1 para 2(9)(d));

(5)   making an arrangement or composition contract with, or granting a trust deed for, their creditors (Sch 1 para 2(9)(e));

(6)   otherwise being unfit to hold office as chair or unable to carry out the functions of that office (Sch 1 para 2(9)(f)).

Service as chair is not service in the civil service of the State: Sch 1 para 2(12). As to discharge from bankruptcy see BANKRUPTCY AND INDIVIDUAL INSOLVENCY vol 5 (2013) PARA 638 et seq; and as to compositions and arrangements with creditors see BANKRUPTCY AND INDIVIDUAL INSOLVENCY vol 5 (2013) PARA 852 et seq.

5   Local Democracy, Economic Development and Construction Act 2009 Sch 1 para 1(1)(b). The term 'ordinary member' is to be construed in accordance with Sch 1 para 1(1)(b): see Sch 1 para 24. The ordinary members are to be appointed by Her Majesty on the recommendation of the Secretary of State: Sch 1 para 1(2). As to the Secretary of State see PARA 2. The following may not be appointed as an ordinary member, however (see Sch 1 para 1(3)):

(1)   a member of a registered party (Sch 1 para 1(3)(a));

(2)   a person who is, or has at any time with the last ten years been, an officer or employee of a registered party or of any accounting unit of such a party (Sch 1 para 1(3)(b));

(3)   a person who holds, or has at any time within the last ten years held, a relevant elective office, within the meaning of the Political Parties, Elections and Referendums Act 2000 s 71, Sch 7 (control of donations to individuals and members associations: see CONSTITUTIONAL LAW AND HUMAN RIGHTS) (Local Democracy, Economic Development and Construction Act 2009 Sch 1 para 1(3)(c));

(4)   a person who has at any time within the last ten years been named as a donor in the register of donations reported under the Political Parties, Elections and Referendums Act 2000 Pt IV Ch III (ss 62–69) (reporting of donations to registered parties) or Pt IV Ch V (s 71) (control of donations to individuals and members associations: see

CONSTITUTIONAL LAW AND HUMAN RIGHTS) (Local Democracy, Economic Development and Construction Act 2009 Sch 1 para 1(3)(d)(i)), or as a participant in the register of recordable transactions reported under the Political Parties, Elections and Referendums Act 2000 Pt IVA (ss 71F–71Y) (regulation of loans and related transactions: see PARA 312; and CONSTITUTIONAL LAW AND HUMAN RIGHTS) (Local Democracy, Economic Development and Construction Act 2009 Sch 1 para 1(3)(d)(ii)). As to the meaning of 'registered party' for these purposes see the Political Parties, Elections and Referendums Act 2000 s 160(1) (cited in PARA 35 note 3); definition applied by the Local Democracy, Economic Development and Construction Act 2009 Sch 1 para 24. As to the meaning of 'accounting unit', in relation to a registered party, see the Political Parties, Elections and Referendums Act 2000 s 160(1) (cited in PARA 253 note 15); definition applied by the Local Democracy, Economic Development and Construction Act 2009 Sch 1 para 24.

A person may not be appointed as an ordinary member for a period of more than five years at any one time (Sch 1 para 1(4)); and no-one may serve as an ordinary member for more than ten years (continuously or otherwise) (Sch 1 para 1(9)). Subject to the provisions of Sch 1 para 1, an ordinary member holds office for the term for which the ordinary member is appointed, and otherwise in accordance with the terms of their appointment: see Sch 1 para 1(5). An ordinary member ceases to hold office if (see Sch 1 para 1(6)):

(a) the ordinary member consents to being nominated as a candidate at a relevant election, within the meaning of the Political Parties, Elections and Referendums Act 2000 Pt II (ss 22–40) (see PARA 253), or to being included in a registered party's list of candidates at such an election (Local Democracy, Economic Development and Construction Act 2009 Sch 1 para 1(6)(a));

(b) the ordinary member takes up any office or employment in or with a registered party or any accounting unit of such a party, with a recognised third party within the meaning of the Political Parties, Elections and Referendums Act 2000 Pt VI (ss 85–100) (controls relating to third party national election campaigns: see PARA 313 note 15), or with a permitted participant within the meaning of Pt VII (ss 101–129) (referendums: see PARA 529) (Local Democracy, Economic Development and Construction Act 2009 Sch 1 para 1(6)(b));

(c) the ordinary member is named as a donor in the register of donations reported under the Political Parties, Elections and Referendums Act 2000 Pt IV Ch III or Pt IV Ch V or in any statement of donations included in a return delivered to the Electoral Commission under s 98 (delivery of returns (recognised third parties): see PARA 322) or s 122 (return delivered to the Commission (permitted participants): see PARA 543) (Local Democracy, Economic Development and Construction Act 2009 Sch 1 para 1(6)(c));

(d) the ordinary member is named as a participant in the register of recordable transactions reported under the Political Parties, Elections and Referendums Act 2000 Pt IVA (Local Democracy, Economic Development and Construction Act 2009 Sch 1 para 1(6)(d)); or

(e) the ordinary member becomes a member of a registered party (Sch 1 para 1(6)(e)).

As to a registered party's list of candidates see PARA 253 et seq.

An ordinary member may, on the member's request, be relieved of office by Her Majesty (Sch 1 para 1(7)); and an ordinary member may, on the recommendation of the Secretary of State, be removed from office by Her Majesty on any of the following grounds (Sch 1 para 1(8)):

(i) failure to discharge the functions of membership for a continuous period of at least three months (Sch 1 para 1(8)(a));

(ii) failure to comply with the terms of appointment (Sch 1 para 1(8)(b));

(iii) conviction of a criminal offence (Sch 1 para 1(8)(c));

(iv) being an undischarged bankrupt or having their estate sequestrated in Scotland and not being discharged (Sch 1 para 1(8)(d));

(v) making an arrangement or composition contract with, or granting a trust deed for, their creditors (Sch 1 para 1(8)(e));

(vi) otherwise being unfit to hold office or unable to carry out the functions of membership (Sch 1 para 1(8)(f)).

Service as an ordinary member is not service in the civil service of the State: Sch 1 para 1(10). The Secretary of State may designate one of the ordinary members of the Commission to be the deputy chair (Sch 1 para 3(1)), who is to act as chair in the event of a vacancy in the office of chair, if the chair is unable to act, and in such other circumstances as the Commission may determine (see Sch 1 para 3(2)). The deputy chair may at any time resign as deputy chair by notice to the Secretary of State: Sch 1 para 3(3).

6   Local Democracy, Economic Development and Construction Act 2009 Sch 1 para 4.

7 See the Local Democracy, Economic Development and Construction Act 2009 Sch 1 para 7(1). However, a person may not be appointed as chief executive of the Commission if, by virtue of Sch 1 para 1(3)(a)–(d) (see note 5), that person may not be appointed as an ordinary member of the Commission (Sch 1 para 7(2)(a)); and a person may not be appointed as any other member of staff of the Commission if, by virtue of Sch 1 para 1(3)(b)–(d) (see note 5), that person may not be appointed as an ordinary member of the Commission (Sch 1 para 7(2)(b)). Subject to the provisions of Sch 1 para 7(5)–(8), employees of the Commission must be appointed on such terms and conditions (including terms and conditions as to remuneration) as the Commission may determine: see Sch 1 para 7(4). The appointment of any member of staff of the Commission terminates (if that person is the chief executive of the Commission) on the occurrence of such an event as is mentioned in any of Sch 1 para 1(6)(a)–(e) (see note 5) (Sch 1 para 7(5)(a)); and, in any other case, on the occurrence of such an event as is mentioned in any of Sch 1 para 1(6)(a)–(d) (see note 5) (Sch 1 para 7(5)(b)). For the purposes of determinations Sch 1 para 7(4), the Commission must have regard to the desirability of keeping the remuneration and other terms or conditions of employment of its employees broadly in line with those applying to persons in the civil service of the State: Sch 1 para 7(6). Although service as chief executive or other employee of the Commission is not service in the civil service of the State (see Sch 1 para 7(3)), service as an employee of the Commission is included in the kinds of employment to which a scheme under the Superannuation Act 1972 s 1 (see CONSTITUTIONAL LAW AND HUMAN RIGHTS vol 8(2) (Reissue) PARA 567) can apply (see the Local Democracy, Economic Development and Construction Act 2009 Sch 1 para 7(7); and see the Superannuation Act 1972 s 1, Sch 1 (amended by the Local Democracy, Economic Development and Construction Act 2009 Sch 1 para 7(7))). The Commission must pay to the Minister for the Civil Service, at such times as the Minister may direct, such sums as the Minister may determine in respect of any increase attributable to Sch 1 para 7(7) in the sums payable out of money provided by Parliament under the Superannuation Act 1972: Local Democracy, Economic Development and Construction Act 2009 Sch 1 para 7(8). As to the Minister for the Civil Service see CONSTITUTIONAL LAW AND HUMAN RIGHTS vol 8(2) (Reissue) PARA 427.

The Superannuation Act 1972 s 1(2) (delegation of functions relating to civil service superannuation schemes by the Minister for the Civil Service to another officer of the Crown etc: see CONSTITUTIONAL LAW AND HUMAN RIGHTS vol 8(2) (Reissue) PARA 567) has effect as if the reference to an officer of the Crown other than a minister included the Commission's chief executive: Local Democracy, Economic Development and Construction Act 2009 Sch 1 para 8(1). Any administration function so conferred on the Commission's chief executive, as it has effect in accordance with Sch 1 para 8(1), may be exercised by (or by employees of) such person as may be authorised in that behalf by the Commission's chief executive: Sch 1 para 8(2). For these purposes, an 'administration function' is a function of administering schemes made under the Superannuation Act 1972 s 1, and schemes for the time being in force: see the Local Democracy, Economic Development and Construction Act 2009 Sch 1 para 8(3). An authorisation given by virtue of Sch 1 para 8(2) may authorise the exercise of an administration function: (1) either wholly or to such extent as may be specified in the authorisation (Sch 1 para 8(4)(a)); (2) either generally or in such cases as may be so specified (Sch 1 para 8(4)(b)); and (3) either unconditionally or subject to the fulfilment of such conditions as may be so specified (Sch 1 para 8(4)(c)). Such an authorisation is to be treated for all purposes as if it were given by virtue of an order under the Deregulation and Contracting Out Act 1994 s 69 (contracting out of functions of ministers and office-holders: see CONSTITUTIONAL LAW AND HUMAN RIGHTS vol 8(2) (Reissue) PARA 364) and may be revoked at any time by the Commission (as well as by the chief executive): see the Local Democracy, Economic Development and Construction Act 2009 Sch 1 para 8(5).

8 Local Democracy, Economic Development and Construction Act 2009 Sch 1 para 5(1). As to membership of such a committee see note 9.

9 Local Democracy, Economic Development and Construction Act 2009 Sch 1 para 5(2). Only a member of the Commission may be a member of one of its committees or sub-committees: Sch 1 para 5(3).

10 Ie subject to the Local Democracy, Economic Development and Construction Act 2009 Sch 1: see Sch 1 para 6(1).

11 Local Democracy, Economic Development and Construction Act 2009 Sch 1 para 6(1).

12 See the Local Democracy, Economic Development and Construction Act 2009 Sch 1 para 6(2).

13 Local Democracy, Economic Development and Construction Act 2009 Sch 1 para 9(1). This provision does not apply, however, to any function of making an order by statutory instrument: Sch 1 para 9(2).

14 Local Democracy, Economic Development and Construction Act 2009 Sch 1 para 9(3).

15 Local Democracy, Economic Development and Construction Act 2009 Sch 1 para 9(4).

16 Local Democracy, Economic Development and Construction Act 2009 Sch 1 para 9(5).

17 The financial year of the Commission is the period of 12 months ending on 31 March: see the Local Democracy, Economic Development and Construction Act 2009 Sch 1 para 10. As to the provision that is made for funding of the Commission's expenditure, including its duty to prepare, and submit to the Speaker's Committee, an estimate of its income and expenditure, see Sch 1 para 11; as to the Commission's duty to prepare a plan setting out its aims and objectives for the period of five years beginning with the financial year to which the estimate relates, and estimated requirements for resources during that five-year period, see Sch 1 para 12; as to annual examinations of the Commission carried out by the Comptroller and Auditor General see Sch 1 para 13; and as to accounts and audit see Sch 1 paras 14–16. As to the Comptroller and Auditor General see CONSTITUTIONAL LAW AND HUMAN RIGHTS vol 8(2) (Reissue) PARAS 724–726. The Local Government Boundary Commission for England is subject also to investigation by the Parliamentary Commissioner for Administration: see the Parliamentary Commissioner Act 1967 s 4, Sch 2; and ADMINISTRATIVE LAW vol 1(1) (2001 Reissue) PARA 41 et seq.

18 Local Democracy, Economic Development and Construction Act 2009 Sch 1 para 17(1).

19 Local Democracy, Economic Development and Construction Act 2009 Sch 1 para 17(2).

20 Local Democracy, Economic Development and Construction Act 2009 Sch 1 para 18(1).

21 Local Democracy, Economic Development and Construction Act 2009 Sch 1 para 18(2).

  The Local Government Boundary Commission for England is a public authority for the purposes of the Freedom of Information Act 2000 (see s 3, Sch I Pt VI: and CONFIDENCE AND DATA PROTECTION vol 8(1) (2003 Reissue) PARA 583 et seq); and the administrative and departmental records of the Local Government Boundary Commission for England are public records as defined for the purposes of the Public Records Act 1958 (see s 10, Sch 1 para 3, Table Pt II; and CONSTITUTIONAL LAW AND HUMAN RIGHTS vol 8(2) (Reissue) PARA 835).

72. The Local Democracy and Boundary Commission for Wales. The Local Government Boundary Commission for Wales was established under the Local Government Act 1972[1] with the functions of carrying out reviews[2] and of making proposals for changes in local government areas in Wales[3]. The body corporate called the Local Government Boundary Commission for Wales was continued in existence by the Local Government (Democracy) (Wales) Act 2013 but it is renamed, and is now known as, the Local Democracy and Boundary Commission for Wales (the 'Welsh Commission')[4].

The Welsh Commission consists of a member to chair the Commission (the 'chairing member'), a member to act as deputy to the chairing member, and not more than three other members[5]. The members of the Welsh Commission must be appointed by the Welsh Ministers[6], on such terms and conditions as the Welsh Ministers may determine (including conditions as to remuneration, allowances and expenses)[7]; and such members hold and vacate office in accordance with the terms and conditions of their respective appointments[8]. The Commission must employ a chief executive[9], who must be appointed by the Welsh Ministers on such terms and conditions as they may determine (including conditions as to remuneration, pension, allowances and expenses)[10]. The Commission may employ staff[11], on terms and conditions determined by the Commission (including conditions as to remuneration, pension, allowances and expenses)[12]; and the Commission may appoint a person (an 'expert') to assist it in the exercise of its functions[13] (so long as the Commission is satisfied that the expert has knowledge, experience or expertise relevant to the exercise of its functions)[14]. The Commission also may appoint a person (an 'assistant commissioner') to whom it may delegate functions[15].

The Commission may do anything which is calculated to facilitate, or is conducive or incidental to, the exercise of its functions[16], except borrow money, acquire land or other property without the consent of the Welsh Ministers, or form and promote companies[17]. The Commission must comply with any direction (general or specific) given to it by the Welsh Ministers[18], and, no later than 30 November after the end of each financial year, the Commission must submit a report to the Welsh Ministers on the discharge of its functions[19].

At any meeting of the Welsh Commission, the quorum is three[20], but the Commission may otherwise regulate its own procedure[21]. The validity of anything done by the Commission is not affected by any defect in the appointment of a member[22]. The Commission may have a seal[23], and a document purporting to be duly executed under the seal of the Commission, or signed on its behalf by the chief executive or another member of staff authorised to do so, is to be received in evidence and taken to be so executed or signed unless the contrary is proved[24]. Provision is made for the Welsh Ministers to pay grants to the Commission of such amounts as they may determine, and subject to any conditions specified by the Welsh Ministers[25]. The Welsh Ministers must designate a person to act as the Commission's accounting officer[26].

It is the duty of the Local Democracy and Boundary Commission for Wales, for the purpose of considering whether it is appropriate to make or recommend changes in the arrangements for local government in Wales[27], to monitor the areas and electoral arrangements relevant to local government in Wales[28]. In pursuance of that duty, the Commission must carry out such reviews[29] as are required under the Local Government (Democracy) (Wales) Act 2013, or under any other enactment, as may be directed by the Welsh Ministers, or as it otherwise considers appropriate[30].

1   See the Local Government Act 1972 s 53(1); and LOCAL GOVERNMENT vol 69 (2009) PARA 77.
2   See LOCAL GOVERNMENT vol 69 (2009) PARA 79 et seq.
3   See LOCAL GOVERNMENT vol 69 (2009) PARA 78. As to the meaning of 'local government area' in relation to Wales see LOCAL GOVERNMENT vol 69 (2009) PARA 22. As to the meaning of 'Wales' see PARA 1 note 1.
4   See the Local Government (Democracy) (Wales) Act 2013 s 2. The Commission is not to be regarded as a servant or agent of the Crown or as enjoying any status, immunity or privilege of the Crown: s 3(1). Nor is the Commission's property to be regarded as property of, or property held on behalf of, the Crown: s 3(2).
5   Local Government (Democracy) (Wales) Act 2013 s 4(1).
6   As to the Welsh Ministers see PARA 2; and see LOCAL GOVERNMENT vol 69 (2009) PARA 97.
7   Local Government (Democracy) (Wales) Act 2013 s 4(2). The Welsh Ministers may not, however, appoint a person who is a member of Parliament, a member of the National Assembly for Wales, a member of a local authority in Wales, an officer of a local authority in Wales, a member of a National Park authority for a National Park in Wales, a police and crime commissioner for a police area in Wales; or a member of the Commission's staff: see s 4(3). 'Local authority' means a principal council or a community council; and 'principal council' means a county council or a county borough council in Wales: see s 72(1). As to the council of a county or county borough in Wales see LOCAL GOVERNMENT vol 69 (2009) PARA 37 et seq; and as to communities and their councils see LOCAL GOVERNMENT vol 69 (2009) PARA 41 et seq.
8   See the Local Government (Democracy) (Wales) Act 2013 s 5.
9   See the Local Government (Democracy) (Wales) Act 2013 s 8(1).
10 See the Local Government (Democracy) (Wales) Act 2013 s 8(2). Before appointing a chief executive the Welsh Ministers must consult the Commission: s 8(3).
11 See the Local Government (Democracy) (Wales) Act 2013 s 9(1).
12 See the Local Government (Democracy) (Wales) Act 2013 s 9(2). The Commission must consult the Welsh Ministers before determining the amounts payable to its staff in respect of remuneration, pensions, allowances and expenses: s 9(3).
13 See the Local Government (Democracy) (Wales) Act 2013 s 10(1). Before appointing an expert the Commission must consult the Welsh Ministers: s 10(2). The Commission may pay the expert such remuneration, allowances or expenses as it may determine (s 10(4)); but the Commission must consult the Welsh Ministers before determining the remuneration or allowances payable to an expert (s 10(5)).
14 See the Local Government (Democracy) (Wales) Act 2013 s 10(3).

15 See the Local Government (Democracy) (Wales) Act 2013 s 11(1). The Commission may delegate to one or more of its members or an assistant commissioner such of its functions under Pt 3 Chs 2–4 (ss 23–36) and Pt 3 Chs 6–7 (ss 45–49) (functions relating to the conduct of reviews of local government or local inquiries) as it may determine to the extent so delegated: s 13(1). This power does not, however, affect the Commission's responsibility for exercise of delegated functions, or its ability to exercise delegated functions: see s 13(2).

The Commission may not appoint an assistant commissioner who is a member of Parliament, a member of the National Assembly for Wales, a member of a local authority in Wales, an officer of a local authority in Wales, a member of a National Park authority for a National Park in Wales, a police and crime commissioner for a police area in Wales; or a member of the Commission's staff: see s 11(2). Before appointing an assistant commissioner the Commission must consult the Welsh Ministers: s 11(3). The Commission may pay an assistant commissioner such remuneration, allowances or expenses as it may determine (s 11(4)); but the Commission must consult the Welsh Ministers before determining the remuneration or allowances payable to an assistant commissioner (s 11(5)).

16 See the Local Government (Democracy) (Wales) Act 2013 s 12(1).

17 See the Local Government (Democracy) (Wales) Act 2013 s 12(2).

18 Local Government (Democracy) (Wales) Act 2013 s 14(1). A direction given by the Welsh Ministers under the Local Government (Democracy) (Wales) Act 2013 may be varied or revoked by a subsequent direction: s 14(2).

19 See the Local Government (Democracy) (Wales) Act 2013 s 20.

20 See the Local Government (Democracy) (Wales) Act 2013 s 6(1).

21 See the Local Government (Democracy) (Wales) Act 2013 s 6(2).

22 Local Government (Democracy) (Wales) Act 2013 s 6(3).

23 See the Local Government (Democracy) (Wales) Act 2013 s 7(1). The application of the seal is authenticated by the signature of a member of the Commission or of another person authorised by the Commission for that purpose: s 7(2).

24 See the Local Government (Democracy) (Wales) Act 2013 s 7(3).

25 See the Local Government (Democracy) (Wales) Act 2013 s 15.

26 See the Local Government (Democracy) (Wales) Act 2013 s 16. The Commission must establish an audit committee (see ss 17, 18); and must for each financial year keep proper accounts and proper records in relation to them, and prepare a statement of accounts (see s 19).

27 Ie for the purpose of considering whether it is appropriate to make or recommend changes under the Local Government (Democracy) (Wales) Act 2013 Pt 3 (ss 21–49) (see PARA 87 et seq; and see LOCAL GOVERNMENT): see s 21(1).

28 Local Government (Democracy) (Wales) Act 2013 s 21(1). For these purposes, 'local government area' means a principal area or a community, and 'principal area' means a county or a county borough in Wales: see s 72(1).

For the purposes of the Local Government (Democracy) (Wales) Act 2013 Pt 3, a reference to the electoral arrangements of a principal area is a reference to:

(1)   the number of members of the council for the principal area (s 29(9)(a));

(2)   the number, type and boundaries of the electoral wards into which the principal area is for the time being divided for the purpose of the election of members (s 29(9)(b));

(3)   the number of members to be elected for any electoral ward in the principal area (s 29(9)(c)); and

(4)   the name of any electoral ward (s 29(9)(d)).

For the purposes of head (2) above, a reference to the type of an electoral ward is a reference to whether the ward is a single or multiple member ward (s 29(10)), where 'electoral ward' means any area for which members are elected to a local authority, 'multiple member ward' means an electoral ward in respect of which a specified number (greater than one) of members are to be elected for that ward, and 'single member ward' means an electoral ward in respect of which only one member is to be elected (s 29(11)). A reference to the electoral arrangements of a community is a reference to:

(a)   the number of members of the council for the community (s 31(7)(a));

(b)   its division into wards (if appropriate) for the purposes of the election of councillors (s 31(7)(b));

(c)   the number and boundaries of any wards (s 31(7)(c));

(d)   the number of members to be elected for any ward (s 31(7)(d));

(e)   the name of any ward (s 31(7)(e)).

As to the election of councillors see PARA 197 et seq; and see LOCAL GOVERNMENT vol 69 (2009) PARA 126 et seq.

29 Ie under the Local Government (Democracy) (Wales) Act 2013 Pt 3: see s 21(2).

30 Local Government (Democracy) (Wales) Act 2013 s 21(2). In carrying out its duties under Pt 3 (and in conducting any review), the Commission must seek to ensure effective and convenient local government: s 21(3).

3. ESTABLISHMENT AND REVIEW OF ELECTORAL BOUNDARIES

(1) THE ESTABLISHMENT OF ELECTORAL BOUNDARIES

73. Establishment of constituencies for the purpose of parliamentary elections. There are for the purpose of parliamentary elections[1] county and borough constituencies[2] which are described in Orders in Council under the Parliamentary Constituencies Act 1986[3], each returning a single member[4].

Provision exists for the continuous review of the distribution of seats by four Boundary Commissions[5] and for machinery to give effect to the recommendations of these Commissions with or without modifications[6].

1 As to the meaning of 'parliamentary election' see PARA 9.
2 Ie, in Scotland, the county and burgh constituencies: see the Parliamentary Constituencies Act 1986 s 1(1). As to the meaning of 'constituency' for these purposes see PARA 9. Constituencies are designated as either county or borough constituencies in the Orders in Council by which they are constituted (see note 4). See further PARLIAMENT vol 78 (2010) PARAS 892–893. The election agent in a county constituency may appoint a sub-agent to represent him in a particular part of that constituency (see PARA 233); and a candidate in a county constituency has a higher limit of election expenses (ie by virtue of a higher additional rate for every entry in the register of electors) under the Representation of the People Act 1983 s 76(2) (see PARA 273).
3 As to the making of Orders in Council under the Parliamentary Constituencies Act 1986 see PARA 78 note 15. Such an order under the Parliamentary Constituencies Act 1986 gives effect, whether with or without modifications, to the recommendations contained in the report of a Boundary Commission: see PARA 78 et seq. Under the Representation of the People Act 1948 Sch 1 (as originally enacted; now repealed), England was allotted 215 county constituencies and 291 borough constituencies, Wales 26 county constituencies and 10 borough constituencies, Scotland 39 county constituencies and 32 burgh constituencies and Northern Ireland 8 county constituencies and 4 borough constituencies. As to the rules for apportioning constituencies in subsequent redistributions see PARA 79 et seq.
4 Parliamentary Constituencies Act 1986 s 1(1).
    The Order in Council currently in force in relation to England is the Parliamentary Constituencies (England) Order 2007, SI 2007/1681 (amended by SI 2009/698). The Order in Council currently in force in relation to Wales is the Parliamentary Constituencies and Assembly Electoral Regions (Wales) Order 2006, SI 2006/1041 (amended by SI 2008/1791; SI 2011/2987). The Parliamentary Voting System and Constituencies Act 2011 has removed the link between Westminster constituencies and National Assembly for Wales constituencies: see PARA 76.
5 As to the permanent Boundary Commissions see PARA 68 et seq. As to the redistribution of seats pursuant to reports made by the Boundary Commissions see PARA 78 et seq.
6 As to the procedure of the Boundary Commissions for these purposes see PARA 82.

74. Establishment of electoral areas for the purpose of local government elections. Councillors for a principal area[1] are elected by the local government electors[2] for that area in accordance with the Local Government Act 1972 and Part I of the Representation of the People Act 1983[3].

For the purposes of the election of councillors in England[4]:

(1)   every non-metropolitan county[5] is divided into electoral divisions[6];
(2)   every metropolitan district[7] is divided into wards[8]; and
(3)   every non-metropolitan district[9] is divided into wards[10].

For the purpose of the election of councillors in Wales[11], every principal area is divided into electoral divisions[12]. In Wales, there must be a separate election for each electoral division[13]; in England, there must be a separate election for each electoral division or ward[14].

For the purposes of the election of London borough councillors[15], every London borough is divided into wards[16], and there must be a separate election for each ward[17].

A local authority in England[18] may, by resolution[19], change the name of any of the authority's electoral areas[20].

Parish or community councillors are elected by the local government electors for the parish[21] or community[22] in accordance with the Local Government Act 1972 and Part I of the Representation of the People Act 1983[23]. Parish councillors must be elected additionally in accordance with relevant electoral arrangements[24].

In England, where a parish is not divided into parish wards, there must be one election of parish councillors for the whole parish[25] but, where a parish is divided into parish wards, there must be a separate election of parish councillors for each ward[26]. In Wales, where a community is not divided into community wards, there must be one election of community councillors for the whole community[27] but, where a community is divided into community wards, there must be a separate election of community councillors for each ward[28]. If the parish has the style of community, the councillors must have the style of 'councillors of the community council'[29]; if the parish has the style of neighbourhood, the councillors must have the style of 'councillors of the neighbourhood council'[30]; if the parish has the style of village, the councillors must have the style of 'councillors of the village council'[31]; and if parishes which have an alternative style are grouped under a common parish council, the provisions as to styling[32] apply to the councillors of that council as the appropriate provision would apply in the case of the council of an individual parish[33].

Provision is made for the continuous review of local government electoral areas in England and Wales[34].

1   As to the meaning of 'principal area' see LOCAL GOVERNMENT vol 69 (2009) PARA 23.
2   For the purposes of the Local Government Act 1972, 'local government elector' means a person registered as a local government elector in the register of electors in accordance with the provisions of the Representation of the People Acts: see the Local Government Act 1972 s 270(1); and LOCAL GOVERNMENT vol 69 (2009) PARA 127. As to the meaning of 'the Representation of the People Acts' see PARA 3 note 1. As to the registration of parliamentary or local government electors see PARA 113 et seq.
3   See the Local Government Act 1972 ss 6(1), 25(1) (both amended by the Representation of the People Act 1983 s 206, Sch 8 para 12). See also LOCAL GOVERNMENT vol 69 (2009) PARA 126 et seq.
4   As to the meaning of 'England' see PARA 1 note 1. The process by which the structure and boundaries of local government are determined in England has been reformed significantly by the Local Government and Public Involvement in Health Act 2007 Pt 1 Ch 1 (ss 1–23) (ie ss 1–7 (change to single tier of local government in England: see LOCAL GOVERNMENT vol 69 (2009) PARAS 57–61), ss 8–10 (boundary change in England: see LOCAL GOVERNMENT vol 69 (2009) PARAS 62–64), ss 11–19 (implementation of changes: see LOCAL GOVERNMENT vol 69 (2009) PARAS 64–67), ss 20–23 (supplementary)). In addition, moves to 'whole council' elections are encouraged, along with single member wards: see Pt 2 Ch 1 (ss 31–54) (power of district councils in England to change electoral scheme: see LOCAL GOVERNMENT vol 69 (2009) PARAS 135–139). The Local Government Act 1992 previously provided comprehensive machinery for the re-organisation of local government by the Secretary of State (or Welsh Ministers) (see LOCAL GOVERNMENT vol 69 (2009) PARA 55 et seq) but this has been superseded largely by the Local Democracy, Economic Development and Construction Act 2009 Pt 3 (ss 55–68) (local government boundary and electoral change: see PARA 83; and LOCAL GOVERNMENT).
5   As to the meaning of 'non-metropolitan county' see LOCAL GOVERNMENT vol 69 (2009) PARA 24.
6   Local Government Act 1972 s 6(2)(a) (amended by the Local Government Act 1985 s 102, Sch 16 para 2; the Local Government Act 2000 s 89(4); the Local Government and Public

Involvement in Health Act 2007 s 22, Sch 1 Pt 2 para 11(1), (2); and the Local Democracy, Economic Development and Construction Act 2009 s 67(1), Sch 4 paras 1, 2(1), (2)). The number of councillors returned for the purposes of head (1) in the text is one councillor for each electoral division, subject to the Local Government Act 1972 s 18, Sch 3 para 3 (division of non-metropolitan counties into districts (number of councillors specified by order): see LOCAL GOVERNMENT vol 69 (2009) PARA 126), the Local Government and Public Involvement in Health Act 2007 s 12(4) (order may provide for an electoral division of a non-metropolitan county to return more than one councillor: see LOCAL GOVERNMENT vol 69 (2009) PARA 61), and the Local Democracy, Economic Development and Construction Act 2009 s 56(8) (power to review electoral arrangements, including the number of councillors to be returned by electoral area: see PARA 83; and LOCAL GOVERNMENT): see s 6(2)(a) (as so amended). The provision made by s 6(2)(a) does not apply where those provisions to which it is subject apply instead.

7 As to the meaning of 'metropolitan district' see LOCAL GOVERNMENT vol 69 (2009) PARA 24.

8 Local Government Act 1972 s 6(2)(b) (substituted by the Local Government and Public Involvement in Health Act 2007 s 58(1), (2)). Each ward referred to in head (2) in the text returns such number of councillors as may be provided as mentioned in the Local Government Act 1972 s 6(3): see s 6(2)(b) (as so substituted). Accordingly, that number of councillors may be provided: (1) under or by virtue of the provisions of s 7 (election of county, metropolitan district, and non-metropolitan district councillors: see LOCAL GOVERNMENT vol 69 (2009) PARAS 128–130); (2) by an order under the Local Government Act 1992 Pt II (ss 12–27) (largely repealed) (local government changes for England: see LOCAL GOVERNMENT vol 69 (2009) PARAS 55–56) or the Local Democracy, Economic Development and Construction Act 2009 Pt 3 (local government boundary and electoral change: see PARA 83; and LOCAL GOVERNMENT); (3) by an order under the Local Government and Rating Act 1997 s 14 (repealed); or (4) by an order under Local Government and Public Involvement in Health Act 2007 Pt 1 (structural and boundary change in England: see LOCAL GOVERNMENT vol 69 (2009) PARA 57 et seq): see the Local Government Act 1972 s 6(3) (added by the Local Government and Rating Act 1997 Sch 3 para 5(b); substituted by the Local Government and Public Involvement in Health Act 2007 s 58(1), (3); and amended by the Local Democracy, Economic Development and Construction Act 2009 Sch 4 paras 1, 2(1), (3)).

9 As to the meaning of 'non-metropolitan district' see LOCAL GOVERNMENT vol 69 (2009) PARA 24.

10 Local Government Act 1972 s 6(2)(c) (amended by the Local Government and Rating Act 1997 s 33(1), Sch 3 para 5(a)). The number of councillors referred to in head (3) in the text may be provided as mentioned in the Local Government Act 1972 s 6(3) (see note 8): see s 6(2)(c) (as so amended).

11 As to the meaning of 'Wales' see PARA 1 note 1.

12 Local Government Act 1972 s 25(2) (substituted by the Local Government (Wales) Act 1994 s 4(1); and amended by the Local Government (Democracy) (Wales) Act 2013 s 73(1), Sch 1 para 1(1), (2)). Each electoral division as is mentioned in the text returns such number of councillors as may be provided by order under the Local Government Act 1972 s 37, Sch 5 para 2 (establishment of new principal councils (electoral divisions): see LOCAL GOVERNMENT vol 69 (2009) PARAS 7, 18) or under or by virtue of the provisions of Pt IV (ss 53–78) (changes in local government areas: see LOCAL GOVERNMENT vol 69 (2009) PARA 77 et seq) or the Local Government (Democracy) (Wales) Act 2013 Pt 3 (ss 21–49) (arrangements for local government: see PARA 87 et seq): see the Local Government Act 1972 s 25(2) (as so substituted and amended).

13 See the Local Government Act 1972 s 25(3) (added by the Local Government (Wales) Act 1994 s 4(1)).

14 See the Local Government Act 1972 s 6(2).

15 The provision made by the Local Government Act 1972 ss 2–7 (principal councils in England) do not apply to London borough councils but the provisions of s 8(1), Sch 2 (see the text and notes 16–17) have effect in relation to them instead: see s 8(1) (amended by the Local Government Act 1985 s 102, Sch 17). As to London boroughs and London borough councils generally, including the election of London borough councillors, see LONDON GOVERNMENT vol 71 (2013) PARA 20 et seq. As to the City of London see PARA 33; and LONDON GOVERNMENT vol 71 (2013) PARA 16 et seq.

16 See the Local Government Act 1972 Sch 2 para 7(1) (amended by the Local Government Act 1985 Sch 17; the Local Government Act 1992 s 27, Sch 3 para 19; the Local Government and Public Involvement in Health Act 2007 Sch 1 Pt 2 para 11(1), (4); and the Local Democracy, Economic Development and Construction Act 2009 Sch 4 paras 1, 4(1), (2)). Each ward as in mentioned in the text returns such number of councillors as is specified in any order under the Local Government Act 1992 Pt II (largely repealed) (local government changes for

England: see LOCAL GOVERNMENT vol 69 (2009) PARAS 55–56), in any order under the Local Government and Public Involvement in Health Act 2007 Pt 1 (structural and boundary change in England: see LOCAL GOVERNMENT vol 69 (2009) PARA 57 et seq), or in any order under the Local Democracy, Economic Development and Construction Act 2009 s 59 (implementation of recommendations following review of electoral areas by Local Government Boundary Commission for England: see PARA 83; and LOCAL GOVERNMENT): see the Local Government Act 1972 Sch 2 para 7(1) (as so amended).

Until provision is made as mentioned in Sch 2 para 7(1) by an order referred to therein, the number of councillors for each ward in a London borough is that specified in the charter for the borough or in an order under the London Government Act 1963 s 1(4), Sch 1 Pt III (repealed) amending the charter, which was in force on the date of the coming into operation of the Local Government Act 1972 Pt IV (ss 53–78) (largely repealed): Sch 2 para 7(2) (amended by the Local Democracy, Economic Development and Construction Act 2009 Sch 4 paras 1, 4(1), (3)).

17 See the Local Government Act 1972 Sch 2 para 7(1) (as amended: see note 16). As to the rules to be observed in relation to the electoral arrangements of a London borough, and in relation to the electoral arrangements of London Assembly constituencies, see PARA 86.

18 For these purposes 'local authority' means a county council in England, a district council in England or a London borough council: see the Local Government and Public Involvement in Health Act 2007 s 59(10).

19 A local authority must comply with the Local Government and Public Involvement in Health Act 2007 s 59(3)–(5) in passing a resolution to change the name of an electoral area: s 59(2). An 'electoral area', in relation to a local authority, means any area for which councillors are elected to the authority: see s 59(10).

Accordingly, the local authority must not pass the resolution unless it has taken reasonable steps to consult such persons as it considers appropriate on the proposed name: s 59(3). The resolution must be passed at a meeting which is specially convened for the purpose of deciding the resolution with notice of the object, and by a majority of at least two thirds of the members (including, in a case where the council is operating a mayor and cabinet executive, the elected mayor of the council) voting on it: see s 59(4), (9). If the name of the electoral area is protected, the resolution may not be passed unless the Local Government Boundary Commission has first agreed to the proposed change: s 59(5) (s 59(5)–(8) amended by the Local Democracy, Economic Development and Construction Act 2009 Sch 4 paras 11, 30(1)–(3)). For these purposes, the name of an electoral area is 'protected' if the name was given to the electoral area by or in pursuance of an order under the Local Government Act 1992 s 17 (recommendations of Local Government Commission:see LOCAL GOVERNMENT vol 69 (2009) PARA 56), an order under the Local Government and Rating Act 1997 s 14 (repealed), or an order under the Local Democracy, Economic Development and Construction Act 2009 s 59 (implementation of recommendations following review of electoral areas by Local Government Boundary Commission for England: see PARA 83; and LOCAL GOVERNMENT), and if that order was made during the period of five years ending with the day on which a resolution to change the name is to be passed: see the Local Government and Public Involvement in Health Act 2007 s 59(8) (as so amended). As to the establishment and constitution of the Local Government Boundary Commission for England see PARA 71.

20 See the Local Government and Public Involvement in Health Act 2007 s 59(1). As soon as practicable after a resolution is passed, the local authority must give notice of the change of name to all of the following: (1) the Local Government Boundary Commission; (2) the Boundary Commission for England; (3) the Office for National Statistics; (4) the Director General of the Ordnance Survey; (5) if the local authority is a county council, the district council (if any) within whose area the electoral area lies; (6) if the local authority is a district council, the county council (if any) within whose area the electoral area lies: see s 59(6) (as amended: see note 19). The change of name does not take effect until the Local Government Boundary Commission has been given notice of the change: s 59(7) (as so amended). As to the Local Government Boundary Commission for England see PARA 71. As to the Office for National Statistics see REGISTRATION CONCERNING THE INDIVIDUAL vol 88 (2012) PARA 334. As to the Director General of the Ordnance Survey see NATIONAL CULTURAL HERITAGE vol 77 (2010) PARA 1110.

21 As to parishes see LOCAL GOVERNMENT vol 69 (2009) PARA 27 et seq.

22 As to communities see LOCAL GOVERNMENT vol 69 (2009) PARA 41 et seq.

23 See the Local Government Act 1972 ss 16(2), 35(1) (ss 16(2), 35(1) amended by the Representation of the People Act 1983 Sch 8 para 12; the Local Government Act 1972 s 16(2) further amended, s 16(2A), (2B) added, by the Local Government and Public Involvement in Health Act 2007 s 101, Sch 5 paras 1, 6(1), (3), (4)).

24 See the Local Government Act 1972 s 16(2) (as amended: see note 23). In their application to the election of parish councillors, the Local Government Act 1972 and the Representation of the People Act 1983 Pt I are subject to the relevant electoral arrangements that apply to the election: Local Government Act 1972 s 16(2A) (as added: see note 23). For these purposes, 'relevant electoral arrangements' means any arrangements about the election of councillors that are made in, or applicable by virtue of, provision made by virtue of the Local Government and Public Involvement in Health Act 2007 s 245(6)(b) (transitional, saving or transitory provision), and any electoral arrangements applicable to the council by virtue of an order under s 7 (implementation of proposals from the Local Government Boundary Commission for England for change to single tier of local government: see LOCAL GOVERNMENT vol 69 (2009) PARA 61), an order under s 10 (implementation of recommendation from the Local Government Boundary Commission for England for boundary change: see LOCAL GOVERNMENT vol 69 (2009) PARA 64) or an order under s 86 (reorganisation of community governance: see LOCAL GOVERNMENT vol 69 (2009) PARA 69): see the Local Government Act 1972 s 16(2B) (as so added).

25 Local Government Act 1972 s 16(4).
26 Local Government Act 1972 s 16(5).
27 Local Government Act 1972 s 35(3).
28 Local Government Act 1972 s 35(4).
29 Local Government Act 1972 s 16(6) (s 16(6)–(9) added by the Local Government and Public Involvement in Health Act 2007 s 75(1), (7)).
30 Local Government Act 1972 s 16(7) (as added: see note 29).
31 Local Government Act 1972 s 16(8) (as added: see note 29).
32 Ie the Local Government Act 1972 s 16(6), (7) or (8) (see the text and notes 29–31), as appropriate: see s 16(9) (as added: see note 29).
33 Local Government Act 1972 s 16(9) (as added: see note 29).
34 See PARA 83 et seq.

75. Establishment of London Assembly constituencies. For the purpose of elections to the London Assembly[1], there are Assembly constituencies, each of which has one constituency member[2]. The Assembly constituencies are the areas, and are to be known by the names, specified in an order made by statutory instrument by the Local Government Boundary Commission for England[3].

Provision is made for the continuous review of London Assembly constituencies[4].

1 As to elections of the members of the London Assembly see PARA 199 et seq; and LONDON GOVERNMENT vol 71 (2013) PARA 76 et seq.
2 See the Greater London Authority Act 1999 s 2(3); and LONDON GOVERNMENT vol 71 (2013) PARA 70. As to the rules to be observed in relation to the electoral arrangements of London Assembly constituencies see LONDON GOVERNMENT vol 71 (2013) PARA 80.
    The Assembly consists of 25 members, of whom 14 are 'constituency members', there being one constituency member for each Assembly constituency (and 11 are members for the whole of Greater London, known as 'London members'): see s 2(2); and LONDON GOVERNMENT vol 71 (2013) PARA 70.
3 See the Greater London Authority Act 1999 s 2(4); and LONDON GOVERNMENT vol 71 (2013) PARA 80. As to the establishment and constitution of the Local Government Boundary Commission for England see PARA 71.
4 See PARA 86.

76. Establishment of constituencies and electoral regions for the purpose of elections to the National Assembly for Wales. The National Assembly for Wales[1] consists of[2]:

(1)   one member for each Assembly constituency ('Assembly constituency members')[3]; and

(2)   members for each Assembly electoral region ('Assembly regional members')[4].

Currently, the Assembly constituencies are those specified as parliamentary constituencies in Wales[5]; there are five Assembly electoral regions[6], and for each Assembly electoral region there are four Assembly seats[7].

1   As to the National Assembly for Wales see CONSTITUTIONAL LAW AND HUMAN RIGHTS.
2   See the Government of Wales Act 2006 s 1(2).
3   Government of Wales Act 2006 s 1(2)(a).
4   Government of Wales Act 2006 s 1(2)(b).
5   See the Government of Wales Act 2006 s 2(1) (substituted by the Parliamentary Voting System
    and Constituencies Act 2011 s 13(1)). Accordingly, the Assembly constituencies are the
    constituencies specified in the Parliamentary Constituencies and Assembly Electoral Regions
    (Wales) Order 2006, SI 2006/1041 (see PARA 73), as amended by:
       (1)   the Parliamentary Constituencies and Assembly Electoral Regions (Wales)
             (Amendment) Order 2008, SI 2008/1791 (Government of Wales Act 2006 s 2(1)(a) (as
             so substituted)); and
       (2)   any Order in Council under the Parliamentary Constituencies Act 1986 giving effect
             (with or without modifications) to a report falling within the Parliamentary Voting
             System and Constituencies Act 2011 s 13(3), (4) (Government of Wales Act 2006
             s 2(1)(b) (as so substituted)).
    Further to head (2) above, transitional provisions applied to reports by the Boundary
    Commission for Wales under the Parliamentary Constituencies Act 1986 relating to interim
    reviews of constituencies that had not been implemented at 16 February 2011 (ie at the time
    when the Parliamentary Voting System and Constituencies Act 2011 Pt 2 (ss 10–14)
    (parliamentary constituencies) came into force): see s 13(3)–(8). Because Assembly
    constituencies now are as specified in heads (1) and (2) above, any future changes to
    Parliamentary constituencies made under the rules introduced by the Parliamentary Voting
    System and Constituencies Act 2011 ss 10–12 (see PARAS 78–82) will not affect Assembly
    constituencies, whose organisation, at the date at which this volume states the law, has been
    frozen pending further legislation and whose review will be subject to a mechanism also under
    new legislation that is yet to be put in place.
6   Government of Wales Act 2006 s 2(2). The Assembly electoral regions are as specified in the
    Parliamentary Constituencies and Assembly Electoral Regions (Wales) Order 2006,
    SI 2006/1041 (see PARA 73): Government of Wales Act 2006 s 2(3).
7   Government of Wales Act 2006 s 2(4).

77.   Establishment of electoral regions for the purpose of European parliamentary elections. There are 73 members of the European Parliament ('MEPs') elected for the United Kingdom[1]. For the purposes of electing those MEPs[2]:

(1)   the area of England[3] and Gibraltar[4] is divided into nine specified electoral regions[5]; and

(2)   Scotland, Wales and Northern Ireland are each single electoral regions[6].

Provision is made for the Secretary of State by notice to require the Electoral Commission to make a recommendation to him as to the distribution of MEPs between the electoral regions[7].

1   See the European Parliamentary Elections Act 2002 s 1(1) (s 1 substituted by the European
    Parliament (Representation) Act 2003 s 1; the European Parliamentary Elections Act 2002 s 1(1)
    amended by the European Union Act 2011 s 16(1), (2)). As to the meaning of 'United Kingdom'
    see PARA 1 note 1.
2   See the European Parliamentary Elections Act 2002 s 1(2) (as substituted: see note 1).
3   As to the meaning of 'England' see PARA 1 note 1.
4   In Application 24833/94 *Matthews v United Kingdom* (1999) 28 EHRR 361, ECtHR, it was
    held that the United Kingdom was responsible for securing for the citizens of Gibraltar the right
    to free elections to the European Parliament, as that body forms part of Gibraltar's legislature.
    Accordingly, Gibraltar is combined with an existing electoral region in England and Wales to
    form a new electoral region (the 'combined region') for the purposes of European parliamentary
    elections taking place after 1 April 2004 (see the European Parliament (Representation)
    Act 2003 s 9); and the provisions of the European Parliamentary Elections Act 2002, other than
    Sch 3 and Sch 4, extend to Gibraltar, accordingly (European Parliament (Representation)
    Act 2003 s 19). (The procedure used to establish the combined region was provided by
    ss 10–13. For these purposes, 'combined region' means the electoral region which includes
    Gibraltar; 'electoral region' means an electoral region of the United Kingdom established under
    the European Parliamentary Elections Act 2002 for the purposes of European parliamentary
    elections; and 'existing electoral region' means an electoral region existing immediately before

8 May 2003 (ie immediately before the passing of the European Parliament (Representation) Act 2003): see s 27(1). In exercise of powers conferred by ss 11–13, 23(2), 25(3) and 26, the European Parliamentary Elections (Combined Region and Campaign Expenditure) (United Kingdom and Gibraltar) Order 2004, SI 2004/366, has been made, extending certain provisions to Gibraltar, making consequential amendments, and specifying that the existing electoral region in England and Wales which is to be combined with Gibraltar to form the combined region for the purposes of the European Parliament (Representation) Act 2003 is the South West electoral region (see the European Parliamentary Elections (Combined Region and Campaign Expenditure) (United Kingdom and Gibraltar) Order 2004, SI 2004/366, art 2). As to the establishment of the combined region, and as to electoral registration and voting in Gibraltar, for elections to the European Parliament see the European Parliament (Representation) Act 2003 Pt II (ss 9–24); the European Parliamentary Elections Regulations 2004, SI 2004/293, regs 5, 12, Sch 4; and PARA 100 note 3. As to the constitution of Gibraltar see COMMONWEALTH vol 13 (2009) PARA 859. As to the meaning of 'Wales' see PARA 1 note 1.

5　European Parliamentary Elections Act 2002 s 1(2)(a) (s 1 as substituted (see note 1); s 1(2)(a) amended by SI 2004/366). The nine electoral regions for England and Gibraltar mentioned in head (1) in the text are listed, and the areas they comprise are specified, in the European Parliamentary Elections Act 2002 Sch 1 (amended by the European Parliament (Representation) Act 2003 s 8(1), (3); and by SI 2004/366; SI 2009/837). Currently, the number of MEPs to be elected for each electoral region mentioned in head (1) in the text is as follows: (1) five for the East Midlands region; (2) seven for the Eastern region; (3) eight for the London region; (4) three for the North East region; (5) eight for the North West region; (6) ten for the South East region; (7) six for the South West region; (8) seven for the West Midlands region; and (9) six for the Yorkshire and the Humber region: see the European Parliamentary Elections Act 2002 s 1(3) (s 1 as so substituted; s 1(3) further substituted by SI 2008/1954; and amended by the European Union Act 2011 s 16(1), (3)).

6　European Parliamentary Elections Act 2002 s 1(2)(b) (as substituted: see note 1). Currently, the number of MEPs to be elected for each electoral region mentioned in head (2) in the text is as follows: (1) six for Scotland; (2) four for Wales; and (3) three for Northern Ireland: see s 1(3) (as substituted and amended: see note 5).

7　See PARA 91 et seq.

(2) THE REVIEW OF ELECTORAL BOUNDARIES

(i) Review of Parliamentary Constituencies

A. PERIODICAL REVIEWS AND REPORTS BY THE BOUNDARY COMMISSIONS

78. Reports of the Boundary Commissions.　Each Boundary Commission[1] must keep under review the representation in the House of Commons of the part of the United Kingdom[2] with which it is concerned and must submit periodical reports[3] with respect to the whole of that part to the Secretary of State[4], either:

(1)　showing the constituencies[5] into which it recommends that the part should be divided in order to give effect to the statutory rules for the distribution of seats[6]; or

(2)　stating that, in the Commission's opinion, no alteration is required to be made in respect of that part of the United Kingdom in order to give effect to those rules[7].

The first report of a Boundary Commission with regard to its area as a whole was submitted in November 1954[8]. Subsequent reports must be submitted periodically[9] before 1 October 2018 (but not before 1 September 2018)[10], and before 1 October of every fifth year after that[11]. A failure by a Boundary Commission to submit a report within the time limit which is appropriate to that report is not, however, to be regarded as invalidating the report for the purposes of any enactment[12].

A report of a Boundary Commission under the Parliamentary Constituencies Act 1986 showing the constituencies into which the Commission recommends that any area should be divided must state, as respects each constituency, the name by which the Commission recommends that it should be known and whether the Commission recommends that it should be a county constituency or a borough constituency[13]. As soon as may be after the report has been submitted to the Secretary of State[14], he must lay it before Parliament[15].

1　As to the constitution of the Boundary Commissions see PARA 68 et seq.

2　As to the meaning of 'United Kingdom' see PARA 1 note 1.

3　Ie in accordance with the Parliamentary Constituencies Act 1986 s 3(2) (see the text and notes 9–11): see s 3(1).

4　See the Parliamentary Constituencies Act 1986 s 3(1). As to the Secretary of State see PARA 2. See also PARLIAMENT vol 78 (2010) PARA 896.

5　As to the meaning of 'constituency' for these purposes see PARA 9.

6　Parliamentary Constituencies Act 1986 s 3(1)(a) (s 3(1)(a), (b) amended by the Parliamentary Voting System and Constituencies Act 2011 ss 10(1), (2), 16, Sch 12 Pt 2). The rules referred to in the text are those set out in the Parliamentary Constituencies Act 1986 s 3(6), Sch 2 (see PARAS 79–81), as read with Sch 2 r 7 (see PARA 81 note 6): see s 3(1)(a) (as so amended). In so far as the working out and application of the rules is not within the discretion of the Commission, it is a matter for Parliament to determine; and it is not for the court to determine whether a particular line of approach which commended itself to the commission was the best: *Harper v Secretary of State for the Home Department* [1955] Ch 238, [1955] 1 All ER 331, CA. The question of the competence of the court in the event of a Commission on the face of its report making recommendations in manifest disregard of the rules was left undecided: see *Harper v Secretary of State for the Home Department* at 251 and 338; and see STATUTES AND LEGISLATIVE PROCESS vol 96 (2012) PARa 1051. See also *Hammersmith Corpn v Boundary Commission for England* (1954) Times, 15 December; *R v Boundary Commission for England, ex p Foot, R v Boundary Commission for England, ex p Gateshead Borough Council* [1983] QB 600, [1983] 1 All ER 1099, CA (the Commission was entrusted with a wide discretion, covering a complex field in which there was no objective standard as to the exercise of that discretion, and as long as the Commission acted honestly and in good faith its recommendations could not be challenged).

　　Once a Boundary Commission has decided what constituencies it proposes to recommend in a report under the Parliamentary Constituencies Act 1986 s 3(1)(a), it must take steps to establish an initial consultation period and cause public hearings to be held during the period beginning with the fifth week of the initial consultation period and ending with the tenth week of it: see s 5; and PARA 82.

7　Parliamentary Constituencies Act 1986 s 3(1)(b) (as amended: see note 6). As to the rules referred to in the text see note 6.

8　See *First Periodical Reports of the Boundary Commissions* presented in November 1954 (Cmd 9311) (England), (Cmd 9313) (Wales), (Cmd 9312) (Scotland), (Cmd 9314) (Northern Ireland), submitted under the House of Commons (Redistribution of Seats) Act 1949 s 2(2)(a) (repealed).

9　Ie reports under the Parliamentary Constituencies Act 1986 s 3(1) (see the text and notes 1–7): see s 3(2) (s 3(2) substituted, s 3(2B), (2C) added, by the Parliamentary Voting System and Constituencies Act 2011 s 10(1), (3), (4)).

　　In relation to any report which a Boundary Commission is required by the Parliamentary Constituencies Act 1986 s 3(2) to submit before a particular date but has not yet submitted (a 'pending boundary report'), the Commission must submit to the Speaker of the House of Commons during the January that begins one year and nine months before that date, and during each subsequent January, a report setting out what progress it has made with the preparation of the pending boundary report, with particular reference to the requirement in s 3(2): see s 3(2B) (as so added). On receiving a report under s 3(2B), the Speaker must lay it before Parliament: s 3(2C) (as so added). As to the Speaker of the House of Commons see PARLIAMENT vol 78 (2010) PARA 931 et seq.

10　Parliamentary Constituencies Act 1986 s 3(2)(a) (s 3(2) as substituted (see note 9); s 3(2)(a) amended by the Electoral Registration and Administration Act 2013 s 6(1)). Because the amendment made by s 6(1) postponed the next boundary review until Autumn 2018, no report was submitted to the Secretary of State, as was previously required, in Autumn 2013 (ie before 1 October 2013).

11　Parliamentary Constituencies Act 1986 s 3(2)(b) (s 3(2) as substituted: see note 9).

12　Parliamentary Constituencies Act 1986 s 3(2A) (added by the Boundary Commissions Act 1992 s 2(1), (4)).

13 Parliamentary Constituencies Act 1986 s 3(4). In Scotland, the recommendation will be that the constituency should be either a county constituency or a burgh constituency: see s 3(4). See also PARA 73.

14 Ie a report under the Parliamentary Constituencies Act 1986 s 3(1) (see the text and notes 1–7): see s 3(5) (s 3(5) substituted, s 3(5A)–(5C) added, by the Parliamentary Voting System and Constituencies Act 2011 s 10(1), (6)).

15 Parliamentary Constituencies Act 1986 s 3(5) (as substituted: see note 14). As soon as may be after the submission of all four reports under the Parliamentary Constituencies Act 1986 s 3(1) (see the text and notes 1–7) that are required by s 3(2) (see the text and notes 9–11) to be submitted before a particular date, the Secretary of State must lay before Parliament the draft of an Order in Council for giving effect to the recommendations contained in them: s 3(5A) (as added: see note 14). Where a Boundary Commission has submitted a report under s 3(1), but no draft under s 3(5A) has yet been laid in relation to the report (s 3(5B)(a) (as so added)), where the Commission notifies the Secretary of State that the recommendations contained in the report are to have effect with specified modifications (s 3(5B)(b) (as so added)), and where the Commission submits to the Secretary of State a statement of the reasons for those modifications (s 3(5B)(c) (as so added)), the draft under s 3(5A) must give effect to the recommendations with those modifications (s 3(5B) (as so added)). The provision made by s 3(5A), (5B) does not apply, however, where each of the reports mentioned in s 3(5) states that no alteration is required to be made in respect of the part of the United Kingdom with which the Commission in question is concerned: s 3(5C) (as so added).

The draft of any Order in Council laid before Parliament by the Secretary of State under the Parliamentary Constituencies Act 1986 for giving effect, whether with or without modifications, to the recommendations contained in the report of a Boundary Commission may make provision for any matters which appear to him to be incidental to, or consequential on, the recommendations: s 4(1). Where any such draft gives effect to any such recommendations with modifications, the Secretary of State must lay before Parliament, together with the draft, the statement submitted under s 3(5B)(c) of the reasons for the modifications: s 4(2) (amended by the Parliamentary Voting System and Constituencies Act 2011 s 10(1), (8)). If any such draft is approved by resolution of each House of Parliament, the Secretary of State must submit it to Her Majesty in Council: Parliamentary Constituencies Act 1986 s 4(3). However, if a motion for the approval of any such draft is rejected by either House of Parliament or withdrawn by leave of the House, the Secretary of State may amend the draft and lay the amended draft before Parliament, and if the draft as so amended is approved by resolution of each House of Parliament, the Secretary of State must submit it to Her Majesty in Council: s 4(4). Where the draft of an Order in Council is so submitted to Her Majesty in Council, Her Majesty in Council may make an order in terms of the draft which comes into force on such date as may be specified in the order and has effect notwithstanding anything in any enactment: s 4(5). However, the coming into force of any such order does not affect any parliamentary election or the constitution of the House of Commons until the dissolution of the Parliament then in being: s 4(6) (amended by the Fixed-term Parliaments Act 2011 s 6(3), Schedule para 17). The validity of any Order in Council purporting to be made under the Parliamentary Constituencies Act 1986 and reciting that a draft of the order has been approved by resolution of each House of Parliament must not be called in question in any legal proceedings whatsoever: s 4(7). See also PARLIAMENT vol 78 (2010) PARA 896.

As to orders that have been made under the Parliamentary Constituencies Act 1986 ss 3, 4, see the Parliamentary Constituencies and Assembly Electoral Regions (Wales) Order 2006, SI 2006/1041 (amended by SI 2008/1791; and SI 2011/2987) (implementing the recommendations of the Boundary Commission for Wales showing the parliamentary constituencies into which it recommends that Wales should be divided); and the Parliamentary Constituencies (England) Order 2007, SI 2007/1681 (amended by SI 2009/698) (implementing recommendations of the Boundary Commission for England showing the parliamentary constituencies into which it recommends that England should be divided).

79.   Rules for distribution of seats: number of constituencies.   The number of constituencies[1] in the United Kingdom[2] is to be 600[3].

The Minister[4] must make arrangements[5]:

(1)   for a committee[6] to carry out a review of the effects of this reduction in the number of constituencies[7]; and

(2)   for the findings of the review to be published[8].

Arrangements under head (1) above must be made no earlier than 1 June 2020 and no later than 30 November 2020[9].

1   As to the meaning of 'constituency' for these purposes see PARA 9.
2   As to the meaning of 'United Kingdom' see PARA 1 note 1.
3   Parliamentary Constituencies Act 1986 s 3(6), Sch 2 r 1 (Sch 2 substituted by the Parliamentary Voting System and Constituencies Act 2011 s 11(1)). The general election in 2010 was conducted on the basis that the number of constituencies in the United Kingdom Parliament was 650. As to rules for the distribution of seats, which fix the size of the House of Commons at 600 members, provide for the number of constituencies in each part of the United Kingdom to be determined by reference to the size of the electorate in each part of the UK, and place a limit on the permitted variation in the number of registered electors for a constituency recommended by a Boundary Commission, see PARAS 80, 81.
4   For these purposes, the 'Minister' means the Lord President of the Council or the Secretary of State: Parliamentary Voting System and Constituencies Act 2011 s 14(4). As to the Secretary of State and the Lord President of the Council see PARA 2.
5   See the Parliamentary Voting System and Constituencies Act 2011 s 14(1).
6   A majority of the members of the committee must be members of the House of Commons: Parliamentary Voting System and Constituencies Act 2011 s 14(2).
7   Parliamentary Voting System and Constituencies Act 2011 s 14(1)(a). Head (1) in the text refers to the reduction in the number of constituencies brought about by s 11 (see the text and notes 1–3): see s 14(1).
8   Parliamentary Voting System and Constituencies Act 2011 s 14(1)(b).
9   Parliamentary Voting System and Constituencies Act 2011 s 14(3) (amended by the Electoral Registration and Administration Act 2013 s 6(3)).

80. Rules for distribution of seats: the parity principle dependent on electoral quota and geographical area. The electorate of any constituency[1] must be[2]:
  (1)   no less than 95 per cent of the United Kingdom electoral quota[3]; and
  (2)   no more than 105 per cent of that quota[4].
This rule[5] does not apply, however, to the 'protected constituencies'[6], namely: (a) the Isle of Wight, where there are two constituencies[7]; and (b) two constituencies in the Scottish islands, namely Orkney and Shetland (comprising the areas of the Orkney Islands Council and the Shetland Islands Council) and Na h-Eileanan an Iar (comprising the area of Comhairle nan Eilean Siar)[8].

A constituency must not have an area of more than 13,000 square kilometres[9].

Nevertheless, a Boundary Commission may take into account, if and to such extent as it thinks fit[10]: (i) special geographical considerations, including in particular the size, shape and accessibility of a constituency[11]; (ii) local government boundaries[12] as they exist on the most recent ordinary council-election day[13] before the review date[14]; (iii) boundaries of existing constituencies[15]; (iv) any local ties that would be broken by changes in constituencies[16]; (v) the inconveniences attendant on such changes[17].

1   For these purposes, the 'electorate' of the United Kingdom, or of a part of the United Kingdom or a constituency, is the total number of persons whose names appear on the relevant version of a register of parliamentary electors in respect of addresses in the United Kingdom, or in that part or that constituency: see the Parliamentary Constituencies Act 1986 s 3(6), Sch 2 r 9(1), (2) (Sch 2 substituted by the Parliamentary Voting System and Constituencies Act 2011 s 11(1)). For this purpose, the relevant version of a register is the version that is required by virtue of the Representation of the People Act 1983 s 13(1) (duty to publish revised version of registers: see PARA 165) to be published no later than the review date, or would be so required but for any power under s 13 to prescribe a later date, or but for s 13(1A) (pending elections: see PARA 165 note 4): see the Parliamentary Constituencies Act 1986 Sch 2 r 9(1), (2) (as so substituted). The 'review date', in relation to a report under s 3(1) that a Boundary Commission is required (by s 3(2)) to submit before a particular date (see PARA 78), is two years and ten months before that date: see Sch 2 r 9(1), (5) (as so substituted). As to the meaning of 'United Kingdom' see PARA 1

note 1. As to the meaning of 'constituency' for these purposes see PARA 9. As to the constitution of the Boundary Commissions see PARA 68 et seq.

2   See the Parliamentary Constituencies Act 1986 Sch 2 r 2(1) (as substituted: see note 1). The provision made by Sch 2 r 2 is subject to Sch 2 r 4(2) (see note 3), Sch 2 r 6(3) (see the text and notes 5–6) and Sch 2 r 7 (see note 10): see Sch 2 r 2(2) (as so substituted).

3   Parliamentary Constituencies Act 1986 Sch 2 r 2(1)(a) (as substituted: see note 1). For these purposes, the 'United Kingdom electoral quota' means U divided by 596, where 'U' is the electorate of the United Kingdom minus the electorate of the 'protected constituencies' (ie the constituencies mentioned in Sch 2 r 6 (see the text and notes 5–8)): see Sch 2 rr 2(3), 9(1), (6) (as so substituted). A constituency does not have to comply with Sch 2 r 2(1)(a), however, if it has an area of more than 12,000 square kilometres, and if the Boundary Commission concerned is satisfied that it is not reasonably possible for the constituency to comply with that rule: Sch 2 r 4(2) (as so substituted). See the text and note 9.

4   Parliamentary Constituencies Act 1986 Sch 2 r 2(1)(b) (as substituted: see note 1).

5   Ie the Parliamentary Constituencies Act 1986 Sch 2 r 2 (see the text and notes 1–4): see Sch 2 r 6(3) (as substituted: see note 1). The rule in Sch 2 r 2 is known as the 'parity principle', being a limit on the geographical size of constituencies, from which four island constituencies are expressly excepted (see heads (a) and (b) in the text). See also note 10.

6   See the Parliamentary Constituencies Act 1986 Sch 2 r 6(3) (as substituted: see note 1). A reference in Sch 2 r 6 to an area is to the area as it existed on 16 February 2011 (ie on the coming into force of the Parliamentary Voting System and Constituencies Act 2011 Pt 2 (ss 10–14) (parliamentary constituencies): see s 19(2)): see the Parliamentary Constituencies Act 1986 Sch 2 r 9(1), (7) (as so substituted).

7   Parliamentary Constituencies Act 1986 Sch 2 r 6(1) (as substituted: see note 1). See note 6.

8   See the Parliamentary Constituencies Act 1986 Sch 2 r 6(2) (as substituted: see note 1). See note 6.

9   Parliamentary Constituencies Act 1986 Sch 2 r 4(1) (as substituted: see note 1). See also Sch 2 r 4(2) (cited in note 3).

10 See the Parliamentary Constituencies Act 1986 Sch 2 r 5(1) (as substituted: see note 1). The provision made by Sch 2 r 5 has effect subject to Sch 2 r 2 (see the text and notes 1–4) and Sch 2 r 4 (see the text and notes 3, 9): see Sch 2 r 5(3) (as so substituted). Where the difference between the electorate of Northern Ireland, and the United Kingdom electoral quota multiplied by the number of seats in Northern Ireland (determined under Sch 2 r 8: see PARA 81), exceeds one third of the United Kingdom electoral quota, and where the Boundary Commission for Northern Ireland considers that having to apply Sch 2 r 2 would unreasonably impair its ability to take into account the factors set out in Sch 2 r 5 (see heads (i) to (v) in the text), Northern Ireland is excepted from Sch 2 r 2: see Sch 2 r 7 (as so substituted).

11 Parliamentary Constituencies Act 1986 Sch 2 r 5(1)(a) (as substituted: see note 1).

12 For these purposes, 'local government boundaries' means, in England, the boundaries of counties and their electoral divisions, districts and their wards, London boroughs and their wards and the City of London; in Wales, the boundaries of counties, county boroughs, electoral divisions, communities and community wards; in Scotland, the boundaries of local government areas and the electoral wards into which they are divided under the Local Governance (Scotland) Act 2004 s 1; and, in Northern Ireland, the boundaries of wards: see the Parliamentary Constituencies Act 1986 Sch 2 r 9(1), (3) (as substituted: see note 1). As to the meanings of 'England' and 'Wales' see PARA 1 note 1. As to the establishment of electoral boundaries see PARA 73 et seq. As to the council of a county, district or London borough in England and the council of a county or county borough in Wales see LOCAL GOVERNMENT vol 69 (2009) PARA 23. As to elections in the City of London see further LONDON GOVERNMENT vol 71 (2013) PARA 24 et seq.

13 For these purposes, 'ordinary council-election day' means, in relation to England and Wales, the ordinary day of election of councillors for local government areas; in relation to Scotland, the day on which the poll is held at ordinary elections of councillors for local government areas; and, in relation to Northern Ireland, the day of an election for any district council (other than an election to fill a casual vacancy): see the Parliamentary Constituencies Act 1986 Sch 2 r 9(1), (4) (as substituted: see note 1). As to the ordinary day of election of councillors for local government areas in England and Wales see PARA 197 et seq.

14 Parliamentary Constituencies Act 1986 Sch 2 r 5(1)(b) (as substituted: see note 1). Additionally, the Boundary Commission for England may take into account, if and to such extent as it thinks fit, boundaries of the electoral regions specified in the European Parliamentary Elections Act 2002 s 1(2), Sch 1 (ignoring Sch 1 para 2(2) and the references to Gibraltar) (see PARA 77 note 5) as it has effect on the most recent ordinary council-election day before the review date: Parliamentary Constituencies Act 1986 Sch 2 r 5(2) (as so substituted).

15 Parliamentary Constituencies Act 1986 Sch 2 r 5(1)(c) (as substituted: see note 1).
16 Parliamentary Constituencies Act 1986 Sch 2 r 5(1)(d) (as substituted: see note 1).
17 Parliamentary Constituencies Act 1986 Sch 2 r 5(1)(e) (as substituted: see note 1). In Sch 2, as it has been substituted by the Parliamentary Voting System and Constituencies Act 2011 s 11(1) (see note 1), the Parliamentary Constituencies Act 1986 Sch 2 r 5(1)(e) does not apply in relation to a report under s 3(1) (see PARA 78) that a Boundary Commission is required by s 3(2) (as it has been substituted by the Parliamentary Voting System and Constituencies Act 2011 s 10(3): see PARA 78) to submit before 1 October 2018: s 11(2) (amended by the Electoral Registration and Administration Act 2013 s 6(2)).

81.   Allocation of constituencies to parts of the United Kingdom. Each constituency[1] must be wholly in one of the four parts of the United Kingdom[2] (England[3], Wales[4], Scotland and Northern Ireland)[5]; and the number of constituencies in each part of the United Kingdom is to be determined in accordance with the specified allocation method[6], which is as follows[7]:

(1)   the first constituency must be allocated to the part of the United Kingdom with the greatest electorate[8];

(2)   the second and subsequent constituencies are allocated in the same way, except that the electorate of a part of the United Kingdom to which one or more constituencies have already been allocated is to be divided by (C multiplied by 2) plus 1, where C is the number of constituencies already allocated to that part[9].

Where the figure given by head (2) above is the same for two or more parts of the United Kingdom, the part to which a constituency is to be allocated must be the one with the smaller or smallest actual electorate[10].

1   As to the meaning of 'constituency' for these purposes see PARA 9.
2   As to the meaning of 'United Kingdom' see PARA 1 note 1.
3   As to the meaning of 'England' see PARA 1 note 1.
4   As to the meaning of 'Wales' see PARA 1 note 1.
5   Parliamentary Constituencies Act 1986 s 3(6), Sch 2 r 3(1) (Sch 2 substituted by the Parliamentary Voting System and Constituencies Act 2011 s 11(1)).
6   Parliamentary Constituencies Act 1986 Sch 2 r 3(2) (as substituted: see note 5). The text refers to the allocation method that is set out in Sch 2 r 8 (see the text and notes 7–10): see Sch 2 r 3(2) (as so substituted). Where the difference between the electorate of Northern Ireland, and the United Kingdom electoral quota multiplied by the number of seats in Northern Ireland (determined under Sch 2 r 8), exceeds one third of the United Kingdom electoral quota, and where the Boundary Commission for Northern Ireland considers that having to apply Sch 2 r 2 (see PARA 80) would unreasonably impair its ability to comply with s 3(2) (see PARA 78), Northern Ireland is excepted from Sch 2 r 2: see Sch 2 r 7 (as so substituted). As to the meaning of the 'United Kingdom electoral quota' see PARA 80 note 3. As to the constitution of the Boundary Commissions see PARA 68 et seq.
7   See the Parliamentary Constituencies Act 1986 Sch 2 r 8(1) (as substituted: see note 5). The allocation method set out in Sch 2 r 8 does not apply to the protected constituencies (ie the constituencies mentioned in Sch 2 r 6: see PARA 80): see Sch 2 r 8(5) (as so substituted). Accordingly, the electorate of England must be treated for the purposes of Sch 2 r 8 as reduced by the electorate of the constituencies mentioned in Sch 2 r 6(1) (ie the protected Isle of Wight constituency) (Sch 2 r 8(5)(a) (as so substituted)); and the electorate of Scotland must be treated for the purposes of Sch 2 r 8 as reduced by the electorate of the constituencies mentioned in Sch 2 r 6(2) (ie the protected Scottish islands constituencies) (Sch 2 r 8(5)(b) (as so substituted)).
8   Parliamentary Constituencies Act 1986 Sch 2 r 8(2) (as substituted: see note 5).
9   Parliamentary Constituencies Act 1986 Sch 2 r 8(3) (as substituted: see note 5).
10 Parliamentary Constituencies Act 1986 Sch 2 r 8(4) (as substituted: see note 5).

B.   PROCEDURE RELATING TO REVIEWS AND PROPOSED RECOMMENDATIONS

82.   Publicity and consultation about Boundary Commission proposals. Once a Boundary Commission[1] has decided what constituencies[2] it proposes to recommend in a report under the Parliamentary Constituencies Act 1986 that its part of the United Kingdom should be divided into[3]:

(1)   the Commission must take such steps as it thinks fit to inform people in each of the proposed constituencies[4]: (a) what the proposals are[5]; (b) that a copy of the proposals is open to inspection at a specified place within the proposed constituency[6]; and (c) that written representations with respect to the proposals may be made to the Commission during a specified period of 12 weeks (the 'initial consultation period')[7];

(2)   the Commission must cause public hearings to be held during the period beginning with the fifth week of the initial consultation period and ending with the tenth week of it[8].

The purpose of a public hearing under head (2) above is to enable representations to be made about any of the proposals with which the hearing is concerned[9]. A public hearing must be completed within two days[10], and it is for the chair of each public hearing[11] to determine the procedure that is to govern that hearing[12]. The chair must, however, make arrangements for a public hearing to begin with an explanation of the proposals with which the hearing is concerned[13], and how written representations about the proposals may be made[14]. The chair of a public hearing also must allow representations to be made by each qualifying party[15], and by any other persons (whether individuals or organisations) considered by the chair to have an interest in any of the proposals with which the hearing is concerned[16]. The chair may put questions, or allow questions to be put, to a person present at the hearing[17].

After the end of the initial consultation period, the Commission[18]:

(i)   must publish, in such manner as it thinks fit, written representations made as mentioned in head (1) above and records of public hearings held under head (2) above[19];

(ii)   must take such steps as it thinks fit to inform people in the proposed constituencies that further written representations with respect to the things published under head (i) above may be made to the Commission during a specified period of four weeks (the 'secondary consultation period')[20].

If, after the end of the secondary consultation period, the Commission is minded to revise its original proposals so as to recommend different constituencies, it must take such steps as it thinks fit to inform people in each of those revised proposed constituencies[21]:

(A)   what the revised proposals are[22];

(B)   that a copy of the revised proposals is open to inspection at a specified place within the revised proposed constituency[23]; and

(C)   that written representations with respect to the revised proposals may be made to the Commission during a specified period of eight weeks[24].

A Boundary Commission must take into consideration written representations duly made to them as mentioned in head (1) above, head (ii) above or head (C) above[25], as well as representations made at public hearings under head (2) above[26].

1   As to the constitution of the Boundary Commissions see PARA 68 et seq.
2   As to the meaning of 'constituency' for these purposes see PARA 9.
3   See the Parliamentary Constituencies Act 1986 s 5(1) (s 5 substituted, Sch 2A added, by the Parliamentary Voting System and Constituencies Act 2011 s 12(1), (2), Sch 11). The report mentioned in the text is one made under the Parliamentary Constituencies Act 1986 s 3(1)(a) (see PARA 78): see s 5 (1) (as so substituted). As to the meaning of 'United Kingdom' see PARA 1 note 1.

4 See the Parliamentary Constituencies Act 1986 s 5(1)(a) (as substituted: see note 3).

5 Parliamentary Constituencies Act 1986 s 5(1)(a)(i) (as substituted: see note 3).

6 Parliamentary Constituencies Act 1986 s 5(1)(a)(ii) (as substituted: see note 3). Head (1)(b) in the text does not apply to a constituency with respect to which no alteration is proposed, however: s 5(2) (as so substituted).

7 Parliamentary Constituencies Act 1986 s 5(1)(a)(iii) (as substituted: see note 3).

8 Parliamentary Constituencies Act 1986 s 5(1)(b) (as substituted: see note 3). Further provision about public hearings under s 5(1)(b) is made by s 5, Sch 2A (see the text and notes 9–17), which has effect: s 5(3) (as so substituted). For the purposes of Sch 2A, 'public hearing' means a hearing under s 5(1)(b): see Sch 2A para 9 (as added: see note 3). Except as provided by s 5 and Sch 2A, a Boundary Commission must not cause any public hearing or inquiry to be held for the purposes of a report under the Parliamentary Constituencies Act 1986: s 5(9) (as so substituted). Where a Boundary Commission publishes general information about how it proposes to carry out its functions (including, in the case of the Boundary Commission for England, information about the extent, if any, to which it proposes to take into account the boundaries mentioned in s 3(6), Sch 2 r 5(2) (boundaries of the electoral regions specified in the European Parliamentary Elections Act 2002 s 1(2), Sch 1: see PARA 80 note 14)) (Parliamentary Constituencies Act 1986 s 5(10)(a) (as so substituted)), or anything else to which s 5(1) (see also the text and notes 1–7), s 5(4) (see the text and notes 18–20) or s 5(5) (see the text and notes 21–24) does not apply (s 5(10)(b) (as so substituted)), it is for the Commission to determine whether to invite representations and, if it decides to do so, the procedure that is to apply (see s 5(10) (as so substituted)).

9 Parliamentary Constituencies Act 1986 Sch 2A para 1 (as added: see note 3). In relation to any particular report under s 3(1)(a) (see PARA 78) (see Sch 2A para 2(1) (as so added)):

    (1)   the Boundary Commission for England must cause at least two and no more than five public hearings to be held in each English region (Sch 2A para 2(1)(a) (as so added));

    (2)   the Boundary Commission for Scotland must cause at least two and no more than five public hearings to be held in Scotland (Sch 2A para 2(1)(b) (as so added));

    (3)   the Boundary Commission for Wales must cause at least two and no more than five public hearings to be held in Wales (Sch 2A para 2(1)(c) (as so added));

    (4)   the Boundary Commission for Northern Ireland must cause at least two and no more than five public hearings to be held in Northern Ireland (Sch 2A para 2(1)(d) (as so added)).

The public hearings in an English region are concerned with proposals for that region, and must between them cover the whole region (Sch 2A para 2(2) (as so added)); the public hearings in Scotland are concerned with proposals for Scotland, and must between them cover the whole of Scotland (Sch 2A para 2(3) (as so added)); the public hearings in Wales are concerned with proposals for Wales, and must between them cover the whole of Wales (Sch 2A para 2(4) (as so added)); and the public hearings in Northern Ireland are concerned with proposals for Northern Ireland, and must between them cover the whole of Northern Ireland (Sch 2A para 2(5) (as so added)). For these purposes, 'English region' means an electoral region specified in the European Parliamentary Elections Act 2002 s 1(2), Sch 1 (ignoring Sch 1 para 2(2) and the references to Gibraltar) (see PARA 77 note 5) as it has effect on the most recent ordinary council-election day before the review date (ie on the day referred to in the Parliamentary Constituencies Act 1986 Sch 2 r 5(2): see PARA 80 note 14): see Sch 2A para 9 (as so added). As to the meanings of 'England' and 'Wales' see PARA 1 note 1.

10 Parliamentary Constituencies Act 1986 Sch 2A para 4 (as added: see note 3).

11 For each public hearing, the Boundary Commission concerned must appoint a person to chair the hearing: Parliamentary Constituencies Act 1986 Sch 2A para 3 (as added: see note 3). For these purposes, the 'chair' means the person appointed under Sch 2A para 3: see Sch 2A para 9 (as so added).

12 Parliamentary Constituencies Act 1986 Sch 2A para 5 (as added: see note 3).

13 Parliamentary Constituencies Act 1986 Sch 2A para 6(a) (as added: see note 3).

14 Parliamentary Constituencies Act 1986 Sch 2A para 6(b) (as added: see note 3). The text refers to written representations that may be made as mentioned in s 5(1)(a) (see head (1) in the text), s 5(4)(b) (see head (ii) in the text) or s 5(5)(c) (see head (C) in the text): see Sch 2A para 6(b) (as so added).

15 Parliamentary Constituencies Act 1986 Sch 2A para 7(1)(a) (as added: see note 3). The chair may restrict the amount of time allowed for representations: (1) by qualifying parties (Sch 2A para 7(2)(a) (as so added)); and (2) by other persons (see the text and note 16) (Sch 2A para 7(2)(b) (as so added)), and need not allow the same amount to each (see Sch 2A para 7(2) (as so added)).

For these purposes, 'qualifying party' means a party that is registered under the Political Parties, Elections and Referendums Act 2000 Pt II (ss 22–40) (see PARA 35 note 3), and either has at least one Member of the House of Commons representing a constituency in the region (or, as the case may be, the part of the United Kingdom) in which the hearing is held, or received at least 10% of the votes cast in that region or part in the most recent parliamentary general election: see the Parliamentary Constituencies Act 1986 Sch 2A para 9 (as so added).

16 Parliamentary Constituencies Act 1986 Sch 2A para 7(1)(b) (as added: see note 3). See note 15. The provision made by Sch 2A para 7(1)(b) has effect subject to Sch 2A para 7(3)(b) (see head (2) below): see Sch 2A para 7(1) (as so added). The chair may determine:
    (1)   the order in which representations are made (Sch 2A para 7(3)(a) (as so added)); and
    (2)   if necessary because of shortage of time, which of those wishing to make representations are not allowed to do so (Sch 2A para 7(3)(b) (as so added)),
in whatever way the chair decides (see Sch 2A para 7(3) (as so added)).

17 Parliamentary Constituencies Act 1986 Sch 2A para 8(1) (as added: see note 3). If questions are allowed to be put, the chair may regulate the manner of questioning or restrict the number of questions a person may ask: Sch 2A para 8(2) (as so added).

18 See the Parliamentary Constituencies Act 1986 s 5(4) (as substituted: see note 3).

19 Parliamentary Constituencies Act 1986 s 5(4)(a) (as substituted: see note 3).

20 Parliamentary Constituencies Act 1986 s 5(4)(b) (as substituted: see note 3). Steps taken under s 5(4) need not be of the same kind as those taken under s 5(1) (see the text and notes 1–8): see s 5(7) (as so substituted).

21 See the Parliamentary Constituencies Act 1986 s 5(5) (as substituted: see note 3). Steps taken under s 5(5) need not be of the same kind as those taken under s 5(1) (see the text and notes 1–8): see s 5(7) (as so substituted). The provision made by s 5(5) does not apply to any proposals to make further revisions: s 5(6) (as so substituted).

22 Parliamentary Constituencies Act 1986 s 5(5)(a) (as substituted: see note 3).

23 Parliamentary Constituencies Act 1986 s 5(5)(b) (as substituted: see note 3).

24 Parliamentary Constituencies Act 1986 s 5(5)(c) (as substituted: see note 3).

25 See the Parliamentary Constituencies Act 1986 s 5(8)(a) (as substituted: see note 3).

26 See the Parliamentary Constituencies Act 1986 s 5(8)(b) (as substituted: see note 3).

(ii) Review of Local Government Electoral Areas

A. ENGLAND

(A) Principal Councils and Parish Councils within the Principal Area

83.   Review of local government areas and recommendations for electoral change by Local Government Boundary Commission for England.   The Local Government Boundary Commission for England[1] must, from time to time[2]:
    (1)   conduct a review of the area of each principal council[3]; and
    (2)   recommend whether a change should be made to the electoral arrangements for that area[4]; and
may, at any time[5]:
    (a)   conduct a review of all or any part of the area of a principal council[6]; and
    (b)   recommend whether a change should be made to the electoral arrangements for the area of the principal council[7].

Where the Local Government Boundary Commission for England recommends[8] that a change should be made to the electoral arrangements for the area of a principal council, the Commission must also recommend whether, in consequence, a change should be made to the electoral arrangements for the area of any parish council, where that area is within the area of the principal council[9].

In relation to the electoral arrangements for the area of a county council[10], the recommendations must secure the following results[11]:
    (i)   an electoral area of the county council must not fall partly inside and partly outside any district[12];

(ii)   every ward of a parish having a parish council (whether separate or common) must lie wholly within a single electoral area of the county council[13]; and

(iii)   every parish which is not divided into parish wards must lie wholly within a single electoral area of the county council[14].

In relation to the electoral arrangements for the area of a district council[15], the recommendations must secure that[16] every ward of a parish having a parish council (whether separate or common) must lie wholly within a single electoral area of the district council[17], and that every parish which is not divided into parish wards must lie wholly within a single electoral area of the district council[18].

In relation to the electoral arrangements for the area of a London borough council[19], the recommendations must secure that[20] every ward of a parish having a parish council (whether separate or common) must lie wholly within a single electoral area of the London borough council[21], and every parish which is not divided into parish wards must lie wholly within a single electoral area of the London borough council[22].

In making any such recommendations in relation to the electoral arrangements for the area of a parish council (including a common parish council)[23], the Local Government Boundary Commission for England must have regard to[24]:

(A)   the need to reflect the identities and interests of local communities[25] (and, in particular, the desirability of fixing boundaries which are and will remain easily identifiable[26], and the desirability of fixing boundaries so as not to break any local ties[27]);

(B)   the need to secure effective and convenient local government[28]; and

(C)   the boundaries of the electoral areas of the principal council or councils in whose area the area of the parish council falls[29].

In making any recommendations as to whether the area of the parish council is to be divided into wards for the election of members of the parish council, the Local Government Boundary Commission for England must have regard to whether the number or distribution of the local government electors in the area is such as to make a single election of the members of the council impracticable or inconvenient[30], and whether it is desirable for any parts of the area of the parish council to be separately represented on the council[31]. In making any recommendations as to the size and boundaries of wards[32], or the number of members of a parish council to be elected for each ward[33], the Local Government Boundary Commission for England must have regard to any change in the number or distribution of the local government electors in the area of the parish council which is likely to take place within the period of five years immediately following the making of the recommendations[34]. In the case of the area of a parish council not divided into wards, in making recommendations as to the number of members to be elected for the parish council, the Local Government Boundary Commission for England must have regard to the number and distribution of the local government electors in the area of the parish council[35], and any change in such number or distribution which is likely to take place within the period of five years immediately following the making of the recommendations[36].

A principal council, which is subject to a scheme for whole-council elections[37] where it is not the case that each of the electoral areas in the council's area returns one member of the council[38], may request the Local Government

Boundary Commission for England to conduct a review of the council's area under head (a) above[39], and make recommendations as to single-member electoral areas under head (b) above[40]. If the Local Government Boundary Commission for England grants such a request, in making its recommendations it must (in addition to the usual matters to be considered on a review of electoral arrangements[41]) have regard to the desirability of securing that each electoral area in the principal council's area should return one member of the council[42]. If the Local Government Boundary Commission for England decides not to grant the principal council's request, however, it must notify the council of its decision and the reasons for it[43].

1   As to the Local Government Boundary Commission for England see PARA 71.
2   See the Local Democracy, Economic Development and Construction Act 2009 s 56(1). Transitional provision is made in relation to anything done previously by the Electoral Commission's Boundary Committee for the purposes of discharging its functions under the Local Government Act 1992 Pt II (ss 12–27) (largely repealed) (local government changes for England: see LOCAL GOVERNMENT vol 69 (2009) PARAS 55–56), which has been superseded largely by the Local Democracy, Economic Development and Construction Act 2009 Pt 3 (ss 55–68): see ss 63, 64, Sch 3. As to the procedure on a review of local government areas by the Local Government Boundary Commission for England and recommendations for electoral change see PARA 84.
3   See the Local Democracy, Economic Development and Construction Act 2009 s 56(1)(a). A principal council must, if requested by the Local Government Boundary Commission for England to do so, provide the Commission, by such date as it may specify, with any information that it may reasonably require in connection with its functions under s 56: see s 56(9). In Pt 3, 'principal council' means a county council in England, a district council, the Council of the Isles of Scilly or a London borough council: see ss 56(3), 68. As to the meaning of 'England' see PARA 1 note 1. As to the council of a county, district or London borough in England see LOCAL GOVERNMENT vol 69 (2009) PARA 23 et seq. As to the Council of the Isles of Scilly see LOCAL GOVERNMENT vol 69 (2009) PARA 36.
4   See the Local Democracy, Economic Development and Construction Act 2009 s 56(1)(b). The Local Government Act 1972 s 6(2)(a) (electoral divisions of non-metropolitan county to return one councillor each: see PARA 74) does not limit the recommendations that may be made under the Local Democracy, Economic Development and Construction Act 2009: s 56(7). In Pt 3, in relation to the area of a principal council, 'electoral arrangements' means the total number of members of the council ('councillors'), the number and boundaries of electoral areas for the purposes of the election of councillors, the number of councillors to be returned by any electoral area in that area, and the name of any electoral area: see ss 56(4), 68. As to the establishment of electoral areas for the purpose of local government elections see PARA 74.
     Further provision relating to recommendations under the Local Democracy, Economic Development and Construction Act 2009 s 56 is made by s 56(8), Sch 2 (see the text and notes 10–36): see s 56(8). The provision made by Sch 2 applies also in relation to the making of recommendations under the Local Government and Public Involvement in Health Act 2007 s 8(6A), where, on a review under s 8(2), the Local Government Boundary Commission for England recommends that a boundary change should be made in relation to any local government area, and the Commission recommends to the Secretary of State that, in consequence, a change should be made to the electoral arrangements of the area of a local authority; or to the electoral arrangements of the area of a parish council: see ss 8–19; and LOCAL GOVERNMENT vol 69 (2009) PARAS 62–67.
5   See the Local Democracy, Economic Development and Construction Act 2009 s 56(2).
6   See the Local Democracy, Economic Development and Construction Act 2009 s 56(2)(a).
7   See the Local Democracy, Economic Development and Construction Act 2009 s 56(2)(b). See note 4.
8   Ie under the Local Democracy, Economic Development and Construction Act 2009 s 56: see s 56(5).
9   Local Democracy, Economic Development and Construction Act 2009 s 56(5). See note 4. A parish council must, if requested by the Local Government Boundary Commission for England to do so, provide the Commission, by such date as it may specify, with any information that it may reasonably require in connection with its functions under s 56: see s 56(9). In Pt 3, in relation to the area of a parish council, 'electoral arrangements' means the total number of members of the parish council ('parish councillors'), arrangements for the division of the parish

or (in the case of a common parish council) any of the parishes into wards for the purposes of the election of parish councillors, the number and boundaries of any wards, the number of parish councillors to be returned by any ward (or, in the case of a common parish council, by each parish), and the name of any ward: see ss 56(6), 68. As to the ordinary elections of parish councillors for any parish see PARA 200. As to parishes see LOCAL GOVERNMENT vol 69 (2009) PARA 27 et seq.

10 Ie the Local Democracy, Economic Development and Construction Act 2009 Sch 2 para 1 applies where the Local Government Boundary Commission for England makes recommendations under s 56 in relation to the electoral arrangements for the area of a county council: see Sch 2 para 1(1).

11 See the Local Democracy, Economic Development and Construction Act 2009 Sch 2 para 1(2). Subject to Sch 2 para 1(2), in making the recommendations, the Local Government Boundary Commission for England must have regard to (see Sch 2 para 1(3)):
    (1)   the need to secure that the ratio of the number of local government electors to the number of members of the county council to be elected is, as nearly as possible, the same in every electoral area of the council (Sch 2 para 1(3)(a));
    (2)   the need to reflect the identities and interests of local communities (see Sch 2 para 1(3)(b)), and in particular: (a) the desirability of fixing boundaries which are and will remain easily identifiable (Sch 2 para 1(3)(b)(i)); and (b) the desirability of not breaking local ties when fixing boundaries (Sch 2 para 1(3)(b)(ii));
    (3)   the need to secure effective and convenient local government (Sch 2 para 1(3)(c)); and
    (4)   the boundaries of the electoral areas of any district council whose area is within the area of the county council (Sch 2 para 1(3)(d)).
    For the purpose of head (1) above, the Local Government Boundary Commission for England must have regard to any change in the number or distribution of local government electors in the area of the county council which is likely to take place within the period of five years immediately following the making of the recommendations: Sch 2 para 1(4). 'Electoral area', in relation to a principal council, means an area for which one or more members of the council are elected; and 'local government elector' has the meaning given in the Local Government Act 1972 s 270(1) (see LOCAL GOVERNMENT vol 69 (2009) PARA 127): see the Local Democracy, Economic Development and Construction Act 2009 Sch 2 para 5.

12 Local Democracy, Economic Development and Construction Act 2009 Sch 2 para 1(2)(a).
13 Local Democracy, Economic Development and Construction Act 2009 Sch 2 para 1(2)(b).
14 Local Democracy, Economic Development and Construction Act 2009 Sch 2 para 1(2)(c).
15 Ie the Local Democracy, Economic Development and Construction Act 2009 Sch 2 para 2 applies where the Local Government Boundary Commission for England makes recommendations under s 56 in relation to the electoral arrangements for the area of a district council: see Sch 2 para 2(1).

16 See the Local Democracy, Economic Development and Construction Act 2009 Sch 2 para 2(2). Subject to Sch 2 para 2(2), in making the recommendations the Local Government Boundary Commission for England must have regard to (see Sch 2 para 2(3)):
    (1)   the need to secure that the ratio of the number of local government electors to the number of members of the district council to be elected is, as nearly as possible, the same in every electoral area of the council (Sch 2 para 2(3)(a));
    (2)   the need to reflect the identities and interests of local communities (Sch 2 para 2(3)(b)), and in particular: (a) the desirability of fixing boundaries which are and will remain easily identifiable (Sch 2 para 2(3)(b)(i)); and (b) the desirability of fixing boundaries so as not to break any local ties (Sch 2 para 2(3)(b)(ii));
    (3)   the need to secure effective and convenient local government (Sch 2 para 2(3)(c)); and
    (4)   in the case of a district council that is subject to a scheme for elections by halves or by thirds, or that has resolved to revert to being subject to such a scheme under the Local Government and Public Involvement in Health Act 2007 Pt 2 Ch 1 (ss 31–54) (electoral arrangements (power of district councils in England to change electoral scheme): see LOCAL GOVERNMENT vol 69 (2009) PARA 135 et seq), the desirability of securing that each electoral area of the district council returns an appropriate number of members of the council (Sch 2 para 2(3)(d)).
    For the purpose of head (1) above, the Local Government Boundary Commission for England must have regard to any change in the number or distribution of local government electors in the area of the district council which is likely to take place within the period of five years immediately following the making of the recommendations: Sch 2 para 2(4). For the purposes of head (4) above: (i) a district council is 'subject to a scheme of elections by halves' if one half (or as nearly as may be) of its members are to be elected in each year in which it holds ordinary elections of members of the council (Sch 2 para 2(5)(a)); (ii) a district council is 'subject to a

scheme of elections by thirds' if one third (or as nearly as may be) of its members are to be
elected in each year in which it holds ordinary elections of members of the council (Sch 2
para 2(5)(b)); and (iii) the number of members of the district council returned by an electoral
area of the council is 'appropriate' (in the case of a scheme for elections by halves) if it is
divisible by two, or (in the case of a scheme for elections by thirds) if it is divisible by three
(Sch 2 para 2(5)(c)).

17 Local Democracy, Economic Development and Construction Act 2009 Sch 2 para 2(2)(a).
18 Local Democracy, Economic Development and Construction Act 2009 Sch 2 para 2(2)(b).
19 Ie the Local Democracy, Economic Development and Construction Act 2009 Sch 2 para 3
    applies where the Local Government Boundary Commission for England makes
    recommendations under s 56 in relation to the electoral arrangements for the area of a London
    borough council: see Sch 2 para 3(1).
20 See the Local Democracy, Economic Development and Construction Act 2009 Sch 2 para 3(2).
    Subject to Sch 2 para 3(2), in making the recommendations the Local Government Boundary
    Commission for England must have regard to (see Sch 2 para 3(3)):
    (1)   the need to secure that the ratio of the number of local government electors to the
           number of members of the London borough council to be elected is, as nearly as
           possible, the same in every electoral area of the council (Sch 2 para 3(3)(a));
    (2)   the need to reflect the identities and interests of local communities (Sch 2 para 3(3)(b)),
           and in particular: (a) the desirability of fixing boundaries which are and will remain
           easily identifiable (Sch 2 para 3(3)(b)(i)); and (b) the desirability of fixing boundaries so
           as not to break any local ties (Sch 2 para 3(3)(b)(ii)); and
    (3)   the need to secure effective and convenient local government (Sch 2 para 3(3)(c)).
    For the purpose of head (1) above, the Local Government Boundary Commission for England
    must have regard to any change in the number or distribution of local government electors in the
    area of the London borough council which is likely to take place within the period of five years
    immediately following the making of the recommendations: Sch 2 para 3(4).
21 Local Democracy, Economic Development and Construction Act 2009 Sch 2 para 3(2)(a).
22 Local Democracy, Economic Development and Construction Act 2009 Sch 2 para 3(2)(b).
23 Ie the Local Democracy, Economic Development and Construction Act 2009 Sch 2 para 4
    applies where the Local Government Boundary Commission for England makes
    recommendations under s 56 in relation to the electoral arrangements for the area of a parish
    council (including a common parish council): see Sch 2 para 4(1).
24 See the Local Democracy, Economic Development and Construction Act 2009 Sch 2 para 4(2).
25 See the Local Democracy, Economic Development and Construction Act 2009 Sch 2
    para 4(2)(a).
26 Local Democracy, Economic Development and Construction Act 2009 Sch 2 para 4(2)(a)(i).
27 Local Democracy, Economic Development and Construction Act 2009 Sch 2 para 4(2)(a)(ii).
28 Local Democracy, Economic Development and Construction Act 2009 Sch 2 para 4(2)(b).
29 Local Democracy, Economic Development and Construction Act 2009 Sch 2 para 4(2)(c).
30 See the Local Democracy, Economic Development and Construction Act 2009 Sch 2
    para 4(3)(a).
31 See the Local Democracy, Economic Development and Construction Act 2009 Sch 2
    para 4(3)(b).
32 See the Local Democracy, Economic Development and Construction Act 2009 Sch 2
    para 4(4)(a).
33 See the Local Democracy, Economic Development and Construction Act 2009 Sch 2
    para 4(4)(b).
34 See the Local Democracy, Economic Development and Construction Act 2009 Sch 2 para 4(4).
35 See the Local Democracy, Economic Development and Construction Act 2009 Sch 2
    para 4(5)(a).
36 See the Local Democracy, Economic Development and Construction Act 2009 Sch 2
    para 4(5)(b).
37 For these purposes, a principal council is 'subject to a scheme for whole-council elections' if, in
    each year in which ordinary elections of members of the council are to be held, all the members
    of the council are to be elected: see the Local Democracy, Economic Development and
    Construction Act 2009 s 57(4). A district council is also 'subject to a scheme for whole-council
    elections' for those purposes if the Local Government and Public Involvement in Health
    Act 2007 s 34 (scheme for whole-council elections: see LOCAL GOVERNMENT vol 69 (2009) PARA
    136) applies to the council but, by virtue of s 34(4A) (temporary continuation of previous
    electoral scheme: see LOCAL GOVERNMENT vol 69 (2009) PARA 135), not all the members of the

council are to be elected in a year in which ordinary elections of members of the council are to be held: see the Local Democracy, Economic Development and Construction Act 2009 s 57(4A) (added by the Localism Act 2011 s 24(7)).

38 See the Local Democracy, Economic Development and Construction Act 2009 s 57(3).

39 See the Local Democracy, Economic Development and Construction Act 2009 s 57(1)(a).

40 See the Local Democracy, Economic Development and Construction Act 2009 s 57(1)(b). Nothing in s 57 prevents the Local Government Boundary Commission for England, when making recommendations as to single-member electoral areas pursuant to s 57(1), from making other recommendations under s 56(2)(b): s 57(7). For these purposes, 'recommendations as to single-member electoral areas' means recommendations, for each electoral area in the area of a principal council, as to whether the electoral area should return one member of the council (see s 57(2)), where references to electoral areas are, in relation to a case where the Local Government Boundary Commission for England makes recommendations for change to the number or boundaries of electoral areas in the area of a principal council, to the recommended electoral areas (see s 57(8)).

41 Ie in addition to the matters to be considered pursuant to the Local Democracy, Economic Development and Construction Act 2009 Sch 2 (see the text and notes 10–36): see s 57(5).

42 Local Democracy, Economic Development and Construction Act 2009 s 57(5). For these purposes, references to electoral areas are, in relation to a case where the Local Government Boundary Commission for England makes recommendations for change to the number or boundaries of electoral areas in the area of a principal council, to the recommended electoral areas: see s 57(8).

43 Local Democracy, Economic Development and Construction Act 2009 s 57(6).

84.   Procedure on review of local government areas and recommendations for electoral change.   As soon as reasonably practicable after deciding to conduct a review of local government areas[1], the Local Government Boundary Commission for England[2] must take such steps as it considers sufficient to secure that persons who may be interested in the review are informed of[3]:

(1)   the fact that the review is to take place[4]; and

(2)   any particular matters to which the review is to relate[5].

In conducting such a review, the Local Government Boundary Commission for England must[6]:

(a)   prepare and publish draft recommendations[7];

(b)   take such steps as it considers sufficient to secure that persons who may be interested in the recommendations are informed of them and of the period within which representations with respect to them may be made[8]; and

(c)   take into consideration any representations made to the Local Government Boundary Commission for England within that period[9].

As soon as practicable after conducting such a review[10], the Local Government Boundary Commission for England must publish a report stating its recommendations[11], and take such steps as it considers sufficient to secure that persons who may be interested in the recommendations are informed of them[12]. Where such a report[13] contains recommendations for electoral changes, the Local Government Boundary Commission for England may by order give effect to all or any of the recommendations[14]. Such an order may in particular include provision as to[15]:

(i)   the total number of members of any principal council or parish council ('councillors')[16];

(ii)   the number and boundaries of electoral areas for the purposes of the election of councillors[17];

(iii)   the number of councillors to be returned by any electoral area[18];

(iv)   the name of any electoral area[19];

(v)   the election of councillors for any electoral area[20];

   (vi)   the order of retirement of councillors[21];

   (vii) the ordinary year of election for a parish council[22].

Such an order may not, however, require or authorise the holding of an election for membership of a principal council otherwise than at an ordinary election for that council[23].

1   Ie under the Local Democracy, Economic Development and Construction Act 2009 s 56 (see PARA 83): see s 58(1).

2   As to the Local Government Boundary Commission for England see PARA 71.

3   See the Local Democracy, Economic Development and Construction Act 2009 s 58(1).

4   Local Democracy, Economic Development and Construction Act 2009 s 58(1)(a).

5   Local Democracy, Economic Development and Construction Act 2009 s 58(1)(b).

6   See the Local Democracy, Economic Development and Construction Act 2009 s 58(2).

7   Local Democracy, Economic Development and Construction Act 2009 s 58(2)(a). The Local Government Boundary Commission for England may at any time before publishing draft recommendations under s 58(2)(a) consult such persons as it considers appropriate: s 58(3).

8   Local Democracy, Economic Development and Construction Act 2009 s 58(2)(b).

9   Local Democracy, Economic Development and Construction Act 2009 s 58(2)(c).

10 Ie under the Local Democracy, Economic Development and Construction Act 2009 s 56 (see PARA 83): see s 58(4).

11 See the Local Democracy, Economic Development and Construction Act 2009 s 58(4)(a).

12 See the Local Democracy, Economic Development and Construction Act 2009 s 58(4)(b).

13 Ie a report under the Local Democracy, Economic Development and Construction Act 2009 s 58(4) (see the text and notes 10–12): see s 59(1).

14 See the Local Democracy, Economic Development and Construction Act 2009 s 59(1). Such an order must be made by statutory instrument (s 59(8)); and a draft of a statutory instrument containing such an order must be laid before Parliament before the instrument is made (s 59(9)). An order under s 59 may contain incidental, consequential, supplementary or transitional provision, or savings (s 59(4)(a)), and may make different provision for different cases, including different provision for different areas or councils (s 59(4)(b)). The provision referred to in s 59(4)(a) may include provision applying any instrument made under an enactment (with or without modifications), extending, excluding or amending any such instrument, or repealing or revoking any such instrument: see s 59(5). See eg the Slough (Electoral Changes) Order 2012, SI 2012/2769 (made in exercise of the power conferred by the Local Democracy, Economic Development and Construction Act 2009 ss 58(4), 59(1) in relation to electoral changes that apply in respect of local government elections to be held on and after the ordinary day of election of councillors in 2014).

    Where the Local Government Boundary Commission for England is satisfied that a mistake has occurred in the preparation of an order under the Local Democracy, Economic Development and Construction Act 2009 s 59(1), and that the mistake is such that it cannot be rectified by a subsequent order under s 59 by virtue of the Interpretation Act 1978 s 14 (implied power to amend: see STATUTES AND LEGISLATIVE PROCESS vol 96 (2012) PARA 1071), the Local Government Boundary Commission for England may by order under the Local Democracy, Economic Development and Construction Act 2009 s 59(6) make such provision as it thinks necessary or expedient for rectifying the mistake: see s 59(6). For this purpose, in relation to an order, 'mistake' includes a provision contained in or omitted from the order in reliance on information supplied by any public body which is inaccurate or incomplete: see s 59(7).

15 See the Local Democracy, Economic Development and Construction Act 2009 s 59(2).

16 Local Democracy, Economic Development and Construction Act 2009 s 59(2)(a).

17 Local Democracy, Economic Development and Construction Act 2009 s 59(2)(b).

18 Local Democracy, Economic Development and Construction Act 2009 s 59(2)(c).

19 Local Democracy, Economic Development and Construction Act 2009 s 59(2)(d).

20 Local Democracy, Economic Development and Construction Act 2009 s 59(2)(e).

21 Local Democracy, Economic Development and Construction Act 2009 s 59(2)(f).

22 Local Democracy, Economic Development and Construction Act 2009 s 59(2)(g).

23 Local Democracy, Economic Development and Construction Act 2009 s 59(3).

85.   Consequential recommendations arising from community governance reviews. A community governance review[1] may make recommendations to the Local Government Boundary Commission for England[2] as to what related alteration (if any) should be made to the boundaries of the electoral areas of any affected principal council[3]; and the Commission may by order give effect to those recommendations[4]. The Commission must notify each relevant principal council of whether or not the Commission has given effect to the recommendations[5] and, where it has done so, it must also send each relevant principal council two copies of the order so made[6].

1   As to the meaning of 'community governance review' see the Local Government and Public Involvement in Health Act 2007 Pt 4 Ch 3 (ss 79–102) (Parishes: Reorganisation); and LOCAL GOVERNMENT vol 69 (2009) PARA 68.
2   Ie under the Local Government and Public Involvement in Health Act 2007 ss 79–91, 93–102 (see LOCAL GOVERNMENT vol 69 (2009) PARAS 68–76): see s 92(1); and LOCAL GOVERNMENT vol 69 (2009) PARA 73. As to the Local Government Boundary Commission for England see PARA 71.
3   See the Local Government and Public Involvement in Health Act 2007 s 92(1), (2); and LOCAL GOVERNMENT vol 69 (2009) PARA 73. For these purposes, 'affected principal council' means any principal council whose area the community governance review relates to (including the council carrying out the review); and 'related' means related to the other recommendations made under Pt 4 Ch 3: see s 92(6); and LOCAL GOVERNMENT vol 69 (2009) PARA 73.
4   See the Local Government and Public Involvement in Health Act 2007 s 92(3); and LOCAL GOVERNMENT vol 69 (2009) PARA 73. Many such orders have been made in exercise of these powers and they are not mentioned further in this work because they have local effect inherently, but see eg the District of Blaby (Electoral Changes) Order 2012, SI 2012/2854.
5   See the Local Government and Public Involvement in Health Act 2007 s 92(4); and LOCAL GOVERNMENT vol 69 (2009) PARA 73.
6   See the Local Government and Public Involvement in Health Act 2007 s 92(5); and LOCAL GOVERNMENT vol 69 (2009) PARA 73. For these purposes, 'relevant principal council', in relation to recommendations under s 92(2), means the principal council that made the recommendations and (if the recommendations are made by a district council for an area for which there is a county council) the county council: see s 92(6); and LOCAL GOVERNMENT vol 69 (2009) PARA 73.

(B) London Assembly Constituencies

86.   Review of London Assembly constituencies.   Under the rules relating to London Assembly constituencies[1], there must be 14 Assembly constituencies[2], each of which must consist of two or more entire London boroughs[3]. The Assembly constituencies, and their areas, are specified in an order made by statutory instrument by the Local Government Boundary Commission for England[4].

Where the boundary of a London borough is altered[5], the Local Government Boundary Commission for England must consider whether to conduct a review of Assembly constituencies in order to ensure that they comply with the statutory rules[6]. The Commission may also conduct a review of Assembly constituencies at any time[7]. In either case, the Commission must inform interested persons that a review is to take place, must consider any representations it receives and must publish any recommendations[8]. The recommendations may be given effect to by statutory instrument, a draft of which must be laid before Parliament[9].

1   Ie the rules contained in the Greater London Authority Act 1999 s 2(5), Sch 1 para 7(1): see LONDON GOVERNMENT vol 71 (2013) PARA 80.
2   See the Greater London Authority Act 1999 Sch 1 para 7(1), r 1; and LONDON GOVERNMENT vol 71 (2013) PARA 80.
3   See the Greater London Authority Act 1999 Sch 1 para 7(1), r 2; and LONDON GOVERNMENT vol 71 (2013) PARA 80. For these purposes, any reference to a London borough includes a reference to the City of London, which for these purposes is taken to include the Inner Temple and the Middle Temple: see Sch 1 para 7(2)(a); and LONDON GOVERNMENT vol 71 (2013) PARA 80. As to the London boroughs see LONDON GOVERNMENT vol 71 (2013) PARA 15. As to the City of London and the Temples see LONDON GOVERNMENT vol 71 (2013) PARAS 16–17.

4   See the Greater London Authority Act 1999 s 2(4); and LONDON GOVERNMENT vol 71 (2013) PARA 80. As to the order that is currently in force see the Greater London Authority (Assembly Constituencies and Returning Officers) Order 1999, SI 1999/3380. As to the Local Government Boundary Commission for England see PARA 71.

5   Ie where the Secretary of State makes an order under the Local Government and Public Involvement in Health Act 2007 s 10 (see LOCAL GOVERNMENT vol 69 (2009) PARA 34) which includes a boundary change (within the meaning of s 8(3)) affecting a London borough.

6   Ie the rules set out in the Greater London Authority Act 1999 Sch 1 para 7 (see note 1). The review is for the purposes of making recommendations as to whether the boundary change requires changes to Assembly constituencies in order to comply with the rules, and if so, what those changes should be: see Sch 1 para 1; and LONDON GOVERNMENT vol 71 (2013) PARA 80.

7   Following such a review, the Local Government Boundary Commission for England may make recommendations, complying with the rules set out in Sch 1 para 7 (see note 1), as to the area into which Greater London should be divided to form the Assembly constituencies, and the name by which each Assembly constituency should be known: see the Greater London Authority Act 1999 Sch 1 para 2; and LONDON GOVERNMENT vol 71 (2013) PARA 80.

8   See the Greater London Authority Act 1999 Sch 1 para 3; and LONDON GOVERNMENT vol 71 (2013) PARA 80.

9   See the Greater London Authority Act 1999 Sch 1 para 4; and LONDON GOVERNMENT vol 71 (2013) PARA 80.

B. WALES

87.   Review of electoral arrangements for principal areas in Wales. It is the duty of the Local Democracy and Boundary Commission for Wales (the 'Welsh Commission')[1] to conduct a review of the electoral arrangements for each principal area[2] at least once in every 'review period'[3] (being the period of ten years beginning with 30 September 2013[4], and each subsequent period of ten years thereafter)[5]. The Commission must, in respect of each review period[6]:

(1)   prepare and publish a programme which sets out its proposed timetable for conducting all the reviews so required during the period[7]; and

(2)   send a copy of the programme to the Welsh Ministers[8].

The Commission must comply with its duties, in respect of the first review period, as soon as possible after it begins, and, in respect of each subsequent review period, before the period begins[9]. The changes that the Commission may recommend in relation to any such review of electoral arrangements for principal areas are[10]:

(a)   such changes to the electoral arrangements for the principal area under review as appears to it appropriate[11]; and

(b)   in consequence of such change: (i) such community boundary changes as it considers appropriate in relation to any community in the principal area[12]; (ii) such community council changes and changes to the electoral arrangements for such a community as it considers appropriate[13]; (iii) such preserved county changes as it considers appropriate[14].

The Commission must not, however, in any period of nine months preceding the day of an ordinary council election under the Local Government Act 1972[15], make or publish any recommendations relating to the electoral arrangements of a principal area[16].

In addition, the Welsh Commission has power, either of its own initiative or at the request of a principal council, to conduct a review of the electoral arrangements for a principal area[17], but the Commission must not conduct such a review at the request of a principal council if it considers that doing so would impede the proper exercise of its functions[18].

Provision is made for the procedure on a review of electoral arrangements, and for implementation following a review[19].

1   The Local Democracy and Boundary Commission for Wales is the body formerly known as the Local Government Boundary Commission for Wales, which has been continued in existence and renamed, by the Local Government (Democracy) (Wales) Act 2013: see s 2; and PARA 72.

2   As to the meanings of 'principal area', and of references to the electoral arrangements of a principal area, see PARA 72 note 28. As to the duty of the Local Democracy and Boundary Commission for Wales, for the purpose of considering whether it is appropriate to make or recommend changes in the arrangements for local government in Wales, to monitor the areas and electoral arrangements relevant to local government in Wales see PARA 72. As well as arising from the Commission's specific duty to review the electoral arrangements for principal areas in Wales, recommendations for electoral arrangements changes may arise also from the Commission's review of principal area boundaries under the Local Government (Democracy) (Wales) Act 2013 Pt 3 Ch 2 (ss 23–28) (see LOCAL GOVERNMENT). The Welsh Ministers also may direct the Welsh Commission to undertake a review of the electoral arrangements for a new local government area: see the Local Government (Wales) Measure 2011 Pt 9 Ch 2 (ss 162–171); and LOCAL GOVERNMENT. As to the Welsh Ministers see PARA 2.

3   Local Government (Democracy) (Wales) Act 2013 s 29(1).

4   Ie the period of ten years beginning with the day on which the Local Government (Democracy) (Wales) Act 2013 s 29 came into force (see s 75(2)(b)): see s 29(3).

5   Local Government (Democracy) (Wales) Act 2013 s 29(3).

6   See the Local Government (Democracy) (Wales) Act 2013 s 29(2).

7   Local Government (Democracy) (Wales) Act 2013 s 29(2)(a).

8   Local Government (Democracy) (Wales) Act 2013 s 29(2)(b).

9   See the Local Government (Democracy) (Wales) Act 2013 s 29(4).

10 See the Local Government (Democracy) (Wales) Act 2013 s 29(7).

11 Local Government (Democracy) (Wales) Act 2013 s 29(7)(a). In considering whether to make recommendations for changes to the electoral arrangements for a principal area in Wales, the Local Democracy and Boundary Commission for Wales must apply s 30 (considerations for a review of principal area electoral arrangements): see PARA 89.

12 Local Government (Democracy) (Wales) Act 2013 s 29(7)(b)(i). As to communities and their councillors see LOCAL GOVERNMENT vol 69 (2009) PARA 41 et seq.

13 Local Government (Democracy) (Wales) Act 2013 s 29(7)(b)(ii).

14 Local Government (Democracy) (Wales) Act 2013 s 29(7)(b)(iii). References to a 'preserved county change' are references to a change in the area of a preserved county: see s 23(4)(d). For the purposes of Pt 3 (ss 21–49), 'preserved county' means any county created by the Local Government Act 1972 as a county in Wales as it stood immediately before the passing of the Local Government (Wales) Act 1994 but subject to any provision of that Act or any provision made under the Local Government Act 1972 or under the Local Government (Democracy) (Wales) Act 2013 redrawing its boundaries: see s 27(4). As to counties or county boroughs in Wales see LOCAL GOVERNMENT vol 69 (2009) PARA 37 et seq.

15 Ie under the Local Government Act 1972 s 26 (elections of councillors: see LOCAL GOVERNMENT vol 69 (2009) PARA 131): see the Local Government (Democracy) (Wales) Act 2013 s 29(8).

16 Local Government (Democracy) (Wales) Act 2013 s 29(8).

17 See the Local Government (Democracy) (Wales) Act 2013 s 29(5).

18 See the Local Government (Democracy) (Wales) Act 2013 s 29(6).

19 As to the procedure for local government reviews see the Local Government (Democracy) (Wales) Act 2013 Pt 3 Ch 4 (ss 34–36); and LOCAL GOVERNMENT. As to implementation following a review see Pt 3 Ch 5 (ss 37–44); and LOCAL GOVERNMENT. As to miscellaneous provision (directions and guidance, local inquiries that may be held, with respect to any local government review) see Pt 3 Ch 7 (ss 48–49); and LOCAL GOVERNMENT.

88.   Review of electoral arrangements for communities in Wales.   It is the duty of each principal council in Wales[1], for the purpose of considering whether it is appropriate to make or recommend changes in the arrangements for local government in Wales[2], to monitor the communities in its area, and the electoral arrangements of such communities[3]. In pursuance of that duty, a principal council must[4]:

(1)   have regard to the Local Democracy and Boundary Commission for Wales's timetable for conducting the reviews of principal areas' electoral arrangements[5]; and

(2) carry out such reviews[6] as are required under the Local Government (Democracy) (Wales) Act 2013, or under any other enactment, as may be directed by the Welsh Ministers, or as it otherwise considers appropriate[7].

A principal council in Wales may conduct a review of the electoral arrangements for a community in its area[8], either of its own initiative[9], or at the request of the community council for the community, or of no fewer than 30 local government electors[10] registered in the community[11]. But a principal council must not conduct such a review at the request of the community council or local government electors if it considers that doing so would impede the proper exercise of its functions[12]. The changes that a principal council may propose and make in relation to such a review of electoral arrangements for communities in Wales are[13]:

(a) such changes to the electoral arrangements for the community as the principal council considers appropriate[14]; and

(b) in consequence of any change to the electoral arrangements for the community, such changes to the electoral arrangements of the principal area as it considers appropriate[15].

The Local Democracy and Boundary Commission for Wales may conduct a review of the electoral arrangements for a community, in any of the following circumstances[16]:

(i) where the Commission has agreed to exercise a principal council's function of conducting reviews[17] pursuant to an agreement entered into between them[18];

(ii) where the Commission has been requested to conduct a review of a community either by the community council, or by no fewer than 30 local government electors from the community[19];

(iii) where a principal council has not complied with a direction by the Welsh Ministers to conduct a review of the electoral arrangements for one or more of its communities[20].

But the Commission must not conduct such a review following a request by a community council, or by local government electors, if it considers that doing so would impede the proper exercise of its functions[21]. The changes that the Commission may recommend in relation to any review of electoral arrangements for communities in Wales are[22]:

(A) such changes to the electoral arrangements for the community that the Commission considers appropriate[23]; and

(B) in consequence of any change to the electoral arrangements for the community, such changes to the electoral arrangements of the principal area as it considers appropriate[24].

Provision is made for the procedure on a review of electoral arrangements, and for implementation following a review[25].

1   As to the meaning of 'principal council' see PARA 72 note 7; and see LOCAL GOVERNMENT vol 69 (2009) PARA 23. As to the meaning of 'Wales' see PARA 1 note 1.

2   Ie for the purpose of considering whether it is appropriate to make or recommend changes under the Local Government (Democracy) (Wales) Act 2013 Pt 3 (ss 21–49): see s 22(1).

3   See the Local Government (Democracy) (Wales) Act 2013 s 22(1). As to the meaning of references to the electoral arrangements of a community see PARA 72 note 28. As well as arising from a principal council's specific duty to review the electoral arrangements for a community in its area, recommendations for changes to electoral arrangements may arise from a principal council's review of communities in its area under the Local Government (Democracy) (Wales) Act 2013 Pt 3 Ch 2 (ss 23–28) (see LOCAL GOVERNMENT). The Welsh Ministers also may direct the Welsh Commission to undertake a review of all electoral arrangements for a new local

government area: see the Local Government (Wales) Measure 2011 Pt 9 Ch 2 (ss 162–171); and LOCAL GOVERNMENT. As to the Welsh Ministers see PARA 2. As to communities see LOCAL GOVERNMENT vol 69 (2009) PARA 41 et seq.

A principal council must, in respect of each reporting period, publish a report describing how it has discharged its duty under the Local Government (Democracy) (Wales) Act 2013 s 22(1) and send a copy of the report to the Local Democracy and Boundary Commission for Wales: s 22(5). For these purposes, 'reporting period' means the period of ten years beginning with the date on which the principal council last published a report under the Local Government Act 1972 s 55(2A) (repealed) or, if earlier, s 57(4A) (repealed), or, in the case of a principal council which has not published such a report before 30 September 2013 (ie before the coming into force of the Local Government (Democracy) (Wales) Act 2013 s 22: see s 75(2)(b)), the period of ten years beginning with 30 September 2013, and each subsequent period of ten years: see s 22(6). A principal council may enter into an agreement with the Local Democracy and Boundary Commission for Wales for the Commission (under s 32: see the text and notes 16–24) to exercise the council's function of conducting reviews under s 31: s 31(5). The agreement may be on such terms and conditions as the principal council and the Commission consider appropriate: s 31(6). A principal council must provide the Commission with such information as it may reasonably require in connection with the exercise of its functions under Pt 3: s 22(4). The Local Democracy and Boundary Commission for Wales is the body formerly known as the Local Government Boundary Commission for Wales, which has been continued in existence and renamed, by the Local Government (Democracy) (Wales) Act 2013: see s 2; and PARA 72.

4   See the Local Government (Democracy) (Wales) Act 2013 s 22(2).
5   Local Government (Democracy) (Wales) Act 2013 s 22(2)(a). Head (1) in the text refers to the requirements imposed on the Local Democracy and Boundary Commission for Wales by s 29(1) (see PARA 87): see s 22(2)(a).
6   Ie under the Local Government (Democracy) (Wales) Act 2013 Pt 3: see s 22(2)(b).
7   Local Government (Democracy) (Wales) Act 2013 s 22(2)(b). In carrying out its duties under Pt 3 (and in conducting any review), a principal council must seek to ensure effective and convenient local government: s 22(3).
8   See the Local Government (Democracy) (Wales) Act 2013 s 31(1).
9   Local Government (Democracy) (Wales) Act 2013 s 31(1)(a).
10 In the Local Government (Democracy) (Wales) Act 2013 Pt 3, 'local government elector' means a person registered as a local government elector in the register of electors in accordance with the provisions of the Representation of the People Acts: see the Local Government (Democracy) (Wales) Act 2013 s 30(4). As to the meaning of 'the Representation of the People Acts' see PARA 3 note 1. As to the registration of parliamentary or local government electors see PARA 113 et seq.
11 Local Government (Democracy) (Wales) Act 2013 s 31(1)(b).
12 Local Government (Democracy) (Wales) Act 2013 s 31(2).
13 See the Local Government (Democracy) (Wales) Act 2013 s 31(3).
14 Local Government (Democracy) (Wales) Act 2013 s 31(3)(a).
15 Local Government (Democracy) (Wales) Act 2013 s 31(3)(b). For these purposes, s 30 (considerations for a review of principal area electoral arrangements: see PARA 89) applies to a principal council as it applies to the Commission: s 31(4). As to the meanings of 'principal area', and of references to the electoral arrangements of a principal area, see PARA 72 note 28.
16 See the Local Government (Democracy) (Wales) Act 2013 s 32(1).
17 Ie under the Local Government (Democracy) (Wales) Act 2013 s 31(5) (see note 3): see s 32(2)(a).
18 Local Government (Democracy) (Wales) Act 2013 s 32(2)(a).
19 Local Government (Democracy) (Wales) Act 2013 s 32(2)(b).
20 Local Government (Democracy) (Wales) Act 2013 s 32(2)(c). As to reviews conducted under a direction by the Welsh Ministers see head (2) in the text. Where the Commission conducts a review in the circumstances described in head (iii) in the text, it may recover the cost of doing so from the principal council: s 32(5). In the event of a disagreement between the Commission and the principal council as to the amount payable to the Commission under s 32(5), the Welsh Ministers may determine that amount: s 32(6). Any sum payable to the Commission in this way is recoverable as a debt due to the Commission: s 32(7).
21 See the Local Government (Democracy) (Wales) Act 2013 s 32(3).
22 See the Local Government (Democracy) (Wales) Act 2013 s 32(4).
23 Local Government (Democracy) (Wales) Act 2013 s 32(4)(a).
24 Local Government (Democracy) (Wales) Act 2013 s 32(4)(b).
25 As to the procedure for local government reviews see the Local Government (Democracy) (Wales) Act 2013 Pt 3 Ch 4 (ss 34–36); and LOCAL GOVERNMENT. As to implementation

following a review see Pt 3 Ch 5 (ss 37–44); and LOCAL GOVERNMENT. As to miscellaneous provision (directions and guidance, local inquiries that may be held, with respect to any local government review) see Pt 3 Ch 7 (ss 48–49); and LOCAL GOVERNMENT.

89.   Considerations for a review of principal area or community electoral arrangements. In considering whether to make recommendations for changes to the electoral arrangements for a principal area in Wales[1], the Local Democracy and Boundary Commission for Wales must[2]:

(1)   seek to ensure that the ratio of local government electors[3] to the number of members of the council to be elected is, as nearly as may be, the same in every electoral ward of the principal area[4];

(2)   have regard to: (a) the desirability of fixing boundaries for electoral wards which are and will remain easily identifiable[5]; (b) the desirability of not breaking local ties when fixing boundaries for electoral wards[6].

Where a principal council[7] is considering making (or, as the case may be, the Commission is considering recommending) changes to the electoral arrangements for a community[8], then, in considering whether a community should be divided into community wards, regard is to be had to[9]:

(i)   whether the number or distribution of the local government electors for the community is such as to make a single election of community councillors impractical or inconvenient[10]; and

(ii)   whether it is desirable that any area of the community should be separately represented on the community council[11].

Where it is decided to divide a community into community wards, in considering the size and boundaries of the wards and in fixing the number of community councillors to be elected for each ward, regard is to be had to[12]:

(A)   any change in the number or distribution of local government electors of the community which is likely to take place within the period of five years immediately following any recommendation[13];

(B)   the desirability of fixing boundaries which are and will remain easily identifiable[14]; and

(C)   any local ties which will be broken by the fixing of any particular boundaries[15].

Where it is decided not to divide a community into community wards, in fixing the number of councillors to be elected for each community, regard is to be had to the number and distribution of local government electors in the community[16], and any change in such number or distribution which is likely to take place within the period of five years immediately following the fixing of the number of community councillors[17].

1   Ie under the Local Government (Democracy) (Wales) Act 2013 s 29 (see PARA 87). As to the meaning of 'Wales' see PARA 1 note 1. As to the meanings of 'principal area', and of references to the electoral arrangements of a principal area, see PARA 72 note 28.

2   See the Local Government (Democracy) (Wales) Act 2013 s 30(1). The Local Democracy and Boundary Commission for Wales is the body formerly known as the Local Government Boundary Commission for Wales, which has been continued in existence and renamed, by the Local Government (Democracy) (Wales) Act 2013 (see s 2; and PARA 72); as to the duty of the Local Democracy and Boundary Commission for Wales, for the purpose of considering whether it is appropriate to make or recommend changes in the arrangements for local government in Wales, to monitor the areas and electoral arrangements relevant to local government in Wales see PARA 72.

3   As to the meaning of 'local government elector' for these purposes see PARA 88 note 10.

4   Local Government (Democracy) (Wales) Act 2013 s 30(1)(a). For the purposes of head (1) in the text, account is to be taken of:

(1)   any discrepancy between the number of local government electors and the number of persons that are eligible to be local government electors (as indicated by relevant official statistics) (s 30(2)(a)); and

(2)   any change to the number or distribution of local government electors in the principal area which is likely to take place in the period of five years immediately following the making of any recommendation (s 30(2)(b)).

For these purposes, 'relevant official statistics' means such official statistics within the meaning of the Statistics and Registration Service Act 2007 s 6 (see REGISTRATION CONCERNING THE INDIVIDUAL vol 88 (2012) PARA 355) as the Commission considers appropriate: Local Government (Democracy) (Wales) Act 2013 s 30(3). As to the meaning of 'principal area' see PARA 72 note 28. As to the establishment of electoral areas for the purpose of local government elections see PARA 74. As to the election of councillors see PARA 197 et seq; and LOCAL GOVERNMENT vol 69 (2009) PARA 126 et seq.

5   Local Government (Democracy) (Wales) Act 2013 s 30(1)(b)(i).
6   Local Government (Democracy) (Wales) Act 2013 s 30(1)(b)(ii).
7   As to the meaning of 'principal council' see PARA 72 note 7; and see LOCAL GOVERNMENT vol 69 (2009) PARA 23.
8   See the Local Government (Democracy) (Wales) Act 2013 s 33(1). As to the meaning of references to the electoral arrangements of a community see PARA 72 note 28. As to communities see LOCAL GOVERNMENT vol 69 (2009) PARA 41 et seq.
9   See the Local Government (Democracy) (Wales) Act 2013 s 33(2).
10   Local Government (Democracy) (Wales) Act 2013 s 33(2)(a). For these purposes, account is to be taken of any discrepancy between the number of local government electors and number of persons that are eligible to be local government electors (as indicated by relevant official statistics): s 33(5). 'Relevant official statistics' means such official statistics within the meaning of the Statistics and Registration Service Act 2007 s 6 (see REGISTRATION CONCERNING THE INDIVIDUAL vol 88 (2012) PARA 355) as the Commission, or as the case may be, principal council considers appropriate: Local Government (Democracy) (Wales) Act 2013 s 33(6).
11   Local Government (Democracy) (Wales) Act 2013 s 33(2)(b).
12   See the Local Government (Democracy) (Wales) Act 2013 s 33(3).
13   Local Government (Democracy) (Wales) Act 2013 s 33(3)(a).
14   Local Government (Democracy) (Wales) Act 2013 s 33(3)(b).
15   Local Government (Democracy) (Wales) Act 2013 s 33(3)(c).
16   Local Government (Democracy) (Wales) Act 2013 s 33(4)(a).
17   Local Government (Democracy) (Wales) Act 2013 s 33(4)(b).

(iii) Review of Welsh Assembly Electoral Regions

90.   Review of Welsh Assembly electoral regions. The provisions of the Government of Wales Act 2006 that set out the mechanism for the review of Welsh Assembly electoral regions and for alterations both in those regions and in the allocation of seats to those regions[1] have been repealed[2] and there is no legislative provision made currently for the future review of Welsh Assembly electoral regions[3].

1   Ie the Government of Wales Act 2006 s 2(5), Sch 1 (alteration of Assembly electoral regions).
2   Ie by the Parliamentary Voting System and Constituencies Act 2011 ss 13(2)(b), 16, Sch 12 Pt 2.
3   Accordingly, the mechanism required for the review of Welsh Assembly electoral regions is currently in abeyance pending new legislation, yet to be formulated. Although not directly on point, the reviews to be conducted by all four Boundary Commissions of the United Kingdom on recommendations for new parliamentary constituencies have been postponed until 2018: see PARA 78 note 10.

(iv) Review of European Parliamentary Electoral Regions

91.   Recommendations by Electoral Commission as to the distribution of United Kingdom MEPs. The Secretary of State[1] may by notice require the Electoral Commission[2] to make a recommendation[3] to him as to the distribution between the electoral regions of[4]: (1) a total number of members of the European Parliament ('MEPs')[5] specified in the notice[6]; or (2) if the notice specifies more than one total number of MEPs, each of the total numbers so specified[7]. The power to give such a notice is exercisable with a view to the implementation of any change or anticipated change under EU law[8] in the total number of MEPs to be elected for the United Kingdom[9]. The Electoral Commission must comply with such a notice within the period specified therein[10]; and, in determining what recommendation to make for the distribution of any total number of MEPs, the Electoral Commission must ensure that: (a) each electoral region is allocated at least three MEPs[11]; and (b) the ratio of electors[12] to MEPs is as nearly as possible the same in each electoral region[13].

1   As to the Secretary of State see PARA 2.
2   As to the establishment and constitution of the Electoral Commission see PARA 34 et seq.
3   A recommendation under the European Parliament (Representation) Act 2003 s 3 must be published by the Electoral Commission and laid before Parliament by the Secretary of State: s 3(5)(a) (amended by SI 2003/1887). Such a recommendation ceases to have effect at the end of the period of one year beginning with the day on which it is made: European Parliament (Representation) Act 2003 s 3(5)(b).
4   See the European Parliament (Representation) Act 2003 s 3(1) (amended by SI 2003/1887). As to the meaning of 'United Kingdom' see PARA 1 note 1; and as to the meaning of 'electoral region' for these purposes see PARA 77 note 4.
5   For these purposes, 'MEP' means a member of the European Parliament: see the European Parliament (Representation) Act 2003 s 27(1). As to MEPs see PARA 13.
6   European Parliament (Representation) Act 2003 s 3(1)(a).
7   European Parliament (Representation) Act 2003 s 3(1)(b).
8   For the purposes of the European Parliament (Representation) Act 2003 Pt 1 (ss 1–8), 'change under EU law', in relation to a change in the number of MEPs to be elected for the United Kingdom, means a change made by (see s 2(1) (amended by SI 2011/1043)):
     (1)   a treaty provision that is part of the EU Treaties (European Parliament (Representation) Act 2003 s 2(1)(a) (s 2(1)(a), (b) amended by SI 2011/1043)); or
     (2)   any provision of a European Council Decision, or of any other instrument, made under a treaty provision that is part of the EU Treaties (European Parliament (Representation) Act 2003 s 2(1)(b) (as so amended)).
     A reference to a treaty provision being part of the EU Treaties is to it being, or being included in provisions which are, specified in the European Communities Act 1972 s 1(2) by virtue of an amendment made by an Act, whether passed before or after the European Parliament (Representation) Act 2003: see s 2(2) (amended by SI 2011/1043). 'Treaty' includes any international agreement (however described) and a protocol or annex to a treaty or other international agreement: European Parliament (Representation) Act 2003 s 2(3). As to the EU Treaties see PARA 6.
9   European Parliament (Representation) Act 2003 s 3(2) (amended by SI 2011/1043).
10   European Parliament (Representation) Act 2003 s 3(3).
11   European Parliament (Representation) Act 2003 s 3(4)(a).
12   For the purposes of the European Parliament (Representation) Act 2003 s 3(4), an 'elector', in relation to an electoral region, is a person whose name appears on the relevant day in (or in any part of) a relevant register which relates to the region: s 4(1). 'Relevant day' means 1 December preceding the day on which the notice under s 3 is given; and ' relevant register' has the same meaning as in the European Parliamentary Elections Act 2002 s 1A, Sch 1A (periodic reviews: see PARA 92 note 6): see the European Parliament (Representation) Act 2003 s 4(2). As to the registration of electors generally see PARA 113 et seq.
13   European Parliament (Representation) Act 2003 s 3(4)(b). In calculating the total number of electors for any electoral region: (1) persons who are registered but have not attained the age of 18 are to be counted as electors (s 4(3)(a)); (2) a citizen of the European Union (not being a Commonwealth citizen or a citizen of the Republic of Ireland) who is registered only for the purposes of local government elections is to be disregarded (s 4(3)(b)); and (3) the Electoral Commission may assume that each relevant register is accurate and that names appearing more than once on registers (or parts of registers) which relate to an electoral region are the names of different electors (s 4(3)(c)).

92.   Periodic reviews by the Electoral Commission of the distribution of MEPs between the electoral regions. As soon as possible after 1 May in a pre-election year[1], the Electoral Commission[2] must carry out a review (the 'periodic review') of the distribution of members of the European Parliament ('MEPs;)[3] between the electoral regions[4], and report its conclusions to the Secretary of State[5]. In carrying out the periodic review, the Commission must consider whether, assuming that each region is entitled to be allocated at least three MEPs, the ratio of electors[6] to MEPs is as nearly as possible the same for every electoral region[7]. If the Commission concludes that such a result is not achieved by the current distribution of MEPs, it must include in its report a recommendation specifying a distribution that would achieve that result[8]. The report must be published by the Commission and laid before Parliament by the Secretary of State[9].

The Commission may not take any step (or further step) in carrying out a periodic review if an order implementing changes in the number of United Kingdom MEPs[10] is made or a 'suspension notice'[11] is given to the Commission: (1) within the period of 12 months ending with 1 May in the pre-election year in question[12]; or (2) after the end of that period but before the Commission makes its report[13], unless and until the duties in relation to carrying out a periodic review revive[14].

1   For these purposes, 'pre-election year' means a year which immediately precedes a year in which a general election of MEPs is to be held; and 'general election of MEPs' means an election required to be held in the United Kingdom by virtue of art 11(2) of the Act annexed to Council Decision 76/787: see the European Parliamentary Elections Act 2002 s 1A, Sch 1A para 6(1) (Sch 1A added by the European Parliament (Representation) Act 2003 s 7(1), (2), Schedule; definition of 'general election of MEPs' in the European Parliamentary Elections Act 2002 Sch 1A para 6(1) amended by SI 2004/1374). The 'Act annexed to Council Decision 76/787' is the Act concerning the election of the representatives of the European Parliament by direct universal suffrage annexed to EEC and Euratom Decision 76/787 (OJ L278, 08.10.76, p 1) (the '1976 Act') (see PARA 6): see the European Parliamentary Elections Act 2002 s 17. As to the meaning of 'United Kingdom' see PARA 1 note 1.

2   As to the establishment and constitution of the Electoral Commission see PARA 34 et seq.

3   As to MEPs see PARA 13.

4   European Parliamentary Elections Act 2002 Sch 1A para 1(1)(a) (as added: see note 1). The provision made by Sch 1A para 1 is subject to that made by Sch 1A para 2 (see the text and notes 10–14): see Sch 1A para 1 (as so added). As to electoral regions established for the purposes of European parliamentary elections see PARA 77.

5   European Parliamentary Elections Act 2002 Sch 1A para 1(1)(b) (as added: see note 1). See note 4. As to the Secretary of State see PARA 2.

6   For the purposes of the European Parliamentary Elections Act 2002 Sch 1A para 1(2), a person is an 'elector', in relation to an electoral region, if his name appears on 1 May in the pre-election year concerned in (or in any part of) a relevant register which relates to the region: Sch 1A para 6(2) (as added: see note 1). 'Relevant register' means: (1) a register of parliamentary electors (Sch 1A para 6(1)(a) (as so added)); (2) a register of local government electors (Sch 1A para 6(1)(b) (as so added)); (3) a register of peers maintained under the Representation of the People Act 1985 s 3 (extension of European parliamentary franchise to peers resident outside the United Kingdom: see PARA 101) (European Parliamentary Elections Act 2002 Sch 1A para 6(1)(c) (as so added)); and (4) a register maintained under the European Parliamentary Elections (Franchise of Relevant Citizens of the Union) Regulations 2001, SI 2001/1184, reg 5 (citizens of the European Union other than Commonwealth and Republic of Ireland citizens: see PARA 143) (European Parliamentary Elections Act 2002 Sch 1A para 6(1)(d) (as so added)). As to the form and content of the register of parliamentary and local government electors see PARA 145.

    In calculating the total number of electors for any electoral region: (a) persons who are registered but have not attained the age of 18 are to be counted as electors (Sch 1A para 6(3)(a) (as so added)); (b) a citizen of the European Union (not being a Commonwealth citizen or a citizen of the Republic of Ireland) who is registered only for the purposes of local government elections is to be disregarded (Sch 1A para 6(3)(b) (as so added)); and (c) the Electoral Commission may assume that each relevant register is accurate and that names appearing more than once on registers (or parts of registers) which relate to an electoral region are the names of different electors (Sch 1A para 6(3)(c) (as so added)). For these purposes, 'citizen of the European Union' is to be determined in accordance with the Treaty on the Functioning of the

European Union (Rome, 25 March 1957; TS 1 (1973); Cmnd 5179) ('TFEU') art 20 (formerly art 17 TEC: see PARA 6 note 1), which states that every person holding the nationality of a member state is a citizen of the Union: see the European Parliamentary Elections Act 2002 s 17; Interpretation Act 1978 s 17(2)(b).

7   European Parliamentary Elections Act 2002 Sch 1A para 1(2) (as added: see note 1).
8   European Parliamentary Elections Act 2002 Sch 1A para 1(3) (as added: see note 1).
9   European Parliamentary Elections Act 2002 Sch 1A para 1(4) (as added: see note 1).
10   Ie an order under the European Parliament (Representation) Act 2003 s 5 (a '2003 Act order') (see PARA 94), which takes effect in relation to the next general election of MEPs after it is made: see the European Parliamentary Elections Act 2002 Sch 1A para 2(3) (as added: see note 1).
11   Ie a notice stating that the Secretary of State considers it likely that a 2003 Act order will be made before the next general election of MEPs: see the European Parliamentary Elections Act 2002 Sch 1A para 2(3) (as added: see note 1).
12   European Parliamentary Elections Act 2002 Sch 1A para 2(1)(a) (as added: see note 1).
13   European Parliamentary Elections Act 2002 Sch 1A para 2(1)(b) (as added: see note 1).
14   See the European Parliamentary Elections Act 2002 Sch 1A para 2(1) (as added: see note 1). The duties under Sch 1A para 1 revive if the Secretary of State withdraws a suspension notice more than nine months before the date of the poll for the next general election of MEPs: see Sch 1A para 2(2) (as so added). Such a revival is subject again to Sch 1A para 2(2): see Sch 1A para 2(2) (as so added). As to the date of the poll at a European parliamentary election see PARA 222.

93.   Implementation of Electoral Commission recommendation following periodic review. Where a recommendation specifying a revised distribution of members of the European Parliament ('MEPs') is made to the Secretary of State[1] following a periodic review[2], the Secretary of State must lay before Parliament a draft of an order giving effect to the recommendation by amending any of the numbers specified in the European Parliamentary Elections Act 2002[3]. If the draft is approved by resolution of each House, the Secretary of State must make an order in the terms of the draft[4], but he must consult the Electoral Commission before laying such an order before Parliament[5].

The Secretary of State may not take any step (or further step) in laying such an order[6] if an order implementing changes in the number of United Kingdom MEPs[7] is made before he would otherwise have taken it[8]. Subject to that, the Secretary of State is not required to take any such step (or such further step) if and so long as he is of the opinion that it is likely that an order implementing changes in the number of United Kingdom MEPs will be made before the next general election of MEPs[9]. However, if he ceases to be of that opinion, the Secretary of State may not make an order[10] on or after the relevant day[11]; and he is not required to take any other step in laying an order[12] if he does not consider that it will be practicable to make an order[13] before the relevant day[14].

1   As to the Secretary of State see PARA 2.
2   Ie a recommendation under the European Parliamentary Elections Act 2002 s 1A, Sch 1A para 1(3) (see PARA 92): see Sch 1A para 3(1) (Sch 1A added by the European Parliament (Representation) Act 2003 s 7(2), Schedule).
3   European Parliamentary Elections Act 2002 Sch 1A para 3(1)(a) (as added: see note 2). The text refers to the numbers specified in s 1(3) (see PARA 77 note 5): see Sch 1A para 3(1)(a) (as so added).
        If a motion for the approval of a draft of an order under Sch 1A para 3 is rejected by either House or withdrawn by leave of the House, the Secretary of State may, after consulting the Electoral Commission, alter the draft order and lay it before Parliament for approval: Sch 1A para 4(1) (as so added). However, the Secretary of State may not, without the consent of the Commission, alter a draft order so as to propose a distribution of MEPs other than that recommended under Sch 1A para 1(3) (see PARA 92): Sch 1A para 4(2) (as so added). The Commission may not give its consent under Sch 1A para 4(2) unless it is satisfied that the distribution of MEPs could have been recommended under Sch 1A para 1(3): Sch 1A para 4(3) (as so added). If an altered draft order is approved by both Houses, the Secretary of State must make an order under Sch 1A para 3 in the terms of the altered draft: Sch 1A para 4(4) (as so

added). Schedule 1A para 4 has effect subject to Sch 1A para 5 (see the text and notes 6–14): Sch 1A para 4(5) (as so added). As to the establishment and constitution of the Electoral Commission see PARA 34 et seq.

4 European Parliamentary Elections Act 2002 Sch 1A para 3(1)(b) (as added: see note 2). Such an order may make consequential, transitional or saving provision (Sch 1A para 3(2) (as so added)); and such provision may modify any enactment (Sch 1A para 3(3) (as so added)). As to the making of orders under the European Parliamentary Elections Act 2002 generally see PARA 13 note 12.

5 European Parliamentary Elections Act 2002 Sch 1A para 3(4) (as added: see note 2). Schedule 1A para 3 has effect subject to Sch 1A para 4 (see note 3) and Sch 1A para 5 (see the text and notes 6–14): Sch 1A para 3(5) (as so added).

6 Ie any step or further step under the European Parliamentary Elections Act 2002 Sch 1A paras 3, 4 (see the text and notes 1–5): see Sch 1A para 5(1) (as added: see note 2).

7 Ie a '2003 Act order' (as to which see PARA 92 note 10): see the European Parliamentary Elections Act 2002 Sch 1A para 5(1) (as added: see note 2). As to the meaning of 'United Kingdom' see PARA 1 note 1.

8 European Parliamentary Elections Act 2002 Sch 1A para 5(1) (as added: see note 2).

9 European Parliamentary Elections Act 2002 Sch 1A para 5(2) (as added: see note 2). As to the meaning of 'general election of MEPs' see PARA 92 note 1.

10 Ie an order under the European Parliamentary Elections Act 2002 Sch 1A para 3 (see the text and notes 1–5): see Sch 1A para 5(3)(a) (as added: see note 2).

11 European Parliamentary Elections Act 2002 Sch 1A para 5(3)(a) (as added: see note 2). For this purpose, the 'relevant day' means the first day of the period of four months ending with the day on which the poll for the next general election of MEPs is to be held: see Sch 1A para 5(4) (as so added).

12 Ie any step or further step under the European Parliamentary Elections Act 2002 Sch 1A paras 3, 4 (see the text and notes 1–5): see Sch 1A para 5(3)(b) (as added: see note 2).

13 Ie an order under the European Parliamentary Elections Act 2002 Sch 1A para 3 (see the text and notes 1–5): see Sch 1A para 5(3)(b) (as added: see note 2).

14 European Parliamentary Elections Act 2002 Sch 1A para 5(3)(b) (as added: see note 2).

94.   Order giving effect to a change under EU law in the number of MEPs to be elected for the United Kingdom.   The Secretary of State[1] may by order[2] give effect to a change under EU law[3] in the number of members of the European Parliament ('MEPs') to be elected for the United Kingdom[4] by amending[5]: (1) the figure specified in the European Parliamentary Elections Act 2002[6] giving the total number of MEPs to be elected for the United Kingdom[7]; and (2) any of the specified figures[8] giving the numbers of MEPs to be elected in the electoral regions[9]. The distribution of MEPs resulting from the provision made under head (2) above must[10] be the distribution proposed in a recommendation of the Electoral Commission[11] which is effective on the day on which the order is made[12].

An order making an amendment to the number of MEPs and electoral regions[13] may be made before the provision making the relevant change[14] has entered into force[15]. If the relevant change is made by a provision of a treaty, an order making such an amendment may also be made before that provision has become part of the EU Treaties and, if the treaty requires ratification, before it is ratified by the United Kingdom[16]. However, no such amendment[17] may be made so as to come into force[18]: (a) if the relevant change is made by any provision of a European Council Decision, or of any other instrument, made under a treaty provision that is part of the EU Treaties[19], before that provision has entered into force[20]; and (b) if the relevant change is made by a treaty provision, before that provision has both entered into force and become part of the EU Treaties[21].

The Secretary of State must consult the Electoral Commission before making such an order giving effect to a change under EU law in the number of MEPs to be elected for the United Kingdom[22].

1 As to the Secretary of State see PARA 2.

2 The power to make an order under the European Parliament (Representation) Act 2003 s 5 is exercisable by statutory instrument: see s 6(1), (2). Such an order may make consequential, transitional or saving provision (s 6(3)); and such provision may modify any enactment (s 6(4)). For these purposes, 'enactment' means a provision of an Act (whether passed before or after the European Parliament (Representation) Act 2003, which was passed on 8 May 2003), including a provision modified by the European Parliament (Representation) Act 2003, or a provision of subordinate legislation (whenever made): see s 27(2). This definition is extended for certain purposes in relation to the Gibraltar franchise: see s 27(3).

If a motion for the approval of a draft order is rejected by either House or withdrawn by leave of the House the Secretary of State may, after consulting the Electoral Commission, alter the draft order: s 6(6) (s 6(6), (7) amended by SI 2003/1887). However, the Secretary of State may not, without the consent of the Electoral Commission, alter any amendments to the European Parliamentary Elections Act 2002 s 1(3) (see PARA 77 note 5) contained in the draft order: European Parliament (Representation) Act 2003 s 6(7) (as so amended). The Electoral Commission may not give its consent under s 6(7) unless it is satisfied that the distribution of members of the European Parliament ('MEPs') proposed by the altered draft order could have been recommended under s 3 (see PARA 91): s 6(8). A statutory instrument containing an order that is not subject to approval in draft under s 6(5) (see note 15) is subject to annulment in pursuance of a resolution of either House of Parliament: s 6(9).

3 As to the meaning of 'change under EU law' see PARA 91 note 8.

4 As to the meaning of 'United Kingdom' see PARA 1 note 1.

5 European Parliament (Representation) Act 2003 s 5(1) (amended by SI 2003/1887; SI 2011/1043).

6 Ie specified in the European Parliamentary Elections Act 2002 s 1(1) (see PARA 77): see the European Parliament (Representation) Act 2003 s 5(1)(a).

7 European Parliament (Representation) Act 2003 s 5(1)(a). As to the latest order made in exercise of the powers conferred under ss 5(1), 6(3) see the European Parliament (Number of MEPs and Distribution between Electoral Regions) (United Kingdom and Gibraltar) Order 2008, SI 2008/1954 (implementing the recommendation of the Electoral Commission made under the European Parliament (Representation) Act 2003 s 3 (see PARA 91) to adjust the distribution between the electoral regions of the changed number of United Kingdom MEPs following the Treaty concerning the accession of the Republic of Bulgaria and Romania to the European Union signed at Luxembourg on 25 April 2005).

8 Ie specified in the European Parliamentary Elections Act 2002 s 1(3) (see PARA 77 note 5): see the European Parliament (Representation) Act 2003 s 5(1)(b).

9 European Parliament (Representation) Act 2003 s 5(1)(b). See note 7. As to electoral regions established for the purposes of European parliamentary elections see PARA 77.

10 Ie subject to the European Parliament (Representation) Act 2003 s 6(6)–(8) (see note 2): see s 5(2).

11 Ie under the European Parliament (Representation) Act 2003 s 3 (see PARA 91): see s 5(2).

12 European Parliament (Representation) Act 2003 s 5(2).

13 Ie any amendment to the European Parliamentary Elections Act 2002 s 1 (see PARA 77): see the European Parliament (Representation) Act 2003 s 5(3).

14 For the purposes of the European Parliament (Representation) Act 2003 s 5(3)–(5) (see the text and notes 15–21), the 'relevant change', in relation to an order under s 5 amending the European Parliamentary Elections Act 2002 s 1 (see PARA 77), means the change under EU law being implemented by the order: European Parliament (Representation) Act 2003 s 5(6) (amended by SI 2011/1043).

15 European Parliament (Representation) Act 2003 s 5(3). However, such an order may not be made unless a draft of it has been laid before, and approved by a resolution of, each House of Parliament: s 6(5).

16 European Parliament (Representation) Act 2003 s 5(4) (amended by SI 2011/1043).

17 Ie no amendment to the European Parliamentary Elections Act 2002 s 1 (see PARA 77): see the European Parliament (Representation) Act 2003 s 5(5).

18 European Parliament (Representation) Act 2003 s 5(5).

19 Ie by a provision mentioned in the European Parliament (Representation) Act 2003 s 2(1)(b) (see PARA 91 note 8): see s 5(5)(a).

20 See the European Parliament (Representation) Act 2003 s 5(5)(a).

21 European Parliament (Representation) Act 2003 s 5(5)(b) (amended by SI 2011/1043).

22 See the European Parliament (Representation) Act 2003 s 5(7) (amended by SI 2003/1887).

4. RIGHT TO VOTE AND REGISTRATION OF ELECTORS

(1) THE RIGHT TO VOTE

(i) Entitlement to Vote in Elections

A. PARLIAMENTARY AND LOCAL GOVERNMENT ELECTIONS

95. Entitlement to vote as parliamentary elector. A person[1] is entitled to vote[2] as an elector at a parliamentary election[3] in any constituency[4] if on the date of the poll[5] he is[6]:

    (1)   registered in the register of parliamentary electors for that constituency[7];

    (2)   not subject to any legal incapacity[8] to vote (age apart)[9];

    (3)   either a Commonwealth citizen[10] or a citizen of the Republic of Ireland[11]; and

    (4)   of voting age[12].

Different qualifications apply in respect of British citizens overseas[13].

A person is not so entitled to vote as an elector more than once[14] in the same constituency at any parliamentary election[15] or in more than one constituency at a general election[16].

1   Under the Interpretation Act 1978, 'person' includes a body of persons corporate or unincorporate: ss 5, 22(1), 23(1), Sch 1, Sch 2 para 4(1)(a). Without prejudice to the provisions of the Interpretation Act 1978, and for the purposes of the Representation of the People Act 1983, unless the context otherwise requires, 'person' includes an association corporate or unincorporate: see s 202(1). For these purposes, the context does otherwise require, and a company is not a person entitled to vote: see *Wills v Tozer* (1904) 53 WR 74.

2   'Voter' means a person voting at an election and includes a person voting as proxy and, except in the parliamentary elections rules, and the rules under the Representation of the People Act 1983 s 36 (see PARA 383), a person voting by proxy; and 'vote' (whether noun or verb) must be construed accordingly, except that in those rules any reference to an elector voting or an elector's vote must include a reference to an elector voting by proxy or an elector's vote given by proxy: see s 202(1). For the purposes of the Representation of the People Act 1983, 'elector', in relation to an election, means any person who has for the time being an entry on the register to be used at that election, but does not include those shown in the register (or, in the case of a person who has an anonymous entry in the register, in the record of anonymous entries) as below voting age on the day fixed for the poll: see s 202(1) (definition amended by the Electoral Administration Act 2006 s 10(2), Sch 1 paras 2, 13(1), (3)). 'Voting age', in the context of parliamentary elections, means 18 years or over: see the Representation of the People Act 1983 s 1(1)(d) (s 1 substituted by the Representation of the People Act 2000 s 1(1)). For the purposes of the Representation of the People Acts, a person is deemed not to have attained a given age until the commencement of the relevant anniversary of the day of his birth: Representation of the People Act 1983 s 202(2). As to the meanings of 'the Representation of the People Acts' and 'election' for these purposes see PARA 3 note 1; as to the meaning of 'anonymous entry' in relation to a register of electors see PARA 148; and as to the meaning of 'parliamentary elections rules' see PARA 383 note 2. As to the form and content of registers of electors and the record of anonymous entries see PARA 145 et seq; and as to applications to vote by proxy see PARA 367 et seq.

3   As to the meaning of 'parliamentary election' see PARA 9.

4   As to the meaning of 'constituency' for these purposes see PARA 9.

5   As to the date of the poll at a parliamentary general election or by-election see PARA 195.

6   See the Representation of the People Act 1983 s 1(1) (as substituted: see note 2).

7   Representation of the People Act 1983 s 1(1)(a) (as substituted: see note 2). As to entitlement to be registered as a parliamentary or local government elector see PARA 113 et seq.

8   'Legal incapacity' includes (in addition, where applicable, to any incapacity by virtue of any subsisting provision of the common law) any disqualification imposed by the Representation of the People Act 1983 or any other Act: see s 202(1) (amended by the Electoral Administration Act 2006 s 73(1), (2)). Similarly, for the purposes of the National Assembly for Wales

(Representation of the People) Order 2007, SI 2007/236, 'legal incapacity' includes (in addition to any incapacity arising by virtue of any subsisting provision of the common law) any disqualification imposed by the National Assembly for Wales (Representation of the People) Order 2007, SI 2007/236, or by any other enactment (see art 2(1)); and, for the purposes of the European Parliamentary Elections Regulations 2004, SI 2004/293, 'legal incapacity' includes (in addition to any incapacity arising by virtue of any subsisting provision of the common law) any disqualification imposed by the European Parliamentary Elections Regulations 2004, SI 2004/293, or by any Act (see reg 2(1) (substituted by SI 2009/186)). As to legal incapacities to vote generally see PARA 109 et seq.

As to the common law rule which formerly provided that a person was subject to a legal incapacity to vote by reason of his mental state see PARA 108. At common law, a peer of Parliament was also legally incapable of voting at a parliamentary election, even though his name may have been placed upon the register without objection: see *Earl Beauchamp v Madresfield* (1872) LR 8 CP 245; 4 Co Inst 2, 15; *Marquis of Bristol v Beck* (1907) 96 LT 55; *Pembroke Boroughs Case* (1901) 5 O'M & H 135 at 142; *Petersfield Case, Stowe v Jolliffe* (1874) LR 9 CP 734 at 750 per Lord Coleridge CJ; *Droitwich Case, Viscount Southwell's Case* (1835) Kn & Omb 44 at 65. See also *Bedford Borough Case, Marquis of Tavistock's Case* (1833) Cockb & Rowe 37 at 95, Per & Kn 112 at 146, explained in *Re Parliamentary Election for Bristol South East* [1964] 2 QB 257 at 281–282, sub nom *Re Bristol South East Parliamentary Election* [1961] 3 All ER 354 at 366–367, DC, per Gorman J. However, by virtue of the House of Lords Act 1999 s 3, the holder of a hereditary peerage is not disqualified by virtue of that peerage (unless excepted under ss 1, 2) for voting at elections to the House of Commons: see PARLIAMENT vol 78 (2010) PARA 897.

9 Representation of the People Act 1983 s 1(1)(b) (as substituted: see note 2).
10 As to who are Commonwealth citizens see BRITISH NATIONALITY vol 4 (2011) PARA 409.
11 Representation of the People Act 1983 s 1(1)(c) (as substituted: see note 2). As to who are citizens of the Republic of Ireland see BRITISH NATIONALITY vol 4 (2011) PARA 410.
12 Representation of the People Act 1983 s 1(1)(d) (as substituted: see note 2). As to voting age see note 2.
13 See PARA 96.
14 The restrictions on voting more than once do not affect the right of an elector to vote by proxy at any relevant election, subject to the rules regarding proxy voting being met in each case: see PARA 367 et seq.
15 Representation of the People Act 1983 s 1(2)(a) (as substituted: see note 2).
16 Representation of the People Act 1983 s 1(2)(b) (as substituted: see note 2). As to usage of the term 'parliamentary general election' see PARA 9 note 1; and as to parliamentary general elections generally see PARA 189 et seq.

96. Extension of parliamentary franchise to British citizens overseas. A person[1] is entitled to vote[2] as an elector[3] at a parliamentary election[4] in any constituency[5] if:

(1) he qualifies as an overseas elector in respect of that constituency on the relevant date[6];

(2) on that date and on the date of the poll[7] he is not subject to any legal incapacity to vote[8] and is a British citizen[9]; and

(3) on the date of the poll he is registered in a register of parliamentary electors[10] for that constituency[11].

A person qualifies as an overseas elector in respect of a constituency on the relevant date[12] if on that date he is not resident in the United Kingdom[13] and if he satisfies one of the following sets of conditions[14]. The first set of conditions is that:

(a) the person was included in a register of parliamentary electors in respect of an address at a place[15] that is situated within the constituency concerned[16];

(b) that entry in the register was made on the basis that he was resident[17] or to be treated for the purposes of registration as resident at that address[18];

(c)   that entry in the register was in force at any time falling within the period of 15 years ending immediately before the relevant date[19]; and

(d)   subsequent to that entry ceasing to have effect, no entry was made in any register of parliamentary electors on the basis that he was resident, or to be treated for the purposes of registration as resident, at any other address[20].

The second set of conditions is that:

(i)   the person was last resident in the United Kingdom within the period of 15 years ending immediately before the relevant date[21];

(ii)   he was by reason only of his age incapable of being included in any register of parliamentary electors in force on the last day on which he was resident in the United Kingdom[22]; and

(iii)   the address at which he was resident on that day was at a place that is situated within the constituency concerned and a parent or guardian of his was included, in respect of that address, in a register of parliamentary electors or a register of local government electors in force on that day[23].

The restrictions on the registration of such persons are described elsewhere in this title[24].

1   The Representation of the People Act 1985 s 1 has effect as if contained in the Representation of the People Act 1983 Pt I (ss 1–66B): see the Representation of the People Act 1985 s 27(2). Accordingly, as to the meaning of 'person' see PARA 95 note 1.
2   As to the meaning of 'vote' see PARA 95 note 2; definition applied by virtue of the Representation of the People Act 1985 s 27(2) (see note 1).
3   As to the meaning of 'elector' see PARA 95 note 2; definition applied by virtue of the Representation of the People Act 1985 s 27(2) (see note 1).
4   As to the meaning of 'parliamentary election' see PARA 9.
5   Ie without prejudice to the qualification set out in the Representation of the People Act 1983 s 1 (see PARA 95). As to the meaning of 'constituency' for these purposes see PARA 9.
6   Representation of the People Act 1985 s 1(1)(a) (s 1 substituted by the Representation of the People Act 2000 s 8, Sch 2 paras 1, 2). The reference in the text to the 'relevant date' is to the date on which a person makes a declaration under and in accordance with the Representation of the People Act 1985 s 2 (an 'overseas elector's declaration') (see PARA 114): see s 1(1)(a) (as so substituted).
7   As to the date of the poll at a parliamentary general election or by-election see PARA 195.
8   Representation of the People Act 1985 s 1(1)(b)(i) (as substituted: see note 6). As to the meaning of 'legal incapacity (to vote)' for these purposes see PARA 95 note 8; definition applied by virtue of s 27(2) (see note 1). However, the reference in s 1(1) to a person being subject to a legal incapacity to vote on the relevant date does not include a reference to his being under the age of 18 on that date: s 1(5) (as so substituted). As to voting age for parliamentary elections see PARA 95 note 2.
9   Representation of the People Act 1985 s 1(1)(b)(ii) (as substituted: see note 6). As to who are British citizens see BRITISH NATIONALITY vol 4 (2011) PARAS 406, 421 et seq. As to the entitlement under which Commonwealth citizens and citizens of the Republic of Ireland are entitled to vote see PARA 95.
10 As to entitlement to be registered as a parliamentary or local government elector see PARA 113 et seq.
11 Representation of the People Act 1985 s 1(1)(c) (as substituted: see note 6).
12 Ie for the purposes of the Representation of the People Act 1983 and the Representation of the People Act 1985: see s 1(2) (as substituted: see note 6).
13 Representation of the People Act 1985 s 1(2)(a) (as substituted: see note 6). For the purposes of s 1, where a person is registered in a register of parliamentary electors for any constituency or part of a constituency in pursuance of an overseas elector's declaration (see note 6), it is conclusively presumed that he was not resident in the United Kingdom on the relevant date: s 2(7) (s 2 substituted by the Representation of the People Act 2000 Sch 2 paras 1, 3). As to the meaning of 'United Kingdom' see PARA 1 note 1.
14 Representation of the People Act 1985 s 1(2)(b) (as substituted: see note 6). In the case of the holder of a hereditary peerage to whom the House of Lords Act 1999 s 3(1) applies (see PARA 95

note 8; and PARLIAMENT vol 78 (2010) PARA 897), any reference in the Representation of the People Act 1985 s 1(3) (see heads (a)–(d) in the text) or s 1(4)(b) (see head (ii) in the text) to a register of parliamentary electors includes any register of local government electors in Great Britain which was required to be published on any date not later than 15 February 2000: see the Holders of Hereditary Peerages (Overseas Electors) (Transitional Provisions) Order 2001, SI 2001/84, art 2. A peer had the right to be registered in the register of local government electors under the Representation of the People Act 1983 s 15: see PARA 126. As to the meaning of 'Great Britain' see PARA 1 note 1.

15 The provision is so worded that the entitlement arises even if the premises in respect of which the person was registered are subsequently destroyed. A person might be included in respect of an address even if the address itself is not shown in the register of electors because the person's name only is included (see PARA 145).

16 Representation of the People Act 1985 s 1(3)(a) (as substituted: see note 6). See note 14.

17 As to the determination of residence for the purposes of registration as a parliamentary or local government elector see PARA 117 et seq; provisions applied by virtue of the Representation of the People Act 1985 s 27(2) (see note 1).

18 Representation of the People Act 1985 s 1(3)(b) (as substituted: see note 6). See note 14.

19 Representation of the People Act 1985 s 1(3)(c) (s 1 as substituted (see note 6); s 1(3)(c), (4)(a) amended by the Political Parties, Elections and Referendums Act 2000 s 141(a)). See note 14. Disenfranchisement, triggered under the Representation of the People Act 1985 s 1(3)(c) after the passing of 15 years' residence overseas (the '15-year rule'), has the legitimate objectives of testing the strength of a British citizen's links with the United Kingdom over a significant period of time and removing the right to vote from those whose links with the United Kingdom had diminished and who were not, for the most part, directly affected by the laws passed there: *R (on the application of Preston) v Lord President of the Council* [2012] EWCA Civ 1378, [2013] QB 687, [2013] 1 All ER 869 (case brought on the basis that the 15 year rule was an unjustified and discriminatory restriction on the exercise of the fundamental right conferred by the Treaty on the Functioning of the European Union for citizens of the EU to move and reside freely within the territory of the member states: see PARA 6).

20 Representation of the People Act 1985 s 1(3)(d) (as substituted: see note 6). An electoral registration officer may have mistakenly included the person in the register as resident at an address even though that person was not resident (or treated for the purposes of registration as resident) there on the qualifying date to which the register relates. See note 14.

21 Representation of the People Act 1985 s 1(4)(a) (as substituted and amended: see note 19).

22 Representation of the People Act 1985 s 1(4)(b) (as substituted: see note 6). See note 14.

23 Representation of the People Act 1985 s 1(4)(c) (as substituted: see note 6). The reference in s 1(4) to a register of local government electors includes a reference to a register of electors prepared for the purposes of local elections (within the meaning of the Electoral Law Act (Northern Ireland) 1962): see the Representation of the People Act 1985 s 1(5) (as so substituted).

24 See PARA 114 et seq.

97. Entitlement to vote as local government elector.

A person[1] is entitled to vote[2] as an elector[3] at a local government election[4] in any electoral area[5] if, on the date of the poll[6], he[7]:

(1) is registered in the register of local government electors for that area[8];

(2) is not subject to any legal incapacity[9] to vote (age apart)[10];

(3) is a Commonwealth citizen[11], a citizen of the Republic of Ireland[12], or a relevant citizen of the Union[13]; and

(4) is of voting age[14].

However, a person is not so entitled to vote as an elector more than once[15] in the same electoral area at any local government election[16] or in more than one electoral area at an ordinary election[17] for a local government area which is not a single electoral area[18].

1 As to the meaning of 'person' see PARA 95 note 1.

2 As to the meaning of 'vote' see PARA 95 note 2.

3 As to the meaning of 'elector' see PARA 95 note 2.

4 As to the meaning of 'local government election' see PARA 11. Local government electors are entitled to vote at a parish or community meeting or at a poll consequent thereon: see PARA 106.

Elections of the Mayor of London and the members of the London Assembly are treated as local government elections for the purposes of the Representation of the People Acts: see PARA 11; and LONDON GOVERNMENT vol 71 (2013) PARA 76 et seq. As to the entitlement to vote in local authority mayoral elections see PARA 98.

5   As to the meaning of 'electoral area' see PARA 11.

6   As to the date of the poll at local government elections (including elections to fill vacancies) see PARAS 206–209.

7   See the Representation of the People Act 1983 s 2(1) (s 2 substituted by the Representation of the People Act 2000 s 1(1)).

8   Representation of the People Act 1983 s 2(1)(a) (as substituted: see note 7). As to the meaning of 'local government area' see PARA 33 note 7. As to entitlement to be registered as a parliamentary or local government elector see PARA 113 et seq.

9   As to the meaning of 'legal incapacity' for these purposes see PARA 95 note 8.

10 Representation of the People Act 1983 s 2(1)(b) (as substituted: see note 7). As to voting age see head (4) in the text.

11 As to who are Commonwealth citizens see BRITISH NATIONALITY vol 4 (2011) PARA 409.

12 As to who are citizens of the Republic of Ireland see BRITISH NATIONALITY vol 4 (2011) PARA 410.

13 Representation of the People Act 1983 s 2(1)(c) (as substituted: see note 7). 'Citizen of the Union' must be construed in accordance with the Treaty on the Functioning of the European Union (Rome, 25 March 1957; TS 1 (1973); Cmnd 5179) ('TFEU') art 20 (formerly art 17 TEC: see PARA 6 note 1), which states that every person holding the nationality of a member state is a citizen of the Union; and 'relevant citizen of the Union' means such a citizen who is not a Commonwealth citizen or a citizen of the Republic of Ireland: see the Representation of the People Act 1983 s 202(1) (definition added by SI 1995/1948); Interpretation Act 1978 s 17(2)(b).

14 Representation of the People Act 1983 s 2(1)(d) (as substituted: see note 7). 'Voting age', for the purposes of local government elections, means 18 years or over: see s 2(1)(d) (as so substituted). A person entitled to vote is, subject to restrictions, entitled to be registered: see PARA 112.

15 The restrictions on voting more than once do not affect the right of an elector to vote by proxy at any relevant election, subject to the rules regarding proxy voting being met in each case: see PARA 367 et seq.

16 Representation of the People Act 1983 s 2(2)(a) (as substituted: see note 7).

17 As to ordinary local government elections see PARA 197 et seq.

18 Representation of the People Act 1983 s 2(2)(b) (as substituted: see note 7).

98.   Entitlement to vote for the return of an elected local authority mayor. The persons[1] entitled to vote as electors at an election for the return of an elected mayor[2] are those who on the day of the poll[3]: (1) would be entitled to vote as electors at an election of councillors[4] for an electoral area[5] which is situated within the area of the local authority concerned[6]; and (2) are registered in the register of local government electors[7] at an address within the authority's area[8].

However, a person is not so entitled as an elector to cast more than one first preference vote, or more than one second preference vote[9], at an election for the return of an elected mayor[10].

1   As to the meaning of 'person' see PARA 95 note 1.

2   In England, 'elected mayor', in relation to a local authority, means an individual elected as mayor of the authority by the local government electors for the authority's area in accordance with the provisions made by or under the Local Government Act 2000 Pt 1A (ss 9B–9R) (added by the Localism Act 2011 s 21, Sch 2 Pt 1 para 1) (arrangements with respect to local authority governance in England): see the Local Government Act 2000 s 9H(1)–(5) (as so added); PARA 10; and LOCAL GOVERNMENT. Elections of the Mayor of London and the members of the London Assembly are treated as local government elections for the purposes of the Representation of the People Acts: see PARA 11; and LONDON GOVERNMENT vol 71 (2013) PARA 76 et seq. In Wales, 'elected mayor', in relation to a local authority, means an individual elected as mayor of the authority by the local government electors for the authority's area in accordance with the provisions made by or under Pt II (ss 10–48A) (ie as it has been amended by the Localism Act 2011 s 22, Sch 3 para 66 so that it confers powers on the Welsh Ministers only):

see the Local Government Act 2000 s 39(1); and LOCAL GOVERNMENT vol 69 (2009) PARA 321. As to the return of an elected mayor for a local authority see further PARA 198 et seq; and LOCAL GOVERNMENT vol 69 (2009) PARA 320 et seq.

3 A poll may be held also for the return of elected executive members (see LOCAL GOVERNMENT vol 69 (2009) PARA 320) but, at the date at which this volume states the law, no regulations had been made in relation to such elections. As to the election of leaders in 'leader and cabinet executive' structures in England see the Local Government Act 2000 ss 9I–9ID; and LOCAL GOVERNMENT.

4 As to local government statutes covering the election of councillors and mayors see PARA 10; and as to the provision for local government elections that is made under the Representation of the People Acts see PARA 11.

5 As to the entitlement to vote as a local government elector in any electoral area see PARA 97.

6 See the Local Government Act 2000 s 9HD(1)(a) (as added: see note 2), s 43(1)(a); and see LOCAL GOVERNMENT vol 69 (2009) PARA 321. As to the meaning of 'local authority' for these purposes see LOCAL GOVERNMENT vol 69 (2009) PARA 23.

7 As to the registers of electors see PARA 145 et seq.

8 See the Local Government Act 2000 s 9HD(1)(b) (as added: see note 2), s 43(1)(b); and LOCAL GOVERNMENT vol 69 (2009) PARA 321.

9 As to preference votes in an election for the return of an elected mayor see PARA 341; and LOCAL GOVERNMENT vol 69 (2009) PARA 322.

10 See the Local Government Act 2000 ss 9HD(2) (as added: see note 2), s 43(2); and LOCAL GOVERNMENT vol 69 (2009) PARA 321.

B. WELSH ASSEMBLY ELECTIONS

99. Entitlement to vote at an election of Welsh Assembly members. The persons[1] entitled to vote at an election of Assembly members[2] (or of an Assembly member) in an Assembly constituency[3] are those who on the day of the poll[4]: (1) would be entitled to vote as electors at a local government election[5] in an electoral area[6] wholly or partly included in the Assembly constituency[7]; and (2) are registered in the register of local government electors[8] at an address within the Assembly constituency[9].

However, a person is not entitled as an elector: (a) to cast more than one constituency vote[10], or more than one electoral region vote[11], in the same Assembly constituency at any general election[12]; (b) to vote in more than one Assembly constituency at any such election[13]; or (c) to cast more than one vote in an election held[14] to fill a vacancy for the seat of an Assembly member returned for an Assembly constituency[15].

1 As to the meaning of 'person' see PARA 95 note 1.
2 As to the meaning of 'Assembly member' see PARA 12.
3 As to Assembly constituencies see PARA 76.

4 See the Government of Wales Act 2006 s 12(1). As to the poll at an election of Assembly members see PARA 213 et seq.
5 As to the entitlement to vote as an elector at a local government election see PARA 97.
6 As to the meaning of 'electoral area' in relation to local government elections see PARA 11.

7 Government of Wales Act 2006 s 12(1)(a).
8 As to the registers of electors see PARA 145 et seq.

9 Government of Wales Act 2006 s 12(1)(b).
10 As to the meaning of 'constituency vote' for this purpose see PARA 364.
11 As to the meaning of 'electoral region vote' for this purpose see PARA 364.
12 Government of Wales Act 2006 s 12(2)(a). As to ordinary Assembly elections see PARA 213 et seq.

13 Government of Wales Act 2006 s 12(2)(b).
14 Ie under the Government of Wales Act 2006 s 10 (see PARA 214): see s 12(2)(c).

15 Government of Wales Act 2006 s 12(2)(c).

C. EUROPEAN PARLIAMENTARY ELECTIONS

100.   Entitlement to vote as European parliamentary elector. A person[1] is entitled to vote as an elector at an election to the European Parliament[2] in an electoral region[3] if he is within any of the following categories[4], namely if:

(1)   on the day of the poll[5], he would be entitled to vote as an elector at a parliamentary election[6] in a parliamentary constituency[7] wholly or partly comprised in the electoral region[8], and: (a) the address in respect of which he is registered in the relevant register of parliamentary electors[9] is within the electoral region[10]; or (b) his registration in the relevant register of parliamentary electors results from an overseas elector's declaration[11] which specifies an address within the electoral region[12];

(2)   he is a peer who on the day of the poll would be entitled to vote at a local government election[13] in an electoral area[14] wholly or partly comprised in the electoral region[15], and the address in respect of which he is registered in the relevant register of local government electors is within the electoral region[16];

(3)   he is entitled to vote in the electoral region by virtue of the provision made which extends the franchise for European parliamentary elections to peers resident outside the United Kingdom[17]; or

(4)   he is entitled to vote in the electoral region by virtue of the provision made for relevant citizens of the European Union[18] (other than Commonwealth citizens and citizens of the Republic of Ireland[19]) to vote as European Parliamentary electors[20].

1   As to the meaning of 'person' see PARA 95 note 1.
2   As to elections to the European Parliament generally see PARA 13 et seq.
3   As to electoral regions constituted for the purposes of European parliamentary elections see PARA 77.
      The entitlement to vote under the European Parliamentary Elections Act 2002 s 8 does not apply to voting in Gibraltar: see s 8(8) (added by the European Parliament (Representation) Act 2003 s 15(3)). However, a person is entitled to vote in Gibraltar as an elector at a European parliamentary election if on the day of the poll he is registered in the Gibraltar register (subject to any enactment which provides for alterations made after a specified date in the register to be disregarded), is not subject to a legal incapacity to vote in Gibraltar at such an election (age apart), is a Commonwealth citizen or a citizen of the European Union (other than a Commonwealth citizen), and is at least 18 years of age: see the European Parliament (Representation) Act 2003 s 15(1), (2). The 'Gibraltar register' is a register of European Parliamentary electors in Gibraltar maintained by the European electoral registration officer for Gibraltar (ie the Clerk of the House of Assembly of Gibraltar who holds the post by virtue of his office): see s 14(1), (2). A person is entitled to be registered in the Gibraltar register if, on the relevant date, he is resident in Gibraltar, is not subject to a legal incapacity to vote in Gibraltar at a European parliamentary election (age apart), is a qualifying Commonwealth citizen or a citizen of the European Union (other than a qualifying Commonwealth citizen), and is at least 18 years of age: see s 16(1). A person is also entitled to be registered in the Gibraltar register if, on the relevant date, he is not resident in Gibraltar but qualifies for registration in Gibraltar as an overseas elector, is not subject to a legal incapacity to vote in Gibraltar at a European parliamentary election (age apart), is a Commonwealth citizen, and is at least 18 years of age: see s 16(2). The provision so made by s 16(1), (2) has effect subject to or in accordance with any provision made under s 17 (regulations relating to ss 14–16): s 16(3). Provision supplementary to s 17 is made by s 18. For these purposes, the 'relevant date' is the date on which an application for registration in the Gibraltar register is made or treated (by virtue of any enactment) as having been made (s 16(4)); and 'qualifying Commonwealth citizen' means a Commonwealth citizen who does not, under the law of Gibraltar, require a permit or certificate to enter or remain in Gibraltar, or who for the time being has (or is by virtue of any provision of the law of Gibraltar to be treated as having) a permit or certificate entitling him to enter or remain in Gibraltar (s 16(5)). The European Parliamentary Elections Regulations 2004,

SI 2004/293, have been made in exercise of the powers conferred, inter alia, by the European Parliament (Representation) Act 2003 s 17, and the European Parliamentary Elections Regulations 2004, SI 2004/293, Sch 4 (amended by SI 2009/186; SI 2009/2054) makes provision as to legal incapacity to vote in Gibraltar as an elector at a European parliamentary election, and entitlement to registration in the Gibraltar register: see the European Parliamentary Elections Regulations 2004, SI 2004/293, reg 12. See the text and notes 11–12. As to the 'combined region' which includes Gibraltar see further PARA 77 note 4. As to who are Commonwealth citizens see BRITISH NATIONALITY vol 4 (2011) PARA 409.

4 Ie if he is within any of the European Parliamentary Elections Act 2002 s 8(2)–(5) (see heads (1) to (4) in the text): see s 8(1). This provision made by s 8(1) has effect subject to any provision of regulations made under the European Parliamentary Elections Act 2002 which provides for alterations made after a specified date in a register of electors to be disregarded: s 8(6). As to the making of regulations under the European Parliamentary Elections Act 2002 generally see PARA 13 note 12.

5 As to the poll at a European parliamentary election see PARA 217 et seq.

6 As to the entitlement to vote as an elector at a parliamentary election see PARA 95 et seq.

7 As to the meaning of 'constituency' for these purposes see PARA 9.

8 See the European Parliamentary Elections Act 2002 s 8(2).

9 As to the registers of electors see PARA 145 et seq.

10 European Parliamentary Elections Act 2002 s 8(2)(a).

11 As to overseas electors' declarations see note 12; and PARA 114 et seq.

12 European Parliamentary Elections Act 2002 s 8(2)(b). An overseas elector's declaration must specify the address in the United Kingdom in respect of which the declarant was registered as an elector: see the Representation of the People Act 1985 s 2(4); and PARA 132. For the purposes of the European Parliamentary Elections Regulations 2004, SI 2004/293, 'overseas elector' means a person falling within the European Parliamentary Elections Act 2002 s 8(2)(b) or, in relation to Gibraltar, a person falling within the European Parliament (Representation) Act 2003 s 16(2) (see note 3); and 'overseas elector's declaration' has the meaning given by the Representation of the People Act 1985 s 2 (see PARA 132) or, in relation to Gibraltar, the European Parliamentary Elections Regulations 2004, SI 2004/293, reg 12, Sch 4 (see note 3): see reg 2(1) (substituted by SI 2009/186).

13 For these purposes, 'local government election' includes a municipal election in the City of London (that is, an election to the office of mayor, alderman, common councilman or sheriff and also the election of any officer elected by the mayor, aldermen and liverymen in common hall): see the European Parliamentary Elections Act 2002 s 8(7). As to municipal elections in the City of London see PARA 33.

14 As to the entitlement to vote at a local government election in an electoral area see PARA 97.

15 See the European Parliamentary Elections Act 2002 s 8(3)(a).

16 See the European Parliamentary Elections Act 2002 s 8(3)(b).

17 European Parliamentary Elections Act 2002 s 8(4). The text refers to provision made under the Representation of the People Act 1985 s 3 (extension of European parliamentary franchise to peers resident outside the United Kingdom: see PARA 101): see the European Parliamentary Elections Act 2002 s 8(4). For the purposes of the European Parliamentary Elections Regulations 2004, SI 2004/293, 'European parliamentary overseas elector' means a person falling within the European Parliamentary Elections Act 2002 s 8(4); and 'European Parliamentary overseas elector's declaration' means a declaration made in pursuance of regulations made under the Representation of the People Act 1985 s 3 (see PARA 101): see the European Parliamentary Elections Regulations 2004, SI 2004/293, reg 2(1) (as substituted: see note 12). As to the meaning of 'United Kingdom' see PARA 1 note 1.

18 As to the meaning of 'citizen of the Union' for these purposes see PARA 92 note 6.

19 As to who are citizens of the Republic of Ireland see BRITISH NATIONALITY vol 4 (2011) PARA 410.

20 European Parliamentary Elections Act 2002 s 8(5). The text refers to provision made under the European Parliamentary Elections (Franchise of Relevant Citizens of the Union) Regulations 2001, SI 2001/1184: see the European Parliamentary Elections Act 2002 s 8(5). The 2001 regulations implement Council Directive (EC) 93/109 of 6 December 1993 (OJ L329, 30.12.1993, p 34) laying down detailed arrangements for the exercise of the right to vote and to stand as a candidate in elections to the European Parliament for citizens of the Union residing in a member state of which they are not nationals: see PARA 6 note 8. As to the provision made for relevant citizens of the European Union to register and to vote as European parliamentary electors see PARA 102; and as to the provision made for relevant citizens of the European Union to stand as candidates at European parliamentary elections see PARA 229.

101. Extension of European parliamentary franchise to peers resident outside the United Kingdom. A person[1] is entitled[2] to vote[3] as an elector[4] at a European parliamentary election[5] in any electoral region if[6]:

(1)   he qualifies in respect of that region on the relevant date[7];

(2)   on that date and on the day appointed for the election[8] he is not subject to any legal incapacity to vote[9] and is a British citizen[10]; and

(3)   on the day so appointed he is registered in the electoral region[11].

A peer so qualifies[12] in respect of an electoral region on the relevant date if on that date he is not resident in the United Kingdom[13] and he satisfies one of the following sets of conditions[14]. The first set of conditions is that:

(a)   the peer was included in a register of local government electors in respect of an address at a place[15] that is situated within the electoral region concerned[16];

(b)   that entry in the register was made on the basis that he was resident[17], or to be treated for the purposes of registration as resident, at that address[18];

(c)   that entry in the register was in force at any time falling within the period of 15 years ending immediately before the relevant date[19]; and

(d)   subsequent to that entry ceasing to have effect, no entry was made in any register of local government electors on the basis that he was resident, or to be treated for the purposes of registration as resident, at any other address[20].

The second set of conditions is that:

(i)   the peer was last resident in the United Kingdom within the period of 15 years ending immediately before the relevant date[21];

(ii)   he was by reason only of his age incapable of being included in any register of local government electors in force on the last day on which he was resident in the United Kingdom[22]; and

(iii)   the address at which he was resident on that day was at a place that is situated within the electoral region concerned and a parent or guardian of his was included, in respect of that address, in a register of parliamentary electors or a register of local government electors in force on that day[23].

The restrictions on the registration of such persons are described elsewhere in this title[24].

1   The Representation of the People Act 1985 s 3 has effect as if contained in the Representation of the People Act 1983 Pt I (ss 1–66B): see the Representation of the People Act 1985 s 27(2). Accordingly, as to the meaning of 'person' see PARA 95 note 1.

2   Ie by virtue of the Representation of the People Act 1985 s 3: see s 3(1) (s 3 substituted by the Representation of the People Act 2000 s 8, Sch 2 paras 1, 4). See also the qualification set out in the European Parliamentary Elections Act 2002 s 8 (entitlement to vote as European parliamentary elector: see PARA 100).

3   As to the meaning of 'vote' see PARA 95 note 2; definition applied by virtue of the Representation of the People Act 1985 s 27(2) (see note 1).

4   As to the meaning of 'elector' see PARA 95 note 2; definition applied by virtue of the Representation of the People Act 1985 s 27(2) (see note 1).

5   As to the meaning of 'European parliamentary election' for these purposes see PARA 21 note 2.

6   See the Representation of the People Act 1985 s 3(1) (as substituted: see note 2). As to electoral regions established for the purpose of European parliamentary elections see PARA 77.

7   See the Representation of the People Act 1985 s 3(1)(a) (as substituted: see note 2). Head (1) in the text refers to qualification under s 3, and the relevant date referred to therein is the date on which a person makes a declaration under and in accordance with regulations under s 3: see s 3(1)(a) (as so substituted). Regulations under s 3 may:

(1)   provide for a person seeking registration under s 3 to make a declaration for the purpose, being a declaration of the prescribed facts and containing the prescribed information (s 3(5)(a) (as so substituted));

(2)   require such declarations to be attested and provide for the charging of fees in respect of their attestation (s 3(5)(b) (as so substituted));

(3)   make provision for and in connection with the cancellation of such declarations (s 3(5)(c) (as so substituted));

(4)   provide for the registration, subject to prescribed exceptions and on satisfying prescribed conditions, of those peers who (apart from the requirements of registration) may be entitled by virtue of s 3 to vote as electors at European parliamentary elections (s 3(6)(a) (as so substituted));

(5)   apply with such modifications or exceptions as may be prescribed any provision in respect of the registration of parliamentary or local government electors made by or under the Representation of the People Act 1983 or the Representation of the People Act 1985 (s 3(6)(b) (as so substituted)).

Such regulations must require each registration officer to prepare and publish, in respect of any year for which any peers are to be registered under s 3, a register of the peers so registered; and any such register must so far as practicable be combined with the registers of parliamentary electors and of local government electors, the entries of peers registered under s 3 being marked to indicate that fact: s 3(7) (s 3 as so substituted; s 3(7) amended by the Electoral Administration Act 2006 s 10(2), Sch 1 para 17(1), (3)). As to persons who have an anonymous entry in a register see note 16. As to the meaning of 'registration officer' see PARA 139 note 1; definition applied by virtue of the Representation of the People Act 1985 s 27(2) (see note 1). As to the registration of parliamentary or local government electors see PARA 112 et seq; and as to the registers of electors see PARA 145 et seq. For these purposes, references to the register of local government elections include a reference to a register of electors prepared for the purposes of local elections or for the purposes of municipal elections in the City of London (ie, elections to the office of mayor, alderman, common councilman or sheriff and also elections of officers elected by the mayor, aldermen and liverymen in common hall): see s 3(8)(c) (as so substituted). As to elections in the City of London see PARA 33.

'Prescribed' means prescribed by regulations: see the Representation of the People Act 1983 s 202(1); definition applied by virtue of the Representation of the People Act 1985 s 27(2) (see note 1). As to the regulations made under s 3 see the Representation of the People (England and Wales) Regulations 2001, SI 2001/341, reg 13, Sch 4, which apply with modifications specified provisions for the registration of European parliamentary overseas electors. For these purposes, the Representation of the People Act 1983 s 4(5) (attainers: see PARA 113), s 9 (register of electors: see PARA 145), s 10A(1)(a), (3), (3A), (4), (9) (maintenance of registers: registration of electors: see PARAS 157, 169), s 13 (publication of registers: see PARA 165), ss 13A–13B (alteration of registers: see PARA 168), s 50 (effect of misdescription: see PARA 150), s 52 (discharge of registration duties: see PARAS 140, 141), s 54 (payment of expenses of registration: see PARA 144), s 56 (registration appeals: see PARA 172), s 63 (breach of official duty: see PARA 737) and the Representation of the People Act 1985 s 2 (registration of British citizens overseas: see PARA 114), s 12 (offences as to declarations etc: see PARA 735) must, subject to any modifications and exceptions specified in relation to those provisions in the Representation of the People (England and Wales) Regulations 2001, SI 2001/341, reg 13(4), Sch 4, apply for the purposes of the registration of peers who (subject to the requirement of registration) are entitled to vote at a European parliamentary election as they apply for the purpose of the registration of parliamentary electors: see reg 13(4), Sch 4 (Sch 4 amended by SI 2009/725). Unless the context otherwise requires, in the provisions applied by the Representation of the People (England and Wales) Regulations 2001, SI 2001/341, Sch 4: (a) any reference to an overseas elector's declaration must be construed as a reference to a European parliamentary overseas elector's declaration; (b) any reference to a constituency must be construed as a reference to an electoral region; (c) any reference to a register of parliamentary electors must be construed as a reference to a register kept under the Representation of the People Act 1985 s 3 and any reference to the register of local government electors must be disregarded; and (d) any reference to a provision which is also applied by the Representation of the People (England and Wales) Regulations 2001, SI 2001/341, Sch 4 must be construed as a reference to such a provision as so applied: see reg 13(5). Regulations 3, 5–8, 11 (general, interpretation and miscellaneous), regs 18–22 (overseas electors' declarations: see PARAS 132–136) and regs 23–25, 27–32, 36(2), (3), 38–43, 45 (registration: see PARA 145 et seq), subject to any modifications specified in reg 13(6), Sch 4A, and subject to reg 13(7), apply also to a European parliamentary overseas elector's declaration and registration in pursuance of it as they apply to an overseas elector's declaration and registration in pursuance of it: see reg 13(6), Sch 4A (reg 13(6) substituted,

Sch 4A added, by SI 2009/725). For the purposes set out in the Representation of the People (England and Wales) Regulations 2001, SI 2001/341, reg 13(6), those regulations, unless the context otherwise requires, have effect as if: (i) any reference to a parliamentary elector were a reference to a peer entitled to vote at a European parliamentary election under the Representation of the People Act 1985 s 3; (ii) any reference to an overseas elector were a reference to a European parliamentary overseas elector; (iii) any reference to an overseas elector's declaration were a reference to a European parliamentary overseas elector's declaration; and (iv) any reference to a provision which is applied by Sch 4 were a reference to that provision as so applied: see reg 13(7). As to a peer's entitlement to be registered for these purposes see reg 13(1) (cited in PARA 115); and as to the duty of the relevant registration officer to so register him see reg 13(2), (3) (cited in PARA 143). As to publication of the register see reg 13(8); and PARA 165. For these purposes, unless the context otherwise requires, 'European parliamentary overseas elector' means a peer who has made a European parliamentary overseas elector's declaration and is registered or is entitled to be registered in pursuance of it; and 'European parliamentary overseas elector's declaration' means a declaration made in pursuance of the Representation of the People Act 1985 s 2 as applied by the Representation of the People (England and Wales) Regulations 2001, SI 2001/341, reg 13 and Sch 4: see reg 2(1).

8	See the Representation of the People Act 1985 s 3(1)(b) (as substituted: see note 2). As to the poll at a European parliamentary election see PARA 222 et seq.

9	Representation of the People Act 1985 s 3(1)(b)(i) (as substituted: see note 2). For these purposes, 'legal incapacity' has the same meaning in relation to Great Britain as it has in the Representation of the People Act 1983 for the purposes of local government elections (see PARA 95 note 8), but the reference in the Representation of the People Act 1985 s 3(1)(b) to a person being subject to a legal incapacity to vote on the relevant date does not include a reference to his being below the age of 18 on that date: see s 3(8)(a) (as so substituted). As to the meaning of 'Great Britain' see PARA 1 note 1. As to the meaning of 'local government election' see PARA 11; definition applied by virtue of s 27(2) (see note 1). As to voting age for local government elections see PARA 97 note 14.

10	Representation of the People Act 1985 s 3(1)(b)(ii) (as substituted: see note 2). As to who are British citizens see BRITISH NATIONALITY vol 4 (2011) PARAS 406, 421 et seq.

11	Representation of the People Act 1985 s 3(1)(c) (as substituted: see note 2). Head (3) in the text refers to a person who is registered in the electoral region in a register under s 3: see s 3(1)(c) (as so substituted).

12	Ie under the Representation of the People Act 1985 s 3, for the purposes of head (1) in the text: see s 3(2) (as substituted: see note 2).

13	Representation of the People Act 1985 s 3(2)(a) (as substituted: see note 2). As to the meaning of 'United Kingdom' see PARA 1 note 1.

14	Representation of the People Act 1985 s 3(2)(b) (as substituted: see note 2). The rules as to the qualification of a peer under s 3 are the same as those for a person to qualify as an overseas elector under s 1 (see PARA 96), but with the substitution of references to the register of local government electors for references to the register of parliamentary electors.

15	The provision is so worded that the entitlement arises even if the premises in respect of which the person was registered are subsequently destroyed. A person might be included in respect of an address even if the address itself is not shown in the register of electors because the person's name only is included (see PARA 145).

16	Representation of the People Act 1985 s 3(3)(a) (as substituted: see note 2). For the purposes of s 3(3)(a), a person who has an anonymous entry in a register of parliamentary electors or local government electors is not to be regarded as being included in that register: s 3(4A) (s 3 as so substituted; s 3(4A) added by the Electoral Administration Act 2006 Sch 1 para 17(1), (2)). As to the meaning of 'anonymous entry' in relation to a register of electors see PARA 148.

17	As to the determination of residence for the purposes of registration as a parliamentary or local government elector see PARA 117 et seq; provisions applied by virtue of the Representation of the People Act 1985 s 27(2) (see note 1).

18	Representation of the People Act 1985 s 3(3)(b) (as substituted: see note 2).

19	Representation of the People Act 1985 s 3(3)(c) (s 3 as substituted (see note 2); s 3(3)(c), s 3(4)(a) amended by the Political Parties, Elections and Referendums Act 2000 s 141(b)).

20	Representation of the People Act 1985 s 3(3)(d) (as substituted: see note 2). An electoral registration officer may have mistakenly included the person in the register as resident at an address even though that person was not resident (or treated for the purposes of registration as resident) there on the qualifying date to which the register relates.

21	Representation of the People Act 1985 s 3(4)(a) (s 3 as substituted (see note 2); s 3(4)(a) as amended (see note 19)).

22	Representation of the People Act 1985 s 3(4)(b) (as substituted: see note 2).

23　Representation of the People Act 1985 s 3(4)(c) (as substituted: see note 2). For the purposes of
　　s 3(4)(c), a person who has an anonymous entry in a register of parliamentary electors or local
　　government electors is not to be regarded as being included in that register: s 3(4A) (s 3 as so
　　substituted; s 3(4A) as added (see note 16)).

24　See PARA 111 et seq.

102.　Entitlement of relevant citizens of the European Union to vote as European parliamentary electors.

A person[1] is entitled to vote as an elector at a European parliamentary election[2] in an electoral region[3] if on the date of the poll[4]:

(1)　he is registered in the region in the register of relevant citizens of the Union[5] entitled to vote at European parliamentary elections[6];

(2)　he is not subject to any legal incapacity[7] to vote (age apart)[8];

(3)　he is a relevant citizen of the Union[9]; and

(4)　he is of voting age[10].

However, a person is not so entitled to vote as an elector more than once in the same electoral region at any European parliamentary election[11], or in more than one electoral region at a European parliamentary general election[12].

The restrictions on the registration of such persons are described elsewhere in this title[13].

1　As to the meaning of 'person' see PARA 95 note 1.

2　Ie by virtue of the European Parliamentary Elections (Franchise of Relevant Citizens of the
　　Union) Regulations 2001, SI 2001/1184 and without prejudice to the qualifications set out in
　　the European Parliamentary Elections Act 2002 s 8 (entitlement to vote as European
　　parliamentary elector: see PARA 100) and the Representation of the People Act 1985 s 3
　　(extension of European parliamentary franchise to peers resident outside the United Kingdom:
　　see PARA 101). As to European parliamentary elections generally see PARA 13 et seq.

3　As to electoral regions established for the purpose of European parliamentary elections see
　　PARA 77.

4　See the European Parliamentary Elections (Franchise of Relevant Citizens of the Union)
　　Regulations 2001, SI 2001/1184, reg 3(1). As to the date of the poll at a European
　　parliamentary election see PARA 222.

5　For these purposes, 'Citizen of the Union' is to be determined in accordance with the Treaty on
　　the Functioning of the European Union (Rome, 25 March 1957; TS 1 (1973); Cmnd 5179)
　　('TFEU') art 20 (formerly art 17 TEC: see PARA 6 note 1), which states that every person holding
　　the nationality of a member state is a citizen of the Union; and 'relevant citizen of the Union'
　　means such a citizen who is not a Commonwealth citizen or a citizen of the Republic of Ireland:
　　see the European Parliamentary Elections (Franchise of Relevant Citizens of the Union)
　　Regulations 2001, SI 2001/1184, reg 1(2); Interpretation Act 1978 s 17(2)(b). As to who are
　　Commonwealth citizens see BRITISH NATIONALITY vol 4 (2011) PARA 409; and as to who are
　　citizens of the Republic of Ireland see BRITISH NATIONALITY vol 4 (2011) PARA 410.

6　European Parliamentary Elections (Franchise of Relevant Citizens of the Union)
　　Regulations 2001, SI 2001/1184, reg 3(1)(a). The text refers to the register maintained under
　　reg 5(2) (see PARA 143): see reg 3(1)(a). The register must, so far as practicable, be combined
　　with the registers of parliamentary and local government electors and with any register of peers
　　kept under the Representation of the People Act 1985 s 3 (extension of European parliamentary
　　franchise to peers resident outside the United Kingdom: see PARA 101), the names of the persons
　　so registered being marked to indicate that fact: see PARA 145.

　　　For the purposes of the registration of relevant citizens of the Union as European
　　parliamentary electors, the Representation of the People Act 1983 s 5 (general residence
　　requirement: see PARA 117), s 6 (deemed residence for merchant seamen: see PARA 118), s 7
　　(deemed residence for persons in mental hospitals who are not detained offenders or on remand:
　　see PARA 119), s 7A (deemed residence for persons on remand: see PARA 120), ss 7B–7C
　　(residence deemed by way of declaration of local connection: see PARAS 121–124), s 9 (register
　　of electors: see PARA 145), ss 9B, 9C (anonymous registration: see PARAS 147, 148, 171), s 10A
　　(maintenance of registers: see PARAS 157, 169), s 13 (publication of registers: see PARA 165), ss 13A–13B (alteration of registers: see PARA 168), s 50 (effect of
　　misdescription: see PARA 150), s 52 (discharge of registration duties: see PARAS 140, 141), s 54
　　(payment of expenses of registration: see PARA 144), s 56 (registration appeals: see PARA 172),

s 62 (offences as to declarations: see PARA 735), s 63 (breach of official duty: see PARA 737), ss 119, 202 (general provisions as to interpretation) and the Representation of the People (England and Wales) Regulations 2001, SI 2001/341, regs 3, 5–8, 11 (general, interpretation and miscellaneous) and regs 24, 27–32A, 36, 36A, 38–41A, 45A–45G (registration: see PARA 145 et seq) apply as they apply for the purposes of the registration of parliamentary and local government electors, subject to any modification and exceptions specified in relation to those provisions in the European Parliamentary Elections (Franchise of Relevant Citizens of the Union) Regulations 2001, SI 2001/1184, reg 9, Schedule, and, unless the context otherwise requires, in the provisions so applied: (1) any reference to a parliamentary elector is a reference to a European parliamentary elector; (2) any reference to a register is to the register maintained under reg 5(2) (see PARA 143); (3) any reference to a constituency is a reference to an electoral region; and (4) any reference in such a provision to another provision which is so applied, is to that provision as so applied: see reg 9, Schedule (reg 9 amended, Schedule substituted, by SI 2009/726).

For the purpose of extending the rights of citizens and nationals of accession states who (subject to the requirements of registration) may vote at local government and European parliamentary elections, reg 9 is applied with modifications: see the Local and European Parliamentary Elections (Registration of Citizens of Accession States) Regulations 2003, SI 2003/1557, reg 6, Sch 1 para 6.

7   For the purposes of the European Parliamentary Elections (Franchise of Relevant Citizens of the Union) Regulations 2001, SI 2001/1184, reg 3, 'legal incapacity' has the same meaning, in relation to European parliamentary elections, as it has in the Representation of the People Act 1983 in relation to parliamentary elections (see PARA 95 note 8): European Parliamentary Elections (Franchise of Relevant Citizens of the Union) Regulations 2001, SI 2001/1184, reg 3(3).

8   European Parliamentary Elections (Franchise of Relevant Citizens of the Union) Regulations 2001, SI 2001/1184, reg 3(1)(b).

9   European Parliamentary Elections (Franchise of Relevant Citizens of the Union) Regulations 2001, SI 2001/1184, reg 3(1)(c).

10 European Parliamentary Elections (Franchise of Relevant Citizens of the Union) Regulations 2001, SI 2001/1184, reg 3(1)(d). For these purposes, 'voting age' is 18 years or over: see reg 3(1)(d).

11 European Parliamentary Elections (Franchise of Relevant Citizens of the Union) Regulations 2001, SI 2001/1184, reg 3(2)(a).

12 European Parliamentary Elections (Franchise of Relevant Citizens of the Union) Regulations 2001, SI 2001/1184, reg 3(2)(b).

13 See PARA 116 et seq.

(ii) Entitlement to Vote in Referendums and Polls

103.   Persons entitled to vote in a referendum under the Political Parties, Elections and Referendums Act 2000.   The framework for referendums to which the Political Parties, Elections and Referendums Act 2000 applies does not make provision for entitlement to vote in any individual referendum[1]. Any such provision must be made by the further legislation that is required to provide for the holding of any particular referendum within the framework[2].

1   See the Political Parties, Elections and Referendums Act 2000 Pt VII (ss 101–129); and PARA 527 et seq.

2   For example, the persons entitled to vote in any referendum held in pursuance of the European Union Act 2011 ss 2, 3 or 6 are the persons who, on the date of the referendum, would be entitled to vote as an elector at a parliamentary election in a constituency in the United Kingdom, or who, on that date, while disqualified by reason of being peers from voting as electors in parliamentary elections, would qualify otherwise under the terms of the European Union Act 2011, or who (where the referendum is also being held in Gibraltar) are the Commonwealth citizens who, on the date of the referendum, would be entitled to vote in Gibraltar at a European parliamentary election in the combined electoral region in which Gibraltar is comprised: see s 11; and PARA 14 note 7.

104. Persons entitled to vote in a local authority referendum under the Local Government Act 2000. The persons[1] entitled to vote in a referendum held by a local authority[2] are those who on the day of the referendum[3]: (1) would be entitled to vote as electors at an election of councillors[4] for an electoral area[5] which is situated within the authority's area[6]; and (2) are registered in the register of local government electors[7] at an address within the authority's area[8].

1 As to the meaning of 'person' see PARA 95 note 1.
2 Ie a referendum held under the Local Government Act 2000 Pt 1A Ch 2 (ss 9C–9ID) (Executive Arrangements (England): see LOCAL GOVERNMENT) or under any provision of Pt II (ss 10–48A) (Executive Arrangements (Wales): see LOCAL GOVERNMENT vol 69 (2009) PARA 314 et seq): see ss 9MG(1), 45(4); and LOCAL GOVERNMENT. As to the meaning of 'local authority' for these purposes see LOCAL GOVERNMENT vol 69 (2009) PARA 23.
3 See the Local Government Act 2000 ss 9MG(1), 45(4); and LOCAL GOVERNMENT.
4 As to entitlement to vote at local government elections see PARA 97. As to the election of councillors generally see LOCAL GOVERNMENT vol 69 (2009) PARA 126 et seq.
5 As to the meaning of 'electoral area' see PARA 11.
6 See the Local Government Act 2000 ss 9MG(1)(a), 45(4)(a); and LOCAL GOVERNMENT.
7 As to the meaning of 'local government elector' for these purposes see LOCAL GOVERNMENT vol 69 (2009) PARA 127. As to the registers of electors see PARA 145 et seq.
8 See the Local Government Act 2000 ss 9MG(1)(b), 45(4)(b); and LOCAL GOVERNMENT.

105. Persons entitled to vote in a poll held to ascertain views about whether or how any of the functions of the Welsh Ministers should be exercised. The persons[1] entitled to vote in a poll for the purpose of ascertaining views about whether or how any of the functions of the Welsh Ministers should be exercised[2] are those who[3]: (1) would be entitled to vote as electors at a local government election[4] in an electoral area[5] wholly or partly included in the area in which the poll is held[6]; and (2) are registered in the register of local government electors[7] at an address within the area in which the poll is held[8].

1 As to the meaning of 'person' see PARA 95 note 1.
2 Ie a poll held under the Government of Wales Act 2006 s 64 (see PARAS 662–664): see s 64(2). As to the Welsh Ministers see PARA 2.
3 See the Government of Wales Act 2006 s 64(2).
4 As to entitlement to vote at local government elections see PARA 97.
5 As to the meaning of 'electoral area' see PARA 11.
6 Government of Wales Act 2006 s 64(2)(a).
7 As to the registers of electors see PARA 145 et seq.
8 Government of Wales Act 2006 s 64(2)(b).

106. Persons entitled to vote in poll consequent on parish or community meeting. A poll consequent on a parish or community meeting[2] is a poll of those entitled to attend the meeting as local government electors[2].

1 As to parish and community meetings generally see LOCAL GOVERNMENT vol 69 (2009) PARA 635 et seq.
2 See the Local Government Act 1972 s 99 (amended by the Local Government Act 1985 s 84, Sch 14 para 14; the Education Reform Act 1988 s 237, Sch 13 Pt I; the Police and Magistrates' Courts Act 1994 s 43, Sch 4 Pt I para 8; the Police Act 1996 s 103, Sch 7 para 1(2)(h); the Police Act 1997 s 88, Sch 6 para 3; the Greater London Authority Act 1999 s 325, Sch 27 para 26; the Criminal Justice and Police Act 2001 ss 128(1), 137, Sch 6 Pt 2 paras 22, 25, Sch 7 Pt 5(1); the Local Democracy, Economic Development and Construction Act 2009 s 119, Sch 6 paras 10, 17; and the Police Reform and Social Responsibility Act 2011 s 99, Sch 16 Pt 3 paras 100, 103); Local Government Act 1972 Sch 12 Pt III para 18(5) (amended by the Representation of the People Act 1983 s 206, Sch 8 para 14); Local Government Act 1972 Sch 12 Pt V para 34(5) (amended by the Representation of the People Act 1983 Sch 8 para 14). As to the entitlement to vote at local government elections see PARA 97.

(iii) Restrictions on Entitlement to Vote

A. DISFRANCHISEMENT OF CERTAIN PARLIAMENTARY AND LOCAL GOVERNMENT ELECTORS

107. Disfranchisement of serving prisoners and detained offenders. Under the Representation of the People Act 1983, during the time that a convicted person[1] is detained in a penal institution[2] in pursuance of his sentence[3], or is unlawfully at large when he would otherwise be so detained, he is legally incapable of voting at any parliamentary[4] or local government election[5]. However, the European Court of Human Rights has found that this restriction, to the extent that it constitutes an absolute bar on voting by any serving prisoner in any circumstances, offends against the principle of proportionality[6].

1   For this purpose, 'convicted person' means any person found guilty of an offence (whether under the law of the United Kingdom or not), including a person found guilty by a court of a service offence within the meaning of the Armed Forces Act 2006 (see ARMED FORCES vol 3 (2011) PARA 569 et seq), but not including a person dealt with by committal or other summary process for contempt of court (see CONTEMPT OF COURT vol 22 (2012) PARA 95 et seq): Representation of the People Act 1983 s 3(2)(a) (definition amended by the Armed Forces Act 2006 s 378(1), Sch 16 para 95). In this definition, the reference to a service offence includes an SDA offence: see the Armed Forces Act 2006 (Transitional Provisions etc) Order 2009, SI 2009/205, art 205, Sch 1 para 24(1). As to the meaning of 'SDA offence' for these purposes see art 2(1), (4). As to the meaning of 'United Kingdom' see PARA 1 note 1.

2   For this purpose, 'penal institution' means an institution to which the Prison Act 1952 applies (see PRISONS AND PRISONERS vol 85 (2012) PARA 403): see the Representation of the People Act 1983 s 3(2)(b).

3   For this purpose, a person detained for default in complying with his sentence is not to be treated as detained in pursuance of the sentence, whether or not the sentence provided for detention in the event of default, but a person detained by virtue of a conditional pardon in respect of an offence is to be treated as detained in pursuance of his sentence: Representation of the People Act 1983 s 3(2)(c).

4   As to the meaning of 'parliamentary election' see PARA 9.

5   Representation of the People Act 1983 s 3(1) (amended by the Representation of the People Act 1985 s 24, Sch 4 para 1). It is immaterial for these purposes whether a conviction or sentence was before or after the passing of the Representation of the People Act 1983 (ie 8 February 1983): s 3(3). As to the meaning of 'local government election' see PARA 11. As to the registration to vote of persons remanded in custody see PARA 120.

6   See Application 74025/01 *Hirst v United Kingdom (No 2)* (2004) 38 EHRR 825, 16 BHRC 409, (2004) Times, 8 April, ECtHR; on appeal (2005) 42 EHRR 849, 19 BHRC 546, (2005) Times, 10 October, ECtHR (Grand Chamber) (the principle of proportionality required a discernible and sufficient link to be made between the sanction of disenfranchisement and the conduct and circumstances of the individual). In particular, the Representation of the People Act 1983 s 3 was found to contravene the Convention for the Protection of Human Rights and Fundamental Freedoms (Rome, 4 November 1950; TS 71 (1953); Cmd 8969; Council of Europe, ETS no 5), First Protocol (Paris, 20 March 1952; TS 46; Cmnd 9221; Council of Europe, ETS no 9) art 3 (see PARA 7; and RIGHTS AND FREEDOMS vol 88A (2013) PARAS 572–593). The United Kingdom intervened in Application 126/05 *Scoppola v Italy (No 3)* (2012) Times, 12 June, [2012] ECHR 126/05, ECtHR, in order to challenge the Grand Chamber's findings in Application 74025/01 *Hirst v United Kingdom (No 2)*, but the Court affirmed its principle that, when disenfranchisement affected a group of people generally, automatically and indiscriminately, based solely on the fact that they were serving a prison sentence, irrespective of the length of the sentence and irrespective of the nature or gravity of their offence and their individual circumstances, it was not compatible with the Convention for the Protection of Human Rights and Fundamental Freedoms First Protocol art 3; but that First Protocol art 3 guaranteed subjective rights, which were not absolute and accordingly afforded the contracting state a wide margin of appreciation, and that the role of the Court was confined to determining whether any restriction affecting all convicted prisoners in custody exceeded any acceptable margin of appreciation, leaving it to the legislature to decide on the choice of means for securing the rights guaranteed by First Protocol art 3. The European Court of Human Rights has considered what remedies, if any, might be appropriate for the continuing lack of

amendment to the Representation of the People Act 1983 s 3, and decided that the finding of a violation constituted sufficient just satisfaction, when viewed in tandem with a direction that the United Kingdom must introduce legislative proposals to amend s 3, and (if appropriate) corresponding provision in the European Parliamentary Elections Act 2002 s 8 (entitlement to vote as European parliamentary elector: see PARA 100), with a view to the enactment of an electoral law to achieve compliance with the court's judgment in Application 74025/01 *Hirst v United Kingdom (No 2)*: see Application 60041/08 *Greens v United Kingdom* (2010) 53 EHRR 710, (2010) Times, 24 November, ECtHR. See also *R (on the application of Chester) v Secretary of State for Justice* [2010] EWCA Civ 1439, [2011] 1 WLR 1436, [2010] All ER (D) 219 (Dec) (an advisory opinion as to what legislation, as yet undrafted, might properly contain or omit would have been quite beyond the pale; the nature and scope of measures amending or replacing the Representation of the People Act 1983 s 3 was likely to be acutely controversial concerning aspects not of the law but of social policy which is a political responsibility, and that was where it should remain); and *R (on the application of Chester) v Secretary of State for Justice, McGeoch v The Lord President of the Council* [2013] UKSC 63, [2013] All ER (D) 174 (Oct), (2013) Times, 22 October (prohibition on prisoners voting in the UK had previously been the subject of a declaration of incompatibility with the ECHR and was, at the instant time, under active consideration by Parliament; in those circumstances, there was no point in making a further declaration of incompatibility and any legislative amendment would not in any case be likely to remedy the prisoner's particular grievance). Accordingly, there are no reasonable grounds in domestic law for bringing a claim for damages or a declaration for being disenfranchised whilst a prisoner: *Tovey v Ministry of Justice* [2011] EWHC 271 (QB), [2011] NLJR 290, [2011] All ER (D) 202 (Feb). As to a claim by a serving prisoner that his disenfranchisement is contrary to his rights under both the Treaty on the Functioning of the European Union (Rome, 25 March 1957; TS 1 (1973); Cmnd 5179) and the Charter of Fundamental Rights of the European Union (OJ C303, 14 12 2007, p 1) (see CONSTITUTIONAL LAW AND HUMAN RIGHTS) see *McGeogh v Lord President of the Council* [2011] CSIH 67, 2012 SC 410, 2012 SLT 224; *McGeogh v Electoral Registration Officer Dumfries and Galloway* [2011] CSOH 65, 2011 SLT 633; and *R (on the application of Chester) v Secretary of State for Justice, McGeoch v The Lord President of the Council* (European law did not incorporate any right to vote paralleling that recognised by the European Court of Human Rights in its case law or any other individual right to vote that was engaged or upon which, if engaged, the claimants were able to rely). As to current law and policy relating to prisoners' voting eligibility and registration see PRISONS AND PRISONERS vol 85 (2012) PARA 551.

108. Disfranchisement of offenders detained in mental hospitals. A person in respect of whom a court has made certain hospital orders or directions on grounds of mental health or insanity[1] is, during the time that he is detained at any place in pursuance of such an order or direction[2], or during the time that he is unlawfully at large when he would otherwise be so detained[3], legally incapable of voting at any parliamentary or local government election[4].

Any rule of the common law which provided that a person is subject to a legal incapacity to vote by reason only of his mental state[5] no longer applies[6].

1 As respects England and Wales, the Representation of the People Act 1983 s 3A applies to:
 (1) any person in respect of whom an order has been made under the Mental Health Act 1983 s 37 (powers of courts to order hospital admission or guardianship: see MENTAL HEALTH AND CAPACITY vol 75 (2013) PARA 864), s 38 (interim hospital orders: see MENTAL HEALTH AND CAPACITY vol 75 (2013) PARA 864), s 44 (committal to hospital for restriction order: see MENTAL HEALTH AND CAPACITY vol 75 (2013) PARA 873) or s 51(5) (hospital order in person's absence and without conviction: see MENTAL HEALTH AND CAPACITY vol 75 (2013) PARA 896) or in respect of whom a direction has been given under s 45A (power of higher courts to direct hospital admission: see MENTAL HEALTH AND CAPACITY vol 75 (2013) PARA 863), s 46 (repealed) or s 47 (removal to hospital of persons serving sentences of imprisonment: see MENTAL HEALTH AND CAPACITY vol 75 (2013) PARA 892) (Representation of the People Act 1983 s 3A(2)(a) (s 3A added by the Representation of the People Act 2000 s 2));
 (2) any person in respect of whom an order has been made under the Criminal Procedure (Insanity) Act 1964 s 5(2)(a) (hospital orders where persons not guilty by reason of insanity or unfit to plead: see MENTAL HEALTH AND CAPACITY vol 75 (2013) PARA 874;

and SENTENCING AND DISPOSITION OF OFFENDERS vol 92 (2010) PARA 332 et seq) (Representation of the People Act 1983 s 3A(2)(b) (as so added)); and

(3)   any person in respect of whom the Court of Appeal has made an order under the Criminal Appeal Act 1968 s 6(2)(a) or s 14(2)(a) (hospital orders where findings of insanity or of unfitness to plead substituted: see MENTAL HEALTH AND CAPACITY vol 75 (2013) PARA 874) (Representation of the People Act 1983 s 3A(2)(c) (as so added)).

The reference in head (1) above to an order under the Mental Health Act 1983 s 37 or 38 includes such an order made by virtue of the Armed Forces Act 2006 s 169, Sch 4 (modifications to the Mental Health Act 1983 where Court Martial makes findings as to insanity of the accused: see ARMED FORCES vol 3 (2011) PARA 650), including the Armed Forces Act 2006 Sch 4 as it is applied by the Court Martial Appeals Act 1968 s 16(2) (application of provisions to Appeal Court as they apply in relation to the Court Martial: see ARMED FORCES vol 3 (2011) PARA 668): Representation of the People Act 1983 s 3A(5) (s 3A as so added; s 3A(5) substituted by the Armed Forces Act 2006 s 378(1), Sch 16 para 96). In the Representation of the People Act 1983 s 3A(5), the reference to the Armed Forces Act 2006 Sch 4 includes the Army Act 1955 ss 116A(2), 116B(2)(d) (repealed), the Air Force Act 1955 ss 116A(2), 116B(2)(d) (repealed), the Naval Discipline Act 1957 ss 63A(2), 63B(2)(d) (repealed) (powers to deal with person unfit to stand trial or not guilty by reason of insanity), and the Courts-Martial (Appeals) Act 1968 s 16 (substitution of finding of insanity or findings of unfitness to stand trial etc: see ARMED FORCES vol 3 (2011) PARA 668) and s 23 (repealed) (substitution of findings of unfitness to stand trial), as those provisions had effect before the amendments made by the Armed Forces Act 2006: see the Armed Forces Act 2006 (Transitional Provisions etc) Order 2009, SI 2009/205, art 205, Sch 1 para 24(2). As to the meaning of 'person' see PARA 95 note 1.

As to the application of the Representation of the People Act 1983 s 3A to Scotland see s 3A(3) (s 3A as so added; s 3A(3) amended by SI 2005/2078; SSI 2005/465); and as to its application as respects Northern Ireland see the Representation of the People Act 1983 s 3A(4) (as so added).

Any reference in s 3A to a person in respect of whom any order or direction falling within s 3A(2)–(4) has been made or given includes a reference to a person in respect of whom any such order or direction is, by virtue of any enactment, to be treated as having been made or given in connection with his transfer to a place in the part of the United Kingdom mentioned in s 3A(2)–(4): s 3A(6) (as so added). Any reference in any of s 3A(2)–(4) to a provision of any Act or order includes a reference to any earlier provision (whether of that Act or order as originally enacted or made or as previously amended, or otherwise) to the like effect: s 3A(7) (as so added).

2   See the Representation of the People Act 1983 s 3A(1)(a) (as added: see note 1).

3   See the Representation of the People Act 1983 s 3A(1)(b) (as added: see note 1).

4   See the Representation of the People Act 1983 s 3A(1) (as added: see note 1). As to the meaning of 'legal incapacity' for the purposes of the Representation of the People Act 1983 see PARA 95 note 8. As to the registration to vote of patients in mental hospitals who are not detained offenders or on remand see PARA 119.

5   See e g *Bedford County Case, Burgess' Case* (1785) 2 Lud EC 381 at 567 (where an objection to the vote of an idiot was made but not proved); and see also *Oakhampton Case, Robins' Case* (1791) 1 Fras 69 at 162; *Bridgewater Case, Tucker's Case* (1803) 1 Peck 101 at 108 (which both related to the capacity of persons suffering from severe mental illness being able to vote in a lucid interval).

6   See the Electoral Administration Act 2006 s 73(1).

B.   INCAPACITIES IMPOSED ON ELECTORS FOR OFFENCES

109.   Incapacity imposed for offences against electoral law during parliamentary or local government election.   A candidate[1] at a parliamentary[2] or local government election[3] or other person[4] reported by an election court[5] as being personally guilty of a corrupt[6] or illegal practice[7] is, for the period beginning with the date of the report and ending five years after that date (where the person is reported personally guilty of a corrupt practice) or for the period beginning with the date of the report and ending three years after that date (where the person is reported personally guilty of an illegal practice), incapable of being registered as an elector[8] or voting[9] at any parliamentary election in the United Kingdom[10] or at any local government election in Great Britain[11]. Such a person is incapable also, during the same relevant period, of being elected to the House of Commons, or of holding any elective office, and if already elected to a seat in the House of Commons, or holding any such elective office, is to vacate the seat or office as from the date of the report[12].

A person convicted of a corrupt practice[13] is, for the period beginning with the date of conviction and ending five years after that date, and a person convicted of an illegal practice[14] is, for the period beginning with the date of conviction and ending three years after that date, incapable of being registered as an elector or voting at any parliamentary election in the United Kingdom or at any local government election in Great Britain[15]. Such a person is incapable also, during the same relevant period, of being elected to the House of Commons, or of holding any elective office, and, if already elected to a seat in the House of Commons, or holding any such elective office, is to vacate the seat or office[16].

1   As to candidacy at a parliamentary or local government election see PARA 224 et seq.
2   As to the meaning of 'parliamentary election' see PARA 9.
3   As to the meaning of 'local government election' see PARA 11.
4   As to the meaning of 'person' see PARA 95 note 1.
5   As to the meaning of 'election court' for these purposes see PARA 761 note 14.
6   The incapacity imposed by the Representation of the People Act 1983 s 160(4)(a)(i) applies only to a candidate or other person reported personally guilty of a corrupt practice under s 60 (personation: see PARA 730), s 62A (offences associated with postal or proxy voting which are corrupt practices: see PARA 731), or s 62B (Scotland): see s 160(4A); and PARA 905 note 9.
7   The incapacity imposed by the Representation of the People Act 1983 s 160(4)(a)(i) applies only to a candidate or other person reported personally guilty of an illegal practice under s 61 (other voting offences: see PARA 700): see s 160(4A); and PARA 905 note 9.
8   As to the meaning of 'elector' see PARA 95 note 2.
9   As to the meaning of 'vote' see PARA 95 note 2.
10 As to the meaning of 'United Kingdom' see PARA 1 note 1.
11 See the Representation of the People Act 1983 s 160(4)(a)(i), (5); and PARA 905. The incapacity so imposed is subject to mitigation or remission under s 174: see PARA 910. As to the meaning of 'Great Britain' see PARA 1 note 1.
12 See the Representation of the People Act 1983 s 160(4)(a)(ii), (iii), (b), (5); and PARA 905. The incapacity so imposed is subject to mitigation or remission under s 174: see PARA 910.
13 The incapacity imposed by the Representation of the People Act 1983 s 173(1)(a)(i) applies only to a person convicted of a corrupt practice under s 60 (personation: see PARA 730), s 62A (offences associated with postal or proxy voting which are corrupt practices: see PARA 731), or s 62B (Scotland): see s 173(2); and PARA 905 note 9.
14 The incapacity imposed by the Representation of the People Act 1983 s 173(1)(a)(i) applies only to a person convicted of an illegal practice under s 61 (other voting offences: see PARA 700): see s 173(2); and PARA 905 note 9.
15 See the Representation of the People Act 1983 s 173(1)(a)(i), (3); and PARA 905.
16 See the Representation of the People Act 1983 s 173(1)(a)(ii), (iii), (3); and PARA 905. The vacation of a seat so imposed is subject to remission under s 174: see PARA 910.

110.   Incapacity imposed for offences against electoral law during Welsh Assembly election.   A candidate at a Welsh Assembly election[1] or other person[2] reported by an election court[3] as being personally guilty of a corrupt[4] or illegal practice[5] is, for the period beginning with the date of the report and ending five years after that date (where the person is reported personally guilty of a corrupt practice) or for the period beginning with the date of the report and ending three years after that date (where the person is reported personally guilty of an illegal practice), incapable of being registered as an elector[6] or voting[7] at any Assembly election, at any election to the House of Commons[8], at any election to the European Parliament[9], at any election to the Scottish Parliament or to the Northern Ireland Assembly, or at any local government election[10]. Such a person is incapable also, during the same relevant period, of being elected to the

Assembly, the House of Commons, the European Parliament, the Scottish Parliament, the Northern Ireland Assembly or as a member of a local authority, and if already elected to a seat in the Assembly or holding another elective office, is to vacate the seat or office as from the date of the report[11].

A person convicted of a corrupt practice[12] is, for the period beginning with the date of conviction and ending five years after that date, and a person convicted of an illegal practice[13] is, for the period beginning with the date of conviction and ending three years after that date, incapable of being registered as an elector or voting at any Assembly election, at any election to the House of Commons, at any election to the European Parliament, at any election to the Scottish Parliament or to the Northern Ireland Assembly, or at any local government election[14]. Such a person is incapable also, during the same relevant period, of being elected to the Assembly, the House of Commons, the European Parliament, the Scottish Parliament, the Northern Ireland Assembly or as a member of a local authority[15] and, if already elected to a seat in the Assembly, or holding any such elective office, is to vacate the seat or office[16].

Persons reported personally guilty of, or convicted of, corrupt or illegal practices at parliamentary elections or local government elections or at European parliamentary elections are also subject[17] to being declared incapable of being registered as an elector or voting at any Assembly election[18].

1 As to candidacy at a Welsh Assembly election see PARA 227. As to the meaning of 'Assembly election' for these purposes see PARA 3 note 2.

2 For these purposes, 'person' includes (without prejudice to the provisions of the Interpretation Act 1978: see PARA 95 note 1) an association corporate or unincorporate: see the National Assembly for Wales (Representation of the People) Order 2007, SI 2007/236, art 2(1).

3 As to the meaning of 'election court' for these purposes see PARA 764 note 6.

4 The incapacities imposed by the National Assembly for Wales (Representation of the People) Order 2007, SI 2007/236, art 110(3)(a) apply only to a candidate or other person reported personally guilty of a corrupt practice under art 14(11) (offences connected with postal or proxy voting: see PARA 731) or art 30 (personation: see PARA 730): see art 110(4); and PARA 907.

5 The incapacities imposed by the National Assembly for Wales (Representation of the People) Order 2007, SI 2007/236, art 110(3)(a) apply only to a candidate or other person reported personally guilty of an illegal practice under art 31 (other voting offences: see PARA 700): see art 110(4); and PARA 907.

6 For these purposes, 'elector' means any person whose name is for the time being on the register to be used at an Assembly election (or in the case of a person who has an anonymous entry in the register, in the record of anonymous entries) but does not include those shown on the register as below voting age on the day fixed for the poll: see the National Assembly for Wales (Representation of the People) Order 2007, SI 2007/236, art 2(1) (definition substituted by SI 2010/2931). As to the meaning of 'anonymous entry' in relation to a register of electors see PARA 148. As to the registers of electors see PARA 143 et seq; and as to the poll at an election of Assembly members see PARA 213 et seq. Voting age is determined by reference to entitlement to vote as an elector at a local government election, ie 18 years (see PARA 97 note 14).

7 For these purposes, 'voter' means a person voting at an Assembly election and includes a person voting as proxy and, except in the National Assembly for Wales (Representation of the People) Order 2007, SI 2007/236, art 17(1), Sch 5 (Assembly election rules: see PARA 383 note 20), a person voting by proxy; and 'vote' (whether noun or verb) must be construed accordingly, except that in Sch 5 any reference to an elector voting or an elector's vote must include a reference to an elector voting by proxy or elector's vote given by proxy, and 'absent vote' must be construed accordingly: see art 2(1). As to voting by proxy see PARA 367 et seq.

8 As to elections to Parliament see PARA 9 et seq.

9 For the purposes of the National Assembly for Wales (Representation of the People) Order 2007, SI 2007/236, 'European parliamentary election' has the same meaning as in the Representation of the People Act 1985 s 27(1) (see PARA 21 note 2): see the National Assembly for Wales (Representation of the People) Order 2007, SI 2007/236, art 2(1).

10 See the National Assembly for Wales (Representation of the People) Order 2007, SI 2007/236, art 110(3)(a), (5); and PARA 907. The incapacity so imposed is subject to mitigation or remission under art 126: see PARA 910. As to the meaning of 'local government election' for these purposes see PARA 17 note 5.

11 See the National Assembly for Wales (Representation of the People) Order 2007, SI 2007/236, art 110(3)(b), (5); and PARA 907. The incapacity so imposed is subject to mitigation or remission under art 126: see PARA 910.

12 The incapacity imposed by the National Assembly for Wales (Representation of the People) Order 2007, SI 2007/236, art 123(1)(a) applies only to a candidate or other person reported personally guilty of a corrupt practice under art 14(11) (offences connected with postal or proxy voting: see PARA 731) or art 30 (personation: see PARA 730): see art 123(3); and PARA 907.

13 The incapacity imposed by the National Assembly for Wales (Representation of the People) Order 2007, SI 2007/236, art 123(1)(a) applies only to a candidate or other person reported personally guilty of an illegal practice under art 31 (other voting offences: see PARA 700): see art 123(3); and PARA 907.

14 See the National Assembly for Wales (Representation of the People) Order 2007, SI 2007/236, art 123(1); and PARA 907.

15 See the National Assembly for Wales (Representation of the People) Order 2007, SI 2007/236, art 123(1); and PARA 907.

16 See the National Assembly for Wales (Representation of the People) Order 2007, SI 2007/236, art 123(2); and PARA 907. The incapacity so imposed is not subject to remission even if a court subsequently determines that the conviction should not be upheld: see art 123(7): see PARA 907 note 17.

17 Ie in addition to being subject to the incapacities set out in the Representation of the People Act 1983 s 160(4) (see PARA 905) or s 173 (see PARA 905) or the European Parliamentary Elections Regulations 2004, SI 2004/293, reg 107 (see PARA 909) (as the case may be). Note that the European Parliamentary Elections Regulations 2004, SI 2004/293, make no provision for incapacity arising from a candidate or other person having been reported by an election court personally guilty of a corrupt practice: see PARA 111.

18 See the National Assembly for Wales (Representation of the People) Order 2007, SI 2007/236, arts 111–112, 124–125; and PARA 907.

111. Incapacity imposed for offences against electoral law during European parliamentary election. A candidate at a European parliamentary election[1] or other person convicted of a corrupt or illegal practice[2] is, during the relevant period[3], incapable of being registered as an elector[4] or voting[5] at any parliamentary[6] or European parliamentary election in the United Kingdom[7] or at any local government election[8] in Great Britain[9]. Such a person is incapable also, during the same relevant period, of being elected to the House of Commons or the European Parliament, or of holding any elective office, and, if already elected to a seat in the House of Commons or the European Parliament, or holding any such elective office, is to vacate the seat or office as from the date of the conviction[10].

1 As to candidacy at a European parliamentary election see PARA 228 et seq.

2 The incapacity imposed by the European Parliamentary Elections Regulations 2004, SI 2004/293, reg 107(1)(a)(i) applies only to a candidate or other person convicted of a corrupt practice under reg 23 (personation: see PARA 730) or of an illegal practice under reg 24 (other voting offences: see PARA 700): see reg 107(2); and PARA 909.

The European Parliamentary Elections Regulations 2004, SI 2004/293, make no provision for incapacity arising from a candidate or other person having been reported by an election court personally guilty of a corrupt or illegal practice; cf the equivalent provisions in the Representation of the People Act 1983 (see PARA 109) or the National Assembly for Wales (Representation of the People) Order 2007, SI 2007/236 (see PARA 110).

3 For these purposes, the relevant period is the period beginning with the date of the conviction and ending, in the case of a person convicted of a corrupt practice, five years after that date or, in the case of a person convicted of an illegal practice, three years after that date: see the European Parliamentary Elections Regulations 2004, SI 2004/293, reg 107(3); and PARA 909.

4 For these purposes, 'elector', in relation to a European parliamentary election, means any person who has for the time being an entry in a register of electors, but does not include those shown in

such a register (or in the case of a person who has an anonymous entry in the register, in the record of anonymous entries) as below voting age on the day fixed for the poll: see the European Parliamentary Elections Regulations 2004, SI 2004/293, reg 2(1) (substituted by SI 2009/186). 'Register of electors' means any part of: (1) a register of parliamentary or, in the case of peers, local government electors; (2) a register under the Representation of the People Act 1985 s 3 (peers resident outside the United Kingdom registered as European parliamentary electors: see PARA 101); (3) a register under the European Parliamentary Elections (Franchise of Relevant Citizens of the Union) Regulations 2001, SI 2001/1184, reg 5 (see PARA 143); and (4) the Gibraltar register (see PARA 116 note 2), in force within an electoral region at the time of a European parliamentary election in that region: see the European Parliamentary Elections Regulations 2004, SI 2004/293, reg 2(1) (as so substituted). As to the registers of electors see PARA 143 et seq; as to electoral regions established for the purposes of European parliamentary elections see PARA 77; and as to the poll at such an election see PARA 217 et seq. 'Voting age' is currently 18 years for all purposes: see PARAS 95 note 2, 97 note 14, 102 note 10.

5   For these purposes, 'voter' means a person voting at a European parliamentary election and includes a person voting as proxy and, except in the European parliamentary elections rules (ie the rules contained in the European Parliamentary Elections Regulations 2004, SI 2004/293, reg 9(1), Sch 1: see PARA 383 note 16), a person voting by proxy; and 'vote' (whether noun or verb) must be construed accordingly, except that, in the European parliamentary elections rules, any reference to an elector voting or an elector's vote includes a reference to an elector voting by proxy or an elector's vote given by proxy: see reg 2(1) (as substituted: see note 4). As to voting by proxy see PARA 367 et seq.

6   As to the meaning of 'parliamentary election' see PARA 9.

7   As to the meaning of 'United Kingdom' see PARA 1 note 1.

8   As to the meaning of 'local government election' see PARA 11.

9   See the European Parliamentary Elections Regulations 2004, SI 2004/293, reg 107(1)(a)(i); and PARA 909. As to the meaning of 'Great Britain' see PARA 1 note 1. Such a person is incapable also of being registered as a European parliamentary elector or voting at any European parliamentary election in Gibraltar: see reg 107(1)(a)(ii); and PARA 909. The incapacity so imposed is subject to mitigation or remission under reg 112: see PARA 910. As to the provision made for registration to vote as a European parliamentary elector at any European parliamentary election in Gibraltar see PARA 100.

10   See the European Parliamentary Elections Regulations 2004, SI 2004/293, reg 107(1)(a)(iii), (iv), (b); and PARA 909. The incapacity so imposed is not subject to remission even if a court subsequently determines that the conviction should not be upheld: see reg 107(6): see PARA 909.

(2) THE REGISTRATION OF ELECTORS

(i) In general

112. General provision made as to registration etc. Provision may be made by regulations under the Representation of the People Act 1983[1]:

(1)   with respect to the form of the register of electors and of any special lists or records required by the Representation of the People Act 1983 in connection with the register or with any election[2];

(2)   with respect to the procedure to be followed in the preparation of the register and the place and manner of its publication[3], and with respect to the procedure to be followed in the preparation of any such special lists or records, and the time, place and manner of their publication[4];

(3)   generally with respect to any matters incidental to the provisions of the Representation of the People Act 1983 so far as those provisions relate to the registration of electors or to voting by post or proxy[5]; and

(4)   for the supply of any such record or special list as is mentioned in heads (1) and (2) above to such persons as are prescribed[6], with respect to any conditions subject to which the supply is made[7], and making it an offence for a person to fail to comply with any such condition[8].

For the purposes of elections for the return of members of the National Assembly for Wales, the power to make provision by order as to the conduct of such elections includes, in particular, the power to make provision about the registration of electors and for disregarding alterations in a register of electors[9]. Entitlement to vote in such elections is otherwise dependent upon entries in the relevant register of local government electors made under the Representation of the People Act 1983[10].

For the purposes of European parliamentary elections, special provision is made for the registration of peers resident outside the United Kingdom[11] and for the registration of relevant citizens of the European Union who are entitled to vote at such elections[12]. Entitlement to vote in such elections is otherwise dependent upon entries in the relevant register made under the Representation of the People Act 1983, that is, the relevant register of parliamentary electors or (if a peer resident in the United Kingdom) the relevant register of local government electors[13].

1   See the Representation of the People Act 1983 s 53(1). As to the making of regulations under the Representation of the People Act 1983 generally see PARA 28 note 16. The following regulations have been made under s 53: the Representation of the People (England and Wales) Regulations 2001, SI 2001/341; the Representation of the People (Form of Canvass) (England and Wales) Regulations 2006, SI 2006/1694 (see PARA 151 et seq); the Representation of the People (Electoral Registration Data Schemes) Regulations 2011, SI 2011/1467 (made in exercise of the powers conferred by the Representation of the People Act 1983 ss 53(1), (3), 201(3), Sch 2 para 10B(1)(a), (2), but in relation to a scheme in an order made in exercise of the powers conferred by the Political Parties and Elections Act 2009 ss 35, 36 (prospectively repealed): see PARA 152); and the Electoral Registration (Disclosure of Electoral Registers) Regulations 2013, SI 2013/760 (see PARA 156).

      Without prejudice to the generality of the Representation of the People Act 1983 s 53(1) (see heads (1) to (3) in the text), regulations made with respect to the matters mentioned in s 53(1) may contain any such provisions as are mentioned in Sch 2 paras 1–13 (amended by the Representation of the People Act 1985 ss 4, 11, 24, 28, Sch 2 Pt I, Sch 4 para 85, Sch 5; the Representation of the People Act 1989 s 5; the Local Government (Wales) Act 1994 s 66(6), Sch 16 para 68(18); the Data Protection Act 1998 s 74(1), Sch 15 para 7; the Representation of the People Act 2000 ss 8, 9(1)–(3), 15(1), Sch 1 paras 1, 24(1)–(7), Sch 6 paras 3, 11(1)–(4); the Electoral Administration Act 2006 ss 10(2), 47, Sch 1 paras 2, 15, 69, 94, 96; and the Electoral Registration and Administration Act 2013 s 2(6), Sch 2 paras 1–4): see the Representation of the People Act 1983 s 53(3) (amended by the Representation of the People Act 1985 Sch 4 para 13). However, before making regulations containing provision under the Representation of the People Act 1983 Sch 2 para 1A, or under Sch 2 para 13(1ZB) so far as relating to Sch 2 para 1A, the Secretary of State must consult the Electoral Commission, the Information Commissioner, and any other person the Secretary of State thinks appropriate: s 53(5) (s 53(5)–(8) added by the Electoral Registration and Administration Act 2013 Sch 2 paras 1, 5). As to transitional provisions in relation to offences added to the Representation of the People Act 1983 Sch 2 para 13(1ZD) by the Electoral Registration and Administration Act 2013 Sch 2 para 4, see s 13(3), (4). The Secretary of State may require the Electoral Commission to prepare a report on specified matters relating to the operation of any provision made under the Representation of the People Act 1983 Sch 2 para 1A, and to give the Secretary of State a copy of the report by no later than a specified date (see s 53(6) (as so added)), and the Secretary of State must publish a copy of the report (s 53(7) (as so added)). A registration officer in Great Britain must comply with any request made by the Electoral Commission for information that it reasonably requires in connection with the preparation of such a report: s 53(8) (as so added). The Representation of the People Act 1983 Sch 2 is further amended by the Political Parties and Elections Act 2009 ss 33(2), (10), (11), 39, Sch 7, as from a date to be appointed under s 43(1), and by the Electoral Registration and Administration Act 2013 ss 2(1)–(4), 13(1), Sch 4 paras 1, 20, as from a date to be appointed under s 27(1). However, at the date at which this volume states the law, no such day had been appointed. As to the meaning of 'Great Britain' see PARA 1 note 1. As to the meaning of 'registration officer' see PARA 139 note 1. As to the Secretary of State see PARA 2. As to the establishment and constitution of the Electoral Commission see PARA 34 et seq. As to the form and content of registers of electors and the record of anonymous entries see PARA 145 et seq; and as to applications to vote by proxy see PARA 367 et seq. As to the Information Commissioner see CONFIDENCE AND INFORMATIONAL PRIVACY vol 19 (2011) PARA 109 et seq.

2   Representation of the People Act 1983 s 53(1)(a) (amended by the Representation of the People Act 2000 s 15(2), Sch 1 paras 1, 13(a), Sch 7 Pt I).

3   Representation of the People Act 1983 s 53(1)(b)(i) (s 53(1)(b) substituted by the Representation of the People Act 2000 Sch 1 paras 1, 13(b)).

4   Representation of the People Act 1983 s 53(1)(b)(ii) (as substituted: see note 3).

5   Representation of the People Act 1983 s 53(1)(c).

6   Representation of the People Act 1983 s 53(4)(a) (s 53(4) added by the Electoral Administration Act 2006 s 74(1), Sch 1 paras 104, 109).

7   Representation of the People Act 1983 s 53(4)(b) (as added: see note 6).

8   Representation of the People Act 1983 s 53(4)(c) (as added: see note 6). The offence mentioned in head (4) in the text is punishable on summary conviction by a fine not exceeding level 5 on the standard scale: see s 53(4)(c) (as so added). As to the standard scale see SENTENCING AND DISPOSITION OF OFFENDERS vol 92 (2010) PARA 142.

9   See PARA 12. As to the regulations made see the National Assembly for Wales (Representation of the People) Order 2007, SI 2007/236.

10 See PARA 99.

11 Peers who are resident outside the United Kingdom may be registered under the Representation of the People Act 1985 s 3: see PARA 101. The register must be published and, so far as practicable, combined with the registers of parliamentary electors and of local government electors, the names of the peers so registered being marked to indicate that fact: see s 3(7); and PARA 101 note 7.

12 A register of relevant citizens of the Union who are entitled to vote at European parliamentary elections is maintained under the European Parliamentary Elections (Franchise of Relevant Citizens of the Union) Regulations 2001, SI 2001/1184, reg 4 (see PARA 116) and reg 5(2) (see PARA 143). As to the meaning of 'relevant citizen of the Union' for these purposes see PARA 102 note 5. The register must, so far as practicable, be combined with the registers of parliamentary electors and of local government electors and with any register of peers kept under the Representation of the People Act 1985 s 3 (see note 11), the names of the persons so registered being marked to indicate that fact: see PARA 145.

13 As to the entitlement to vote as European parliamentary elector generally see PARA 100.

(ii) Entitlement to Registration

A. GENERAL ENTITLEMENT

113. Entitlement to be registered as a parliamentary or local government elector. A person[1] is entitled to be registered in the register of parliamentary electors[2] for any constituency[3] or part of a constituency if on the relevant date[4]:

(1)   he is resident[5] in the constituency or that part of it[6];

(2)   he is not subject to any legal incapacity[7] to vote (age apart)[8];

(3)   he is either a qualifying Commonwealth citizen or a citizen of the Republic of Ireland[9]; and

(4)   he is of voting age[10].

A person is entitled to be registered in the register of local government electors for any electoral area[11] if on the relevant date[12]:

(a)   he is resident in that area[13];

(b)   he is not subject to any legal incapacity to vote (age apart)[14];

(c)   he is a qualifying Commonwealth citizen, a citizen of the Republic of Ireland or a relevant citizen of the European Union[15]; and

(d)   he is of voting age[16].

These provisions[17] have effect: (i) subject to any enactment imposing a disqualification for registration as a parliamentary or (as the case may be) local government elector[18] and compliance with any prescribed[19] requirements[20]; and (ii) (as respects registration as a parliamentary elector) without prejudice to the provisions regarding the registration of British citizens overseas[21].

A person otherwise qualified is entitled[22] to be registered in a register of parliamentary electors or local government electors if he will attain voting age before the end of the period of 12 months beginning with 1 December next following the relevant date[23]. However, his entry in the register must give the date on which he will attain that age[24] and until the date given in the entry he must not by virtue of the entry be treated as an elector for any purposes other than those of an election the date of the poll for which is the date so given or any later date[25].

1 As to the meaning of 'person' see PARA 95 note 1.

2 As to the meaning of 'elector' for these purposes see PARA 95 note 2. As to the registers of electors see PARA 145 et seq.

3 As to the meaning of 'constituency' for these purposes see PARA 9.

4 See the Representation of the People Act 1983 s 4(1) (s 4 substituted by the Representation of the People Act 2000 s 1(2)). For these purposes, 'the relevant date', in relation to a person, means: (1) the date on which an application for registration is made or, by virtue of the Representation of the People Act 1983 s 10A(2) (see PARA 157), is treated as having been made, by him; (2) in the case of a person applying for registration in pursuance of a declaration of local connection or a service declaration, the date on which the declaration was made: see s 4(6) (as so substituted). As to declarations of local connection see PARA 121 et seq; as to service declarations see PARA 125 et seq; and as to applications for registration see PARA 157 et seq.

   Because the annual canvass for 2013 to be conducted under the Representation of the People Act 1983 s 10(1) (see PARA 151) has been postponed, the reference in s 4(6) to s 10A(2) must be treated as a reference to s 10A(2) as subject to the modification in the Electoral Registration (Postponement of 2013 Annual Canvass) Order 2013, SI 2013/794, art 2: see art 2(4). The Representation of the People Act 2000 changed the system for the registration of parliamentary and local government electors, removing the requirement for residence on a qualifying date for inclusion in a register of electors which had effect for one year and replacing it with a system of registration under which the registers of electors have continuing effect, subject to amendment ('rolling registration'). As to the system of individual electoral registration which, at the date at which this volume states the law, is likely to provide the basis for the register in use at the 2015 general election and beyond, however, see PARA 152 et seq.

5 As to the determination of residence for the purposes of registration as a parliamentary or local government elector see PARA 117 et seq.

6 Representation of the People Act 1983 s 4(1)(a) (as substituted: see note 4).

7 As to the meaning of 'legal incapacity' for these purposes see PARA 95 note 8.

8 Representation of the People Act 1983 s 4(1)(b) (as substituted: see note 4).

9 Representation of the People Act 1983 s 4(1)(c) (as substituted: see note 4). For these purposes, 'qualifying Commonwealth citizen' means a Commonwealth citizen who: (1) is not a person who requires leave under the Immigration Act 1971 to enter or remain in the United Kingdom (see IMMIGRATION AND ASYLUM vol 57 (2012) PARA 5 et seq); or (2) is such a person but for the time being has, or is, by virtue of any enactment, to be treated as having, any description of such leave: see the Representation of the People Act 1983 s 4(6) (as so substituted). As to the meaning of 'United Kingdom' see PARA 1 note 1. As to who are Commonwealth citizens see BRITISH NATIONALITY vol 4 (2011) PARA 409. As to who are citizens of the Republic of Ireland see BRITISH NATIONALITY vol 4 (2011) PARA 410.

10 Representation of the People Act 1983 s 4(1)(d) (as substituted: see note 4). As to voting age for the purposes of parliamentary elections see PARA 95 note 2.

11 As to the meaning of 'electoral area' see PARA 11.

12 See the Representation of the People Act 1983 s 4(3) (as substituted: see note 4).

13 Representation of the People Act 1983 s 4(3)(a) (as substituted: see note 4).

14 Representation of the People Act 1983 s 4(3)(b) (as substituted: see note 4).

15 Representation of the People Act 1983 s 4(3)(c) (as substituted: see note 4). As to the meaning of 'relevant citizen of the Union' for these purposes see PARA 97 note 13.

   For the purposes of extending the rights of citizens and nationals of accession states who (subject to the requirements of registration) may vote at local government and European parliamentary elections, s 4(3) is applied with modifications: see the Local and European Parliamentary Elections (Registration of Citizens of Accession States) Regulations 2003, SI 2003/1557, reg 2(1), (2), (3)(a).

16 Representation of the People Act 1983 s 4(3)(d) (as substituted: see note 4).

17 Ie the Representation of the People Act 1983 s 4(1)–(3) (see the text and notes 1–16): see s 4(4) (as substituted: see note 4).

18 Representation of the People Act 1983 s 4(4)(a)(i) (as substituted: see note 4). As to restrictions on the entitlement to vote see PARA 107 et seq.

19 For these purposes, 'prescribed' means prescribed by regulations: see the Representation of the People Act 1983 s 202(1). As to the making of regulations under the Representation of the People Act 1983 generally see PARA 28 note 16. As to the regulations made under s 4 see the Representation of the People (England and Wales) Regulations 2001, SI 2001/341, Pt III (regs 23–45H) (registration); and PARA 141 et seq.

20 Representation of the People Act 1983 s 4(4)(a)(ii) (as substituted: see note 4).

21 Representation of the People Act 1983 s 4(4)(b) (as substituted: see note 4). The provisions referred to in the text are those contained in the Representation of the People Act 1985 s 2(1) (see PARA 114): see the Representation of the People Act 1983 s 4(4)(b) (as so substituted).

22 Ie despite the Representation of the People Act 1983 s 4(1)(d) (see head (4) in the text) or s 4(3)(d) (see head (d) in the text), as the case may be: see s 4(5) (as substituted: see note 4).

23 Representation of the People Act 1983 s 4(5) (as substituted: see note 4). For the purposes of extending the rights of peers who (subject to the requirement of registration) may vote at European parliamentary elections, s 4(5) is applied with modifications: see the Representation of the People (England and Wales) Regulations 2001, SI 2001/341, reg 13(4), Sch 4; and PARA 101 note 7.

24 Representation of the People Act 1983 s 4(5)(a) (as substituted: see note 4). If a person entitled to be registered by virtue of s 4(5) has an anonymous entry in the register, the references in s 4(5)(a) and s 4(5)(b) (see the text and note 25) to his entry in the register are to be read as references to his entry in the record of anonymous entries prepared in pursuance of s 53(1), Sch 2 para 8A (provisions requiring the registration officer to prepare a record of those persons with anonymous entries in the register: see PARA 112): s 4(5A) (added by the Electoral Administration Act 2006 s 10(2), Sch 1 paras 2, 3). As to the meaning of 'anonymous entry' in relation to a register of electors see PARA 148.

25 Representation of the People Act 1983 s 4(5)(b) (as substituted: see note 4). See note 24. As to the date of the poll at a parliamentary general election or by-election see PARA 195; and as to the date of the poll at local government elections (including elections to fill vacancies) see PARAS 206–209.

114. Entitlement to be registered as an overseas parliamentary elector. A person[1] is entitled to be registered in a register of parliamentary electors[2] in pursuance of a declaration (an 'overseas elector's declaration') made by him[3] if: (1) the register is for the constituency[4] or part of the constituency within which is situated the place in the United Kingdom[5] specified in the declaration[6] as having been the address in respect of which he was registered, or at which he was resident[7], as the case may be[8]; and (2) the registration officer[9] concerned is satisfied that, on the relevant date[10], he qualifies as an overseas elector in respect of that constituency for which that register is prepared[11].

1 The Representation of the People Act 1985 ss 1–12 have effect as if contained in the Representation of the People Act 1983 Pt I (ss 1–66B): see the Representation of the People Act 1985 s 27(2). Accordingly, as to the meaning of 'person' see PARA 95 note 1; definition applied by virtue of s 27(2).

2 As to the meaning of 'elector' see PARA 95 note 2; definition applied by virtue of the Representation of the People Act 1985 s 27(2) (see note 1). As to the registers of electors see PARA 145 et seq.

3 See the Representation of the People Act 1985 s 2(1) (s 2 substituted by the Representation of the People Act 2000 s 8, Sch 2 paras 1, 3). The text refers to a declaration made under and in accordance with the Representation of the People Act 1985 s 2: see s 2(1) (as so substituted). As to the formalities of such a declaration see PARA 132.

   For the purposes of extending the rights of peers who (subject to the requirement of registration) may vote at European parliamentary elections, s 2 is applied with modifications: see the Representation of the People (England and Wales) Regulations 2001, SI 2001/341, reg 13(4), Sch 4; and PARA 101 note 7.

4 As to the meaning of 'constituency' for these purposes see PARA 9.

5 As to the meaning of 'United Kingdom' see PARA 1 note 1.

6	Ie in accordance with the Representation of the People Act 1985 s 2(4) (see PARA 132): see s 2(1)(a) (as substituted: see note 3).
7	As to the determination of residence for the purposes of registration as a parliamentary or local government elector see PARA 117 et seq; provisions applied by virtue of the Representation of the People Act 1985 s 27(2) (see note 1).
8	See the Representation of the People Act 1985 s 2(1)(a) (as substituted: see note 3). See note 3.
9	As to the meaning of 'registration officer' see PARA 139 note 1; definition applied by virtue of the Representation of the People Act 1985 s 27(2) (see note 1).
10	For these purposes, 'the relevant date' has the meaning given by the Representation of the People Act 1985 s 1(1)(a) (see PARA 96 note 6): see s 2(8) (as substituted: see note 3). See note 3.
11	Representation of the People Act 1985 s 2(1)(b) (as substituted: see note 3). See note 3. As to the expiry or removal of such entries see PARA 169. For the purposes of the Representation of the People (England and Wales) Regulations 2001, SI 2001/341, 'overseas elector' means a person who has made an overseas elector's declaration and is registered or entitled to be registered as a parliamentary elector in pursuance of it: see reg 3(1).

115. Entitlement of peer to be registered as an overseas European parliamentary elector. A peer who, apart from the requirement of registration, is entitled[1] to vote as an elector at a European parliamentary election[2] in a particular electoral region[3] is entitled to be registered in a register[4] prepared and published by a registration officer[5].

1	Ie by virtue of the Representation of the People Act 1985 s 3 (see PARA 101): see the Representation of the People (England and Wales) Regulations 2001, SI 2001/341, reg 13(1).
2	As to European parliamentary elections generally see PARA 13 et seq.
3	As to electoral regions constituted for the purposes of European parliamentary elections see PARA 77.
4	Ie a register under the Representation of the People Act 1985 s 3 (see PARA 101): see the Representation of the People (England and Wales) Regulations 2001, SI 2001/341, reg 13(1).
5	Representation of the People (England and Wales) Regulations 2001, SI 2001/341, reg 13(1). As to the meaning of 'registration officer' see PARA 139 note 1. The register mentioned in the text must be prepared and published in accordance with reg 13 and the provisions applied by it: see reg 13(1). As to the provisions so applied see PARA 101 note 7.

116. Entitlement of relevant citizen of the European Union to be registered as a European parliamentary elector. A person is entitled to be registered in the register of relevant citizens of the Union[1] entitled to vote at European parliamentary elections[2] for part of an electoral region[3] if on the relevant date[4]:
(1)	he is resident in that part of the region[5];
(2)	he is not subject to any legal incapacity to vote (age apart)[6];
(3)	he is a relevant citizen of the Union[7]; and
(4)	he is of voting age[8].
The registration officer[9] must also have received in respect of that person an application and declaration duly made[10]. These provisions[11] have effect subject to: (a) any enactment[12] imposing a disqualification for registration as a European parliamentary elector[13]; and (b) compliance with the requirements of the European Parliamentary Elections (Franchise of Relevant Citizens of the Union) Regulations 2001[14] and any provision applied by those regulations[15].
A person otherwise qualified is[16] entitled to be registered in a register of relevant citizens of the Union entitled to vote at European parliamentary elections[17] if he will attain voting age before the end of the period of 12 months beginning with 1 December next following the relevant date[18]. However, his entry in the register must give the date on which he will attain that age[19] and, until the date given in the entry, he must not by virtue of the entry be treated as an elector for any purposes other than those of an election the date of the poll for which is the date so given or any later date[20].

1 As to the meaning of 'relevant citizen of the Union' for these purposes see PARA 102 note 5.
2 Ie the register maintained under the European Parliamentary Elections (Franchise of Relevant Citizens of the Union) Regulations 2001, SI 2001/1184, reg 5(2) (see PARA 143): see reg 4(1). As to the entitlement of relevant citizens of the Union to vote at European parliamentary elections see PARA 102. A person resident in Gibraltar is, subject to his satisfying the requirements for entitlement to vote in and register for European parliamentary elections, entitled to be registered in the register of European parliamentary electors in Gibraltar ('the Gibraltar register'), which is maintained by the European electoral registration officer for Gibraltar: see the European Parliament (Representation) Act 2003 ss 14, 16–18; and PARA 100 note 3.
3 As to electoral regions constituted for the purposes of European parliamentary elections see PARA 77.
4 See the European Parliamentary Elections (Franchise of Relevant Citizens of the Union) Regulations 2001, SI 2001/1184, reg 4(1). For this purpose, 'the relevant date' means the date on which the application and declaration required by the reg 6(1), (2) (see PARA 159) were made: see reg 4(5). For the purposes of extending the rights of citizens and nationals of accession states who (subject to the requirements of registration) may vote at local government and European parliamentary elections, reg 4 is applied with modifications: see the Local and European Parliamentary Elections (Registration of Citizens of Accession States) Regulations 2003, SI 2003/1557, reg 6, Sch 1 para 2.
5 European Parliamentary Elections (Franchise of Relevant Citizens of the Union) Regulations 2001, SI 2001/1184, reg 4(1)(a). See note 4.
6 European Parliamentary Elections (Franchise of Relevant Citizens of the Union) Regulations 2001, SI 2001/1184, reg 4(1)(b). See note 4.
7 European Parliamentary Elections (Franchise of Relevant Citizens of the Union) Regulations 2001, SI 2001/1184, reg 4(1)(c). See note 4.
8 European Parliamentary Elections (Franchise of Relevant Citizens of the Union) Regulations 2001, SI 2001/1184, reg 4(1)(d). See note 4. 'Voting age' is currently 18 years for these purposes: see PARA 102 note 10.
9 As to the registration officer see PARA 139.
10 See the European Parliamentary Elections (Franchise of Relevant Citizens of the Union) Regulations 2001, SI 2001/1184, reg 4(1). The text refers to an application and declaration duly made in accordance with reg 6(1), (2) (see PARA 159): see reg 4(1). See note 4. As to the expiry or removal of entries pursuant to such a declaration see PARA 169.
11 Ie reg 4(1) (see the text and notes 1–10): see reg 4(3).
12 For these purposes, 'enactment' includes any provision of an Act, and any provision of subordinate legislation (within the meaning of the Interpretation Act 1978: see STATUTES AND LEGISLATIVE PROCESS vol 96 (2012) PARA 609): see the European Parliamentary Elections (Franchise of Relevant Citizens of the Union) Regulations 2001, SI 2001/1184, reg 4(5). See note 4.
13 European Parliamentary Elections (Franchise of Relevant Citizens of the Union) Regulations 2001, SI 2001/1184, reg 4(3)(a). See note 4.
14 Ie the European Parliamentary Elections (Franchise of Relevant Citizens of the Union) Regulations 2001, SI 2001/1184: see reg 4(3)(b).
15 European Parliamentary Elections (Franchise of Relevant Citizens of the Union) Regulations 2001, SI 2001/1184, reg 4(3)(b). See note 4.
16 Ie despite the European Parliamentary Elections (Franchise of Relevant Citizens of the Union) Regulations 2001, SI 2001/1184, reg 4(1)(d) (see head (4) in the text): see reg 4(4).
17 Ie in a register maintained under the European Parliamentary Elections (Franchise of Relevant Citizens of the Union) Regulations 2001, SI 2001/1184, reg 5(2) (see PARA 143): see reg 4(4).
18 European Parliamentary Elections (Franchise of Relevant Citizens of the Union) Regulations 2001, SI 2001/1184, reg 4(4). See note 4.
19 European Parliamentary Elections (Franchise of Relevant Citizens of the Union) Regulations 2001, SI 2001/1184, reg 4(4)(a). See note 4.
20 European Parliamentary Elections (Franchise of Relevant Citizens of the Union) Regulations 2001, SI 2001/1184, reg 4(4)(b). See note 4. As to the date of the poll at a European parliamentary election see PARA 222.

B. THE RESIDENCE REQUIREMENT

117. Determination of residence for registration as a parliamentary or local government elector. For the purposes of ascertaining the entitlement of a person[1] to be registered as a parliamentary or local government elector[2], where the question as to whether a person is resident at a particular address on the relevant date[3] falls to be determined[4], regard must be had, in particular, to the purpose and other circumstances, as well as to the fact, of his presence at, or absence from, the address on that date[5]. For example, where at a particular time a person is staying at any place otherwise than on a permanent basis, he may in all the circumstances be taken to be at that time resident there if he has no home elsewhere, or not resident there if he does have a home elsewhere[6]. At common law, it has been held that a person's residence is by implication that person's home[7], where at least he has a sleeping apartment[8] or shares one, although merely sleeping on the premises is not conclusive of residence[9]. A person may reside on premises as a guest[10], or as a trespasser[11] or otherwise unlawfully[12]. When a person has a country and a town house, it is a mere question of fact whether he has two residences or only one residence[13]. A short-stay visitor is not resident[14]. One test of residence that has been applied is whether the person's presence at the address had, on the relevant date, a considerable degree of permanence[15]. However, permanence, like most aspects of residence, is a question of fact and degree[16].

A person may be resident at an address even though he is temporarily absent from it[17]. His residence will, however, be interrupted if he is unable to return at will without the breach of a legal obligation, subject to the statutory provisions mentioned below[18]. For the statutory purpose of determining whether a person is resident in a dwelling[19] on the relevant date[20], his residence in the dwelling is not deemed for registration purposes to have been interrupted by reason of his absence in the performance of any duty arising from or incidental to any office, service or employment[21] held or undertaken by him[22] if: (1) he intends to resume actual residence within six months of giving up such residence, and will not be prevented from doing so by the performance of that duty[23]; or (2) the dwelling serves as a permanent place of residence (whether for himself or for himself and other persons) and he would be in actual residence there but for his absence in the performance of that duty[24]. Special provision is made for the registration of persons by way of a declaration of local connection for which an address must be provided by the declarant so that the registration officer concerned or the returning officer may correspond with him (unless he is willing to collect such correspondence periodically from the registration officer's office)[25]. A person who is detained at any place in legal custody is not, by reason of his presence there, to be treated as resident for the purposes of registration[26].

1   As to the meaning of 'person' see PARA 95 note 1.

2   Ie for the purposes of the Representation of the People Act 1983 s 4 (see PARA 113). As to the meaning of 'elector' see PARA 95 note 2. As to the registers of electors see PARA 145 et seq.

3   As to the relevant date for this purpose see PARA 113 note 4. The scheme introduced by the Representation of the People Act 2000, which makes a person's registration dependent upon residence at a relevant date ('rolling registration'), operates in contrast to the schemes under the Representation of the People Act 1918 (and earlier enactments, all of which are now repealed) whereby a person had to be resident for a qualifying period before he was entitled to be registered or under the Representation of the People Act 1948 (now repealed) which required a person to be resident on a (fixed) qualifying date. As to the system of individual electoral registration which, at the date at which this volume states the law, is likely to provide the basis for the register in use at the 2015 general election and beyond see PARA 152 et seq.

4   See the Representation of the People Act 1983 s 5(1) (s 5 substituted by the Representation of the People Act 2000 s 3).

    For the purposes of relevant citizens of the Union who (subject to the requirement of registration) may vote at European parliamentary elections, the Representation of the People Act 1983 s 5 is applied with modifications: see the European Parliamentary Elections (Franchise of Relevant Citizens of the Union) Regulations 2001, SI 2001/1184, reg 9, Schedule; and PARA 102 note 6. As to the meaning of 'relevant citizen of the Union' for these purposes see PARA 102 note 5.

5   See the Representation of the People Act 1983 s 5(2) (as substituted: see note 4). See note 4.

6   See the Representation of the People Act 1983 s 5(2) (as substituted: see note 4). See note 4.

7   *Barlow v Smith* (1892) 9 TLR 57 at 58, DC; *R v Hammond* (1852) 17 QB 772 at 780–783.

8   *Tewkesbury Case, Whithorn v Thomas* (1844) Bar & Arn 259; *R v Exeter Corpn, Wescomb's Case* (1868) LR 4 QB 110; *R v Exeter Corpn, Dipstale's Case* (1868) LR 4 QB 114.

9   *R v Exeter Corpn, Dipstale's Case* (1868) LR 4 QB 114; *Oldham Case, Baxter's Case* (1869) 20 LT 302 at 308.

10 *Bath Case* (1857) Wolfe & D 148; *Horsham Case, Andrews' Case* (1866) 14 LT 274.

11 *Beal v Ford* (1877) 3 CPD 73, DC.

12 *Hipperson v Newbury District Electoral Registration Officer* [1985] QB 1060 at 1075, [1985] 2 All ER 456 at 463, CA, per Sir John Donaldson MR (protesters unlawfully camping outside air force base were entitled to be registered; the submission was rejected that the franchise is affected by the fact that the qualifying residence is illegal or, a fortiori, unlawful).

13 *R v Exeter Corpn, Wescomb's Case* (1868) LR 4 QB 110 at 113 per Blackburn J; *Bond v St George, Hanover Square, Overseers* (1870) LR 6 CP 312.

14 *Fox v Stirk and Bristol Electoral Registration Officer* [1970] 2 QB 463 at 475, [1970] 3 All ER 7 at 12, CA, per Lord Denning MR (obiter). Similarly a guest who stays for the weekend is not resident.

15 *Fox v Stirk and Bristol Electoral Registration Officer* [1970] 2 QB 463 at 475, [1970] 3 All ER 7 at 12, CA, per Lord Denning MR (university students in halls of residence or colleges entitled to be registered as voters).

16 *Hipperson v Newbury District Electoral Registration Officer* [1985] QB 1060 at 1073, [1985] 2 All ER 456 at 462, CA, per Sir John Donaldson MR (protesters who had been camping outside an air force base for a substantial period entitled to be registered notwithstanding that they might, in theory, be required to leave shortly after the qualifying date).

17 *Taylor v St Mary Abbott Overseers* (1870) LR 6 CP 309; *Bond v St George, Hanover Square, Overseers* (1870) LR 6 CP 312; *Ipswich Case, Pisey's Case* (1838) Falc & Fitz 271.

18 *Kidderminster Case, Powell v Guest* (1864) 18 CBNS 72, a case of imprisonment without the option of a fine, in which it was suggested that imprisonment on civil process or for non-payment of a fine would not interrupt the residence. See also *Ford v Pye* (1873) LR 9 CP 269 (exchange of livings); *Durant v Carter* (1873) LR 9 CP 261 (occupation of rectory by locum tenens); *Ford v Drew* (1879) 5 CPD 59 (absence while articled to a solicitor); *Ford v Hart* (1873) LR 9 CP 273 (absence while on duty in armed forces).

19 For these purposes, 'dwelling' includes any part of a building where that part is occupied separately as a dwelling: see the Representation of the People Act 1983 s 202(1) (definition substituted, for definition of 'dwelling house', by the Representation of the People Act 2000 s 8, Sch 1 paras 1, 22(a)). See *Thompson v Ward, Ellis v Burch* (1871) LR 6 CP 327; *Stribling v Halse* (1885) 16 QBD 246; *Barnett v Hickmott* [1895] 1 QB 691; *Clutterbuck v Taylor* [1896] 1 QB 395, CA; *M'Quade v Charlton* [1904] 2 IR 383; *Ladd v O'Toole* [1904] 2 IR 389, CA; *M'Daid v Balmer* [1907] 2 IR 345.

20 Ie for the purposes of the Representation of the People Act 1983 s 4 (see PARA 113): see s 5(3) (as substituted: see note 4).

21 For the purposes of the Representation of the People Act 1983 s 5(3), any temporary period of unemployment is disregarded: s 5(4) (as substituted: see note 4). See note 4.

22 See the Representation of the People Act 1983 s 5(3) (as substituted: see note 4). The provision made by s 5(3) applies in relation to a person's absence by reason of his attendance on a course provided by an educational institution as it applies in relation to a person's absence in the performance of any duty such as is mentioned in s 5(3): see s 5(5) (as so substituted). See note 4. In relation to a person who: (1) is not a member of the forces as defined by s 59(1) for the purposes of the parliamentary and local government franchise (see PARA 125 note 2); but (2) is, in the performance of his duty as a member of Her Majesty's reserve or auxiliary forces, absent on the relevant date for the purposes of s 4 (see PARA 113) from an address at which he has been residing, any question arising under s 5(3) as to whether his residence at that address has been interrupted on the relevant date by his absence in the performance of that duty is to be determined as if the performance of that duty did not prevent his resuming actual residence at any time after that date: see s 59(2) (amended by the Representation of the People Act 2000 s 8, Sch 1 paras 1, 16).

23 Representation of the People Act 1983 s 5(3)(a) (as substituted: see note 4). See note 4.

24 Representation of the People Act 1983 s 5(3)(b) (as substituted: see note 4). See note 4. See also
   Lister v Edinburgh Electoral Registration Officer 1963 SLT (Sh Ct) 9 (residence abroad
   necessitated by applicant's particular employment and could not be avoided without giving up
   her employment).
25 See PARA 121 et seq.
26 Representation of the People Act 1983 s 5(6) (as substituted: see note 4). This provision is
   subject to the provisions which help to determine the residence of patients in mental hospitals
   who are not detained offenders or on remand (see s 7; and PARA 119) or of persons remanded in
   custody etc (see s 7A; and PARA 120): see s 5(6) (as so substituted). See note 4.

118.   Residence of merchant seamen may be deemed. For the purposes of
entitlement to be registered as a parliamentary or local government elector[1], a
merchant seaman[2], at any time when he is not resident[3] in the United Kingdom[4],
and would have been resident there but for the nature of his occupation, is
entitled to be treated as a resident[5]: (1) at any place at which he would have been
resident but for the nature of his occupation[6]; or (2) at any hostel or club
providing accommodation for merchant seamen at which he commonly stays in
the course of his occupation[7].

1 Ie for the purposes of the Representation of the People Act 1983 s 4 (see PARA 113): see s 6
   (amended by the Representation of the People Act 2000 s 8, Sch 1 paras 1, 2). As to the meaning
   of 'elector' see PARA 95 note 2.
      For the purposes of relevant citizens of the Union who (subject to the requirement of
   registration) may vote at European parliamentary elections, s 6 is applied with modifications:
   see the European Parliamentary Elections (Franchise of Relevant Citizens of the Union)
   Regulations 2001, SI 2001/1184, reg 9, Schedule; and PARA 102 note 6. As to the meaning of
   'relevant citizen of the Union' for these purposes see PARA 102 note 5.
2 For these purposes, 'merchant seaman' means any person not having a service qualification
   whose employment or the greater part of it is carried out on board seagoing ships, and includes
   any such person while temporarily without employment: see the Representation of the People
   Act 1983 s 6. As to the meaning of 'person' see PARA 95 note 1. As to the service qualification
   see PARA 125 et seq.
3 As to the general requirements for residence for the purposes of registration as a parliamentary
   or local government elector see PARA 117.
4 As to the meaning of 'United Kingdom' see PARA 1 note 1.
5 See the Representation of the People Act 1983 s 6 (as amended: see note 1). See note 1.
6 Representation of the People Act 1983 s 6(a). See note 1.
7 Representation of the People Act 1983 s 6(b). See note 1.

**119.   Deemed residence of patients in mental hospitals who are not detained
offenders or on remand.** For the purposes of ascertaining entitlement to be
registered as a parliamentary or local government elector[1], a person[2]:

(1)   who is a patient in a mental hospital[3] (whether or not he is liable to be
       detained there)[4]; but
(2)   who is not a detained offender[5] or on remand[6],

must be regarded as resident at the mental hospital in question if the length of
the period which he is likely to spend at the hospital is sufficient for him to be
regarded as being resident there for the purposes of electoral registration[7].

1 Ie for the purposes of the Representation of the People Act 1983 s 4 (see PARA 113): see s 7(2)
   (s 7 substituted by the Representation of the People Act 2000 s 4). As to the meaning of 'elector'
   see PARA 95 note 2.
      For the purposes of relevant citizens of the Union who (subject to the requirements of
   registration) may vote at European parliamentary elections, the Representation of the People
   Act 1983 s 7 is applied with modifications: see the European Parliamentary Elections (Franchise
   of Relevant Citizens of the Union) Regulations 2001, SI 2001/1184, reg 9, Schedule; and PARA
   102 note 6. As to the meaning of 'relevant citizen of the Union' for these purposes see PARA 102
   note 5.

2 Ie a person to whom the Representation of the People Act 1983 s 7 applies (that is, a person falling within s 7(1): see heads (1) and (2) in the text): see s 7(2) (as substituted: see note 1). As to the meaning of 'person' see PARA 95 note 1.

3 For these purposes, 'mental hospital' means any establishment (or part of an establishment) maintained wholly or mainly for the reception and treatment of persons suffering from any form of mental disorder: see the Representation of the People Act 1983 s 7(6) (as substituted: see note 1). 'Mental disorder', in relation to England or Wales, has the same meaning as in the Mental Health Act 1983 (see MENTAL HEALTH AND CAPACITY vol 75 (2013) PARA 761): Representation of the People Act 1983 s 7(6)(a) (as so substituted). As to the meanings of 'England' and 'Wales' see PARA 1 note 1.

4 Representation of the People Act 1983 s 7(1)(a) (as substituted: see note 1). See note 1. The text refers to a person who may be a voluntary patient in a mental hospital.

5 Ie he is not a person to whom the Representation of the People Act 1983 s 3A (disfranchisement of offenders detained in mental hospitals: see PARA 108) applies: see s 7(1)(b) (as substituted: see note 1). See note 1.

6 Representation of the People Act 1983 s 7(1)(b) (as substituted: see note 1). The text refers to a person on remand, to whom s 7A (deemed residence of persons remanded in custody: see PARA 120) applies: see s 7(1)(b) (as so substituted). See note 1.

7 See the Representation of the People Act 1983 s 7(2) (as substituted: see note 1). However, s 7(2) must not be taken as precluding the registration of a person to whom s 7 applies (see heads (1) and (2) in the text), either:
    (1)   by virtue of his residence at some place other than the mental hospital in which he is a patient (s 7(5)(a) (as so substituted)); or
    (2)   in pursuance of a declaration of local connection (s 7(5)(b) (as so substituted)).
See note 1. As to declarations of local connection see PARA 121; and as to the removal from the register of entries made in pursuance of a deemed residence see PARA 169.

120. Deemed residence of persons remanded in custody. For the purposes of ascertaining entitlement to be registered as a parliamentary or local government elector[1], a person[2] who is detained at any place pursuant to a relevant order or direction[3] and is so detained otherwise than after[4]:

    (1)   being convicted of any offence[5]; or

    (2)   a finding in criminal proceedings that he did the act or made the omission charged[6],

must be regarded as resident at the place at which he is detained if the length of the period which he is likely to spend at that place is sufficient for him to be regarded as being resident there for the purposes of electoral registration[7].

1 Ie for the purposes of the Representation of the People Act 1983 s 4 (see PARA 113): see s 7A(2) (s 7A added by the Representation of the People Act 2000 s 5). As to the meaning of 'elector' see PARA 95 note 2.
    For the purposes of relevant citizens of the Union who (subject to the requirements of registration) may vote at European parliamentary elections, the Representation of the People Act 1983 s 7A is applied with modifications: see the European Parliamentary Elections (Franchise of Relevant Citizens of the Union) Regulations 2001, SI 2001/1184, reg 9, Schedule; and PARA 102 note 6. As to the meaning of 'relevant citizen of the Union' for these purposes see PARA 102 note 5.

2 Ie a person to whom the Representation of the People Act 1983 s 7A applies (that is, a person falling within s 7A(1): see heads (1) and (2) in the text): see s 7A(2) (as added: see note 1). As to the meaning of 'person' see PARA 95 note 1.

3 For these purposes, a 'relevant order or direction' means a remand or committal in custody, a remand to a hospital under the Mental Health Act 1983 s 35 (remand for report on accused's mental condition: see MENTAL HEALTH AND CAPACITY vol 75 (2013) PARA 862) or s 36 (remand of accused person to hospital for treatment: see MENTAL HEALTH AND CAPACITY vol 75 (2013) PARA 862) or a direction for removal to a hospital under s 48 (removal to hospital of certain prisoners: see MENTAL HEALTH AND CAPACITY vol 75 (2013) PARA 893): see the Representation of the People Act 1983 s 7A(6) (as added: see note 1).

4 See the Representation of the People Act 1983 s 7A(1) (as added: see note 1). See note 1.

5 Representation of the People Act 1983 s 7A(1)(a) (as added: see note 1). See note 1. As to the disenfranchisement of serving prisoners and detained offenders see PARA 107.

6 Representation of the People Act 1983 s 7A(1)(b) (as added: see note 1). See note 1.

7   See the Representation of the People Act 1983 s 7A(2) (as added: see note 1). However, s 7A(2) must not be taken as precluding the registration of a person to whom s 7A applies (see heads (1) and (2) in the text), either:
    (1)   by virtue of his residence at some place other than the place at which he is detained (s 7A(5)(a) (as so added)); or
    (2)   in pursuance of a declaration of local connection (s 7A(5)(b) (as so added)).
    As to the application and modification of these provisions see note 1. As to declarations of local connection see PARA 121; and as to the removal from the register of entries made in pursuance of a deemed residence see PARA 169.

121. Notional residence deemed by way of declaration of local connection. A declaration of local connection may be made by any person[1] who on the date when he makes such a declaration is[2]:

(1)   a person who is a patient in a mental hospital[3] (whether or not he is liable to be detained there) but who is not a detained offender or on remand[4] and who would not be entitled to be registered by virtue of residence[5] at any place other than the mental hospital at which he is a patient[6]; or

(2)   a person who is detained at any place pursuant to a relevant committal, custodial or hospital order or direction[7] and is so detained otherwise than after being convicted of any offence, or a finding in criminal proceedings that he did the act or made the omission charged[8] and who would not be entitled to be registered by virtue of residence at any place other than the place at which he is detained[9]; or

(3)   a person who does not fall within head (1) or head (2) above (and is not otherwise in legal custody) and who is not, for the purposes of ascertaining his entitlement to be registered as a parliamentary or local government elector[10], resident at any address in the United Kingdom[11] (a 'homeless person')[12].

Such a declaration may be made only by a person to whom head (1), head (2) or head (3) above applies[13], but may be made by such a person despite the fact that by reason of his age he is not entitled to vote[14].

A declaration of local connection may be cancelled at any time by the declarant[15].

1   Ie a person to whom the Representation of the People Act 1983 s 7B applies (that is, a person falling within s 7B(2): see heads (1) to (3) in the text): see s 7B(1)(a) (s 7B added by the Representation of the People Act 2000 s 6). As to the meaning of 'person' see PARA 95 note 1.
        For the purposes of relevant citizens of the Union who (subject to the requirements of registration) may vote at European parliamentary elections, the Representation of the People Act 1983 s 7B is applied with modifications: see the European Parliamentary Elections (Franchise of Relevant Citizens of the Union) Regulations 2001, SI 2001/1184, reg 9, Schedule; and PARA 102 note 6. As to the meaning of 'relevant citizen of the Union' for these purposes see PARA 102 note 5.
2   See the Representation of the People Act 1983 s 7B(2) (as added: see note 1). There is no attestation required for a declaration of local connection, as this might be difficult for eg a homeless person to comply with; cf the formalities associated with service declarations (cited in PARA 127) or certain overseas electors' declarations (cited in PARA 134).
3   As to the meaning of 'mental hospital' see PARA 119 note 3.
4   Ie a person to whom the Representation of the People Act 1983 s 7 (deemed residence for persons in mental hospitals who are not detained offenders or on remand: see PARA 119) applies: see s 7B(2)(a) (as added: see note 1). The text refers to the second limb of the test as to whether s 7 applies or not, ie that the person is not a person to whom s 3A (disfranchisement of offenders detained in mental hospitals: see PARA 108) or s 7A (deemed residence of persons remanded in custody: see PARA 120) applies: see s 7(1)(b); and PARA 119.
5   As to the general requirements for residence for the purposes of registration as a parliamentary or local government elector see PARA 117.

6 Representation of the People Act 1983 s 7B(2)(a) (as added: see note 1). The reference in the text is to a mental hospital within the meaning of s 7 (see note 3): see s 7B(2)(a) (as so added).
7 As to the relevant orders or directions referred to in the text see PARA 120 note 3.
8 Ie a person to whom the Representation of the People Act 1983 s 7A (deemed residence of persons remanded in custody: see PARA 120) applies: see s 7B(2)(b) (as added: see note 1).
9 Representation of the People Act 1983 s 7B(2)(b) (as added: see note 1). The text refers to the place at which the person in question is detained as mentioned in s 7A(1) (see PARA 120): see s 7B(2)(b) (as so added).
10 Ie for the purposes of the Representation of the People Act 1983 s 4 (see PARA 113): see s 7B(2)(c) (as added: see note 1). As to the meaning of 'elector' see PARA 95 note 2.
11 As to the meaning of 'United Kingdom' see PARA 1 note 1.
12 Representation of the People Act 1983 s 7B(2)(c) (as added: see note 1).
13 Representation of the People Act 1983 s 7B(1)(a) (as added: see note 1). As to offences associated with declarations of local connection see PARA 735.
14 Representation of the People Act 1983 s 7B(1)(b) (as added: see note 1). As to entitlement to vote see PARA 95 et seq.
15 Representation of the People Act 1983 s 7B(9) (as added: see note 1). A cancellation as mentioned in the text terminates the entitlement to vote in pursuance of a declaration of local connection: see PARA 170.

122. Formalities associated with declaration of local connection. A declaration of local connection[1] must state:

(1) the name of the declarant and either an address to which correspondence for him from either the registration officer[2] concerned or the returning officer can be delivered[3], or that he is willing to collect such correspondence periodically from the registration officer's office[4];

(2) the date of the declaration[5];

(3) that on the date of the declaration the declarant falls into one of the categories of persons who may make such a declaration[6], specifying the category in question[7], and (in the case of a person[8] whose category is not that of a homeless person) the name and address of the mental hospital[9] at which he is a patient or (as the case may be) of the place at which he is detained[10];

(4) the required address[11];

(5) that on the date of the declaration the declarant is a Commonwealth citizen[12] or a citizen of the Republic of Ireland[13] or (if the declaration is made for the purposes only of local government elections[14]) a relevant citizen of the Union[15];

(6) whether the declarant has on the date of the declaration attained the age of 18 years, and, if he has not, the date of his birth[16].

1 By virtue of the Representation of the People Act 1983 s 7B(2), a declaration of local connection may be made by a person who would not be entitled to be registered by virtue of residence at any place other than the mental hospital at which he is a patient, or other than the place at which he is detained, or by a person who is not resident at any address in the United Kingdom (a 'homeless person'): see PARA 121. As to its effect see PARA 124. As to the meaning of 'United Kingdom' see PARA 1 note 1.
2 As to the meaning of 'registration officer' see PARA 139 note 1.
3 Representation of the People Act 1983 s 7B(3)(a)(i) (s 7B added by the Representation of the People Act 2000 s 6). As to returning officers see PARA 350.
     For the purposes of extending the rights of relevant citizens of the Union who (subject to the requirement of registration) may vote at European parliamentary elections, and of citizens and nationals of accession states who (subject to the requirement of registration) may vote at local government and European parliamentary elections, the Representation of the People Act 1983 s 7B is applied with modifications: see the European Parliamentary Elections (Franchise of Relevant Citizens of the Union) Regulations 2001, SI 2001/1184, reg 9, Schedule (cited in PARA 102 note 6); and the Local and European Parliamentary Elections (Registration of Citizens of

Accession States) Regulations 2003, SI 2003/1557, reg 2(1), (3)(b), (c). As to the meaning of 'relevant citizen of the Union' for these purposes see PARA 102 note 5.

4 Representation of the People Act 1983 s 7B(3)(a)(ii) (as added: see note 3). See note 3.

5 Representation of the People Act 1983 s 7B(3)(b) (as added: see note 3). See note 3.

6 Ie one of the categories of persons to whom the Representation of the People Act 1983 s 7B applies (see note 1): see s 7B(3)(c)(i) (as added: see note 3).

7 Representation of the People Act 1983 s 7B(3)(c)(i) (as added: see note 3). See note 3.

8 Ie a person falling within the Representation of the People Act 1983 s 7B(2)(a) (ie a person to whom s 7 (deemed residence for persons in mental hospitals who are not detained offenders or on remand: see PARA 119) applies: see PARA 121) or s 7B(2)(b) (ie a person to whom s 7A (deemed residence of persons remanded in custody: see PARA 120) applies: see PARA 121): see s 7B(3)(c)(ii) (as added: see note 3). See note 3.

9 As to the meaning of 'mental hospital' see PARA 119 note 3.

10 Representation of the People Act 1983 s 7B(3)(c)(ii) (as added: see note 3). See note 3. The text refers to the place at which the person in question is detained as mentioned in s 7A(1) (deemed residence of persons remanded in custody: see PARA 120).

11 Representation of the People Act 1983 s 7B(3)(d) (as added: see note 3). For these purposes, the 'required address' is:

(1) in the case of a person falling within s 7B(2)(a), (b) (see PARA 121): (a) the address in the United Kingdom where he would be residing if he were not such a patient, or detained, as mentioned in that provision (s 7B(4)(a)(i) (as so added)); or (b) if he cannot give such an address, an address in the United Kingdom at which he has resided (s 7B(4)(a)(ii) (as so added));

(2) in the case of a homeless person, the address of, or which is nearest to, a place in the United Kingdom where he commonly spends a substantial part of his time (whether during the day or at night) (s 7B(4)(b) (as so added)).

Where a declaration of local connection made by a homeless person is delivered to the registration officer concerned during the period:

(i) beginning with the date when a vacancy occurs: (A) in the seat for the parliamentary constituency within which the required address falls (s 7B(6)(a)(i) (as so added)); or (B) in the seat for any National Assembly for Wales constituency within which it falls (s 7B(6)(a)(ii) (as so added)); and

(ii) ending on the final nomination day, within the meaning of s 13B (alteration of registers (pending elections): see PARA 168), for the parliamentary by-election, or (as the case may be) the election under the Government of Wales Act 2006 s 10 (election to fill a vacancy for the seat of an Assembly member returned for an Assembly constituency: see PARA 214) held in respect of that vacancy (Representation of the People Act 1983 s 7B(6)(b) (s 7B as so added; s 7B(6)(b) amended by SI 2007/1388)),

the declaration must state that, during the period of three months ending on the date of the declaration, the declarant has commonly been spending a substantial part of his time (whether during the day or at night) at, or near, the required address (see the Representation of the People Act 1983 s 7B(6) (as so added)). See note 3.

Irregularities in stating the required address (ie stating more than one address or stating different addresses on more than one declaration bearing the same date) render the declaration or declarations void: see PARA 123.

12 As to who are Commonwealth citizens see BRITISH NATIONALITY vol 4 (2011) PARA 409.

13 As to who are citizens of the Republic of Ireland see BRITISH NATIONALITY vol 4 (2011) PARA 410.

14 As to the meaning of 'local government election' see PARA 11.

15 Representation of the People Act 1983 s 7B(3)(e) (as added: see note 3). See note 3. As to the meaning of 'relevant citizen of the Union' for these purposes see PARA 97 note 13.

16 Representation of the People Act 1983 s 7B(3)(f) (as added: see note 3). See note 3.

123.   Invalid declaration of local connection.   If a person:

(1)   makes a declaration of local connection[1] stating more than one address[2]; or

(2)   makes more than one declaration of local connection bearing the same date and stating different addresses[3],

the declaration or declarations are void[4].

A declaration of local connection is of no effect unless it is received by the registration officer[5] concerned within the period of three months beginning with the date of the declaration[6].

1   See PARAS 121–122.
2   Representation of the People Act 1983 s 7B(8)(a) (s 7B added by the Representation of the People Act 2000 s 6). The text refers to the address stated under the Representation of the People Act 1983 s 7B(3)(d) (see PARA 122): see s 7B(8)(a) (as so added).

     For the purposes of extending the rights of relevant citizens of the Union who (subject to the requirement of registration) may vote at European parliamentary elections, and of citizens and nationals of accession states who (subject to the requirement of registration) may vote at local government and European parliamentary elections, the Representation of the People Act 1983 s 7B is applied with modifications: see the European Parliamentary Elections (Franchise of Relevant Citizens of the Union) Regulations 2001, SI 2001/1184, reg 9, Schedule (cited in PARA 102 note 6); and the Local and European Parliamentary Elections (Registration of Citizens of Accession States) Regulations 2003, SI 2003/1557, reg 2(1), (3)(b), (c). As to the meaning of 'relevant citizen of the Union' for these purposes see PARA 102 note 5.
3   Representation of the People Act 1983 s 7B(8)(b) (as added: see note 2).
4   See the Representation of the People Act 1983 s 7B(8) (as added: see note 2). As to offences associated with declarations of local connection see PARA 735.
5   As to the meaning of 'registration officer' see PARA 139 note 1.
6   Representation of the People Act 1983 s 7B(10) (as added: see note 2).

124.   Effect of declaration of local connection.   Where a person's declaration of local connection is in force[1] when he applies for registration[2], he must be regarded for the purposes[3] of ascertaining his entitlement to be registered as a parliamentary or local government elector[4] as resident on the date of the declaration at the address stated in it[5].

No declaration of local connection may be specially made by a person for the purposes of local government elections[6], and any such declaration made for the purposes of parliamentary elections[7] is to have effect also for the purposes of local government elections[8]. However, a declaration of local connection may be made for the purposes only of local government elections by a person who is as a peer subject to a legal incapacity to vote at parliamentary elections[9] or by a relevant citizen of the Union[10] and, where so made, must be marked to show that it is available for local government elections only (but must in all other respects be the same as other declarations of local connection)[11].

1   As to the formalities associated with making a declaration of local connection see PARA 122; and as to the removal from the register of entries made in pursuance of such a declaration see PARA 169. As to the registration officer's duty to send reminders to electors registered pursuant to a declaration see PARA 141.
2   As to applications for registration see PARA 157 et seq.
3   Ie for the purposes of the Representation of the People Act 1983 s 4 (see PARA 113): see the Representation of the People Act 1983 s 7C(1) (ss 7B, 7C added by the Representation of the People Act 2000 s 6).

     For the purposes of extending the rights of relevant citizens of the Union who (subject to the requirement of registration) may vote at European parliamentary elections, and of citizens and nationals of accession states who (subject to the requirement of registration) may vote at local government and European parliamentary elections, s 7B and s 7C are applied with modifications: see the European Parliamentary Elections (Franchise of Relevant Citizens of the Union) Regulations 2001, SI 2001/1184, reg 9, Schedule (cited in PARA 102 note 6); and the Local and European Parliamentary Elections (Registration of Citizens of Accession States) Regulations 2003, SI 2003/1557, reg 2(1), (3)(b), (c). As to the meaning of 'relevant citizen of the Union' for these purposes see PARA 102 note 5.
4   See the Representation of the People Act 1983 s 7C(1) (as added: see note 3). See note 3. As to the meaning of 'elector' see PARA 95 note 2.
5   Representation of the People Act 1983 s 7C(1)(a) (as added: see note 3). The text refers to the address stated in accordance with the Representation of the People Act 1983 s 7B(3)(d) (see

PARA 122): see s 7C(1)(a) (as so added). The provisions of s 7C must not be taken as precluding the registration of a person falling within s 7B(2)(a), (b) (see PARA 121) in pursuance of an application made by virtue of s 7(2) (deemed residence for persons in mental hospitals who are not detained offenders or on remand: see PARA 119) or s 7A(2) (deemed residence of persons remanded in custody: see PARA 120): s 7C(4) (as so added). See note 3.

6 As to the meaning of 'local government election' see PARA 11.
7 As to parliamentary elections see PARA 189 et seq.
8 Representation of the People Act 1983 s 7B(7) (as added: see note 3). See note 3.
9 See PARA 95 note 8.
10 Representation of the People Act 1983 s 7B(7)(a) (as added: see note 3). See note 3. As to the meaning of 'relevant citizen of the Union' for these purposes see PARA 97 note 13.
11 Representation of the People Act 1983 s 7B(7)(b) (as added: see note 3). See note 3.

C. SERVICE QUALIFICATION AND SERVICE DECLARATIONS

125. Service qualification. For the purposes of the Representation of the People Act 1983, a person has a service qualification who[1]:

(1) is a member of the forces[2];

(2) (not being such a member) is employed in the service of the Crown in a post outside the United Kingdom of any prescribed class or description[3];

(3) is employed by the British Council[4] in a post outside the United Kingdom[5];

(4) is the spouse or civil partner of a member of the forces[6];

(5) is the spouse or civil partner of a person mentioned in head (2) or head (3) above and is residing outside the United Kingdom to be with his or her spouse or civil partner[7].

Where a person leaves the United Kingdom to take up employment or residence as mentioned in heads (1) to (5) above, or returns to the United Kingdom at the end of such employment or residence, the employment or residence is deemed to begin from the time of leaving or to continue until the time of returning, as the case may be[8].

Statutory guidance must be made available to persons having a service qualification by virtue of heads (1) to (3) above[9].

1 See the Representation of the People Act 1983 s 14(1). As to the meaning of 'person' see PARA 95 note 1.
2 Representation of the People Act 1983 s 14(1)(a). For the purposes of Pt I (ss 1–66B), 'member of the forces' means a person serving on full pay as a member of any of the naval, military or air forces of the Crown raised in the United Kingdom: s 59(1)(a). However, that expression does not include either a person serving only as a member of a reserve or auxiliary force (except in so far as regulations provide that it includes persons so serving during a period of emergency) or a member of the regular army whose terms of service are such that, except for the purpose of training, he is required to serve only in Northern Ireland: see s 59(1)(b) (amended by the Representation of the People Act 1993 s 1). As to the meaning of 'United Kingdom' see PARA 1 note 1. As to the making of regulations under the Representation of the People Act 1983 generally see PARA 28 note 16. At the date at which this volume states the law, no regulations had been made under s 59. As to the position of members of the reserve and auxiliary forces in relation to residence for registration purposes see PARA 117 note 22.
3 Representation of the People Act 1983 s 14(1)(b). 'Prescribed' means prescribed by regulations: see s 202(1). A person falls within the class or description referred to in s 14(1)(b) if he is required to devote his whole working time to the duties of that post and the remuneration of it is paid wholly out of money provided by Parliament: Representation of the People (England and Wales) Regulations 2001, SI 2001/341, reg 14. If a declarant does not fall within reg 14, his declaration should be returned: see PARA 129.
4 As to the British Council see NATIONAL CULTURAL HERITAGE vol 77 (2010) PARA 966.
5 Representation of the People Act 1983 s 14(1)(c).
6 Representation of the People Act 1983 s 14(1)(d) (amended by the Civil Partnership Act 2004 s 261(1), Sch 27 para 80(1), (2)).

7   Representation of the People Act 1983 s 14(1)(e) (substituted by the Civil Partnership Act 2004 Sch 27 para 80(1), (3)).
8   See the Representation of the People Act 1983 s 14(1).
9   See PARA 131.

126. Service declaration. A service declaration may be made only by a person who has a service qualification[1], or by a person about to leave the United Kingdom[2] in such circumstances as to acquire a service qualification[3]. A service declaration may be made by such a person notwithstanding the fact that by reason of his age he is not yet entitled to vote[4].

A service declaration may at any time be cancelled by the declarant[5].

1   Representation of the People Act 1983 s 15(1)(a). As to the persons who have a service qualification see PARA 125. If a service declaration fails to comply with the requirements of s 15, it should be returned to the declarant: see PARA 129.
2   As to the meaning of 'United Kingdom' see PARA 1 note 1.
3   Representation of the People Act 1983 s 15(1)(b). Conditions may be prescribed in respect of a person about to leave the United Kingdom in such circumstances as to acquire a service qualification: see s 15(1)(b). 'Prescribed' means prescribed by regulations: see s 202(1). As to the making of regulations under the Representation of the People Act 1983 generally see PARA 28 note 16. At the date at which this volume states the law, no regulations had been made under s 15(1)(b).
4   Representation of the People Act 1983 s 15(1). As to entitlement to vote see PARA 95 et seq.
     For the purposes of the Representation of the People Act 1983, 'service voter' means a person who has made a service declaration and is registered or entitled to be registered in pursuance of it: see s 202(1). Similarly, for the purposes of the European Parliamentary Elections Regulations 2004, SI 2004/293, and the National Assembly for Wales (Representation of the People) Order 2007, SI 2007/236, 'service voter' means a person who has made such a service declaration and is registered or entitled to be registered in pursuance of it: European Parliamentary Elections Regulations 2004, SI 2004/293, reg 2(1) (substituted by SI 2009/186); National Assembly for Wales (Representation of the People) Order 2007, SI 2007/236, art 2(1).
5   Representation of the People Act 1983 s 15(7) (amended by the Representation of the People Act 2000 ss 8, 15(2), Sch 1 paras 1, 8(1), (3), Sch 7 Pt I). A cancellation as mentioned in the text terminates the entitlement to vote in pursuance of a service declaration: see PARA 170.

127. Formalities associated with service declarations. A service declaration[1] must state:

(1)   the date of the declaration[2];
(2)   that on that date the declarant is (or, but for the circumstances entitling him to make the declaration, would have been) residing in the United Kingdom[3];
(3)   the address where the declarant is (or, as the case may be, would have been) residing in the United Kingdom or, if he cannot give any such address, an address at which he has resided in the United Kingdom[4];
(4)   that on the date of the declaration the declarant is a Commonwealth citizen[5] or a citizen of the Republic of Ireland[6] or a relevant citizen of the Union[7];
(5)   whether the declarant had on the date of the declaration attained the age of 18 years, and, if he had not, the date of his birth[8];
(6)   such particulars, if any, of the declarant's identity and service qualification as may be prescribed[9].

Except where the declarant is a member of the forces or the spouse or civil partner of such a member, a service declaration must be attested in the manner prescribed[10].

1   As to service declarations see PARA 126.
2   Representation of the People Act 1983 s 16(a).

3   Representation of the People Act 1983 s 16(b) (s 16(b), (d) amended by the Representation of the People Act 2000 ss 8, 15(2), Sch 1 paras 1, 9, Sch 7 Pt I). As to the meaning of 'United Kingdom' see PARA 1 note 1.

4   Representation of the People Act 1983 s 16(d) (as amended: see note 3). Examples might assist to explain the variety of possible circumstances envisaged by this provision: a declarant who is, for example, a member of the forces might be serving in the United Kingdom at the time of making the declaration and therefore residing at an address here; or although at that time he is serving abroad, he can give an address at which he will reside on his return to the United Kingdom (notwithstanding that he has possibly not resided there in the past); or he might be able to give an address at which he would have been residing but for his service elsewhere; finally if he has permanently left his previous home in the United Kingdom because of his service with the forces, he must give an address at which he has resided here.

     Irregularities in stating the required address (ie declaring to more than one address or making more than one service declaration bearing the same date and declaring to different addresses) render the declaration or declarations void: see PARA 129.

5   As to who are Commonwealth citizens see BRITISH NATIONALITY vol 4 (2011) PARA 409.

6   As to who are citizens of the Republic of Ireland see BRITISH NATIONALITY vol 4 (2011) PARA 410.

7   Representation of the People Act 1983 s 16(e) (amended by SI 1995/1948). As to the meaning of 'relevant citizen of the Union' for these purposes see PARA 97 note 13.

     For the purposes of extending the rights of citizens and nationals of accession states who (subject to the requirement of registration) may vote at local government and European parliamentary elections, the Representation of the People Act 1983 s 16(e) is applied with modifications: see the Local and European Parliamentary Elections (Registration of Citizens of Accession States) Regulations 2003, SI 2003/1557, reg 2(1), (3)(e).

8   Representation of the People Act 1983 s 16(f).

9   Representation of the People Act 1983 s 16(g). 'Prescribed' means prescribed by regulations: see s 202(1). Accordingly, in addition to the matters specified in s 16(a)–(f) (see heads (1)–(5) in the text), a service declaration must state (see the Representation of the People (England and Wales) Regulations 2001, SI 2001/341, reg 15(1)):

     (1)   the declarant's full name and present address (reg 15(1)(a)), the grounds on which the declarant claims a service declaration (reg 15(1)(b)), and such of the particulars specified in heads (2), (3) or (4) below as are relevant to the service qualification claimed by the declarant (reg 15(1)(c));

     (2)   where the declarant claims a service qualification on the grounds that he is a member of the forces (within the meaning of the Representation of the People Act 1983 s 59(1): see PARA 125 note 2) or the spouse or civil partner of such a member, the service declaration must state the service (whether naval, military or air forces) in which that member serves, the rank or rating of that member, and the service number of that member, and where that member serves in the military forces, the service declaration must in addition state the regiment or corps in which he serves (see the Representation of the People (England and Wales) Regulations 2001, SI 2001/341, reg 15(2) (reg 15(2)–(4) amended by SI 2005/2114));

     (3)   where the declarant claims a service qualification on the grounds that he is a Crown servant to whom the Representation of the People (England and Wales) Regulations 2001, SI 2001/341, reg 14 applies (see PARA 125 note 3) or the spouse or civil partner of such a servant, the service declaration must state the name of the government department in which that servant works and a description of the post of that servant (see reg 15(3) (as so amended));

     (4)   where the declarant claims a service qualification on the grounds that he is a British Council employee or the spouse or civil partner of such an employee, the service declaration must state a description of the post of that employee (see reg 15(4) (as so amended)).

     For these purposes, 'British Council employee' means a person employed by the British Council in a post outside the United Kingdom; and 'Crown servant' means a person who is employed in a post falling within the class or description set out in reg 14 (see PARA 125 note 3): see reg 3(1). As to the British Council see NATIONAL CULTURAL HERITAGE vol 77 (2010) PARA 966.

     If a declaration fails to contain the required particulars, it should be returned to the declarant: see PARA 129.

10   Representation of the People Act 1983 s 16 (amended by the Civil Partnership Act 2004 s 261(1), Sch 27 para 81). At the date at which this volume states the law, no regulations had been made regarding the manner in which a service declaration must be attested.

128. Transmission of service declaration. A service declaration[1] made by a member of the forces or his spouse or civil partner must be transmitted to the appropriate registration officer[2].

A service declaration made by a person who is or will be a Crown servant[3] or by his spouse or civil partner must be transmitted by the declarant to the government department under which that person or his spouse is or will be employed or to an officer designated by that department, and transmitted by that department or officer to the appropriate registration officer[4].

A service declaration made by a person who is or will be a British Council employee[5] or by his spouse or civil partner must be transmitted by the declarant to the British Council and transmitted by the British Council to the appropriate registration officer[6].

Where the registration officer is satisfied that the declaration is duly made, he is required so to notify the declarant[7].

1 As to the making of service declarations see PARAS 126–127.
2 Representation of the People (England and Wales) Regulations 2001, SI 2001/341, reg 16(1) (reg 16(1)–(3) amended by SI 2005/2114). For these purposes, 'appropriate registration officer' means the registration officer for the area within which is situated the address specified in the declaration in accordance with the Representation of the People Act 1983 s 16(d) (see PARA 127): Representation of the People (England and Wales) Regulations 2001, SI 2001/341, reg 16(4). As to the meaning of 'registration officer' see PARA 139 note 1. Where a declaration is transmitted too late for the declarant's name to be included in the electors' lists, it is treated as a claim to be registered: see PARA 157.
3 See PARA 125 note 3. As to the meaning of 'Crown servant' see PARA 127 note 9.
4 Representation of the People (England and Wales) Regulations 2001, SI 2001/341, reg 16(2) (as amended: see note 2). If the declaration is sent direct to the registration officer by the declarant, it should be returned to the declarant: see PARA 129.
5 As to the meaning of 'British Council employee' see PARA 127 note 9.
6 Representation of the People (England and Wales) Regulations 2001, SI 2001/341, reg 16(3) (as amended: see note 2). If the declaration is sent direct to the registration officer by the declarant, it should be returned to the declarant: see PARA 129.
7 Representation of the People (England and Wales) Regulations 2001, SI 2001/341, reg 17(1).

129. Invalid service declaration. A service declaration[1] is of no effect unless it is received by the registration officer[2] concerned within the period of three months beginning with the date of the declaration[3].

If a person makes a service declaration declaring to more than one address[4] or makes more than one service declaration bearing the same date and declaring to different addresses[5], the declaration or declarations are void[6].

Where the registration officer rejects an application for registration[7] in pursuance of a service declaration because it either does not contain the required particulars[8] or because it does not comply with the requirements as to the service qualification[9] or as to the making of service declarations[10] (or, where appropriate, the qualification for Crown servants[11]), or as to the transmission of such declarations[12], he must return the declaration to the declarant setting out his reasons for so doing[13].

1 As to the making and transmission of service declarations see PARAS 126–128.
2 As to the meaning of 'registration officer' see PARA 139 note 1.
3 Representation of the People Act 1983 s 15(8) (added by the Representation of the People Act 2000 s 8, Sch 1 paras 1, 8(1), (4)). As to stating the date of the declaration see PARA 127.
4 See the Representation of the People Act 1983 s 15(6)(a). The text refers to the address specified in the declaration in accordance with s 16(d) (see PARA 127).
5 See the Representation of the People Act 1983 s 15(6)(b). See note 4.
6 See the Representation of the People Act 1983 s 15(6). As to offences associated with declarations of local connection see PARA 735.

7   As to applications for registration see PARA 157 et seq.

8   Ie the particulars required in the Representation of the People Act 1983 s 16(a)–(f) (see PARA 127) and the Representation of the People (England and Wales) Regulations 2001, SI 2001/341, reg 15 (see PARA 127 note 9): see reg 17(2).

9   Ie the requirements of the Representation of the People Act 1983 s 14 (see PARA 125): see the Representation of the People (England and Wales) Regulations 2001, SI 2001/341, reg 17(2).

10 Ie the requirements of the Representation of the People Act 1983 s 15 (see PARA 126): see the Representation of the People (England and Wales) Regulations 2001, SI 2001/341, reg 17(2).

11 Ie the requirements of the Representation of the People (England and Wales) Regulations 2001, SI 2001/341, reg 14 (see PARA 125 note 3): see reg 17(2). As to the meaning of 'Crown servant' see PARA 127 note 9.

12 Ie the requirements of the Representation of the People (England and Wales) Regulations 2001, SI 2001/341, reg 16 (see PARA 128): see reg 17(2).

13 See the Representation of the People (England and Wales) Regulations 2001, SI 2001/341, reg 17(2).

130. Effect of service declaration. Where a person's service declaration[1] is in force when he applies for registration[2], he must be regarded for the purposes of ascertaining his entitlement to be registered as a parliamentary or local government elector[3] as resident on the date of the declaration at the address specified in it[4] and, until the contrary is proved, as being a Commonwealth citizen[5] or a citizen of the Republic of Ireland[6] or a relevant citizen of the Union[7] of the age appearing from the declaration[8] and as not being subject to any legal incapacity[9] except as so appearing[10]. Where a service declaration appearing to be properly made out[11] and (where required) attested is transmitted to the registration officer in the proper manner[12], then until the contrary is proved the declarant must be treated for the purposes of registration as having had from the date of the declaration, or such later date, if any, as appears from it[13], and as continuing to have, a service qualification[14].

A service declaration made for the purpose of parliamentary elections has effect also for the purpose of local government elections[15]. Accordingly, no service declaration may be specially made for the purpose of local government elections[16], except by a peer who is subject to a legal incapacity to vote at parliamentary elections or by a relevant citizen of the Union[17]; in such a case, the declaration must be marked to show that it is available for local government elections only but must in other respects be the same as other service declarations[18].

1   As to the making and transmission of service declarations see PARAS 126–128.

2   As to applications for registration see PARA 157 et seq.

3   Ie for the purposes of the Representation of the People Act 1983 s 4 (see PARA 113): see s 17(1) (substituted by the Representation of the People Act 2000 s 8, Sch 1 paras 1, 10). As to the meaning of 'elector' see PARA 95 note 2.

4   Representation of the People Act 1983 s 17(1)(a) (as substituted: see note 3). The text refers to the address specified in the declaration in accordance with s 16(d) (see PARA 127): see s 17(1)(a) (as so substituted).

    For the purposes of extending the rights of citizens and nationals of accession states who (subject to the requirement of registration) may vote at local government and European parliamentary elections, s 15(5) (see the text and notes 15–18) and s 17(1) are applied with modifications: see the Local and European Parliamentary Elections (Registration of Citizens of Accession States) Regulations 2003, SI 2003/1557, reg 2(1), (3)(d), (f).

5   As to who are Commonwealth citizens see BRITISH NATIONALITY vol 4 (2011) PARA 409.

6   As to who are citizens of the Republic of Ireland see BRITISH NATIONALITY vol 4 (2011) PARA 410.

7   As to the meaning of 'relevant citizen of the Union' for these purposes see PARA 97 note 13.

8   If the declarant has not attained the age of 18 years, he must state his date of birth: see PARA 127.

9   As to the meaning of 'legal incapacity' for these purposes see PARA 95 note 8.

10 Representation of the People Act 1983 s 17(1)(c) (as substituted: see note 3). See note 4.
11 As to invalid declarations see PARA 129.
12 As to the prescribed manner of transmission of a service declaration see PARA 128. At the date at which this volume states the law, no regulations had been made regarding the manner in which a service declaration must be attested: see PARA 127.
13 This applies where the declarant has not attained the age of 18 years when making the declaration: see PARA 127.
14 Representation of the People Act 1983 s 17(2).
15 See the Representation of the People Act 1983 s 15(5). See note 4. As to the meaning of 'local government election' see PARA 11.
16 See the Representation of the People Act 1983 s 15(5). See note 4.
17 See the Representation of the People Act 1983 s 15(5)(a) (amended by SI 1995/1948). See note 4.
18 Representation of the People Act 1983 s 15(5)(b). See note 4.

131. Guidance for service voters. Arrangements must be made by the appropriate government department[1] for securing that every person having a service qualification[2] either as a member of the forces[3] or on account of his or her employment in the service of the Crown in a post outside the United Kingdom[4] has (so far as circumstances permit) an effective opportunity of exercising from time to time as occasion may require the rights conferred on him or her by the Representation of the People Act 1983 in relation to[5]:

(1)   registration in a register of electors (and in particular in relation to the making and cancellation of service declarations)[6];
(2)   the making and cancellation of appointments of a proxy[7]; and
(3)   voting in person, by post or by proxy[8].

Arrangements must be made also by the appropriate government department for securing that every such person receives such instructions as to the effect of the Representation of the People Act 1983 and any regulations made under it, and such other assistance, as may be reasonably sufficient in connection with the exercise by that person and any spouse or civil partner of that person of any rights conferred on them as mentioned in heads (1) to (3) above[9]. The Ministry of Defence must maintain, in relation to each member of the forces who provides information relating to his registration as an elector, a record of such information[10]; and it must make arrangements to enable each member of the forces to update annually the information so recorded[11].

In relation to British Council employees[12] and their spouses and partners, the British Council has obligations with regard to the making of arrangements, corresponding to those imposed on the appropriate government department[13].

1 For the purposes of the Representation of the People Act 1983 s 59(3), (3A), 'appropriate government department' means, in relation to members of the forces, the Ministry of Defence and, in relation to any other person, means the government department under which he is employed in the employment giving the service qualification: see s 59(3B) (s 59(3) substituted, s 59(3A)–(3D) added, by the Electoral Administration Act 2006 s 13(2)). As to the meaning of 'member of the forces' see PARA 125 note 2. As to the Ministry of Defence see ARMED FORCES vol 3 (2011) PARA 302; and CONSTITUTIONAL LAW AND HUMAN RIGHTS vol 8(2) (Reissue) PARA 438 et seq.
2 As to the making and cancellation of service declarations see PARA 126.
3 Ie by virtue of the Representation of the People Act 1983 s 14(1)(a) (see PARA 125): see s 59(3) (as substituted: see note 1).
4 Ie by virtue of the Representation of the People Act 1983 s 14(1)(b) (see PARA 125): see s 59(3) (as substituted: see note 1). As to the meaning of 'United Kingdom' see PARA 1 note 1.
5 See the Representation of the People Act 1983 s 59(3) (as substituted: see note 1).
6 Representation of the People Act 1983 s 59(3)(a) (as substituted: see note 1). As to the meaning of 'elector' see PARA 95 note 2. As to registration as an elector see PARA 157 et seq.
7 Representation of the People Act 1983 s 59(3)(b) (as substituted: see note 1). As to the manner of voting see PARA 363 et seq; and as to the appointment of proxies see PARA 374 et seq.

For the purposes of the National Assembly for Wales Referendum (Assembly Act Provisions) (Referendum Question, Date of Referendum Etc) Order 2010, SI 2010/2837 (see STATUTES AND LEGISLATIVE PROCESS vol 96 (2012) PARA 602), the Representation of the People Act 1983 s 59(3)(b), (c) are to be construed as including a reference to the National Assembly for Wales Referendum (Assembly Act Provisions) (Referendum Question, Date of Referendum Etc) Order 2010, SI 2010/2837, in connection with the right so conferred on a person having a service qualification by virtue of the Representation of the People Act 1983 s 14(1)(a), (b) (see PARA 125) in relation to the making and cancellation of appointments of a proxy and in relation to voting in person, by post or by proxy; and the Representation of the People Act 1983 s 59(3A) is to be similarly construed: see the National Assembly for Wales Referendum (Assembly Act Provisions) (Referendum Question, Date of Referendum Etc) Order 2010, SI 2010/2837, art 7(1), Sch 1 Pt 3 para 25.

8 Representation of the People Act 1983 s 59(3)(c) (as substituted: see note 1). See note 7. As to applications to vote by post see PARA 367 et seq.

9 Representation of the People Act 1983 s 59(3A) (as added: see note 1). See note 7.

10 Representation of the People Act 1983 s 59(3C) (as added: see note 1).

11 Representation of the People Act 1983 s 59(3D) (as added: see note 1).

12 Ie persons having a service qualification by virtue of the Representation of the People Act 1983 s 14(1)(c) (see PARA 125): see s 59(4) (amended by the Electoral Administration Act 2006 s 13(3)). As to the meaning of 'British Council employee' see PARA 127 note 9.

13 Representation of the People Act 1983 s 59(4) (as amended: see note 12). The provision made by s 59(4) refers to an obligation corresponding to that imposed by s 59(3) and s 59(3A) (see the text and notes 1–9): see s 59(4) (as so amended).

D. OVERSEAS ELECTORS DECLARATIONS

132. Formalities associated with overseas elector's declarations. An overseas elector's declaration[1] must:

(1) state: (a) the date of the declaration[2]; (b) that the declarant is a British citizen[3]; (c) that the declarant will not be resident in the United Kingdom[4] on the relevant date[5]; and (d) when he ceased to be so resident or, in the case of a person relying on registration in pursuance of a service declaration[6], when he ceased to have a service qualification[7] or, if later, ceased to be so resident[8];

(2) show which of the two sets of statutory conditions for qualification as an overseas elector[9] the declarant claims to satisfy[10]; and (a) in the case of the first set of conditions, specify the address in respect of which he was registered[11]; and (b) in the case of the second set of conditions, specify: (i) the date of the declarant's birth[12]; (ii) the address in the United Kingdom at which he was resident[13]; and (iii) the name of the parent or guardian on whose registration in respect of that address he relies, and whether the person named was a parent or guardian[14].

The declaration must contain such other information and satisfy such other requirements as may be prescribed[15]. Accordingly, in addition to the information required by heads (1) and (2) above, an overseas elector's declaration must state the declarant's full name and present address[16] and certain other information[17] where appropriate[18].

An overseas elector's declaration may be cancelled at any time by the declarant[19].

1 As to the meaning of 'overseas elector's declaration' see PARA 114.

2 Representation of the People Act 1985 s 2(3)(a) (s 2 substituted by the Representation of the People Act 2000 s 8, Sch 2 paras 1, 3).

For the purposes of the registration of peers who (subject to the requirement of registration) may vote at European parliamentary elections, the Representation of the People Act 1985 s 2 is applied with modifications: see the Representation of the People (England and Wales) Regulations 2001, SI 2001/341, reg 13(4), Sch 4; and PARA 101 note 7.

3   Representation of the People Act 1985 s 2(3)(b) (as substituted: see note 2). See note 2. As to who are British citizens see BRITISH NATIONALITY vol 4 (2011) PARAS 406, 421 et seq.
4   As to the meaning of 'United Kingdom' see PARA 1 note 1.
5   Representation of the People Act 1985 s 2(3)(c) (as substituted: see note 2). See note 2. As to the relevant date for these purposes see PARAS 96 note 6, 114 note 10.
6   As to service declarations see PARA 125 et seq.
7   As to when a person ceases to have a service qualification see PARAS 126, 129.
8   Representation of the People Act 1985 s 2(3)(d) (as substituted: see note 2). See note 2. This date is relevant for the purposes of the registration officer determining whether the conditions as to qualification as an overseas elector are satisfied (see PARA 96).
9   Ie the conditions in the Representation of the People Act 1985 s 1(3), (4) (see PARA 96): see s 2(4)(a) (as substituted: see note 2).
10   Representation of the People Act 1985 s 2(4)(a) (as substituted: see note 2). See note 2.
11   Representation of the People Act 1985 s 2(4)(b) (as substituted: see note 2). It is with reference to this address that the declarant claims to be registered (see PARA 114). An overseas elector's declaration may not, in the case of either set of conditions, specify more than one such address: see s 2(4); and PARA 136. See note 2.
12   Representation of the People Act 1985 s 2(4)(c)(i) (as substituted: see note 2). See note 2.
13   Representation of the People Act 1985 s 2(4)(c)(ii) (as substituted: see note 2). See note 2. See also note 11.
14   Representation of the People Act 1985 s 2(4)(c)(iii) (as substituted: see note 2). See note 2. The text refers to the name of the parent or guardian upon whose registration a declarant must rely where he cannot rely upon his own previous inclusion in a register of parliamentary electors on account of his age and where the conditions specified in s 1(4) (the 'second set of conditions': see PARA 96) apply.
15   See the Representation of the People Act 1985 s 2(3) (as substituted: see note 2). The requirements prescribed as mentioned in the text may include requirements for declarations to be attested and for the charging of fees in respect of their attestation: see s 2(3) (as so substituted). The Representation of the People Act 1985 ss 1–12 have effect as if contained in the Representation of the People Act 1983 Pt I (ss 1–66B): see the Representation of the People Act 1985 s 27(2). Accordingly, 'prescribed' means prescribed by regulations: see the Representation of the People Act 1983 s 202(1); applied by virtue of the Representation of the People Act 1985 s 27(2). As to the making of regulations under the Representation of the People Act 1985 generally see PARA 28 note 16; and as to the regulations made for the purposes of s 2(3) see the Representation of the People (England and Wales) Regulations 2001, SI 2001/341; the text and notes 16–18; and PARA 133. See note 2. As to the attestation of overseas elector's declarations see further PARA 134.
16   See the Representation of the People (England and Wales) Regulations 2001, SI 2001/341, reg 18(1).
17   Ie any extra information required by the Representation of the People (England and Wales) Regulations 2001, SI 2001/341, reg 18(2)–(7) (see PARA 133): see reg 18(1).
18   See the Representation of the People (England and Wales) Regulations 2001, SI 2001/341, reg 18(1). By virtue of reg 13(6), (7), reg 18 applies to registration in pursuance of a European parliamentary overseas elector's declaration as it applies to registration in pursuance of an overseas elector's declaration: see PARA 101 note 7.
19   Representation of the People Act 1985 s 2(5) (as substituted: see note 2). See note 2. A cancellation as mentioned in the text terminates the entitlement to vote in pursuance of an overseas elector's declaration: see PARA 170.

133.   Additional information required to be stated in overseas elector's declaration in appropriate circumstances.   An overseas elector's declaration must contain, as a minimum, certain specified information[1] and it must satisfy such other requirements as may be prescribed, including, where appropriate, the following additional information[2].

If the declarant was last registered in pursuance of a service or other declaration[3] (rather than actual residence at an address specified in an overseas elector's declaration)[4] and if he no longer had connection with that address at the time at which he was so registered[5], the declaration must include a statement that the declarant was so registered[6]; and if the declarant claims that his name has changed since he was last registered in respect of the address specified in an overseas elector's declaration[7], that declaration must set out the name in respect of which the declarant was last previously registered[8], and give the reason for the change of name[9].

If a declarant has on a previous occasion been registered in a register of parliamentary electors[10] in pursuance of an overseas elector's declaration[11], and has not, since being so registered, been registered in such a register[12] by virtue of being resident or treated for the purposes of registration as resident at an address in the United Kingdom[13], his overseas elector's declaration must state those facts and indicate when he was last registered in pursuance of an overseas elector's declaration[14]; and if a declarant has not made an overseas elector's declaration in pursuance of which he was registered in a register of parliamentary electors since being included in such a register[15] by virtue of being resident or treated for the purposes of registration as resident at an address in the United Kingdom, or has never made such a declaration, his overseas elector's declaration must state[16]:

(1)   in the case of a declarant who is the bearer of a British passport which describes his national status as 'British citizen', the number of that passport together with its date and place of issue[17]; or

(2)   in the case of a declarant who is not the bearer of such a passport, but who was born in the United Kingdom before 1 January 1983, those facts[18]; or

(3)   in the case of a declarant to whom neither head (1) nor head (2) above applies, when and how he acquired the status of British citizen, together with the date, place and country of his birth[19].

In the case of a declarant who is required to transmit a copy of his birth certificate together with his declaration[20], if his name on his birth certificate is not the same as his name as given in his overseas elector's declaration, that declaration must state the reason for the change of name[21]; and if such a declarant relies on the registration of either: (a) a parent whose name in the register of parliamentary or local government electors in force on the relevant date[22] is not the same as the name of that parent as given in either the declarant's birth certificate or overseas elector's declaration[23]; or (b) a guardian whose name in the relevant register[24] is not the same as the name of that guardian as given in the declarant's overseas elector's declaration[25], that declaration must state the name of the parent or, as the case may be, guardian as given in the relevant register[26] and, where known, the reason for the change or, as the case may be, changes of name or, where such reason (or reasons) is not known, a statement to that effect[27].

1   Ie the information required by the Representation of the People Act 1985 s 2(3): see PARA 132. As to the meaning of 'overseas elector's declaration' see PARA 114.

2   See the Representation of the People (England and Wales) Regulations 2001, SI 2001/341, reg 18(1); and PARA 132. The text refers to the information that is prescribed as being required by reg 18(2)–(7) (see the text and notes 3–27): see reg 18(1); and PARA 132. By virtue of reg 13(6), (7), reg 18 applies to registration in pursuance of a European parliamentary overseas elector's declaration as it applies to registration in pursuance of an overseas elector's declaration: see PARA 101 note 7.

3   As to registration in pursuance of a declaration of local connection see PARA 121 et seq; and as to registration in pursuance of a service declaration see PARA 125 et seq.

4   Representation of the People (England and Wales) Regulations 2001, SI 2001/341, reg 18(2)(a). The text refers to an address specified in pursuance of the Representation of the People Act 1985 s 2(4)(b) (see PARA 132): see the Representation of the People (England and Wales) Regulations 2001, SI 2001/341, reg 18(2)(a). See note 2. In the case of a person registered in pursuance of a service or other declaration, the address might not have been included in the register of electors and the elector's name included under the heading 'Other electors' at the end of the relevant section of the register: see PARA 145.

5 Representation of the People (England and Wales) Regulations 2001, SI 2001/341, reg 18(2)(b). See note 2.
6 See the Representation of the People (England and Wales) Regulations 2001, SI 2001/341, reg 18(2). See note 2.
7 Ie the address specified in the overseas elector's declaration in accordance with the Representation of the People Act 1985 s 2(4)(b) (see PARA 132): see the Representation of the People (England and Wales) Regulations 2001, SI 2001/341, reg 18(3). See note 4.
8 Representation of the People (England and Wales) Regulations 2001, SI 2001/341, reg 18(3)(a). See note 2.
9 Representation of the People (England and Wales) Regulations 2001, SI 2001/341, reg 18(3)(b). See note 2.
10 As to the entitlement to be registered as a parliamentary elector see PARA 113.
11 Representation of the People (England and Wales) Regulations 2001, SI 2001/341, reg 18(4)(a). See note 2.
12 For the purposes of its application in relation to a European parliamentary overseas elector's declaration (ie by virtue of the Representation of the People (England and Wales) Regulations 2001, SI 2001/341, reg 13(6): see note 2), reg 18(4) has effect as if, in addition to the modifications made by reg 13(6), the words 'a register of local government electors' were substituted for the words 'such a register': see reg 18(4). A peer's entitlement is based on his registration as a local government elector, previously having been denied registration as a parliamentary elector (see PARA 101).
13 Representation of the People (England and Wales) Regulations 2001, SI 2001/341, reg 18(4)(b). See note 2. As to the meaning of 'United Kingdom' see PARA 1 note 1.
14 lSee the Representation of the People (England and Wales) Regulations 2001, SI 2001/341, reg 18(4). See note 2.
15 For the purposes of its application in relation to a European parliamentary overseas elector's declaration (ie by virtue of the Representation of the People (England and Wales) Regulations 2001, SI 2001/341, reg 13(6): see note 2), reg 18(5) has effect as if, in addition to the modifications made by reg 13(6), the words 'a register of local government electors' were substituted for the words 'such a register': see reg 18(5). See note 2.
16 See the Representation of the People (England and Wales) Regulations 2001, SI 2001/341, reg 18(5). See note 2.
17 Representation of the People (England and Wales) Regulations 2001, SI 2001/341, reg 18(5)(a). See note 2. As to who are British citizens see BRITISH NATIONALITY vol 4 (2011) PARAS 406, 421 et seq.
18 Representation of the People (England and Wales) Regulations 2001, SI 2001/341, reg 18(5)(b). See note 2.
19 Representation of the People (England and Wales) Regulations 2001, SI 2001/341, reg 18(5)(c). See note 2.
20 Ie in the case of a declarant to whom the Representation of the People (England and Wales) Regulations 2001, SI 2001/341, reg 19 applies (and who is accordingly required to transmit a copy of his birth certificate together with his declaration) (see PARA 135): see reg 18(6).
21 See the Representation of the People (England and Wales) Regulations 2001, SI 2001/341, reg 18(6). See note 2.
22 Ie the register (and the relevant date) referred to in the Representation of the People Act 1985 s 1(4)(c) (see PARA 96): see the Representation of the People (England and Wales) Regulations 2001, SI 2001/341, reg 18(7)(a). For the purposes of its application in relation to a European parliamentary overseas elector's declaration (ie by virtue of the Representation of the People (England and Wales) Regulations 2001, SI 2001/341, reg 13(6): see note 2), reg 18(7) has effect as if, in addition to the modifications made by reg 13(6), a reference to the Representation of the People Act 1985 s 3(4)(c) (see PARA 101) were substituted for the references to s 1(4)(c), in each place where those references occur: see the Representation of the People (England and Wales) Regulations 2001, SI 2001/341, reg 18(7). See note 2.
23 Representation of the People (England and Wales) Regulations 2001, SI 2001/341, reg 18(7)(a). The text refers to the name of the parent upon whose registration a declarant must rely in accordance with the Representation of the People Act 1985 s 2(4)(c)(iii) (see PARA 132): see the Representation of the People (England and Wales) Regulations 2001, SI 2001/341, reg 18(7)(a). See note 2.
24 Ie the register (and the relevant date) referred to in the Representation of the People Act 1985 s 1(4)(c) (see PARA 96): see the Representation of the People (England and Wales) Regulations 2001, SI 2001/341, reg 18(7)(b).
25 Representation of the People (England and Wales) Regulations 2001, SI 2001/341, reg 18(7)(b). The text refers to the name of the guardian upon whose registration a declarant must rely in

accordance with the Representation of the People Act 1985 s 2(4)(c)(iii) (see PARA 132): see the Representation of the People (England and Wales) Regulations 2001, SI 2001/341, reg 18(7)(b). See note 2.

26 Ie the register referred to in the Representation of the People Act 1985 s 1(4)(c) (see PARA 96): see the Representation of the People (England and Wales) Regulations 2001, SI 2001/341, reg 18(7).

27 See the Representation of the People (England and Wales) Regulations 2001, SI 2001/341, reg 18(7). See note 2.

134. Attestation of certain overseas electors' declarations. An overseas elector's declaration[1] must be attested by the bearer of a British passport which described his national status as a 'British citizen'[2] who:

(1)   is not resident in the United Kingdom[3];

(2)   is aged 18 years or over[4]; and

(3)   is not the spouse, civil partner, parent, grandparent, brother, sister, child or grandchild of the declarant[5].

A person must not attest an overseas elector's declaration unless he is satisfied, to the best of his knowledge and belief, that the declarant is a British citizen who is not resident in the United Kingdom on the date of the declaration[6].

A person attesting an overseas elector's declaration must record on it:

(a)   his full name and address[7];

(b)   that he is the bearer of a British passport which describes his national status as 'British citizen' and the number of that passport together with its date and place of issue[8];

(c)   that he is aged 18 years or over[9];

(d)   that he is not resident in the United Kingdom on the date of the declaration[10];

(e)   that he is not the spouse, civil partner, parent, grandparent, brother, sister, child or grandchild of the declarant[11]; and

(f)   that, to the best of his knowledge and belief, the declarant is a British citizen who is not resident in the United Kingdom on the date of the declaration[12].

A person attesting an overseas elector's declaration must sign the declaration[13].

However, an overseas elector's declaration need not be attested in accordance with these provisions[14] where the declarant has on a previous occasion made such a declaration in pursuance of which he was registered in a register of parliamentary electors and, since being so registered, he has not been included in any register of parliamentary electors by virtue of being resident (or treated for the purposes of registration as resident) at an address in the United Kingdom[15].

1   As to overseas elector's declarations see PARA 114.

2   As to who are British citizens see BRITISH NATIONALITY vol 4 (2011) PARAS 406, 421 et seq.

3   Representation of the People (England and Wales) Regulations 2001, SI 2001/341, reg 20(2)(a). As to the meaning of 'United Kingdom' see PARA 1 note 1. As to the circumstances when a person is treated for the purposes of registration as resident see PARA 117 et seq. By virtue of reg 13(6), (7), reg 20 applies to registration in pursuance of a European parliamentary overseas elector's declaration as it applies to registration in pursuance of an overseas elector's declaration: see PARA 101 note 7.

4   Representation of the People (England and Wales) Regulations 2001, SI 2001/341, reg 20(2)(b). See note 3.

5   Representation of the People (England and Wales) Regulations 2001, SI 2001/341, reg 20(2)(c) (amended by SI 2005/2114). See note 3.

6   Representation of the People (England and Wales) Regulations 2001, SI 2001/341, reg 20(3). See note 3.

7   Representation of the People (England and Wales) Regulations 2001, SI 2001/341, reg 20(4)(a). See note 3.

8   Representation of the People (England and Wales) Regulations 2001, SI 2001/341, reg 20(4)(b). See note 3.
9   Representation of the People (England and Wales) Regulations 2001, SI 2001/341, reg 20(4)(c) See note 3.
10   Representation of the People (England and Wales) Regulations 2001, SI 2001/341, reg 20(4)(d). See note 3.
11   Representation of the People (England and Wales) Regulations 2001, SI 2001/341, reg 20(4)(e) (amended by SI 2005/2114). See note 3.
12   Representation of the People (England and Wales) Regulations 2001, SI 2001/341, reg 20(4)(f). See note 3.
13   See the Representation of the People (England and Wales) Regulations 2001, SI 2001/341, reg 20(4). See note 3.
14   Ie in accordance with the Representation of the People (England and Wales) Regulations 2001, SI 2001/341, reg 20(2)–(4) (see the text and notes 1–13): see reg 20(1).
15   Representation of the People (England and Wales) Regulations 2001, SI 2001/341, reg 20(1). As to registration as an elector see PARA 157 et seq. For the purposes of its application in relation to a European parliamentary overseas elector's declaration (ie by virtue of the Representation of the People (England and Wales) Regulations 2001, SI 2001/341, reg 13(6): see note 3), reg 20(1) has effect as if, in addition to the modifications made by reg 13(6), the words 'local government' were substituted for the word 'parliamentary' in the second place where it occurs: see reg 20(1). A peer's entitlement to vote as an overseas European parliamentary elector is based on his registration as a local government elector, previously having been denied registration as a parliamentary elector: see PARA 101.

135. Transmission of overseas elector's declaration. An overseas elector's declaration[1] must be transmitted to the registration officer[2] for that part of the constituency within which is situated the address specified in the declaration as the address in respect of which the declarant was registered[3]. Where a person: (1) has made an overseas elector's declaration in which he claims to be qualified as an overseas elector by virtue of the conditions set out in relation to persons not previously registered in a register of parliamentary electors on account of age only[4]; and (2) has not on a previous occasion made an overseas elector's declaration in pursuance of which he was registered in a register of parliamentary electors[5], a declarant must transmit together with his overseas elector's declaration a copy of his birth certificate which shows the names of either or both of his parents as well as his date of birth[6].

Where the registration officer is satisfied that the declarant qualifies as an overseas elector[7], he must so notify the applicant[8].

1   As to overseas elector's declarations see PARA 114.
2   As to the meaning of 'registration officer' see PARA 139 note 1.
3   Representation of the People (England and Wales) Regulations 2001, SI 2001/341, reg 21. The text refers to the address specified in the declaration in accordance with the Representation of the People Act 1985 s 2(4) (see PARA 132): see the Representation of the People (England and Wales) Regulations 2001, SI 2001/341, reg 21. Under the Representation of the People Act 1985 s 2(4), the declarant is required to include in an overseas elector's declaration the address either in respect of where the declarant had been registered previously (s 2(4)(b)) or in respect of which he was resident, if not registered previously (s 2(4)(c)): see PARA 132. Where a declaration is transmitted too late for the declarant's name to be included in the electors' lists, it is treated as a claim to be registered: see PARA 157.
     By virtue of the Representation of the People (England and Wales) Regulations 2001, SI 2001/341, reg 13(6), (7), reg 19 (see the text and notes 4–6) and reg 21 apply to registration in pursuance of a European parliamentary overseas elector's declaration as they apply to registration in pursuance of an overseas elector's declaration: see PARA 101 note 7.
4   See the Representation of the People (England and Wales) Regulations 2001, SI 2001/341, reg 19(1). The text refers to qualification as an overseas elector by a declarant who cannot rely upon his own previous inclusion in a register of parliamentary electors on account of his age and who satisfies the other conditions specified in the Representation of the People Act 1985 s 1(4) (the 'second set of conditions': see PARA 96): see the Representation of the People (England and Wales) Regulations 2001, SI 2001/341, reg 19(1). For the purpose of the application of the

Representation of the People (England and Wales) Regulations 2001, SI 2001/341, reg 19 by reg 13(6) (see note 3), reg 19(1) has effect as if, in addition to the modifications made by reg 13(6), a reference to the Representation of the People Act 1985 s 3(4) (see PARA 101) were substituted for the reference to s 1(4): see the Representation of the People (England and Wales) Regulations 2001, SI 2001/341, reg 19(1). As to registration as an elector see PARA 157 et seq.

5 See the Representation of the People (England and Wales) Regulations 2001, SI 2001/341, reg 19(1). See note 3.

6 Representation of the People (England and Wales) Regulations 2001, SI 2001/341, reg 19(2). See note 3.

7 Ie under the provisions of the Representation of the People Act 1985 s 1 (extension of parliamentary franchise to British citizens overseas: see PARA 96) and s 2 (registration of British citizens overseas: see PARA 114 et seq): see the Representation of the People (England and Wales) Regulations 2001, SI 2001/341, reg 22(1).

For the purposes of its application in relation to a European parliamentary overseas elector's declaration (ie by virtue of the Representation of the People (England and Wales) Regulations 2001, SI 2001/341, reg 13(6): see note 3), reg 22(1) has effect as if, in addition to the modifications made by reg 13(6), references in reg 22(1) to the Representation of the People Act 1985 s 2 and s 3 (extension of European parliamentary franchise to peers resident outside the United Kingdom: see PARA 101) were substituted for the references to s 1 and s 2: see the Representation of the People (England and Wales) Regulations 2001, SI 2001/341, reg 22(3).

8 Representation of the People (England and Wales) Regulations 2001, SI 2001/341, reg 22(1). See note 3.

136. Invalid declarations. An overseas elector's declaration[1] is of no effect unless it is received by the registration officer[2] concerned within the period of three months beginning with the relevant date[3].

An overseas elector's declaration may not specify more than one address as the address in respect of which the declarant is registered[4]; and if the declarant makes more than one such declaration bearing the same date and specifying different addresses in the United Kingdom[5] as the address in respect of which he was registered the declarations are void[6].

Where the registration officer[7] rejects an application for registration in pursuance of an overseas elector's declaration because:

(1) in his opinion the declarant does not qualify as an overseas elector in respect of a parliamentary constituency[8]; or

(2) the declaration does not satisfy the requirements in relation to registration as such an elector[9], or in relation to the contents of the declaration[10] or in relation to its attestation[11]; or

(3) in the case of a declarant who is required to transmit a copy of his birth certificate together with his declaration[12], that requirement has not been complied with[13],

he must return the declaration to the declarant and set out his reasons for rejecting the application for registration[14].

1 As to the meaning of 'overseas elector's declaration' see PARA 114.
2 As to the meaning of 'registration officer' see PARA 139.
3 Representation of the People Act 1985 s 2(6) (s 2 substituted by the Representation of the People Act 2000 s 8, Sch 2 paras 1, 3). The reference in the text to the 'relevant date' is to the date on which a person makes a declaration under and in accordance with the Representation of the People Act 1985 s 2 (an 'overseas elector's declaration'): see PARA 114.

For the purposes of the registration of peers who (subject to the requirement of registration) may vote at European parliamentary elections, s 2 is applied with modifications: see the Representation of the People (England and Wales) Regulations 2001, SI 2001/341, reg 13(4), Sch 4; and PARA 101 note 7.
4 See the Representation of the People Act 1985 s 2(4) (as substituted: see note 3). See note 3. The text refers to the address which a declarant is required to include in an overseas elector's declaration either in respect of where the declarant had been registered previously, where the

'first' set of conditions applies (s 2(4)(b) (as so substituted)), or in respect of which he was resident, if not registered previously, where the 'second' set of conditions applies (s 2(4)(c) (as so substituted)): see PARA 132.

5   As to the meaning of 'United Kingdom' see PARA 1 note 1.

6   See the Representation of the People Act 1985 s 2(4) (as substituted: see note 3).

7   As to the meaning of 'registration officer' for these purposes see PARA 139 note 1.

8   Representation of the People (England and Wales) Regulations 2001, SI 2001/341, reg 22(2)(a). The text refers to qualification as an overseas elector in respect of a parliamentary constituency under the Representation of the People Act 1985 s 1 (extension of parliamentary franchise to British citizens overseas: see PARA 96): see the Representation of the People (England and Wales) Regulations 2001, SI 2001/341, reg 22(2)(a). By virtue of reg 13(6), (7), reg 22 applies to registration in pursuance of a European parliamentary overseas elector's declaration as it applies to registration in pursuance of an overseas elector's declaration: see PARA 101 note 7. For the purpose of the application of reg 22 by reg 13(6), reg 22(2) has effect as if, in addition to the modifications made by reg 13(6), the reference in reg 22(2) to the Representation of the People Act 1985 s 1 was substituted by a reference to s 3 (extension of European parliamentary franchise to peers resident outside the United Kingdom: see PARA 101): see the Representation of the People (England and Wales) Regulations 2001, SI 2001/341, reg 22(3).

9   Ie the requirements of the Representation of the People Act 1985 s 2 (see PARAS 114 et seq, 137): see the Representation of the People (England and Wales) Regulations 2001, SI 2001/341, reg 22(2)(b). See note 8.

10   Ie the requirements of the Representation of the People (England and Wales) Regulations 2001, SI 2001/341, reg 18 (see PARAS 132–133): see reg 22(2)(b). See note 8.

11   Representation of the People (England and Wales) Regulations 2001, SI 2001/341, reg 22(2)(b). The text refers to the attestation required for certain overseas elector's declarations under reg 20 (see PARA 134): see reg 22(2)(b). See note 8.

12   Ie in the case of a declarant to whom the Representation of the People (England and Wales) Regulations 2001, SI 2001/341, reg 19 applies (see PARA 135): see reg 22(2)(c). See note 8.

13   Representation of the People (England and Wales) Regulations 2001, SI 2001/341, reg 22(2)(c). See note 8.

14   See the Representation of the People (England and Wales) Regulations 2001, SI 2001/341, reg 22(2). See note 8.

137. Effect of overseas elector's declaration. Where a person is registered in a register of parliamentary electors for any constituency or part of a constituency in pursuance of an overseas elector's declaration[1], it is conclusively presumed for the purposes of entitlement to vote as an overseas elector at a parliamentary election[2] that he was not resident in the United Kingdom on the relevant date[3].

1   As to the meaning of 'overseas elector's declaration' see PARA 114.

2   Ie for the purposes of the Representation of the People Act 1985 s 1 (extension of parliamentary franchise to British citizens overseas: see PARA 96): see s 2(7).

3   Representation of the People Act 1985 s 2(7). For the purposes of the registration of peers who (subject to the requirement of registration) may vote at European parliamentary elections, s 2 is applied with modifications: see the Representation of the People (England and Wales) Regulations 2001, SI 2001/341, reg 13(4), Sch 4; and PARA 101 note 7.

E.   OFFENCES

138. Offences associated with voters' declarations. A person who makes a declaration of local connection[1] or a service declaration[2] when he is not authorised to do so, or (except as permitted by the Representation of the People Act 1983) when he knows that he is subject to a legal incapacity to vote[3], or when he knows that the declaration contains a statement which is false, is guilty of an offence[4]. A person who makes an overseas elector's declaration[5] (or a declaration purporting to be such a declaration) when he knows that he is subject to a legal incapacity, or when he knows that the declaration contains a statement which is false, is guilty of an offence[6].

A person who attests a service declaration[7] or an overseas elector's declaration[8] (or a declaration purporting to be an overseas elector's declaration) when he knows that he is not authorised to attest such a declaration, or when he knows that the declaration contains a statement which is false, is guilty of an offence also[9].

1   As to declarations of local connection see PARA 121 et seq.
2   As to service declarations see PARA 125 et seq.
3   As to the meaning of 'legal incapacity' for these purposes see PARA 95 note 8.
4   See the Representation of the People Act 1983 s 62(1)(a); and PARA 735.
5   As to overseas elector's declarations see PARA 114 et seq.
6   See the Representation of the People Act 1985 s 12(1); and PARA 735.
7   As to the attestation of a service declaration see PARA 127.
8   As to the attestation of an overseas elector's declaration see PARA 134.
9   See the Representation of the People Act 1983 s 62(1)(b); the Representation of the People Act 1985 s 12(2); and PARA 735.

(iii) Registration Officers

139.   Registration officers. Electoral registration officers ('registration officers') are appointed for the registration of parliamentary and local government electors[1]. In England, the council of every district[2] and London borough[3] must appoint an officer of the council to be registration officer for any constituency or part of a constituency coterminous with or situated in the district or borough, except that, in relation to any constituency part of which consists of some or all of the area of the City of London[4] and the Inner and Middle Temples[5], the Common Council of the City of London[6] must appoint an officer to be registration officer for that part of the constituency[7]. In Wales, the council of every county[8] or county borough[9] must appoint an officer of the council to be registration officer for any constituency or part of a constituency coterminous with or situated in the area of the council[10].

The officer who is the registration officer for any such area in England or Wales[11] is the registration officer also for the area in question for the purposes of the registration of relevant citizens of the Union[12] as European parliamentary electors[13].

1   See the Representation of the People Act 1983 s 8(1). Any reference in any Act, whenever passed, to the registration officer for the registration of parliamentary or local government electors is to be taken as a reference to the registration officer appointed under the Representation of the People Act 1983: see s 206, Sch 7 para 11. As to the application of Sch 7 para 11 see PARA 145 note 45. As to the entitlement to registration as a parliamentary or local government elector see PARA 113. For the purposes of the Representation of the People (England and Wales) Regulations 2001, SI 2001/341, 'registration officer' means the electoral registration officer (see reg 3(1)); and 'registration area' means the area for which a registration officer acts (see reg 3(1) (definition added by SI 2002/1871)).

   For the purposes of the European Parliamentary Elections Regulations 2004, SI 2004/293, 'registration officer' means an officer appointed under the Representation of the People Act 1983 s 8 or, in relation to Gibraltar, the European electoral registration officer for Gibraltar; and 'relevant registration officer', except where otherwise provided, means: (1) the registration officer of the local authority in whose area the election is held; or (2) if the local counting area comprises any part of the area of more than one local authority, the registration officer of the local authority in whose area the greater or greatest (as the case may be) number of electors are registered to vote at European parliamentary elections; or (3) in relation to the City of London, the registration officer for the London borough of Westminster; or (4) in relation to the Scottish electoral region, the returning officer designated under the European Parliamentary Elections Act 2002 s 6(3) (returning officer for Scotland); or (5) the European electoral registration officer for Gibraltar as regards documents issued for use in Gibraltar: see the European Parliamentary Elections Regulations 2004, SI 2004/293, reg 2(1) (substituted by SI 2009/186). For these purposes, 'local counting area' means a parliamentary constituency wholly or partly comprised in an electoral region in England or in Wales, or a local government area in Scotland, or Gibraltar: see the European Parliamentary Elections Regulations 2004, SI 2004/293, reg 2(1) (as so substituted). As to the meanings of 'England' and 'Wales' see PARA 1 note 1. As to the meaning of 'constituency' for the purpose of parliamentary elections see PARA 9. As to electoral regions established for the purposes of European parliamentary elections see PARA 77; and as to the European electoral registration officer for Gibraltar see PARA 100.

For the purposes of the National Assembly for Wales (Representation of the People) Order 2007, SI 2007/236, 'registration officer' means an electoral registration officer; and 'relevant registration officer' is to be construed in accordance with the Electoral Administration Act 2006 ss 42(1), 44(1)–(3), (5) (retention and inspection of documents relating to certain local elections: see PARA 505): see the National Assembly for Wales (Representation of the People) Order 2007, SI 2007/236, art 2(1).

The expression 'relevant registration officer' is defined also for the purposes of the parliamentary elections rules (see the Representation of the People Act 1983 s 23(1), Sch 1 r 55(1A); and PARA 496 note 3); and the local government elections rules (see the Local Elections (Principal Areas) (England and Wales) Rules 2006, SI 2006/3304, r 3, Sch 2 r 52(2); the Local Elections (Parishes and Communities) (England and Wales) Rules 2006, SI 2006/3305, r 3, Sch 2 r 52(2); and PARA 498 note 4). It is defined for other more limited purposes: see eg the Representation of the People (England and Wales) Regulations 2001, SI 2001/341, reg 13 ('the list of overseas electors'); and PARA 143 note 10.

2 As to districts in England and their councils see LOCAL GOVERNMENT vol 69 (2009) PARA 24 et seq.

3 As to London boroughs and their councils see LOCAL GOVERNMENT vol 69 (2009) PARA 35; LONDON GOVERNMENT vol 71 (2013) PARAS 15, 20 et seq.

4 As to elections in the City of London see PARA 33.

5 As to the Temples see LONDON GOVERNMENT vol 71 (2013) PARA 17.

6 As to the Common Council of the City of London see LONDON GOVERNMENT vol 71 (2013) PARA 34 et seq.

7 See the Representation of the People Act 1983 s 8(2) (amended by the Local Government (Wales) Act 1994 s 66(6), (8), Sch 16 para 68(1), Sch 18; and the Parliamentary Voting System and Constituencies Act 2011 s 11(4)). A registration officer appointed under the Representation of the People Act 1983 s 8(2), or under s 8(2A), (3) (see the text and notes 8–11), is disqualified for membership of the House of Commons: see the House of Commons Disqualification Act 1975 s 1(1), Sch 1 Pt III; and PARLIAMENT vol 78 (2010) PARAS 905, 908.

8 As to counties in Wales and their councils see LOCAL GOVERNMENT vol 69 (2009) PARA 37 et seq.

9 As to county boroughs in Wales and their councils see LOCAL GOVERNMENT vol 69 (2009) PARA 37 et seq.

10 Representation of the People Act 1983 s 8(2A) (added by the Local Government (Wales) Act 1994 Sch 16 para 68(1)). See note 7.

11 Ie the officer who under the Representation of the People Act 1983 s 8(2) or s 8(2A) (see the text and notes 2–10) is the registration officer for any of the areas referred to in s 8(2) or s 8(2A), as the case may be, for the purposes of the Representation of the People Act 1983: see the European Parliamentary Elections (Franchise of Relevant Citizens of the Union) Regulations 2001, SI 2001/1184, reg 5(1)(a). The provision made by reg 5(1)(a) also includes references to the Representation of the People Act 1983 s 8(3) (substituted by the Local Government etc (Scotland) Act 1994 s 180(1), Sch 13 para 130(2)) (Scotland) and the Representation of the People Act 1983 s 8(4) (Northern Ireland): see the European Parliamentary Elections (Franchise of Relevant Citizens of the Union) Regulations 2001, SI 2001/1184, reg 5(1)(a). See note 7. Provision is made also for the officer who is appointed registration officer for the Isles of Scilly for the purposes of the Representation of the People Act 1983: see the European Parliamentary Elections (Franchise of Relevant Citizens of the Union) Regulations 2001, SI 2001/1184, reg 5(1)(b). As to the registration officer for the Isles of Scilly see PARA 11 note 17.

For the purposes of extending the rights of citizens and nationals of accession states who (subject to the requirements of registration) may vote at local government and European parliamentary elections, reg 5 is applied with modifications: see the Local and European Parliamentary Elections (Registration of Citizens of Accession States) Regulations 2003, SI 2003/1557, reg 6, Sch 1 para 3.

12 As to the meaning of 'relevant citizen of the Union' for these purposes see PARA 102 note 5.

13 European Parliamentary Elections (Franchise of Relevant Citizens of the Union) Regulations 2001, SI 2001/1184, reg 5(1). As to the registration of relevant citizens of the Union as European parliamentary electors see PARA 116.

140. Deputies and assistants. Any of the powers and duties of a registration officer may be performed and exercised by a deputy for the time being approved by the council which appointed the registration officer[1].

Where there is a vacancy in the office of registration officer, or in the event of his incapacity to act, any acts authorised or required to be done by, or with respect to, the registration officer may be done by or with respect to the proper officer[2] of the council by which the registration officer was appointed[3].

A district council[4] or London borough council[5] in England[6], or a county council[7] or county borough council[8] in Wales[9], must assign such officers to assist the registration officer as may be required for carrying out his functions[10].

1   See the Representation of the People Act 1983 s 52(2) (s 52(2), (3) amended, s 52(4) substituted, by the Representation of the People Act 1985 ss 24, 28, Sch 4 para 12, Sch 5); National Assembly for Wales (Representation of the People) Order 2007, SI 2007/236, art 28(2); European Parliamentary Elections Regulations 2004, SI 2004/293, reg 19(1). The provisions of the Representation of the People Act 1983, or the National Assembly for Wales (Representation of the People) Order 2007, SI 2007/236, or the European Parliamentary Elections Regulations 2004, SI 2004/293, as the case may be, apply to any such deputy as is mentioned in the text so far as respects any duties or powers to be performed or exercised by him as they apply to the registration officer: see the Representation of the People Act 1983 s 52(2) (as so amended); National Assembly for Wales (Representation of the People) Order 2007, SI 2007/236, art 28(2); European Parliamentary Elections Regulations 2004, SI 2004/293, reg 19(1). As to the appointment of registration officers see PARA 139; and as to the penalties for breach of official duty by a deputy or assistant see PARA 737.

The functions of a registration officer under the Representation of the People Act 1985 ss 2, 3, 6–9 are included in any reference to a registration officer's functions under the Representation of the People Act 1983 because those provisions have effect as if they were contained in Pt I (ss 1–66B): see the Representation of the People Act 1985 s 27(2). The Representation of the People Act 1983 s 52 is applied and modified for the purpose of local authority mayoral elections in England and Wales by the Local Authorities (Mayoral Elections) (England and Wales) Regulations 2007, SI 2007/1024, reg 3(2)–(5), Sch 2 Table 1: see PARA 11 note 14. As to the meanings of 'England' and 'Wales' see PARA 1 note 1.

The provision made by the European Parliamentary Elections Regulations 2004, SI 2004/293, reg 19 is applied with modifications as respects the European parliamentary electoral registration officer for Gibraltar: see reg 19(4) (amended by SI 2009/186). As to the European electoral registration officer for Gibraltar see PARA 100 note 3. For the purposes of extending the rights of peers and of relevant citizens of the Union who (subject to the requirement of registration) may vote at European parliamentary elections, the Representation of the People Act 1983 s 52 is applied with modifications: see the Representation of the People (England and Wales) Regulations 2001, SI 2001/341, reg 13(4), Sch 4 (cited in PARA 101 note 7); and the European Parliamentary Elections (Franchise of Relevant Citizens of the Union) Regulations 2001, SI 2001/1184, reg 9, Schedule (cited in PARA 102 note 6).

2   The 'proper officer' means any officer appointed for the purpose by the council (or, in relation to the Greater London Authority, the Authority or a functional body): see the Local Government Act 1972 s 270(3), (4); Greater London Authority Act 1999 s 424(1), (2); Representation of the People Act 1983 s 202(1) (definition substituted by the Greater London Authority Act 1999 s 17, Sch 3 paras 1, 38(1), (2)(c)); European Parliamentary Elections Regulations 2004, SI 2004/293, reg 2(1) (substituted by SI 2009/186). 'Proper officer' is not defined expressly for the purposes of the National Assembly for Wales (Representation of the People) Order 2007, SI 2007/236, but it is submitted that the provision made by the Local Government Act 1972 s 270(3), (4) suffices. As to the Greater London Authority see LONDON GOVERNMENT vol 71 (2013) PARA 67 et seq.

3   Representation of the People Act 1983 s 52(3) (as amended: see note 1); National Assembly for Wales (Representation of the People) Order 2007, SI 2007/236, art 28(3); European Parliamentary Elections Regulations 2004, SI 2004/293, reg 19(2). See note 1.

4   As to districts in England and their councils see LOCAL GOVERNMENT vol 69 (2009) PARA 24 et seq.

5   As to London boroughs and their councils see LOCAL GOVERNMENT vol 69 (2009) PARA 35;
    LONDON GOVERNMENT vol 71 (2013) PARAS 15, 20 et seq.
6   See the Representation of the People Act 1983 s 52(4)(a) (s 52(4) as substituted (see note 1);
    s 52(4)(a) amended, s 52(4)(aa) added, by the Local Government (Wales) Act 1994 s 66(6), (8),
    Sch 16 para 68(12), Sch 18); European Parliamentary Elections Regulations 2004, SI 2004/293,
    reg 19(3)(a). See note 1.
7   As to counties in Wales and their councils see LOCAL GOVERNMENT vol 69 (2009) PARA 37 et
    seq.
8   As to county boroughs in Wales and their councils see LOCAL GOVERNMENT vol 69 (2009) PARA
    37 et seq.
9   See the Representation of the People Act 1983 s 52(4)(aa) (s 52(4) as substituted (see note 1);
    s 52(4)(aa) as added (see note 6)); National Assembly for Wales (Representation of the People)
    Order 2007, SI 2007/236, art 28(4); European Parliamentary Elections Regulations 2004,
    SI 2004/293, reg 19(3)(b). See note 1.
10 See the Representation of the People Act 1983 s 52(4) (as substituted: see note 1); National
    Assembly for Wales (Representation of the People) Order 2007, SI 2007/236, art 28(4);
    European Parliamentary Elections Regulations 2004, SI 2004/293, reg 19(3). See note 1. As to
    Scotland see the Representation of the People Act 1983 s 52(4)(b) (s 52(4) as so substituted;
    s 52(4)(b) amended by the Local Government etc (Scotland) Act 1994 s 180(1), Sch 13
    para 130(5)).

141.   Duty to secure relevant registration objectives.   Each registration officer[1]
must take all steps that are necessary for the purpose of complying with his duty[2]
to maintain the registers of electors[3] and, in administering the registers, he must
have regard to data protection provisions[4]. It is also the duty of the registration
officer, during the relevant period[5], to send to a person registered in pursuance
of[6]:

(1)   a service declaration[7];

(2)   a declaration of local connection[8]; and

(3)   an overseas elector's declaration[9],

a reminder of the need to make a fresh declaration if he wishes to remain
registered as an elector in pursuance of such a declaration[10]; and, in relation to
each person who has an anonymous entry in the register[11], the registration
officer must, during the relevant period[12], send a reminder[13]:

(a)   that his entitlement to registration will terminate at the end of the
      period of 12 months beginning with the date on which his entry in the
      register first took effect[14];

(b)   that, if he wishes to remain entered in the register after that period, he
      must make a fresh application for registration in accordance with the
      requirements prescribed for the purposes[15]; and

(c)   that, if he wishes to remain entered in the register anonymously, the
      application for registration must be accompanied by a fresh application
      for an anonymous entry[16].

A registration officer must also compile records of absent voters and of their
proxies[17], a list of overseas electors[18], and lists of rooms which candidates are
entitled to use for election meetings[19].

A registration officer must comply with any general or special directions given
by the Secretary of State with respect to the arrangements to be made by the
registration officer for carrying out his functions under the Representation of the
People Act 1983[20]; and an electoral registration officer must take such steps as
he thinks appropriate to encourage the participation by electors in the electoral
process in the area for which he acts[21] and, in so doing, he must have regard to
any guidance issued by the Electoral Commission[22].

1   As to the appointment of registration officers see PARA 139.

2   Ie under the Representation of the People Act 1983 s 9(1) (see PARA 143): see s 9A(1) (s 9A added by the Electoral Administration Act 2006 s 9(1)).

3   Representation of the People Act 1983 s 9A(1) (as added: see note 2). As to the meaning of 'elector' see PARA 95 note 2. As to the compilation and maintenance of registers of electors see PARA 145 et seq.

The steps referred to in the text include:

(1)   sending more than once to any address the form to be used for the canvass under s 10 (see PARA 151) (s 9A(2)(a) (as so added));

(2)   making on one or more occasions house to house inquiries under s 10(5) (see PARA 151) (s 9A(2)(b) (as so added));

(3)   making contact by such other means as the registration officer thinks appropriate with persons who do not have an entry in a register (s 9A(2)(c) (as so added));

(4)   inspecting any records held by any person which he is permitted to inspect under or by virtue of any enactment or rule of law (s 9A(2)(d) (as so added));

(5)   providing training to persons under his direction or control in connection with the carrying out of the duty (s 9A(2)(e) (as so added)).

Regulations made by the Secretary of State may amend s 9A(2) by varying or repealing any of the paragraphs therein or by inserting any paragraph: see s 9A(3) (as so added). As to the Secretary of State see PARA 2. As to the making of regulations under the Representation of the People Act 1983 generally see PARA 28 note 16. At the date at which this volume states the law, no regulations had been made under s 9A. As to the powers available to a registration officer to require information about electors and to inspect certain records for the purposes of registration see PARA 142. A registration officer also has power to make inquiries of electors who have been granted applications to vote by proxy on certain grounds: see PARAS 368–369.

As from a day to be appointed under the Electoral Registration and Administration Act 2013 s 27(1), the Representation of the People Act 1983 s 9A(1) is amended so that the purpose for taking the specified steps is extended to include the purpose of securing that, so far as is reasonably practicable, persons who are entitled to be registered in a register (and no others) are registered in it: see s 9A(1) (s 9A as so added; s 9A(1) prospectively amended by the Electoral Registration and Administration Act 2013 s 13(1), Sch 4 paras 1, 6(1), (2)). Head (1) above is amended also so that the reference to the Representation of the People Act 1983 s 10 is repealed and a reference to s 9D added (registration officers' duty to conduct annual canvass in Great Britain compatible with system of individual registration: see PARA 154) (and so the reference in head (2) above becomes a reference to s 9D(5), instead of s 10(5), accordingly): see s 9A(2)(a) (s 9A as so added; s 9A(2)(a) prospectively amended by the Electoral Registration and Administration Act 2013 Sch 4 paras 1, 6(1), (3)). However, at the date at which this volume states the law, no such day had been appointed.

As from a day to be appointed under the Political Parties and Elections Act 2009 s 43(1), the Representation of the People Act 1983 s 10ZB (added by the Northern Ireland (Miscellaneous Provisions) Act 2006 s 4) (relevant registration objectives (Northern Ireland)) is prospectively amended by the Political Parties and Elections Act 2009 ss 33(2), (4), 39, Sch 7 (and extended to England and Wales and Scotland, accordingly). As from such a day, the relevant registration objectives are to secure, so far as reasonably practicable:

(a)   that every person who is entitled to be registered in a register is registered in it (Representation of the People Act 1983 s 10ZB(1)(a) (as so added));

(b)   that no person who is not entitled to be registered in a register is registered in it (s 10ZB(1)(b) (as so added)); and

(c)   that none of the required information relating to any person registered in a register is false (s 10ZB(1)(c) (as so added)).

However, in applying s 10ZB(1), the registrations of the persons mentioned in s 10(3) (registrations with which a canvass is not concerned: see PARA 151) must be disregarded: see s 10ZB(2) (as so added and extended). For these purposes, 'register' means a register maintained by a registration officer under s 9 (see PARA 143) (see s 10ZB(3) (s 10ZB as so added; s 10ZB(3)–(5) prospectively amended by the Political Parties and Elections Act 2009 s 33(2), (4)); and 'false', in relation to a signature, means that the signature is not the usual signature of, or was written by a person other than, the person whose signature it purports to be (see the Representation of the People Act 1983 s 10ZB(7) (as so added and extended)). The 'required information' means the following (as appearing in the register or other records of the registration officer concerned) (see s 10ZB(4) (s 10ZB as so added; s 10ZB(4) prospectively amended)):

(i)   the person's name (s 10ZB(4)(a) (as so added));

(ii)   the person's qualifying address (s 10ZB(4)(b) (as so added));

(iii) the person's date of birth (s 10ZB(4)(c) (as so added));

(iv)   subject to s 10ZB(5), the person's signature (s 10ZB(4)(d) (as so added));
(v)   the person's national insurance number or a statement that he does not have one (s 10ZB(4)(e) (as so added)).
However, the required information does not include the person's signature if the registration officer concerned has dispensed with the requirement to provide a signature: see s 10ZB(5) (s 10ZB as so added; s 10ZB(5) prospectively amended). However, as from a day to be appointed under the Electoral Registration and Administration Act 2013 s 27(1), the Political Parties and Elections Act 2009 s 33 is repealed by the Electoral Registration and Administration Act 2013 s 13(1), Sch 4 para 24(b). At the date at which this volume states the law, no such day had been appointed for either purpose.

4   Electoral registration officers must administer the register having regard to Council Directive (EC) 95/46 (OJ L281, 23.11.95, p 31) on the protection of individuals with regard to the processing of personal data and on the free movement of such data ('the Data Protection Directive') (see CONFIDENCE AND INFORMATIONAL PRIVACY vol 19 (2011) PARA 95 et seq) and the Data Protection Act 1998 s 11 (right to prevent processing for purposes of direct marketing: see CONFIDENCE AND INFORMATIONAL PRIVACY vol 19 (2011) PARA 122); and the Representation of the People Act 1983 must be construed so as to be compliant and consistent with those provisions: *R (on the application of Robertson) v Wakefield Metropolitan District Council* [2001] EWHC Admin 915, [2002] QB 1052, [2002] LGR 286. As to the Data Protection Directive see CONFIDENCE AND INFORMATIONAL PRIVACY vol 19 (2011) PARA 95 et seq. As to the restrictions placed on registration officers and other persons regarding the supply of registers and disclosure of the information contained in them see PARA 179 et seq.

5   See the Representation of the People (England and Wales) Regulations 2001, SI 2001/341, reg 25(2). For these purposes, the 'relevant period' means the period beginning nine months after the date when the existing entry in a register of the person in question first takes effect and ending ten months after that date, except that, in the case of a person who is a member of the forces, or who is the spouse or civil partner of a member of the forces (ie a person who is mentioned in the Representation of the People Act 1983 s 14(1)(a) or s 14(1)(d): see PARA 125), and is registered in pursuance of a service declaration, the 'relevant period' means the period beginning 57 months after the date when the existing entry in a register of the person in question first takes effect and ending 58 months after that date: see the Representation of the People (England and Wales) Regulations 2001, SI 2001/341, reg 25(3) (substituted by SI 2006/3406; amended by SI 2010/882). By virtue of the Representation of the People (England and Wales) Regulations 2001, SI 2001/341, reg 13(6), (7), reg 25 applies to registration in pursuance of a European parliamentary overseas elector's declaration as it applies to registration in pursuance of an overseas elector's declaration: see PARA 101 note 7. As to registration in pursuance of an overseas elector's declaration see PARA 114 et seq.
    Where the day or last day of the time allowed by the Representation of the People (England and Wales) Regulations 2001, SI 2001/341, for the doing of any thing falls on a Saturday, Sunday, Christmas Eve, Christmas Day, Good Friday or a bank holiday, that time must be extended until the next following day which is not one of those days: see reg 8(1), (3) (reg 8(3) amended by SI 2006/2910). For this purpose, 'bank holiday' means a day which, under the Banking and Financial Dealings Act 1971, is a bank holiday in England and Wales (see TIME vol 97 (2010) PARA 321): see the Representation of the People (England and Wales) Regulations 2001, SI 2001/341, reg 8(4). As to registration in pursuance of a service declaration see PARA 125 et seq. By virtue of reg 13(6), (7), reg 8 applies to registration in pursuance of a European parliamentary overseas elector's declaration as it applies to registration in pursuance of an overseas elector's declaration (see PARA 101 note 7); and for the purposes of relevant citizens of the Union who (subject to the requirement of registration) may vote at European parliamentary elections, reg 8 applies with modifications (see the European Parliamentary Elections (Franchise of Relevant Citizens of the Union) Regulations 2001, SI 2001/1184, reg 9, Schedule; and PARA 102 note 6). The Representation of the People (England and Wales) Regulations 2001, SI 2001/341, reg 8 is also applied and modified, in relation to Wales, by the Local Authorities (Conduct of Referendums) (Wales) Regulations 2008, SI 2008/1848, reg 8(2), Sch 4 Table 5, and, in relation to England, by the Local Authorities (Conduct of Referendums) (England) Regulations 2012, SI 2012/323, regs 8(2), 11–13, Sch 4 Table 6: see PARA 15 note 2.

6   See the Representation of the People (England and Wales) Regulations 2001, SI 2001/341, reg 25(1).

7   Representation of the People (England and Wales) Regulations 2001, SI 2001/341, reg 25(1)(a).

8   Representation of the People (England and Wales) Regulations 2001, SI 2001/341, reg 25(1)(b). As to registration in pursuance of a declaration of local connection see PARA 121 et seq.

9   Representation of the People (England and Wales) Regulations 2001, SI 2001/341, reg 25(1)(c).

10 See the Representation of the People (England and Wales) Regulations 2001, SI 2001/341, reg 25(2). This provision does not apply in respect of a person registered in pursuance of a service declaration, a declaration of local connection or an overseas elector's declaration, however, where the registration officer has already received from that person a fresh declaration, or where information which the registration officer has received indicates that that person is no longer entitled to make the relevant declaration: see reg 25(4).

11 See the Representation of the People (England and Wales) Regulations 2001, SI 2001/341, reg 25A(1) (reg 25A added by SI 2006/2910). As to anonymous registration see PARA 148.

12 For these purposes, the 'relevant period' must be construed in accordance with the Representation of the People (England and Wales) Regulations 2001, SI 2001/341, reg 25(3) (see note 5): reg 25A(4) (as added: see note 11).

13 Representation of the People (England and Wales) Regulations 2001, SI 2001/341, reg 25A(2) (as added: see note 11). This provision does not apply, however, where the registration officer has already received from that person a fresh application for registration made in accordance with the requirements prescribed for the purposes of the Representation of the People Act 1983 s 10A(1)(a) (see PARA 157) which is accompanied by a fresh application for an anonymous entry: Representation of the People (England and Wales) Regulations 2001, SI 2001/341, reg 25A(3) (as so added).

14 Representation of the People (England and Wales) Regulations 2001, SI 2001/341, reg 25A(2)(a) (as added: see note 11).

15 Representation of the People (England and Wales) Regulations 2001, SI 2001/341, reg 25A(2)(b) (as added: see note 11). Head (b) in the text refers to the requirements prescribed for the purposes of the Representation of the People Act 1983 s 10A(1)(a) (see PARA 157): see the Representation of the People (England and Wales) Regulations 2001, SI 2001/341, reg 25A(2)(b) (as so added).

16 Representation of the People (England and Wales) Regulations 2001, SI 2001/341, reg 25A(2)(c) (as added: see note 11).

17 See PARA 367 et seq. The registration officer must also every year by 31 January send every person who remains an absent voter (and whose signature held on the personal identifiers record is more than five years old) a notice in writing requiring him to provide a fresh signature and informing him of the date on which he would cease to be entitled to vote by post or by proxy in the event of a failure or refusal to provide a fresh signature: see PARA 366.

18 See PARA 146.

19 See PARA 336.

20 Representation of the People Act 1983 s 52(1) (amended by the Representation of the People Act 1985 s 24, Sch 4 para 12(a)). Without prejudice to the generality of the Representation of the People Act 1983 s 52(1), the directions which may be given thereunder include directions requiring a registration officer to maintain his registers in a specified electronic form: see s 52(1A) (added by the Political Parties, Elections and Referendums Act 2000 s 158(1), Sch 21 para 6(1), (5)). Any such directions may in particular specify:

(1) the software which is to be used in connection with the maintenance of the registers in that form (Representation of the People Act 1983 s 52(1A)(a) (as so added));

(2) the standards in accordance with which that software is to be maintained and updated (s 52(1A)(b) (as so added));

(3) how information required (by or under any enactment) to be included in the registers is to be recorded and stored in that form (s 52(1A)(c) (as so added)).

The function of giving directions under s 52(1) is exercisable only on, and in accordance with, a recommendation of the Electoral Commission: see the Political Parties, Elections and Referendums Act 2000 s 8(1); and PARA 56. In relation to Welsh Assembly elections, a registration officer must comply with any general or specific directions which may be given by the Secretary of State, in accordance with and on the recommendation of the Electoral Commission, with respect to the arrangements to be made by the registration officer in carrying out his functions under the National Assembly for Wales (Representation of the People) Order 2007, SI 2007/236: see art 28(1). As to the Electoral Commission see PARA 34 et seq.

For the purposes of extending the rights of peers and of relevant citizens of the Union who (subject to the requirement of registration) may vote at European parliamentary elections, the Representation of the People Act 1983 s 52 is applied with modifications: see the Representation of the People (England and Wales) Regulations 2001, SI 2001/341, reg 13(4), Sch 4 (cited in PARA 101 note 7); and the European Parliamentary Elections (Franchise of Relevant Citizens of the Union) Regulations 2001, SI 2001/1184, reg 9, Schedule (cited in PARA 102 note 6). The Representation of the People Act 1983 s 52 is applied and modified also for the purpose of local authority mayoral elections in England and Wales by the Local Authorities (Mayoral Elections)

(England and Wales) Regulations 2007, SI 2007/1024, reg 3(2)–(5), Sch 2 Table 1: see PARA 11 note 14. As to the meanings of 'England' and 'Wales' see PARA 1 note 1.

21 See the Electoral Administration Act 2006 s 69(1), (8)(a). The provision made by s 69 is applied and modified for the purpose of local authority mayoral elections in England and Wales by the Local Authorities (Mayoral Elections) (England and Wales) Regulations 2007, SI 2007/1024, reg 3(2)–(5), Sch 2 Table 5 (see PARA 11 note 14); and for the purposes of local authority referendums, in relation to Wales, by the Local Authorities (Conduct of Referendums) (Wales) Regulations 2008, SI 2008/1848, reg 8(2), Sch 4 Table 4; and, in relation to England, by the Local Authorities (Conduct of Referendums) (England) Regulations 2012, SI 2012/323, regs 8(2), 11–13, Sch 4 Table 5 (see PARA 15 note 2).

22 Electoral Administration Act 2006 s 69(2). See note 21.

142. Registration officer's powers to require information about electors and to inspect certain records. A registration officer[1] may require any person to give information required for the purposes of that officer's duties in maintaining registers of parliamentary and local government electors[2]. If any person fails to comply with any such requisition of the registration officer[3], that person is liable to a penalty[4].

Except where an application for registration is made in pursuance of a service declaration[5], a registration officer who has doubts about a person's age or nationality may require that person to produce for the purposes of registration the following specified evidence[6]:

(1)   a birth certificate or a statutory declaration as to the person's date of birth[7];

(2)   a certificate of naturalisation[8];

(3)   where a person has made an overseas elector's declaration[9], further evidence of his status as a British citizen[10] including a document showing that he has become a British citizen by virtue of registration[11];

(4)   in any other case, either a document showing that he has become a Commonwealth citizen[12] by virtue of registration[13] or a statutory declaration that he is a qualifying Commonwealth citizen[14] or citizen of the Republic of Ireland[15] or a relevant citizen of the Union[16].

Except where the declarant has, or has applied for, an anonymous entry[17], any such declaration must be made available for inspection at the registration officer's office until the determination of the application for registration and of any objections duly made to it[18]. If any fee is payable in connection with the making of a declaration for these purposes, the registration officer must pay that fee and it is to be treated as part of his registration expenses[19].

A registration officer is authorised to inspect, for the purpose of his registration duties, records kept (in whatever form) by[20]: (a) the council by which he was appointed[21] and any registrar of births and deaths[22]; or (b) any person providing services to, or authorised to exercise any function of, any such council or registrar[23]. A registration officer is authorised also to make copies of information contained in such records[24].

1   As to registration officers see PARA 139.

2   Representation of the People (England and Wales) Regulations 2001, SI 2001/341, reg 23(1). A registration officer is under a duty to require persons to give information required for the purposes of that officer's duty under the Juries Act 1974 s 3(1) (electoral register as basis of jury selection: see JURIES vol 61 (2010) PARA 812): Representation of the People (England and Wales) Regulations 2001, SI 2001/341, reg 23(2). By virtue of reg 13(6), (7), regs 23, 24 (see the text and notes 3–19) apply to registration in pursuance of a European parliamentary overseas elector's declaration as they apply to registration in pursuance of an overseas elector's declaration: see PARA 101 note 7. As to the duty of registration officers to maintain, prepare and publish registers of electors see PARA 141.

3　Ie any such requisition as is mentioned in the Representation of the People (England and Wales) Regulations 2001, SI 2001/341, reg 23 (see the text and notes 1–2): see reg 23(3) (amended by SI 2006/2910); and PARA 733.

4　See the Representation of the People (England and Wales) Regulations 2001, SI 2001/341, reg 23(3) (as amended: see note 3); and PARA 733. The penalty as mentioned in the text is a fine, on summary conviction, not exceeding level 3 on the standard scale: see reg 23(3) (as so amended); and PARA 733. See note 2. As to the standard scale see SENTENCING AND DISPOSITION OF OFFENDERS vol 92 (2010) PARA 142.

5　See the Representation of the People (England and Wales) Regulations 2001, SI 2001/341, reg 24(5). See note 2. As to service declarations see PARA 125 et seq.

　　For the purposes of extending the rights of relevant citizens of the Union who (subject to the requirement of registration) may vote at European parliamentary elections, and of citizens and nationals of accession states who (subject to the requirement of registration) may vote at local government and European parliamentary elections, reg 24 applies with modifications: see the European Parliamentary Elections (Franchise of Relevant Citizens of the Union) Regulations 2001, SI 2001/1184, reg 9, Schedule (cited in PARA 102 note 6); and the Local and European Parliamentary Elections (Registration of Citizens of Accession States) Regulations 2003, SI 2003/1557, reg 7, Sch 2 para 1(1), (3)(a).

6　See the Representation of the People (England and Wales) Regulations 2001, SI 2001/341, reg 24(1). See notes 2, 5.

7　Representation of the People (England and Wales) Regulations 2001, SI 2001/341, reg 24(2)(a). See notes 2, 5.

8　Representation of the People (England and Wales) Regulations 2001, SI 2001/341, reg 24(2)(b). See notes 2, 5. As to certificates of naturalisation see BRITISH NATIONALITY vol 4 (2011) PARA 484.

9　As to overseas elector's declarations see PARA 114 et seq.

10　As to who are British citizens see BRITISH NATIONALITY vol 4 (2011) PARAS 406, 421 et seq.

11　Representation of the People (England and Wales) Regulations 2001, SI 2001/341, reg 24(2)(c). See notes 2, 5.

12　As to who are Commonwealth citizens see BRITISH NATIONALITY vol 4 (2011) PARA 409.

13　Representation of the People (England and Wales) Regulations 2001, SI 2001/341, reg 24(2)(d)(i). See notes 2, 5.

14　For this purpose, 'qualifying Commonwealth citizen' has the same meaning as in the Representation of the People Act 1983 s 4 (entitlement to be registered as parliamentary or local government elector: see PARA 113 note 9): Representation of the People (England and Wales) Regulations 2001, SI 2001/341, reg 24(6). See notes 2, 5.

15　As to who are citizens of the Republic of Ireland see BRITISH NATIONALITY vol 4 (2011) PARA 410.

16　Representation of the People (England and Wales) Regulations 2001, SI 2001/341, reg 24(2)(d)(ii). See notes 2, 5. As to the entitlement of relevant citizens of the Union to be registered as European parliamentary electors see PARA 116.

17　See the Representation of the People (England and Wales) Regulations 2001, SI 2001/341, reg 24(4A) (added by SI 2006/2910). See notes 2, 5. As to anonymous registration see PARA 148.

18　Representation of the People (England and Wales) Regulations 2001, SI 2001/341, reg 24(4). See notes 2, 5. For these purposes, 'available for inspection' means available for inspection during ordinary office hours: see reg 3(1). Where a document (but not the full register) is made available for inspection under the Representation of the People (England and Wales) Regulations 2001, SI 2001/341, any person may make a copy (whether handwritten or by other means) of the whole or any part of it: see reg 7(1), (2) (reg 7(1) renumbered, and reg 7(2) added, by SI 2002/1871). As to the meaning of 'full register' see PARA 167 note 2. As to the determination of applications for registration and the making of objections see PARA 157 et seq.

19　Representation of the People (England and Wales) Regulations 2001, SI 2001/341, reg 24(3). The text refers to 'registration expenses' within the meaning of the Representation of the People Act 1983 s 54(1) (see PARA 144): see the Representation of the People (England and Wales) Regulations 2001, SI 2001/341, reg 24(3). See notes 2, 5.

20　See the Representation of the People (England and Wales) Regulations 2001, SI 2001/341, reg 35(1).

21　See the Representation of the People (England and Wales) Regulations 2001, SI 2001/341, reg 35(1)(a), (2)(a).

22　See the Representation of the People (England and Wales) Regulations 2001, SI 2001/341, reg 35(1)(a), (2)(b). As to registrars of births and deaths see REGISTRATION CONCERNING THE INDIVIDUAL vol 88 (2012) PARA 338.

23 Representation of the People (England and Wales) Regulations 2001, SI 2001/341, reg 35(1)(b).
24 Representation of the People (England and Wales) Regulations 2001, SI 2001/341, reg 35(3).

143. Discharge of duties by registration officer. It is the duty of each registration officer[1] to maintain:

(1)   a register of parliamentary electors[2] for each constituency or part of a constituency[3] in the area for which he acts[4];

(2)   a register of local government electors for the local government areas[5] or parts of local government areas included in the area for which he acts[6];

(3)   a register of any person or persons entitled to be registered as a relevant citizen of the Union[7] for the purposes of European parliamentary elections[8].

The registration officer must also prepare and publish a list of the names of each person who appears to him to be entitled to be registered in pursuance of an overseas elector's declaration ('the list of overseas electors')[9]; and it is the duty of the relevant registration officer[10] to prepare and publish a register[11] in respect of any year for which any peer who is entitled to vote as a European parliamentary elector is entitled to be registered[12]. As far as is reasonably practicable, the registration officer must combine the registers[13]. The registration officer also must keep a record of anonymous entries[14].

1   As to the appointment of registration officers see PARA 139.
2   As to the registers of electors see PARA 145 et seq.
3   As to the meaning of 'constituency' for these purposes see PARA 9. Where, under the Representation of the People Act 1983 s 9, two or more registration officers maintain registers of parliamentary electors in respect of different parts of the same constituency, then in relation to that constituency any reference in the Representation of the People Act 1983 (whether express or implied) to the register of parliamentary electors for a constituency must be read either as a reference to one of those registers or, in relation to one of those registration officers, as the register maintained by him, as the context may require: see s 9(7) (s 9 substituted by the Representation of the People Act 2000 s 8, Sch 1 paras 1, 3). For these purposes, any reference, in relation to a registration officer, to 'his' registers is a reference to the registers maintained by him under the Representation of the People Act 1983 s 9: see s 9(8)(a) (as so substituted). As to constituencies established for the purpose of Welsh Assembly elections see note 4.

     The functions of a registration officer under the Representation of the People Act 1985 ss 2, 3, 6–9 are included in any reference to a registration officer's functions under the Representation of the People Act 1983 because those provisions have effect as if they were contained in Pt I (ss 1–66B): see the Representation of the People Act 1985 s 27(2).

     For the purposes of extending the rights of peers and of relevant citizens of the Union who (subject to the requirement of registration) may vote at European parliamentary elections, the provisions of the Representation of the People Act 1983 s 9(1)–(4), (7), (8) are applied with modifications: see the Representation of the People (England and Wales) Regulations 2001, SI 2001/341, reg 13(4), Sch 4 (cited in PARA 101 note 7); and the European Parliamentary Elections (Franchise of Relevant Citizens of the Union) Regulations 2001, SI 2001/1184, reg 9, Schedule (cited in PARA 102 note 6).

4   Representation of the People Act 1983 s 9(1)(a) (as substituted: see note 3). See note 3. A returning officer for a parliamentary election, or for a local government election in England and Wales (within the meaning of the Representation of the People Act 1983: see PARA 11), may take such steps as he thinks appropriate to remedy any act or omission on his part, or on the part of an electoral registration officer, which arises in connection with any function the returning officer or relevant person has in relation to the election, and which is not in accordance with the rules or any other requirements applicable to the election: see the Electoral Administration Act 2006 s 46; and PARAS 530 note 26, 354 note 25.

     Each electoral registration officer for the Parliamentary constituencies and the Assembly electoral regions affected by the Parliamentary Constituencies and Assembly Electoral Regions (Wales) (Amendment) Order 2008, SI 2008/1791 (see PARA 76), must make such re-arrangement or adaptation of the registers of parliamentary electors as may be necessary to give effect to that Order: see art 3; and PARA 76.

5　As to the meaning of 'local government area' see PARA 33 note 7.

6　Representation of the People Act 1983 s 9(1)(b) (as substituted: see note 3). See notes 3, 4.

7　As to the meaning of 'relevant citizen of the Union' for these purposes see PARA 102 note 5.

8　European Parliamentary Elections (Franchise of Relevant Citizens of the Union) Regulations 2001, SI 2001/1184, reg 5(2). The text refers to entitlement to registration under reg 4 (see PARA 116): see reg 5(2).

9　See the Representation of the People (England and Wales) Regulations 2001, SI 2001/341, reg 45(1). The 'list of overseas electors' means the list prepared under reg 45: see reg 3(1). The registration officer must include in the list of overseas electors the address specified in the overseas elector's declaration in accordance with the Representation of the People Act 1985 s 2(4) (overseas elector's declarations: see PARA 132) and the Representation of the People (England and Wales) Regulations 2001, SI 2001/341, reg 18(1) (contents of overseas elector's declarations: see PARA 132): see reg 45(1). As to the form and content of the list of overseas electors see PARA 146; and as to publication see PARA 165 et seq. By virtue of reg 13(6), (7), reg 45 applies to registration in pursuance of a European parliamentary overseas elector's declaration as it applies to registration in pursuance of an overseas elector's declaration: see PARA 101 note 7.

10　Ie the officer appointed under the Representation of the People Act 1983 s 8 (see PARA 139): see the Representation of the People (England and Wales) Regulations 2001, SI 2001/341, reg 13(2). For the purposes of reg 13(2), the 'relevant registration officer' is the officer who acts for the area within which is situated the place specified in the declaration in accordance with the Representation of the People Act 1985 s 2(4) (overseas elector's declarations: see PARA 132), as that provision is applied by the Representation of the People (England and Wales) Regulations 2001, SI 2001/341, reg 13 (see note 3), as having been the address in respect of which the declarant was previously registered or, as the case may be, at which he was resident: see reg 13(3).

11　Ie under the Representation of the People Act 1985 s 3 (entitlement of peers to vote as European parliamentary electors: see PARA 101): see the Representation of the People (England and Wales) Regulations 2001, SI 2001/341, reg 13(2).

12　See the Representation of the People (England and Wales) Regulations 2001, SI 2001/341, reg 13(2). The relevant registration officer also must take reasonable steps to obtain information required by him for the purpose: see reg 13(2).

13　See PARA 145. The registers of parliamentary electors, of local government electors, of peers overseas registered as European parliamentary overseas electors and of relevant citizens of the Union registered as European parliamentary electors should all be combined, as far as is reasonably practicable: see the Representation of the People Act 1985 s 3(7) (cited in PARA 101); and the Representation of the People (England and Wales) Regulations 2001, SI 2001/341, reg 13(2).

14　Representation of the People (England and Wales) Regulations 2001, SI 2001/341, reg 45A(1) (added by SI 2006/2910). As to the form and content of the record of anonymous entries see PARA 145.

144. Payment of expenses of registration officer.　Any expenses properly incurred by a registration officer[1] in the performance of his functions[2] must be paid by the local authority[3] by whom he was appointed[4]. These expenses are referred to as 'registration expenses'[5].

Any fees paid to the registration officer[6] must be accounted for by him and paid to the local authority by which he was appointed[7].

On the request of a registration officer for an advance on account of registration expenses the local authority by which he was appointed may, if it thinks fit, make such an advance to him of such an amount and subject to such conditions as it may approve[8].

The Secretary of State[9] may reimburse an electoral registration officer in respect of any expenditure incurred by the officer for the purposes of encouraging electoral participation[10].

1　As to the appointment of registration officers see PARA 139.

2　Ie under the Representation of the People Act 1983, or the European Parliamentary Elections Regulations 2004, SI 2004/293, or the National Assembly for Wales (Representation of the People) Order 2007, SI 2007/236 (as the case may be): see the Representation of the People

Act 1983 s 54(1) (amended by the Representation of the People Act 1985 s 24, Sch 4 para 14(a)); the European Parliamentary Elections Regulations 2004, SI 2004/293, reg 20(1); and the National Assembly for Wales (Representation of the People) Order 2007, SI 2007/236, art 29(1). As from a day to be appointed under the Electoral Registration and Administration Act 2013 s 27(1), the Representation of the People Act 1983 s 54(1) is further amended so that a registration officer's functions under the Electoral Registration and Administration Act 2013 are included in the expenses properly incurred which must be paid as mentioned in the text: see the Representation of the People Act 1983 s 54(1) (prospectively amended by the Electoral Registration and Administration Act 2013 s 13(1), Sch 4 paras 1, 17). At the date at which this volume states the law, no such day had been appointed.

The functions of a registration officer under the Representation of the People Act 1985 ss 2, 3, 6–9 are included in any reference to a registration officer's functions under the Representation of the People Act 1983 because those provisions have effect as if they were contained in Pt I (ss 1–66B): see the Representation of the People Act 1985 s 27(2). However, the European Parliamentary Elections Regulations 2004, SI 2004/293, reg 20 does not apply to the European parliamentary electoral registration officer for Gibraltar: reg 20(5). As to the European electoral registration officer for Gibraltar see PARA 100 note 3.

For the purposes of extending the rights of peers and of relevant citizens of the Union who (subject to the requirement of registration) may vote at European parliamentary elections, the Representation of the People Act 1983 s 54 is applied with modifications: see the Representation of the People (England and Wales) Regulations 2001, SI 2001/341, reg 13(4), Sch 4 (cited in PARA 101 note 7); and the European Parliamentary Elections (Franchise of Relevant Citizens of the Union) Regulations 2001, SI 2001/1184, reg 9, Schedule (cited in PARA 102 note 6).

The Representation of the People Act 1983 s 54 is applied and modified for the purpose of local authority mayoral elections in England and Wales by the Local Authorities (Mayoral Elections) (England and Wales) Regulations 2007, SI 2007/1024, reg 3(2)–(5), Sch 2 Table 1: see PARA 11 note 14.

3   In the Representation of the People Act 1983, unless the context otherwise requires, 'local authority' means the Greater London Authority, a county council, a county borough council, a district council, a London borough council or a parish or community council: see s 203(1) (definition amended by the Local Government Act 1985 ss 18(1), 19, 102(2), Sch 9 Pt I, Sch 17; the Education Reform Act 1988 s 237, Sch 13 Pt I; the Local Government (Wales) Act 1994 s 66(6), Sch 16 para 68(16); and the Greater London Authority Act 1999 s 17, Sch 3 paras 1, 39(1), (4)(a)). In the National Assembly for Wales (Representation of the People) Order 2007, SI 2007/236, art 29, the county or county borough councils are specifically referred to in place of the more general term 'local authority': see art 29(1)–(3); and see also the text and notes 6–8. As to districts, counties and county boroughs, and their councils, see LOCAL GOVERNMENT vol 69 (2009) PARA 23 et seq. As to London boroughs and their councils see LOCAL GOVERNMENT vol 69 (2009) PARA 35; LONDON GOVERNMENT vol 71 (2013) PARAS 15, 20 et seq. As to parishes and their councils see LOCAL GOVERNMENT vol 69 (2009) PARA 27 et seq; and as to communities and their councils see LOCAL GOVERNMENT vol 69 (2009) PARA 41 et seq. As to the Greater London Authority see LONDON GOVERNMENT vol 71 (2013) PARA 67 et seq.

4   Representation of the People Act 1983 s 54(1) (as amended: see note 2); European Parliamentary Elections Regulations 2004, SI 2004/293, reg 20(1); National Assembly for Wales (Representation of the People) Order 2007, SI 2007/236, art 29(1). See note 2.

5   See the Representation of the People Act 1983 s 54(1) (as amended: see note 2); the European Parliamentary Elections Regulations 2004, SI 2004/293, reg 20(1); and the National Assembly for Wales (Representation of the People) Order 2007, SI 2007/236, art 29(1). Any reference in any Act, whenever passed, to registration expenses in connection with the registration of parliamentary and local government electors is to be taken as a reference to registration expenses under the Representation of the People Act 1983: see s 206, Sch 7 para 12. As to the application of Sch 7 para 12 see PARA 145 note 45. See note 2.

Any registration expenses (or contributions to them) paid by the Common Council of the City of London must be paid out of the general rate and any sums paid to the Common Council under these provisions must be paid to the credit of that rate: Representation of the People Act 1983 s 54(5); European Parliamentary Elections Regulations 2004, SI 2004/293, reg 20(4). As to elections in the City of London see PARA 33. As to the Common Council of the City of London see LONDON GOVERNMENT vol 71 (2013) PARA 34 et seq.

6   Ie under the Representation of the People Act 1983, or the European Parliamentary Elections Regulations 2004, SI 2004/293, or the National Assembly for Wales (Representation of the People) Order 2007, SI 2007/236, as the case may be: see the Representation of the People Act 1983 s 54(3) (amended by the Representation of the People Act 1985 s 24, Sch 4

para 14(b)); the European Parliamentary Elections Regulations 2004, SI 2004/293, reg 20(2); and the National Assembly for Wales (Representation of the People) Order 2007, SI 2007/236, art 29(2). Such fees are paid to the registration officer on the sale of the register of electors: see further PARA 188.

7   See the Representation of the People Act 1983 s 54(3) (as amended: see note 6); the European Parliamentary Elections Regulations 2004, SI 2004/293, reg 20(2); and the National Assembly for Wales (Representation of the People) Order 2007, SI 2007/236, art 29(2). See notes 2, 3.

8   See the Representation of the People Act 1983 s 54(4)(a); the European Parliamentary Elections Regulations 2004, SI 2004/293, reg 20(3); and the National Assembly for Wales (Representation of the People) Order 2007, SI 2007/236, art 29(3). See notes 2, 3.

9   As to the Secretary of State see PARA 2.

10 Electoral Administration Act 2006 s 69(4), (8)(a). The text refers to the electoral registration officer's duty of encouraging electoral participation under s 69 (see PARA 141): see s 69(4), (8)(a). The amount paid under s 69(4) must not in any year exceed such amount as is determined in accordance with regulations made by the Secretary of State: s 69(5). The power to make such regulations is exercisable by statutory instrument subject to annulment in pursuance of a resolution of either House of Parliament (s 69(6)); and such regulations may make different provision for different purposes (s 69(7)). Accordingly, the Encouraging Electoral Participation (Reimbursement of Expenses) (England and Wales) Regulations 2006, SI 2006/2972, which come into force on 1 April 2007, have been made, and provide that the total amount that may be paid to local electoral officers in England and Wales in pursuance of the Electoral Administration Act 2006 s 69(4) in the year ending on 31 March 2008 and each successive year is £2,500,000: Encouraging Electoral Participation (Reimbursement of Expenses) (England and Wales) Regulations 2006, SI 2006/2972, reg 2. For these purposes, 'year' means a period of 12 months ending on 31 March (reg 1(2)); and 'local electoral officer' means an electoral registration officer (Electoral Administration Act 2006 s 69(8)(a)). The Electoral Administration Act 2006 s 69 is applied and modified for the purpose of local authority mayoral elections in England and Wales by the Local Authorities (Mayoral Elections) (England and Wales) Regulations 2007, SI 2007/1024, reg 3(2)–(5), Sch 2 Table 5 (see PARA 11 note 14); and for the purposes of local authority referendums, in relation to Wales, by the Local Authorities (Conduct of Referendums) (Wales) Regulations 2008, SI 2008/1848, reg 8(2), Sch 4 Table 4, and, in relation to England, by the Local Authorities (Conduct of Referendums) (England) Regulations 2012, SI 2012/323, regs 8(2), 11–13, Sch 4 Table 5 (see PARA 15 note 2).

(iv) Records of Electors

A. THE REGISTER OF ELECTORS AND LIST OF OVERSEAS ELECTORS

145. Form and content of registers of electors. Each register of electors[1] must contain[2]:

(1) the names of the persons appearing to the registration officer to be entitled to be registered in it, subject to their complying with any prescribed[3] requirements[4];

(2) subject to any prescribed exceptions, the qualifying addresses[5] of the persons registered in it[6]; and

(3) in relation to each such person, that person's electoral number[7].

A person's 'electoral number' is such number (with or without any letters[8]) as is for the time being allocated by the registration officer to that person as his electoral number for the purposes of the register in question[9]. Electoral numbers must be allocated by a registration officer in such a way as to ensure, so far as is reasonably practicable, that in each separate part of a register the numbers run consecutively[10]. An anonymous entry of a person consists of that person's electoral number together with the letter 'N'[11]; and the registration officer must enter in the record of anonymous entries each person who is entered in the register with such an entry[12].

The register must be framed in separate parts for each parliamentary polling district[13], except that, where a parliamentary polling district is contained in more than one electoral area[14], there must be a separate part of the register for each part of the polling district contained in each electoral area[15]. There must be a different letter or letters in the register for each parliamentary polling district and such letter or letters are deemed to form part of an elector's number in the register[16]. The names and addresses of each separate part of the register must be arranged in street order[17]. However, if the registration officer determines for any part of the register that street order is not reasonably practicable, the names and addresses must be arranged either in alphabetical order or partly in street order and partly in alphabetical order[18]. The name of any person whose qualifying address is not contained in a register[19] must be grouped together in alphabetical order[20] at the end of that part of the register to which the address relates[21], beneath the heading 'Other electors'[22], and without giving that address[23]. An anonymous entry of a person is to be entered in the register[24] at the end of the part of the register which relates to the qualifying address of the person entitled to the entry[25], under the heading of 'Other electors'[26], and following the names grouped together under that heading[27].

The registers of parliamentary electors and local government elector[28] must so far as practicable be combined, the entries of persons registered only as parliamentary electors or local government electors being marked to indicate that fact[29]. As far as practicable, a register of peers entitled to be registered as European parliamentary electors[30] must[31] be combined with the register of parliamentary and local government electors, the names of peers so registered being marked to indicate that fact[32]; and a register of relevant citizens of the Union[33] who are registered as European parliamentary electors must so far as practicable be combined both with the registers of parliamentary and local government electors[34] and with any register of peers entitled to be registered as European parliamentary electors[35], the names of persons registered as relevant citizens of the Union being marked to indicate that fact[36]. The marks specified to appear against a person's entry in the register to indicate that he is registered in one or more of the four registers which are required to be combined[37] are as follows[38]:

(a)   to indicate that a relevant citizen of the Union is registered only in the register of local government electors, the letter 'G' must be placed against his entry[39];

(b)   to indicate that such a citizen is registered in both that register and the register of such citizens registered as European parliamentary electors, the letter 'K' must be placed against his entry[40];

(c)   to indicate that any other person is registered only in the register of local government electors, the letter 'L' must be placed against his entry[41];

(d)   to indicate that an overseas elector is registered only in the register of parliamentary electors, the letter 'F' must be placed against his entry[42];

(e)   to indicate that a European parliamentary overseas elector is registered only in the register of such electors, the letter 'E' must be placed against his entry[43].

Where no mark appears against a person's entry in the register of electors, this indicates that he is registered in the registers of parliamentary and local government electors[44].

Any reference in any Act, whenever passed, whatever the terms used in the reference[45], to the register of parliamentary and local government electors, or to the register of parliamentary electors, or to the register of local government electors, or to the electors' lists for any such register, is to be taken as a reference to the register kept under the Representation of the People Act 1983, or to that register so far as it relates to either parliamentary electors or local government electors, or to the electors' lists for such a register, as the case may be; and references in any Act to a parliamentary or local government elector must be construed accordingly[46]. However, in relation to a person shown in a register or electors' list as attaining voting age[47] on a specified date, these references do not apply except for the purposes of an election at which the day fixed for the poll falls on or after that date[48].

1 As to the duty of registration officers to maintain, prepare and publish registers of electors see PARA 141. As to the form and content of the list of overseas electors see PARA 146. As far as is practicable, all such registers should be combined: see the text and notes 28–36.

2 Representation of the People Act 1983 s 9(2) (s 9 substituted by the Representation of the People Act 2000 s 8, Sch 1 paras 1, 3; the Representation of the People Act 1983 s 9(2) amended by the Electoral Administration Act 2006 s 10(2), Sch 1 paras 2, 4(1), (2)). The Representation of the People Act 1983 s 9(2) currently is subject only to s 9B(3) (test for anonymous entry in the register: see PARA 148): see s 9(2) (as so substituted and amended). However, as from a day to be appointed under the Electoral Registration and Administration Act 2013 s 27(1), the amendments made by the Electoral Administration Act 2006 Sch 1 paras 2, 4(1), (2) are repealed, and the Representation of the People Act 1983 s 9(2) amended, so that it is subject to any other provision of the Representation of the People Act 1983: see s 9(2) (as so substituted; prospectively amended by the Electoral Registration and Administration Act 2013 s 13(1), Sch 4 paras 1, 5(a), 23). At the date at which this volume states the law, no such day had been appointed.

   For the purposes of extending the rights of peers and of relevant citizens of the Union who (subject to the requirement of registration) may vote at European parliamentary elections, the provisions of the Representation of the People Act 1983 s 9(1)–(4), (7), (8) are applied with modifications: see the Representation of the People (England and Wales) Regulations 2001, SI 2001/341, reg 13(4), Sch 4 (cited in PARA 101 note 7); and the European Parliamentary Elections (Franchise of Relevant Citizens of the Union) Regulations 2001, SI 2001/1184, reg 9, Schedule (cited in PARA 102 note 6).

3 For these purposes, 'prescribed' means prescribed by regulations: see the Representation of the People Act 1983 s 202(1). As to the making of regulations under the Representation of the People Act 1983 generally see PARA 28 note 16. As to the regulations made under s 9(2) see the Representation of the People (England and Wales) Regulations 2001, SI 2001/341, regs 38–45H; and see also PARAS 143, 146.

4 Representation of the People Act 1983 s 9(2)(a) (as substituted: see note 2). As from a day to be appointed under the Electoral Registration and Administration Act 2013 s 27(1), the Representation of the People Act 1983 s 9(2)(a) is substituted so that head (1) in the text specifies that each register must contain the names of persons who appear to the registration officer to be entitled to be registered in it and in respect of whom a successful application for registration has been made: see s 9(2)(a) (s 9 as so substituted; s 9(2)(a) prospectively substituted by the Electoral Registration and Administration Act 2013 Sch 4 paras 1, 5(b)). At the date at which this volume states the law, no such day had been appointed. See note 2.

5 In the Representation of the People Act 1983, 'qualifying address', in relation to a person registered in a register of electors, is the address in respect of which he is entitled to be so registered: see s 9(8)(b) (as substituted: see note 2); s 202(1) (definition added by the Representation of the People Act 2000 Sch 1 paras 1, 22(b)). See note 2.

6 Representation of the People Act 1983 s 9(2)(b) (as substituted: see note 2). See note 2. As to the meaning of 'prescribed' see note 3. According to the exceptions prescribed as mentioned in the text, s 9(2)(b) does not apply to an address:

   (1) where it appears to the registration officer that a service voter in his service declaration, or a person who has made a declaration of local connection, has given that address in such a declaration as an address at which he has resided, but which is not an address at which he is or would be residing but for the circumstances entitling him to make such a declaration (Representation of the People (England and Wales) Regulations 2001, SI 2001/341, reg 40(1)(a), (2));

   (2) given in a declaration of local connection in accordance with the Representation of the People Act 1983 s 7B(4)(b) (required address given by a homeless person: see PARA 122 note 11) (Representation of the People (England and Wales) Regulations 2001, SI 2001/341, reg 40(1)(a), (3)); or

(3)   which is specified in an overseas elector's declaration in accordance with the Representation of the People Act 1985 s 2(4)(b) or s 2(4)(c)(ii) (see PARA 132) (Representation of the People (England and Wales) Regulations 2001, SI 2001/341, reg 40(1)(b)).

As to overseas elector's declarations see PARA 114 et seq; as to declarations of local connection see PARA 121 et seq; and as to service declarations see PARA 125 et seq.

For the purposes of extending the rights of relevant citizens of the Union who (subject to the requirement of registration) may vote at European parliamentary elections, regs 38–41 are applied with modification: see the European Parliamentary Elections (Franchise of Relevant Citizens of the Union) Regulations 2001, SI 2001/1184, reg 9, Schedule; and PARA 102 note 6. By virtue of the Representation of the People (England and Wales) Regulations 2001, SI 2001/341, reg 13(6), (7), regs 38–42 apply with modifications to registration in pursuance of a European parliamentary overseas elector's declaration as they apply to registration in pursuance of an overseas elector's declaration: see PARA 101 note 7.

7   Representation of the People Act 1983 s 9(2)(c) (as substituted: see note 2). See note 2.
8   As to the letters which are used to mark entries in the registers see the text and notes 11, 37–44.
9   Representation of the People Act 1983 s 9(3) (as substituted: see note 2). See note 2.
10   Representation of the People Act 1983 s 9(4) (as substituted: see note 2). See note 2.
11   Representation of the People (England and Wales) Regulations 2001, SI 2001/341, reg 41A(1) (regs 41A, 45A, 45G added by SI 2006/2910).
12   Representation of the People (England and Wales) Regulations 2001, SI 2001/341, reg 45A(2) (as added: see note 11). The entry in the record referred to in the text must contain:
    (1)   the full name of the person to whom the entry relates (reg 45A(3)(a) (as so added));
    (2)   his electoral number (reg 45A(3)(b) (as so added));
    (3)   his qualifying address (reg 45A(3)(c) (as so added));
    (4)   where he has given in his application for an anonymous entry an address other than his qualifying address to which correspondence should be sent, that address (reg 45A(3)(d) (as so added));
    (5)   the date on which the anonymous entry in the register took effect (reg 45A(3)(e) (as so added)).

Where the application of a person with an anonymous entry to vote by post is granted, the registration officer must also enter in the record the address to which the postal ballot paper should be sent as given in the application (ie in accordance with reg 51(2)(d): see PARA 367): reg 45A(4) (as so added). As to the registration officer's duty to keep a record of anonymous entries see PARA 141.

Where a registration officer enters a person in the record of anonymous entries, he must issue to that person a certificate of anonymous registration: reg 45G(1) (as added: see note 11). A certificate of anonymous registration must be in writing and signed by the registration officer (reg 45G(2) (as so added)); and it must state:
    (a)   the name of the area for which the registration officer acts (reg 45G(3)(a) (as so added));
    (b)   the name, electoral number and qualifying address of the person who has the anonymous entry (reg 45G(3)(b) (as so added));
    (c)   the date on which the anonymous entry took effect (reg 45G(3)(c) (as so added));
    (d)   that, unless a fresh application for an anonymous entry is made, the entitlement to remain registered anonymously will terminate no later than at the end of the period of 12 months beginning with the date stated in accordance with head (c) above (reg 45G(3)(d) (as so added)).

A 'certificate of anonymous registration' means a certificate issued in pursuance of reg 45G: see reg 3(1) (definition added by SI 2006/2910).

13   Representation of the People (England and Wales) Regulations 2001, SI 2001/341, reg 38(1). See note 6. As to polling districts at parliamentary elections see PARA 343.
14   As to the meaning of 'electoral area' see PARA 11.
15   Representation of the People (England and Wales) Regulations 2001, SI 2001/341, reg 38(2). See note 6.

Where a Welsh Assembly constituency is not coterminous with, or wholly situated in, a county or county borough, the registration officer for any part of the Assembly constituency must, if he is not the returning officer for the constituency, consult him concerning the form of so much of the register, or the electors' lists, as relates to the constituency, in order to ensure that, so far as practicable, it is in a form similar to that in use elsewhere in the constituency: National Assembly for Wales (Representation of the People) Order 2007, SI 2007/236, art 140(a)(i), (ii). As to the meanings of 'Assembly constituency' and 'Assembly election' for these purposes see PARA 3 note 2; and as to the meaning of 'constituency returning officer' see

PARA 18 note 2. As to Assembly constituencies see PARA 76; as to the electors' lists see PARA 151 et seq; and as to returning officers for Welsh Assembly elections see PARA 357 et seq. As to counties and county boroughs in Wales see LOCAL GOVERNMENT vol 69 (2009) PARA 37 et seq.

16 Representation of the People (England and Wales) Regulations 2001, SI 2001/341, reg 39. See note 6.

17 Representation of the People (England and Wales) Regulations 2001, SI 2001/341, reg 41(1). See note 6.

18 Representation of the People (England and Wales) Regulations 2001, SI 2001/341, reg 41(2). See note 6.

19 Ie by virtue of the Representation of the People (England and Wales) Regulations 2001, SI 2001/341, reg 40 (see note 6): see reg 41(3).

20 Representation of the People (England and Wales) Regulations 2001, SI 2001/341, reg 41(3). See note 6.

21 Representation of the People (England and Wales) Regulations 2001, SI 2001/341, reg 41(3)(a). See note 6.

22 Representation of the People (England and Wales) Regulations 2001, SI 2001/341, reg 41(3)(b). See note 6.

23 Representation of the People (England and Wales) Regulations 2001, SI 2001/341, reg 41(3)(c). See note 6.

24 See the Representation of the People (England and Wales) Regulations 2001, SI 2001/341, reg 41A(2) (as added: see note 11).

25 Representation of the People (England and Wales) Regulations 2001, SI 2001/341, reg 41A(2)(a) (as added: see note 11).

26 Representation of the People (England and Wales) Regulations 2001, SI 2001/341, reg 41A(2)(b) (as added: see note 11). The text refers to the heading of 'Other electors' as mentioned in reg 41(3)(b) (see the text and note 22): see reg 41A(2)(b) (as so added).

27 Representation of the People (England and Wales) Regulations 2001, SI 2001/341, reg 41A(2)(c) (as added: see note 11). The text refers to the names grouped together under the heading of 'Other electors' in pursuance of reg 41(3) (see the text and notes 19–23): see reg 41A(2)(c) (as so added).

28 As to the duty of each registration officer to maintain registers of parliamentary electors and local government electors see PARA 143.

29 Representation of the People Act 1983 s 9(5) (s 9 as substituted (see note 2); s 9(5) amended by the Electoral Administration Act 2006 Sch 1 paras 2, 4(1), (3)). See note 2. As to anonymous entries in the register of electors see PARA 147 et seq.

30 As to the register of peers entitled to be registered as European parliamentary electors see PARA 143.

31 Ie under the Representation of the People Act 1985 s 3(7) (see PARA 101 note 7): see the Representation of the People (England and Wales) Regulations 2001, SI 2001/341, reg 13(2); and PARA 143.

32 See the Representation of the People Act 1985 s 3(7) (cited in PARA 101 note 7); and the Representation of the People (England and Wales) Regulations 2001, SI 2001/341, reg 13(2) (cited in PARA 143).

33 As to the meaning of 'relevant citizen of the Union' for these purposes see PARA 102 note 5.

34 European Parliamentary Elections (Franchise of Relevant Citizens of the Union) Regulations 2001, SI 2001/1184, reg 5(3)(a).
For the purposes of extending the rights of citizens and nationals of accession states who (subject to the requirements of registration) may vote at local government and European parliamentary elections, reg 5 is applied with modifications: see the Local and European Parliamentary Elections (Registration of Citizens of Accession States) Regulations 2003, SI 2003/1557, reg 6, Sch 1 para 3.

35 European Parliamentary Elections (Franchise of Relevant Citizens of the Union) Regulations 2001, SI 2001/1184, reg 5(3)(b). The text refers to any register of peers kept under the Representation of the People Act 1985 s 3(7) (see PARA 101 note 7): see the European Parliamentary Elections (Franchise of Relevant Citizens of the Union) Regulations 2001, SI 2001/1184, reg 5(3)(b). See note 34.

36 European Parliamentary Elections (Franchise of Relevant Citizens of the Union) Regulations 2001, SI 2001/1184, reg 5(3). The text refers to the names of persons registered under reg 5 (see PARA 143): see reg 5(3) See note 34.

37 Ie those of parliamentary electors, of local government electors, of peers overseas registered as European parliamentary overseas electors and of relevant citizens of the Union registered as European parliamentary electors: see the Representation of the People (England and Wales) Regulations 2001, SI 2001/341, reg 42(1) (reg 42(1)–(7) amended by SI 2006/2910). A

registration officer must also prepare a list of the names of each person who appears to him to be entitled to be registered in pursuance of an overseas elector's declaration ('the list of overseas electors'): see reg 45; and PARA 146.

38 Representation of the People (England and Wales) Regulations 2001, SI 2001/341, reg 42(1) (as amended: see note 37). The marks are specified in reg 42(3)–(7): see heads (a)–(e) in the text. See note 6. Letters may appear against a person's entry in versions of the register other than for the purposes of combining them. To indicate that an elector or his proxy is entitled to vote by post and is for that reason not entitled to vote in person, the letter 'A' is placed against the entry of that elector in any copy of the register, or part of it, provided for a polling station: see reg 62; and PARAS 377, 382. In any copy of the full register (or any copy of a notice of alteration) which is sold to prescribed government departments or to credit reference agencies, the letter 'Z' is placed against the entry of any person whose entry is not included in the edited version of the register: see reg 111; and PARA 188 note 8. As to the meaning of 'full register' see PARA 167 note 2; and as to the meaning of 'edited register' see PARA 167 note 4.

39 Representation of the People (England and Wales) Regulations 2001, SI 2001/341, reg 42(3) (as amended: see note 37).

For the purposes of extending the rights of citizens and nationals of accession states who (subject to the requirements of registration) may vote at local government and European parliamentary elections, reg 42(3) is applied with modifications: see the Local and European Parliamentary Elections (Registration of Citizens of Accession States) Regulations 2003, SI 2003/1557, reg 7, Sch 2 para 1(1), (3)(c). See also note 6.

40 Representation of the People (England and Wales) Regulations 2001, SI 2001/341, reg 42(4) (as amended: see note 37). See note 6.

41 Representation of the People (England and Wales) Regulations 2001, SI 2001/341, reg 42(5) (as amended: see note 37). See note 6.

42 Representation of the People (England and Wales) Regulations 2001, SI 2001/341, reg 42(6) (as amended: see note 37). See note 6.

43 Representation of the People (England and Wales) Regulations 2001, SI 2001/341, reg 42(7) (as amended: see note 37). See note 6.

44 Representation of the People (England and Wales) Regulations 2001, SI 2001/341, reg 42(2) (as amended: see note 37). See note 6.

45 The provisions of the Representation of the People Act 1983 Sch 7 paras 10–12 (see the text and notes 46–48; PARA 139 note 1; and PARA 144 note 5) apply to a reference both to any of the matters mentioned in them (whatever the terms used in the reference), and to any other matter which was to be construed as a reference to any of those matters by virtue of an enactment repealed by the Representation of the People Act 1948: see the Representation of the People Act 1983 Sch 7 para 13(1). Those provisions, so far as they relate to the Representation of the People Act 1983, or any other Act passed after 30 July 1948 (ie after the date when the Representation of the People Act 1948 was passed), do not apply where the context otherwise requires, however (see the Representation of the People Act 1983 Sch 7 para 13(2)); and, so far as Sch 7 paras 10–12 relate to Acts passed before 30 July 1948, those provisions may be excluded in whole or in part by an order of the Secretary of State in any particular case where they appear to him to be inappropriate: see the Representation of the People Act 1983 Sch 7 para 13(3)–(6). Functions of the Secretary of State under Sch 7 para 13, and any instrument having effect under it, are to be exercised concurrently with the Lord President of the Council: see the Lord President of the Council Order 2010, SI 2010/1837, art 3(1)(a), (2)–(9). As to the Secretary of State see PARA 2. At the date at which this volume states the law, no such order had been made.

46 See the Representation of the People Act 1983 s 206, Sch 7 para 10(1). See note 45.

47 For the purposes of parliamentary and local government elections, voting age is currently 18 years: see PARA 95 note 2.

48 Representation of the People Act 1983 Sch 7 para 10(2). See note 45.

146. Form and content of list of overseas electors. The list of overseas electors[1] must have a separate part in respect of each constituency[2] which is wholly or partly comprised in the area for which the registration officer acts[3]. The names of the persons included in each part must be listed in alphabetical order[4]; and the name of a person appearing to the registration officer to be entitled to be registered in pursuance of a European parliamentary overseas elector's declaration[5] must be marked with the letter 'E'[6].

1   As to the meaning of 'list of overseas electors' see PARA 143 note 9.
2   As to the meaning of 'constituency' for these purposes see PARA 9.
3   See the Representation of the People (England and Wales) Regulations 2001, SI 2001/341, reg 45(2). By virtue of reg 13(6), (7), reg 45 applies to registration in pursuance of a European parliamentary overseas elector's declaration as it applies to registration in pursuance of an overseas elector's declaration: see PARA 101 note 7. As to registration officers and the areas for which they act see PARA 139.
4   See the Representation of the People (England and Wales) Regulations 2001, SI 2001/341, reg 45(2).
5   Ie and included in the list of overseas electors by virtue of the Representation of the People (England and Wales) Regulations 2001, SI 2001/341, reg 13(6) (see note 3): see reg 45(4).
6   Representation of the People (England and Wales) Regulations 2001, SI 2001/341, reg 45(4). As to the entries associated with overseas electors in the registers of electors see PARA 145.

147. Applications for anonymous entry in register. Until a day to be appointed[1], an application for registration in a register of parliamentary electors or local government electors[2] may be made[3] and accompanied by[4]:

(1)   an application for anonymous registration[5] made in accordance with prescribed[6] requirements ('an application for an anonymous entry')[7];

(2)   a declaration made in accordance with such requirements for the purposes of such an application[8]; and

(3)   such evidence in support of the application for an anonymous entry as may be prescribed[9].

An application for an anonymous entry must state[10]:

(a)   the applicant's full name[11];

(b)   the address in respect of which the applicant applies to be registered and at which he is resident on the date of the application[12];

(c)   the reason for the application[13]; and

(d)   the date of the application[14].

The application must be in writing and signed by the applicant[15]; and must be accompanied by evidence of the nature prescribed[16], being either evidence of relevant court orders or injunctions[17] or evidence by attestation of the risk to the safety of the applicant or of another person of the same household as the applicant[18].

The application must be accompanied by a declaration made by the applicant[19]:

(i)   that the particulars given in accordance with heads (a) to (d) above are true[20];

(ii)   that, so far as he is aware, the evidence provided as mentioned in head (3) above[21] is genuine; and

(iii) that, where the evidence so provided relates not to the applicant but to another person of the same household as the applicant[22], the person to whom the evidence relates is a person of the same household of the applicant[23] and, so far as he is aware, the evidence so provided[24] is genuine[25].

The application may give an address to which the registration officer must send correspondence, other than the address given in accordance with head (b) above[26].

Where the registration officer[27] determines[28] that the applicant for an anonymous entry is entitled to be registered[29], and where the application for an anonymous entry is made in accordance with the prescribed[30] requirements[31], he must also determine whether the safety test is satisfied[32]. The safety test is satisfied if the safety of the applicant for an anonymous entry or that of any other person of the same household would be at risk if the register contains the name of the applicant or his qualifying address[33]. Accordingly, the registration officer must determine that the safety test is satisfied (and so allow the application for an anonymous entry) where he is satisfied[34]: (A) that the evidence provided in support of the application[35] constitutes evidence of the nature prescribed[36]; and (B) in the case of an application where the evidence so provided relates not to the applicant but to another person of the same household as the applicant[37], that the evidence so provided establishes that the person in question is a person of the same household as the applicant[38].

1 As from a day to be appointed under the Electoral Registration and Administration Act 2013 s 27(1), the Representation of the People Act 1983 s 9B (added by the Electoral Administration Act 2006 s 10(1)) is amended so that s 9B(1), (2) is substituted (see the text and notes 2–9, 27–29), and s 9(1A) added, by the Electoral Registration and Administration Act 2013 s 13(1), Sch 4 paras 1, 7(1), (2). At the date at which this volume states the law, no such day had been appointed. However, as from such a day, an application under the Representation of the People Act 1983 s 9B (an 'application for an anonymous entry') may be made by any person, in conjunction with an application for registration under s 10ZC (not yet in force) (see PARA 163), or by a person who already has an anonymous entry, for the purposes of remaining registered with such an entry (see s 9C(3); and PARA 171): see s 9B(1) (s 9B as so added; s 9B(1) prospectively substituted). An application for an anonymous entry must be made in accordance with prescribed requirements and must be accompanied by a declaration made in accordance with prescribed requirements, and by such evidence in support as may be prescribed: see s 9B(1A) (s 9B as so added; s 9B(1A) prospectively added).

2 As to the register of parliamentary and local government electors see PARA 145.

3 Ie in accordance with the requirements prescribed for the purposes of the Representation of the People Act 1983 s 10A(1)(a) (see PARA 157): see s 9B(1) (as added: see note 1). See note 1.

4 See the Representation of the People Act 1983 s 9B(1) (as added: see note 1). See note 1.

5 Ie an application under the Representation of the People Act 1983 s 9B: see s 9B(1)(a) (as added: see note 1). See note 1.

6 For these purposes, 'prescribed' means prescribed by regulations: see the Representation of the People Act 1983 s 202(1). As to the making of regulations under the Representation of the People Act 1983 generally see PARA 28 note 16. As to the regulations made for the purposes of s 9B see the text and notes 10–26.

7 Representation of the People Act 1983 s 9B(1)(a) (as added: see note 1). See note 1.The requirements referred to in the text are prescribed under the Representation of the People (England and Wales) Regulations 2001, SI 2001/341, reg 31G(1)–(4), (6): see the text and notes 10–16, 26.

8 Representation of the People Act 1983 s 9B(1)(b) (as added: see note 1). See note 1. The requirements referred to in the text are prescribed under the Representation of the People (England and Wales) Regulations 2001, SI 2001/341, reg 31G(5): see the text and notes 19–25.

9 Representation of the People Act 1983 s 9B(1)(c) (as added: see note 1). See note 1. The evidence referred to in the text is prescribed under the Representation of the People (England and Wales) Regulations 2001, SI 2001/341, regs 31I, 31J: see the text and notes 17, 18.

10 See the Representation of the People (England and Wales) Regulations 2001, SI 2001/341, reg 31G(1) (regs 31G–31J added by SI 2006/2910).

11 Representation of the People (England and Wales) Regulations 2001, SI 2001/341, reg 31G(1)(a) (as added: see note 10).

12 Representation of the People (England and Wales) Regulations 2001, SI 2001/341, reg 31G(1)(b) (as added: see note 10). The text refers to the address given in accordance with reg 26(1)(b) (applications for registration: see PARA 158): see reg 31G(1)(b) (as so added).

13 Representation of the People (England and Wales) Regulations 2001, SI 2001/341, reg 31G(1)(c) (as added: see note 10).

14 Representation of the People (England and Wales) Regulations 2001, SI 2001/341, reg 31G(1)(d) (as added: see note 10).

15 See the Representation of the People (England and Wales) Regulations 2001, SI 2001/341, reg 31G(2) (as added: see note 10).

16 See the Representation of the People (England and Wales) Regulations 2001, SI 2001/341, reg 31G(3) (as added: see note 10). The text refers to the evidence prescribed under reg 31I (see the text and note 17) or reg 31J (see the text and note 18): see reg 31G(3) (as so added). Where the evidence mentioned in reg 31G(3) relates not to the applicant, but to another person of the

same household as the applicant, the application must be accompanied by evidence that that person is of that household: reg 31G(4) (as so added).

17   Evidence which meets the following conditions is prescribed for the purposes of the Representation of the People (England and Wales) Regulations 2001, SI 2001/341, reg 31G(3) and reg 31H(2)(a) (see head (A) in the text) (see reg 31I(1) (as added: see note 10)):

   (1)   the first condition is that the evidence is, or is a copy of, a relevant order or injunction (reg 31I(2) (as so added));

   (2)   the second condition is that the relevant order or injunction is made for the protection, or otherwise for the benefit, of the applicant for an anonymous entry, or of another person of the same household as him (see reg 31I(4) (as so added));

   (3)   the third condition is that the relevant order or injunction is in force on the day on which the application for an anonymous entry is made (reg 31I(5) (as so added)).

For these purposes, a relevant order or injunction is an injunction for the purpose of restraining a person from pursuing any conduct which amounts to harassment granted in proceedings under the Protection from Harassment Act 1997 s 3 (see TORT vol 97 (2010) PARA 557), an injunction granted under s 3A(2) (see TORT vol 97 (2010) PARA 557), a restraining order made under s 5(1) (see SENTENCING AND DISPOSITION OF OFFENDERS vol 92 (2010) PARA 349), a restraining order on acquittal made under s 5A(1) (see SENTENCING AND DISPOSITION OF OFFENDERS vol 92 (2010) PARA 349) or a non-molestation order made under the Family Law Act 1996 s 42(2) (see MATRIMONIAL AND CIVIL PARTNERSHIP LAW vol 73 (2009) PARA 716 et seq): see the Representation of the People (England and Wales) Regulations 2001, SI 2001/341, reg 31I(3) (as so added).

18   An attestation within the meaning of the Representation of the People (England and Wales) Regulations 2001, SI 2001/341, reg 31J is prescribed for the purposes of reg 31G(3) and reg 31H(2)(a) (see head (A) in the text): see reg 31J(1) (as added: see note 10). The attestation:

   (1)   must certify that the safety of the applicant, or of another named person of the same household as him, would be at risk if the register contained the name of the applicant or his qualifying address (reg 31J(2)(a) (as so added));

   (2)   must state the date on which it is made (reg 31J(2)(b) (as so added)); and

   (3)   must be in writing and signed by a qualifying officer (reg 31J(2)(c) (as so added)).

For these purposes, 'qualifying officer' means a police officer of or above the rank of superintendent of any police force in England and Wales, the Director General of the Security Service, the Director General of the National Crime Agency, any director of adult social services in England within the meaning of the Local Authority Social Services Act 1970 s 6(A1) (see SOCIAL SERVICES AND COMMUNITY CARE vol 44(2) (Reissue) PARA 1007), any director of children's services in England within the meaning of the Children Act 2004 s 18 (see CHILDREN AND YOUNG PERSONS vol 9 (2012) PARA 207) and, in relation to Wales, any director of social services in Wales within the meaning of the Local Authority Social Services Act 1970 s 6(1) (see SOCIAL SERVICES AND COMMUNITY CARE vol 44(2) (Reissue) PARA 1007): see the Representation of the People (England and Wales) Regulations 2001, SI 2001/341, reg 31J(4) (s 31J as so added; s 31J(4) amended by SI 2009/725). The attestation must state the period for which it has effect, being a period of between one and five years beginning with the date on which the attestation is made: Representation of the People (England and Wales) Regulations 2001, SI 2001/341, reg 31J(3) (as so added). As to the meanings of 'England' and 'Wales' see PARA 1 note 1. Under the Local Authority Social Services Act 1970 s 6(A1), a local authority in England must appoint an officer, to be known as the director of adult social services, for the purposes of its social services functions, other than those for which the authority's director of children's services is responsible under the Children Act 2004 s 18: see SOCIAL SERVICES AND COMMUNITY CARE vol 44(2) (Reissue) PARA 1007. As to the Security Service see CONSTITUTIONAL LAW AND HUMAN RIGHTS vol 8(2) (Reissue) PARA 471; and as to ranks that may be held in a police force in England and Wales see POLICE AND INVESTIGATORY POWERS vol 84 (2013) PARA 169 et seq. As to the National Crime Agency (which absorbed and replaced the Serious Organised Crime Agency with effect from 1 October 2013) see the Crime and Courts Act 2013 Pt 1 (ss 1–16); and POLICE AND INVESTIGATORY POWERS.

19   See the Representation of the People (England and Wales) Regulations 2001, SI 2001/341, reg 31G(5) (as added: see note 10).

20   Representation of the People (England and Wales) Regulations 2001, SI 2001/341, reg 31G(5)(a) (as added: see note 10).

21   Representation of the People (England and Wales) Regulations 2001, SI 2001/341, reg 31G(5)(b) (as added: see note 10). The text refers to the evidence provided in pursuance of reg 31G(3) (see the text and notes 16–18): see reg 31G(5)(b) (as so added).

22 Ie where the evidence is provided in pursuance of the Representation of the People (England and Wales) Regulations 2001, SI 2001/341, reg 31G(4) (see note 16): see reg 31G(5)(c) (as added: see note 10).

23 Representation of the People (England and Wales) Regulations 2001, SI 2001/341, reg 31G(5)(c)(i) (as added: see note 10).

24 Ie in pursuance of the Representation of the People (England and Wales) Regulations 2001, SI 2001/341, reg 31G(4) (see note 16): see reg 31G(5)(c)(ii) (as added: see note 10).

25 Representation of the People (England and Wales) Regulations 2001, SI 2001/341, reg 31G(5)(c)(ii) (as added: see note 10).

26 Representation of the People (England and Wales) Regulations 2001, SI 2001/341, reg 31G(6) (as added: see note 10).

27 As to registration officers see PARA 139.

28 For the purposes of the Representation of the People Act 1983 s 9B, 'determines' means determines in accordance with regulations: see s 9B(11) (as added: see note 1). As to the regulations made see the Representation of the People (England and Wales) Regulations 2001, SI 2001/341, reg 31H; and the text and notes 29–38.

29 See the Representation of the People Act 1983 s 9B(2) (as added: see note 1); and the Representation of the People (England and Wales) Regulations 2001, SI 2001/341, reg 31H(1)(a) (as added: see note 10). See note 28.

30 Ie in accordance with the Representation of the People (England and Wales) Regulations 2001, SI 2001/341, reg 31G(1), (2) (see the text and notes 10–15) and reg 31G(5) (see the text and notes 19–25): see reg 31H(1)(b) (as added: see note 10).

31 Representation of the People (England and Wales) Regulations 2001, SI 2001/341, reg 31H(1)(b) (as added: see note 10).

32 See the Representation of the People Act 1983 s 9B(2) (as added: see note 1).
    As from a day to be appointed under the Electoral Registration and Administration Act 2013 s 27(1), the Representation of the People Act 1983 s 9B(2) is substituted so that a registration officer who receives an application for an anonymous entry must determine whether the safety test is satisfied (unless, in the case of an application under s 9B(1)(a) (see note 1), the person's application for registration has been rejected otherwise than by virtue of s 9B): see s 9B(2) (s 9B as so added; s 9B(2) prospectively substituted (see note 1)). At the date at which this volume states the law, no such day had been appointed.

33 Representation of the People Act 1983 s 9B(10) (as added: see note 1). As to the meaning of 'qualifying address' see PARA 145 note 5.

34 See the Representation of the People (England and Wales) Regulations 2001, SI 2001/341, reg 31H(2) (as added: see note 10).

35 Ie in pursuance of the Representation of the People (England and Wales) Regulations 2001, SI 2001/341, reg 31G(3) (see the text and note 16): see reg 31H(2)(a) (as added: see note 10).

36 Representation of the People (England and Wales) Regulations 2001, SI 2001/341, reg 31H(2)(a) (as added: see note 10). The text refers to evidence of the nature prescribed in reg 31I (evidence of relevant court orders or injunctions: see the text and note 17) or reg 31J (evidence by attestation: see the text and note 18): see reg 31H(2)(a) (as so added).

37 Ie where the Representation of the People (England and Wales) Regulations 2001, SI 2001/341, reg 31G(4) applies (see note 16): see reg 31H(2)(b) (as added: see note 10).

38 Representation of the People (England and Wales) Regulations 2001, SI 2001/341, reg 31H(2)(b) (as added: see note 10).

148. Procedure for determining applications for anonymous entry. If the registration officer[1], in considering an application for an anonymous entry[2] in a register of parliamentary electors[3] or local government electors[4], determines[5] that the person is entitled to be registered, he must also determine whether the safety test is satisfied[6].

If the registration officer does not determine that the safety test is satisfied, no entry is to be made in respect of him in the register[7]; but this does not affect any other entry in the register for the person[8] or the determination of any further application for registration which is made by the person[9].

If the registration officer determines that the safety test is satisfied then the usual requirements for a register entry[10] do not apply in relation to the person[11], and the person's entry in the register instead contains letters in the prescribed form and his electoral number (an 'anonymous entry')[12]. If an anonymous entry is made in respect of a person, the registration officer must remove any other entry in the register for that person[13]. Any communication sent by a registration officer or the returning officer[14] for any election to a person who has an anonymous entry must be sent in an envelope or other form of covering so as not to disclose to any other person that the person has an anonymous entry[15].

1   As to registration officers and the areas for which they act see PARA 139.
2   As to applications for an anonymous entry in a register of electors see PARA 147.
3   As to the register of parliamentary electors see PARA 145.
4   As to the register of local government electors see PARA 145.
5   As to the meaning of 'determines' for this purpose see PARA 147 note 28.
6   See the Representation of the People Act 1983 s 9B(2); and PARA 147.
7   Representation of the People Act 1983 s 9B(6) (s 9B added by the Electoral Administration Act 2006 s 10(1)). The text refers to no entry being made, whether an anonymous entry (see the text and note 12) or otherwise: see s 9B(6) (as so added).
    As from a day to be appointed under the Electoral Registration and Administration Act 2013 s 27(1), the Representation of the People Act 1983 s 9B(6) is substituted so that if a person makes an application under s 9B(1)(a) ('an application for an anonymous entry': see PARA 147) and the registration officer determines that the safety test is not satisfied, no entry is to be made in the register as a result of the person's application under s 10ZC (not yet in force) (see PARA 163), whether an anonymous entry or otherwise: see s 9B(6) (s 9B as so added; s 9B(6) prospectively substituted by the Electoral Registration and Administration Act 2013 s 13(1), Sch 4 paras 1, 7(1), (4)). At the date at which this volume states the law, no such day had been appointed.
8   See the Representation of the People Act 1983 s 9B(7)(a) (as added: see note 7).
9   See the Representation of the People Act 1983 s 9B(7)(b) (as added: see note 7). Until a day to be appointed, the determination of any further application for registration made by the person which is treated as having been made by him by virtue of s 10A(2) (see PARA 157) is not affected by s 9B(6): see s 9B(7)(b) (as so added). However, as from a day to be appointed under the Electoral Registration and Administration Act 2013 s 27(1), the Representation of the People Act 1983 s 9B(7)(b) is amended so that this caveat is repealed: see s 9B(7)(b) (s 9B as so added; s 9B(7)(b) amended by the Electoral Registration and Administration Act 2013 Sch 4 paras 1, 7(1), (5)). At the date at which this volume states the law, no such day had been appointed.
10 Ie the requirements of the Representation of the People Act 1983 s 9(2) (see PARA 145): see s 9B(3)(a) (as added: see note 7).
11 Representation of the People Act 1983 s 9B(3)(a) (as added: see note 7).
12 See the Representation of the People Act 1983 s 9B(3)(b), (4) (as added: see note 7). For these purposes, 'anonymous entry', in relation to a register of electors, must be construed in accordance with s 9B; and the 'record of anonymous entries' means the record prepared in pursuance of regulations made by virtue of s 53(1), Sch 2 para 8A (provisions requiring the registration officer to prepare a record of those persons with anonymous entries in the register: see PARA 112): see s 202(1) (definitions added by the Electoral Administration Act 2006 s 10(2), Sch 1 paras 2, 13(1), (2)). As to a person's electoral number see PARA 145.
13 Representation of the People Act 1983 s 9B(5) (as added: see note 7).
    As from a day to be appointed under the Electoral Registration and Administration Act 2013 s 27(1), the Representation of the People Act 1983 s 9B(5) is amended so that it applies to the circumstance where an anonymous entry is made in respect of a person as the result of an application under s 9B(1)(a) ('an application for an anonymous entry': see PARA 147): see s 9B(5) (s 9B as so added; s 9B(5) prospectively amended by the Electoral Registration and Administration Act 2013 Sch 4 paras 1, 7(1), (3)). At the date at which this volume states the law, no such day had been appointed.
14 As to returning officers see PARA 350.
15 Representation of the People Act 1983 s 9B(8) (as added: see note 7).

149.   Effect of register entries and list of proxies.   If any entry in the register of electors[1] gives a date as that on a which the person named will attain voting age[2], the entry is conclusive[3] that until the date given in the entry he is not of voting age nor entitled to be treated as an elector except for purposes of an election[4] at which the day fixed for the poll is that or a later date[5].

A person registered as an elector[6] or entered in the list of proxies[7] cannot be excluded from voting on any of the following grounds[8], namely that:

(1)   he is not of voting age[9];

(2)   that he is not or, on the relevant date[10] (or the date of his appointment, as the case may be, was not)[11]: (a) a Commonwealth citizen[12]; (b) a citizen of the Republic of Ireland[13]; (c) in the case of a person registered as a parliamentary elector or as a European parliamentary elector (as the case may be) in pursuance of an overseas elector's declaration[14], a British citizen[15]; and (d) in the case of a person registered as a local government elector or entered in the list of proxies by virtue of being a relevant citizen of the Union[16], a relevant citizen of the Union[17]; or

(3)   that he is or, on the relevant date (or the date of his appointment, as the case may be) was, otherwise subject to any other legal incapacity to vote[18].

This, however, does not prevent the rejection of the vote on a scrutiny[19] or affect the person's liability to any penalty for voting[20].

1   Ie (1) in relation to parliamentary and local government elections, the register of parliamentary or local government electors (see the Representation of the People Act 1983 s 49(4)); (2) in relation to European parliamentary elections, any part of: (a) a register of parliamentary or, in the case of peers, local government electors; (b) a register under the Representation of the People Act 1985 s 3 (peers resident outside the United Kingdom registered as European parliamentary electors: see PARA 101); (c) a register under the European Parliamentary Elections (Franchise of Relevant Citizens of the Union) Regulations 2001, SI 2001/1184, reg 5 (see PARA 143); and (d) the Gibraltar register (see PARA 116 note 2), in force within an electoral region at the time of a European parliamentary election in that region (see the European Parliamentary Elections Regulations 2004, SI 2004/293, reg 2(1); and PARA 111 note 4); and (3) in relation to Welsh Assembly elections, the register of local government electors (see the National Assembly for Wales (Representation of the People) Order 2007, SI 2007/236, art 2(1)). As to the meaning of 'United Kingdom' see PARA 1 note 1. As to electoral regions established for the purposes of European parliamentary elections see PARA 77; and as to the registers of electors generally see PARA 143 et seq.

     For the purposes of extending the rights of citizens and nationals of accession states who (subject to the requirements of registration) may vote at local government and European parliamentary elections, the Representation of the People Act 1983 s 49, and the National Assembly for Wales (Representation of the People) Order 2007, SI 2007/236, art 26, are applied with modifications: see the Local and European Parliamentary Elections (Registration of Citizens of Accession States) Regulations 2003, SI 2003/1557, regs 2(1), (4), 7, Sch 2 para 6(1), (3); and the Interpretation Act 1978 s 17(2)(b).

     The Representation of the People Act 1983 s 49(4), (5) has been applied and modified also in order to make provision for the conduct of local authority referendums, in relation to Wales, by the Local Authorities (Conduct of Referendums) (Wales) Regulations 2008, SI 2008/1848, reg 8(2), Sch 4 Table 1, and, in relation to England, by the Local Authorities (Conduct of Referendums) (England) Regulations 2012, SI 2012/323, regs 8(2), 11–13, Sch 4 Table 1: see PARA 15 note 2. As to the meanings of 'England' and 'Wales' see PARA 1 note 1.

2   'Voting age' is currently 18 years for all purposes: see PARAS 95 note 2, 97 note 14, 102 note 10.

3   Ie for any purpose of the Representation of the People Act 1983 Pt I (ss 1–66B), or the European Parliamentary Elections Regulations 2004, SI 2004/293, Pt 1 (regs 1–30), or the National Assembly for Wales (Representation of the People) Order 2007, SI 2007/236, Pt 2 (arts 3–36), relating to the person named as elector: see the Representation of the People Act 1983 s 49(4); the European Parliamentary Elections Regulations 2004, SI 2004/293, reg 17(1); and the National Assembly for Wales (Representation of the People) Order 2007, SI 2007/236, art 26(1). See note 1.

4   As to the meaning of 'election' see PARA 3 note 1.

5   Representation of the People Act 1983 s 49(4); European Parliamentary Elections Regulations 2004, SI 2004/293, reg 17(1); National Assembly for Wales (Representation of the People) Order 2007, SI 2007/236, art 26(1). See note 1. The Representation of the People Act 1983 s 49(4), the European Parliamentary Elections Regulations 2004, SI 2004/293, reg 17(1), and the National Assembly for Wales (Representation of the People) Order 2007,

SI 2007/236, art 26(1), all apply to an entry in the record of anonymous entries as each applies to an entry in the register of electors: Representation of the People Act 1983 s 49(4A) (added by the Electoral Administration Act 2006 s 10(2), Sch 1 paras 2, 7); European Parliamentary Elections Regulations 2004, SI 2004/293, reg 17(1A) (added by SI 2009/186); National Assembly for Wales (Representation of the People) Order 2007, SI 2007/236, art 26(5). As to the meaning of the 'record of anonymous entries' see PARA 148 note 12.

6 Ie in relation to parliamentary and local government elections, as a parliamentary or local government elector (see the Representation of the People Act 1983 s 49(5) (substituted by SI 1995/1948)), in relation to European parliamentary elections, as any person whose name is for the time being on the register of electors (see note 1), but not including those shown in the register as below voting age on the day fixed for the poll (see the European Parliamentary Elections Regulations 2004, SI 2004/293, reg 2(1) (substituted by SI 2009/186)), and in relation to Welsh Assembly elections, as a local government elector only (see the National Assembly for Wales (Representation of the People) Order 2007, SI 2007/236, art 26(2)).

7 As to the meaning of the 'list of proxies' see PARA 373 note 14.

8 See the Representation of the People Act 1983 s 49(5) (as substituted: see note 6); the European Parliamentary Elections Regulations 2004, SI 2004/293, reg 17(2); and the National Assembly for Wales (Representation of the People) Order 2007, SI 2007/236, art 26(2). See note 1.

9 Representation of the People Act 1983 s 49(5)(a) (as substituted: see note 6); European Parliamentary Elections Regulations 2004, SI 2004/293, reg 17(2)(a); National Assembly for Wales (Representation of the People) Order 2007, SI 2007/236, art 26(3)(a). See note 1.

10 For these purposes, the 'relevant date' means, in relation to a person registered in the register in question (see note 1) as published in accordance with the Representation of the People Act 1983 s 13(1) (see PARA 165), the 15 October immediately preceding the date of publication of the register or, in relation to any other person registered in the register in question, the 'relevant date' for the purposes of s 4 (entitlement to be registered as parliamentary or local government elector: see PARA 113 note 4): s 49(6) (added by the Representation of the People Act 2000 s 8, Sch 1 paras 1, 12(1), (4)); European Parliamentary Elections Regulations 2004, SI 2004/293, reg 17(3); National Assembly for Wales (Representation of the People) Order 2007, SI 2007/236, art 26(4). In relation to a person entered in the Gibraltar register, the 'relevant date' means the date on which an application for registration is made or treated as having been made by virtue of the European Parliamentary Elections Regulations 2004, SI 2004/293, reg 12, Sch 4 para 6 (see PARA 100 note 3): see reg 17(3). See note 1.

As from a day to be appointed under the Electoral Registration and Administration Act 2013 s 27(1), the Representation of the People Act 1983 s 49(5)(b), (c) is amended, and s 49(6) repealed, by the Electoral Registration and Administration Act 2013 s 13(1), Sch 4 paras 1, 16(1)–(3), and the amendments made by the Representation of the People Act 2000 Sch 1 paras 1, 12(1), (3), (4) are repealed accordingly by the Electoral Registration and Administration Act 2013 Sch 4 paras 1, 22. At the date at which this volume states the law, no such day had been appointed.

11 Representation of the People Act 1983 s 49(5)(b) (s 49 as substituted (see note 6); s 49(5)(b) amended by the Representation of the People Act 2000 Sch 1 paras 1, 12(1), (3)); European Parliamentary Elections Regulations 2004, SI 2004/293, reg 17(2)(b); National Assembly for Wales (Representation of the People) Order 2007, SI 2007/236, art 26(3)(b). See note 1.

As from a day to be appointed under the Electoral Registration and Administration Act 2013 s 27(1), the Representation of the People Act 1983 s 49(5)(b) is amended so that it applies simply to a person who is not or was not at any particular time falling within s 49(5)(b)(i)–(iv) (see heads (2)(a) to (2)(d) in the text): see s 49(5)(b) (prospectively amended by the Electoral Registration and Administration Act 2013 Sch 4 paras 1, 16(1), (2)(a), 22). See note 10. At the date at which this volume states the law, no such day had been appointed.

12 Representation of the People Act 1983 s 49(5)(b)(i) (as substituted: see note 6); European Parliamentary Elections Regulations 2004, SI 2004/293, reg 17(2)(b)(i); National Assembly for Wales (Representation of the People) Order 2007, SI 2007/236, art 26(3)(b)(i). See note 1. As to who are Commonwealth citizens see BRITISH NATIONALITY vol 4 (2011) PARA 409.

13 Representation of the People Act 1983 s 49(5)(b)(ii) (as substituted: see note 6); European Parliamentary Elections Regulations 2004, SI 2004/293, reg 17(2)(b)(ii); National Assembly for Wales (Representation of the People) Order 2007, SI 2007/236, art 26(3)(b)(ii). The provision made by the European Parliamentary Elections Regulations 2004, SI 2004/293, reg 17(2)(b)(ii), does not apply in relation to a person registered in the Gibraltar register: see reg 17(4)(a). See note 1. As to who are citizens of the Republic of Ireland see BRITISH NATIONALITY vol 4 (2011) PARA 410.

14 For these purposes, 'overseas elector's declaration' has the meaning given by the Representation of the People Act 1985 s 2 (see PARA 114): see the Representation of the People Act 1983 s 202(1) (definition added by the Representation of the People Act 1985 s 4(5), Sch 2 Pt I).

15 Representation of the People Act 1983 s 49(5)(b)(iii) (as substituted: see note 6); European Parliamentary Elections Regulations 2004, SI 2004/293, reg 17(2)(b)(iii). In relation to a person entered in the Gibraltar register, reg 17(2)(b)(iii) is modified so that it refers to a Commonwealth citizen rather than a British citizen: see reg 17(4)(b). See note 1. As to who are British citizens see BRITISH NATIONALITY vol 4 (2011) PARAS 406, 421 et seq.

16 For the purposes of the European Parliamentary Elections Regulations 2004, SI 2004/293, 'citizen of the Union' must be construed in accordance with the Treaty on the Functioning of the European Union (Rome, 25 March 1957; TS 1 (1973); Cmnd 5179) ('TFEU') art 20 (formerly art 17 TEC: see PARA 6 note 1), which states that every person holding the nationality of a member state is a citizen of the Union; and 'relevant citizen of the Union' means such a citizen who is not a Commonwealth citizen or a citizen of the Republic of Ireland: see the European Parliamentary Elections Regulations 2004, SI 2004/293, reg 2(1) (substituted by SI 2009/186). As to the meaning of 'relevant citizen of the Union' in relation to the Representation of the People Act 1983 see PARA 97 note 13.

17 Representation of the People Act 1983 s 49(5)(b)(iv) (as substituted: see note 6); European Parliamentary Elections Regulations 2004, SI 2004/293, reg 17(2)(b)(iv); National Assembly for Wales (Representation of the People) Order 2007, SI 2007/236, art 26(3)(b)(iii). For the purposes of the National Assembly for Wales (Representation of the People) Order 2007, SI 2007/236, 'relevant citizen of the Union' means a citizen of the Union who is not a qualifying Commonwealth citizen or a citizen of the Republic of Ireland; and 'citizen of the Union' must be construed in accordance with the Treaty on the Functioning of the European Union (Rome, 25 March 1957; TS 1 (1973); Cmnd 5179) ('TFEU') art 20 (formerly art 17 TEC: see PARA 6 note 1), which states that every person holding the nationality of a member state is a citizen of the Union: see the National Assembly for Wales (Representation of the People) Order 2007, SI 2007/236, art 2(1) (definition amended by SI 2012/1809). For these purposes, 'qualifying Commonwealth citizen' means a Commonwealth citizen who is either: (1) not a person who requires leave under the Immigration Act 1971 to enter or remain in the United Kingdom (see IMMIGRATION AND ASYLUM vol 57 (2012) PARA 5 et seq); or (2) is such a person but for the time being has (or is, by virtue of any enactment, to be treated as having) indefinite leave to remain within the meaning of the Immigration Act 1971 (see IMMIGRATION AND ASYLUM vol 57 (2012) PARAS 17, 140), but a person is not a 'qualifying Commonwealth citizen' for these purposes, if he does not require leave to enter or remain in the United Kingdom by virtue only of the Immigration Act 1971 s 8 (exemptions to requirement for leave in special cases: see IMMIGRATION AND ASYLUM vol 57 (2012) PARA 22 et seq): see the National Assembly for Wales (Representation of the People) Order 2007, SI 2007/236, art 2(1). See note 1.

18 Representation of the People Act 1983 s 49(5)(c) (s 49 as substituted (see note 6); s 49(5)(c) amended by the Representation of the People Act 2000 Sch 1 paras 1, 12(1), (3)); European Parliamentary Elections Regulations 2004, SI 2004/293, reg 17(2)(c); National Assembly for Wales (Representation of the People) Order 2007, SI 2007/236, art 26(3)(c). See note 1. As to the meaning of 'legal incapacity (to vote)' see PARA 95 note 8.

As from a day to be appointed under the Electoral Registration and Administration Act 2013 s 27(1), the Representation of the People Act 1983 s 49(5)(c) is amended so that it applies simply to a person who is or was at any particular time otherwise subject to any other legal incapacity to vote: see s 49(5)(c) (prospectively amended by the Electoral Registration and Administration Act 2013 Sch 4 paras 1, 16(1), (2)(b), 22). See note 10. At the date at which this volume states the law, no such day had been appointed.

19 As to the rejection, on a scrutiny, of votes given by persons under a legal incapacity to vote see PARA 841.

20 See the Representation of the People Act 1983 s 49(5) (as substituted: see note 6); the European Parliamentary Elections Regulations 2004, SI 2004/293, reg 17(2); and the National Assembly for Wales (Representation of the People) Order 2007, SI 2007/236, art 26(2). See note 1.

150. Effect of misdescription in documents published by registration officer.

No misnomer or inaccurate description of any person or place named[1]:

(1) in the register of parliamentary electors[2];

(2) in the register of local government electors[3];

(3) in the register of peers[4] overseas registered as European parliamentary overseas electors[5];

(4)   in the register of relevant citizens of the Union[6] registered as European parliamentary electors[7]; or

(5)   in any required list, record, proxy paper, nomination paper, ballot paper, notice or other document[8],

affects the full operation of the document with respect to that person or place in any case where the description of the person or place is such as to be commonly understood[9].

1   See the Representation of the People Act 1983 s 50; the European Parliamentary Elections Regulations 2004, SI 2004/293, reg 18; and the National Assembly for Wales (Representation of the People) Order 2007, SI 2007/236, art 27.

     For the purposes of extending the rights of peers and of relevant citizens of the Union who (subject to the requirement of registration) may vote at European parliamentary elections, the Representation of the People Act 1983 s 50 is applied with modifications: see the Representation of the People (England and Wales) Regulations 2001, SI 2001/341, reg 13(4), Sch 4 (cited in PARA 101 note 7); and the European Parliamentary Elections (Franchise of Relevant Citizens of the Union) Regulations 2001, SI 2001/1184, reg 9, Schedule (cited in PARA 102 note 6).

     The Representation of the People Act 1983 s 50 is applied and modified for the purpose of local authority mayoral elections in England and Wales by the Local Authorities (Mayoral Elections) (England and Wales) Regulations 2007, SI 2007/1024, reg 3(2)–(5), Sch 2 Table 1: see PARA 11 note 14. As to the meanings of 'England' and 'Wales' see PARA 1 note 1.

2   Representation of the People Act 1983 s 50(a); European Parliamentary Elections Regulations 2004, SI 2004/293, regs 2(1), 18(a) (reg 2(1) substituted by SI 2009/186). See note 1. As to the meaning of 'register of electors', for the purposes of the European Parliamentary Elections Regulations 2004, SI 2004/293, see PARA 111 note 4. As to the register of parliamentary electors see PARA 143.

3   Representation of the People Act 1983 s 50(b); European Parliamentary Elections Regulations 2004, SI 2004/293, regs 2(1), 18(a); National Assembly for Wales (Representation of the People) Order 2007, SI 2007/236, arts 2(1), 27(a). See note 1. As to the register of local government electors see PARA 143.

4   Ie a register under the Representation of the People Act 1985 s 3 (extension of European parliamentary franchise to peers resident outside the United Kingdom: see PARA 101): see the European Parliamentary Elections Regulations 2004, SI 2004/293, regs 2(1), 18(a).

5   See the European Parliamentary Elections Regulations 2004, SI 2004/293, regs 2(1), 18(a).

6   Ie a register under the European Parliamentary Elections (Franchise of Relevant Citizens of the Union) Regulations 2001, SI 2001/1184, reg 5 (see PARA 143): see the European Parliamentary Elections Regulations 2004, SI 2004/293, regs 2(1), 18(a). As to the meaning of 'relevant citizen of the Union' for these purposes see PARA 149 note 16.

7   See the European Parliamentary Elections Regulations 2004, SI 2004/293, regs 2(1), 18(a). The Gibraltar register (see PARA 116 note 2) is also included in the list: see regs 2(1), 18(a).

8   Representation of the People Act 1983 s 50(c); European Parliamentary Elections Regulations 2004, SI 2004/293, reg 18(b); National Assembly for Wales (Representation of the People) Order 2007, SI 2007/236, art 27(b). Head (5) in the text refers to any list, record, proxy paper, nomination paper, ballot paper, notice or other document required for the purposes of the Representation of the People Act 1983 Pt I (ss 1–66B), and the parliamentary elections rules, for the purposes of the European Parliamentary Elections Regulations 2004, SI 2004/293, Pt 1 (regs 1–30), or for the purposes of the National Assembly for Wales (Representation of the People) Order 2007, SI 2007/236, as the case may be: see the Representation of the People Act 1983 s 50(c); the European Parliamentary Elections Regulations 2004, SI 2004/293, reg 18(b); and the National Assembly for Wales (Representation of the People) Order 2007, SI 2007/236, art 27(b). See note 1. As to the meaning of 'parliamentary elections rules' see PARA 383 note 2. As to nomination papers see PARA 255 et seq; as to proxy papers see PARA 367 et seq; and as to ballot papers see PARA 386 et seq.

9   See the Representation of the People Act 1983 s 50; the European Parliamentary Elections Regulations 2004, SI 2004/293, reg 18; and the National Assembly for Wales (Representation of the People) Order 2007, SI 2007/236, art 27. See note 1. As to the offence of providing false information for any purpose connected with the registration of electors see the Representation of the People Act 1983 s 13D; and PARA 735.

B. MAINTENANCE OF ELECTORAL RECORDS

(A) System of Registration based on Annual Canvass

151. Annual canvass. Until a day to be appointed[1], each registration officer in Great Britain[2] must conduct an annual canvass in relation to the area for which he acts[3] for the purpose of ascertaining the persons who are for the time being entitled to be, or to remain, registered in his registers[4]. The canvass for any year must be conducted by reference to residence[5] on 15 October in that year[6]. A canvass is not, however, concerned with[7]:

(1)   the registration of persons in respect of residence in penal institutions[8] or mental hospitals[9] or other places at which certain persons[10] may be detained under a relevant order or direction[11];

(2)   the registration of persons in pursuance of declarations of local connection[12], service declarations[13], or overseas electors' declarations[14]; or

(3)   the registration of persons with anonymous entries in the register[15].

The form to be used for the purposes of a canvass must be either a form prescribed for those purposes[16] or a form to the same effect[17].

In connection with a canvass, a registration officer may[18], for the purpose of supplementing the information obtained by the use of any such form[19] or, where any such form has not been returned, obtaining any information designed to be obtained by the use of the form[20], make such house to house inquiries as he thinks fit[21].

On the conclusion of a canvass, a registration officer must make such alterations in his registers as fall to be made[22] as a result of the canvass[23].

1   As from a day to be appointed under the Electoral Registration and Administration Act 2013 s 27(1), the Representation of the People Act 1983 s 10 (substituted by the Representation of the People Act 2000 s 8, Sch 1 paras 1, 4) is amended by the Electoral Registration and Administration Act 2013 s 13(1), Sch 4 paras 1, 9, so that its effect is limited to Northern Ireland only. Amendments made to the Representation of the People Act 1983 s 10(3) by the Electoral Administration Act 2006 s 10(2), Sch 1 paras 2, 5 (see the text and note 15) are repealed by the Electoral Registration and Administration Act 2013 Sch 4 paras 1, 23 accordingly. The provision made by the prospectively amended Representation of the People Act 1983 s 10 will then complement s 10ZA (added by the Northern Ireland (Miscellaneous provisions) Act 2006 s 3) (Northern Ireland: timing of canvass). However, at the date at which this volume states the law, no such day had been appointed. Because the prospective amendments apply to Northern Ireland only, their effect is not set out in any detail. As to reform of the system of registration based on an annual canvass of households see PARA 152; as to the power to abolish or amend the annual canvass in Great Britain see PARA 153; and as to the registration officers' duty to conduct an annual canvass in Great Britain compatible with the system of individual registration see PARA 154.

2   As to the meaning of 'Great Britain' see PARA 1 note 1. As to registration officers see PARA 139.

3   As to the area for which a registration officer acts see PARA 139.

4   Representation of the People Act 1983 s 10(1) (s 10 as substituted (see note 1); s 10(1) amended by the Northern Ireland (Miscellaneous provisions) Act 2006 s 2(1), (2)). As to references, in relation to a registration officer, to 'his' registers see PARA 143 note 3. As to the duty of registration officers to maintain, prepare and publish registers of electors see PARA 143.

      As from a day to be appointed under the Electoral Registration and Administration Act 2013 s 27(1), the Representation of the People Act 1983 s 10(1) is repealed by the Electoral Registration and Administration Act 2013 Sch 4 paras 1, 9(1), (2) (see note 1). However, at the date at which this volume states the law, no such day had been appointed.

5   For these purposes, 'residence' means residence for the purposes of the Representation of the People Act 1983 s 4 (entitlement to be registered as parliamentary or local government elector: see PARA 113): s 10(7) (as substituted: see note 1).

6   Representation of the People Act 1983 s 10(2) (s 10 as substituted (see note 1); s 10(2) amended by the Northern Ireland (Miscellaneous provisions) Act 2006 s 2(1), (4)).

As from a day to be appointed under the Electoral Registration and Administration Act 2013 s 27(1), the Representation of the People Act 1983 s 10(2) is amended by the Electoral Registration and Administration Act 2013 Sch 4 paras 1, 9(1), (3) so that its effect is limited to the Representation of the People Act 1983 s 10(1A) (added by the Northern Ireland (Miscellaneous provisions) Act 2006 s 2(1), (3)), excluding the Representation of the People Act 1983 s 10(1) (prospectively repealed) (see notes 1, 4). However, at the date at which this volume states the law, no such day had been appointed.

As part of the transitional arrangements for the implementation of individual electoral registration under the Electoral Registration and Administration Act 2013 (see PARA 156), the Representation of the People Act 1983 s 10(2) does not apply in respect of the annual canvass for 2013 (ie the annual canvass which, but for the Electoral Registration (Postponement of 2013 Annual Canvass) Order 2013, SI 2013/794, each registration officer would be required under the Representation of the People Act 1983 s 10(2) to conduct by reference to residence on 15 October 2013) in any area in Great Britain: see the Electoral Registration (Postponement of 2013 Annual Canvass) Order 2013, SI 2013/794, art 4(1)(a). Accordingly, the annual canvass for 2013 to be conducted under the Representation of the People Act 1983 s 10(1) is postponed, and a registration officer must not conduct any part of that canvass before 1 October 2013: see the Electoral Registration (Postponement of 2013 Annual Canvass) Order 2013, SI 2013/794, art 2(1), (2). That canvass must be conducted instead within the period starting on 1 October 2013 and ending on 17 February 2014 in relation to England and on 10 March 2014 in relation to Scotland and Wales: see art 2(3). As to the meanings of 'England' and 'Wales' see PARA 1 note 1.

7 See the Representation of the People Act 1983 s 10(3) (as substituted: see note 1).
    As from a day to be appointed under the Electoral Registration and Administration Act 2013 s 27(1), the Representation of the People Act 1983 s 10(3) is amended, and s 10(3)(c) (see head (3) in the text) repealed, by the Electoral Registration and Administration Act 2013 Sch 4 paras 1, 9(1), (4) (see note 1). However, at the date at which this volume states the law, no such day had been appointed.

8 Ie within the meaning of the Representation of the People Act 1983 s 3 (see PARA 107 note 2): see s 10(3)(a) (as substituted: see note 1).

9 Ie within the meaning of the Representation of the People Act 1983 s 7 (see PARA 119 note 3): see s 10(3)(a) (as substituted: see note 1).

10 Ie persons to whom the Representation of the People Act 1983 s 7A (deemed residence of persons remanded in custody: see PARA 120) applies: see s 10(3)(a) (as substituted: see note 1).

11 Representation of the People Act 1983 s 10(3)(a) (as substituted: see note 1). As to the orders or directions referred to in the text see PARA 120 note 3.

12 Representation of the People Act 1983 s 10(3)(b)(i) (as substituted: see note 1). As to declarations of local connection see PARA 121 et seq.

13 Representation of the People Act 1983 s 10(3)(b)(ii) (as substituted: see note 1). As to service declarations see PARA 125 et seq.

14 Representation of the People Act 1983 s 10(3)(b)(iii) (as substituted: see note 1). As to the meaning of 'overseas elector's declaration' see PARA 149 note 14. As to registration in the register of parliamentary electors in pursuance of an overseas elector's declaration see PARA 114 et seq.

15 Representation of the People Act 1983 s 10(3)(c) (s 10 as substituted (see note 1); s 10(3)(c) added by the Electoral Administration Act 2006 s 10(2), Sch 1 paras 2, 5). As to anonymous entries in a register of electors see PARA 147 et seq.
    As from a day to be appointed under the Electoral Registration and Administration Act 2013 s 27(1), the Representation of the People Act 1983 s 10(3)(c) is repealed by the Electoral Registration and Administration Act 2013 Sch 1 para 23, Sch 4 paras 1, 9(1), (4) (see notes 1, 7). However, at the date at which this volume states the law, no such day had been appointed.

16 For these purposes, 'prescribed' means prescribed by regulations: see the Representation of the People Act 1983 s 202(1). As to the making of regulations under the Representation of the People Act 1983 generally see PARA 28 note 16. As to the regulations made under s 10(4) see the Representation of the People (Form of Canvass) (England and Wales) Regulations 2006, SI 2006/1694. The form prescribed for use for the purposes of the canvass which is required to be conducted by the Representation of the People Act 1983 s 10 is set out in the Representation of the People (Form of Canvass) (England and Wales) Regulations 2006, SI 2006/1694, accordingly: see regs 3, 4, Schedule Pts 1, 2 (Form of Canvass and Form of Words about the Two Versions of the Register). As to modifications made to the Schedule, following the postponement of the annual canvass for 2013 (see note 6), see the Electoral Registration (Postponement of 2013 Annual Canvass) Order 2013, SI 2013/794, art 4(2).

17 Representation of the People Act 1983 s 10(4) (as substituted: see note 1).

As from a day to be appointed under the Electoral Registration and Administration Act 2013 s 27(1), the Representation of the People Act 1983 s 10(4) is substituted, and the substitution of s 10(4),and the incidental addition of s 10(4C), (4D), by the Political Parties and Elections Act 2009 s 33(2), (3) (not yet in force) are repealed (see PARA 152), by the Electoral Registration and Administration Act 2013 Sch 4 paras 1, 9(1), (5), 24 (see note 1). However, at the date at which this volume states the law, no such day had been appointed.

18 See the Representation of the People Act 1983 s 10(5) (as substituted: see note 1).

As from a day to be appointed under the Electoral Registration and Administration Act 2013 s 27(1), the Representation of the People Act 1983 s 10(5) is amended so that the reference to a registration officer becomes a reference to the Chief Electoral Officer for Northern Ireland: see s 10(5) (prospectively amended by the Electoral Registration and Administration Act 2013 Sch 4 paras 1, 9(1), (7)). See note 1. However, at the date at which this volume states the law, no such day had been appointed.

19 Representation of the People Act 1983 s 10(5)(a) (as substituted: see note 1).

20 Representation of the People Act 1983 s 10(5)(b) (as substituted: see note 1).

21 See the Representation of the People Act 1983 s 10(5) (as substituted: see note 1). See note 18. As to the registration officer's general powers to require information about electors and to inspect certain records see PARA 142.

22 Ie in accordance with the Representation of the People Act 1983 s 10A (maintenance of the registers (registration of electors): see PARA 157): see s 10(6) (as substituted: see note 1).

23 Representation of the People Act 1983 s 10(6) (as substituted: see note 1).

As from a day to be appointed under the Electoral Registration and Administration Act 2013 s 27(1), the Representation of the People Act 1983 s 10(6) is amended so that the reference to a registration officer becomes a reference to the Chief Electoral Officer for Northern Ireland: see s 10(6) (prospectively amended by the Electoral Registration and Administration Act 2013 Sch 4 paras 1, 9(1), (8)). See note 1. However, at the date at which this volume states the law, no such day had been appointed.

152. Reform of the system of registration based on annual canvass of households. The electoral registration system based on an annual canvass of households[1] dates from the early part of the twentieth century and relies upon an unsupported declaration from those who register to vote that they are indeed eligible[2]. Egregious examples of voter fraud[3] prompted Parliament to pass legislation that paved the way for, and then introduced, a system of Individual Electoral Registration, requiring each individual elector to apply to register to vote, and for each elector to provide personal identifiers allowing any such application to be verified before a name is added to the register[4].

Part 2 of the Electoral Administration Act 2006 had already taken some steps to improve the completeness and accuracy of registers by imposing a new duty on EROs to identify as many eligible electors as possible and to register them, and by establishing a scheme of anonymous registration for people whose safety would be threatened by publication on the electoral register[5]; Part 3 of that Act introduced a requirement for persons applying to vote by post or proxy to supply personal identifiers as a measure against fraud[6]. Part 4 of the Political Parties and Elections Act 2009 provided for the phased implementation of individual electoral registration in Great Britain, with additional identifying information (National Insurance (NI) number, date of birth, signature) being provided on a voluntary basis by those wishing to register from 2010 to 2015, and on a compulsory basis from 2015 (including information gathered from other public sector databases for the purpose of maintaining a complete and accurate electoral register by means of 'data-matching' schemes), subject to a positive recommendation by the Electoral Commission and Parliament that the system is ready for the change[7].

However, it was not until 2011 that a White Paper was published announcing a compulsory scheme of individual electoral registration, with the stated aims of reducing electoral fraud and restoring voters' confidence in the system by improving the completeness, accuracy and security of the register, as well as making the registration system more accessible to all by providing the means for eligible people to register themselves more easily[8]. Part 1 of the Electoral Registration and Administration Act 2013 makes provision, including transitional arrangements, for the register of electors to be published under a new individual electoral registration system (likely to be the register used for the 2015 general election), for the use of data matching to check entries on the register, and for an annual canvass which is compatible with the new system[9] (together with a power to amend or abolish the annual canvass in future, subject to a report by the Electoral Commission and an order requiring the approval by a resolution of each House of Parliament)[10]. The Electoral Registration and Administration Act 2013 also repeals those provisions in Part 4 of the Political Parties and Elections Act 2009 concerning the previous voluntary and compulsory schemes of individual electoral registration in Great Britain which are replaced by the 2013 Act, and the previous powers on data schemes, which will be superseded by those contained in the 2013 Act[11].

1   Ie whereby each household is asked to provide a list of eligible electors at that address (subject to provision made, outside of the annual canvass process, for an individual elector to submit this information on a 'rolling registration' application form): see PARA 151.

2   See PARA 151. Although no evidence of eligibility to vote is required by the canvass form, an electoral registration officer (ERO) who has doubts about a person's age or nationality may require that person to produce for the purposes of registration certain specified evidence: see PARA 142. However, the system is largely paper based and lacks efficiency.

3   See eg *In the Matter of Local Government Elections for the Aston and Bordesley Green Wards of the Birmingham City Council held on 10 June 2004, Akhtar v Jahan, Iqbal v Islam* [2005] All ER (D) 15 (Apr), Election Ct (revsd in part: *R (on the application of Afzal) v Election Court* [2005] EWCA Civ 647, [2005] LGR 823, [2005] All ER (D) 415 (May)); *Re Central Ward, Slough Election Petition, Simmons v Khan* [2008] EWHC B4 (QB), Election Ct; and PARA 754.

4   See the text and notes 5–11.

5   See the Electoral Administration Act 2006 Pt 2 (ss 9–13); and PARAS 147, 148, 169.

6   See the Electoral Administration Act 2006 Pt 3 (ss 14–15); and PARAS 363 et seq, 735.

7   See the Political Parties and Elections Act 2009 Pt 4 (ss 28–37) (Electoral Registration); and the text and note 11. Many of those provisions will be repealed without having been commenced: see the text and note 11.

8   See *Individual Electoral Registration* (June 2011) (Cm 8108) (which included draft legislation and was accompanied by a programme for consultation).

9   See the Electoral Registration and Administration Act 2013 Pt 1 (ss 1–13, Schs 1–5) (individual electoral registration in Great Britain); and PARA 153 et seq. As to transitional arrangements see s 13, Sch 5; and PARA 156.

10   See the Electoral Registration and Administration Act 2013 ss 7–11; and PARA 153.

11   The Political Parties and Elections Act 2009 ss 30–34 (electoral registration: provision of identifying information), 35, 36 (data schemes for the purpose of maintaining a complete and accurate electoral register and ensuring that any other information held on electors is accurate) and s 37 (interpretation) are all prospectively repealed by the Electoral Registration and Administration Act 2013 s 13(1), Sch 4 paras 1, 24. See also the Electoral Registration Data Schemes Order 2011, SI 2011/1466 (revoked by SI 2012/1944); the Representation of the People (Electoral Registration Data Schemes) Regulations 2011, SI 2011/1467 (made in exercise of the powers conferred by the Representation of the People Act 1983 ss 53(1), (3), 201(3), Sch 2 para 10B(1)(a), (2), but in relation to a scheme in an order made in exercise of the powers conferred by the Political Parties and Elections Act 2009 ss 35, 36 authorising or requiring a person to provide information to an electoral registration officer, that officer may pass a copy of an electoral register that they have compiled (or part of it) to another person in order for the register to be compared with information kept by the person authorised or required to provide information under the scheme); the Electoral Registration Data Schemes Order 2012, SI 2012/1944 (made in exercise of the powers conferred by the Political Parties and Elections Act 2009 ss 35, 36, establishing schemes for the Secretary of State for Work and Pensions to provide data to specified electoral registration officers, in order to assist them in meeting the registration objectives set out at s 31(8)); and the Electoral Registration Data Schemes (No 2)

Order 2012, SI 2012/3232 (made in exercise of the powers conferred by the Political Parties and Elections Act 2009 ss 35, 36, establishing schemes for the provision of data to specified electoral registration officers, in order to assist them in meeting the registration objectives set out at s 31(8)). See also the Lord President of the Council Order 2010, SI 2010/1837. The remainder of the Political Parties and Elections Act 2009 Pt 4 (ie ss 28, 29) dealt with the schemes made in connection with the co-ordinated on-line record of electors ('CORE'), established by the Electoral Administration Act 2006 Pt 1 (ss 1–8), which is repealed by the Electoral Registration and Administration Act 2013 s 23(1): see the Electoral Registration and Administration Act 2013 (Commencement No 2) Order 2013, SI 2013/702, art 3(e).

153.   Power to abolish or amend the annual canvass in Great Britain.   As from a day to be appointed[1], the Minister[2] may by order[3]:

(1)   make provision for the purposes of assisting registration officers in Great Britain to ascertain[4]: (a) the names and addresses of persons who are not registered in a register but who are entitled to be registered[5]; (b) those persons who are registered in a register but who are not entitled to be registered[6];

(2)   modify the provision made by the Representation of the People Act 1983 that imposes a duty to conduct an annual canvass in Great Britain[7] (or any other provision relating to such a canvass)[8], and abolish that duty to conduct a canvass[9].

If the duty to conduct a canvass is abolished under head (2) above, then the provision that may be made under head (1) above includes provision reinstating the duty[10].

Such an order may be made so as to have effect in relation to a specified period[11] (referred to for these purposes as a 'pilot scheme')[12]. The Minister may make a pilot scheme applying in relation to an area, however, only if the registration officer for that area has proposed the making of a pilot scheme in relation to that area, and has agreed to any modifications made by the Minister to the proposal[13]. A pilot scheme may be replaced by a further pilot scheme[14].

The Minister may by order[15] make provision for the purpose of testing, for a specified period and in relation to a specified area, how the changes made by any registration provision work in practice[16]; but he may make such an order in relation to an area only if the registration officer for that area has proposed the making of an order in relation to that area, and has agreed to any modifications made by the Minister to the proposal[17].

1   The Electoral Registration and Administration Act 2013 ss 7–12 come into force as from a day to be appointed under s 27(1). At the date at which this volume states the law, such a day had been appointed in relation to s 10 (ie 2 April 2013: see the Electoral Registration and Administration Act 2013 (Commencement No 2) Order 2013, SI 2013/702, art 3(a)) (see the text and notes 15–17), and in relation to the Electoral Registration and Administration Act 2013 s 11 (ie 25 March 2013: see the Electoral Registration and Administration Act 2013 (Commencement No 2) Order 2013, SI 2013/702, art 2) (see note 3), but not in relation to the Electoral Registration and Administration Act 2013 ss 7–9.

2   Ie the Secretary of State or the Lord President of the Council: see the Electoral Registration and Administration Act 2013 s 25(1). As to the Secretary of State and the Lord President of the Council see PARA 2.

3   See the Electoral Registration and Administration Act 2013 s 7(1), (2) (not yet in force: see note 1). Any order made under Pt 1 (ss 1–13) (individual electoral registration in Great Britain) is to be made by statutory instrument (s 11(1)); but a statutory instrument containing such an order (whether alone or with other provision) may not be made unless a draft of the instrument has been laid before and approved by a resolution of each House of Parliament (s 11(2)). Such an order may make consequential, supplementary, incidental, transitional or saving provision (s 11(3)), may modify any other Act or subordinate legislation, whenever passed or made (s 11(4)), may apply generally or only in specified cases, circumstances or areas, and may make different provision for different cases, circumstances or areas (see s 11(5)). For these purposes,

'modify' includes amend, repeal or revoke; and 'subordinate legislation' has the same meaning as in the Interpretation Act 1978 (see STATUTES AND LEGISLATIVE PROCESS vol 96 (2012) PARA 609): see the Electoral Registration and Administration Act 2013 s 12 (not yet in force). The provision made by s 13(2), Sch 5 para 28 (power to bring forward effect of Sch 5 para 6 (removal of existing registrations after the third new canvass): see PARA 156) contains an exception to s 11(2): see s 11(2), Sch 5 para 28(3).

An order under s 7 may confer power to make subordinate legislation and, if it does so, must provide that the subordinate legislation is to be made by statutory instrument, and that the instrument may not be made unless a draft of it has been laid before and approved by a resolution of each House of Parliament: see s 7(5) (not yet in force). An order under s 7 also may create offences punishable on summary conviction by a fine not exceeding level 5 on the standard scale: s 7(4) (not yet in force). As to the standard scale see SENTENCING AND DISPOSITION OF OFFENDERS vol 92 (2010) PARA 142.

If the Minister consults the Electoral Commission about a proposal to make an order under s 7, the Commission must prepare a report assessing the extent to which the objective in s 8(2) is met, the extent to which the objective would be met if the order were made, and the merits of alternative ways of achieving the objective: see s 8(1) (not yet in force). The objective is to assist registration officers in Great Britain to ascertain (see s 8(2) (not yet in force)):

(1)   the names and addresses of persons who are not registered in a register but who are entitled to be registered (s 8(2)(a) (not yet in force));

(2)   those persons who are registered in a register but who are not entitled to be registered (s 8(2)(b) (not yet in force)).

A registration officer in Great Britain must comply with any request made by the Electoral Commission for information that it reasonably requires in connection with the preparation of a report under s 8: see s 8(5) (not yet in force). The Electoral Commission must give a copy of the report to the Minister by the specified date (being a date to be specified by the Minister which must not be before the end of the period of three months beginning with the day on which the Commission is consulted): see s 8(3), (4) (not yet in force). When a draft of a statutory instrument containing an order under s 7 is laid before Parliament (see s 11), it must be accompanied by a report under s 8, unless the instrument contains provision only for the purpose of reinstating the duty to conduct a canvass as mentioned in s 7(3) (see the text and note 10): s 8(6). For these purposes, 'register' means a register of parliamentary electors or local government electors maintained by a registration officer in Great Britain; and 'registration officer' has the same meaning as in the Representation of the People Act 1983(see s 8; and PARA 139): see the Electoral Registration and Administration Act 2013 s 12 (not yet in force). As to the meaning of 'Great Britain' see PARA 1 note 1. As to registration officers see PARA 139; and as to the duty of registration officers to maintain, prepare and publish registers of electors see PARA 143. As to the establishment and constitution of the Electoral Commission see PARA 34 et seq.

4   See the Electoral Registration and Administration Act 2013 s 7(1) (not yet in force: see note 1).

5   Electoral Registration and Administration Act 2013 s 7(1)(a) (not yet in force: see note 1). As to the entitlement to be registered as an elector see PARA 113 et seq.

6   Electoral Registration and Administration Act 2013 s 7(1)(b) (not yet in force: see note 1).

7   Ie modify the Representation of the People Act 1983 s 9D (not yet in force) (registration officers' duty to conduct annual canvass in Great Britain compatible with system of individual registration: see PARA 154): see the Electoral Registration and Administration Act 2013 s 7(2)(a) (not yet in force: see note 1).

8   Electoral Registration and Administration Act 2013 s 7(2)(a) (not yet in force: see note 1).

9   Electoral Registration and Administration Act 2013 s 7(2)(b) (not yet in force: see note 1).

10   Electoral Registration and Administration Act 2013 s 7(3) (not yet in force: see note 1).

11   See the Electoral Registration and Administration Act 2013 s 9(1) (not yet in force: see note 1). The provision that may be made in a pilot scheme by virtue of s 11(3) (see note 3) includes, in particular, provision in connection with the expiry of the specified period: s 9(5) (not yet in force).

12   See the Electoral Registration and Administration Act 2013 s 9(2) (not yet in force: see note 1). The provision made by s 8 (see note 3) does not apply in relation to a pilot scheme: s 9(4) (not yet in force).

13   See the Electoral Registration and Administration Act 2013 s 9(3) (not yet in force: see note 1). If a pilot scheme is made, the Electoral Commission must prepare a report on the pilot scheme, and, by no later than a date to be specified in the pilot scheme, give a copy of the report to the Minister and to the registration officer for the area concerned (or the officer for each area concerned): see s 9(7) (not yet in force). A registration officer in Great Britain must comply with any request made by the Electoral Commission for information that it reasonably requires in

connection with the preparation of a report under s 9: see s 9(10) (not yet in force). The Electoral Commission's report must contain a description of the pilot scheme, an assessment of the extent to which the objective in s 8(2) (see note 3) was met in the area or areas concerned immediately before the specified period, an assessment of the extent to which the objective was met in the area or areas concerned during the specified period, and an assessment of the extent to which the scheme resulted in savings of time and costs, or the opposite: see s 9(8) (not yet in force). The Minister must publish the Electoral Commission's report: s 9(9) (not yet in force).

14 Electoral Registration and Administration Act 2013 s 9(6) (not yet in force: see note 1).
15 An order under the Electoral Registration and Administration Act 2013 s 10 may, in particular, make provision the effect of which corresponds to the effect of the amendments made by any registration provision (or the subordinate legislation that may be made by virtue of any registration provision): s 10(2). For these purposes, 'registration provision' means any provision of s 1 and Sch 1 (see PARAS 163, 164, 169), s 2 and Sch 2 (see PARA 112), and s 13, Sch 4 (related amendments): s 10(3).
16 Electoral Registration and Administration Act 2013 s 10(1). The provision that may be made in an order under s 10 by virtue of s 11(3) (see note 3) includes, in particular, provision in connection with the expiry of the specified period: s 10(5). An order under s 10 also may make provision modifying s 13, Sch 5 (transitional provision: see PARA 156), for example, to modify the meaning of 'new application for registration': s 10(6).
17 See the Electoral Registration and Administration Act 2013 s 10(4).

(B) System of Individual Electoral Registration in Great Britain

154. Registration officers' duty to conduct annual canvass in Great Britain compatible with system of individual registration. As from a day to be appointed[1], each registration officer in Great Britain[2] must conduct an annual canvass in relation to the area for which the officer acts[3]. The purpose of the canvass is to ascertain[4]:

(1) the names and addresses of persons who are entitled to be registered in a register maintained by the officer but who are not registered[5];

(2) those persons who are registered in such a register but who are not entitled to be registered[6].

The canvass is to be conducted in a manner to be set out in regulations[7] (which may confer functions on the Electoral Commission)[8]; but a registration officer may make house to house inquiries for the purposes of the canvass[9], for example:

(a) to obtain information before sending out a canvass form[10];

(b) to supplement information provided on a canvass form[11]; or

(c) to obtain information where no canvass form is returned[12].

However, nothing in this provision[13] applies in relation to[14]: (i) the registration of persons in respect of residence in penal institutions[15] or mental hospitals[16] or other places at which certain persons[17] may be detained under a relevant order or direction[18]; (ii) the registration of persons in pursuance of declarations of local connection[19], service declarations[20], or overseas electors' declarations[21]; or (iii) the registration of persons with anonymous entries in the register[22].

1 The Representation of the People Act 1983 s 9D is added by the Electoral Registration and Administration Act 2013 s 4, as from a day to be appointed under s 27(1). At the date at which this volume states the law, no such day had been appointed.
2 As to the meaning of 'Great Britain' see PARA 1 note 1. As to registration officers see PARA 139.
3 Representation of the People Act 1983 s 9D(1) (prospectively added: see note 1). As to the areas for which registration officers act see PARA 139.
    Although s 9D restates (with modification) the requirement to conduct an annual canvass in a manner set out in regulations, the Electoral Registration and Administration Act 2013 ss 7–11 (partly in force) give a power to abolish or amend the annual canvass in Great Britain, subject to the specified procedure (see PARA 153).
4 See the Representation of the People Act 1983 s 9D(2) (prospectively added: see note 1).

5   Representation of the People Act 1983 s 9D(2)(a) (prospectively added: see note 1). As to the duty of registration officers to maintain, prepare and publish registers of electors see PARA 143.
6   Representation of the People Act 1983 s 9D(2)(b) (prospectively added: see note 1).
7   See the Representation of the People Act 1983 s 9D(3) (prospectively added: see note 1).
8   See the Representation of the People Act 1983 s 9D(4) (prospectively added: see note 1). For example, the Commission may be required to design a canvass form: see s 9D(4) (prospectively added). As to the establishment and constitution of the Electoral Commission see PARA 34 et seq.
9   See the Representation of the People Act 1983 s 9D(5) (prospectively added: see note 1).
10   Representation of the People Act 1983 s 9D(5)(a) (prospectively added: see note 1).
11   Representation of the People Act 1983 s 9D(5)(b) (prospectively added: see note 1).
12   Representation of the People Act 1983 s 9D(5)(c) (prospectively added: see note 1).
13   Ie nothing in the Representation of the People Act 1983 s 9D: see s 9D(6) (prospectively added: see note 1).
14   See the Representation of the People Act 1983 s 9D(6) (prospectively added: see note 1).
15   Ie within the meaning of the Representation of the People Act 1983 s 3 (see PARA 107 note 2): see s 9D(6)(a) (prospectively added: see note 1).
16   Ie within the meaning of the Representation of the People Act 1983 s 7 (see PARA 119 note 3): see s 9D(6)(a) (prospectively added: see note 1).
17   Ie persons to whom the Representation of the People Act 1983 s 7A (deemed residence of persons remanded in custody: see PARA 120) applies: see s 9D(6)(a) (prospectively added: see note 1).
18   Representation of the People Act 1983 s 9D(6)(a) (prospectively added: see note 1). As to the orders or directions referred to in the text see PARA 120 note 3.
19   As to declarations of local connection see PARA 121 et seq.
20   As to service declarations see PARA 125 et seq.
21   Representation of the People Act 1983 s 9D(6)(b) (prospectively added: see note 1). As to the meaning of 'overseas elector's declaration' see PARA 149 note 14. As to registration in the register of parliamentary electors in pursuance of an overseas elector's declaration see PARA 114 et seq.
22   Representation of the People Act 1983 s 9D(6)(c) (prospectively added: see note 1). As to anonymous entries in a register of electors see PARA 147 et seq.

155.   Registration officers' duty to invite unregistered persons to apply for registration. As from a day to be appointed[1], a registration officer in Great Britain[2] must give a person an invitation to apply for registration in a register maintained by the officer if[3]:

(1)   the officer is aware of the person's name and address[4];
(2)   the person is not registered in the register[5]; and
(3)   the officer has reason to believe that the person may be entitled to be registered in the register[6].

Regulations may make provision about such invitations[7], including: (a) provision about the form and contents of invitations[8]; (b) provision about the giving of invitations[9]; (c) provision requiring invitations to be accompanied by, or combined with, application forms or other documents (including partially completed application forms)[10]; and such regulations may confer functions on the Electoral Commission[11].

A registration officer who gives a person such an invitation may subsequently require the person to make an application for registration by a specified date[12] (although this is of no effect if the person is not entitled to be registered[13]); and a registration officer may impose a civil penalty on a person who fails to comply with a requirement imposed by the officer in this way[14].

1   The Representation of the People Act 1983 s 9E is added by the Electoral Registration and Administration Act 2013 s 5(1), as from a day to be appointed under s 27(1). At the date at which this volume states the law, no such day had been appointed.
2   As to the meaning of 'Great Britain' see PARA 1 note 1. As to registration officers see PARA 139.

3   See the Representation of the People Act 1983 s 9E(1) (prospectively added: see note 1). As to the duty of registration officers to maintain, prepare and publish registers of electors see PARA 143.
4   Representation of the People Act 1983 s 9E(1)(a) (prospectively added: see note 1).
5   Representation of the People Act 1983 s 9E(1)(b) (prospectively added: see note 1).
6   Representation of the People Act 1983 s 9E(1)(c) (prospectively added: see note 1).
7   See the Representation of the People Act 1983 s 9E(2) (prospectively added: see note 1).
8   Representation of the People Act 1983 s 9E(2)(a) (prospectively added: see note 1).
9   Representation of the People Act 1983 s 9E(2)(b) (prospectively added: see note 1). For example, provision may be made under head (b) in the text about the manner in which invitations must be given or how often they must be given: see s 9E(2)(b) (prospectively added).
10   Representation of the People Act 1983 s 9E(2)(c) (prospectively added: see note 1).
11   See the Representation of the People Act 1983 s 9E(3) (prospectively added: see note 1). For example, the Commission may be required to design an invitation: see s 9E(3) (prospectively added). As to the establishment and constitution of the Electoral Commission see PARA 34 et seq.
12   See the Representation of the People Act 1983 s 9E(4) (prospectively added: see note 1). Regulations may make provision about requirements under s 9E(4), including provision for them to be cancelled in specified circumstances, and may specify steps that a registration officer must take before imposing a requirement: see s 9E(6) (prospectively added). As to the making of regulations under the Representation of the People Act 1983 generally see PARA 28 note 16.
13   See the Representation of the People Act 1983 s 9E(5) (prospectively added: see note 1).
14   See the Representation of the People Act 1983 s 9E(7) (prospectively added: see note 1). As to the civil penalty that may be imposed for a failure to make an application for registration when required by the registration officer see s 9E(8), Sch ZA1 (not yet in force); and PARA 756.

156. Transitional arrangements made for introduction of individual registration. Arrangements are required to manage the transitional period after the date appointed for the relevant Electoral Registration and Administration Act 2013 provisions that govern individual electoral registration in Great Britain[1] to come fully into force[2]. These arrangements provide for:

(1)   the checking of old entries and confirmation of entitlement to remain registered, including by means of data matching[3];

(2)   the removal of all registrations made under the annual canvass system by the end of the third new canvass[4];

(3)   the encouragement of new applications from those with existing registrations whose entitlement to remain registered is not confirmed under head (1) above[5];

(4)   the restriction of applications to vote by post or proxy to those registered under the new system (whether by making an application under the new system or by having their entry confirmed under head (1) above)[6];

(5)   providing for persons registered as a result of a declaration of local connection, a service declaration or an overseas elector's declaration, and people registered anonymously[7];

(6)   providing for persons registered who are considered to be resident as a patient in a mental hospital[8] or at a place where they are being detained[9] pursuant to a relevant order or direction otherwise than after being convicted of any offence, or a finding in criminal proceedings that he did the act or made the omission charged[10].

Supplementary provision is also made[11].

1   Ie the Electoral Registration and Administration Act 2013 Pt 1 (ss 1–13, Schs 1–5) (individual electoral registration in Great Britain): see PARAS 153 et seq, 157 et seq. As to the meaning of 'Great Britain' see PARA 1 note 1.
2   See the Electoral Registration and Administration Act 2013 s 13(2), Sch 5; and the text and notes 3–11. Apart from Sch 5 para 28 (power to bring forward effect of Sch 5 para 6 (removal

of existing registrations after the third new canvass)), which came into force at the end of the period of two months beginning with the day on which the Electoral Registration and Administration Act 2013 was passed (ie two months beginning with 31 January 2013: see s 27(2)), the provision made by Sch 5 comes into force as from a day to be appointed under s 27(1). At the date at which this volume states the law, such a day had been appointed in relation to Sch 5 para 4(4) ((application of the Representation of the People Act 1983 s 53(5)–(8)), and in relation to the Electoral Registration and Administration Act 2013 Sch 5 para 9(1), (5)–(7) (powers to delay canvasses and timing of canvasses) (ie 5 February 2013: see the Electoral Registration and Administration Act 2013 (Commencement No 1) Order 2013, SI 2013/219, art 2). However, at the date at which this volume states the law, no such day had been appointed in relation to Sch 5 paras 1–3, 4(1)–(3), (5), 5–8, 9(2)–(4), 10–27, 29, 30.

3 See the Electoral Registration and Administration Act 2013 Sch 5 Pt 1 (paras 1–4) (Sch 5 paras 1–3, 4(1)–(3), (5) not yet in force: see note 2). For these purposes, a person's entitlement to remain registered has been 'confirmed' if, having taken specified steps to check whether each person who has an entry in a register maintained by the officer is entitled to remain registered, the registration officer is satisfied that there is evidence of a specified kind to support the person's entitlement to be registered: see Sch 5 para 4(1), (2) (not yet in force). See also the Electoral Registration (Disclosure of Electoral Registers) Regulations 2013, SI 2013/760 (made by the Lord President of the Council in exercise of the powers conferred on him by the Representation of the People Act 1983 s 53(1), (3), Sch 2 paras 1A, 13(1ZB), (2)) (cited in PARA 112).

4 See the Electoral Registration and Administration Act 2013 Sch 5 Pt 2 (paras 5–7) (not yet in force: see note 2). For these purposes, the 'third new canvass' means the third canvass under the Representation of the People Act 1983 s 9D (not yet in force) (see PARA 154): see the Electoral Registration and Administration Act 2013 Sch 5 para 30(1) (not yet in force).

5 See the Electoral Registration and Administration Act 2013 Sch 5 Pt 3 (paras 8–15) (Sch 5 paras 8, 9(2)–(4), 10 not yet in force: see note 2). For these purposes, a person makes a 'new application for registration' in a register maintained by a registration officer in Great Britain if an application for registration in the register under the Representation of the People Act 1983 s 10ZC (not yet in force) (see PARA 163) is made in respect of that person, or if an application for alteration of the register under s 10ZD (not yet in force) (see PARA 164) is made in respect of him: see the Electoral Registration and Administration Act 2013 Sch 5 para 3(1) (not yet in force).

   See also the Electoral Registration (Postponement of 2013 Annual Canvass) Order 2013, SI 2013/794 (made by the Lord President of the Council in exercise of the powers conferred by the Electoral Registration and Administration Act 2013 ss 11(3), (4), (5), 25(1), and Sch 5 para 9(1)) (cited in PARA 151 note 6).

6 See the Electoral Registration and Administration Act 2013 Sch 5 Pt 4 (paras 16–19) (not yet in force: see note 2).

7 See the Electoral Registration and Administration Act 2013 Sch 5 Pt 5 (paras 20–23) (not yet in force: see note 2). As to declarations of local connection see PARA 121 et seq; and as to service declarations see PARA 125 et seq. As to the meaning of 'overseas elector's declaration' see PARA 149 note 14. As to registration in the register of parliamentary electors in pursuance of an overseas elector's declaration see PARA 114 et seq. As to anonymous entries in a register of electors see PARA 147 et seq.

8 Ie persons registered by virtue of an application under the Representation of the People Act 1983 s 7(2) (see PARA 119): see the Electoral Registration and Administration Act 2013 Sch 5 para 24 (not yet in force: see note 2).

9 Ie persons registered by virtue of an application under the Representation of the People Act 1983 s 7A(2) (see PARA 120): see the Electoral Registration and Administration Act 2013 Sch 5 para 24 (not yet in force: see note 2).

10 See the Electoral Registration and Administration Act 2013 Sch 5 Pt 6 (paras 24–27) (not yet in force: see note 2).

11 See the Electoral Registration and Administration Act 2013 Sch 5 Pt 7 (paras 28–30) (Sch 5 paras 29, 30 not yet in force: see note 2).

C. APPLICATIONS FOR ENTRY ON REGISTER TO BE ADDED OR ALTERED

(A) Applications for Entry on Register derived from Annual Canvass

157. Registration officer to determine applications for registration and alteration. Until a day to be appointed[1], a registration officer[2] must determine[3] all applications for registration which are[4]:

(1) made to him in accordance with the prescribed[5] requirements[6]; or

(2) treated as made to him in respect of any address[7] in circumstances where[8]: (a) in connection with an annual canvass[9], the form completed in respect of such an address[10] specifies any person as a person who is entitled to be registered in a register[11]; and (b) that person is not for the time being registered in the register in respect of that address[12].

This duty[13] applies to applications asking for[14]:

(i) the omission, insertion or alteration of a date as that on which a person will become of voting age and entitled to registration[15]; or

(ii) the alteration of the qualifying address in respect of which a person is registered[16],

as it applies to applications for registration[17].

1 As from a day to be appointed under the Electoral Registration and Administration Act 2013 s 27(1), the Representation of the People Act 1983 s 10A (added by the Representation of the People Act 2000 s 8, Sch 1 paras 1, 4) is amended by the Electoral Registration and Administration Act 2013 s 13(1), Sch 4 paras 1, 10, so that its effect is limited to Northern Ireland only. The provision made by the prospectively amended Representation of the People Act 1983 s 10A will then complement the prospectively amended s 10 (maintenance of registers: duty to conduct canvass in Northern Ireland) (see PARA 151). However, at the date at which this volume states the law, no such day had been appointed. Because the prospective amendments apply to Northern Ireland only, their effect is not set out in any detail. As to the duty of a registration officer in Great Britain to determine applications for the individual registration of electors after such a day is appointed see PARA 163.

2 As to registration officers see PARA 139. As from a day to be appointed under the Electoral Registration and Administration Act 2013 s 27(1), the Representation of the People Act 1983 s 10A(1) is amended so that the reference to a registration officer becomes a reference to the Chief Electoral Officer for Northern Ireland: see s 10A(1) (prospectively amended by the Electoral Registration and Administration Act 2013 Sch 4 paras 1, 10(1), (2)). See note 1. However, at the date at which this volume states the law, no such day had been appointed.

3 For this purpose, 'determines' means determines in accordance with regulations: Representation of the People Act 1983 s 10A(9) (as added: see note 1). As to the making of regulations under the Representation of the People Act 1983 generally see PARA 28 note 16. As to the regulations which provide for the determination of applications for registration see PARA 162.

4 See the Representation of the People Act 1983 s 10A(1) (as added: see note 1). See note 1

5 For these purposes, 'prescribed' means prescribed by regulations: see the Representation of the People Act 1983 s 202(1). As to the regulations so made see PARA 158.

6 Representation of the People Act 1983 s 10A(1)(a) (as added: see note 1). See note 1. The registration officer must supply free of charge as many forms for use in connection with s 10A(1)(a) as appear to that officer reasonable in the circumstances to any person who satisfies that officer of his intention to use the forms in connection with an election: see the Representation of the People (England and Wales) Regulations 2001, SI 2001/341, reg 4(1)(a). The provision made by reg 4 is applied and modified, in relation to Wales, by the Local Authorities (Conduct of Referendums) (Wales) Regulations 2008, SI 2008/1848, reg 8(2), Sch 4 Table 5, and, in relation to England, by the Local Authorities (Conduct of Referendums) (England) Regulations 2012, SI 2012/323, regs 8(2), 11–13, Sch 4 Table 6: see PARA 15 note 2.

The Representation of the People Act 1983 s 10A(1C), (1D), which makes further provision about information to be obtained in relation to applications for registration, is prospectively added by the Political Parties and Elections Act 2009 s 33(2), (5)(d), as from a day to be appointed under s 43(1), but the amendment prospectively made is repealed by the Electoral Registration and Administration Act 2013 Sch 4 paras 1, 24, as from a day to be appointed under s 27(1) (see note 1).At the date at which this volume states the law, no such day had been appointed in respect of either amendment.

7 Ie by virtue of the Representation of the People Act 1983 s 10A(2) (see the text and notes 8–12): see s 10A(1)(b) (as added: see note 1). The application referred to in s 10A(2) is to be treated as made on the 15 October in the year in question: see s 10A(2A) (s 10A as so added; s 10A(2A) added by the Political Parties and Elections Act 2009 Sch 6 para 1(1), (3)). However, because the annual canvass for 2013 to be conducted under the Representation of the People Act 1983 s 10(1) (see PARA 151) has been postponed, s 10A(2) applies to that canvass as if the reference to 15 October were a reference to the date the canvass form was received by the registration officer: see the Electoral Registration (Postponement of 2013 Annual Canvass) Order 2013, SI 2013/794, art 2(4). See note 1. See further PARA 169 note 8.

At the date at which this volume states the law, the Representation of the People Act 1983 s 10A(2A) is subject to s 13BB (added by the Political Parties and Elections Act 2009 s 23(1)) (which applies where notice is published of an election to which the Representation of the People Act 1983 s 13B (alteration of registers (pending election): see PARA 168) applies that is to be held in an area which includes the relevant address, during the period starting with 1 July in the year of the canvass and ending with 1 December in that year). However, s 13BB is repealed by the Electoral Registration and Administration Act 2013 Sch 4 paras 1, 14, 24, as from a day to be appointed under s 27(1); and the reference in the Representation of the People Act 1983 s 10A(2A) to s 13BB is repealed accordingly by the Electoral Registration and Administration Act 2013 Sch 4 paras 1, 10(1), (3), as from a day to be appointed under s 27(1). However, at the date at which this volume states the law, no such day had been appointed in respect of either amendment.

8 See the Representation of the People Act 1983 s 10A(2) (s 10A as added (see note 1); s 10A(2) amended by the Political Parties and Elections Act 2009 s 39, Sch 6 para 1(1), (2), Sch 7). See note 1.

9 Ie under the Representation of the People Act 1983 s 10 (see PARA 151): see s 10A(2)(a) (as added: see note 1). See note 1.

10 As to the form to be used for the purposes of a canvass see PARA 151 note 16.

11 Representation of the People Act 1983 s 10A(2)(a) (as added: see note 1). As to the registers of electors see PARA 145. See note 1.

The Representation of the People Act 1983 s 10A(2)(a) is amended by the Political Parties and Elections Act 2009 s 33(2), (5)(e), as from a day to be appointed under s 43(1), but the amendment prospectively so made is repealed by the Electoral Registration and Administration Act 2013 Sch 4 paras 1, 24, as from a day to be appointed under s 27(1) (see note 1). At the date at which this volume states the law, no such day had been appointed in respect of either amendment.

12 Representation of the People Act 1983 s 10A(2)(b) (as added: see note 1).

13 Ie the Representation of the People Act 1983 s 10A(1) (see the text and notes 1–7): see s 10A(4) (as added: see note 1).

14 See the Representation of the People Act 1983 s 10A(4) (as added: see note 1). See note 1.

As from a day to be appointed under the Electoral Registration and Administration Act 2013 s 27(1), the Representation of the People Act 1983 s 10A(4) is amended so that it applies to applications in Northern Ireland only: see s 10A(4) (prospectively amended by the Electoral Registration and Administration Act 2013 Sch 4 paras 1, 10(1), (6)). See note 1. However, at the date at which this volume states the law, no such day had been appointed.

15 Representation of the People Act 1983 s 10A(4)(a) (as added: see note 1). See note 1. 'Voting age' is currently 18 years for all purposes: see PARAS 95 note 2, 97 note 14, 102 note 10. As to the entitlement to be registered as an elector see PARA 113 et seq.

16 Representation of the People Act 1983 s 10A(4)(b) (as added: see note 1). See note 1. As to the meaning of 'qualifying address' see PARA 145 note 5.

17 See the Representation of the People Act 1983 s 10A(4) (as added: see note 1). See note 1.

158. Form of application for registration as a parliamentary or local government elector. An application for registration[1] as a parliamentary[2] or local government elector[3] or both ('an application for registration') must state[4]:

(1)   the applicant's full name[5];

(2)   the address in respect of which the applicant applies to be registered and at which he is resident on the date of the application[6];

(3)   any address in respect of which the applicant is currently registered as an elector, if he has ceased to reside at that address[7];

(4) in the case of an applicant who has not attained the age of 18 years, his date of birth[8];

(5) in the case of an applicant who is 70 years of age or older, that fact[9];

(6) in the case of an applicant whose application is not accompanied by an application for an anonymous entry and who wishes his name and address to be omitted from the edited version of the register, that request[10];

(7) except in the case of a person applying to be registered in pursuance of an overseas elector's declaration[11], the applicant's nationality[12];

(8) in the case of an applicant whose application is accompanied by an application for an anonymous entry, that fact[13].

In the case of a person applying to be registered as a parliamentary or local government elector (or both) in pursuance of a service declaration[14], a declaration of local connection[15] or an overseas elector's declaration, the declaration in question must accompany the application[16].

An application for registration must include a declaration made by the applicant that[17]:

(a) the particulars given in accordance with heads (1) to (8) above are true[18];

(b) in the case of an application by a relevant citizen of the Union for registration as a local government elector[19], he is such a citizen[20]; and

(c) in any other case, he is a Commonwealth citizen[21] or citizen of the Republic of Ireland[22].

An application for registration must be made in writing[23] to the registration officer and must be signed[24] and dated by the applicant[25]. An application for registration must be made available for inspection[26] at the registration officer's office until the application has been determined by the registration officer[27].

Where the registration officer provides the form on which an application for registration is made[28], the form of words about the two versions of the register (the full register and the edited register)[29] or a form of words to the same effect, must form part of the application form[30]. Where an application for registration is made otherwise than on a form provided by the registration officer, that officer must, on or before the determination of the application[31], send to the applicant the form of words about the two versions of the register and must, at the same time, inform the applicant, in writing, that he may, before the end of the period of 21 days, starting with the day on which the officer sends that form of words to the applicant[32], make a request, in writing, to the registration officer that he wishes his name and address to be excluded from the edited version of the register[33]. Where an applicant does not reply to the registration officer within the period of 21 days, the registration officer must assume that the applicant does not request that his name and address be excluded from the edited version of the register[34]; but, where an applicant does reply to the registration officer within the period of 21 days, and in his response requests that his name and address be excluded from the edited version register, that request must be treated as part of the application for registration[35].

1 Ie under the Representation of the People Act 1983 s 10A(1)(a) (see PARA 157) or s 13A(1)(a) (see PARA 168): see the Representation of the People (England and Wales) Regulations 2001, SI 2001/341, reg 26(1) (amended by SI 2002/1871).

2 As to the entitlement to be registered as a parliamentary elector see PARA 113.

3 As to the entitlement to be registered as a local government elector see PARA 113.

4 See the Representation of the People (England and Wales) Regulations 2001, SI 2001/341, reg 26(1) (as amended: see note 1).

For the purposes of extending the rights of citizens and nationals of accession states who (subject to the requirements of registration) may vote at local government and European parliamentary elections, the Representation of the People (England and Wales) Regulations 2001, SI 2001/341, reg 26 is applied with modifications: see the Local and European Parliamentary Elections (Registration of Citizens of Accession States) Regulations 2003, SI 2003/1557, reg 7, Sch 2 para 1(1), (3)(b).

5   Representation of the People (England and Wales) Regulations 2001, SI 2001/341, reg 26(1)(a). See note 4.
6   Representation of the People (England and Wales) Regulations 2001, SI 2001/341, reg 26(1)(b). See note 4.
7   Representation of the People (England and Wales) Regulations 2001, SI 2001/341, reg 26(1)(c). See note 4. Where a registration officer receives an application for registration which includes a statement given in accordance with reg 26(1)(c), and where the address given in the statement received by the registration officer ('the new registration officer') is in an area for which another registration officer ('the former registration officer') acts, the new registration officer must as soon as practicable notify the former registration officer that the applicant no longer resides in his area: see reg 37(1), (2). As to registration officers and the areas for which they act see PARA 139.
8   Representation of the People (England and Wales) Regulations 2001, SI 2001/341, reg 26(1)(d). See note 4.
9   Representation of the People (England and Wales) Regulations 2001, SI 2001/341, reg 26(1)(e). See note 4.
10 Representation of the People (England and Wales) Regulations 2001, SI 2001/341, reg 26(1)(g) (substituted by SI 2002/1871; and amended by SI 2006/2910). See note 4. As to applications for an anonymous entry in a register of electors see PARA 147.
11 As to registration in pursuance of an overseas elector's declaration see PARA 114 et seq.
12 Representation of the People (England and Wales) Regulations 2001, SI 2001/341, reg 26(1)(h) (added by SI 2006/752). See note 4.
13 Representation of the People (England and Wales) Regulations 2001, SI 2001/341, reg 26(1)(i) (added by SI 2006/2910). See note 4.
14 As to registration in pursuance of a service declaration see PARA 125 et seq.
15 As to registration in pursuance of a declaration of local connection see PARA 121 et seq.
16 Representation of the People (England and Wales) Regulations 2001, SI 2001/341, reg 26(2) (amended by SI 2002/1871). See note 4.
17 See the Representation of the People (England and Wales) Regulations 2001, SI 2001/341, reg 26(3) (amended by SI 2002/1871). See note 4.
18 Representation of the People (England and Wales) Regulations 2001, SI 2001/341, reg 26(3)(a). See note 4.
19 As to the entitlement to vote as a local government elector see PARA 97.
20 Representation of the People (England and Wales) Regulations 2001, SI 2001/341, reg 26(3)(b). This requirement does not apply to a person applying to be registered in pursuance of a service declaration or an overseas elector's declaration: see reg 26(5). See note 4.
21 As to who are Commonwealth citizens see BRITISH NATIONALITY vol 4 (2011) PARA 409.
22 Representation of the People (England and Wales) Regulations 2001, SI 2001/341, reg 26(3)(c). This requirement does not apply to a person applying to be registered in pursuance of a service declaration or an overseas elector's declaration: see reg 26(5). See note 4. As to who are citizens of the Republic of Ireland see BRITISH NATIONALITY vol 4 (2011) PARA 410.
23 The requirement in the Representation of the People (England and Wales) Regulations 2001, SI 2001/341 that any application, notice, representation or objection should be in writing is satisfied where (apart from the usual meaning of that expression) the text of it is transmitted by electronic means, is received in legible form, and is capable of being used for subsequent reference: see reg 5 (amended by SI 2006/2910).

By virtue of the Representation of the People (England and Wales) Regulations 2001, SI 2001/341, reg 13(6), (7), reg 5 and reg 6 (see note 24) apply to registration in pursuance of a European parliamentary overseas elector's declaration as they apply to registration in pursuance of an overseas elector's declaration (see PARA 101 note 7); and for the purposes of extending the rights of relevant citizens of the Union who (subject to the requirements of registration) may vote at European parliamentary elections, reg 5 and reg 6 are applied with modifications (see the European Parliamentary Elections (Franchise of Relevant Citizens of the Union) Regulations 2001, SI 2001/1184, reg 9, Schedule; and PARA 102 note 6).

The Representation of the People (England and Wales) Regulations 2001, SI 2001/341, reg 5 and reg 6 are applied and modified also, in relation to Wales, by the Local Authorities (Conduct of Referendums) (Wales) Regulations 2008, SI 2008/1848, reg 8(2), Sch 4 Table 5, and, in relation to England, by the Local Authorities (Conduct of Referendums) (England) Regulations 2012, SI 2012/323, regs 8(2), 11–13, Sch 4 Table 6: see PARA 15 note 2.

24 A requirement in the Representation of the People (England and Wales) Regulations 2001, SI 2001/341 for an application, notice, representation or objection to be signed is satisfied (as an alternative to the signature given by hand) where there is both an electronic signature incorporated into or logically associated with a particular electronic communication and the certification by any person of such a signature: see reg 6(1) (amended by SI 2006/2910). For these purposes, an electronic signature is so much of anything in electronic form as: (1) is incorporated into or otherwise logically associated with any electronic communication or both; and (2) purports to be so incorporated or associated for the purpose of being used in establishing the authenticity of the communication, the integrity of the communication or both (see the Representation of the People (England and Wales) Regulations 2001, SI 2001/341, reg 6(2)); and an electronic signature incorporated into or associated with a particular electronic communication is certified by any person if that person (whether before or after the making of the communication) has made a statement confirming that the signature, a means of producing, communicating or verifying the signature or a procedure applied to the signature, is (either alone or in combination with other factors) a valid means of establishing the authenticity of the communication, the integrity of the communication or both (see reg 6(3)). See note 23.

25 Representation of the People (England and Wales) Regulations 2001, SI 2001/341, reg 26(4). See note 4.

26 As to the meaning of 'available for inspection' see PARA 142 note 18. As to provision made for the inspection of documents see PARA 168 note 12.

27 Representation of the People (England and Wales) Regulations 2001, SI 2001/341, reg 28(1) (reg 28(1) renumbered, reg 28(2) added, by SI 2006/2910). This provision does not apply, however, to an application for registration which is accompanied by an application for an anonymous entry: Representation of the People (England and Wales) Regulations 2001, SI 2001/341, reg 28(2) (as so added).
    By virtue of the Representation of the People (England and Wales) Regulations 2001, SI 2001/341, reg 13(6), (7), reg 28 applies to registration in pursuance of a European parliamentary overseas elector's declaration as it applies to registration in pursuance of an overseas elector's declaration (see PARA 101 note 7); and for the purposes of extending the rights of relevant citizens of the Union who (subject to the requirements of registration) may vote at European parliamentary elections, reg 28 is applied with modifications (see the European Parliamentary Elections (Franchise of Relevant Citizens of the Union) Regulations 2001, SI 2001/1184, reg 9, Schedule; and PARA 102 note 6).

28 Ie in connection with the Representation of the People Act 1983 s 10A(1)(a) (see PARA 157) or s 10A(3) (see PARA 160): see the Representation of the People (England and Wales) Regulations 2001, SI 2001/341, reg 26(6) (added by SI 2002/1871; and amended by SI 2006/1694).

29 Ie the form of words in the Representation of the People (Form of Canvass) (England and Wales) Regulations 2006, SI 2006/1694, reg 4, Schedule Pt 2 (Form of Words about the Two Versions of the Register) (see PARA 151 note 16): see the Representation of the People (England and Wales) Regulations 2001, SI 2001/341, reg 26(6) (as added and amended: see note 28).

30 Representation of the People (England and Wales) Regulations 2001, SI 2001/341, reg 26(6) (as added and amended: see note 28). The provisions of reg 26(6)–(9) (see also notes 31–35) do not apply to an application for registration which is accompanied by an application for an anonymous entry: reg 26(10) (added by SI 2006/2910). See note 4.

31 As to the procedure for determining applications see PARA 162.

32 As to the calculation of periods of time for the purposes of the Representation of the People (England and Wales) Regulations 2001, SI 2001/341 see PARA 141 note 5.

33 Representation of the People (England and Wales) Regulations 2001, SI 2001/341, reg 26(7) (added by SI 2002/1871). See notes 4, 30. As to requests for an applicant's name and address to be excluded from the edited version of the register see PARA 167.

34 Representation of the People (England and Wales) Regulations 2001, SI 2001/341, reg 26(8) (added by SI 2002/1871). See notes 4, 30.

35 Representation of the People (England and Wales) Regulations 2001, SI 2001/341, reg 26(9) (added by SI 2002/1871). See notes 4, 30.

159.   Form of application by relevant citizen of the Union for registration as European parliamentary elector. An application for registration as European parliamentary elector[1] may be made by a relevant citizen of the Union[2] ('the applicant'), must be signed and dated by him[3], and must state[4]:

(1)   the full name of the applicant[5];

(2)   the address in respect of which the applicant claims to be registered and whether he is resident there on the relevant date[6];

(3)   if the applicant is not resident on the relevant date at the address in respect of which he claims to be registered, whether he has made a declaration of local connection[7];

(4)   if the applicant is a merchant seaman on the relevant date, that fact[8]; and

(5)   either that the applicant is aged 18 or over or, if not, the date of his birth[9].

Such an application must include a declaration stating[10]:

(a)   the nationality of the applicant[11];

(b)   the applicant's address in the United Kingdom[12], if different from the address given under head (2) above[13];

(c)   where the applicant's name has been entered in a register of electors in a locality or constituency[14] in the member state of which he is a national, the name of the locality or constituency where, so far as he knows, his name was last so entered[15]; and

(d)   that the applicant will exercise any right which he has to vote at European parliamentary elections at any such election only in the United Kingdom during the period for which any entry in the register of electors made in pursuance of his application remains in force[16].

Such a declaration may be cancelled at any time by the declarant[17].

The registration officer[18] must supply free of charge as many copies of forms for use in connection with such applications and declarations as appear to that officer reasonable in the circumstances to any person who satisfies that officer of his intention to use the forms in connection with the registration of relevant citizens of the Union as European parliamentary electors[19]. An application and a declaration are of no effect unless they are received by the registration officer concerned within the period of three months beginning with the date on which they are made[20].

As soon as practicable after the registration officer has registered the name of a relevant citizen of the Union in the register maintained for the purpose[21], in circumstances where the relevant citizen would be entitled to vote at a European parliamentary general election in pursuance of the registration, he must send information contained in the application[22] and declaration[23] by virtue of which he entered the name in the register to the person shown as the representative of the state in respect of which the applicant is a national in a direction containing a list of such representatives issued by the Lord Chancellor[24].

A person who makes a statement which he knows to be false, either in such an application for registration as a European parliamentary elector[25], or in the related declaration[26], is guilty of an offence and liable on summary conviction to a fine[27].

1   Ie an application under the European Parliamentary Elections (Franchise of Relevant Citizens of the Union) Regulations 2001, SI 2001/1184, reg 6 (as required by reg 4(1): see PARA 116): see reg 6(1).

2   As to the meaning of 'relevant citizen of the Union' for these purposes see PARA 102 note 5.

3   As to offences associated with voting declarations see PARA 735.

4   See the European Parliamentary Elections (Franchise of Relevant Citizens of the Union) Regulations 2001, SI 2001/1184, reg 6(1).

    For the purposes of extending the rights of citizens and nationals of accession states who (subject to the requirements of registration) may vote at local government and European parliamentary elections, reg 6 is applied with modifications: see the Local and European Parliamentary Elections (Registration of Citizens of Accession States) Regulations 2003, SI 2003/1557, reg 6, Sch 1 para 4.

5   European Parliamentary Elections (Franchise of Relevant Citizens of the Union) Regulations 2001, SI 2001/1184, reg 6(1)(a). See note 4.

6   European Parliamentary Elections (Franchise of Relevant Citizens of the Union) Regulations 2001, SI 2001/1184, reg 6(1)(b). For these purposes, 'relevant date' has the same meaning as in reg 4 (see PARA 116 note 4): see reg 6(6). See note 4.

7   European Parliamentary Elections (Franchise of Relevant Citizens of the Union) Regulations 2001, SI 2001/1184, reg 6(1)(d). See note 4. As to registration in pursuance of a declaration of local connection see PARA 121 et seq.

8   European Parliamentary Elections (Franchise of Relevant Citizens of the Union) Regulations 2001, SI 2001/1184, reg 6(1)(e). See note 4. As to deemed residence for merchant seamen see PARA 118.

9   European Parliamentary Elections (Franchise of Relevant Citizens of the Union) Regulations 2001, SI 2001/1184, reg 6(1)(f). See note 4.

10 See the European Parliamentary Elections (Franchise of Relevant Citizens of the Union) Regulations 2001, SI 2001/1184, reg 6(2). See note 4.

11 European Parliamentary Elections (Franchise of Relevant Citizens of the Union) Regulations 2001, SI 2001/1184, reg 6(2)(a). See note 4.

12 As to the meaning of 'United Kingdom' see PARA 1 note 1.

13 European Parliamentary Elections (Franchise of Relevant Citizens of the Union) Regulations 2001, SI 2001/1184, reg 6(2)(b). See note 4.

14 For these purposes, 'locality or constituency' has the same meaning as it has in Council Directive (EC) 93/109 of 6 December 1993 (OJ L329, 30.12.1993, p 34) laying down detailed arrangements for the exercise of the right to vote and to stand as a candidate in elections to the European Parliament for citizens of the Union residing in a member state of which they are not nationals (as to which see PARA 6 note 8): see the European Parliamentary Elections (Franchise of Relevant Citizens of the Union) Regulations 2001, SI 2001/1184, reg 6(6). See note 4. There is no separate definition of 'locality or constituency' made in Council Directive (EC) 93/109 of 6 December 1993 (OJ L329, 30.12.1993, p 34), although reference is made in the definition for 'electoral roll' (see art 2(7)), and sporadic references appear in context in the substantive articles.

15 European Parliamentary Elections (Franchise of Relevant Citizens of the Union) Regulations 2001, SI 2001/1184, reg 6(2)(c). See note 4.

16 European Parliamentary Elections (Franchise of Relevant Citizens of the Union) Regulations 2001, SI 2001/1184, reg 6(2)(d). See note 4.

17 See the European Parliamentary Elections (Franchise of Relevant Citizens of the Union) Regulations 2001, SI 2001/1184, reg 10(1). A cancellation as mentioned in the text terminates the entitlement to vote in pursuance of such a declaration: see PARA 170.

    For the purposes of extending the rights of citizens and nationals of accession states who (subject to the requirements of registration) may vote at local government and European parliamentary elections, reg 10 is applied with modifications: see the Local and European Parliamentary Elections (Registration of Citizens of Accession States) Regulations 2003, SI 2003/1557, Sch 1 para 7.

18 As to the registration officer see PARA 139.

19 European Parliamentary Elections (Franchise of Relevant Citizens of the Union) Regulations 2001, SI 2001/1184, reg 6(3). See note 4.

20 European Parliamentary Elections (Franchise of Relevant Citizens of the Union) Regulations 2001, SI 2001/1184, reg 6(4). See note 4.

21 Ie the register maintained under the European Parliamentary Elections (Franchise of Relevant Citizens of the Union) Regulations 2001, SI 2001/1184, reg 5(2) (see PARA 143): see reg 8(1) (amended by SI 2003/1557; SI 2009/726).

22 Ie an application made under the European Parliamentary Elections (Franchise of Relevant Citizens of the Union) Regulations 2001, SI 2001/1184, reg 6(1) (see the text and notes 1–9): see reg 8(1) (as amended: see note 21).

23 Ie a declaration made under the European Parliamentary Elections (Franchise of Relevant Citizens of the Union) Regulations 2001, SI 2001/1184, reg 6(2) (see the text and notes 10–16): see reg 8(1) (as amended: see note 21).

24 See the European Parliamentary Elections (Franchise of Relevant Citizens of the Union) Regulations 2001, SI 2001/1184, reg 8(1), (2) (reg 8(1) as amended: see note 21). The Lord Chancellor must issue directions identifying the representative for each member state of the European Union to whom the information referred to in the text is to be sent: reg 8(3) (added by

SI 2003/1557; amended by SI 2009/726). As to the Lord Chancellor see PARA 2; and see, more generally, CONSTITUTIONAL LAW AND HUMAN RIGHTS vol 8(2) (Reissue) PARA 477 et seq.

For the purposes of extending the rights of citizens and nationals of accession states who (subject to the requirements of registration) may vote at local government and European parliamentary elections, the European Parliamentary Elections (Franchise of Relevant Citizens of the Union) Regulations 2001, SI 2001/1184, reg 8 is applied with modifications: see the Local and European Parliamentary Elections (Registration of Citizens of Accession States) Regulations 2003, SI 2003/1557, Sch 1 para 5.

25 Ie in an application required by the European Parliamentary Elections (Franchise of Relevant Citizens of the Union) Regulations 2001, SI 2001/1184, reg 6(1) (see the text and notes 1–9): see reg 7(1); and PARA 736.

26 Ie in a declaration required by the European Parliamentary Elections (Franchise of Relevant Citizens of the Union) Regulations 2001, SI 2001/1184, reg 6(2) (see the text and notes 10–16): see reg 7(1); and PARA 736.

27 See the European Parliamentary Elections (Franchise of Relevant Citizens of the Union) Regulations 2001, SI 2001/1184, reg 7(1); and PARA 736. The penalty is a fine not exceeding level 3 on the standard scale: see reg 7(1); and PARA 736. As to the standard scale see SENTENCING AND DISPOSITION OF OFFENDERS vol 92 (2010) PARA 142.

160. Registration officer to determine objections to registration. Until a day to be appointed[1], a registration officer[2] must determine[3] all objections to a person's registration[4] made in accordance with the prescribed[5] requirements by another person whose name appears in the register in question[6]. This duty[7] applies to objections asking for[8]:

(1) the omission, insertion or alteration of a date as that on which a person will become of voting age and entitled to registration[9]; or

(2) the alteration of the qualifying address in respect of which a person is registered[10],

as it applies to objections to a person's registration[11].

1 As from a day to be appointed under the Electoral Registration and Administration Act 2013 s 27(1), the Representation of the People Act 1983 s 10A (added by the Representation of the People Act 2000 s 8, Sch 1 paras 1, 4) is amended by the Electoral Registration and Administration Act 2013 s 13(1), Sch 4 paras 1, 10, so that its effect is limited to Northern Ireland only. The Representation of the People Act 1983 s 10A(3B) (see note 4) is repealed by the Electoral Registration and Administration Act 2013 Sch 4 paras 1, 10(1), (5), 23 accordingly. The provision made by the prospectively amended Representation of the People Act 1983 s 10A will then complement the prospectively amended s 10 (maintenance of registers: duty to conduct canvass in Northern Ireland) (see PARA 151). However, at the date at which this volume states the law, no such day had been appointed. Because the prospective amendments apply to Northern Ireland only, their effect is not set out in any detail.

2 As to registration officers see PARA 139. As from a day to be appointed under the Electoral Registration and Administration Act 2013 s 27(1), the Representation of the People Act 1983 s 10A(3) is amended so that the reference to a registration officer becomes a reference to the Chief Electoral Officer for Northern Ireland and the reference to a person's registration (see the text and note 4) becomes a reference to a person's registration in Northern Ireland: see s 10A(3) (s 10A as added (see note 1); s 10A(3) prospectively amended by the Electoral Registration and Administration Act 2013 Sch 4 paras 1, 10(1), (4)). See note 1. However, at the date at which this volume states the law, no such day had been appointed.

3 As to the meaning of 'determine' for these purposes see PARA 157 note 3.

4 The Representation of the People Act 1983 s 10A(3) applies to an objection to a person's registration whether the objection is made before or after the person is registered in the register: s 10A(3A) (s 10A as added (see note 1); s 10A(3A) added by the Electoral Administration Act 2006 s 12(4)). However, no objection to a person's registration may be made if the person has an anonymous entry in the register: Representation of the People Act 1983 s 10A(3B) (s 10A as so added; s 10A(3B) added by the Electoral Administration Act 2006 s 10(2), Sch 1 paras 2, 6(1), (2)). As to the meaning of 'anonymous entry' in relation to a register of electors see PARA 148. As to the determination of objections to registration see PARAS 161–162.

   As from a day to be appointed under the Electoral Registration and Administration Act 2013 s 27(1), the Representation of the People Act 1983 s 10A(3B) is repealed by the Electoral

Registration and Administration Act 2013 Sch 4 paras 1, 10(1), (5), 23. See note 1. However, at the date at which this volume states the law, no such day had been appointed.

5 For these purposes, 'prescribed' means prescribed by regulations: see the Representation of the People Act 1983 s 202(1). As to the regulations so made see PARA 161.

6 Representation of the People Act 1983 s 10A(3) (as added: see note 1). See notes 1, 2. The registration officer must supply free of charge as many forms for use in connection with the Representation of the People Act 1983 s 10A(3) as appear to that officer reasonable in the circumstances to any person who satisfies that officer of his intention to use the forms in connection with an election: see the Representation of the People (England and Wales) Regulations 2001, SI 2001/341, reg 4(1)(a). The provision made by reg 4 is applied and modified, in relation to Wales, by the Local Authorities (Conduct of Referendums) (Wales) Regulations 2008, SI 2008/1848, reg 8(2), Sch 4 Table 5, and, in relation to England, by the Local Authorities (Conduct of Referendums) (England) Regulations 2012, SI 2012/323, regs 8(2), 11–13, Sch 4 Table 6: see PARA 15 note 2.

7 Ie the Representation of the People Act 1983 s 10A(3) (see the text and notes 1–6): see s 10A(4) (as added: see note 1). See note 1.

8 See the Representation of the People Act 1983 s 10A(4) (as added: see note 1). See note 1.

As from a day to be appointed under the Electoral Registration and Administration Act 2013 s 27(1), the Representation of the People Act 1983 s 10A(4) is amended so that it applies to applications in Northern Ireland only: see s 10A(4) (prospectively amended by the Electoral Registration and Administration Act 2013 Sch 4 paras 1, 10(1), (6)). See note 1. However, at the date at which this volume states the law, no such day had been appointed.

9 Representation of the People Act 1983 s 10A(4)(a) (as added: see note 1). See note 1. 'Voting age' is currently 18 years for all purposes: see PARAS 95 note 2, 97 note 14, 102 note 10. As to the entitlement to be registered as an elector see PARA 113 et seq.

10 Representation of the People Act 1983 s 10A(4)(b) (as added: see note 1). See note 1. As to the meaning of 'qualifying address' see PARA 145 note 5.

11 See the Representation of the People Act 1983 s 10A(4) (as added: see note 1). See note 1.

161. Form of objection to registration. Any objection to a person's registration[1] must state[2]:

(1)   the name of the person against whom the objection is made[3];

(2)   in the case of an objection made before that person is entered in the register, the address of that person as given in the application for registration[4] (or, in the case of an objection made after that person is entered in the register, the electoral number and qualifying address of that person contained in the register)[5];

(3)   the grounds of the objection[6];

(4)   the name of the objector and his address as shown in the register (if so shown) together with the address to which correspondence should be sent if that address is different or if no address is shown in the register[7]; and

(5)   the electoral number of the objector[8].

An objection must be made in writing[9] and must be signed[10] and dated by the person objecting[11].

Any objection to a person's registration must be made available for inspection at the registration officer's office[12] until the objection has been determined by the registration officer[13].

1 See the Representation of the People Act 1983 s 10A(1)(a); and PARA 157. For the purposes of the Representation of the People (England and Wales) Regulations 2001, SI 2001/341, Pt III (regs 23–45H), 'objection' includes representations made against an application for registration under the Representation of the People Act 1983 s 13A(1)(a) (see PARA 168): Representation of the People (England and Wales) Regulations 2001, SI 2001/341, reg 27(3).

By virtue of reg 13(6), (7), reg 27 and reg 28 (see the text and notes 12–13) apply to registration in pursuance of a European parliamentary overseas elector's declaration as they apply to registration in pursuance of an overseas elector's declaration (see PARA 101 note 7); and for the purposes of extending the rights of relevant citizens of the Union who (subject to the requirements of registration) may vote at European parliamentary elections, reg 27 and reg 28 are applied with modifications (see the European Parliamentary Elections (Franchise of Relevant Citizens of the Union) Regulations 2001, SI 2001/1184, reg 9, Schedule; and PARA 102 note 6).

2   See the Representation of the People (England and Wales) Regulations 2001, SI 2001/341, reg 27(1). See note 1.

3   Representation of the People (England and Wales) Regulations 2001, SI 2001/341, reg 27(1)(a). See note 1.

4   Representation of the People (England and Wales) Regulations 2001, SI 2001/341, reg 27(1)(b) (reg 27(1)(b) amended, reg 27(1)(ba) added, by SI 2006/2910). See note 1.

5   Representation of the People (England and Wales) Regulations 2001, SI 2001/341, reg 27(1)(ba) (as added: see note 4). See note 1. As to the meaning of 'qualifying address' for these purposes see PARA 145 note 5. As to a person's electoral number see PARA 145.

6   Representation of the People (England and Wales) Regulations 2001, SI 2001/341, reg 27(1)(c). See note 1.

7   Representation of the People (England and Wales) Regulations 2001, SI 2001/341, reg 27(1)(d). See note 1.

8   Representation of the People (England and Wales) Regulations 2001, SI 2001/341, reg 27(1)(e). See note 1.

9   As to the requirement for an objection to be in writing see PARA 158 note 23.

10 As to the requirement for an objection to be signed see PARA 158 note 24.

11 Representation of the People (England and Wales) Regulations 2001, SI 2001/341, reg 27(2). See note 1.

12 As to the meaning of 'available for inspection' see PARA 142 note 18. As to the registration officer see PARA 139; and as to provision made for the inspection of documents see PARA 168 note 12.

13 Representation of the People (England and Wales) Regulations 2001, SI 2001/341, reg 28(1) (reg 28(1) renumbered, reg 28(2) added, by SI 2006/2910). This provision does not apply, however, to an application for registration which is accompanied by an application for an anonymous entry: Representation of the People (England and Wales) Regulations 2001, SI 2001/341, reg 28(2) (as so added). See note 1. As to applications for anonymous registration see PARA 147; and as to the procedure for determining objections see PARA 162.

162.   Procedure for determining applications for registration and objections.
A registration officer[1] must discharge his functions of determining an application for registration[2] and an objection[3] in accordance with the statutory provisions[4]. The registration officer must keep separate lists[5] of:

(1)   applications for registration[6];

(2)   objections made before the person against whom the objection is made is entered in the register[7];

(3)   objections made after the person against whom the objection is made is entered in the register[8].

On receipt of an application, the registration officer must enter the name of the applicant and the address claimed as his qualifying address[9] in the list he keeps in pursuance of head (1) above[10]. On receipt of an objection made before the person against whom the objection is made is entered in the register, the registration officer must enter, in the list he keeps in pursuance of head (2) above, the name and qualifying address of the objector together with the name of the applicant and the address claimed as his qualifying address[11] and, in the list he keeps in pursuance of head (1) above, the particulars of the objection[12]. On receipt of any other objection, the registration officer must enter the name and qualifying address of the objector together with the name of the applicant and the address claimed as his qualifying address in the list he keeps in pursuance of head (3) above[13]. The registration officer may ask for further information and take no further action until such information is supplied, if he is of opinion that the particulars given in the application or objection are insufficient[14].

The registration officer may allow an application without a hearing provided that no objection is made within the period of five days beginning with the day following the entry of the application in the list of applications[15]. The registration officer may disallow an objection if he is of the opinion that the objector is not entitled to object[16]; and he must so inform the objector[17]. Furthermore, he may disallow an objection without a hearing if he is of the opinion that the objection is clearly without merit[18]. The registration officer may send to the applicant or objector a notice stating his opinion that an application or objection cannot be allowed either because the matter has been concluded by the decision of a court[19] or because the particulars given in the application or objection do not entitle the applicant or objector to succeed[20]. In such cases, the registration officer must state the grounds for his opinion, and that he intends to disallow the application or objection unless that person gives the registration officer notice within three days from the date of the registration officer's notice that he requires the application or objection to be heard[21]. If the registration officer receives no such notice within that time, he may disallow the application or objection[22].

Unless the registration officer allows or disallows the application or objection without a hearing[23], he must send a notice[24] to the person making the application (in the case of an application)[25] and to both the objector and the person objected to (in the case of an objection)[26], stating the time and place at which he proposes to hear the application or objection[27] (plus the name and address of the objector and the grounds of the objection, in the case of a notice sent to a person objected to)[28]. The time fixed for the hearing of an application or objection must not be earlier than the third day or later than the seventh day after the date of the notice[29]. The persons entitled to appear and be heard at the hearing of applications and objections are as follows[30]:

(a)   on an application, the applicant[31];

(b)   on an objection, the objector and the person objected to[32];

(c)   on an application or an objection, any other person who appears to the registration officer to be interested[33].

The registration officer may, at the request of any person entitled to appear and be heard or, if he thinks fit, without such a request, require that the evidence tendered by any person be given on oath and he may administer the oath for the purpose[34].

Where the registration officer is able to determine an objection before an alteration to the register is due to take effect[35] and where he allows the objection[36], the application is to be treated as if it had been disallowed[37]. Where the registration officer is not able to determine an objection before the alteration to the register is due to take effect, the objection is to be treated as if it was made after the person against whom it is made is entered in the register[38].

1   As to registration officers and the areas for which they act see PARA 139.
2   Ie under the Representation of the People Act 1983 s 10A(1) (see PARA 157) or s 13A(1)(a) (see PARA 168): see the Representation of the People (England and Wales) Regulations 2001, SI 2001/341, reg 29(1) (amended by SI 2006/2910).
3   Ie under the Representation of the People Act 1983 s 10A(3) (see PARA 160): see the Representation of the People (England and Wales) Regulations 2001, SI 2001/341, reg 29(1) (as amended: see note 2).
4   Representation of the People (England and Wales) Regulations 2001, SI 2001/341, reg 29(1) (as amended: see note 2). The statutory provisions referred to in the text are regs 29–31A (see the text and notes 5–38): see reg 29(1) (as so amended).
       By virtue of reg 13(6), (7), the provisions of reg 6, reg 8 (see note 15), and regs 29–31A, apply to registration in pursuance of a European parliamentary overseas elector's declaration as they apply to registration in pursuance of an overseas elector's declaration (see PARA 101 note 7); and for the purposes of extending the rights of relevant citizens of the Union who (subject to the requirements of registration) may vote at European parliamentary elections, regs 6, 8, 29–31A are applied with modifications (see the European Parliamentary Elections

(Franchise of Relevant Citizens of the Union) Regulations 2001, SI 2001/1184, reg 9, Schedule; and PARA 102 note 6). In any case where the registration officer is not required to notify the applicant of the result of an application under the provisions applied by reg 9, he must so notify the applicant under the European Parliamentary Elections (Franchise of Relevant Citizens of the Union) Regulations 2001, SI 2001/1184: reg 6(5). For the purposes of extending the rights of citizens and nationals of accession states who (subject to the requirements of registration) may vote at local government and European parliamentary elections, reg 6 is applied with modifications: see the Local and European Parliamentary Elections (Registration of Citizens of Accession States) Regulations 2003, SI 2003/1557, reg 6, Sch 1 para 4.

5 See the Representation of the People (England and Wales) Regulations 2001, SI 2001/341, reg 29(2) (reg 29(2) substituted, reg 29(2A)–(2D) added, by SI 2006/2910). See note 4.

6 Representation of the People (England and Wales) Regulations 2001, SI 2001/341, reg 29(2)(a) (as substituted: see note 5). See note 4.

7 Representation of the People (England and Wales) Regulations 2001, SI 2001/341, reg 29(2)(b) (as substituted: see note 5). See note 4.

8 Representation of the People (England and Wales) Regulations 2001, SI 2001/341, reg 29(2)(c) (as substituted: see note 5). See note 4.

9 For this purpose, 'qualifying address' includes the address specified in an overseas elector's declaration in accordance with the Representation of the People Act 1985 s 2(4)(b) or s 2(4)(c)(ii) (see PARA 132): Representation of the People (England and Wales) Regulations 2001, SI 2001/341, reg 29(8) (added by SI 2006/2910). As to the application and modification of these provisions see note 4. As to overseas elector's declarations see PARA 114 et seq.

10 Representation of the People (England and Wales) Regulations 2001, SI 2001/341, reg 29(2A) (as added: see note 5). The provision made by reg 29(2A) does not apply to an application accompanied by an application for an anonymous entry, however: reg 29(2B) (as so added). As to the application and modification of these provisions see note 4. As to applications for anonymous registration see PARA 147.

11 Representation of the People (England and Wales) Regulations 2001, SI 2001/341, reg 29(2C)(a) (as added: see note 5). The text refers to the requirement for the name and qualifying address of the objector to be entered together with the particulars referred to in reg 29(2A) (see the text and notes 9–10): see reg 29(2C)(a) (as so added). See note 4.

12 Representation of the People (England and Wales) Regulations 2001, SI 2001/341, reg 29(2C)(b) (as added: see note 5). See note 4.

13 Representation of the People (England and Wales) Regulations 2001, SI 2001/341, reg 29(2D) (as added: see note 5). The text refers to the requirement for the name and qualifying address of the objector to be entered together with the particulars referred to in reg 29(2A) (see the text and notes 9–10): see reg 29(2D) (as so added). See note 4.

14 Representation of the People (England and Wales) Regulations 2001, SI 2001/341, reg 29(3). See note 4.

15 Representation of the People (England and Wales) Regulations 2001, SI 2001/341, reg 29(4) (reg 29(4) amended, reg 29(4A) added, by SI 2006/2910). In the case of an application for registration accompanied by an application for an anonymous entry, however, the registration officer may allow the former application without a hearing at any time: Representation of the People (England and Wales) Regulations 2001, SI 2001/341, reg 29(4A) (as so added). As to the application and modification of these provisions see note 4. Subject to reg 56(6) (closing date for application for absent vote: see PARA 367 note 6), in computing any period of not more than seven days for the purposes of the Representation of the People (England and Wales) Regulations 2001, SI 2001/341, a Saturday, Sunday, Christmas Eve, Christmas Day, Good Friday or a bank holiday is to be disregarded: see reg 8(2), (3) (reg 8(3) amended by SI 2006/2910). For this purpose, 'bank holiday' means a day which under the Banking and Financial Dealings Act 1971 is a bank holiday in England and Wales (see TIME vol 97 (2010) PARA 321): Representation of the People (England and Wales) Regulations 2001, SI 2001/341, reg 8(4). As to the meanings of 'England' and 'Wales' see PARA 1 note 1.

By virtue of reg 13(6), (7), reg 8 applies to registration in pursuance of a European parliamentary overseas elector's declaration as it applies to registration in pursuance of an overseas elector's declaration (see PARA 101 note 7); and for the purposes of relevant citizens of the Union who (subject to the requirement of registration) may vote at European parliamentary elections, reg 8 applies with modifications (see the European Parliamentary Elections (Franchise of Relevant Citizens of the Union) Regulations 2001, SI 2001/1184, reg 9, Schedule; and PARA 102 note 6). The Representation of the People (England and Wales) Regulations 2001, SI 2001/341, reg 8 is also applied and modified, in relation to Wales, by the Local Authorities (Conduct of Referendums) (Wales) Regulations 2008, SI 2008/1848, reg 8(2), Sch 4 Table 5, and, in relation to England, by the Local Authorities (Conduct of Referendums) (England) Regulations 2012, SI 2012/323, regs 8(2), 11–13, Sch 4 Table 6: see PARA 15 note 2.

16 See the Representation of the People (England and Wales) Regulations 2001, SI 2001/341, reg 29(5) (amended by SI 2006/2910). See note 4.

17 See the Representation of the People (England and Wales) Regulations 2001, SI 2001/341, reg 29(5) (as amended: see note 16). See note 4.

18 Representation of the People (England and Wales) Regulations 2001, SI 2001/341, reg 29(5A) (reg 29(5A)–(5D) added by SI 2006/2910). Where the registration officer disallows an objection in this way without a hearing, he must send to the objector a notice stating that the application has been disallowed on that basis and the grounds for his opinion: Representation of the People (England and Wales) Regulations 2001, SI 2001/341, reg 29(5B) (as so added). An objector may require the objection to be heard by giving notice to the registration officer within three days from the date of the notice given under reg 29(5B): reg 29(5C) (as so added). A notification under reg 29(5C) is not to prevent the application to which the objection relates from being allowed: reg 29(5D) (as so added). As to the application and modification of these provisions see note 4.

19 Representation of the People (England and Wales) Regulations 2001, SI 2001/341, reg 29(6)(a). See note 4.

20 Representation of the People (England and Wales) Regulations 2001, SI 2001/341, reg 29(6)(b). See note 4.

21 See the Representation of the People (England and Wales) Regulations 2001, SI 2001/341, reg 29(7). See note 4.

22 See the Representation of the People (England and Wales) Regulations 2001, SI 2001/341, reg 29(7). See note 4.

23 Ie under the Representation of the People (England and Wales) Regulations 2001, SI 2001/341, reg 29 (see the text and notes 15, 18): see reg 30(1).

24 See the Representation of the People (England and Wales) Regulations 2001, SI 2001/341, reg 30(1). See note 4.

25 See the Representation of the People (England and Wales) Regulations 2001, SI 2001/341, reg 30(1)(a). See note 4.

26 See the Representation of the People (England and Wales) Regulations 2001, SI 2001/341, reg 30(1)(b). See note 4.

27 Representation of the People (England and Wales) Regulations 2001, SI 2001/341, reg 30(1)(b)(i). See note 4.

28 Representation of the People (England and Wales) Regulations 2001, SI 2001/341, reg 30(1)(b)(ii). See note 4.

29 Representation of the People (England and Wales) Regulations 2001, SI 2001/341, reg 30(2). See note 4.

30 See the Representation of the People (England and Wales) Regulations 2001, SI 2001/341, reg 31(1). Any person entitled to appear and be heard may do so either in person or by any other person on his behalf: reg 31(3). The right to appear and be heard includes the right to make written representations: reg 31(2). See note 4.

31 Representation of the People (England and Wales) Regulations 2001, SI 2001/341, reg 31(1)(a). See note 4.

32 Representation of the People (England and Wales) Regulations 2001, SI 2001/341, reg 31(1)(b). See note 4.

33 Representation of the People (England and Wales) Regulations 2001, SI 2001/341, reg 31(1)(c). See note 4.

34 Representation of the People (England and Wales) Regulations 2001, SI 2001/341, reg 31(4). See note 4.

35 See the Representation of the People (England and Wales) Regulations 2001, SI 2001/341, reg 31A(2)(a) (reg 31A added by SI 2006/2910). The text refers to circumstances where:

(1) an application for registration has been allowed (whether without or following a hearing) (Representation of the People (England and Wales) Regulations 2001, SI 2001/341, reg 31A(1)(a) (as so added)); and

(2) either: (a) an objection is later made to that application (reg 31A(1)(b)(i) (as so added)); or (b) an objector whose objection in respect of that application has been disallowed without a hearing in pursuance of reg 29(5A) (see the text and note 18) notifies the registration officer, in accordance with reg 29(5C) (see note 18), that he requires the objection to be heard (reg 31A(1)(b)(ii) (as so added)); and

(3) no alteration to the register has yet taken effect in respect of that application by virtue of the Representation of the People Act 1983 s 13(5) (see PARA 165), s 13A(2) (see

PARA 168) or s 13B(3) (see PARA 168) (Representation of the People (England and Wales) Regulations 2001, SI 2001/341, reg 31A(1)(c) (as so added)).

36 See the Representation of the People (England and Wales) Regulations 2001, SI 2001/341, reg 31A(2)(b) (as added: see note 35).

37 See the Representation of the People (England and Wales) Regulations 2001, SI 2001/341, reg 31A(2) (as added: see note 35).

38 Representation of the People (England and Wales) Regulations 2001, SI 2001/341, reg 31A(3) (as added: see note 35). Where reg 31A(3) applies, the registration officer must transfer the entry relating to the objection from the list he keeps in pursuance of head (2) in the text to the list he keeps in pursuance of head (3) in the text: reg 31A(4) (as so added).

(B) Applications for Entry on Register derived from Individual Electoral Registration

163. Registration officer to determine applications for individual registration of electors. As from a day to be appointed[1], a registration officer in Great Britain[2] must enter a person[3] ('P') in a register maintained by the officer[4]:

(1) if an application for registration is made by someone who appears to the officer to be P[5];

(2) if any requirements imposed by or under the Representation of the People Act 1983 in relation to the application are met[6]; and

(3) if P appears to the officer to be entitled to be registered in the register[7].

In determining such an application, the officer must consider any objection made in accordance with the prescribed[8] requirements by another person whose name appears in the register[9]. Regulations may make provision about the procedure for determining such applications[10].

1 The Representation of the People Act 1983 s 10ZC is added by the Electoral Registration and Administration Act 2013 s 1(1), as from a day to be appointed under s 27(1). At the date at which this volume states the law, no such day had been appointed.

2 As to the meaning of 'Great Britain' see PARA 1 note 1. As to registration officers see PARA 139.

3 As to the meaning of 'person' see PARA 95 note 1.

4 See the Representation of the People Act 1983 s 10ZC(1) (prospectively added: see note 1). As to the duty of registration officers to maintain, prepare and publish registers of electors see PARA 143.

5 Representation of the People Act 1983 s 10ZC(1)(a) (prospectively added: see note 1).

6 Representation of the People Act 1983 s 10ZC(1)(b) (prospectively added: see note 1).

7 Representation of the People Act 1983 s 10ZC(1)(c) (prospectively added: see note 1). As to the entitlement to be registered as an elector see PARA 113 et seq.

8 For these purposes, 'prescribed' means prescribed by regulations: see the Representation of the People Act 1983 s 202(1). As to the making of regulations under the Representation of the People Act 1983 generally see PARA 28 note 16. At the date at which this volume states the law, no such regulations had been made under s 10ZC.

9 Representation of the People Act 1983 s 10ZC(2) (prospectively added: see note 1).
   Registration officers in Great Britain must have regard to any guidance given by the Minister about the determination of applications under s 10ZC (Electoral Registration and Administration Act 2013 s 1(3)); and the guidance that may be given includes guidance about the process for determining whether the conditions in the Representation of the People Act 1983 s 10C(1) (see heads (1) to (3) in the text) are met and the relative weight to be given to different kinds of evidence (Electoral Registration and Administration Act 2013 s 1(4)). The provision made by s (3), (4) ceases to have effect at the end of the period of five years beginning with the day on which it comes fully into force: s 1(5). For these purposes, the 'Minister' means the Secretary of State or the Lord President of the Council: see s 25(1). As to the Secretary of State and the Lord President of the Council see PARA 2.

10 Representation of the People Act 1983 s 10ZC(3) (prospectively added: see note 1).

164.   Alterations to entries on register of electors derived from individual registration.   As from a day to be appointed[1], a registration officer in Great Britain[2] must alter the name or address in respect of which a person[3] ('P') is registered in a register maintained by the officer[4]:

(1)   if an application for alteration is made by someone who appears to the officer to be P[5];

(2)   if any requirements imposed by or under the Representation of the People Act 1983 in relation to the application are met[6]; and

(3)   if P appears to the officer to be entitled to be registered in the register in respect of the new name or the new address (as the case may be)[7].

In determining such an application, the officer must consider any objection made in accordance with the prescribed[8] requirements by another person whose name appears in the register[9]. Regulations may make provision about the procedure for determining such applications[10].

1   The Representation of the People Act 1983 s 10ZD is added by the Electoral Registration and Administration Act 2013 s 1(2), Sch 1 para 1, as from a day to be appointed under s 27(1). At the date at which this volume states the law, no such day had been appointed.
2   As to the meaning of 'Great Britain' see PARA 1 note 1. As to registration officers see PARA 139.
3   As to the meaning of 'person' see PARA 95 note 1.
4   See the Representation of the People Act 1983 s 10ZD(1) (prospectively added: see note 1). As to the duty of registration officers to maintain, prepare and publish registers of electors see PARA 143.
5   Representation of the People Act 1983 s 10ZD(1)(a) (prospectively added: see note 1).
6   Representation of the People Act 1983 s 10ZD(1)(b) (prospectively added: see note 1).
7   Representation of the People Act 1983 s 10ZD(1)(c) (prospectively added: see note 1). As to the entitlement to be registered as an elector see PARA 113 et seq.
8   For these purposes, 'prescribed' means prescribed by regulations: see the Representation of the People Act 1983 s 202(1). As to the making of regulations under the Representation of the People Act 1983 generally see PARA 28 note 16. At the date at which this volume states the law, no such regulations had been made under s 10ZD.
9   Representation of the People Act 1983 s 10ZD(2) (prospectively added: see note 1)
    Registration officers in Great Britain must have regard to any guidance given by the Minister about the determination of applications under s 10ZD (Electoral Registration and Administration Act 2013 Sch 1 para 2(1)); and the guidance that may be given includes guidance about the process for determining whether the conditions in the Representation of the People Act 1983 s 10D(1) (see heads (1) to (3) in the text) are met and the relative weight to be given to different kinds of evidence (Electoral Registration and Administration Act 2013 Sch 1 para 2(2)). The provision made by Sch 1 para 2(1), (2) ceases to have effect at the end of the period of five years beginning with the day on which it comes fully into force: Sch 1 para 2(3). For these purposes, the 'Minister' means the Secretary of State or the Lord President of the Council: see s 25(1). As to the Secretary of State and the Lord President of the Council see PARA 2.
10   Representation of the People Act 1983 s 10ZD(3) (prospectively added: see note 1).

165.   Publication of revised version of registers and list of overseas electors. Following the conclusion of the canvass conducted by a registration officer[1] for any year[2], each such officer must for each year publish a revised version of his registers[3] (if there is a canvass in his area in that year) during the period starting with the end of the canvass in that year and ending with 1 December in that year or such later date as may be prescribed[4]. The revised versions of the registers must incorporate all the alterations which are required to be made in them as a result of the annual canvass[5] and any alterations which are required to be made by virtue of the statutory provisions which relate to the alteration of the registers[6]. A registration officer may in addition, if he thinks fit, publish a revised version of either of his registers at any time between[7] the time when the register was last published following the conclusion of the annual canvass[8] and the time when it is due to be next so published[9]. However, a registration officer proposing to publish a revised version of a register in this way[10] must publish notice of his intention to do so by such time and in such manner as may be prescribed[11]. A register of peers resident outside the United Kingdom who are registered as European parliamentary electors[12] may be published by means of a notice making additions to the registers of parliamentary electors and of local government electors with which it must be combined[13].

When revising a register for publication, the registration officer must make such changes affecting the electoral numbers[14] of persons registered in the register as he considers necessary in order to comply with the requirement[15] that the numbers should, so far as is reasonably practicable, run consecutively in each separate part of a register[16].

Where a revised version of a register is published at any time in this way, the register has effect in the form in which it is so published as from that time until the time when[17] a revised version is next so published[18] or, if earlier, any alteration to the register takes effect under the statutory provisions which relate to the alteration of the registers[19]. The revised version of a register[20] must be kept published until the coming into force of the next revised version of it[21].

At the time when the registration officer publishes a revised version of the register following the conclusion of the annual canvass[22], he must publish also the list of overseas electors[23] by making a copy of it available for inspection under supervision at his office[24]; and the list must be kept so published until the next revised version of the register is published following the conclusion of the annual canvass[25].

1   As to registration officers and the areas for which they act see PARA 139.
2   Ie under the Representation of the People Act 1983 s 10: see PARA 151.
3   See the Representation of the People Act 1983 s 13(1) (s 13 substituted by the Representation of the People Act 2000 s 8, Sch 1 paras 1, 6; the Representation of the People Act 1983 s 13(1) substituted by the Northern Ireland (Miscellaneous Provisions) Act 2006 s 5(1)). The registers referred to in the text are the registers of parliamentary electors and local government electors. As to references, in relation to a registration officer, to 'his' registers see PARA 143 note 3. For the purposes of extending the rights of peers and of relevant citizens of the Union who (subject to the requirement of registration) may vote at European parliamentary elections, the Representation of the People Act 1983 s 13 is applied with modifications: see the Representation of the People (England and Wales) Regulations 2001, SI 2001/341, reg 13(4), Sch 4 (cited in PARA 101 note 7); and the European Parliamentary Elections (Franchise of Relevant Citizens of the Union) Regulations 2001, SI 2001/1184, reg 9, Schedule (cited in PARA 102 note 6).

    Any reference in the Representation of the People Act 1983 s 13 to the publication of a revised version of the register is to its publication in accordance with regulations made in pursuance of s 53(1), Sch 2 para 10A (copies of the register etc to be made available for inspection by the public) and Sch 2 para 10B(1)(a) (registration officer to supply copies of the register etc to prescribed persons) (see PARA 112): s 13(6) (as so substituted). Accordingly, the manner in which each revised version of the full register is to be published under s 13(1) and s 13(3) (see the text and notes 7–11) is by the registration officer:
    (1)   making a copy of it available for inspection under supervision at his office, and at such places, if any, in his registration area as allow members of the public in that area reasonable facilities for that purpose (Representation of the People (England and Wales) Regulations 2001, SI 2001/341, reg 43(1)(a) (reg 43(1) numbered and substituted, reg 43(1A) added, by SI 2002/1871)); and
    (2)   supplying copies of it in accordance with the Representation of the People (England and Wales) Regulations 2001, SI 2001/341, Pt VI (regs 92–115) (see PARA 179 et seq) (reg 43(1)(b) (as so substituted)).
    Where a copy of the full register is made available pursuant to head (1) above by providing the register on a computer screen or otherwise in data form, the registration officer must ensure that

the manner in, and equipment on, which that copy is provided do not permit any person consulting that copy to search it by electronic means by reference to the name of any person or to copy or transmit any part of that copy by electronic, or any other, means: reg 43(1A) (as so added). The permitted purpose for which a copy of the full register is made available for inspection under supervision in this way does not include direct marketing: see PARA 179 note 18. As to the meaning of 'full register' see PARA 167 note 2. As to the meaning of 'available for inspection' see PARA 142 note 18; and as to provision made for the inspection of documents see PARA 168 note 12. As to the making of regulations under the Representation of the People Act 1983 generally see PARA 28 note 16. By virtue of the Representation of the People (England and Wales) Regulations 2001, SI 2001/341, reg 13(6), (7), reg 43 applies to registration in pursuance of a European parliamentary overseas elector's declaration as it applies to registration in pursuance of an overseas elector's declaration: see PARA 101 note 7.

4   See the Representation of the People Act 1983 s 13(1)(a) (as substituted: see note 3). This provision has effect, however, in the case of a registration officer acting for an area in which (or in part of which) an election to which s 13B applies (alteration of registers (pending elections): see PARA 168) is held during the period, starting with 1 July in the year in question and ending with 1 December in that year, as if for '1 December in that year' there were substituted '1 February in the following year': see s 13(1A) (s 13 as so substituted; s 13(1A) added by the Political Parties and Elections Act 2009 s 23(2)). See note 3. For these purposes, 'prescribed' means prescribed by regulations: see the Representation of the People Act 1983 s 202(1).

     Because the annual canvass for 2013 to be conducted under the Representation of the People Act 1983 s 10(1) (see PARA 151) has been postponed, s 13(1) and s 13(1A) does not apply to registration officers in Great Britain for 2013 (see the Electoral Registration (Postponement of 2013 Annual Canvass) Order 2013, SI 2013/794, art 4(1)(b)); and any other provision of the Representation of the People Act 1983 which refers to a register published under s 13(1)(a) applies in the same way to a register published in Great Britain under the Electoral Registration (Postponement of 2013 Annual Canvass) Order 2013, SI 2013/794, art 3 (see art 4(1)(c)). Accordingly, each registration officer in England must publish a revised version of his registers by 17 February 2014; and each registration officer in Scotland and Wales must publish a revised version of his registers by 10 March 2014: see art 3(1), (2). As to the meanings of 'England' and 'Wales' see PARA 1 note 1. As to the system of individual electoral registration which, at the date at which this volume states the law, is likely to provide the basis for the register in use at the 2015 general election and beyond, see PARA 152 et seq.

5   Representation of the People Act 1983 s 13(2)(a) (as substituted: see note 3). The text refers to alterations which are required to be made as mentioned in s 10(6) (see PARA 151): see s 13(2)(a) (as so substituted). See note 3.

6   Representation of the People Act 1983 s 13(2)(b) (as substituted: see note 3). The text refers to alterations which are required to be made by virtue of s 13A(3) (see PARA 168): see s 13(2)(b) (as so substituted). See note 3.

     As from a day to be appointed under the Electoral Registration and Administration Act 2013 s 27(1), the Representation of the People Act 1983 s 13(2)(b) is amended so that it refers to alterations which are required to be made by virtue of s 13A(3) or s 13(3A) (see PARA 168): see s 13(2)(b) (s 13 as so substituted; s 13(2)(b) prospectively amended by the Electoral Registration and Administration Act 2013 s 13(1), Sch 4 paras 1, 11(1), (2)). However, at the date at which this volume states the law, no such day had been appointed.

7   See the Representation of the People Act 1983 s 13(3) (as substituted: see note 3). See note 3.

8   Representation of the People Act 1983 s 13(3)(a) (as substituted: see note 3). The text refers to the time when the register was last published in accordance with s 13(1) (see the text and notes 1–4): see s 13(3)(a) (as so substituted). See note 3.

9   Representation of the People Act 1983 s 13(3)(b) (as substituted: see note 3). See note 3.

10   Ie in accordance with the Representation of the People Act 1983 s 13(3): see s 13(3) (as substituted: see note 3).

11   See the Representation of the People Act 1983 s 13(3) (as substituted: see note 3). See note 3. As to the meaning of 'prescribed' see note 4. Accordingly, a notice under s 13(3) must be published:

    (1)   not less than 14 days before the publication of the revised version of the register to which it relates (Representation of the People (England and Wales) Regulations 2001, SI 2001/341, reg 36(1)(a));

    (2)   in a newspaper circulating in the area for which the registration officer acts (reg 36(1)(b)); and

    (3)   by posting a copy of it at his office and in some conspicuous place or places in that area (reg 36(1)(c)).

     For the purposes of extending the rights of relevant citizens of the Union who (subject to the requirements of registration) may vote at European parliamentary elections, the Representation of the People (England and Wales) Regulations 2001, SI 2001/341, reg 36 is applied with modifications: see the European Parliamentary Elections (Franchise of Relevant Citizens of the Union) Regulations 2001, SI 2001/1184, reg 9, Schedule; and PARA 102 note 6.

12 Ie a register under the Representation of the People Act 1985 s 3, which has been prepared and published in accordance with the Representation of the People (England and Wales) Regulations 2001, SI 2001/341, reg 13, and the provisions applied by it (see PARA 101): see reg 13(8).

13 Representation of the People (England and Wales) Regulations 2001, SI 2001/341, reg 13(8). As to the combination of registers see PARA 145.

14 As to electoral numbers see PARA 145.

15 Ie the requirement in the Representation of the People Act 1983 s 9(4) (see PARA 145): see s 13(4) (as substituted: see note 3).

16 Representation of the People Act 1983 s 13(4) (as substituted: see note 3). See note 3. As to the framing of a register in parts see PARA 145.

17 See the Representation of the People Act 1983 s 13(5) (as substituted: see note 3). See note 3.

18 Representation of the People Act 1983 s 13(5)(a) (as substituted: see note 3). See note 3.

19 Representation of the People Act 1983 s 13(5)(b) (s 13 as substituted (see note 3); s 13(5)(b) amended by the Political Parties and Elections Act 2009 s 39, Sch 6 para 2). The text refers to alterations which take effect under any of the Representation of the People Act 1983 s 13A (see PARA 168), s 13AB (not yet in force) (see PARA 168), s 13B (see PARA 168), s 13BA (alteration of registers in Northern Ireland) or s 13BB (prospectively repealed) (election falling within canvass period: see PARA 157 note 7): see s 13(5)(b) (as so substituted and amended). See note 3.

As from a day to be appointed under the Electoral Registration and Administration Act 2013 s 27(1), the Representation of the People Act 1983 s 13(5)(b) is amended so that the reference to s 13BB (prospectively repealed) is repealed: see s 13(5)(b) (as so substituted and amended; s 13(5)(b) prospectively further amended by the Electoral Registration and Administration Act 2013 Sch 4 paras 1, 11(1), (3)). However, at the date at which this volume states the law, no such day had been appointed.

20 Ie the revised version of a register published under the Representation of the People Act 1983 s 13(1) (see the text and notes 1–4) or s 13(3) (see the text and notes 7–11): see the Representation of the People (England and Wales) Regulations 2001, SI 2001/341, reg 43(2).

21 Representation of the People (England and Wales) Regulations 2001, SI 2001/341, reg 43(2). See note 3.

22 Ie under the Representation of the People Act 1983 s 13(1) (see the text and notes 1–4): see the Representation of the People (England and Wales) Regulations 2001, SI 2001/341, reg 45(3) (amended by SI 2002/1871).

23 As to the meaning of 'list of overseas electors' see PARA 143 note 9.

24 See the Representation of the People (England and Wales) Regulations 2001, SI 2001/341, reg 45(3) (as amended: see note 22). As to the meaning of 'available for inspection' see PARA 142 note 18. By virtue of the Representation of the People (England and Wales) Regulations 2001, SI 2001/341, reg 13(6), (7), reg 45 applies to registration in pursuance of a European parliamentary overseas elector's declaration as it applies to registration in pursuance of an overseas elector's declaration: see PARA 101 note 7.

25 See the Representation of the People (England and Wales) Regulations 2001, SI 2001/341, reg 45(3) (as amended: see note 22). The text refers to the time when the next revised version of the register is published under the Representation of the People Act 1983 s 13(1) (see the text and notes 1–4): see the Representation of the People (England and Wales) Regulations 2001, SI 2001/341, reg 45(3) (as so amended). See note 24.

166. Supply of electoral information following publication of revised register.
As soon as practicable after the publication of a revised version of the register[1] following the conclusion of the annual canvass[2], the registration officer[3] must supply to the Secretary of State[4] a document setting out the information about electors which is required as follows[5]:

(1) the name of the constituency[6] (and, if only part of the constituency is situated in the area for which the registration officer acts, that fact) must be stated and the following total numbers of electors in that constituency or part thereof listed, namely[7]:

(a) parliamentary electors (including those referred to in head (1)(d) below)[8];

(b)   local government electors (including those referred to in head (1)(d) below)[9];

(c)   those local government electors who are ineligible to vote at parliamentary elections[10]; and

(d)   those registered before attaining voting age[11];

(2)   the following totals must be set out separately as respects those electors referred to in head (1)(a) and head (1)(d) above, namely[12]:

      (a)   those registered by virtue of residence at a qualifying address[13];

      (b)   those registered in pursuance of a service declaration[14];

      (c)   those registered in pursuance of an overseas elector's declaration[15]; and

      (d)   those registered in pursuance of a declaration of local connection[16];

(3)   in respect of each relevant area[17] in the constituency, there must be stated[18]:

      (a)   its name or number[19];

      (b)   the letters[20] for each parliamentary polling district in each relevant area (or part thereof)[21]; and

      (c)   if only part of the relevant area is situated in the constituency, that fact[22],

and the following total numbers of electors in that area or part thereof must be listed, namely[23]:

      (i)   parliamentary electors (including those referred to in head (ii) below)[24];

      (ii)   those registered before attaining voting age[25]; and

      (iii)   those local government electors who are ineligible to vote at parliamentary elections[26];

(4)   the total number of electors who have an anonymous entry must be stated[27].

1   As to the meaning of references to publication of a revised version of the register see PARA 165 note 3.

2   Ie under the Representation of the People Act 1983 s 13(1) (see PARA 165): see the Representation of the People (England and Wales) Regulations 2001, SI 2001/341, reg 44(1) (reg 44(1) amended, reg 44(6) added, by SI 2006/2910).

3   As to registration officers and the areas for which they act see PARA 139.

4   As to the Secretary of State see PARA 2.

5   See the Representation of the People (England and Wales) Regulations 2001, SI 2001/341, reg 44(1) (as amended: see note 2).

6   As to the meaning of 'constituency' for these purposes see PARA 9.

7   See the Representation of the People (England and Wales) Regulations 2001, SI 2001/341, reg 44(2).

8   Representation of the People (England and Wales) Regulations 2001, SI 2001/341, reg 44(2)(a). As to the entitlement to vote as a parliamentary elector see PARA 95.

9   Representation of the People (England and Wales) Regulations 2001, SI 2001/341, reg 44(2)(b). As to the entitlement to vote as a local government elector see PARA 97.

10   Representation of the People (England and Wales) Regulations 2001, SI 2001/341, reg 44(2)(c).

11   Representation of the People (England and Wales) Regulations 2001, SI 2001/341, reg 44(2)(d). The text refers to those registered in pursuance of the Representation of the People Act 1983 s 4(5) (attainers: see PARA 113): see the Representation of the People (England and Wales) Regulations 2001, SI 2001/341, reg 44(2)(d).

12   See the Representation of the People (England and Wales) Regulations 2001, SI 2001/341, reg 44(3).

13   Representation of the People (England and Wales) Regulations 2001, SI 2001/341, reg 44(3)(a). As to registration by virtue of residence at a qualifying address see PARA 113.

14   Representation of the People (England and Wales) Regulations 2001, SI 2001/341, reg 44(3)(b). As to registration in pursuance of a service declaration see PARA 125 et seq.

15 Representation of the People (England and Wales) Regulations 2001, SI 2001/341, reg 44(3)(c). As to registration in pursuance of an overseas elector's declaration see PARA 114 et seq.

16 Representation of the People (England and Wales) Regulations 2001, SI 2001/341, reg 44(3)(d). As to registration in pursuance of a declaration of local connection see PARA 121 et seq.

17 For these purposes, 'relevant area' means, in England, a ward of a district, of a London borough or of the City of London and, in Wales, an electoral division of a county or county borough: see the Representation of the People (England and Wales) Regulations 2001, SI 2001/341, reg 44(5). As to the City of London see PARA 33. As to districts in England and their councils see LOCAL GOVERNMENT vol 69 (2009) PARA 24 et seq. As to London boroughs and their councils see LOCAL GOVERNMENT vol 69 (2009) PARA 35; LONDON GOVERNMENT vol 71 (2013) PARAS 15, 20 et seq. As to counties in Wales and their councils see LOCAL GOVERNMENT vol 69 (2009) PARA 37 et seq; and as to county boroughs in Wales and their councils see LOCAL GOVERNMENT vol 69 (2009) PARA 37 et seq.

18 See the Representation of the People (England and Wales) Regulations 2001, SI 2001/341, reg 44(4).

19 Representation of the People (England and Wales) Regulations 2001, SI 2001/341, reg 44(4)(a).

20 Ie the different letters for each parliamentary polling district referred to in the Representation of the People (England and Wales) Regulations 2001, SI 2001/341, reg 39 (see PARA 145): see reg 44(4)(b).

21 Representation of the People (England and Wales) Regulations 2001, SI 2001/341, reg 44(4)(b).

22 Representation of the People (England and Wales) Regulations 2001, SI 2001/341, reg 44(4)(c).

23 See the Representation of the People (England and Wales) Regulations 2001, SI 2001/341, reg 44(4).

24 Representation of the People (England and Wales) Regulations 2001, SI 2001/341, reg 44(4)(i).

25 Representation of the People (England and Wales) Regulations 2001, SI 2001/341, reg 44(4)(ii). The text refers to those registered in pursuance of the Representation of the People Act 1983 s 4(5) (attainers: see PARA 113): see the Representation of the People (England and Wales) Regulations 2001, SI 2001/341, reg 44(4)(ii).

26 Representation of the People (England and Wales) Regulations 2001, SI 2001/341, reg 44(4)(iii).

27 See the Representation of the People (England and Wales) Regulations 2001, SI 2001/341, reg 44(6) (as added: see note 2).

167. Publication of edited version of register. At the time when the registration officer[1] publishes a version of the register (the 'full register')[2], he must also publish[3] a version of the register (the 'edited register')[4], which must omit the name and address of any elector whose details are included in the full register, if a request has been duly made[5] by or on behalf of that elector for his name and address to be excluded from the edited register[6]. The edited register also must omit all anonymous entries in the register, and any information relating to them[7]. In other respects, the edited register must be identical to the full register and, accordingly, must include any mark or date which is required to be recorded against the name of any elector[8].

The manner in which each revised version of the edited register is to be published in this way is by the registration officer making a copy of it available for inspection at his office[9] and by such other means (if any) as he thinks appropriate[10]. Each revised version of the edited register must be kept published until the coming into force of the next revised version of it[11].

1 As to registration officers and the areas for which they act see PARA 139.

2 Ie a revised version of the register published under the Representation of the People Act 1983 s 13(1) or (3) (see PARA 165): see the Representation of the People (England and Wales) Regulations 2001, SI 2001/341, reg 93(1) (reg 93 added by SI 2002/1871). Unless the context otherwise requires, 'full register' has the meaning given in the Representation of the People (England and Wales) Regulations 2001, SI 2001/341, reg 93(1) (see reg 3(1) (definition added by SI 2002/1871)); and, unless the contrary intention appears, any reference in the Representation of the People (England and Wales) Regulations 2001, SI 2001/341, to the register is to the full register (see reg 93(5) (as so added)).

3 Ie under the Representation of the People (England and Wales) Regulations 2001, SI 2001/341, reg 93: see reg 93(1) (as added: see note 2).

4   Representation of the People (England and Wales) Regulations 2001, SI 2001/341, reg 93(1) (as added: see note 2). Unless the context otherwise requires, 'edited register' has the meaning given in reg 93(1): see reg 3(1) (definition added by SI 2002/1871).

5   Ie in the form referred to in the Representation of the People Act 1983 s 10(4) (see PARA 151) or in accordance with the Representation of the People (England and Wales) Regulations 2001, SI 2001/341, reg 26 (see PARA 158): see reg 93(2) (as added: see note 2).

6   Representation of the People (England and Wales) Regulations 2001, SI 2001/341, reg 93(2) (as added: see note 2). Notwithstanding the omission of names and addresses in accordance with reg 93(2), reg 41 (order of names: see PARA 145) applies to the edited register as it applies to the full register: reg 93(4) (as so added).

7   Representation of the People (England and Wales) Regulations 2001, SI 2001/341, reg 93(2A) (reg 93 as added (see note 2); reg 93(2A) added by SI 2006/2910).

8   Representation of the People (England and Wales) Regulations 2001, SI 2001/341, reg 93(3) (as added: see note 2). As to the marks and dates which must be recorded against the name of any elector in the register see PARA 145.

9   See the Representation of the People (England and Wales) Regulations 2001, SI 2001/341, reg 93(6)(a) (as added: see note 2). As to the meaning of 'available for inspection' see PARA 142 note 18. The usual provision made under the Representation of the People (England and Wales) Regulations 2001, SI 2001/341 for inspecting a document (see reg 7(1); and PARA 142 note 18) does not apply to the full register: reg 7(2) (reg 7(2)–(5) added by SI 2002/1871). A person inspecting the full register may not make copies of any part of it, or record any particulars included in it, otherwise than by means of handwritten notes: see the Representation of the People (England and Wales) Regulations 2001, SI 2001/341, reg 7(3) (as so added). A person who inspects the full register and makes a copy of it or records any particulars included in it otherwise than by means of handwritten notes is guilty of an offence and liable on summary conviction to a fine not exceeding level 5 on the standard scale: see reg 7(4) (as so added); and PARA 734. For these purposes, 'full register' includes any part of it and also includes any notice published under the Representation of the People Act 1983 s 13A(2) (see PARA 168), s 13B(3) (see PARA 168), s 13B(3B) (see PARA 168) or s 13B(3D) (see PARA 168) altering the register: see the Representation of the People (England and Wales) Regulations 2001, SI 2001/341, reg 7(5) (as so added; amended by SI 2006/2910). As to registration offences generally see further PARA 733 et seq. As to the standard scale see SENTENCING AND DISPOSITION OF OFFENDERS vol 92 (2010) PARA 142.

By virtue of the Representation of the People (England and Wales) Regulations 2001, SI 2001/341, reg 13(6), (7), reg 7 is applied with modifications to registration in pursuance of a European parliamentary overseas elector's declaration as it applies to registration in pursuance of an overseas elector's declaration (see PARA 101 note 7); and for the purposes of extending the rights of relevant citizens of the Union who (subject to the requirements of registration) may vote at European parliamentary elections, reg 7 is applied with modifications (see the European Parliamentary Elections (Franchise of Relevant Citizens of the Union) Regulations 2001, SI 2001/1184, reg 9, Schedule; and PARA 102 note 6).

10   Representation of the People (England and Wales) Regulations 2001, SI 2001/341, reg 93(6)(b) (as added: see note 2).

11   Representation of the People (England and Wales) Regulations 2001, SI 2001/341, reg 93(7) (as added: see note 2).

168. Notice of alteration of published register. Where, at any time ('the relevant time') after the publication of a revised version of a register[1] by a registration officer in Great Britain[2], the registration officer[3]:

(1)   on an application for registration being made by any person in accordance with the prescribed[4] requirements, determines[5] that that person is entitled to be so registered[6];

(2)   is required, by virtue of any provision of the Representation of the People Act 1983 relating to the franchise and its exercise[7], to remove a person's entry from the register[8];

(3)   is notified of any decision on an appeal[9] which duly requires any alteration in the register[10]; or

(4)   determines that the register contains any clerical error[11],

the registration officer must issue, in the prescribed manner, a notice[12] specifying the appropriate alteration in the register[13]. The notice must be so issued by him either on the first day of the month which follows that in which the relevant time falls[14] or (if that day is less than 14 days after that time) on the first day of the month immediately following that month[15]. However, a registration officer is not so required to issue a notice in a case where the notice is required to be issued either at the beginning of the month containing the date on which a revised version of the register is next due to be published[16], or at the beginning of either of the two months preceding that containing the date on which a revised version of the register is next due to be published following the conclusion of the annual canvass[17]. In such a case, the alteration in question must be made in that revised version of the register[18]. The alteration in question has effect as from the beginning of the day on which the notice is issued[19].

However, if an alteration in a published version of a register is due to take effect[20] after the fifth day before the date of the poll[21] for a parliamentary election[22], an election to the European Parliament[23], a Welsh Assembly election[24], a local government election in England or Wales[25] or elections of police and crime commissioners[26] ('a relevant election'), the alteration does not have effect for the purposes of that election[27]. In circumstances where:

(a)   at any time before the appropriate publication date[28] in the case of such an election, the registration officer has to issue a notice specifying an appropriate alteration in the register[29] in connection with a determination, requirement or decision falling within any of heads (1) to (4) above[30];

(b)   in consequence of the determination, requirement or decision, an entry relating to a person falls to be made in (or removed from) the register in respect of an address in the relevant election area[31]; and

(c)   no alteration made in consequence of that determination, requirement or decision has already taken effect, or is due to take effect, on or before the fifth day before the date of the poll[32],

the registration officer must issue, in the prescribed manner, a notice specifying the appropriate alteration in the register[33]. The notice must be so issued by him on the appropriate publication date[34] and the alteration takes effect as from the beginning of that day[35]. In circumstances where:

(i)   at any time on or after the appropriate publication date in the case of a relevant election but before the prescribed time on the day of the poll[36], the registration officer must issue, in the prescribed manner, a notice specifying the appropriate alteration in the register[37] in connection with a notification mentioned in head (3) above[38]; and

(ii)   in consequence of the notification either an entry relating to that person falls to be made in the register in respect of an address in the relevant election area[39] or his entry in the register requires to be altered[40],

the registration officer must issue, in the prescribed manner, a notice specifying the appropriate alteration in the register[41]. The notice must be so issued by him when he receives the notification[42] and the alteration takes effect as from the beginning of the day on which the notice is issued[43]. In circumstances where:

(A)   at any time on or after the appropriate publication date in the case of a relevant election but before the prescribed time on the day of the poll[44], the registration officer must issue, in the prescribed manner, a notice specifying the appropriate alteration in the register[45] in connection with a determination falling within head (4) above[46]; and

(B) the determination was made following a representation[47] made by or on behalf of a person to the registration officer[48]; and

(C) in consequence of the determination, either an entry relating to that person falls to be made in the register in respect of an address in the relevant election area[49] or his entry in the register requires to be altered[50],

the registration officer must issue, in the prescribed manner, a notice specifying the appropriate alteration in the register[51]. The notice must be so issued by him when he makes the determination[52] and the alteration takes effect as from the beginning of the day on which the notice is issued[53].

As from a day to be appointed[54], on the interim publication date[55], where[56]:

(aa) at any time before the interim publication date, the registration officer has to issue a notice specifying an appropriate alteration in the register[57] in connection with a determination, requirement or decision falling within any of heads (1) to (4) above[58];

(bb) in consequence of the determination, requirement or decision, an entry relating to a person falls to be made in (or removed from) the register in respect of an address in the relevant election area[59]; and

(cc) no alteration made in consequence of that determination, requirement or decision has already taken effect, or is due to take effect, under a relevant provision[60] on or before the interim publication date[61],

the registration officer must issue, in the prescribed manner[62], a notice specifying the appropriate alteration in the register[63]; and the alteration takes effect from the beginning of the interim publication date[64].

No alteration affecting a published version of a register of electors is to be made otherwise than in accordance with the provisions set out above[65].

1 Any reference in the Representation of the People Act 1983 s 13 (see PARA 165) or s 13A to the publication of a revised version of the register is to its publication in accordance with regulations made in pursuance of s 53(1), Sch 2 para 10A (copies of the register etc to be made available for inspection by the public) and Sch 2 para 10B(1)(a) (registration officer to supply copies of the register etc to prescribed persons) (see PARA 112): see s 13(6); and PARA 165 note 3. As to the manner in which each revised version of the full register is to be published under s 13(1) and s 13(3) see the Representation of the People (England and Wales) Regulations 2001, SI 2001/341, reg 43; and PARA 165 note 3.

2 As to the meaning of 'Great Britain' see PARA 1 note 1. As to registration officers and the areas for which they act see PARA 139. As to references, in relation to a registration officer, to 'his' registers see PARA 143 note 3.

3 See the Representation of the People Act 1983 s 13A(1) (ss 13A, 13B added by the Representation of the People Act 2000 s 8, Sch 1 paras 1, 6).

For the purposes of extending the rights of peers and relevant citizens of the Union who (subject to the requirement of registration) may vote at European parliamentary elections, the Representation of the People Act 1983 s 13A and s 13B are applied with modifications: see the Representation of the People (England and Wales) Regulations 2001, SI 2001/341, reg 13(4), Sch 4 (cited in PARA 101 note 7); and the European Parliamentary Elections (Franchise of Relevant Citizens of the Union) Regulations 2001, SI 2001/1184, reg 9, Schedule (cited in PARA 102 note 6). The Representation of the People Act 1983 s 13B has been applied and modified in order to make provision for the conduct of local authority referendums, in relation to Wales, by the Local Authorities (Conduct of Referendums) (Wales) Regulations 2008, SI 2008/1848, reg 8(2), Sch 4 Table 1; and, in relation to England, by the Local Authorities (Conduct of Referendums) (England) Regulations 2012, SI 2012/323, regs 8(2), 11–13, Sch 4 Table 1: see PARA 15 note 2. As to the meanings of 'England' and 'Wales' see PARA 1 note 1.

4 For these purposes, 'prescribed' means prescribed by regulations: see the Representation of the People Act 1983 s 202(1). As to the making of regulations under the Representation of the People Act 1983 generally see PARA 28 note 16. As to the regulations that have been made for the purposes of s 13A see the Representation of the People (England and Wales) Regulations 2001, SI 2001/341; and PARA 158.

5   For these purposes, 'determines' means determines in accordance with regulations: see the Representation of the People Act 1983 s 13A(6) (as added: see note 3). See note 3. As to the regulations that have been made under s 13A(6) see the Representation of the People (England and Wales) Regulations 2001, SI 2001/341; and PARA 162.

6   Representation of the People Act 1983 s 13A(1)(a) (as added: see note 3). See note 3. As from a day to be appointed under the Electoral Registration and Administration Act 2013 s 27(1), the Representation of the People Act 1983 s 13A(1)(a) is amended by the Electoral Registration and Administration Act 2013 s 13(1), Sch 4 paras 1, 12(1), (2)(b), so that its effect is limited to Northern Ireland only. The Representation of the People Act 1983 s 13A(1)(za) is added, accordingly, to accommodate circumstances where the registration officer is required by s 10ZC(1) (not yet in force) (registration officer to determine applications for individual registration of electors: see PARA 163) to enter a person in the register: see s 13A(1)(za) (prospectively added by the Electoral Registration and Administration Act 2013 Sch 4 paras 1, 12(1), (2)(a)). However, at the date at which this volume states the law, no such day had been appointed.

7   Ie by virtue of any provision of the Representation of the People Act 1983 Pt I (ss 1–66B): see s 13A(1)(b) (as added: see note 3). See note 3.

8   Representation of the People Act 1983 s 13A(1)(b) (as added: see note 3). See note 3. As from a day to be appointed under the Electoral Registration and Administration Act 2013 s 27(1), the Representation of the People Act 1983 s 13A(1)(zb) is added to accommodate circumstances where the registration officer is required by s 10ZD(1) (not yet in force) (alterations to entries on register of electors derived from individual registration: see PARA 164) to alter a person's entry in the register: see s 13A(1)(zb) (prospectively added by the Electoral Registration and Administration Act 2013 Sch 4 paras 1, 12(1), (2)(a)). However, at the date at which this volume states the law, no such day had been appointed.

9   Ie by virtue of the Representation of the People Act 1983 s 56 (see PARA 172 et seq): see s 13A(1)(c) (as added: see note 3). See note 3.

10 Representation of the People Act 1983 s 13A(1)(c) (as added: see note 3). Head (3) in the text refers to any such alteration in the register as is mentioned in s 56(4) (see PARA 178): see s 13A(1)(c) (as so added). See note 3.

11 Representation of the People Act 1983 s 13A(1)(d) (as added: see note 3). See note 3. As from a day to be appointed under the Electoral Registration and Administration Act 2013 s 27(1), the Representation of the People Act 1983 s 13A(1)(d) is amended so that it applies, in the case of a registration officer in Great Britain, where he determines that the register contains any information that is incorrect: see s 13A(1)(d) (prospectively amended by the Electoral Registration and Administration Act 2013 s 1(2), Sch 1 para 3). However, at the date at which this volume states the law, no such day had been appointed.

12 A notice under the Representation of the People Act 1983 s 13A(2) or under s 13B(3) (see the text and notes 33–35), s 13B(3B) (see the text and notes 41–43) or s 13B(3D) (see the text and notes 51–53) must be issued (see the Representation of the People (England and Wales) Regulations 2001, SI 2001/341, reg 36(2) (amended by SI 2006/2910)):

    (1)   by making a copy of it available for inspection under supervision at the registration officer's office and at such places, if any, in his registration area as allow members of the public in that area reasonable facilities for that purpose (Representation of the People (England and Wales) Regulations 2001, SI 2001/341, reg 36(2)(a) (reg 36(2)(a) substituted, reg 36(2)(aa) added, by SI 2002/1871));

    (2)   by supplying copies of it in accordance with the Representation of the People (England and Wales) Regulations 2001, SI 2001/341, Pt VI (regs 92–115) (see PARA 179 et seq) (reg 36(2)(aa) (as so added)); and

    (3)   except in a case falling within reg 31C(2)(d) (death of elector: see PARA 169), by sending a copy of it to any person affected by its contents (reg 36(2)(b) (amended by SI 2006/2910)).

    As to the meaning of 'available for inspection' see PARA 142 note 18. See also note 32.
         By virtue of the Representation of the People (England and Wales) Regulations 2001, SI 2001/341, reg 13(6), (7), reg 36(2) applies to registration in pursuance of a European parliamentary overseas elector's declaration as it applies to registration in pursuance of an overseas elector's declaration (see PARA 101 note 7); and for the purposes of extending the rights of relevant citizens of the Union who (subject to the requirement of registration) may vote at European parliamentary elections, reg 36(2) is applied with modifications (see the European Parliamentary Elections (Franchise of Relevant Citizens of the Union) Regulations 2001, SI 2001/1184, reg 9, Schedule; and PARA 102 note 6).

13 Representation of the People Act 1983 s 13A(2) (as added: see note 3). See note 3. This is subject to s 13A(3) (see the text and notes 16–18): see s 13A(2) (as so added). See also note 32.

14 Representation of the People Act 1983 s 13A(2)(a)(i) (as added: see note 3). Periods of time must be calculated in accordance with s 119 (see PARA 230 note 11), which applies for the purposes of s 13A(2)(a) as if it were contained in Pt II (ss 67–119) (the election campaign: see PARA 230 et seq): s 13A(6) (as so added). As to the application and modification of these provisions see note 3.

15 Representation of the People Act 1983 s 13A(2)(a)(ii) (as added: see note 3). See note 3. See also note 14.

As from a day to be appointed under the Electoral Registration and Administration Act 2013 s 27(1), the Representation of the People Act 1983 s 13A(3A) is added to provide s 13A(2)(a)(ii) also does not require a registration officer in Great Britain to issue a notice under s 13A(2) in a case where the month which follows that in which the relevant time falls is the month containing the date on which a revised version of the register is next due to be published in accordance with s 13(1)(a) (see PARA 165); and in such a case the alteration in question must be made in that revised version of the register: see s 13A(3A) (prospectively added by the Electoral Registration and Administration Act 2013 Sch 4 paras 1, 12(1), (3)). However, at the date at which this volume states the law, no such day had been appointed.

16 Representation of the People Act 1983 s 13A(3)(a) (as added: see note 3). The text refers to a revised version of the register next due to be published in accordance with s 13(1) or s 13(3) (see PARA 165): see s 13A(3)(a) (as so added). See note 3.

17 Representation of the People Act 1983 s 13A(3)(b) (as added: see note 3). The text refers to the time when the register is next due to be published in accordance with s 13(1)(a) (see PARA 165): see s 13A(3)(b) (as so added). See note 3.

18 See the Representation of the People Act 1983 s 13A(3) (as added: see note 3). See note 3.

19 Representation of the People Act 1983 s 13A(2)(b) (as added: see note 3). This provision is subject to s 13B(1) (see the text and notes 20–21): see s 13A(2)(b) (as so added). See note 3.

20 Ie by virtue of the Representation of the People Act 1983 s 13A(2) (see the text and notes 12–15, 19): see s 13B(1) (s 13B as added (see note 3); s 13B(1) substituted by the Electoral Administration Act 2006 s 11(1), (2)).

21 See the Representation of the People Act 1983 s 13B(1) (s 13B as added (see note 3); s 13B(1) as substituted (see note 20)). For these purposes, s 119 (see PARA 230 note 11) applies as if it were contained in Pt II (the election campaign: see PARA 230 et seq) and as if each of the days referred to in s 13B were the day on which anything is required or permitted to be done by or in pursuance of Pt II: see s 13B(6) (as so added). As to the application and modification of s 13B see note 3.

22 Representation of the People Act 1983 s 13B(4)(a) (as added: see note 3). See note 3. As to the date of the poll at a parliamentary general election or by-election see PARA 195.

23 Representation of the People Act 1983 s 13B(4)(b) (as added: see note 3). See note 3. As to the date of the poll at a European parliamentary election see PARA 222.

24 Representation of the People Act 1983 s 13B(4)(d) (as added: see note 3). See note 3. An alteration in a published version of a register of electors under s 13A does not have effect for the purposes of an Assembly election if it is to take effect after the fifth day before the date of the poll: National Assembly for Wales (Representation of the People) Order 2007, SI 2007/236, art 4. As to the meaning of 'Assembly election' see PARA 3 note 2. As to the date of the poll at Welsh Assembly elections (including elections to fill vacancies in an Assembly constituency) see PARAS 213–214.

25 Representation of the People Act 1983 s 13B(4)(f) (as added: see note 3). See note 3. As to the date of the poll at local government elections (including elections to fill vacancies) see PARAS 206–209.

26 Representation of the People Act 1983 s 13B(4)(g) (s 13B as added (see note 3); s 13B(4)(g) added by the Police Reform and Social Responsibility Act 2011 s 74, Sch 10 para 3). See note 3. As to elections of police and crime commissioners see POLICE AND INVESTIGATORY POWERS vol 84 (2013) PARA 62 et seq.

27 See the Representation of the People Act 1983 s 13B(1) (s 13B as added (see note 3); s 13B(1) as substituted (see note 20)). See notes 3, 21.

28 For these purposes, the 'appropriate publication date', in relation to a registration officer and an election to which the Representation of the People Act 1983 s 13B applies (see the text and notes 22–26), means either the sixth or the fifth day before the date of the poll, as the registration officer may determine: see s 13B(5) (as added: see note 3). As to the application and modification of these provisions see note 3.

29 Ie where the Representation of the People Act 1983 s 13A applies to a registration officer by virtue of s 13A(1) (see the text and notes 1–11): see s 13B(2)(a) (s 13B as added (see note 3); s 13B(2) substituted by the Electoral Administration Act 2006 s 11(1), (3)).

30　Representation of the People Act 1983 s 13B(2)(a) (s 13B as added (see note 3); s 13B(2) as substituted (see note 29)). See notes 3, 21. As from a day to be appointed under the Electoral Registration and Administration Act 2013 s 27(1), the Representation of the People Act 1983 s 13B(2)(a) is amended so that it applies, in connection with a determination, requirement or decision falling within any of s 13A(1)(za) (not yet in force) (see note 6), s 13A(1)(zb) (not yet in force) (see note 8), or s 13A(1)(b)–(d) (see heads (2) to (4) in the text): see s 13B(2)(a) (prospectively amended by the Electoral Registration and Administration Act 2013 Sch 4 paras 1, 13). However, at the date at which this volume states the law, no such day had been appointed.

31　Representation of the People Act 1983 s 13B(2)(b) (s 13B as added (see note 3); s 13B(2) as substituted (see note 29)). For these purposes, 'the relevant election area', in relation to a registration officer and an election to which s 13B applies (see the text and notes 22–26), means either the area for which the registration officer acts or, if the election is held in only part of that area, the part of that area in question: see s 13B(5) (as so added). As to the application and modification of these provisions see notes 3, 21.

32　See the Representation of the People Act 1983 s 13B(2)(c) (s 13B as added (see note 3); s 13B(2) as substituted (see note 29)). The text refers to alterations taking effect under s 13A(2) (see the text and notes 12–15, 19): see s 13B(2)(c) (s 13B as so added, s 13B(2) as so substituted). As from a day to be appointed under the Electoral Registration and Administration Act 2013 s 27(1), the Representation of the People Act 1983 s 13B(2)(c) is amended so that it applies where no alteration takes effect under s 13A(2) or under s 13AB(3) (not yet in force) (see the text and note 64): see s 13B(2)(c) (s 13B as so added, s 13B(2) as so substituted; s 13B(2)(c) prospectively amended by the Electoral Registration and Administration Act 2013 s 16(1), (4)). However, at the date at which this volume states the law, no such day had been appointed. As to the application and modification of these provisions see notes 3, 21.

33　See the Representation of the People Act 1983 s 13B(3) (as added: see note 3). In a case where s 13B(3), s 13B(3B) (see the text and notes 41–43) or s 13B(3D) (see the text and notes 51–53) requires a registration officer to issue a notice, he is not required to issue a notice under s 13A(2) (see the text and notes 12–15), however: s 13A(4) (s 13A as added (see note 3); s 13A(4) amended by the Electoral Administration Act 2006 s 11(6), Sch 1 paras 31, 32). As from a day to be appointed under the Electoral Registration and Administration Act 2013 s 27(1), the Representation of the People Act 1983 s 13A(4) is amended so that it applies in a case where s 13AB(2) (see the text and notes 62–63), s 13B(3), s 13B(3B) (see the text and notes 41–43) or s 13B(3D) (see the text and notes 51–53) requires a registration officer to issue a notice: see s 13A(4) (s 13A as so added, s 13A(4) as so amended and prospectively further amended by the Electoral Registration and Administration Act 2013 s 16(1), (2)(a)). However, at the date at which this volume states the law, no such day had been appointed.

34　Representation of the People Act 1983 s 13B(3)(a) (as added: see note 3).

35　Representation of the People Act 1983 s 13B(3)(b) (as added: see note 3).

36　For the purposes of the Representation of the People Act 1983 s 13B(3A), the prescribed time on the day of the poll is 9 pm: see the Representation of the People (England and Wales) Regulations 2001, SI 2001/341, reg 36(3) (added by SI 2006/2910); and the European Parliamentary Elections Regulations 2004, SI 2004/293, Sch 1 para 47(7) (Sch 1 substituted by SI 2009/186).

37　Ie where the Representation of the People Act 1983 s 13A applies to a registration officer by virtue of s 13A(1) (see the text and notes 1–11): see s 13B(3A)(a) (s 13B(3A)–(3E) added by the Electoral Administration Act 2006 s 11(1), (4)). See notes 3, 21.

38　Representation of the People Act 1983 s 13B(3A)(a) (as added: see note 37). See notes 3, 21.

39　Representation of the People Act 1983 s 13B(3A)(b)(i) (as added: see note 37). See notes 3, 21.

40　Representation of the People Act 1983 s 13B(3A)(b)(ii) (as added: see note 37). See notes 3, 21.

41　Representation of the People Act 1983 s 13B(3B) (as added: see note 37). See notes 3, 21. As to the notice referred to in the text see note 33. Where a notice is issued under s 13B(3B) on the day of the poll, the registration officer must take reasonable steps to ensure that the notice comes to the attention of the relevant registration officer (in the case of a parliamentary election) or the appropriate registration officer (in the case of a European parliamentary election): Representation of the People (England and Wales) Regulations 2001, SI 2001/341, reg 36A(1) (reg 36A added by SI 2006/2910); European Parliamentary Elections Regulations 2004, SI 2004/293, Sch 1 para 47(4) (Sch 1 as substituted: see note 36). Such steps may include communicating the notice to the presiding officer by telephone, in which case the presiding officer must make a written record of that notice: see the Representation of the People (England and Wales) Regulations 2001, SI 2001/341, reg 36A(2), (3) (as so added); and the European Parliamentary Elections Regulations 2004, SI 2004/293, Sch 1 para 47(5), (6) (Sch 1 as so substituted). The presiding officer must keep a list of persons to whom ballot papers are delivered in consequence of an alteration to the register made by virtue of the Representation of the People Act 1983 s 13B(3B) which takes effect on the day of the poll: see Sch 1 r 41A; the European Parliamentary Elections Regulations 2004, SI 2004/293, Sch 1 para 47(1); the Local Elections (Principal Areas) (England and Wales) Rules 2006, SI 2006/3304, Sch 2 r 41; the Local Elections (Parishes and Communities) (England and Wales) Rules 2006, SI 2006/3305, Sch 2 r 41; the National Assembly for Wales (Representation of the People) Order 2007, SI 2007/236, Sch 5 para 51; the Local Authorities (Mayoral Elections) (England and Wales) Regulations 2007, SI 2007/1024, Sch 1 r 43; the Greater London Authority Elections Rules 2007, SI 2007/3541, Sch 1 r 44(1), Sch 2 r 45(1), Sch 3 r 44(1); and PARA 399 note 5. See also the Local Authorities (Conduct of Referendums) (Wales) Regulations 2008, SI 2008/1848, Sch 3 r 32; the Local Authorities (Conduct of Referendums) (England) Regulations 2012, SI 2012/323, Sch 3 r 32. As to the appointment of presiding officers see PARA 393.

Where any other ordinary London Authority election in the Assembly constituency is contested, the same list may be used for the election and each Authority election, and where it is so used, an entry in that list must be taken to mean that ballot papers were delivered in respect of each Authority election, unless the list identifies the election for which a tendered ballot paper was delivered: see the Greater London Authority Elections Rules 2007, SI 2007/3541, Sch 1 r 44(2), Sch 2 r 45(2), Sch 3 r 44(2).

42   Representation of the People Act 1983 s 13B(3B)(a) (as added: see note 37). See notes 3, 21.

43   Representation of the People Act 1983 s 13B(3B)(b) (as added: see note 37). See notes 3, 21.

44   For the purposes of the Representation of the People Act 1983 s 13B(3C), the prescribed time on the day of the poll is 9 pm: see the Representation of the People (England and Wales) Regulations 2001, SI 2001/341, reg 36(3) (as added: see note 36); and the European Parliamentary Elections Regulations 2004, SI 2004/293, Sch 1 para 47(7) (Sch 1 as substituted: see note 36).

45   Ie where the Representation of the People Act 1983 s 13A applies to a registration officer by virtue of s 13A(1) (see the text and notes 1–11): see s 13B(3C)(a) (as added: see note 37). See note 3.

46   Representation of the People Act 1983 s 13B(3C)(a) (as added: see note 37). See note 3.

47   For this purpose, 'representation' means a representation made in accordance with prescribed requirements to the effect that the register contains a clerical error: see the Representation of the People Act 1983 s 13B(3E) (as added: see note 37). See notes 3, 21. For the purposes of s 13B(3C), a representation may be made orally or in writing: see the Representation of the People (England and Wales) Regulations 2001, SI 2001/341, reg 32A(1) (reg 32A added by SI 2006/2910); and the European Parliamentary Elections Regulations 2004, SI 2004/293, Sch 1 para 47(2) (Sch 1 as substituted: see note 36). Where a representation is made in a polling station to a presiding officer, the presiding officer must as soon as practicable communicate that representation to the relevant registration officer (in the case of a parliamentary election) or to the appropriate registration officer (in the case of a European parliamentary election): see the Representation of the People (England and Wales) Regulations 2001, SI 2001/341, reg 32A(2) (as so added); and the European Parliamentary Elections Regulations 2004, SI 2004/293, Sch 1 para 47(3) (Sch 1 as so substituted).

48   Representation of the People Act 1983 s 13B(3C)(b) (as added: see note 37). See notes 3, 21.

49   Representation of the People Act 1983 s 13B(3C)(c)(i) (as added: see note 37). See notes 3, 21.

50   Representation of the People Act 1983 s 13B(3C)(c)(ii) (as added: see note 37). See notes 3, 21.

51   Representation of the People Act 1983 s 13B(3D) (as added: see note 37). See notes 3, 21. As to the notice referred to in the text see note 33. Where a notice is issued under s 13B(3D) on the day of the poll, the registration officer must take reasonable steps to ensure that the notice comes to the attention of the relevant presiding officer: see the Representation of the People (England and Wales) Regulations 2001, SI 2001/341, reg 36A(1) (reg 36A as added: see note 41); and the European Parliamentary Elections Regulations 2004, SI 2004/293, Sch 1 para 47(4) (Sch 1 as substituted: see note 36). Such steps may include communicating the notice to the presiding officer by telephone, in which case the presiding officer must make a written record of that notice: see the Representation of the People (England and Wales) Regulations 2001, SI 2001/341, reg 36A(2), (3) (as so added); and the European Parliamentary Elections Regulations 2004, SI 2004/293, Sch 1 para 47(5), (6) (Sch 1 as so substituted). The presiding officer must keep a list of persons to whom ballot papers are delivered in consequence of an alteration to the register made by virtue of the Representation of the People Act 1983 s 13B(3D) which takes effect on the day of the poll: see Sch 1 r 41A; the European Parliamentary Elections Regulations 2004, SI 2004/293, Sch 1 para 47(1); the Local Elections (Principal Areas) (England and Wales) Rules 2006, SI 2006/3304, Sch 2 r 41; the Local Elections (Parishes and Communities) (England and Wales) Rules 2006, SI 2006/3305, Sch 2 r 41; the National Assembly for Wales (Representation of the People) Order 2007, SI 2007/236, Sch 5 para 51; the

Local Authorities (Mayoral Elections) (England and Wales) Regulations 2007, SI 2007/1024, Sch 1 r 43; the Greater London Authority Elections Rules 2007, SI 2007/3541, Sch 1 r 44(1), Sch 2 r 45(1), Sch 3 r 44(1); and PARA 399 note 5. See also the Local Authorities (Conduct of Referendums) (Wales) Regulations 2008, SI 2008/1848, Sch 3 r 32; the Local Authorities (Conduct of Referendums) (England) Regulations 2012, SI 2012/323, Sch 3 r 32.

52 Representation of the People Act 1983 s 13B(3D)(a) (as added: see note 37). See notes 3, 21.
53 Representation of the People Act 1983 s 13B(3D)(b) (as added: see note 37). See notes 3, 21.
54 The Representation of the People Act 1983 s 13AB is added by the Electoral Registration and Administration Act 2013 s 16(1), (3), as from a day to be appointed under s 27(1). However, at the date at which this volume states the law, no such day had been appointed.
55 In relation to a registration officer and an election to which the Representation of the People Act 1983 s 13AB applies, there are two interim publication dates (see s 13AB(4) (prospectively added: see note 54)):
    (1) the first interim publication date is the last day on which nomination papers may be delivered to the returning officer for the purposes of the election (s 13AB(5) (prospectively added));
    (2) the second interim publication date is to be determined by the registration officer, but must be a day after the first interim publication date and before the appropriate publication date (s 13AB(6) (prospectively added)).
    The 'appropriate publication date', in relation to a registration officer and an election to which s 13AB applies, means either the sixth or the fifth day before the date of the poll, as the registration officer may determine: see s 13B(5) (as added: see note 3); applied by s 13AB(9) (prospectively added). The provision made by s 13A(6) (see note 14) applies for the purposes of s 13AB as it applies for the purposes of s 13A: see s 13AB(9) (prospectively added). For these purposes, the elections to which s 13AB applies are parliamentary elections in England, Wales or Scotland, elections in England, Wales or Scotland to the European Parliament, elections to the Scottish Parliament or National Assembly for Wales, local government elections in England, Wales or Scotland and elections of police and crime commissioners in England and Wales: see s 13AB(8) (prospectively added).
56 See the Representation of the People Act 1983 s 13AB(1), (2) (prospectively added: see note 54).
57 Ie where the Representation of the People Act 1983 s 13A applies to a registration officer by virtue of s 13A(1) (see the text and notes 1–11): see s 13AB(1)(a) (prospectively added: see note 54).
58 Representation of the People Act 1983 s 13AB(1)(a) (prospectively added: see note 54). Head (aa) in the text applies in connection with a determination, requirement or decision falling within any of s 13B(1)(za) (not yet in force) (see note 6), s 13B(1)(zb) (not yet in force) (see note 8), or s 13B(b)–(d) (see heads (2) to (4) in the text): see s 13AB(1)(a) (prospectively added).
59 Representation of the People Act 1983 s 13AB(1)(b) (prospectively added: see note 54). For these purposes, 'the relevant election area', in relation to a registration officer and an election to which s 13AB applies (see note 55), means either the area for which the registration officer acts or, if the election is held in only part of that area, the part of that area in question: see s 13B(5) (as added: see note 3); applied by s 13AB(9) (prospectively added).
60 For this purpose, 'relevant provision' means (in relation to the first interim publication date) the Representation of the People Act 1983 s 13A(2) (see the text and notes 12–15, 19) and (in relation to the second interim publication date) s 13A(2) and s 13A(3) (see the text and notes 16–18) as it applies in relation to the first interim publication date: see s 13AB(7) (prospectively added: see note 54).
61 Representation of the People Act 1983 s 13AB(1)(c) (prospectively added: see note 54).
62 For these purposes, 'prescribed' means prescribed by regulations: see the Representation of the People Act 1983 s 202(1). At the date at which this volume states the law, no such regulations had been prescribed.
63 See the Representation of the People Act 1983 s 13AB(2) (prospectively added: see note 54).
64 See the Representation of the People Act 1983 s 13AB(3) (prospectively added: see note 54).
65 Representation of the People Act 1983 s 13A(5) (s 13A as added (see note 3); s 13A(5) amended by the Political Parties and Elections Act 2009 s 39, Sch 6 para 3). The text refers to the provisions of the Representation of the People Act 1983 s 13A (see the text and notes 1–19), s 13AB (see the text and notes 54–64), s 13B (see the text and notes 20–53), and s 13BB (prospectively repealed) (election falling within canvass period: see PARA 157 note 7): see s 13A(5) (s 13A as so added, s 13A(5) as so amended). As from a day to be appointed under the Electoral Registration and Administration Act 2013 s 27(1), the Representation of the People Act 1983 s 13A(5) is amended so that it applies to the provisions of s 13A, s 13AB or s 13B only: see s 13A(5) (s 13A as so added, s 13A(5) as so amended and prospectively further

amended by the Electoral Registration and Administration Act 2013 s 16(1), (2)(b), Sch 4 paras 12(1), (4)). However, at the date at which this volume states the law, no such day had been appointed.

(v) Termination of Entitlement to Registration

169. Termination of entitlement to be registered as parliamentary or local government elector. Until a day to be appointed[1], where a person ('the elector') is entered in a register in respect of any address[2], the elector is entitled to remain registered in the register in respect of that address until such time as the registration officer[3] concerned[4]:

(1) determines[5], on the conclusion of an annual canvass[6], that the elector was not resident[7] at that address on the 15 October in question[8], or that either because the form used for the purposes of the canvass[9] was not returned in respect of that address[10] or because, for any other reason, insufficient information was obtained as to whether the elector was resident at that address on that date[11], the registration officer is unable to satisfy himself that the elector was then so resident at that address[12]; or

(2) determines that the elector was not entitled to be registered in respect of that address or that he has ceased to be resident at that address or has otherwise ceased to satisfy the conditions for registration as a parliamentary or local government elector[13].

Where the entitlement of a person to remain registered in a register in respect of any address terminates by virtue of head (1) or head (2) above[14], the registration officer concerned must remove that person's entry from the register once the officer has satisfied any prescribed requirements applying in relation to the removal of that entry[15]. However, this duty to remove a person's entry from the register of parliamentary or local government electors does not apply in circumstances where[16]:

(a) on the conclusion of an annual canvass[17] the registration officer is unable to satisfy himself that a person duly entered in a register in respect of any address was, on the 15 October in question, resident at that address either because the form used for the purposes of the canvass[18] was not returned in respect of that address or because, for any other reason, insufficient information was obtained as to whether that person was resident at that address on that date[19];

(b) the registration officer has no information which suggests that that person is no longer so resident[20]; and

(c) that person was registered at that address otherwise than by virtue of notional residence as a patient in a mental hospital[21] or as a person remanded in custody[22] or in pursuance of a declaration of local connection, a service declaration or an overseas elector's declaration[23].

Where the circumstances set out in heads (a) to (c) above apply, the registration officer is authorised to retain the entry of the person concerned in such a register for the period expiring with the publication of a revised version of the register[24] in the year next following that in which the canvass referred to in head (a) above was conducted[25].

As from a day to be appointed[26], where a person is entered in a register in respect of any address in Great Britain, the person is entitled to remain registered until the registration officer concerned determines[27] that the person:

(i) was not entitled to be registered in respect of the address[28];

(ii)   has ceased to be resident at the address or has otherwise ceased to satisfy the conditions for registration[29]; or

(iii)   was registered as the result of an application for individual electoral registration[30] made by some other person (or that the person's entry has been altered as the result of an application[31] made by some other person)[32].

Where a person's entitlement to remain registered terminates by virtue of any of heads (i) to (iii) above[33], the officer must remove that person's entry from the register[34]. Regulations may make provision about the procedure for making determinations under heads (i) to (iii) above[35], which may include provision requiring an officer to take prescribed steps before making a determination[36]. However, a registration officer in Great Britain may make house to house inquiries for the purpose[37]; and such an officer must consider whether to make such a determination[38] if the officer either receives an objection to a person's registration in a register maintained by the officer[39], or otherwise becomes aware of information that causes the officer to suspect that a condition in any of heads (i) to (iii) above may be met in relation to a person's entry in such a register[40]. Nothing in these provisions relating to individual electoral registration[41] applies in relation to[42]: (A) the registration of persons in respect of residence in mental hospitals[43] or other places at which certain persons[44] may be detained under a relevant order or direction[45]; or (B) the registration of persons in pursuance of declarations of local connection, service declarations, or overseas electors' declarations[46].

1   As from a day to be appointed under the Electoral Registration and Administration Act 2013 s 27(1), the Representation of the People Act 1983 s 10A (added by the Representation of the People Act 2000 s 8, Sch 1 paras 1, 4) is amended by the Electoral Registration and Administration Act 2013 s 13(1), Sch 4 paras 1, 10, so that its effect is limited to Northern Ireland only. However, at the date at which this volume states the law, no such day had been appointed. Because the prospective amendments apply to Northern Ireland only, their effect is not set out in any detail. The provisions that will apply in Great Britain after such a day are set out in the text and notes 26–46. As to the meaning of 'Great Britain' see PARA 1 note 1.

2   As to the entitlement to be registered as an elector generally see PARA 113 et seq. As to the meaning of 'person' see PARA 95 note 1.

3   As to registration officers and the areas for which they act see PARA 139.

4   See the Representation of the People Act 1983 s 10A(5) (s 10A as added (see note 1); s 10A(5) amended by the Electoral Administration Act 2006 ss 10(2), 12(5)(a), 74(2), Sch 1 paras 2, 6(1), (3), Sch 2). As from a day to be appointed under the Electoral Registration and Administration Act 2013 s 27(1), the Representation of the People Act 1983 s 10A(5) is amended so that the reference to any address becomes limited to any address in Northern Ireland, and the reference to the registration officer concerned becomes a reference to the Chief Electoral Officer for Northern Ireland: see s 10A(5) (as so added and amended; prospectively further amended by the Electoral Registration and Administration Act 2013 Sch 4 paras 1, 10(1), (7)(a), (b)). However, at the date at which this volume states the law, no such day had been appointed. See note 1.

    Nothing in the Representation of the People Act 1983 s 10A(5), or in s 10A(6) (see the text and notes 14–15), applies in relation to the registration of persons (see s 10A(8) (as so added)):

    (1)   in pursuance of applications for registration made by virtue of s 7(2) (notional residence of patients in mental hospitals who are not detained offenders or on remand: see PARA 119) or s 7A(2) (notional residence of persons remanded in custody: see PARA 120) (s 10A(8)(a) (as so added)); or

    (2)   in pursuance of declarations falling within s 10(3)(b) (ie a declaration of local connection, a service declaration or an overseas elector's declaration: see PARA 151) (s 10A(8)(b) (as so added)).

    As to the termination of registration made by virtue of head (1) or head (2) above see PARA 170. As to the meaning of 'overseas elector's declaration' see PARA 149 note 14. As to registration in the register of parliamentary electors in pursuance of an overseas elector's declaration see PARA 114 et seq; as to declarations of local connection see PARA 121 et seq; and as to service declarations see PARA 125 et seq.

5   For this purpose, 'determines' means determines in accordance with regulations: see the Representation of the People Act 1983 s 10A(9) (as added: see note 1). As to the making of regulations under the Representation of the People Act 1983 generally see PARA 28 note 16. As to the annual canvass see PARA 151; and as to the regulations made in connection with the annual canvass see PARA 157 et seq. As to reform of the system of registration based on an annual canvass of households see PARA 152; as to the power to abolish or amend the annual canvass in Great Britain see PARA 153; and as to the registration officers' duty to conduct an annual canvass in Great Britain compatible with the system of individual registration see PARA 154.

6   Ie under the Representation of the People Act 1983 s 10 (see PARA 151): see s 10A(5)(a) (as added: see note 1).

7   For this purpose, 'resident' means resident for the purposes of the Representation of the People Act 1983 s 4 (entitlement to be registered as parliamentary or local government elector: see PARA 113): see s 10A(9) (as added: see note 1).

8   See the Representation of the People Act 1983 s 10A(5)(a) (as added: see note 1). The date mentioned in the text (ie 15 October) is the date in relation to which the annual canvass takes place: see PARA 151. However, because the annual canvass for 2013 to be conducted under s 10(1) (see PARA 151) has been postponed, s 10A(2) (see PARA 157) applies to that canvass as if the reference to 15 October were a reference to the date the canvass form was received by the registration officer (see PARA 157 note 7), and s 10A(5)(a) applies to that canvass as if the reference to 15 October were omitted: see the Electoral Registration (Postponement of 2013 Annual Canvass) Order 2013, SI 2013/794, art 2(4), (5).

9   Ie the form mentioned in the Representation of the People Act 1983 s 10(4) (see PARA 151): see s 10A(5)(a)(i) (as added: see note 1).

10   See the Representation of the People Act 1983 s 10A(5)(a)(i) (as added: see note 1).
     As from a day to be appointed under the Political Parties and Elections Act 2009 s 43(1), the Representation of the People Act 1983 s 10A(5)(a)(i) is substituted by the Political Parties and Elections Act 2009 s 33(2), (5)(f), but the amendment prospectively so made is repealed by the Electoral Registration and Administration Act 2013 Sch 4 paras 1, 24, as from a day to be appointed under s 27(1). At the date at which this volume states the law, no such day had been appointed in respect of either amendment. See further note 1.

11   See the Representation of the People Act 1983 s 10A(5)(a)(ii) (as added: see note 1). As to the determination of residence for registration as a parliamentary or local government elector generally see PARA 117 et seq.

12   See the Representation of the People Act 1983 s 10A(5)(a) (as added: see note 1). See note 1.
     As from a day to be appointed under the Electoral Registration and Administration Act 2013 s 27(1), the Representation of the People Act 1983 s 10A(5)(a) is amended so that the reference to the registration officer becomes a reference simply to the officer: see s 10A(5)(a) (prospectively amended by the Electoral Registration and Administration Act 2013 Sch 4 paras 1, 10(1), (7)(c)). At the date at which this volume states the law, no such day had been appointed. See note 1.

13   Representation of the People Act 1983 s 10A(5)(b) (s 10A as added (see note 1); s 10A(5)(b) substituted by the Electoral Administration Act 2006 s 12(5)(b)). The text refers to the conditions for registration set out in the Representation of the People Act 1983 s 4 (entitlement to be registered as parliamentary or local government elector: see PARA 113): see s 10A(5)(b) (s 10A as so added, s 10A(5)(b) as so substituted). A registration officer may, for the purpose of obtaining any information relevant to a determination under s 10A(5)(b), make such house to house inquiries as he thinks fit: s 10A(5B) (s 10A as so added, s 10A(5B) added by the Electoral Administration Act 2006 s 12(6)). As from a day to be appointed under the Electoral Registration and Administration Act 2013 s 27(1), the Representation of the People Act 1983 s 10A(5B) is amended so that the reference to a registration officer becomes a reference to the Chief Electoral Officer for Northern Ireland: see s 10A(5B) (s 10A as so added; s 10A(5B) as so substituted, and prospectively amended by the Electoral Registration and Administration Act 2013 Sch 4 paras 1, 10(1), (9)). See note 1. However, at the date at which this volume states the law, no such day had been appointed.
     A registration officer must discharge his function under the Representation of the People Act 1983 s 10A(5)(b) (ie the function of determining whether a person either was entitled to be registered or has ceased to be resident at the address in respect of which he is entered in the register or otherwise ceased to satisfy the conditions for registration set out in s 4) in accordance with the procedure set out in the Representation of the People (England and Wales)

Regulations 2001, SI 2001/341, regs 31C–31F: see reg 31B(1), (2)(b) (regs 31B, 31C added by SI 2006/2910). However, the registration officer may determine whether a person has ceased to be resident at the address in respect of which he is entered in the register (or has otherwise ceased to satisfy the conditions for registration set out in the Representation of the People Act 1983 s 4) without following the procedure set out in the Representation of the People (England and Wales) Regulations 2001, SI 2001/341, regs 31D–31F (ie the procedure for reviewing entitlement to registration in respect of a person entered in the register: see PARA 170) (see reg 31C(1) (as so added)) in circumstances where the registration officer:

(1)   has received an application under reg 26 (see PARA 158) which includes a statement that the applicant has ceased to reside at any address in respect of which the applicant is currently registered as an elector (ie a statement under reg 26(1)(c): see PARA 158) (reg 31C(2)(a) (as so added));

(2)   has received a notice under reg 37 (ie where the address given in accordance with reg 26(1)(c) is in an area for which another registration officer acts: see PARA 158) (reg 31C(2)(b) (as so added));

(3)   has been given information by the elector that he has ceased to reside at the address in question or has otherwise ceased to satisfy the conditions for registration set out in the Representation of the People Act 1983 s 4 (Representation of the People (England and Wales) Regulations 2001, SI 2001/341, reg 31C(2)(c) (as so added));

(4)   has been notified by a relative or executor of the elector or by the registrar of births and deaths that the elector has died (reg 31C(2)(d) (as so added)).

For these purposes, 'elector' means a person who is duly entered in a register in respect of an address; and 'relative' means a spouse, civil partner, parent, grandparent, brother, sister, child or grandchild: see reg 31C(3) (as so added).

14 Ie by virtue of the Representation of the People Act 1983 s 10A(5) (see the text and notes 1–13): see s 10A(6) (as added: see note 1).

15 Representation of the People Act 1983 s 10A(6) (as added: see note 1). This provision does not apply, however, if, or to the extent that, regulations so provide in relation to any prescribed circumstances (see the text and notes 16–25); and regulations may, in particular, authorise a registration officer to retain entries in his registers for the prescribed period if he thinks fit in cases where the form mentioned in s 10(4) (ie the form used for the purposes of the canvass: see PARA 151) has not been returned in respect of any address: s 10A(7) (as so added).

As from a day to be appointed under the Electoral Registration and Administration Act 2013 s 27(1), the Representation of the People Act 1983 s 10A(6), (7) is amended so that the references to registration officers become references to the Chief Electoral Officer for Northern Ireland: see s 10A(6), (7) (s 10A as so added, s 10A(6), (7) prospectively amended by the Electoral Registration and Administration Act 2013 Sch 4 paras 1, 10(1), (10), (11)). The Representation of the People Act 1983 s 10A(7) is amended also by the Political Parties and Elections Act 2009 s 33(2), (5)(h), as from a day to be appointed under s 43(1), but the amendment prospectively so made is repealed by the Electoral Registration and Administration Act 2013 Sch 4 paras 1, 24, as from a day to be appointed under s 27(1). See note 1. At the date at which this volume states the law, no such day had been appointed in respect of any of these amendments, however.

16 Representation of the People (England and Wales) Regulations 2001, SI 2001/341, reg 34(1).

17 Ie under the Representation of the People Act 1983 s 10 (see PARA 151): see the Representation of the People (England and Wales) Regulations 2001, SI 2001/341, reg 34(2)(a).

18 Ie the form mentioned in the Representation of the People Act 1983 s 10(4) (see PARA 151): see the Representation of the People (England and Wales) Regulations 2001, SI 2001/341, reg 34(2)(a).

19 Representation of the People (England and Wales) Regulations 2001, SI 2001/341, reg 34(2)(a). See note 8.

20 Representation of the People (England and Wales) Regulations 2001, SI 2001/341, reg 34(2)(b).

21 Ie in pursuance of an application made by virtue of the Representation of the People Act 1983 s 7(2) (notional residence of patients in mental hospitals who are not detained offenders or on remand: see PARA 119): see the Representation of the People (England and Wales) Regulations 2001, SI 2001/341, reg 34(2)(c) (substituted by SI 2006/2910).

22 Ie in pursuance of an application made by virtue of the Representation of the People Act 1983 s 7A(2) (notional residence of persons remanded in custody: see PARA 120): see the Representation of the People (England and Wales) Regulations 2001, SI 2001/341, reg 34(2)(c) (as substituted: see note 21).

23 Representation of the People (England and Wales) Regulations 2001, SI 2001/341, reg 34(2)(c) (as substituted: see note 21).

24 Ie as published under the Representation of the People Act 1983 s 13(1) (see PARA 165): see the Representation of the People (England and Wales) Regulations 2001, SI 2001/341, reg 34(3).

25 Representation of the People (England and Wales) Regulations 2001, SI 2001/341, reg 34(3).

26 As from a day to be appointed under the Electoral Registration and Administration Act 2013 s 27(1), the Representation of the People Act 1983 s 10ZE is added by the Electoral Registration and Administration Act 2013 s 1(2), Sch 1 para 1. However, at the date at which this volume states the law, no such day had been appointed.

27 See the Representation of the People Act 1983 s 10ZE(1) (prospectively added: see note 26). See note 5.

28 Representation of the People Act 1983 s 10ZE(1)(a) (prospectively added: see note 26).

29 Representation of the People Act 1983 s 10ZE(1)(b) (prospectively added: see note 26). Head (ii) in the text refers to the conditions for registration set out in s 4 (entitlement to be registered as parliamentary or local government elector: see PARA 113): see s 10ZE(1)(b) (prospectively added). For these purposes, 'resident' means resident for the purposes of s 4: see s 10ZE(8) (prospectively added).

30 Ie under the Representation of the People Act 1983 s 10ZC (not yet in force) (see PARA 163): see s 10ZE(1)(c) (prospectively added: see note 26).

31 Ie under the Representation of the People Act 1983 s 10ZD (not yet in force) (see PARA 164): see s 10ZE(1)(c) (prospectively added: see note 26).

32 Representation of the People Act 1983 s 10ZE(1)(c) (prospectively added: see note 26).

33 Ie by virtue of the Representation of the People Act 1983 s 10ZE(1) (see the text and notes 27–32): see s 10ZE(2) (prospectively added: see note 26).

34 See the Representation of the People Act 1983 s 10ZE(2) (prospectively added: see note 26).

35 Ie under the Representation of the People Act 1983 s 10ZE(1) (see the text and notes 27–32): see s 10ZE(4) (prospectively added: see note 26).

36 See the Representation of the People Act 1983 s 10ZE(4) (prospectively added: see note 26).

37 See the Representation of the People Act 1983 s 10ZE(3) (prospectively added: see note 26). The text refers to the purpose of deciding whether or not to make a determination under s 10ZE(1) (see the text and notes 27–32): see s 10ZE(3) (prospectively added).

38 Ie under the Representation of the People Act 1983 s 10ZE(1) (see the text and notes 27–32): see s 10ZE(5) (prospectively added: see note 26).

39 Representation of the People Act 1983 s 10ZE(5)(a) (prospectively added: see note 26). This provision applies only if the objection to the person's registration is made in accordance with the prescribed requirements by someone whose name appears in the register, and it does not apply if the person has an anonymous entry in the register: see s 10ZE(6) (prospectively added). As to anonymous entries in a register of electors see PARA 147 et seq.

40 Representation of the People Act 1983 s 10ZE(5)(b) (prospectively added: see note 26).

41 Ie nothing in the Representation of the People Act 1983 s 10ZE: see s 10ZE(7) (prospectively added: see note 26).

42 See the Representation of the People Act 1983 s 10ZE(7) (prospectively added: see note 26).

43 Ie within the meaning of the Representation of the People Act 1983 s 7(2) (see PARA 119 note 3): see s 10ZE(7)(a) (prospectively added: see note 26).

44 Ie persons to whom the Representation of the People Act 1983 s 7A(2) (deemed residence of persons remanded in custody: see PARA 120) applies: see s 10ZE(7)(a) (prospectively added: see note 26).

45 Representation of the People Act 1983 s 10ZE(7)(a) (prospectively added: see note 26). As to the orders or directions referred to in the text see PARA 120 note 3. As to the termination of registration made in relation to persons mentioned in head (A) in the text see PARA 170.

46 Representation of the People Act 1983 s 10ZE(7)(b) (prospectively added: see note 26). As to the termination of registration made in relation to persons mentioned in head (B) in the text see PARA 170.

170. Termination of entitlement to be registered by virtue of notional residence or in pursuance of voter's declaration. A person registered in the register of electors[1] in pursuance of an application for registration made by virtue of deemed residence as a patient in a mental hospital[2] or deemed residence as a person remanded in custody[3] or in pursuance of a declaration of local connection[4] or a service declaration[5] or an overseas elector's declaration[6] is entitled to remain so registered until[7]:

    (1)   the end of the period of 12 months beginning with the date when the entry in the register first takes effect[8];

(2)	the registration officer[9] determines in accordance with regulations[10] that the person was not entitled to be registered[11];

(3)	as from a day to be appointed[12], the registration officer determines in accordance with regulations that the person was registered as the result of an application for individual electoral registration[13] made by some other person, or that the person's entry has been altered as the result of an application[14] made by some other person[15];

(4)	another entry made in respect of him in any register of electors takes effect[16]; or

(5)	in the case of registration in pursuance of a declaration of local connection or a service declaration or an overseas elector's declaration, the declaration is cancelled[17],

whichever first occurs[18]. For the purposes of making a determination in accordance with head (2) above, a registration officer may conduct a review in respect of a person entered in the register[19]. Where the registration officer is not satisfied that the subject of the review is entitled to be registered, he must send to that person such notice[20] as he considers appropriate[21], enter the review in the list kept of such reviews[22] and make his determination either with a hearing[23] or, in certain circumstances, without a hearing[24].

Where the entitlement of a person to remain registered terminates by virtue of any of heads (1) to (5) above[25], the registration officer concerned must remove that person's entry from the register, unless he is entitled to remain registered in pursuance of a further application for registration made by virtue of deemed residence[26] or in pursuance of a further declaration of local connection or a further service declaration or a further overseas elector's declaration (whichever applies)[27]. The registration officer has a continuing duty to send to a person registered in pursuance of a declaration of local connection, a service declaration or an overseas elector's declaration a reminder of the need to make a fresh declaration if he wishes to remain registered as an elector in pursuance of such a declaration[28].

A relevant citizen of the Union[29] registered in a register of electors maintained in the register of relevant citizens of the Union entitled to vote at European parliamentary elections[30] is entitled to remain so registered until[31]:

(a)	the end of the period of 12 months beginning with the date when the entry in the register first takes effect[32];

(b)	the declaration which accompanies any application for such registration[33] is cancelled[34];

(c)	the citizen applies for his name to be removed[35];

(d)	any entry made in respect of him in any other register of electors[36] takes effect[37],

whichever occurs first[38]. Where the entitlement of such a person to remain registered terminates in such a way[39], the registration officer concerned must remove that person's entry from the register, unless he is entitled to remain registered in pursuance of a further application and declaration[40]. The registration officer also must remove the name of a relevant citizen of the Union from the register of relevant citizens of the Union entitled to vote at European parliamentary elections[41] if the Secretary of State sends to that officer a copy of any information provided by the member state of which that citizen is a national to show that he has lost the right to vote there[42].

1	Ie the register of parliamentary or local government electors. As to the register of electors see PARA 145 et seq.

2   Ie an application for registration in the register of parliamentary or local government electors made by virtue of the Representation of the People Act 1983 s 7(2) (notional residence of patients in mental hospitals who are not detained offenders or on remand: see PARA 119): see s 7(3) (s 7 substituted by the Representation of the People Act 2000 s 4).

3   Ie an application for registration in the register of parliamentary or local government electors made by virtue of the Representation of the People Act 1983 s 7A(2) (notional residence of persons remanded in custody: see PARA 120): see s 7A(3) (s 7A added by the Representation of the People Act 2000 s 5).

4   Ie an application for registration in the register of parliamentary or local government electors in pursuance of a declaration of local connection made under the Representation of the People Act 1983 s 7B (see PARA 121 et seq): see s 7C(2) (s 7C added by the Representation of the People Act 2000 s 6).

5   Ie an application for registration in the register of parliamentary or local government electors in pursuance of a service declaration made under the Representation of the People Act 1983 s 15 (see PARA 126): see s 15(2) (s 15(2), (3) substituted by the Representation of the People Act 2000 s 8, Sch 1 paras 1, 8(1), (2)).

6   Ie an registration in the register of parliamentary electors in pursuance of an overseas elector's declaration made under the Representation of the People Act 1985 s 2 (see PARA 114 et seq): see s 2(2) (s 2 substituted by the Representation of the People Act 2000 s 8, Sch 2 paras 1, 3). As to the meaning of 'overseas elector's declaration' see PARA 149 note 14.

7   Representation of the People Act 1983 s 7(3) (as substituted: see note 2); s 7A(3) (as added: see note 3); s 7C(2) (as added: see note 4); s 15(2) (as substituted: see note 5); Representation of the People Act 1985 s 2(2) (as substituted: see note 6).

     For the purpose of extending the rights of peers who (subject to the requirement of registration) may vote at European parliamentary elections, the Representation of the People Act 1985 s 2 is applied with modifications (see the Representation of the People (England and Wales) Regulations 2001, SI 2001/341, reg 13(4), Sch 4; and PARA 101 note 7); for the purposes of extending the rights of relevant citizens of the Union who (subject to the requirement of registration) may vote at European parliamentary elections, the Representation of the People Act 1983 s 7 and ss 7A–7C are applied with modifications (see the European Parliamentary Elections (Franchise of Relevant Citizens of the Union) Regulations 2001, SI 2001/1184, reg 9, Schedule; and PARA 102 note 6); and for the purposes of extending the rights of citizens and nationals of accession states who (subject to the requirement of registration) may vote at local government and European parliamentary elections, the Representation of the People Act 1983 s 7B and s 15 are applied with modifications (see the Local and European Parliamentary Elections (Registration of Citizens of Accession States) Regulations 2003, SI 2003/1557, reg 2(1), (3)(b)–(d)).

8   Representation of the People Act 1983 s 7(3)(a) (as substituted: see note 2); s 7A(3)(a) (as added: see note 3); s 7C(2)(a) (as added: see note 4); s 15(2)(a) (as substituted: see note 5); Representation of the People Act 1985 s 2(2)(a) (as substituted: see note 6).

     The Secretary of State may by order provide that, in relation to a person who is a member of the forces or who is the spouse or civil partner of a member of the forces (ie a person who is mentioned in the Representation of the People Act 1983 s 14(1)(a) or s 14(1)(d): see PARA 125), s 15(2)(a) has effect as if for the period of 12 months there were substituted such other period (not exceeding five years) as he thinks appropriate: s 15(9) (s 15(9)–(12) added by the Electoral Administration Act 2006 s 13(1)). As to the Secretary of State see PARA 2. The power to make such an order is exercisable by statutory instrument, which may contain such incidental or consequential provision as the Secretary of State thinks appropriate: Representation of the People Act 1983 s 15(10) (as so added). However, no such order may be made unless the Secretary of State first consults the Electoral Commission and unless a draft of the instrument containing the order is laid before, and approved by a resolution of, each House of Parliament: s 15(11) (as so added). If the period substituted by such an order is longer than the period for the time being in force, the longer period has effect in relation to any person who immediately before the order was made was entitled to remain in a register by virtue of s 15(2): s 15(12) (as so added). Accordingly, s 15(2)(a) has effect as regards the persons mentioned in s 14(1)(a) or s 14(1)(d) as if for 'the period of 12 months' there were substituted 'the period of 5 years': Service Voters' Registration Period Order 2010, SI 2010/882, art 2. As to the application and modification of these provisions see note 7. As to the establishment and constitution of the Electoral Commission see PARA 34 et seq.

9   As to registration officers and the areas for which they act see PARA 139.

10   The regulations referred to in the text are the Representation of the People (England and Wales) Regulations 2001, SI 2001/341, regs 31B–31F (see the text and notes 11, 19–24). As to the

making of regulations under the Representation of the People Act 1983 generally (and, by virtue of the Representation of the People Act 1985 s 27(2), under the Representation of the People Act 1985) see PARA 28 note 16.

11 Representation of the People Act 1983 s 7(3)(aa) (s 7 as substituted (see note 2); s 7(3)(aa) added by the Electoral Administration Act 2006 s 12(1)); Representation of the People Act 1983 s 7A(3)(aa) (s 7A as added (see note 3); s 7A(3)(aa) added by the Electoral Administration Act 2006 s 12(2)); Representation of the People Act 1983 s 7C(2)(aa) (s 7C as added (see note 4); s 7C(2)(aa) added by the Electoral Administration Act 2006 s 12(3)); Representation of the People Act 1983 s 15(2)(aa) (s 15(2) as substituted (see note 5); s 15(2)(aa) added by the Electoral Administration Act 2006 s 12(7)); Representation of the People Act 1985 s 2(2)(aa) (s 2 as substituted (see note 6); s 2(2)(aa) added by the Electoral Administration Act 2006 s 12(9)). As to the application and modification of these provisions see note 7.

A registration officer must discharge his function of determining whether a person was entitled to be registered under the Representation of the People Act 1983 s 7(3)(aa), s 7A(3)(aa), s 7C(2)(aa), s 15(2)(aa) or under the Representation of the People Act 1985 s 2(2)(aa) in accordance with the procedure set out in the Representation of the People (England and Wales) Regulations 2001, SI 2001/341, regs 31D–31F (see the text and notes 19–24): see reg 31B(1), (2)(a) (regs 31B, 31D–31F added by SI 2006/2910). A registration officer must also discharge his function under the Representation of the People Act 1983 s 10A(5)(b) in accordance with the procedure set out in the Representation of the People (England and Wales) Regulations 2001, SI 2001/341, regs 31D–31F, unless reg 31C applies: see reg 31B(1), (2)(b); and PARA 169.

12 As from a day to be appointed under the Electoral Registration and Administration Act 2013 s 27(1), the Representation of the People Act 1983 s 7(3)(ab), 7A(3)(ab), s 7C(2)(ab), s 15(2)(ab), and the Representation of the People Act 1985 s 2(2)(ab), are added by the Electoral Registration and Administration Act 2013 s 13(1), Sch 4 paras 1–4, 15, 21. However, at the date at which this volume states the law, no such day had been appointed.

13 Ie under the Representation of the People Act 1983 s 10ZC (not yet in force) (see PARA 163).

14 Ie under the Representation of the People Act 1983 s 10ZD (not yet in force) (see PARA 164).

15 Representation of the People Act 1983 s 7(3)(ab) (s 7 as substituted (see note 2); s 7(3)(ab) prospectively added (see note 12)); s 7A(3)(ab) (s 7A as added (see note 3); s 7A(3)(ab) prospectively added (see note 12)); s 7C(2)(ab) (s 7C as added (see note 4); s 7C(2)(ab) prospectively added (see note 12)); s 15(2)(ab) (s 15(2) as substituted (see note 5); s 15(2)(ab) prospectively added (see note 12)); Representation of the People Act 1985 s 2(2)(ab) (s 2 as substituted (see note 6); s 2(2)(ab) prospectively added (see note 12)).

16 Representation of the People Act 1983 s 7(3)(b) (as substituted: see note 2); s 7A(3)(b) (as added: see note 3); s 7C(2)(c) (as added: see note 4); s 15(2)(c) (as substituted: see note 5); Representation of the People Act 1985 s 2(2)(c) (as substituted: see note 6). As to the application and modification of these provisions see note 7. The text refers to another entry taking effect whether or not in pursuance of an application for registration made by virtue of deemed residence or in pursuance of a declaration of local connection or a service declaration; and, in the case of an overseas elector's declaration, it refers to another entry taking effect otherwise than in pursuance of an overseas elector's declaration.

17 Representation of the People Act 1983 s 7C(2)(b) (as added: see note 4); s 15(2)(b) (as substituted: see note 5); Representation of the People Act 1985 s 2(2)(b) (as substituted: see note 6). As to the application and modification of these provisions see note 7. The text refers to a cancellation under the Representation of the People Act 1983 s 7B(9) (cancellation of declaration of local connection: see PARA 121), s 15(7) (cancellation of service declaration: see PARA 126) or the Representation of the People Act 1985 s 2(5) (cancellation of overseas elector's declaration: see PARA 132).

18 Representation of the People Act 1983 s 7(3) (as substituted: see note 2); s 7A(3) (as added: see note 3); s 7C(2) (as added: see note 4); s 15(2) (as substituted: see note 5); Representation of the People Act 1985 s 2(2) (as substituted: see note 6). As to the application and modification of these provisions see note 7.

19 Representation of the People (England and Wales) Regulations 2001, SI 2001/341, reg 31D(1) (as added: see note 11). For these purposes, 'review' must be construed in accordance with reg 31D(1); and the 'subject of the review' means the person in respect of whom the review is conducted: see reg 31D(10) (as so added).

20 Ie of a kind specified in the Representation of the People (England and Wales) Regulations 2001, SI 2001/341, reg 31D(4): see reg 31D(2) (as added: see note 11). A notice is specified for the purposes of reg 31D(4) if:

    (1)   it states that the registration officer is of the opinion that the subject of the review is not entitled to be registered and the grounds for his opinion (reg 31D(4)(a) (as so added));

(2) it states the reason for the review and requires the subject of the review to provide such further information as might be specified in the notice or requires him to make a declaration under reg 24 (evidence as to age or nationality: see PARA 142) or both (reg 31D(4)(b) (as so added)); or

(3) it states the reason for the review and that the registration officer intends to conduct a hearing of it (reg 31D(4)(c) (as so added)).

Where the registration officer determines that a hearing of the review should be conducted, the notice given under reg 31D(4)(c) (see head (3) above) must also state the time and place at which he proposes to hear the review: reg 31F(1) (as so added).

21 Representation of the People (England and Wales) Regulations 2001, SI 2001/341, reg 31D(2)(a) (as added: see note 11).

22 Representation of the People (England and Wales) Regulations 2001, SI 2001/341, reg 31D(2)(b) (as added: see note 11). The text refers to the list kept in pursuance of reg 31E, which the registration officer must keep: reg 31E(1) (as so added). The list must contain, in relation to each review, the full name of the subject of the review, his electoral number, his qualifying address, and the reason for the review (see reg 31E(2) (as so added)); and the list must be made available for inspection at the registration officer's office (reg 31E(3) (as so added)). However, reg 31E does not apply to any review where the subject of the review has an anonymous entry (reg 31E(4) (as so added)); nor does the provision made by reg 31D(2)(b) apply where the subject of the review has an anonymous entry (reg 31D(3) (as so added)). As to the meaning of 'available for inspection' see PARA 142 note 18. As to provision made for the inspection of documents see PARA 168 note 12. As to a person's electoral number see PARA 145; and as to applications for an anonymous entry in the register see PARA 147.

23 Ie in accordance with the Representation of the People (England and Wales) Regulations 2001, SI 2001/341, reg 31F.

Where the subject of the review requires the review to be heard, the registration officer must send to that person a notice stating the time and place at which he proposes to hear the review: reg 31F(2) (as added: see note 11). The time fixed for the hearing must not be earlier than the third day after the date of the notice in which that time is stated (reg 31F(3) (as so added)); and the persons entitled to appear and be heard are the subject of the review and any other person who appears to the registration officer to be interested (see reg 31F(4) (as so added)). The procedure which applies to the hearing of an application for registration or objection (ie reg 31(2)–(4): see PARA 162) applies to the hearing of a review see reg 31F(5) (as so added). The registration officer may determine that the subject of the review was not entitled to be registered or, as the case may be, has ceased to satisfy the conditions for registration set out in the Representation of the People Act 1983 s 4 (entitlement to be registered as parliamentary or local government elector: see PARA 113), despite the failure of that person (or any other person entitled to appear and be heard) to attend: Representation of the People (England and Wales) Regulations 2001, SI 2001/341, reg 31F(6) (as so added). In making a determination under reg 31F(6), the registration officer must take into account any written representations made to him by the subject of the review and may take into account the written representations of any other person who appears to him to be interested: reg 31F(7) (as so added).

24 Ie in accordance with the Representation of the People (England and Wales) Regulations 2001, SI 2001/341, reg 31D(5)–(9).

Where the registration officer sends to the subject of the review a notice in the form specified in reg 31D(4)(a) (see note 20), and where that person does not, within 14 days beginning with the date of that notice, notify the registration officer that he requires the review to be heard, the registration officer may determine without a hearing that the subject of the review was not entitled to be registered or, as the case may be, has ceased to satisfy the conditions for registration set out in the Representation of the People Act 1983 s 4 (entitlement to be registered as parliamentary or local government elector: see PARA 113): see the Representation of the People (England and Wales) Regulations 2001, SI 2001/341, reg 31D(5) (as added: see note 11).

Where the registration officer sends to the subject of the review a notice in the form specified in reg 31D(4)(b) (see note 20), and where that person does not respond to the registration officer's satisfaction, or at all, within the period of 28 days beginning with the date of that notice (see reg 31D(6) (as so added)), the registration officer may send a notice to the subject of the review which states that he is not satisfied that that person is entitled to be registered, and the grounds for his opinion (reg 31D(7) (as so added)). Where the registration officer sends to the subject of the review a notice in pursuance of reg 31D(7), and where the subject of the review does not, within the period of 14 days beginning with the date of that notice, notify the registration officer that he requires the review to be heard, the registration officer may determine without a hearing that the subject of the review was not entitled to be registered or, as the case may be, has ceased to satisfy the conditions for registration set out in the Representation of the

People Act 1983 s 4 (see PARA 113): see the Representation of the People (England and Wales) Regulations 2001, SI 2001/341, reg 31D(8) (as so added).

In making a determination under either reg 31D(5) or reg 31D(8), the registration officer must take into account any written representations made to him by the subject of the review and may take into account the written representations of any other person who appears to him to be interested: reg 31D(9) (as so added).

25 Ie by virtue of the Representation of the People Act 1983 s 7(3), s 7A(3), s 7C(2), s 15(2), or the Representation of the People Act 1985 s 2(2) (as the case may be): see the text and notes 1–18.

26 Ie a further application made by virtue of the Representation of the People Act 1983 s 7(2) (deemed residence of patients in mental hospitals who are not detained offenders or on remand: see PARA 119) or s 7A(2) (deemed residence of persons remanded in custody: see PARA 120).

27 Representation of the People Act 1983 s 7(4) (as substituted: see note 2); s 7A(4) (as added: see note 3); s 7C(3) (as added: see note 4); s 15(3) (as substituted: see note 5); Representation of the People Act 1985 s 2(2) (as substituted: see note 6). As to the application and modification of these provisions see note 7.

28 See the Representation of the People (England and Wales) Regulations 2001, SI 2001/341, reg 25; and PARA 141.

29 As to the meaning of 'relevant citizen of the Union' for these purposes see PARA 102 note 5.

30 Ie the register maintained under the European Parliamentary Elections (Franchise of Relevant Citizens of the Union) Regulations 2001, SI 2001/1184, reg 5(2) (see PARA 143): see reg 10(2).

31 See the European Parliamentary Elections (Franchise of Relevant Citizens of the Union) Regulations 2001, SI 2001/1184, reg 10(2).

For the purposes of extending the rights of citizens and nationals of accession states who (subject to the requirement of registration) may vote at local government and European parliamentary elections, reg 10 is applied with modifications: see the Local and European Parliamentary Elections (Registration of Citizens of Accession States) Regulations 2003, SI 2003/1557, reg 6, Sch 1 para 7.

32 European Parliamentary Elections (Franchise of Relevant Citizens of the Union) Regulations 2001, SI 2001/1184, reg 10(2)(a). See note 31.

33 Ie the declaration under the European Parliamentary Elections (Franchise of Relevant Citizens of the Union) Regulations 2001, SI 2001/1184, reg 6(2) (see PARA 159): see reg 10(2)(b). See note 31.

34 European Parliamentary Elections (Franchise of Relevant Citizens of the Union) Regulations 2001, SI 2001/1184, reg 10(2)(b). The text refers to cancellation under reg 10(1) (see PARA 159): see reg 10(2)(b). See note 31.

35 European Parliamentary Elections (Franchise of Relevant Citizens of the Union) Regulations 2001, SI 2001/1184, reg 10(2)(c). See note 31.

36 Ie any other register maintained under the European Parliamentary Elections (Franchise of Relevant Citizens of the Union) Regulations 2001, SI 2001/1184, reg 5(2) (see PARA 143): see reg 10(2)(d). See note 31.

37 European Parliamentary Elections (Franchise of Relevant Citizens of the Union) Regulations 2001, SI 2001/1184, reg 10(2)(d). See note 31.

38 See the European Parliamentary Elections (Franchise of Relevant Citizens of the Union) Regulations 2001, SI 2001/1184, reg 10(2). See note 31.

39 Ie by virtue of the European Parliamentary Elections (Franchise of Relevant Citizens of the Union) Regulations 2001, SI 2001/1184, reg 10(2) (see the text and notes 29–38): see reg 10(3). See note 31.

40 European Parliamentary Elections (Franchise of Relevant Citizens of the Union) Regulations 2001, SI 2001/1184, reg 10(3). The text refers to a further application and declaration under reg 6(1), (2) (see PARA 159): see reg 10(3). See note 31.

41 Ie from the register maintained under the European Parliamentary Elections (Franchise of Relevant Citizens of the Union) Regulations 2001, SI 2001/1184, reg 5(2) (see PARA 143): see reg 10(4). See note 31.

42 European Parliamentary Elections (Franchise of Relevant Citizens of the Union) Regulations 2001, SI 2001/1184, reg 10(4). See note 31.

171. Termination of entitlement to anonymous entry in register. If a person has an anonymous entry in a register[1], his entitlement to remain registered in pursuance of an application for an anonymous entry[2] terminates[3]:

(1) at the end of the period of 12 months beginning with the date when the entry in the register first takes effect[4]; or

(2)   if the declaration made for the purposes of an application for an anonymous entry is cancelled at any time before the expiry of that 12 month period, at the time when the declaration is cancelled[5].

If a person's entitlement to remain registered terminates in such a way[6], the registration officer concerned must remove that person's entry from the register, unless he is entitled to remain registered with an anonymous entry in pursuance of a further application for registration accompanied by a further application for an anonymous entry[7].

1   As to the meaning of 'anonymous entry' in relation to a register of electors see PARA 148.
2   Ie in pursuance of the application for registration mentioned in the Representation of the People Act 1983 s 9B(1) (see PARA 147): see s 9C(1) (s 9C added by the Electoral Administration Act 2006 s 10(1)). As to the prospective amendment of the Representation of the People Act 1983 s 9C(1) see note 3.
3   See the Representation of the People Act 1983 s 9C(1) (as added: see note 2).
     As from a day to be appointed under the Electoral Registration and Administration Act 2013 s 27(1), the Representation of the People Act 1983 s 9C(1) is amended so that the reference to 'in pursuance of the application for registration mentioned in the Representation of the People Act 1983 s 9B(1)' is repealed: see s 9C(1) (s 9C as so added, s 9C(1) prospectively amended by the Electoral Registration and Administration Act 2013 Sch 4 paras 1, 8(1), (2)). However, at the date at which this volume states the law, no such day had been appointed.
4   Representation of the People Act 1983 s 9C(1)(a) (as added: see note 2). The provision made by s 9C(1) does not affect the application of any other provision of the Representation of the People Act 1983 or of the Representation of the People Act 1985 which has the effect that the person's entitlement to registration terminates before the expiry of the 12-month period mentioned in the Representation of the People Act 1983 s 9C(1) or before the cancellation of the declaration made for the purposes of s 9B (as to which see PARA 147): s 9C(2) (as so added)
5   Representation of the People Act 1983 s 9C(1)(b) (as added: see note 2).
6   Ie by virtue of the Representation of the People Act 1983 s 9C(1) (see the text and notes 1–5): see s 9C(3) (as added: see note 2).
7   Representation of the People Act 1983 s 9C(3) (as added: see note 2). The text refers to a further application for registration accompanied by a further application under s 9B (see PARA 147): see s 9C(3) (as so added).
     As from a day to be appointed under the Electoral Registration and Administration Act 2013 s 27(1), the Representation of the People Act 1983 s 9C(3) is amended so that the reference to 'a further application for registration accompanied by' is repealed and the reference simply becomes one to 'in pursuance of a further application under s 9B': see s 9C(3) (s 9C as so added, s 9C(3) prospectively amended by the Electoral Registration and Administration Act 2013 Sch 4 paras 1, 8(1), (3)). However, at the date at which this volume states the law, no such day had been appointed.

(vi) Registration Appeals

172. Decisions from which registration appeals lie. An appeal relating to the registration of electors lies to the county court in the following cases[1]:

(1)   until a day to be appointed[2], from any decision of the registration officer[3] under the Representation of the People Act 1983 on any application for registration or objection to a person's registration made to and considered by him[4];

(2)   until a day to be appointed[5], from any decision under the Representation of the People Act 1983 of the registration officer (other than on an application for registration or objection to a person's registration) that a person registered in respect of any address was not entitled to be registered in respect of that address or that he has ceased to be resident at that address or has otherwise ceased to satisfy the conditions for registration as a parliamentary or local government elector[6];

(3)   as from a day to be appointed[7], from any decision of a registration officer to register a person following an application for individual electoral registration[8] in a case where an objection has been duly made[9];

(4)   as from a day to be appointed[10], from any decision of a registration officer not to alter a register derived from individual electoral registration following an application duly made[11] to alter the name or address in respect of which a person is so registered[12];

(5)   as from a day to be appointed[13], from any decision of a registration officer to alter a register derived from individual electoral registration following an application[14] in a case where an objection has been duly made[15];

(6)   as from a day to be appointed[16], from any determination of a registration officer[17], as a result of which a person's entitlement to remain registered in a register derived from individual electoral registration terminates[18];

(7)   from a determination of the registration officer on an application for an anonymous entry in the register of electors[19];

(8)   from any decision of the registration officer under the Representation of the People Act 1983, or under regulations, disallowing a person's application to vote by proxy or by post as elector, or to vote by post as proxy, in any case where the application is not made for a particular election only[20].

No such appeal lies, however, where a person desiring to appeal has not availed himself of a prescribed[21] right to be heard by, or make representations to, the registration officer on the matter which is the subject of the appeal[22] or has not given the prescribed notice of appeal within the prescribed time[23].

1   See the Representation of the People Act 1983 s 56(1). In any Act, unless the context otherwise requires, 'county court' means, in relation to England and Wales, a court held for a district under the County Courts Act 1984: Interpretation Act 1978 s 5, Sch 1 (definition amended by the County Courts Act 1984 s 148(1), Sch 2 para 68; and SI 1980/397). In the case of Gibraltar, for the purposes of the European Parliamentary Elections Regulations 2004, SI 2004/293, reg 21 (see the text and see notes 20–23; and PARAS 173, 175 et seq), the appropriate court is the Gibraltar court (ie the court determined by or under the law of Gibraltar to be the court for that purpose): see reg 21(8). As to the meanings of 'England' and 'Wales' see PARA 1 note 1. See further COURTS AND TRIBUNALS vol 24 (2010) PARA 758 et seq. As to the procedure on appeal see CPR PD 52D—*Statutory Appeals and Appeals Subject to Special Provision*; and PARA 173 et seq.
      For the purposes of extending the rights of peers and of relevant citizens of the Union who (subject to the requirement of registration) may vote at European parliamentary elections, the Representation of the People Act 1983 s 56 is applied with modifications: see the Representation of the People (England and Wales) Regulations 2001, SI 2001/341, reg 13(4), Sch 4 (cited in PARA 101 note 7); and the European Parliamentary Elections (Franchise of Relevant Citizens of the Union) Regulations 2001, SI 2001/1184, reg 9, Schedule (cited in PARA 102 note 6).

2   As from a day to be appointed under the Electoral Registration and Administration Act 2013 s 27(1), the Representation of the People Act 1983 s 56(1)(a), (aa) is substituted, and s 56(aza)–(azd) added, by the Electoral Registration and Administration Act 2013 s 13(1), Sch 4 paras 1, 18: see the text and notes 3–18. However, at the date at which this volume states the law, no such day had been appointed.

3   As to registration officers and the areas for which they act see PARA 139.

4   Representation of the People Act 1983 s 56(1)(a) (amended by the Representation of the People Act 2000 s 8, Sch 1 paras 1, 14(1), (2)(a)). As to such decisions see PARA 157 et seq.
      As from a day to be appointed under the Electoral Registration and Administration Act 2013 s 27(1), the Representation of the People Act 1983 s 56(1)(a) is substituted so that a ground for appeal lies from any decision of a registration officer not to register a person following an application under s 10ZC (not yet in force) (registration officer to determine applications for individual registration of electors: see PARA 163): see s 56(1)(a) (prospectively substituted by the

Electoral Registration and Administration Act 2013 Sch 4 paras 1, 18). However, at the date at which this volume states the law, no such day had been appointed. See note 2.

5   See note 2.

6   Representation of the People Act 1983 s 56(1)(aa) (added by the Electoral Administration Act 2006 s 12(8)). The text refers to the conditions for registration set out in the Representation of the People Act 1983 s 4 (entitlement to be registered as parliamentary or local government elector: see PARA 113): see s 56(1)(aa) (as so added).

As from a day to be appointed under the Electoral Registration and Administration Act 2013 s 27(1), the Representation of the People Act 1983 s 56(1)(aa) is substituted so that a ground for appeal lies from any decision of a registration officer not to make a determination under s 10ZE(1) following an objection under s 10ZE(5)(a) (not yet in force) (removal of electors from register: see PARA 169): see s 56(1)(aa) (prospectively substituted by the Electoral Registration and Administration Act 2013 Sch 4 paras 1, 18). However, at the date at which this volume states the law, no such day had been appointed. See note 2.

7   See note 2.

8   Ie following an application under the Representation of the People Act 1983 s 10ZC (not yet in force) (see PARA 163): see s 56(1)(aza) (prospectively added by the Electoral Registration and Administration Act 2013 Sch 4 paras 1, 18). See note 2.

9   Representation of the People Act 1983 s 56(1)(aza) (prospectively added: see note 8). The text refers to an objection that has been made under s 10ZC (not yet in force) (see PARA 163): see s 56(1)(aza) (prospectively added). See note 2.

10   See note 2.

11   Ie following an application under the Representation of the People Act 1983 s 10ZD (not yet in force) (alterations to entries on register of electors derived from individual registration: see PARA 164): see s 56(1)(azb) (prospectively added by the Electoral Registration and Administration Act 2013 Sch 4 paras 1, 18). See note 2.

12   Representation of the People Act 1983 s 56(1)(azb) (prospectively added: see note 11). See note 2.

13   See note 2.

14   Ie following an application under the Representation of the People Act 1983 s 10ZD (not yet in force) (alterations to entries on register of electors derived from individual registration: see PARA 164): see s 56(1)(azc) (prospectively added by the Electoral Registration and Administration Act 2013 Sch 4 paras 1, 18). See note 2.

15   Representation of the People Act 1983 s 56(1)(azc) (prospectively added: see note 14). The text refers to an objection that has been made under s 10ZD (not yet in force) (see PARA 164): see s 56(1)(azc) (prospectively added). See note 2.

16   See note 2.

17   Ie any decision of a registration officer under the Representation of the People Act 1983 s 10ZE (not yet in force) (removal of electors from register: see PARA 169), or under any other provision of the Representation of the People Act 1983: see s 56(1)(azd) (prospectively added by the Electoral Registration and Administration Act 2013 Sch 4 paras 1, 18). See note 2.

18   Representation of the People Act 1983 s 56(1)(azd) (prospectively added: see note 17). See note 2.

19   Representation of the People Act 1983 s 56(1)(ab) (added by the Electoral Administration Act 2006 s 10(2), Sch 1 paras 2, 8). The text refers to a determination of the registration officer under the Representation of the People Act 1983 s 9B(2) (see PARA 147): see s 56(1)(ab) (as so added).

20   Representation of the People Act 1983 s 56(1)(b) (amended by the Representation of the People Act 1985 s 11, Sch 2 para 1); National Assembly for Wales (Representation of the People) Order 2007, SI 2007/236, art 5(1); European Parliamentary Elections Regulations 2004, SI 2004/293, reg 21(1) (substituted by SI 2009/186). This provision, as enacted under the Representation of the People Act 1983, applies to applications for parliamentary or local government elections since the provisions in the Representation of the People Act 1985 which concern such applications have effect as if contained in the Representation of the People Act 1983 Pt I (ss 1–66B): see the Representation of the People Act 1985 s 27(2). The National Assembly for Wales (Representation of the People) Order 2007, SI 2007/236, art 5(1) applies where the application is not made for a particular Assembly election only and is subject to giving notice of the appeal in accordance with Sch 1 para 9(1) (see PARA 173): see art 5(1). The European Parliamentary Elections Regulations 2004, SI 2004/293, reg 21(1) applies also to a decision under the European Parliamentary Elections Regulations 2004, SI 2004/293, of the registration officer to remove a person's entry from the lists of postal voters or of proxy postal voters, in any case where the entry is not related to a particular election only: see reg 21(1) (as so substituted). See note 1. As to the meaning of 'election' see PARA 3 note 1. As to the meaning

of 'Assembly election' for these purposes see PARA 3 note 2. As to applications to vote by proxy or by post (other than for a particular election) see PARA 367 et seq; and as to applications to vote by post as proxy (other than for a particular election) see PARA 378.

21 Ie prescribed by regulations: see the Representation of the People Act 1983 s 202(1). As to the making of regulations under the Representation of the People Act 1983 generally see PARA 28 note 16. For the purposes of the European Parliamentary Elections Regulations 2004, SI 2004/293, reg 21(2), 'prescribed' means prescribed by Sch 2 para 28: see reg 21(7). As to the regulations so made see notes 22–23; and PARAS 173, 175 et seq.

22 As to the right to be heard or make representations on the hearing of a claim or objection with respect to the right to be registered see PARA 162.

23 See the Representation of the People Act 1983 s 56(1); and the European Parliamentary Elections Regulations 2004, SI 2004/293, reg 21(2). See note 1. As to the giving of notice of appeal see PARA 173.

It has been held that the appeal must be brought by the person affected: *Registration Officer for the Parliamentary County of Hants v Ainslie* (1933) 148 LT 496, CA. That appeal, however, turned on the wording of the county court rules for registration appeals then in force.

173. Notice of appeal. A person desiring to appeal:

(1) from the decision of a registration officer[1] regarding an application for registration made to and considered by him[2]; or

(2) from the decision of a registration officer[3] that a person was not entitled to be registered or, as the case may be, has ceased to satisfy the conditions for registration[4]; or

(3) from a determination of the registration officer made in relation to an application for an anonymous entry in the register[5]; or

(4) against the decision of a registration officer disallowing a person's application to vote by proxy or by post as elector (or to vote by post as proxy in any case where the application is not made for a particular election only)[6],

must give notice of appeal to the registration officer[7]: (a) in the case of an application for registration, when the decision is given or within 14 days thereafter[8]; or (b) in the case of an application for an absent vote, within 14 days of the receipt of the notice refusing such an application[9]. The grounds of such an appeal must be specified[10]. No appeal lies if the prescribed notice of appeal is not given within the time mentioned above[11].

The respondents to the appeal are the registration officer[12] and, if the decision of the registration officer was given in favour of any other person than the person who has given notice of such an appeal, that other person[13].

Where the prescribed notice of appeal from a decision of a registration officer is duly given, the registration officer must forward any such notice to the appropriate county court in accordance with rules of court together, in each case, with a statement of the material facts which in his opinion have been established in the case and with his decision upon the whole case, and on any point which may be specified as a ground of appeal[14].

1 As to registration officers and the areas for which they act see PARA 139.

2 Ie under the Representation of the People Act 1983 s 56(1)(a) (see PARA 172), from the decision of a registration officer regarding an application for registration: see the Representation of the People (England and Wales) Regulations 2001, SI 2001/341, reg 32(1)(a) (reg 32(1) substituted by SI 2006/2910).

By virtue of the Representation of the People (England and Wales) Regulations 2001, SI 2001/341, reg 13(6), (7), reg 32 applies to registration in pursuance of a European parliamentary overseas elector's declaration as it applies to registration in pursuance of an overseas elector's declaration (see PARA 101 note 7); and for the purposes of extending the rights of relevant citizens of the Union who (subject to the requirements of registration) may vote at European parliamentary elections, reg 32 is applied with modifications (see the European

Parliamentary Elections (Franchise of Relevant Citizens of the Union) Regulations 2001, SI 2001/1184, reg 9, Schedule; and PARA 102 note 6).

3   Ie an appeal made in accordance with the Representation of the People (England and Wales) Regulations 2001, SI 2001/341, regs 31C–31F (see PARAS 169–170): see reg 32(1)(b) (as substituted: see note 2).

4   Ie under the Representation of the People Act 1983 s 56(1)(aa) (see PARA 172): Representation of the People (England and Wales) Regulations 2001, SI 2001/341, reg 32(1)(b) (as substituted: see note 2). The text refers to the conditions for registration set out in the Representation of the People Act 1983 s 4 (entitlement to be registered as parliamentary or local government elector: see PARA 113): see the Representation of the People (England and Wales) Regulations 2001, SI 2001/341, reg 32(1)(b) (as so substituted). As to the application and modification of reg 32 see note 2.

5   Ie under the Representation of the People Act 1983 s 56(1)(ab) (see PARA 172): Representation of the People (England and Wales) Regulations 2001, SI 2001/341, reg 32(1)(c) (as substituted: see note 2). The text refers to a determination under the Representation of the People Act 1983 s 9B(2) (see PARA 147), made under the Representation of the People (England and Wales) Regulations 2001, SI 2001/341, reg 31H (see PARA 147): see reg 32(1)(c) (as so substituted). As to the application and modification of reg 32 see note 2.

6   Ie under the Representation of the People Act 1983 s 56(1)(b) (see the Representation of the People (England and Wales) Regulations 2001, SI 2001/341, reg 58(1)) or under the European Parliamentary Elections Regulations 2004, SI 2004/293, reg 21(1) (see Sch 2 para 28(1) (Sch 2 substituted by SI 2009/186)) or under the National Assembly for Wales (Representation of the People) Order 2007, SI 2007/236, art 5(1) (see Sch 1 para 9(1)). See PARA 172. As to applications to vote by proxy or by post (other than for a particular election) see PARA 367 et seq.

7   Representation of the People (England and Wales) Regulations 2001, SI 2001/341, regs 32(2)(a), 58(1); European Parliamentary Elections Regulations 2004, SI 2004/293, Sch 2 para 28(1) (as substituted: see note 6); National Assembly for Wales (Representation of the People) Order 2007, SI 2007/236, Sch 1 para 9(1). As to the application and modification of the Representation of the People (England and Wales) Regulations 2001, SI 2001/341, reg 32 see note 2. CPR 52.4 (appellant's notice: see CIVIL PROCEDURE vol 12 (2009) PARA 1663) does not apply to an appeal to which CPR PD 52D—*Statutory Appeals and Appeals Subject to Special Provision* para 31 applies (see the text and notes 13–14): CPR PD 52D—*Statutory Appeals and Appeals Subject to Special Provision* para 31.1(6).

     The Representation of the People (England and Wales) Regulations 2001, SI 2001/341, reg 58, has effect for the purposes of local authority referendums, subject to the modifications specified, in relation to Wales, by the Local Authorities (Conduct of Referendums) (Wales) Regulations 2008, SI 2008/1848, reg 8(2), Sch 4 Table 5, and, in relation to England, by the Local Authorities (Conduct of Referendums) (England) Regulations 2012, SI 2012/323, regs 8(2), 11–13, Sch 4 Table 6 (see PARA 15 note 2).

8   Representation of the People (England and Wales) Regulations 2001, SI 2001/341, reg 32(2)(a). In such a case, notice of appeal must be given also to the opposite party (if any): see reg 32(2)(a). As to the application and modification of reg 32 see note 2.

9   Representation of the People (England and Wales) Regulations 2001, SI 2001/341, reg 58(1); European Parliamentary Elections Regulations 2004, SI 2004/293, Sch 2 para 28(1) (as substituted: see note 6); National Assembly for Wales (Representation of the People) Order 2007, SI 2007/236, Sch 1 para 9(1). The notice referred to in the text is the notice given under the Representation of the People (England and Wales) Regulations 2001, SI 2001/341, reg 57(4), under the European Parliamentary Elections Regulations 2004, SI 2004/293, Sch 2 para 27(3), or under the National Assembly for Wales (Representation of the People) Order 2007, SI 2007/236, Sch 1 para 8(4) (as the case may be) (see PARA 367).

10   Representation of the People (England and Wales) Regulations 2001, SI 2001/341, regs 32(2)(b), 58(1); European Parliamentary Elections Regulations 2004, SI 2004/293, Sch 2 para 28(1) (as substituted: see note 6); National Assembly for Wales (Representation of the People) Order 2007, SI 2007/236, Sch 1 para 9(1). As to the application and modification of the Representation of the People (England and Wales) Regulations 2001, SI 2001/341, reg 32 see note 2.

11   See the Representation of the People Act 1983 s 56(1); the European Parliamentary Elections Regulations 2004, SI 2004/293, reg 21(2); and see PARA 172. In *Game v City of London Deputy Registration Officer* [1950] CLY 1309, it was held that the county court had no power to extend the prescribed time for giving notice of appeal to the registration officer.

12   See the Representation of the People Act 1983 s 56(5); the European Parliamentary Elections Regulations 2004, SI 2004/293, reg 21(6); the National Assembly for Wales (Representation of

the People) Order 2007, SI 2007/236, art 5(6); and CPR PD 52D—*Statutory Appeals and Appeals Subject to Special Provision* para 31.1(1), (3). The registration officer must undertake such duties: (1) in connection with appeals brought by virtue of the Representation of the People Act 1983 s 56 as may be prescribed by regulations (see s 56(5)); and (2) in connection with appeals brought by virtue of the European Parliamentary Elections Regulations 2004, SI 2004/293, reg 21, as are set out in Sch 2 para 28 (see reg 21(6)). The National Assembly for Wales (Representation of the People) Order 2007, SI 2007/236, art 5(7) provides for the application and modification of CPR Sch 2 CCR Ord 45 r 2 (revoked by SI 2007/2204), which has been replaced by CPR PD 52D—*Statutory Appeals and Appeals Subject to Special Provision* para 31. It is submitted therefore that references in para 31 to 'regulations made under the Representation of the People Act 1983 s 53' (see note 14) are to be construed as including a reference to the National Assembly for Wales (Representation of the People) Order 2007, SI 2007/236, Sch 1 para 9: see art 5(7).

Where a person wishes to appeal against the inclusion of names in the register, the appeal can only bind those persons who have been made respondents to the appeal: *R v Judge Hurst, ex p Smith* [1960] 2 QB 133, [1960] 2 All ER 385, DC.

13 See CPR PD 52D—*Statutory Appeals and Appeals Subject to Special Provision* para 31.1(1), (3).

In the case of an appeal to a county court to which para 31.1 applies, if a party to the appeal is a person whose entry in the register is an anonymous entry, or who has applied for such an entry, the appellant may indicate in the appeal notice that an application for an anonymous entry has been applied for, or that the entry in the register is an anonymous entry: see CPR PD 52D—*Statutory Appeals and Appeals Subject to Special Provision* para 31.2(2), (4). For these purposes, 'anonymous entry' has the meaning given by the Representation of the People Act 1983 s 9B(4) (see PARA 148); and 'appeal notice' means the notice required by the Representation of the People (England and Wales) Regulations 2001, SI 2001/341, reg 32 (see the text and notes 1–10): see CPR PD 52D—*Statutory Appeals and Appeals Subject to Special Provision* para 31.2(1). The respondent or any other person who applies to become a party to the proceedings may indicate in a respondent's notice or an application to join the proceedings that the entry in the register is an anonymous entry, or that an application has been made for an anonymous entry: CPR PD 52D—*Statutory Appeals and Appeals Subject to Special Provision* para 31.2(5). Where the appellant gives such an indication in the appeal notice, the court will refer the matter to a district judge for directions about the further conduct of the proceedings, and, in particular, directions about how the matter should be listed in the court list: CPR PD 52D—*Statutory Appeals and Appeals Subject to Special Provision* para 31.2(6). Where the court otherwise becomes aware that a party to the appeal is a person whose entry in the register is an anonymous entry, or who has applied for such an entry, the court will give notice to the parties that no further step is to be taken until the court has given any necessary directions for the further conduct of the matter: CPR PD 52D—*Statutory Appeals and Appeals Subject to Special Provision* para 31.2(7). The provision made by para 31.2 applies also to an appeal to the Court of Appeal from a decision of a county court in an appeal to which para 31.1 applies: see para 31.2(3); and PARA 176 note 2.

14 Representation of the People (England and Wales) Regulations 2001, SI 2001/341, regs 32(3), 58(2); European Parliamentary Elections Regulations 2004, SI 2004/293, Sch 2 para 28(2) (as substituted: see note 6); National Assembly for Wales (Representation of the People) Order 2007, SI 2007/236, Sch 1 para 9(2). In the case of Gibraltar, the appropriate court is the Gibraltar court (ie the court determined by or under the law of Gibraltar to be the court for that purpose): see the European Parliamentary Elections Regulations 2004, SI 2004/293, reg 5(2), Sch 2 para 28(2) (Sch 2 as so substituted). As to the application and modification of the Representation of the People (England and Wales) Regulations 2001, SI 2001/341, reg 32 see note 2.

In relation to an appeal against a decision of a registration officer, being a decision referred to in the Representation of the People Act 1983 s 56(1) (see PARA 172), where a person ('the appellant') has given notice of such an appeal in accordance with the relevant requirements of s 56, and of the regulations made under s 53 ('the Regulations'), the registration officer must, within seven days after the appellant receives the notice, forward the notice, and the statement required by the Regulations, by post to the county court: see CPR PD 52D—*Statutory Appeals and Appeals Subject to Special Provision* para 31.1(1), (2).

174. Consolidation of appeals and test cases. Where it appears to the registration officer[1] that any notices of appeal given to him[2] are based on similar

grounds, he must inform the county court of the fact for the purpose of enabling the court, if it thinks fit, to consolidate the appeals or select one of them as a test case[3].

Accordingly, where two or more appeals against decisions of registration officers involve the same point of law, the court may direct that one appeal ('the test-case appeal') is to be heard first as a test case[4]. The court must then send a notice of the direction to each party to all of those appeals[5]. If such a notice is served on any party to an appeal (other than the test-case appeal), that party may (within seven days after the notice is served on that party) give notice to the court requesting the appeal to be heard[6]. The court must then hear that appeal after the test-case appeal is disposed of[7], giving the parties to that appeal notice of the day on which it will be heard[8]. If no such notice is given within that limited time period, the decision on the test-case appeal binds the parties to each of the other appeals[9], and the court must make, in each other appeal, an order similar to the order in the test-case appeal without further hearing[10].

1 As to registration officers and the areas for which they act see PARA 139.
2 As to the giving of notice of appeal see PARA 173.
3 Representation of the People (England and Wales) Regulations 2001, SI 2001/341, regs 32(4), 58(3); European Parliamentary Elections Regulations 2004, SI 2004/293, Sch 2 para 28(4) (Sch 2 substituted by SI 2009/186); National Assembly for Wales (Representation of the People) Order 2007, SI 2007/236, Sch 1 para 9(3). In the case of Gibraltar, the appropriate court is the Gibraltar court (ie the court determined by or under the law of Gibraltar to be the court for that purpose): see the European Parliamentary Elections Regulations 2004, SI 2004/293, reg 5(2), Sch 2 para 28(4) (Sch 2 as so substituted). As to the application of the National Assembly for Wales (Representation of the People) Order 2007, SI 2007/236, see PARA 173 note 12.
    By virtue of the Representation of the People (England and Wales) Regulations 2001, SI 2001/341, reg 13(6), (7), reg 32 applies to registration in pursuance of a European parliamentary overseas elector's declaration as it applies to registration in pursuance of an overseas elector's declaration (see PARA 101 note 7); and for the purposes of extending the rights of relevant citizens of the Union who (subject to the requirements of registration) may vote at European parliamentary elections, reg 32 is applied with modifications (see the European Parliamentary Elections (Franchise of Relevant Citizens of the Union) Regulations 2001, SI 2001/1184, reg 9, Schedule; and PARA 102 note 6).
4 CPR PD 52D—*Statutory Appeals and Appeals Subject to Special Provision* para 31.3(1). The text refers specifically to an appeal to which para 31.1 applies (ie an appeal against a decision of a registration officer, being a decision referred to in the Representation of the People Act 1983 s 56(1) (see PARA 172)): see CPR PD 52D—*Statutory Appeals and Appeals Subject to Special Provision* para 31.3(1).
5 CPR PD 52D—*Statutory Appeals and Appeals Subject to Special Provision* para 31.3(2).
6 CPR PD 52D—*Statutory Appeals and Appeals Subject to Special Provision* para 31.3(3).
7 CPR PD 52D—*Statutory Appeals and Appeals Subject to Special Provision* para 31.3(3)(a).
8 CPR PD 52D—*Statutory Appeals and Appeals Subject to Special Provision* para 31.3(3)(b).
9 CPR PD 52D—*Statutory Appeals and Appeals Subject to Special Provision* para 31.3(4)(a). This provision does not affect the right to appeal to the Court of Appeal (see PARA 176) of any party to an appeal other than the test-case appeal: para 31.3(5).
10 CPR PD 52D—*Statutory Appeals and Appeals Subject to Special Provision* para 31.3(4)(b).

175. Hearing of appeal and costs. On the hearing of an appeal[1] in relation to the decision of a registration officer[2], the statement forwarded to the court by the registration officer and any document containing information furnished to the court by the registration officer[3] are admissible as evidence of the facts stated therein[4]. The court has power to draw any inference of fact which might have been drawn by the registration officer[5], and to give any decision and make any order which ought to have been given or made by the registration officer[6].

A respondent to an appeal, other than the registration officer, is not liable for or entitled to costs, unless he appears before the court in support of the registration officer's decision[7]. Any expenses properly incurred by the registration officer arising out of an appeal are included in the registration expenses payable to him[8].

In test cases[9], the party to each other appeal who is in the same interest as the unsuccessful party to the selected appeal is liable for the costs of the test-case appeal in the same manner and to the same extent as the unsuccessful party to that appeal and an order directing the party to pay such costs may be made and enforced accordingly[10]. Any party who gave notice requesting a separate hearing to be held after the hearing of the selected appeal[11] is not entitled to receive any costs occasioned by the separate hearing of that appeal, unless the judge otherwise directs[12].

1 Ie an appeal to a county court to which CPR PD 52D—*Statutory Appeals and Appeals Subject to Special Provision* para 31.1 applies: see PARA 173.

2 As to registration officers and the areas for which they act see PARA 139. As to the decisions from which an appeal lies see PARA 172.

3 Ie pursuant to regulations made under the Representation of the People Act 1983 s 53, Sch 2 (see PARA 112): see CPR PD 52D—*Statutory Appeals and Appeals Subject to Special Provision* para 31.1(4)(a). As the regulations make provision only for a statement of the material facts which have been established in the case and with the officer's decision upon the whole case, and on any point which may be specified as a ground of appeal (see PARA 173), *quaere* whether a document containing information provided by the registration officer, other than the statement given pursuant to regulations, is admissible as evidence of the facts stated therein.

4 CPR PD 52D—*Statutory Appeals and Appeals Subject to Special Provision* para 31.1(4)(a).

5 CPR PD 52D—*Statutory Appeals and Appeals Subject to Special Provision* para 31.1(4)(b)(i).

6 CPR PD 52D—*Statutory Appeals and Appeals Subject to Special Provision* para 31.1(4)(b)(ii).

7 CPR PD 52D—*Statutory Appeals and Appeals Subject to Special Provision* para 31.1(5).

8 See the Representation of the People Act 1983 s 56(5); the European Parliamentary Elections Regulations 2004, SI 2004/293, reg 21(6); and the National Assembly for Wales (Representation of the People) Order 2007, SI 2007/236, art 5(6). As to the payment of the expenses of registration see PARA 144. As to the application of the National Assembly for Wales (Representation of the People) Order 2007, SI 2007/236, see PARA 173 note 12.

For the purposes of the extension of the rights of peers and of relevant citizens of the Union who (subject to the requirement of registration) may vote at European parliamentary elections, the Representation of the People Act 1983 s 56 is applied with modifications: see the Representation of the People (England and Wales) Regulations 2001, SI 2001/341, reg 13(4), Sch 4 (cited in PARA 101 note 7); and the European Parliamentary Elections (Franchise of Relevant Citizens of the Union) Regulations 2001, SI 2001/1184, reg 9, Schedule (cited in PARA 102 note 6).

9 As to the court's power to select a test case see PARA 174.

10 CPR PD 52D—*Statutory Appeals and Appeals Subject to Special Provision* para 31.3(4)(c).

11 As to the procedure where a separate hearing is desired see PARA 174.

12 CPR PD 52D—*Statutory Appeals and Appeals Subject to Special Provision* para 31.3(3)(c).

176. Appeal to Court of Appeal.

On general principles, if any party to the proceedings[1] in a county court is dissatisfied with the determination of the judge, he may appeal from it to the Court of Appeal[2].

No appeal lies from the decision of the Court of Appeal on appeal from a decision of the county court on a registration appeal[3].

1 A person who is not a party to the proceedings might apply to the High Court for judicial review where the county court has acted without jurisdiction: *R v Judge Sir Donald Hurst, ex p Smith* [1960] 2 QB 133, [1960] 2 All ER 385, DC (where a county court judge had ordered that the names of 90 members of a college, who were not parties to the proceedings, should be struck off the register after allowing an objection in respect of four other members of that college who had been parties, he had acted without jurisdiction and his directions were quashed on an application for an order of certiorari).

2   See the County Courts Act 1984 s 77; and CIVIL PROCEDURE vol 12 (2009) PARA 1679. In the case of Gibraltar, for the purposes of the European Parliamentary Elections Regulations 2004, SI 2004/293, reg 21, the reference to the Court of Appeal must be construed as a reference to the Gibraltar Court of Appeal: see reg 21(8).

     CPR PD 52D—*Statutory Appeals and Appeals Subject to Special Provision* para 31.2 (see PARA 173) applies to an appeal to the Court of Appeal from a decision of a county court in an appeal to which para 31.1 (see PARA 173 note 13) applies: see para 31.2(3).

3   Representation of the People Act 1983 s 56(2); European Parliamentary Elections Regulations 2004, SI 2004/293, reg 21(3); National Assembly for Wales (Representation of the People) Order 2007, SI 2007/236, art 5(2). The decisions referred to in the text are those in relation to registration as a parliamentary or local government elector under the Representation of the People Act 1983 s 56, those in relation to registration as a Welsh Assembly elector under the National Assembly for Wales (Representation of the People) Order 2007, SI 2007/236, art 5 or those in relation to registration as a European parliamentary elector under the European Parliamentary Elections Regulations 2004, SI 2004/293, reg 21 (whichever applies) (see PARA 172). As to the application of the National Assembly for Wales (Representation of the People) Order 2007, SI 2007/236, see PARA 173 note 12.

     For the purposes of the extension of the rights of peers and of relevant citizens of the Union who (subject to the requirement of registration) may vote at European parliamentary elections, the Representation of the People Act 1983 s 56 is applied with modifications: see the Representation of the People (England and Wales) Regulations 2001, SI 2001/341, reg 13(4), Sch 4 (cited in PARA 101 note 7); and the European Parliamentary Elections (Franchise of Relevant Citizens of the Union) Regulations 2001, SI 2001/1184, reg 9, Schedule (cited in PARA 102 note 6).

177. Appeals pending when notice of election given. An appeal to the county court or Court of Appeal as to a registration officer's decision[1] which is pending when notice of an election is given[2] does not prejudice the operation, as respects the election, of the decision appealed against, and anything done in pursuance of the decision is as good as if no such appeal had been brought and is not affected by the decision of the appeal[3]. This rule does not apply to an election, however, where, as a result of the decision on the appeal, an alteration in the register of electors is made[4] on or before the date of the poll[5].

1   Ie by virtue of, in relation to a parliamentary or local government election, the Representation of the People Act 1983 s 56 or, in relation to a European parliamentary election, the European Parliamentary Elections Regulations 2004, SI 2004/293, reg 21 or, in relation to a Welsh Assembly election, the National Assembly for Wales (Representation of the People) Order 2007, SI 2007/236, art 5 (whichever applies) (see PARA 172). As to registration officers and the areas for which they act see PARA 139.

2   As to the date when notice of election is to be given at a parliamentary election see PARA 196; as to notice of the date at a local government election see PARA 211; as to notice of the date at a Welsh Assembly election see PARA 216; and as to notice of the date at a European parliamentary election see PARA 223.

3   Representation of the People Act 1983 s 56(3); European Parliamentary Elections Regulations 2004, SI 2004/293, reg 21(4); National Assembly for Wales (Representation of the People) Order 2007, SI 2007/236, art 5(3).

     For the purposes of the extension of the rights of peers and of relevant citizens of the Union who (subject to the requirement of registration) may vote at European parliamentary elections, the Representation of the People Act 1983 s 56 is applied with modifications: see the Representation of the People (England and Wales) Regulations 2001, SI 2001/341, reg 13(4), Sch 4 (cited in PARA 101 note 7); and the European Parliamentary Elections (Franchise of Relevant Citizens of the Union) Regulations 2001, SI 2001/1184, reg 9, Schedule (cited in PARA 102 note 6).

4   Ie in pursuance of the Representation of the People Act 1983 s 56(4) (see PARA 178), taking effect under s 13(5) (see PARA 165), s 13A(2) (see PARA 168), s 13B(3) (see PARA 168) or s 13B(3B) (see PARA 168), or under the National Assembly for Wales (Representation of the People) Order 2007, SI 2007/236, art 5 (as the case may be). See note 5.

5   Representation of the People Act 1983 s 56(4A) (added by the Representation of the People Act 1985 s 24, Sch 4 para 16(b); amended by the Representation of the People Act 2000 s 8, Sch 1 paras 1, 14(1), (4); and the Electoral Administration Act 2006 s 11(1), (5)); National

Assembly for Wales (Representation of the People) Order 2007, SI 2007/236, art 5(5) (amended by SI 2010/2931). See note 3. As to the last day on which nomination papers nominating candidates at an election may be delivered at an election see PARA 260.

As from a day to be appointed under the Electoral Registration and Administration Act 2013 s 27(1), the Representation of the People Act 1983 s 56(4A) is amended to include an alteration in the register made in pursuance of s 56(4) (see PARA 178) taking effect under s 13AB (not yet in force) (see PARA 168): see s 56(4A) (as so added and amended; prospectively further amended by the Electoral Registration and Administration Act 2013 s 16(1), (5)(b)). However, at the date at which this volume states the law, no such day had been appointed.

178. Notification to registration officer and alteration of register. Notice of the decision of the county court or of the Court of Appeal on any registration appeal[1] must be sent to the registration officer[2] in manner provided by rules of court[3]. The registration officer must make such alterations in the register[4] or relevant records[5] as may be required to give effect to the decision[6].

1　Ie the decision in relation to registration as a parliamentary or local government elector under the Representation of the People Act 1983 s 56, in relation to registration as a European parliamentary elector under the European Parliamentary Elections Regulations 2004, SI 2004/293, reg 21, or in relation to registration as a Welsh Assembly elector under the National Assembly for Wales (Representation of the People) Order 2007, SI 2007/236, art 5 (whichever applies) (see PARA 172).

2　As to registration officers and the areas for which they act see PARA 139.

3　Representation of the People Act 1983 s 56(4); European Parliamentary Elections Regulations 2004, SI 2004/293, reg 21(5); National Assembly for Wales (Representation of the People) Order 2007, SI 2007/236, art 5(4). See further CIVIL PROCEDURE.

For the purposes of the extension of the rights of peers and of relevant citizens of the Union who (subject to the requirement of registration) may vote at European parliamentary elections, the Representation of the People Act 1983 s 56 is applied with modifications: see the Representation of the People (England and Wales) Regulations 2001, SI 2001/341, reg 13(4), Sch 4 (cited in PARA 101 note 7); and the European Parliamentary Elections (Franchise of Relevant Citizens of the Union) Regulations 2001, SI 2001/1184, reg 9, Schedule (cited in PARA 102 note 6).

4　Ie in accordance with the Representation of the People Act 1983 s 13A (see PARA 168) and s 13B (see PARA 168). As to the register see PARA 143 et seq.

5　Ie the record which is kept under the National Assembly for Wales (Representation of the People) Order 2007, SI 2007/236, art 8(3) of those whose applications for an absent vote at Assembly elections for a particular or an indefinite period have been granted (see PARA 370) or the record kept under art 12(6) of those whose applications to vote as a proxy at Assembly elections (whether for an indefinite period or for a particular period) have been granted (see PARA 379). See note 6.

6　Representation of the People Act 1983 s 56(4) (amended by the Representation of the People Act 2000 ss 8, 15(2), Sch 1 paras 1, 14(1), (3), Sch 7 Pt I); National Assembly for Wales (Representation of the People) Order 2007, SI 2007/236, art 5(4). See note 3.

As from a day to be appointed under the Electoral Registration and Administration Act 2013 s 27(1), the Representation of the People Act 1983 s 56(4) is amended to include an alteration in the register made in accordance with s 13AB (not yet in force) (see PARA 168): see s 56(4) (as so amended; prospectively further amended by the Electoral Registration and Administration Act 2013 s 16(1), (5)(a)). However, at the date at which this volume states the law, no such day had been appointed.

(vii) Supply and Sale of Electoral Records and Restrictions on Use

179. General restriction on supply of electoral records and disclosure of information. Persons with access to the full register of electors[1], or to the information contained in it, may not supply to any other person a copy of the full register[2], disclose any information which is contained in it (and which is not contained in the edited register)[3], or make use of any such information[4], otherwise than as follows:

(1)　the registration officer[5], any deputy registration officer[6], and any person appointed to assist any such officer (or who in the course of his employment is assigned to assist any such officer in his registration duties)[7] may not so supply, disclose or make use of such registers or such information otherwise than in accordance with an enactment[8];

(2)   any officer[9] to whom copies of the register are delivered for the purpose of summoning jurors[10], and any other person to whom a copy of the full register has been supplied or to whom information contained in it has been disclosed for the purpose of summoning jurors[11], may not so supply, disclose or make use of such registers or such information otherwise than for the purpose of summoning jurors[12];

(3)   any person to whom a copy of the full register has been supplied in pursuance of a relevant provision[13], under which a copy of the full register is to be supplied (or information from that register disclosed for a particular purpose)[14], any person to whom information contained in the full register has been disclosed in pursuance of such a provision[15], any person to whom either such person has supplied a copy of the full register (or information contained in it) for the purposes (express or implied) of such a provision[16], and any person who has obtained access to a copy of the full register (or information contained in it) by any other means[17], may not so supply, disclose or make use of such registers or such information other than for a permitted purpose[18].

The restrictions contained in heads (1) and (2) above apply to a person to whom the full register is duly supplied, or to whom any information contained in it (that is not contained in the edited register) is duly disclosed, as they apply to the original recipient of the data[19].

The registration officer, any deputy registration officer and any person appointed to assist any such officer (or who in the course of his employment is assigned to assist such officer in his registration duties)[20] may not[21] supply to any person a copy of the record of anonymous entries[22], disclose information contained in it[23] or make use of such information[24], otherwise than in accordance with an enactment[25] or in accordance with the order of any court or tribunal made at any hearing or during the course of any proceedings[26]. All such persons must take proper precautions for the safe custody of the record[27]. The registration officer must, at the request in writing of any person to whom a copy of the full register has been supplied or to whom information contained in it has been disclosed for the purpose of summoning jurors[28], supply to that person a copy of the record of anonymous entries[29]. No person who has been supplied with a copy of the record of anonymous entries for these purposes[30] may supply a copy of the record of anonymous entries[31], disclose any information contained in it[32] or make use of any such information[33], other than for the purpose of summoning jurors[34]; and such persons must take proper precautions for the safe custody of the record[35].

1   As to the meaning of 'full register' see PARA 167 note 2. For the purposes of the Representation of the People (England and Wales) Regulations 2001, SI 2001/341, Pt VI (regs 92–115), 'register' includes: (1) any part of the register referred to; and (2) any notice altering the register published under the Representation of the People Act 1983 s 13A(2), s 13B(3), s 13B(3B) or s 13B(3D) (see PARA 168): see the Representation of the People (England and Wales) Regulations 2001, SI 2001/341, reg 92(1) (regs 92, 94–96 added by SI 2002/1871; the Representation of the People (England and Wales) Regulations 2001, SI 2001/341, reg 92(1) amended by SI 2006/2910). However, head (2) above does not apply either in the context of the Representation of the People (England and Wales) Regulations 2001, SI 2001/341, reg 93

(edited version of the register: see PARA 167), or in the context of the supply by the registration officer of the register and notices altering the register (see PARA 168): see reg 92(1) (as so added and amended).

2 Representation of the People (England and Wales) Regulations 2001, SI 2001/341, reg 94(3)(a) (as added: see note 1).

3 Representation of the People (England and Wales) Regulations 2001, SI 2001/341, reg 94(3)(b) (as added: see note 1). As to the meaning of 'edited register' see PARA 167 note 4.

4 Representation of the People (England and Wales) Regulations 2001, SI 2001/341, reg 94(3)(c) (as added: see note 1).

5 Representation of the People (England and Wales) Regulations 2001, SI 2001/341, reg 94(1)(a) (as added: see note 1). Where the registration officer is also the returning officer or acting returning officer at any election or the counting officer at a referendum held by or under an Act of Parliament (and thereby has access to the full register without being supplied with a copy of it), reg 94 also applies to:

   (1) the registration officer acting in that other capacity (reg 94(2)(a) (as so added));
   (2) any deputy returning officer, deputy acting returning officer or deputy counting officer (reg 94(2)(b) (as so added)); and
   (3) any person appointed to assist any person mentioned in head (1) or head (2) above or who in the course of his employment is assigned to assist any such officer in his duties in respect of the election or referendum in question (reg 94(2)(c) (as so added)).

As to the meaning of 'registration officer' for these purposes see PARA 139 note 1. As to the appointment of deputies of and assistants to the registration officer see PARA 140; as to returning officers and their deputies and assistants see PARA 350 et seq; and as to counting officers and their deputies see PARA 553 et seq.

6 Representation of the People (England and Wales) Regulations 2001, SI 2001/341, reg 94(1)(b) (as added: see note 1).

7 Representation of the People (England and Wales) Regulations 2001, SI 2001/341, reg 94(1)(c) (as added: see note 1).

8 Representation of the People (England and Wales) Regulations 2001, SI 2001/341, reg 94(3) (as added: see note 1). For the purposes of Pt VI, 'enactment' has the same meaning as in the Representation of the People Act 2000 s 17(2) (see PARA 521 note 8) (see the Representation of the People (England and Wales) Regulations 2001, SI 2001/341, reg 92(2)(a) (reg 92 as added: see note 1)); and for the purposes of reg 94, it includes the Representation of the People (England and Wales) Regulations 2001, SI 2001/341 (see reg 94(3) (as so added)). Nothing in reg 94(3) applies to the supply or disclosure by a person mentioned in head (1) in the text to another such person in connection with his registration duties or for the purposes of an election or referendum, however: reg 94(4) (as so added). A person who contravenes reg 94(3) is guilty of an offence and liable on summary conviction to a fine not exceeding level 5 on the standard scale: see reg 115; and PARA 734. As to the standard scale see SENTENCING AND DISPOSITION OF OFFENDERS vol 92 (2010) PARA 142.

9 Ie any officer designated under the Juries Act 1974 s 3(1) (electoral register as basis of jury selection: see JURIES vol 61 (2010) PARA 812): see the Representation of the People (England and Wales) Regulations 2001, SI 2001/341, reg 95(1)(a) (as added: see note 1).

10 Representation of the People (England and Wales) Regulations 2001, SI 2001/341, reg 95(1)(a) (as added: see note 1).

11 Representation of the People (England and Wales) Regulations 2001, SI 2001/341, reg 95(1)(b) (as added: see note 1).

12 Representation of the People (England and Wales) Regulations 2001, SI 2001/341, reg 95(2) (as added: see note 1). A person who contravenes reg 95(2) is guilty of an offence and liable on summary conviction to a fine not exceeding level 5 on the standard scale: see reg 115; and PARA 734.

13 Ie any enactment, except the Juries Act 1974 (see head (2) in the text), and the Representation of the People (England and Wales) Regulations 2001, SI 2001/341: see reg 96(3) (as added: see note 1).

14 See the Representation of the People (England and Wales) Regulations 2001, SI 2001/341, reg 96(1)(a), (3) (as added: see note 1).

15 Representation of the People (England and Wales) Regulations 2001, SI 2001/341, reg 96(1)(b) (as added: see note 1).

16 Representation of the People (England and Wales) Regulations 2001, SI 2001/341, reg 96(1)(c) (as added: see note 1).

17 Representation of the People (England and Wales) Regulations 2001, SI 2001/341, reg 96(1)(d) (as added: see note 1).

18 Representation of the People (England and Wales) Regulations 2001, SI 2001/341, reg 96(2) (reg 96 as added (see note 1); reg 96(2) amended, reg 96(2A) added, by SI 2006/752). 'Permitted purpose' must be construed in accordance with the Representation of the People (England and Wales) Regulations 2001, SI 2001/341, reg 96(2A), as follows (see reg 96(2) (as so added and amended)):

   (1)   where the copy was supplied or the information obtained in pursuance of a relevant provision, it means the particular purpose for which the copy was supplied or the information disclosed to the person in question pursuant to the relevant provision (reg 96(2A)(a) (as so added)); and

   (2)   where the copy was not supplied or the information was not disclosed in pursuance of a relevant provision (see reg 96(2A)(b) (as so added)):

      (a)   in the case of a person to whom the copy of the full register was made available for inspection under supervision in accordance with reg 43(1)(a) (see PARA 165 note 3), reg 97(2)(a), (3) (see PARA 180), reg 97A(4)(a), (b) (see PARA 180), reg 99(4)(a) (see PARA 187) and reg 109A(6)(a), (b) (see PARA 181), it does not include direct marketing within the meaning of the Data Protection Act 1998 s 11(3) (see CONFIDENCE AND INFORMATIONAL PRIVACY vol 19 (2011) PARA 122) (see the Representation of the People (England and Wales) Regulations 2001, SI 2001/341, reg 96(2A)(b)(i) (as so added)); and

      (b)   in any other case, it means any purpose for which the person to whom reg 96 applies could have obtained a copy of the register or the information contained in it pursuant to any enactment, including the Representation of the People (England and Wales) Regulations 2001, SI 2001/341 (see reg 96(2A)(b)(ii) (as so added)).

   A person who contravenes reg 96(2) is guilty of an offence and liable on summary conviction to a fine not exceeding level 5 on the standard scale: see reg 115; and PARA 734. As to the meaning of 'available for inspection' see PARA 142 note 18. The provision made by reg 96(2) is modified by the Representation of the People (Electoral Registration Data Schemes) Regulations 2011, SI 2011/1467, art 4, 5 (made in exercise of the powers conferred by the Representation of the People Act 1983 ss 53(1), (3), 201(3), Sch 2 para 10B(1)(a), (2), but in relation to a scheme in an order made in exercise of the powers conferred by the Political Parties and Elections Act 2009 ss 35, 36 (prospectively repealed): see PARAS 112 note 1, 152).

   In *R (on the application of Robertson) v Wakefield Metropolitan District Council* [2001] EWHC Admin 915, [2002] QB 1052, [2002] LGR 286, the previous practice of selling the electoral register for direct marketing purposes without affording an individual elector a right of objection was held to be a disproportionate interference with the individual's right to respect for private life under the Convention for the Protection of Human Rights and Fundamental Freedoms (Rome, 4 November 1950; TS 71 (1953); Cmd 8969) art 8 and, to the extent that the prevailing regulations made the right to vote conditional upon acquiescence in the practice with no right of objection, they also involved an unjustified and disproportionate restriction on the right to vote by reference to the First Protocol (Paris, 20 March 1952; Cmnd 9221) art 3 (see PARA 7).

   The restrictions on the supply, disclosure and use of the full register in the Representation of the People (England and Wales) Regulations 2001, SI 2001/341, regs 94 and 96 apply to information covered by reg 61(1)(a), (b) (see PARA 185 note 11), to information covered by the European Parliamentary Elections Regulations 2004, SI 2004/293, reg 10, Sch 2 para 32(1)(a), (b) (see PARA 185 note 12), and to information covered by the National Assembly for Wales (Representation of the People) Order 2007, SI 2007/236, art 15(2), Sch 1 para 13(1)(a), (b) (see PARA 185 note 13), as the case may be, as they apply to the full register, except that the permitted purpose means either research purposes within the meaning of that term in the Data Protection Act 1998 s 33 (see CONFIDENCE AND INFORMATIONAL PRIVACY vol 19 (2011) PARA 144), or electoral purposes: see the Representation of the People (England and Wales) Regulations 2001, SI 2001/341, reg 61A (added by SI 2006/2910); the European Parliamentary Elections Regulations 2004, SI 2004/293, reg Sch 2 para 33 (Sch 2 substituted by SI 2009/186); and the National Assembly for Wales (Representation of the People) Order 2007, SI 2007/236, Sch 1 para 14.

19 See the Representation of the People (England and Wales) Regulations 2001, SI 2001/341, reg 92(10) (reg 92 as added (see note 1); reg 92(10) amended by SI 2006/752).

20 See the Representation of the People (England and Wales) Regulations 2001, SI 2001/341, reg 45B(1) (regs 45B, 45D added by SI 2006/2910). Where the registration officer is also the returning officer or acting returning officer at any election or counting officer at any referendum (and in consequence has access to the record of anonymous entries without being supplied with a copy of it), the Representation of the People (England and Wales) Regulations 2001,

SI 2001/341, reg 45B applies to the registration officer acting in that other capacity, to any deputy returning officer, deputy acting returning officer or deputy counting officer, and to any person appointed to assist any such officer or who in the course of his employment is assigned to assist any such officer in his duties in respect of the election or referendum in question: see reg 45B(2) (as so added). For these purposes, 'counting officer' means the counting officer at a referendum held by or under any Act: see reg 45B(6) (as so added). As to the duty of the registration officer to keep a record of anonymous entries see PARA 143 et seq.

21 See the Representation of the People (England and Wales) Regulations 2001, SI 2001/341, reg 45B(3) (as added: see note 20). Nothing in reg 45B(3) (see the text and notes 22–24) applies to the supply or disclosure by a person to whom reg 45B applies (see the text and note 20) to another such person in connection with his registration duties or for the purposes of an election or referendum: reg 45B(4) (as so added).

22 Representation of the People (England and Wales) Regulations 2001, SI 2001/341, reg 45B(3)(a) (as added: see note 20).

23 Representation of the People (England and Wales) Regulations 2001, SI 2001/341, reg 45B(3)(b) (as added: see note 20).

24 Representation of the People (England and Wales) Regulations 2001, SI 2001/341, reg 45B(3)(c) (as added: see note 20).

25 Ie including the Representation of the People (England and Wales) Regulations 2001, SI 2001/341: see reg 45B(3) (as added: see note 20). For these purposes, 'enactment' has the same meaning as in the Representation of the People Act 2000 s 17(2) (see PARA 521 note 8): see the Representation of the People (England and Wales) Regulations 2001, SI 2001/341, reg 45B(6) (as so added).

26 Representation of the People (England and Wales) Regulations 2001, SI 2001/341, reg 45B(3) (as added: see note 20).

27 Representation of the People (England and Wales) Regulations 2001, SI 2001/341, reg 45B(5) (as added: see note 20).

28 Ie other than a designated officer within the meaning of the Juries Act 1974 s 3(1) (electoral register as basis of jury selection: see JURIES vol 61 (2010) PARA 812): see the Representation of the People (England and Wales) Regulations 2001, SI 2001/341, reg 45D(1) (as added: see note 20).

29 See the Representation of the People (England and Wales) Regulations 2001, SI 2001/341, reg 45D(1), (2) (as added: see note 20).

30 Ie either in accordance with the Representation of the People (England and Wales) Regulations 2001, SI 2001/341, reg 45D(2) (see the text and notes 28–29), or in accordance with the Juries Act 1974 s 3(1A) (see JURIES vol 61 (2010) PARA 801 et seq): see the Representation of the People (England and Wales) Regulations 2001, SI 2001/341, reg 45D(3) (as added: see note 20).

31 Representation of the People (England and Wales) Regulations 2001, SI 2001/341, reg 45D(4)(a) (as added: see note 20). A person who contravenes reg 45D(4) is guilty of an offence and liable on summary conviction to a fine not exceeding level 5 on the standard scale: see reg 115; and PARA 734.

32 Representation of the People (England and Wales) Regulations 2001, SI 2001/341, reg 45D(4)(b) (as added: see note 20). As to relevant offences see note 31.

33 Representation of the People (England and Wales) Regulations 2001, SI 2001/341, reg 45D(4)(c) (as added: see note 20). As to relevant offences see note 31.

34 Representation of the People (England and Wales) Regulations 2001, SI 2001/341, reg 45D(4) (as added: see note 20). As to relevant offences see note 31.

35 Representation of the People (England and Wales) Regulations 2001, SI 2001/341, reg 45D(5) (as added: see note 20).

180.   Supply of electoral records to national libraries.   Each registration officer in England or Wales (as the case may be)[1] must supply, free of charge and on publication[2], one printed copy and one data copy of any revised version of the register[3], and one printed copy of any list of overseas electors[4], to the national libraries[5]. No person employed by such a library may[6]:

(1)   supply a copy of the full register other than to another such person or to a person using the library to inspect it under supervision[7];

(2)　disclose any information contained in it (that is not contained in the edited register) otherwise than by allowing a person using the library to inspect it under supervision[8]; or

(3)　make use of any such information[9].

However, a person employed by the library is not prohibited from supplying a copy of, or disclosing information contained in, a version of the full register where: (a) more than ten years have expired since that version of the register was first published[10]; and (b) the supply or disclosure is for research purposes in compliance with the relevant conditions[11].

Where a copy of the full register is made available for inspection by providing the register on a computer screen or otherwise in data form, the library must ensure that the manner in, and equipment on, which that copy is provided do not permit any person consulting that copy either to search it by electronic means by reference to the name of any person[12], or to copy or transmit any part of that copy by electronic means[13]. A person who inspects the copy of the full register held by the library, whether a printed copy or in data form, may not[14] make copies of any part of it[15] or record any particulars included in it[16], otherwise than by means of handwritten notes[17]. No person who obtains a copy of the full register (or to whom information contained in it that is not contained in the edited register is disclosed under the circumstances described in heads (a) and (b) above) may supply a copy of it[18], disclose any such information[19] or make use of any such information[20], otherwise than for research purposes in compliance with the relevant conditions[21]. The restrictions on supply and disclosure thereby imposed on a recipient of the data apply equally to any person to whom the full register is duly supplied or to whom any information contained in it (that is not contained in the edited register) is duly disclosed as they apply to the original recipient[22].

1　As to the meaning of 'registration officer' for these purposes see PARA 139 note 1. As to the meanings of 'England' and 'Wales' see PARA 1 note 1.

2　See the Representation of the People (England and Wales) Regulations 2001, SI 2001/341, reg 97(1) (regs 92, 97 added by SI 2002/1871; the Representation of the People (England and Wales) Regulations 2001, SI 2001/341, reg 97(1) amended by SI 2006/752); and the Representation of the People (England and Wales) Regulations 2001, SI 2001/341, reg 97A(1), (2) (reg 97A added by SI 2006/752).

　　Subject to any direction of the Secretary of State under the Representation of the People Act 1983 s 52(1) (discharge of registration duties: see PARA 141), any duty on a registration officer to supply data under the Representation of the People (England and Wales) Regulations 2001, SI 2001/341, Pt VI (regs 92–115) imposes only a duty to supply data in the form in which he holds it (reg 92(5) (as so added)), and he must not supply data which includes information not included in the printed version of the full register otherwise than under a provision in an enactment (reg 92(6) (as so added)). For these purposes, 'data' means information which is recorded with the intention that it should be processed by means of equipment operating automatically in response to instructions given for that purpose: see reg 3(1) (definition substituted by SI 2001/1700). As to the meaning of 'enactment' see PARA 179 note 8. As to the meaning of 'full register' see PARA 167 note 2. As to the meaning of 'register' see PARA 179 note 1. As to the Secretary of State see PARA 2.

3　Representation of the People (England and Wales) Regulations 2001, SI 2001/341, reg 97(1)(a) (reg 97 as added (see note 2); reg 97(1)(a) amended by SI 2006/752); Representation of the People (England and Wales) Regulations 2001, SI 2001/341, reg 97A(1)(a), (2)(a) (as added: see note 2). The text refers to the revised version of a register published under the Representation of the People Act 1983 s 13(1) or s 13(3) (see PARA 165). The duty of a registration officer in England to supply one copy of any revised version of the register to the National Library of Wales is a duty to supply a data copy unless, prior to publication, the National Library of Wales has requested in writing a printed copy instead: reg 97A(3) (as so added).

4　Representation of the People (England and Wales) Regulations 2001, SI 2001/341, reg 97(1)(b) (reg 97 as added (see note 2); reg 97(1)(b) amended by SI 2006/752); Representation of the

People (England and Wales) Regulations 2001, SI 2001/341, reg 97A(1)(b), (2)(b) (as added: see note 2). As to the meaning of 'list of overseas electors' see PARA 143 note 9.

5   Representation of the People (England and Wales) Regulations 2001, SI 2001/341, reg 97(1) (as added: see note 2); Representation of the People (England and Wales) Regulations 2001, SI 2001/341, reg 97A(1), (2) (as added: see note 2). For these purposes, the national libraries referred to in the text are the British Library and the National Library of Wales (as the case may be). As to the British Library and the National Library of Wales see NATIONAL CULTURAL HERITAGE vol 77 (2010) PARA 906 et seq.

6   Representation of the People (England and Wales) Regulations 2001, SI 2001/341, reg 97(2) (reg 97 as added (see note 2); reg 97(2) amended by SI 2006/752); Representation of the People (England and Wales) Regulations 2001, SI 2001/341, reg 97A(4) (as added: see note 2). This provision is expressed to be subject to reg 97(5) or reg 97A(7) (as the case may be) (see the text and notes 10–11): see reg 97(2) (as so added and amended); reg 97A(4) (as so added). For the purposes of Pt VI, any reference to an employee of any person who has access to a copy of the full register is deemed to include any person working or providing services for the purposes of that person or employed by or on behalf of, or working for, any person who is so working or who is supplying such a service: see reg 92(3) (as added: see note 2).

A person who contravenes reg 97(2) or reg 97A(4) is guilty of an offence and liable on summary conviction to a fine not exceeding level 5 on the standard scale: see reg 115; and PARA 734. As to the standard scale see SENTENCING AND DISPOSITION OF OFFENDERS vol 92 (2010) PARA 142.

7   Representation of the People (England and Wales) Regulations 2001, SI 2001/341, reg 97(2)(a) (as added: see note 2); reg 97A(4)(a) (as added: see note 2). The permitted purpose for which a copy of the full register is made available for inspection under supervision in this way does not include direct marketing: see PARA 179 note 18.

8   Representation of the People (England and Wales) Regulations 2001, SI 2001/341, reg 97(2)(b), (3) (reg 97 as added (see note 2); reg 97(3) amended by SI 2006/752); Representation of the People (England and Wales) Regulations 2001, SI 2001/341, reg 97A(4)(b) (as added: see note 2). In the case of the British Library, the prohibition on the disclosure of information which is contained in the full register (that is not contained in the edited register) otherwise than by allowing a person using the library to inspect it under supervision is also expressed as a general prohibition, subject to reg 97(5) (see the text and notes 10–11): see reg 97(3) (as so added and amended). As to the meaning of 'edited register' see PARA 167 note 4. As to the permitted purpose for which a copy of the full register may be made available see note 7.

9   Representation of the People (England and Wales) Regulations 2001, SI 2001/341, reg 97(2)(c) (as added: see note 2); reg 97A(4)(c) (as added: see note 2).

10 Representation of the People (England and Wales) Regulations 2001, SI 2001/341, reg 97(5)(a) (reg 97 as added (see note 2); reg 97(5), (6) added by SI 2006/752); Representation of the People (England and Wales) Regulations 2001, SI 2001/341, reg 97A(7)(a) (as added: see note 2). The text refers to that version of the register first published in accordance with reg 43 (see PARA 165 note 3).

11 Representation of the People (England and Wales) Regulations 2001, SI 2001/341, reg 97(5)(b) (as added: see note 10); reg 97A(7)(b) (as added: see note 2). 'Research purposes' must be construed in accordance with the Data Protection Act 1998 s 33(1) (research, history and statistics: see CONFIDENCE AND INFORMATIONAL PRIVACY vol 19 (2011) PARA 144); and 'relevant conditions' has the same meaning as in s 33(1): see the Representation of the People (England and Wales) Regulations 2001, SI 2001/341, reg 92(2)(c), (d) (reg 92 as added (see note 2); reg 92(2)(c), (d) added by SI 2006/752).

Any person who has obtained or is entitled to obtain a copy of the full register under the Representation of the People (England and Wales) Regulations 2001, SI 2001/341, reg 97(5) or reg 97A(7) may supply a copy of the full register to a processor for the purpose of processing the information contained in the register, or he may procure that a processor processes and provides to him any copy of the register which the processor has obtained under the Representation of the People (England and Wales) Regulations 2001, SI 2001/341, for use in respect of the purposes for which that person is entitled to obtain such copy or information (as the case may be): see reg 92(7) (reg 92 as so added; reg 92(7) amended by SI 2006/752). The processor may not disclose the full register or the information contained in it except to the person who supplied it to the processor or an employee of that person or to a person who is entitled to obtain a copy of the full register under the Representation of the People (England and Wales) Regulations 2001, SI 2001/341, or any employee of such a person: reg 92(9) (as so added). For these purposes, 'processor' means any person who provides a service which consists of putting information into data form or processing information in data form and any reference to a processor includes a reference to his employees (see reg 92(2)(b) (as so added)); and 'data form' means information which is in a form which is capable of being processed by means of equipment operating automatically in response to instructions given for that purpose (see reg 3(1) (definition added by SI 2002/1871)). A person who contravenes the Representation of the People (England and Wales) Regulations 2001, SI 2001/341, reg 92(9) is guilty of an offence and liable on summary conviction to a fine not exceeding level 5 on the standard scale: see reg 115; and PARA 734. As to the restriction on the transfer of personal data to a country or territory outside the European Economic Area see CONFIDENCE AND INFORMATIONAL PRIVACY vol 19 (2011) PARA 108.

12 Representation of the People (England and Wales) Regulations 2001, SI 2001/341, reg 97(3A)(a) (reg 97 as added (see note 2); reg 97(3A) added by SI 2006/752); Representation of the People (England and Wales) Regulations 2001, SI 2001/341, reg 97A(5)(a) (as added: see note 2).

13 Representation of the People (England and Wales) Regulations 2001, SI 2001/341, reg 97(3A)(b) (as added: see note 12); reg 97A(5)(b) (as added: see note 2). As to the meaning of 'available for inspection' see PARA 142 note 18.

14 Representation of the People (England and Wales) Regulations 2001, SI 2001/341, reg 97(4) (reg 97 as added (see note 2); reg 97(4) amended by SI 2006/752); Representation of the People (England and Wales) Regulations 2001, SI 2001/341, reg 97A(6) (as added: see note 2). A person who contravenes reg 97(4) or reg 97A(6) is guilty of an offence and liable on summary conviction to a fine not exceeding level 5 on the standard scale: see reg 115; and PARA 734.

15 Representation of the People (England and Wales) Regulations 2001, SI 2001/341, reg 97(4)(a) (as added: see note 2); reg 97A(6)(a) (as added: see note 2).

16 Representation of the People (England and Wales) Regulations 2001, SI 2001/341, reg 97(4)(b) (as added: see note 2); reg 97A(6)(b) (as added: see note 2).

17 Representation of the People (England and Wales) Regulations 2001, SI 2001/341, reg 97(4) (as added: see note 2); reg 97A(6) (as added: see note 2).

18 Representation of the People (England and Wales) Regulations 2001, SI 2001/341, reg 97(6)(a) (as added: see note 10); reg 97A(8)(a) (as added: see note 2).

19 Representation of the People (England and Wales) Regulations 2001, SI 2001/341, reg 97(6)(b) (as added: see note 10); reg 97A(8)(b) (as added: see note 2).

20 Representation of the People (England and Wales) Regulations 2001, SI 2001/341, reg 97(6)(c) (as added: see note 10); reg 97A(8)(c) (as added: see note 2).

21 Representation of the People (England and Wales) Regulations 2001, SI 2001/341, reg 97(6) (as added: see note 10); reg 97A(8) (as added: see note 2). A person who contravenes reg 97(6) or reg 97A(8) is guilty of an offence and liable on summary conviction to a fine not exceeding level 5 on the standard scale: see reg 115; and PARA 734.

22 Representation of the People (England and Wales) Regulations 2001, SI 2001/341, reg 92(10) (reg 92 as added (see note 2); reg 92(10) amended by SI 2006/752). The text refers to the restrictions contained in the Representation of the People (England and Wales) Regulations 2001, SI 2001/341, reg 97(6) (see the text and notes 18–21) and reg 97A(8) (see the text and notes 18–21): see reg 92(10) (as so added and amended).

181. Supply of electoral records to public libraries and local authority archives service. A public library[1] or a local authority archives service[2] may request the registration officer[3] to supply free of charge the relevant part[4] of any revised version of the register[5], any notice altering the published register[6] or any list of overseas electors[7]. Such a request must be made in writing[8], and must:

(1) specify the documents requested[9];

(2) state whether the request is made only in respect of the current documents or whether it includes a request for the supply of any subsequent document on publication[10]; and

(3) state whether a printed copy of any of the documents is requested instead of the version in data form[11].

The registration officer must supply the relevant part of any documents so requested in accordance with a request that has been duly made[12]. No person employed by the public library or the local authority archives service may[13]:

(a) supply a copy of the full register[14] other than to another such person or to a person using the library or the archives service to inspect it under supervision[15];

(b) disclose any information contained in it (that is not contained in the edited register[16]) otherwise than by allowing a person using the library or the archives service to inspect it under supervision[17]; or

(c)   make use of any such information[18].

However, the public library or local authority archives service is not prohibited from supplying a copy of, or disclosing information contained in, a version of the full register where: (i) more than ten years have expired since that version of the register was first published[19]; and (ii) the supply or disclosure is for research purposes in compliance with the relevant conditions[20].

Where a copy of the full register is made available for inspection[21], in accordance with head (a) or head (b) above, by providing the register on a computer screen or otherwise in data form, the library or the archives service must ensure that the manner in, and equipment on, which that copy is provided do not permit any person consulting that copy either to search it by electronic means by reference to the name of any person[22], or to copy or transmit any part of that copy by electronic means[23]. A person who inspects the copy of the full register, whether a printed copy or in data form, may not[24] either make copies of any part of it[25], or record any particulars included in it[26], otherwise than by means of handwritten notes[27]. No person who obtains a copy of the full register (or to whom information contained in it that is not contained in the edited register is disclosed under the circumstances described in heads (i) and (ii) above) may supply a copy of it[28], disclose any such information[29] or make use of any such information[30], otherwise than for research purposes in compliance with the relevant conditions[31]. The restrictions on supply and disclosure thereby imposed on an original recipient of the data apply equally to a person to whom the full register is duly supplied or to whom any information contained in it (that is not contained in the edited register) is duly disclosed as they apply to the original recipient[32].

1   For these purposes, 'public library' means a library maintained by a library authority, where 'library authority' has the same meaning as in the Local Government Act 1972 s 206 (public libraries and museums (England)) and the Public Libraries and Museums Act 1964 s 4 (library authorities and areas) (see NATIONAL CULTURAL HERITAGE vol 77 (2010) PARA 926): see the Representation of the People (England and Wales) Regulations 2001, SI 2001/341, reg 109A(11) (reg 109A added by SI 2006/752).

2   For these purposes, 'local authority archives service' means an archives service established by a county council, a county borough council, a district council, a London borough council, the Common Council of the City of London, or the Council of the Isles of Scilly, in exercise of its functions under the Local Government (Records) Act 1962 (see LOCAL GOVERNMENT vol 69 (2009) PARA 541): see the Representation of the People (England and Wales) Regulations 2001, SI 2001/341, reg 109A(11) (as added: see note 1). As to districts in England and counties and county boroughs in Wales, and their councils, see LOCAL GOVERNMENT vol 69 (2009) PARAS 24 et seq, 37 et seq. As to London boroughs and their councils see LOCAL GOVERNMENT vol 69 (2009) PARA 35; LONDON GOVERNMENT vol 71 (2013) PARAS 15, 20 et seq. As to the Common Council of the City of London see LONDON GOVERNMENT vol 71 (2013) PARA 34 et seq. As to the Council of the Isles of Scilly see LOCAL GOVERNMENT vol 69 (2009) PARA 36.

3   As to the meaning of 'registration officer' for these purposes see PARA 139 note 1.

4   See the Representation of the People (England and Wales) Regulations 2001, SI 2001/341, reg 109A(1) (as added: see note 1). The text refers to the relevant part within the meaning of reg 109A(2): see reg 109A(1) (as so added). Accordingly, for these purposes, the relevant part of the documents listed in reg 109A(1) is so much of them as a public library or local authority archives service has been given responsibility for keeping by a library authority or local authority respectively: reg 109A(2) (as so added).

5   Representation of the People (England and Wales) Regulations 2001, SI 2001/341, reg 109A(1)(a) (as added: see note 1). The text refers to the revised version of a register published under the Representation of the People Act 1983 s 13(1) or s 13(3) (see PARA 165): see the Representation of the People (England and Wales) Regulations 2001, SI 2001/341, reg 109A(1)(a) (as so added).

6 Representation of the People (England and Wales) Regulations 2001, SI 2001/341, reg 109A(1)(b) (reg 109A as added (see note 1); reg 109A(1)(b) amended by SI 2006/2910). The text refers to a notice of alteration published under the Representation of the People Act 1983 s 13A(2), s 13B(3), s 13B(3B) or s 13B(3D) (see PARA 168): see the Representation of the People (England and Wales) Regulations 2001, SI 2001/341, reg 109A(1)(b) (as so added and amended).

7 Representation of the People (England and Wales) Regulations 2001, SI 2001/341, reg 109A(1)(c) (as added: see note 1). As to the meaning of 'list of overseas electors' see PARA 143 note 9.

8 See the Representation of the People (England and Wales) Regulations 2001, SI 2001/341, reg 109A(3) (as added: see note 1).

9 Representation of the People (England and Wales) Regulations 2001, SI 2001/341, reg 109A(3)(a) (as added: see note 1).

10 Representation of the People (England and Wales) Regulations 2001, SI 2001/341, reg 109A(3)(b) (as added: see note 1).

11 Representation of the People (England and Wales) Regulations 2001, SI 2001/341, reg 109A(3)(c) (as added: see note 1). Unless a request has been made in advance of supply under reg 109A(3)(c), the copy of a document supplied under reg 109A is to be in data form: reg 109A(4) (as so added). As to the meaning of 'data form' see PARA 180 note 11. As to general aspects of the duty on a registration officer to supply data under Pt VI (regs 92–115) see PARA 180 note 2.

12 Representation of the People (England and Wales) Regulations 2001, SI 2001/341, reg 109A(5) (as added: see note 1).

13 See the Representation of the People (England and Wales) Regulations 2001, SI 2001/341, reg 109A(6) (as added (see note 1). This provision is expressed to be subject to reg 109A(9) (see the text and notes 19–20): see reg 109A(6) (as so added). As to references to employees of any person who has access to a copy of the full register see PARA 180 note 6. A person who contravenes regs 109A(6), (8) (see the text and notes 24–27) or reg 109A(10) (see the text and notes 28–31) is guilty of an offence and liable on summary conviction to a fine not exceeding level 5 on the standard scale: see reg 115; and PARA 734. As to the standard scale see SENTENCING AND DISPOSITION OF OFFENDERS vol 92 (2010) PARA 142.

14 As to the meaning of 'full register' see PARA 167 note 2. As to the meaning of 'register' see PARA 179 note 1.

15 Representation of the People (England and Wales) Regulations 2001, SI 2001/341, reg 109A(6)(a) (as added: see note 1). See note 13. The permitted purpose for which a copy of the full register is made available for inspection under supervision in this way does not include direct marketing: see PARA 179 note 18.

16 As to the meaning of 'edited register' see PARA 167 note 4.

17 Representation of the People (England and Wales) Regulations 2001, SI 2001/341, reg 109A(6)(b) (as added: see note 1). See note 13. As to the permitted purpose for which a copy of the full register may be made available see note 15.

18 Representation of the People (England and Wales) Regulations 2001, SI 2001/341, reg 109A(6)(c) (as added: see note 1). See note 13.

19 Representation of the People (England and Wales) Regulations 2001, SI 2001/341, reg 109A(9)(a) (as added: see note 1). The text refers to that version of the register first published in accordance with reg 43 (see PARA 165 note 3): see reg 109A(9)(a) (as so added).

20 Representation of the People (England and Wales) Regulations 2001, SI 2001/341, reg 109A(9)(b) (as added: see note 1). As to the meanings of 'research purposes' and 'relevant conditions' see PARA 180 note 11.

21 As to the meaning of 'available for inspection' see PARA 142 note 18.

22 Representation of the People (England and Wales) Regulations 2001, SI 2001/341, reg 109A(7)(a) (as added: see note 1).

23 Representation of the People (England and Wales) Regulations 2001, SI 2001/341, reg 109A(7)(b) (as added: see note 1).

24 See the Representation of the People (England and Wales) Regulations 2001, SI 2001/341, reg 109A(8) (as added: see note 1). See note 13.

25 Representation of the People (England and Wales) Regulations 2001, SI 2001/341, reg 109A(8)(a) (as added: see note 1). See note 13.

26 Representation of the People (England and Wales) Regulations 2001, SI 2001/341, reg 109A(8)(b) (as added: see note 1). See note 13.

27 See the Representation of the People (England and Wales) Regulations 2001, SI 2001/341, reg 109A(8) (as added: see note 1). See note 13.

28 Representation of the People (England and Wales) Regulations 2001, SI 2001/341, reg 109A(10)(a) (as added: see note 1). See note 13.

29 Representation of the People (England and Wales) Regulations 2001, SI 2001/341, reg 109A(10)(b) (as added: see note 1). See note 13.

30 Representation of the People (England and Wales) Regulations 2001, SI 2001/341, reg 109A(10)(c) (as added: see note 1). See note 13.

31 See the Representation of the People (England and Wales) Regulations 2001, SI 2001/341, reg 109A(10) (as added: see note 1). See note 13.

32 Representation of the People (England and Wales) Regulations 2001, SI 2001/341, reg 92(10) (reg 92 as added (see note 1); reg 92(10) amended by SI 2006/752). See note 13. Any person who has obtained or is entitled to obtain a copy of the full register under the Representation of the People (England and Wales) Regulations 2001, SI 2001/341, reg 109A(9) may supply a copy of the full register to a processor for the purpose of processing the information contained in the register, or he may procure that a processor processes and provides to him any copy of the register which the processor has obtained under the Representation of the People (England and Wales) Regulations 2001, SI 2001/341, for use in respect of the purposes for which that person is entitled to obtain such copy or information (as the case may be): see reg 92(7) (reg 92 as so added; reg 92(7) amended by SI 2006/752); and see PARA 180 note 11.

182.   Supply of electoral records to holders of electoral office.   Each registration officer[1] must supply, free of charge and on publication[2], one copy of any revised version of the register[3] and one copy of any notice altering the published register[4] to the following persons[5]:

(1)   the returning officer for a non-metropolitan county[6];

(2)   the persons or officers who are the returning officers at an election of members of the London Assembly and of the Mayor of London[7];

(3)   the returning officer appointed for elections to each parish or community council within the electoral area[8].

As soon as practicable after the relevant event[9], a registration officer who is not the acting returning officer for a constituency wholly or partly in his registration area[10] must supply free of charge to that officer as many printed copies of[11]:

(a)   the latest revised version of the register[12];

(b)   any notice setting out an alteration to that version of the register[13]; and

(c)   the most recent list of overseas electors[14],

as the returning officer may reasonably require for the purposes of a parliamentary election[15]. As soon as practicable after the relevant date[16], a registration officer who is not designated as a local returning officer for part of a European parliamentary electoral region[17] which falls wholly or partly in his registration area must supply free of charge to that officer as many printed copies of the documents[18] referred to in heads (a), (b) and (c) above as the local returning officer may reasonably require for the purposes of a European parliamentary election[19]. Where a registration officer is not the returning officer for any Welsh Assembly election in respect of any constituency or region[20] wholly or partly within his registration area, he must supply free of charge to that officer as many printed copies of the documents referred to in head (a) or head (b) above, together with one copy of each in data form, as the returning officer may reasonably require for the purposes of such an election[21].

No person to whom a copy of the register has been duly supplied[22] may supply a copy of the full register[23], disclose any information contained in it (that is not contained in the edited register)[24] or make use of any such information[25], other than for the purposes of an election[26]. The restrictions on supply and disclosure imposed on the original recipient apply equally to any person to whom the full register is duly supplied or to whom any information contained in it (that is not contained in the edited register) is duly disclosed as they apply to the original recipient[27].

Whenever the registration officer supplies a copy of the full register, or any part of it, to a returning officer or counting officer[28], the registration officer must supply, together with the copy of the register, a copy of the record of anonymous entries[29] and, together with any part of the register, a copy of the record so far as it relates to that part[30]. A registration officer also may supply a copy of the record to a returning officer or counting officer at any other time[31]. No person to whom a copy of the record has been supplied in such a way may supply a copy of the record[32], disclose any information contained in it[33] or make use of any such information[34], other than for the purposes of an election or referendum (as the case may be)[35]. Each person supplied with a copy of the record in this way[36] must take proper precautions for its safe custody[37].

1   As to the meaning of 'registration officer' for these purposes see PARA 139 note 1.
2   See the Representation of the People (England and Wales) Regulations 2001, SI 2001/341, reg 98(1) (regs 92, 98 added by SI 2002/1871). For these purposes, the duty to supply one copy of the register is a duty to supply it in data form unless, prior to publication, the officer or person to whom it is to be supplied has requested in writing a printed copy instead: Representation of the People (England and Wales) Regulations 2001, SI 2001/341, reg 98(3) (as so added). As to the meaning of 'data form' see PARA. As to the meaning of 'register' see PARA 179 note 1. As to general aspects of the duty on a registration officer to supply data under Pt VI (regs 92–115) see PARA 180 note 2.
3   Representation of the People (England and Wales) Regulations 2001, SI 2001/341, reg 98(1)(a) (as added: see note 2). The text refers to the revised version of a register published under the Representation of the People Act 1983 s 13(1) or (3) (see PARA 165): see the Representation of the People (England and Wales) Regulations 2001, SI 2001/341, reg 98(1)(a) (as so added).
4   Representation of the People (England and Wales) Regulations 2001, SI 2001/341, reg 98(1)(b) (reg 98 as added (see note 2); reg 98(1)(b) amended by SI 2006/2910). The text refers to a notice of alteration published under the Representation of the People Act 1983 s 13A(2), s 13B(3), s 13B(3B) or s 13B(3D) (see PARA 168): see the Representation of the People (England and Wales) Regulations 2001, SI 2001/341, reg 98(1)(b) (as so added and amended).
5   See the Representation of the People (England and Wales) Regulations 2001, SI 2001/341, reg 98(1) (as added: see note 2).
6   Representation of the People (England and Wales) Regulations 2001, SI 2001/341, reg 98(2)(a) (as added: see note 2). As to the meaning of 'non-metropolitan county' see LOCAL GOVERNMENT vol 69 (2009) PARA 24. As to returning officers see PARA 350 et seq.
7   Representation of the People (England and Wales) Regulations 2001, SI 2001/341, reg 98(2)(b) (as added: see note 2). The text refers to the persons or officers appointed under the Representation of the People Act 1983 s 35(2B) (returning officer at an election of a constituency member of the London Assembly) and s 35(2C) (returning officer at election of the Mayor of London and the London members of the London Assembly) (see PARA 354): see the Representation of the People (England and Wales) Regulations 2001, SI 2001/341, reg 98(2)(b) (as so added).
8   Representation of the People (England and Wales) Regulations 2001, SI 2001/341, reg 98(2)(c) (as added: see note 2). The text refers to the officers appointed pursuant to the Representation of the People Act 1983 s 35(1) (returning officer for elections of councillors of parishes) and s 35(1A) (returning officer for elections of councillors of communities) (see PARA 354), as the case may be: see the Representation of the People (England and Wales) Regulations 2001, SI 2001/341, reg 98(2)(c) (as so added). As to the meaning of 'electoral area' see PARA 11. As to parishes see LOCAL GOVERNMENT vol 69 (2009) PARA 27 et seq; and as to communities see LOCAL GOVERNMENT vol 69 (2009) PARA 41 et seq.
9   For these purposes, the 'relevant event' means either the announcement of Her Majesty's intention to dissolve Parliament (see PARA 189 et seq) or the occurrence of a vacancy in the relevant constituency (see PARA 191): see the Representation of the People (England and Wales) Regulations 2001, SI 2001/341, reg 98(5)(a) (as added: see note 2).
10 As to returning officers generally see PARA 350 et seq. As to the meaning of 'registration area' see PARA 139 note 1. As to the meaning of 'constituency' for these purposes see PARA 9.

11　See the Representation of the People (England and Wales) Regulations 2001, SI 2001/341, reg 98(4) (as added: see note 2). For these purposes, the duty to supply as many printed copies of the register, notices and list of overseas electors as the returning officer may reasonably require (see heads (a) to (c) in the text) includes a duty to supply one copy of each in data form: reg 98(5)(b) (as so added). As to the meaning of 'list of overseas electors' see PARA 143 note 9.

12　Representation of the People (England and Wales) Regulations 2001, SI 2001/341, reg 98(4)(a) (as added: see note 2). The text refers to the latest revised version of the register published under either the Representation of the People Act 1983 s 13(1) or s 13(3), as the case may be (see PARA 165): see the Representation of the People (England and Wales) Regulations 2001, SI 2001/341, reg 98(4)(a) (as so added). See note 11.

13　Representation of the People (England and Wales) Regulations 2001, SI 2001/341, reg 98(4)(b) (reg 98 as added (see note 2); reg 98(4)(b) amended by SI 2006/2910). The text refers to a notice of alteration published under the Representation of the People Act 1983 s 13A(2), s 13B(3), s 13B(3B) or s 13B(3D) (see PARA 168): see the Representation of the People (England and Wales) Regulations 2001, SI 2001/341, reg 98(4)(b) (as so added and amended). See note 11.

14　Representation of the People (England and Wales) Regulations 2001, SI 2001/341, reg 98(4)(c) (as added: see note 2). See note 11.

15　See the Representation of the People (England and Wales) Regulations 2001, SI 2001/341, reg 98(4) (as added: see note 2).

16　For these purposes, the 'relevant date' means (in the case of a general election of members of the European Parliament) the date which is two months before the day appointed by order of the Secretary of State for the poll (see PARA 222) or (where the Secretary of State has made an order appointing a day for the poll at a by-election) the date on which that order was made (see PARA 218): Representation of the People (England and Wales) Regulations 2001, SI 2001/341, reg 98(7)(a) (as added: see note 2). As to the Secretary of State see PARA 2.

17　As to electoral regions established for these purposes see PARA 77; and as to the designation of local returning officers see PARA 360.

18　For these purposes, the duty to supply as many printed copies of the register, notices and list of overseas electors as the local returning officer may reasonably require includes a duty to supply one copy of each in data form: Representation of the People (England and Wales) Regulations 2001, SI 2001/341, reg 98(7)(b) (as added: see note 2).

19　Representation of the People (England and Wales) Regulations 2001, SI 2001/341, reg 98(6) (as added: see note 2).

20　As to the meanings of 'constituency election' and 'regional election' for these purposes see PARA 3 note 2.

21　Representation of the People (England and Wales) Regulations 2001, SI 2001/341, reg 98(8) (as added: see note 2).

22　le supplied under the Representation of the People (England and Wales) Regulations 2001, SI 2001/341, reg 98: see reg 98(9) (as added: see note 2).

23　Representation of the People (England and Wales) Regulations 2001, SI 2001/341, reg 98(9)(a) (as added: see note 2). As to the meaning of 'full register' see PARA 167 note 2.

24　Representation of the People (England and Wales) Regulations 2001, SI 2001/341, reg 98(9)(b) (as added: see note 2). As to the meaning of 'edited register' see PARA 167 note 4.

25　Representation of the People (England and Wales) Regulations 2001, SI 2001/341, reg 98(9)(c) (as added: see note 2).

26　See the Representation of the People (England and Wales) Regulations 2001, SI 2001/341, reg 98(9) (as added: see note 2). A person who contravenes reg 98(9) is guilty of an offence and liable on summary conviction to a fine not exceeding level 5 on the standard scale: see reg 115; and PARA 734. As to the standard scale see SENTENCING AND DISPOSITION OF OFFENDERS vol 92 (2010) PARA 142.

27　Representation of the People (England and Wales) Regulations 2001, SI 2001/341, reg 92(10) (reg 92 as added (see note 2); reg 92(10) amended by SI 2006/752). However, any person who has obtained or is entitled to obtain a copy of the full register under the Representation of the People (England and Wales) Regulations 2001, SI 2001/341, reg 98 (see the text and notes 1–26) may supply a copy of the full register to a processor for the purpose of processing the information contained in the register, or he may procure that a processor processes and provides to him any copy of the register which the processor has obtained under the Representation of the People (England and Wales) Regulations 2001, SI 2001/341, for use in respect of the purposes for which that person is entitled to obtain such copy or information (as the case may be): see reg 92(7) (reg 92 as so added; reg 92(7) amended by SI 2006/752); and see PARA 180 note 11.

28 See the Representation of the People (England and Wales) Regulations 2001, SI 2001/341, reg 45C(1) (reg 45C added by SI 2006/2910). As to the meaning of 'counting officer' see PARA 179 note 20.

29 Representation of the People (England and Wales) Regulations 2001, SI 2001/341, reg 45C(2)(a) (as added: see note 28). As to the duty of the registration officer to keep a record of anonymous entries see PARA 143 et seq.

30 Representation of the People (England and Wales) Regulations 2001, SI 2001/341, reg 45C(2)(b) (as added: see note 28).

31 Representation of the People (England and Wales) Regulations 2001, SI 2001/341, reg 45C(3) (as added: see note 28).

32 Representation of the People (England and Wales) Regulations 2001, SI 2001/341, reg 45C(4)(a) (as added: see note 28). A person who contravenes reg 45C(4) is guilty of an offence and liable on summary conviction to a fine not exceeding level 5 on the standard scale: see reg 115; and PARA 734.

33 Representation of the People (England and Wales) Regulations 2001, SI 2001/341, reg 45C(4)(b) (as added: see note 28). As to relevant offences see note 32.

34 Representation of the People (England and Wales) Regulations 2001, SI 2001/341, reg 45C(4)(c) (as added: see note 28). As to relevant offences see note 32.

35 Representation of the People (England and Wales) Regulations 2001, SI 2001/341, reg 45C(4) (as added: see note 28). As to relevant offences see note 32.

36 Ie under the Representation of the People (England and Wales) Regulations 2001, SI 2001/341, reg 45C: see reg 45C(5) (as added: see note 28).

37 Representation of the People (England and Wales) Regulations 2001, SI 2001/341, reg 45C(5) (as added: see note 28).

183. Supply of electoral records to Electoral Commission. Each registration officer[1] must supply, free of charge and on publication[2], one copy of any revised version of the register[3], one copy of any notice altering the published register[4] and one copy of any list of overseas electors[5], to the Electoral Commission[6].

Neither the Electoral Commissioners[7] nor any person employed by the Electoral Commission may[8]:

(1)   supply a copy of the full register[9] other than to an Electoral Commissioner or another such person[10];

(2)   disclose any information contained in it (that is not contained in the edited register[11]) otherwise than in accordance with heads (a) and (b) below[12]; or

(3)   make use of any such information otherwise than in connection with their statutory functions under, or by virtue of, the Political Parties, Elections and Referendums Act 2000[13].

The full register or any information contained in it and not in the edited register may not be disclosed otherwise than[14]:

(a)   where necessary to carry out the Electoral Commission's duties in relation to the statutory rules on permissible donors[15]; or

(b)   by publishing information about electors which does not include the name or address of any elector[16].

The restrictions on supply and disclosure imposed on the Electoral Commissioners and on any person employed by the Electoral Commission[17] apply equally to any person to whom the full register is duly supplied or to whom any information contained in it (that is not contained in the edited register) is duly disclosed as they apply to the Electoral Commissioners and to employees of the Electoral Commission[18].

1 As to the meaning of 'registration officer' for these purposes see PARA 139 note 1.
2 See the Representation of the People (England and Wales) Regulations 2001, SI 2001/341, reg 100(1) (regs 92, 100 added by SI 2002/1871). For these purposes, the duty to supply is a duty to supply in data form unless, prior to publication, the Electoral Commission has requested in writing a printed copy instead: Representation of the People (England and Wales)

Regulations 2001, SI 2001/341, reg 100(2) (as so added). As to the meaning of 'data form' see PARA 180 note 11. As to the Electoral Commission see PARA 34 et seq; and as to general aspects of the duty on a registration officer to supply data under Pt VI (regs 92–115) see PARA 180 note 2.

3   Representation of the People (England and Wales) Regulations 2001, SI 2001/341, reg 100(1)(a) (as added: see note 2). The text refers to the revised version of a register published under the Representation of the People Act 1983 s 13(1) or s 13(3) (see PARA 165): see the Representation of the People (England and Wales) Regulations 2001, SI 2001/341, reg 100(1)(a) (as so added). As to the meaning of 'register' see PARA 179 note 1.

4   Representation of the People (England and Wales) Regulations 2001, SI 2001/341, reg 100(1)(b) (reg 100 as added (see note 2); reg 100(1)(b) amended by SI 2006/2910). The text refers to a notice of alteration published under the Representation of the People Act 1983 s 13A(2), s 13B(3), s 13B(3B) or s 13B(3D) (see PARA 168): see the Representation of the People (England and Wales) Regulations 2001, SI 2001/341, reg 100(1)(b) (as so added and amended).

5   Representation of the People (England and Wales) Regulations 2001, SI 2001/341, reg 100(1)(c) (as added: see note 2). As to the meaning of 'list of overseas electors' see PARA 143 note 9.

6   See the Representation of the People (England and Wales) Regulations 2001, SI 2001/341, reg 100(1) (as added: see note 2).

7   For these purposes, 'Electoral Commissioner' includes a Deputy Electoral Commissioner and an Assistant Electoral Commissioner: Representation of the People (England and Wales) Regulations 2001, SI 2001/341, reg 100(4) (as added: see note 2). However, Deputy Electoral Commissioners were appointed under the Political Parties, Elections and Referendums Act 2000 s 15, which has been repealed by the Local Democracy, Economic Development and Construction Act 2009 ss 61(1), (2)(b), 146(1), Sch 7 Pt 3: see PARA 71. As to the Electoral Commissioners see PARA 35 et seq; and as to the appointment of Assistant Electoral Commissioners see PARA 40.

8   See the Representation of the People (England and Wales) Regulations 2001, SI 2001/341, reg 100(3) (as added: see note 2). As to references to employees of any person who has access to a copy of the full register see PARA 180 note 6. A person who contravenes reg 100(3) is guilty of an offence and liable on summary conviction to a fine not exceeding level 5 on the standard scale: see reg 115; and PARA 734. As to the standard scale see SENTENCING AND DISPOSITION OF OFFENDERS vol 92 (2010) PARA 142.

9   As to the meaning of 'full register' see PARA 167 note 2.

10 Representation of the People (England and Wales) Regulations 2001, SI 2001/341, reg 100(3)(a) (as added: see note 2). See note 8.

11 As to the meaning of 'edited register' see PARA 167 note 4.

12 Representation of the People (England and Wales) Regulations 2001, SI 2001/341, reg 100(3)(b) (as added: see note 2). See note 8.

13 Representation of the People (England and Wales) Regulations 2001, SI 2001/341, reg 100(3)(c) (as added: see note 2). See note 8. As to the functions of the Electoral Commissioners see PARA 51 et seq.

14 See the Representation of the People (England and Wales) Regulations 2001, SI 2001/341, reg 100(5) (as added: see note 2). A person who contravenes reg 100(5) is guilty of an offence and liable on summary conviction to a fine not exceeding level 5 on the standard scale: see reg 115; and PARA 734.

15 Representation of the People (England and Wales) Regulations 2001, SI 2001/341, reg 100(5)(a) (as added: see note 2). The text refers to the duties of the Electoral Commission in relation to the rules on permissible donors in the Political Parties, Elections and Referendums Act 2000 (as to which see PARA 288 et seq): see the Representation of the People (England and Wales) Regulations 2001, SI 2001/341, reg 100(5)(a) (as so added). As to related offences see note 14.

16 Representation of the People (England and Wales) Regulations 2001, SI 2001/341, reg 100(5)(b) (as added: see note 2). As to related offences see note 14.

17 Ie the restriction contained in the Representation of the People (England and Wales) Regulations 2001, SI 2001/341, reg 100(3) (see the text and notes 7–13): see reg 92(10) (reg 92 as added (see note 2); reg 92(10) amended by SI 2006/752).

18 Representation of the People (England and Wales) Regulations 2001, SI 2001/341, reg 92(10) (as added and amended: see note 17). However, any person who has obtained or is entitled to obtain a copy of the full register under reg 100 may supply a copy of the full register to a processor for the purpose of processing the information contained in the register, or he may procure that a processor processes and provides to him any copy of the register which the processor has obtained under the Representation of the People (England and Wales) Regulations 2001, SI 2001/341, for use in respect of the purposes for which that person is

entitled to obtain such copy or information (as the case may be): see reg 92(7) (reg 92 as so added; reg 92(7) amended by SI 2006/752); and see PARA 180 note 11.

184. Supply of electoral records to the Boundary Commissions. Each registration officer in England[1] must supply, free of charge and on publication[2]:

(1)   one copy of any revised version of the register[3];

(2)   one copy of any notice altering the published register[4]; and

(3)   one copy of any list of overseas electors[5],

to the Boundary Commission for England[6]; and each registration officer in Wales[7] must similarly supply, free of charge and on publication, one copy of each of the documents listed in heads (1) to (3) above to the Boundary Commission for Wales and the Local Democracy and Boundary Commission for Wales[8].

Neither a member of the Commission in question[9], nor a person appointed to assist the Commission in question to carry out its functions[10], nor any person employed by the Commission in question[11], may:

(a)   supply a copy of the full register[12] other than to another such person[13];

(b)   disclose any information contained in it (that is not contained in the edited register[14]) otherwise than by publishing information about electors which does not include the name and address of any elector[15]; or

(c)   process or make use of any such information other than in connection with their statutory functions[16].

The restrictions on supply and disclosure imposed on a member of such a Commission or on any person appointed to assist it or on any person employed by it[17] apply to any person to whom the full register is duly supplied or to whom any information contained in it (that is not contained in the edited register) is duly disclosed as they apply to any such member or to any such person[18].

1   As to the meaning of 'registration officer' for these purposes see PARA 139 note 1. As to the meaning of 'England' see PARA 1 note 1.

2   See the Representation of the People (England and Wales) Regulations 2001, SI 2001/341, reg 101(1) (regs 92, 101 added by SI 2002/1871). For these purposes, the duty to supply is a duty to supply in data form unless, prior to publication, the Commission to whom it is to be supplied has requested in writing a printed copy instead: see the Representation of the People (England and Wales) Regulations 2001, SI 2001/341, reg 101(4) (as so added). As to the meaning of 'data form' see PARA 180 note 11. As to general aspects of the duty on a registration officer to supply data under Pt VI (regs 92–115) see PARA 180 note 2.

3   See the Representation of the People (England and Wales) Regulations 2001, SI 2001/341, reg 101(1), (3)(a) (as added: see note 2). The text refers to the revised version of a register published under the Representation of the People Act 1983 s 13(1) or (3) (see PARA 165): see the Representation of the People (England and Wales) Regulations 2001, SI 2001/341, reg 101(3)(a) (as so added). As to the meaning of 'register' see PARA 179 note 1.

4   See the Representation of the People (England and Wales) Regulations 2001, SI 2001/341, reg 101(1), (3)(b) (reg 101 as added (see note 2); reg 101(3)(b) amended by SI 2006/2910). The text refers to a notice of alteration published under the Representation of the People Act 1983 s 13A(2), s 13B(3), s 13B(3B) or s 13B(3D) (see PARA 168): see the Representation of the People (England and Wales) Regulations 2001, SI 2001/341, reg 101(3)(b) (as so added).

5   See the Representation of the People (England and Wales) Regulations 2001, SI 2001/341, reg 101(1), (3)(c) (as added: see note 2). As to the meaning of 'list of overseas electors' see PARA 143 note 9.

6   See the Representation of the People (England and Wales) Regulations 2001, SI 2001/341, reg 101(1) (as added: see note 2). As to the Boundary Commission for England see PARA 68.

7   As to the meaning of 'Wales' see PARA 1 note 1.

8   See the Representation of the People (England and Wales) Regulations 2001, SI 2001/341, reg 101(2) (as added: see note 2). For these purposes, the duty to supply is a duty to supply in data form unless, prior to publication, the Commission to whom it is to be supplied has requested in writing a printed copy instead: see reg 101(4) (as so added). As to the Boundary

Commission for Wales see PARA 68. The Local Democracy and Boundary Commission for Wales is the body formerly known as the Local Government Boundary Commission for Wales, which has been continued in existence and renamed, by the Local Government (Democracy) (Wales) Act 2013: see s 2; and PARA 72.

9   See the Representation of the People (England and Wales) Regulations 2001, SI 2001/341, reg 101(5)(a) (as added: see note 2).

10   See the Representation of the People (England and Wales) Regulations 2001, SI 2001/341, reg 101(5)(b) (as added: see note 2).

11   See the Representation of the People (England and Wales) Regulations 2001, SI 2001/341, reg 101(5)(c) (as added: see note 2). As to references to employees of any person who has access to a copy of the full register see PARA 180 note 6.

12   As to the meaning of 'full register' see PARA 167 note 2.

13   Representation of the People (England and Wales) Regulations 2001, SI 2001/341, reg 101(6)(a) (as added: see note 2). A person who contravenes reg 101(6) is guilty of an offence and liable on summary conviction to a fine not exceeding level 5 on the standard scale: see reg 115; and PARA 734. As to the standard scale see SENTENCING AND DISPOSITION OF OFFENDERS vol 92 (2010) PARA 142.

14   As to the meaning of 'edited register' see PARA 167 note 4.

15   Representation of the People (England and Wales) Regulations 2001, SI 2001/341, reg 101(6)(b) (as added: see note 2). As to related offences see note 13.

16   Representation of the People (England and Wales) Regulations 2001, SI 2001/341, reg 101(6)(c) (as added: see note 2). As to related offences see note 13.

17   Ie the restriction contained in the Representation of the People (England and Wales) Regulations 2001, SI 2001/341, reg 101(6) (see the text and notes 12–16): see reg 92(10) (reg 92 as added (see note 2); reg 92(10) amended by SI 2006/752).

18   Representation of the People (England and Wales) Regulations 2001, SI 2001/341, reg 92(10) (as added and amended: see note 17). However, any person who has obtained or is entitled to obtain a copy of the full register under reg 101 (see the text and notes 1–16) may supply a copy of the full register to a processor for the purpose of processing the information contained in the register, or he may procure that a processor processes and provides to him any copy of the register which the processor has obtained under the Representation of the People (England and Wales) Regulations 2001, SI 2001/341, for use in respect of the purposes for which that person is entitled to obtain such copy or information (as the case may be): see reg 92(7) (reg 92 as so added; reg 92(7) amended by SI 2006/752); and see PARA 180 note 11.

185.   Supply of electoral records to elected officials, holders of offices, candidates. The persons or organisations falling within heads (a) to (q) below[1] may request the registration officer[2] to supply free of charge the relevant part[3] of a revised version of the register[4], the relevant part of any notice altering the published register[5] or the relevant part of a list of overseas electors[6]. Such a request must be made in writing[7], and must:

(1)   specify the documents requested[8];

(2)   state whether the request is made only in respect of the current documents or whether it includes a request for the supply of any subsequent document on publication for as long as the person making the request falls within the category of person entitled to receive such copies[9]; and

(3)   state whether a printed copy of any of the documents is requested instead of the version in data form[10].

The following persons or organisations may make such a request:

(a)   the member of Parliament for any constituency wholly or partly within the registration area[11];

(b)   each member of the European Parliament for an electoral region in which the registration area is situated[12];

(c)   each member of the National Assembly for Wales for any constituency or region wholly or partly within the registration area[13];

(d)   each councillor for an electoral area falling within the registration area[14];

(e)   the Mayor of London and the London members of the London Assembly, where the registration area falls wholly or partly within Greater London[15];

(f)   the constituency members of the London Assembly, where the registration area falls wholly or partly within an Assembly constituency[16];

(g)   an elected mayor[17] where the registration area falls wholly or partly within the area of the local authority for which the mayor is elected[18];

(h)   the holder of an elective office which is subject to the statutory controls relating to donations[19];

(i)   a candidate for election at a parliamentary, local government or London Authority election[20];

(j)   any person nominated by the registered nominating officer[21] of a registered political party to act for the purpose of requesting such documents on behalf of a particular constituency[22];

(k)   a registered political party, other than a minor party[23];

(l)   a recognised third party, other than a registered political party[24];

(m)   a permitted participant, other than a registered political party[25];

(n)   the local authority by which the registration officer was appointed[26];

(o)   a local authority whose area falls wholly or partly within the registration area of that local authority, other than a parish council or community council falling within head (p) below[27];

(p)   a parish council or community council[28]; and

(q)   a candidate at a parliamentary or European parliamentary election[29], at an election to the National Assembly of Wales[30], at a local government election[31] and at an election of a mayor under the Local Government Act 2000[32], where any part of the area in respect of which the candidate stands for election includes the whole or part of a registration area[33].

In accordance with any such request that has been duly made, the registration officer must supply the relevant part of the document or documents[34]. A person who obtains a copy of any document in this way may use it for any purpose for which that person would be entitled to obtain that document[35] but any restrictions which apply for that purpose[36] apply to any such use[37]. The restrictions imposed on the original recipient[38] apply to a person to whom the full register[39] is duly supplied or to whom any information contained in it (that is not contained in the edited register) is duly disclosed as they apply to the original recipient[40].

No such person as is mentioned in heads (a) to (g) above may supply a copy of the full register to any person[41], disclose any information contained in it that is not contained in the edited register[42] or make use of any such information[43], otherwise than for purposes in connection with the office by virtue of which he is entitled to the full register or for electoral purposes[44]. No person to whom either head (h) or head (i) above applies may supply a copy of the full register to any person[45], disclose any information contained in it that is not contained in the edited register[46] or make use of any such information[47], otherwise than for the purpose of complying with the statutory controls on donations[48]. No person to whom head (j) above applies may supply a copy of the full register to any person[49], disclose any information contained in it that is not contained in the edited register[50] or make use of any such information[51], otherwise than for electoral purposes or the purposes of electoral registration[52]. No person employed by, or assisting (whether or not for reward) a registered political party to which head (k) applies, or a recognised third party to which head (l) above applies, and to which a copy of the register has been supplied, may supply a copy of the full register to any person[53], disclose any information contained in it that is not contained in the edited register[54] or make use of any such information[55], otherwise than for electoral purposes[56] or for the purpose of complying with the controls on donations to registered parties[57]. No person employed by, or assisting (whether or not for reward) a permitted participant to which head (m) above applies, and to which a copy of the register has been supplied, may supply a copy of the full register to any person[58], disclose any information contained in it that is not contained in the edited register[59] or make use of any such information[60], otherwise than for purposes in connection with the campaign in respect of the referendum[61] or for the purpose of complying with the controls on donations to permitted participants[62].

No councillor or employee of a local authority mentioned in either head (n) or head (o) above may supply a copy of the full register to any person other than to another councillor of or employee of the same local authority[63], disclose any information contained in it that is not included in the edited register[64] or make use of any such information[65]. No parish or community councillor, person employed by or otherwise assisting (whether or not for reward) a parish or community council mentioned in head (p) above, and to which a copy of the register has been supplied, may supply a copy of the full register to any person[66], disclose any information contained in it that is not contained in the edited register[67] or make use of any such information[68], otherwise than for the purpose of establishing whether any person is entitled to attend and participate in a meeting of, or take any action on behalf of, the parish or community, as the case may be, or for the purposes of a local poll under the Local Government Act 2003[69].

No candidate or election agent to whom a copy of the register has been supplied by virtue of head (q) above may supply a copy of the full register to any person[70], disclose any information contained in it that is not contained in the edited register[71] or make use of any such information[72], other than for electoral purposes[73].

1   Ie the persons or organisations falling within the Representation of the People (England and Wales) Regulations 2001, SI 2001/341, regs 103–108 (see heads (a)–(q) in the text): see reg 102(1) (regs 92, 102–108 added by SI 2002/1871). As to the persons or organisations falling within the Representation of the People (England and Wales) Regulations 2001, SI 2001/341, regs 108A, 109, to which reg 102 also applies, see PARA 186.

2   As to registration officers and the areas for which they act see PARA 139.

3   See the Representation of the People (England and Wales) Regulations 2001, SI 2001/341, reg 102(1) (as added: see note 1). The relevant part of a document is defined discretely for each of the purposes in the Representation of the People (England and Wales) Regulations 2001, SI 2001/341, regs 103–108: see the text and notes 11–33.

4   Representation of the People (England and Wales) Regulations 2001, SI 2001/341, reg 102(1)(a) (as added: see note 1). The text refers to the revised version of a register published under the Representation of the People Act 1983 s 13(1) or s 13(3) (see PARA 165): see the Representation of the People (England and Wales) Regulations 2001, SI 2001/341, reg 102(1)(a) (as so added). As to the meaning of 'register' see PARA 179 note 1.

5   Representation of the People (England and Wales) Regulations 2001, SI 2001/341, reg 102(1)(b) (reg 102 as added (see note 1); reg 102(1)(b) amended by SI 2006/2910). The text refers to a notice of alteration published under the Representation of the People Act 1983 s 13A(2), s 13B(3), s 13B(3B) or s 13B(3D) (see PARA 168): see the Representation of the People (England and Wales) Regulations 2001, SI 2001/341, reg 102(1)(b) (as so added and amended).

6   Representation of the People (England and Wales) Regulations 2001, SI 2001/341, reg 102(1)(c) (as added: see note 1). As to the meaning of 'list of overseas electors' see PARA 143 note 9.

7 See the Representation of the People (England and Wales) Regulations 2001, SI 2001/341, reg 102(2) (as added: see note 1).

8 Representation of the People (England and Wales) Regulations 2001, SI 2001/341, reg 102(2)(a) (as added: see note 1).

9 Representation of the People (England and Wales) Regulations 2001, SI 2001/341, reg 102(2)(b) (as added: see note 1). A person falling within reg 108 (ie candidates at certain elections specified therein: see head (q) in the text) may not make a request for the supply of any subsequent document on publication, however: reg 102(5) (as so added).

10 Representation of the People (England and Wales) Regulations 2001, SI 2001/341, reg 102(2)(c) (as added: see note 1). Unless a request has been made in advance of supply under reg 102(2)(c), the copy of a document supplied under reg 102 is to be in data form: reg 102(3) (as so added). As to the meaning of 'data form' see PARA 180 note 11. As to general aspects of the duty on a registration officer to supply data under Pt VI (regs 92–115) see PARA 180 note 2.

11 Representation of the People (England and Wales) Regulations 2001, SI 2001/341, reg 103(1)(a) (as added: see note 1). In the case of a member of Parliament, the relevant part of the documents for the purposes of reg 102(1) (see the text and notes 1–6) is so much of them as relates to the whole or any part of the constituency which he represents as falls within the registration area: see reg 103(2)(a) (as so added). As to the meaning of 'registration area' see PARA 139 note 1. As to members of Parliament and parliamentary constituencies see PARA 9.

Persons who are entitled to copies of the full register in accordance with the provisions of reg 103 (see also the text and notes 12–18), reg 105 (see the text and notes 21–22), reg 106 (see the text and notes 23–25) and reg 108 (see the text and notes 29–33) are also entitled, subject to regs 61, 61A, to request that the registration officer supply free of charge the relevant parts of a copy of any of the following information which he keeps, namely the current version of the information which would, in the event of a particular parliamentary of local government election, be included in the postal voters lists, the list of proxies or the proxy postal voters lists which he is required to keep under the Representation of the People Act 2000 s 12, Sch 4 para 5 (see PARA 373) or Sch 4 para 7(8) (see PARA 381), and the current or final version of the postal voters list, the list of proxies or the proxy postal voters list kept under Sch 4 para 5 or Sch 4 para 7(8): see the Representation of the People (England and Wales) Regulations 2001, SI 2001/341, reg 61 (substituted by SI 2006/2910). As to restrictions on the data so supplied see the Representation of the People (England and Wales) Regulations 2001, SI 2001/341, reg 61A; and PARA 179 note 18. A person who contravenes reg 61(3) or reg 61(14) is guilty of an offence and liable on summary conviction to a fine not exceeding level 5 on the standard scale: see reg 115; and PARA 734. As to the standard scale see SENTENCING AND DISPOSITION OF OFFENDERS vol 92 (2010) PARA 142.

12 Representation of the People (England and Wales) Regulations 2001, SI 2001/341, reg 103(1)(b) (as added: see note 1). In the case of a member of the European Parliament, the relevant part of the documents for the purposes of reg 102(1) (see the text and notes 1–6) is all parts of them: reg 103(2)(b) (as so added). As to members of the European Parliament and electoral regions established for the purposes of European parliamentary elections see PARAS 13 et seq, 77 et seq.

Specified persons who are entitled to copies of the full register in accordance with the provisions of reg 103 (see also the text and notes 11, 13–18), reg 105 (see the text and notes 21–22), reg 106 (see the text and notes 23–25) and reg 108 (see the text and notes 29–33) are also entitled, subject to the European Parliamentary Elections Regulations 2004, SI 2004/293, reg 10, Sch 2 paras 32, 33, to request that the registration officer supply free of charge the relevant parts of a copy of any of the following information which he keeps, namely the current version of the information which would, in the event of a particular European parliamentary election, be included in the postal voters lists, the list of proxies or the proxy postal voters lists which he is required to keep under Sch 2 para 5 (see PARA 373) or Sch 2 para 7(8) (see PARA 381), and the current or final version of the postal voters list, the list of proxies or the proxy postal voters list kept under Sch 2 para 5 or Sch 2 para 7(8): see Sch 2 para 32 (Sch 2 substituted by SI 2009/186). As to restrictions on the data so supplied see the European Parliamentary Elections Regulations 2004, SI 2004/293, Sch 2 para 33; and PARA 179 note 18.

13 Representation of the People (England and Wales) Regulations 2001, SI 2001/341, reg 103(1)(c) (as added: see note 1). In the case of a member of the National Assembly for Wales, the relevant part of the documents for the purposes of reg 102(1) (see the text and notes 1–6) is so much of them as relates to the whole or any part of the constituency or region which he represents as falls within the registration area: see reg 103(2)(a) (as so added). As to constituency members and regional members of the National Assembly for Wales see PARA 12.

Specified persons who are entitled to copies of the full register in accordance with the provisions of reg 103 (see also the text and notes 11–12, 14–18), reg 105 (see the text and notes 21–22), reg 106 (see the text and notes 23–25) and reg 108 (see the text and notes 29–33) are also entitled, subject to the National Assembly for Wales (Representation of the People) Order 2007, SI 2007/236, art 15(2), Sch 1 paras 13, 14, to request that the registration officer supply free of charge the relevant parts of a copy of any of the following information which he keeps, namely the current version of the information which would, in the event of a particular Assembly election, be included in the postal voters lists, the list of proxies or the proxy postal voters lists which he is required to keep under art 10 (see PARA 373) or art 12(8) (see PARA 381), and the current or final version of the postal voters list, the list of proxies or the proxy postal voters list kept under art 10 or art 12(8): see Sch 1 para 13 (amended by SI 2010/2931). As to restrictions on the data so supplied see the National Assembly for Wales (Representation of the People) Order 2007, SI 2007/236, Sch 1 para 14; and PARA 179 note 18.

14 Representation of the People (England and Wales) Regulations 2001, SI 2001/341, reg 103(1)(d) (as added: see note 1). In the case of a councillor for an electoral area, the relevant part of the documents for the purposes of reg 102(1) (see the text and notes 1–6) is so much of them as relates to that area: reg 103(2)(c) (as so added). As to the meaning of 'electoral area' see PARA 11.

15 Representation of the People (England and Wales) Regulations 2001, SI 2001/341, reg 103(1)(e) (as added: see note 1). In the case of the Mayor of London and a London member of the London Assembly, the relevant part of the documents for the purposes of reg 102(1) (see the text and notes 1–6) is so much of them as relates to the Greater London area: reg 103(2)(d) (as so added). As to the election of the Mayor of London and London members of the London Assembly see PARA 199 et seq. As to the administrative area of Greater London see LONDON GOVERNMENT vol 71 (2013) PARA 14.

16 Representation of the People (England and Wales) Regulations 2001, SI 2001/341, reg 103(1)(f) (as added: see note 1). The text refers to an Assembly constituency within the meaning of the Greater London Authority Act 1999 (see s 2(4), (5); and LONDON GOVERNMENT vol 71 (2013) PARA 80): see the Representation of the People (England and Wales) Regulations 2001, SI 2001/341, reg 103(1)(f) (as so added). In the case of a constituency member of the London Assembly, the relevant part of the documents for the purposes of reg 102(1) (see the text and notes 1–6) is so much of them as relates to any part of the Assembly constituency which he represents as falls within the registration area: reg 103(2)(e) (as so added).

17 Ie within the meaning of the Local Government Act 2000 s 39(1) (see LOCAL GOVERNMENT vol 69 (2009) PARA 320): see the Representation of the People (England and Wales) Regulations 2001, SI 2001/341, reg 103(1)(g) (as added: see note 1). The Local Government Act 2000 Pt 2 (ss 10–48A) (Local authorities in Wales: arrangements with respect to executives etc) has been amended by the Localism Act 2011 s 22, Sch 3 so that it applies only to local authorities in Wales: see LOCAL GOVERNMENT vol 69 (2009) PARA 303 et seq. It is submitted that a reference to an elected mayor within the meaning of the Local Government Act 2000 s 9H(1) (ie an individual elected as mayor of a local authority by the local government electors for the authority's area in accordance with the provisions made by or under Pt 1A (ss 9B–9R) (arrangements with respect to local governance in England): see LOCAL GOVERNMENT) is to be read into the Representation of the People (England and Wales) Regulations 2001, SI 2001/341, reg 103(1)(g), accordingly.

18 Representation of the People (England and Wales) Regulations 2001, SI 2001/341, reg 103(1)(g) (as added: see note 1). In the case of a mayor falling within reg 103(1)(g), the relevant part of the documents for the purposes of reg 102(1) (see the text and notes 1–6) is so much of them as relates to any part of the area of the local authority for which he is elected as falls within the registration area: reg 103(2)(f) (as so added).

19 Representation of the People (England and Wales) Regulations 2001, SI 2001/341, reg 104(1)(a) (as added: see note 1). The text refers to the holder of a relevant elective office within the meaning of the Political Parties, Elections and Referendums Act 2000 s 71, Sch 7 para 1(8) (see CONSTITUTIONAL LAW AND HUMAN RIGHTS): see the Representation of the People (England and Wales) Regulations 2001, SI 2001/341, reg 104(1)(a) (as so added). In the case of such a person, the relevant part of the documents for the purposes of reg 102(1) (see the text and notes 1–6) is the whole of them: see reg 104(2) (as so added).

20 Representation of the People (England and Wales) Regulations 2001, SI 2001/341, reg 104(1)(b) (as added: see note 1). For these purposes, 'candidate' has the same meaning as in the Representation of the People Act 1983 s 118A (see PARA 230): see the Representation of the People (England and Wales) Regulations 2001, SI 2001/341, reg 3(1) (definition substituted by SI 2002/1871). In the case of such a candidate, the relevant part of the documents for the purposes of the Representation of the People (England and Wales) Regulations 2001, SI 2001/341, reg 102(1) (see the text and notes 1–6) is the whole of them: see reg 104(2) (as so added). As to the meaning of 'Authority election' see PARA 11.

21 Ie within the meaning of the Political Parties, Elections Referendums Act 2000 s 24 (see PARA 253; and CONSTITUTIONAL LAW AND HUMAN RIGHTS): see the Representation of the People (England and Wales) Regulations 2001, SI 2001/341, reg 105(1) (as added: see note 1).

22 Representation of the People (England and Wales) Regulations 2001, SI 2001/341, reg 105(1) (as added: see note 1). Not more than one person for the same constituency may be nominated under reg 105(1) in respect of the same registered political party and registration area: reg 105(2) (as so added). In the case of a person duly nominated, the relevant part of the documents for the purposes of reg 102(1) (see the text and notes 1–6) is so much of them as relates to the whole or any part of the constituency in question as falls within the registration area: reg 105(3) (as so added).

23 Representation of the People (England and Wales) Regulations 2001, SI 2001/341, reg 106(1)(a) (as added: see note 1). The text refers to a registered political party other than a minor party within the meaning of the Political Parties, Elections and Referendums Act 2000 s 160(1) (see PARA 253): see the Representation of the People (England and Wales) Regulations 2001, SI 2001/341, reg 106(1)(a) (as so added). In the case of such a party, the relevant part of the documents for the purposes of reg 102(1) (see the text and notes 1–6) is the whole of them: see reg 106(2) (as so added).

24 Representation of the People (England and Wales) Regulations 2001, SI 2001/341, reg 106(1)(b) (as added: see note 1). The text refers to a 'recognised third party' within the meaning of the Political Parties, Elections and Referendums Act 2000 s 85(5) (control of expenditure by third parties in national parliamentary election campaigns: see PARA 313 note 15): see the Representation of the People (England and Wales) Regulations 2001, SI 2001/341, reg 106(1)(b) (as so added). In the case of such a party, the relevant part of the documents for the purposes of reg 102(1) (see the text and notes 1–6) is the whole of them: see reg 106(2) (as so added).

25 Representation of the People (England and Wales) Regulations 2001, SI 2001/341, reg 106(1)(c) (as added: see note 1). The text refers to a 'permitted participant' within the meaning of the Political Parties, Elections and Referendums Act 2000 s 105(1) (permitted participant for the purpose of referendums: see PARA 529): see the Representation of the People (England and Wales) Regulations 2001, SI 2001/341, reg 106(1)(c) (as so added). In the case of such a participant, the relevant part of the documents for the purposes of reg 102(1) (see the text and notes 1–6) is the whole of them: see reg 106(2) (as so added).

26 Representation of the People (England and Wales) Regulations 2001, SI 2001/341, reg 107(1)(a) (reg 107 as added (see note 1); reg 107(1) substituted by SI 2006/752). The relevant part of the documents for the purposes of the Representation of the People (England and Wales) Regulations 2001, SI 2001/341, reg 102(1) (see the text and notes 1–6) is so much of them as relates to the area of the local authority concerned: see reg 107(2) (reg 107 as so added; reg 107(2), (5) amended by SI 2006/752). For this purpose, 'local authority' has the meaning given by the Local Government Act 2003 s 116 (see PARA 557 note 1): see the Representation of the People (England and Wales) Regulations 2001, SI 2001/341, reg 107(5) (as so added and amended).

27 Representation of the People (England and Wales) Regulations 2001, SI 2001/341, reg 107(1)(b) (as added and substituted: see note 26). The relevant part of the documents for the purposes of reg 102(1) (see the text and notes 1–6) is so much of them as relates to the area of the local authority concerned: see reg 107(2) (as added and amended: see note 26). As to parishes and their councils see LOCAL GOVERNMENT vol 69 (2009) PARA 27 et seq; and as to communities and their councils see LOCAL GOVERNMENT vol 69 (2009) PARA 41 et seq.

28 Representation of the People (England and Wales) Regulations 2001, SI 2001/341, reg 107(6) (as added: see note 1). The text refers to parish councils as established by the Local Government Act 1972 s 9(4) (see LOCAL GOVERNMENT vol 69 (2009) PARA 28) and community councils as referred to in s 27(2) (see LOCAL GOVERNMENT vol 69 (2009) PARA 41): see the Representation of the People (England and Wales) Regulations 2001, SI 2001/341, reg 107(6) (as so added). The relevant part of the documents for the purposes of reg 102(1) (see the text and notes 1–6) is so much of them as relates to the parish or community concerned: reg 107(7) (as so added).

29 Representation of the People (England and Wales) Regulations 2001, SI 2001/341, reg 108(1)(a) (as added: see note 1).

30 Representation of the People (England and Wales) Regulations 2001, SI 2001/341, reg 108(1)(b) (as added: see note 1).

31 Representation of the People (England and Wales) Regulations 2001, SI 2001/341, reg 108(1)(c) (as added: see note 1).

32 Representation of the People (England and Wales) Regulations 2001, SI 2001/341, reg 108(1)(d) (as added: see note 1). The text refers to an election under the Local Government Act 2000 Pt II

for the return of an elected mayor (see PARA 198 et seq): see the Representation of the People (England and Wales) Regulations 2001, SI 2001/341, reg 108(1)(d) (as so added). See, however, note 17.

33 See the Representation of the People (England and Wales) Regulations 2001, SI 2001/341, reg 108(1) (as added: see note 1). For these purposes, 'candidate' includes a candidate at an election of a mayor under the Local Government Act 2000 Pt II (see note 32) and an individual candidate at a European parliamentary election, or at an election in an electoral region for the National Assembly for Wales: see the Representation of the People (England and Wales) Regulations 2001, SI 2001/341, reg 108(2) (as so added). In the case of a registered political party which submits a list of candidates at a European parliamentary election, at an election of the London members of the London Assembly or at an election in an electoral region for the National Assembly for Wales, the entitlement otherwise conferred by reg 108 on a candidate is conferred on the election agent of that party: reg 108(3) (as so added). In relation to the candidates mentioned in head (q) in the text, the relevant part of the documents for the purposes of reg 102(1) (see the text and notes 1–6) is so much of them as relate to the area for which the candidate is standing: reg 108(4) (as so added). As to candidates and election agents generally see PARA 230 et seq. As to individual candidates and list candidates in European parliamentary elections, elections of the London members of the London Assembly and elections in an electoral region for the National Assembly for Wales see PARA 340 et seq.

34 See the Representation of the People (England and Wales) Regulations 2001, SI 2001/341, reg 102(4) (as added: see note 1).

35 Ie any entitlement under the Representation of the People (England and Wales) Regulations 2001, SI 2001/341: see reg 102(6) (reg 102 as added (see note 1); reg 102(6) amended by the Counter-Terrorism Act 2008 s 20(4), Sch 1 para 2(1), (3)). This means that the data supplied to a recipient for one of the authorised purposes may be used by that recipient for any other of the authorised purposes without any further notification being made.

36 Ie any restrictions which apply for the purpose under whichever of the Representation of the People (England and Wales) Regulations 2001, SI 2001/341, regs 103–108 (see the text and notes 11–33, 41–73) or reg 109 (see PARA 186) entitles that person to obtain that document: see reg 102(6) (as added and amended: see note 35).

37 Representation of the People (England and Wales) Regulations 2001, SI 2001/341, reg 102(6) (as added and amended: see note 35).

38 Ie the restrictions contained in the Representation of the People (England and Wales) Regulations 2001, SI 2001/341, reg 103(3) (see the text and notes 41–44), reg 104(3) (see the text and notes 45–48), reg 105(4) (see the text and notes 49–52), reg 106(3) (see the text and notes 53–62), reg 107(3) (see the text and notes 63–65), reg 107(8) (see the text and notes 66–69), reg 108(5) (see the text and notes 70–73) and reg 109(3) (see PARA 186): see reg 92(10) (reg 92 as added (see note 1); reg 92(10) amended by SI 2006/752).

39 As to the meaning of 'full register' see PARA 167 note 2.

40 Representation of the People (England and Wales) Regulations 2001, SI 2001/341, reg 92(10) (as added and amended: see note 38). However, any person who has obtained or is entitled to obtain a copy of the full register under reg 103, reg 105, reg 106 (see the text and notes 11–18, 21–25) or reg 109 (see PARA 186) may supply a copy of the full register to a processor for the purpose of processing the information contained in the register, or he may procure that a processor processes and provides to him any copy of the register which the processor has obtained under the Representation of the People (England and Wales) Regulations 2001, SI 2001/341, for use in respect of the purposes for which that person is entitled to obtain such copy or information (as the case may be): see reg 92(7) (reg 92 as so added; reg 92(7) amended by SI 2006/752); and see PARA 180 note 11.

41 Representation of the People (England and Wales) Regulations 2001, SI 2001/341, reg 103(3)(a) (as added: see note 1). A person who contravenes reg 103(3) is guilty of an offence and liable on summary conviction to a fine not exceeding level 5 on the standard scale: see reg 115; and PARA 734.

42 Representation of the People (England and Wales) Regulations 2001, SI 2001/341, reg 103(3)(b) (as added: see note 1). As to the meaning of 'edited register' see PARA 167 note 4. As to relevant offences see note 41.

43 Representation of the People (England and Wales) Regulations 2001, SI 2001/341, reg 103(3)(c) (as added: see note 1). As to relevant offences see note 41.

44 See the Representation of the People (England and Wales) Regulations 2001, SI 2001/341, reg 103(3) (as added: see note 1). As to relevant offences see note 41.

45 Representation of the People (England and Wales) Regulations 2001, SI 2001/341, reg 104(3)(a) (as added: see note 1). A person who contravenes reg 104(3) is guilty of an offence and liable on summary conviction to a fine not exceeding level 5 on the standard scale: see reg 115; and PARA 734.

46 Representation of the People (England and Wales) Regulations 2001, SI 2001/341, reg 104(3)(b) (as added: see note 1) As to relevant offences see note 45.

47 Representation of the People (England and Wales) Regulations 2001, SI 2001/341, reg 104(3)(c) (as added: see note 1) As to relevant offences see note 45.

48 See the Representation of the People (England and Wales) Regulations 2001, SI 2001/341, reg 104(3), (4) (as added: note 1) The text refers to the controls on donations contained in the Representation of the People Act 1983 s 71A, Sch 2A (see PARA 286 et seq) or in the Political Parties, Elections and Referendums Act 2000 Sch 7 (see CONSTITUTIONAL LAW AND HUMAN RIGHTS), as the case may be: see the Representation of the People (England and Wales) Regulations 2001, SI 2001/341, reg 104(4) (as so added). As to relevant offences see note 45.

49 Representation of the People (England and Wales) Regulations 2001, SI 2001/341, reg 105(4)(a) (as added: see note 1). A person who contravenes reg 105(4) is guilty of an offence and liable on summary conviction to a fine not exceeding level 5 on the standard scale: see reg 115; and PARA 734.

50 Representation of the People (England and Wales) Regulations 2001, SI 2001/341, reg 105(4)(b) (as added: see note 1). As to relevant offences see note 49.

51 Representation of the People (England and Wales) Regulations 2001, SI 2001/341, reg 105(4)(c) (as added: see note 1). As to relevant offences see note 49.

52 See the Representation of the People (England and Wales) Regulations 2001, SI 2001/341, reg 105(4) (as added: see note 1). As to relevant offences see note 49.

53 Representation of the People (England and Wales) Regulations 2001, SI 2001/341, reg 106(3)(a) (as added: see note 1). As to references to employees of any person who has access to a copy of the full register see PARA 180 note 6. A person who contravenes reg 106(3) is guilty of an offence and liable on summary conviction to a fine not exceeding level 5 on the standard scale: see reg 115; and PARA 734.

54 Representation of the People (England and Wales) Regulations 2001, SI 2001/341, reg 106(3)(b) (as added: see note 1). As to relevant offences see note 53.

55 Representation of the People (England and Wales) Regulations 2001, SI 2001/341, reg 106(3)(c) (as added: see note 1). As to relevant offences see note 53.

56 See the Representation of the People (England and Wales) Regulations 2001, SI 2001/341, reg 106(3), (4)(a)(i) (as added: see note 1). As to relevant offences see note 53.

57 See the Representation of the People (England and Wales) Regulations 2001, SI 2001/341, reg 106(3), (4)(a)(ii) (as added: see note 1). The text refers to the controls on donations under the Political Parties, Elections and Referendums Act 2000 Pt IV (ss 50–71) (control of donations to registered parties, individuals and members associations: see CONSTITUTIONAL LAW AND HUMAN RIGHTS) or, as the case may be, s 95, Sch 11 (control of donations to recognised third parties: see PARA 325 et seq): see the Representation of the People (England and Wales) Regulations 2001, SI 2001/341, reg 106(3), (4)(a)(ii) (as so added). As to relevant offences see note 53.

58 Representation of the People (England and Wales) Regulations 2001, SI 2001/341, reg 106(3)(a) (as added: see note 1). As to relevant offences see note 53.

59 Representation of the People (England and Wales) Regulations 2001, SI 2001/341, reg 106(3)(b) (as added: see note 1). As to relevant offences see note 53.

60 Representation of the People (England and Wales) Regulations 2001, SI 2001/341, reg 106(3)(c) (as added: see note 1). As to relevant offences see note 53.

61 See the Representation of the People (England and Wales) Regulations 2001, SI 2001/341, reg 106(3), (4)(b)(i) (as added: see note 1). The text refers to the referendum identified in the declaration made to the Electoral Commission by the participant under the Political Parties, Elections and Referendums Act 2000 s 106 (see PARA 529): see the Representation of the People (England and Wales) Regulations 2001, SI 2001/341, reg 106(3), (4)(b)(i) (as so added). As to the Electoral Commission see PARA 34 et seq. As to relevant offences see note 53.

62 See the Representation of the People (England and Wales) Regulations 2001, SI 2001/341, reg 106(3), (4)(b)(ii) (as added: see note 1). The text refers to the controls on donations under the Political Parties, Elections and Referendums Act 2000 s 119, Sch 15 (control of donations to permitted participants: see PARA 546 et seq): see the Representation of the People (England and Wales) Regulations 2001, SI 2001/341, reg 106(3), (4)(b)(ii) (as so added). As to relevant offences see note 53.

63 Representation of the People (England and Wales) Regulations 2001, SI 2001/341, reg 107(3)(a) (reg 107 as added (see note 1); reg 107(3)(a), (4), (4)(a) amended, reg 107(4)(aa) added, by

SI 2006/752). A councillor or employee of the local authority may supply a copy of the register, or disclose or make use of information contained in it that is not contained in the edited register (see the Representation of the People (England and Wales) Regulations 2001, SI 2001/341, reg 107(4) (as so added and amended)):

(1)   where necessary for the discharge of a statutory function of the local authority or any other local authority relating to security, law enforcement and crime prevention (reg 107(4)(a) (as so added and amended)); or

(2)   for the purposes of a poll under the Local Government Act 2003 s 116 (local poll: see PARA 557) (Representation of the People (England and Wales) Regulations 2001, SI 2001/341, reg 107(4)(aa) (as so added)); or

(3)   for statistical purposes, in which case no information is to be disclosed which includes the name and address of any elector (whether that name or address appears in the edited register or only in the full register) (reg 107(4)(b) (as so added)).

A person who contravenes reg 107(3) or reg 107(8) (see the text and notes 66–69) is guilty of an offence and liable on summary conviction to a fine not exceeding level 5 on the standard scale: see reg 115; and PARA 734.

64   Representation of the People (England and Wales) Regulations 2001, SI 2001/341, reg 107(3)(b) (as added: see note 1). As to relevant offences see note 63.

65   Representation of the People (England and Wales) Regulations 2001, SI 2001/341, reg 107(3)(c) (as added: see note 1). As to relevant offences see note 63.

66   Representation of the People (England and Wales) Regulations 2001, SI 2001/341, reg 107(8)(a) (as added: see note 1). As to relevant offences see note 63.

67   Representation of the People (England and Wales) Regulations 2001, SI 2001/341, reg 107(8)(b) (as added: see note 1). As to relevant offences see note 63.

68   Representation of the People (England and Wales) Regulations 2001, SI 2001/341, reg 107(8)(c) (as added: see note 1). As to relevant offences see note 63.

69   Representation of the People (England and Wales) Regulations 2001, SI 2001/341, reg 107(8) (reg 107 as added (see note 1); reg 107(8) amended by SI 2006/752). The text refers to a local poll under the Local Government Act 2003 s 116 (local polls: see PARA 557): see the Representation of the People (England and Wales) Regulations 2001, SI 2001/341, reg 107(8) (as so added and amended). As to relevant offences see note 63.

70   Representation of the People (England and Wales) Regulations 2001, SI 2001/341, reg 108(5)(a) (as added: see note 1). A person who contravenes reg 108(5) is guilty of an offence and liable on summary conviction to a fine not exceeding level 5 on the standard scale: see reg 115; and PARA 734.

71   Representation of the People (England and Wales) Regulations 2001, SI 2001/341, reg 108(5)(b) (as added: see note 1). As to relevant offences see note 70.

72   Representation of the People (England and Wales) Regulations 2001, SI 2001/341, reg 108(5)(c) (as added: see note 1). As to relevant offences see note 70.

73   See the Representation of the People (England and Wales) Regulations 2001, SI 2001/341, reg 108(5) (as added: see note 1). As to relevant offences see note 70.

186.   Supply of electoral records to security and intelligence services, police forces, etc. The Security Service[1], the Government Communications Headquarters[2], and the Secret Intelligence Service[3], or any police force in Great Britain[4], the National Crime Agency[5], the Police Information Technology Organisation[6], or any body of constables established under an Act of Parliament[7], may request the registration officer[8] to supply free of charge the relevant part[9] of a revised version of the register[10], the relevant part of any notice altering the published register[11] or the relevant part of a list of overseas electors[12]. Such a request must be made in writing[13], and must:

(1)   specify the documents requested[14];

(2)   state whether the request is made only in respect of the current documents or whether it includes a request for the supply of any subsequent document on publication for as long as the person making the request falls within the category of person entitled to receive such copies[15]; and

(3)   state whether a printed copy of any of the documents is requested instead of the version in data form[16].

In accordance with any such request that has been duly made, the registration officer must supply the relevant part of the document or documents[17]. A person who obtains a copy of any document in this way may use it for any purpose for which that person would be entitled to obtain that document[18] but any restrictions which apply for that purpose[19] apply to any such use[20]. The restrictions imposed on the original recipient[21] apply to a person to whom the full register[22] is duly supplied or to whom any information contained in it (that is not contained in the edited register) is duly disclosed as they apply to the original recipient[23].

No person serving whether as a constable, officer or employee in any of the specified police forces and organisations[24] may supply a copy of the full register to any person[25], disclose any information contained in it that is not contained in the edited register[26] or make use of any such information[27], otherwise than for the purposes[28] of the prevention and detection of crime and the enforcement of the criminal law (whether in England and Wales or elsewhere) or for the vetting of a relevant person[29] for the purpose of safeguarding national security[30].

Where the registration officer supplies a copy of the full register to the Security Service, to the Government Communications Headquarters or to the Secret Intelligence Service[31], the registration officer must supply a copy of the record of anonymous entries together with the register[32].

The registration officer also must supply a copy of the record of anonymous entries, at the request in writing of a senior officer[33], to any police force in Great Britain[34], the Police Information Technology Organisation[35], any body of constables established under an Act of Parliament[36], or the National Crime Agency[37]. No person serving whether as a constable, officer or employee of any such force or organisation may supply to any person a copy of the record[38], disclose any information contained in it[39] or make use of any such information[40], otherwise than for the purposes of[41] the prevention and detection of crime and the enforcement of the criminal law (whether in England and Wales or elsewhere)[42] or the vetting of a relevant person[43] for the purpose of safeguarding national security[44]. Each person supplied with a copy of the record in this way[45] must take proper precautions for its safe custody[46].

1 Representation of the People (England and Wales) Regulations 2001, SI 2001/341, reg 108A(1)(a) (reg 108A added by the Counter-Terrorism Act 2008 s 20(4), Sch 1 para 2(1), (4)). In relation to the services to which the Representation of the People (England and Wales) Regulations 2001, SI 2001/341, reg 108A, applies, the relevant part of the documents for the purposes of reg 102(1) (see the text and notes 8–9) is the whole of them: reg 108A(2) (as so added). As to the Security Service see CONSTITUTIONAL LAW AND HUMAN RIGHTS vol 8(2) (Reissue) PARA 471.

2 Representation of the People (England and Wales) Regulations 2001, SI 2001/341, reg 108A(1)(b) (as added: see note 1). As to the relevant part of the documents for these purposes see note 1. As to the Government Communications Headquarters see CONSTITUTIONAL LAW AND HUMAN RIGHTS vol 8(2) (Reissue) PARA 473.

3 Representation of the People (England and Wales) Regulations 2001, SI 2001/341, reg 108A(1)(c) (as added: see note 1). As to the relevant part of the documents for these purposes see note 1. As to the Secret Intelligence Service see CONSTITUTIONAL LAW AND HUMAN RIGHTS vol 8(2) (Reissue) PARA 472.

4 Representation of the People (England and Wales) Regulations 2001, SI 2001/341, reg 109(1)(a) (regs 92, 102, 109 added by SI 2002/1871). In relation to the police forces and organisations to which the Representation of the People (England and Wales) Regulations 2001, SI 2001/341, reg 109, applies, the relevant part of the documents for the purposes of reg 102(1) (see the text and notes 8–9) is the whole of them: reg 109(2) (as so added). As to the meaning of 'Great Britain' see PARA 1 note 1. As to the administration of police areas and police forces in England and Wales see POLICE AND INVESTIGATORY POWERS vol 84 (2013) PARA 52 et seq.

5 Representation of the People (England and Wales) Regulations 2001, SI 2001/341, reg 109(1)(c) (reg 109 as added (see note 4); reg 109(1)(c) substituted by SI 2006/594). As to the relevant part of the documents for these purposes see note 4. As to the National Crime Agency (which absorbed and replaced the Serious Organised Crime Agency with effect from 1 October 2013) see the Crime and Courts Act 2013 Pt 1 (ss 1–16); and POLICE AND INVESTIGATORY POWERS.

6 Representation of the People (England and Wales) Regulations 2001, SI 2001/341, reg 109(1)(e) (reg 109 as added (see note 4); reg 109(1)(e) amended by SI 2006/752). As to the relevant part of the documents for these purposes see note 4. The Police Information Technology Organisation was subsumed into the National Policing Improvement Agency (NPIA) on 1 April 2007, but the information and communications technology function of the NPIA has been transferred to the Police ICT company, which was incorporated in 2012 with the Home Office and Association of Chief Police Officers as joint owners: see POLICE AND INVESTIGATORY POWERS vol 84 (2013) PARA 160. At the date at which this volume states the law, the Police ICT company is not yet fully operational, however.

7 Representation of the People (England and Wales) Regulations 2001, SI 2001/341, reg 109(1)(f) (as added: see note 4). As to the relevant part of the documents for these purposes see note 4. As to the office of constable see POLICE AND INVESTIGATORY POWERS vol 84 (2013) PARA 1 et seq.

8 As to registration officers and the areas for which they act see PARA 139.

9 See the Representation of the People (England and Wales) Regulations 2001, SI 2001/341, reg 102(1) (as added: see note 4). The relevant part of a document is defined discretely for each of the purposes in regs 108A, 109: see notes 1, 4. As to the persons or organisations falling within regs 103–108, to which reg 102 also applies, see PARA 185.

10 Representation of the People (England and Wales) Regulations 2001, SI 2001/341, reg 102(1)(a) (as added: see note 4). The text refers to the revised version of a register published under the Representation of the People Act 1983 s 13(1) or s 13(3) (see PARA 165): see the Representation of the People (England and Wales) Regulations 2001, SI 2001/341, reg 102(1)(a) (as so added). As to the meaning of 'register' see PARA 179 note 1.

11 Representation of the People (England and Wales) Regulations 2001, SI 2001/341, reg 102(1)(b) (reg 102 as added (see note 4); reg 102(1)(b) amended by SI 2006/2910). The text refers to a notice of alteration published under the Representation of the People Act 1983 s 13A(2), s 13B(3), s 13B(3B) or s 13B(3D) (see PARA 168): see the Representation of the People (England and Wales) Regulations 2001, SI 2001/341, reg 102(1)(b) (as so added and amended).

12 Representation of the People (England and Wales) Regulations 2001, SI 2001/341, reg 102(1)(c) (as added: see note 4). As to the meaning of 'list of overseas electors' see PARA 143 note 9.

13 See the Representation of the People (England and Wales) Regulations 2001, SI 2001/341, reg 102(2) (as added: see note 4).

14 Representation of the People (England and Wales) Regulations 2001, SI 2001/341, reg 102(2)(a) (as added: see note 4).

15 Representation of the People (England and Wales) Regulations 2001, SI 2001/341, reg 102(2)(b) (as added: see note 4).

16 Representation of the People (England and Wales) Regulations 2001, SI 2001/341, reg 102(2)(c) (as added: see note 4). Unless a request has been made in advance of supply under reg 102(2)(c), the copy of a document supplied under reg 102 is to be in data form: reg 102(3) (as so added). As to the meaning of 'data form' see PARA 180 note 11. As to general aspects of the duty on a registration officer to supply data under Pt VI (regs 92–115) see PARA 180 note 2.

17 See the Representation of the People (England and Wales) Regulations 2001, SI 2001/341, reg 102(4) (as added: see note 4).

18 Ie any entitlement under the Representation of the People (England and Wales) Regulations 2001, SI 2001/341: see reg 102(6) (reg 102 as added (see note 4); reg 102(6) amended by the Counter-Terrorism Act 2008 Sch 1 para 2(1), (3)). This means that the data supplied to a recipient for one of the authorised purposes may be used by that recipient for any other of the authorised purposes without any further notification being made.

19 Ie any restrictions which apply for the purpose under whichever of the Representation of the People (England and Wales) Regulations 2001, SI 2001/341, regs 103–108 (see PARA 185) or reg 109 (see the text and notes 4–7) entitles that person to obtain that document: see reg 102(6) (as added and amended: see note 18).

20 Representation of the People (England and Wales) Regulations 2001, SI 2001/341, reg 102(6) (as added and amended: see note 18). This provision does not apply any restrictions associated with the purpose of reg 108A (see the text and notes 1–3) which entitles a person to obtain the document: see reg 102(6) (as so added and amended).

21 Ie the restrictions contained in the Representation of the People (England and Wales) Regulations 2001, SI 2001/341, reg 103(3) (see PARA 185), reg 104(3) (see PARA 185), reg 105(4) (see PARA 185), reg 106(3) (see PARA 185), reg 107(3) (see PARA 185), reg 107(8) (see

PARA 185), reg 108(5) (see PARA 185) and reg 109(3) (see the text and notes 24–28): see reg 92(10) (reg 92 as added (see note 4); reg 92(10) amended by SI 2006/752).

22 As to the meaning of 'full register' see PARA 167 note 2.

23 Representation of the People (England and Wales) Regulations 2001, SI 2001/341, reg 92(10) (as added and amended: see note 21). However, any person who has obtained or is entitled to obtain a copy of the full register under reg 103, reg 105, reg 106 (see PARA 185) or reg 109 (see the text and notes 4–7) may supply a copy of the full register to a processor for the purpose of processing the information contained in the register, or he may procure that a processor processes and provides to him any copy of the register which the processor has obtained under the Representation of the People (England and Wales) Regulations 2001, SI 2001/341, for use in respect of the purposes for which that person is entitled to obtain such copy or information (as the case may be): see reg 92(7) (reg 92 as so added; reg 92(7) amended by SI 2006/752); and see PARA 180 note 11.

24 Ie in any of the forces and organisations to which the Representation of the People (England and Wales) Regulations 2001, SI 2001/341, reg 109, applies (see the text and notes 4–7): see reg 109(3) (as added: see note 4). A person who contravenes reg 109(3) is guilty of an offence and liable on summary conviction to a fine not exceeding level 5 on the standard scale: see reg 115; and PARA 734.

25 Representation of the People (England and Wales) Regulations 2001, SI 2001/341, reg 109(3)(a) (as added: see note 4). As to relevant offences see note 24.

26 Representation of the People (England and Wales) Regulations 2001, SI 2001/341, reg 109(3)(b) (as added: see note 4). As to relevant offences see note 24.

27 Representation of the People (England and Wales) Regulations 2001, SI 2001/341, reg 109(3)(c) (as added: see note 4). As to relevant offences see note 24.

28 See the Representation of the People (England and Wales) Regulations 2001, SI 2001/341, reg 109(3) (reg 109 as added (see note 4); reg 109(3) amended by SI 2006/752). The text refers to the purposes specified in the Representation of the People (England and Wales) Regulations 2001, SI 2001/341, reg 109(4) (see the text and notes 29–30): see reg 109(3) (as so added and amended). As to relevant offences see note 24.

29 For these purposes, 'relevant person' means either a constable or officer or prospective constable or officer of the force or organisation, or an employee of (or applicant for employment by) the force or organisation: see the Representation of the People (England and Wales) Regulations 2001, SI 2001/341, reg 109(5) (reg 109 as added (see note 4); reg 109(4), (5) added by SI 2006/752).

30 See the Representation of the People (England and Wales) Regulations 2001, SI 2001/341, reg 109(4) (reg 109(4) as added (see note 29); amended by the Counter-Terrorism Act 2008 s 99, Sch 1 para 2(1), (5), Sch 9 Pt 2). As to relevant offences see note 24.

31 See the Representation of the People (England and Wales) Regulations 2001, SI 2001/341, reg 45E(1) (regs 45E, 45F added by SI 2006/2910).

32 See the Representation of the People (England and Wales) Regulations 2001, SI 2001/341, reg 45E(2) (as added: see note 31). As to the duty of the registration officer to keep a record of anonymous entries see PARA 143 et seq.

33 See the Representation of the People (England and Wales) Regulations 2001, SI 2001/341, reg 45F(1) (as added: see note 31). In the case of any police force in Great Britain, the Police Information Technology Organisation and any body of constables established under an Act of Parliament, 'senior officer' means, for these purposes, an officer of a rank senior to that of superintendent and, in the case of the National Crime Agency, it means the Director General of that Agency: see the Representation of the People (England and Wales) Regulations 2001, SI 2001/341, reg 45F(2) (as so added). As to the National Crime Agency see note 5; and as to the Police Information Technology Organisation see note 6.

34 Representation of the People (England and Wales) Regulations 2001, SI 2001/341, reg 45F(1)(a) (as added: see note 31).

35 Representation of the People (England and Wales) Regulations 2001, SI 2001/341, reg 45F(1)(c) (as added: see note 31).

36 Representation of the People (England and Wales) Regulations 2001, SI 2001/341, reg 45F(1)(d) (as added: see note 31).

37 Representation of the People (England and Wales) Regulations 2001, SI 2001/341, reg 45F(1)(e) (as added: see note 31). As to the National Crime Agency see note 5.

38 Representation of the People (England and Wales) Regulations 2001, SI 2001/341, reg 45F(3)(a) (as added: see note 31). A person who contravenes reg 45F(3) is guilty of an offence and liable on summary conviction to a fine not exceeding level 5 on the standard scale: see reg 115; and PARA 734.

39 Representation of the People (England and Wales) Regulations 2001, SI 2001/341, reg 45F(3)(b) (as added: see note 31). As to relevant offences see note 38.
40 Representation of the People (England and Wales) Regulations 2001, SI 2001/341, reg 45F(3)(c) (as added: see note 31). As to relevant offences see note 38.
41 See the Representation of the People (England and Wales) Regulations 2001, SI 2001/341, reg 45F(3) (as added: see note 31). The text refers to the purposes specified in reg 45F(4) (see the text and notes 42–44): see reg 45F(3) (as so added). As to relevant offences see note 38.
42 Representation of the People (England and Wales) Regulations 2001, SI 2001/341, reg 45F(4)(a) (as added: see note 31).
43 For these purposes, 'relevant person' means either a constable or officer or prospective constable or officer of the force or organisation or an employee of (or applicant for employment by) the force or organisation: see the Representation of the People (England and Wales) Regulations 2001, SI 2001/341, reg 45F(5) (as added: see note 31).
44 Representation of the People (England and Wales) Regulations 2001, SI 2001/341, reg 45F(4)(b) (as added: see note 31).
45 Ie under the Representation of the People (England and Wales) Regulations 2001, SI 2001/341, reg 45F: see reg 45F(6) (as added: see note 31).
46 Representation of the People (England and Wales) Regulations 2001, SI 2001/341, reg 45F(6) (as added: see note 31).

187. Supply of electoral records to Statistics Board. Each registration officer[1] must supply, free of charge and on publication[2], one copy of any revised version of the register[3], one copy of any notice altering the published register[4], and one copy of any list of overseas electors[5], to the Statistics Board ('the Board')[6]. No person employed by the Board may[7]:

(1) supply a copy of the full register other than to another such person[8];
(2) disclose any information contained in it (that is not contained in the edited register[9]) otherwise than in accordance with heads (a) and (b) below[10]; or
(3) make use of any such information other than for statistical purposes[11].

No information which is contained in the full register and not in the edited register may be disclosed otherwise than[12]:

(a) by allowing a person using the premises of the Board to inspect it under supervision[13]; and
(b) by publishing information about electors which does not include the name or address of any elector[14].

However, a person employed by the Board is not prohibited from supplying a copy of, or disclosing information contained in, a version of the full register where[15]:

(i) more than ten years have expired since that version of the register was first published[16]; and
(ii) the supply or disclosure is for research purposes in compliance with the relevant conditions[17].

Where a copy of the full register is made available for inspection[18] by providing the register on a computer screen or otherwise in data form, the Board must ensure that the manner in, and equipment on, which that copy is provided do not permit any person consulting that copy either to search it by electronic means by reference to the name of any person, or to copy or transmit any part of that copy by electronic means[19]. A person who inspects the copy of the full register held by the Board, whether a printed copy or in data form, may not[20] either make copies of any part of it[21], or record any particulars included in it[22], otherwise than by means of handwritten notes[23]. No person who obtains a copy of the full register (or to whom information contained in it that is not contained in the edited register is disclosed under the circumstances described in heads (i) and (ii) above) may supply a copy of it[24], disclose any such information[25], or make use of any such information[26], otherwise than for research purposes in compliance with the relevant conditions[27].

1   As to the meaning of 'registration officer' for these purposes see PARA 139 note 1.
2   See the Representation of the People (England and Wales) Regulations 2001, SI 2001/341, reg 99(1) (reg 99 added by SI 2002/1871; the Representation of the People (England and Wales) Regulations 2001, SI 2001/341, reg 99(1), (2) amended by SI 2009/725). For these purposes, the duty to supply is a duty to supply in data form unless, prior to publication, the Statistics Board has requested in writing a printed copy instead: Representation of the People (England and Wales) Regulations 2001, SI 2001/341, reg 99(2) (as so added and amended). As to the meaning of 'data form' see PARA 180 note 11. As to general aspects of the duty on a registration officer to supply data under Pt VI (regs 92–115) see PARA 180 note 2. As to the Statistics Board see REGISTRATION CONCERNING THE INDIVIDUAL vol 88 (2012) PARA 334.
3   Representation of the People (England and Wales) Regulations 2001, SI 2001/341, reg 99(1)(a) (as added: see note 2). The text refers to the revised version of a register published under the Representation of the People Act 1983 s 13(1) or s 13(3) (see PARA 165): see the Representation of the People (England and Wales) Regulations 2001, SI 2001/341, reg 99(1)(a) (as so added). As to the meaning of 'register' see PARA 179 note 1.
4   Representation of the People (England and Wales) Regulations 2001, SI 2001/341, reg 99(1)(b) (reg 99 as added (see note 2); reg 99(1)(b) amended by SI 2006/2910). The text refers to a notice of alteration published under the Representation of the People Act 1983 s 13A(2), s 13B(3), s 13B(3B) or s 13B(3D) (see PARA 168): see the Representation of the People (England and Wales) Regulations 2001, SI 2001/341, reg 99(1)(b) (as so added and amended).
5   Representation of the People (England and Wales) Regulations 2001, SI 2001/341, reg 99(1)(c) (as added: see note 2). As to the meaning of 'list of overseas electors' see PARA 143 note 9.
6   See the Representation of the People (England and Wales) Regulations 2001, SI 2001/341, reg 99(1) (as added and amended: see note 2).
7   See the Representation of the People (England and Wales) Regulations 2001, SI 2001/341, reg 99(3) (reg 99 as added (see note 2); reg 99(3) amended by SI 2006/752; SI 2009/725). This provision is expressed to be subject to the Representation of the People (England and Wales) Regulations 2001, SI 2001/341, reg 99(6) (see the text and notes 15–17): see reg 99(3) (as so added and amended). As to references to employees of any person who has access to a copy of the full register see PARA 180 note 6. A person who contravenes reg 99(3) is guilty of an offence and liable on summary conviction to a fine not exceeding level 5 on the standard scale: see reg 115; and PARA 734. As to the standard scale see SENTENCING AND DISPOSITION OF OFFENDERS vol 92 (2010) PARA 142.
8   Representation of the People (England and Wales) Regulations 2001, SI 2001/341, reg 99(3)(a) (as added: see note 2). As to relevant offences see note 7. As to the meaning of 'full register' see PARA 167 note 2.
9   As to the meaning of 'edited register' see PARA 167 note 4.
10 Representation of the People (England and Wales) Regulations 2001, SI 2001/341, reg 99(3)(b) (as added: see note 2). As to relevant offences see note 7.
11 Representation of the People (England and Wales) Regulations 2001, SI 2001/341, reg 99(3)(c) (as added: see note 2). As to relevant offences see note 7.
12 See the Representation of the People (England and Wales) Regulations 2001, SI 2001/341, reg 99(4) (reg 99 as added (see note 2); reg 99(4) amended by SI 2006/752). This provision is expressed to be subject to the Representation of the People (England and Wales) Regulations 2001, SI 2001/341, reg 99(6) (see the text and notes 15–17): see reg 99(4) (as so added and amended).
13 Representation of the People (England and Wales) Regulations 2001, SI 2001/341, reg 99(4)(a) (reg 99 as added (see note 2); reg 99(4)(a) amended by SI 2009/725). The permitted purpose for which a copy of the full register is made available for inspection under supervision in this way does not include direct marketing: see PARA 179 note 18.
14 Representation of the People (England and Wales) Regulations 2001, SI 2001/341, reg 99(4)(b) (as added: see note 2).
15 See the Representation of the People (England and Wales) Regulations 2001, SI 2001/341, reg 99(6) (reg 99 as added (see note 2); reg 99(6), (7) added by SI 2006/752; the Representation of the People (England and Wales) Regulations 2001, SI 2001/341, reg 99(6) amended by SI 2009/725).
16 Representation of the People (England and Wales) Regulations 2001, SI 2001/341, reg 99(6)(a) (as added: see note 15). The text refers to that version of the register first published in accordance with reg 43 (see PARA 165 note 3): see reg 99(6)(a) (as so added).

17 Representation of the People (England and Wales) Regulations 2001, SI 2001/341, reg 99(6)(b) (as added: see note 15). As to the meanings of 'research purposes' and 'relevant conditions' see PARA 180 note 11.

18 As to the meaning of 'available for inspection' see PARA 142 note 18.

19 See the Representation of the People (England and Wales) Regulations 2001, SI 2001/341, reg 99(4A) (reg 99 as added (see note 2); reg 99(4A) added by SI 2006/752; and amended by SI 2009/725).

20 See the Representation of the People (England and Wales) Regulations 2001, SI 2001/341, reg 99(5) (reg 99 as added (see note 2); reg 99(5) amended by SI 2006/752). A person who contravenes the Representation of the People (England and Wales) Regulations 2001, SI 2001/341, reg 99(5) is guilty of an offence and liable on summary conviction to a fine not exceeding level 5 on the standard scale: see reg 115; and PARA 734.

21 Representation of the People (England and Wales) Regulations 2001, SI 2001/341, reg 99(5)(a) (as added: see note 2). As to relevant offences see note 20.

22 Representation of the People (England and Wales) Regulations 2001, SI 2001/341, reg 99(5)(b) (as added: see note 2). As to relevant offences see note 20.

23 See the Representation of the People (England and Wales) Regulations 2001, SI 2001/341, reg 99(5) (as added and amended: see note 20). As to relevant offences see note 20.

24 Representation of the People (England and Wales) Regulations 2001, SI 2001/341, reg 99(7)(a) (as added: see note 15). A person who contravenes the Representation of the People (England and Wales) Regulations 2001, SI 2001/341, reg 99(7) is guilty of an offence and liable on summary conviction to a fine not exceeding level 5 on the standard scale: see reg 115; and PARA 734.

25 Representation of the People (England and Wales) Regulations 2001, SI 2001/341, reg 99(7)(b) (as added: see note 15). As to relevant offences see note 24.

26 Representation of the People (England and Wales) Regulations 2001, SI 2001/341, reg 99(7)(c) (as added: see note 15). As to relevant offences see note 24.

27 See the Representation of the People (England and Wales) Regulations 2001, SI 2001/341, reg 99(7) (as added: see note 15). As to relevant offences see note 24.

188. Sale of edited and full versions of register etc. The registration officer[1] must supply a copy of the edited register[2] to any person on payment of a fee[3]. However, the registration officer may not sell a copy of the full register[4], or a copy of any notice altering the register ('a relevant notice')[5], or a copy of the list of overseas electors[6], except to a person who is entitled[7] to purchase them[8]. A fee is payable for any sale of the full register[9].

A request for a copy of the full register, or of any published notice altering that register, as the case may be, must be made in writing[10], and must:

(1) specify the documents requested[11];

(2) state whether the request is made only in respect of the current documents or whether it includes a request for the supply of any subsequent documents on publication for as long as the person making the request pays for them[12]; and

(3) state whether a printed copy of any of the documents is requested instead of the version in data form[13].

However, the registration officer must not supply a printed copy of the full register if to do so would result in his having insufficient copies of it for the purposes of any requirement made by or under any enactment[14]. Subject to this proviso, the registration officer must supply, on request and on payment of a fee[15], a copy of a relevant document to[16]:

(a) a government department[17];

(b) the Environment Agency[18];

(c) the Financial Services Authority[19];

(d) any body not falling within heads (a) to (c) above which carries out the vetting of any person for the purpose of safeguarding national security[20];

(e) a credit reference agency which is registered under Part III of the

Consumer Credit Act 1974[21], and which is carrying on the business of providing credit reference services[22].

No person in an organisation mentioned in heads (a) to (e) above to which a copy of the register has been supplied[23] may:

(i)   supply a copy of the full register to any person[24];

(ii)   disclose any information contained in it that is not contained in the edited register[25]; or

(iii)   make use of any such information[26],

other than for the purpose set out in the provision by virtue of which the full register has been supplied[27]. These restrictions (the 'relevant restrictions') apply to a person to whom a copy of the full register is duly supplied or to whom information contained in it is duly disclosed as they apply to the original recipient in the organisation to which the copy of the full register was supplied under the provision in question[28].

In the case of a body falling within heads (a) to (c) above, the relevant restrictions apply except for the purpose of the prevention and detection of crime and the enforcement of the criminal law (whether in England and Wales or elsewhere)[29], the vetting of employees and applicants for employment where such vetting is required pursuant to any enactment[30], the vetting of any person where such vetting is for the purpose of safeguarding national security[31], and the supply and disclosure of information by a government department to an authorised person[32]. In the case of a body falling within head (d) above, the relevant restrictions apply except for the purpose of the vetting of any person where such vetting is for the purpose of safeguarding national security[33]. In the case of an agency falling within head (e) above, the relevant restrictions apply except for the purpose of vetting applications for credit[34] or applications that can result in the giving of credit or the giving of any guarantee, indemnity or assurance in relation to the giving of credit[35], meeting any obligations contained in statutory provisions or rules relating to money laundering[36], and statistical analysis of credit risk assessment in a case where no person whose details are included in the full register is referred to by name or necessary implication[37].

1   As to the meaning of 'registration officer' for these purposes see PARA 139 note 1.

2   As to the meaning of 'edited register' see PARA 167 note 4. As to the meaning of 'register' see PARA 179 note 1.

3   Representation of the People (England and Wales) Regulations 2001, SI 2001/341, reg 110(1) (regs 110–114 added by SI 2002/1871). The fee is calculated in accordance with the Representation of the People (England and Wales) Regulations 2001, SI 2001/341, reg 110(2): see reg 110(1) (as so added). Accordingly:

     (1)   in the case of the register in data form, the fee is at the rate of £20 plus £1.50 for each 1,000 entries (or remaining part of 1,000 entries) in it (reg 110(2)(a) (as so added)); and

     (2)   in the case of the register in printed form, the fee is at the rate of £10 plus £5 for each 1,000 entries (or remaining part of 1,000 entries) in it (reg 110(2)(b) (as so added)).

As to the meaning of 'data form' see PARA 180 note 11. As to general aspects of the duty on a registration officer to supply data under Pt VI (regs 92–115) see PARA 180 note 2.

4   Representation of the People (England and Wales) Regulations 2001, SI 2001/341, reg 111(1)(a) (as added: see note 3). As to the meaning of 'full register' see PARA 167 note 2.

5   Representation of the People (England and Wales) Regulations 2001, SI 2001/341, reg 111(1)(b) (reg 111 as added (see note 3); reg 111(1)(b) amended by SI 2006/2910). The text refers to a notice of alteration published under the Representation of the People Act 1983 s 13A(2), s 13B(3), s 13B(3B) or s 13B(3D) (see PARA 168): see the Representation of the People (England and Wales) Regulations 2001, SI 2001/341, reg 111(1)(b) (as so added and amended).

6   Representation of the People (England and Wales) Regulations 2001, SI 2001/341, reg 111(1)(c) (as added: see note 3). As to the meaning of 'list of overseas electors' see PARA 143 note 9.

7　Ie entitled under the Representation of the People (England and Wales) Regulations 2001, SI 2001/341, reg 113 (see heads (a)–(d) in the text) or reg 114 (see head (e) in the text): see reg 111(1) (as added: see note 3).

8　Representation of the People (England and Wales) Regulations 2001, SI 2001/341, reg 111(1) (as added: see note 3). In any copy of the full register, or any copy of a notice under the Representation of the People Act 1983 s 13A(2), s 13B(3), s 13B(3B) or s 13B(3D) which is sold in accordance with the Representation of the People (England and Wales) Regulations 2001, SI 2001/341, regs 112–114 (see the text and notes 10–37), the letter 'Z' must be placed against the entry of any person whose entry is not included in the edited version of the register: reg 111(7) (reg 111 as so added; reg 111(7) amended by SI 2006/752; SI 2006/2910).

9　Representation of the People (England and Wales) Regulations 2001, SI 2001/341, reg 111(2) (as added: see note 3). The fee for such sale is to be calculated in accordance with reg 111(3)–(6): see reg 111(2) (as so added). Accordingly:
　　(1)　in the case of the register or a relevant notice in data form, the fee is at the rate of £20 plus £1.50 for each 1,000 entries (or remaining part of 1,000 entries) in it (reg 111(5)(a) (as so added)); and
　　(2)　in the case of the register or a relevant notice in printed form, the fee is at the rate of £10 plus £5 for each 1,000 entries (or remaining part of 1,000 entries) in it (reg 111(5)(b) (as so added)).

Where a person purchases the full register together with any relevant notices which are published at that time altering the register, the register and the notices must be treated as the same document for the purposes of the calculations set out in reg 111(5); and any entry in the register which is deleted by a notice must be ignored for the purposes of the calculation: see reg 111(3) (as so added). However, where a person purchases a relevant notice separately from the full register, the calculations set out in reg 111(5) must be applied to that notice: reg 111(4) (as so added).

　　In the case of the list of overseas electors:
　　(a)　where the list is purchased in data form, the fee is at the rate of £20 plus £1.50 for each 100 entries (or remaining part of 100 entries) in it (reg 111(6)(a) (as so added)); and
　　(b)　where the list is purchased in printed form, the fee is at the rate of £10 plus £5 for each 100 entries (or remaining part of 100 entries) in it (reg 111(6)(b) (as so added)).

10　See the Representation of the People (England and Wales) Regulations 2001, SI 2001/341, reg 112(1), (7) (reg 112 as added (see note 3); reg 112(1), (7) amended by SI 2006/2910). The text refers to any notice of alteration published under the Representation of the People Act 1983 s 13A(2), s 13B(3), s 13B(3B) or s 13B(3D) (see PARA 168): see the Representation of the People (England and Wales) Regulations 2001, SI 2001/341, reg 112(1), (7) (as so added and amended).

11　Representation of the People (England and Wales) Regulations 2001, SI 2001/341, reg 112(7)(a) (as added: see note 3).

12　Representation of the People (England and Wales) Regulations 2001, SI 2001/341, reg 112(7)(b) (as added: see note 3).

13　Representation of the People (England and Wales) Regulations 2001, SI 2001/341, reg 112(7)(c) (as added: see note 3).

14　Representation of the People (England and Wales) Regulations 2001, SI 2001/341, reg 112(2) (as added: see note 3). As to the meaning of 'enactment' see PARA 179 note 8.

15　Ie a fee calculated in accordance with the Representation of the People (England and Wales) Regulations 2001, SI 2001/341, reg 111 (see note 9): see regs 113(1), 114(1) (as added: see note 3).

16　See the Representation of the People (England and Wales) Regulations 2001, SI 2001/341, regs 113(1), 114(1) (regs 113, 114 as added (see note 3); reg 113(1) amended by the Counter-Terrorism Act 2008 s 20(4), Sch 1 para 2(1), (6)(a)). The provision made by the Representation of the People (England and Wales) Regulations 2001, SI 2001/341, reg 113(1) does not apply to a department to which reg 108A (see PARA 186) applies: see reg 113(1) (as so added and amended).

　　For the purposes of reg 113 and reg 114, a 'relevant document' means the full register published under the Representation of the People Act 1983 s 13(1) or s 13(3) (see PARA 165), any notice published under s 13A(2), s 13B(3), s 13B(3B) or s 13B(3D) (see PARA 168) amending that register, and the list of overseas electors: see the Representation of the People (England and Wales) Regulations 2001, SI 2001/341, reg 112(6) (reg 112 as added (see note 3); reg 112(6) amended by SI 2006/2910).

17　Representation of the People (England and Wales) Regulations 2001, SI 2001/341, reg 113(1)(a) (reg 113 as added (see note 3); reg 113(1)(a)–(d) added by SI 2006/752).

18 Representation of the People (England and Wales) Regulations 2001, SI 2001/341, reg 113(1)(b) (as added: see note 17). As to the Environment Agency see ENVIRONMENTAL QUALITY AND PUBLIC HEALTH vol 45 (2010) PARA 68 et seq.

19 Representation of the People (England and Wales) Regulations 2001, SI 2001/341, reg 113(1)(c) (as added: see note 17). The Financial Services Authority was abolished with effect from 19 December 2012, and responsibility for financial regulation vested in the Financial Conduct Authority and the Prudential Regulation Authority: see the Financial Services and Markets Act 2000 ss 1A–3S (substituted by the Financial Services Act 2012 s 6(1)); and FINANCIAL SERVICES AND INSTITUTIONS vol 48 (2008) PARA 5 et seq.

20 Representation of the People (England and Wales) Regulations 2001, SI 2001/341, reg 113(1)(d) (as added: see note 17).

21 Ie a credit reference agency registered under the Consumer Credit Act 1974 Pt III (ss 21–41ZB), by virtue of s 147 (see CONSUMER CREDIT vol 21 (2011) PARA 30): see the Representation of the People (England and Wales) Regulations 2001, SI 2001/341, reg 114(1) (as added: see note 3).

22 Representation of the People (England and Wales) Regulations 2001, SI 2001/341, reg 114(1) (as added: see note 3). The registration officer may require a credit reference agency to provide such evidence that it is carrying on the business of providing credit reference services as he reasonably requires: reg 114(4) (as so added). For these purposes, 'credit reference services' means the furnishing of persons with information relevant to the financial standing of individuals, which is information collected by the person furnishing it for the purpose of so furnishing it: see reg 114(5) (as so added). A company running a low cost identity verification and credit-vetting service which did not fall within reg 114 applied for judicial review seeking, inter alia, declaratory relief to the effect that, if it were to modify its business, it would come within that regulation; however, the application was dismissed on the ground, inter alia, that declaratory relief directed to the company's proposals would be contrary to principle: see *R (on the application of I-CD Publishing Ltd) v Office of the Deputy Prime Minister* [2003] EWHC 1761 (Admin), (2003) Times, 11 August, [2003] All ER (D) 343 (Jul). The sale of the full register to credit reference agencies has been held not to violate the right to vote by reference to the Convention for the Protection of Human Rights and Fundamental Freedoms (Rome, 4 November 1950; TS 71 (1953); Cmd 8969), First Protocol (Paris, 20 March 1952; Cmnd 9221) art 3 (see PARA 7): *R (on the application of Robertson) v Lord Chancellor's Department* [2003] EWHC 1760 (Admin), (2003) Times, 11 August, [2003] All ER (D) 340 (Jul) (it was permissible to conclude that the public interest in the facilitation of credit and in the control of fraud outweighed the very modest interference with the right to vote involved with the sale of the full register to credit reference agencies). The sale of full registers for direct marketing purposes is not permitted, however: see PARA 179 note 18.

23 Ie supplied under the Representation of the People (England and Wales) Regulations 2001, SI 2001/341, reg 113 or reg 114 (see the text and notes 15–22): see reg 112(4) (as added: see note 3).

24 Representation of the People (England and Wales) Regulations 2001, SI 2001/341, reg 112(4)(a) (as added: see note 3).

25 Representation of the People (England and Wales) Regulations 2001, SI 2001/341, reg 112(4)(b) (as added: see note 3).

26 Representation of the People (England and Wales) Regulations 2001, SI 2001/341, reg 112(4)(c) (as added: see note 3).

27 See the Representation of the People (England and Wales) Regulations 2001, SI 2001/341, reg 112(4) (as added: see note 3). The restrictions set out in reg 112(4), (5) (see also the text and note 28) are referred to as the 'relevant restrictions': see reg 112(3) (as so added).
   Any person who has obtained or is entitled to obtain a copy of the full register under reg 113 (see heads (a)–(d) in the text) or reg 114 (see head (e) in the text) may supply a copy of the full register to a processor for the purpose of processing the information contained in the register, or he may procure that a processor processes and provides to him any copy of the register which the processor has obtained under the Representation of the People (England and Wales) Regulations 2001, SI 2001/341, for use in respect of the purposes for which that person is entitled to obtain such copy or information (as the case may be): see reg 92(7) (reg 92 as so added; reg 92(7) amended by SI 2006/752); and see PARA 180 note 11. A person who contravenes the Representation of the People (England and Wales) Regulations 2001, SI 2001/341, reg 112(4), is guilty of an offence and liable on summary conviction to a fine not exceeding level 5 on the standard scale: see reg 115; and PARA 734. As to the standard scale see SENTENCING AND DISPOSITION OF OFFENDERS vol 92 (2010) PARA 142.

28 See the Representation of the People (England and Wales) Regulations 2001, SI 2001/341, reg 112(5) (as added: see note 3). The restrictions set out in reg 112(4), (5) (see also the text and notes 23–27) are referred to as the 'relevant restrictions': see reg 112(3) (as so added). A person

who contravenes reg 112(5) is guilty of an offence and liable on summary conviction to a fine not exceeding level 5 on the standard scale: see reg 115; and PARA 734.

29 Representation of the People (England and Wales) Regulations 2001, SI 2001/341, reg 113(2)(a)(i) (reg 113 as added (see note 3); reg 113(2) substituted by SI 2006/752).

30 Representation of the People (England and Wales) Regulations 2001, SI 2001/341, reg 113(2)(a)(ii) (reg 113 as added (see note 3); reg 113(2) as substituted (see note 29)).

31 Representation of the People (England and Wales) Regulations 2001, SI 2001/341, reg 113(2)(a)(iii) (reg 113 as added (see note 3); reg 113(2) as substituted (see note 29)).

32 Representation of the People (England and Wales) Regulations 2001, SI 2001/341, reg 113(2)(a)(iv) (reg 113 as added (see note 3); reg 113(2) as substituted (see note 29)). The supply and disclosure mentioned in the text must take place in accordance with reg 113(3)–(6): reg 113(2)(a)(iv) (as so added and substituted). Accordingly, a government department, other than one mentioned in reg 108A (see PARA 186), may supply, whether or not on payment, a copy of the full register to a person ('an authorised person'), who may only disclose information contained in the full register to any person falling within regs 103–108 (see PARA 185) and for use for the purposes for which such a person could obtain a register under the regulation concerned: see reg 113(3), (5) (reg 113 as so added; reg 113(3) amended by the Counter-Terrorism Act 2008 Sch 1 para 2(1), (6)(b); and by SI 2006/752). The restrictions in the Representation of the People (England and Wales) Regulations 2001, SI 2001/341, regs 103–108 apply to a person to whom information contained in the full register is disclosed under reg 113(5) as it applies to a person to whom a copy of the register is supplied under regs 103–108: see reg 113(6) (as so added). The Queen's Printers copy of reg 113(6) refers to 'a person to whom a copy of the register is applied' but it is submitted that 'a person to whom a copy of the register is supplied' is intended. For these purposes, any reference to an authorised person includes a reference to his employees: see reg 113(4) (as so added). As to references to employees of any person who has access to a copy of the full register see PARA 180 note 6. A person who contravenes reg 113(5) or reg 113(6) is guilty of an offence and liable on summary conviction to a fine not exceeding level 5 on the standard scale: see reg 115; and PARA 734.

33 Representation of the People (England and Wales) Regulations 2001, SI 2001/341, reg 113(2)(b) (reg 113 as added (see note 3); reg 113(2) as substituted (see note 29)).

34 For these purposes, 'application for credit' includes an application to refinance or reschedule an existing credit agreement; and 'credit' includes a cash loan and any other form of financial accommodation: see the Representation of the People (England and Wales) Regulations 2001, SI 2001/341, reg 114(5) (as added: see note 3).

35 See the Representation of the People (England and Wales) Regulations 2001, SI 2001/341, reg 114(2), (3)(a) (as added: see note 3).

36 See the Representation of the People (England and Wales) Regulations 2001, SI 2001/341, reg 114(2), (3)(b) (reg 114 as added (see note 3); reg 114(3)(b) amended by SI 2003/3075; SI 2007/2157). The text refers to the Money Laundering Regulations 2007, SI 2007/2157 (see CRIMINAL LAW vol 26 (2010) PARA 742 et seq) and any money laundering rules made pursuant to the Financial Services and Markets Act 2000 s 146 (see FINANCIAL SERVICES AND INSTITUTIONS vol 48 (2008) PARA 30): see the Representation of the People (England and Wales) Regulations 2001, SI 2001/341, reg 114(2), (3)(b) (as so added and amended).

37 See the Representation of the People (England and Wales) Regulations 2001, SI 2001/341, reg 114(2), (3)(c) (as added: see note 3).

5. PROCEDURE FOR CONDUCTING ELECTIONS

(1) INITIATING AN ELECTION

(i) Initiating a Parliamentary Election

A. PARLIAMENTARY GENERAL ELECTION

189. Commanding of elections for new parliament. A new Parliament is summoned by means of a royal proclamation made with the advice of the Privy Council[1].

The prerogative power to dissolve Parliament before the maximum five-year period dictated by the Septennial Act 1715[2], exercised conventionally by Her Majesty with the advice of the Privy Council, has been abolished, however, by the Fixed-term Parliaments Act 2011[3], which fixes the day for the poll at a parliamentary general election so that it falls ordinarily on the first Thursday in May every five years counting from 2010[4], although provision is made for an early call if circumstances require[5]. Once the polling day for the next parliamentary general election is set in this way[6], the provisions of the Fixed-term Parliaments Act 2011 require that the Parliament then in existence dissolves at the beginning of the seventeenth working day[7] before that day[8]; and Parliament cannot otherwise be dissolved[9].

The procedure then becomes governed in the usual way by the Parliamentary Elections Rules, and by the parliamentary elections timetable in particular, which requires the writs for parliamentary elections to be issued as soon as practicable after the dissolution of Parliament by the Fixed-term Parliaments Act 2011[10]. Accordingly, once Parliament dissolves, the Lord Chancellor (and, in relation to Northern Ireland, the Secretary of State) have the authority to have the writs for the election sealed and issued[11]; and Her Majesty may issue the proclamation summoning the new Parliament[12]. The Fixed-term Parliaments Act 2011 does not affect the way in which the sealing of a proclamation summoning a new Parliament may be authorised[13]; nor does it affect Her Majesty's power to prorogue Parliament[14].

1   See PARLIAMENT vol 78 (2010) PARA 998; and see also note 10. As to royal proclamations see CONSTITUTIONAL LAW AND HUMAN RIGHTS vol 8(2) (Reissue) PARA 917.

2   The Parliament Act 1911 s 7 amended the Septennial Act 1715 so that five years was substituted for seven years as the time fixed for the maximum duration of Parliament. As to the repeal of these provisions see note 3.

3   The Septennial Act 1715, and the Parliament Act 1911 s 7, have been repealed by the Fixed-term Parliaments Act 2011: see s 6(3), Schedule paras 2, 4. See also the Succession to the Crown Act 1707 s 7, the Representation of the People Act 1867 s 51, and the Regency Act 1937 s 6(1) (all amended by the Fixed-term Parliaments Act 2011 Schedule paras 1, 3, 5); and PARLIAMENT vol 78 (2010) PARA 1014. An amendment or repeal made by the Fixed-term Parliaments Act 2011 has the same extent as the enactment or relevant part of the enactment to which the amendment or repeal relates: se s 7(3).

     The Fixed-term Parliaments Act 2011 received Royal Assent on 15 September 2011 (see Preamble), and came into force on the day that it was passed (see s 7(2)). The Prime Minister must make arrangements for a committee to carry out a review of the operation of the Fixed-term Parliaments Act 2011 and, if appropriate in consequence of its findings, to make recommendations for the repeal or amendment of that Act, and for the publication of the committee's findings and recommendations (if any): see s 7(4). A majority of the members of the committee are to be members of the House of Commons: s 7(5). The subject matter of the Fixed-term Parliaments Act 2011 is reserved for the purpose of the Scotland Act 1998, non-devolved for the purpose of the Government of Wales Act 2006, and excepted for the purpose of the Northern Ireland Act 1998: see CONSTITUTIONAL LAW AND HUMAN RIGHTS.

4   See the Fixed-term Parliaments Act 2011 s 1; and PARA 195. The Prime Minister has a limited power by order to defer the date thus set for up to two months, subject to approval of the statutory instrument making the order being approved by both Houses of Parliament: see s 1(5)–(7); and PARA 195. The general elections for the National Assembly for Wales, which were scheduled to take place on 7 May 2015, were re-scheduled to take place instead on 5 May 2016, with subsequent ordinary general elections scheduled to be held on the first Thursday in May in the fourth calendar year after May 2016: see s 5 (explaining the effect of the Government of Wales Act 2006 s 3(1)); and PARA 213. Similar provision was made in relation to the general elections for the Scottish Parliament which were scheduled to take place on 7 May 2015: see the Fixed-term Parliaments Act 2011 s 4.

5   See the Fixed-term Parliaments Act 2011 s 2; and PARA 195.

6   Ie determined under the Fixed-term Parliaments Act 2011 s 1, or appointed under s 2(7) (see PARA 195): see s 3(1) (prospectively amended: see note 7).

7   For these purposes, 'working day' means any day other than a Saturday or Sunday, a Christmas Eve, Christmas Day or Good Friday, a day which is a bank holiday under the Banking and Financial Dealings Act 1971 in any part of the United Kingdom (see TIME vol 97 (2010) PARA 321), or a day appointed for public thanksgiving or mourning: see the Fixed-term Parliaments Act 2011 s 3(5). However, if on a day (the 'relevant day') one or more working days are fixed or appointed as bank holidays or days for public thanksgiving or mourning, and if, as a result, the day for the dissolution of a Parliament would, apart from s 3(6), be brought forward from what it was immediately before the relevant day to a day that is earlier than 30 days after the relevant day, the day or days in question are to continue to be treated as working days (even if the polling day is subsequently changed): see s 3(6). As to the meaning of 'United Kingdom' see PARA 1 note 1.

   As from a day to be appointed under the Electoral Registration and Administration Act 2013 s 27(1), the Fixed-term Parliaments Act 2011 s 3(1) is amended so that the reference to 'the seventeenth working day' becomes a reference to 'the twenty-fifth working day' (with the effect of extending the electoral timetable to 25 days): see s 3(1) (prospectively amended by the Electoral Registration and Administration Act 2013 s 14(1)). However, at the date at which this volume states the law, no such day had been appointed.

8   Fixed-term Parliaments Act 2011 s 3(1) (prospectively amended: see note 7). Previously, the dissolution of Parliament was an incident of the royal proclamation summoning a new Parliament (see the text and note 1).

9   Fixed-term Parliaments Act 2011 s 3(2).

10 See the Representation of the People Act 1983 Sch 1 r 1 (Timetable); and PARA 192. The timetable refers specifically to the dissolution of Parliament by the Fixed-term Parliaments Act 2011 s 3(1) (see the text and notes 6–8): see the Representation of the People Act 1983 Sch 1 r 1; and PARA 192. As to the meaning of 'parliamentary elections rules' see PARA 383 note 2.

   Prior to the Fixed-term Parliaments Act 2011, the proclamation made by Her Majesty announced at the same time that orders have been given for writs to be issued by the Lord Chancellor in due form for the summoning of a new Parliament, and appointed a day and place for the meeting of the new Parliament: see PARLIAMENT vol 78 (2010) PARAS 998, 1022. As to the Lord Chancellor see PARA 2; and see, more generally, CONSTITUTIONAL LAW AND HUMAN RIGHTS vol 8(2) (Reissue) PARA 477 et seq.

11 See the Fixed-term Parliaments Act 2011 s 3(3). See further the Representation of the People Act 1983 Sch 1 r 3; and PARA 192 et seq.

12 See the Fixed-term Parliaments Act 2011 s 3(4). The proclamation may:
    (1)   appoint the day for the first meeting of the new Parliament (s 3(4)(a)); and
    (2)   deal with any other matter which was normally dealt with before 15 September 2011 (ie before the passing of the Fixed-term Parliaments Act 2011: see note 3) by proclamations summoning new Parliaments (except a matter dealt with by s 3(1) (see the text and notes 6–8) or s 3(3) (see the text and note 11)) (s 3(4)(b)).
    The demise of the Crown does not affect any proclamation summoning a new Parliament issued before the demise, or any other matter relating to a parliamentary election or the summoning of a new Parliament: see the Representation of the People Act 1985 s 20; and PARA 190.

13 See the Fixed-term Parliaments Act 2011 s 6(2). The sealing of a proclamation to be issued under s 2(7) (see PARA 195) may be authorised in the same way: see s 6(2). The traditional way in which the sealing of a proclamation summoning a new Parliament under the Great Seal of the

Realm is authorised is by Order in Council rather than a warrant under the Royal Sign Manual. As to Writs under the Great Seal see CONSTITUTIONAL LAW AND HUMAN RIGHTS vol 8(2) (Reissue) PARA 919.

14   See the Fixed-term Parliaments Act 2011 s 6(1). See the text and note 1. As to prorogation by exercise of the royal prerogative see further PARLIAMENT vol 78 (2010) PARAS 998, 1018.

190. Effect of demise of the Crown occurring on or after dissolution of a Parliament. The demise of the Crown[1] does not affect any proclamation summoning a new Parliament issued before the demise[2], or any other matter relating to a parliamentary election or the summoning of a new Parliament[3]. However, if the demise occurs[4]:

(1)   on the day of the dissolution of a Parliament under the Fixed-term Parliaments Act 2011[5]; or

(2)   after that day, but before the polling day for the next parliamentary general election after the dissolution as determined or appointed under the Fixed-term Parliaments Act 2011 ('the current election')[6],

then, in relation to the current election, for the purposes of the parliamentary elections timetable[7], as set out in the parliamentary elections rules[8]: (a) the polling day must be the fourteenth day after the day which would otherwise have been the polling day[9], or (if the fourteenth day is not a working day[10]) the next working day after the fourteenth day[11]; (b) any working day within the period of 13 days beginning with the day after the demise must be disregarded in computing any period of time[12], and is not to be treated as a day for the purpose of any proceedings before the polling day[13]. The provisions which limit the amount of election expenses incurred by an individual or party candidate[14] have effect in relation to any candidate at the election as if the maximum amount specified[15] were increased by one-half[16].

If the proclamation summoning the new Parliament after the current election was issued before the demise, the meeting of the new Parliament must (subject to any prorogation subsequent to the demise) take place on the fourteenth day after the day appointed in the proclamation for the meeting[17], or (if the fourteenth day is not a working day) the next working day after the fourteenth day[18].

If the demise occurs within the period of seven days before the day of the dissolution of a Parliament determined under the Fixed-term Parliaments Act 2011[19], these provisions[20] have effect as if the demise occurred on that day[21].

1   The term 'demise of the Crown' refers to the death of a monarch, and is used to describe the transfer of the kingdom to his or her successor: see CROWN AND ROYAL FAMILY vol 12(1) (Reissue) PARA 15.

2   As to the issue of a royal proclamation summoning a new Parliament see the Fixed-term Parliaments Act 2011 s 3(4); and PARA 189.

3   Representation of the People Act 1985 s 20(1) (s 20 substituted by the Fixed-term Parliaments Act 2011 s 6(3), Schedule paras 14, 16). The provision made by the Representation of the People Act 1985 s 20(1) is expressed to be subject to s 20(2)–(8) (see the text and notes 4–21): see s 20(1) (as so substituted). As to the effect of the demise of the Crown generally see CROWN AND ROYAL FAMILY vol 12(1) (Reissue) PARA 15 et seq.

4   See the Representation of the People Act 1985 s 20(2) (as substituted: see note 3). The provision made by s 20(3)–(6) (see the text and notes 7–18) applies if either condition set out in s 20(2) (see also the text and notes 5–6) is met; and any relevant writ, notice or other document is to be issued or, if already issued, read accordingly: see s 20(2) (as so substituted).

5   Representation of the People Act 1985 s 20(2)(a) (as substituted: see note 3). The text refers to the day of the dissolution of a Parliament by the Fixed-term Parliaments Act 2011 s 3(1) (see PARA 189): see the Representation of the People Act 1985 s 20(2)(a) (as so substituted).

6   Representation of the People Act 1985 s 20(2)(b) (as substituted: see note 3). The text refers to the dissolution as determined under the Fixed-term Parliaments Act 2011 s 1 (see PARA 195), or appointed under s 2(7) (see PARA 195): see the Representation of the People Act 1985 s 20(2)(b) (as so substituted). As to the date of the poll at a parliamentary general election see PARA 195.

7   Ie for the purposes of the timetable in the Representation of the People Act 1983 Sch 1 r 1 (see
    PARA 192): see the Representation of the People Act 1985 s 20(3) (as so substituted).

8   See the Representation of the People Act 1985 s 20(3) (as substituted: see note 3). As to the
    meaning of 'parliamentary elections rules' see PARA 383 note 2.

9   Representation of the People Act 1985 s 20(3)(a)(i) (as substituted: see note 3). If the polling day
    for the current election was appointed under the Fixed-term Parliaments Act 2011 s 2(7) (see
    PARA 195) (ie rather than determined under s 1: see PARA 195), the reference to the polling day
    in s 1(4) (see PARA 195) is to be read, in relation to the current election, as a reference to the new
    polling day under head (a) in the text: s 20(4) (as so substituted).

10 For these purposes, 'working day' means any day other than one to which the Representation of
    the People Act 1983 Sch 1 r 2 (computation of time: see PARA 195 note 27) applies in relation to
    the current election (or would have applied had it fallen before the polling day): see the
    Representation of the People Act 1985 s 20(8) (as substituted: see note 3).

11 Representation of the People Act 1985 s 20(3)(a)(ii) (as substituted: see note 3). See note 9.

12 Representation of the People Act 1985 s 20(3)(b)(i) (as substituted: see note 3).

13 Representation of the People Act 1985 s 20(3)(b)(ii) (as substituted: see note 3). The proceedings
    referred to in the text might include eg applications for an absent vote at a particular election,
    which must be received by the registration officer before a set date: see PARA 371.

14 Ie the Representation of the People Act 1983 s 76 (see PARA 273): see the Representation of the
    People Act 1985 s 20(5) (as substituted: see note 3).

15 Ie the maximum amount specified in the Representation of the People Act 1983 s 76(2)(a) (see
    PARA 273): see the Representation of the People Act 1985 s 20(5) (as substituted: see note 3).

16 Representation of the People Act 1985 s 20(5) (as substituted: see note 3).

17 See the Representation of the People Act 1985 s 20(6)(a) (as substituted: see note 3). As to the
    subject matter of a proclamation see the Fixed-term Parliaments Act 2011 s 3(4); and PARA 189.

18 See the Representation of the People Act 1985 s 20(6)(b) (as substituted: see note 3).

19 Ie the day of the dissolution of a Parliament determined by the Fixed-term Parliaments Act 2011
    s 3(1) (see PARA 189): see the Representation of the People Act 1985 s 20(7) (as substituted: see
    note 3).

20 Ie the Representation of the People Act 1985 s 20(2)–(6) (see the text and notes 4–18): see
    s 20(7) (as substituted: see note 3).

21 Representation of the People Act 1985 s 20(7) (as substituted: see note 3).

B. PARLIAMENTARY BY-ELECTION

191.   Power of House of Commons to fill vacant seats.   When the House of
Commons is sitting and a seat becomes vacant by reason of the death of a
member, or for any other cause[1], the House, upon motion made, orders the
Speaker to issue his warrant empowering the Clerk of the Crown in Chancery to
make out a new writ to fill the vacancy[2]. Where a vacancy is caused during a
prorogation of Parliament or adjournment of the House of Commons, the
procedure for issuing the warrant is subject to special provision[3].

1   As to methods of retirement from the House of Commons see PARLIAMENT vol 78 (2010) PARA
    894.

2   See PARLIAMENT vol 78 (2010) PARA 1094. As to the Clerk of the Crown in Chancery see
    CONSTITUTIONAL LAW AND HUMAN RIGHTS vol 8(2) (Reissue) PARA 921.

3   See the Recess Elections Act 1975; and PARLIAMENT vol 78 (2010) PARA 1095.

C. WRITS AND NOTICE OF PARLIAMENTARY ELECTION

192.   Issue and conveyance of writs for parliamentary elections.   Writs for a
parliamentary general election must be issued as soon as practicable after the
dissolution of Parliament[1]; the writ for a parliamentary by-election must be
issued as soon as practicable after the issue of the warrant for the writ[2].

Each writ must be issued in the prescribed form[3], and must be directed to the
returning officer, in each constituency[4] in which an election is to be held, by the
title of his office (and not by his name), and each writ must be conveyed to him[5].

Delivery of the writ to a person for the time being authorised by law to act as deputy for the officer who by virtue of his office is returning officer is as good as delivery to the returning officer[6]. For a parliamentary election in a constituency in England[7] and Wales[8], the writ is conveyed to the acting returning officer if[9]:

(1)   the returning officer has, by notice in the form prescribed[10], so requested and the notice is received by the Clerk of the Crown in Chancery one month or more before the issue of the writ[11]; and

(2)   the notice has not been revoked by a further notice in the form prescribed[12] and received within such time[13].

Such a notice has effect in relation to all constituencies of which the person giving the notice is returning officer at the time of giving it[14] or of which he or a successor in office becomes returning officer by virtue of that office[15].

1   See the Representation of the People Act 1983 Sch 1 r 1 (Sch 1 r 1 amended by the Fixed-term Parliaments Act 2011 s 6(3), Schedule paras 6, 10(1), (2)). The text refers to the dissolution of Parliament by the Fixed-term Parliaments Act 2011 s 3(1) (see PARA 189): see the Representation of the People Act 1983 Sch 1 r 1 (as so amended).

     Writs for parliamentary elections continue to be sealed and issued in accordance with the practice of the office of the Clerk of the Crown existing when the Representation of the People Act 1983 was enacted: Sch 1 r 3(1). See PARLIAMENT vol 78 (2010) PARA 998. In the Representation of the People Act 1983, the expression 'Clerk of the Crown' means the Clerk of the Crown in Chancery: s 202(1). As to the Clerk of the Crown in Chancery see CONSTITUTIONAL LAW AND HUMAN RIGHTS vol 8(2) (Reissue) PARA 921.

2   See the Representation of the People Act 1983 Sch 1 r 1. As to the issue of the warrant for the writ in the case of a by-election see PARA 191.

     Where a vacancy occurs before or immediately after the first meeting of a new Parliament, the writ to fill the vacancy will not be issued until the time for presenting election petitions has expired; and if an election petition claiming the seat is pending, the writ will not be issued until after the petition has been tried or withdrawn: see PARLIAMENT vol 78 (2010) PARA 1094.

3   See the Representation of the People Act 1983 Sch 1 r 3(2). The form of the writ is set out in Sch 1, Appendix of Forms (Form of writ) (Form of writ amended by the Fixed-term Parliaments Act 2011 Schedule paras 6, 13): see the Representation of the People Act 1983 Sch 1 r 3(2). Any form in the Appendix may be adapted so far as circumstances require: Sch 1, Appendix of Forms (Note).

4   As to the meaning of 'constituency' for the purposes of parliamentary elections see PARA 9. As to returning officers for parliamentary elections generally see PARA 350 et seq.

5   See the Representation of the People Act 1983 Sch 1 r 3(2), Appendix of Forms (Form of writ (as amended: see note 3); Label or direction of writ). Her Majesty may by Order in Council:

(1)   specify the manner in which writs are to be conveyed, whether by post, by an officer appointed by the Lord Chancellor or otherwise, and make different provision for different classes of writs (Sch 1 r 3(3)(a)); and

(2)   provide for the giving of receipts for writs by persons to whom they are delivered or who may receive them in the course of their conveyance (Sch 1 r 3(3)(b))

Such an order may:

(a)   require a returning officer to provide an address to which writs are to be conveyed and any change of that address (Sch 1 r 3(5)(a)); and

(b)   provide for recording those addresses (Sch 1 r 3(5)(b)); and

(c)   provide that the delivery of a writ to a person found in and for the time being in charge of a place so recorded as the office of a returning officer is as good as delivery to that returning officer (Sch 1 r 3(5)(c)).

A draft of such an order must be laid before Parliament, and any such order may provide for any incidental or supplemental matter: Sch 1 r 3(7). As to the order made see the Parliamentary Writs Order 1983, SI 1983/605; the text and notes 10–12; and PARAS 193–194. Where by virtue of the Representation of the People Act 1983 Sch 1 r 4 (see the text and notes 7–15) writs are conveyed to the acting returning officer, Sch 1 r 3(5) applies in relation to him as it applies in relation to a returning officer: Sch 1 r 4(3).

6   Representation of the People Act 1983 Sch 1 r 3(4).

7   As to the meaning of 'England' see PARA 1 note 1.

8   As to the meaning of 'Wales' see PARA 1 note 1.

9   See the Representation of the People Act 1983 Sch 1 r 4(1). This provision applies notwithstanding anything in Sch 1 r 3 (see the text and notes 3–6): see Sch 1 r 4(1). Any duty

imposed on a returning officer for a parliamentary election under Sch 1 r 3 is not to be discharged by the registration officer as acting returning officer (see s 28(2)(a); and PARA 351) but Sch 1 r 4 provides for the conveyance of a writ to the acting returning officer in certain cases notwithstanding anything set out in Sch 1 r 3 (see Sch 1 r 4(1)). See also the text and notes 5–6. As to the electoral registration officer see PARA 139 et seq.

10 Ie by notice in the form prescribed by an Order in Council under the Representation of the People Act 1983 Sch 1 r 3: see Sch 1 r 4(1)(a). The form of notice by a returning officer requesting that the writ be conveyed to the acting returning officer is prescribed by the Parliamentary Writs Order 1983, SI 1983/605, art 3(1), Schedule para 1 (Form of notice by returning officer requesting that the writ be conveyed to the acting returning officer) (amended in relation to England by SI 2002/1057). A form to the like effect may be used: see the Parliamentary Writs Order 1983, SI 1983/605, art 3(1).

Any notice which was given under the Parliamentary Writs Order 1944, SR & O 1944/334 (revoked by the Parliamentary Writs Order 1983, SI 1983/605, art 12(1)), which was in force at the coming into operation of the Parliamentary Writs Order 1983, SI 1983/605, continues to have effect as if made under the latter order: art 12(2).

11 Representation of the People Act 1983 Sch 1 r 4(1)(a). The returning officer must forthwith send a copy of the notice to the appropriate acting returning officer so that the latter may comply with the duty in the Parliamentary Writs Order 1983, SI 1983/605, art 5(2) to provide to the relevant universal postal service provider an address at which the writ may be conveyed: art 4. As to the duty to provide such an address see PARA 193.

12 The form of notice by a returning officer revoking the notice requesting that the writ be conveyed to the acting returning officer is prescribed by the Parliamentary Writs Order 1983, SI 1983/605, art 3(2), Schedule para 2 (Form of notice by returning officer revoking the notice set out in paragraph 1 above) (amended in relation to England by SI 2002/1057). A form to the like effect may be used: see the Parliamentary Writs Order 1983, SI 1983/605, art 3(2).

13 Representation of the People Act 1983 Sch 1 r 4(1)(b). See also note 10.

14 Representation of the People Act 1983 Sch 1 r 4(2)(a).

15 Representation of the People Act 1983 Sch 1 r 4(2)(b).

193.   Parliamentary writs list. Every returning officer for a constituency[1] must provide to the relevant universal postal service provider[2] an address at which the writ for a parliamentary election may be conveyed to him[3]:

(1)   if he is requested by the relevant universal postal service provider so to do[4]; or

(2)   on the revocation of any notice requesting the writ to be conveyed to the acting returning officer[5].

Where the writ is to be conveyed to the acting returning officer by virtue of such a notice[6], he must:

(a)   on being informed that it has been given[7]; or

(b)   if requested by the relevant universal postal service provider so to do[8], provide to the relevant universal postal service provider such an address[9]. On any change of that address, the returning officer (or, as the case may be, acting returning officer) must as soon as possible provide to the relevant universal postal service provider a new address at which the writ may be conveyed[10].

The relevant universal postal service provider is required to keep a list called the 'parliamentary writs list' setting out[11], by the title of his office, each returning officer[12] or acting returning officer[13] to whom a writ is required to be conveyed and recording as the office of that officer the address last provided by him[14]. The relevant universal postal service provider must also assign to an appointed postal official, in respect of each returning officer or acting returning officer set out in the parliamentary writs list, the duty of securing the delivery of any writ required to be delivered to that officer[15]. The designation and address of the official so appointed is to be entered in the list together with a reference to the officer to whom he is required to secure the delivery of any such writ[16]. As soon as practicable after: (i) a new parliamentary writs list has been prepared[17]; or (ii) alterations have been made to such a list[18], the relevant universal postal service provider must send a copy of the list or, as the case may be, the alterations to the Clerk of the Crown in Chancery[19].

1   As to the meaning of 'constituency' for the purposes of parliamentary elections see PARA 9. As to returning officers for parliamentary elections generally see PARA 350 et seq.
2   For these purposes, the 'relevant universal postal service provider' means the universal service provider, within the meaning of the Postal Services Act 2011 Pt 3 (ss 27–67) (regulation of postal services) (see POSTAL SERVICES vol 85 (2012) PARA 252), responsible for conveying writs: see the Parliamentary Writs Order 1983, SI 1983/605, art 2 (definition added by SI 2001/1149; amended by SI 2011/2085).
3   See the Parliamentary Writs Order 1983, SI 1983/605, art 5(1) (amended by SI 2001/1149). As to the issue and conveyance of writs for parliamentary elections see PARA 192.
4   Parliamentary Writs Order 1983, SI 1983/605, art 5(1)(a) (amended by SI 2001/1149).
5   Parliamentary Writs Order 1983, SI 1983/605, art 5(1)(b). The text refers to a notice given under the Representation of the People Act 1983 Sch 1 r 4(1)(a) which may be revoked by a notice under Sch 1 r 4(1)(b) (see PARA 192): see the Parliamentary Writs Order 1983, SI 1983/605, art 5(1)(b).
6   Ie a notice given under the Representation of the People Act 1983 Sch 1 r 4(1)(a) (see PARA 192): see the Parliamentary Writs Order 1983, SI 1983/605, art 5(2).
7   Parliamentary Writs Order 1983, SI 1983/605, art 5(2)(a). The returning officer is required forthwith to copy the notice to the acting returning officer so that the duty in art 5(2) may be complied with: see PARA 192 note 11.
8   Parliamentary Writs Order 1983, SI 1983/605, art 5(2)(b) (amended by SI 2001/1149).
9   Parliamentary Writs Order 1983, SI 1983/605, art 5(2) (amended by SI 2001/1149).
10 See the Parliamentary Writs Order 1983, SI 1983/605, art 5(1), (2) (as amended: see notes 3, 9).
11 See the Parliamentary Writs Order 1983, SI 1983/605, art 6 (amended by SI 2001/1149). For these purposes, 'parliamentary writs list' means the list prepared and kept in accordance with the Parliamentary Writs Order 1983, SI 1983/605, art 6: see art 2.
12 Ie in respect of whom a notice given under the Representation of the People Act 1983 Sch 1 r 4(1)(a) is not in force (see PARA 192): see the Parliamentary Writs Order 1983, SI 1983/605, art 6(a).
13 Ie in respect of whom a notice given under the Representation of the People Act 1983 Sch 1 r 4(1)(a) is in force (see PARA 192): see the Parliamentary Writs Order 1983, SI 1983/605, art 6(b).
14 See the Parliamentary Writs Order 1983, SI 1983/605, art 6(a), (b). The text refers to the last address provided by the returning officer under art 5(1) (see the text and notes 1–5, 10) (see art 6(a)) or by the acting returning officer under art 5(2) (see the text and notes 6–10) (see art 6(b)), as the case may be.
15 See the Parliamentary Writs Order 1983, SI 1983/605, art 7(1) (amended by SI 2001/1149). The text refers to any writ for a parliamentary election required to be conveyed to the officer under the Representation of the People Act 1983 Sch 1 r 3 (see PARA 192) or Sch 1 r 4 (see PARA 192): see the Parliamentary Writs Order 1983, SI 1983/605, art 7(1) (as so amended).
16 Parliamentary Writs Order 1983, SI 1983/605, art 7(2).
17 Parliamentary Writs Order 1983, SI 1983/605, art 8(a).
18 Parliamentary Writs Order 1983, SI 1983/605, art 8(b).
19 Parliamentary Writs Order 1983, SI 1983/605, art 8 (amended by SI 2001/1149). As to the Clerk of the Crown in Chancery see CONSTITUTIONAL LAW AND HUMAN RIGHTS vol 8(2) (Reissue) PARA 921.

194.   Conveyance of writs for parliamentary elections. As soon as may be after the issue of a writ for a parliamentary election[1], the Clerk of the Crown in Chancery[2] must cause to be sent by the registered post service of the relevant universal postal service provider[3] to the postal official appearing from the parliamentary writs list to be charged with the duty of securing the delivery of the writ (the 'appropriate official')[4], a package containing the writ[5], instructions from the relevant universal postal service provider to him as to the delivery of the writ[6] and a form of receipt to be signed by the person to whom the writ is delivered[7]. On receipt of this package, the appropriate official must forthwith convey the writ, or cause it to be conveyed, to the returning officer[8] or, as the case may be, acting returning officer[9] to whom it is addressed[10]. The person to whom the writ is so delivered is required to sign the form of receipt and deliver the receipt to the appropriate official or the person acting on his behalf[11]. He must also endorse the writ with a statement signed by him as to the date on which he received it[12]. The appropriate official must as soon as practicable send by the registered post service of the relevant universal postal service provider to the Clerk of the Crown in Chancery the receipt for the delivery of the writ[13].

1   As to the issue and conveyance of writs for parliamentary elections see PARA 192.
2   As to the Clerk of the Crown in Chancery see CONSTITUTIONAL LAW AND HUMAN RIGHTS vol 8(2) (Reissue) PARA 921.
3   For these purposes, 'registered post service' means a postal service which provides for the registration of postal packets in connection with their transmission by post and for the payment of compensation for any loss or damage: see the Postal Services Act 2000 s 125(1); definition applied by the Parliamentary Writs Order 1983, SI 1983/605, art 2 (definition added by SI 2001/1149). As to the meaning of 'relevant universal postal service provider' see PARA 193 note 2.
4   As to the appointment of postal officials see PARA 193.
5   See the Parliamentary Writs Order 1983, SI 1983/605, arts 9, 10(1) (art 10(1) amended by SI 2001/1149).
6   See the Parliamentary Writs Order 1983, SI 1983/605, arts 9, 10(2)(a) (art 10(2)(a) amended by SI 2001/1149).
7   See the Parliamentary Writs Order 1983, SI 1983/605, arts 9, 10(2)(b).
8   As to returning officers for parliamentary elections generally see PARA 350 et seq.
9   As to the appointment of acting returning officers to whom the writ must be conveyed see PARA 192.
10 See the Parliamentary Writs Order 1983, SI 1983/605, arts 9, 11(1). Delivery of the writ to a person found in or for the time being in charge of the place which is recorded in the parliamentary writs lists as being the office of the returning officer or, as the case may be, acting returning officer is as good as delivery to that officer: see arts 9, 11(1).
11 See the Parliamentary Writs Order 1983, SI 1983/605, arts 9, 11(2).
12 Representation of the People Act 1983 Sch 1 r 3(6), Appendix of Forms (Endorsement).
13 See the Parliamentary Writs Order 1983, SI 1983/605, arts 9, 11(3) (art 11(3) amended by SI 2001/1149).

195. Polling days for parliamentary elections. In the case of a parliamentary general election[1], the day of polling is the day either determined or appointed under the Fixed-term Parliaments Act 2011[2]. Accordingly, the polling day for the next parliamentary general election after 15 September 2011[3] is to be 7 May 2015[4], and the polling day for each subsequent parliamentary general election is to be the first Thursday in May in the fifth calendar year following that in which the polling day for the previous parliamentary general election fell[5]. These timings are modified, however, if the polling day for the previous parliamentary general election was appointed under the Fixed-term Parliaments Act 2011[6], and if, in the calendar year in which it fell, that polling day fell before the first Thursday in May[7]. The Prime Minister may by order made by statutory instrument[8] provide that the polling day for a parliamentary general election in a specified calendar year is to be later than the day determined in this way[9], but may not be more than two months later[10].

Notwithstanding this provision[11], an early parliamentary general election may take place if[12]:

(1)   the House of Commons passes a motion in the form[13]: 'That there shall be an early parliamentary general election'[14]; and
(2)   if the motion is passed on a division, the number of members who vote in favour of the motion is a number equal to or greater than two thirds of the number of seats in the House (including vacant seats)[15].

An early parliamentary general election is also to take place if[16]:

(a)   the House of Commons passes a motion in the form[17]: 'That this House has no confidence in Her Majesty's government'[18]; and

(b)   the period of 14 days after the day on which that motion is passed ends without the House passing a motion in the form[19]: 'That this House has confidence in Her Majesty's government'[20].

For the purposes of the parliamentary elections timetable[21], as set out in the parliamentary elections rules[22], if a parliamentary general election is to take place as provided for by the Fixed-term Parliaments Act 2011[23], the polling day for the election is to be the day appointed by Her Majesty by proclamation on the recommendation of the Prime Minister[24] (and, accordingly, the appointed day replaces the day which would otherwise have been the polling day for the next election determined under the Fixed-term Parliaments Act 2011)[25].

In the case of a parliamentary by-election, the day of polling is fixed by the returning officer[26] and must not be earlier than the ninth nor later than the eleventh day after the last day for delivery of nomination papers[27].

1   As to parliamentary elections, and as to use of the term 'parliamentary general election', see PARA 9.
2   See the Representation of the People Act 1983 Sch 1 r 1 (amended by the Fixed-term Parliaments Act 2011 s 6(3), Schedule paras 6, 10(1), (4)). The text refers to the day determined under the Fixed-term Parliaments Act 2011 s 1 (see the text and notes 3–10), or appointed under s 2(7) (see the text and notes 23–25): see the Representation of the People Act 1983 Sch 1 r 1 (as so amended). The Fixed-term Parliaments Act 2011 s 1 applies for the purposes of the timetable in the Representation of the People Act 1983 Sch 1 r 1 and is subject to the Fixed-term Parliaments Act 2011 s 2 (see the text and notes 11–25): s 1(1).
3   Ie after the passing of the Fixed-term Parliaments Act 2011: see s 1(2). The Fixed-term Parliaments Act 2011 received Royal Assent on 15 September 2011 (see Preamble), and came into force on the day that it was passed (see s 7(2)).
4   Fixed-term Parliaments Act 2011 s 1(2). A general election for the National Assembly for Wales is not to fall on the same date as a parliamentary general election under s 1(2): see s 5; and PARA 189 note 4. Similar provision is made in relation to general elections for the Scottish Parliament: see s 4; and PARA 189 note 4.
5   Fixed-term Parliaments Act 2011 s 1(3).
6   Ie appointed under the Fixed-term Parliaments Act 2011 s 2(7) (see the text and notes 23–25): see s 1(4).
7   See the Fixed-term Parliaments Act 2011 s 1(4). In the circumstances described in the text, s 1(3) has effect as if for 'fifth' there were substituted 'fourth': see s 1(4). In other words, if the early election is held before the first Thursday in May in an election year, the next general election will be held on the first Thursday in May in the fourth year from the previous election.
8   A statutory instrument containing an order under the Fixed-term Parliaments Act 2011 s 1(5) may not be made unless a draft has been laid before and approved by a resolution of each House of Parliament: s 1(6). The draft laid before Parliament must be accompanied by a statement setting out the Prime Minister's reasons for proposing the change in the polling day: s 1(7). It is intended that the power for the Prime Minister to defer the date of a scheduled parliamentary general election would accommodate short term crises or other conditions which might make it inappropriate to hold the election on the scheduled date (e g a repeat of the foot and mouth crisis which led to the postponement of the local elections in 2001): see Explanatory Notes to the Fixed-term Parliaments Act 2011 para 26.
9   Ie determined under the Fixed-term Parliaments Act 2011 s 1(2) (see the text and notes 3–4) or s 1(3) (see the text and note 5): see s 1(5).
10   Fixed-term Parliaments Act 2011 s 1(5).
11   Ie notwithstanding the Fixed-term Parliaments Act 2011 s 1: see the text and notes 3–10.
12   See the Fixed-term Parliaments Act 2011 s 2(1).
13   Fixed-term Parliaments Act 2011 s 2(1)(a). The form of the motion must be that set out in s 2(2) (see the text and note 14): see s 2(1)(a).
14   See the Fixed-term Parliaments Act 2011 s 2(2).
15   Fixed-term Parliaments Act 2011 s 2(1)(b).
16   See the Fixed-term Parliaments Act 2011 s 2(3).
17   Fixed-term Parliaments Act 2011 s 2(3)(a). The form of the motion must be that set out in s 2(4) (see the text and note 18): see s 2(3)(a).

18 See the Fixed-term Parliaments Act 2011 s 2(4).

19 Fixed-term Parliaments Act 2011 s 2(3)(b). The form of the motion must be that set out in s 2(5) (see the text and note 20): see s 2(3)(b).

20 See the Fixed-term Parliaments Act 2011 s 2(5).

21 Ie for the purposes of the timetable in the Representation of the People Act 1983 Sch 1 r 1 (see the text and notes 1–2): see the Fixed-term Parliaments Act 2011 s 2(6).

22 See the Fixed-term Parliaments Act 2011 s 2(6). As to the parliamentary elections rules see PARA 383.

23 Ie as provided for by the Fixed-term Parliaments Act 2011 s 1(2) (see the text and notes 3–4) or s 1(3) (see the text and note 5): see s 2(7).

24 As to the issue of a royal proclamation summoning a new Parliament see the Fixed-term Parliaments Act 2011 s 3(4); and PARA 189.

25 See the Fixed-term Parliaments Act 2011 s 2(7). The text refers to the day which would otherwise have been the polling day for the next election determined under s 1 (see the text and notes 3–10): see s 2(7).

26 As to returning officers for parliamentary elections generally see PARA 350 et seq.

27 See the Representation of the People Act 1983 Sch 1 r 1 (amended by the Representation of the People Act 1985 s 24, Sch 4 para 73). As from a day to be appointed under the Electoral Registration and Administration Act 2013 s 27(1), the 'Polling' entry in the timetable set out in the Representation of the People Act 1983 Sch 1 r 1 is amended so that the day fixed by the returning officer 'must not be earlier than the seventeenth nor later than the nineteenth day': see Sch 1 r 1 (prospectively amended by the Electoral Registration and Administration Act 2013 s 14(2)). However, at the date at which this volume states the law, no such day had been appointed. As to the delivery of nomination papers for candidates at parliamentary by-elections see PARA 260.

In computing any period of time for the purposes of the timetable in the Representation of the People Act 1983 Sch 1 r 1, the following must be disregarded (see Sch 1 r 2(1) (amended by the Fixed-term Parliaments Act 2011 Schedule paras 6, 11(1), (2))):

(1) a Saturday or Sunday (Representation of the People Act 1983 Sch 1 r 2(1)(a));

(2) Christmas Eve, Christmas Day, Good Friday or a bank holiday (Sch 1 r 2(1)(b) (substituted by the Representation of the People Act 1985 s 19; and amended by the Electoral Administration Act 2006 ss 20, 74(2), Sch 1 paras 49, 52, Sch 2)); or

(3) a day appointed for public thanksgiving or mourning (Representation of the People Act 1983 Sch 1 r 2(1)(c)).

For these purposes, 'bank holiday' means:

(a) in relation to a general election, a day which is a bank holiday under the Banking and Financial Dealings Act 1971 in any part of the United Kingdom (see TIME vol 97 (2010) PARA 321) (Representation of the People Act 1983 Sch 1 r 2(2)(a));

(b) in relation to a by-election, a day which is a bank holiday under the Banking and Financial Dealings Act 1971 in that part of the United Kingdom in which the constituency is situated (Representation of the People Act 1983 Sch 1 r 2(2)(b)),

but head (b) above and not head (a) above applies at a general election in relation to any proceedings commenced afresh by reason of a candidate's death (see Sch 1 r 2(2) (amended by the Fixed-term Parliaments Act 2011 Schedule paras 6, 11(1), (4))). In relation to a general election, any day within heads (1) to (3) above is not to be treated as a day for the purpose of any proceedings in the timetable before the polling day (Representation of the People Act 1983 Sch 1 r 2(1A) (Sch 1 r 2(1A), (1B), (2A) added by the Fixed-term Parliaments Act 2011 Schedule, paras 6, 11(1), (3), (5))); and, in relation to a by-election, any day within heads (1) to (3) above is not to be treated as a day for the purpose of any proceedings in the timetable up to the completion of the poll nor is the returning officer obliged to proceed with the counting of the votes on such a day (Representation of the People Act 1983 Sch 1 r 2(1B) (as so added)). In relation to a general election, Sch 1 r 2 does not apply to a day which is a bank holiday, or a day appointed for public thanksgiving or mourning, if the day was not fixed or appointed as such before the dissolution of Parliament by the Fixed-term Parliaments Act 2011 s 1 (see the text and notes 3–10), or if the day is one that is treated as a working day by s 3(6) (see PARA 189 note 7) (see the Representation of the People Act 1983 Sch 1 r 2(2A) (as so added)). However, in relation to any proceedings commenced afresh by reason of a candidate's death, Sch 1 r 2(2A) is to be ignored: see Sch 1 r 2(2A) (as so added). As to the meaning of 'United Kingdom' see PARA 1 note 1. As to writs for by-elections see PARA 191. As to the counting of votes at a parliamentary election see PARA 425. As to proceedings commenced afresh by reason of a candidate's death see PARA 515.

196.   Notice of election at parliamentary election. Not later than 4 pm on the second day after that on which the writ for a parliamentary general election or parliamentary by-election is received[1], the returning officer[2] must publish notice of the election[3]. The notice must state:

(1)   the place and times at which nomination papers are to be delivered[4], and that forms of nomination papers may be obtained at that place and those times[5];

(2)   the date of the poll in the event of a contest[6];

(3)   the date by which[7] applications to vote by post or by proxy[8], and other applications and notices about postal or proxy voting[9], must reach the electoral registration officer in order that they may be effective for the election[10]; and

(4)   the arrangements which apply for the payment of the deposit[11] to be made by means of the electronic transfer of funds[12].

1   See the Representation of the People Act 1983 Sch 1 r 1. As to the computation of time for the purposes of Sch 1 r 1 see PARA 195 note 27. As to the conveyance of writs for parliamentary elections see PARA 194.

2   As to returning officers for parliamentary elections generally see PARA 350 et seq.

3   Representation of the People Act 1983 Sch 1 rr 1, 5(1) (r 5(1) amended by the Representation of the People Act 1985 ss 24, 28, Sch 4 para 74, Sch 5). As to the giving of public notices by a returning officer for a parliamentary election see PARA 350.

4   Representation of the People Act 1983 Sch 1 r 5(1)(a). As to the nomination of candidates at parliamentary elections see PARA 224 et seq.

5   See the Representation of the People Act 1983 Sch 1 r 5(1).

6   Representation of the People Act 1983 Sch 1 r 5(1)(b). As to the date of the poll at a parliamentary election see PARA 195.

7   Ie except in such circumstances as may be prescribed: see the Representation of the People Act 1983 Sch 1 r 5(2) (amended by the Representation of the People Act 2000 s 15(1), Sch 6 paras 3, 10(1), (2)). 'Prescribed' means prescribed by regulations: see the Representation of the People Act 1983 s 202(1). As to the making of regulations under the Representation of the People Act 1983 generally see PARA 28 note 16. At the date at which this volume states the law, no such regulations had been made under Sch 1 r 5.

8   See the Representation of the People Act 1983 Sch 1 r 5(2)(a) (amended by the Representation of the People Act 1985 s 11, Sch 2 para 4). As to applications to vote by post or by proxy see PARA 367 et seq.

9   See the Representation of the People Act 1983 Sch 1 r 5(2)(b).

10 See the Representation of the People Act 1983 Sch 1 r 5(2). As to the electoral registration officer see PARA 139 et seq.

11 Ie the deposit required by the Representation of the People Act 1983 Sch 1 r 9 (see PARA 259): see Sch 1 r 5(1A) (added by the Electoral Administration Act 2006 s 19(1), (3)).

12 Representation of the People Act 1983 Sch 1 r 5(1A) (as added: see note 11).

(ii)   Initiating a Local Government Election

A.   ORDINARY ELECTIONS

197.   Ordinary election of councillors for local government principal areas. In England[1]:

(1)   county councillors are elected every four years[2] and serve a four-year term, retiring on the fourth day after the election of their successors[3];

(2)   metropolitan district councillors[4], elected in every year other than a year of election of county councillors[5], serve a four-year term, and one-third of the whole number of councillors in each ward, being those who have been councillors for the longest time without re-election, retire in every ordinary year of election of such councillors on the fourth day after the day of the election[6]; and

(3)   non-metropolitan district councillors[7] are elected for a term of office lasting four years[8], with the years of election being every fourth year[9] except where an order is made for a district to have elections by thirds, in which case the elections take place in the year when that order comes into force and in every year thereafter which is not a county council election year[10].

Further to head (3) above, where whole-council elections are in force, the whole number of non-metropolitan district councillors retire simultaneously in every ordinary year of election of such councillors on the fourth day after the ordinary day of election[11]. Where election by thirds is in force, one-third of the non-metropolitan district councillors, being those who have served longest without re-election, retire in every ordinary year of election of such councillors on the fourth day after the ordinary day of election[12].

The ordinary elections of London borough councillors[13] take place at four-yearly intervals[14]. The term of office of London borough councillors is four years; the councillors retire together in every fourth year on the fourth day after the ordinary day of election[15]. If a municipal election in a London borough is not held on the appointed day or within the appointed time or becomes void, the municipal corporation is not thereby dissolved or disabled from acting[16].

In Wales[17], the ordinary elections of councillors of principal councils[18] take place in every fourth year[19]. The term of office of every such councillor is four years[20]. The persons who were councillors immediately before any ordinary election retire on the fourth day after the election[21].

In all cases newly-elected councillors come into office on the day on which their predecessors retire[22].

1   As to the meaning of 'England' see PARA 1 note 1. As to the establishment of electoral areas for the purpose of local government elections in England see PARA 74.

2   County councillors were elected in 1973 and are elected in every fourth year thereafter.: see the Local Government Act 1972 s 7(1); and LOCAL GOVERNMENT vol 69 (2009) PARA 128. As to counties in England see LOCAL GOVERNMENT vol 69 (2009) PARA 24 et seq. Consequent on the abolition of metropolitan councils in England by the Local Government Act 1985, such elections take place only in non-metropolitan counties: see LOCAL GOVERNMENT vol 69 (2009) PARA 17.

3   See the Local Government Act 1972 s 7(1); and LOCAL GOVERNMENT vol 69 (2009) PARA 128.

4   As to districts in England see LOCAL GOVERNMENT vol 69 (2009) PARA 24.

5   See the Local Government Act 1972 s 7(2), which specifies that the elections are to take place in every year other than 1977 and every fourth year thereafter. See further LOCAL GOVERNMENT vol 69 (2009) PARA 129.

6   See the Local Government Act 1972 s 7(3); and LOCAL GOVERNMENT vol 69 (2009) PARA 129.

7   As to the meaning of 'non-metropolitan district' see LOCAL GOVERNMENT vol 69 (2009) PARA 24.

8   See the Local Government Act 1972 s 7(9)(a); and LOCAL GOVERNMENT vol 69 (2009) PARA 130.

9   See the Local Government Act 1972 s 7(8)(a); and LOCAL GOVERNMENT vol 69 (2009) PARA 130. Such elections took place in 1979 and have taken place at four-yearly intervals thereafter.

10 See the Local Government Act 1972 s 7(8)(b); and LOCAL GOVERNMENT vol 69 (2009) PARA 130.

11 See the Local Government Act 1972 s 7(9)(b); and LOCAL GOVERNMENT vol 69 (2009) PARA 130.

12 See the Local Government Act 1972 s 7(9)(c); and LOCAL GOVERNMENT vol 69 (2009) PARA 130. Where the number of councillors in a non-metropolitan district ward is not divisible by three and where election by thirds operates, as nearly as may be one-third of the councillors, being those who have served longest without re-election, are to retire: see s 7(9)(c); and LOCAL GOVERNMENT vol 69 (2009) PARA 130.

13 As to the London boroughs and their councils see LOCAL GOVERNMENT vol 69 (2009) PARA 35; LONDON GOVERNMENT vol 71 (2013) PARA 15 et seq.

14 See the Local Government Act 1972 s 8(1), Sch 2 para 6(3); and LONDON GOVERNMENT vol 71 (2013) PARA 21. Such elections took place in 1974 and take place at four-yearly intervals thereafter: see Sch 2 para 6(3); and LONDON GOVERNMENT vol 71 (2013) PARA 21.
15 See the Local Government Act 1972 Sch 2 para 6(3); and LONDON GOVERNMENT vol 71 (2013) PARA 21.
16 See the Representation of the People Act 1983 s 39(9); and PARA 670.
17 As to the meaning of 'Wales' see PARA 1 note 1. As to the establishment of electoral areas for the purpose of local government elections in Wales see PARA 74.
18 As to the meaning of 'principal council' see LOCAL GOVERNMENT vol 69 (2009) PARA 23.
19 See the Local Government Act 1972 s 26(1); and LOCAL GOVERNMENT vol 69 (2009) PARA 131. Such elections took place in 2004 and are to take place at four-yearly intervals thereafter: see s 26(1); and LOCAL GOVERNMENT vol 69 (2009) PARA 131.
20 See the Local Government Act 1972 s 26(2); and LOCAL GOVERNMENT vol 69 (2009) PARA 131.
21 See the Local Government Act 1972 s 26(3)(a); and LOCAL GOVERNMENT vol 69 (2009) PARA 131.
22 See the Local Government Act 1972 ss 7(1), (3), (9)(b), (c), 26(3)(b), Sch 2 para 6(3); and LOCAL GOVERNMENT vol 69 (2009) PARAS 128–131; LONDON GOVERNMENT vol 71 (2013) PARA 21.

198.   Ordinary election of local authority mayor. The Secretary of State in England[1], or, in Wales, the Welsh Ministers[2], may by regulations make provision[3]:

(1)   as to the dates on which and years in which elections for the return of elected mayors may or must take place[4];

(2)   as to the intervals between elections for the return of elected mayors[5]; and

(3)   as to the term of office of elected mayors[6].

Subject to head (3) above, the term of office of an elected mayor of a local authority is to be four years[7].

Accordingly, the election for the return of an elected mayor in England takes place[8] on the ordinary day of election[9] in a year in which ordinary elections of councillors of the local authority are held, as may be specified in or determined under the local authority's executive arrangements[10]. Such an election may not take place before the end of the period of 23 months beginning with the date on which the first election for the return of an elected mayor of that authority took place[11], but it must take place no later than 67 months beginning with the date on which that first election took place[12].

Special provision is made: (a) for elections held after a referendum[13] has approved proposals to change executive arrangements[14]; and (b) for elections after the second election held otherwise than in accordance with the above provisions[15].

An individual elected as mayor comes into office on the fourth day after the election at which he or she was elected and, unless he or she resigns or otherwise ceases to hold office, holds office until his or her successor comes into office[16].

1   As to the meaning of 'England' see PARA 1 note 1. As to the Secretary of State for these purposes see PARA 2.
2   As to the meaning of 'Wales' see PARA 1 note 1. As to the Welsh Ministers see PARA 2.
3   See the Local Government Act 2000 ss 9HB, 41; and LOCAL GOVERNMENT vol 69 (2009) PARA 320. As to the regulations made under s 9HB see the Local Authorities (Elected Mayors) (Elections, Terms of Office and Casual Vacancies) (England) Regulations 2012, SI 2012/336. At the date at which this volume states the law, no regulations had been made under the Local Government Act 2000 s 41 in relation to Wales.
4   See the Local Government Act 2000 ss 9HB(a), 41(a); and LOCAL GOVERNMENT vol 69 (2009) PARA 320. For these purposes, 'elected mayor', in relation to a local authority, means an individual elected as mayor of the authority by the local government electors for the authority's area in accordance with the provisions made by or under either the Local Government Act 2000 Pt 1A (ss 9B–9R) (arrangements with respect to local governance in England) or Pt II

(ss 10–48A) (Local authorities in Wales: arrangements with respect to executives etc) (see LOCAL GOVERNMENT vol 69 (2009) PARA 303 et seq), as the case may be: see ss 9H(1), 39(1); and LOCAL GOVERNMENT vol 69 (2009) PARA 320. As to the election and term of office of leaders in 'leader and cabinet executive' structures in England see ss 9I–9ID; and LOCAL GOVERNMENT. The provision made by Pt II has been amended by the Localism Act 2011 s 22, Sch 3 so that it confers powers on the Welsh Ministers only: see LOCAL GOVERNMENT vol 69 (2009) PARA 320.

5	See the Local Government Act 2000 ss 9HB(b), 41(b); and LOCAL GOVERNMENT vol 69 (2009) PARA 320.

6	See the Local Government Act 2000 ss 9HB(c), 41(c); and LOCAL GOVERNMENT vol 69 (2009) PARA 320.

7	See the Local Government Act 2000 ss 9H(7), 39(6); and LOCAL GOVERNMENT vol 69 (2009) PARA 322. As to the filling of vacancies in the office of elected mayor see PARA 203.

8	Ie any election which takes place after the first election has been held in accordance with the Local Authorities (Elected Mayors) (Elections, Terms of Office and Casual Vacancies) (England) Regulations 2012, SI 2012/336, reg 3. For these purposes, 'election', except in reg 9 (see PARA 203), does not include an election to fill a casual vacancy: see reg 2(1).

9	For these purposes, the 'ordinary day of election', in relation to any year, means the day in that year on which, in accordance with the Representation of the People Act 1983 s 37 (see PARA 206), councillors are elected for local government areas: see the Local Authorities (Elected Mayors) (Elections, Terms of Office and Casual Vacancies) (England) Regulations 2012, SI 2012/336, reg 2(1).

10	See the Local Authorities (Elected Mayors) (Elections, Terms of Office and Casual Vacancies) (England) Regulations 2012, SI 2012/336, reg 4(1).

11	See the Local Authorities (Elected Mayors) (Elections, Terms of Office and Casual Vacancies) (England) Regulations 2012, SI 2012/336, reg 4(2).

12	See the Local Authorities (Elected Mayors) (Elections, Terms of Office and Casual Vacancies) (England) Regulations 2012, SI 2012/336, reg 4(3).

13	Ie held under the Local Government Act 2000 Pt 1A Ch 4 (ss 9K–9OA) (changing governance arrangements: see LOCAL GOVERNMENT).

14	See the Local Authorities (Elected Mayors) (Elections, Terms of Office and Casual Vacancies) (England) Regulations 2012, SI 2012/336, regs 5, 6.

15	Ie elections other than elections held under the Local Authorities (Elected Mayors) (Elections, Terms of Office and Casual Vacancies) (England) Regulations 2012, SI 2012/336, regs 3–6 (see the text and notes 8–14): see reg 7.

16	See the Local Authorities (Elected Mayors) (Elections, Terms of Office and Casual Vacancies) (England) Regulations 2012, SI 2012/336, reg 8(1). This is subject to the provisions of reg 8(2), (3) which deal with circumstances:

   (1)	where a local authority which operates a mayor and cabinet executive passes a resolution to make a change in governance arrangements of the kind set out in the Local Government Act 2000 s 9K or 9KA (see LOCAL GOVERNMENT) (see the Local Authorities (Elected Mayors) (Elections, Terms of Office and Casual Vacancies) (England) Regulations 2012, SI 2012/336, reg 8(2)); or

   (2)	where the result of a further referendum is to reject the continuation of the existing mayor and cabinet executive (reg 8(3)).

'Further referendum' means a referendum held in pursuance of the order of an election court under the Local Authorities (Conduct of Referendums) (England) Regulations 2012, SI 2012/323, reg 17(5) (determination of referendum petitions, and subsequent procedures: see PARA 866); and 'referendum' means a referendum held under the Local Government Act 2000 s 9M (referendum in cases where change of governance arrangements is subject to approval: see LOCAL GOVERNMENT), or by virtue of regulations or an order made under any provision of Pt 1A (see LOCAL GOVERNMENT), other than a further referendum: see the Local Authorities (Elected Mayors) (Elections, Terms of Office and Casual Vacancies) (England) Regulations 2012, SI 2012/336, reg 2(1). As to executive and alternative arrangements and referendums for the approval of such arrangements generally see LOCAL GOVERNMENT vol 69 (2009) PARA 303 et seq.

**199.	London Assembly or London Mayoral ordinary elections.**	The Mayor of London[1] and members of the London Assembly[2] are returned in accordance with provision made in or by virtue of the Greater London Authority Act 1999 for the holding of ordinary elections[3] of the Mayor, the constituency members and the London members[4]. The term of office of the Mayor and Assembly members returned at an ordinary election begins on the second day after the day on which the last of the successful candidates at the ordinary election is declared to be returned[5], and it ends on the second day after the day on which the last of the successful candidates at the next ordinary election is declared to be returned[6].

The poll at each ordinary Authority election is held in the fourth calendar year following that in which the previous ordinary election was held[7].

1   As to the Mayor of London see LONDON GOVERNMENT vol 71 (2013) PARA 69.
2   As to the London Assembly, constituency members of the London Assembly, and London members of the London Assembly, see LONDON GOVERNMENT vol 71 (2013) PARA 70.
3   An ordinary election involves the holding of an election for the return of the Mayor, an election for the return of the London members and elections for the return of the constituency members: see the Greater London Authority Act 1999 s 2(7); and LONDON GOVERNMENT vol 71 (2013) PARA 77.
4   See the Greater London Authority Act 1999 s 2(6)(a); and LONDON GOVERNMENT vol 71 (2013) PARA 82. As to the filling of vacancies arising in the office of Mayor of London or in membership of the London Assembly see PARA 204.
5   See the Greater London Authority Act 1999 s 2(8)(a); and LONDON GOVERNMENT vol 71 (2013) PARA 82.
6   See the Greater London Authority Act 1999 s 2(8)(b); and LONDON GOVERNMENT vol 71 (2013) PARA 82.
7   See the Greater London Authority Act 1999 s 3(2); and LONDON GOVERNMENT vol 71 (2013) PARA 77. The Secretary of State retains a power to make an order fixing a day other than the first Thursday in May as the day of the poll: see the Representation of the People Act 1983 ss 37(2), 37A (applied by the Greater London Authority Act 1999 s 3(3)); and PARA 206. The poll at the first ordinary election was held on 4 May 2000 but provision was made for the Secretary of State to provide for a later date by order: see s 3(1).

200. Election of councillors for parish or community councils and of chairman for parish meetings. The ordinary elections of parish councillors in England[1], or community councillors in Wales[2], take place at four-yearly intervals[3]. Their term of office is four years[4]. The number of parish councillors for each parish must not be less than five[5]. The whole number of parish or community councillors retire together in every ordinary year of election of such councillors on the fourth day after the ordinary day of election, and the newly elected councillors come into office on the day on which their predecessors retire[6].

Where, at an ordinary election of parish or community councillors in England and Wales, an insufficient number of persons are or remain validly nominated[7] to fill the vacancies in respect of which the election is held[8], then, unless the number of newly elected members of the council in question is less than the number that constitutes a quorum for meetings of the council[9]:

(1)   those members may co-opt any person or persons to fill the vacancy or vacancies remaining unfilled[10];

(2)   in relation to any vacancy or vacancies that are not so filled, the district council[11] or, in the case of a community council, the county council or county borough council[12] may by order make any appointment or do anything which appears to it necessary or expedient for the proper holding of an election of a parish or community councillor or councillors or the first meeting of a parish or community council after an ordinary election of parish or community councillors and properly constituting the council, and may, if it appears necessary, direct the holding of an election or meeting and fix the date for it[13].

However, the powers mentioned in head (2) above must not be exercised before the expiry of the period of 35 days[14] beginning with the day on which the election is held[15].

In a parish not having a separate parish council, the chairman of a parish meeting is elected at its annual assembly and continues in office until his successor is elected[16]. A poll may be demanded before the conclusion of a parish or community meeting on any question arising[17] and, in the case of a parish meeting, such a question may involve appointment to any office[18].

1   As to the meaning of 'England' see PARA 1 note 1. As to parishes generally see LOCAL GOVERNMENT vol 69 (2009) PARA 27 et seq.

2   As to the meaning of 'Wales' see PARA 1 note 1. As to communities generally see LOCAL GOVERNMENT vol 69 (2009) PARA 41 et seq.

3   See the Local Government Act 1972 s 16(3), s 35(2); and LOCAL GOVERNMENT vol 69 (2009) PARAS 132–133. Such parish elections took place in 1979 and take place at four-yearly intervals thereafter; and such community elections took place in 2004 and are to take place at four-yearly intervals thereafter. As to the appointment of community youth representatives by community councils see the Local Government (Wales) Measure 2011 Pt 7 Ch 4 (ss 118–121); and LOCAL GOVERNMENT.

4   See the Local Government Act 1972 s 16(3), s 35(2A); and LOCAL GOVERNMENT vol 69 (2009) PARAS 132–133.

5   See the Local Government Act 1972 s 16(1); and LOCAL GOVERNMENT vol 69 (2009) PARA 33. There is no provision corresponding to this in respect of community councillors.

6   See the Local Government Act 1972 s 16(3), s 35(2B); and LOCAL GOVERNMENT vol 69 (2009) PARAS 132–133.

7   As to the procedure where a poll is not necessary see PARA 482.

8   See the Representation of the People Act 1985 s 21(1). As to the filling of casual vacancies in parish or community councils see PARA 205.

9   See the Representation of the People Act 1985 s 21(2). Subject to the provision which applies where more than one-third of the members of a local authority become disqualified at the same time (see the Local Government Act 1972 s 99, Sch 12 para 45; and LOCAL GOVERNMENT vol 69 (2009) PARA 630), no business may be transacted at a meeting of a parish or community council unless at least one-third of the whole number of members are present; but notwithstanding anything in that provision in no case may the quorum be less than three: see Sch 12 paras 12, 28; and LOCAL GOVERNMENT vol 69 (2009) PARA 634.

10   Representation of the People Act 1985 s 21(2)(a). As to the requirement of public notice where vacancies in community council membership are to be filled by co-option see the Local Government (Wales) Measure 2011 ss 116, 117; and LOCAL GOVERNMENT.

11   As to the council of a district in England see LOCAL GOVERNMENT vol 69 (2009) PARA 24 et seq. In the case of a common parish council under which are grouped, by virtue of the Local Government Act 1972 s 11(5) (see LOCAL GOVERNMENT vol 69 (2009) PARA 29), parishes situated in different districts, the reference to the district council is to be construed as a reference to the council of the district in which there is the greater number of local electors for the parishes in the group: see the Representation of the People Act 1983 s 39(7); applied by the Representation of the People Act 1985 s 21(3).

12   See the Representation of the People Act 1985 s 21(2)(b) (amended by the Local Government (Wales) Act 1994 s 66(6), (8), Sch 16 para 74(2), Sch 18). As to the council of a county or county borough in Wales see LOCAL GOVERNMENT vol 69 (2009) PARA 37 et seq.

13   Representation of the People Act 1983 s 39(4) (amended by the Local Government (Wales) Act 1994 Sch 16 para 68(11)); applied by the Representation of the People Act 1985 s 21(2)(b) (as amended: see note 12).

14   The Representation of the People Act 1983 s 40(3) applies for the purposes of computing this period of 35 days as it applies for the purposes of s 39(1) (see PARA 209 note 7): see the Representation of the People Act 1985 s 21(2), (3).

15   See the Representation of the People Act 1985 s 21(2). The duty of the returning officer under the Representation of the People Act 1983 s 39(1) (see PARA 209) to order an election is disapplied: Representation of the People Act 1985 s 21(2)(c).

16   See the Local Government Act 1972 s 15(10); and LOCAL GOVERNMENT vol 69 (2009) PARA 146. In a parish having a separate parish council the chairman of the parish council, if present, presides at a parish meeting and if he is absent the vice-chairman (if any), if present, presides: see s 99, Sch 12 para 17(1); and LOCAL GOVERNMENT vol 69 (2009) PARA 637. In a parish which does not have a separate parish council the chairman chosen for the year in question under s 15(10) or s 88(3) (filling of casual vacancy: see LOCAL GOVERNMENT vol 69 (2009) PARA 148), if present, presides: see Sch 12 para 17(2); and LOCAL GOVERNMENT vol 69 (2009) PARA 637. If the chairman and the vice-chairman of the parish council or the chairman of the parish meeting,

as the case may be, is absent from an assembly of the parish meeting, the parish meeting may appoint a person to take the chair, and that person has, for the purposes of that meeting, the powers and authority of the chairman: see Sch 12 para 17(3); and LOCAL GOVERNMENT vol 69 (2009) PARA 637. As to community meetings see ss 27, 32; and LOCAL GOVERNMENT vol 69 (2009) PARA 46. In a community for which there is a community council, the chairman of the council, if present, presides at a community meeting (see Sch 12 para 33(1); and LOCAL GOVERNMENT vol 69 (2009) PARA 637); and in any other case a community meeting appoints a person to be chairman at that meeting (see Sch 12 para 33(2); and LOCAL GOVERNMENT vol 69 (2009) PARA 637).

17 See the Local Government Act 1972 Sch 12 paras 18, 34; and LOCAL GOVERNMENT vol 69 (2009) PARA 638. As to polls consequent on a parish or community meeting on a question not involving appointment to office see PARA 556 et seq.

18 See further LOCAL GOVERNMENT vol 69 (2009) PARA 638. There is no provision corresponding to this in respect of community meetings.

201. Insufficient nominations at ordinary election of parish and community councillors. Where, at an ordinary election of parish councillors in England[1], or community councillors in Wales[2], an insufficient number of persons are or remain validly nominated to fill the vacancies in respect of which the election is held[3], then, unless the number of newly elected members of the council in question is less than the number that constitutes a quorum for meetings of the council[4]:

(1) those members may co-opt any person or persons to fill the vacancy or vacancies remaining unfilled[5];

(2) in relation to any vacancy or vacancies that are not so filled, the district council[6] or, in the case of a community council, the county council or county borough council[7] may by order make any appointment or do anything which appears to it necessary or expedient for the proper holding of an election of a parish or community councillor or councillors or the first meeting of a parish or community council after an ordinary election of parish or community councillors and properly constituting the council[8], and may, if it appears necessary, direct the holding of an election or meeting and fix the date for it[9].

However, the powers mentioned in head (2) above must not be exercised before the expiry of the period of 35 days[10] beginning with the day on which the election is held[11].

1 As to the ordinary elections of parish councillors see PARA 200. As to the meaning of 'England' see PARA 1 note 1. As to parishes generally see LOCAL GOVERNMENT vol 69 (2009) PARA 27 et seq.

2 As to the ordinary elections of community councillors see PARA 200. As to the meaning of 'Wales' see PARA 1 note 1. As to communities generally see LOCAL GOVERNMENT vol 69 (2009) PARA 41 et seq.

3 See the Representation of the People Act 1985 s 21(1). As to the procedure where a poll is not necessary see PARA 482.

4 See the Representation of the People Act 1985 s 21(2). Subject to the provision which applies where more than one-third of the members of a local authority become disqualified at the same time (see the Local Government Act 1972 s 99, Sch 12 para 45; and LOCAL GOVERNMENT vol 69 (2009) PARA 630), no business may be transacted at a meeting of a parish or community council unless at least one-third of the whole number of members are present; but notwithstanding anything in that provision in no case may the quorum be less than three: see Sch 12 paras 12, 28; and LOCAL GOVERNMENT vol 69 (2009) PARA 634.

5 Representation of the People Act 1985 s 21(2)(a). As to the requirement of public notice where vacancies in community council membership are to be filled by co-option see the Local Government (Wales) Measure 2011 ss 116, 117; and LOCAL GOVERNMENT.

6 As to the council of a district in England see LOCAL GOVERNMENT vol 69 (2009) PARA 24 et seq. In the case of a common parish council under which are grouped, by virtue of the Local Government Act 1972 s 11(5) (see LOCAL GOVERNMENT vol 69 (2009) PARA 29), parishes

situated in different districts, the reference to the district council is to be construed as a reference to the council of the district in which there is the greater number of local electors for the parishes in the group: Representation of the People Act 1983 s 39(7); applied by the Representation of the People Act 1985 s 21(3).

7 As to the council of a county or county borough in Wales see LOCAL GOVERNMENT vol 69 (2009) PARA 37 et seq.

8 Representation of the People Act 1983 s 39(4)(i); applied by the Representation of the People Act 1985 s 21(2)(b) (amended by the Local Government (Wales) Act 1994 s 66(6), (8), Sch 16 para 74(2), Sch 18).

9 Representation of the People Act 1983 s 39(4)(ii); applied by the Representation of the People Act 1985 s 21(2)(b) (as amended: see note 8).

10 The period of 35 days is to be computed in accordance with the Representation of the People Act 1983 s 40 (see PARA 209 note 7): see the Representation of the People Act 1985 s 21(2). The Representation of the People Act 1983 s 40(3) applies for the purposes of the Representation of the People Act 1985 s 21(2) as it applies for the purposes of the Representation of the People Act 1983 s 39(1) (see PARA 209 note 7): see the Representation of the People Act 1985 s 21(3).

11 See the Representation of the People Act 1985 s 21(2). The duty of the returning officer under the Representation of the People Act 1983 s 39(1) (see PARA 209) to order an election is also disapplied: Representation of the People Act 1985 s 21(2)(c).

B. FILLING OF VACANCIES

202. Vacancies in the office of councillor for a principal area. On a casual vacancy[1] occurring in the office of a councillor for any principal area[2], an election to fill the vacancy must be held[3]:

(1) in a case in which the High Court or the council has declared the office to be vacant[4], within 35 days from the date of the declaration[5]; and

(2) in any other case within 35 days after written notice of the vacancy has been given to the proper officer[6] of the authority by two local government electors for the area[7].

Where a casual vacancy occurs within six months before the day on which the councillor whose office is vacant would regularly have retired, an election is not to be held to fill the vacancy, unless on the occurrence of the vacancy (or in the case of a number of simultaneous vacancies, the occurrence of the vacancies) the total number of unfilled vacancies in the membership of the council exceeds one-third of the whole number of members; where an election is not held, the vacancy is filled at the next ordinary election[8].

Where more than one casual vacancy in the office of councillor of a district in which councillors are elected by thirds is filled at the same election[9], the person elected by the smallest number of votes is deemed to be elected in place of the councillor who would regularly have first retired, and the person elected by the next smallest number of votes is deemed to be elected in place of the councillor who would regularly have next retired, and so with respect to the others; and if there has not been a contested election, or if any doubt arises, the order of retirement is determined by lot[10].

Where an election to fill one or more casual vacancies in the office of councillor of a district in which councillors are elected by thirds is combined with an ordinary election of councillors[11], and the election is contested, the persons who are elected by the smallest number of votes are deemed elected to fill the casual vacancies[12]; in the case of an equality of votes between the persons who are elected by the smallest number of votes, the persons who are elected to fill the casual vacancies are determined by lot[13]. If the persons elected to fill the casual vacancies will hold office for different periods, the person elected by the smallest number of votes, or, if the votes are equal, such person as is determined by lot, holds office for the shorter period[14]. Where the election is not contested, those declared elected (if fewer than the vacancies to be filled) are deemed elected to fill the vacancies in which they will hold office for the longest periods[15]. Where there are two or more persons declared elected and they are to fill vacancies in which they will hold office for different periods, any retiring councillors elected are deemed elected to fill the vacancies in which they will hold office for the longest period; the question which of the persons declared elected who are not retiring councillors is to be deemed elected to fill any of the vacancies not filled by retiring councillors must be determined by lot[16].

Where any question is required to be determined by lot in this way[17], then, in the case of a contested election, the lot must be drawn by the returning officer immediately after the question has arisen[18]. In any other case, the lot must be drawn at the next meeting of the council after the question has arisen and the drawing must be conducted under the direction of the person presiding at the meeting[19].

A person elected or appointed in England or Wales to fill any casual vacancy holds office until the date upon which the person in whose place he is elected or appointed would regularly have retired, and he must then retire[20].

1   As to the date on which such a vacancy is deemed to have occurred and as to the public notice of such a vacancy that must be given see the Local Government Act 1972 s 87; and LOCAL GOVERNMENT vol 69 (2009) PARA 299.
2   As to the meaning of 'principal area' see LOCAL GOVERNMENT vol 69 (2009) PARA 23.
3   See the Local Government Act 1972 s 89(1); and LOCAL GOVERNMENT vol 69 (2009) PARA 140.
4   As to such declarations see LOCAL GOVERNMENT vol 69 (2009) PARAS 298, 301.
5   See the Local Government Act 1972 s 89(1)(a); and LOCAL GOVERNMENT vol 69 (2009) PARA 140. The period of time referred to in the text is to be computed in accordance with s 243(4) (see LOCAL GOVERNMENT vol 69 (2009) PARA 128): see s 89(1)(a); and LOCAL GOVERNMENT vol 69 (2009) PARA 140.
6   As to the meaning of 'proper officer' see LOCAL GOVERNMENT vol 69 (2009) PARA 431.
7   See the Local Government Act 1972 s 89(1)(b); and LOCAL GOVERNMENT vol 69 (2009) PARA 140. As to fixing the day of election see PARA 208. As to the meaning of 'local government elector' see LOCAL GOVERNMENT vol 69 (2009) PARA 127.
8   See the Local Government Act 1972 s 89(3); and LOCAL GOVERNMENT vol 69 (2009) PARA 140.
9   As to elections where councillors are elected by thirds at the same election see PARA 197. As to districts in England see LOCAL GOVERNMENT vol 69 (2009) PARA 24.
10   See the Local Government Act 1972 s 89(4); and LOCAL GOVERNMENT vol 69 (2009) PARA 140.
11   As to combined polls at elections generally see PARA 16 et seq.
12   See the Local Government Act 1972 s 89(5)(a)(i); and LOCAL GOVERNMENT vol 69 (2009) PARA 140.
13   See the Local Government Act 1972 s 89(5)(a)(i); and LOCAL GOVERNMENT vol 69 (2009) PARA 140.
14   See the Local Government Act 1972 s 89(5)(a)(ii); and LOCAL GOVERNMENT vol 69 (2009) PARA 140.
15   See the Local Government Act 1972 s 89(5)(b)(i); and LOCAL GOVERNMENT vol 69 (2009) PARA 140.
16   See the Local Government Act 1972 s 89(5)(b)(ii); and LOCAL GOVERNMENT vol 69 (2009) PARA 140.
17   Ie under the Local Government Act 1972 s 89 (see LOCAL GOVERNMENT vol 69 (2009) PARA 140).
18   See the Local Government Act 1972 s 89(7)(a); and LOCAL GOVERNMENT vol 69 (2009) PARA 140.
19   See the Local Government Act 1972 s 89(7)(b); and LOCAL GOVERNMENT vol 69 (2009) PARA 140.
20   See the Local Government Act 1972 s 90; and LOCAL GOVERNMENT vol 69 (2009) PARA 142.

203.   **Vacancies in the office of elected mayor.** The Secretary of State in England[1], or, in Wales, the Welsh Ministers[2], may by regulations make provision[3] as to the filling of vacancies in the office of elected mayor[4].

Accordingly, on a casual vacancy occurring in the office of elected mayor in England[5], an election to fill the vacancy must be held[6]:

(1)   in a case in which the High Court or the local authority has declared the office to be vacant[7], within 35 days from the date of the declaration[8]; or

(2)   in any other case, within 35 days[9] after notice in writing of the vacancy has been given to the proper officer of the authority by two local government electors for the area[10].

However, a casual vacancy in the office of elected mayor[11]: (a) must not be filled if the authority has passed a resolution to make a change in governance arrangements[12]; and (b) if it occurs within six months before the day on which the elected mayor would have retired, must be filled at the next ordinary election for the return of an elected mayor[13].

A person elected to fill a casual vacancy in the office of elected mayor holds office until the date on which the person in whose place he or she is elected would have ceased[14] to hold office[15].

1   As to the meaning of 'England' see PARA 1 note 1. As to the Secretary of State for these purposes see PARA 2.

2   As to the meaning of 'Wales' see PARA 1 note 1. As to the Welsh Ministers see PARA 2.

3   See the Local Government Act 2000 ss 9HB, 41; and LOCAL GOVERNMENT vol 69 (2009) PARA 320. As to the regulations made under s 9HB see the Local Authorities (Elected Mayors) (Elections, Terms of Office and Casual Vacancies) (England) Regulations 2012, SI 2012/336. At the date at which this volume states the law, no regulations had been made under the Local Government Act 2000 s 41 in relation to Wales. The provision made by Pt II (ss 10–48A) (Local authorities in Wales: arrangements with respect to executives etc) (see LOCAL GOVERNMENT vol 69 (2009) PARA 303 et seq), has been amended by the Localism Act 2011 s 22, Sch 3 so that it confers powers on the Welsh Ministers only: see LOCAL GOVERNMENT vol 69 (2009) PARA 320.

4   See the Local Government Act 2000 ss 9HB(d), 41(d); and LOCAL GOVERNMENT vol 69 (2009) PARA 320. As to the meaning of 'elected mayor' for these purposes see PARA 198 note 4. As to the power to make provision for the filling of vacancies in the office of executive leader of a 'leader and cabinet executive' structure in England see s 9ID; and LOCAL GOVERNMENT.

5   As to the date on which such a vacancy is to be taken to have occurred see the Local Authorities (Elected Mayors) (Elections, Terms of Office and Casual Vacancies) (England) Regulations 2012, SI 2012/336, reg 10(1); and as to the giving of public notice of such a vacancy see reg 10(2).

6   See the Local Authorities (Elected Mayors) (Elections, Terms of Office and Casual Vacancies) (England) Regulations 2012, SI 2012/336, reg 9(1).

7   As to such declarations see LOCAL GOVERNMENT vol 69 (2009) PARAS 298, 301.

8   Local Authorities (Elected Mayors) (Elections, Terms of Office and Casual Vacancies) (England) Regulations 2012, SI 2012/336, reg 9(1)(a). The day of election under reg 9(1) must be fixed by the returning officer and in computing a period for that purpose the following must be disregarded:
    (1)   a Saturday or Sunday (reg 9(3)(a));
    (2)   Christmas Eve, Christmas Day, Good Friday or a day which is a bank holiday under the Banking and Financial Dealings Act 1971 in England (see TIME vol 97 (2010) PARA 321) (Local Authorities (Elected Mayors) (Elections, Terms of Office and Casual Vacancies) (England) Regulations 2012, SI 2012/336, reg 9(3)(b)); and
    (3)   any day appointed as a day of public thanksgiving or mourning (reg 9(3)(c)).
    Where, between the giving of a notice of the poll and the completion of the poll, a day is declared to be a bank holiday or day of public thanksgiving or mourning, reg 9(3) does not operate to invalidate any act which would have been valid apart from that provision: reg 9(4).

9   As to the calculation of time for these purposes see the Local Authorities (Elected Mayors) (Elections, Terms of Office and Casual Vacancies) (England) Regulations 2012, SI 2012/336, reg 9(3); and note 8.

10 Local Authorities (Elected Mayors) (Elections, Terms of Office and Casual Vacancies) (England) Regulations 2012, SI 2012/336, reg 9(1)(b). As to the meaning of 'local government elector' see LOCAL GOVERNMENT vol 69 (2009) PARA 127; and as to the meaning of 'proper officer' see LOCAL GOVERNMENT vol 69 (2009) PARA 431.

11 See the Local Authorities (Elected Mayors) (Elections, Terms of Office and Casual Vacancies) (England) Regulations 2012, SI 2012/336, reg 9(2).

12 Local Authorities (Elected Mayors) (Elections, Terms of Office and Casual Vacancies) (England) Regulations 2012, SI 2012/336, reg 9(2)(a). The text refers to a change in governance arrangements of the kind set out in the Local Government Act 2000 s 9K (a local authority may cease to operate its existing form of governance, and start to operate a different form of governance: see LOCAL GOVERNMENT) or s 9KA (a local authority which operates executive arrangements may vary the arrangements so that they provide for a different form of executive, and, if it makes such a variation, vary the arrangements in such other respects (if any) as it considers appropriate: see LOCAL GOVERNMENT): see the Local Authorities (Elected Mayors) (Elections, Terms of Office and Casual Vacancies) (England) Regulations 2012, SI 2012/336, reg 9(2)(a).

13 Local Authorities (Elected Mayors) (Elections, Terms of Office and Casual Vacancies) (England) Regulations 2012, SI 2012/336, reg 9(2)(b). The text refers to the election held on the day determined by reference to the applicable provision of reg 4, reg 6 or, as the case may be, reg 7 (see PARA 198), or by the Local Government Act 2000 s 9H(6) (elections for the return of an elected mayor are to take place on the ordinary day of election in each of the relevant election years.: see LOCAL GOVERNMENT): see the Local Authorities (Elected Mayors) (Elections, Terms of Office and Casual Vacancies) (England) Regulations 2012, SI 2012/336, reg 9(2)(b).

14 Ie in accordance with the Local Authorities (Elected Mayors) (Elections, Terms of Office and Casual Vacancies) (England) Regulations 2012, SI 2012/336, reg 8 (see PARA 198): see reg 11.

15 Local Authorities (Elected Mayors) (Elections, Terms of Office and Casual Vacancies) (England) Regulations 2012, SI 2012/336, reg 11.

204. Vacancies arising in the office of Mayor of London or in membership of the London Assembly. Where a vacancy occurs in the office of Mayor of London[1] an election must be held to fill the vacancy[2]. At the election to fill the vacancy each person entitled to vote as an elector[3] at the election has a mayoral vote[4]. The date of the poll at the election is fixed by the Greater London returning officer[5] and must be no later than 35 days[6] after the date of the relevant event[7]. The term of office of the person returned as the Mayor at the election begins immediately upon his being declared to be returned as the Mayor[9], and ends at the time when it would have ended had he been returned as the Mayor at the previous ordinary election[10].

Where the office of an Assembly member[11] returned for an Assembly constituency[12] is vacant[13] an election must be held in the Assembly constituency to fill the vacancy[14]. At the election to fill the vacancy, each person entitled to vote at the election has a constituency vote[15], and the Assembly member for the Assembly constituency is returned under the simple majority system[16]. The date of the poll at the election is fixed by the constituency returning officer[17] and must be no later than 35 days[18] after the date of the relevant event[19]. A person may not be a candidate at an election to fill a vacancy if he is the Mayor of London[20], an Assembly member[21], or a candidate in another such election[22]. The term of office of the person returned at the election begins immediately upon his being declared to be returned as the constituency member[23], and ends at the time when it would have ended had he been returned as the constituency member at the previous ordinary election[24].

Where the office of a London member[25] who was returned as an individual candidate[26] is vacant, the vacancy must remain unfilled until the next ordinary election[27]. Where the office of a London member who was returned from a registered political party's list[28] is vacant, the Greater London returning officer must notify the Chair of the London Assembly[29] of the name of the person who is to fill the vacancy[30]. As soon as practicable after the Greater London returning officer (the 'GLRO') has identified the person who is to fill the vacancy, he must invite him to attend at his office to sign the declaration of acceptance of office[31]. Where a person's name has been notified[32], his term of office as a London member begins on the day on which the notification is received[33] and ends at the time when it would have ended had he been returned as a London member at the previous ordinary election[34]. Where a vacancy in the office of a London member who was returned from a registered political party's list is not so filled[35], the vacancy must remain unfilled until the next ordinary election[36].

1   See the Greater London Authority Act 1999 s 16(1); and LONDON GOVERNMENT vol 71 (2013) PARA 99. As to the Mayor of London see LONDON GOVERNMENT vol 71 (2013) PARA 69; as to the circumstances in which vacancies in the office of Mayor may arise see LONDON GOVERNMENT vol 71 (2013) PARAS 89–94; and as to provision made for an acting Mayor during a vacancy in the office of Mayor of London see LONDON GOVERNMENT vol 71 (2013) PARAS 95–98.

2   See the Greater London Authority Act 1999 s 16(2); and LONDON GOVERNMENT vol 71 (2013) PARA 99. The requirement to hold an election is subject to the proviso that, if the vacancy occurs within the period of six months preceding an ordinary election, it must be left unfilled until that election: see s 16(9); and LONDON GOVERNMENT vol 71 (2013) PARA 99. As to London mayoral and Assembly ordinary elections see PARA 199. A vacancy may arise in an Assembly constituency if a person who is a candidate in an election to fill a vacancy in the office of Mayor is also a candidate in an election to fill a vacancy in an Assembly constituency and that person is returned in both elections: see s 16(10); and the text and notes 11–24. As to the establishment of London Assembly constituencies see PARA 75.

3   As to the meaning of 'elector' for these purposes see LONDON GOVERNMENT vol 71 (2013) PARA 73.

4   See the Greater London Authority Act 1999 s 16(3); and LONDON GOVERNMENT vol 71 (2013) PARA 99. As to the meaning of 'mayoral vote' see LONDON GOVERNMENT vol 71 (2013) PARA 78.

5   See the Greater London Authority Act 1999 s 16(5); and LONDON GOVERNMENT vol 71 (2013) PARA 99. As to the meaning of 'Greater London returning officer' see LONDON GOVERNMENT vol 71 (2013) PARA 81.

6   The Local Government Act 1972 s 243(4) (computation of time for electoral purposes) applies for the purpose of computing the period of 35 days referred to in the Greater London Authority Act 1999 s 16(6) as it applies for the purposes of the Local Government Act 1972 s 89(1) (see PARA 202 note 5): see the Greater London Authority Act 1999 s 16(8); and LONDON GOVERNMENT vol 71 (2013) PARA 99.

7   See the Greater London Authority Act 1999 s 16(6); and LONDON GOVERNMENT vol 71 (2013) PARA 99. For this purpose, the 'relevant event' means:
    (1)   in a case where the High Court or the proper officer of the Greater London Authority has declared the office to be vacant (see LONDON GOVERNMENT vol 71 (2013) PARAS 90, 93), the making of that declaration (see s 16(7)(a); and LONDON GOVERNMENT vol 71 (2013) PARA 99); or
    (2)   in any other case, the giving of notice of the vacancy to the proper officer of the Authority by two or more local government electors for Greater London (see s 16(7)(b); and LONDON GOVERNMENT vol 71 (2013) PARA 99).
    As to the meanings of 'notice' and 'proper officer' see LONDON GOVERNMENT vol 71 (2013) PARA 71. As to the meaning of 'local government elector' see LONDON GOVERNMENT vol 71 (2013) PARA 73.

9   See the Greater London Authority Act 1999 s 16(11)(a); and LONDON GOVERNMENT vol 71 (2013) PARA 99.

10 See the Greater London Authority Act 1999 s 16(11)(b); and LONDON GOVERNMENT vol 71 (2013) PARA 99.

11 As to the meaning of 'Assembly member' see LONDON GOVERNMENT vol 71 (2013) PARA 70.

12 As to elections for the return of constituency members of the London Assembly see PARA 199 et seq. See also LONDON GOVERNMENT vol 71 (2013) PARAS 70, 80, 85.

13 See the Greater London Authority Act 1999 s 10(1); and LONDON GOVERNMENT vol 71 (2013) PARA 111. As to the London Assembly see LONDON GOVERNMENT vol 71 (2013) PARA 70; as to notice to be given regarding a vacancy in membership of the London Assembly see LONDON GOVERNMENT vol 71 (2013) PARA 103; and as to the circumstances in which vacancies in membership of the London Assembly may arise see LONDON GOVERNMENT vol 71 (2013) PARAS 104–110.

14 See the Greater London Authority Act 1999 s 10(2); and LONDON GOVERNMENT vol 71 (2013) PARA 111. The requirement to hold an election is subject to the proviso that if the vacancy occurs within the period of six months preceding an ordinary election, it must be left unfilled

until that election unless, on the occurrence of the vacancy (or, in the case of a number of simultaneous vacancies, the occurrence of the vacancies) the total number of unfilled vacancies in the membership of the Assembly exceeds one-third of the whole number of Assembly members: see s 10(8), (9); and LONDON GOVERNMENT vol 71 (2013) PARA 111.

15 See the Greater London Authority Act 1999 s 10(3)(a); and LONDON GOVERNMENT vol 71 (2013) PARA 111. As to the meaning of 'constituency vote' see LONDON GOVERNMENT vol 71 (2013) PARA 78.

16 See the Greater London Authority Act 1999 s 10(3)(b); and LONDON GOVERNMENT vol 71 (2013) PARA 111. As to the voting systems used in balloting see PARAS 339–341.

17 See the Greater London Authority Act 1999 s 10(4); and LONDON GOVERNMENT vol 71 (2013) PARA 111. As to the constituency returning officer see LONDON GOVERNMENT vol 71 (2013) PARAS 79, 111.

18 The Local Government Act 1972 s 243(4) (computation of time for electoral purposes) applies for the purpose of computing the period of 35 days referred to in the Greater London Authority Act 1999 s 10(5) as it applies for the purposes of the Local Government Act 1972 s 89(1) (see PARA 202 note 5): see the Greater London Authority Act 1999 s 10(7); and LONDON GOVERNMENT vol 71 (2013) PARA 111.

19 See the Greater London Authority Act 1999 s 10(5); and LONDON GOVERNMENT vol 71 (2013) PARA 111. For this purpose, the 'relevant event' means:
    (1)   in a case where the High Court or the proper officer of the Greater London Authority has declared the office to be vacant (see LONDON GOVERNMENT vol 71 (2013) PARAS 209, 211), the making of that declaration (see s 10(6)(a); and LONDON GOVERNMENT vol 71 (2013) PARA 111); or
    (2)   in any other case, the giving of notice of the vacancy to the proper officer of the Authority by two or more local government electors for the Assembly constituency concerned (see s 10(6)(b); and LONDON GOVERNMENT vol 71 (2013) PARA 111).

20 See the Greater London Authority Act 1999 s 10(10)(a); and LONDON GOVERNMENT vol 71 (2013) PARA 111.

21 See the Greater London Authority Act 1999 s 10(10)(b); and LONDON GOVERNMENT vol 71 (2013) PARA 111.

22 See the Greater London Authority Act 1999 s 10(10)(c); and LONDON GOVERNMENT vol 71 (2013) PARA 111.

23 See the Greater London Authority Act 1999 s 10(11)(a); and LONDON GOVERNMENT vol 71 (2013) PARA 111.

24 See the Greater London Authority Act 1999 s 10(11)(b); and LONDON GOVERNMENT vol 71 (2013) PARA 111.

25 As to London members of the London Assembly see LONDON GOVERNMENT vol 71 (2013) PARA 70.

26 As to individual candidates to be London members see LONDON GOVERNMENT vol 71 (2013) PARA 81. As to elections for the return of London members of the London Assembly see PARA 199 et seq. See also LONDON GOVERNMENT vol 71 (2013) PARA 86.

27 See the Greater London Authority Act 1999 s 11(1), (2); and LONDON GOVERNMENT vol 71 (2013) PARA 112.

28 Ie returned under the Greater London Authority Act 1999 s 11 or s 4, Sch 2 Pt II paras 5–8 (see LONDON GOVERNMENT vol 71 (2013) PARAS 81, 86). As to the meaning of 'registered political party' see LONDON GOVERNMENT vol 71 (2013) PARA 78. As to party lists see LONDON GOVERNMENT vol 71 (2013) PARA 81.

29 As to the Chair of the Assembly see LONDON GOVERNMENT vol 71 (2013) PARA 72.

30 See the Greater London Authority Act 1999 s 11(1), (3); and LONDON GOVERNMENT vol 71 (2013) PARA 112. As to the qualification requirements and disqualification for such a vacancy see ss 11(4)–(6), 20; and LONDON GOVERNMENT vol 71 (2013) PARA 112.
    As soon as the office of a London member who was returned from a registered party's list becomes vacant, the Greater London returning officer ('GLRO') (see PARA 211 note 8) must simultaneously give or send to the party's nominating officer, and to the person whose name would, in accordance with s 11(6), and on the assumption that he satisfies the conditions in s 11(4) (see LONDON GOVERNMENT vol 71 (2013) PARA 112), be so notified, written notice (a 'paragraph (1) notice') of the matters specified in the Greater London Authority Elections Rules 2007, SI 2007/3541, Sch 2 r 65(2) (see heads (1) to (3) below): see Sch 2 r 65(1). Accordingly, the matters specified to be included in such a notice are:
    (1)   the vacancy (Sch 2 r 65(2)(a));
    (2)   that the nominating officer may, by notice in writing delivered to the GLRO not later than one month after the date of the paragraph (1) notice, give the notice referred to in the Greater London Authority Act 1999 s 11(4)(c), (5)(b) (notice by party to the GLRO

withdrawing a person's name as the person who is to fill the vacancy: see LONDON GOVERNMENT vol 71 (2013) PARA 112) (Greater London Authority Elections Rules 2007, SI 2007/3541, Sch 2 r 65(2)(b)); and

(3)   that the person must, by notice in writing delivered to the GLRO not later than one month after the date of the paragraph (1) notice, indicate whichever of the following apply to him (Sch 2 r 65(2)(c)): (a) that he is willing to serve as a London member ('notice of willingness') (Sch 2 r 65(2)(c)(i)); (b) that he is not willing to serve as a London member (Sch 2 r 65(2)(c)(ii)); or (c) that he is a dual candidate (Sch 2 r 65(2)(c)(iii)).

For the purposes of Sch 2 Pt 7 (rr 63–67), 'nominating officer', in relation to a registered party and a vacancy in the office of a London member, means the person who holds that office in the party at the time at which the vacancy arises; and 'dual candidate' means a person whose name, subject to Sch 2 r 65, falls to be notified as mentioned in the Greater London Authority Act 1999 s 11(6) (see LONDON GOVERNMENT vol 71 (2013) PARA 112) and who is a candidate (otherwise than at an ordinary election) for election as the Mayor of London or as a constituency member: see the Greater London Authority Elections Rules 2007, SI 2007/3541, Sch 2 r 63. Where the GLRO receives a notice under head (3)(b) above, or under the Greater London Authority Act 1999 s 11(5)(b), he must again send a paragraph (1) notice, but with the substitution, for the name of the person to whom the first such notice was sent, of the name of the person who, on the same assumption, would be the next person whose name would be notified in accordance with s 11(6); and so on until, in respect of such a person, no notice is given under s 11(5)(b), and a notice of willingness has been received: see the Greater London Authority Elections Rules 2007, SI 2007/3541, Sch 2 r 66.

The GLRO must not notify the Chair of the Assembly as mentioned in the Greater London Authority Act 1999 s 11(3) until:

(i)   the period mentioned in head (2) above has elapsed (Greater London Authority Elections Rules 2007, SI 2007/3541, Sch 2 r 65(3)(a)); and

(ii)   he has received a notice of willingness (Sch 2 r 65(3)(b)); and

(iii)   if the person by whom notice of willingness has been given is a dual candidate, the result of the election at which he is a mayoral or constituency member candidate has been declared (Sch 2 r 65(3)(c)).

Where a person whose name is for the time being included in a party list is elected (otherwise than at an ordinary election) either as the Mayor of London, or as a constituency member, his name is removed from that list: see Sch 2 r 64(1). For these purposes, the name of a person to whom Sch 2 r 64(1) applies is treated as ceasing to be included in the list from the date on which he is returned as the Mayor, or as a constituency member, as the case may be (even if his return is void): Sch 2 r 64(2). Where proof is given to the GLRO's satisfaction that a person whose name is for the time being included in a party list has died, then the GLRO must remove that person's name from that list: Sch 2 r 64(3).

As to the equivalent rules for filling vacancies in the office of a London member who was returned from a registered party's list, where an Authority election is combined with a relevant election or referendum see the Greater London Authority Elections Rules 2007, SI 2007/3541, Sch 6 r 65.

31 Greater London Authority Elections Rules 2007, SI 2007/3541, Sch 2 r 67(1). In a case to which the Greater London Authority Act 1999 s 11(3) applies (see the text and notes 28–30), as soon as practicable after the declaration of acceptance of office has been signed, the GLRO must notify the Chair of the Assembly as mentioned therein: Greater London Authority Elections Rules 2007, SI 2007/3541, Sch 2 r 67(2).

32 Ie under the Greater London Authority Act 1999 s 11(3) (see the text and notes 28–30).

33 See the Greater London Authority Act 1999 s 11(7)(a); and LONDON GOVERNMENT vol 71 (2013) PARA 112. The Greater London Authority Act 1999 applies as if the person had been declared to be returned as a London member on the day on which the notification is so received: see s 11(7); and LONDON GOVERNMENT vol 71 (2013) PARA 112.

34 See the Greater London Authority Act 1999 s 11(7)(b); and LONDON GOVERNMENT vol 71 (2013) PARA 112. See note 33.

35 Ie in accordance with the Greater London Authority Act 1999 s 11(3)–(7) (see the text and notes 28–34).

36 See the Greater London Authority Act 1999 s 11(2); and LONDON GOVERNMENT vol 71 (2013) PARA 112.

205. Vacancies in parish or community councils. A request may be made for an election to fill a casual vacancy in the office of a parish or community councillor[1]. Any such request must be made[2]:

(1)   to the proper officer of the council of the district[3] in which the parish is situate or the county or county borough[4] in which the community is situate[5];

(2)   by ten persons who are named on the register in use at the time of the request as local government electors[6] for the electoral area in which the vacancy has occurred[7]; and

(3)   within 14 days[8] after public notice of the vacancy has been given in accordance with the Local Government Act 1972[9].

An election must be held, if so requested, if the casual vacancy in the office of the parish or community councillor occurs other than within six months before the day on which that councillor would regularly have retired[10]; and such an election, if so required, must be held on a day appointed by the returning officer[11], being a day falling within the period of 60 days[12] beginning with the day on which public notice of the vacancy was given[13].

Where a casual vacancy in any such office is not required to be filled by election, the parish or community council must (or, if the vacancy occurs within six months of the date on which the parish or community councillor would regularly have retired, may[14]), as soon as practicable after the expiry of the period of 14 days referred to in head (3) above, co-opt a person to fill the vacancy[15].

A person elected or appointed in England or Wales to fill any such casual vacancy holds office until the date upon which the person in whose place he is elected or appointed would regularly have retired, and he must then retire[16].

1   Local Elections (Parishes and Communities) (England and Wales) Rules 2006, SI 2006/3305, r 5(1). Such a request must be made in accordance with r 5(2) (see the text and notes 2–9): see r 5(1). As to the situation where, at an ordinary election of parish or community councillors, an insufficient number of persons are or remain validly nominated to fill the vacancies in respect of which the election is held see PARA 201. As to parishes and their councillors generally see LOCAL GOVERNMENT vol 69 (2009) PARA 27 et seq; and as to communities and their councillors generally see LOCAL GOVERNMENT vol 69 (2009) PARA 41 et seq.

     The Local Government Act 1972 provides that a casual vacancy among parish or community councillors is to be filled by election or by the parish or community council in accordance with rules made under the Representation of the People Act 1983 s 36 (see PARA 383): see the Local Government Act 1972 s 89(6); and LOCAL GOVERNMENT vol 69 (2009) PARAS 132, 133, 140. The relevant rules and provisions for these purposes are those contained in the Local Elections (Parishes and Communities) (England and Wales) Rules 2006, SI 2006/3305.

2   See the Local Elections (Parishes and Communities) (England and Wales) Rules 2006, SI 2006/3305, r 5(2).

3   As to the meaning of 'proper officer' see LOCAL GOVERNMENT vol 69 (2009) PARA 431. As to the council of a district in England see LOCAL GOVERNMENT vol 69 (2009) PARA 24 et seq.

4   As to the council of a county or county borough in Wales see LOCAL GOVERNMENT vol 69 (2009) PARA 37 et seq.

5   Local Elections (Parishes and Communities) (England and Wales) Rules 2006, SI 2006/3305, r 5(2)(a).

6   As to the meaning of 'local government elector' see LOCAL GOVERNMENT vol 69 (2009) PARA 127. As to entitlement to vote as a local government elector see PARA 97.

7   Local Elections (Parishes and Communities) (England and Wales) Rules 2006, SI 2006/3305, r 5(2)(b). As to electoral areas established for these purposes see PARA 11 et seq.

8   Ie to be computed in accordance with the Local Elections (Parishes and Communities) (England and Wales) Rules 2006, SI 2006/3305, Sch 2 r 2 (see PARA 211 note 1): see r 5(2)(c).

9   Local Elections (Parishes and Communities) (England and Wales) Rules 2006, SI 2006/3305, r 5(2)(c). The text refers to the public notice that must be given in accordance with the Local Government Act 1972 s 87(2) (see LOCAL GOVERNMENT vol 69 (2009) PARA 299): see the Local

Elections (Parishes and Communities) (England and Wales) Rules 2006, SI 2006/3305, r 5(2)(c). As to the requirement of public notice where vacancies in community council membership are to be filled by co-option see note 15.

10 Local Elections (Parishes and Communities) (England and Wales) Rules 2006, SI 2006/3305, r 5(3). As to the normal term of office of a councillor such as is mentioned in the text see PARA 200.

11 As to returning officers appointed for the purposes of local government elections see PARA 354 et seq.

12 See note 8.

13 Local Elections (Parishes and Communities) (England and Wales) Rules 2006, SI 2006/3305, r 5(4).

14 See the Local Elections (Parishes and Communities) (England and Wales) Rules 2006, SI 2006/3305, r 5(6). Any vacancy that is not so filled must be filled at the next ordinary election: see r 5(6).

15 See the Local Elections (Parishes and Communities) (England and Wales) Rules 2006, SI 2006/3305, r 5(5). As to the requirement of public notice where vacancies in community council membership are to be filled by co-option see the Local Government (Wales) Measure 2011 ss 116, 117; and LOCAL GOVERNMENT.

16 See the Local Government Act 1972 s 90; and LOCAL GOVERNMENT vol 69 (2009) PARA 142.

C. FIXING DAY OF ELECTION AND GIVING OF NOTICE

206. Ordinary day of local government election. In every year, the ordinary day of election of councillors is the same for all local government areas[1], and is either:

(1) the first Thursday in May[2]; or

(2) such other day as may be fixed by the Secretary of State by order[3] made not later than 1 February in the year preceding the year (or, in the case of an order affecting more than one year, the first year) in which the order is to take effect[4].

The poll at each ordinary Authority election held subsequent to the first[5] is held on the first Thursday in May in the fourth calendar year following that in which the previous ordinary election was held[6]. However, this is subject to any order made by virtue of the power conferred by head (2) above[7], which, as respects Authority elections, includes power to make an order fixing a day other than the first Thursday in May as the day on which the poll is to be held at an ordinary election other than the first[8], and the power to make an order providing that, in a year in which a European Parliamentary general election is to be held, the day on which the poll at an Authority election is to be held at an ordinary election must be changed so as to be the same as the date of the poll at the European Parliamentary general election[9].

When the day thereby fixed[10] is a Saturday, Sunday, Christmas Eve, Christmas Day, Good Friday, bank holiday or a day appointed for public thanksgiving or mourning, the date of election is postponed to the first day thereafter which is not one of those days[11].

1 See the Representation of the People Act 1983 s 37(1) (s 37(1) renumbered by the Greater London Authority Act 1999 s 17, Sch 3 paras 1, 5(1), (2)). As to the meaning of 'local government area' see PARA 33 note 7.

The Representation of the People Act 1983 s 37(1) is subject to any order under either s 37A (power to change date of local elections to date of European parliamentary general election (England): see note 3) or s 37B (power to change date of local elections to date of European parliamentary general election (Wales): see note 3): see s 37(2A) (ss 37(2A), 37A, 37B added by Local Government and Public Involvement in Health Act 2007 s 60(1), (2)). As to European parliamentary general elections see PARA 217 et seq.

Until a day to be appointed under the Electoral Registration and Administration Act 2013 s 27(1), where the ordinary day of election of councillors for local government areas is the same as the date on which the poll at a parliamentary or European parliamentary general election is to be held, any poll at an election of parish or community councillors must be postponed for three weeks: see the Representation of the People Act 1985 s 16(1) (prospectively repealed by the Electoral Registration and Administration Act 2013 s 15(1)); and PARA 25. As to parliamentary general elections see PARA 9.

2   Representation of the People Act 1983 s 37(1)(a) (as renumbered: see note 1).

3   The power to make an order under the Representation of the People Act 1983 s 37 is exercisable by statutory instrument: s 37(3) (renumbered by the Greater London Authority Act 1999 Sch 3 paras 1, 5(1), (3), (4)).

The Secretary of State in England, or, in Wales, the Welsh Ministers, also may by order provide that in a year in which a European Parliamentary general election is to be held (see the Representation of the People Act 1983 ss 37A(1), 37B(1) (ss 37A, 37B as added: see note 1)):

(1)   the ordinary day of election of councillors for counties in England, districts and London boroughs (s 37A(1)(a) (as so added));

(2)   the ordinary day of election of councillors for counties in Wales and county boroughs (s 37B(1)(a) (as so added));

(3)   the ordinary day of election of councillors for parishes (s 37A(1)(b) (as so added));

(4)   the ordinary day of election of councillors for communities (s 37B(1)(b) (as so added)); and

(5)   as respects Authority elections, the day on which the poll is to be held at an ordinary election (s 37A(1)(c) (as so added)),

must be changed so as to be the same as the date of the poll at the European Parliamentary general election (see ss 37A(1), 37B(1) (as so added)). Such an order must be made by statutory instrument (ss 37A(9), 37B(9) (as so added)), but may not be made unless a draft of the instrument has been laid before and approved by a resolution of each House of Parliament or by a resolution of the National Assembly for Wales, as the case may be (ss 37A(10), 37B(10) (as so added)). As to the meanings of 'England' and 'Wales' see PARA 1 note 1. As to the meaning of 'Authority election' see PARA 11. As to the meaning of 'European parliamentary general election' see PARA 21 note 2. As to the Secretary of State for these purposes, and as to the Welsh Ministers, see PARA 2. As to the council of a district in England see LOCAL GOVERNMENT vol 69 (2009) PARA 24 et seq; and as to parishes and their councillors generally see LOCAL GOVERNMENT vol 69 (2009) PARA 27 et seq. As to the London boroughs and their councils see LOCAL GOVERNMENT vol 69 (2009) PARA 35; LONDON GOVERNMENT vol 71 (2013) PARA 15 et seq. As to the council of a county or county borough in Wales see LOCAL GOVERNMENT vol 69 (2009) PARA 37 et seq; and as to communities and their councillors generally see LOCAL GOVERNMENT vol 69 (2009) PARA 41 et seq. As to the National Assembly for Wales see CONSTITUTIONAL LAW AND HUMAN RIGHTS.

An order under the Representation of the People Act 1983 s 37A(1) may make provision under all of heads (1), (3), (5) above, or under one or more of those heads (see s 37A(2) (as so added)); and an order under s 37B(1) may make provision under heads (2) and (4) above, or under one of those heads (see s 37B(2) (as so added)). Either such order must relate to a single year, and must be made at least six months before the local election day in that year (or, if earlier, the date of the poll at the European Parliamentary general election in that year): see ss 37A(3), 37B(3) (as so added). For this particular purpose, the 'local election day' in a particular year is either the first Thursday in May, or, if an order has been made under s 37(1)(b) (power to change date of council and Assembly elections: see also the text and note 4) in relation to that year, the day specified in the order: see ss 37A(4), 37B(4) (as so added). Where the Welsh Ministers make an order under s 37B, the Secretary of State may by order make such consequential provision in relation to elections in England as he thinks fit (s 37A(7) (as so added)); and, where the Secretary of State makes an order under s 37A, the Welsh Ministers may by order make such consequential provision in relation to elections in Wales as they think fit (s 37B(7) (as so added)). An order under either s 37A(1) or s 37B(1) may make incidental, supplementary or consequential provision or savings (see ss 37A(6), 37B(6) (as so added)); and the powers under s 37A(6), (7), and under s 37B(6), (7), as the case may be, include power to make different provision for different purposes, and to make provision disapplying or modifying the application of an enactment or an instrument made under an enactment (see ss 37A(8), 37B(8) (as so added)). Before making such an order, the Secretary of State in England, or, in Wales, the Welsh Ministers, must consult the Electoral Commission, and such other persons as he, or they, consider appropriate: ss 37A(5), 37B(5) (as so added). As to the establishment and constitution of the Electoral Commission see PARA 34 et seq. At the date at which this volume states the law, no such order had been made under s 37B, but, under s 37A, the Local Elections (Ordinary Day of Elections in 2014) Order 2013, SI 2013/2277, had been made, changing the ordinary day of election of councillors in England for counties, districts and London boroughs, and for parishes, in 2014, so as to be the same as the date of the poll at the European Parliamentary general election held in that year, and making related provision.

4   Representation of the People Act 1983 s 37(1)(b) (s 37(1) as renumbered (see note 1); s 37(1)(b) amended by the Representation of the People Act 1985 s 18(2)).

5   The poll at the first ordinary election was held on 4 May 2000 but provision was made for the Secretary of State to provide for a later date by order: see the Greater London Authority Act 1999 s 3(1).

6   See the Greater London Authority Act 1999 s 3(2); and LONDON GOVERNMENT vol 71 (2013) PARA 77.

7   Ie is subject to any order made by virtue of the Representation of the People Act 1983 s 37(2) (see the text and note 8) or s 37A (see note 3): see the Greater London Authority Act 1999 s 3(3); and LONDON GOVERNMENT vol 71 (2013) PARA 77.

8   See the Representation of the People Act 1983 s 37(2) (added by the Greater London Authority Act 1999 Sch 3 paras 1, 5(1), (5)).

9   See the Representation of the People Act 1983 s 37A; and note 3.

10 Ie when the day on which anything is required to be done by the Representation of the People Act 1983 s 37 (see the text and notes 1–4, 7–8), or the Greater London Authority Act 1999 s 3 (see the text and notes 5–6): see the Representation of the People Act 1983 s 40(1) (amended by the Representation of the People Act 1985 ss 16(2), 19(1), 28(1), Sch 5; the Greater London Authority Act 1999 Sch 3 paras 1, 7(1), (2); the Electoral Administration Act 2006 ss 20, 74(2), Sch 1 paras 49, 50, Sch 2; and the Electoral Registration and Administration Act 2013 s 15(3)).

11 Representation of the People Act 1983 s 40(1) (as amended: see note 10). Where the day of election is postponed under s 40(1), the day to which it is postponed must be treated as the day of election for the purposes of the Representation of the People Act 1983, for the purposes of the Local Government Act 1972 and (in the case of an Authority election) for the purposes of the Greater London Authority Act 1999: Representation of the People Act 1983 s 40(2) (amended by the Education Reform Act 1988 s 237, Sch 12 para 51; and the Greater London Authority Act 1999 Sch 3 paras 1, 7(1), (3)).

The Representation of the People Act 1983 s 40 is applied and modified for the purpose of local authority mayoral elections in England and Wales by the Local Authorities (Mayoral Elections) (England and Wales) Regulations 2007, SI 2007/1024, reg 3(2)–(5), Sch 2 Table 1: see PARA 11 note 14.

207.   Day of poll consequent on a parish meeting.   The day of a poll consequent on a parish meeting[1] must be fixed by the returning officer[2] and must not be earlier than the fourteenth day nor later than the twenty-fifth day after the day on which the poll was demanded[3].

1   Ie on a question involving appointment to office: see PARA 200.
2   As to the returning officer at a poll consequent on parish meeting see PARA 356.
3   See the Parish and Community Meetings (Polls) Rules 1987, SI 1987/1, Schedule r 1 (Timetable).

208.   Day of election at certain local government elections to fill casual vacancy.   The day of election to fill a casual vacancy in the office of councillor for any principal area[1] must be fixed by the returning officer[2].

1   As to the meaning of 'principal area' see LOCAL GOVERNMENT vol 69 (2009) PARA 23. As to vacancies in the office of councillor for a principal area see PARA 202. As to casual vacancies in parish and community councils and (where appropriate) the day of election see PARA 205.
2   See the Local Government Act 1972 s 89(1), (2); and LOCAL GOVERNMENT vol 69 (2009) PARA 140. As to returning officers for local government elections see PARA 354 et seq.

209.   Day of local government election if vacancies not filled.   If, at a local government election in England and Wales[1], other than an election for the return of the London members of the London Assembly[2]:

(1)   the poll is abandoned or countermanded for any reason[3]; or

(2)   no person is or remains, or an insufficient number of persons are or remain, validly nominated to fill the vacancy or vacancies in respect of which the election is held[4],

the returning officer[5] must order an election to fill any vacancy which remains unfilled to be held on a day appointed by him[6]. The day of election must fall within the period of 35 days beginning with the day fixed as the day of election for the first election[7]. If for any other reason an election to an office under the Local Government Act 1972 or the Greater London Authority Act 1999, other than that of chairman of a parish or community council or parish meeting, or parish or community councillor[8], is not held on the appointed day, or within the appointed time, or fails either wholly or in part or becomes void, the High Court may order an election to be held on a day appointed by the court[9].

Where an election is ordered to be held in this way[10], the relevant elections rules[11] relating to the notice to be given of an election and the manner in which an election is to be conducted apply in relation to the election so ordered to be held as they applied or would have applied in relation to the election which had not been duly held or has failed or become void[12]; and no fresh nomination is necessary in the case of a candidate who remains validly nominated for the election[13].

1   As to the meanings of 'England' and 'Wales' see PARA 1 note 1. As to the meaning of 'local government election' see PARA 11.
2   See the Representation of the People Act 1983 s 39(1) (amended by the Greater London Authority Act 1999 s 17, Sch 3 paras 1, 6(1), (2)). As to the meaning of 'London member', in relation to the London Assembly, see PARA 11 note 5. As to elections for the return of the London members of the London Assembly see PARA 199 et seq.
    The Representation of the People Act 1983 ss 39, 40 are applied and modified for the purpose of local authority mayoral elections in England and Wales by the Local Authorities (Mayoral Elections) (England and Wales) Regulations 2007, SI 2007/1024, reg 3(2)–(5), Sch 2 Table 1: see PARA 11 note 14.
3   Representation of the People Act 1983 s 39(1)(a). As to the countermand or abandonment of the poll at a local government election by reason of the death of a candidate see PARA 516 et seq.
4   Representation of the People Act 1983 s 39(1)(b). As to nominations and their validity see PARA 255 et seq.
5   As to returning officers for local government elections generally see PARA 354 et seq.
6   See the Representation of the People Act 1983 s 39(1) (amended by the Local Government Act 1985 s 102(2), Sch 17). This duty does not apply where, at an ordinary election of parish or community councillors, an insufficient number of persons is or remains validly nominated, unless the number of newly elected members of the council is less than the number that constitutes a quorum for meetings of the council: see the Representation of the People Act 1985 s 21(1), (2)(c); and PARA 200.
7   See the Representation of the People Act 1983 s 39(1) (amended by the Representation of the People Act 1985 s 19(2)). The period mentioned in the text must be computed according to the Representation of the People Act 1983 s 40: see s 39(1) (as so amended). Accordingly, when the day fixed by the Representation of the People Act 1983 s 39(1) is a Saturday, Sunday, Christmas Eve, Christmas Day, Good Friday, bank holiday or a day appointed for public thanksgiving or mourning, the date of election is postponed to the first day thereafter which is not one of those days: s 40(1) (amended by the Representation of the People Act 1985 ss 16(2), 19(1), 28(1), Sch 5; and the Electoral Administration Act 2006 ss 20, 74(2), Sch 1 paras 49, 50, Sch 2). Where the day of election is so postponed under the Representation of the People Act 1983 s 40(1), the day to which it is postponed must be treated as the day of election for the purposes of the Representation of the People Act 1983 and the Local Government Act 1972: Representation of the People Act 1983 s 40(2) (amended by the Education Reform Act 1988 s 237, Sch 12 para 51). In computing any period of time for the purpose of the Representation of the People Act 1983 s 39, a Saturday, Sunday, Christmas Eve, Christmas Day, Good Friday, bank holiday or a day appointed for public thanksgiving or mourning must be disregarded but where, between the giving of a notice of election and the completion of the poll, a day is declared to be a bank holiday or day of public thanksgiving or mourning (and is accordingly disregarded), the requirement to disregard such a day is not to operate to invalidate any act which would have been valid apart from that requirement: see s 40(1), (3) (s 40(1) as so amended). As to the giving of notice of a local government election see PARA 211.
8   As to the election of parish or community councillors see PARA 200 et seq.

9   Representation of the People Act 1983 s 39(2) (amended by the Local Government Act 1985
    ss 18(1), 19, Sch 9 Pt I; the Education Reform Act 1988 s 237, Sch 13 Pt I; and the Greater
    London Authority Act 1999 Sch 3 paras 1, 6(1), (3)). The High Court may order that the costs
    incurred by any person in connection with proceedings under the Representation of the People
    Act 1983 s 39(2) are to be paid by the local authority concerned: s 39(3). Where the High Court
    orders an election to be held, such an order may include such modifications of Pt I (ss 1–66A),
    including the elections rules made under s 36 (see PARA 383) and the Local Government
    Act 1972 or the Greater London Authority Act 1999, as appear to the High Court necessary or
    expedient for carrying the order into effect: Representation of the People Act 1983 s 39(6)(a)
    (amended by the Local Government Act 1985 Sch 9 Pt I; the Education Reform Act 1988 Sch 13
    Pt I; and the Greater London Authority Act 1999 Sch 3 paras 1, 6(1), (4)). As to the meaning of
    'local authority' for these purposes see PARA 144 note 3.
10 Ie under the Representation of the People Act 1983 s 39: see s 39(5).
11 Ie the relevant rules made under the Representation of the People Act 1983 s 36 (see PARA 383):
    see s 39(5)(a).
12 Representation of the People Act 1983 s 39(5)(a).
13 Representation of the People Act 1983 s 39(5)(b).

**210.   Abortive parish or community election or poll consequent on a parish or
community meeting.** If any difficulty arises with respect to an election of parish
or community councillors or of an individual parish or community councillor[1],
or if, because an election is not held or is defective or for any other reason[2], a
parish or community council is not properly constituted[3], the district council in
England[4], or the county or county borough council in Wales[5], may by order[6]
make any appointment or do any thing which appears to it necessary or
expedient for the proper holding of such an election and properly constituting
the council[7] and may, if it appears to it necessary, direct the holding of an
election and fix the date for it[8]. Where an election is ordered to be held in this
way[9], the relevant elections rules[10] relating to the notice to be given of an
election and the manner in which an election is to be conducted apply in relation
to the election so ordered to be held as they applied or would have applied in
relation to the election which had not been duly held or has failed or become
void[11]; and no fresh nomination is necessary in the case of a candidate who
remains validly nominated for the election[12].

Where a poll consequent on a parish or community meeting[13] is
countermanded or abandoned by reason of the death of a candidate[14], the
district council for the area in which the parish or community is situated may by
order make any appointment or make provision for the holding of a parish
meeting or do such other thing as appears to it to be expedient in the
circumstances[15].

1   See the Representation of the People Act 1983 s 39(4)(a). As to the election of parish or
    community councillors see PARA 200 et seq.
        The Representation of the People Act 1983 s 39 is applied and modified for the purpose of
    local authority mayoral elections in England and Wales by the Local Authorities (Mayoral
    Elections) (England and Wales) Regulations 2007, SI 2007/1024, reg 3(2)–(5), Sch 2 Table 1: see
    PARA 11 note 14.
2   As to the countermand or abandonment of polls at local government elections see PARA 516.
3   See the Representation of the People Act 1983 s 39(4)(b).
4   As to the meaning of 'England' see PARA 1 note 1. As to the councils of districts in England see
    LOCAL GOVERNMENT vol 69 (2009) PARA 24 et seq.
        In the case of a common parish council under which are grouped, by virtue of the Local
    Government Act 1972 s 11(5) (see LOCAL GOVERNMENT vol 69 (2009) PARA 29), parishes
    situated in different districts, the reference to the district council is to be construed as a reference
    to the council of the district in which there is the greater number of local government electors
    for the parishes in the group: Representation of the People Act 1983 s 39(7). As to the meaning
    of 'elector' for these purposes see PARA 95 note 2.

5   See the Representation of the People Act 1983 s 39(4) (amended by the Local Government (Wales) Act 1994 s 66(6), Sch 16 para 68(11)). As to the meaning of 'Wales' see PARA 1 note 1. As to the council of a county or county borough in Wales see LOCAL GOVERNMENT vol 69 (2009) PARA 37 et seq.

6   Such an order may include such modifications of the Representation of the People Act 1983 Pt I (ss 1–66A), including the elections rules made under s 36 (see PARA 383), and the Local Government Act 1972 or the Greater London Authority Act 1999, as appear to the district council or Welsh county or county borough council necessary or expedient for carrying the order into effect: Representation of the People Act 1983 s 39(6)(a) (amended by the Local Government Act 1985 ss 18(1), 19, Sch 9 Pt I; the Education Reform Act 1988 s 237, Sch 13 Pt I; the Local Government (Wales) Act 1994 s 66(6), Sch 16 para 68(11)(a); and the Greater London Authority Act 1999 Sch 3 paras 1, 6(1), (4)). Such an order may also modify the provisions of the Representation of the People Act 1983 and the rules with respect to parish or community council elections under s 36 (see PARA 383) and any other enactment relating to such elections: s 39(6)(b) (amended by the Local Government (Wales) Act 1994 s 66(8), Sch 16 para 68(11)(b), Sch 18).

7   Representation of the People Act 1983 s 39(4)(i). This provision does not apply if s 39(1) (returning officer to order local government election to be held if vacancies not filled: see PARA 209) applies: see s 39(4).

8   Representation of the People Act 1983 s 39(4)(ii). See note 7.

9   Ie under the Representation of the People Act 1983 s 39.

10 Ie the relevant rules made under the Representation of the People Act 1983 s 36 (see PARA 383).

11 Representation of the People Act 1983 s 39(5)(a).

12 Representation of the People Act 1983 s 39(5)(b).

13 See PARA 200 et seq.

14 See the Parish and Community Meetings (Polls) Rules 1987, SI 1987/1, Schedule r 37; and PARA 516.

15 See the Parish and Community Meetings (Polls) Rules 1987, SI 1987/1, Schedule r 37(4); and PARA 516.

211. Notice of local government election. Not later than the twenty-fifth day before the day of a principal area, or parish or community council, election, or before the day of a local authority mayoral election[1], the returning officer[2] must publish notice of the election[3]. Not later than the thirtieth day before the day of a London Mayoral election[4], or an Authority election for the return of constituency members[5], or London members[6], of the London Assembly[7], the Greater London returning officer[8] or the constituency returning officer[9] (as the case may be) must publish notice of the election[10].

Such a notice must state:

(1)   the place and times at which nomination papers are to be delivered[11] and that forms of nomination papers (and party lists, in the case of a London members election) may be obtained at that place and those times[12];

(2)   the date of the poll in the event of a contest[13]; and

(3)   the date by which applications to vote by post or by proxy[14], and other applications and notices about postal or proxy voting[15], must reach the electoral registration officer[16] in order that they may be effective for the election[17].

Such a notice, in the case of a local authority mayoral election, or a London Authority election (including a London Mayoral election), must also state the arrangements, if any, which apply for the payment of the required deposit[18] to be made by means of the electronic transfer of funds[19].

1   Local Elections (Principal Areas) (England and Wales) Rules 2006, SI 2006/3304, Sch 2 r 1; Local Elections (Parishes and Communities) (England and Wales) Rules 2006, SI 2006/3305, Sch 2 r 1; Local Authorities (Mayoral Elections) (England and Wales) Regulations 2007, SI 2007/1024, Sch 1 r 3.

In computing any period of time for the purposes of the timetable in the Local Elections (Principal Areas) (England and Wales) Rules 2006, SI 2006/3304, Sch 2 r 1, or in the Local Elections (Parishes and Communities) (England and Wales) Rules 2006, SI 2006/3305, Sch 2 r 1, or in the Local Authorities (Mayoral Elections) (England and Wales) Regulations 2007, SI 2007/1024, Sch 1 r 3, the following must be disregarded:

(1)   a Saturday or Sunday (Local Elections (Principal Areas) (England and Wales) Rules 2006, SI 2006/3304, Sch 2 r 2(1)(a); Local Elections (Parishes and Communities) (England and Wales) Rules 2006, SI 2006/3305, Sch 2 r 2(1)(a); Local Authorities (Mayoral Elections) (England and Wales) Regulations 2007, SI 2007/1024, Sch 1 r 4(1)(a));

(2)   Christmas Eve, Christmas Day, Good Friday or a bank holiday (Local Elections (Principal Areas) (England and Wales) Rules 2006, SI 2006/3304, Sch 2 r 2(1)(b); Local Elections (Parishes and Communities) (England and Wales) Rules 2006, SI 2006/3305, Sch 2 r 2(1)(b); Local Authorities (Mayoral Elections) (England and Wales) Regulations 2007, SI 2007/1024, Sch 1 r 4(1)(b));

(3)   a day appointed for public thanksgiving or mourning (Local Elections (Principal Areas) (England and Wales) Rules 2006, SI 2006/3304, Sch 2 r 2(1)(c); Local Elections (Parishes and Communities) (England and Wales) Rules 2006, SI 2006/3305, Sch 2 r 2(1)(c); Local Authorities (Mayoral Elections) (England and Wales) Regulations 2007, SI 2007/1024, Sch 1 r 4(1)(c)).

Any such day is not to be treated as a day for the purpose of any proceedings up to the completion of the poll nor is the returning officer obliged to proceed with the counting of the votes on such a day: Local Elections (Principal Areas) (England and Wales) Rules 2006, SI 2006/3304, Sch 2 r 2(1); Local Elections (Parishes and Communities) (England and Wales) Rules 2006, SI 2006/3305, Sch 2 r 2(1); Local Authorities (Mayoral Elections) (England and Wales) Regulations 2007, SI 2007/1024, Sch 1 r 4(1). For these purposes, 'bank holiday' means a day which is a bank holiday under the Banking and Financial Dealings Act 1971 in England and Wales (see TIME vol 97 (2010) PARA 321): Local Elections (Principal Areas) (England and Wales) Rules 2006, SI 2006/3304, Sch 2 r 2(2); Local Elections (Parishes and Communities) (England and Wales) Rules 2006, SI 2006/3305, Sch 2 r 2(2); Local Authorities (Mayoral Elections) (England and Wales) Regulations 2007, SI 2007/1024, Sch 1 r 4(2). As to the meanings of 'England' and 'Wales' see PARA 1 note 1.

As to the counting of votes at a local government election (except a London Authority election) see PARA 425; in relation to a local authority mayoral election see PARA 436; in relation to a London Authority election see PARA 444; and in relation to a London mayoral election see PARA 451.

Identical provision is made by the Representation of the People Act 1983 s 40(3), which states that, in computing any period of time for the purpose of any rules under s 36 (see PARA 383), a Saturday or Sunday, Christmas Eve, Christmas Day, Good Friday, or a bank holiday or a day appointed for public thanksgiving or mourning must be disregarded but this provision, so far as it relates to any such rules, has effect subject to the provisions of those rules: see s 40(1), (3) (s 40(1) amended by the Representation of the People Act 1985 ss 16(2), 19(1), 28(1), Sch 5; and the Electoral Administration Act 2006 ss 20, 74(2), Sch 1 paras 49, 50, Sch 2). Since the rules do not make provision different from that in the Representation of the People Act 1983 s 40(3), it is arguable that that provision, as well as the provision in the rules, applies to determine the computation of time for the purposes of the rules. In that event, the further provision made in s 40(3) applies so that where, between the giving of a notice of election and the completion of the poll a day is declared to be a bank holiday or day of public thanksgiving or mourning (and is accordingly disregarded), the requirement to disregard such a day is not to operate to invalidate any act which would have been valid apart from that requirement: see s 40(3). The provision made by s 40 is applied and modified for the purpose of local authority mayoral elections in England and Wales by the Local Authorities (Mayoral Elections) (England and Wales) Regulations 2007, SI 2007/1024, reg 3(2)–(5), Sch 2 Table 1: see PARA 11 note 14.

As to local government principal area or parish or community council elections, when they are combined with any other relevant election or referendum, see the Local Elections (Principal Areas) (England and Wales) Rules 2006, SI 2006/3304, r 4, Sch 3; the Local Elections (Parishes and Communities) (England and Wales) Rules 2006, SI 2006/3305, r 4, Sch 3; and PARA 22 et seq.

2   As to returning officers for local government elections generally see PARA 354 et seq.

3   Local Elections (Principal Areas) (England and Wales) Rules 2006, SI 2006/3304, Sch 2 r 3(1); Local Elections (Parishes and Communities) (England and Wales) Rules 2006, SI 2006/3305,

Sch 2 r 3(1); Local Authorities (Mayoral Elections) (England and Wales) Regulations 2007, SI 2007/1024, Sch 1 r 5(1). As to the giving of public notices for the purposes of a local government election see PARA 354.

4   As to the Mayor of London see LONDON GOVERNMENT vol 71 (2013) PARA 69.

In computing any period of time for the purposes of the timetable in the Greater London Authority Elections Rules 2007, SI 2007/3541, Sch 1 Sch 2 r 3, or Sch 3 r 3, the following must be disregarded:

(1)   a Saturday or Sunday (Sch 1 r 4(1)(a), Sch 2 r 4(1)(a), Sch 3 r 4(1)(a));

(2)   Christmas Eve, Christmas Day, Maundy Thursday, Good Friday or a bank holiday (Sch 1 r 4(1)(b), Sch 2 r 4(1)(b), Sch 3 r 4(1)(b)); or

(3)   a day appointed for public thanksgiving or mourning (Sch 1 r 4(1)(c), Sch 2 r 4(1)(c), Sch 3 r 4(1)(c)).

Any such day is not to be treated as a day for the purpose of any proceedings up to the completion of the poll nor is the constituency returning officer (see note 9) obliged to proceed with the counting of the votes on such a day: Sch 1 r 4(1), Sch 2 r 4(1), Sch 3 r 4(1). For these purposes, 'bank holiday' means a day which is a bank holiday under the Banking and Financial Dealings Act 1971 in England and Wales (see TIME vol 97 (2010) PARA 321): Greater London Authority Elections Rules 2007, SI 2007/3541, Sch 1 r 4(2), Sch 2 r 4(2), Sch 3 r 4(2).

5   As to the meaning of 'constituency member', in relation to the London Assembly, see PARA 11 note 6; definition applied by virtue of the Greater London Authority Elections Rules 2007, SI 2007/3541, r 2(2). As to ordinary elections of constituency members of the London Assembly see PARA 199 et seq. As to the London Assembly, constituency members of the London Assembly, and London members of the London Assembly, see LONDON GOVERNMENT vol 71 (2013) PARA 70.

6   As to the meaning of 'London member', in relation to the London Assembly, see PARA 11 note 5; definition applied by virtue of the Greater London Authority Elections Rules 2007, SI 2007/3541, r 2(2). As to ordinary elections of London members of the London Assembly see PARA 199 et seq.

7   See the Greater London Authority Elections Rules 2007, SI 2007/3541, Sch 1 Sch 2 r 3, Sch 3 r 3.

8   Ie in the case of an Authority election for the return of a Mayor of London and of Authority elections for the return of London members of the London Assembly. For these purposes, 'Greater London returning officer' ('GLRO') means the person who is for the time being the proper officer of the Greater London Authority for the purposes of the Representation of the People Act 1983 s 35(2C) (returning officer at the election of the Mayor and London Members: see PARA 354): see the Greater London Authority Elections Rules 2007, SI 2007/3541, r 2(1). References in the rules to the GLRO include references to any person appointed by him under the Representation of the People Act 1983 s 35(4) (returning officers for local elections in England and Wales: see PARA 354): see the Greater London Authority Elections Rules 2007, SI 2007/3541, r 2(2)(b). As to the meaning of 'Greater London returning officer' see also LONDON GOVERNMENT vol 71 (2013) PARA 81.

9   Ie in the case of Authority elections for the return of constituency members of the London Assembly. For these purposes, 'constituency returning officer' ('CRO'), in relation to an Assembly constituency and an election, means the person, or a person of the description, for the time being designated by order under the Representation of the People Act 1983 s 35(2B) (see PARA 354): see the Greater London Authority Elections Rules 2007, SI 2007/3541, r 2(1). References in the rules to the CRO include references to any person appointed by him under the Representation of the People Act 1983 s 35(4) (returning officers for local elections in England and Wales: see PARA 354): see the Greater London Authority Elections Rules 2007, SI 2007/3541, r 2(2)(a). As to the meaning of 'Assembly constituency', in relation to the London Assembly, see PARA 11 note 6. As to the constituency returning officer see also LONDON GOVERNMENT vol 71 (2013) PARAS 79, 111.

10   Greater London Authority Elections Rules 2007, SI 2007/3541, Sch 1 r 5(1), Sch 2 r 5(1), Sch 3 r 5(1). In the case of elections for the return of London members and of the London Mayor, publication must take place in each Assembly constituency: see Sch 2 r 5(1), Sch 2 r 5(1).

11   Local Elections (Principal Areas) (England and Wales) Rules 2006, SI 2006/3304, Sch 2 r 3(1)(a); Local Elections (Parishes and Communities) (England and Wales) Rules 2006, SI 2006/3305, Sch 2 r 3(1)(a); Local Authorities (Mayoral Elections) (England and Wales) Regulations 2007, SI 2007/1024, Sch 1 r 5(1)(a); Greater London Authority Elections Rules 2007, SI 2007/3541, Sch 1 r 5(1)(a), Sch 2 r 5(1)(a), Sch 3 r 5(1)(a). As to the nomination of candidates at elections see PARA 253 et seq.

12   Local Elections (Principal Areas) (England and Wales) Rules 2006, SI 2006/3304, Sch 2 r 3(1); Local Elections (Parishes and Communities) (England and Wales) Rules 2006, SI 2006/3305,

Sch 2 r 3(1); Local Authorities (Mayoral Elections) (England and Wales) Regulations 2007, SI 2007/1024, Sch 1 r 5(1); Greater London Authority Elections Rules 2007, SI 2007/3541, Sch 1 r 5(1), Sch 2 r 5(1), Sch 3 r 5(1). As to the forms of nomination papers see PARA 255.

13 Local Elections (Principal Areas) (England and Wales) Rules 2006, SI 2006/3304, Sch 2 r 3(1)(b); Local Elections (Parishes and Communities) (England and Wales) Rules 2006, SI 2006/3305, Sch 2 r 3(1)(b); Local Authorities (Mayoral Elections) (England and Wales) Regulations 2007, SI 2007/1024, Sch 1 r 5(1)(b); Greater London Authority Elections Rules 2007, SI 2007/3541, Sch 1 r 5(1)(b), Sch 2 r 5(1)(b), Sch 3 r 5(1)(b). As to the date of the poll at local government elections (including elections to fill vacancies) see PARAS 206–209; and as to the procedure uncontested elections see PARA 475.

14 Local Elections (Principal Areas) (England and Wales) Rules 2006, SI 2006/3304, Sch 2 r 3(2)(a); Local Elections (Parishes and Communities) (England and Wales) Rules 2006, SI 2006/3305, Sch 2 r 3(2)(a); Local Authorities (Mayoral Elections) (England and Wales) Regulations 2007, SI 2007/1024, Sch 1 r 5(3)(a); Greater London Authority Elections Rules 2007, SI 2007/3541, Sch 1 r 5(3)(a), Sch 2 r 5(3)(a), Sch 3 r 5(3)(a). As to applications to vote by post or by proxy see PARA 367 et seq.

15 Local Elections (Principal Areas) (England and Wales) Rules 2006, SI 2006/3304, Sch 2 r 3(2)(b); Local Elections (Parishes and Communities) (England and Wales) Rules 2006, SI 2006/3305, Sch 2 r 3(2)(b); Local Authorities (Mayoral Elections) (England and Wales) Regulations 2007, SI 2007/1024, Sch 1 r 5(3)(b); Greater London Authority Elections Rules 2007, SI 2007/3541, Sch 1 r 5(3)(b), Sch 2 r 5(3)(b), Sch 3 r 5(3)(b).

16 As to the electoral registration officer see PARA 139 et seq.

17 Local Elections (Principal Areas) (England and Wales) Rules 2006, SI 2006/3304, Sch 2 r 3(2); Local Elections (Parishes and Communities) (England and Wales) Rules 2006, SI 2006/3305, Sch 2 r 3(2); Local Authorities (Mayoral Elections) (England and Wales) Regulations 2007, SI 2007/1024, Sch 1 r 5(3) (amended by SI 2012/2059); Greater London Authority Elections Rules 2007, SI 2007/3541, Sch 1 r 5(3), Sch 2 r 5(3), Sch 3 r 5(3).

18 Ie the deposit required by the Local Authorities (Mayoral Elections) (England and Wales) Regulations 2007, SI 2007/1024, Sch 1 r 10 (see Sch 1 r 5(2)), or by the Greater London Authority Elections Rules 2007, SI 2007/3541, Sch 1 r 8, Sch 2 r 10, Sch 3 r 9 (see Sch 1 r 5(2), Sch 2 r 5(2), Sch 3 r 5(2)) (see PARA 259).

19 Local Authorities (Mayoral Elections) (England and Wales) Regulations 2007, SI 2007/1024, Sch 1 r 5(2); Greater London Authority Elections Rules 2007, SI 2007/3541, Sch 1 r 5(2), Sch 2 r 5(2), Sch 3 r 5(2).

212. Notice of poll consequent on a parish meeting taken on a question of appointment to office. If a poll consequent on a parish or community meeting is required to be taken[1], the chairman of the meeting must notify the district council in which the parish or community is situate of the fact[2]; and the chairman of the meeting must give the returning officer[3] such particulars as will enable him to give notice of the poll[4].

Not later than the fifth day before the day of the poll[5], the returning officer must give public notice of the poll which refers to the parish or community meeting at which a poll was demanded[6]. Such a notice must state:

(1) the day and hours fixed for the poll[7];

(2) if the poll is taken on the question of appointment to any office[8], the name of the office, the number of vacancies, the particulars of each candidate who has not withdrawn (the order of the names of the candidates and particulars being the same as in the ballot papers) and the name of the proposer of each candidate[9]; and

(3) the situation of each polling station and the description of the persons entitled to vote there[10].

1 As to how polls consequent on a parish or community meeting come about see PARA 200.

2 See the Parish and Community Meetings (Polls) Rules 1987, SI 1987/1, r 4(1). As to the council of a district in England see LOCAL GOVERNMENT vol 69 (2009) PARA 24 et seq; and as to parishes and their councillors generally see LOCAL GOVERNMENT vol 69 (2009) PARA 27 et seq.

As to the council of a county or county borough in Wales see LOCAL GOVERNMENT vol 69 (2009) PARA 37 et seq; and as to communities and their councillors generally see LOCAL GOVERNMENT vol 69 (2009) PARA 41 et seq.

3   The council must appoint an officer of the council to be returning officer: see the Parish and Community Meetings (Polls) Rules 1987, SI 1987/1, r 4(1); and PARA 356.

4   Parish and Community Meetings (Polls) Rules 1987, SI 1987/1, r 4(2).

5   Parish and Community Meetings (Polls) Rules 1987, SI 1987/1, Schedule r 1. In computing any period of time for the purposes of the timetable in Schedule r 1, the following must be disregarded:

    (1)   a Saturday or a Sunday (Schedule r 2(1)(a));

    (2)   Christmas Eve, Christmas Day, Maundy Thursday, Good Friday or a bank holiday (Schedule r 2(1)(b)); or

    (3)   a day appointed for public thanksgiving or mourning (Schedule r 2(1)(c)).

However, any such day must not be treated as a day for the purpose of any proceedings up to the completion of the poll nor is the returning officer obliged to proceed with the counting of votes on such a day: see Schedule r 2(1). For these purposes, 'bank holiday' means a day which is a bank holiday under the Banking and Financial Dealings Act 1971 in England and Wales (see TIME vol 97 (2010) PARA 321): Parish and Community Meetings (Polls) Rules 1987, SI 1987/1, Schedule r 2(2). Although Maundy Thursday is still specified under head (2) above, this day has been removed from similar lists which are applicable to other local elections: see PARA 211 notes 1, 4.

6   See the Parish and Community Meetings (Polls) Rules 1987, SI 1987/1, Schedule r 8; and PARA 388.

7   See the Parish and Community Meetings (Polls) Rules 1987, SI 1987/1, Schedule r 8(a); and PARA 388.

8   As to polls consequent on a parish meeting not involving a question of appointment to any office see PARA 556 et seq.

9   See the Parish and Community Meetings (Polls) Rules 1987, SI 1987/1, Schedule r 8(b); and PARA 388.

10   See the Parish and Community Meetings (Polls) Rules 1987, SI 1987/1, Schedule r 8(d); and PARA 388. As to polling districts and polling places see PARA 343 et seq.

(iii) Initiating a Welsh Assembly Election

A. ORDINARY GENERAL ELECTION

213.   Ordinary general election for the National Assembly for Wales. The poll at an ordinary general election for the National Assembly for Wales[1] is to be held on the first Thursday in May in the fourth calendar year following that in which the previous ordinary general election was held[2], unless provision is made for the day of the poll by an order[3].

If the poll is to be held on the first Thursday in May, the Assembly:

(1)   is dissolved[4] at the beginning of the minimum period which ends with that day[5]; and

(2)   must meet within the period of seven days beginning immediately after the day of the poll[6].

However, if:

(a)   the Assembly resolves that it should be dissolved[7]; and

(b)   the resolution of the Assembly is passed on a vote in which the number of Assembly members voting in favour of it is not less than two-thirds of the total number of Assembly seats[8]; or

(c)   any period during which the Assembly is required[9] to nominate an Assembly member for appointment as the First Minister[10] ends without such a nomination being made[11],

the Secretary of State must propose a day for the holding of a poll at an extraordinary general election[12]. If the Secretary of State proposes such a day, Her Majesty may by Order in Council:

(i)   dissolve the Assembly and require an extraordinary general election to be held[13];

(ii)   require the poll at the election to be held on the day proposed[14]; and

(iii)   require the Assembly to meet within the period of seven days beginning immediately after the day of the poll[15].

If a poll for an extraordinary general election is held in this way[16] within the period of six months ending with the day on which the poll at the next ordinary general election would be held[17], that ordinary general election is not to be held[18].

1   As to the National Assembly for Wales see CONSTITUTIONAL LAW AND HUMAN RIGHTS.

2   The poll at the first ordinary general election for the National Assembly for Wales was held on 6 May 1999. The provisions of the Government of Wales Act 2006 came into force on 4 May 2007 (ie immediately following the date on which the ordinary election in 2007 was held under the Government of Wales Act 1998 s 3: see CONSTITUTIONAL LAW AND HUMAN RIGHTS): see the Government of Wales Act 2006 s 161(1), (4), (5).

3   Government of Wales Act 2006 s 3(1). The text refers to provision made by an order under the Government of Wales Act 2006 s 4: see s 3(1). Accordingly, the Secretary of State may by order provide for the poll at an ordinary general election to be held on a day which is neither more than one month earlier, nor more than one month later, than the first Thursday in May: see s 4(1). Such an order must make provision for the Assembly:
    (1)   to be dissolved on a day specified in the order (s 4(2)(a)); and
    (2)   to meet within the period of seven days beginning immediately after the day of the poll (s 4(2)(b)).
    In calculating any period of days for the purposes of provision made by virtue of head (2) above, the following days are to be disregarded:
    (a)   Saturday and Sunday (s 4(3)(a));
    (b)   Good Friday (s 4(3)(b));
    (c)   any day which is a bank holiday in Wales under the Banking and Financial Dealings Act 1971 (see TIME vol 97 (2010) PARA 321) (Government of Wales Act 2006 s 4(3)(c)), and
    (d)   any day appointed for public thanksgiving or mourning (s 4(3)(d)).
    Such an order may make provision for any provision of, or made under, the Representation of the People Acts, or any other enactment relating to the election of Assembly members, to have effect with such modifications or exceptions as the Secretary of State considers appropriate in connection with the alteration of the day of the poll: s 4(4). No such order is to be made, however, unless the Secretary of State has consulted the Welsh Ministers about it (s 4(5)); and a statutory instrument containing such an order is subject to annulment in pursuance of a resolution of either House of Parliament (s 4(6)). As to the meaning of 'Assembly members' for these purposes see PARA 12; and as to the meaning of 'Wales' see PARA 1 note 1. As to the Secretary of State see PARA 2. As to the meaning of 'the Representation of the People Acts' see PARA 3 note 1. As to the Welsh Ministers see CONSTITUTIONAL LAW AND HUMAN RIGHTS.
       A general election for the National Assembly for Wales is not to fall on the same date as a parliamentary general election under the Fixed-term Parliaments Act 2011 s 1(2) (see PARA 195): see s 5 (explaining the effect of the Government of Wales Act 2006 s 3(1)); and see PARAS 189, 195.

4   Ie by virtue of the Government of Wales Act 2006 s 3: see s 3(2)(a).

5   Government of Wales Act 2006 s 3(2)(a). For these purposes, the 'minimum period' means the period determined in accordance with an order under s 13 (power to make provision about elections etc: see PARA 12 note 16): s 3(3). Accordingly, the 'minimum period' for this purpose is a period of 21 days, computed in accordance with the National Assembly for Wales (Representation of the People) Order 2007, SI 2007/236, Sch 5 para 2: art 148. In computing any period of time for the purposes of the timetable set out in Sch 5 para 1, the following must be disregarded:
    (1)   a Saturday or a Sunday (Sch 5 para 2(a));
    (2)   Christmas Eve, Christmas Day or Good Friday (Sch 5 para 2(b));
    (3)   a day which is a bank holiday in Wales under the Banking and Financial Dealings Act 1971 (see TIME vol 97 (2010) PARA 321) (National Assembly for Wales (Representation of the People) Order 2007, SI 2007/236, Sch 5 para 2(c)); or
    (4)   a day appointed for public thanksgiving or mourning (Sch 5 para 2(d)).

Any such day is not to be treated as a day for the purpose of any proceedings up to the completion of the poll nor shall a constituency returning officer be obliged to proceed with the counting of votes on such a day: see Sch 5 para 2. The National Assembly for Wales (Representation of the People) Order 2007, SI 2007/236, was made in exercise of the powers conferred by the Government of Wales Act 1998 s 11, but is treated as if made under the Government of Wales Act 2006 s 13, by virtue of the Interpretation Act 1978 s 17(2). As to the meaning of 'constituency returning officer' see PARA 18 note 2. As to returning officers appointed for the purposes of Welsh Assembly elections see PARA 357 et seq.

6   Government of Wales Act 2006 s 3(2)(b). In calculating any period of days for the purposes of s 3(2)(b), the following days are to be disregarded:
     (1)   Saturday and Sunday (s 3(4)(a));
     (2)   any day which is a bank holiday in Wales under the Banking and Financial Dealings Act 1971 (see TIME vol 97 (2010) PARA 321) (Government of Wales Act 2006 s 3(4)(b)); and
     (3)   any day appointed for public thanksgiving or mourning (s 3(4)(c)).

7   Government of Wales Act 2006 s 5(2)(a).
8   Government of Wales Act 2006 s 5(2)(b).
9   Ie required under the Government of Wales Act 2006 s 47 (see CONSTITUTIONAL LAW AND HUMAN RIGHTS): see s 5(3).
10   As to the First Minister see CONSTITUTIONAL LAW AND HUMAN RIGHTS.
11   Government of Wales Act 2006 s 5(3).
12   See the Government of Wales Act 2006 s 5(1).
13   Government of Wales Act 2006 s 5(4)(a).
14   Government of Wales Act 2006 s 5(4)(b).
15   Government of Wales Act 2006 s 5(4)(c). In calculating any period of days for the purposes of s 5(4)(c), the following days are to be disregarded:
     (1)   Saturday and Sunday (s 5(7)(a));
     (2)   Christmas Eve, Christmas Day and Good Friday (s 5(7)(b));
     (3)   any day which is a bank holiday in Wales under the Banking and Financial Dealings Act 1971 (see TIME vol 97 (2010) PARA 321) (Government of Wales Act 2006 s 5(7)(c)); and
     (4)   any day appointed for public thanksgiving or mourning (s 5(7)(d)).
16   Ie under the Government of Wales Act 2006 s 5: see s 5(5).
17   Ie disregarding the Government of Wales Act 2006 s 4 (as to which see note 3): see s 5(5).
18   Government of Wales Act 2006 s 5(5). This provision does not affect the year in which the subsequent ordinary general election is to be held: s 5(6).

B. BY-ELECTIONS AND THE FILLING OF VACANCIES

214.   Vacancies in constituency seats in the National Assembly for Wales.   If the seat of an Assembly constituency member[1] returned for an Assembly constituency[2] is vacant[3], an election must be held in the Assembly constituency to fill the vacancy[4]. At the election, each person entitled to vote only has a constituency vote[5]; and the Assembly constituency member for the Assembly constituency is to be returned under the simple majority system[6].

The date of the poll at the election must be fixed by the presiding officer of the Assembly[7]; and the date must fall within the period of three months beginning with the occurrence of the vacancy[8]. Where the date of the poll to fill a vacant seat for an Assembly constituency is fixed by the presiding officer in this way, he must forthwith send a notice to the returning officer[9] for the Assembly constituency stating[10] both that the vacancy exists[11] and the date fixed for the poll to fill that vacancy[12]. However, the election must not be held if it appears to the presiding officer that the latest date which may be fixed for the poll would fall within the period of three months ending with the day on which the poll at the next ordinary general election would be held[13].

1   As to the meaning of 'Assembly constituency members' for these purposes see PARA 12.
2   As to the meaning of 'Assembly constituency' see PARA 3 note 2. As to the establishment of constituencies for the purpose of Welsh Assembly elections see PARA 76.

3   See the Government of Wales Act 2006 s 10(1).

4   See the Government of Wales Act 2006 s 10(2). This provision is expressed to be subject to s 10(7) (see the text and note 13): see s 10(2).

5   See the Government of Wales Act 2006 s 10(3). As to the meaning of 'constituency vote' see PARA 364.

6   See the Government of Wales Act 2006 s 10(3). A person may not be a candidate in an election to fill a vacancy if the person is an Assembly member or if the person is a candidate in another such election: see s 10(9). As to the voting systems used in balloting at a constituency election see PARA 339.

7   Government of Wales Act 2006 s 10(4). As to the presiding officer of the National Assembly for Wales see CONSTITUTIONAL LAW AND HUMAN RIGHTS.

8   Government of Wales Act 2006 s 10(5). If the vacancy does not come to the presiding officer's notice within the period of one month beginning with its occurrence, the date must fall within the period of three months beginning when it does come to the presiding officer's notice: s 10(6). Standing orders must make provision for determining the date on which a vacancy occurs for these purposes: s 10(8). As to the standing orders referred to see s 31 (Assembly proceedings to be regulated by standing orders); and CONSTITUTIONAL LAW AND HUMAN RIGHTS.

9   As to the returning officer for an Assembly constituency see PARA 357 et seq.

10 See the National Assembly for Wales (Representation of the People) Order 2007, SI 2007/236, Sch 5 para 77. Where the Presiding Officer of the Assembly sends a notice under Sch 5 para 77, he must record in the returns book the fact of the vacancy in the Assembly constituency concerned: see Sch 5 para 79(2). As to the returns book see PARA 215 note 42.

11 National Assembly for Wales (Representation of the People) Order 2007, SI 2007/236, Sch 5 para 77(a).

12 National Assembly for Wales (Representation of the People) Order 2007, SI 2007/236, Sch 5 para 77(b).

13 Government of Wales Act 2006 s 10(7). The text refers to the day on which the poll at the next ordinary general election would be held disregarding s 4 (see PARA 213 note 3): see s 10(7). Where a vacancy in an Assembly constituency cannot be filled because, under the relevant enactment, an election to fill that vacancy must not be held, the Presiding Officer of the Assembly must record in the returns book that (see Sch 5 para 79(4)):

    (1)   there is a vacancy in the Assembly constituency concerned (Sch 5 para 79(4)(a)); and

    (2)   under the relevant enactment, the seat is to remain vacant until the next Assembly general election (Sch 5 para 79(4)(b)).

In relation to a vacancy occurring after the 2007 Assembly general election in an Assembly constituency, the 'relevant enactment' means the Government of Wales Act 2006 s 10(7): see Sch 5 para 79(7)(a).

215.   Vacancies in electoral region seats in the National Assembly for Wales. If the seat of an Assembly regional member[1] returned for an Assembly electoral region[2] is vacant[3], and if the Assembly regional member was returned[4] from the list of a registered political party[5], the regional returning officer[6] must notify to the Presiding Officer of the National Assembly for Wales[7] the name of the person who is to fill the vacancy[8]. A person's name may only be so notified, however, if the person[9]:

    (1)   is included on the list submitted by the registered political party for the last general election[10];

    (2)   is willing to serve as an Assembly regional member for the Assembly electoral region[11]; and

    (3)   does not fall within the following criteria[12], namely that he is not a member of the registered political party[13], and that the registered political party has given notice to the regional returning officer that the person's name is not to be notified to the Presiding Officer as the name of the person who is to fill the vacancy[14].

If there is more than one person who satisfies the conditions set out in heads (1) to (3) above, the regional returning officer may only notify the name of whichever of them was the higher, or the highest, on that list[15].

Accordingly, where it comes to the notice of the Presiding Officer that the seat of an Assembly member returned from a party list for an Assembly electoral region is vacant, he must[16] forthwith send a notice to the returning officer for the Assembly electoral region[17]. Such a notice must:

(a)   state that a vacancy exists[18]; and

(b)   set out the name of the person who had been returned to fill that seat, together with the name of the registered political party[19] on whose list he was included[20].

Where a regional returning officer receives such a notice, he must ascertain from the list submitted at the previous Assembly general election by the registered political party named in the notice the name and address of the person whose name appears highest on that list (the 'prospective member')[21]. The regional returning officer must take such steps as appear to him to be reasonable[22]:

(i)   to contact the prospective member to ask whether he will state that he is willing to serve as an Assembly member for the Assembly electoral region[23]; and

(ii)   to contact the registered nominating officer of the registered political party[24] on whose list that person is included and notify that officer of the action he is taking under head (i) above[25].

Where, within such period as the regional returning officer considers reasonable[26]:

(A)   he decides that the steps he has taken to contact the prospective member have been unsuccessful[27]; or

(B)   he has not received from the prospective member a statement in writing that he is willing to serve as an Assembly member for the Assembly electoral region[28]; or

(C)   the prospective member has stated he is not willing to so serve as an Assembly member[29]; or

(D)   the regional returning officer is satisfied that the prospective member is not a member of the registered political party on whose list he is included[30], and where he receives notice signed by the registered nominating officer of that party that the prospective member's name is not to be notified to the presiding officer of the Assembly as the name of the person who is to fill the vacancy[31],

the prospective member must be treated as ceasing to be included on that list for the purposes of filling that vacancy[32]. Where a person is so treated, the regional returning officer must repeat the procedure required by heads (i) and (ii) above in respect of the person (if any) whose name and address appears next highest on that list[33]. The regional returning officer must continue to repeat the procedure until he has notified to the Presiding Officer of the Assembly the name of the person who is to fill the vacancy or until the names on that list are exhausted[34]. Subject to head (D) above, where a prospective member states in writing in response to the question from the regional returning officer under head (i) above[35] that he is willing to serve as an Assembly member for the Assembly electoral region, the regional returning officer must forthwith notify to the Presiding Officer of the Assembly the name of that person as the person to fill the vacancy[36].

A person whose name is notified to the Presiding Officer of the Assembly in this way[37] is to be treated as having been declared to be returned as an Assembly regional member for the Assembly electoral region on the day on which notification of the person's name is received by the presiding officer[38]. The regional returning officer must forthwith give public notice of the name of the member to be returned[39] and the name of the registered political party for which such a member was a party list candidate[40].

However, the seat remains vacant until the next general election if the Assembly regional member was returned as an individual candidate[41], or if that Assembly regional member was returned from the list of a registered political party but there is no-one who satisfies the conditions set out in heads (1) to (3) above[42].

1   As to the meaning of 'Assembly regional member' see PARA 12.
2   As to the meaning of 'Assembly electoral region' see PARA 3 note 2.
3   See the Government of Wales Act 2006 s 11(1).
4   Ie returned under the Government of Wales Act 2006 s 9 (ie at an ordinary general election: see PARA 340) or under s 11 (ie to fill an electoral regional vacancy): see s 11(2).
5   As to the meaning of 'registered political party' for these purposes see PARA 227 note 4.
6   As to the meaning of 'regional returning officer' see PARA 18 note 2.
7   As to the presiding officer of the National Assembly for Wales see CONSTITUTIONAL LAW AND HUMAN RIGHTS.
8   See the Government of Wales Act 2006 s 11(2).
9   See the Government of Wales Act 2006 s 11(3).
10 Government of Wales Act 2006 s 11(3)(a). For these purposes, a person included on the list submitted by a registered political party for the last general election who:
    (1)   was returned as an Assembly regional member under s 9 at that election (ie at an ordinary general election: see PARA 340), even if the return was void (s 11(8)(a));
    (2)   has subsequently been a candidate in an election held under s 10 (ie to fill an Assembly constituency vacancy: see PARA 214), whether or not returned (s 11(8)(b)); or
    (3)   has subsequently been returned under s 11, even if the return was void (s 11(8)(c)),
   is treated on and after the return of the person, or of the successful candidate at the election, as not having been included on the list (see s 11(8)).
11 Government of Wales Act 2006 s 11(3)(b).
12 Government of Wales Act 2006 s 11(3)(c). The text refers to a person to whom s 11(4) (see the text and notes 13–14) does not apply: see s 11(3)(c).
13 Government of Wales Act 2006 s 11(4)(a).
14 Government of Wales Act 2006 s 11(4)(b).
15 Government of Wales Act 2006 s 11(5).
16 Ie other than where the National Assembly for Wales (Representation of the People) Order 2007, SI 2007/236, art 101 (regional election determined to be void by election court: see PARA 863) applies: see Sch 5 para 78(1).
17 See the National Assembly for Wales (Representation of the People) Order 2007, SI 2007/236, Sch 5 para 78(1). The notice referred to in the text must be in accordance with Sch 5 para 78(2) (see the text and notes 18–20): see Sch 5 para 78(1). Where the Presiding Officer of the Assembly sends a notice under Sch 5 para 78(1), he must record in the returns book the fact of the vacancy in the Assembly electoral region concerned: see Sch 5 para 79(2). As to the returns book see note 42.
18 National Assembly for Wales (Representation of the People) Order 2007, SI 2007/236, Sch 5 para 78(2)(a).
19 For these purposes, 'registered political party' means a party which was registered under the Political Parties, Elections and Referendums Act 2000 Pt II (ss 22–40) (registration of political parties: see PARA 253) on the day (the 'relevant day') which is two days before the last day for delivery of nomination papers at the election in accordance with the timetable set out in the National Assembly for Wales (Representation of the People) Order 2007, SI 2007/236, Sch 5 para 1(1) (see PARA 216): see Sch 5 para 80(1). For these purposes, any day mentioned in Sch 5 para 2 (see PARA 213 note 5) should be disregarded: see Sch 5 para 80(3).
20 National Assembly for Wales (Representation of the People) Order 2007, SI 2007/236, Sch 5 para 78(2)(b).
21 National Assembly for Wales (Representation of the People) Order 2007, SI 2007/236, Sch 5 para 78(3).
22 See the National Assembly for Wales (Representation of the People) Order 2007, SI 2007/236, Sch 5 para 78(4).
23 National Assembly for Wales (Representation of the People) Order 2007, SI 2007/236, Sch 5 para 78(4)(a).

24 As to the nominating officer of a registered political party see PARA 253. A registered nominating officer for a registered political party may, in writing, appoint one or more persons to discharge all or any of his functions conferred or imposed by the National Assembly for Wales (Representation of the People) Order 2007, SI 2007/236, Sch 5: see Sch 5 para 81(1). Where an appointment is made under Sch 5 para 81(1), a copy of the document which records the writing required by Sch 5 para 81(1) must be delivered:

    (1)   to the constituency returning officer, in the case of a constituency election (Sch 5 para 81(2)(a));

    (2)   to the regional returning officer, in the case of a regional election (Sch 5 para 81(2)(b)); and

    (3)   to each constituency returning officer for an Assembly constituency in the Assembly electoral region, in the case of a regional election (Sch 5 para 81(2)(c)).

Where a returning officer does not receive a copy of the document required to be delivered to him under Sch 5 para 81(2), he is entitled to treat any function of the registered nominating officer purportedly exercised (or to be exercised) on his behalf by another person as not so exercised (or exercisable): Sch 5 para 81(3). As to the meaning of 'constituency returning officer' see PARA 18 note 2.

25 National Assembly for Wales (Representation of the People) Order 2007, SI 2007/236, Sch 5 para 78(4)(b).

26 See the National Assembly for Wales (Representation of the People) Order 2007, SI 2007/236, Sch 5 para 78(5).

27 National Assembly for Wales (Representation of the People) Order 2007, SI 2007/236, Sch 5 para 78(5)(a).

28 National Assembly for Wales (Representation of the People) Order 2007, SI 2007/236, Sch 5 para 78(5)(b).

29 National Assembly for Wales (Representation of the People) Order 2007, SI 2007/236, Sch 5 para 78(5)(c).

30 National Assembly for Wales (Representation of the People) Order 2007, SI 2007/236, Sch 5 para 78(5)(d)(i).

31 National Assembly for Wales (Representation of the People) Order 2007, SI 2007/236, Sch 5 para 78(5)(d)(ii).

32 See the National Assembly for Wales (Representation of the People) Order 2007, SI 2007/236, Sch 5 para 78(5).

33 See the National Assembly for Wales (Representation of the People) Order 2007, SI 2007/236, Sch 5 para 78(6). The requirements of Sch 5 para 78(5), (6) (see also the text and note 32) also apply with respect to the person mentioned in the text: see Sch 5 para 78(6).

34 National Assembly for Wales (Representation of the People) Order 2007, SI 2007/236, Sch 5 para 78(7).

35 Ie in response to the question under the National Assembly for Wales (Representation of the People) Order 2007, SI 2007/236, Sch 5 para 78(4)(a), including that provision as applied by Sch 5 para 78(6) (see note 33): see Sch 5 para 78(8).

36 National Assembly for Wales (Representation of the People) Order 2007, SI 2007/236, Sch 5 para 78(8). Where the Presiding Officer of the Assembly is notified under Sch 5 para 78(8) of the name of the person who is to fill an Assembly electoral region vacancy, he must record in the returns book the name of that person, the name of the relevant Assembly electoral region and also the date on which he received that notification: Sch 5 para 79(3). As to the returns book see note 42.

37 Ie under the Government of Wales Act 2006 s 11(2) (see the text and notes 4–8): see s 11(6).

38 Government of Wales Act 2006 s 11(6).

39 National Assembly for Wales (Representation of the People) Order 2007, SI 2007/236, Sch 5 para 78(9)(a).

40 National Assembly for Wales (Representation of the People) Order 2007, SI 2007/236, Sch 5 para 78(9)(b).

41 Government of Wales Act 2006 s 11(7)(a). As to the meaning of 'individual candidate' at a Welsh Assembly regional election see PARA 230 note 19. As to the form and contents of an election petition which may be issued to challenge such a return see PARA 780.

    Where it comes to the notice of the Presiding Officer of the Assembly that:

    (1)   the seat of an Assembly member returned for an Assembly electoral region is vacant (National Assembly for Wales (Representation of the People) Order 2007, SI 2007/236, Sch 5 para 79(5)(a)); and

    (2)   the person was returned as an individual candidate (Sch 5 para 79(5)(b)),

he must record in the returns book (see Sch 5 para 79(5)):

(a) that there is a vacancy in the Assembly electoral region concerned (Sch 5 para 79(5)(i)); and

(b) that, under the relevant enactment, the seat is to remain vacant until the next Assembly general election (Sch 5 para 79(5)(ii)).

In relation to a vacancy occurring after the 2007 Assembly general election in an Assembly electoral region for which an individual candidate was the member, the 'relevant enactment' means the Government of Wales Act 2006 s 11(7)(a): see the National Assembly for Wales (Representation of the People) Order 2007, SI 2007/236, Sch 5 para 79(7)(b).

42 Government of Wales Act 2006 s 11(7)(b).

Where, following the application of the National Assembly for Wales (Representation of the People) Order 2007, SI 2007/236, Sch 5 para 78 (see the text and notes 16–40), the seat continues to be vacant the regional returning officer must forthwith (see Sch 5 para 78(10)):

(1) give public notice that the vacancy cannot be filled and that the seat will remain vacant until the next Assembly general election by virtue of the relevant enactment (Sch 5 para 78(10)(a));

(2) complete a certificate in the form set out in English and Welsh in art 134(3), Sch 10 (Form CT: Form of certificate: electoral region; seat to remain vacant until next Assembly general election) (Sch 5 para 78(10)(b)); and

(3) deliver it, or cause it to be delivered, to the Clerk (Sch 5 para 78(10)(c)).

In respect of vacancies occurring after the 2007 Assembly general election, the 'relevant enactment' referred to in head (1) above means the Government of Wales Act 2006 s 11(7)(b): see the National Assembly for Wales (Representation of the People) Order 2007, SI 2007/236, Sch 5 para 78(11). On receipt of a certificate delivered under Sch 5 para 78(10), the Clerk must enter the information contained in the certificate in a book kept for that purpose at the Assembly (the 'returns book'): Sch 5 para 79(1). The returns book must be open to public inspection at reasonable times and any person may, on payment of a reasonable fee, obtain copies from the book: Sch 5 para 79(6). The 'Clerk' must be construed in accordance with the Government of Wales Act 2006 s 26 (see CONSTITUTIONAL LAW AND HUMAN RIGHTS): see the National Assembly for Wales (Representation of the People) Order 2007, SI 2007/236, art 2(1).

C. NOTICE OF ELECTION

216. Notice of Welsh Assembly election. Not later than the twenty-fifth day before the day of an Assembly election[1], the constituency returning officer[2] (in the case of an Assembly constituency election[3]) must publish, and the regional returning officer[4] (in the case of an Assembly regional election[5]) must prepare, notice of the election[6]. Such a notice must state:

(1) the place (or places, in the case of a regional election) and times at which nomination papers are to be delivered[7], and that forms of nomination papers may be obtained at that place (or at those places) and at those times[8];

(2) the date of the poll in the event of a contest[9];

(3) the arrangements which apply for the payment of the required deposit[10] to be made by means of the electronic transfer of funds[11]; and

(4) the date by which applications to vote by post or by proxy[12], and other applications and notices about postal or proxy voting[13], must reach the electoral registration officer[14] in order that they may be effective for the election[15].

In the case of a regional election, the regional returning officer must deliver, or cause to be delivered, the prepared notice to each constituency returning officer for an Assembly constituency in the Assembly electoral region[16]; and, on receipt of such a notice by these means, a constituency returning officer must publish it[17].

1 See the National Assembly for Wales (Representation of the People) Order 2007, SI 2007/236, Sch 5 para 1(1). As to the meaning of 'Assembly election' see PARA 3 note 2. As to the computation of any period of time for the purposes of the timetable in Sch 5 para 1 see PARA 213 note 5. As to the day of election see PARA 213 et seq.

2   As to the meaning of 'constituency returning officer' see PARA 18 note 2. As to returning officers appointed for the purposes of Welsh Assembly elections see PARA 357 et seq.

3   As to the meaning of 'Assembly constituency election' see PARA 3 note 2.

4   As to the meaning of 'regional returning officer' see PARA 18 note 2.

5   As to the meaning of 'Assembly regional election' see PARA 3 note 2.

6   See the National Assembly for Wales (Representation of the People) Order 2007, SI 2007/236, Sch 5 para 3(1), (2).

7   National Assembly for Wales (Representation of the People) Order 2007, SI 2007/236, Sch 5 para 3(1)(a), (2)(a). The forms referred to in the text are forms of individual nomination papers in the case of a constituency election and forms of individual or party nomination papers in the case of a regional election: see PARA 255 et seq.

8   National Assembly for Wales (Representation of the People) Order 2007, SI 2007/236, Sch 5 para 3(1)(b), (2)(b). See note 7.

9   National Assembly for Wales (Representation of the People) Order 2007, SI 2007/236, Sch 5 para 3(1)(c), (2)(c). As the date of the poll at Welsh Assembly elections (including elections to fill vacancies in an Assembly constituency) see PARAS 213–214.

10 Ie the deposit required by the National Assembly for Wales (Representation of the People) Order 2007, SI 2007/236, Sch 5 para 10 (see PARA 259): see Sch 5 para 3(3)(a).

11 National Assembly for Wales (Representation of the People) Order 2007, SI 2007/236, Sch 5 para 3(3)(a).

12 National Assembly for Wales (Representation of the People) Order 2007, SI 2007/236, Sch 5 para 3(3)(b)(i). As to applications to vote by post or by proxy see PARA 367 et seq.

13 National Assembly for Wales (Representation of the People) Order 2007, SI 2007/236, Sch 5 para 3(3)(b)(ii).

14 As to the electoral registration officer see PARA 139 et seq.

15 See the National Assembly for Wales (Representation of the People) Order 2007, SI 2007/236, Sch 5 para 3(3)(b).

16 See the National Assembly for Wales (Representation of the People) Order 2007, SI 2007/236, Sch 5 para 3(2). As to the meanings of 'Assembly constituency' and 'Assembly electoral region' see PARA 3 note 2.

17 See the National Assembly for Wales (Representation of the People) Order 2007, SI 2007/236, Sch 5 para 3(4).

(iv) Initiating a European Parliamentary Election

A. GENERAL ELECTIONS

217.   European parliamentary general elections.   The Treaty on European Union[1] provides that members of the European Parliament are elected for a fixed term of five years[2]. The five-year term for which members of the European Parliament are elected begins at the opening of the first session following each election[3] and the term of office of each representative begins and ends at the same time as that period[4]. Elections take place in the period determined by the European Council in the last year of the five-year period[5].

1   Ie the Treaty on European Union signed at Maastricht on 7 February 1992 ('TEU') (Cm 1934); and taking effect on 1 November 1993 (OJ L293, 27.11.1993, p 61). The European Union is founded on this treaty together with the Treaty establishing the European Atomic Energy Community (Rome, 25 March 1957; TS 1 (1973) Cmnd 5179) ('Euratom Treaty': see ENERGY AND CLIMATE CHANGE vol 44 (2011) PARAS 761–763) and the Treaty on the Functioning of the European Union (Rome, 25 March 1957; TS 1 (1973); Cmnd 5179) ('TFEU'). TFEU was formerly cited as the Treaty Establishing the European Community (Rome, 25 March 1957; TS 1 (1973); Cmnd 5179) ('TEC'), to which the United Kingdom acceded by virtue of the Act of Accession 1972. The Treaty has been renamed since and its provisions renumbered: (1) by the Treaty of Amsterdam (ie the Treaty of Amsterdam Amending the Treaty on European Union, the Treaties Establishing the European Communities and Related Acts (Amsterdam, 2 October 1997, ECS 14 (1997); Cm 3780)): see *Treaty Citation (No 2) (Note)* [1999] All ER (EC) 646, ECJ; and (2) by the Treaty of Lisbon (ie the Treaty of Lisbon Amending the Treaty Establishing the European Union and the Treaty Establishing the European Community (Lisbon, 13 December 2007, ECS 13 (2007); Cm 7294)). As to the meaning of 'United Kingdom' see PARA 1 note 1.

2 See TEU art 14(3) (formerly art 190(1), (3) TEC: see note 1). See further PARA 6.

3 1976 Act concerning the election of the representatives of the European Parliament by direct universal suffrage (OJ L278, 08.10.76, p 5) (the '1976 Act') art 5(1) (amended and renumbered by EC and Euratom Decision 2002/772 (OJ L283, 21.10.2002, p 1)). The five-year period may be extended or curtailed in certain circumstances: see the 1976 Act art 11(2); and note 5. As to the 1976 Act and as to the elections that are required under European law see PARA 6.

4 1976 Act art 5(2) (as amended and renumbered: see note 3).

5 See the 1976 Act art 11(2) (as amended and renumbered: see note 3). Should it prove impossible to hold the elections during the period so determined, the Council acting unanimously must, after consulting the Parliament, determine, at least one month before the end of the five-year term referred to in the 1976 Act art 5 (see the text and notes 3–4), another electoral period which must not be more than two months before or one month after the period originally determined: see art 11(2) (as so amended and renumbered). As to fixing the date for the holding of such elections see PARA 222.

B. BY-ELECTIONS AND THE FILLING OF VACANCIES

218. Provision for the procedure to be followed for the filling of vacant seats.
A seat falls vacant when the mandate of a member of the European Parliament ('MEP') ends as a result of resignation, death or withdrawal of the mandate[1]. Each member state must lay down appropriate procedures for filling any seat which falls vacant during the five-year term of office[2] for the remainder of that period[3]. Where the law of a member state makes explicit provision for the withdrawal of the mandate of a member of the European Parliament[4], that mandate ends pursuant to those legal provisions and the competent national authorities must so inform the European Parliament[5]. Where a seat falls vacant as a result of resignation or death, the President of the European Parliament must immediately so inform the competent authorities of the member state concerned[6].

For the purposes of filling the seat of an MEP elected for the United Kingdom which is or becomes vacant, the Secretary of State must by regulations[7] make provision prescribing the procedure to be followed[8]. Such regulations may:

(1) include provision requiring a by-election to be held in specified circumstances[9]; and

(2) require a seat last filled from a party's list of candidates[10] to be filled, in specified circumstances, from such a list (without a by-election)[11].

Where regulations provide for a by-election to be held, the poll must take place on a day, appointed by order of the Secretary of State, within such period as may be specified in the regulations[12] (although the regulations may enable the Secretary of State to decline to appoint a day in certain circumstances[13]).

1 1976 Act concerning the election of the representatives of the European Parliament by direct universal suffrage (OJ L278, 08.10.76, p 5) (the '1976 Act') art 13(1) (art 13 substituted and renumbered by EC and Euratom Decision 2002/772 (OJ L283, 21.10.2002, p 1)). As to the 1976 Act and as to the elections that are required under European law see PARA 6.

2 Ie the five-year term of office referred to in the 1976 Act art 5 (see PARA 217): see art 13(2) (as substituted and renumbered: see note 1).

3 1976 Act art 13(2) (as substituted and renumbered: see note 1). This provision is subject to the other provisions of the 1976 Act: see art 13(2) (as so substituted and renumbered).

4 As to the national provisions which govern European parliamentary elections in the United Kingdom see PARA 13 et seq.

5 1976 Act art 13(3) (as substituted and renumbered: see note 1). In the case of the United Kingdom, the competent national authority referred to in the text is the Secretary of State: see PARA 219. As to the meaning of 'United Kingdom' see PARA 1 note 1. As to the Secretary of State see PARA 2.

6 1976 Act art 13(4) (as substituted and renumbered: see note 1).

7   As to the making of regulations under the European Parliamentary Elections Act 2002 see PARA 13 note 12. As to the regulations so made see the European Parliamentary Elections Regulations 2004, SI 2004/293, regs 82–85; and PARAS 219–221.
8   See the European Parliamentary Elections Act 2002 s 5(1). See further PARA 219.
9   European Parliamentary Elections Act 2002 s 5(2)(a). Such provision may modify s 2 (voting system for European parliamentary general elections in Great Britain and Gibraltar: see PARA 340) in its application to by-elections: see s 5(2)(a). See further PARA 221.
10   As to the system of candidature whereby registered parties submit lists of candidates see PARA 340.
11   European Parliamentary Elections Act 2002 s 5(2)(b). See further PARA 220.
12   European Parliamentary Elections Act 2002 s 5(3)(a). See further PARA 221.
13   European Parliamentary Elections Act 2002 s 5(3)(b). See further PARA 221.

219. Initial response to vacancies. As soon as practicable after the Secretary of State has[1] either:

(1)   received information from the President of the European Parliament[2] of a vacancy in the seat of a member of the European Parliament ('MEP')[3]; or

(2)   informed the European Parliament[4] that a vacancy exists[5],

he must send a notice to the returning officer for the electoral region in which the vacancy exists[6]. Such a notice must:

(a)   state that a vacancy exists[7]; and

(b)   set out the name of the person who was returned in the seat which is vacant, together with the name of the registered party[8] on whose list[9] his name was included[10].

However, the requirement to send such a notice does not apply: (i) where it appears from the declaration of the result of the election that the person whose seat is now vacant was an individual candidate[11]; or (ii) where the event referred to in head (1) or head (2) above occurred less than six months before the Thursday of the period of the next general election of MEPs[12].

1   Ie subject to the European Parliamentary Elections Regulations 2004, SI 2004/293, reg 82(2) (see the text and note 11) and reg 82(5) (see the text and note 12): see reg 82(1). As to the Secretary of State see PARA 2.
2   Ie pursuant to the 1976 Act concerning the election of the representatives of the European Parliament by direct universal suffrage (OJ L278, 08.10.76, p 5) (the '1976 Act') art 13(4) (see PARA 218): see the European Parliamentary Elections Regulations 2004, SI 2004/293, reg 82(1)(a). As to the 1976 Act see PARA 6.
3   European Parliamentary Elections Regulations 2004, SI 2004/293, reg 82(1)(a).
4   Ie pursuant to the 1976 Act art 13(3) (see PARA 218): see the European Parliamentary Elections Regulations 2004, SI 2004/293, reg 82(1)(b).
5   European Parliamentary Elections Regulations 2004, SI 2004/293, reg 82(1)(b).
6   See the European Parliamentary Elections Regulations 2004, SI 2004/293, reg 82(1). The notice referred to in the text must be in accordance with reg 82(4) (see the text and notes 7–10): see reg 82(1). As to returning officers appointed for the purposes of elections to the European Parliament see PARA 360.
7   European Parliamentary Elections Regulations 2004, SI 2004/293, reg 82(4)(a).
8   As to the meaning of 'registered party' for these purposes see PARA 230 note 29.
9   As to the meaning of 'list' for these purposes see PARA 230 note 29. As to the system of candidature whereby registered parties submit lists of candidates see PARA 340.
10   European Parliamentary Elections Regulations 2004, SI 2004/293, reg 82(4)(b).
11   See the European Parliamentary Elections Regulations 2004, SI 2004/293, reg 82(2). Subject to reg 85(2) (see PARA 221), a by-election must be held in the circumstances described in reg 82(2) to fill the vacancy, and the period within which the poll at that election must take place is six months from the occurrence of the event specified in head (1) or head (2) in the text, as the case may be: reg 82(3). As to the meaning of 'individual candidate' at a European parliamentary election see PARA 230 note 32.
12   See the European Parliamentary Elections Regulations 2004, SI 2004/293, reg 82(5). For the purpose of reg 82(5) and reg 83(1) (see PARA 220), the period of the next general election of

MEPs is that during which the next general election would take place in accordance with the 1976 Act (see PARA 218): see the European Parliamentary Elections Regulations 2004, SI 2004/293, reg 82(6).

220. Filling of vacancies from a registered party's list. On receipt of a notice of a vacancy in the seat of a member of the European Parliament ('MEP')[1], the returning officer[2] must ascertain from the list submitted by the registered party named in the notice[3] (the 'relevant list') the name and address of the person whose name appears highest on that list (the 'first choice'), disregarding the name of any person who has been returned as an MEP or who has died[4]. The returning officer must take such steps as appear to him to be reasonable to contact the first choice to ask whether he will:

(1) state in writing that he is willing and able to be returned as an MEP[5]; and

(2) deliver a certificate signed by or on behalf of the nominating officer of the registered party[6] which submitted the relevant list stating that he may be returned as that party's MEP[7].

Where, within such period as the returning officer considers reasonable, he decides that the steps he has taken to contact the first choice have been unsuccessful[8], or he has not received from the first choice the statement referred to in head (1) above and the certificate referred to in head (2) above[9], or where the first choice has stated in writing that he is not willing or able to be returned as an MEP[10], or has failed to deliver the certificate referred to in head (2) above[11], the returning officer must repeat the procedure set out in heads (1) and (2) above[12] in respect of the person (if any) whose name and address appears next in the relevant list (the 'second choice') or, where that person does not satisfy the necessary conditions[13], in respect of the person (if any) whose name and address appear next highest after the second choice in that list[14]. The returning officer must continue to repeat the procedure until the seat is filled or until the names in the list are exhausted[15].

Where a person whose name appears on the relevant list provides the statement referred to in head (1) above and the certificate referred to in head (2) above, the returning officer must declare in writing that person to be returned as an MEP[16]. The returning officer must give public notice of such a declaration and send a copy of it to the Secretary of State[17]. However, where the returning officer is unable to fill the seat[18], he must notify the Secretary of State that he is unable to do so[19].

1 Ie on receipt of a notice under the European Parliamentary Elections Regulations 2004, SI 2004/293, reg 82(4) (see PARA 219): see reg 83(1).

2 As to returning officers appointed for the purposes of elections to the European Parliament see PARA 360.

3 As to the meanings of 'list' and 'registered party' for these purposes see PARA 230 note 29. As to the system of candidature whereby registered parties submit lists of candidates see PARA 340.

4 European Parliamentary Elections Regulations 2004, SI 2004/293, reg 83(1).

5 European Parliamentary Elections Regulations 2004, SI 2004/293, reg 83(2)(a).

6 For these purposes, 'nominating officer' means the person registered under the Political Parties, Elections and Referendums Act 2000 as the officer with responsibility for the matters referred to in s 24(3) (see PARA 253) in respect of a registered party: see the European Parliamentary Elections Regulations 2004, SI 2004/293, reg 2(1) (substituted by SI 2009/186).

7 European Parliamentary Elections Regulations 2004, SI 2004/293, reg 83(2)(b). As to the nominating officer of a registered party see PARA 253.

8 European Parliamentary Elections Regulations 2004, SI 2004/293, reg 83(3)(a)(i).

9 European Parliamentary Elections Regulations 2004, SI 2004/293, reg 83(3)(a)(ii).

10 European Parliamentary Elections Regulations 2004, SI 2004/293, reg 83(3)(b)(i).

11   European Parliamentary Elections Regulations 2004, SI 2004/293, reg 83(3)(b)(ii).

12   Ie the procedure required by the European Parliamentary Elections Regulations 2004, SI 2004/293, reg 83(2) (see the text and notes 5–7): see reg 83(4).

13   Ie where the European Parliamentary Elections Regulations 2004, SI 2004/293, reg 83(3)(a) (see the text and notes 8–9) or reg 83(3)(b) (see the text and notes 10–11) applies in respect of that person: see reg 83(4).

14   See the European Parliamentary Elections Regulations 2004, SI 2004/293, reg 83(4).

15   See the European Parliamentary Elections Regulations 2004, SI 2004/293, reg 83(4).

16   European Parliamentary Elections Regulations 2004, SI 2004/293, reg 83(5). However, where the returning officer has, in accordance with reg 83(4) (see the text and notes 12–15), asked a second or other subsequent choice the questions in reg 83(2) (see heads (1) and (2) in the text) (reg 83(6)(a)), and where the person who was previously asked those questions then provides the statement and certificate referred to in reg 83(2) (reg 83(6)(b)), that statement and certificate has no effect unless and until the circumstances described in reg 83(3)(a) (see the text and notes 8–9) or reg 83(3)(b) (see the text and notes 10–11) apply in respect of the second or other subsequent choice (see reg 83(6)).

17   European Parliamentary Elections Regulations 2004, SI 2004/293, reg 83(7). As to the Secretary of State see PARA 2. As to public notice by a returning officer for a European parliamentary election that is required to be given by or under the European Parliamentary Elections Regulations 2004, SI 2004/293, see PARA 239 note 23.

18   Ie under the European Parliamentary Elections Regulations 2004, SI 2004/293, reg 83 (see the text and notes 1–17): see reg 83(8).

19   European Parliamentary Elections Regulations 2004, SI 2004/293, reg 83(8).

221. By-elections held to fill vacancies. Where the Secretary of State[1] has received a notice from a returning officer[2] that he is unable to fill a vacant seat from the registered party's list[3], a by-election must be held to fill that vacancy[4]. The period within which the poll at any such by-election must take place is six months from the date on which the Secretary of State receives the notice[5]. However, where the latest date for the poll for a by-election would fall on or after the Thursday of the period of the next general election of members of the European Parliament ('MEPs')[6], the requirement to hold a by-election does not apply[7] and the Secretary of State may not appoint a day for the poll for a by-election[8].

1   As to the Secretary of State see PARA 2.

2   As to returning officers appointed for the purposes of elections to the European Parliament see PARA 360.

3   The text refers to a notice received under the European Parliamentary Elections Regulations 2004, SI 2004/293, reg 83(8) (see PARA 220): see reg 84(1). As to the meanings of 'list' and 'registered party' for these purposes see PARA 230 note 29. As to the system of candidature whereby registered parties submit lists of candidates see PARA 340.

4   European Parliamentary Elections Regulations 2004, SI 2004/293, reg 84(1).

5   European Parliamentary Elections Regulations 2004, SI 2004/293, reg 84(2).

6   European Parliamentary Elections Regulations 2004, SI 2004/293, reg 85(1). The text refers to the period of the next general election of MEPs within the meaning of reg 82(6) (see PARA 219 note 12): see reg 85(1).

7   Ie in the circumstances in which the European Parliamentary Elections Regulations 2004, SI 2004/293, reg 85 applies (see the text and note 6), reg 82(3) (see PARA 219 note 11) and reg 84(1) (see the text and notes 1–4) do not apply: see reg 85(2).

8   European Parliamentary Elections Regulations 2004, SI 2004/293, reg 85(2).

C. DATE AND NOTICE OF ELECTION

222. The date of a European parliamentary general election. Under European Union legislation, elections to the European Parliament[1] are held on the date and at the times fixed by each member state[2] but for all member states this date must fall within the same period starting on a Thursday morning and ending on the following Sunday[3].

In the United Kingdom[4], the poll at each general election of members of the European Parliament ('MEPs') is held on a day appointed by order of the Secretary of State[5].

1   As to the elections that are required under European law see PARA 6.
2   See the 1976 Act concerning the election of the representatives of the European Parliament by direct universal suffrage (OJ L278, 08.10.76, p 5) (the '1976 Act') art 10(1) (art 10 amended and renumbered by EC and Euratom Decision 2002/772 (OJ L283, 21.10.2002, p 1)). As to the 1976 Act see PARA 6.
3   See the 1976 Act art 10(1) (as amended and renumbered: see note 2). Member states may not officially make public the results of their count until after the close of polling in the member state whose electors are the last to vote within the period referred to in art 10(1): see art 10(2) (as amended and renumbered: see note 2). See also note 5.
4   As to the meaning of 'United Kingdom' see PARA 1 note 1.
5   See the European Parliamentary Elections Act 2002 s 4. As to the Secretary of State see PARA 2; and as to the making of orders under the European Parliamentary Elections Act 2002 see PARA 13 note 12. At the date at which this volume states the law, the most recent date appointed for a poll for the general election of MEPs in the United Kingdom and Gibraltar has been 22 May 2014: see the European Parliamentary Elections (Appointed Day of Poll) Order 2013, SI 2013/2063. This Order was made in exercise of the powers conferred by the European Parliamentary Elections Act 2002 s 4, pursuant to Council Decision (EU, Euratom) 2013/299 of 14 June 2013 (OJ L169, 21.06.2013, p 69) fixing the period for the eighth election of representatives to the European Parliament by direct universal suffrage (setting 22–25 May 2014 as the period for elections of Members of the European Parliament in 2014). As to the national provisions which govern European parliamentary elections in the United Kingdom see PARA 13 et seq.

223.   Notice of European parliamentary election. Not later than the twenty-fifth day before the date of the poll at a European parliamentary election[1], the returning officer must publish notice of the election[2]. Such a notice must state:

(1)   the place and times at which nomination papers are to be delivered[3], and that forms of nomination papers may be obtained at that place and at those times[4];

(2)   the date of the poll in the event of a contest[5];

(3)   the arrangements which apply for the payment of the required deposit[6] to be made by means of the electronic transfer of funds[7]; and

(4)   the date by which applications to vote by post or by proxy[8], and other applications and notices about postal or proxy voting[9], must reach the electoral registration officer[10] in order that they may be effective for the election[11].

The returning officer must send a copy of the notice to the local returning officer for each local counting area[12] in the electoral region[13]; and each local returning officer must publish the copy of the notice at a place within the area in which he acts[14].

1   See the European Parliamentary Elections Regulations 2004, SI 2004/293, reg 9, Sch 1 para 1 (Sch 1 substituted by SI 2009/186). As to the date of the poll at a European parliamentary general election see PARA 222.
      In computing any period of time for the purposes of the timetable in the European Parliamentary Elections Regulations 2004, SI 2004/293, Sch 1 para 1, the following must be disregarded:
      (1)   a Saturday or Sunday (Sch 1 para 2(1)(a) (as so substituted));
      (2)   Christmas Eve, Christmas Day, Good Friday or a bank holiday (Sch 1 para 2(1)(b) (as so substituted)); or
      (3)   a day appointed for public thanksgiving or mourning (Sch 1 para 2(1)(c) (as so substituted)).

Any such day must not be treated as a day for the purpose of any proceedings up to the completion of the poll nor is the returning officer or local returning officer obliged to proceed with the counting of votes on such a day: see Sch 1 para 2(1) (as so substituted). For these purposes, 'bank holiday' means:

    (a)   in relation to a general election in the combined region, a day which is a bank holiday under the Banking and Financial Dealings Act 1971 in any part of the United Kingdom (see TIME vol 97 (2010) PARA 321) or a bank or public holiday in Gibraltar not otherwise falling within head (2) above (European Parliamentary Elections Regulations 2004, SI 2004/293, Sch 1 para 2(2)(a) (as so substituted));

    (b)   in relation to a by-election in the combined region, a day which is a bank holiday under the Banking and Financial Dealings Act 1971 in England and Wales or a bank or public holiday in Gibraltar not otherwise falling within head (2) above (European Parliamentary Elections Regulations 2004, SI 2004/293, Sch 1 para 2(2)(b) (as so substituted));

    (c)   in relation to a general election in a region other than the combined region, a day which is a bank holiday under the Banking and Financial Dealings Act 1971 in any part of the United Kingdom (European Parliamentary Elections Regulations 2004, SI 2004/293, Sch 1 para 2(2)(c) (as so substituted)); and

    (d)   in relation to a by-election in a region other than the combined region, a day which is a bank holiday under the Banking and Financial Dealings Act 1971 in that part of the United Kingdom in which the region is situated (European Parliamentary Elections Regulations 2004, SI 2004/293, Sch 1 para 2(2)(d) (as so substituted)).

However, head (b) or head (d) above, and not head (a) or head (c) above, applies at a general election in relation to any proceedings extending, by reason of riot or open violence, beyond the time laid down by the timetable in Sch 1 para 1: see Sch 1 para 2(2). As to the meanings of 'England', 'Wales' and 'United Kingdom' see PARA 1 note 1. As to the establishment of electoral regions (including the 'combined region') for the purpose of elections to the European Parliament see PARA 77; and as to returning officers and local returning officers appointed for such purposes see PARA 360.

2   See the European Parliamentary Elections Regulations 2004, SI 2004/293, Sch 1 para 3(1) (as substituted: see note 1).

3   European Parliamentary Elections Regulations 2004, SI 2004/293, Sch 1 para 3(1)(a) (as substituted: see note 1). As to the nomination of candidates at elections see PARA 253 et seq.

4   See the European Parliamentary Elections Regulations 2004, SI 2004/293, Sch 1 para 3(1) (as substituted: see note 1).

5   European Parliamentary Elections Regulations 2004, SI 2004/293, Sch 1 para 3(1)(b) (as substituted: see note 1).

6   Ie as required by the European Parliamentary Elections Regulations 2004, SI 2004/293, Sch 1 para 10 (see PARA 259): see Sch 1 para 3(2) (as substituted: see note 1).

7   European Parliamentary Elections Regulations 2004, SI 2004/293, Sch 1 para 3(2) (as substituted: see note 1).

8   European Parliamentary Elections Regulations 2004, SI 2004/293, Sch 1 para 3(3)(a) (as substituted: see note 1). As to applications to vote by post or by proxy see PARA 367 et seq.

9   European Parliamentary Elections Regulations 2004, SI 2004/293, Sch 1 para 3(3)(b) (as substituted: see note 1).

10 As to the electoral registration officer see PARA 139 et seq.

11 European Parliamentary Elections Regulations 2004, SI 2004/293, Sch 1 para 3(3) (as substituted: see note 1).

12 As to the meaning of 'local counting area' see PARA 139 note 1.

13 See the European Parliamentary Elections Regulations 2004, SI 2004/293, Sch 1 para 3(4) (as substituted: see note 1).

14 See the European Parliamentary Elections Regulations 2004, SI 2004/293, Sch 1 para 3(4) (as substituted: see note 1).

(2) CANDIDACY FOR ELECTIONS

(i) Standing in Parliamentary Elections

224. Disqualification for membership of the House of Commons. A person is disqualified for membership of the House of Commons if, on the day on which he is nominated as a candidate[1], he has not attained the age of 18[2]. If a person so disqualified is elected as a member of that House his election is void[3]. Persons, other than citizens of the Republic of Ireland[4] and qualifying Commonwealth citizens[5], who are born outside Great Britain and Ireland and the dominions are also disqualified for membership of the House of Commons[6]. If a person so disqualified[7] is elected as a member of that House his election is void[8]. In most circumstances, the disqualification of persons elected as members of Parliament on grounds subsisting at the time of election may be determined through presentation of an election petition[9].

A person may be disqualified for membership of the House of Commons by virtue of vocation or status[10], through incapacity[11] or by office or service[12]. Provision is made to determine questions arising otherwise than through an election petition in relation to the qualification of any member of Parliament or any person elected to be such a member[13].

1   As to the nomination of candidates at a parliamentary election see PARA 253 et seq.

2   Electoral Administration Act 2006 s 17(1).

3   Electoral Administration Act 2006 s 17(2). This provision is subject to an order made by the House of Commons under the House of Commons Disqualification Act 1975 s 6(2) (order that disqualification be disregarded: see PARLIAMENT vol 78 (2010) PARA 910) as applied by the Electoral Administration Act 2006 s 17(3): see s 17(2). The House of Commons Disqualification Act 1975 s 6(2)–(4) (see PARLIAMENT vol 78 (2010) PARA 910) and s 7 (jurisdiction of Privy Council as to disqualification: see PARLIAMENT vol 78 (2010) PARA 912) apply in the case of a person disqualified by the Electoral Administration Act 2006 s 17(1) as they apply in the case of a person disqualified by the House of Commons Disqualification Act 1975; and references in s 6(2)–(4) and s 7 to a person disqualified by the House of Commons Disqualification Act 1975 must be construed as including references to a person disqualified by the Electoral Administration Act 2006 s 17(1): see s 17(3).

4   As to who are citizens of the Republic of Ireland see BRITISH NATIONALITY vol 4 (2011) PARA 410.

5   For these purposes, a person is a qualifying Commonwealth citizen if he is a Commonwealth citizen who either:

     (1)   is not a person who requires leave under the Immigration Act 1971 to enter or remain in the United Kingdom (see IMMIGRATION AND ASYLUM vol 57 (2012) PARA 10) (Electoral Administration Act 2006 s 18(2)(a)); or

     (2)   is such a person but for the time being has (or is, by virtue of any enactment, to be treated as having) indefinite leave to remain within the meaning of the Immigration Act 1971 (see IMMIGRATION AND ASYLUM vol 57 (2012) PARAS 17, 140) (Electoral Administration Act 2006 s 18(2)(b)).

   However, a person is not a qualifying Commonwealth citizen by virtue of head (1) above if he does not require leave to enter or remain in the United Kingdom by virtue only of the Immigration Act 1971 s 8 (exceptions to requirement for leave in special cases: see IMMIGRATION AND ASYLUM vol 57 (2012) PARA 22 et seq): see the Electoral Administration Act 2006 s 18(3). As to the meaning of 'United Kingdom' see PARA 1 note 1. As to who are Commonwealth citizens see BRITISH NATIONALITY vol 4 (2011) PARA 409.

6   See the Act of Settlement (1700) s 3, as modified by the Electoral Administration Act 2006 s 18(1). See also BRITISH NATIONALITY vol 4 (2011) PARAS 409, 410; PARLIAMENT vol 78 (2010) PARA 899. As to the meaning of 'Great Britain' see PARA 1 note 1.

   For the avoidance of doubt, the repeal in the Electoral Administration Act 2006 s 18(7) of the entry in the British Nationality Act 1981 Sch 7 (entry which modified certain disqualifications imposed by the Act of Settlement (1700) s 3) applied only so far as the modification made by that entry related to membership of the House of Commons, or to anything from which a person is disqualified by virtue of a disqualification from membership of that House; and s 3 has effect accordingly, and has done so since 1 January 2007 (ie since the coming into force of the Electoral Administration Act 2006 s 18: see s 77(2); and the Electoral Administration Act 2006 (Commencement No 2, Transitional and Savings Provisions) Order 2006, SI 2006/3412, art 3, Sch 1, para 14(e)): see the Constitutional Reform and Governance Act 2010 s 47(1), (2).

7   Ie by virtue of the Act of Settlement (1700) s 3, as modified by the Electoral Administration Act 2006 s 18(1) (see note 6): see s 18(4)(a).

8   Electoral Administration Act 2006 s 18(4)(a). If a person being a member of that House becomes disqualified for membership as mentioned in the text, his seat is vacated: s 18(4)(b). Section 18(4) is subject to an order made by the House of Commons under the House of Commons Disqualification Act 1975 s 6(2) (order that disqualification be disregarded: see PARLIAMENT vol 78 (2010) PARA 910) as applied by the Electoral Administration Act 2006 s 18(5): see s 18(4). The House of Commons Disqualification Act 1975 s 6(2)–(4) (see PARLIAMENT vol 78 (2010) PARA 910) and s 7 (jurisdiction of Privy Council as to disqualification: see PARLIAMENT vol 78 (2010) PARA 912) apply in the case of a person disqualified as mentioned in the Electoral Administration Act 2006 s 18(4) as they apply in the case of a person disqualified by the House of Commons Disqualification Act 1975; and references in s 6(2)–(4) and s 7 to a person disqualified by the House of Commons Disqualification Act 1975 must be construed as including references to a person disqualified as mentioned in the Electoral Administration Act 2006 s 18(4): see s 18(5).

9   As to election petitions generally see PARA 780 et seq. See also PARLIAMENT vol 78 (2010) PARA 913.

10   As to disqualification of peers see PARLIAMENT vol 78 (2010) PARA 897; as to disqualification of aliens see PARLIAMENT vol 78 (2010) PARA 899; and as to disqualification of bankrupts see PARLIAMENT vol 78 (2010) PARA 903.

11   As to the disqualification of election offenders see PARAS 905, 910; and PARLIAMENT vol 78 (2010) PARA 901. As to disqualification of minors (persons under the age of 18) see PARLIAMENT vol 78 (2010) PARA 898; as to disqualification for mental disorder see PARLIAMENT vol 78 (2010) PARA 900; and as to disqualification of criminal offenders see PARLIAMENT vol 78 (2010) PARA 902.

12   See the House of Commons Disqualification Act 1975; and PARLIAMENT vol 78 (2010) PARAS 905–910. As to the armed forces and parliamentary candidature see ARMED FORCES vol 3 (2011) PARA 327.

13   See PARLIAMENT vol 78 (2010) PARAS 911, 912. Numerous Acts which formerly afforded an opportunity for courts of law to determine a question of disqualification as a result of actions brought to recover statutory penalties from members of Parliament for sitting or voting while disqualified have now been abolished; however, a statutory penalty may be imposed still for each day on which a candidate successful at an election sits or votes in the House of Commons while disqualified on the grounds of having failed to transmit the return and declarations as to election expenses within the time limited for that purpose: see the Representation of the People Act 1983 s 85(1); PARA 755; and PARLIAMENT vol 78 (2010) PARA 914.

(ii) Standing in Local Government Elections

225. Qualification for membership of local authority. Unless disqualified[1], a person is qualified to be elected[2] and to be a member of a local authority[3], if he is a qualifying Commonwealth citizen[4] or a citizen of the Republic of Ireland[5] or a relevant citizen of the European Union[6] and on the relevant day[7] he has attained the age of 18 years[8], and:

(1)   on that day he is and thereafter continues to be a local government elector[9] for the area of the authority[10]; or

(2)   he has during the whole of the 12 months preceding that day occupied as an owner or tenant any land or other premises in that area[11]; or

(3)   his principal or only place of work during that 12 months has been in that area[12]; or

(4)   he has during the whole of those 12 months resided in that area[13]; or

(5)   in the case of a member of a parish or community council, he has during the whole of those 12 months resided either in the parish or community or within three miles of it[14].

On ceasing to hold office he is eligible for re-election, unless disqualified or not qualified[15].

1   Ie by virtue of the Local Government Act 1972 or any other enactment (see LOCAL GOVERNMENT vol 69 (2009) PARA 119): see s 79(1); and LOCAL GOVERNMENT vol 69 (2009) PARA 117. As to the armed forces and local government office see ARMED FORCES vol 3 (2011) PARA 327.

2   As to local government elections see PARA 197 et seq.

3   As to the meaning of 'local authority' for these purposes see LOCAL GOVERNMENT vol 69 (2009) PARA 23.

4   For these purposes, a person is a qualifying Commonwealth citizen if he is a Commonwealth citizen who either:

   (1)   is not a person who requires leave under the Immigration Act 1971 to enter or remain in the United Kingdom (see IMMIGRATION AND ASYLUM vol 57 (2012) PARA 10) (see the Local Government Act 1972 s 79(2B)(a); and LOCAL GOVERNMENT vol 69 (2009) PARA 117); or

   (2)   is such a person but for the time being has (or is, by virtue of any enactment, to be treated as having) indefinite leave to remain within the meaning of the Immigration Act 1971 (see IMMIGRATION AND ASYLUM vol 57 (2012) PARAS 17, 140) (see the Local Government Act 1972 s 79(2B)(b); and LOCAL GOVERNMENT vol 69 (2009) PARA 117).

   However, a person is not a qualifying Commonwealth citizen by virtue of head (1) above if he does not require leave to enter or remain in the United Kingdom by virtue only of the Immigration Act 1971 s 8 (exceptions to requirement for leave in special cases: see IMMIGRATION AND ASYLUM vol 57 (2012) PARA 22 et seq): see the Local Government Act 1972 s 79(2C); and LOCAL GOVERNMENT vol 69 (2009) PARA 117. As to who are Commonwealth citizens see BRITISH NATIONALITY vol 4 (2011) PARA 409.

5   As to who are citizens of the Republic of Ireland see BRITISH NATIONALITY vol 4 (2011) PARA 410.

6   The Local Government Act 1972 s 79 uses the expression 'citizen of the Union' which must be construed in accordance with the Treaty on the Functioning of the European Union (Rome, 25 March 1957; TS 1 (1973); Cmnd 5179) ('TFEU') art 20 (formerly art 17 TEC: see PARA 6 note 1), which states that every person holding the nationality of a member state is a citizen of the Union; and 'relevant citizen of the Union' means such a citizen who is not a qualifying Commonwealth citizen or a citizen of the Republic of Ireland: see the Local Government Act 1972 s 79(2A); and LOCAL GOVERNMENT vol 69 (2009) PARA 117.

7   The 'relevant day' in relation to any candidate means, except in the case of an election not preceded by the nomination of candidates, the day on which he is nominated as a candidate and also, if there is a poll, the day of election: see the Local Government Act 1972 s 79(2)(a); and LOCAL GOVERNMENT vol 69 (2009) PARA 117. In that excepted case, the 'relevant day' is the day of election: see s 79(2)(b); and LOCAL GOVERNMENT vol 69 (2009) PARA 117.

8   See the Local Government Act 1972 s 79(1); and LOCAL GOVERNMENT vol 69 (2009) PARA 117.

9   As to the meaning of 'local government elector' for these purposes see LOCAL GOVERNMENT vol 69 (2009) PARA 127.

10 See the Local Government Act 1972 s 79(1)(a); and LOCAL GOVERNMENT vol 69 (2009) PARA 117. As to areas and authorities in England see LOCAL GOVERNMENT vol 69 (2009) PARA 24 et seq; and as to areas and authorities in Wales see LOCAL GOVERNMENT vol 69 (2009) PARA 37 et seq.

11 See the Local Government Act 1972 s 79(1)(b); and LOCAL GOVERNMENT vol 69 (2009) PARA 117.

12 See the Local Government Act 1972 s 79(1)(c); and LOCAL GOVERNMENT vol 69 (2009) PARA 117. The phrase 'principal or only place of work' is to be given its natural and ordinary meaning and has a wider meaning than 'business' or 'employment'; constituency work may suffice, as the phrase 'principal or only place of work' does not impose a requirement that the candidate should have a personal interest in the area: *Parker v Yeo* (1992) 90 LGR 645, CA ('work' may include duties performed by a candidate as a previously-elected councillor of the local authority).

13 See the Local Government Act 1972 s 79(1)(d); and LOCAL GOVERNMENT vol 69 (2009) PARA 117. The word 'residence' does not have a technical meaning, but will generally connote a degree of permanence; it is possible for a person to have several residences, but a temporary residence at a place does not make a person a resident of that place; similarly, temporary absence from a place does not deprive a person of his residency of that place: *Fox v Stirk and Bristol Electoral Registration Officer* [1970] 2 QB 463, [1970] 3 All ER 7, CA. See also *R v Mayor of Exeter (Wescomb's Case)* (1868) LR 4 QB 110, DC; *R v Mayor of Exeter (Dipstale's Case)* (1868) LR 4 QB 114, DC; *Tewkesbury Case, Whithorn v Thomas* (1844) 9 JP 89; *R v Vicar and Churchwardens of Bredwarding, ex p Burton-Phillipson* [1920] 1 KB 47; *Barlow v Smith* (1892) 9 TLR 57, DC; *Stanford v Williams* (1899) 80 LT 490, DC; and see *Hipperson v Newbury District Electoral Registration Officer* [1985] QB 1060 at 1075, [1985] 2 All ER 456 at 463, CA, per Sir John Donaldson MR (protesters unlawfully camping outside air force base were entitled to be registered; the submission was rejected that the franchise is affected by the fact that the qualifying residence is illegal or, a fortiori, unlawful).

14   See the Local Government Act 1972 s 79(1)(e); and LOCAL GOVERNMENT vol 69 (2009) PARA 117.

15   This is the effect of the Local Government Act 1972 s 79(1): see LOCAL GOVERNMENT vol 69 (2009) PARA 117.

226.   Candidacy for elections to be a member of the London Assembly or to be the Mayor of London. A person is qualified[1] to be elected and to be the Mayor of London[2] or an Assembly member[3] if he satisfies the following requirements[4], namely that:

(1)   he is a qualifying Commonwealth citizen[5], a citizen of the Republic of Ireland[6] or a relevant citizen of the Union[7];

(2)   on the relevant day[8], he has attained the age of 18 years[9]; and

(3)   he satisfies at least one of the conditions relating to his residence, employment or entitlement to vote in Greater London[10].

These provisions apply in relation to being returned as a London member[11] otherwise than at an election following a vacancy arising in such an office[12] as they apply in relation to being elected[13].

At an ordinary election[14], a person may not be a candidate to be the London Assembly member for more than one Assembly constituency[15]. Any registered political party[16] may submit to the Greater London returning officer[17] a list of candidates to be London members[18]. The list has effect in relation to the ordinary election and any vacancies among the London members[19] which occur after that election and before the next ordinary election[20]. The list must not include more than 25 persons (but may include only one)[21], and must not include a person: (a) who is a candidate to be a constituency member but who is not a candidate of that party[22]; (b) who is included on any other list submitted for the election of London members[23]; or (c) who is an individual candidate to be a London member[24]. Similarly, a person may not be an individual candidate to be a London member if: (i) he is included on a list submitted by a registered political party for the election of London members[25]; or (ii) he is a candidate of any registered political party to be the Mayor of London or a constituency member[26].

1   Ie subject to any disqualification by virtue of the Greater London Authority Act 1999 or any other enactment: see s 20(1); and LONDON GOVERNMENT vol 71 (2013) PARA 73. As to such disqualification generally see LONDON GOVERNMENT vol 71 (2013) PARA 74 et seq. The acts and proceedings of any person elected to an office under the Greater London Authority Act 1999 and acting in that office are, notwithstanding his want of qualification, as valid and effectual as if he had been qualified: see s 22; and LONDON GOVERNMENT vol 71 (2013) PARA 73.

2   As to the Mayor of London see LONDON GOVERNMENT vol 71 (2013) PARA 69.

3   As to the meaning of 'Assembly member' and as to the London Assembly see LONDON GOVERNMENT vol 71 (2013) PARA 70.

4   See the Greater London Authority Act 1999 s 20(1); and LONDON GOVERNMENT vol 71 (2013) PARA 73.

5   See the Greater London Authority Act 1999 s 20(2)(a); and LONDON GOVERNMENT vol 71 (2013) PARA 73.

    For these purposes, a person is a qualifying Commonwealth citizen if he is a Commonwealth citizen who either:

(1)   is not a person who requires leave under the Immigration Act 1971 to enter or remain in the United Kingdom (see IMMIGRATION AND ASYLUM vol 57 (2012) PARA 10) (see the Greater London Authority Act 1999 s 20(7A)(a); and LONDON GOVERNMENT vol 71 (2013) PARA 73); or

(2)   is such a person but for the time being has (or is, by virtue of any enactment, to be treated as having) indefinite leave to remain within the meaning of the Immigration Act 1971 (see IMMIGRATION AND ASYLUM vol 57 (2012) PARAS 17, 140) (see the Greater London Authority Act 1999 s 20(7A)(b); and LONDON GOVERNMENT vol 71 (2013) PARA 73).

However, a person is not a qualifying Commonwealth citizen by virtue of head (1) above if he does not require leave to enter or remain in the United Kingdom by virtue only of the Immigration Act 1971 s 8 (exceptions to requirement for leave in special cases: see IMMIGRATION AND ASYLUM vol 57 (2012) PARA 22 et seq): see the Greater London Authority Act 1999 s 20(7B); and LONDON GOVERNMENT vol 71 (2013) PARA 73. As to who are Commonwealth citizens see BRITISH NATIONALITY vol 4 (2011) PARA 409.

6 See the Greater London Authority Act 1999 s 20(2)(b); and LONDON GOVERNMENT vol 71 (2013) PARA 73. As to who are citizens of the Republic of Ireland see BRITISH NATIONALITY vol 4 (2011) PARA 410.

7 See the Greater London Authority Act 1999 s 20(2)(c); and LONDON GOVERNMENT vol 71 (2013) PARA 73. For this purpose, 'citizen of the Union' is to be construed in accordance with the Treaty on the Functioning of the European Union (Rome, 25 March 1957; TS 1 (1973); Cmnd 5179) ('TFEU') art 20 (formerly art 17 TEC: see PARA 6 note 1), which states that every person holding the nationality of a member state is a citizen of the Union; and 'relevant citizen of the Union' means such a citizen who is not a qualifying Commonwealth citizen or a citizen of the Republic of Ireland: see the Greater London Authority Act 1999 s 20(8); and LONDON GOVERNMENT vol 71 (2013) PARA 73.

8 The 'relevant day', in relation to any candidate, means: (1) the day on which he is nominated as a candidate and also, if there is a poll, the day of the election; or (2) if the election is not preceded by the nomination of candidates, the day of the election: see the Greater London Authority Act 1999 s 20(8); and LONDON GOVERNMENT vol 71 (2013) PARA 73.

9 See the Greater London Authority Act 1999 s 20(3); and LONDON GOVERNMENT vol 71 (2013) PARA 73.

10 See the Greater London Authority Act 1999 s 20(4); and LONDON GOVERNMENT vol 71 (2013) PARA 73. The conditions to be satisfied are that:

(1) on the relevant day the person is, and from that day continues to be, a local government elector for Greater London (see s 20(4)(a); and LONDON GOVERNMENT vol 71 (2013) PARA 73);

(2) the person has, during the whole of the 12 months preceding that day, occupied as owner or tenant any land or other premises in Greater London (see s 20(4)(b); and LONDON GOVERNMENT vol 71 (2013) PARA 73);

(3) the person's principal or only place of work during that 12 months has been in Greater London (see s 20(4)(c); and LONDON GOVERNMENT vol 71 (2013) PARA 73);

(4) the person has during the whole of that 12 months resided in Greater London (see s 20(4)(d); and LONDON GOVERNMENT vol 71 (2013) PARA 73).

'Local government elector' means a person registered as a local government elector in the register of electors in accordance with the provisions of the Representation of the People Acts (see PARA 145 et seq): see the Greater London Authority Act 1999 s 29; and LONDON GOVERNMENT vol 71 (2013) PARA 73. As to the meaning of 'the Representation of the People Acts' see PARA 3 note 1. 'Elector' has the same meaning as in the Representation of the People Act 1983 s 202(1) (see PARA 95 note 2): see the Greater London Authority Act 1999 s 29; and LONDON GOVERNMENT vol 71 (2013) PARA 73. As to the meaning of 'vote' for these purposes see LONDON GOVERNMENT vol 71 (2013) PARA 84. As to Greater London see LONDON GOVERNMENT vol 71 (2013) PARA 14.

11 As to London members of the London Assembly see LONDON GOVERNMENT vol 71 (2013) PARA 70.

12 Ie under the Greater London Authority Act 1999 s 11 (see PARA 204): see s 20(5); and LONDON GOVERNMENT vol 71 (2013) PARA 112.

13 See the Greater London Authority Act 1999 s 20(5); and LONDON GOVERNMENT vol 71 (2013) PARA 112. References in s 20 to 'election' must accordingly be construed as if a London member so returned were elected at an election on the day on which he is to be treated as returned (see s 20(6); and LONDON GOVERNMENT vol 71 (2013) PARA 112); and in the application of s 20 by virtue of s 20(5), any reference to the day on which a person is nominated as a candidate must be taken as a reference to the day on which notification of the person's name is given under s 11(3) (see PARA 204) by the Greater London returning officer (see s 20(7); and LONDON GOVERNMENT vol 71 (2013) PARA 112). As to the meaning of 'Greater London returning officer' for these purposes see LONDON GOVERNMENT vol 71 (2013) PARA 81.

14 As to London Assembly ordinary elections see PARA 199; and see LONDON GOVERNMENT vol 71 (2013) PARA 76 et seq.

15 See the Greater London Authority Act 1999 s 4(9); and LONDON GOVERNMENT vol 71 (2013) PARA 78. As to the meaning of 'Assembly constituency', in relation to the London Assembly, see PARA 11 note 6. As to constituency members of the London Assembly see LONDON GOVERNMENT vol 71 (2013) PARA 70.

16   For these purposes, 'registered political party' means a party registered under the Political Parties, Elections and Referendums Act 2000 Pt II (ss 22–40) (registration of political parties: see PARA 253): see the Greater London Authority Act 1999 s 4(11); and LONDON GOVERNMENT vol 71 (2013) PARA 81.

17   See the Greater London Authority Act 1999 s 4(6), Sch 2 para 5(2); and LONDON GOVERNMENT vol 71 (2013) PARA 81.

18   See the Greater London Authority Act 1999 Sch 2 para 5(1); and LONDON GOVERNMENT vol 71 (2013) PARA 81. The London members are returned via 'London votes', i e the votes which may be given for a registered political party which has submitted a list of candidates to be London members or for an individual who is a candidate to be a London member: see s 4(1)(c), (5); and PARA 340 note 9.

19   As to vacancies arising in membership of the London Assembly see PARA 204.

20   See the Greater London Authority Act 1999 Sch 2 para 5(3); and LONDON GOVERNMENT vol 71 (2013) PARA 81.

21   See the Greater London Authority Act 1999 Sch 2 para 5(4); and LONDON GOVERNMENT vol 71 (2013) PARA 81).

22   See the Greater London Authority Act 1999 Sch 2 para 5(5)(a); and LONDON GOVERNMENT vol 71 (2013) PARA 81.

23   See the Greater London Authority Act 1999 Sch 2 para 5(5)(b); and LONDON GOVERNMENT vol 71 (2013) PARA 81.

24   See the Greater London Authority Act 1999 Sch 2 para 5(5)(c); and LONDON GOVERNMENT vol 71 (2013) PARA 81.

25   See the Greater London Authority Act 1999 Sch 2 para 5(6)(a); and LONDON GOVERNMENT vol 71 (2013) PARA 81.

26   See the Greater London Authority Act 1999 Sch 2 para 5(6)(b); and LONDON GOVERNMENT vol 71 (2013) PARA 81.

(iii) Standing in Welsh Assembly Elections

227. Candidacy for Welsh Assembly elections. At a general election for the National Assembly for Wales[1]:

(1)   a person may not be a candidate to be the Assembly constituency member[2] for more than one Assembly constituency[3];

(2)   any registered political party[4] may submit a list of candidates[5] for return as Assembly regional members[6] for a particular Assembly electoral region[7].

Such a list as is mentioned in head (2) above must be submitted to the regional returning officer[8]; and must not include more than 12 persons (but may include only one)[9]. A person must not be included in such a list: (a) who is included on any other list submitted for the Assembly electoral region or any list submitted for another Assembly electoral region[10]; (b) who is an individual candidate to be an Assembly member for the Assembly electoral region[11] or another Assembly electoral region[12]; (c) who is a candidate to be the Assembly constituency member for an Assembly constituency[13]. A person may not be an individual candidate to be an Assembly regional member for the Assembly electoral region if that person is: (i) included on a list submitted by a registered political party for the Assembly electoral region or another Assembly electoral region[14]; (ii) an individual candidate to be an Assembly regional member for another Assembly electoral region[15]; (iii) a candidate to be the Assembly constituency member for an Assembly constituency[16].

A person is disqualified from being an Assembly member if that person:

(A)   is disqualified from being a member of the House of Commons[17];

(B)   holds any of the offices for the time being designated by Order in Council as offices disqualifying persons from being Assembly members[18];

(C)   holds the office of Auditor General[19];

(D) holds the office of Public Services Ombudsman for Wales[20]; or

(E) is employed as a member of the staff of the Assembly[21].

A person who holds office as lord-lieutenant, lieutenant or high sheriff of any area in Wales[22] is disqualified from being an Assembly member for any Assembly constituency or Assembly electoral region wholly or partly included in that area[23].

1 As to an ordinary general election for the National Assembly for Wales see PARA 213. As to the National Assembly for Wales see CONSTITUTIONAL LAW AND HUMAN RIGHTS.

2 As to the meanings of 'Assembly constituency member' and 'Assembly member' for these purposes see PARA 12.

3 See the Government of Wales Act 2006 s 7(1). As to the establishment of constituencies for the purpose of Welsh Assembly elections see PARA 76 et seq.

4 For the purposes of the Government of Wales Act 2006, 'registered political party' means a party registered under the Political Parties, Elections and Referendums Act 2000 Pt II (ss 22–40) (registration of political parties: see PARA 253): see the Government of Wales Act 2006 s 6(6).

5 As to the system of candidature whereby registered parties submit lists of candidates see PARA 340.

6 As to the meaning of 'Assembly regional members' see PARA 12.

7 See the Government of Wales Act 2006 s 7(2). As to the establishment of electoral regions for the purpose of Welsh Assembly elections see PARA 76 et seq.

8 Government of Wales Act 2006 s 7(3). As to the meaning of 'regional returning officer' for these purposes see PARA 12 note 9.

9 Government of Wales Act 2006 s 7(4).

10 Government of Wales Act 2006 s 7(5)(a).

11 As to individual candidates for Assembly electoral regions see PARA 12.

12 Government of Wales Act 2006 s 7(5)(b).

13 Government of Wales Act 2006 s 7(5)(c).

14 Government of Wales Act 2006 s 7(6)(a). In the Queen's Speech 2013, HM Government announced plans to allow political parties and candidates the option to stand in both a constituency and on a regional list during Welsh Assembly elections; and to ensure that Assembly Members cannot be an MP at the same time.

15 Government of Wales Act 2006 s 7(6)(b).

16 Government of Wales Act 2006 s 7(6)(c).

17 Government of Wales Act 2006 s 16(1)(a). The text refers to disqualification under the House of Commons Disqualification Act 1975 s 1(1)(a)–(e) (judges, civil servants, members of the armed forces, members of police forces and members of foreign legislatures: see PARLIAMENT vol 78 (2010) PARAS 905–908): see the Government of Wales Act 2006 s 16(1)(a). Subject to s 17(1), (2) (exceptions and relief from disqualification: see CONSTITUTIONAL LAW AND HUMAN RIGHTS), a person is also disqualified from being an Assembly member if that person is disqualified otherwise than under the House of Commons Disqualification Act 1975 (either generally or in relation to a particular constituency) from being a member of the House of Commons or from sitting and voting in it: Government of Wales Act 2006 s 16(2). For these purposes, the references to the Republic of Ireland in the Representation of the People Act 1981 s 1 (disqualification of offenders detained in, or unlawfully at large from detention in, the British Islands or the Republic of Ireland: see PARA 263 note 11) are to be treated as references to any member state (other than the United Kingdom): see the Government of Wales Act 2006 s 16(3). See also PARA 264. As to the meaning of 'United Kingdom' see PARA 1 note 1. As to membership of the House of Commons generally see PARLIAMENT vol 78 (2010) PARA 897 et seq.

18 Government of Wales Act 2006 s 16(1)(b). As to the making of such orders see s 16(5), (6); and CONSTITUTIONAL LAW AND HUMAN RIGHTS. As to the order made under s 16(1), (5) see the National Assembly for Wales (Disqualification) Order 2010, SI 2010/2969.

19 Government of Wales Act 2006 s 16(1)(c). As to the Comptroller and Auditor General see CONSTITUTIONAL LAW AND HUMAN RIGHTS vol 8(2) (Reissue) PARAS 724–726.

20 Government of Wales Act 2006 s 16(1)(d). As to the Public Services Ombudsman for Wales see CONSTITUTIONAL LAW AND HUMAN RIGHTS.

21 Government of Wales Act 2006 s 16(1)(e).

22 As to the meaning of 'Wales' see PARA 1 note 1.

23 Government of Wales Act 2006 s 16(4).

(iv) Standing in European Parliamentary Elections

228.   Candidacy for elections to the office of member of the European Parliament. The Secretary of State[1] must by regulations[2]:

(1)   make provision for the nomination of registered parties in relation to an election of members of the European Parliament ('MEPs') in a European parliamentary electoral region[3]; and

(2)   require a nomination under head (1) above to be accompanied by a list of candidates numbering no more than the number of MEPs to be elected for the region[4].

A person is disqualified for the office of MEP if he is disqualified for membership of the House of Commons[5]. A person is disqualified for the office of MEP for a particular electoral region if he is disqualified[6] for membership of the House of Commons for any parliamentary constituency[7] wholly or partly comprised in that region[8]. A person who is a citizen of the European Union[9], and is not a Commonwealth citizen[10] or a citizen of the Republic of Ireland[11], is disqualified for the office of MEP if he is disqualified for that office through a criminal law or civil law decision[12] under the law of the member state of which he is a national[13]. If a person who is returned as an MEP for an electoral region[14] is so disqualified either for the office of MEP[15] or for the office of MEP for that region[16], his return is void and his seat vacant[17]. If an MEP becomes so disqualified for the office of MEP, or for the office of MEP for the electoral region for which he was returned, his seat is to be vacated[18].

Any person may apply to the appropriate court[19] for a declaration that a person who purports to be an MEP for a particular electoral region is disqualified[20] (whether generally or for that region)[21], or was so disqualified at the time when, or at some time since, he was returned as an MEP[22]. On such an application, the person in respect of whom the application is made is to be the respondent[23] and the applicant must give such security for the costs or expenses of the proceedings, not exceeding £5,000, as the court may direct[24]. The decision of the court on such an application is final[25]. Any declaration made by the court on such an application must be certified in writing to the Secretary of State immediately by the court[26]. However, no declaration is to be made in respect of any person on grounds which subsisted at the time of his election if there is pending, or has been tried, an election petition in which his disqualification on those grounds is, or was, in issue[27].

1   As to the Secretary of State see PARA 2.

2   See the European Parliamentary Elections Act 2002 s 2(2). As to the making of regulations under the European Parliamentary Elections Act 2002 see PARA 13 note 12. As to the regulations made for these purposes see the European Parliamentary Elections Regulations 2004, SI 2004/293.

3   European Parliamentary Elections Act 2002 s 2(2)(a). As to electoral regions constituted for the purposes of European parliamentary elections see PARA 77; and as to the nomination of individual candidates and registered parties which are to stand for election at a European parliamentary election see PARA 255 et seq.

4   European Parliamentary Elections Act 2002 s 2(2)(b). As to the number of MEPs to be elected for the United Kingdom see PARA 13.

5   European Parliamentary Elections Act 2002 s 10(1)(a) (amended by the Constitutional Reform Act 2005 ss 145, 146, Sch 17 Pt 2 para 32, Sch 18 Pt 5). See also the European Parliamentary Elections Regulations 2004, SI 2004/293, reg 9, Sch 1 para 18 (cited in PARA 263 note 54), which deals with disqualification under the Representation of the People Act 1981 (as it applies in respect of the office of MEP by virtue of the European Parliamentary Elections Act 2002 s 10(1)(a)) for the purposes of the nomination of candidates.

A person is not disqualified for the office of MEP under the European Parliamentary Elections Act 2002 s 10(1)(a) merely because:

(1)	he is a peer (s 10(2)(a));
(2)	he is a Lord Spiritual (s 10(2)(b));
(3)	he holds an office mentioned in the House of Commons Disqualification Act 1975 s 4 (stewardship of Chiltern Hundreds etc: see PARLIAMENT vol 78 (2010) PARA 895) (European Parliamentary Elections Act 2002 s 10(2)(c)); or
(4)	he holds any of the offices described in the House of Commons Disqualification Act 1975 s 4, Sch 1 Pt II (bodies of which all members are disqualified: see PARLIAMENT vol 78 (2010) PARA 908) or Sch 1 Pt 3 (other disqualifying offices: see PARLIAMENT vol 78 (2010) PARA 908) which are designated by order by the Secretary of State for the purposes of the European Parliamentary Elections Act 2002 s 10 (s 10(2)(d)).

Nor is a citizen of the European Union who is resident in the United Kingdom or Gibraltar disqualified for the office of MEP under s 10(1)(a) merely because he is disqualified for membership of the House of Commons under the Act of Settlement (1700) s 3 (disqualification of persons, other than qualifying Commonwealth and Republic of Ireland citizens, who are born outside Great Britain and Ireland and the dominions: see PARLIAMENT vol 78 (2010) PARA 899): European Parliamentary Elections Act 2002 s 10(3) (amended by the European Parliament (Representation) Act 2003 s 21(1)(a); and the Electoral Administration Act 2006 s 18(6), Sch 1 para 41(1), (2)). As to the meaning of 'United Kingdom' see PARA 1 note 1. As to the meaning of 'citizen of the European Union' for these purposes see PARA 92 note 6. As to membership of the House of Commons generally see PARLIAMENT vol 78 (2010) PARA 897 et seq.

The European Parliamentary Elections Act 2002 s 10(1) is without prejudice to the 1976 Act concerning the election of the representatives of the European Parliament by direct universal suffrage, art 6(1), (2) (incompatibility of office of MEP with certain offices in or connected with EU institutions: see PARA 6 note 5): European Parliamentary Elections Act 2002 10(8) (amended by SI 2004/1374; SI 2011/1043). From the European Parliament elections in 2004, the office of member of the European Parliament is incompatible with that of member of a national parliament; however, by way of derogation, members of the United Kingdom Parliament who were also members of the European Parliament during the five-year term preceding election to the European Parliament in 2004 may have held a dual mandate until the European Parliament elections in 2009: see the 1976 Act concerning the election of the representatives of the European Parliament by direct universal suffrage (OJ L278, 08.10.76, p 5) (the '1976 Act') art 7(2) (added and renumbered by EC and Euratom Decision 2002/772 (OJ L283, 21.10.2002, p 1)). As to the 1976 Act see PARA 6. A life peer who, on or after the date of the first general election of MEPs held after 15 July 2008 (ie after the coming into force of the European Parliament (House of Lords Disqualification) Regulations 2008, SI 2008/1647: see reg 1), is either declared returned as an MEP in accordance with the European Parliamentary Elections Regulations 2004, SI 2004/293, reg 83(5) (filling of vacancies from a registered party's list: see PARA 220), or declared elected as an MEP in accordance with Sch 1 para 61(1), (2) (see PARA 493), is disqualified from sitting or voting in the House of Lords, and from sitting or voting in a committee of the House of Lords or a joint committee of both Houses of Parliament, at any time during which he remains an MEP: European Parliament (House of Lords Disqualification) Regulations 2008, SI 2008/1647, regs 3, 4(1); Interpretation Act 1978 s 17(2). No writ of summons may be issued to a life peer while disqualified under this provision: see the European Parliament (House of Lords Disqualification) Regulations 2008, SI 2008/1647, reg 4(2). Where such a life peer is declared elected or returned as an MEP, the returning officer must notify the Speaker of the House of Lords: reg 5. For these purposes, 'life peer' means a person upon whom a peerage has been conferred under the Life Peerages Act 1958 s 1 (see PEERAGES AND DIGNITIES vol 79 (2008) PARA 824): see the European Parliament (House of Lords Disqualification) Regulations 2008, SI 2008/1647, reg 2.

As to the power of the Secretary of State to provide for persons of a description connected to Gibraltar to be disqualified from the office of MEP see the European Parliamentary Elections Act 2002 s 10(3A), (3B), (4A), (4B), (7A)–(7C) (s 10(3A), (3B), (7A)–(7C) added, s 10(4A) amended, by the Electoral Administration Act 2006 Sch 1 para 41(1), (3)–(5); the European Parliamentary Elections Act 2002 s 10(4A), (4B) added by the European Parliament (Representation) Act 2003 s 21(1)(b)); and the European Parliament (Disqualification) (United Kingdom and Gibraltar) Order 2009, SI 2009/190 (made under the European Parliamentary Elections Act 2002 s 10(4A)).

6	Ie under the House of Commons Disqualification Act 1975 s 1(2) (disqualification of persons holding named offices: see PARLIAMENT vol 78 (2010) PARA 908): see the European Parliamentary Elections Act 2002 s 10(4).

7	As to the meaning of 'constituency' for the purpose of parliamentary elections see PARA 9.

8   European Parliamentary Elections Act 2002 s 10(4).

9   European Parliamentary Elections Act 2002 s 10(5)(a).

10   As to who are Commonwealth citizens see BRITISH NATIONALITY vol 4 (2011) PARA 409.

11   European Parliamentary Elections Act 2002 s 10(5)(b). As to who are citizens of the Republic of Ireland see BRITISH NATIONALITY vol 4 (2011) PARA 410.

12   For these purposes, 'criminal law or civil law decision' has the same meaning as in Council Directive (EC) 93/109 of 6 December 1993 (OJ L329, 30.12.1993, p 34) laying down detailed arrangements for the exercise of the right to vote and to stand as a candidate in elections to the European Parliament for citizens of the Union residing in a member state of which they are not nationals (see PARA 6 note 8): see the European Parliamentary Elections Act 2002 s 10(5).

13   See the European Parliamentary Elections Act 2002 s 10(5).

14   Ie under the European Parliamentary Elections Act 2002 s 2 (general election: see the text and notes 1–4) or s 5 (filling vacant seats: see PARA 218): see s 10(6).

15   European Parliamentary Elections Act 2002 s 10(6)(a).

16   European Parliamentary Elections Act 2002 s 10(6)(b).

17   See the European Parliamentary Elections Act 2002 s 10(6).

18   European Parliamentary Elections Act 2002 s 10(7). As to filling vacant seats see PARA 218.

19   For these purposes, if the electoral region concerned is an electoral region in England and Wales or the combined region, the appropriate court is the High Court: see the European Parliamentary Elections Act 2002 s 11(2)(a) (amended by SI 2004/366). As to the meanings of 'England' and 'Wales' see PARA 1 note 1. As to the establishment of electoral regions (including the 'combined region') for the purpose of elections to the European Parliament see PARA 77.

20   Ie under the European Parliamentary Elections Act 2002 s 10 (see the text and notes 5–18): see s 11(1)(a).

21   European Parliamentary Elections Act 2002 s 11(1)(a).

22   European Parliamentary Elections Act 2002 s 11(1)(b). The text refers to a person returned as an MEP under either s 2 (general election: see the text and notes 1–4) or s 5 (filling vacant seats: see PARA 218): see s 11(1)(b).

23   European Parliamentary Elections Act 2002 s 11(4)(a).

24   European Parliamentary Elections Act 2002 s 11(4)(b). The Secretary of State may by order substitute another figure for the figure in s 11(4)(b) (s 11(5)(a) (s 11(5)(a) renumbered, s 11(5)(b) added, by the European Parliament (Representation) Act 2003 s 21(2))) and prescribe a different figure for applications where the electoral region concerned is the combined region (European Parliamentary Elections Act 2002 s 11(5)(b) (as so added)). At the date at which this volume states the law, no such order had been made.

25   European Parliamentary Elections Act 2002 s 11(3).

26   European Parliamentary Elections Act 2002 s 11(7).

27   European Parliamentary Elections Act 2002 s 11(6). As to election petitions questioning European parliamentary elections see PARA 765 et seq.

229. Candidature at European parliamentary election by a relevant citizen of the Union. Where the candidate at a European parliamentary election[1] is a relevant citizen of the Union[2], he is not validly nominated[3] as an individual candidate[4] or as a candidate on a registered party's list[5] unless[6]:

(1)   a declaration made by or on behalf of the candidate[7]; and

(2)   a certificate made by the competent administrative authorities[8] in the member state of which the candidate is a national[9],

are delivered at the place and within the time for the delivery of nomination papers[10].

The declaration referred to in head (1) above, which must be made by or on behalf of the candidate, must state, in addition to the candidate's name[11]:

(a)   his nationality[12];

(b)   his home address in the United Kingdom[13] in full[14];

(c)   that he is not standing as a candidate for election to the European Parliament in any other member state at elections held in the same period[15]; and

(d)   where his name has been entered in a register of electors in a locality or constituency[16] in the member state of which he is a national, the name of the locality or constituency where, so far as he knows, his name was last entered[17].

The certificate referred to in head (2) above, which must be made by the competent administrative authorities in the member state of which the candidate is a national, must state either that the candidate has not been deprived of his right to stand as a candidate in the member state of which he is a national or that no such disqualification is known to the competent administrative authorities[18].

As soon as practicable after publication of the statement of parties and individual candidates nominated[19], the returning officer[20] must send to the Secretary of State[21] a copy of the declaration so made by any candidate who stands nominated either by virtue of the list of candidates which accompanied a registered party's nomination or as an individual candidate[22].

A person is guilty of an offence if he makes a statement which he knows to be false in the declaration that is required as mentioned in head (1) above[23].

1   As to European parliamentary elections see PARA 217 et seq. As to the meaning of 'candidate' generally see PARA 230.
2   As to the meaning of 'relevant citizen of the Union' for these purposes see PARA 149 note 16.
3   As to the nomination of individual candidates and registered parties which are to stand for election at a European parliamentary election see PARA 255 et seq.
4   As to the meaning of 'individual candidate' at a European parliamentary election see PARA 230 note 32.
5   As to the meanings of 'list' and 'registered party' for these purposes see PARA 230 note 29. As to the system of candidature whereby registered parties submit lists of candidates see PARA 340.
6   See the European Parliamentary Elections Regulations 2004, SI 2004/293, reg 9, Sch 1 para 9(1) (Sch 1 substituted by SI 2009/186).
7   Ie a declaration under the European Parliamentary Elections Regulations 2004, SI 2004/293, Sch 1 para 9(2) (see the text and notes 11–17): see Sch 1 para 9(1) (as substituted: see note 6).
8   For these purposes, 'competent administrative authorities' has the same meaning as in Council Directive (EC) 93/109 of 6 December 1993 (OJ L329, 30.12.1993, p 34) laying down detailed arrangements for the exercise of the right to vote and to stand as a candidate in elections to the European Parliament for citizens of the Union residing in a member state of which they are not nationals (see PARA 6 note 8): see the European Parliamentary Elections Regulations 2004, SI 2004/293, Sch 1 para 9(5) (as substituted: see note 6).
9   Ie a certificate under the European Parliamentary Elections Regulations 2004, SI 2004/293, Sch 1 para 9(3) (see the text and note 18): see Sch 1 para 9(1) (as substituted: see note 6).
10 See the European Parliamentary Elections Regulations 2004, SI 2004/293, Sch 1 para 9(1) (as substituted: see note 6). As to the delivery of nomination papers see PARA 260.
11 See the European Parliamentary Elections Regulations 2004, SI 2004/293, Sch 1 para 9(2) (as substituted: see note 6).
12 European Parliamentary Elections Regulations 2004, SI 2004/293, Sch 1 para 9(2)(a) (as substituted: see note 6).
13 As to the meaning of 'United Kingdom' see PARA 1 note 1. For the purposes of European parliamentary elections held in the combined region (as to which see PARA 77), a home address in Gibraltar may be specified: see the European Parliamentary Elections Regulations 2004, SI 2004/293, Sch 1 para 9(2)(b) (as substituted: see note 6).
14 European Parliamentary Elections Regulations 2004, SI 2004/293, Sch 1 para 9(2)(b) (as substituted: see note 6).
15 European Parliamentary Elections Regulations 2004, SI 2004/293, Sch 1 para 9(2)(c) (as substituted: see note 6).
16 For these purposes, 'locality or constituency' has the same meaning as in Council Directive (EC) 93/109 of 6 December 1993 (OJ L329, 30.12.1993, p 34) laying down detailed arrangements for the exercise of the right to vote and to stand as a candidate in elections to the European Parliament for citizens of the Union residing in a member state of which they are not nationals (see PARA 6 note 8): see the European Parliamentary Elections Regulations 2004, SI 2004/293, Sch 1 para 9(5) (as substituted: see note 6). There is no separate definition of 'locality or constituency' made in Council Directive (EC) 93/109 of 6 December 1993 (OJ L329, 30.12.1993, p 34), although reference is made in the definition for 'electoral roll' (see art 2(7)), and sporadic references appear in context in the substantive articles.

17 European Parliamentary Elections Regulations 2004, SI 2004/293, Sch 1 para 9(2)(d) (as substituted: see note 6).
18 European Parliamentary Elections Regulations 2004, SI 2004/293, Sch 1 para 9(3) (as substituted: see note 6).
19 As to the meaning of 'statement of parties and individual candidates nominated' see PARA 267 note 3.
20 As to returning officers for European parliamentary elections see PARA 360 et seq.
21 As to the Secretary of State see PARA 2.
22 European Parliamentary Elections Regulations 2004, SI 2004/293, Sch 1 para 9(4) (as substituted: see note 6).
23 See the European Parliamentary Elections Regulations 2004, SI 2004/293, reg 28(1); and PARA 736.

(3) THE ELECTION CAMPAIGN

(i) The Candidate and Election Agent

A. THE CANDIDATE

230. Meaning of 'candidate'. For the purposes of the Representation of the People Act 1983, in so far as it provides for parliamentary and local government election campaigns[1] and for legal proceedings in connection with such elections[2], and unless the context otherwise requires[3]:

(1) a person becomes a candidate at a parliamentary election[4]:

    (a) on the date of the dissolution of Parliament[5] (or, in the case of a by-election, on the date of the occurrence of the vacancy)[6], in consequence of which the writ for the election is issued[7], if on or before that date he is declared by himself or by others to be a candidate at the election[8]; and

    (b) otherwise, on the day on which he is so declared by himself or by others or on which he is nominated as a candidate at the election (whichever is the earlier)[9];

(2) a person becomes a candidate at an election under the local government Act[10]:

    (a) on the last day for publication of notice of the election[11], if on or before that day he is declared by himself or by others to be a candidate at the election[12]; and

    (b) otherwise, on the day on which he is so declared by himself or by others or on which he is nominated as a candidate at the election (whichever is the earlier)[13],

or, in the case of a person included in a list of candidates submitted by a registered political party in connection with an election of the London members of the London Assembly at an ordinary election[14], on the day on which the list is submitted by the party[15].

For the purposes of the provisions that govern Welsh Assembly elections[16], in so far as they provide for the election campaign[17] and for legal proceedings in connection with such elections[18] and unless the context otherwise requires, a person becomes a constituency or individual candidate in relation to an Assembly election[19]:

    (i) on the date of the dissolution of the National Assembly for Wales[20] (or, in the case of an election to fill a casual vacancy, of the occurrence of the vacancy if on or before that date he is declared by himself or others to be a candidate at the election)[21]; and

(ii) otherwise, on the day on which he is so declared by himself or others or on which he is nominated as a candidate at the election (whichever is the earlier)[22],

or, in the case of a party list candidate[23], on the day on which the list is submitted by the party to the regional returning officer[24].

For the purposes of the provisions that govern European parliamentary elections[25], in so far as they provide for the election campaign[26] and for legal proceedings in connection with such elections[27] and unless the context otherwise requires, a person becomes a candidate at such an election[28]:

(A) in the case of a person included in the list of candidates of a registered party[29] to accompany its nomination for election[30], on the day on which the list is submitted by the party[31]; or

(B) in the case of a person not included in the list of candidates of a registered party to accompany its nomination for election[32], on the last day for publication of the notice of the election[33] if on or before that day he is declared by himself or by others to be a candidate at the election[34] and, otherwise, on the day on which he is so declared by himself or by others or on which he is nominated as a candidate at the election (whichever is the earlier)[35].

Where a person has been declared by others to be a candidate at a parliamentary election, or at a Welsh Assembly election, as the case may be, without his consent, no liability is imposed on that person[36] unless he has afterwards given his assent to the declaration, or unless he has been nominated[37]. However, a candidate may be guilty of bribery or treating, and election expenses may be incurred on his behalf, even though the bribery or treating takes place, or the expenses are incurred, before he comes within the statutory definition of 'candidate'[38].

1 Ie in the Representation of the People Act 1983 Pt II (ss 67–119) (see PARA 231 et seq). See note 3.

2 Ie in the Representation of the People Act 1983 Pt III (ss 120–186) (see PARA 761 et seq). See note 3.

3 See the Representation of the People Act 1983 s 118A(1) (s 118A added by the Political Parties, Elections and Referendums Act 2000 s 135(2), (3)). 'Candidate' must be construed for the purposes of the Representation of the People Act 1983 Pt II, unless the context otherwise requires, in accordance with s 118A (see s 118 (definition substituted by the Political Parties, Elections and Referendums Act 2000 s 135(1), (3)); Representation of the People Act 1983 s 118A(1) (as so added)); and 'candidate' has the same meaning, unless the context otherwise requires, for the purposes of the Representation of the People Act 1983 Pt III, as in Pt II (see s 185). See also note 37. 'Candidate' can bear a more limited meaning, eg, for the purposes of sending an election address free of charge where a person is not deemed to be a candidate unless certain conditions are met: see PARA 330.

   The Representation of the People Act 1983 s 118A is applied and modified for the purpose of local authority mayoral elections in England and Wales by the Local Authorities (Mayoral Elections) (England and Wales) Regulations 2007, SI 2007/1024, reg 3(2)–(5), Sch 2 Table 1: see PARA 11 note 14. For the purposes of the Local Authorities (Mayoral Elections) (England and Wales) Regulations 2007, SI 2007/1024, 'candidate' means a candidate to be an elected mayor: see reg 2(1). As to the meanings of 'England' and 'Wales' see PARA 1 note 1.

4 See the Representation of the People Act 1983 s 118A(2) (as added: see note 3). As to parliamentary elections see PARA 9 et seq.

5 Representation of the People Act 1983 s 118A(2)(a)(i) (as added: see note 3). As to the dissolution of Parliament see PARA 189.

6 Representation of the People Act 1983 s 118A(2)(a)(ii) (as added: see note 3). As to parliamentary by-elections see PARA 191.

7 As to the issue of writs for parliamentary elections see PARA 192.

8 Representation of the People Act 1983 s 118A(2)(a) (as added: see note 3). As to the nomination and declaration of candidates see PARA 253 et seq.

9   Representation of the People Act 1983 s 118A(2)(b) (as added: see note 3).

10   See the Representation of the People Act 1983 s 118A(3) (as added: see note 3). As to the meaning of 'election under the local government Act' see PARA 11 note 2. As to elections in the City of London see PARA 33.

11   As to publication of the notice for a local government election see PARA 211. Where the day or last day on which anything is required or permitted to be done by or in pursuance of the Representation of the People Act 1983 Pt II is a Saturday, Sunday, Christmas Eve, Christmas Day, Good Friday, a bank holiday or a day appointed for public thanksgiving or mourning (see s 119(1), (2) (s 119(2), (3) substituted by the Representation of the People Act 1985 s 19(4); the Representation of the People Act 1983 s 119(2) amended by the Electoral Administration Act 2006 ss 20, 74(2), Sch 1 paras 49, 51, Sch 2)):

     (1)   the requirement or permission is deemed to relate to the first day thereafter which is not one of those days (Representation of the People Act 1983 s 119(1)(a)); and

     (2)   in computing any period of not more than seven days for the purposes of Pt II, any of the days so mentioned must be disregarded (s 119(1)(b)).

For these purposes, 'bank holiday', in relation to any election, means a day which is a bank holiday in the part of the United Kingdom in which the constituency or, as the case may be, electoral area is situated: see s 119(3) (as so substituted). In relation to a parliamentary general election, the list of excluded days does not include any day to which Sch 1 r 2 does not apply by virtue of Sch 1 r 2(2A) (computation of time: see PARA 195 note 27): see s 119(2) (as so substituted and amended; and further amended by the Fixed-term Parliaments Act 2011 s 6(3), Schedule paras 6, 9). As to the meaning of 'constituency' for the purposes of parliamentary elections see PARA 9; as to the meaning of 'electoral area' for the purposes of local government elections see PARA 11; and as to the meaning of 'United Kingdom' see PARA 1 note 1.

     The Representation of the People Act 1983 s 119 has effect for the purposes of local authority referendums, subject to the modifications specified, in relation to Wales, by the Local Authorities (Conduct of Referendums) (Wales) Regulations 2008, SI 2008/1848, reg 8(2), Sch 4 Table 1, and, in relation to England, by the Local Authorities (Conduct of Referendums) (England) Regulations 2012, SI 2012/323, regs 8(2), 11–13, Sch 4 Table 1: see PARA 15 note 2.

12   Representation of the People Act 1983 s 118A(3)(a) (as added: see note 3).

13   Representation of the People Act 1983 s 118A(3)(b) (as added: see note 3).

14   Any reference in the Representation of the People Act 1983 to a registered political party submitting a list of candidates to be London members of the London Assembly at an ordinary election must be construed in accordance with the Greater London Authority Act 1999 s 4(5)(a), (6), Sch 2 Pt II paras 5–8 (see LONDON GOVERNMENT vol 71 (2013) PARAS 78, 81 et seq); and related expressions must be construed accordingly: Representation of the People Act 1983 s 203(1B) (added by the Greater London Authority Act 1999 s 17, Sch 3 para 39(1), (5)). As to London Assembly ordinary elections see PARA 199; and see LONDON GOVERNMENT vol 71 (2013) PARA 76 et seq. As to the meaning of 'London member', in relation to the London Assembly, see PARA 11 note 5; and see LONDON GOVERNMENT vol 71 (2013) PARA 70.

15   See the Representation of the People Act 1983 s 118A(3) (as added: see note 3).

16   Ie the National Assembly for Wales (Representation of the People) Order 2007, SI 2007/236. As to the meaning of 'Assembly election' see PARA 3 note 2. As to Welsh Assembly elections generally see PARA 12 et seq. As to the National Assembly for Wales see CONSTITUTIONAL LAW AND HUMAN RIGHTS.

17   Ie in the National Assembly for Wales (Representation of the People) Order 2007, SI 2007/236, Pt 3 (arts 37–85) (see PARA 235 et seq). See note 19.

18   Ie in the National Assembly for Wales (Representation of the People) Order 2007, SI 2007/236, Pt 4 (arts 86–138) (see PARA 764 et seq). See note 19.

19   See the National Assembly for Wales (Representation of the People) Order 2007, SI 2007/236, art 84(2). The text refers to a candidate at any Assembly election subsequent to the 2007 Assembly general election: see art 84(2). 'Candidate' must be construed for the purposes of Pt 3, except where the context otherwise requires, in accordance with art 84(2) (see art 84(1)); and 'candidate' has the same meaning, unless the context otherwise requires, for the purposes of Pt 4, as in Pt 3 (see art 137(1)). See also note 37. For the purposes of the National Assembly for Wales (Representation of the People) Order 2007, SI 2007/236, 'candidate' means a constituency candidate, an individual candidate or a party list candidate, where 'constituency candidate' means a candidate at an Assembly constituency election; and 'individual candidate' means a candidate at an Assembly regional election other than a party list candidate: see art 2(1). As to the meanings of 'constituency election' and 'regional election' for these purposes see PARA 3 note 2. As to the meaning of 'party list candidate' see note 23.

20 National Assembly for Wales (Representation of the People) Order 2007, SI 2007/236, art 84(2(b)(i)(aa). Where the day or last day on which anything is required or permitted to be done by or in pursuance of Pt 3 is (see art 85(1)):
   (1)   a Saturday or a Sunday (art 85(2)(a));
   (2)   Christmas Eve, Christmas Day or Good Friday (art 85(2)(b));
   (3)   a day which is a bank holiday in Wales under the Banking and Financial Dealings Act 1971 (see TIME vol 97 (2010) PARA 321) (National Assembly for Wales (Representation of the People) Order 2007, SI 2007/236, art 85(2)(c)); or
   (4)   a day appointed for public thanksgiving or mourning (art 85(2)(d)),
   then:
   (a)   the requirement or permission is deemed to relate to the first day thereafter which is not one of those days (art 85(1)(a)); and
   (b)   in computing any period of not more than seven days for the purposes of Pt 3, any of the days so mentioned must be disregarded (art 85(1)(b)).
21 National Assembly for Wales (Representation of the People) Order 2007, SI 2007/236, art 84(2(b)(i)(bb).
22 National Assembly for Wales (Representation of the People) Order 2007, SI 2007/236, art 84(2(b)(ii).
23 For these purposes, 'party list candidate' means a candidate included on a party list; and 'party list' means a list of not more than 12 candidates (but it may be a list of only one candidate) to be Assembly members for an Assembly electoral region which is to be or has been submitted to a regional returning officer by a registered political party: see the National Assembly for Wales (Representation of the People) Order 2007, SI 2007/236, art 2(1). 'Registered political party' means (subject to Sch 5 para 80 (references in Sch 5 to a registered political party: see PARA 215 note 19)) a party registered under the Political Parties, Elections and Referendums Act 2000 Pt II (ss 22–40) (registration of political parties: see PARA 253): see the National Assembly for Wales (Representation of the People) Order 2007, SI 2007/236, art 2(1). As to the meanings of 'Assembly electoral region' and 'Assembly members' see PARA 3 note 2. As to the meaning of 'regional returning officer' see PARA 18 note 2. As to returning officers for Welsh Assembly elections see PARA 357 et seq.
24 See the National Assembly for Wales (Representation of the People) Order 2007, SI 2007/236, Sch 5 para 7; and PARA 255.
25 Ie the European Parliamentary Elections Regulations 2004, SI 2004/293. As to European parliamentary elections generally see PARA 13 et seq.
26 Ie in the European Parliamentary Elections Regulations 2004, SI 2004/293, Pt 2 (regs 31–81). See note 28.
27 Ie in the European Parliamentary Elections Regulations 2004, SI 2004/293, Pt 4 (regs 86–122). See note 28.
28 See the European Parliamentary Elections Regulations 2004, SI 2004/293, reg 31(2). 'Candidate' must be construed for the purposes of Pt 2, except where the context otherwise requires, in accordance with reg 31(2) (see reg 31(1)); and 'candidate' has the same meaning, unless the context otherwise requires, for the purposes of Pt 4, as in Pt 2 (see reg 86(1)).
29 For these purposes, 'list' means a list of candidates submitted by a registered party to accompany its nomination for election; and 'registered party' means a party registered under the Political Parties, Elections and Referendums Act 2000 Pt II (see PARA 253): see the European Parliamentary Elections Regulations 2004, SI 2004/293, reg 2(1) (substituted by SI 2009/186).
30 As to the system of candidature whereby registered parties submit lists of candidates see PARA 340.
31 European Parliamentary Elections Regulations 2004, SI 2004/293, reg 31(2)(a).
   Where the day or last day on which anything is required or permitted to be done by or in pursuance of Pt 2 is a Saturday, Sunday, Christmas Eve, Christmas Day, Good Friday, a bank holiday or a day appointed for public thanksgiving or mourning (see reg 32(1), (2) (reg 32(2) amended by SI 2009/186)):
   (1)   the requirement or permission is deemed to relate to the first day thereafter which is not one of those days (European Parliamentary Elections Regulations 2004, SI 2004/293, reg 32(1)(a)); and
   (2)   in computing any period of not more than seven days for the purposes of Pt 2, any of the days so mentioned must be disregarded (reg 32(1)(b)).
   For these purposes, 'bank holiday', in relation to any European parliamentary election, means:
   (a)   in relation to the combined region, a day which is a bank holiday under the Banking and Financial Dealings Act 1971 in England and Wales (see TIME vol 97 (2010) PARA 321) or a bank or public holiday in Gibraltar not otherwise falling within the European Parliamentary Elections Regulations 2004, SI 2004/293, reg 32(2) (see reg 32(3)(a));

   (b)   in relation to an electoral region other than the combined region, a day which is a bank holiday under the Banking and Financial Dealings Act 1971 in that part of the United Kingdom in which the region is situated (see the European Parliamentary Elections Regulations 2004, SI 2004/293, reg 32(3)(b)).

As to the establishment of electoral regions for the purpose of elections to the European Parliament, and as to the combined region, see PARA 77.

32   See the European Parliamentary Elections Regulations 2004, SI 2004/293, reg 31(2)(b). In Pt 2, unless the context otherwise requires, a person to whom reg 31(2)(b) applies is known as an 'individual candidate': reg 31(1).

33   As to the date of the publication of notice of a European parliamentary election see PARA 223.

34   European Parliamentary Elections Regulations 2004, SI 2004/293, reg 31(2)(b)(i).

35   European Parliamentary Elections Regulations 2004, SI 2004/293, reg 31(2)(b)(ii).

36   Ie by virtue of the Representation of the People Act 1983 Pt II (see note 1) or for the purposes of the National Assembly for Wales (Representation of the People) Order 2007, SI 2007/236, Pt 3 (see note 17).

37   See the Representation of the People Act 1983 s 117(1); the National Assembly for Wales (Representation of the People) Order 2007, SI 2007/236, art 83(1); and PARA 258. The saving in the Representation of the People Act 1983 s 117(1) applies in relation to Pt III (see note 3) as in relation to Pt II (see s 185); and the saving in the National Assembly for Wales (Representation of the People) Order 2007, SI 2007/236, art 83(1) applies in relation to Pt 4 (see note 19) as in relation to Pt 3 (see art 137(1)). No such saving is made for the purposes of the European Parliamentary Elections Regulations 2004, SI 2004/293, however.

38   As to election expenses see PARA 269 et seq; as to bribery see PARAS 709–720; and as to treating see PARAS 721–722.

B.   APPOINTMENT AND DUTIES OF ELECTION AGENT

231.   Appointment of election agent for parliamentary and local government elections.   At a parliamentary election[1] or local government election[2] (other than an election of parish or community councillors)[3], a person must be named by or on behalf of each candidate as the candidate's election agent[4] and his name and address must be declared in writing by the candidate, or by some other person on his behalf, to the appropriate officer[5] not later than the latest time for the delivery of notices of withdrawals[6] for an election[7]. A candidate may name himself as election agent, in which case he is then, upon doing so, subject, so far as circumstances admit, to the provisions of the Representation of the People Act 1983 both as a candidate and as an election agent[8].

One election agent only must be appointed for each candidate, but, whether the election agent appointed is the candidate himself or not, the appointment may be revoked[9]. If (whether before, during or after the election) the appointment (or deemed appointment) of an election agent is revoked, or if an election agent dies, another election agent must be appointed forthwith and his name and address declared in writing to the appropriate officer[10]. The declaration as a candidate's election agent of a person other than the candidate is of no effect unless it is made and signed by that person or is accompanied by a written declaration of acceptance signed by him[11]. Upon the name and address of an election agent being declared to the appropriate officer, the appropriate officer must forthwith give public notice of that name and address[12].

1   As to parliamentary elections see PARA 9 et seq.

2   As to the meaning of 'local government election' see PARA 11. As to elections in the City of London see PARA 33.

3   A candidate at:
    (1)   an election of parish councillors in England, or of community councillors in Wales (Representation of the People Act 1983 s 71(a)); or
    (2)   any election under the local government Act which is not a local government election (see PARAS 10, 11) (Representation of the People Act 1983 s 71(b)),

need not have an election agent and accordingly the Representation of the People Act 1983 ss 67–70A (see the text and notes 7–12; and PARAS 232–234) do not apply to those elections (see s 71). Similarly, there is no provision made for election agents to be appointed at a poll consequent on a parish meeting on a question involving appointment to office. See also note 5. As to the meanings of 'England' and 'Wales' see PARA 1 note 1; and as to the meaning of 'candidate' see PARA 230. As to the election of parish and community councillors see PARA 200 et seq.

4   A sub-agent may be appointed for a parliamentary election in a county constituency or for an Authority election: see PARA 233. An election agent may act gratuitously or for remuneration (ie as a declared expense used for the purposes of the candidate's election: see PARA 269).

5   In the Representation of the People Act 1983 Pt II (ss 67–119), the 'appropriate officer' means:
    (1)   in relation to a parliamentary election, the returning officer (s 67(7)(a));
    (2)   in relation to an Authority election, the returning officer for that election as determined under s 35(2B) (returning officer at an election of a constituency member of the London Assembly: see PARA 354) or, as the case may be, s 35(2C)(a), (b) (returning officer at election of the Mayor of London and the London members of the London Assembly: see PARA 354) (s 67(7)(aa) (added by the Greater London Authority Act 1999 s 17, Sch 3 paras 1, 12(1), (6)(a)));
    (3)   in relation to any other local government election, the proper officer of the authority for which the election is held (Representation of the People Act 1983 s 67(7)(b) (amended by the Greater London Authority Act 1999 Sch 3 paras 1, 12(1), (6)(b))).
As to the meaning of 'Authority election' see PARA 11; and as to the meaning of the 'proper officer' see PARA 140 note 2. As to returning officers for parliamentary and local elections generally see PARA 350 et seq.
    The Representation of the People Act 1983 Pt II is applied and modified for the purposes of an election of parish or community councillors, and for an election of the chairman of a parish or community council or a parish meeting, by virtue of the Representation of the People Act 1983 s 187(1) (amended by the Representation of the People Act 1985 ss 24, 28, Sch 4 para 64, Sch 5); and the Local Authorities (Parishes and Communities) (England and Wales) Rules 2006, SI 2006/3305, r 6(a), (b). See also note 3.The Representation of the People Act 1983 s 67 is also applied and modified for the purpose of local authority mayoral elections in England and Wales by the Local Authorities (Mayoral Elections) (England and Wales) Regulations 2007, SI 2007/1024, reg 3(2)–(5), Sch 2 Table 1: see PARA 11 note 14.

6   As to the latest time for the withdrawal of a notice of election see PARA 266.

7   Representation of the People Act 1983 s 67(1). Any person before whom a declaration is authorised to be made under the Representation of the People Act 1983 may take the declaration: s 200(2).
    Where a registered political party submits a list of candidates to be London members of the London Assembly at an ordinary election, the requirements of s 67(1) in relation to those candidates are that not later than the time there mentioned (see s 67(1A) (added by the Greater London Authority Act 1999 Sch 3 paras 1, 12(1), (2))):
    (1)   a person must be named by or on behalf of the party as the election agent of all of those candidates (Representation of the People Act 1983 s 67(1A)(a) (as so added)); and
    (2)   the declaration required by s 67(1) must be made by or on behalf of the party (s 67(1A)(b) (as so added)).
For these purposes, 'registered political party' means a party registered under the Political Parties, Elections and Referendums Act 2000 Pt II (ss 22–40) (registration of political parties: see PARA 253): see the Representation of the People Act 1983 s 202(1) (definition added by the Greater London Authority Act 1999 Sch 3 paras 1, 38(1), (3); and amended by the Political Parties, Elections and Referendums Act 2000 s 158(1), Sch 21 para 6(1), (8)). As to references to a registered political party submitting a list of candidates to be London members of the London Assembly at an ordinary election see PARA 230 note 14. As to London Assembly ordinary elections see PARA 199; and see LONDON GOVERNMENT vol 71 (2013) PARA 76 et seq. As to the meaning of 'London member', in relation to the London Assembly, see PARA 11 note 5; and see LONDON GOVERNMENT vol 71 (2013) PARA 70.

8   See the Representation of the People Act 1983 s 67(2). If the candidate names himself as election agent, references in the Representation of the People Act 1983 to an election agent must, except where the context otherwise requires, be construed to refer to the candidate acting in his capacity as election agent: see s 67(2). As to the effect of default in the appointment of an election agent for parliamentary and local government elections see PARA 232.
    Where a registered political party submits a list of candidates to be London members of the London Assembly at an ordinary election, a candidate included in the list (see s 67(2A) (added by the Greater London Authority Act 1999 Sch 3 paras 1, 12(1), (3))):

(1)   must not under the Representation of the People Act 1983 s 67(2) name himself as his own election agent (s 67(2A)(a) (as so added)); but

(2)   may be named by or on behalf of the party as the election agent of all the candidates included in the list (s 67(2A)(b) (as so added)),

and the provisions which have effect by virtue of s 67(2) in relation to a candidate upon his naming himself as election agent also have effect in relation to a candidate upon his being named as election agent by virtue of head (2) above (see s 67(2A) (as so added)).

9   Representation of the People Act 1983 s 67(3) (s 67(3) amended, s 67(3A) added, by the Greater London Authority Act 1999 Sch 3 paras 1, 12(1), (4)). The Representation of the People Act 1983 s 67(3) is subject to s 67(3A): see s 67(3) (as so amended).

Where a registered political party submits a list of candidates to be London members of the London Assembly at an ordinary election (see s 67(3A) (as so added)):

(1)   the same person must be appointed as election agent for all the candidates included in the list (s 67(3A)(a) (as so added)); and

(2)   any such appointment may only be revoked by or on behalf of the party and in respect of all the candidates (s 67(3A)(b) (as so added)).

10   Representation of the People Act 1983 s 67(4) (amended by the Representation of the People Act 1985 s 24, Sch 4 para 20).

11   Representation of the People Act 1983 s 67(5).

Where a registered political party submits a list of candidates to be London members of the London Assembly at an ordinary election, s 67(5) applies in relation to the candidates included in that list as if the reference to a person other than the candidate were a reference to a person other than the candidate whose name appears highest on the list: s 67(5A) (added by the Greater London Authority Act 1999 Sch 3 paras 1, 12(1), (5)).

12   Representation of the People Act 1983 s 67(6).

A public notice required by or under the Representation of the People Act 1983 to be given by a returning officer for a parliamentary election, or by the proper officer of a local authority at a local government election (ie by the 'appropriate officer': see note 5) must be given by the notice being posted in some conspicuous place or places in the constituency at a parliamentary election or in the local government area at a local government election; and may also be given in such other manner as the appropriate officer thinks desirable for publicising it: see s 200(1), (1A) (s 200(1) substituted, s 200(1A) added, by the Representation of the People Act 1985 Sch 4 para 68). As to the meaning of 'local government area' see PARA 33 note 7. The Representation of the People Act 1983 s 200 has effect for the purposes of local authority referendums, subject to the modifications specified, in relation to Wales, by the Local Authorities (Conduct of Referendums) (Wales) Regulations 2008, SI 2008/1848, reg 8(2), Sch 4 Table 1, and, in relation to England, by the Local Authorities (Conduct of Referendums) (England) Regulations 2012, SI 2012/323, regs 8(2), 11–13, Sch 4 Table 1: see PARA 15 note 2.

232.   Effect of default in appointment of election agent for parliamentary and local government elections.   If, at the latest time for delivery of notices of withdrawals from a parliamentary or local government election[1], no person's name and address is duly given[2] as the election agent[3] of a candidate[4] who remains validly nominated[5], the candidate is deemed at that time to have named himself as election agent and to have revoked any appointment of another person as his election agent[6]. If the person whose name and address have been so given as those of the candidate's election agent (not being the candidate himself) dies[7], and if a new appointment is not made on the day of the death or on the following day[8], the candidate is deemed to have appointed himself as from the time of the death[9]. If the appointment of a candidate's election agent is revoked without a new appointment being made, the candidate himself is deemed to have been appointed (or re-appointed) election agent[10]. The deemed appointment of a candidate as his own election agent may be revoked as if it were an actual appointment[11]. Where, by virtue of these provisions, a candidate is to be treated as his own election agent, he is deemed to have his office:

(1)   at his address as given in the statement as to persons nominated[12]; or

(2)   if that address is outside the permitted area for the office[13], at the qualifying address of the person (or first person) named in that statement as his proposer[14].

On being satisfied that a candidate is by virtue of these provisions to be treated as his own election agent, the appropriate officer[15] must forthwith proceed to publish notice of the name and address of the candidate and of the address of his office in the same manner as if notice of these had been duly given[16].

The above provisions[17] do not apply where a registered political party submits a list of candidates to be London members of the London Assembly at an ordinary election[18]. Rather, if no person's name and address is given as required[19] as the election agent of all of the candidates included in the list who remain validly nominated at the latest time for delivery of notices of withdrawals[20]:

(a)   the candidate whose name appears highest on the list is deemed at that time to have been named on behalf of the party as election agent for all of the candidates[21]; and

(b)   any appointment of another person as election agent for those candidates is deemed to have been revoked[22].

If the person whose name and address have been so given as those of the election agent for the candidates dies[23], and if a new appointment is not made on the day of the death or on the following day[24], the candidate whose name appears highest on the list is deemed to have been named on behalf of the party as election agent for all of the candidates as from the time of death[25]. If the appointment of the election agent for the candidates is revoked without a new appointment being made, the candidate whose name appears highest on the list is deemed to have been appointed (or re-appointed) election agent[26]. The deemed appointment of a candidate as election agent may be revoked as if it were an actual appointment[27]. Where a candidate included in the list is[28] to be treated as election agent, he is deemed to have his office either at his address as given in the statement as to persons nominated[29] or (if that address is outside the permitted area for the office) at the qualifying address of the person (or first person) named in that statement as his proposer[30]. The appropriate officer, on being satisfied that a candidate is[31] to be treated as election agent, must forthwith proceed to publish the like notice as if the name and address of the candidate and the address of his office had been duly given to him[32].

1   As to the latest time for the withdrawal of a notice of election see PARA 266. As to the meaning of 'local government election' see PARA 11. As to parliamentary elections see PARA 9 et seq; and as to elections in the City of London see PARA 33.

2   Ie given as required by the Representation of the People Act 1983 s 67 (see PARA 231): see s 70(1).

3   As to the appointment of an election agent for parliamentary and local government elections see PARA 231; and as to elections where election agents are not needed see PARA 231 note 3.

4   As to the meaning of 'candidate' see PARA 230.

5   As to the nomination of candidates at elections see PARA 255 et seq.

6   Representation of the People Act 1983 s 70(1). Under this provision, a purported appointment of an election agent would be revoked, however, if notice of that appointment had not been given to the appropriate officer in accordance with the provisions described in PARA 231.

7   Representation of the People Act 1983 s 70(2)(a).

8   Representation of the People Act 1983 s 70(2)(b).

9   See the Representation of the People Act 1983 s 70(2).

10   Representation of the People Act 1983 s 70(3).

11   Representation of the People Act 1983 s 70(3A) (added by the Representation of the People Act 1985 s 24, Sch 4 para 23).

12   Representation of the People Act 1983 s 70(4)(a) (s 70(4)(a) amended, s 70(7) added, by the Political Parties and Elections Act 2009 s 39, Sch 6 para 5(1)–(3)). In the case of a parliamentary election, where the address is not given on the statement referred to in head (1) in the text, the

address as given under the Representation of the People Act 1983 Sch 1 r 6(4) (home address form: see PARA 256) must be used: see s 70(4)(a) (as so amended). As to the statement of persons nominated see PARA 267.

13   As to the permitted area mentioned in the text see PARA 234.

14   Representation of the People Act 1983 s 70(4)(b).

15   As to the meaning of 'appropriate officer' in relation to a parliamentary or local government election see PARA 231 note 5.

16   Representation of the People Act 1983 s 70(6). The text refers to the way that the name and address of an election agent must be given under s 67 (see PARA 231) and s 69 (see PARA 234): see s 70(6). In the case of a parliamentary election, s 70(6) applies whether or not a statement has been made under Sch 1 r 6(5) (address in home address form not to be made public: see PARA 256), requiring the candidate's home address not to be made public: s 70(7) (as added: see note 12). As to the manner in which public notice that is required by or under the Representation of the People Act 1983 is to be given by the appropriate officer see PARA 231 note 12.

17   Ie the Representation of the People Act 1983 s 70 (see the text and notes 1–16): see s 70A(1)(a) (s 70A added by the Greater London Authority Act 1999 s 17, Sch 3 paras 1, 15).

18   See the Representation of the People Act 1983 s 70A(1)(a) (as added: see note 17). Where a registered political party submits a list of candidates to be London members of the London Assembly at an ordinary election, s 70A(2)–(7) (see the text and notes 19–32) have effect in place of s 70 (see the text and notes 1–16): see s 70A(1)(b) (as so added). As to references to a registered political party submitting a list of candidates to be London members of the London Assembly at an ordinary election see PARA 230 note 14. As to London Assembly ordinary elections see PARA 199; and see LONDON GOVERNMENT vol 71 (2013) PARA 76 et seq. As to the meaning of 'London member', in relation to the London Assembly, see PARA 11 note 5; and see LONDON GOVERNMENT vol 71 (2013) PARA 70.

19   Ie as required by virtue of the Representation of the People Act 1983 s 67(1A) (see PARA 231 note 7): see s 70A(2) (as added: see note 17). See note 18.

20   See the Representation of the People Act 1983 s 70A(2) (as added: see note 17). See note 18.

21   Representation of the People Act 1983 s 70A(2)(a) (as added: see note 17). See note 18.

22   Representation of the People Act 1983 s 70A(2)(b) (as added: see note 17). See note 18.

23   Representation of the People Act 1983 s 70A(3)(a) (as added: see note 17). See note 18.

24   Representation of the People Act 1983 s 70A(3)(b) (as added: see note 17). See note 18.

25   See the Representation of the People Act 1983 s 70A(3) (as added: see note 17). See note 18.

26   Representation of the People Act 1983 s 70A(4) (as added: see note 17). See note 18.

27   Representation of the People Act 1983 s 70A(5) (as added: see note 17). See note 18.

28   Ie by virtue of the Representation of the People Act 1983 s 70A: see s 70A(6) (as added: see note 17). See note 18.

29   Representation of the People Act 1983 s 70A(6)(a) (as added: see note 17). See note 18.

30   Representation of the People Act 1983 s 70A(6)(b) (as added: see note 17). See note 18.

31   Ie by virtue of the Representation of the People Act 1983 s 70A: see s 70A(7) (as added: see note 17). See note 18.

32   Representation of the People Act 1983 s 70A(7) (as added: see note 17). The text refers to the way that the name and address of an election agent must be given under s 67 (see PARA 231) and his office's address must be given under s 69 (see PARA 234). see s 70A(7) (as so added). See note 18.

233. Nomination of sub-agent at certain parliamentary and local government elections.

In the case of a parliamentary election for a county constituency[1] or, in relation to a London Authority election[2], an election agent[3] for a candidate[4] may appoint one, but not more than one, deputy election agent (called a 'sub-agent') to act in any part of the constituency or electoral area[5]. As regards matters in a part of the constituency or electoral area for which there is a sub-agent, the election agent may act by the sub-agent[6], and anything done for the purposes of the Representation of the People Act 1983 by or to the sub-agent in his part of the constituency or electoral area is deemed to be done by or to the election agent[7].

Not later than the second day before the day of the poll[8], the election agent must declare in writing the name and address of every sub-agent to the returning officer[9], and the returning officer must forthwith give public notice[10] of the name and address of every sub-agent so declared[11].

The appointment of a sub-agent is not vacated by the election agent who appointed him ceasing to be election agent, but may be revoked by the candidate's election agent for the time being[12]; and in the event of the revocation of the appointment or of the death of a sub-agent, another sub-agent may be appointed, and his name and address must be forthwith declared in writing to the returning officer[13], who must forthwith give public notice of the same[14]. The declaration to be made to the returning officer[15] and the public notice to be given by him[16], must specify the part of the constituency or electoral area within which any sub-agent is appointed to act[17].

1   Representation of the People Act 1983 s 68(1)(a) (renumbered by the Greater London Authority Act 1999 s 17, Sch 3 paras 1, 13(1), (2)(a)). As to the distinction between county constituencies and borough constituencies at parliamentary elections see PARA 73. There are no sub-agents in borough constituencies.

2   Representation of the People Act 1983 s 68(1)(b) (added by the Greater London Authority Act 1999 Sch 3 paras 1, 13(1), (2)(b)). As to the meaning of 'Authority election' see PARA 11.

3   As to the appointment of an election agent for parliamentary and local government elections see PARA 231; and as to elections where election agents are not needed see PARA 231 note 3.

4   As to the meaning of 'candidate' see PARA 230.

5   See the Representation of the People Act 1983 s 68(1) (amended by the Greater London Authority Act 1999 Sch 3 paras 1, 13(1), (2)(c)). A sub-agent must have an office: see PARA 234. As to the meaning of 'electoral area' see PARA 11.

    Where a registered political party submits a list of candidates to be London members of the London Assembly at an ordinary election (see the Representation of the People Act 1983 s 68(4A) (added by the Greater London Authority Act 1999 Sch 3 paras 1, 13(1), (4))):

    (1)   the election agent for those candidates must, if he appoints a sub-agent for any part of the electoral area in the case of any of those candidates, appoint the same person as sub-agent for that part of the electoral area in the case of all of the candidates (Representation of the People Act 1983 s 68(4A)(a) (as so added)); and

    (2)   any such appointment may only be revoked in respect of all of the candidates (s 68(4A)(b) (as so added)).

    As to revocation see s 68(4); and the text and notes 12–14. As to references to a registered political party submitting a list of candidates to be London members of the London Assembly at an ordinary election see PARA 230 note 14. As to London Assembly ordinary elections see PARA 199; and see LONDON GOVERNMENT vol 71 (2013) PARA 76 et seq. As to the meaning of 'London member', in relation to the London Assembly, see PARA 11 note 5; and see LONDON GOVERNMENT vol 71 (2013) PARA 70.

6   See the Representation of the People Act 1983 s 68(2) (amended by the Greater London Authority Act 1999 Sch 3 paras 1, 13(1), (3)).

7   Representation of the People Act 1983 s 68(2)(a) (amended by the Greater London Authority Act 1999 Sch 3 paras 1, 13(1), (3)). Any act or default of a sub-agent which, if he were the election agent, would be an illegal practice or other offence against the Representation of the People Act 1983 is an illegal practice and offence against the Representation of the People Act 1983 committed by the sub-agent; and the sub-agent is liable to punishment accordingly: s 68(2)(b). The candidate is to suffer the like incapacity as if the act or default in question had been the act or default of the election agent: s 68(2)(c). As to a candidate's liability for the illegal practices of his agents see PARAS 244, 894; and as to the punishment of illegal practices see PARA 888.

8   As to the day of the poll at a parliamentary election see PARA 195; and as to the day of the poll at a local government election see PARA 206.

9   Ie as the 'appropriate officer' (see PARA 231 note 5): see the Representation of the People Act 1983 s 68(3) (amended by the Representation of the People Act 1985 s 24, Sch 4 para 21). As to declarations made under the Representation of the People Act 1983 see PARA 231 note 7. As to returning officers for parliamentary and local elections generally see PARA 350 et seq.

10 As to the manner in which public notice that is required by or under the Representation of the People Act 1983 is to be given by the appropriate officer see PARA 231 note 12.

11 Representation of the People Act 1983 s 68(3) (as amended: see note 9). The Representation of the People Act 1983 s 68(3) re-enacts a requirement originally imposed by the Corrupt and Illegal Practices Prevention Act 1883 s 25(3) (repealed), which used the words 'one clear day'

instead of 'not later than the second day'; the effect of a failure to comply with the requirement to notify was considered in *Northumberland, Berwick-upon-Tweed Division, Case* (1923) 7 O'M & H 1 at 26–27, 38–39 per Sankey J, where it was decided (at 38–39) that the failure to notify the returning officer of the names of the sub-agents did not invalidate the appointment. Importance was attached to the fact that notification was so close to the day of the poll (at 26–27, 38) and the view was expressed (at 38) that 'the object of that sub-section was to place it beyond doubt who were sub-agents in order that a person should have no difficulty in future proceedings against either such sub-agents or the candidate in proving the sub-agency'. It was held that an act lawfully done by the sub-agent could hardly be rendered illegal because the name of the sub-agent was not notified in time: see *Northumberland, Berwick-upon-Tweed Division, Case* at 39.

12 See the Representation of the People Act 1983 s 68(4).
13 Ie as the 'appropriate officer' (see PARA 231 note 5): see the Representation of the People Act 1983 s 68(4).
14 See the Representation of the People Act 1983 s 68(4).
15 Ie as the 'appropriate officer' (see PARA 231 note 5): see the Representation of the People Act 1983 s 68(5) (amended by the Greater London Authority Act 1999 Sch 3 paras 1, 13(1), (5)).
16 Ie the declaration to be made under the Representation of the People Act 1983 s 68(3) (see the text and notes 8–11) and the notice to be given under s 68(4) (see the text and note 14): see s 68(5) (as amended: see note 15).
17 Representation of the People Act 1983 s 68(5) (as amended: see note 15).

234.   Office of agents for parliamentary and local government elections. Every election agent[1] and every sub-agent[2] appointed for parliamentary and local government elections must have an office to which all claims, notices, legal process and other documents may be sent[3].

The address of the office must be declared to the appropriate officer[4] at the same time as the appointment of the agent[5] is declared to him[6], and it must be stated in the public notice of the name of the agent[7].

The office of the election agent for a parliamentary election must be within the constituency[8] (or an adjoining constituency) or in a Welsh county or county borough[9], or in a London borough[10] or district, which is partly comprised in or adjoins the constituency[11]. The office of a sub-agent for a parliamentary election must be in the area within which he is appointed to act[12].

The office of an election agent for a local government election must be within the local government area[13], or in the constituency (or one of the constituencies in which the area is comprised), or in a Welsh county or county borough, or London borough or district, which adjoins it[14]. The office of a sub-agent for a local government election must be in the area within which he is appointed to act[15].

Any claim, notice, legal process or other document delivered at the office of the election agent or sub-agent, and addressed to him, is deemed to have been served on him, and every such agent or sub-agent may, in respect of any matter connected with the election in which he is acting, be sued in any court having jurisdiction at the place where his office is situated[16].

1   As to the appointment of an election agent for parliamentary and local government elections see PARA 231; and as to elections where election agents are not needed see PARA 231 note 3. As to the meaning of 'local government election' see PARA 11. As to parliamentary elections see PARA 9 et seq; and as to elections in the City of London see PARA 33.
2   As to the appointment of election sub-agents for certain parliamentary and local government elections see PARA 233.
3   Representation of the People Act 1983 s 69(1) (amended by the Political Parties, Elections and Referendums Act 2000 s 138, Sch 18 paras 1, 19(1)(a)).
4   As to the meaning of 'appropriate officer' in relation to a parliamentary or local government election see PARA 231 note 5.
5   'Agent' includes sub-agent where sub-agents may be appointed: see PARA 233.

6 Representation of the People Act 1983 s 69(1)(a) (amended by the Representation of the People Act 1985 s 24, Sch 4 para 22).
7 Representation of the People Act 1983 s 69(1)(b). As to the public notice of agents which the appropriate officer is required to give see PARAS 231–233.
8 As to the meaning of 'constituency' for the purposes of parliamentary elections see PARA 9.
9 As to a county or county borough in Wales see LOCAL GOVERNMENT vol 69 (2009) PARA 37 et seq.
10 As to the London boroughs and their councils see LOCAL GOVERNMENT vol 69 (2009) PARA 35; LONDON GOVERNMENT vol 71 (2013) PARA 15 et seq.
11 See the Representation of the People Act 1983 s 69(2)(a) (s 69(2)(a), (b) amended by the Local Government (Wales) Act 1994 s 66(6), Sch 16 para 68(13)).
12 See the Representation of the People Act 1983 s 69(2)(a).
13 As to the meaning of 'local government area' see PARA 33 note 7.
14 See the Representation of the People Act 1983 s 69(2)(b) (as amended: see note 11).
15 See the Representation of the People Act 1983 s 69(2)(b) (amended by the Greater London Authority Act 1999 s 17, Sch 3 paras 1, 14).
16 Representation of the People Act 1983 s 69(3) (amended by the Political Parties, Elections and Referendums Act 2000 Sch 18 paras 1, 19(1)(b)).

235. Appointment of election agent for Welsh Assembly Elections. At a Welsh Assembly election[1], a person must be named by or on behalf of[2]:

(1) each constituency candidate[3], in the case of a constituency election[4]; and
(2) each individual candidate[5], in the case of a regional election[6],

as the candidate's election agent not later than the latest time for delivery of notices of withdrawal of candidature[7]. The name and address of the candidate's election agent must be declared in writing by the candidate, or by some other person on his behalf, to the appropriate returning officer[8] not later than that time[9]. A candidate at a constituency election or an individual candidate at a regional election may name himself as election agent[10].

At a regional election, not later than the latest time for delivery of notices of withdrawal of candidature, a person must be named by, or on behalf of, each registered political party submitting a party list[11] as the election agent for that party in relation to that list, and that person's name and address must be declared in writing by or on behalf of that party's registered nominating officer[12] to the regional returning officer[13] not later than that time[14]. A candidate included on a registered political party's party list may be named as election agent for that party in relation to that party list[15].

One election agent only may be appointed for[16]:

(a) each candidate at a constituency election[17];
(b) each individual candidate at a regional election[18]; and
(c) each registered political party that has submitted a party list at a regional election[19].

However, the appointment, whether the election agent appointed is the candidate himself or not, may be revoked[20]; and if (whether before, during or after the election) the appointment (or deemed appointment) of an election agent is revoked, or if an election agent dies, another election agent must be appointed forthwith and his name and address declared in writing to the appropriate returning officer[21]. The declaration as an election agent of a person, other than: (i) a constituency candidate, or an individual candidate[22]; or (ii) in relation to a registered political party that has submitted a party list, the candidate whose name appears first on the list[23], is of no effect[24] unless it is made and signed by that person, or is accompanied by a written declaration of acceptance signed by him[25]. Upon the name and address of an election agent being declared to the appropriate returning officer[26]: (A) the appropriate returning officer must forthwith give public notice of that name and address[27]; and (B) in the case of a regional election, the regional returning officer must forthwith give notice of that name and address to the constituency returning officer for each Assembly constituency in the Assembly electoral region[28].

Where a candidate has been named or has named himself as an election agent, so far as circumstances permit, he is subject to the provisions that govern Welsh Assembly elections[29] both as a candidate and as an election agent and, except where the context otherwise requires, any reference in those provisions to an election agent must be construed to refer to the candidate acting in his capacity as election agent[30].

1   As to the meaning of 'Assembly election' see PARA 3 note 2.
2   See the National Assembly for Wales (Representation of the People) Order 2007, SI 2007/236, art 37(1).
3   As to the meanings of 'candidate' and 'constituency candidate' for these purposes see PARA 230 note 19.
4   National Assembly for Wales (Representation of the People) Order 2007, SI 2007/236, art 37(1)(a). As to the meaning of 'constituency election' see PARA 3 note 2.
5   As to the meaning of 'individual candidate' at a Welsh Assembly regional election see PARA 230 note 19.
6   National Assembly for Wales (Representation of the People) Order 2007, SI 2007/236, art 37(1)(b). As to the meaning of 'regional election' see PARA 3 note 2.
7   See the National Assembly for Wales (Representation of the People) Order 2007, SI 2007/236, art 37(1). As to the latest time for the withdrawal of a notice of election see PARA 266.
8   As to the meaning of 'appropriate returning officer' see PARA 18 note 2.
9   See the National Assembly for Wales (Representation of the People) Order 2007, SI 2007/236, art 37(1). Any person before whom a declaration is authorised to be made under the National Assembly for Wales (Representation of the People) Order 2007, SI 2007/236, may take the declaration: art 143(2).
10   National Assembly for Wales (Representation of the People) Order 2007, SI 2007/236, art 37(2).
11   As to the meaning of 'registered political party' see PARA 215 note 19; and as to the meaning of 'party list' see PARA 230 note 23.
12   As to the nominating officer of a registered party see PARA 253. A registered nominating officer for a registered political party may, in writing, appoint one or more persons to discharge all or any of his functions conferred or imposed by the National Assembly for Wales (Representation of the People) Order 2007, SI 2007/236, Sch 5: see Sch 5 para 81(1); and PARA 215 note 24.
13   As to the meaning of 'regional returning officer' see PARA 18 note 2.
14   National Assembly for Wales (Representation of the People) Order 2007, SI 2007/236, art 37(3).
15   National Assembly for Wales (Representation of the People) Order 2007, SI 2007/236, art 37(4).
16   See the National Assembly for Wales (Representation of the People) Order 2007, SI 2007/236, art 37(6).
17   National Assembly for Wales (Representation of the People) Order 2007, SI 2007/236, art 37(6)(a).
18   National Assembly for Wales (Representation of the People) Order 2007, SI 2007/236, art 37(6)(b).
19   National Assembly for Wales (Representation of the People) Order 2007, SI 2007/236, art 37(6)(c).
20   See the National Assembly for Wales (Representation of the People) Order 2007, SI 2007/236, art 37(6).
21   National Assembly for Wales (Representation of the People) Order 2007, SI 2007/236, art 37(7).
22   National Assembly for Wales (Representation of the People) Order 2007, SI 2007/236, art 37(8)(a).
23   National Assembly for Wales (Representation of the People) Order 2007, SI 2007/236, art 37(8)(b).
24   Ie is of no effect under the National Assembly for Wales (Representation of the People) Order 2007, SI 2007/236, art 37: see art 37(8).
25   National Assembly for Wales (Representation of the People) Order 2007, SI 2007/236, art 37(8).

26 See the National Assembly for Wales (Representation of the People) Order 2007, SI 2007/236,
    art 37(9).
27 National Assembly for Wales (Representation of the People) Order 2007, SI 2007/236,
    art 37(9)(a). A public notice required by or under the National Assembly for Wales
    (Representation of the People) Order 2007, SI 2007/236, to be given by a constituency or
    regional returning officer at an Assembly election must be given by posting the notice in some
    conspicuous place or places in the Assembly constituency (in the case of a constituency election),
    and in each Assembly constituency in the Assembly electoral region for which the election is
    held (in the case of regional election): see art 143(1). Such notice may also be given in such other
    manner as the appropriate returning officer thinks desirable for publicising it: see art 143(1). As
    to the meanings of 'Assembly constituency' and 'Assembly electoral region' see PARA 3 note 2.
28 National Assembly for Wales (Representation of the People) Order 2007, SI 2007/236,
    art 37(9)(b). As to the meaning of 'constituency returning officer' see PARA 18 note 2.
29 Ie is subject to the provisions of the National Assembly for Wales (Representation of the People)
    Order 2007, SI 2007/236: see art 37(5).
30 National Assembly for Wales (Representation of the People) Order 2007, SI 2007/236,
    art 37(5).

**236. Effect of default in appointment of election agent for Welsh Assembly
Elections.** If, at the latest time for delivery of notices of withdrawal of
candidature for a Welsh Assembly election[1], no person's name and address is
given as required[2] as the election agent[3] of a constituency candidate[4] or
individual candidate[5] who remains validly nominated[6], or in respect of a
registered political party that has submitted a party list at a regional election[7]:

(1) in the case of a candidate at a constituency election[8], or an individual
     candidate at a regional election, the candidate is deemed at that time to
     have named himself as election agent, and to have revoked any
     appointment of another person as his election agent[9]; and

(2) in the case of a registered political party that has submitted a party list
     at a regional election, the candidate whose name appears first on the list
     is deemed at that time to have been named as election agent, and any
     appointment of another person as that party's election agent is deemed
     to have been revoked[10].

If the person dies whose name and address have been so given as those of an
election agent for a candidate at a constituency election or for an individual
candidate (not being the candidate himself) or for a registered political party[11],
and if a new appointment is not made on the day of the death or on the
following day[12], then:

(a) in the case of a candidate at a constituency election or an individual
     candidate at a regional election, he is deemed to have appointed himself
     as from the time of death[13]; and

(b) in the case of the death of an election agent for a registered political
     party at a regional election[14], the candidate whose name appears first on
     the list is deemed to have been appointed from the time of death[15] (or, in
     the case of the death of such a candidate, the candidate whose name
     appears next highest on the list is deemed to have been appointed from
     the time of death)[16].

If the appointment of an election agent is revoked without a new appointment
being made[17], then:

(i)   in the case of a candidate at a constituency election or an individual
      candidate at a regional election, the candidate himself is deemed to have
      been appointed (or re-appointed) election agent[18]; and

(ii) in the case of a registered political party, the candidate whose name
      appears first on that party's list is deemed to have been appointed (or
      re-appointed) election agent[19].

The deemed appointment of an election agent may be revoked as if it were an actual appointment[20].

Where a candidate is[21] to be treated as an election agent, he is deemed to have his office at his address as given for that purpose in his consent to nomination[22]. The appropriate returning officer[23], on being satisfied that a person is[24] to be treated as an election agent, must forthwith proceed to give such like notice as if the name and address of the person and the address of his office had been duly given to him[25].

1   As to the meaning of 'Assembly election' see PARA 3 note 2. As to the latest time for the withdrawal of a notice of election see PARA 266.
2   Ie given as required by the National Assembly for Wales (Representation of the People) Order 2007, SI 2007/236, art 37 (see PARA 235): see art 40(1), (2).
3   As to the appointment of an election agent for Welsh Assembly elections see PARA 235.
4   As to the meanings of 'candidate' and 'constituency candidate' for these purposes see PARA 230 note 19.
5   As to the meaning of 'individual candidate' at a Welsh Assembly regional election see PARA 230 note 19.
6   As to the nomination of candidates at elections see PARA 255 et seq.
7   See the National Assembly for Wales (Representation of the People) Order 2007, SI 2007/236, art 40(1), (2). As to the meaning of 'regional election' see PARA 3 note 2. As to the meaning of 'registered political party' see PARA 215 note 19; and as to the meaning of 'party list' see PARA 230 note 23.
8   As to the meaning of 'constituency election' see PARA 3 note 2.
9   See the National Assembly for Wales (Representation of the People) Order 2007, SI 2007/236, art 40(1).
10 See the National Assembly for Wales (Representation of the People) Order 2007, SI 2007/236, art 40(2).
11 National Assembly for Wales (Representation of the People) Order 2007, SI 2007/236, art 40(3)(a).
12 National Assembly for Wales (Representation of the People) Order 2007, SI 2007/236, art 40(3)(b).
13 National Assembly for Wales (Representation of the People) Order 2007, SI 2007/236, art 40(4)(a).
14 See the National Assembly for Wales (Representation of the People) Order 2007, SI 2007/236, art 40(4)(b).
15 National Assembly for Wales (Representation of the People) Order 2007, SI 2007/236, art 40(4)(b)(i).
16 National Assembly for Wales (Representation of the People) Order 2007, SI 2007/236, art 40(4)(b)(ii).
17 See the National Assembly for Wales (Representation of the People) Order 2007, SI 2007/236, art 40(5).
18 National Assembly for Wales (Representation of the People) Order 2007, SI 2007/236, art 40(5)(a).
19 National Assembly for Wales (Representation of the People) Order 2007, SI 2007/236, art 40(5)(b).
20 National Assembly for Wales (Representation of the People) Order 2007, SI 2007/236, art 40(6).
21 Ie by virtue of the National Assembly for Wales (Representation of the People) Order 2007, SI 2007/236, art 40: see art 40(7).
22 National Assembly for Wales (Representation of the People) Order 2007, SI 2007/236, art 40(7). The text refers to the consent to nomination under Sch 5 para 9, which requires a candidate's consent given under that rule to state an address within the relevant area that may be deemed to be his office as an election agent for the purposes of art 40(7) (see Sch 5 para 9(4)(b); and PARA 258): see art 40(7).
23 As to the meaning of 'appropriate returning officer' at a Welsh Assembly election see PARA 18 note 2.
24 Ie by virtue of the National Assembly for Wales (Representation of the People) Order 2007, SI 2007/236, art 40: see art 40(8).
25 National Assembly for Wales (Representation of the People) Order 2007, SI 2007/236, art 40(8). The text refers to the way that the name and address of an election agent, and his

office's address, must be given under art 37 (see PARA 235) and art 39 (see PARA 238): see art 40(8). As to the manner in which notice is to be given see PARA 235 note 27.

237.   Nomination of sub-agent for Welsh Assembly Elections.   At a Welsh Assembly election[1], an election agent[2] may[3] appoint one, but not more than one, deputy election agent (referred to as a 'sub-agent') to act in[4] any part of the Assembly constituency[5] (in the case of a constituency election)[6], or in any part of the Assembly electoral region[7] (in the case of a regional election)[8]. As regards matters in the part of an Assembly constituency or electoral region for which there is a sub-agent, the election agent may act by the sub-agent[9]; and anything done by or to the sub-agent in his part of the Assembly constituency or electoral region for the purposes of the statutory rules which govern Welsh Assembly elections[10] is deemed to be done by or to the election agent[11]. Not later than the second day before the day of the poll[12], the election agent must declare in writing the name and address of every sub-agent to the appropriate returning officer[13], and:

(1)   the returning officer must forthwith give public notice of the name and address of every sub-agent so declared[14]; and

(2)   in the case of a regional election, the regional returning officer[15] must forthwith give notice of that name and address to the constituency returning officer[16] for each Assembly constituency in any part of which the sub-agent is appointed to act[17].

The appointment of a sub-agent is not vacated by the election agent who appointed him ceasing to be election agent[18] but such appointment may be revoked by whoever is for the time being the election agent[19]. In the event of the revocation of the appointment, or of the death of a sub-agent, another sub-agent may be appointed, and his name and address must be forthwith declared in writing to the appropriate returning officer, who must forthwith give the like notice required by head (1) above and, if applicable, head (2) above[20].

1   As to the meaning of 'Assembly election' see PARA 3 note 2.
2   As to the appointment of an election agent for Welsh Assembly elections see PARA 235.
3   Ie subject to the provisions of the National Assembly for Wales (Representation of the People) Order 2007, SI 2007/236, art 38: see art 38(1).
4   See the National Assembly for Wales (Representation of the People) Order 2007, SI 2007/236, art 38(1).
5   As to the meaning of 'Assembly constituency' see PARA 3 note 2.
6   National Assembly for Wales (Representation of the People) Order 2007, SI 2007/236, art 38(1)(a). As to the meaning of 'constituency election' see PARA 3 note 2.
7   As to the meaning of 'Assembly electoral region' see PARA 3 note 2.
8   National Assembly for Wales (Representation of the People) Order 2007, SI 2007/236, art 38(1)(b). As to the meaning of 'regional election' see PARA 3 note 2.
9   See the National Assembly for Wales (Representation of the People) Order 2007, SI 2007/236, art 38(2).
10   Ie anything done for the purposes of the National Assembly for Wales (Representation of the People) Order 2007, SI 2007/236: see art 38(2)(a).
11   National Assembly for Wales (Representation of the People) Order 2007, SI 2007/236, art 38(2)(a). Any act or default of a sub-agent which, if he were the election agent, would be an illegal practice or other offence against the National Assembly for Wales (Representation of the People) Order 2007, SI 2007/236, is an illegal practice and offence against that order committed by the sub-agent; and the sub-agent is liable to punishment accordingly: see art 38(2)(b). A candidate suffers the like incapacity as if that act or default had been the election agent's act or default: art 38(2)(c). As to the meaning of 'candidate' for these purposes see PARA 230 note 19. As to a candidate's liability for the illegal practices of his agents see PARAS 244, 894; and as to the punishment of illegal practices see PARA 888.
12   As to the day of the poll at a Welsh Assembly election see PARA 213; and as to the computation of the period mentioned in the text see PARA 230 note 20.

13 National Assembly for Wales (Representation of the People) Order 2007, SI 2007/236, art 38(3). The declaration to be made to the appropriate returning officer, and such notice to be given by him, under art 38(3) must specify the part of the Assembly constituency or electoral region within which any sub-agent is appointed to act: see art 38(5). As to the meaning of 'appropriate returning officer' at a Welsh Assembly election see PARA 18 note 2. As to the making of declarations for these purposes see PARA 235 note 9.

14 National Assembly for Wales (Representation of the People) Order 2007, SI 2007/236, art 38(3)(a). See note 13. As to the manner in which public notice is to be given see PARA 235 note 27.

15 As to the meaning of 'regional returning officer' see PARA 18 note 2.

16 As to the meaning of 'constituency returning officer' see PARA 18 note 2.

17 National Assembly for Wales (Representation of the People) Order 2007, SI 2007/236, art 38(3)(b). See note 13.

18 National Assembly for Wales (Representation of the People) Order 2007, SI 2007/236, art 38(4)(a).

19 National Assembly for Wales (Representation of the People) Order 2007, SI 2007/236, art 38(4)(b).

20 See the National Assembly for Wales (Representation of the People) Order 2007, SI 2007/236, art 38(4). The declaration to be made to the appropriate returning officer, and such notice to be given by him, under art 38(4) must specify the part of the Assembly constituency or electoral region within which any sub-agent is appointed to act: see art 38(5).

238. Office of agents for Welsh Assembly Elections. Every election agent[1] and every sub-agent[2] appointed for a Welsh Assembly election[3] must have an office to which all claims, notices, legal processes and other documents may be sent[4]. The address of the office must be:

(1)   declared to the appropriate returning officer[5] at the same time as the appointment of the agent is declared to him[6];

(2)   stated in the public notice that is required to be given by the appropriate returning officer upon the name and address of an election agent or sub-agent being declared to him[7]; and

(3)   in the case of a regional election[8], stated in the notice that is given by the regional returning officer to the constituency returning officers[9].

The office of an election agent for a constituency election[10] must be[11]: (a) in the Assembly constituency[12] for which the election is held (or in an adjoining Assembly constituency)[13]; or (b) in a county or county borough[14] which is partly comprised in or adjoins the first mentioned Assembly constituency[15]. The office of an election agent for a regional election must be[16] in Wales[17], and the office of a sub-agent must be in the area within which he is appointed to act[18].

Any claim, notice, legal process or other document delivered at the office of the election agent or sub-agent, and addressed to him, is deemed to have been served on him; and every election agent or sub-agent may, in respect of any matter connected with the election in which he is acting, be sued in any court having jurisdiction at the place where his office is situated[19].

1   As to the appointment of an election agent for Welsh Assembly elections see PARA 235.

2   As to the appointment of an election sub-agent for Welsh Assembly elections see PARA 237.

3   As to the meaning of 'Assembly election' see PARA 3 note 2.

4   See the National Assembly for Wales (Representation of the People) Order 2007, SI 2007/236, art 39(1).

5   As to the meaning of 'appropriate returning officer' at a Welsh Assembly election see PARA 18 note 2.

6   National Assembly for Wales (Representation of the People) Order 2007, SI 2007/236, art 39(1)(a). As to the making of declarations for these purposes see PARA 235 note 9.

7   National Assembly for Wales (Representation of the People) Order 2007, SI 2007/236, art 39(1)(b). The text refers to the public notice that is required under art 37(9)(a) (see PARA 235) or art 38(3)(a) (see PARA 237): see art 39(1)(b).

8   As to the meaning of 'regional election' see PARA 3 note 2.

9   National Assembly for Wales (Representation of the People) Order 2007, SI 2007/236, art 39(1)(c). The text refers to the notice that is required to be given to the constituency returning officer under art 37(9)(b) (see PARA 235) or art 38(3)(b) (see PARA 237): see art 39(1)(c). As to the meanings of 'constituency returning officer' and 'regional returning officer' see PARA 18 note 2.

10   As to the meaning of 'constituency election' see PARA 3 note 2.

11   Ie subject to the National Assembly for Wales (Representation of the People) Order 2007, SI 2007/236, art 40(7), whereby a candidate treated as an election agent is deemed to have his office at his address as given for that purpose in his consent to nomination: see PARA 236.

12   As to the meaning of 'Assembly constituency' see PARA 3 note 2.

13   National Assembly for Wales (Representation of the People) Order 2007, SI 2007/236, art 39(2)(a)(i).

14   As to a county or county borough in Wales see LOCAL GOVERNMENT vol 69 (2009) PARA 37 et seq.

15   National Assembly for Wales (Representation of the People) Order 2007, SI 2007/236, art 39(2)(a)(ii).

16   See note 11.

17   National Assembly for Wales (Representation of the People) Order 2007, SI 2007/236, art 39(2)(b) (amended by SI 2010/2931). As to the meaning of 'Wales' see PARA 1 note 1.

18   National Assembly for Wales (Representation of the People) Order 2007, SI 2007/236, art 39(2)(c).

19   National Assembly for Wales (Representation of the People) Order 2007, SI 2007/236, art 39(3).

239.   Appointment of election agent for European parliamentary elections.
Where, at a general election of members of the European Parliament ('MEPs')[1], the nominating officer[2] of a registered party[3] nominates (or authorises the nomination of) that party to stand for election in more than one electoral region[4], the nominating officer must name himself or some other person as the party's national election agent not later than the latest date for the delivery of notices of withdrawal for an election[5]. The name and address of the person so named must be declared in writing by or on behalf of the party's nominating officer to the Secretary of State[6] not later than that time[7]. One national election agent only may be appointed for each registered party[8]. However, the appointment (whether or not the national election agent appointed is the party's nominating officer) may be revoked[9]; and if (whether before, during or after the general election of MEPs) the appointment (or deemed appointment) of a national election agent is revoked, or if a national election agent dies, another national election agent must be appointed forthwith and his name and address declared to the Secretary of State[10]. The declaration as a party's national election agent of a person other than the nominating officer of that party is of no effect unless it is made and signed by that person or is accompanied by a written declaration of acceptance signed by him[11]. Upon the name and address of a national election agent being declared to the Secretary of State, the Secretary of State must forthwith give public notice of that name and address[12].

Where a registered party is nominated for election in one electoral region only[13], the nominating officer of a registered party[14] must name himself or some other person as the party's election agent not later than the latest date for the delivery of notices of withdrawal for an election[15]. The name and address of the person so named must be declared in writing by or on behalf of the party's nominating officer to the appropriate officer[16] not later than that time[17]. One election agent only may be appointed for each registered party[18]. However, the appointment (whether or not the election agent appointed is the party's nominating officer) may be revoked[19]; and if (whether before, during or after the election) the appointment (or deemed appointment) of an election agent is revoked, or if an election agent dies, another election agent must be appointed forthwith and his name and address declared to the appropriate officer[20]. The declaration as a party's election agent of a person other than the nominating officer of that party is of no effect[21] unless it is made and signed by that person or is accompanied by a written declaration of acceptance signed by him[22]. Upon the name and address of an election agent being declared to the appropriate officer, the appropriate officer must forthwith give public notice of that name and address[23].

A person must be named by or on behalf of each individual candidate at a European parliamentary election[24] as the individual candidate's election agent, and the name and address of the individual candidate's election agent must be declared in writing by the individual candidate or some other person on his behalf to the appropriate officer not later than the latest time for the delivery of notices of withdrawals for an election[25]. An individual candidate may name himself as election agent, and upon doing so is, so far as circumstances admit, subject to the provisions that govern European parliamentary elections[26] both as an individual candidate and as an election agent, and, except where the context otherwise requires, any reference in those provisions[27] to an election agent must be construed to refer to the individual candidate acting in his capacity of election agent[28]. One election agent only may be appointed for each individual candidate[29]. However, the appointment (whether the election agent appointed is the individual candidate himself or not) may be revoked[30]; and if (whether before, during or after the election) the appointment (or deemed appointment) of an election agent is revoked, or if an election agent dies, another election agent must be appointed forthwith and his name and address declared in writing to the appropriate officer[31]. The declaration as an individual candidate's election agent of a person other than the individual candidate is of no effect[32] unless it is made and signed by that person or is accompanied by a written declaration of acceptance signed by him[33]. Upon the name and address of an election agent being declared to the appropriate officer, the appropriate officer must forthwith give public notice of that name and address[34].

1   As to European parliamentary general elections see PARA 217 et seq.

2   As to the meaning of 'nominating officer' see PARA 220 note 6. Where for any reason the nominating officer of a registered party is unable to act, functions conferred on him by the European Parliamentary Elections Regulations 2004, SI 2004/293, reg 33, must be discharged by the person registered as leader of that party under the Political Parties, Elections and Referendums Act 2000 (see PARA 253) or, where that person is also the nominating officer, the person who holds some other office in the party and is registered in pursuance of it under s 24 (see PARA 253): see the European Parliamentary Elections Regulations 2004, SI 2004/293, reg 33(8). As to the meaning of 'registered party' for these purposes see PARA 230 note 29.

3   Ie in accordance with the European parliamentary elections rules: see the European Parliamentary Elections Regulations 2004, SI 2004/293, reg 33(1). As to the meaning of 'European parliamentary elections rules' see PARA 383 note 16.

4   See the European Parliamentary Elections Regulations 2004, SI 2004/293, reg 33(1). As to the establishment of electoral regions for the purpose of elections to the European Parliament see PARA 77.

5   See the European Parliamentary Elections Regulations 2004, SI 2004/293, reg 33(2). Accordingly, 'national election agent' means the person appointed under reg 33: see reg 2(1) (substituted by SI 2009/186). In the European Parliamentary Elections Regulations 2004, SI 2004/293, regs 34–126 (except regs 38–41), any reference to an election agent must, in the case of a registered party to which reg 33 applies, be construed as a reference to a national election agent; and any reference to the election agent of a candidate must, in the case of a registered party to which reg 33 applies, be construed as a reference to that party's national election agent: see reg 33(9). As to the latest time for the withdrawal of a notice of election see PARA 266.

6   As to the Secretary of State see PARA 2.
7   European Parliamentary Elections Regulations 2004, SI 2004/293, reg 33(3). Any person before
    whom a declaration is authorised to be made under the European Parliamentary Elections
    Regulations 2004, SI 2004/293, may take the declaration: reg 123(3).
8   See the European Parliamentary Elections Regulations 2004, SI 2004/293, reg 33(4).
9   See the European Parliamentary Elections Regulations 2004, SI 2004/293, reg 33(4).
10 European Parliamentary Elections Regulations 2004, SI 2004/293, reg 33(5).
11 European Parliamentary Elections Regulations 2004, SI 2004/293, reg 33(6).
12 European Parliamentary Elections Regulations 2004, SI 2004/293, reg 33(7).
13 See the European Parliamentary Elections Regulations 2004, SI 2004/293, reg 34(1).
14 Where for any reason the nominating officer of a registered party is unable to act, functions
    conferred on him by the European Parliamentary Elections Regulations 2004, SI 2004/293,
    reg 34 must be discharged by the person registered as leader of that party under the Political
    Parties, Elections and Referendums Act 2000 (see PARA 253) or, where that person is also the
    nominating officer, the person who holds some other office in the party and is registered in
    pursuance of it under s 24 (see PARA 253): see the European Parliamentary Elections
    Regulations 2004, SI 2004/293, reg 33(8); applied by reg 34(8).
15 European Parliamentary Elections Regulations 2004, SI 2004/293, reg 34(2). In regs 35–126
    (except regs 38–41), any reference to the election agent of a candidate must, in the case of a
    registered party to which reg 34 applies, be construed as a reference to that party's election
    agent: see reg 34(9).
16 In the European Parliamentary Elections Regulations 2004, SI 2004/293, Pt 2 (regs 31–81),
    unless the context otherwise requires, 'appropriate officer' means the returning officer: see
    reg 31(1). As to returning officers for European parliamentary elections see PARA 360 et seq.
17 European Parliamentary Elections Regulations 2004, SI 2004/293, reg 34(3).
18 See the European Parliamentary Elections Regulations 2004, SI 2004/293, reg 34(4).
19 See the European Parliamentary Elections Regulations 2004, SI 2004/293, reg 34(4).
20 European Parliamentary Elections Regulations 2004, SI 2004/293, reg 34(5).
21 Ie under the European Parliamentary Elections Regulations 2004, SI 2004/293, reg 34: see
    reg 34(6).
22 European Parliamentary Elections Regulations 2004, SI 2004/293, reg 34(6).
23 European Parliamentary Elections Regulations 2004, SI 2004/293, reg 34(7).
        A public notice required by or under the European Parliamentary Elections
    Regulations 2004, SI 2004/293, to be given by a returning officer for a European parliamentary
    election must be given by posting the notice in some conspicuous place or places in the electoral
    region, and may also be given in such other manner as he thinks desirable for publicising it:
    reg 123(1). In the application of reg 123(1) to the combined region, the notice must be given by
    posting it in some conspicuous place or places in that part of the combined region which is in
    the United Kingdom and in some conspicuous place or places in that part which is in Gibraltar:
    reg 123(4). A public notice required by or under the European Parliamentary Elections
    Regulations 2004, SI 2004/293, to be given by a local returning officer must be given by posting
    the notice in some conspicuous place or places in the local counting area and may also be given
    in such other manner as he thinks fit: reg 123(2). In relation to any document which by virtue of
    the European Parliamentary Elections Regulations 2004, SI 2004/293, is required or authorised
    to be given to voters or displayed in any place for the purposes of a European parliamentary
    election, the person who is required or authorised to give or display the document must, as he
    thinks appropriate (see reg 122A(1), (2), (3) (reg 122A added by SI 2009/186)):
    (1)   give or display or otherwise make available, in such form as he thinks appropriate, the
          document in Braille, the document in languages other than English, graphical
          representations of the information contained in the document, and other means of
          making the information contained in the document accessible to persons who might not
          otherwise have reasonable access to the information (see the European Parliamentary
          Elections Regulations 2004, SI 2004/293, reg 122A(2) (as so added)); and also
    (2)   make available the information contained in the document in such audible form as he
          thinks appropriate (see reg 122A(3) (as so added)).
    Heads (1) and (2) above do not apply to the nomination paper and the ballot paper (see PARAS
    260, 386): see reg 122A(4); and PARAS 260 note 60, 386 note 3. As to the meaning of 'United
    Kingdom' see PARA 1 note 1. As to the meaning of 'local counting area' for the purposes of a
    European parliamentary election see PARA 139 note 1. As to the establishment of electoral
    regions (including the 'combined region') for the purpose of elections to the European
    Parliament see PARA 77. As to local returning officers appointed for the purposes of elections to
    the European Parliament see PARA 360.

24 As to the meaning of 'individual candidate' at a European parliamentary election see PARA 230 note 32.
25 European Parliamentary Elections Regulations 2004, SI 2004/293, reg 38(1).
26 Ie is subject to the provisions of the European Parliamentary Elections Regulations 2004, SI 2004/293: see reg 38(2).
27 Ie any reference in the European Parliamentary Elections Regulations 2004, SI 2004/293: see reg 38(2).
28 European Parliamentary Elections Regulations 2004, SI 2004/293, reg 38(2).
29 See the European Parliamentary Elections Regulations 2004, SI 2004/293, reg 38(3).
30 See the European Parliamentary Elections Regulations 2004, SI 2004/293, reg 38(3).
31 European Parliamentary Elections Regulations 2004, SI 2004/293, reg 38(4).
32 Ie is of no effect under the European Parliamentary Elections Regulations 2004, SI 2004/293, reg 38: see reg 38(5).
33 European Parliamentary Elections Regulations 2004, SI 2004/293, reg 38(5).
34 European Parliamentary Elections Regulations 2004, SI 2004/293, reg 38(6). As to public notice required by or under the European Parliamentary Elections Regulations 2004, SI 2004/293, to be given by a returning officer see note 23.

240. Effect of default in appointment of election agent for European parliamentary elections. If, by the latest time for delivery of notices of withdrawals[1], no person's name and address are given as required as the national election agent[2] of a registered party[3], or as the election agent[4] of a registered party for an electoral region[5], the nominating officer is deemed to have named himself as the national election agent (or, as the case may be, the election agent) and to have revoked any appointment of another person as that agent[6]. If the person whose name and address have been so given as those of the party's national election agent (or, as the case may be, election agent), not being the party's nominating officer[7], dies[8], and if a new appointment is not made on the day of the death or the following day[9], the party's nominating officer is deemed to have appointed himself as from the time of the death to the office in question[10]. If the appointment of a party's national election agent (or, as the case may be, election agent) is revoked without a new appointment being made, the party's nominating officer is deemed to have been appointed (or re-appointed) to the office in question[11]. The deemed appointment of a nominating officer as his party's national election agent (or, as the case may be, election agent) may be revoked as if it were an actual appointment[12]. On being satisfied that a party's nominating officer[13] is[14] to be treated as the party's national election agent[15], or as the party's election agent[16], the Secretary of State[17] or the appropriate officer[18] (as the case may be) must forthwith proceed to publish the like notice as if that officer's name and address and the address of his office had been duly given to him[19].

If no person's name and address is given so required[20] as the election agent of an individual candidate[21] who remains validly nominated[22] at the latest time for delivery of notices of withdrawals, the individual candidate is deemed at that time to have named himself as election agent and to have revoked any appointment of another person as his election agent[23]. If the person whose name and address have been so given as those of the individual candidate's election agent (not being the individual candidate himself) dies[24], and if a new appointment is not made on the day of the death or on the following day[25], the individual candidate is deemed to have appointed himself as from the time of death[26]. If the appointment of an individual candidate's election agent is revoked without a new appointment being made, the individual candidate himself is deemed to have been appointed (or re-appointed) election agent[27]. The deemed appointment of an individual candidate as his own election agent may be revoked as if it were an actual appointment[28]. Where an individual candidate is[29] to be treated as his own election agent, he is deemed to have his office at his address as given in the statement as to persons nominated[30]. The appropriate officer, on being satisfied that an individual candidate is[31] to be treated as his own election agent, must forthwith proceed to publish the like notice as if the name and address of the individual candidate and the address of his office had been duly given to him[32].

1   See the European Parliamentary Elections Regulations 2004, SI 2004/293, reg 37(1). As to the latest time for the withdrawal of candidature see PARA 266.
2   Ie as required by the European Parliamentary Elections Regulations 2004, SI 2004/293, reg 33 (see PARA 239): see reg 37(1)(a). As to the meaning of 'national election agent' for the purposes of a European parliamentary election see PARA 239 note 5.
3   See the European Parliamentary Elections Regulations 2004, SI 2004/293, reg 37(1)(a). As to the meaning of 'registered party' for these purposes see PARA 230 note 29.
4   Ie as required by the European Parliamentary Elections Regulations 2004, SI 2004/293, reg 34, where reg 33 does not apply (see PARA 239): see reg 37(1)(b). As to references to the election agent of a candidate at a European parliamentary election see PARA 239 note 15.
5   See the European Parliamentary Elections Regulations 2004, SI 2004/293, reg 37(1)(b). As to the establishment of electoral regions for the purpose of elections to the European Parliament see PARA 77.
6   See the European Parliamentary Elections Regulations 2004, SI 2004/293, reg 37(1).
7   As to the meaning of 'nominating officer' for the purposes of a European parliamentary election see PARA 239 note 2.
8   European Parliamentary Elections Regulations 2004, SI 2004/293, reg 37(2)(a).
9   European Parliamentary Elections Regulations 2004, SI 2004/293, reg 37(2)(b).
10 European Parliamentary Elections Regulations 2004, SI 2004/293, reg 37(2). Where for any reason the nominating officer of a registered party is unable to act, functions conferred on him by reg 37 must be discharged by the person registered as leader of that party under the Political Parties, Elections and Referendums Act 2000 (see PARA 253) or, where that person is also the nominating officer, the person who holds some other office in the party and is registered in pursuance of it under s 24 (see PARA 253): see the European Parliamentary Elections Regulations 2004, SI 2004/293, reg 33(8); applied by reg 37(5). Where a party's nominating officer or officer determined under reg 33(8), as applied by reg 37(5), is by virtue of reg 37 to be treated as the party's national election agent (or, as the case may be, election agent), he is deemed to have his office at the address registered under the Political Parties, Elections and Referendums Act 2000 (see PARA 253) as the party's headquarters (or, if it has no headquarters, the address to which communications to the party may be sent): European Parliamentary Elections Regulations 2004, SI 2004/293, reg 37(6).
11 European Parliamentary Elections Regulations 2004, SI 2004/293, reg 37(3). See note 10.
12 European Parliamentary Elections Regulations 2004, SI 2004/293, reg 37(4).
13 Ie or other officer determined under the European Parliamentary Elections Regulations 2004, SI 2004/293, reg 37(5) (see note 10): see reg 37(7).
14 Ie by virtue of the European Parliamentary Elections Regulations 2004, SI 2004/293, reg 37: see reg 37(7).
15 European Parliamentary Elections Regulations 2004, SI 2004/293, reg 37(7)(a).
16 European Parliamentary Elections Regulations 2004, SI 2004/293, reg 37(7)(b).
17 As to the Secretary of State see PARA 2.
18 As to the meaning of the 'appropriate officer' in relation to a European parliamentary election see PARA 239 note 16.
19 European Parliamentary Elections Regulations 2004, SI 2004/293, reg 37(7). The text refers to the way that the name and address of a national election agent must be given under reg 33 (see PARA 239) and the office address given under reg 36 (see PARA 242), and the way that the name and address of an election agent must be given under reg 34 (see PARA 239) and the office address given under reg 36: see reg 37(7). As to the manner in which notice is to be given see PARA 239 note 23.
20 Ie as required by the European Parliamentary Elections Regulations 2004, SI 2004/293, reg 38 (see PARA 239): see reg 41(1).
21 As to the meaning of 'individual candidate' at a European parliamentary election see PARA 230 note 32.
22 As to the nomination of candidates see PARA 253 et seq.

23 European Parliamentary Elections Regulations 2004, SI 2004/293, reg 41(1).

24 European Parliamentary Elections Regulations 2004, SI 2004/293, reg 41(2)(a).

25 European Parliamentary Elections Regulations 2004, SI 2004/293, reg 41(2)(b).

26 See the European Parliamentary Elections Regulations 2004, SI 2004/293, reg 41(2).

27 European Parliamentary Elections Regulations 2004, SI 2004/293, reg 41(3).

28 European Parliamentary Elections Regulations 2004, SI 2004/293, reg 41(4).

29 Ie by virtue of the European Parliamentary Elections Regulations 2004, SI 2004/293, reg 41: see reg 41(5).

30 European Parliamentary Elections Regulations 2004, SI 2004/293, reg 41(5). As to the statement of persons nominated see PARA 267.

31 Ie by virtue of the European Parliamentary Elections Regulations 2004, SI 2004/293, reg 41: see reg 41(6).

32 European Parliamentary Elections Regulations 2004, SI 2004/293, reg 41(6). The text refers to the way that the name and address of an election agent for an individual candidate must be given under reg 38 (see PARA 239) and the office address given under reg 40 (see PARA 242): see reg 41(6).

241.   Nomination of sub-agent for European parliamentary elections.   A national election agent[1] or a person authorised by him may appoint one, but not more than one, deputy election agent (referred to as a 'sub-agent') to act in any electoral region[2] and one, but not more than one, deputy election agent to act in any part of a European parliamentary electoral region[3]. An election agent of a registered party[4] may appoint one, but not more than one, deputy election agent (also referred to as a 'sub-agent') to act in any part of the electoral region[5]. As regards matters in the area for which there is a sub-agent, the election agent (including the national election agent), may act by the sub-agent[6]; and anything done for the purposes of the provisions that govern European parliamentary elections[7] by or to the sub-agent in his area is deemed to be done by or to the election agent (including the national election agent)[8].

Not later than the fifth day before the day of the poll[9], the national election agent or a person acting on his behalf (or, as the case may be, the election agent) must declare in writing to the returning officer[10] the name and address of every sub-agent[11] and the area for which he is appointed to act[12]. The appointment of a sub-agent is not vacated by the national election agent (or, as the case may be, the election agent) who appointed him ceasing to be such an agent[13]; but the appointment of a sub-agent may be revoked by whoever is for the time being the national election agent (or, as the case may be, election agent)[14]. Where the appointment of a sub-agent is revoked, or if the sub-agent dies, another sub-agent may be appointed, and the national election agent or a person acting on his behalf (or, as the case may be, the election agent) must forthwith declare in writing to the returning officer[15] the name and address of the sub-agent[16], and the area for which he is appointed to act[17]. On receipt of such a declaration (either in the normal course of events[18] or upon the revocation of a sub-agent's appointment or where the sub-agent dies[19]), the returning officer must forthwith give public notice of the name, address and area so declared[20].

An election agent for an individual candidate at a European parliamentary election[21] may appoint to act in any part of the electoral region one, but not more than one, deputy election agent (referred to as a 'sub-agent')[22]. As regards matters in a part of the electoral region for which there is a sub-agent, the election agent[23] may act by the sub-agent[24]; and anything done for the purposes of the provisions that govern European parliamentary elections[25] by or to the sub-agent in his part of the electoral region is deemed to be done by or to the election agent[26].

Not later than the fifth day before the day of the poll, the election agent must declare in writing the name and address of every sub-agent to the appropriate officer[27], and the appropriate officer must forthwith give public notice of the name and address of every sub-agent so declared[28]. The appointment of a sub-agent is not vacated by the election agent who appointed him ceasing to be election agent[29], but may be revoked by whoever is for the time being the individual candidate's election agent[30]. In the event of the revocation of the appointment or of the death of a sub-agent, another sub-agent may be appointed, and his name and address must be forthwith declared in writing to the appropriate officer, who must forthwith give public notice of the name and address so declared[31].

1   As to the meaning of 'national election agent' for the purpose of elections to the European Parliament see PARA 239 note 5.
2   As to the establishment of electoral regions for the purpose of elections to the European Parliament see PARA 77.
3   See the European Parliamentary Elections Regulations 2004, SI 2004/293, reg 35(1).
4   References in the European Parliamentary Elections Regulations 2004, SI 2004/293, reg 35 to an election agent are to the election agent of a registered party: see reg 35(9). As to the meaning of 'registered party' for these purposes see PARA 230 note 29.
5   European Parliamentary Elections Regulations 2004, SI 2004/293, reg 35(2).
6   European Parliamentary Elections Regulations 2004, SI 2004/293, reg 35(3).
7   Ie for the purposes of the European Parliamentary Elections Regulations 2004, SI 2004/293: see reg 35(3)(a).
8   European Parliamentary Elections Regulations 2004, SI 2004/293, reg 35(3)(a). Any act or default of a sub-agent which, if he were the election agent (including the national election agent), would be an illegal practice or other offence against the European Parliamentary Elections Regulations 2004, SI 2004/293, is an illegal practice and offence against the European Parliamentary Elections Regulations 2004, SI 2004/293, committed by the sub-agent; and the sub-agent is liable to punishment accordingly: reg 35(3)(b).
9   Ie calculated in accordance with the European Parliamentary Elections Regulations 2004, SI 2004/293, reg 32 (see PARA 230 note 31): see reg 35(4). As to the day of the poll at a European parliamentary election see PARA 222.
10 See the European Parliamentary Elections Regulations 2004, SI 2004/293, reg 35(4). As to the making of declarations see PARA 239 note 7; and as to returning officers for European parliamentary elections see PARA 360 et seq.
11 European Parliamentary Elections Regulations 2004, SI 2004/293, reg 35(4)(a).
12 European Parliamentary Elections Regulations 2004, SI 2004/293, reg 35(4)(b).
13 European Parliamentary Elections Regulations 2004, SI 2004/293, reg 35(5).
14 European Parliamentary Elections Regulations 2004, SI 2004/293, reg 35(6).
15 See the European Parliamentary Elections Regulations 2004, SI 2004/293, reg 35(7).
16 European Parliamentary Elections Regulations 2004, SI 2004/293, reg 35(7)(a).
17 European Parliamentary Elections Regulations 2004, SI 2004/293, reg 35(7)(b).
18 Ie under the European Parliamentary Elections Regulations 2004, SI 2004/293, reg 35(4) (see the text and notes 9–12): see reg 35(8).
19 Ie under the European Parliamentary Elections Regulations 2004, SI 2004/293, reg 35(7) (see the text and notes 15–17): see reg 35(8).
20 European Parliamentary Elections Regulations 2004, SI 2004/293, reg 35(8). As to public notice by a returning officer for a European parliamentary election that is required to be given by or under the European Parliamentary Elections Regulations 2004, SI 2004/293, see PARA 239 note 23.
21 As to the meaning of 'individual candidate' at a European parliamentary election see PARA 230 note 32.
22 European Parliamentary Elections Regulations 2004, SI 2004/293, reg 39(1).
23 For the purposes of the European Parliamentary Elections Regulations 2004, SI 2004/293, reg 39(2)–(4) (see the text and notes 24–31), references to an election agent are to an election agent of an individual candidate: see reg 39(6).
24 European Parliamentary Elections Regulations 2004, SI 2004/293, reg 39(2).
25 Ie for the purposes of the European Parliamentary Elections Regulations 2004, SI 2004/293: see reg 39(2)(a).

26 European Parliamentary Elections Regulations 2004, SI 2004/293, reg 39(2)(a). Any act or default of a sub-agent which, if he were the election agent, would be an illegal practice or other offence against the European Parliamentary Elections Regulations 2004, SI 2004/293, is an illegal practice and offence against the European Parliamentary Elections Regulations 2004, SI 2004/293,committed by the sub-agent; and the sub-agent is liable to punishment accordingly: reg 39(2)(b).

27 As to the meaning of the 'appropriate officer' in relation to a European parliamentary election see PARA 239 note 16.

28 European Parliamentary Elections Regulations 2004, SI 2004/293, reg 39(3). The declaration mentioned in the text to be made to the appropriate officer, and the notice to be given by him, under reg 39(3) must specify the part of the electoral region within which any sub-agent is appointed to act: see reg 39(5). As to references to an election agent for these purposes see note 23.

29 See the European Parliamentary Elections Regulations 2004, SI 2004/293, reg 39(4)(a). As to references to an election agent for these purposes see note 23.

30 See the European Parliamentary Elections Regulations 2004, SI 2004/293, reg 39(4)(b).

31 See the European Parliamentary Elections Regulations 2004, SI 2004/293, reg 39(4). The declaration to be made to the appropriate officer, and the notice to be given by him, under reg 39(4) must specify the part of the electoral region within which any sub-agent is appointed to act: see reg 39(5).

242.   Office of agents for European parliamentary elections. Every national election agent[1], every election agent[2] and every sub-agent[3] of a registered party[4] must have an office to which all claims, notices, legal process and other documents may be sent[5]. The office of a national election agent must be in the United Kingdom[6]. That office must be declared to the Secretary of State[7] at the same time as the appointment of the agent is declared to him[8], and it must be stated in the public notice of the name of the agent[9]. The office of the election agent or sub-agent of a registered party also must be within the United Kingdom[10]. That office must be declared to the appropriate officer[11] at the same time as the appointment of the agent is declared to him[12] and it must be stated in the public notice of the name of the agent[13]. Any claim, notice, legal process or other document delivered at the address of the national election agent, election agent or sub-agent and addressed to him, is deemed to have been served on him; and every national election agent, election agent or sub-agent may in respect of any matter connected with the election in which he is acting be sued in any court having jurisdiction at the place where his office is situated[14].

Every election agent and every sub-agent of an individual candidate[15] must have an office to which all claims, notices, writs, summonses and legal process and other documents may be sent[16]. The address of the office must be declared to the appropriate officer at the same time as the appointment of the agent is declared to him[17] and it must be stated in the public notice of the name of the agent[18]. The office of the election agent or sub-agent must be within the United Kingdom[19]. Any claim, notice, writ, summons or legal process or other document delivered at the office of the election agent or sub-agent and addressed to him, is deemed to have been served on him; and every election agent or sub-agent may in respect of any matter connected with the election in which he is acting be sued in any court having jurisdiction at the place where his office is situated[20].

1 As to the meaning of 'national election agent' for the purposes of a European parliamentary election see PARA 239 note 5.

2 As to references to the election agent of a candidate at a European parliamentary election see PARA 239 note 15.

3 As to the meaning of 'sub-agent' see PARA 241.

4 As to the meaning of 'registered party' for the purposes of European parliamentary elections for these purposes see PARA 230 note 29.

5   European Parliamentary Elections Regulations 2004, SI 2004/293, reg 36(1) (reg 36(1), (4) amended by SI 2009/186).

6   See the European Parliamentary Elections Regulations 2004, SI 2004/293, reg 36(2). As to the meaning of 'United Kingdom' see PARA 1 note 1.

7   As to the Secretary of State see PARA 2.

8   See the European Parliamentary Elections Regulations 2004, SI 2004/293, reg 36(2)(a). As to the making of declarations see PARA 239 note 7.

9   See the European Parliamentary Elections Regulations 2004, SI 2004/293, reg 36(2)(b). As to the public notice mentioned in the text see PARAS 239, 241.

10 European Parliamentary Elections Regulations 2004, SI 2004/293, reg 36(3). In the case of a party standing for election in the combined region, the office must be in Gibraltar: see reg 36(3). As to the establishment of electoral regions (including the 'combined region') for the purpose of elections to the European Parliament see PARA 77.

11 As to the meaning of the 'appropriate officer' in relation to a European parliamentary election see PARA 239 note 16.

12 See the European Parliamentary Elections Regulations 2004, SI 2004/293, reg 36(3)(a).

13 See the European Parliamentary Elections Regulations 2004, SI 2004/293, reg 36(3)(b).

14 European Parliamentary Elections Regulations 2004, SI 2004/293, reg 36(4) (as amended: see note 5).

15 For the purposes of the European Parliamentary Elections Regulations 2004, SI 2004/293, reg 40, references to an election agent and sub-agent are to an election agent or sub-agent of an individual candidate: reg 40(4). As to the meaning of 'individual candidate' at a European parliamentary election see PARA 230 note 32.

16 European Parliamentary Elections Regulations 2004, SI 2004/293, reg 40(1). In order to be consistent with reg 36 (as amended: see the text and notes 1–5), 'all claims, notices, writs, summonses and legal process and other documents' ought to read 'all claims, notices, legal process (which would include writs and summonses) and other documents' but, at the date at which this volume states the law, the necessary amendment has not been made to reg 40.

17 See the European Parliamentary Elections Regulations 2004, SI 2004/293, reg 40(1)(a).

18 See the European Parliamentary Elections Regulations 2004, SI 2004/293, reg 40(1)(b).

19 European Parliamentary Elections Regulations 2004, SI 2004/293, reg 40(2). In the case of a candidate standing for election in the combined region, the office must be in Gibraltar: see reg 40(2).

20 European Parliamentary Elections Regulations 2004, SI 2004/293, reg 40(3). See note 16.

243.   Duties of election agent.   The duties of an election agent[1] with respect to the authorising and incurring of election expenses, the payment of all claims, and the return and declarations respecting such expenses, are dealt with elsewhere in this title[2]. All books, accounts and documents should be carefully preserved until after any possible election petition[3]. The election agent must take all reasonable steps for preventing the commission of corrupt and illegal practices at the election[4].

The election agent may appoint unpaid polling or counting agents[5] and may do or assist in doing anything which a polling or counting agent is authorised to do; and anything required or authorised to be done in the presence of the polling or counting agents may be done in the presence of an election agent instead of the polling or counting agents[6].

1   As to the requirement to appoint election agents see PARA 231 et seq.

2   See PARA 269 et seq.

3   This is prudent practice. For examples of the problems and consequences if documents are destroyed see eg *Dorsetshire, Eastern Division, Case* (1910) 6 O'M & H 22 at 37 per Lawrence J; *Cork, Eastern Division, Case* (1911) 6 O'M & H 318 at 343 per Gibson J.

4   See the Representation of the People Act 1983 s 158(3)(b); and PARA 901.

5   See PARA 394.

6   See PARA 394.

C. ELECTORAL AGENCY

244. Candidate's liability. A candidate's liability to have his election avoided under the doctrines of election agency[1] is distinct from, and wider than, his liability under the criminal[2] or civil law of agency[3]. Once the agency is established, a candidate is liable to have his election avoided[4] for corrupt or illegal practices committed by his agents even though the act was not authorised by the candidate or was expressly forbidden[5]. The reason for this stringent law is that candidates put forward agents to act for them; and if it were permitted that these agents should play foul, and that the candidate should have all the benefit of their foul play without being responsible for it in the way of losing his seat, great mischief would arise[6]. In this respect the relationship between candidate and agent resembles that of employer and employee[7]. Other comparisons of the relationship between candidate and agent that have been made are that between the sheriff and his bailiffs[8], or that of a yachtsman who is responsible in a yacht race for the conduct of every person who is on board his vessel[9] or that of the owner of a racehorse and the jockey he employs[10].

An agent may be employed to act generally or in some particular transaction[11]. Similarly a canvasser may be employed to canvass only particular voters. A candidate's liability for corrupt or illegal practices committed by such an agent is limited to acts within the agent's authority, and thus if a canvasser is employed to canvass particular voters, his illegal acts in respect of other voters will not affect the candidate[12].

An agent may turn an innocent act into a guilty act by the manner of his doing it[13].

1   The doctrines originated in the principles, practice and rules on which committees of the House of Commons acted in dealing with election petitions and which have to be followed, as far as may be, by election courts: see PARA 771. In particular the principles and rules with regard to agency are to be observed, as far as may be, in the case of a petition questioning an election under the Local Government Act 1972 as in the case of a petition questioning a parliamentary election: see PARA 817.

2   A candidate's liability to penalties for corrupt practices committed by an agent is, it seems, in general the same as that of a principal under the ordinary criminal law relating to agency (see AGENCY vol 1 (2008) PARA 155; CRIMINAL LAW vol 25 (2010) PARA 316); the candidate is liable only on proof that the agent acted on the candidate's express or implied authority or that the candidate ratified the act after it was done or appointed the agent to do all acts legal or illegal which he might think proper to support the candidate's interest: see *Cooper v Slade* (1858) 27 LJQB 449 at 464 (a decision under enactments now replaced by the Representation of the People Act 1983 s 113(2), cited in PARA 709); and see also *Norwich Case, Tillett v Stracey* (1869) 1 O'M & H 8 at 10. For statutory provisions limiting the candidate's liability for the acts of his agents in particular cases see the Representation of the People Act 1983 s 61(7)(b) (cited in PARA 700); s 75(5)(ii) (cited in PARAS 687, 707); s 86(5) (cited in PARA 688); s 106(2) (cited in PARA 680); s 189(2) (cited in PARA 700); and s 90, Sch 4 para 1(2) (cited in PARA 675).

3   *Greenock Case* (1869) 1 O'M & H 247 at 251; *Norfolk, Northern Division, Case* (1869) 1 O'M & H 236 at 240; *Taunton Borough Case* (1874) 2 O'M & H 66.

4   See PARAS 894–898.

5   *Taunton Case, Williams and Mellor v Cox* (1869) 1 O'M & H 181; *Great Yarmouth Borough Case* (1906) 5 O'M & H 176 at 179 per Channell J; *Norwich Case, Tillett v Stracey* (1869) 1 O'M & H 8 at 10; *Lichfield Case, Anson v Dyott* (1869) 1 O'M & H 22; *Barnstaple Case* (1874) 2 O'M & H 105; *Harwich Borough Case* (1880) 3 O'M & H 61 at 69; *Sligo Borough Case* (1869) 1 O'M & H 300 at 302. For a recent case in which the election of a councillor was avoided for corrupt or illegal practices and general corruption committed by a candidate and by his agents see *Re Central Ward, Slough Election Petition, Simmons v Khan* [2008] EWHC B4 (QB), Election Ct. As to examples of agency see PARAS 247–250.

6   *Staleybridge Case, Ogden, Woolley and Buckley v Sidebottom, Gilbert's Case* (1869) 1 O'M & H 66 at 67. See also *Coventry Case, Berry v Eaton and Hill* (1869) 1 O'M & H 97; and see (1869) 20 LT 405 at 409 per Willes J ('I shall ever hold it to be [...] a wise and beneficial rule

of constitutional law that for the purpose of securing purity and freedom of election candidates shall be answerable for the acts of their agents as well as for their own acts').

7   *Westminster Borough Case* (1869) 1 O'M & H 89 at 95; *Norwich Case* (1869) 1 O'M & H 8 at 10–11; *Aylesbury Case* (1886) 4 O'M & H 59 at 62; *Shoreditch, Haggerston Division, Case, Cremer v Lowles* (1896) 5 O'M & H 68 at 70, 84.

8   *Harwich Borough Case* (1880) 3 O'M & H 61 at 69.

9   *Westbury Case, Laverton v Phipps, Harrop's Case* (1869) 1 O'M & H 47 at 55; *Tamworth Case, Hill and Walton v Peel and Bulwer* (1869) 1 O'M & H 75 at 81; *Coventry Case, Berry v Eaton and Hill* (1869) 1 O'M & H 97 at 107; *Blackburn Case* (1869) 1 O'M & H 198 at 202; *Wigan Case, Spencer and Prestt v Powell* (1881) 4 O'M & H 1 at 11.

10 *Coventry Case, Berry v Eaton and Hill* (1869) 1 O'M & H 97 at 107; *Blackburn Case* (1869) 1 O'M & H 198 at 202; *Wigan Case, Spencer and Prestt v Powell* (1881) 4 O'M & H 1 at 11.

11 *Harwich Borough Case* (1880) 3 O'M & H 61 at 69; *Plymouth, Drake Division, Case* (1929) 7 O'M & H 101 at 126.

12 *Bodmin Case* (1869) 1 O'M & H 117 at 120; *Sligo Borough Case* (1869) 1 O'M & H 300 at 302. On the other hand the candidate cannot escape liability by confining the agent's authority to lawful acts: see *Sligo Borough Case*.

13 *Boston Borough Case, Malcolm v Parry* (1874) LR 9 CP 610, where an act intended by the candidate to be an act of charity became bribery.

245.   Evidence of agency.

In order to prove agency it is not necessary to show that the person was actually appointed by the candidate[1] or that he was paid[2]. The crucial test is whether there has been employment or authorisation of the agent by the candidate to do some election work or the adoption of his work when done[3]. The candidate, however, is liable not only for the acts of the agents whom he has himself appointed or authorised, but also for the acts of agents employed by his election agent or by any other agent having authority to employ others[4]. He may be liable even though his election agent refused to employ the agent[5].

In the absence of authorisation or ratification the candidate must be proved either by himself or by his acknowledged agents to have employed the agent to act on his behalf, or to have to some extent put himself in the agent's hands, or to have made common measure with him for the purpose of promoting the candidate's election[6]. The candidate must have entrusted the alleged agent with some material part of the business of the election[7]. Mere non-interference on the candidate's part with persons who, feeling interested in the candidate's success, may act in support of his canvass is not sufficient to saddle the candidate with any unlawful acts of theirs of which the candidate and his election agent are ignorant[8]. Employment in the business of the election is a question of degree[9], but it has never yet been distinctly and precisely defined what degree of evidence is required to establish such a relationship between the candidate and the person guilty of corruption as should constitute agency. No one yet has been able to go further than to say that, as to some cases, enough has been established, but as to others, enough has not been established, to vacate the seat[10]. All the circumstances of the case must be taken into consideration, and the evidence may be regarded cumulatively as establishing the agency[11]. Agency at a previous election is not admissible in itself to prove agency at a subsequent election[12], but where there has been organized bribery by a person as a candidate's agent at a previous election and the person has canvassed for the same candidate at a subsequent election and bribed voters, it is difficult, if not impossible, for the candidate to prove that the person was not his agent at the subsequent election[13].

1   *Harwich Borough Case* (1880) 3 O'M & H 61. For the current statutory definition of 'candidate' see PARA 230.

2   *Bewdley Case* (1869) 1 O'M & H 16 at 17.

3   *Great Yarmouth Borough Case* (1906) 5 O'M & H 176 at 189; *Plymouth, Drake Division, Case* (1929) 7 O'M & H 101. For the ratification to be effective the candidate must be fully aware of the character of the act at the time when he ratifies it: *Tamworth Case, Hill and Walton v Peel and Bulwer* (1869) 1 O'M & H 75 at 81.

4   *Bewdley Case* (1869) 1 O'M & H 16; *Staleybridge Case, Ogden, Woolley and Buckley v Sidebottom, Gilbert's Case* (1869) 1 O'M & H 66; *Plymouth Case* (1880) 3 O'M & H 107; *Hartlepools Case* (1910) 6 O'M & H 1; *Sunderland Borough Case* (1896) 5 O'M & H 53; *Barnstaple Case* (1874) 2 O'M & H 105; *Cashel Borough Case* (1869) 1 O'M & H 286.

5   *Stroud Case, Holloway v Brand* (1874) 3 O'M & H 7 at 11.

6   *Taunton Borough Case* (1874) 2 O'M & H 66 at 74; *Wakefield Case* (1874) 2 O'M & H 100 at 102. For a recent case in which agency was found see *Re Central Ward, Slough Election Petition, Simmons v Khan* [2008] EWHC B4 (QB), Election Ct (a large number of bogus names had been deliberately and fraudulently entered on the electoral register shortly before the election, most of which had been used to cast postal votes to secure the councillor's election).

7   *Dungannon Borough Case* (1880) 3 O'M & H 101.

8   *Taunton Borough Case* (1874) 2 O'M & H 66 at 74.

9   *Hereford Borough Case* (1869) 1 O'M & H 194 at 195.

10 *Bridgewater Case* (1869) 1 O'M & H 112 at 115.

11 *Bewdley Case* (1869) 1 O'M & H 16 at 18; *Staleybridge Case, Ogden, Woolley and Buckley v Sidebottom, Gilbert's Case* (1869) 1 O'M & H 66 at 70; *Wakefield Case* (1874) 2 O'M & H 100 at 102; *Tewkesbury Case, Collins v Price* (1880) 3 O'M & H 97 at 99; *Bridgewater Case* (1869) 1 O'M & H 112 at 115; *Taunton Case, Williams and Mellor v Cox* (1869) 1 O'M & H 181; *Hereford Borough Case* (1869) 1 O'M & H 194 at 195.

12 *Ashburton Case* (1859) Wolf & B 1.

13 *Waterford Borough Case* (1870) 2 O'M & H 1.

246.   Agency where only one act of corruption. It would appear that stricter evidence of agency is required where only one act of corruption has been committed. In strict logic, if a man would be an agent if he was shown to have corrupted one hundred people by paying them £5 each, then, if he corrupts only a single man by giving him a glass of beer, he ought to be regarded as an agent equally[1]. Nevertheless it would appear that where there is satisfactory proof that it was intended that an election should be conducted honestly and in accordance with the law, strong evidence of agency is required in order to fix the candidate with the responsibility for a single unlawful act on the agent's part[2]. It would not, however, suffice for the candidate merely to say that he did not contemplate the acts that were done or did not intend that anything illegal should be done[3].

1   *Hastings Case, Calthorpe and Sutton v Brassey and North* (1869) 1 O'M & H 217 at 218.

2   *Barnstaple Case* (1874) 2 O'M & H 105 at 106; *Wigan Case* (1869) 1 O'M & H 188 at 192; *Hastings Case, Calthorpe and Sutton v Brassey and North, Foster's Case* (1869) 21 LT 234 at 237, 1 O'M & H 217 at 218; *Taunton Borough Case* (1874) 2 O'M & H 66 at 75; *Great Yarmouth Borough Case* (1895) 5 O'M & H 1/6 at 179; but see *Shrewsbury Case* (1870) 2 O'M & H 36 at 37. The distinction appears to be that a single act of bribery if proved will suffice to avoid an election: see PARA 720. An election court, however, will be unwilling to upset an otherwise honest election because of an isolated and insignificant act of bribery. Accordingly the court will require clear evidence both of the act of bribery and of the person bribing acting as an agent of the candidate.

3   *Sligo Borough Case* (1869) 1 O'M & H 300 at 302.

247.   Canvassers as agents. A canvasser is a person who solicits and persuades individual voters, although not necessarily one by one separately, to vote for a candidate[1]. General canvassing is strong evidence of agency, and evidence which requires a very strong case to rebut it, if it can be rebutted[2]. On the other hand, a voluntary canvasser who canvasses without authority is not an agent[3]. A person who, although nominally called a canvasser, is in substance not a man whose influence is relied on, but is a mere messenger sent round for information as to how voters intend to vote rather than with a view to his exercising any influence, either personally or by his powers of persuasion, is not necessarily an agent[4]. Merely introducing voters to the candidate does not constitute agency[5].

1   *Plymouth, Drake Division, Case* (1929) 7 O'M & H 101 at 125. See also the Representation of the People Act 1983 s 100(1) (cited in PARA 747), which prevents canvassing by members of the police force who may not 'by word, message, writing or in any other manner, endeavour to persuade any person to give, or dissuade any person from giving, his vote'.

2   *Wigan Case, Spencer and Prestt v Powell* (1881) 4 O'M & H 1 at 13; *Westbury Case, Laverton v Phipps, Harrop's Case* (1869) 1 O'M & H 47 at 55; *Lichfield Case, Anson v Dyott* (1869) 1 O'M & H 22 at 25.

3   *Bolton Case* (1874) 2 O'M & H 138 at 141; *Harwich Borough Case* (1880) 3 O'M & H 61 at 69; *Westbury Case* (1880) 3 O'M & H 78.

4   *Bodmin Case* (1869) 1 O'M & H 117 at 120; *Plymouth, Drake Division, Case* (1929) 7 O'M & H 101 at 125.

5   *Shrewsbury Case* (1870) 2 O'M & H 36; *Salisbury Case, Rigden v Edwards and Grenfell* (1880) 3 O'M & H 130; but see *Bewdley Case* (1869) 19 LT 676, 1 O'M & H 16; *Rochester Borough Case* (1892) Day 98 at 102.

248.   Member of election committee as agent.   Being a member of a candidate's election committee is strong evidence of agency[1]. Agency cannot be evaded merely by not appointing a committee; persons who do what members of the committee generally do are just as much members of the committee as if they were expressly called so for that reason[2], but a member of a self-constituted voluntary committee does not become an agent of the candidate[3]. Evidence of agency may be rebutted[4].

1   In the *Dublin City Case* (1869) 1 O'M & H 270 at 272, it was proved that there were district committees in all the wards which were sent instructions by the election agent; it was held that all the members of these committees were agents. In the *Southampton Borough Case* (1895) 5 O'M & H 17, a person who was a chairman of a ward Conservative association and a member of the candidate's committee was held to be an agent. See also *Huddersfield Borough Case* (1853) 2 Pow R & D 124 at 128; *Liverpool Case* (1853) 2 Pow R & D 248; *Tynemouth Case* (1853) 2 Pow R & D 181; *Nottingham Town Case (No 2)* (1843) Bar & Arn 136 at 156; *Preston Case* (1859) Wolf & B 71.

2   *Lichfield Case, Anson v Dyott* (1869) 1 O'M & H 22 at 25; *Wakefield Case* (1874) 2 O'M & H 100; *Shoreditch, Haggerston Division, Case, Cremer v Lowles* (1895) 5 O'M & H 68; *Rochester Borough Case* (1892) 4 O'M & H 156, Day 98.

3   *Westminster Borough Case* (1869) 1 O'M & H 89 at 92; *Drogheda Borough Case* (1857) Wolf & D 206 at 209; *Staleybridge Case, Ogden, Woolley and Buckley v Sidebottom, Gilbert's Case* (1869) 1 O'M & H 66; *Wareham Case* (1857) Wolf & D 85 at 95.

4   In *Windsor Case, Herbert v Gardiner* (1874) 31 LT 133, 2 O'M & H 88, the only evidence of a person being an agent was that he was a member of a candidate's election committee: it was not proved who put him on the committee, what his duties were or what he did; his own statement was that he understood he was to do his best for the candidate. He was held not to be an agent.

249.   Political associations as agents.   It has been recognised that there may be a political association existing for the purpose of a political party, advocating the cause of a particular candidate and largely contributing to his success, yet in no privity with the candidate or his agents, and an independent agency and acting on its own behalf[1]. It has been said that such an association would not be one for whose acts the candidate would be responsible[2]. There may, on the other hand, be a political association advocating the views of a candidate of which that candidate is not a member, to the funds of which he does not subscribe, and with which he personally is not ostensibly connected, but at the same time in intimate relationship with his agents respecting the canvassing of voters, and the conduct of the election, and largely contributing to the result. Such an association could be held to be one for whose acts the candidate was responsible[3].

An association representing one of the political parties may further the general interests of the party it represents, including work in connection with the preparation of the electors' lists, without necessarily becoming an agent of a candidate; but the moment it appears that the candidate or his election agent adopts, either individually or collectively, the work that is done by that association in such a manner as to benefit by its agency regarding the election, the association will become the candidate's agent[4].

1 *Bewdley Case, Spencer v Harrison* (1880) 3 O'M & H 145 at 146.
2 *Bewdley Case, Spencer v Harrison* (1880) 3 O'M & H 145 at 146; and see e g *Westbury Case* (1880) 3 O'M & H 78 (cited in note 4).
3 *Bewdley Case, Spencer v Harrison* (1880) 3 O'M & H 145 at 146.
4 *Cork, Eastern Division, Case* (1911) 6 O'M & H 318 at 342; *Worcester Borough Case, Glaszard and Turner v Allsopp* (1892) 4 O'M & H 153; *Walsall Borough Case* (1892) 4 O'M & H 123; *Northumberland, Hexham Division, Case, Hudspeth and Lyal v Clayton* (1892) Day 90 at 91. In *Rochester Borough Case* (1892) 4 O'M & H 156 at 160, Cave J approved the practice of political associations suspending their activities as soon as an election commences. In *Northumberland, Berwick-upon-Tweed Division, Case* (1923) 7 O'M & H 1, a political association was founded by an agent of the candidate and wholly financed by the candidate, and expenses were incurred by it in paying an organiser on the candidate's behalf and were continued even after it had been nominally dissolved; the court decided that payments made by it from the date when the election was held to have begun ought to have been returned by the candidate. In *Westbury Case* (1880) 3 O'M & H 78, a political association invited a candidate to become its representative, and he attended some of its meetings to expound his political views, but there was no further substantial connection between them; the court decided that members of the association had not become agents of the candidate. On the other hand, in *Bewdley Case, Spencer v Harrison* (1880) 3 O'M & H 145, an association had been formed before the election to promote the candidature of a certain candidate and was subsequently in constant communication with his election agent who attended the association's meetings, supplied its minute book at the candidate's expense, from time to time reported progress to the association and used, in common with the association, a marked register of voters, and the leading members of the association were actively engaged in the conduct of the election; the court held that members of the association were agents of the candidate. In *Taunton Case, Williams and Mellor v Cox* (1869) 1 O'M & H 181, during an election people met at the rooms of a Conservative Association, papers and circulars were sent out by it and members of the association canvassed; the court held that members of the association were agents of the candidate. In *St George's Division, Tower Hamlets, Case* (1896) 5 O'M & H 89 at 97, it was stated that if the object of a political association was simply to secure the election of a particular individual, it would be difficult, if not impossible, for the candidate to take part in its operations without becoming responsible for its acts during the election; and if its object were to procure the election of some candidate professing the political views of one of the two great parties which were supposed to divide the country, and the candidate attended its meetings and availed himself of its assistance, its officers would probably be held to constitute his agents. See also *Westminster Borough Case* (1869) 1 O'M & H 89; *Gravesend Case* (1880) 44 LT 64, 3 O'M & H 81.

250. Other examples of agents. Priests may become agents of a candidate[1].

An association (other than a political association) which holds meetings to promote its own views does not necessarily become an agent of a candidate, even though it incidentally promotes his interests[2].

A circular urging all persons to aid in securing a certain candidate's return has been held to make every person the candidate's agent who acted on it and took up his interests[3].

The mere fact that the alleged agent is a brother of the candidate[4] or the business partner[5] or son[6] of an authorised agent is not sufficient to establish agency. A confidential employee, even though active in the election, is not necessarily an agent[7].

The fact that the candidate and a person are closely associated in philanthropic work and that the candidate accepts a testimonial from that person does not necessarily make that person an agent of the candidate[8]. If there are joint candidates, as may happen at local government elections, the agents of the one would thereby become the agents of the other[9], unless it was made clear that an agent was acting on behalf of one candidate only[10]. One candidate does not, however, become liable for the previously committed acts of an agent of the other candidate where he was not aware of those acts[11].

1   *Limerick Borough Case* (1869) 1 O'M & H 260 at 262; *Galway County Case* (1872) 2 O'M & H 46; *Galway Borough Case* (1874) 2 O'M & H 196; *Meath, Southern Division, Case* (1892) 4 O'M & H 130; *Meath, Northern Division, Case* (1892) 4 O'M & H 185. As to spiritual influence amounting to undue influence at election see PARA 726.
2   *Walsall Borough Case* (1892) 4 O'M & H 123 (licensed victuallers' association). However, where a candidate who knew that a procession was being formed on behalf of a licensed victuallers' association for political electioneering purposes got into the vehicle at the head of it on the invitation of the organizer, the candidate was held to have made the organizer his agent: *West Bromwich Case* (1911) 6 O'M & H 256 at 278.
3   *Blackburn Case* (1869) 1 O'M & H 198. In a later case, however, it was held by one judge (the other judge dissenting) that a letter addressed to 5,000 persons who had signed a letter requesting the candidate to stand, and which asked the recipients to enter heartily into the contest and secure the votes and interest of others, did not make the persons receiving and acting upon it the candidate's agents: *Norwich Case, Birbeck v Bullard* (1886) 4 O'M & H 84.
4   *Ipswich Case* (1857) Wolf & D 173 at 178; and see *Dorsertshire, Eastern Division, Case* (1911) 6 O'M & H 22.
5   *Mallow Borough Case* (1870) 2 O'M & H 18 at 21.
6   *Westminster Borough Case* (1869) 1 O'M & H 89 at 96.
7   *Cockermouth Case* (1853) 2 Pow R & D 167 at 170.
8   *Plymouth, Drake Division, Case* (1929) 7 O'M & H 101 at 107, 118.
9   *North Norfolk Case* (1869) 1 O'M & H 236 at 240.
10 *Norwich Case* (1871) 23 LT 701, 2 O'M & H 38.
11 *Malcolm v Parry (2nd Case)* (1875) LR 10 CP 168, sub nom *Boston Case, Malcolm v Ingram and Parry* (1875) 31 LT 845.

251.   Termination of agency.   An ordinary agency will be taken to have terminated when the election is over[1] unless the candidate's privity is shown[2]. The agency may also be terminated by the repudiation and withdrawal of the agent's authority[3]. Statements made by an ordinary agent after the election is over are not admissible as evidence against the candidate[4]. Evidence of acts done after the election may be admitted if the acts are connected with, or throw light on, some transaction which took place during the election[5].

1   *King's Lynn Case, Armes and Holditch v Bourke* (1896) 1 O'M & H 206 at 208; *North Norfolk Case* (1869) 1 O'M & H 236 at 243; *Longford Case* (1870) 2 O'M & H 6 at 12.
2   *Salford Case* (1869) 1 O'M & H 133 at 140. This rule does not apply to the election agent who has certain duties to perform in connection with election expenses after the election is over: *Salford Case* at 140.
3   *Taunton Case, Williams and Mellor v Cox* (1869) 1 O'M & H 181 at 183.
4   *Harwich Borough Case* (1880) 3 O'M & H 61 at 64; *Cheltenham Borough Election Case* (1880) 3 O'M & H 86 at 88; *Bodmin Case* (1869) 1 O'M & H 117 at 119; *Taunton Borough Case* (1874) 2 O'M & H 66 at 69. It has been stated that the election is not over until the declaration of the result is made: *Galway County Case* (1872) 2 O'M & H 46 at 49.
5   *Southampton Case* (1869) 1 O'M & H 222.

252.   Statutory prohibition on agency by election officials and canvassing by police officers.   Any returning officer or any officer or clerk appointed under elections rules[1], or any partner or clerk of any such a person who acts as a candidate's agent in the conduct or management of the election is guilty of an offence[2].

Any member of a police force who canvasses any person to give his vote at any election held wholly or partly within the police area is also guilty of an offence[3].

1   Ie the rules made for parliamentary and local government elections, for European parliamentary elections or for Welsh Assembly elections (see PARA 383). As to returning officers for parliamentary elections generally see PARA 350 et seq. As to the appointment of presiding officers and their clerks by returning officers see PARA 393.
2   See the Representation of the People Act 1983 s 99; and PARA 746.
3   See the Representation of the People Act 1983 s 100; and PARA 747.

(ii) Nomination of Candidates

253. Registration of party and officials as condition precedent to participation in election. No nomination may be made in relation to a relevant election (that is, in relation to a parliamentary election[1], any local government election[2] except a parish or community election[3], the election of a police and crime commissioner[4], a Welsh Assembly election[5], or an election to the European Parliament[6]) unless the nomination is in respect of[7]:

   (1)   a person who stands for election in the name of a qualifying registered party[8]; or

   (2)   a person who does not purport to represent any party[9]; or

   (3)   a qualifying registered party, where the election is one for which registered parties may be nominated[10].

A party may not be registered unless a person has been registered as its leader, as its nominating officer and as its treasurer[11]. The person registered as a party's nominating officer has responsibility for the arrangements for the submission by representatives of the party of lists of candidates for the purpose of elections[12], the issuing of a certificate giving the party's authorised description[13] and the approval of descriptions and emblems used on nomination and ballot papers at elections[14]. The person registered as a party's treasurer is responsible for the party's compliance with the provisions relating to accounting requirements[15], the control of donations and the regulation of loans and related transactions[16] and, unless a person is registered as the party's campaigns officer[17], with the provisions relating to control of campaign expenditure[18], controls relating to third party national election campaign expenditure[19] and referendums[20] as well[21]. The registers of political parties are maintained by the Electoral Commission[22].

A broadcaster is prohibited from including in its broadcasting services any party political broadcast made on behalf of a party which is not a registered party under the Political Parties, Elections and Referendums Act 2000[23].

1   See the Political Parties, Elections and Referendums Act 2000 s 22(1), (5)(a). As to the meaning of 'parliamentary election' see PARA 9.
2   See the Political Parties, Elections and Referendums Act 2000 s 22(1), (5)(f). As to the meaning of 'local government election' see PARA 11.
3   See the Political Parties, Elections and Referendums Act 2000 s 22(4). For these purposes, a 'parish or community election' means an election of councillors for a parish in England or a community in Wales: see s 40(1). As to the meanings of 'England' and 'Wales' see PARA 1 note 1. As to the election of councillors for parish or community councils see PARA 200 et seq. As to parishes generally see LOCAL GOVERNMENT vol 69 (2009) PARA 27 et seq; and as to communities generally see LOCAL GOVERNMENT vol 69 (2009) PARA 41 et seq.
4   See the Political Parties, Elections and Referendums Act 2000 s 22(1), (5)(ea) (s 22(5)(ea) added by SI 2012/1917). As to the election of police and crime commissioners see POLICE AND INVESTIGATORY POWERS vol 84 (2013) PARA 62 et seq.

5   See the Political Parties, Elections and Referendums Act 2000 s 22(1), (5)(d). As to Welsh Assembly elections see PARA 12 et seq.

6   See the Political Parties, Elections and Referendums Act 2000 s 22(1), (5)(b). As to elections to the European Parliament see PARA 13 et seq.

7   See the Political Parties, Elections and Referendums Act 2000 s 22(1).

8   Political Parties, Elections and Referendums Act 2000 s 22(1)(a). For these purposes, a person stands for election in the name of a registered party if his nomination paper includes a description authorised by a certificate issued by or on behalf of the registered nominating officer of the party: see ss 22(6), 160(3). A party (other than a minor party) is a 'qualifying registered party' in relation to a relevant election (other than a European parliamentary election) if the constituency, police area, local government area or electoral region in which the election is held is in England or Wales, and the party was, on the day (the 'relevant day') which is two days before the last day for the delivery of nomination papers at that election, registered in respect of that part of Great Britain in the Great Britain register maintained by the Electoral Commission under s 23 (new registers of political parties: see CONSTITUTIONAL LAW AND HUMAN RIGHTS): see s 22(2)(a) (amended by the Electoral Administration Act 2006 s 52(4), (5)(a); and by SI 2012/1917). For these purposes, any day falling within the Representation of the People Act 1983 Sch 1 r 2(1) subject to Sch 1 r 2(2A) (computation of time: see PARA 195 note 27) is disregarded: Political Parties, Elections and Referendums Act 2000 s 22(2A) (added by the Electoral Administration Act 2006 s 52(4), (6); amended by the Fixed-term Parliaments Act 2011 s 6(3), Schedule paras 18, 19). In relation to a European parliamentary election, a party is a 'qualifying registered party' if the electoral region in which the election is held is in England or Wales, or is the electoral region of Wales, and the party was, on the last day for publication of notice of the election, registered in respect of that part of Great Britain in the Great Britain register maintained by the Commission under the Political Parties, Elections and Referendums Act 2000 s 23 (see CONSTITUTIONAL LAW AND HUMAN RIGHTS): see s 22(2)(a) (as so amended). For the purposes of Pt II (ss 22–40), 'party' includes any organisation or person; and 'registered' (unless the context otherwise requires) means registered under Pt II: see s 40(1). For these purposes, 'minor party' means (in accordance with s 34(1): see CONSTITUTIONAL LAW AND HUMAN RIGHTS) a party registered in the Great Britain register in pursuance of a declaration falling within s 28(2)(d) (see CONSTITUTIONAL LAW AND HUMAN RIGHTS); and the 'Great Britain register' means the register of political parties referred to in s 23(2)(a) (ie a register of parties that intend to contest relevant elections in one or more of England, Scotland and Wales: see CONSTITUTIONAL LAW AND HUMAN RIGHTS): s 160(1). As to applications for the registration of political parties for these purposes see ss 28–29, Sch 4; and CONSTITUTIONAL LAW AND HUMAN RIGHTS. The registration of minor parties in various respects to that of other parties: see s 34; and CONSTITUTIONAL LAW AND HUMAN RIGHTS. As to the requirement for certain party office holders to be registered see the text and note 11. On receipt of a request made by the Secretary of State, the Electoral Commission must send a copy of the Great Britain register, or any parts of it specified in the request, to the Secretary of State, or to any other person so specified: see s 35; and CONSTITUTIONAL LAW AND HUMAN RIGHTS. As to the meaning of 'Great Britain' see PARA 1 note 1. As to the meaning of 'Assembly electoral region' in relation to Welsh Assembly elections see PARA 3 note 2; as to the meaning of 'constituency' for the purposes of parliamentary elections see PARA 9; and as to the meaning of 'local government area' see PARA 33 note 7. As to the establishment of electoral regions for the purpose of elections to the European Parliament see PARA 77. As to publication of the notice for a local government election see PARA 211; and as to nomination papers related to candidature at elections see PARA 255 et seq. As to the Electoral Commission see PARA 34 et seq. As to police areas see POLICE AND INVESTIGATORY POWERS vol 84 (2013) PARA 52 et seq.

9   Political Parties, Elections and Referendums Act 2000 s 22(1)(b). For these purposes, a person does not purport to represent any party if the description of the candidate given in his nomination paper is 'Independent' (or where the candidate is the Speaker of the House of Commons seeking re-election, 'The Speaker seeking re-election') or if no description of the candidate is given in his nomination paper: see s 22(3). See also the National Assembly for Wales (Elections: Nomination Papers) (Welsh Form) Order 2001, SI 2001/2914, art 2(1), which prescribes the form of words in Welsh to be used instead of the word 'Independent' specified by the Political Parties, Elections and Referendums Act 2000 s 22(3).

10 Political Parties, Elections and Referendums Act 2000 s 22(1)(c).

11 See the Political Parties, Elections and Referendums Act 2000 s 24(1); and CONSTITUTIONAL LAW AND HUMAN RIGHTS. The person registered as leader may also be registered as nominating officer or treasurer (or both): see s 24(1); and CONSTITUTIONAL LAW AND HUMAN RIGHTS. As to who may be registered as a party's leader see s 24(2); and CONSTITUTIONAL LAW AND HUMAN

RIGHTS. As to offences created in relation to false statements made in connection with the registration of political parties see s 39; and CONSTITUTIONAL LAW AND HUMAN RIGHTS.

12 As to the system of candidature whereby registered parties submit lists of candidates see PARA 340.

13 Ie as mentioned in the Political Parties, Elections and Referendums Act 2000 s 22(6) (see note 8): see s 24(3); and CONSTITUTIONAL LAW AND HUMAN RIGHTS.

14 See the Political Parties, Elections and Referendums Act 2000 s 24(3); and CONSTITUTIONAL LAW AND HUMAN RIGHTS. A party may request the registration of up to 12 descriptions to be used by it on nomination papers or ballot papers and up to three emblems to be used by it on ballot papers: see ss 28A, 28B, 29; and CONSTITUTIONAL LAW AND HUMAN RIGHTS.

15 Ie the Political Parties, Elections and Referendums Act 2000 Pt III (ss 41–49) (see CONSTITUTIONAL LAW AND HUMAN RIGHTS). In the case of a party with accounting units, the person registered as the party's treasurer, in relation to the provisions of Pt III, is responsible for compliance on the part of the party's central organisation (rather than of the party): see s 24(5); and CONSTITUTIONAL LAW AND HUMAN RIGHTS. For these purposes, a registered party is a 'party with accounting units' if the party's scheme under s 26 identifies the party as being taken to consist of a central organisation and one or more separate accounting units, that is to say constituent or affiliated organisations each of which is to be responsible for its own financial affairs and transactions for the purposes of Pt III; 'accounting unit' means such a constituent or affiliated organisation; and, in the case of such a party, the 'central organisation' of the party is the central organisation so referred to: see ss 26(2)(b), (11), 160(1); and CONSTITUTIONAL LAW AND HUMAN RIGHTS. A party may not be registered unless it has adopted a scheme which sets out the arrangements for regulating the financial affairs of the party and which has been approved by the Electoral Commission: see s 26; and CONSTITUTIONAL LAW AND HUMAN RIGHTS. As to accounting units see further s 27; and CONSTITUTIONAL LAW AND HUMAN RIGHTS. As to assistance that may be provided by the Electoral Commission for existing parties to meet or reduce expenses falling initially to be incurred by them in order to comply with Pt III see s 36; and CONSTITUTIONAL LAW AND HUMAN RIGHTS.

16 Ie the Political Parties, Elections and Referendums Act 2000 Pt IV (ss 50–71C) (control of donations to registered parties and their members etc: see CONSTITUTIONAL LAW AND HUMAN RIGHTS), Pt IVA (ss 71F–71Z2) (regulation of loans and related transactions: see CONSTITUTIONAL LAW AND HUMAN RIGHTS). As to weekly reporting of donations made to registered parties during election periods see PARA 311; and CONSTITUTIONAL LAW AND HUMAN RIGHTS. As to weekly reporting of regulated transactions involving registered parties during election periods see PARA 312; and CONSTITUTIONAL LAW AND HUMAN RIGHTS. As to assistance that may be provided by the Electoral Commission for existing parties to meet or reduce expenses falling initially to be incurred by them in order to comply with Pt IV see s 36; and CONSTITUTIONAL LAW AND HUMAN RIGHTS. As to the control of donations to individual candidates during elections see PARA 286 et seq.

17 A person may be registered as a party's campaigns officer in accordance with the Political Parties, Elections and Referendums Act 2000 s 25 (parties with campaign officers: see CONSTITUTIONAL LAW AND HUMAN RIGHTS).

18 Ie the Political Parties, Elections and Referendums Act 2000 Pt V (ss 72–84) (see PARA 299 et seq).

19 Ie the Political Parties, Elections and Referendums Act 2000 Pt VI (ss 85–100) (see PARA 313 et seq).

20 Ie the Political Parties, Elections and Referendums Act 2000 Pt VII (ss 101–129) (see PARA 527 et seq).

21 See the Political Parties, Elections and Referendums Act 2000 s 24(4); and CONSTITUTIONAL LAW AND HUMAN RIGHTS.

22 See the Political Parties, Elections and Referendums Act 2000 ss 23(1), 160(1); and CONSTITUTIONAL LAW AND HUMAN RIGHTS. As to maintenance of the registers (changes, cessation of registration, etc) see ss 30–33; and CONSTITUTIONAL LAW AND HUMAN RIGHTS.

23 See the Political Parties, Elections and Referendums Act 2000 s 37; PARA 332; and CONSTITUTIONAL LAW AND HUMAN RIGHTS.

254. Selection of candidates by political parties. Electoral law does not regulate the procedures by which political parties select candidates to stand at an election.

Previously, however, both the Sex Discrimination Act 1975 (repealed) and the Race Relations Act 1976 (repealed) had been held to apply in limited ways to the selection of candidates by political parties[1]. The Equality Act 2010 has replaced discrimination law in England and Wales almost in its entirety, creating a common regime that applies, with certain variations and exceptions, to discrimination of all types and in all contexts[2], including provision that allows registered political parties to make arrangements in relation to the selection of election candidates to address the under-representation of people with particular. protected characteristics in elected bodies (for example, by means of single-sex shortlists and, where proportionate, shortlists for people with a specific 'protected characteristic', such as race or disability)[3].

It seems that a political party otherwise has discretion to select its own candidates to stand at elections, at least in so far as the rules which govern the party empower an administrative authority of the party to intervene, if necessary by the deselection and imposition of candidates[4].

1   As to discrimination on grounds of gender see *Jepson and Dyas-Elliot v Labour Party* [1996] IRLR 116 (a political party's ability to take positive action to increase, in that case, the number of women elected to the House of Commons was constrained under the Sex Discrimination Act 1975 and other measures); but see now the text and notes 2–3. As to discrimination on grounds of race see *Ali v McDonagh* [2002] EWCA Civ 93, [2002] ICR 1026, [2002] IRLR 489 (party's selection of a candidate or acceptance of a nomination for candidacy was for its own political purposes and did not confer an authorisation or qualification falling within the terms of the Race Relations Act 1976), overruling *Sawyer v Ahsan* [2000] ICR 1, [1999] IRLR 609, EAT (Labour Party discriminated against applicant on racial grounds by failing to select him as a candidate for the office of local government councillor contrary to the Race Relations Act 1976); and *Watt (formerly Carter) v Ahsan (sued on behalf of the Labour Party)* [2007] UKHL 51, [2008] 1 AC 696, sub nom *Ahsan v Watt (formerly Carter)* [2008] 1 All ER 869 (the Race Relations Act 1976 provided a remedy against discrimination by an association whose admission to membership is so conducted that the members do not constitute a section of the public, a formula which was capable of application to the Labour Party).

2   As to the Equality Act 2010 generally see DISCRIMINATION.

3   See the Equality Act 2010 ss 104, 105; and DISCRIMINATION. See also s 106 (not yet in force) (responding to a recommendation, made by the Speaker's Conference on parliamentary representation, that registered political parties be required to publish anonymised information on the diversity of their candidate selections, as a means of encouraging broader representation and increasing involvement of all groups in the democratic process); and DISCRIMINATION. The Sex Discrimination (Election Candidates) Act 2002, which made similar provision to that of the Equality Act 2010 s 104, has been amended by ss 105(3), (4), 211(2), Sch 27 Pt 1 (as amended by SI 2010/2279), so that its current application is restricted to Northern Ireland only. The Equality Act 2010 does not apply to Northern Ireland, with the exceptions of s 82 (offshore work), s 105(3), (4) (expiry of the Sex Discrimination (Election Candidates) Act 2002) and the Equality Act 2010 s 199 (abolition of presumption of advancement): see s 217.

4   See *Choudhry v Triesman* [2003] EWHC 1203 (Ch), [2003] 22 LS Gaz R 29, (2003) Times, 2 May (candidates whose selection was impugned on the basis of 'unsound' procedures used in certain wards applied for injunctive relief to ensure that their names were presented to the returning officer and for declaratory relief to the effect that their selections be allowed to stand; the applications failed as the judge declined to compel a registered political party to allow candidates to stand if the party had genuine and substantial concerns as to the regularity and honesty of the procedure for their selection). See also *Nattrass v UK Independence Party* [2013] EWHC 3017 (Ch), [2013] All ER (D) 111 (Oct) (despite a possibly flawed pre-selection process, an injunction to stop a national selection ballot among party members founded on any implied contractual term or other wrong done to a 'de-selected' sitting MEP was refused on the balance of convenience; a duty of natural justice could not be read into the party's process, and it would be inappropriate for the court to interfere with a process that has achieved its aim of producing 60 potential candidates for election). As to legal challenges to election proceedings see PARA 665 et seq.

255.   Form and supply of nomination papers.   Each candidate[1] at a parliamentary election[2] must be nominated by a separate nomination paper, the form of which is prescribed[3]. The returning officer[4] must supply any elector[5] with a form of nomination paper at the place and during the time for delivery of nomination papers[6], but it is not necessary for a nomination to be on a form supplied by the returning officer[7]. At any such elector's request, the returning officer must prepare a nomination paper for signature[8].

Each candidate[9] at a local government election[10] must be nominated by a separate nomination paper, the form of which is prescribed[11]. The returning officer[12] must supply any elector[13] with as many forms of nomination papers as may be required[14] at the place and during the time for delivery of nomination papers[15], but it is not necessary for a nomination to be on a form supplied by the returning officer[16]. At the request of any such elector, the returning officer must prepare a nomination paper for signature[17]. A registered party which is a qualifying party[18] and which is to stand at the election of London members of the London Assembly[19] must be nominated by a nomination paper in the appropriate form[20] which is duly delivered to the Greater London returning officer[21] by the party's registered nominating officer[22] or by a person authorised in writing by him[23].

Each candidate at a Welsh Assembly constituency election[24], and each individual candidate[25] at a Welsh Assembly regional election[26], must be nominated by a separate nomination paper, the form of which is prescribed[27]. The constituency returning officer[28] or the regional returning officer[29] (as the case may be) must supply any person upon request with a form of the appropriate nomination paper[30] at the place, and during the time, for delivery of nomination papers but it is not necessary for any such nomination to be on a form supplied by the relevant returning officer[31]. A registered political party[32] may stand for election at a regional election if it is a qualifying party[33] in relation to that region and if it is nominated by a separate nomination paper (a 'party nomination paper') in the appropriate form[34] which is duly delivered by that party's registered nominating officer[35] to the regional returning officer[36]. The regional returning officer must supply any person on request with a form of party nomination paper at the place, and during the time, for delivery of individual or party nomination papers, but it is not necessary for a party nomination paper to be on a form supplied by the regional returning officer[37].

Each individual candidate at a European parliamentary election[38] must be nominated by a separate nomination paper[39]. A registered party[40] which is to stand for election at a European parliamentary general election in an electoral region[41] must be nominated by a nomination paper delivered to the returning officer[42] by the party's nominating officer[43] or by a person authorised in writing by him[44].

1   As to the meaning of 'candidate' see PARA 230.
2   As to the meaning of 'parliamentary election' see PARA 9.
3   See the Representation of the People Act 1983 Sch 1 r 6(1). As to the prescribed form see Sch 1, Appendix of Forms (Form of nomination paper) (amended by the Political Parties, Elections and Referendums Act 2000 s 38(1), (4); the Representation of the People Act 2000 ss 8, 15(2), Sch 1 paras 1, 23(1), (3), Sch 7 Pt I; the Electoral Administration Act 2006 s 21(1), (4), (5); and the Political Parties and Elections Act 2009 s 39, Sch 6 para 8(1), (6)); and see PARA 256. Any form in the Representation of the People Act 1983 Sch 1, Appendix of Forms may be adapted so far as circumstances require: see Sch 1, Appendix of Forms (Note). A Welsh version of the form that may be used at elections in Wales has also been prescribed: see the Parliamentary Elections (Welsh Forms) Order 2007, SI 2007/1014, arts 4(3)–(5), 5(c), Sch 1 (Form 3 (Ffurflen 3: Ffurt y Papur Enwebu)) (art 4(3), Sch 1 Form 3 amended by SI 2010/1078). The form so prescribed may be used with such adaptations as the circumstances may require: see the Parliamentary Elections (Welsh Forms) Order 2007, SI 2007/1014, art 7. As to the meaning of 'Wales' see PARA 1 note 1.
4   As to returning officers for parliamentary elections see PARA 350 et seq.

5   'Elector' in this context means a person who is registered in the register of parliamentary electors for the constituency on the last day for publication of notice of the election: see the Representation of the People Act 1983 Sch 1 r 7(6)(a) (Sch 1 r 7(6) substituted by the Representation of the People Act 2000 s 8, Sch 1 paras 1, 23(1), (2)). This includes a person then shown in that register as below voting age if (but only if) it appears from the register that he will be of voting age on the day fixed for the poll: see the Representation of the People Act 1983 Sch 1 r 7(6)(b) (as so substituted). However, for these purposes, 'elector' does not include a person who has an anonymous entry in the register: see Sch 1 r 7(7) (added by the Electoral Administration Act 2006 s 10(2), Sch 1 paras 2, 14(1), (2)). As to the meaning of 'constituency' for the purposes of parliamentary elections see PARA 9; as to voting age for parliamentary elections see PARA 95 note 2; as to registration as a parliamentary elector see PARA 113 et seq; and as to the registers of electors see PARA 145 et seq. As to the meaning of 'anonymous entry' in relation to a register of electors see PARA 148. As to the date of the poll at a parliamentary general election or by-election see PARA 195; and as to publication of the notice for a parliamentary election see PARA 196.

6   See the Representation of the People Act 1983 Sch 1 r 7(4)(a). As to the timetable for the delivery of nomination papers see PARA 260.

7   See the Representation of the People Act 1983 Sch 1 r 7(4).

8   See the Representation of the People Act 1983 Sch 1 r 7(4)(b).

9   Ie each 'individual candidate' in the case of an election of London members of the London Assembly: see the Greater London Authority Elections Rules 2007, SI 2007/3541, Sch 2 r 6(1). As to the meaning of 'London member', in relation to the London Assembly, see PARA 11 note 5. In such elections, party lists operate and the term 'individual candidate' is used to indicate a person standing for election who is not included in the list of candidates of a registered party (see notes 18–23). As to elections for the return of the London members of the London Assembly see PARA 199 et seq. As to individual candidates to be London members see LONDON GOVERNMENT vol 71 (2013) PARA 81.

10   Ie an election of councillors for any electoral area, or any London Authority election, with general references to 'local government elections' being taken to include local authority mayoral elections: see PARA 11. There is no provision for the nomination of candidates at a poll consequent on a parish meeting (as to which see PARA 200 et seq) because they will already have been nominated at the meeting. As to when no fresh nomination is necessary in the event that a local government election has not been held or has failed or become void see PARA 209. As to elections for the return of elected local authority mayors see PARA 198 et seq.

11   Local Elections (Principal Areas) (England and Wales) Rules 2006, SI 2006/3304, Sch 2 r 4(1); Local Elections (Parishes and Communities) (England and Wales) Rules 2006, SI 2006/3305, Sch 2 r 4(1); Local Authorities (Mayoral Elections) (England and Wales) Regulations 2007, SI 2007/1024, Sch 1 r 6(1), (2); Greater London Authority Elections Rules 2007, SI 2007/3541, Sch 1 r 6(1)(a), Sch 2 r 6(1)(a), Sch 3 r 6(1)(a).

As to the form prescribed for principal area elections see the Local Elections (Principal Areas) (England and Wales) Rules 2006, SI 2006/3304, Sch 2 Appendix of Forms (Form of nomination paper); and where such elections are taken together with another relevant election or referendum see Sch 3 Appendix of Forms (Form of nomination paper). As to the form prescribed for parish or community elections see the Local Elections (Parishes and Communities) (England and Wales) Rules 2006, SI 2006/3305, Sch 2 Appendix of Forms (Form of nomination paper); and where such elections are taken together with another relevant election or referendum see Sch 3 Appendix of Forms (Form of nomination paper). As to the form prescribed for the return of an elected local authority mayor see the Local Authorities (Mayoral Elections) (England and Wales) Regulations 2007, SI 2007/1024, Sch 1, Appendix of Forms (Form 1: form of nomination paper); and as to the forms prescribed for the election of the Mayor of London and of members of the London Assembly see the Greater London Authority Elections Rules 2007, SI 2007/3541, r 9, Sch 10 r 2 (Form 1: constituency member and London member (individual) candidates (form of nomination paper)); Form 3: candidate to be the Mayor of London (form of nomination paper)) (Forms 1, 3 substituted by SI 2012/198). Any of these forms may be adapted so far as circumstances require.

As to the Welsh version of the form that may be used at principal area elections in Wales see the Local Elections (Principal Areas) (Welsh Forms) Order 2007, SI 2007/1015, art 6(b), Sch 2 (Form 2 (Ffurflen 2: Etholiadau Llywodraeth Leol; Ffurf y Papur Enwebu)); and as to the Welsh version of the form which is prescribed to be used at community elections in Wales see the Local Elections (Communities) (Welsh Forms) Order 2007, SI 2007/1013, art 6(b), Sch 2 (Form 2 (Ffurflen 2: Etholiadau Cymunedol; Ffurf y Papur Enwebu)). The forms so prescribed may be used with such adaptations as the circumstances may require: see the Elections (Principal Areas)

(Welsh Forms) Order 2007, SI 2007/1015, art 10; and the Local Elections (Communities) (Welsh Forms) Order 2007, SI 2007/1013, art 10.

12 As to returning officers for local government elections see PARA 354 et seq. The Greater London returning officer is specified in relation to a London Mayoral election: see the Greater London Authority Elections Rules 2007, SI 2007/3541, Sch 3 r 7(4). The duty imposed on a returning officer to supply nomination papers at a local election does not seem to apply at a London Constituency members election or in relation to a London members election, as Sch 1, Sch 2 do not provide provision equivalent to Sch 3 r 7(4) etc (see the text and notes 13–17). As to the meaning of the 'Greater London returning officer' see PARA 211 note 8.

13 For these purposes, in relation to local government elections (including elections for the return of an elected local authority or London mayor but excluding the other London Authority elections), 'elector' means a person who is registered in the register of local government electors for the electoral area in question on the last day for the publication of notice of the election: Local Elections (Principal Areas) (England and Wales) Rules 2006, SI 2006/3304, Sch 2 r 6(7)(a), Appendix of Forms (Form of nomination paper, note 7(a)); Local Elections (Parishes and Communities) (England and Wales) Rules 2006, SI 2006/3305, Sch 2 r 6(7)(a), Appendix of Forms (Form of nomination paper, note 6(a)); Local Authorities (Mayoral Elections) (England and Wales) Regulations 2007, SI 2007/1024, Sch 1 r 8(5)(a), Appendix of Forms (Form 1: Form of nomination paper, note 6(a)); Greater London Authority Elections Rules 2007, SI 2007/3541, Sch 10 r 2 (Form 3: candidate to be the Mayor of London, note 7(a)). This includes a person then shown in the register as below voting age if (but only if) it appears from the register that he will be of voting age on the day fixed for the poll: Local Elections (Principal Areas) (England and Wales) Rules 2006, SI 2006/3304, Sch 2 r 6(7)(b), Appendix of Forms (Form of nomination paper, note 7(b)); Local Elections (Parishes and Communities) (England and Wales) Rules 2006, SI 2006/3305, Sch 2 r 6(7)(b), Appendix of Forms (Form of nomination paper, note 6(b)); Local Authorities (Mayoral Elections) (England and Wales) Regulations 2007, SI 2007/1024, Sch 1 r 8(5)(b), Appendix of Forms (Form 1: Form of nomination paper, note 6(b)); Greater London Authority Elections Rules 2007, SI 2007/3541, Sch 10 r 2 (Form 3: candidate to be the Mayor of London, note 7(b)). However, in relation to local government elections for principal areas, parishes and communities, and in relation to elections for the return of an elected local authority mayor, 'elector' does not include a person who has an anonymous entry in the register and accordingly such a person may not nominate a candidate for such elections: Local Elections (Principal Areas) (England and Wales) Rules 2006, SI 2006/3304, Sch 2 r 6(8), Appendix of Forms (Form of nomination paper, note 8); Local Elections (Parishes and Communities) (England and Wales) Rules 2006, SI 2006/3305, Sch 2 r 6(8), Appendix of Forms (Form of nomination paper, note 7); Local Authorities (Mayoral Elections) (England and Wales) Regulations 2007, SI 2007/1024, Sch 1 r 8(6), Appendix of Forms (Form 1: form of nomination paper, note 7). In relation to a London Mayoral election, 'elector' means a person named as a local government elector in the register being used at the election in that London Assembly constituency and includes a person shown in the register as below voting age if it appears from the register that he will be of voting age on the day fixed for the poll: Greater London Authority Elections Rules 2007, SI 2007/3541, Sch 3 r 7(5). This definition does not include, however, a person who has an anonymous entry in the register: see Sch 3 r 7(5). There is no equivalent provision made to define 'elector' for the purposes of a London Assembly Constituency members election or in relation to a London Assembly members election in Sch 1, Sch 2. As to the meaning of 'Assembly constituency' in relation to the London Assembly, and as to the meaning of 'electoral area' generally, see PARA 11. As to voting age for local government elections see PARA 97 note 14; as to entitlement to vote at local authority mayoral elections see PARA 98; and as to registration as a local government elector see PARA 113 et seq. As to the date of the poll at an election for the return of a local authority elected mayor see PARA 198; and as to the date of the poll at local government elections (including elections to fill vacancies) see PARAS 206–209. As to publication of the notice for a local government election (including an election for the return of an elected local authority mayor) see PARA 211.

14 This duty applies equally to the supply of forms of the candidate's consent to nomination: see PARA 258.

15 Local Elections (Principal Areas) (England and Wales) Rules 2006, SI 2006/3304, Sch 2 r 6(4)(a); Local Elections (Parishes and Communities) (England and Wales) Rules 2006, SI 2006/3305, Sch 2 r 6(4)(a); Local Authorities (Mayoral Elections) (England and Wales) Regulations 2007, SI 2007/1024, Sch 1 r 8(4)(a); Greater London Authority Elections Rules 2007, SI 2007/3541, Sch 3 r 7(4)(a). As to the delivery of nomination papers see PARA 260.

16 Local Elections (Principal Areas) (England and Wales) Rules 2006, SI 2006/3304, Sch 2 r 6(4); Local Elections (Parishes and Communities) (England and Wales) Rules 2006, SI 2006/3305,

Sch 2 r 6(4); Local Authorities (Mayoral Elections) (England and Wales) Regulations 2007, SI 2007/1024, Sch 1 r 8(4); Greater London Authority Elections Rules 2007, SI 2007/3541, Sch 3 r 7(4). See note 13.

17 Local Elections (Principal Areas) (England and Wales) Rules 2006, SI 2006/3304, Sch 2 r 6(4)(b); Local Elections (Parishes and Communities) (England and Wales) Rules 2006, SI 2006/3305, Sch 2 r 6(4)(b); Local Authorities (Mayoral Elections) (England and Wales) Regulations 2007, SI 2007/1024, Sch 1 r 8(4)(b); Greater London Authority Elections Rules 2007, SI 2007/3541, Sch 3 r 7(4)(b). See note 13.

18 For these purposes, a registered political party is a qualifying party if, on the relevant day, the party was registered in respect of England in the Great Britain register maintained under the Political Parties, Elections and Referendums Act 2000 Pt II (ss 22–40) (registration of political parties: see PARA 253) (see the Greater London Authority Elections Rules 2007, SI 2007/3541, Sch 2 r 7(5)(b)); and 'registered party' means a party which was registered under the Political Parties, Elections and Referendums Act 2000 Pt II on the day (the 'relevant day'), which is two days before the last day for delivery of nomination papers and party lists at that election (see the Greater London Authority Elections Rules 2007, SI 2007/3541, Sch 2 r 7(5)(a)). As to the meaning of 'England' see PARA 1 note 1. As to the meaning of 'Great Britain register' see PARA 253 note 8. As to the meaning of 'registered political party' see also LONDON GOVERNMENT vol 71 (2013) PARA 78.

19 As to the meaning of 'London member', in relation to the London Assembly, see PARA 11 note 5; definition applied by virtue of the Greater London Authority Elections Rules 2007, SI 2007/3541, r 2(3). As to elections for the return of London members of the London Assembly see PARA 199 et seq. See also LONDON GOVERNMENT vol 71 (2013) PARA 86. As to London members of the London Assembly generally see LONDON GOVERNMENT vol 71 (2013) PARA 70.

20 As to the form mentioned in the text see the Greater London Authority Elections Rules 2007, SI 2007/3541, Sch 10 r 2 (Form 2: London member (party list) candidates (form of nomination paper)) (Form 2 substituted by SI 2012/198).

21 Ie in accordance with the Greater London Authority Elections Rules 2007, SI 2007/3541, Sch 2 rr 7(2)–(5), 8 (see PARAS 256, 257): see Sch 2 r 7(1).

22 As to a party's nominating officer see PARA 253.

23 Greater London Authority Elections Rules 2007, SI 2007/3541, Sch 2 r 7(1). Accordingly, for the purposes of Sch 2 rr 9–68, unless the context indicates otherwise, 'nomination paper' includes both a reference to the nomination paper of a registered party delivered under Sch 2 r 7(1) (see also the text and notes 18–22), and a reference to the nomination paper of an individual candidate delivered under Sch 2 r 6(1) (see the text and notes 9–11); and 'nomination paper of a registered party' includes a reference to a party list delivered under Sch 2 r 7(2) (see PARA 256: see Sch 2 r 8(5). As to party lists see LONDON GOVERNMENT vol 71 (2013) PARA 81.

24 Ie each candidate at a constituency election: see the National Assembly for Wales (Representation of the People) Order 2007, SI 2007/236, Sch 5 para 4(1). As to the meaning of 'constituency election' for the purposes of Welsh Assembly elections see PARA 3 note 2; and as to the meanings of 'candidate' and 'constituency candidate' for these purposes see PARA 230 note 19.

25 As to the meaning of 'individual candidate' at a Welsh Assembly regional election see PARA 230 note 19.

26 As to the meaning of 'regional election' for the purposes of Welsh Assembly elections see PARA 3 note 2.

27 National Assembly for Wales (Representation of the People) Order 2007, SI 2007/236, Sch 5 paras 4(1), 6(1). The forms prescribed as mentioned in the text are set out in English and in Welsh in art 142, Sch 10 Appendix of Forms (Form CE: Form of nomination paper (constituency election); Form CH: Form of individual nomination paper (regional election)): see Sch 5 paras 4(1), 6(1).

Except in relation to the forms of ballot paper to be used at constituency and regional elections set out in Sch 10, the forms set out in the National Assembly for Wales (Representation of the People) Order 2007, SI 2007/236, may be used with such variations as the circumstances may require: see art 142(1), (2). Without prejudice to the power conferred by art 142(1), where any form to which art 142(1) applies is set out in English and Welsh in the National Assembly for Wales (Representation of the People) Order 2007, SI 2007/236, so that it is set out in English first and then in Welsh, that form may be varied so that the English and Welsh parts are combined or so that it is set out in Welsh first and then in English: see art 142(3). Where any form is required to be completed by any person, and it is a form set out as referred to in art 142(3), such form may be validly completed by completion of either the English or Welsh parts: see art 142(4).

28 Ie in the case of a constituency election: see the National Assembly for Wales (Representation of the People) Order 2007, SI 2007/236, Sch 5 para 4(6). As to the meaning of 'constituency returning officer' for the purposes of Welsh Assembly elections see PARA 18 note 2.

29 Ie in the case of a regional election: see the National Assembly for Wales (Representation of the People) Order 2007, SI 2007/236, Sch 5 para 6(5). As to the meaning of 'regional returning officer' for the purposes of Welsh Assembly elections see PARA 18 note 2.

30 Ie a form of constituency nomination paper (in the case of constituency elections) or a form of individual nomination paper (in the case of a regional election): see the National Assembly for Wales (Representation of the People) Order 2007, SI 2007/236, Sch 5 paras 4(6), 6(5).

31 National Assembly for Wales (Representation of the People) Order 2007, SI 2007/236, Sch 5 paras 4(6), 6(5). As to the relevant returning officers see the text and notes 28, 29.

32 As to the meaning of 'registered political party' see PARA 215 note 19.

33 For these purposes, a registered political party is a qualifying party in relation to a Welsh Assembly constituency or electoral region if, on the relevant day, the party was registered in respect of Wales in the Great Britain register maintained under the Political Parties, Elections and Referendums Act 2000 Pt II (ss 22–40) (registration of political parties: see PARA 253): see the National Assembly for Wales (Representation of the People) Order 2007, SI 2007/236, Sch 5 para 80(2). As to the meaning of the 'relevant day' for these purposes see Sch 5 para 80(1); and PARA 215 note 19.

34 Ie in the form that is set out in English and in Welsh in the National Assembly for Wales (Representation of the People) Order 2007, SI 2007/236, Sch 10 Appendix of Forms (Form CI: Form of party nomination paper (regional election)): see Sch 5 para 7(1).

35 As to the nominating officer see PARA 253. A registered nominating officer for a registered political party may, in writing, appoint one or more persons to discharge all or any of his functions conferred or imposed by the National Assembly for Wales (Representation of the People) Order 2007, SI 2007/236, Sch 5: see Sch 5 para 81(1); and PARA 215 note 24.

36 National Assembly for Wales (Representation of the People) Order 2007, SI 2007/236, Sch 5 para 7(1). As to the delivery of nomination papers see PARA 260.

37 National Assembly for Wales (Representation of the People) Order 2007, SI 2007/236, Sch 5 para 7(7).

38 As to the meaning of 'individual candidate' at a European parliamentary election see PARA 230 note 32. As to European parliamentary elections see further PARA 13 et seq.

39 European Parliamentary Elections Regulations 2004, SI 2004/293, Sch 1 para 4(1) (Sch 1 substituted by SI 2009/186). The form of a nomination paper for a European parliamentary election is not prescribed.

40 As to the meaning of 'registered party' for these purposes see PARA 230 note 29.

41 As to the establishment of electoral regions for the purpose of elections to the European Parliament see PARA 77.

42 As to returning officers appointed for the purposes of elections to the European Parliament see PARA 360.

43 As to the meaning of 'nominating officer' for the purposes of a European parliamentary election see PARA 239 note 2.

44 European Parliamentary Elections Regulations 2004, SI 2004/293, Sch 1 para 6(1) (Sch 1 as substituted: see note 39).

256. Particulars required in nomination papers. The nomination paper for a parliamentary election[1] must state the candidate's full names and[2], if desired, description[3]. The description, if any, must consist of either a properly-authorised description relating to a registered political party[4], or the word 'Independent'[5]. Any such nomination paper may not include a description of a candidate, however, which is likely to lead electors to associate the candidate with a registered political party[6] (or with two or more registered political parties) unless the party (or each of the parties) is a qualifying party in relation to the constituency[7], and the description (or registered description, in the case of two or more parties) is authorised by a certificate[8]. The certificate must be[9]:

(1)   issued by or on behalf of the registered nominating officer of the party (or of each of the parties, as the case may be)[10]; and

(2)   received by the returning officer at some time during the period for delivery of nomination papers[11].

The nomination paper for a parliamentary election must be accompanied by a form (the 'home address form') which states the candidate's full names[12], and the candidate's home address in full[13]. The home address form may contain a statement made and signed by the candidate that he requires the home address not to be made public[14] and, if it does so, the home address form must state the constituency within which that address is situated (or, if that address is outside the United Kingdom[15], the country within which it is situated)[16].

The nomination paper at a local government election for principal areas, parishes and communities[17], a local authority mayoral election[18], and a London Authority election where individual candidates are standing[19], must state the candidate's full names[20], the candidate's home address in full[21], and, if desired, description[22]. Except at local government elections for parishes and communities[23], or at an election of individual candidates to be London members of the London Assembly[24], the description, if any, must consist of either a properly-authorised description relating to a registered political party[25] or the word 'Independent'[26]; and any such nomination paper may not include a description of a candidate that is likely to lead electors to associate the candidate with a registered political party (or with two or more registered political parties)[27] unless the party (or of each of the parties, if there is more than one) is a qualifying party in relation to the electoral area[28], and the description (or registered description, in the case of two or more parties) is authorised by a certificate[29]. The certificate must be:

(a)   issued by or on behalf of the registered nominating officer of the party (or of each of the parties, if there is more than one)[30]; and

(b)   received by the returning officer[31] before the last time for the delivery of nomination papers[32].

For the purposes of a London Authority election for the return of London members, a registered party's nomination paper[33] must state the authorised description by which the registered party is to stand for election[34]; it must include a statement, signed by the person issuing the paper[35], that it is issued either by the party's registered nominating officer[36], or on behalf of the party's registered nominating officer by a person authorised in writing by him[37]; and it must be accompanied by a party list which sets out the full names and home addresses of each candidate included in that list[38].

The nomination paper for each candidate at a Welsh Assembly constituency election[39] ('constituency nomination paper'), and for each individual candidate at a Welsh Assembly regional election[40] ('individual nomination paper'), must state the candidate's full names[41], the candidate's home address in full[42], and, if desired, a description[43]. The description may consist of the word 'Independent' (or 'Annibynnol', or both)[44], although, at a constituency election, the description, if any, alternatively may consist of a description relating to a registered political party which is properly authorised[45]. A constituency nomination paper may not include a description of a candidate which is likely to lead voters to associate the candidate with a registered political party (or with two or more registered political parties)[46] unless the party (or of each of the parties, if there is more than one) is a qualifying party in relation to the constituency[47] and the description (or registered description, in the case of two or more parties) is authorised by a certificate in the prescribed form[48]. The certificate must be:

(i)   issued by the registered nominating officer of the party (or of each of the parties, if there is more than one)[49]; and

(ii) received by the constituency returning officer[50] at some time during the period for the delivery of nomination papers[51].

A party nomination paper[52] must include[53] either the registered name (or names) of the party[54], or a registered description of the party[55]; and it must include also the list ('party list') of candidates ('party list candidates') submitted by the party for that regional election[56]. The party nomination paper is the nomination paper for each candidate on that list[57]. In respect of each party list candidate, the party list must state the candidate's full names[58], and the candidate's home address in full[59].

The nomination paper for an individual candidate at a European parliamentary election[60] must state the candidate's full names[61], the candidate's home address in full[62] and, if desired, description[63]. The description, if any, must consist of the word 'Independent'[64] (or, in the case of an individual candidate standing on behalf of a registered party[65] at a by-election[66], the registered name of the party[67], or an authorised description of the party)[68]. The nomination paper of an individual candidate standing on behalf of a registered party at a by-election may not include a description of an individual candidate which is likely to lead voters to associate the candidate with a registered political party (or with two or more registered political parties)[69] unless the individual candidate is standing on behalf of a registered party (or on behalf of two or more registered parties) at a European parliamentary by-election[70], the party (or each of the parties, if there is more than one) is a qualifying party in relation to the electoral region[71] and the description (or registered description, in the case of two or more parties) is authorised by a certificate[72]. The certificate must be:

(A) issued by or on behalf of the party's registered nominating officer of the party (or of each of the parties, if there is more than one)[73]; and

(B) received by the returning officer[74] before the last time for the delivery of nomination papers[75].

The nomination paper for a registered party that is to stand for election at a European parliamentary general election in an electoral region must state the registered name of the party[76], and may state the description by which the registered party is to stand for election[77]. Such a nomination paper must include a statement that the party is nominated by or on behalf of the nominating officer of the registered party in question (and the statement must be signed by the person making it)[78]. The nomination paper must be accompanied by a list of candidates[79] which sets out the full names and home addresses in full of each candidate[80]. The number of candidates in such a list must not exceed the number of members of the European Parliament ('MEPs') to be elected in the electoral region at the general election[81].

No misnomer[82] or inaccurate description of any person or place named in any nomination paper affects the full operation of that document with respect to that person or place in any case where the description of the person or place is such as to be commonly understood[83]. Thus it has been held that a mere mis-spelling of a surname, not calculated to mislead electors, does not give good ground for objection[84]; nor does the use in an address of an outdated street name which had been recently changed[85]. It has also been held that the use of a contraction of a Christian name which is well known and in ordinary use as representing that name, such as 'Wm' for 'William', is permissible instead of setting out the forename in full[86].

1 As to the meaning of 'parliamentary election' see PARA 9. As to the form and supply of nomination papers see PARA 255.

2   Representation of the People Act 1983 Sch 1 r 6(2)(a) (amended by the Political Parties and
     Elections Act 2009 s 39, Sch 6 para 8(1), (2)). There appears to be no case law on what is meant
     by the 'full names' of a person but as to the statutory effect of misnomers or inaccurate
     descriptions in nomination papers see the text and notes 82–86. As to the meaning of
     'candidate' generally see PARA 230.
          The surname must be placed first in the list of the candidate's names: Representation of the
     People Act 1983 Sch 1 r 6(2). Where a candidate is commonly known by some title, he may be
     described by his title as if it were his surname: Sch 1, Appendix of Forms (Form of nomination
     paper, note 2). If a candidate commonly uses either a surname which is different from any other
     surname he has, or a forename which is different from any other forename he has, the
     nomination paper may state the commonly used surname or forename in addition to the other
     name: Sch 1 r 6(2A) (added by the Electoral Administration Act 2006 s 21(1), (2)). Where a
     candidate's commonly used name appears on the nomination paper in this way, that name
     (instead of any other name) will appear on the ballot paper: Representation of the People
     Act 1983 Sch 1, Appendix of Forms (Form of nomination paper, note 2A) (Form of nomination
     paper, notes 2A, 2B added by the Electoral Administration Act 2006 s 21(1), (5)). However, the
     ballot paper will show the other name if the returning officer thinks either that the use of the
     commonly used name may be likely to mislead or confuse electors, or that the commonly used
     name is obscene or offensive: Representation of the People Act 1983 Sch 1, Appendix of Forms
     (Form of nomination paper, note 2B) (as so added). As to the meaning of 'elector' for these
     purposes see PARA 95 note 2. As to decisions regarding the validity of nomination papers see
     PARA 263. As to returning officers for parliamentary elections see PARA 350 et seq. Names likely
     to mislead or confuse electors may constitute a fraudulent device under applicable electoral law:
     see PARA 727.
3   Representation of the People Act 1983 Sch 1 r 6(2)(c).
4   Representation of the People Act 1983 Sch 1 r 6(3)(a) (Sch 1 r 6(3) substituted by the Political
     Parties, Elections and Referendums Act 2000 s 38(1), (2); Representation of the People Act 1983
     Sch 1 r 6(3)(a) amended by the Electoral Administration Act 2006 ss 19(1), (4), 74(2), Sch 2).
     The description must be authorised as mentioned in the text under either the Representation of
     the People Act 1983 Sch 1 r 6A(1) or Sch 1 r 6A(1B) (see the text and notes 6–11): see Sch 1
     r 6(3)(a) (Sch 1 r 6(3) as so substituted, Sch 1 r 6(3)(a) as so amended). As to the meaning of
     'registered political party' for these purposes see note 6; and as to the authorised description
     specifically see note 8.
5   Representation of the People Act 1983 Sch 1 r 6(3)(b) (as substituted: see note 4). 'Annibynnol'
     is prescribed as the form of words in Welsh for the word 'Independent' which is specified for use
     as the description of a candidate in a nomination paper by Sch 1 r 6(3)(b); and the word in
     Welsh so prescribed may be used as well as or in place of the equivalent word in English at a
     parliamentary election in Wales: see the Parliamentary Elections (Welsh Forms) Order 2007,
     SI 2007/1014, art 4(3), (5) (art 4(3) amended by SI 2010/1078). As to the meaning of 'Wales' see
     PARA 1 note 1.
          Where the candidate at a parliamentary election is the Speaker of the House of Commons
     seeking re-election, the words 'The Speaker seeking re-election' may be used as the description:
     see the Representation of the People Act 1983 Sch 1 r 6(3)(b) (as so substituted). 'Y Llefarydd yn
     ailymgeisio' is prescribed as the form of words in Welsh for the words 'The Speaker seeking
     re-election' which is specified for use as the description of a candidate in a nomination paper
     by Sch 1 r 6(3)(b); and the forms of words in Welsh so prescribed may be used as well as or in
     place of the equivalent words in English at a parliamentary election in Wales: see the
     Parliamentary Elections (Welsh Forms) Order 2007, SI 2007/1014, art 4(4), (5).
6   For these purposes, 'registered political party' means a party which was registered under the
     Political Parties, Elections and Referendums Act 2000 Pt II (ss 22–40) (registration of political
     parties: see PARA 253) on the day (the 'relevant day') which is two days before the last day for
     the delivery of nomination papers at that election (see PARA 260): Representation of the People
     Act 1983 Sch 1 r 6A(3)(a) (Sch 1 r 6A added by the Registration of Political Parties Act 1998
     s 13, Sch 2 para 2; Representation of the People Act 1983 Sch 1 r 6A(3) substituted by the
     Political Parties, Elections and Referendums Act 2000 s 38(1), (3)(b); Representation of the
     People Act 1983 Sch 1 r 6A(3)(a) amended by the Electoral Administration Act 2006
     s 52(1), (2)(a)). For these purposes, any day is disregarded which falls within the Representation
     of the People Act 1983 Sch 1 r 2(1) subject to Sch 1 r 2(2A) (computation of time: see PARA 195
     note 27): Sch 1 r 6A(4) (Sch 1 r 6A as so added; Sch 1 r 6A(4) added by the Electoral
     Administration Act 2006 s 52(1), (3), and amended by the Fixed-term Parliaments Act 2011
     s 6(3), Schedule paras 6, 12).
7   For these purposes, a registered political party is a qualifying party in relation to a constituency
     if the constituency is in England or Wales and the party was on the relevant day (see note 6)

registered in respect of that part of Great Britain in the Great Britain register maintained under the Political Parties, Elections and Referendums Act 2000 Pt II (registration of political parties: see PARA 253): Representation of the People Act 1983 Sch 1 r 6A(3)(b) (Sch 1 r 6A as added, Sch 1 r 6A(3) as substituted (see note 6); Sch 1 r 6A(3)(b) amended by the Electoral Administration Act 2006 s 52(1), (2)(b)). As to the meaning of 'constituency' for the purposes of parliamentary elections see PARA 9. As to the meanings of 'England' and 'Great Britain' see PARA 1 note 1; and as to the meaning of the 'Great Britain register' see PARA 253 note 8.

8   Representation of the People Act 1983 Sch 1 r 6A(1) (Sch 1 r 6A as added (see note 6); Sch 1 r 6A(1) amended by the Political Parties, Elections and Referendums Act 2000 s 38(1), (3)(a); and by the Electoral Administration Act 2006 s 74(1), Sch 1 paras 104, 129(1), (2)); Representation of the People Act 1983 Sch 1 r 6A(1B) (Sch 1 r 6A as so added; Sch 1 r 6A(1A)–(1C) added by the Electoral Administration Act 2006 s 49(3)). For the purposes of the Representation of the People Act 1983 Sch 1 r 6A(1), an authorised description may be either the name of the party registered under the Political Parties, Elections and Referendums Act 2000 s 28 (registration of parties: see CONSTITUTIONAL LAW AND HUMAN RIGHTS) or a description of the party registered under s 28A (descriptions: see CONSTITUTIONAL LAW AND HUMAN RIGHTS): Representation of the People Act 1983 Sch 1 r 6A(1A) (as so added). For the purposes of Sch 1 r 6A(1B), a description is a registered description if it is a description registered for use by the parties under the Political Parties, Elections and Referendums Act 2000 s 28B (joint descriptions: see CONSTITUTIONAL LAW AND HUMAN RIGHTS): Representation of the People Act 1983 Sch 1 r 6A(1C) (as so added).

    In *R (on the application of De Beer) v Balabanoff* [2002] EWHC 670 (Admin), (2002) Times, 25 April, [2002] All ER (D) 34 (Apr), a returning officer's decision to reject nomination papers on which the description was not as authorised by a certificate (for the purposes of what is now the Local Elections (Principal Areas) (England and Wales) Rules 2006, SI 2006/3304, Sch 2 r 5(1), (3): see the text and notes 27–32) was held to be reasonable and he was not in error in failing to look beyond those papers when exercising his judgment on the matter; Parliament has conferred duties (but not discretions) on returning officers and has made express provisions as to how any decision of a returning officer might be challenged, namely by petition before an election court after the election (as to which see PARA 761 et seq).

9   See the Representation of the People Act 1983 Sch 1 r 6A(1) (Sch 1 r 6A as added (see note 6); Sch 1 r 6A(1) as amended (see note 8)); and Sch 1 r 6A(1B) (as added: see note 8).

10   Representation of the People Act 1983 Sch 1 r 6A(1)(a) (as added: see note 6); Sch 1 r 6A(1B)(a) (as added: see note 8). See note 8. A person is guilty of a corrupt practice if he fraudulently purports to be authorised to issue a certificate under Sch 1 r 6A(1) or Sch 1 r 6A(1B) on behalf of a registered political party's nominating officer: see Sch 1 r 6A(2); and PARA 706. As to the registered nominating officer of a party see PARA 253.

11   Representation of the People Act 1983 Sch 1 r 6A(1)(b) (as added: see note 6); Sch 1 r 6A(1B)(b) (as added: see note 8). See also note 8. As to the period for delivery of nomination papers see PARA 260.

12   Representation of the People Act 1983 Sch 1 r 6(4)(a) (Sch 1 r 6(4), (5) added by the Political Parties and Elections Act 2009 s 24(1), (2)(b)).

13   Representation of the People Act 1983 Sch 1 r 6(4)(b) (as added: see note 12). As to the meaning of 'home address' see note 21.

14   Representation of the People Act 1983 Sch 1 r 6(5)(a) (as added: see note 12).

15   As to the meaning of 'United Kingdom' see PARA 1 note 1.

16   Representation of the People Act 1983 Sch 1 r 6(5)(b) (as added: see note 12).

17   As to the meaning of 'local government election' see PARA 11. As to the ordinary election of councillors for local government principal areas see PARA 197 et seq; and as to ordinary elections of councillors for parishes or communities see PARA 200 et seq.

18   As to elections for the return of an elected local authority mayor see PARA 198 et seq.

19   Ie at a London Assembly Constituency members election or a London Mayoral election or at an election of London members of the London Assembly (insofar as the nomination relates to an individual candidate): see the Greater London Authority Elections Rules 2007, SI 2007/3541, Sch 1 r 6(2), Sch 2 r 6(2), Sch 3 r 6(2). As to the meaning of 'Authority election' see PARA 11. As to the meaning of 'London member', in relation to the London Assembly, see PARA 11 note 5; definition applied by virtue of r 2(2). As to the meaning of 'constituency member', in relation to the London Assembly, see PARA 11 note 6; definition applied by virtue of r 2(2). As to the meaning of 'Assembly constituency', in relation to the London Assembly, see PARA 11 note 6. As to elections for the return of the members of the London Assembly, and for the return of an elected Mayor of London, see PARA 199 et seq. As to the London Assembly see LONDON GOVERNMENT vol 71 (2013) PARA 70; as to constituency members of the London Assembly see

further LONDON GOVERNMENT vol 71 (2013) PARA 80; and as to individual candidates to be London members of the London Assembly see further LONDON GOVERNMENT vol 71 (2013) PARA 81.

20 Local Elections (Principal Areas) (England and Wales) Rules 2006, SI 2006/3304, Sch 2 r 4(2)(a); Local Elections (Parishes and Communities) (England and Wales) Rules 2006, SI 2006/3305, Sch 2 r 4(2)(a); Local Authorities (Mayoral Elections) (England and Wales) Regulations 2007, SI 2007/1024, Sch 1 r 6(3)(a); Greater London Authority Elections Rules 2007, SI 2007/3541, Sch 1 r 6(2)(a), Sch 2 r 6(2)(a), Sch 3 r 6(2)(a). The surname must be placed first in the list of the candidate's names: Local Elections (Principal Areas) (England and Wales) Rules 2006, SI 2006/3304, Sch 2 r 4(2); Local Elections (Parishes and Communities) (England and Wales) Rules 2006, SI 2006/3305, Sch 2 r 4(2); Local Authorities (Mayoral Elections) (England and Wales) Regulations 2007, SI 2007/1024, Sch 1 r 6(3); Greater London Authority Elections Rules 2007, SI 2007/3541, Sch 1 r 6(2), Sch 2 r 6(2), Sch 3 r 6(2).

Where a candidate is commonly known by some title, he may be described by his title as if it were his surname (or part of his surname, in the case of a London Authority election): Local Elections (Principal Areas) (England and Wales) Rules 2006, SI 2006/3304, Sch 2 Appendix of Forms (Form of nomination paper, note 2); Local Elections (Parishes and Communities) (England and Wales) Rules 2006, SI 2006/3305, Sch 2 Appendix of Forms (Form of nomination paper, note 2); Local Authorities (Mayoral Elections) (England and Wales) Regulations 2007, SI 2007/1024, Sch 1 Appendix of Forms (Form 1: form of nomination paper, note 2); Greater London Authority Elections Rules 2007, SI 2007/3541, Sch 10 r 2 (Form 1: constituency member and London member (individual) candidates (form of nomination paper), note 2; Form 3: candidate to be the Mayor of London (form of nomination paper), note 2) (Forms 1, 3 substituted by SI 2012/198). If a candidate commonly uses either a surname which is different from any other surname he has, or a forename which is different from any other forename he has, the nomination paper may state the commonly used surname and/or forename in addition to the other name: Local Elections (Principal Areas) (England and Wales) Rules 2006, SI 2006/3304, Sch 2 r 4(3); Local Elections (Parishes and Communities) (England and Wales) Rules 2006, SI 2006/3305, Sch 2 r 4(3); Local Authorities (Mayoral Elections) (England and Wales) Regulations 2007, SI 2007/1024, Sch 1 r 6(4); Greater London Authority Elections Rules 2007, SI 2007/3541, Sch 1 r 6(3), Sch 2 r 8(1), (2), Sch 3 r 6(3). Where a candidate's commonly used name appears on the nomination paper in this way, that name (instead of any other name) will appear on the ballot paper: Local Elections (Principal Areas) (England and Wales) Rules 2006, SI 2006/3304, Sch 2 Appendix of Forms (Form of nomination paper, note 3); Local Elections (Parishes and Communities) (England and Wales) Rules 2006, SI 2006/3305, Sch 2 Appendix of Forms (Form of nomination paper, note 3); Local Authorities (Mayoral Elections) (England and Wales) Regulations 2007, SI 2007/1024, Sch 1 Appendix of Forms (Form 1: form of nomination paper, note 3); Greater London Authority Elections Rules 2007, SI 2007/3541, Sch 10 r 2 (Form 1: constituency member and London member (individual) candidates (form of nomination paper), note 3; Form 3: candidate to be the Mayor of London (form of nomination paper), note 3). However, the ballot paper will show the other name if the returning officer thinks either that the use of the commonly used name may be likely to mislead or confuse electors, or that the commonly used name is obscene or offensive: Local Elections (Principal Areas) (England and Wales) Rules 2006, SI 2006/3304, Sch 2 Appendix of Forms (Form of nomination paper, note 4); Local Elections (Parishes and Communities) (England and Wales) Rules 2006, SI 2006/3305, Sch 2 Appendix of Forms (Form of nomination paper, note 4); Local Authorities (Mayoral Elections) (England and Wales) Regulations 2007, SI 2007/1024, Sch 1 Appendix of Forms (Form 1: form of nomination paper, note 4); Greater London Authority Elections Rules 2007, SI 2007/3541, Sch 10 r 2 (Form 1: constituency member and London member (individual) candidates (form of nomination paper), note 4; Form 3: candidate to be the Mayor of London (form of nomination paper), note 4). As to returning officers for local government elections see PARA 354 et seq. In elections for the return of constituency members of the London Assembly, the reference is to the constituency returning officer ('CRO'); in other London Assembly elections (ie for London members and in the case of a London Mayoral election), the reference is to the Greater London returning officer ('GLRO'). As to the meaning of the 'Greater London returning officer' see PARA 211 note 8; and as to the meaning of the 'constituency returning officer' in this context see PARA 211 note 9.

21 Local Elections (Principal Areas) (England and Wales) Rules 2006, SI 2006/3304, Sch 2 r 4(2)(b); Local Elections (Parishes and Communities) (England and Wales) Rules 2006, SI 2006/3305, Sch 2 r 4(2)(b); Local Authorities (Mayoral Elections) (England and Wales) Regulations 2007, SI 2007/1024, Sch 1 r 6(3)(b); Greater London Authority Elections Rules 2007, SI 2007/3541, Sch 1 r 6(2)(b), Sch 2 r 6(2)(b), Sch 3 r 6(2)(b).

A person's home address is the place where he lives with his family and sleeps at night and is not his place of business, even if the proprietor is better known by his place of business than by his place of residence: *R v Hammond* (1852) 17 QB 772, 21 LJQB 153 (election of borough councillors). The object of the statutory provisions is to give one address by which the candidate can be easily identified: *Allen v Greensill* (1847) 4 CB 100; *R v Hammond*. See also the cases on the meaning of 'residence' cited at PARA 225 note 13.As to the statutory effect of inaccurate descriptions of places in nomination papers see the text and notes 82–86. For a case where a person was twice nominated, once by a correct and once by an incorrect address, see PARA 263 note 9.

22 Local Elections (Principal Areas) (England and Wales) Rules 2006, SI 2006/3304, Sch 2 r 4(2)(c); Local Elections (Parishes and Communities) (England and Wales) Rules 2006, SI 2006/3305, Sch 2 r 4(2)(c); Local Authorities (Mayoral Elections) (England and Wales) Regulations 2007, SI 2007/1024, Sch 1 r 6(3)(c); Greater London Authority Elections Rules 2007, SI 2007/3541, Sch 1 r 6(2)(c), Sch 2 r 6(2)(c), Sch 3 r 6(2)(c). As to the limited descriptions allowed at local government elections for parishes and communities, and at an election of individual candidates to be London members of the London Assembly, see notes 23, 24.

23 In relation to local government elections for parishes and communities, the description, if any, must not exceed six words in length, and need not refer to the candidate's rank, profession or calling so long as, with the candidate's other particulars, it is sufficient to identify him: Local Elections (Parishes and Communities) (England and Wales) Rules 2006, SI 2006/3305, Sch 2 r 4(4).

24 In the case of an individual candidate at an election of London members of the London Assembly, the only description allowed is a description consisting of the word 'Independent': see the Greater London Authority Elections Rules 2007, SI 2007/3541, Sch 2 r 6(2)(c). At an election of London members of the London Assembly, the only use of a properly-authorised description relating to a registered political party occurs in relation to party lists: see the text and notes 33–38.

25 Local Elections (Principal Areas) (England and Wales) Rules 2006, SI 2006/3304, Sch 2 r 4(4)(a); Local Authorities (Mayoral Elections) (England and Wales) Regulations 2007, SI 2007/1024, Sch 1 r 6(5)(a); Greater London Authority Elections Rules 2007, SI 2007/3541, Sch 1 r 6(4)(a), Sch 3 r 6(4)(a). The description referred to in the text must be authorised under the Local Elections (Principal Areas) (England and Wales) Rules 2006, SI 2006/3304, Sch 2 r 5(1) or Sch 2r 5(3), the Local Authorities (Mayoral Elections) (England and Wales) Regulations 2007, SI 2007/1024, Sch 1 r 7(1) or Sch 1 r 7(3), or under the Greater London Authority Elections Rules 2007, SI 2007/3541, Sch 1 r 6(5) or Sch 1 r 6(7), Sch 3 r 6(5) or Sch 3 r 6(7), as the case may be (see the text and notes 27–32). As to the meaning of 'registered political party' for these purposes see note 27; and as to the authorised description specifically see note 29.

26 Local Elections (Principal Areas) (England and Wales) Rules 2006, SI 2006/3304, Sch 2 r 4(4)(b); Local Authorities (Mayoral Elections) (England and Wales) Regulations 2007, SI 2007/1024, Sch 1 r 6(5)(b); Greater London Authority Elections Rules 2007, SI 2007/3541, Sch 1 r 6(4)(b), Sch 3 r 6(4)(b). 'Annibynnwr' is prescribed as the form of words in Welsh for the word 'Independent' which is specified for use as the description of a candidate in a nomination paper by the Local Elections (Principal Areas) (England and Wales) Rules 2006, SI 2006/3304, Sch 2 r 4(4)(b), Sch 3 r 4(4)(b); and the word in Welsh so prescribed may be used as well as or in place of the equivalent word in English at a principal area election: see the Elections (Principal Areas) (Welsh Forms) Order 2007, SI 2007/1015, art 4(3), (4).

27 Local Elections (Principal Areas) (England and Wales) Rules 2006, SI 2006/3304, Sch 2 r 5(1), (3); Local Elections (Parishes and Communities) (England and Wales) Rules 2006, SI 2006/3305, Sch 2 r 5(1), (3); Local Authorities (Mayoral Elections) (England and Wales) Regulations 2007, SI 2007/1024, Sch 1 r 7(1), (3); Greater London Authority Elections Rules 2007, SI 2007/3541, Sch 1 r 6(5), (7), Sch 3 r 6(5), (7).

For these purposes, 'registered political party' means a party which was registered under the Political Parties, Elections and Referendums Act 2000 Pt II (ss 22–40) (registration of political parties: see PARA 253) on the day (the 'relevant day') which is two days before the last day for the delivery of nomination papers at that election (see PARA 260): Local Elections (Principal Areas) (England and Wales) Rules 2006, SI 2006/3304, Sch 2 r 5(6)(a); Local Elections (Parishes and Communities) (England and Wales) Rules 2006, SI 2006/3305, Sch 2 r 5(6)(a); Local Authorities (Mayoral Elections) (England and Wales) Regulations 2007, SI 2007/1024, Sch 1 r 7(6)(a); Greater London Authority Elections Rules 2007, SI 2007/3541, Sch 1 r 6(10)(a), Sch 3 r 6(10)(a). For these purposes, any day is disregarded which falls, in relation to a local government election for principal areas, within the Local Elections (Principal Areas) (England

and Wales) Rules 2006, SI 2006/3304, Sch 2 r 2(1) or, in relation to a local government election for parishes and communities, within the Local Elections (Parishes and Communities) (England and Wales) Rules 2006, SI 2006/3305, Sch 2 r 2(1), or, in relation to a local authority mayoral election, within the Local Authorities (Mayoral Elections) (England and Wales) Regulations 2007, SI 2007/1024, Sch 1 r 4(1), or, in relation to a London Authority election, within the Greater London Authority Elections Rules 2007, SI 2007/3541, Sch 1 r 4(1), Sch 3 r 4(1) (see PARA 211 note 1): Local Elections (Principal Areas) (England and Wales) Rules 2006, SI 2006/3304, Sch 2 r 5(7); Local Elections (Parishes and Communities) (England and Wales) Rules 2006, SI 2006/3305, Sch 2 r 5(7); Local Authorities (Mayoral Elections) (England and Wales) Regulations 2007, SI 2007/1024, Sch 1 r 7(7); Greater London Authority Elections Rules 2007, SI 2007/3541, Sch 1 r 6(11), Sch 3 r 6(11).

28　Local Elections (Principal Areas) (England and Wales) Rules 2006, SI 2006/3304, Sch 2 r 5(1), (3); Local Elections (Parishes and Communities) (England and Wales) Rules 2006, SI 2006/3305, Sch 2 r 5(1), (3); Local Authorities (Mayoral Elections) (England and Wales) Regulations 2007, SI 2007/1024, Sch 1 r 7(1), (3); Greater London Authority Elections Rules 2007, SI 2007/3541, Sch 1 r 6(5)(a), (7), Sch 3 r 6(5)(a), (7). For these purposes, a registered political party is a qualifying party in relation to an electoral area if the electoral area is in England or Wales and the party was on the relevant day (see note 27) registered in respect of that part of Great Britain in the Great Britain register maintained under the Political Parties, Elections and Referendums Act 2000 Pt II: Local Elections (Principal Areas) (England and Wales) Rules 2006, SI 2006/3304, Sch 2 r 5(6)(b); Local Elections (Parishes and Communities) (England and Wales) Rules 2006, SI 2006/3305, Sch 2 r 5(6)(b); Local Authorities (Mayoral Elections) (England and Wales) Regulations 2007, SI 2007/1024, Sch 1 r 7(6)(b); Greater London Authority Elections Rules 2007, SI 2007/3541, Sch 1 r 6(10)(b), Sch 3 r 6(10)(b). In relation to a London Mayoral election, the reference to an electoral area is to be read in all instances as a reference to Greater London: see Sch 3 r 6(5)(a), Sch 3 r 6(7), Sch 3 r 6(10)(b). As to the meaning of 'electoral area' generally see PARA 11.

29　Local Elections (Principal Areas) (England and Wales) Rules 2006, SI 2006/3304, Sch 2 r 5(1), (3); Local Elections (Parishes and Communities) (England and Wales) Rules 2006, SI 2006/3305, Sch 2 r 5(1), (3); Local Authorities (Mayoral Elections) (England and Wales) Regulations 2007, SI 2007/1024, Sch 1 r 7(1), (3); Greater London Authority Elections Rules 2007, SI 2007/3541, Sch 1 r 6(5)(b), (7), Sch 3 r 6(5)(b), (7). See *R (on the application of De Beer) v Balabanoff* [2002] EWHC 670 (Admin), (2002) Times, 25 April, [2002] All ER (D) 34 (Apr); and note 8.

　　For the purposes of the Local Elections (Principal Areas) (England and Wales) Rules 2006, SI 2006/3304, Sch 2 r 5(1), the Local Elections (Parishes and Communities) (England and Wales) Rules 2006, SI 2006/3305, Sch 2 r 5(1), the Local Authorities (Mayoral Elections) (England and Wales) Regulations 2007, SI 2007/1024, Sch 1 r 7(1), or the Greater London Authority Elections Rules 2007, SI 2007/3541, Sch 1 r 6(5), Sch 3 r 6(5), an authorised description may be either the name of the party registered under the Political Parties, Elections and Referendums Act 2000 s 28 (registration of parties: see CONSTITUTIONAL LAW AND HUMAN RIGHTS) or a description of the party registered under s 28A (descriptions: see CONSTITUTIONAL LAW AND HUMAN RIGHTS): Local Elections (Principal Areas) (England and Wales) Rules 2006, SI 2006/3304, Sch 2 r 5(2); Local Elections (Parishes and Communities) (England and Wales) Rules 2006, SI 2006/3305, Sch 2 r 5(2); Local Authorities (Mayoral Elections) (England and Wales) Regulations 2007, SI 2007/1024, Sch 1 r 7(2); Greater London Authority Elections Rules 2007, SI 2007/3541, Sch 1 r 6(6), Sch 3 r 6(6). For the purposes of the Local Elections (Principal Areas) (England and Wales) Rules 2006, SI 2006/3304, Sch 2 r 5(3), the Local Elections (Parishes and Communities) (England and Wales) Rules 2006, SI 2006/3305, Sch 2 r 5(3), the Local Authorities (Mayoral Elections) (England and Wales) Regulations 2007, SI 2007/1024, Sch 1 r 7(3), or the Greater London Authority Elections Rules 2007, SI 2007/3541, Sch 1 r 6(7), Sch 3 r 6(7), a description is a registered description if it is a description registered for use by the parties under the Political Parties, Elections and Referendums Act 2000 s 28B (joint descriptions: see CONSTITUTIONAL LAW AND HUMAN RIGHTS): Local Elections (Principal Areas) (England and Wales) Rules 2006, SI 2006/3304, Sch 2 r 5(4); Local Elections (Parishes and Communities) (England and Wales) Rules 2006, SI 2006/3305, Sch 2 r 5(4); Local Authorities (Mayoral Elections) (England and Wales) Regulations 2007, SI 2007/1024, Sch 1 r 7(4); Greater London Authority Elections Rules 2007, SI 2007/3541, Sch 1 r 6(8), Sch 3 r 6(8).

30　Local Elections (Principal Areas) (England and Wales) Rules 2006, SI 2006/3304, Sch 2 r 5(1)(a), (3)(a); Local Elections (Parishes and Communities) (England and Wales) Rules 2006, SI 2006/3305, Sch 2 r 5(1)(a), (3)(a); Local Authorities (Mayoral Elections) (England and Wales) Regulations 2007, SI 2007/1024, Sch 1 r 7(1)(a), (3)(a); Greater London Authority Elections Rules 2007, SI 2007/3541, Sch 1 r 6(5)(b)(i), (7)(a), Sch 3 r 6(5)(b)(i), (7)(a).

A person is guilty of a corrupt practice if he fraudulently purports to be authorised to so issue a certificate on behalf of a registered political party's nominating officer: see the Local Elections (Principal Areas) (England and Wales) Rules 2006, SI 2006/3304, Sch 2 r 5(5); the Local Elections (Parishes and Communities) (England and Wales) Rules 2006, SI 2006/3305, Sch 2 r 5(5); the Local Authorities (Mayoral Elections) (England and Wales) Regulations 2007, SI 2007/1024, Sch 1 r 7(5); the Greater London Authority Elections Rules 2007, SI 2007/3541, Sch 1 r 6(9), Sch 3 r 6(9); and PARA 706.

31 In the case of elections for the return of constituency members of the London Assembly, the constituency returning officer ('CRO') is specified (see the Greater London Authority Elections Rules 2007, SI 2007/3541, Sch 1 r 6(5)(b)(ii), (7)(b)); and in the case of a London Mayoral election, the Greater London returning officer ('GLRO') is specified (see Sch 3 r 6(5)(b)(ii), (7)(b)). As to the meaning of the 'Greater London returning officer' see PARA 211 note 8; and as to the meaning of the 'constituency returning officer' in this context see PARA 211 note 9.

32 Local Elections (Principal Areas) (England and Wales) Rules 2006, SI 2006/3304, Sch 2 r 5(1)(b), (3)(b); Local Elections (Parishes and Communities) (England and Wales) Rules 2006, SI 2006/3305, Sch 2 r 5(1)(b), (3)(b); Local Authorities (Mayoral Elections) (England and Wales) Regulations 2007, SI 2007/1024, Sch 1 r 7(1)(b), (3)(b); Greater London Authority Elections Rules 2007, SI 2007/3541, Sch 1 r 6(5)(b)(ii), (7)(b), Sch 3 r 6(5)(b)(ii), (7)(b). As to the time for the delivery of nomination papers in relation to local government elections see PARA 260.

33 As to references to nomination papers and party lists in elections for the return of London members of the London Assembly see PARA 255 note 23.

34 Greater London Authority Elections Rules 2007, SI 2007/3541, Sch 2 r 7(2)(a). An authorised description for the purposes of Sch 2 r 7(2)(a) may be either the name of the party registered under the Political Parties, Elections and Referendums Act 2000 s 28 (registration of parties: see CONSTITUTIONAL LAW AND HUMAN RIGHTS) or a description of the party registered under s 28A (descriptions: see CONSTITUTIONAL LAW AND HUMAN RIGHTS): see the Greater London Authority Elections Rules 2007, SI 2007/3541, Sch 2 r 7(3).

35 Greater London Authority Elections Rules 2007, SI 2007/3541, Sch 2 r 7(2)(b).

36 Greater London Authority Elections Rules 2007, SI 2007/3541, Sch 2 r 7(2)(b)(i).

37 Greater London Authority Elections Rules 2007, SI 2007/3541, Sch 2 r 7(2)(b)(ii). A person is guilty of a corrupt practice if he fraudulently purports to be authorised to make the statement required by Sch 2 r 7(2)(b) on behalf of a registered political party's nominating officer: see Sch 2 r 7(4); and PARA 706.

38 Greater London Authority Elections Rules 2007, SI 2007/3541, Sch 2 r 7(2)(c). Where a candidate included on a party list is commonly known by some title, he may be described by his title as if it were part of his surname: Sch 10 r 2 (Form 2: London member (party list) candidates (form of nomination paper), note 2) (Form 2 substituted by SI 2012/198). If a candidate included on a party list commonly uses either a surname which is different from any other surname he has, or a forename which is different from any other forename he has, the party list may state the commonly used surname and/or forename in addition to the other name: see the Greater London Authority Elections Rules 2007, SI 2007/3541, Sch 2 r 8(1), (2). Where a candidate's commonly used name appears on the party list in this way, that name (instead of any other name) will appear on the ballot paper: Sch 10 r 2 (Form 2: London member (party list) candidates (form of nomination paper), note 3). However, the ballot paper will show the other name if the GLRO thinks either that the use of the commonly used name may be likely to mislead or confuse electors, or that the commonly used name is obscene or offensive: Sch 10 r 2 (Form 2: London member (party list) candidates (form of nomination paper), note 4).

39 As to the meaning of 'constituency election' for the purposes of Welsh Assembly elections see PARA 3 note 2; and as to the meanings of 'candidate' and 'constituency candidate' for these purposes see PARA 230 note 19.

40 As to the meaning of 'regional election' for the purposes of Welsh Assembly elections see PARA 3 note 2; and as to the meaning of 'individual candidate' at a Welsh Assembly regional election see PARA 230 note 19.

41 National Assembly for Wales (Representation of the People) Order 2007, SI 2007/236, Sch 5 paras 4(2)(a), 6(2)(a).
The surname must be placed first in the list of the candidate's names: Sch 5 paras 4(2), 6(2). Where a candidate is commonly known by some title, that title may be used as if it were his surname: Sch 10 Appendix of Forms (Form CE: Form of nomination paper (constituency election), note 2; Form CH: Form of individual nomination paper (regional election), note 2). If a candidate commonly uses either a surname which is different from any other surname he has, or a forename which is different from any other forename he has, the nomination paper may state the commonly used surname or forename in addition to the other name: Sch 5 paras 4(3),

6(3). Where a candidate's commonly used name appears on the nomination paper in this way, that name (instead of any other name) will appear on the ballot paper: Sch 10 Appendix of Forms (Form CE: Form of nomination paper (constituency election), note 3; Form CH: Form of individual nomination paper (regional election), note 3). However, the ballot paper will show the other name if the returning officer thinks either that the use of the commonly used name may be likely to mislead or confuse electors, or that the commonly used name is obscene or offensive: Sch 10 Appendix of Forms (Form CE: Form of nomination paper (constituency election), note 4; Form CH: Form of individual nomination paper (regional election), note 4).

42 National Assembly for Wales (Representation of the People) Order 2007, SI 2007/236, Sch 5 paras 4(2)(b), 6(2)(b).

43 National Assembly for Wales (Representation of the People) Order 2007, SI 2007/236, Sch 5 paras 4(2)(c), 6(2)(c). This provision made by Sch 5 para 4(2)(c) is subject to Sch 5 para 4(4) (see the text and notes 44–45): see Sch 5 para 4(2)(c).

44 National Assembly for Wales (Representation of the People) Order 2007, SI 2007/236, Sch 5 paras 4(4)(b), 6(2)(c).

45 National Assembly for Wales (Representation of the People) Order 2007, SI 2007/236, Sch 5 para 4(4)(a). The description must be authorised as mentioned in the text under Sch 5 para 5(1) or Sch 5 para 5(3) (see the text and notes 46–51): see Sch 5 para 4(4)(a). As to the meaning of 'registered political party' for these purposes see PARA 215 note 19; and as to the authorised description specifically see note 48.

46 See the National Assembly for Wales (Representation of the People) Order 2007, SI 2007/236, Sch 5 para 5(1), (3).

47 As to the meaning of 'qualifying party in relation to an Assembly constituency' see PARA 255 note 33.

48 See the National Assembly for Wales (Representation of the People) Order 2007, SI 2007/236, Sch 5 para 5(1), (3). The form prescribed as mentioned in the text is set out in English and in Welsh in Sch 10 Appendix of Forms (Form CF: Form of certificate referred to in rule 5(1); Form CG: Form of certificate referred to in rule 5(3)): see Sch 5 para 5(1), (3). A certificate issued under Sch 5 para 5(1) or Sch 5 para 5(3) may be combined with a constituency nomination paper delivered under Sch 5 para 4(1) (see PARA 260): Sch 5 para 5(6). For the purposes of Sch 5 para 5(1), an authorised description may be either the name of the party registered under the Political Parties, Elections and Referendums Act 2000 s 28 (registration of parties: see CONSTITUTIONAL LAW AND HUMAN RIGHTS) or a description of the party registered under s 28A (descriptions: see CONSTITUTIONAL LAW AND HUMAN RIGHTS): National Assembly for Wales (Representation of the People) Order 2007, SI 2007/236, Sch 5 para 5(2). For the purposes of Sch 5 para 5(3), a description is a registered description if it is a description registered for use by the parties under the Political Parties, Elections and Referendums Act 2000 s 28B (joint descriptions: see CONSTITUTIONAL LAW AND HUMAN RIGHTS): National Assembly for Wales (Representation of the People) Order 2007, SI 2007/236, Sch 5 para 5(4). If it is proposed that the party's registered emblem (or, as the case may be, one of the party's registered emblems) is to be shown on the ballot paper against the candidate's particulars, a certificate issued under Sch 5 para 5(1) or Sch 5 para 5(3) must request that it be so shown (Sch 5 para 5(5)), except that:

(1) in a case in which a party has more than one registered emblem, only one of its emblems may be requested to be shown on the ballot paper (Sch 5 para 5(5)(a)); and

(2) in a case to which Sch 5 para 5(3) applies (ie two or more registered political parties), the registered emblem of only one of the parties may be requested to be shown on the ballot paper (Sch 5 para 5(5)(b)).

49 National Assembly for Wales (Representation of the People) Order 2007, SI 2007/236, Sch 5 para 5(1)(a), (3)(a). A person is guilty of a corrupt practice if he fraudulently purports to be authorised, by virtue of Sch 5 para 81 (registered nominating officer may appoint one or more persons to discharge all or any of his functions: see PARA 215 note 24), to issue a certificate under Sch 5 para 5(1) or Sch 5 para 5(3) on behalf of a party's registered nominating officer: see Sch 5 para 5(7); and PARA 706.

50 As to the meaning of 'constituency returning officer' for the purposes of Welsh Assembly elections see PARA 18 note 2.

51 National Assembly for Wales (Representation of the People) Order 2007, SI 2007/236, Sch 5 para 5(1)(b), (3)(b). As to the time for the delivery of nomination papers in relation to Welsh Assembly elections see PARA 260.

52 As to the meaning of 'party nomination paper' at a Welsh Assembly regional election see PARA 255.

53 Ie in accordance with the National Assembly for Wales (Representation of the People) Order 2007, SI 2007/236, Sch 5 para 8: see Sch 5 para 7(2). Accordingly, the name (or, as the

case may be, names) or description required by Sch 5 para 7(2) to be contained in a party nomination paper must be authorised by a certificate in the form set out in English and Welsh (ie in the form set out in Sch 10 Appendix of Forms (Form CJ: Form of certificate referred to in rule 8(1))) issued by the registered nominating officer of the registered political party: Sch 5 para 8(1). If it is proposed that the party's registered emblem is to be shown on the ballot paper against the party's name or description the certificate issued under Sch 5 para 8(1) must request that it be so shown; but so that in a case in which a party has more than one registered emblem, only one of its emblems may be requested to be shown on the ballot paper: Sch 5 para 8(2). A certificate issued under Sch 5 para 8(1) must be combined with the party nomination paper delivered under Sch 5 para 7(1) (see PARA 255): Sch 5 para 8(3). A person is guilty of a corrupt practice if he fraudulently purports to be authorised, by virtue of Sch 5 para 81 (registered nominating officer may appoint one or more persons to discharge all or any of his functions: see PARA 215 note 24), to issue a certificate under Sch 5 para 8(1) on behalf of a party's registered nominating officer: see Sch 5 para 8(4); and PARA 706.

54 National Assembly for Wales (Representation of the People) Order 2007, SI 2007/236, Sch 5 para 7(2)(a). The text refers to the name (or names) of the party registered under the Political Parties, Elections and Referendums Act 2000 s 28 (registration of parties: see CONSTITUTIONAL LAW AND HUMAN RIGHTS): see the National Assembly for Wales (Representation of the People) Order 2007, SI 2007/236, Sch 5 para 7(2)(a). See note 53.

55 National Assembly for Wales (Representation of the People) Order 2007, SI 2007/236, Sch 5 para 7(2)(b). The text refers to a description of the party registered for use under the Political Parties, Elections and Referendums Act 2000 s 28B (joint descriptions: see CONSTITUTIONAL LAW AND HUMAN RIGHTS) see the National Assembly for Wales (Representation of the People) Order 2007, SI 2007/236, Sch 5 para 7(2)(b). See note 53.

56 See the National Assembly for Wales (Representation of the People) Order 2007, SI 2007/236, Sch 5 para 7(3). As to the meanings of 'party list' and 'party list candidate' at a Welsh Assembly regional election see PARA 230 note 19.

57 See the National Assembly for Wales (Representation of the People) Order 2007, SI 2007/236, Sch 5 para 7(3).

58 National Assembly for Wales (Representation of the People) Order 2007, SI 2007/236, Sch 5 para 7(4)(a). The surname of each candidate to be included on a party list must be placed first in the list of his names: Sch 5 para 7(4). Where a party list candidate is commonly known by some title, that title may be used as if it were his surname: Sch 10 Appendix of Forms (Form CI: Form of party nomination paper (regional election), note 2). If a party list candidate commonly uses either a surname which is different from any other surname he has, or a forename which is different from any other forename he has, the party list may state the commonly used surname or forename in addition to the other name: Sch 5 para 7(5). Where a party list candidate's commonly used name appears on the party nomination paper in this way, that name (instead of any other name) will appear on the ballot paper: Sch 10 Appendix of Forms (Form CI: Form of party nomination paper (regional election), note 3). However, the ballot paper will show the other name if the returning officer thinks either that the use of the commonly used name may be likely to mislead or confuse electors, or that the commonly used name is obscene or offensive: Sch 10 Appendix of Forms (Form CI: Form of party nomination paper (regional election), note 4).

59 National Assembly for Wales (Representation of the People) Order 2007, SI 2007/236, Sch 5 para 7(4)(b).

60 As to the meaning of 'individual candidate' at a European parliamentary election see PARA 230 note 32. As to European parliamentary elections see PARA 13 et seq.

61 European Parliamentary Elections Regulations 2004, SI 2004/293, Sch 1 para 4(2)(a) (Sch 1 substituted by SI 2009/186). The candidate's surname must be placed first in the list of his names: European Parliamentary Elections Regulations 2004, SI 2004/293, Sch 1 para 4(2) (as so substituted). If an individual candidate commonly uses either a surname which is different from any other surname he has, or a forename which is different from any other forename he has, the nomination paper may state the commonly used surname or forename in addition to the other name: Sch 1 para 4(3) (as so substituted). The form of a nomination paper for a European parliamentary election is not prescribed.

62 European Parliamentary Elections Regulations 2004, SI 2004/293, Sch 1 para 4(2)(b) (as substituted: see note 61).

63 European Parliamentary Elections Regulations 2004, SI 2004/293, Sch 1 para 4(2)(c) (as substituted: see note 61).

64 European Parliamentary Elections Regulations 2004, SI 2004/293, Sch 1 para 4(4)(b) (as substituted: see note 61). 'Annibynnol' is prescribed as the form of words in Welsh for the word 'Independent' which is prescribed for use as the description of an individual candidate in a

nomination paper by Sch 1 para 4(4)(b); and the form of words so prescribed may be used as
well as or in place of the equivalent word in English at a European parliamentary election in
Wales: see the European Parliamentary Elections (Welsh Forms) Order 2009, SI 2009/781,
art 4(3), (4).

65 See note 67.

66 As to European parliamentary by-elections see PARA 218 et seq.

67 European Parliamentary Elections Regulations 2004, SI 2004/293, Sch 1 para 4(4)(a) (as
substituted: see note 61). The text refers to the name of the party registered under the Political
Parties, Elections and Referendums Act 2000 s 28 (registration of parties: see CONSTITUTIONAL
LAW AND HUMAN RIGHTS): see the European Parliamentary Elections Regulations 2004,
SI 2004/293, Sch 1 para 4(4)(a) (as so substituted). The nomination paper of an individual
candidate standing on behalf of a registered party at a by-election must state the name of the
party registered under the Political Parties, Elections and Referendums Act 2000 s 28: see the
European Parliamentary Elections Regulations 2004, SI 2004/293, Sch 1 para 5(1) (as so
substituted). For these purposes, 'registered party' means a party which was registered under the
Political Parties, Elections and Referendums Act 2000 Pt II (registration of political parties: see
PARA 253) on the day (the 'relevant day') which is two days before the last day for the delivery
of nomination papers at that election (see PARA 260): European Parliamentary Elections
Regulations 2004, SI 2004/293, Sch 1 para 5(7)(a) (as so substituted). For these purposes, any
day is disregarded which falls, within Sch 1 para 2(1) (see PARA 223 note 1): Sch 1 para 5(8) (as
so substituted).

68 European Parliamentary Elections Regulations 2004, SI 2004/293, Sch 1 para 4(4)(a) (as
substituted: see note 61). The text refers to a description of the party which is authorised as
mentioned in Sch 1 para 5(2) or Sch 1 para 5(4) (see the text and notes 69–75): see Sch 1
para 4(4)(a) (as so substituted).

69 European Parliamentary Elections Regulations 2004, SI 2004/293, Sch 1 para 5(2), (4) (as
substituted: see note 61).

70 European Parliamentary Elections Regulations 2004, SI 2004/293, Sch 1 para 5(2)(a), (4)(a) (as
substituted: see note 61).

71 European Parliamentary Elections Regulations 2004, SI 2004/293, Sch 1 para 5(2)(b), (4)(b) (as
substituted: see note 61). For these purposes, a registered political party is a qualifying party in
relation to a European parliamentary electoral region if the region is in England (including the
combined region) or is Wales and the party was on the relevant day (see note 67) registered in
respect of that part of Great Britain (or the combined region) in the Great Britain register
maintained under the Political Parties, Elections and Referendums Act 2000 Pt II: European
Parliamentary Elections Regulations 2004, SI 2004/293, Sch 1 para 5(7)(b) (as so substituted).
As to the establishment of electoral regions (including the combined region) for the purpose of
elections to the European Parliament see PARA 77.

72 See the European Parliamentary Elections Regulations 2004, SI 2004/293, Sch 1 para 5(2)(c),
(4)(c) (as substituted: see note 61). For these purposes of Sch 1 para 5(2), an authorised
description must be a description of the party registered under the Political Parties, Elections and
Referendums Act 2000 s 28A (descriptions: see CONSTITUTIONAL LAW AND HUMAN RIGHTS):
European Parliamentary Elections Regulations 2004, SI 2004/293, Sch 1 para 5(3) (as so
substituted). For the purposes of Sch 1 para 5(4), an authorised description is a registered
description if it is a description registered for use by the parties under the Political Parties,
Elections and Referendums Act 2000 s 28B (joint descriptions: see CONSTITUTIONAL LAW AND
HUMAN RIGHTS): European Parliamentary Elections Regulations 2004, SI 2004/293, Sch 1
para 5(5) (as so substituted).

73 European Parliamentary Elections Regulations 2004, SI 2004/293, Sch 1 para 5(2)(c)(i), (4)(c)(i)
(as substituted: see note 61). A person is guilty of a corrupt practice if he fraudulently purports
to be authorised to issue a certificate under Sch 1 para 5(2) or Sch 1 para 5(4) on behalf of a
registered party's nominating officer: see Sch 1 para 5(6); and PARA 706.

74 As to returning officers at European parliamentary elections see PARA 360 et seq.

75 European Parliamentary Elections Regulations 2004, SI 2004/293, Sch 1 para 5(2)(c)(ii),
(4)(c)(ii) (as substituted: see note 61). As to the time for the delivery of nomination papers in
relation to European parliamentary by-elections see PARA 260.

76 European Parliamentary Elections Regulations 2004, SI 2004/293, Sch 1 para 6(2) (as
substituted: see note 61). The text refers to the name of the party registered under the Political
Parties, Elections and Referendums Act 2000 s 28 (registration of parties: see CONSTITUTIONAL
LAW AND HUMAN RIGHTS): see the European Parliamentary Elections Regulations 2004,
SI 2004/293, Sch 1 para 6(2) (as so substituted).

77 European Parliamentary Elections Regulations 2004, SI 2004/293, Sch 1 para 6(3) (as
substituted: see note 61). The description must be a description of the party registered for use

under the Political Parties, Elections and Referendums Act 2000 s 28A (descriptions: see CONSTITUTIONAL LAW AND HUMAN RIGHTS) see the European Parliamentary Elections Regulations 2004, SI 2004/293, Sch 1 para 6(4) (as so substituted).

78 European Parliamentary Elections Regulations 2004, SI 2004/293, Sch 1 para 6(6) (as substituted: see note 61). A person is guilty of a corrupt practice if he fraudulently purports to be authorised to make the statement required by Sch 1 para 6(6) on behalf of a registered party's nominating officer: see Sch 1 para 6(8); and PARA 706.

79 European Parliamentary Elections Regulations 2004, SI 2004/293, Sch 1 para 6(5) (as substituted: see note 61). The text refers to a list of candidates which complies with Sch 1 para 7 (see the text and notes 80–81): see Sch 1 para 6(5) (as so substituted).

80 European Parliamentary Elections Regulations 2004, SI 2004/293, Sch 1 para 7(2) (as substituted: see note 61). If a person on the list of a registered party's candidates commonly uses either a surname which is different from any other surname he has, or a forename which is different from any other forename he has, the list may state the person's commonly used surname or forename in addition to the other name: see Sch 1 para 7(3) (as so substituted)

81 European Parliamentary Elections Regulations 2004, SI 2004/293, Sch 1 para 7(1) (as substituted: see note 61).

82 In *R v Plenty* (1869) LR 4 QB 346, the use of 'W' for 'William' in a voting paper was held to be a misnomer that was cured by the statutory provision on misnomers. It was agreed in *Mather v Brown* (1876) 1 CPD 596 that the use of an initial instead of setting out the name in full ('Robert V Mather' for 'Robert Vicars Mather') was a misnomer but it was held that the statutory provision about misnomers did not apply to misnomers in nomination papers.

83 See the Representation of the People Act 1983 s 50; the European Parliamentary Elections Regulations 2004, SI 2004/293, reg 18; and the National Assembly for Wales (Representation of the People) Order 2007, SI 2007/236, art 27. As to the effect of misdescription in documents published by the registration officer see PARA 150.

In the context of the conduct of elections, it has been held that the addition of 'Junior' is not part of a person's real name: *Gledhill v Crowther* (1889) 23 QBD 136, DC (nomination paper for the election of a county councillor was valid, being signed with the ordinary signature of the nominator, who was generally known as 'James Sykes, junior', although his father was dead, and although the word 'junior' did not appear against the nominator's name in the register of county electors). In *R v Casey* [1914] 2 IR 243, a candidate for councillor described himself in nomination papers as Michael B Walsh, the letter 'B' being assumed, his mother's name being Barry, for use in the register of voters and transactions requiring his signature in order to distinguish him from other persons in the neighbourhood also called Michael Walsh. Kenny J stated that 'on the evidence we hold that the relator is known in the district as Michael B Walsh. Even if his full name is Michael Barry Walsh, he is entitled to call himself Michael B Walsh and has done so for many years'. See also *R v Fox* (1887) 16 Cox CC 166 (man applied to the presiding officer for a ballot paper in a name which appeared on the register of voters, and which was inserted therein by the overseers in the belief that it was the name of the applicant, and for the purpose of putting him on the register; no offence of personation).

Where a nomination paper gives an address which is not the candidate's home address, the nomination is invalid: *R v Election Court, ex p Sheppard* [1975] 2 All ER 723, [1975] 1 WLR 1319, DC; *R v Coward* (1851) 16 QB 819 (election of a town councillor whose place of residence had been in a different ward; the inaccurate description of a right place may be cured by the statutory provision but not the accurate description of a wrong place); *R v Deighton* (1844) 5 QB 896 (inaccurate description of party's place of abode in voting papers commonly understood to be that of the party but vote avoided). See also *R v Gregory* (1853) 1 E & B 600, 22 LJQB 120 (vote was improperly rejected on the ground of misdescription in circumstances where a corner house had two doors which each opened onto different streets and where a voting ticket was signed with one of the addresses but the burgess roll gave the address in the other street; it was held that the description in the burgess roll and that in the voting paper would both be commonly understood to mean the proper address).

As to the implications of particulars that are deliberately misleading, especially as to whether they may amount to a fraudulent device, see PARA 727.

84 *Miller v Everton* (1895) 64 LJQB 692, DC.

85 *Soper v Basingstoke Corpn* (1877) 2 CPD 440 (property of seconder of candidate was sufficiently described as no one had been or could be misled by the description).

86 *R v Bradley* (1861) 3 E & E 634, 3 LT 853; *R v Plenty* (1869) LR 4 QB 346, 20 LT 521; *Henry v Armitage* (1883) 12 QBD 257, 50 LT 4, CA; *R v Casey* [1914] 2 IR 243.

257. Subscription of nomination paper. The nomination paper[1] to be delivered at an election must be subscribed, except at the election of constituency members or London members of the London Assembly[2].

The nomination paper for a parliamentary or local government election (except a London mayoral election[3]) must be subscribed by two electors[4] as proposer and seconder[5], and by a specified number of other electors as assenting to the nomination[6] (except that assent is not required where councillors are being elected for a parish or community[7]). The particulars of the candidate should be filled in first; then the paper should be signed by the proposer and seconder; and then it should be signed by the persons assenting (where applicable)[8]. In all cases, the nomination paper must give the electoral number[9] of each person subscribing it[10]; and a person whose name is entered in the appropriate register may not subscribe a nomination paper if the entry gives as the date on which he will become of voting age[11] a date later than the day fixed for the poll[12]. Where a nomination paper bears the signatures of more than the required number of persons as proposing or seconding (and, where applicable, assenting to) the nomination of a candidate[13], the signature (or signatures, up to the required number[14]) appearing first on the paper in each category must be taken into account to the exclusion of any others in that category[15]. A person must not subscribe more than one nomination paper at the same parliamentary election[16], or at the same London mayoral election[17]; and, at an election of councillors for principal areas, parishes or communities, a person must not subscribe more nomination papers than there are vacancies to be filled in the electoral area[18]. A person is not so prevented from subscribing such a nomination paper by reason only of his having subscribed that of a candidate who has died or withdrawn before delivery of the first mentioned paper[19]; but otherwise, his signature is inoperative on all but the paper[20] first delivered[21].

Each nomination paper for a candidate at a Welsh Assembly constituency election[22] (that is, each 'constituency nomination paper'), and each nomination paper for an individual candidate at a Welsh Assembly regional election[23] (that is, each 'individual nomination paper'), which is duly delivered[24], and each party nomination paper at a Welsh Assembly regional election[25], must be subscribed by one person who must also (if he is not the candidate himself or a party list candidate[26], as the case may be) set out his full name and address[27].

Each separate nomination paper for an individual candidate at a European parliamentary election[28] must be signed by the individual candidate himself or by a person authorised in writing by him[29]. The nomination paper for a registered party that is to stand for election at a European parliamentary general election in an electoral region must include a statement that the party is nominated by or on behalf of the nominating officer of the registered party in question (and the statement must be signed by the person making it)[30].

1   As to the form and supply of nomination papers and the particulars required see PARA 255 et seq.
2   Accordingly, subscription is required for a parliamentary election, a local government election (with general references to 'local government election' being taken to include a local authority mayoral election), an election for the return of an elected Mayor of London, a Welsh Assembly constituency or regional election, and a European parliamentary election. As to the meanings of 'constituency election' and 'regional election' for the purposes of Welsh Assembly elections see PARA 3 note 2; as to the meaning of 'parliamentary election' see PARA 9; as to the meaning of 'local government election' see PARA 11. As to European parliamentary elections see PARA 217 et seq.
3   The nomination paper of a candidate for a London mayoral election must be subscribed by at least 330 persons each of whom is entitled to vote at the election: see the Greater London

Authority Elections Rules 2007, SI 2007/3541, Sch 3 r 7(1). In relation to each London borough and the City of London, at least ten of the subscribers must be electors who are ordinarily resident in the borough or, as the case may be, the City: see Sch 3 r 7(1). Although the provision is not so expressed, it is submitted that the 330 persons are subscribed as assenting to the nomination of the candidate to elected as Mayor of London: see Sch 3 r 7(2); and the text and notes 13–15. As to the meaning of 'elector' in this context in relation to any election of the Mayor of London see PARA 255 note 13. As to the London boroughs and the City of London generally see LOCAL GOVERNMENT vol 69 (2009) PARA 35; LONDON GOVERNMENT vol 71 (2013) PARA 15 et seq.

4 As to the meaning of 'elector' in this context for the purposes of a parliamentary election see PARA 255 note 5; and as to the meaning of 'elector' in this context in relation to local government elections and elections for the return of an elected local authority mayor see PARA 255 note 13.

5 Representation of the People Act 1983 Sch 1 r 7(1); Local Elections (Principal Areas) (England and Wales) Rules 2006, SI 2006/3304, Sch 2 r 6(1); Local Elections (Parishes and Communities) (England and Wales) Rules 2006, SI 2006/3305, Sch 2 r 6(1); Local Authorities (Mayoral Elections) (England and Wales) Regulations 2007, SI 2007/1024, Sch 1 r 8(1).

6 Eight other electors must assent in the case of a parliamentary election or principal area local government election: see the Representation of the People Act 1983 Sch 1 r 7(1); and the Local Elections (Principal Areas) (England and Wales) Rules 2006, SI 2006/3304, Sch 2 r 6(1). The requirement for assent does not appear in the Local Elections (Parishes and Communities) (England and Wales) Rules 2006, SI 2006/3305, Sch 2, although proposer and seconder are required. For the return of an elected local authority mayor, 28 other electors must be subscribed as assenting to the nomination: see the Local Authorities (Mayoral Elections) (England and Wales) Regulations 2007, SI 2007/1024, Sch 1 r 8(1). As to the election of councillors for local government principal areas see PARA 197 et seq; and as to the election of parish or community councillors see PARA 200 et seq.

The nomination paper may bear the ordinary signatures of the proposer, seconder and assenters: *Gothard v Clarke* (1880) 5 CPD 253 at 262 per Grove J; *Re Melton Mowbray (Egerton Ward) UDC Election* [1969] 1 QB 192, [1968] 3 All ER 761, DC. The proposer, seconder and assenters need not give their full names: *Bowden v Besley* (1888) 21 QBD 309, DC. Nor is it necessary that their names should be given in the precise form of the register: *Re Melton Mowbray (Egerton Ward) UDC Election*; *Bowden v Besley*; *Gledhill v Crowther* (1889) 23 QBD 136, DC; *Harding v Cornwell* (1889) 60 LT 959, DC. In *Moorhouse v Linney* (1885) 15 QBD 273, DC, two electors were entered in the register as Joseph Burman and Charles Burman. Charles Burman subscribed a nomination paper as Charles Arthur Burman which was his full name and added his correct number in the register; the court held the nomination paper to be invalid apparently on the ground that the person subscribing the nomination paper must subscribe in the same name as appeared on the register as otherwise voters might be misled into thinking that Charles Burman and Charles Arthur Burman were father and son, that the addition of the number on the register did not assist, and that this was not a misnomer which could be cured by the statutory provision as to misnomers (see PARA 256). It is not easy to reconcile this case with the later cases cited.

7 See note 6.

8 *Harmon v Park* (1881) 7 QBD 369, DC. However, the order in which the nomination paper was completed or when any alterations were made is unlikely to be known to the returning officer unless, as in *Harmon v Park*, the alteration takes place at his office. The observation in *Re Melton Mowbray (Egerton Ward) UDC Election* [1969] 1 QB 192 at 198, [1968] 3 All ER 761 at 763 per Paull J that the returning officer has the opportunity to make such enquiries as he may think right was doubted by Wien J in *Greenway-Stanley v Paterson* [1977] 2 All ER 663 at 671, DC, and he thought that if the returning officer has a right to investigate it must be solely because the nomination paper on its face value puts him on enquiry (see *Greenway-Stanley v Paterson* at 671).

It is not clear to what extent subsequent alterations or the filling in and signing of a nomination paper in any order invalidate the nomination paper: see *Harmon v Park* (where an alteration was made after delivery to the town clerk by substituting another burgess as proposer in the absence of the seconder and assenting burgesses, the nomination paper was held invalid on the ground that the persons assenting should be able to see who were the proposer and seconder); *Cox v Davies* [1898] 2 QB 202, DC (where only a proposer and seconder were required, a nomination paper in which the name of the candidate was inserted after the proposer and seconder had signed the nomination paper was held valid); *Howes v Turner* (1876) 1 CPD 670 (where an alteration made after delivery of the nomination paper to the town clerk to correct a supposed mistake was held in itself unobjectionable). As to decisions as to the validity of nomination papers see further PARAS 262–264.

9 As to the meaning of 'electoral number' generally see PARA 145. In relation to London mayoral election, 'electoral number' means a person's number in the register to be used at the election (including the distinctive letter of the parliamentary polling district in which he is registered) except that before publication of the register his number (if any) in the electors' lists for that register must be used instead: see the Greater London Authority Elections Rules 2007, SI 2007/3541, Sch 3 r 7(5), Sch 10 r 2 (Form 3: candidate to be the Mayor of London, note 5).

10 Representation of the People Act 1983 Sch 1 r 7(3); Local Elections (Principal Areas) (England and Wales) Rules 2006, SI 2006/3304, Sch 2 r 6(3); Local Elections (Parishes and Communities) (England and Wales) Rules 2006, SI 2006/3305, Sch 2 r 6(3); Local Authorities (Mayoral Elections) (England and Wales) Regulations 2007, SI 2007/1024, Sch 1 r 8(3); Greater London Authority Elections Rules 2007, SI 2007/3541, Sch 3 r 7(3).

It has been held that the giving of a wrong electoral number invalidates the nomination paper and the same result would apparently have followed if the electoral number had been omitted: *Gothard v Clarke* (1880) 5 CPD 253; *Baldwin v Ellis* [1929] 1 KB 273, DC. In *Gothard v Clarke*, a wrong electoral number was given contrary to the requirement of a note to the prescribed form of nomination paper, at the date of that case there being no express requirement in the relevant rules that the electoral number must be stated, the requirement deriving from the prescribed form of nomination paper. Without expressly deciding the point Grove J thought that the note was mandatory and not directory. Although the use of a form to the like effect was permitted, Grove J and Lopes J decided that the use of a wrong number was not to the like effect as the right number although Grove J thought that a clerical error such as the substitution of '0' for '9' might perhaps be treated differently. They also decided that there was no power to remedy the mistake because the only power to remedy mistakes then in question, which was a provision corresponding to the Representation of the People Act 1983 ss 23(3), 48(1) (see PARA 667), did not apply to decisions on nomination papers by the returning officer. In *Baldwin v Ellis*, there was a rule requiring a candidate at an election of rural district councillors to state, in addition to his description, his qualification as a local government elector for a particular parish. A candidate merely stated in his nomination paper that he was a local government elector without stating, as required, for which parish he was qualified. The returning officer held the nomination paper invalid and the court held that this was right on the ground that there had been no compliance with the rule. The court also held that the rule corresponding to the Representation of the People Act 1983 s 50 (see PARA 256), relating to misnomers or inaccurate descriptions, did not apply because the omission of the name of the parish for which the candidate was qualified as a local government elector was neither a misnomer nor an inaccurate description of the candidate but a failure to comply with the rule.

11 'Voting age' is currently 18 years for all purposes: see PARAS 95 note 2, 97 note 14, 102 note 10.

12 Representation of the People Act 1983 Sch 1 Appendix of Forms (Form of nomination paper, note 5) (Form of nomination paper, note 5 amended by the Representation of the People Act 2000 ss 8, 15(2), Sch 1 paras 1, 23(1), (3)(b), Sch 7 Pt I); Local Elections (Principal Areas) (England and Wales) Rules 2006, SI 2006/3304, Sch 2 Appendix of Forms (Form of nomination paper, note 7(b) (ie definition of 'elector': see PARA 255 note 13)); Local Elections (Parishes and Communities) (England and Wales) Rules 2006, SI 2006/3305, Sch 2 Appendix of Forms (Form of nomination paper, note 6(b) (ie definition of 'elector': see PARA 255 note 13)); Local Authorities (Mayoral Elections) (England and Wales) Regulations 2007, SI 2007/1024, Sch 1 Appendix of Forms (Form 1: Form of nomination paper, note 6(b) (ie definition of 'elector': see PARA 255 note 13)); Greater London Authority Elections Rules 2007, SI 2007/3541, Sch 10 r 2 (Form 3: candidate to be the Mayor of London, note 7(b) (ie definition of 'elector': see PARA 255 note 13)).

13 At a London Mayoral election, the signatures subscribed on a nomination form are limited to persons as assenting to the nomination of a candidate: see the Greater London Authority Elections Rules 2007, SI 2007/3541, Sch 3 r 7(2); and see note 3. As to the meaning of 'candidate' generally see PARA 230.

14 Only one signature is specified in the case of a parish or community council election: see the Local Elections (Parishes and Communities) (England and Wales) Rules 2006, SI 2006/3305, Sch 2 r 6(2).

15 Representation of the People Act 1983 Sch 1 r 7(2); Local Elections (Principal Areas) (England and Wales) Rules 2006, SI 2006/3304, Sch 2 r 6(2); Local Elections (Parishes and Communities) (England and Wales) Rules 2006, SI 2006/3305, Sch 2 r 6(2); Local Authorities (Mayoral Elections) (England and Wales) Regulations 2007, SI 2007/1024, Sch 1 r 8(2); Greater London Authority Elections Rules 2007, SI 2007/3541, Sch 3 r 7(2).

16 Representation of the People Act 1983 Sch 1 r 7(5), Sch 1 Appendix of Forms (Form of nomination paper, note 4).
17 Greater London Authority Elections Rules 2007, SI 2007/3541, Sch 3 r 7(3A) (Sch 3 r 7(3A), (3B) added by SI 2012/198), Greater London Authority Elections Rules 2007, SI 2007/3541, Sch 10 r 2 (Form 3: candidate to be the Mayor of London, note 6).
18 Local Elections (Principal Areas) (England and Wales) Rules 2006, SI 2006/3304, Sch 2 r 6(5), Appendix of Forms (Form of nomination paper, note 6(a)); Local Elections (Parishes and Communities) (England and Wales) Rules 2006, SI 2006/3305, Sch 2 r 6(5), Appendix of Forms (Form of nomination paper, note 5(a)). Nor may a person subscribe any nomination paper in respect of an election in any other electoral area of the same local government principal area (ie in the same county, district, London borough or county borough) or in any other ward of the same parish or community (where such an area is divided into wards) whilst the election in the first-mentioned electoral area or ward is taking place: Local Elections (Principal Areas) (England and Wales) Rules 2006, SI 2006/3304, Sch 2 r 6(5), Appendix of Forms (Form of nomination paper, note 6(b)); Local Elections (Parishes and Communities) (England and Wales) Rules 2006, SI 2006/3305, Sch 2 r 6(5), Appendix of Forms (Form of nomination paper, note 5(b)). As to the meaning of 'electoral area' see PARA 11; and as to the meaning of 'local government area' see PARA 33 note 7.
19 Representation of the People Act 1983 Sch 1 r 7(5); Local Elections (Principal Areas) (England and Wales) Rules 2006, SI 2006/3304, Sch 2 r 6(5); Local Elections (Parishes and Communities) (England and Wales) Rules 2006, SI 2006/3305, Sch 2 r 6(5); Greater London Authority Elections Rules 2007, SI 2007/3541, Sch 3 r 7(3B) (as added: see note 17).
20 Ie or papers, up to the permitted number, where applicable: see the Local Elections (Principal Areas) (England and Wales) Rules 2006, SI 2006/3304, Sch 2 r 6(6); and the Local Elections (Parishes and Communities) (England and Wales) Rules 2006, SI 2006/3305, Sch 2 r 6(6). As to London mayoral elections see note 13.
21 Representation of the People Act 1983 Sch 1 r 7(5); Local Elections (Principal Areas) (England and Wales) Rules 2006, SI 2006/3304, Sch 2 r 6(6); Local Elections (Parishes and Communities) (England and Wales) Rules 2006, SI 2006/3305, Sch 2 r 6(6). This provision does not appear in the Greater London Authority Elections Rules 2007, SI 2007/3541, Sch 3 r 7. As to the delivery of nomination papers see PARA 260.
22 As to the meaning of 'constituency election' for the purposes of Welsh Assembly elections see PARA 3 note 2; and as to the meanings of 'candidate' and 'constituency candidate' for these purposes see PARA 230 note 19.
23 As to the meaning of 'regional election' for the purposes of Welsh Assembly elections see PARA 3 note 2; and as to the meaning of 'individual candidate' at a Welsh Assembly regional election see PARA 230 note 19.
24 Ie delivered under the National Assembly for Wales (Representation of the People) Order 2007, SI 2007/236, Sch 5 para 4 (nomination paper for candidates at a constituency election) or Sch 5 para 6 (nomination paper for individual candidates at a regional election), as the case may be (see PARA 260): see Sch 5 paras 4(5), 6(4).
25 As to the meaning of 'party nomination paper' at a Welsh Assembly regional election see PARA 255.
26 As to the meaning of 'party list candidate' at a Welsh Assembly regional election see PARA 230 note 23.
27 See the National Assembly for Wales (Representation of the People) Order 2007, SI 2007/236, Sch 5 paras 4(5), 6(4), 7(6).
28 As to the meaning of 'individual candidate' at a European parliamentary election see PARA 230 note 32.
29 See the European Parliamentary Elections Regulations 2004, SI 2004/293, Sch 1 para 4(1) (Sch 1 substituted by SI 2009/186).
30 See the European Parliamentary Elections Regulations 2004, SI 2004/293, Sch 1 para 6(6); and PARA 256.

258. Consent of candidate to nomination. A person is not validly nominated[1] for a parliamentary election[2] unless his consent to nomination[3]:

(1)   is given in writing on or within one month before the day fixed as the last day for the delivery of nomination papers[4];

(2)   is attested by one witness[5]; and

(3)   is delivered at the place and within the time for the delivery of nomination papers[6].

However, if the returning officer for such an election[7] is satisfied that, owing to the absence of a person from the United Kingdom[8], it has not been reasonably practicable for his consent in writing to be given in this way, a telegram (or any similar means of communication) consenting to his nomination and purporting to have been sent by him is deemed for these purposes to be consent in writing given by him on the day on which it purports to have been sent, and attestation of his consent is not required[9]. A parliamentary candidate's consent additionally must state the day, month and year of his birth[10], must state both that he is aware of the provisions of the House of Commons Disqualification Act 1975[11] and that, to the best of his knowledge and belief, he is not disqualified for membership of the House of Commons[12], and he must state that he is not a candidate[13] at an election for any other constituency[14] the poll for which is to be held on the same day as that for the election to which the consent relates[15].

A person is not validly nominated for a local government election[16] unless his consent to nomination[17]:

(a)   is given in writing on, or within one month before, the last day for the delivery of nomination papers[18];

(b)   is in the prescribed form (or a form to the like effect)[19];

(c)   is attested by one witness[20]; and

(d)   is delivered at the place and within the time for the delivery of nomination papers[21].

A person is not validly nominated at a Welsh Assembly constituency election[22], or at a Welsh Assembly regional election[23] (whether as an individual or party list candidate[24]), unless his consent to nomination[25]:

(i)   is given and dated in writing on, or within one month before, the day fixed as the last day for the delivery of nomination papers[26];

(ii)   is attested by one witness[27]; and

(iii) is delivered at the place, and within the time, for the delivery of nomination papers[28].

However, if the appropriate returning officer[29] is satisfied that, owing to the absence of a person from the United Kingdom, it has not been reasonably practicable for his consent in writing to be so given, a facsimile communication (or any similar means of communication) consenting to his nomination and purporting to have been sent by him is deemed for these purposes to be consent in writing by him on the day on which it purports to have been sent, and attestation of his consent is not required[30]. A candidate's consent, given either at a Welsh Assembly constituency election or at a Welsh Assembly regional election[31], additionally must state[32]:

(A)   the day, month and year of his birth[33];

(B)   an address within the relevant area[34] that is deemed (where a candidate is to be treated as an election agent[35]) to be his office as an election agent[36];

(C)   that he is aware of the statutory provisions that govern disqualification from being an Assembly member[37] and that, to the best of his knowledge and belief, he is not disqualified for membership of the National Assembly for Wales[38];

(D)   in the case of a candidate at a constituency election, that he is not a candidate at an election for any other constituency, the poll for which is to be held on the same day as that for the election to which the consent relates (or, in the case of an election to fill a casual vacancy, that he is not an Assembly member)[39];

(E)   in the case of an individual candidate at a regional election, that he is not a party list candidate in the election for that region[40], nor a candidate at a constituency election[41], nor an individual or party list candidate at an election for any other region[42], the poll for which is to be held on the same day as that for the election to which the consent relates[43]; and

(F)   in the case of a party list candidate at a regional election, that he is not an individual candidate or a candidate on any other party list in the election for that region[44], nor a candidate at a constituency election[45], nor an individual or party list candidate at an election for any other region[46], the poll for which is to be held on the same day as that for the election to which the consent relates[47].

A candidate at a Welsh Assembly is required to give his consent in this way[48] notwithstanding that he has subscribed the nomination paper by virtue of which he is nominated[49].

A person is not validly nominated at a European parliamentary election[50], as either an individual candidate[51], or as a candidate on a registered party's list[52], unless his consent to nomination[53]:

(aa)   is given in writing on or within one month before the day fixed as the last day for the delivery of nomination papers[54];

(bb)   is attested by one witness[55];

(cc)   in the case of a candidate on a registered party's list, identifies the party in question[56]; and

(dd)   is delivered at the place and within the time for the delivery of nomination papers[57].

However, if the returning officer[58] is satisfied that, owing to the absence of a person from the United Kingdom[59], it has not been reasonably practicable for his consent in writing so to be given, a telegram (or any similar means of communication) consenting to his nomination and purporting to have been sent by him is deemed for these purposes to be consent in writing given by him on the day on which it purports to have been sent, and attestation of his consent is not required[60]. A candidate's consent given at a European parliamentary election[61] additionally must state the day, month and year of his birth[62], and must state both that he is aware of the provisions relating to disqualification from being a member of the European Parliament ('MEP')[63] and that, to the best of his knowledge and belief, he is not disqualified for membership of that office[64].

Where a person has been declared by others to be a candidate at a parliamentary or local government election, or at a Welsh Assembly election, without his consent nothing in the provisions relating to the election campaign[65] is to be construed to impose any liability on that person, unless he has afterwards given his assent to the declaration, or has been nominated[66].

1   As to the form and supply of nomination papers, the particulars required, and subscription, see PARAS 255–257.
2   As to the meaning of 'parliamentary election' see PARA 9.
3   See the Representation of the People Act 1983 Sch 1 r 8(1). The provision made by Sch 1 r 8(1) is subject to Sch 1 r 8(2) (see the text and notes 7–9): see Sch 1 r 8(1).
4   Representation of the People Act 1983 Sch 1 r 8(1)(a).
5   Representation of the People Act 1983 Sch 1 r 8(1)(b).
6   Representation of the People Act 1983 Sch 1 r 8(1)(c). As to the delivery of nomination papers see PARA 260.
7   As to the returning officer for parliamentary elections see PARA 350 et seq.
8   As to the meaning of 'United Kingdom' see PARA 1 note 1.
9   Representation of the People Act 1983 Sch 1 r 8(2).

10 Representation of the People Act 1983 Sch 1 r 8(3)(a).
11 Representation of the People Act 1983 Sch 1 r 8(3)(b)(i). As to the provisions of the House of
    Commons Disqualification Act 1975 see PARLIAMENT vol 78 (2010) PARA 905 et seq.
12 Representation of the People Act 1983 Sch 1 r 8(3)(b)(ii). As to disqualification for membership
    of the House of Commons see PARA 224.
13 As to the meaning of 'candidate' generally see PARA 230.
14 As to the meaning of 'constituency' for the purposes of parliamentary elections see PARA 9.
15 Representation of the People Act 1983 Sch 1 r 8(3)(c) (added by the Electoral Administration
    Act 2006 s 22).
16 Ie an election of councillors for any electoral area, or any London Authority election, with
    general references to 'local government election' being taken to include a local authority
    mayoral election: see PARA 11. As to the meanings of 'Authority election ' and 'electoral area' see
    PARA 11. As to the election of councillors for local government principal areas see PARA 197 et
    seq; as to elections for the return of a local authority mayor see PARA 198; as to London
    Authority elections, including for the return of an elected Mayor of London, see PARA 199 et
    seq; and as to the ordinary elections of parish or community councillors see PARA 200 et seq.
        The validity of a person's nomination under the Greater London Authority Elections
    Rules 2007, SI 2007/3541, Sch 2 r 9 (see the text and notes 17–21) applies to a person whether
    as an individual candidate or a list candidate at elections for the return of London members: see
    Sch 2 r 9(1). As to the meaning of 'London member', in relation to the London Assembly, see
    PARA 11 note 5; definition applied by virtue of r 2(2). As to the meaning of 'constituency
    member', in relation to the London Assembly, see PARA 11 note 6; definition applied by virtue of
    r 2(2). As to references to nomination papers and to party lists in elections for the return of
    London members of the London Assembly see PARA 255 note 23. As to the London Assembly
    see LONDON GOVERNMENT vol 71 (2013) PARA 70; as to constituency members of the London
    Assembly see further LONDON GOVERNMENT vol 71 (2013) PARA 80; and as to individual
    candidates to be London members of the London Assembly see further LONDON GOVERNMENT
    vol 71 (2013) PARA 81.
17 Local Elections (Principal Areas) (England and Wales) Rules 2006, SI 2006/3304, Sch 2 r 7;
    Local Elections (Parishes and Communities) (England and Wales) Rules 2006, SI 2006/3305,
    Sch 2 r 7; Local Authorities (Mayoral Elections) (England and Wales) Regulations 2007,
    SI 2007/1024, Sch 1 r 9; Greater London Authority Elections Rules 2007, SI 2007/3541, Sch 1
    r 7(1), Sch 2 r 9(1), Sch 3 r 8(1).
18 Local Elections (Principal Areas) (England and Wales) Rules 2006, SI 2006/3304, Sch 2 r 7(a);
    Local Elections (Parishes and Communities) (England and Wales) Rules 2006, SI 2006/3305,
    Sch 2 r 7(a); Local Authorities (Mayoral Elections) (England and Wales) Regulations 2007,
    SI 2007/1024, Sch 1 r 9(a); Greater London Authority Elections Rules 2007, SI 2007/3541,
    Sch 1 r 7(1)(a), Sch 2 r 9(1)(a), Sch 3 r 8(1)(a).
19 Local Elections (Principal Areas) (England and Wales) Rules 2006, SI 2006/3304, Sch 2 r 7(b);
    Local Elections (Parishes and Communities) (England and Wales) Rules 2006, SI 2006/3305,
    Sch 2 r 7(b); Local Authorities (Mayoral Elections) (England and Wales) Regulations 2007,
    SI 2007/1024, Sch 1 r 9(b); Greater London Authority Elections Rules 2007, SI 2007/3541,
    Sch 1 r 7(1)(a), Sch 2 r 9(1)(a), Sch 3 r 8(1)(a). As to the forms so prescribed see the Local
    Elections (Principal Areas) (England and Wales) Rules 2006, SI 2006/3304, Appendix of Forms
    (Form of candidate's consent to nomination) (Form amended by SI 2011/1043); the Local
    Elections (Parishes and Communities) (England and Wales) Rules 2006, SI 2006/3305,
    Appendix of Forms (Form of candidate's consent to nomination); the Local Authorities
    (Mayoral Elections) (England and Wales) Regulations 2007, SI 2007/1024, Appendix of Forms
    (Form 2: Form of candidate's consent to nomination) (Form 2 amended by SI 2011/1043); and
    the Greater London Authority Elections Rules 2007, SI 2007/3541, Sch 10 r 2 (Form 4:
    candidate's consent to nomination), as the case may be. As to the Welsh version of the form that
    may be used at principal area elections in Wales see the Local Elections (Principal Areas) (Welsh
    Forms) Order 2007, SI 2007/1015, art 6(c), Sch 2 (Form 3 (Ffurflen 3: Ffurf ar Gydsyniad
    Ymgeisydd i'w Enwebu)); and as to the Welsh version of the form which is prescribed to be used
    at community elections in Wales see the Local Elections (Communities) (Welsh Forms)
    Order 2007, SI 2007/1013, art 6(c), Sch 2 (Form 3 (Ffurflen 3: Ffurf ar Gydsyniad Ymgeisydd
    i'w Enwebu)). The forms so prescribed may be used with such adaptations as the circumstances
    may require: see the Elections (Principal Areas) (Welsh Forms) Order 2007, SI 2007/1015,
    art 10; and the Local Elections (Communities) (Welsh Forms) Order 2007, SI 2007/1013, art 10.
    The returning officer for a local government principal area or parish or community election, or
    local authority mayoral election, must supply any elector with as many forms of consent to
    nomination as may be required at the place and during the time for delivery of nomination
    papers (see PARA 260), but it is not necessary for a consent to nomination to be on a form

supplied by the returning officer: Local Elections (Principal Areas) (England and Wales) Rules 2006, SI 2006/3304, Sch 2 r 6(4); Local Elections (Parishes and Communities) (England and Wales) Rules 2006, SI 2006/3305, Sch 2 r 6(4); Local Authorities (Mayoral Elections) (England and Wales) Regulations 2007, SI 2007/1024, Sch 1 r 8(4).

Amongst other things, the forms for local government principal area and parish or community elections require the candidate to declare that, to the best of his knowledge and belief, he is not disqualified for being elected by reason of any disqualification set out in the Local Government Act 1972 ss 80, 81 (disqualification for election and holding office as member of local authority: see LOCAL GOVERNMENT vol 69 (2009) PARA 119), or any decision made under the Local Government Act 2000 s 79 (case tribunal decisions regarding compliance with code of conduct of relevant authority: see LOCAL GOVERNMENT vol 69 (2009) PARA 283), copies of which provisions must be included with the consent to nomination form: see the Local Elections (Principal Areas) (England and Wales) Rules 2006, SI 2006/3304, Sch 2 r 7(b), Appendix of Forms (Form of candidate's consent to nomination) (Form as so amended); and the Local Elections (Parishes and Communities) (England and Wales) Rules 2006, SI 2006/3305, Sch 2 r 7(b), Appendix of Forms (Form of candidate's consent to nomination). The consent form for a local authority mayoral election candidate requires the candidate to declare that, to the best of his knowledge and belief, he is not disqualified for being elected by reason of any disqualification set out in the Local Government Act 1972 s 80 and the Local Government Act 2000 s 79, copies of which provisions must be included with the consent to nomination form, also that the candidate does not hold a politically-restricted post within the meaning of the Local Government and Housing Act 1989 Pt I (ss 1–21) under a local authority also within the meaning of Pt I (local authority members. officers, staff and committees etc) (see LOCAL GOVERNMENT vol 69 (2009) PARA 122): see the Local Authorities (Mayoral Elections) (England and Wales) Regulations 2007, SI 2007/1024, Sch 1 r 9(b), Appendix of Forms (Form 2: Form of candidate's consent to nomination) (Form 2 as so amended). The candidate's consent given under the Greater London Authority Elections Rules 2007, SI 2007/3541, Sch 1 r 7, Sch 2 r 9, or Sch 3 r 8, as the case may be, must state the day, month and year of his birth, and must contain a statement that, to the best of the candidate's knowledge and belief, he is not disqualified from being elected by reason of any disqualification set out in the Greater London Authority Act 1999 s 21 (disqualification for office of Mayor of London or member of the London Assembly: see LONDON GOVERNMENT vol 71 (2013) PARA 74), or by reason of any decision made under the Local Government Act 2000 s 79: see the Greater London Authority Elections Rules 2007, SI 2007/3541, Sch 1 r 7(2), Sch 2 r 9(2)(a), (c), Sch 3 r 8(2). In the case of an individual candidate or a list candidate at elections for the return of London members of the London Assembly, the candidate's consent additionally must contain a statement that he has read whichever of the Greater London Authority Act 1999 s 4(6), Sch 2 para 5(5), (6) applies in his case (ie persons who may not be included in a registered party's list of candidates or who may not stand as an individual candidate to be a London member: see PARA 226; and LONDON GOVERNMENT vol 71 (2013) PARA 81): Greater London Authority Elections Rules 2007, SI 2007/3541, Sch 2 r 9(2)(b). Accordingly, the consent form used for London Assembly elections requires the candidate to declare that, to the best of his knowledge and belief, he is not disqualified for being elected by reason of any disqualification set out in the Greater London Authority Act 1999 s 21, or specified in any order under s 21(1)(b), or any decision made under the Local Government Act 2000 s 79: see the Greater London Authority Elections Rules 2007, SI 2007/3541, Sch 10 r 2 (Form 4: candidate's consent to nomination).

20 Local Elections (Principal Areas) (England and Wales) Rules 2006, SI 2006/3304, Sch 2 r 7(c); Local Elections (Parishes and Communities) (England and Wales) Rules 2006, SI 2006/3305, Sch 2 r 7(c); Local Authorities (Mayoral Elections) (England and Wales) Regulations 2007, SI 2007/1024, Sch 1 r 9(c); Greater London Authority Elections Rules 2007, SI 2007/3541, Sch 1 r 7(1)(b), Sch 2 r 9(1)(b), Sch 3 r 8(1)(b). For the purposes of London Assembly elections, it is specified that the attesting witness's name and address must be given: see Sch 1 r 7(1)(b), Sch 2 r 9(1)(b), Sch 3 r 8(1)(b).

21 Local Elections (Principal Areas) (England and Wales) Rules 2006, SI 2006/3304, Sch 2 r 7(d); Local Elections (Parishes and Communities) (England and Wales) Rules 2006, SI 2006/3305, Sch 2 r 7(d); Local Authorities (Mayoral Elections) (England and Wales) Regulations 2007, SI 2007/1024, Sch 1 r 9(d); Greater London Authority Elections Rules 2007, SI 2007/3541, Sch 1 r 7(1)(c), Sch 2 r 9(1)(c), Sch 3 r 8(1)(c).

22 As to the meaning of 'constituency election' for the purposes of Welsh Assembly elections see PARA 3 note 2. As to the meaning of 'Assembly constituency' for these purposes see PARA 3 note 2.

23 As to the meaning of 'regional election' for the purposes of Welsh Assembly elections see PARA 3 note 2. As to the meaning of 'Assembly electoral region' for these purposes see PARA 3 note 2.

24 As to the meanings of 'candidate' and 'individual candidate' see PARA 230 note 19; and as to the meaning of 'party list candidate' see PARA 230 note 23.

25 See the National Assembly for Wales (Representation of the People) Order 2007, SI 2007/236, Sch 5 para 9(1), (2). The provision made by Sch 5 para 9(1), (2) is subject to Sch 5 para 9(3) (see the text and notes 29–30): see Sch 5 para 9(1), (2).

26 See the National Assembly for Wales (Representation of the People) Order 2007, SI 2007/236, Sch 5 para 9(1)(a), (2)(a). In the case of a constituency election, the reference is to the delivery of constituency nomination papers (see Sch 5 para 9(1)(a)); and, in the case of a regional election, the reference is to the delivery of either individual nomination papers or party nomination papers (see Sch 5 para 9(2)(a), (c)). As to the meanings of 'constituency nomination paper' and 'individual nomination paper' see PARA 256; and as to the meaning of 'party nomination paper' at a Welsh Assembly regional election see PARA 255. As to the time for the delivery of nomination papers at a Welsh Assembly election see PARA 260.

27 See the National Assembly for Wales (Representation of the People) Order 2007, SI 2007/236, Sch 5 para 9(1)(b), (2)(b).

28 See the National Assembly for Wales (Representation of the People) Order 2007, SI 2007/236, Sch 5 para 9(1)(c), (2)(c). As to references to nomination papers see note 26.

29 As to the meaning of 'appropriate returning officer' at a Welsh Assembly election see PARA 18 note 2.

30 National Assembly for Wales (Representation of the People) Order 2007, SI 2007/236, Sch 5 para 9(3).

31 Ie a candidate's consent given under the National Assembly for Wales (Representation of the People) Order 2007, SI 2007/236, Sch 5 para 9: see Sch 5 para 9(4).

32 See the National Assembly for Wales (Representation of the People) Order 2007, SI 2007/236, Sch 5 para 9(4).

33 National Assembly for Wales (Representation of the People) Order 2007, SI 2007/236, Sch 5 para 9(4)(a).

34 For these purposes, the 'relevant area' is to be construed in accordance with the National Assembly for Wales (Representation of the People) Order 2007, SI 2007/236, art 39(2)(a) (in relation to a constituency election), or in accordance with art 39(2)(b) (in relation to a regional election) (office of agents for Welsh Assembly Elections: see PARA 238): see Sch 5 para 9(6).

35 Ie for the purposes of the National Assembly for Wales (Representation of the People) Order 2007, SI 2007/236, art 40(7) (see PARA 236): see Sch 5 para 9(4)(b).

36 National Assembly for Wales (Representation of the People) Order 2007, SI 2007/236, Sch 5 para 9(4)(b).

37 National Assembly for Wales (Representation of the People) Order 2007, SI 2007/236, Sch 5 para 9(4)(c)(i), (7). The provisions referred to in the text are the Government of Wales Act 2006 ss 16–19 (see PARA 227; and CONSTITUTIONAL LAW AND HUMAN RIGHTS) and any Order in Council made under s 16(1)(b) (as to which see the National Assembly for Wales (Disqualification) Order 2010, SI 2010/2969; and PARA 227): see the National Assembly for Wales (Representation of the People) Order 2007, SI 2007/236, Sch 5 para 9(4)(c)(i), (7).

38 National Assembly for Wales (Representation of the People) Order 2007, SI 2007/236, Sch 5 para 9(4)(c)(ii). As to the National Assembly for Wales see CONSTITUTIONAL LAW AND HUMAN RIGHTS.

39 National Assembly for Wales (Representation of the People) Order 2007, SI 2007/236, Sch 5 para 9(4)(d).

40 National Assembly for Wales (Representation of the People) Order 2007, SI 2007/236, Sch 5 para 9(4)(e)(i).

41 National Assembly for Wales (Representation of the People) Order 2007, SI 2007/236, Sch 5 para 9(4)(e)(ii).

42 National Assembly for Wales (Representation of the People) Order 2007, SI 2007/236, Sch 5 para 9(4)(e)(iii).

43 See the National Assembly for Wales (Representation of the People) Order 2007, SI 2007/236, Sch 5 para 9(4)(e).

44 National Assembly for Wales (Representation of the People) Order 2007, SI 2007/236, Sch 5 para 9(4)(f)(i).

45 National Assembly for Wales (Representation of the People) Order 2007, SI 2007/236, Sch 5 para 9(4)(f)(ii).

46 National Assembly for Wales (Representation of the People) Order 2007, SI 2007/236, Sch 5 para 9(4)(f)(iii).

47 See the National Assembly for Wales (Representation of the People) Order 2007, SI 2007/236, Sch 5 para 9(4)(f).

48 Ie under the National Assembly for Wales (Representation of the People) Order 2007, SI 2007/236, Sch 5 para 9: see Sch 5 para 9(5).
49 National Assembly for Wales (Representation of the People) Order 2007, SI 2007/236, Sch 5 para 9(5).
50 As to European parliamentary elections see PARA 217 et seq.
51 As to the meaning of 'individual candidate' at a European parliamentary election see PARA 230 note 32.
52 As to the meanings of 'list' and 'registered party' for these purposes see PARA 230 note 29. As to the system of candidature whereby registered parties submit lists of candidates see PARA 340.
53 See the European Parliamentary Elections Regulations 2004, SI 2004/293, Sch 1 para 8(1) (Sch 1 substituted by SI 2009/186).
54 European Parliamentary Elections Regulations 2004, SI 2004/293, Sch 1 para 8(1)(a) (as substituted: see note 53). As to the time for the delivery of nomination papers at a European parliamentary by-election see PARA 260.
55 European Parliamentary Elections Regulations 2004, SI 2004/293, Sch 1 para 8(1)(b) (as substituted: see note 53).
56 European Parliamentary Elections Regulations 2004, SI 2004/293, Sch 1 para 8(1)(c) (as substituted: see note 53).
57 European Parliamentary Elections Regulations 2004, SI 2004/293, Sch 1 para 8(1)(d) (as substituted: see note 53). The provision made by Sch 1 para 8(1)(d) is subject to Sch 1 para 8(2) (see the text and notes 58–60): see Sch 1 para 8(1)(d) (as so substituted).
58 As to returning officers at European parliamentary elections see PARA 360 et seq.
59 Ie or from Gibraltar, as the case may be for the purposes of elections held in the combined region (see PARA 77): see the European Parliamentary Elections Regulations 2004, SI 2004/293, Sch 1 para 8(2) (as substituted: see note 53).
60 European Parliamentary Elections Regulations 2004, SI 2004/293, Sch 1 para 8(2) (as substituted: see note 53).
61 Ie given under the European Parliamentary Elections Regulations 2004, SI 2004/293, Sch 1 para 8: see Sch 1 para 8(3) (as substituted: see note 53).
62 European Parliamentary Elections Regulations 2004, SI 2004/293, Sch 1 para 8(3) (as substituted: see note 53).
63 European Parliamentary Elections Regulations 2004, SI 2004/293, Sch 1 para 8(3)(a) (as substituted: see note 53). The text refers to the provisions of the European Parliamentary Elections Act 2002 s 10 (disqualification for the office of MEP: see PARA 228): see the European Parliamentary Elections Regulations 2004, SI 2004/293, Sch 1 para 8(3)(a) (as so substituted).
64 European Parliamentary Elections Regulations 2004, SI 2004/293, Sch 1 para 8(3)(b) (as substituted: see note 53). For these purposes, a candidate is not disqualified for the office of MEP by virtue of his being a life peer at the time of his nomination: Sch 1 para 8(4) (as so substituted).
65 Ie nothing in the Representation of the People Act 1983 Pt II (ss 67–119) (see s 117(1)), or in the National Assembly for Wales (Representation of the People) Order 2007, SI 2007/236, Pt 3 (arts 37–85) (see art 83(1)). No such saving is made for the purposes of European parliamentary elections in the European Parliamentary Elections Regulations 2004, SI 2004/293.
66 Representation of the People Act 1983 ss 117(1), 187(1) (amended by the Representation of the People Act 1985 ss 24, 28, Sch 4 para 64, Sch 5; and the Electoral Administration Act 2006 s 74(1), Sch 1 Pt 7 paras 104, 124); National Assembly for Wales (Representation of the People) Order 2007, SI 2007/236, art 83(1). As to candidacy and liability see also PARA 230.

259. Requirement for deposit at certain elections. A person is not validly nominated as a candidate[1] at a parliamentary[2] or local government election[3] unless the required sum[4] is deposited by him or on his behalf[5] with the returning officer at the place and during the time for delivery of nomination papers[6]. The deposit may be made either by the deposit of any legal tender[7], or by means of a banker's draft[8], or, with the returning officer's consent, in any other manner, including by means of a debit or credit card or the electronic transfer of funds[9].

A person is not validly nominated as a candidate[10] at a Welsh Assembly constituency election[11], or as an individual candidate at a Welsh Assembly regional election[12], unless the sum of £500 is deposited by him or deposited on his behalf[13] with the appropriate returning officer at the place (or, at a regional election, a place) and during the time for delivery of nomination papers[14]. A registered political party[15], and each of the party list candidates[16] on the list it has submitted, may not be validly nominated at a regional election unless the sum of £500 is deposited by the party's registered nominating officer[17] (or by or on behalf of one of the party list candidates)[18] with the regional returning officer at the place (or a place) and during the time for delivery of a party list[19]. In any of these cases, the deposit may be made either by the deposit of any legal tender[20], or by means of a banker's draft[21], or, with the consent of the appropriate returning officer, in any other manner, including by means of a debit or credit card or the electronic transfer of funds[22].

A person is not validly nominated as an individual candidate at a European parliamentary election[23] unless the sum of £5,000 is deposited by him or on his behalf[24] with the returning officer[25] at the place and during the time for delivery of nomination papers[26]. A registered party[27] is not validly nominated for these purposes unless the sum of £5,000 is deposited on its behalf[28] with the returning officer at the place and during the time for the delivery of nomination papers[29]. The deposit may be made either by the deposit of any legal tender[30], or by means of a banker's draft[31], or, with the returning officer's consent, in any other manner, including by means of a debit or credit card or the electronic transfer of funds[32].

1   As to the meaning of 'candidate' generally see PARA 230.
2   As to the meaning of 'parliamentary election' see PARA 9.
3   Ie an election of councillors for any electoral area, or any London Authority election, with general references to 'local government election' being taken to include a local authority mayoral election: see PARA 11. As to the meanings of 'Authority election ' and 'electoral area' see PARA 11. As to the election of councillors for local government principal areas see PARA 197 et seq; as to elections for the return of a local authority mayor see PARA 198; as to London Authority elections, including for the return of an elected Mayor of London, see PARA 199 et seq; and as to the ordinary elections of parish or community councillors see PARA 200 et seq.
    At an election for the return of London members of the London Assembly, the reference is either to a person as an individual candidate at the election or to a registered party (and anyone on its party list): see the Greater London Authority Elections Rules 2007, SI 2007/3541, Sch 2 r 10(1), (2). As to the meaning of 'London member', in relation to the London Assembly, see PARA 11 note 5; definition applied by virtue of r 2(2). As to references to nomination papers and to party lists in elections for the return of London members of the London Assembly see PARA 255 note 23. As to the London Assembly see LONDON GOVERNMENT vol 71 (2013) PARA 70; and as to individual candidates to be London members of the London Assembly see further LONDON GOVERNMENT vol 71 (2013) PARA 81.
4   The sum required as a deposit at each parliamentary or local government election is specified as follows:
    (1)   at a parliamentary election, £500 (Representation of the People Act 1983 Sch 1 r 9(1) (amended by the Representation of the People Act 1985 s 13));
    (2)   at a local authority mayoral election, £500 (Local Authorities (Mayoral Elections) (England and Wales) Regulations 2007, SI 2007/1024, Sch 1 r 10(1));
    (3)   at an election for the return of constituency members of the London Assembly, £1,000 (Greater London Authority Elections Rules 2007, SI 2007/3541, Sch 1 r 8(1));
    (4)   at an election for the return of London members of the London Assembly, £5,000, whether relating to an individual candidate or a registered party (Sch 2 r 10(1), (2)); and
    (5)   for the return of an elected Mayor of London, £10,000 (Sch 3 r 9(1)).
    No deposit is required for candidates nominated at a local government principal area or parish or community election. As to the meaning of 'constituency member', in relation to the London Assembly, see PARA 11 note 6; definition applied by virtue of r 2(2). As to constituency members of the London Assembly see further LONDON GOVERNMENT vol 71 (2013) PARA 80.
5   Where the deposit is made on behalf of the candidate, the person making the deposit must, at the time he makes it, give his name and address to the returning officer, unless those details have previously been given to him under the Representation of the People Act 1983 s 67 (appointment of election agent for parliamentary and local government elections: see PARA 231) or (in the case of a parliamentary election only) under Sch 1 r 6(4) (home address form: see

PARA 256): Sch 1 r 9(3) (added by the Representation of the People Act 1985 s 24, Sch 4 para 75; amended by the Political Parties and Elections Act 2009 s 39, Sch 6 para 8(1), (3)); Local Authorities (Mayoral Elections) (England and Wales) Regulations 2007, SI 2007/1024, Sch 1 r 10(3); Greater London Authority Elections Rules 2007, SI 2007/3541, Sch 1 r 8(3), Sch 2 r 10(4), Sch 3 r 9(3). In the case of a London members election, a deposit can be made only on behalf of a registered party (see Sch 2 r 10(2)); and Sch 2 r 10(4) applies only where the deposit is made on behalf of an individual candidate (see Sch 2 r 10(4)). In elections for the return of constituency members of the London Assembly, any reference to the returning officer is to the constituency returning officer ('CRO') (see Sch 1 r 8(1)–(3)); in other London Assembly elections (ie for London members and in the case of a London Mayoral election), the reference is to the Greater London returning officer ('GLRO') (see Sch 2 r 10(1)–(4), Sch 3 r 9(1)–(3)). As to the meaning of the 'Greater London returning officer' see PARA 211 note 8; and as to the meaning of the 'constituency returning officer' in this context see PARA 211 note 9. As to returning officers for parliamentary elections see PARA 350 et seq; and as to returning officers for local government elections generally see PARA 354 et seq.

6   Representation of the People Act 1983 Sch 1 r 9(1) (as amended: see note 4); Local Authorities (Mayoral Elections) (England and Wales) Regulations 2007, SI 2007/1024, Sch 1 r 10(1); Greater London Authority Elections Rules 2007, SI 2007/3541, Sch 1 r 8(1), Sch 2 r 10(1), (2), Sch 3 r 9(1). In the case of a London members election, the reference in Sch 2 r 10(1), (2) is to the time for delivery of nomination papers and party lists: see Sch 2 r 10(1), (2). As to references to the returning officer see note 5. As to the delivery of nomination papers see PARA 260.

7   Representation of the People Act 1983 Sch 1 r 9(2)(a); Local Authorities (Mayoral Elections) (England and Wales) Regulations 2007, SI 2007/1024, Sch 1 r 10(2)(a); Greater London Authority Elections Rules 2007, SI 2007/3541, Sch 1 r 8(2)(a), Sch 2 r 10(3)(a), Sch 3 r 9(2)(a). As to legal tender see FINANCIAL SERVICES AND INSTITUTIONS vol 49 (2008) PARA 1278 et seq.

8   Representation of the People Act 1983 Sch 1 r 9(2)(b); Local Authorities (Mayoral Elections) (England and Wales) Regulations 2007, SI 2007/1024, Sch 1 r 10(2)(b); Greater London Authority Elections Rules 2007, SI 2007/3541, Sch 1 r 8(2)(b), Sch 2 r 10(3)(b), Sch 3 r 9(2)(b). The returning officer may refuse to accept a deposit sought to be made by means of a banker's draft, however, if he does not know that the drawer carries on business as a banker in the United Kingdom: Representation of the People Act 1983 Sch 1 r 9(2); Local Authorities (Mayoral Elections) (England and Wales) Regulations 2007, SI 2007/1024, Sch 1 r 10(2); Greater London Authority Elections Rules 2007, SI 2007/3541, Sch 1 r 8(2), Sch 2 r 10(3), Sch 3 r 9(2). As to references to the returning officer see note 5. As to the meaning of 'United Kingdom' see PARA 1 note 1.

9   Representation of the People Act 1983 Sch 1 r 9(2)(c) (amended by the Electoral Administration Act 2006 s 19(1), (5)); Local Authorities (Mayoral Elections) (England and Wales) Regulations 2007, SI 2007/1024, Sch 1 r 10(2)(c); Greater London Authority Elections Rules 2007, SI 2007/3541, Sch 1 r 8(2)(c), Sch 2 r 10(3)(c), Sch 3 r 9(2)(c). As to references to the returning officer see note 5.

10   As to the meaning of 'candidate' for these purposes generally see PARA 230 note 19.

11   As to the meanings of 'constituency election' and 'Assembly election' see PARA 3 note 2. As to Welsh Assembly elections generally see PARA 12 et seq.

12   As to the meaning of 'regional election' for the purposes of Welsh Assembly elections see PARA 3 note 2. As to the meaning of 'individual candidate' at a Welsh Assembly regional election see PARA 230 note 19.

13   Where the deposit is made on behalf of a candidate at a constituency election, or an individual candidate at a regional election, the person making the deposit must at the time he makes it give his name and address to the appropriate returning officer unless that information has previously been given to him under the National Assembly for Wales (Representation of the People) Order 2007, SI 2007/236, art 37 (appointment of election agent for Welsh Assembly elections: see PARA 235): Sch 5 para 10(5). As to the meaning of 'appropriate returning officer' for these purposes see PARA 18 note 2.

14   National Assembly for Wales (Representation of the People) Order 2007, SI 2007/236, Sch 5 para 10(1), (2). In the case of a person nominated as a candidate at a constituency election, the reference is to the delivery of constituency nomination papers (see Sch 5 para 10(1)); and, in the case of a person nominated as an individual candidate at a regional election, the reference is to the delivery of individual nomination papers (see Sch 5 para 10(2)). As to the meanings of 'constituency nomination paper' and 'individual nomination paper' see PARA 256. As to the time for the delivery of nomination papers at a Welsh Assembly election see PARA 260.

15   As to the meaning of 'registered political party' for these purposes see PARA 215 note 19.

16   As to the meaning of 'party list candidate' at a Welsh Assembly regional election see PARA 230 note 23.

17 As to the registered nominating officer for a registered political party see PARA 253. A registered nominating officer for a registered political party may, in writing, appoint one or more persons to discharge all or any of his functions conferred or imposed by the National Assembly for Wales (Representation of the People) Order 2007, SI 2007/236, Sch 5: see Sch 5 para 81(1); and PARA 215 note 24.

18 Where the deposit is made on behalf of a registered political party and its party list candidates at a regional election, the person making the deposit must at the time he makes it (see the National Assembly for Wales (Representation of the People) Order 2007, SI 2007/236, Sch 5 para 10(6)):

    (1)   if he is the registered political party's registered nominating officer, state that fact to the regional returning officer (Sch 5 para 10(6)(a)); or

    (2)   if he is not the registered political party's registered nominating officer, give his name and address to the regional returning officer unless that information has previously been given to him under art 37 (appointment of election agent for Welsh Assembly elections: see PARA 235) (Sch 5 para 10(6)(b)).

As to the meanings of 'constituency returning officer' and 'regional returning officer' see PARA 18 note 2.

19 National Assembly for Wales (Representation of the People) Order 2007, SI 2007/236, Sch 5 para 10(3).

20 National Assembly for Wales (Representation of the People) Order 2007, SI 2007/236, Sch 5 para 10(4)(a).

21 National Assembly for Wales (Representation of the People) Order 2007, SI 2007/236, Sch 5 para 10(4)(b). The appropriate returning officer may refuse to accept a deposit sought to be made by means of a banker's draft if he does not know that the drawer carries on business as a banker in the United Kingdom: Sch 5 para 10(4).

22 National Assembly for Wales (Representation of the People) Order 2007, SI 2007/236, Sch 5 para 10(4)(c).

23 As to the meaning of 'individual candidate' at a European parliamentary election see PARA 230 note 32. As to European parliamentary elections see PARA 217 et seq.

24 Where the deposit is made on behalf of an individual candidate, the person making the deposit must at the time he makes it give his name and address to the returning officer, unless they have previously been given to him under the European Parliamentary Elections Regulations 2004, SI 2004/293, reg 38 (appointment of election agent for individual candidate: see PARA 239): see Sch 1 para 10(4) (Sch 1 substituted by SI 2009/186).

25 As to returning officers at European parliamentary elections see PARA 360 et seq.

26 European Parliamentary Elections Regulations 2004, SI 2004/293, Sch 1 para 10(1) (as substituted: see note 24). As to the time for the delivery of nomination papers at a European parliamentary by-election see PARA 260.

27 As to the meaning of 'registered party' for these purposes see PARA 230 note 29. As to the system of candidature whereby registered parties submit lists of candidates see PARA 340.

28 Where the deposit is made on behalf of the registered party, the person making the deposit must at the time he makes it give his name and address to the returning officer, unless they have previously been given to him under the European Parliamentary Elections Regulations 2004, SI 2004/293 reg 33 (appointment of national election agent of registered party: see PARA 239) or reg 34 (appointment of election agent by a registered party standing in one electoral region only: see PARA 239): see Sch 1 para 10(4) (as substituted: see note 24).

29 European Parliamentary Elections Regulations 2004, SI 2004/293, Sch 1 para 10(2) (as substituted: see note 24).

30 European Parliamentary Elections Regulations 2004, SI 2004/293, Sch 1 para 10(3)(a) (as substituted: see note 24).

31 European Parliamentary Elections Regulations 2004, SI 2004/293, Sch 1 para 10(3)(b) (as substituted: see note 24). The returning officer may refuse to accept a deposit sought to be made by means of a banker's draft if he does not know that the drawer carries on business as a banker in the United Kingdom (or Gibraltar, as the case may be for the purposes of elections held in the combined region: see PARA 77): see: Sch 1 para 10(3) (as so substituted).

32 European Parliamentary Elections Regulations 2004, SI 2004/293, Sch 1 para 10(3)(c) (as substituted: see note 24).

260. Delivery of nomination papers. Nomination papers[1] for a parliamentary general election[2] must be delivered between the hours of ten in the morning and four in the afternoon on any day after the date of publication of the notice of election[3], but not later than the sixth day after the date of the dissolution of

Parliament[4]. For a parliamentary by-election[5], the timetable is the same as for a parliamentary general election, except that the last day is a day fixed by the returning officer[6], and this must be not earlier than the third day after the date of publication of the notice of election, nor later than the seventh day after that on which the writ for the by-election is received[7]. In either case, the nomination paper must be delivered, either by or on behalf of the candidate himself[8], or by his proposer or seconder[9], to the returning officer at the place fixed for the purpose[10]. If the paper is delivered by anybody else, the candidate will not have been validly nominated[11]. The returning officer must fix the place at which nomination papers are to be delivered to him[12], and he must attend there during the time for their delivery and for the making of objections to them[13]. The returning officer has no power to extend the time for delivery of nomination papers[14].

Nomination papers for a local government election[15] must be delivered not later than noon on the nineteenth day before the day of election[16], except in the case of London Authority election, when the time limit for delivery is not later than noon on the twenty-fourth day before the day of election[17]. The papers[18] must be delivered before the last time specified for their delivery, and at the place fixed for the purpose by the appropriate returning officer[19]. No further provision is made in relation to the place fixed for the purposes of elections taking place in a parish or community[20], but, in relation to the other local government elections, the place so fixed must be:

(1)   for the purposes of council elections taking place in principal areas, at the offices of the council of the district or London borough[21] in which the electoral area wholly or mainly lies[22];

(2)   for the purposes of local authority mayoral elections, at the offices of the council of the county, county borough, district or London borough in which the electoral area wholly or mainly lies[23];

(3)   for the purposes of London Authority elections for the return of constituency members, at the offices of a local authority within the Assembly constituency[24]; and

(4)   for the purposes of London Authority elections for the return of London members, or for the return of an elected Mayor of London, at one of the offices of the Greater London Authority[25].

All nomination papers for a Welsh Assembly election[26] must be delivered between the hours of ten in the morning and four in the afternoon on any day after the date of publication of notice of election[27] (but before the nineteenth day before the day of election)[28], and between the hours of ten in the morning and noon on the nineteenth day before the day of election[29]. The separate nomination paper for each candidate at a constituency election[30] must be delivered, either by or on behalf of the candidate himself[31], or (where a certificate authorising a candidate's description has been issued[32] and delivered) by the registered nominating officer[33] of a registered political party[34], to the constituency returning officer at the place fixed for the purpose[35]. That place must be fixed by the constituency returning officer himself[36], and it must be either in the Assembly constituency itself[37], or in the registration area[38] that includes the whole or any part of any Assembly constituency[39]. The constituency returning officer must attend there during the time for the delivery of constituency nomination papers[40], and for the making of objections to them[41]. An individual nomination paper for each individual candidate at a regional election[42] must be delivered by or on behalf of the candidate himself[43], and a party nomination paper[44] must be delivered by the registered political party's registered nominating officer[45], to the regional returning officer at the place or a place fixed for the purpose[46]. That place (or those places) must be fixed by the regional returning officer himself[47]; and it (or, as the case may be, they) must be in the Assembly electoral region[48]. The regional returning officer must attend there during the time for the delivery of individual nomination, or party nomination, papers, and for the making of objections to them[49].

Nomination papers and lists of candidates of registered parties[50] for European parliamentary elections[51] must be delivered between the hours of ten in the morning and four in the afternoon in the United Kingdom[52] on any day after the date of the publication of the notice of election[53], but not later than the nineteenth day before the date of the poll[54]. Each separate nomination paper for an individual candidate[55] must be delivered by the individual candidate himself or by a person authorised in writing by him[56]. A nomination paper for each registered party which is to stand for election in the electoral region[57] must be delivered to the returning officer[58], at the place which he has fixed for the purpose, by the party's nominating officer or by a person authorised in writing by him[59]. The returning officer must fix the place in the electoral region at which nomination papers are to be delivered to him, and he must attend there during the time for their delivery, and for the making of objections to them[60].

1 As to the form and supply of nomination papers and the particulars required see PARA 255 et seq.
2 As to the meanings of 'general election' and 'parliamentary election' see PARA 9. As to parliamentary general elections see PARA 189 et seq.
3 As to the publication of the notice of election at a parliamentary election see PARA 196. As to the calculation of dates for these purposes see PARA 195 note 27.
4 See the Representation of the People Act 1983 Sch 1 r 1 (amended by the Fixed-term Parliaments Act 2011 s 6(3), Schedule paras 6, 10(1), (3)). The text refers to the dissolution of Parliament by the Fixed-term Parliaments Act 2011 s 3(1) (see PARA 189): see the Representation of the People Act 1983 Sch 1 r 1 (as so amended).
5 As to parliamentary by-elections see PARA 191 et seq.
6 As to the returning officer for parliamentary elections see PARA 350 et seq.
7 See the Representation of the People Act 1983 Sch 1 r 1. As to the issue and conveyance of writs for parliamentary by-elections see PARA 192.
8 Representation of the People Act 1983 Sch 1 r 6(1)(a). The paper may be so delivered on the candidate's behalf by his election agent if the agent's name and address have been previously given to the returning officer as required by s 67 (appointment of election agent for parliamentary and local government elections: see PARA 231), or are so given at the time the paper is delivered: see Sch 1 r 6(1). As to the meaning of 'candidate' generally see PARA 230. As to the appointment of an election agent for parliamentary elections see PARA 231.
9 Representation of the People Act 1983 Sch 1 r 6(1)(b). As to the subscription of nomination papers see PARA 257.
10 See the Representation of the People Act 1983 Sch 1 r 6(1). The provision made in Sch 1 r 6(1) about delivery of the nomination paper applies also to the home address form: see Sch 1 r 6(4) (added by the Political Parties and Elections Act 2009 s 24(1), (2)(b)). As to the requirement for a nomination paper at a parliamentary election to be accompanied by a home address form see PARA 256.
11 *Monks v Jackson* (1876) 1 CPD 683.
12 For these purposes, the place must be in:
    (1)   the constituency (Representation of the People Act 1983 Sch 1 r 10(2)(a)); or
    (2)   the registration area which includes the constituency (Sch 1 r 10(2)(b)); or
    (3)   unless the constituency is a borough constituency, in a district or Welsh county or county borough adjoining the constituency or registration area (Sch 1 r 10(2)(c) (amended by the Local Government (Wales) Act 1994 s 66(6), Sch 16 para 68(17))).
For the purposes of head (2) above, 'registration area' means the area of two or more constituencies in England and Wales which have the same registration officer: see the Representation of the People Act 1983 Sch 1 r 10(2)(i). As to the meanings of 'England' and 'Wales' see PARA 1 note 1; and as to the meaning of 'constituency' for the purposes of

parliamentary elections see PARA 9. As to the distinction between county constituencies and borough constituencies at parliamentary elections see PARA 73; and as to registration officers and the areas for which they act see PARA 139 et seq. As to districts in England see LOCAL GOVERNMENT vol 69 (2009) PARA 24 et seq; and as to counties and county boroughs in Wales see LOCAL GOVERNMENT vol 69 (2009) PARA 37 et seq.

13   Representation of the People Act 1983 Sch 1 r 10(1). As to the time for the making of objections to nomination papers see PARA 262.

14   *Howes v Turner* (1876) 1 CPD 670; *Cutting v Windsor* (1924) 40 TLR 395.

15   Ie an election of councillors for any electoral area, or any London Authority election, with general references to 'local government election' being taken to include a local authority mayoral election: see PARA 11. As to the meanings of 'Authority election ' and 'electoral area' see PARA 11. As to the election of councillors for local government principal areas see PARA 197 et seq; as to elections for the return of a local authority mayor see PARA 198; as to London Authority elections, including for the return of an elected Mayor of London, see PARA 199 et seq; and as to the ordinary elections of parish or community councillors see PARA 200 et seq.

16   Local Elections (Principal Areas) (England and Wales) Rules 2006, SI 2006/3304, Sch 2 r 1; Local Elections (Parishes and Communities) (England and Wales) Rules 2006, SI 2006/3305, Sch 2 r 1; Local Authorities (Mayoral Elections) (England and Wales) Regulations 2007, SI 2007/1024, Sch 1 r 3. As to the date of the poll at a local authority mayoral election see PARA 198; and as to the date of the poll at other local government elections (including elections to fill vacancies) see PARAS 206–209. As to the calculation of time for these purposes see PARA 211 note 1.

It is the nominee's duty to present valid nomination papers in time and the rules do not raise a legitimate expectation that the returning officer's duty to assess their validity (as to which see PARA 263) will identify any errors in them within the time limits: *R (on the application of De Beer) v Balabanoff* [2002] EWHC 670 (Admin), (2002) Times, 25 April, [2002] All ER (D) 34 (Apr), applied in *R (on the application of Begum) v Tower Hamlets London Borough Council* [2006] EWCA Civ 733, [2006] LGR 674, [2006] All ER (D) 19 (May) (deputy returning officer's filing error was causative of the fact that putative nominees were not able to stand in the election but the invalidity of the papers arose from the nominees' actions whose duty to present valid nomination papers in time had not been transferred to the returning officer).

17   Greater London Authority Elections Rules 2007, SI 2007/3541, Sch 1 Sch 2 r 3, Sch 3 r 3.

18   Ie, generally, the nomination papers for each election, as they apply (see the text and notes 15–17). However, in the case of an election for the return of London members of the London Assembly, and for the purposes of the Greater London Authority Elections Rules 2007, SI 2007/3541, Sch 2 rr 9–68 specifically, unless the context indicates otherwise, 'nomination paper' includes both a reference to the nomination paper of a registered party delivered under Sch 2 r 7(1) (see PARA 255), and a reference to the nomination paper of an individual candidate delivered under Sch 2 r 6(1) (see PARA 255); and 'nomination paper of a registered party' includes a reference to a party list delivered under Sch 2 r 7(2) (see PARA 256): see Sch 2 r 8(5); and PARA 255 note 23. As to the meaning of 'London member' see PARA 11 note 5; definition applied by virtue of r 2(2). As to the meaning of 'registered political party' in this context see PARA 256 note 27. As to the London Assembly see LONDON GOVERNMENT vol 71 (2013) PARA 70; and as to party lists, and as to individual candidates to be London members, see further LONDON GOVERNMENT vol 71 (2013) PARA 81.

19   Local Elections (Principal Areas) (England and Wales) Rules 2006, SI 2006/3304, Sch 2 r 4(1); Local Elections (Parishes and Communities) (England and Wales) Rules 2006, SI 2006/3305, Sch 2 r 4(1); Local Authorities (Mayoral Elections) (England and Wales) Regulations 2007, SI 2007/1024, Sch 1 r 6(1); Greater London Authority Elections Rules 2007, SI 2007/3541, Sch 1 r 6(1)(b), Sch 2 rr 6(1)(b), 8(3), Sch 3 r 6(1)(b). The provisions as to the time and place for the delivery of nomination papers are mandatory: *R v Soothill, ex p Ashdown* (1955) Times, 21 April. However, there is no limitation (as there is in the case of parliamentary or European parliamentary elections or Welsh Assembly elections) on the person delivering the nomination paper nor is it necessary for the nomination paper to be delivered to the returning officer. As to returning officers for local government elections generally see PARA 354 et seq. In elections for the return of constituency members of the London Assembly, any reference to the returning officer is to the constituency returning officer ('CRO') (see the Greater London Authority Elections Rules 2007, SI 2007/3541, Sch 1 r 6(1)(b)); in other London Assembly elections (ie for London members and in the case of a London Mayoral election), the reference is to the Greater London returning officer ('GLRO') (see Sch 2 rr 6(1)(b), 8(3), Sch 3 r 6(1)(b)). As to the meaning of the 'Greater London returning officer' see PARA 211 note 8; and as to the meaning of

the 'constituency returning officer' in this context see PARA 211 note 9. As to the meaning of 'constituency member', in relation to the London Assembly, see PARA 11 note 6; definition applied by virtue of r 2(2).

20 See the Local Elections (Parishes and Communities) (England and Wales) Rules 2006, SI 2006/3305, Sch 2 r 4(1).

21 As to the London boroughs and their councils see LOCAL GOVERNMENT vol 69 (2009) PARA 35; LONDON GOVERNMENT vol 71 (2013) PARA 15 et seq.

22 See the Local Elections (Principal Areas) (England and Wales) Rules 2006, SI 2006/3304, Sch 2 r 4(1).

23 See the Local Authorities (Mayoral Elections) (England and Wales) Regulations 2007, SI 2007/1024, Sch 1 r 6(1).

24 See the Greater London Authority Elections Rules 2007, SI 2007/3541, Sch 1 r 6(1)(b). As to the meaning of 'Assembly constituency', in relation to the London Assembly, see PARA 11 note 6.

25 See the Greater London Authority Elections Rules 2007, SI 2007/3541, Sch 2 rr 6(1)(b), 8(3), Sch 3 r 6(1)(b). Head (4) in the text refers, in the case of a London members election, to the place specified by the GLRO in the notice of election, which must be at one of the offices of the Greater London Authority: see Sch 2 r 8(3). At a London members election, the nomination paper must be delivered in accordance with Sch 2 rr 6, 8 (see Sch 2 rr 6(1)(b)); and, where a nomination paper (and/or party list: see note 18) is delivered in respect of the same registered party, or in respect of the same individual candidate, after an earlier nomination paper (and/or party list) has been delivered, that later paper (and/or list) is deemed to supersede the earlier paper (and/or party list) (see Sch 2 r 8(4)). As to the Greater London Authority see LONDON GOVERNMENT vol 71 (2013) PARA 67 et seq.

26 As to the meaning of 'Assembly election' see PARA 3 note 2. As to Welsh Assembly elections generally see PARA 12 et seq.

27 As to the publication of the notice of Welsh Assembly election see PARA 216.

28 As to the date of the poll at Welsh Assembly elections (including elections to fill vacancies in an Assembly constituency) see PARAS 213–214.

29 National Assembly for Wales (Representation of the People) Order 2007, SI 2007/236, Sch 5 para 1(1). As to the calculation of time for these purposes see PARA 213 note 5.

30 As to the meaning of 'constituency election' for the purposes of Welsh Assembly elections see PARA 3 note 2. As to the meaning of 'candidate' for these purposes generally see PARA 230 note 19.

31 National Assembly for Wales (Representation of the People) Order 2007, SI 2007/236, Sch 5 para 4(1)(a). The paper may be so delivered on the candidate's behalf by his election agent, if the agent's name and address have been previously given to the constituency returning officer as required under art 37 (appointment of election agent for Welsh Assembly elections: see PARA 235), or are so given at the time the nomination paper is delivered: see Sch 5 para 4(1). As to the meaning of 'constituency returning officer' for these purposes see PARA 18 note 2. As to the appointment of an election agent for Welsh Assembly elections see PARA 235.

32 Ie issued under the National Assembly for Wales (Representation of the People) Order 2007, SI 2007/236, Sch 5 para 5(1) or Sch 5 para 5(3) (see PARA 256): see Sch 5 para 4(1)(b).

33 As to the registered nominating officer of a party see PARA 253.

34 National Assembly for Wales (Representation of the People) Order 2007, SI 2007/236, Sch 5 para 4(1)(b). As to the meaning of 'registered political party' for these purposes see PARA 215 note 19.

35 See the National Assembly for Wales (Representation of the People) Order 2007, SI 2007/236, Sch 5 para 4(1).

36 See the National Assembly for Wales (Representation of the People) Order 2007, SI 2007/236, Sch 5 para 11(1).

37 National Assembly for Wales (Representation of the People) Order 2007, SI 2007/236, Sch 5 para 11(2)(a). As to the meaning of 'Assembly constituency' see PARA 3 note 2.

38 For these purposes, 'registration area' means the area of two or more Assembly constituencies which have the same registration officer: see the National Assembly for Wales (Representation of the People) Order 2007, SI 2007/236, Sch 5 para 11(5). As to electoral registration officers, and the areas for which they act, see PARA 139 et seq.

39 National Assembly for Wales (Representation of the People) Order 2007, SI 2007/236, Sch 5 para 11(2)(b).

40 As to the meaning of 'constituency nomination paper' see PARA 256.

41 See the National Assembly for Wales (Representation of the People) Order 2007, SI 2007/236, Sch 5 para 11(1).

42   As to the meaning of Welsh Assembly 'regional election' see PARA 3 note 2; and as to the meaning of 'individual candidate' for these purposes see PARA 230 note 19. As to the meaning of 'individual nomination paper' see PARA 256.

43   See the National Assembly for Wales (Representation of the People) Order 2007, SI 2007/236, Sch 5 para 6(1). An individual nomination paper may be so delivered on the candidate's behalf by his election agent, if the agent's name and address have been previously given to the regional returning officer as required under art 37 (appointment of election agent for Welsh Assembly elections: see PARA 235), or are so given at the time the nomination paper is delivered: see Sch 5 para 6(1). As to the meaning of 'regional returning officer' for these purposes see PARA 18 note 2.

44   As to the meaning of 'party nomination paper' at a Welsh Assembly regional election see PARA 255.

45   See the National Assembly for Wales (Representation of the People) Order 2007, SI 2007/236, Sch 5 para 7(1).

46   See the National Assembly for Wales (Representation of the People) Order 2007, SI 2007/236, Sch 5 paras 6(1), 7(1).

47   See the National Assembly for Wales (Representation of the People) Order 2007, SI 2007/236, Sch 5 para 11(3).

48   National Assembly for Wales (Representation of the People) Order 2007, SI 2007/236, Sch 5 para 11(4).

49   See the National Assembly for Wales (Representation of the People) Order 2007, SI 2007/236, Sch 5 para 11(3).

50   As to the meanings of 'list' and 'registered party' for these purposes see PARA 230 note 29. As to the system of candidature whereby registered parties submit lists of candidates see PARA 340.

51   As to European parliamentary elections see PARA 217 et seq.

52   As to the meaning of 'United Kingdom' see PARA 1 note 1.

53   As to publication of the notice of a European parliamentary election see PARA 223.

54   European Parliamentary Elections Regulations 2004, SI 2004/293, Sch 1 para 1 (Sch 1 substituted by SI 2009/186). As to the date of the poll at a European parliamentary election see PARA 222.

55   As to the meaning of 'individual candidate' at a European parliamentary election see PARA 230 note 32.

56   European Parliamentary Elections Regulations 2004, SI 2004/293, Sch 1 para 4(1) (as substituted: see note 54). Where an individual nomination paper is delivered in respect of the same person after an earlier paper in respect of that person has been delivered, that later paper is deemed to supersede the earlier one: Sch 1 para 4(5) (as so substituted).

57   As to the establishment of electoral regions for the purpose of elections to the European Parliament see PARA 77.

58   As to returning officers at European parliamentary elections see PARA 360 et seq.

59   European Parliamentary Elections Regulations 2004, SI 2004/293, Sch 1 para 6(1) (as substituted: see note 54). Where a nomination paper and list of candidates are delivered in respect of the same registered party after an earlier paper and list have been delivered in respect of that party, that later paper and list must be deemed to supersede the earlier ones: Sch 1 para 6(7) (as so substituted).

60   European Parliamentary Elections Regulations 2004, SI 2004/293, Sch 1 para 11 (as substituted: see note 54).

     The usual provisions that require any document which, by virtue of the European Parliamentary Elections Regulations 2004, SI 2004/293, is required or authorised to be displayed in public, to be made readily accessible (ie reg 122A(1)–(3): see PARA 239 note 23) do not apply to the nomination paper: see reg 122A(4)(a) (reg 122A added by SI 2009/186).

261. Nomination proceedings and the inspection of papers. At a parliamentary election[1], except for the purpose of delivering a nomination paper[2], or of assisting the returning officer[3], no person is entitled to attend the proceedings during the time for delivery of nomination papers, or for the making of objections to them[4], unless he is[5]:

    (1)   a person standing nominated as a candidate[6]; or

    (2)   the election agent[7], proposer or seconder of such a person[8]; or

(3)   a representative of the Electoral Commission who is entitled[9] to attend certain election proceedings and to observe the working practices of certain electoral officials[10].

Except in relation to a person mentioned in head (3) above[11], the right to attend nomination proceedings so conferred includes the right to inspect, and to object to the validity of, any nomination paper and associated home address form[12]. One other person chosen by the candidate is entitled to be present at the delivery of the candidate's nomination, and may afterwards, so long as the candidate stands nominated, attend the nomination proceedings during the time for delivery of nomination papers or for making objections to them, but without any such right to inspect, or to object to, the validity of any nomination paper[13].

At a local government election[14], any person may inspect and take copies of, or extracts from, nomination papers and consents to nomination[15] during ordinary office hours on any day, other than an excepted day[16], before the date of the poll, the allowed period of inspection starting with the latest time for delivery of nomination papers (or 24 hours after that time, at a London Authority election)[17].

For the purposes of a Welsh Assembly constituency election[18] or regional election[19], except for the purpose of delivering a nomination paper[20], or of assisting the returning officer[21], no person is entitled to attend the proceedings during the time for delivery of nomination papers, or for making objections to them, unless he is[22]:

(a)   a person standing nominated as a candidate[23];

(b)   the election agent of such a person[24] (or, at a regional election, the election agent in respect of a party list)[25];

(c)   (at a regional election only) a party list candidate[26];

(d)   the registered nominating officer of a registered political party[27];

(e)   a representative of the Electoral Commission who is entitled[28] to attend certain election proceedings and to observe the working practices of certain electoral officials[29].

Except in relation to a person mentioned in head (e) above[30], the right to attend nomination proceedings so conferred includes the right to inspect, and to object to the validity of, any nomination paper[31]. One other person chosen by the candidate is entitled to be present at the delivery of the nomination paper by which that candidate is nominated, and may afterwards, so long as the candidate stands nominated, attend the nomination proceedings during the time for delivery of nomination papers or for making objections to them, but without any such right to inspect, or to object to, the validity of any nomination paper[32].

At a European parliamentary election[33], except for the purpose of delivering a nomination paper, or of assisting the returning officer[34], no person is entitled to attend the proceedings during the time for delivery of nomination papers, or for making objections to them, unless he is[35]:

(i)   a person standing nominated as an individual candidate[36] or included in a list of candidates[37];

(ii)   the election agent either of an individual candidate, or of a registered party which has submitted a nomination[38]; or

(iii)   a person authorised in writing to deliver a nomination paper[39];

(iv)   a representative of the Electoral Commission who is entitled[40] to attend certain election proceedings and to observe the working practices of certain electoral officials[41].

Except in relation to a person mentioned in head (iv) above[42], the right to attend nomination proceedings so conferred includes the right to inspect, and to object to the validity of, any nomination paper or list of candidates[43]. One other person chosen by each candidate is entitled to be present at the delivery of the candidate's nomination, and may afterwards, so long as the candidate stands nominated, attend the proceedings during the time for delivery of nomination papers, or for making objections to them, but without any right to inspect, or to object to the validity of, any nomination paper[44].

Where the proceedings for or in connection with nomination at a parliamentary election, a Welsh Assembly election, or a European parliamentary election, are on any day interrupted or obstructed by riot or open violence, the proceedings must be abandoned for that day[45]. If that day is the last day for the delivery of nomination papers[46], the proceedings must be continued on the next day as if that were the last day for their delivery[47]; and that day is treated for these purposes as being the last day for such delivery unless there is further interruption or obstruction[48]. Where proceedings are abandoned in this way, nothing may be done after they are continued if the time for doing it had passed at the time of the abandonment[49]; and nothing done before the abandonment is invalidated by reason of the abandonment[50].

1   As to the meaning of 'parliamentary election' see PARA 9.
2   As to the time and place for the delivery of nomination papers see PARA 260.
3   As to the returning officer for parliamentary elections and his duties see PARA 350 et seq.
4   As to the making of objections to nomination papers at a parliamentary election see PARA 262.
5   See the Representation of the People Act 1983 Sch 1 r 11(1). The provision made by Sch 1 r 11 is subject to Sch 1 r 11(4) (see the text and note 13): see Sch 1 r 11(1).
6   Representation of the People Act 1983 Sch 1 r 11(1)(a). As to the meaning of 'candidate' generally see PARA 230. As to the nomination of candidates see PARA 253 et seq.
7   As to the appointment of an election agent for parliamentary elections see PARA 231. Where a candidate acts as his own election agent, he may name one other person who is entitled to attend in place of his election agent: see the Representation of the People Act 1983 Sch 1 r 11(1).
8   Representation of the People Act 1983 Sch 1 r 11(1)(b). Where a person stands nominated by more than one nomination paper, only the persons subscribing as proposer and seconder to such one of those papers as he may select, or, in default of such a selection, to that one of those papers which is first delivered, is entitled to attend as his proposer and seconder: see Sch 1 r 11(2). As to the subscription of nomination papers see PARA 257.
9   Ie by virtue of the Political Parties, Elections and Referendums Act 2000 ss 6A, 6B (see PARA 53): see the Representation of the People Act 1983 Sch 1 r 11(1)(c) (added by the Electoral Administration Act 2006 s 47, Sch 1 paras 69, 83(1), (2)).
10 Representation of the People Act 1983 Sch 1 r 11(1)(c) (as added: see note 9). As to the Electoral Commission see PARA 34 et seq.
11 The rights conferred by the Representation of the People Act 1983 Sch 1 r 11(3) (see the text and note 12) do not apply to a person mentioned in Sch 1 r 11(1)(c) (see head (3) in the text): Sch 1 r 11(3A) (added by the Electoral Administration Act 2006 Sch 1 paras 69, 83(1), (3)).
12 See the Representation of the People Act 1983 Sch 1 r 11(3) (Sch 1 r 11(3) amended, Sch 1 r 11(5) added, by the Political Parties and Elections Act 2009 s 24(1), (3)). The returning officer may not permit a home address form to be inspected otherwise than in accordance with the Representation of the People Act 1983 Sch 1 r 11, or for some other purpose authorised by law: Sch 1 r 11(5) (as so added). As to the requirement for a nomination paper at a parliamentary election to be accompanied by a home address form see PARA 256.
13 Representation of the People Act 1983 Sch 1 r 11(4) (amended by the Electoral Administration Act 2006 Sch 1 paras 69, 83(1), (4)).
14 Ie an election of councillors for any electoral area, or any London Authority election, with general references to 'local government election' being taken to include a local authority mayoral election: see PARA 11. As to the meanings of 'Authority election ' and 'electoral area' see PARA 11. As to the election of councillors for local government principal areas see PARA 197 et seq; as to elections for the return of a local authority mayor see PARA 198; as to London Authority elections, including for the return of an elected Mayor of London, see PARA 199 et seq; and as to the ordinary elections of parish or community councillors see PARA 200 et seq.

15 As to a candidate's consent to nomination see PARA 258.

16 Ie other than a day specified in the Local Elections (Principal Areas) (England and Wales) Rules 2006, SI 2006/3304, Sch 2 r 2(1), the Local Elections (Parishes and Communities) (England and Wales) Rules 2006, SI 2006/3305, Sch 2 r 2(1), the Local Authorities (Mayoral Elections) (England and Wales) Regulations 2007, SI 2007/1024, Sch 1 r 4(1), or the Greater London Authority Elections Rules 2007, SI 2007/3541, Sch 1 r 4(1), Sch 2 r 4(1), Sch 3 r 4(1), as the case may be (as to which see PARA 211 note 1).

17 Local Elections (Principal Areas) (England and Wales) Rules 2006, SI 2006/3304, Sch 2 r 11; Local Elections (Parishes and Communities) (England and Wales) Rules 2006, SI 2006/3305, Sch 2 r 11; Local Authorities (Mayoral Elections) (England and Wales) Regulations 2007, SI 2007/1024, Sch 1 r 13; Greater London Authority Elections Rules 2007, SI 2007/3541, Sch 1 r 12(1), (2), Sch 2 r 14(1), (2), Sch 3 r 13(1), (2). In the case of a London Authority election, it is specified that the period of inspection begins 24 hours after the latest time for delivery of the nomination papers: see Sch 1 r 12(1), Sch 2 r 14(1), Sch 3 r 13(1). As to the date of the poll at an election for the return of a local authority elected mayor see PARA 198; and as to the date of the poll at local government elections (including elections to fill vacancies) see PARAS 206–209.

18 As to the meanings of 'Assembly election' and 'constituency election' see PARA 3 note 2.

19 As to the meaning of 'regional election' for these purposes see PARA 3 note 2.

20 As to the time for delivery of nomination papers see PARA 260. At a Welsh Assembly constituency election, the paper referred to is a constituency nomination paper (see the National Assembly for Wales (Representation of the People) Order 2007, SI 2007/236, Sch 5 para 12(1)); and, at a Welsh Assembly regional election, the paper referred to is either an individual nomination paper or a party nomination paper (see Sch 5 para 12(2)). As to the meaning of 'party nomination paper' at a Welsh Assembly regional election see PARA 255; and as to the meanings of 'constituency nomination paper' and 'individual nomination paper' see PARA 256.

21 At a Welsh Assembly constituency election, the constituency returning officer is the returning officer referred to in the text (see the National Assembly for Wales (Representation of the People) Order 2007, SI 2007/236, Sch 5 para 12(1)); and at a Welsh Assembly regional election, it is the regional returning officer (see Sch 5 para 12(2)). As to the meanings of 'constituency returning officer' and 'regional returning officer' for the purposes of Welsh Assembly elections see PARA 18 note 2.

22 See the National Assembly for Wales (Representation of the People) Order 2007, SI 2007/236, Sch 5 para 12(1), (2). The provision made by Sch 5 para 12(1), (2) is subject o Sch 5 para 12(6) (see the text and note 32): see Sch 5 para 12(1), (2).

23 National Assembly for Wales (Representation of the People) Order 2007, SI 2007/236, Sch 5 para 12(1)(a), (2)(a). In the case of a regional election, the person referred to in the text is a person standing nominated as an individual candidate: see Sch 5 para 12(2)(a). As to the meanings of 'candidate' and 'individual candidate' see PARA 230 note 19.

24 National Assembly for Wales (Representation of the People) Order 2007, SI 2007/236, Sch 5 para 12(1)(b), (2)(b). However, where a constituency candidate acts as his own election agent, he may name one other person who is entitled to attend in place of his election agent (see Sch 5 para 12(1)); and where an individual candidate acts as his own election agent at a regional election, he may name one other person who is entitled to attend in place of his election agent (see Sch 5 para 12(2)). As to the meaning of 'constituency candidate' for these purposes see PARA 230 note 19. As to the appointment of an election agent for Welsh Assembly elections see PARA 235.

25 National Assembly for Wales (Representation of the People) Order 2007, SI 2007/236, Sch 5 para 12(2)(d). The text refers to the election agent of a registered political party that has submitted a party list at a regional election: see Sch 5 para 12(2)(d). As to the meaning of 'registered political party' for these purposes see PARA 215 note 19. As to the meaning of 'party list' see PARA 230 note 23.

26 National Assembly for Wales (Representation of the People) Order 2007, SI 2007/236, Sch 5 para 12(2)(c). However, where a party list candidate acts as election agent for that party in relation to that list, he may name one other person who is entitled to attend in place of the election agent for that party (see Sch 5 para 12(2)). As to the meaning of 'party list candidate' at a Welsh Assembly regional election see PARA 230 note 23.

27 National Assembly for Wales (Representation of the People) Order 2007, SI 2007/236, Sch 5 para 12(1)(c), (2)(d). At a Welsh Assembly constituency election, head (d) in the text refers to the registered nominating officer of a registered political party that has delivered a certificate in respect of a candidate under Sch 5 para 5(1) or Sch 5 para 5(3) (ie a certificate authorising the description of a candidate at a constituency election: see PARA 256) (see Sch 5 para 12(1)(c)); and, at a Welsh Assembly regional election, head (d) in the text refers to the registered

nominating officer of a registered political party that has submitted a party list (see Sch 5 para 12(2)(d)). As to the registered nominating officer of a party see PARA 253.

28 Ie by virtue of the Political Parties, Elections and Referendums Act 2000 ss 6A, 6B (see PARA 53): see the National Assembly for Wales (Representation of the People) Order 2007, SI 2007/236, Sch 5 para 12(1)(d), (2)(e).

29 National Assembly for Wales (Representation of the People) Order 2007, SI 2007/236, Sch 5 para 12(1)(d), (2)(e).

30 The rights conferred by the National Assembly for Wales (Representation of the People) Order 2007, SI 2007/236, Sch 5 para 12(3), (4) (see the text and note 31) do not apply to a person mentioned in Sch 5 para 12(1)(d) or Sch 5 para 12(2)(e) (see head (e) in the text): Sch 5 para 12(5).

31 National Assembly for Wales (Representation of the People) Order 2007, SI 2007/236, Sch 5 para 12(3), (4). At a Welsh Assembly constituency election, the paper referred to is a constituency nomination paper (see Sch 5 para 12(3)); and, at a Welsh Assembly regional election, the paper referred to is either an individual nomination paper or a party nomination paper (including the nomination of any party list candidate on the party list submitted with that party nomination paper) (see Sch 5 para 12(4)).

32 National Assembly for Wales (Representation of the People) Order 2007, SI 2007/236, Sch 5 para 12(6).

33 As to European parliamentary elections see PARA 217 et seq.

34 As to returning officers at European parliamentary elections see PARA 360 et seq.

35 See the European Parliamentary Elections Regulations 2004, SI 2004/293, Sch 1 para 12(1) (Sch 1 substituted by SI 2009/186). See, however, the European Parliamentary Elections Regulations 2004, SI 2004/293, Sch 1 para 12(4); and the text and note 44.

36 As to the meaning of 'individual candidate' at a European parliamentary election see PARA 230 note 32.

37 European Parliamentary Elections Regulations 2004, SI 2004/293, Sch 1 para 12(1)(a) (as substituted: see note 35). The text refers to inclusion in a list of candidates under Sch 1 para 7 (see PARA 256): see Sch 1 para 12(1)(a) (as so substituted).

38 European Parliamentary Elections Regulations 2004, SI 2004/293, Sch 1 para 12(1)(b) (as substituted: see note 35). As to the meaning of 'registered party' for these purposes see PARA 230 note 29. As to the appointment of the election agent of a registered party or for an individual candidate at a European parliamentary election see PARA 239.

39 European Parliamentary Elections Regulations 2004, SI 2004/293, Sch 1 para 12(1)(c) (as substituted: see note 35).

40 Ie by virtue of the Political Parties, Elections and Referendums Act 2000 ss 6A, 6B (see PARA 53): see the European Parliamentary Elections Regulations 2004, SI 2004/293, Sch 1 para 12(1)(d) (as substituted: see note 35).

41 European Parliamentary Elections Regulations 2004, SI 2004/293, Sch 1 para 12(1)(d) (as substituted: see note 35).

42 The rights conferred by the European Parliamentary Elections Regulations 2004, SI 2004/293, Sch 1 para 12(2) (see the text and note 43) do not apply to a person mentioned in Sch 1 para 12(1)(d) (see head (iv) in the text): Sch 1 para 12(3) (as so substituted).

43 European Parliamentary Elections Regulations 2004, SI 2004/293, Sch 1 para 12(2) (as substituted: see note 35).

44 European Parliamentary Elections Regulations 2004, SI 2004/293, Sch 1 para 12(4) (as substituted: see note 35).

45 Representation of the People Act 1983 Sch 1 r 16(1)(a); European Parliamentary Elections Regulations 2004, SI 2004/293, Sch 1 para 19(1)(a) (as substituted: see note 35); National Assembly for Wales (Representation of the People) Order 2007, SI 2007/236, Sch 5 para 20(1)(a).

46 Ie constituency nomination papers, in the case of a Welsh Assembly constituency election (National Assembly for Wales (Representation of the People) Order 2007, SI 2007/236, Sch 5 para 20(b)(i)); or individual and party nomination papers, in the case of a Welsh Assembly regional election (Sch 5 para 20(b)(ii)).

47 Representation of the People Act 1983 Sch 1 r 16(1)(b); European Parliamentary Elections Regulations 2004, SI 2004/293, Sch 1 para 19(1)(b) (as substituted: see note 35); National Assembly for Wales (Representation of the People) Order 2007, SI 2007/236, Sch 5 para 20(1).

48 Representation of the People Act 1983 Sch 1 r 16(1); European Parliamentary Elections Regulations 2004, SI 2004/293, Sch 1 para 19(1) (as substituted: see note 35); National Assembly for Wales (Representation of the People) Order 2007, SI 2007/236, Sch 5 para 20(1).

49　Representation of the People Act 1983 Sch 1 r 16(2)(a); European Parliamentary Elections Regulations 2004, SI 2004/293, Sch 1 para 19(2)(a) (as substituted: see note 35); National Assembly for Wales (Representation of the People) Order 2007, SI 2007/236, Sch 5 para 20(2)(a).

50　Representation of the People Act 1983 Sch 1 r 16(2)(b); European Parliamentary Elections Regulations 2004, SI 2004/293, Sch 1 para 19(2)(b) (as substituted: see note 35); National Assembly for Wales (Representation of the People) Order 2007, SI 2007/236, Sch 5 para 20(2)(b). Accordingly, objections made, and decisions taken, before the proceedings are abandoned are preserved.

262. Nominations duly made stand unless and until candidate withdraws or dies or nomination held to be invalid. Where a nomination paper[1] and consent to nomination[2] of a candidate standing in his own right at an election are delivered[3] (along with any additional documents that may be required[4] and, also where required, a deposit made[5]) in accordance with the relevant election rules, the candidate is deemed to stand nominated unless and until[6]:

(1)　the returning officer[7] decides that the nomination paper is invalid[8]; or

(2)　proof is given, to the returning officer's satisfaction, of the candidate's death[9]; or

(3)　the candidate withdraws[10].

Where the nomination paper of a registered party[11], and the consent to nomination of each candidate included in that party's list[12], are delivered for the purposes of an election of London members of the London Assembly, and a deposit made in accordance with the London members election rules[13], that party, and each candidate on its list, are deemed to stand nominated unless and until the Greater London returning officer ('GLRO') decides that the nomination paper is invalid[14]. Where, in respect of a candidate included in such a party list, proof is given, to the GLRO's satisfaction, of his death[15], or where he withdraws (or his candidature is withdrawn)[16]; the GLRO must delete the name and address of that candidate from the list[17].

Where a party nomination paper at a Welsh Assembly regional election[18], together with its party list[19] and the consent to nomination of each candidate in that list, is delivered, and a deposit made in accordance with the Welsh Assembly election rules[20], that party, and each candidate on its list, are deemed to stand nominated unless and until the regional returning officer decides that the party nomination paper is invalid[21]. Where, in respect of a party list candidate[22], proof is given, to the regional returning officer's satisfaction, of his death[23], or if he withdraws (or his candidature is withdrawn)[24], the candidate ceases to stand nominated[25].

Where a registered political party's nomination paper[26] and list of candidates[27] are delivered at a European parliamentary election, and a deposit is made in accordance with the European parliamentary election rules[28], the party and the candidates on its list are deemed to stand nominated unless and until the returning officer determines that the nomination paper or list is invalid[29].

It is submitted that a returning officer could refuse to include in the statement of persons nominated[30] a candidate who on the foregoing grounds has not been validly nominated[31]; but it is doubtful that a returning officer is able to declare a candidate not validly nominated on other grounds[32].

1　As to the form and supply of nomination papers and the particulars required see PARA 255 et seq. At an election for the return of London members of the London Assembly, the reference is to an individual nomination paper: see the Greater London Authority Elections Rules 2007, SI 2007/3541, Sch 2 r 11(1); and see note 3; PARA 260 note 18. As to the meaning of 'London member' see PARA 11 note 5; definition applied by virtue of r 2(2). At a Welsh Assembly constituency election, the reference is to a constituency nomination paper and, at a Welsh Assembly regional election, the reference is to an individual nomination paper: see the National Assembly for Wales (Representation of the People) Order 2007, SI 2007/236, Sch 5 para 13 (heading). As to the meanings of 'constituency election' and 'regional election', in relation to a Welsh Assembly election, see PARA 3 note 2; and as to the meanings of 'constituency nomination paper' and 'individual nomination paper' see PARA 256.

2   As to the consent to nomination required of a candidate see PARA 258.

3   As to the delivery of nomination papers see PARA 260. As to the meaning of 'candidate' generally see PARA 230. At a London members election, the reference is to an individual candidate (and hence the reference to a nomination paper is to an 'individual nomination paper': see note 1): see the Greater London Authority Elections Rules 2007, SI 2007/3541, Sch 2 r 11(1). At a European parliamentary election, the reference is also to an individual candidate: see the European Parliamentary Elections Regulations 2004, SI 2004/293, Sch 1 para 13(1) (Sch 1 substituted by SI 2009/186). As to the meaning of 'individual candidate' at a European parliamentary election see PARA 230 note 32. As the discussion of a registered political party's nomination to be a candidate at elections (where such a party can stand) and candidates included in such a party's list see the text and notes 11–29.

4   At a parliamentary election, the home address form must be delivered along with the nomination paper and the candidate's consent to it: see the Representation of the People Act 1983 Sch 1 r 12(1) (amended by the Political Parties and Elections Act 2009 s 24(1), (4)(a)). Such a candidate's nomination may be invalidated, in addition to the grounds listed at heads (1) to (3) in the text, if the returning officer decides that the home address form does not comply with the Representation of the People Act 1983 Sch 1 r 6(4) (see PARA 256): Sch 1 r 12(1)(aa) (added by the Political Parties and Elections Act 2009 s 24(1), (4)(b)). As to the requirement for a nomination paper at a parliamentary election to be accompanied by a home address form see PARA 256.

At a European parliamentary election, a declaration and certificate may be required under the European Parliamentary Elections Regulations 2004, SI 2004/293, Sch 1 para 9(2), (3) where the individual candidate standing is a relevant citizen of the Union (see PARA 229): see Sch 1 para 13(1) (as substituted: see note 3). As to the meaning of 'relevant citizen of the Union' for these purposes see PARA 149 note 16.

5   A deposit is required to be made by candidates at a parliamentary election, at any London Authority election, at a Welsh Assembly election (constituency or regional), and at a European parliamentary election: see PARA 259; and see *Boyce v White* (1905) 92 LT 240, DC; *Brown v Benn* (1889) 53 JP 167, DC. A deposit is also required at a local authority mayoral election, by virtue of the Local Authorities (Mayoral Elections) (England and Wales) Regulations 2007, SI 2007/1024, Sch 1 r 10 (see PARA 259), although Sch 1 r 11(1) makes no mention of this. No deposit is required for candidates nominated at a local government principal area or parish or community election: see PARA 259.

6   Representation of the People Act 1983 Sch 1 r 12(1) (as amended: see note 4); European Parliamentary Elections Regulations 2004, SI 2004/293, Sch 1 para 13(1) (as substituted: see note 3); Local Elections (Principal Areas) (England and Wales) Rules 2006, SI 2006/3304, Sch 2 r 8(1); Local Elections (Parishes and Communities) (England and Wales) Rules 2006, SI 2006/3305, Sch 2 r 8(1); National Assembly for Wales (Representation of the People) Order 2007, SI 2007/236, Sch 5 para 13(1); Local Authorities (Mayoral Elections) (England and Wales) Regulations 2007, SI 2007/1024, Sch 1 r 11(1); Greater London Authority Elections Rules 2007, SI 2007/3541, Sch 1 r 9(1), Sch 2 r 11(1), Sch 3 r 10(1).

7   As to returning officers for parliamentary elections see PARA 350 et seq; as to returning officers for local government elections see PARA 354 et seq; and as to returning officers at European parliamentary elections see PARA 360 et seq. In elections for the return of constituency members of the London Assembly, any reference to the returning officer is to the constituency returning officer ('CRO') (see the Greater London Authority Elections Rules 2007, SI 2007/3541, Sch 1 r 9(1)); in other London Assembly elections (ie for London members and in the case of a London Mayoral election), the reference is to the Greater London returning officer ('GLRO') (see Sch 2 rr 11(1), (2), 15(4), Sch 3 r 10(1)). As to the meaning of the 'Greater London returning officer' see PARA 211 note 8; and as to the meaning of the 'constituency returning officer' in this context see PARA 211 note 9. As to the meaning of 'constituency member', in relation to the London Assembly, see PARA 11 note 6; definition applied by virtue of r 2(2). At a Welsh Assembly election, the reference is to the 'appropriate returning officer' (which means a constituency returning officer in relation to a constituency election and a regional returning officer in relation to a regional election: see the National Assembly for Wales (Representation of the People) Order 2007, SI 2007/236, art 2(1); and PARA 18 note 2): see Sch 5 para 13(1)(a), (b).

As to the meanings of 'constituency returning officer' and 'regional returning officer' for the purposes of Welsh Assembly elections see PARA 18 note 2.

8　Representation of the People Act 1983 Sch 1 r 12(1)(a); European Parliamentary Elections Regulations 2004, SI 2004/293, Sch 1 para 13(1)(a) (as substituted: see note 3); Local Elections (Principal Areas) (England and Wales) Rules 2006, SI 2006/3304, Sch 2 r 8(1)(a); Local Elections (Parishes and Communities) (England and Wales) Rules 2006, SI 2006/3305, Sch 2 r 8(1)(a); National Assembly for Wales (Representation of the People) Order 2007, SI 2007/236, Sch 5 para 13(1)(a); Local Authorities (Mayoral Elections) (England and Wales) Regulations 2007, SI 2007/1024, Sch 1 r 11(1)(a); Greater London Authority Elections Rules 2007, SI 2007/3541, Sch 1 r 9(1)(a), Sch 2 r 11(1)(a), Sch 3 r 10(1)(a). In relation to a parliamentary election, see also note 4. As to the grounds upon which a returning officer might hold a nomination paper to be invalid see PARA 263.

9　Representation of the People Act 1983 Sch 1 r 12(1)(b); European Parliamentary Elections Regulations 2004, SI 2004/293, Sch 1 para 13(1)(b) (as substituted: see note 3); Local Elections (Principal Areas) (England and Wales) Rules 2006, SI 2006/3304, Sch 2 r 8(1)(b); Local Elections (Parishes and Communities) (England and Wales) Rules 2006, SI 2006/3305, Sch 2 r 8(1)(b); National Assembly for Wales (Representation of the People) Order 2007, SI 2007/236, Sch 5 para 13(1)(b); Local Authorities (Mayoral Elections) (England and Wales) Regulations 2007, SI 2007/1024, Sch 1 r 11(1)(b); Greater London Authority Elections Rules 2007, SI 2007/3541, Sch 1 r 9(1)(b), Sch 2 r 11(1)(b), Sch 3 r 10(1)(b). Where, before the result of an election of London members is declared, proof is given, to the GLRO's satisfaction, that an individual candidate who is named (or is to be named) in the ballot papers has died, then, in addition to complying with any other requirement of the Greater London Authority Elections Rules 2007, SI 2007/3541, relevant to that event, the GLRO must inform each CRO of that fact (Sch 2 r 15(4)); and the CRO must provide each polling station with a notice of any such death that has been passed on to him in accordance with Sch 2 r 15(4) (see Sch 2 r 29(3)(d); and PARA 391 note 23).

10　Representation of the People Act 1983 Sch 1 r 12(1)(c); European Parliamentary Elections Regulations 2004, SI 2004/293, Sch 1 para 13(1)(c) (as substituted: see note 3); Local Elections (Principal Areas) (England and Wales) Rules 2006, SI 2006/3304, Sch 2 r 8(1)(c); Local Elections (Parishes and Communities) (England and Wales) Rules 2006, SI 2006/3305, Sch 2 r 8(1)(c); National Assembly for Wales (Representation of the People) Order 2007, SI 2007/236, Sch 5 para 13(1)(c); Local Authorities (Mayoral Elections) (England and Wales) Regulations 2007, SI 2007/1024, Sch 1 r 11(1)(c); Greater London Authority Elections Rules 2007, SI 2007/3541, Sch 1 r 9(1)(c), Sch 2 r 11(1)(c), Sch 3 r 10(1)(c). As to withdrawal of a candidate see PARA 266.

11　As to the meaning of 'registered political party' for these purposes see PARA 226 note 16.

12　As to references to party lists in elections for the return of London members of the London Assembly see PARA 255 note 23. As to party lists at the election of London members see further LONDON GOVERNMENT vol 71 (2013) PARA 81.

13　Ie in accordance with the Greater London Authority Elections Rules 2007, SI 2007/3541: see Sch 2 r 11(2).

14　Greater London Authority Elections Rules 2007, SI 2007/3541, Sch 2 r 11(2). This provision is subject to Sch 2 r 11(6) (see the text and notes 15–17; and PARA 263): see Sch 2 r 11(2). As to decisions regarding the validity of party lists see PARA 263.

15　Greater London Authority Elections Rules 2007, SI 2007/3541, Sch 2 r 11(6)(a). Where, before the result of an election of London members is declared, proof is given, to the GLRO's satisfaction, that a candidate whose name appears on a party list has died, then, in addition to complying with any other requirement of the Greater London Authority Elections Rules 2007, SI 2007/3541, relevant to that event, the GLRO must remove that person's name from that list: see Sch 2 r 15(4). See also note 9.

16　Greater London Authority Elections Rules 2007, SI 2007/3541, Sch 2 r 11(6)(b). The text refers to a candidature being withdrawn in accordance with Sch 2 r 15 (see PARA 266): see Sch 2 r 11(6)(b).

17　Greater London Authority Elections Rules 2007, SI 2007/3541, Sch 2 r 11(6). The grounds listed under Sch 2 r 11(6)(a), (b) are supplemented by grounds where:

　(1)　any candidate included in a party list submits particulars in that list that are not as required by law (see Sch 2 r 11(6)(c); and PARA 263);

　(2)　his consent to nomination is not delivered in accordance with Sch 2 r 9 (see PARA 258) (see Sch 2 r 11(6)(d); and PARA 263).

18　As to the meaning of 'party nomination paper' at a Welsh Assembly regional election see PARA 255.

19　As to the meaning of 'party list' at a Welsh Assembly regional election see PARA 230 note 23.

20 Ie in accordance with the National Assembly for Wales (Representation of the People) Order 2007, SI 2007/236: see Sch 5 para 14(1).

21 National Assembly for Wales (Representation of the People) Order 2007, SI 2007/236, Sch 5 r 14(1). The provision made by Sch 5 r 14(1) is subject to Sch 5 r 14(3), (4) (see the text and notes 22–25; and PARA 263 note 50): see Sch 5 r 14(1).

22 As to the meaning of 'party list candidate' at a Welsh Assembly regional election see PARA 230 note 23.

23 National Assembly for Wales (Representation of the People) Order 2007, SI 2007/236, Sch 5 r 14(3)(a).

24 National Assembly for Wales (Representation of the People) Order 2007, SI 2007/236, Sch 5 r 14(3)(b). The text refers to a candidature being withdrawn in accordance with Sch 5 r 15(4) (see PARA 266): see Sch 5 r 14(3)(b).

25 National Assembly for Wales (Representation of the People) Order 2007, SI 2007/236, Sch 5 r 14(3).

26 As to the meaning of 'registered political party' for these purposes see PARA 230 note 29.

27 Ie the list of a registered political party's candidates that must accompany its nomination paper under the European Parliamentary Elections Regulations 2004, SI 2004/293, Sch 1 para 7 (see PARA 256): see Sch 1 para 13(2) (as substituted: see note 3). As to the meaning of 'list' for these purposes see PARA 230 note 29.

28 Ie in accordance with the European Parliamentary Elections Regulations 2004, SI 2004/293: see Sch 1 para 13(2) (as substituted: see note 3).

29 European Parliamentary Elections Regulations 2004, SI 2004/293, Sch 1 para 13(2) (as substituted: see note 3). The provision made by Sch 1 r 13(2) is subject to Sch 1 r 13(5) (see PARA 263): see Sch 1 r 13(2) (as so substituted).

30 As to the statement of persons nominated see PARA 267.

31 *Monks v Jackson* (1876) 1 CPD 683; *Cutting v Windsor* (1924) 40 TLR 395; and see *R v Soothill, ex p Ashdown* (1955) Times, 21 April. In *Howes v Turner* (1876) 1 CPD 670 (a decision under the Municipal Elections Act 1875 s 1 (repealed)), where the notice of the last day for delivery of nomination papers was erroneous, it was argued that the mayor had no power to deal with objections based on the ground that nomination papers were delivered too late; although the headnote to the case states that the mayor had no power to deal with such objections, this appears to go beyond the actual decision of the court which was that the statutory provision in question, namely, that the decision of the mayor disallowing an objection to a nomination paper should be final (cf PARA 263), was limited to objections to the form of a nomination paper (cf PARA 263) and that his decision on other matters, e g the time of delivery, was open to review on an election petition; in this case the court held the election void by reason of the erroneous notice. *Monks v Jackson* is express authority for the view that a mayor should not declare to be duly nominated candidates who have failed to comply with the statutory provisions relating to nomination. In *Cutting v Windsor*, the mayor decided that he had no jurisdiction to entertain an objection based on the ground that a nomination paper was delivered too late; while the court did not express an opinion on this point, Avory J stated that the town clerk had no discretion to receive the nomination paper.

It would appear that the returning officer's decision on these questions to include or to refuse to include a candidate's name on the ground of the alleged validity or invalidity of his nomination is not final and may be questioned on an election petition: see PARA 265. See also *Brown v Benn* (1889) 53 JP 167, DC; *Boyce v White* (1905) 92 LT 240, DC. Where there is only one opponent and that opponent is not validly nominated, a candidate might apply to the High Court for judicial review to order the returning officer to declare that candidate elected: *R v Soothill, ex p Ashdown*. However, a court will hesitate to intervene in a contested election which is ongoing, except on limited grounds, preferring to leave the candidates to the remedies available once polling has finished: see e g PARA 254.

32 Eg if the candidate's nomination paper did not conform to the prescribed form, as this is not a ground on which the returning officer can declare a nomination paper invalid: see PARA 263. In *Marton v Gorill* (1889) 23 QBD 139, DC, the name of the electoral division had been omitted from a nomination paper at a county council election. The returning officer held the nomination paper invalid, but the High Court held that the defect was cured by a statutory provision that an election should not be invalidated by a mistake in the use of a form. This provision does not now apply to elections. The omission of the name of the constituency or electoral area would not be a misnomer or inaccurate description which could be cured by the Representation of the People Act 1983 s 50 (see PARA 256; and see *Baldwin v Ellis* [1929] 1 KB 273, DC); nor would the Representation of the People Act 1983 ss 23(3), 48(1) (see PARA 667) apply to nominations (*Gothard v Clarke* (1880) 5 CPD 253; *Baldwin v Ellis*).

263. Grounds upon which returning officer might hold nomination paper to be invalid. In relation to a candidate[1] standing in his own right at a parliamentary[2] or local government election (except a London Authority election)[3], the returning officer[4] is entitled to hold his nomination paper[5] invalid only on one of the following grounds[6]:

(1)   that the particulars of the candidate[7] or of the persons subscribing the paper[8] are not as required by law[9];

(2)   that the paper is not subscribed as so required[10]; and

(3)   in the case of a parliamentary election, that the candidate is disqualified by the Representation of the People Act 1981[11].

At a London Authority election[12], the returning officer[13] is entitled to hold an individual nomination paper[14] invalid only on the grounds[15] that the particulars of the candidate on the nomination paper are not as required by law[16], or, additionally:

(a)   in the case of a London Mayoral election, that the particulars of the persons subscribing the paper[17] are not as required by law[18], or that the paper is not subscribed as so required[19]; and

(b)   in the case of a London members or London Mayoral election, that the paper breaks one of the rules regarding any description of the candidate that is likely to lead electors to associate the candidate with one or more registered political parties[20].

The Greater London returning officer ('GLRO')is entitled to hold the nomination paper of a registered political party[21], however, invalid only on one of the following grounds[22]:

(i)   that the authorised description by which the registered party is to stand for election[23] is not a registered name or registered description of the party[24];

(ii)   that the nomination paper does not contain the statement[25], signed by the person issuing the paper, that it is issued either by the party's registered nominating officer[26], or on behalf of the party's registered nominating officer by a person authorised in writing by him[27];

(iii)   that the number of candidates on the list is greater than 25[28].

The GLRO must delete the name and address of any candidate included in a party list[29] whose particulars in that list are not as required by law[30], or whose consent to nomination is not delivered in the required manner[31].

At a Welsh Assembly constituency or regional election[32], the appropriate returning officer[33] is entitled to hold a constituency or individual nomination paper[34] invalid only on one of the following grounds[35]:

(A)   that the particulars of the candidate[36] are not as required by law[37];

(B)   that the paper is not subscribed as so required[38];

(C)   that the candidate is disqualified by the Representation of the People Act 1981[39]; or

(D)   that he is excluded from being such a candidate by the Government of Wales Act 2006[40].

At a regional election, the regional returning officer is entitled to hold a party nomination paper invalid only on one of the following grounds[41]:

(aa)   that it does not include the registered name or registered description of the party[42], or does not include the party list of candidates[43] submitted by the party[44];

(bb)   that the name so required is not duly authorised[45] or that the certificate authorising the name has not been combined with the party nomination paper[46] when it was delivered[47];

(cc)   that it is not subscribed as so required[48];

(dd)   that the party list includes more than 12 persons[49]; or

(ee)   that each candidate included on the party list has ceased to stand nominated[50].

The returning officer at a European parliamentary election[51] is entitled to hold a nomination paper of an individual candidate[52] invalid only on the ground that the particulars of the candidate are not as required by law[53] or on the ground that the candidate is disqualified by the Representation of the People Act 1981[54]. The returning officer is entitled to hold a nomination paper of a registered party[55], together with the list of candidates accompanying it[56], invalid only on the ground that the contents of the nomination paper are not as required by law[57], or on the ground that the number of candidates in the list exceeds the number of members of the European Parliament ('MEPs') to be elected in the electoral region at the election[58]. The returning officer must delete from such a list the name and address of any candidate whose particulars are not as required by law[59], where the consent to nomination of any such candidate is not delivered in accordance with the rules[60], or where any such candidate is a relevant citizen of the Union[61], and the required declaration and certificate have not been duly delivered[62].

1   As to the meaning of 'candidate' generally see PARA 230.
2   As to the meaning of 'parliamentary election' see PARA 9.
3   Ie an election of councillors for any electoral area (and, usually, any London Authority election), with general references to 'local government election' being taken to include a local authority mayoral election: see PARA 11. As to the meanings of 'Authority election ' and 'electoral area' see PARA 11. As to the election of councillors for local government principal areas see PARA 197 et seq; as to elections for the return of a local authority mayor see PARA 198; as to London Authority elections see PARA 199 et seq; and as to the ordinary elections of parish or community councillors see PARA 200 et seq.
4   As to the returning officer for parliamentary elections and the performance of his duties see PARA 350 et seq; and as to returning officers for local government elections see PARA 354 et seq.
5   As to the nomination of candidates at an election see PARA 253 et seq.
6   Representation of the People Act 1983 Sch 1 r 12(2); Local Elections (Principal Areas) (England and Wales) Rules 2006, SI 2006/3304, Sch 2 r 8(2); Local Elections (Parishes and Communities) (England and Wales) Rules 2006, SI 2006/3305, Sch 2 r 8(2); Local Authorities (Mayoral Elections) (England and Wales) Regulations 2007, SI 2007/1024, Sch 1 r 11(2). As to a returning officer's decisions regarding the validity of nomination papers see PARA 264.
7   As to the particulars required in nomination papers see PARA 256.
8   As to the subscription of nomination papers see PARA 257.
9   Representation of the People Act 1983 Sch 1 r 12(2)(a); Local Elections (Principal Areas) (England and Wales) Rules 2006, SI 2006/3304, Sch 2 r 8(2)(a); Local Elections (Parishes and Communities) (England and Wales) Rules 2006, SI 2006/3305, Sch 2 r 8(2)(a); Local Authorities (Mayoral Elections) (England and Wales) Regulations 2007, SI 2007/1024, Sch 1 r 11(2)(a).
    When considering whether to hold a nomination paper invalid on this ground, the returning officer's duty includes, if he so wishes, a check to see whether the electoral numbers of those who propose, second and assent to the nomination as given on the nomination paper are the same as those numbers as given in the register of electors: see *Greenway-Stanley v Paterson* [1977] 2 All ER 663 at 670, DC, per O'Connor J. However, the returning officer is not entitled to investigate the facts underlying a name given in the particulars which, on their face, are unobjectionable (*Greenway-Stanley v Paterson* at 670 per O'Connor J) or an address which is given (*R v Election Court, ex p Sheppard* [1975] 2 All ER 723, [1975] 1 WLR 1319, DC). A possible exception might arise where the nomination on its face puts the returning officer on enquiry: *Greenway-Stanley v Paterson* at 671 per Wien J (who nevertheless expressly disapproved the view in *Re Melton Mowbray (Egerton Ward) UDC Election* [1969] 1 QB 192 at 198, [1968] 3 All ER 761 at 763, DC, per Paull J, that the returning officer has the

opportunity to make such enquiries as he may think right). A returning officer at a parliamentary election may correct obvious spelling mistakes in the candidate's details or minor errors as to a person's electoral number: see PARA 265.

The phrase 'as required by law' may be assumed to refer to the law relating to nomination at elections, although in *Sanders v Chichester* [1995] 03 LS Gaz R 37, (1994) Times, 2 December, a case considering a potentially misleading party description used at a European parliamentary election before such matters were regulated (see PARA 253), the phrase was given a wider meaning to embrace descriptions that might contravene the general law or involve the returning officer in a breach of the law (where, for instance, the particulars given were obscene, racist or an incitement to crime). The scope for particulars of the candidate or of persons subscribing the paper to be 'not as required by law' in this wider sense seems limited, although false, deliberately misleading or mischievously-chosen particulars may constitute a fraudulent device or contrivance under the Representation of the People Act 1983 s 115(2)(b) (see PARA 723).

Where a person is twice nominated, once by a nomination paper with correct and once by a nomination paper with incorrect particulars, the incorrect nomination does not avoid the correct nomination: *Northcote v Pulsford* (1875) LR 10 CP 476; and see PARA 267.

10 Representation of the People Act 1983 Sch 1 r 12(2)(b); Local Elections (Principal Areas) (England and Wales) Rules 2006, SI 2006/3304, Sch 2 r 8(2)(b); Local Elections (Parishes and Communities) (England and Wales) Rules 2006, SI 2006/3305, Sch 2 r 8(2)(b); Local Authorities (Mayoral Elections) (England and Wales) Regulations 2007, SI 2007/1024, Sch 1 r 11(2)(b).

11 Representation of the People Act 1983 Sch 1 r 12(2)(c). If it appears to the returning officer that any of the persons nominated might be disqualified by the Representation of the People Act 1981, he must, as soon as practicable after the expiry of the time allowed for the delivery of nomination papers, prepare and publish a draft of the statement required under the Representation of the People Act 1983 Sch 1 r 14 (statement of persons nominated: see PARA 267): Sch 1 r 15(1). The draft must be headed 'Draft statement of persons nominated' and it must omit the names of the persons subscribing the papers but must contain a notice stating that any person who wishes to object to the nomination of any candidate on the ground that he is disqualified for nomination under the Representation of the People Act 1981 may do so between the hours of ten in the morning and four in the afternoon on the day and at the place specified in the notice: Representation of the People Act 1983 Sch 1 r 15(2). The day so specified is to be the day next after the last day for the delivery of nomination papers: Sch 1 para 15(2).

Under the Representation of the People Act 1981, a person found guilty of one or more offences, whether before or after 2 July 1981 (ie the date on which the Act received Royal Assent) and whether in the United Kingdom or elsewhere, and sentenced or ordered to be imprisoned or detained indefinitely, or for more than one year, is disqualified for membership of the House of Commons while detained anywhere in the British Islands or the Republic of Ireland in pursuance of the sentence or order or while unlawfully at large at a time when he would otherwise be so detained: s 1. See note 39. If such a person is nominated for election as a member of the House of Commons, his nomination is void: s 2(1). 'British Islands' means the United Kingdom, the Channel Islands and the Isle of Man: Interpretation Act 1978 s 5, Sch 1. There is no statutory definition of the 'Channel Islands'. As to the meaning of 'United Kingdom' see PARA 1 note 1. As to the effect of disqualification under the Representation of the People Act 1981 see PARLIAMENT vol 78 (2010) PARA 902.

12 Ie at a London constituency members election, a London members election, or a London Mayoral election. As to the meaning of 'London member' see PARA 11 note 5; definition applied by virtue of the Greater London Authority Elections Rules 2007, SI 2007/3541, r 2(2). As to the meaning of 'constituency member', in relation to the London Assembly, see PARA 11 note 6; definition applied by virtue of r 2(2).

13 In elections for the return of constituency members of the London Assembly, any reference to the returning officer is to the constituency returning officer ('CRO') (see the Greater London Authority Elections Rules 2007, SI 2007/3541, Sch 1 r 9(2)); in other London Assembly elections (ie for London members and in the case of a London Mayoral election), the reference is to the Greater London returning officer ('GLRO') (see Sch 2 r 11(2), (4)–(6), Sch 3 r 10(2), (2A)). As to the meaning of the 'Greater London returning officer' see PARA 211 note 8; and as to the meaning of the 'constituency returning officer' in this context see PARA 211 note 9.

14 Ie an individual nomination paper for a London members election (see the Greater London Authority Elections Rules 2007, SI 2007/3541, Sch 2 r 9(4)), or simply a nomination paper for either a London constituency members or London Mayoral election (see Sch 1 r 9(2), Sch 3 r 10(2)). As to references to nomination papers in elections for the return of London members of the London Assembly see PARA 260 note 18.

15 See the Greater London Authority Elections Rules 2007, SI 2007/3541, Sch 1 r 9(2), Sch 2 r 11(4), Sch 3 r 10(2).

16 Greater London Authority Elections Rules 2007, SI 2007/3541, Sch 1 r 9(2)(a), Sch 2 r 11(4), Sch 3 r 10(2)(a).

17 The nomination paper of a candidate for a London mayoral election must be subscribed by at least 330 persons entitled to vote at the election, who must not subscribe more than one such nomination paper at the same election: see the Greater London Authority Elections Rules 2007, SI 2007/3541, Sch 3 r 7(1), (3A); and PARA 257. No subscription of a nomination paper is required at the election of constituency members or London members of the London Assembly: see PARA 257.

18 Greater London Authority Elections Rules 2007, SI 2007/3541, Sch 3 r 10(2)(a).

19 Greater London Authority Elections Rules 2007, SI 2007/3541, Sch 3 r 10(2)(b). If, contrary to Sch 3 r 7(3A) (see note 17; and PARA 257), a person subscribes more than one nomination paper the GLRO, in determining whether a paper is subscribed as so required under Sch 3 r 10(2)(b) must only take the person's signature into account in respect of the first nomination paper delivered under Sch 3 r 6(1)(b) (see PARA 260) on which the person's signature appears, and must, where the person's signature appears on a nomination paper delivered subsequently, find that the paper is not subscribed as so required if the signature appears within the first 330 signatures on the paper, regardless of whether the paper contains more than 330 signatures: see Sch 3 r 10(2A) (added by SI 2012/198).

20 Greater London Authority Elections Rules 2007, SI 2007/3541, Sch 1 r 9(2)(b), Sch 3 r 10(2)(c). Head (b) in the text refers to a nomination paper that:
    (1)   at a London constituency members election, breaks Sch 1 r 6(5), (7) (see PARA 256) (see Sch 1 r 9(2)(b));
    (2)   at a London Mayoral election, breaks Sch 3 r 6(5), (7) (see PARA 256) (see Sch 3 r 10(2)(c)).
As to the consequences where a paper is found to break these rules see further PARA 264 note 8.

21 As to the meaning of 'registered political party' for these purposes see PARA 256 note 27.

22 Greater London Authority Elections Rules 2007, SI 2007/3541, Sch 2 r 11(5).

23 Ie the authorised description stated under the Greater London Authority Elections Rules 2007, SI 2007/3541, Sch 2 r 7(2)(a) (see PARA 256): see Sch 2 r 11(5)(a).

24 Greater London Authority Elections Rules 2007, SI 2007/3541, Sch 2 r 11(5)(a). The text refers to a description stated under Sch 2 r 7(2)(a) that breaches Sch 2 r 7(3) (see PARA 256): see Sch 2 r 11(5)(a).

25 Ie the statement referred to in the Greater London Authority Elections Rules 2007, SI 2007/3541, Sch 2 r 7(2)(b) (see PARA 256): see Sch 2 r 11(5)(b).

26 As to the registered nominating officer of a party see PARA 253.

27 Greater London Authority Elections Rules 2007, SI 2007/3541, Sch 2 r 11(5)(b).

28 Greater London Authority Elections Rules 2007, SI 2007/3541, Sch 2 r 11(5)(c).

29 Ie supplementary to the grounds that:
    (1)   proof is given to the GLRO's satisfaction of the candidate's death (see the Greater London Authority Elections Rules 2007, SI 2007/3541, Sch 2 r 11(6)(a); and PARA 262);
    (2)   the candidate withdraws, or his candidature is withdrawn in accordance with Sch 2 r 15 (see PARA 266) (see Sch 2 r 11(6)(b); and PARA 262).
The GLRO must, as soon as practicable after each nomination paper has been delivered, examine it and decide whether each candidate included in a registered party's list has been validly nominated: see Sch 2 r 11(3). As to references to party lists in elections for the return of London members of the London Assembly see PARA 255 note 23.

30 Greater London Authority Elections Rules 2007, SI 2007/3541, Sch 2 r 11(6)(c).

31 Greater London Authority Elections Rules 2007, SI 2007/3541, Sch 2 r 11(6)(d). The reference in the text is to delivery of the consent to nomination in accordance with Sch 2 r 9 (see PARA 258): see Sch 2 r 11(6)(d).

32 As to the meanings of 'Assembly election', and 'constituency election' and 'regional election', in relation to a Welsh Assembly election, see PARA 3 note 2.

33 For these purposes, 'appropriate returning officer' means a constituency returning officer in relation to a constituency election and a regional returning officer in relation to a regional election: see the National Assembly for Wales (Representation of the People) Order 2007, SI 2007/236, art 2(1); and PARA 18 note 2. As to the meanings of 'constituency returning officer' and 'regional returning officer' see PARA 18 note 2.

34 At a Welsh Assembly constituency election, the reference is to a constituency nomination paper and, at a Welsh Assembly regional election, the reference is to an individual nomination paper:

see the National Assembly for Wales (Representation of the People) Order 2007, SI 2007/236, Sch 5 para 13 (heading). As to the meanings of 'constituency nomination paper' and 'individual nomination paper' see PARA 256.

35 See the National Assembly for Wales (Representation of the People) Order 2007, SI 2007/236, Sch 5 para 13(2).

36 The National Assembly for Wales (Representation of the People) Order 2007, SI 2007/236, Sch 5 para 13 applies to both a constituency candidate and an individual candidate: Sch 5 para 13(9). As to the meanings of 'constituency candidate' at a Welsh Assembly constituency election, and 'individual candidate' at a Welsh Assembly regional election, see PARA 230 note 19.

37 National Assembly for Wales (Representation of the People) Order 2007, SI 2007/236, Sch 5 para 13(2)(a). Head (A) in the text includes the ground, at a constituency election, that a nomination paper breaches Sch 5 para 5(1) or Sch 5 para 5(13) (candidate unduly associated with one or more registered political parties: see PARA 256): see Sch 5 para 13(2)(a). As to the consequences where a paper is found to break these rules see further PARA 264 note 18.

38 National Assembly for Wales (Representation of the People) Order 2007, SI 2007/236, Sch 5 para 13(2)(b).

39 National Assembly for Wales (Representation of the People) Order 2007, SI 2007/236, Sch 5 para 13(2)(c). If it appears to the appropriate returning officer that any person nominated as a constituency candidate or as an individual candidate or as a party list candidate might be disqualified by the Representation of the People Act 1981 (as it is applied and modified by the Government of Wales Act 2006 s 16(3): see PARA 227 note 17), he must, as soon as practicable after the expiry of the time allowed for the delivery of constituency nomination papers (at a constituency election), or for the delivery of individual nomination papers or party nomination papers (in the case of a regional election), prepare and publish a draft of the statement required by the National Assembly for Wales (Representation of the People) Order 2007, SI 2007/236, Sch 5 para 16 or Sch 5 para 17 (statements of parties and other persons nominated: see PARA 267): Sch 5 para 19(1). The draft must be headed (in the case of a constituency election) 'Draft statement of persons nominated/datganiad drafft o'r personau a enwebwyd' or (in the case of a regional election) 'Draft statement of registered political parties and other persons nominated/datganiad drafft y pleidiau gwleidyddol cofrestredig a phobl eraill a enwebwyd', and it must contain a notice stating that any person who wishes to object to the nomination of any candidate on the ground that he is disqualified for nomination under the Representation of the People Act 1981 (as so applied and modified) may do so between the hours of ten in the morning and four in the afternoon on the day and at the place specified in the notice: National Assembly for Wales (Representation of the People) Order 2007, SI 2007/236, Sch 5 para 19(2). The day to be so specified is the day next after the last day for the delivery nomination papers: see Sch 5 para 19(2). As to the meaning of 'party nomination paper' see PARA 255. As to the meanings of 'party list' and 'party list candidate' at a Welsh Assembly regional election see PARA 230 note 23.

40 National Assembly for Wales (Representation of the People) Order 2007, SI 2007/236, Sch 5 para 13(2)(d), (e), (8). Head (D) in the text refers to candidature that is in breach of either:

(1)	the Government of Wales Act 2006 s 7(6) (ie a person may not be an individual candidate at a region election if he is included on a list submitted by a registered political party for the Assembly electoral region or another Assembly electoral region, is an individual candidate to be an Assembly regional member for another Assembly electoral region, or is a candidate to be the Assembly constituency member for an Assembly constituency: see PARA 227) (see the National Assembly for Wales (Representation of the People) Order 2007, SI 2007/236, Sch 5 para 13(2)(d), (8)); or

(2)	the Government of Wales Act 2006 s 7(1) or 10(9) (ie a person may not be a candidate to be the Assembly constituency member for more than one Assembly constituency, and may not be a candidate in a constituency election to fill a vacancy if the person is an Assembly member, or is a candidate in another such election: see PARAS 214, 227) (see the National Assembly for Wales (Representation of the People) Order 2007, SI 2007/236, Sch 5 para 13(2)(e), (8)).

As to the meanings of 'Assembly constituency' and 'Assembly electoral region' see PARA 3 note 2.

41 See the National Assembly for Wales (Representation of the People) Order 2007, SI 2007/236, Sch 5 para 14(2).

42 Ie the party nomination paper breaches the National Assembly for Wales (Representation of the People) Order 2007, SI 2007/236, Sch 5 para 7(2) (see PARA 256): see Sch 5 para 14(2)(a).

43 Ie the party nomination paper breaches the National Assembly for Wales (Representation of the People) Order 2007, SI 2007/236, Sch 5 para 7(3) (see PARA 256): see Sch 5 para 14(2)(a).

44   See the National Assembly for Wales (Representation of the People) Order 2007, SI 2007/236, Sch 5 para 14(2)(a).

45   Ie the party nomination paper breaches the National Assembly for Wales (Representation of the People) Order 2007, SI 2007/236, Sch 5 para 8(1) (see PARA 256): see Sch 5 para 14(2)(b).

46   Ie the party nomination paper breaches the National Assembly for Wales (Representation of the People) Order 2007, SI 2007/236, Sch 5 para 8(3) (see PARA 256): see Sch 5 para 14(2)(b).

47   National Assembly for Wales (Representation of the People) Order 2007, SI 2007/236, Sch 5 para 14(2)(b).

48   National Assembly for Wales (Representation of the People) Order 2007, SI 2007/236, Sch 5 para 14(2)(c).

49   National Assembly for Wales (Representation of the People) Order 2007, SI 2007/236, Sch 5 para 14(2)(d).

50   National Assembly for Wales (Representation of the People) Order 2007, SI 2007/236, Sch 5 para 14(2)(e). Head (ee) in the text refers to each candidate having ceased to stand nominated in accordance with Sch 5 para 14(3) and Sch 5 para 14(4): see Sch 5 para 14(2)(e). Where, in respect of a party list candidate at a Welsh Assembly regional election, proof is given, to the regional returning officer's satisfaction, of his death, or if he withdraws or his candidature is withdrawn in accordance with Sch 5 r 15(4) (see PARA 266), the candidate automatically ceases to stand nominated: see Sch 5 r 14(3); and PARA 262. The regional returning officer is entitled to hold that a party list candidate ceases to stand nominated, however, where (see Sch 5 para 14(4)):

     (1)   the candidate's particulars are not as required by law (Sch 5 para 14(4)(a)); or

     (2)   he is disqualified by the Representation of the People Act 1981 (see note 39) (National Assembly for Wales (Representation of the People) Order 2007, SI 2007/236, Sch 5 para 14(4)(b)); or

     (3)   his candidatures is in breach of the Government of Wales Act 2006 s 7(5) (ie a party list may not include a person who is included on any other list submitted for the Assembly electoral region or any list submitted for another Assembly electoral region, who is an individual candidate to be an Assembly regional member for the Assembly electoral region or another Assembly electoral region, or who is a candidate to be the Assembly constituency member for an Assembly constituency: see PARA 227) (National Assembly for Wales (Representation of the People) Order 2007, SI 2007/236, Sch 5 para 14(4)(c), (11)).

Where a party list candidate ceases to stand nominated by virtue of Sch 5 para 14(4), (11), it does not of itself prevent any other candidate included on the party list from continuing to stand nominated: Sch 5 para 14(5).

51   As to European parliamentary elections see PARA 217 et seq; and as to returning officers at European parliamentary elections see PARA 360 et seq.

52   As to the meaning of 'individual candidate' at a European parliamentary election see PARA 230 note 32.

53   See the European Parliamentary Elections Regulations 2004, SI 2004/293, Sch 1 para 13(3)(a) (Sch 1 substituted by SI 2009/186).

54   See the European Parliamentary Elections Regulations 2004, SI 2004/293, Sch 1 para 13(3)(b) (as substituted: see note 53). The text refers to the Representation of the People Act 1981 as it applies in respect of the office of member of the European Parliament ('MEP') by virtue of the European Parliamentary Elections Act 2002 s 10(1)(a) (see PARA 228), and, for the purposes of the combined region (as to which see PARA 77), the text includes disqualification under any corresponding provision in respect of detained offenders in Gibraltar made under s 10(4A) (Secretary of State may by order provide for persons of a description connected to Gibraltar to be disqualified from the office of MEP: see PARA 228): see the European Parliamentary Elections Regulations 2004, SI 2004/293, Sch 1 para 13(3)(b) (as so substituted).

     If it appears to the returning officer that any of the persons nominated as an individual candidate might be disqualified by the Representation of the People Act 1981 (as so applied), or by any corresponding provision so made in respect of Gibraltar, he must, as soon as practicable after the expiry of the time allowed for the delivery of nomination papers, prepare and publish a draft of that part of the statement of parties and individual candidates nominated as is required by the European Parliamentary Elections Regulations 2004, SI 2004/293, Sch 1 para 15(1)(b) (see PARA 267): Sch 1 para 18(1) (as so substituted). The draft must be headed 'Draft statement of individual candidates nominated' and it must contain a notice stating that any person who wishes to object to the nomination of any individual candidate on the ground that he is disqualified for nomination under the Representation of the People Act 1981 (as so applied), or under any corresponding provision so made in respect of Gibraltar, may do so between the hours of ten in the morning and four in the afternoon on the day and at the place specified in the notice: European Parliamentary Elections Regulations 2004, SI 2004/293, Sch 1 para 18(2) (as so substituted). The day to be so specified is the day after the last day for the delivery of nomination papers: see Sch 1 para 18(2) (as so substituted). As to the meaning of 'statement of parties and individual candidates nominated' see PARA 267 note 3.

55 As to the meaning of 'registered party' for these purposes see PARA 230 note 29.
56 Ie the list of a registered political party's candidates that must accompany its nomination paper under the European Parliamentary Elections Regulations 2004, SI 2004/293, Sch 1 para 7: see PARA 256. As to the meaning of 'list' for these purposes see PARA 230 note 29.
57 See the European Parliamentary Elections Regulations 2004, SI 2004/293, Sch 1 para 13(4)(a) (as substituted: see note 53).
58 See the European Parliamentary Elections Regulations 2004, SI 2004/293, Sch 1 para 13(4)(b) (as substituted: see note 53). The text refers to the number of candidates in the list breaching Sch 1 para 7(1) (see PARA 256): see Sch 1 para 13(4)(b) (as so substituted). As to the establishment of electoral regions for the purpose of elections to the European Parliament see PARA 77.
59 See the European Parliamentary Elections Regulations 2004, SI 2004/293, Sch 1 para 13(5)(a) (as substituted: see note 53).
60 See the European Parliamentary Elections Regulations 2004, SI 2004/293, Sch 1 para 13(5)(b) (as substituted: see note 53).
61 As to the meaning of 'relevant citizen of the Union' for these purposes see PARA 149 note 16.
62 See the European Parliamentary Elections Regulations 2004, SI 2004/293, Sch 1 para 13(5)(c) (as substituted: see note 53). The text refers to the declaration and certificate duly delivered under Sch 1 para 9(2), (3) where the candidate at a European parliamentary election is a relevant citizen of the Union (see PARA 229): see Sch 1 para 13(5)(c) (as so substituted).

264. Returning officer's decisions regarding the validity of nomination papers. The returning officer at a parliamentary election[1] must give his decision on any objection to a nomination paper[2]:

(1) as soon as practicable after it is made[3]; and

(2) in any event, before the end of the period of 24 hours starting with the close of the period for delivery of nomination papers[4].

At a local government election[5], the returning officer[6] is obliged to examine each nomination paper as soon as practicable after it has been delivered and then decide whether the candidate (and, in the case of a London members election, each registered party and each candidate included on that party's list[7]) has been validly nominated[8].

The appropriate returning officer at a Welsh Assembly constituency or regional election[9], must give his decision on any objection to a constituency nomination paper[10], individual nomination paper[11], party nomination paper[12], or party list candidate[13]:

(a) as soon as practicable after it is made[14]; and

(b) in any event, before the end of the period of 24 hours starting with the close of the period for delivery of nomination papers[15].

The returning officer at a European parliamentary election[16] must give his decision on any objection to a nomination paper:

(i) as soon as practicable after it is made[17]; and

(ii) in any event, before the end of the period of 24 hours starting with the close of the period for delivery of nomination papers[18].

Where the returning officer[19] decides that a nomination paper[20] is invalid, he must endorse on the paper that fact and the reasons for his decision, and he must sign the paper[21]; and, where he deletes any name from the list of candidates of a registered party[22], he must endorse that fact on the nomination paper also, and the reasons for his decision, and he also must sign the paper[23].

The returning officer's decision on the validity of a nomination paper (or accompanying party list or party list candidature, where applicable)[24] is final and must not be questioned in any proceeding whatsoever[25], except that nothing in the provisions that allow a returning officer to decide on the validity of a nomination prevents the validity of a nomination being questioned on an election petition[26].

1   As to the meaning of 'parliamentary election' see PARA 9. As to the returning officer for parliamentary elections and the performance of his duties see PARA 350 et seq.

2   See the Representation of the People Act 1983 Sch 1 r 12(3) (amended by the Registration of Political Parties Act 1998 s 13, Sch 2 para 3(2)).
    The extent of the returning officer's jurisdiction in relation to objections to a nomination paper which have not been specifically raised by persons attending the nomination is not clear. In *R v Taylor* (1895) 59 JP 393 (a municipal election case), Lord Russell CJ said that it was not the duty of the returning officer to look for objections and still less to point out possible objections to rival candidates for that would shake the confidence which the electors ought to have in his impartiality. At local government elections, there is no provision for candidates to attend the nomination and to object, and the obligation on the returning officer to examine the nomination papers and to satisfy himself that they are valid is more explicitly stated: see the text and notes 5–8.

3   Representation of the People Act 1983 Sch 1 r 12(3)(a) (Sch 1 r 12(3)(a), (b) added by the Electoral Administration Act 2006 s 19(1), (6)). In the case of a parliamentary general election or by-election, objections to nomination papers must be made during the hours allowed for delivery of nomination papers on the last day for their delivery and the hour following: Representation of the People Act 1983 Sch 1 r 1. However, no objection may be made in the afternoon of that last day except to a nomination paper delivered within 24 hours of the last time for its delivery and, in the case of a nomination paper so delivered, no objection may be so made to the sufficiency or nature of the particulars of a candidate unless made at or immediately after the time of the delivery of the nomination paper: Sch 1 r 1(a). This timetable does not apply to objections made in pursuance of Sch 1 r 15(2) (disqualification under the Representation of the People Act 1981: see PARA 263 note 11), however, for which separate provision is made: Representation of the People Act 1983 Sch 1 r 1(b). See also note 4.

4   Representation of the People Act 1983 Sch 1 r 12(3)(b) (as added: see note 3). The provision made by Sch 1 r 12(3) is subject to Sch 1 r 12(3A): see Sch 1 r 12(3) (as amended: see note 2). Accordingly, if, in the returning officer's opinion, a nomination paper breaks the rule in Sch 1 r 6A(1) or Sch 1 r 6A(1B) (candidate associated with a registered political party: see PARA 256), he must give a decision to that effect as soon as practicable after delivery of the nomination paper and, in any event, before the end of the period of 24 hours starting with the close of the period for delivery of nomination papers set out in Sch 1 r 1 (see PARA 260): see Sch 1 r 12(3A) (added by the Registration of Political Parties Act 1998 s 13, Sch 2 para 3(3); amended by the Electoral Administration Act 2006 ss 19(1), (7), 74(1), Sch 1 paras 104, 130). As to the delivery of nomination papers see PARA 260.

5   Ie an election of councillors for any electoral area, or any London Authority election, with general references to 'local government election' being taken to include a local authority mayoral election: see PARA 11. As to the meanings of 'Authority election ' and 'electoral area' see PARA 11. As to the election of councillors for local government principal areas see PARA 197 et seq; as to elections for the return of a local authority mayor see PARA 198; as to London Authority elections see PARA 199 et seq; and as to the ordinary elections of parish or community councillors see PARA 200 et seq.

6   As to returning officers for local government elections see PARA 354 et seq. In elections for the return of constituency members of the London Assembly, any reference to the returning officer is to the constituency returning officer ('CRO') (see the Greater London Authority Elections Rules 2007, SI 2007/3541, Sch 1 r 9(3), (4)); in other London Assembly elections (ie for London members and in the case of a London Mayoral election), the reference is to the Greater London returning officer ('GLRO') (see Sch 2 r 11(3), Sch 3 r 10(4)). As to the meaning of the 'Greater London returning officer' see PARA 211 note 8; and as to the meaning of the 'constituency returning officer' in this context see PARA 211 note 9.

7   As to references to party lists in elections for the return of London members of the London Assembly see PARA 255 note 23. As to the meaning of 'registered political party' for these purposes see PARA 256 note 27.

8   Local Elections (Principal Areas) (England and Wales) Rules 2006, SI 2006/3304, Sch 2 r 8(3); Local Elections (Parishes and Communities) (England and Wales) Rules 2006, SI 2006/3305, Sch 2 r 8(3); Local Authorities (Mayoral Elections) (England and Wales) Regulations 2007, SI 2007/1024, Sch 1 r 11(3); Greater London Authority Elections Rules 2007, SI 2007/3541,

Sch 1 r 9(3), Sch 2 r 11(3), Sch 3 r 10(3). This is subject to the proviso that, where the returning officer is entitled to hold a nomination paper invalid on the ground that, in his opinion, the nomination paper:

(1)   at an election of councillors for local government principal areas, breaks the Local Elections (Principal Areas) (England and Wales) Rules 2006, SI 2006/3304, Sch 2 r 5(1) or Sch 2 r 5(3) (candidate unduly associated with one or more registered political parties: see PARA 256) (see Sch 2 r 8(4));

(2)   at an ordinary election of parish or community councillors, breaks the Local Elections (Parishes and Communities) (England and Wales) Rules 2006, SI 2006/3305, Sch 2 r 5(1) or Sch 2 r 5(3) (candidate unduly associated with one or more registered political parties: see PARA 256) (see Sch 2 r 8(4));

(3)   at an election for the return of a local authority mayor, breaks the Local Authorities (Mayoral Elections) (England and Wales) Regulations 2007, SI 2007/1024, Sch 1 r 7(1) or Sch 1 r 7(3) (candidate unduly associated with one or more registered political parties: see PARA 256) (see Sch 1 r 11(4));

(4)   at a London constituency members election, breaks the Greater London Authority Elections Rules 2007, SI 2007/3541, Sch 1 r 6(5) or Sch 1 r 6(7) (candidate unduly associated with one or more registered political parties: see PARA 256) (see Sch 1 r 9(4));

(5)   at a London Mayoral election, breaks Sch 3 r 6(5) or Sch 3 r 6(7) (candidate unduly associated with one or more registered political parties: see PARA 256) (see Sch 3 r 10(4)),

the returning officer must give a decision to that effect, as soon as practicable after the delivery of the nomination paper, and, in any event, before the end of the period of 24 hours starting with the close of the timetabled period for delivery of nomination papers (whichever period properly applies: see PARA 260): Local Elections (Principal Areas) (England and Wales) Rules 2006, SI 2006/3304, Sch 2 r 8(4); Local Elections (Parishes and Communities) (England and Wales) Rules 2006, SI 2006/3305, Sch 2 r 8(4); Local Authorities (Mayoral Elections) (England and Wales) Regulations 2007, SI 2007/1024, Sch 1 r 11(4); Greater London Authority Elections Rules 2007, SI 2007/3541, Sch 1 r 9(4), Sch 3 r 10(4). At a London members election, the GLRO is entitled to hold an individual nomination paper invalid only on the grounds that the particulars of the candidate on the nomination paper are not as required by law: see Sch 2 r 11(4); and PARA 263. Where, however, in the GLRO's opinion, the nomination paper of a registered party at such an election is invalid on the grounds that:

(a)   the authorised description stated under the Greater London Authority Elections Rules 2007, SI 2007/3541, Sch 2 r 7(2)(a) breaches Sch 2 r 7(3) (see PARA 256) (see Sch 2 r 11(5)(a), (9); and PARA 263); or

(b)   the nomination paper does not contain the statement referred to in Sch 2 r 7(2)(b) (see PARA 256) (see Sch 2 r 11(5)(b), (9); and PARA 263),

then he must give a decision to that effect, as soon as practicable after the delivery of the nomination paper, and, in any event, before the end of the period of 24 hours starting with the end of the period for the delivery of nomination papers set out in the timetable in Sch 2 r 3 (see PARA 260): see Sch 2 r 11(9).

9   For these purposes, 'appropriate returning officer' means a constituency returning officer in relation to a constituency election and a regional returning officer in relation to a regional election: see the National Assembly for Wales (Representation of the People) Order 2007, SI 2007/236, art 2(1); and PARA 18 note 2. As to the meanings of 'Assembly election', and 'constituency election' and 'regional election', in relation to a Welsh Assembly election, see PARA 3 note 2; and as to the meanings of 'constituency returning officer' and 'regional returning officer' see PARA 18 note 2.

10   As to the meaning of 'constituency nomination paper' see PARA 256.

11   As to the meaning of 'individual nomination paper' see PARA 256.

12   As to the meaning of 'party nomination paper' see PARA 255.

13   As to the meanings of 'party list' and 'party list candidate' at a Welsh Assembly regional election see PARA 230 note 23.

14   National Assembly for Wales (Representation of the People) Order 2007, SI 2007/236, Sch 5 paras 13(3)(a), 14(6)(a). At an Assembly election, objections to nomination papers must be made during the hours allowed for delivery of nomination papers on the last day for their delivery and the hour following: Sch 5 para 1(1). However, no objection may be made in the afternoon of that last day except to a nomination paper delivered within 24 hours of the last time for its delivery and, in the case of a nomination paper so delivered, no objection may be so made to the sufficiency or nature of the particulars of a candidate unless made at or immediately after the time of the delivery of the nomination paper: Sch 5 para 1(1)(a). The timetable set out in Sch 5 para 1 does not apply to objections made under Sch 5 para 19(2) (disqualification

under the Representation of the People Act 1981: see PARA 263 note 39), for which separate provision is made: National Assembly for Wales (Representation of the People) Order 2007, SI 2007/236, Sch 5 para 1(1)(b). For these purposes, the making of an objection to a party nomination paper includes the making of an objection to the nomination of any party list candidate on the list of candidates accompanying a party nomination paper (see PARA 255): see Sch 5 para 1(2).

15 National Assembly for Wales (Representation of the People) Order 2007, SI 2007/236, Sch 5 paras 13(3)(b), 14(6)(b). Although Sch 5 para 13 applies to both a constituency candidate and an individual candidate, Sch 5 para 13(3) specifies the period for delivery of constituency nomination papers set out in Sch 5 para 1(1) (which does not in fact make a distinction between the nomination papers: see PARA 260): see Sch 5 para 13(3). As to the meanings of 'constituency candidate' at a Welsh Assembly constituency election, and 'individual candidate' at a Welsh Assembly regional election, see PARA 230 note 19.

If, in the constituency returning officer's opinion, an individual nomination paper breaches Sch 5 para 5(1) or Sch 5 para 5(3) (candidate unduly associated with one or more registered political parties: see PARA 256), or if, in the regional returning officer's opinion, a party nomination paper breaches Sch 5 para 7(2) (authorised description by which the registered party is to stand for election is not a registered name or registered description of the party: see PARA 256), Sch 5 para 8(1) (name or description of the party not duly authorised: see PARA 256) or Sch 5 para 8(3) (certificate authorising party name or description not combined with party nomination paper: see PARA 256), he must give a decision to that effect as soon as practicable after the delivery of the nomination paper (see PARA 260), and, in any event, before the end of the period of 24 hours starting with the close of the period for delivery of nomination papers: see Sch 5 paras 13(4), 14(7).

16 As to European parliamentary elections see PARA 217 et seq; and as to returning officers at European parliamentary elections see PARA 360 et seq.

17 European Parliamentary Elections Regulations 2004, SI 2004/293, Sch 1 para 13(6)(a) (Sch 1 substituted by SI 2009/186). Objections to nomination papers or to the list of candidates of a registered party must be made during the hours allowed for delivery of nomination papers and list of candidates on the last day for their delivery and the hour following: European Parliamentary Elections Regulations 2004, SI 2004/293, Sch 1 para 1 (as so substituted). However, no objection may be made in the afternoon of that last day except to a nomination paper delivered within 24 hours of the last time for its delivery and, in the case of a nomination paper so delivered, no objection may be so made to the sufficiency or nature of the particulars of a registered party or candidate on the party's list or individual candidate unless made at or immediately after the time of the delivery of the nomination paper: Sch 1 para 1(a) (as so substituted). The timetable set out in Sch 1 para 1 does not apply to objections made in pursuance of Sch 1 para 18(2) (disqualification under the Representation of the People Act 1981: see PARA 263 note 54), for which separate provision is made: European Parliamentary Elections Regulations 2004, SI 2004/293, Sch 1 para 1(b) (as so substituted). As to the meanings of 'registered political party' and 'list' for these purposes see PARA 230 note 29.

18 European Parliamentary Elections Regulations 2004, SI 2004/293, Sch 1 para 13(6)(b) (as substituted: see note 17). If, however, in the returning officer's opinion, a nomination paper breaches Sch 1 para 5(2) or Sch 1 para 5(4) (individual candidate unduly associated with one or more registered political parties: see PARA 256), he must give a decision to that effect as soon as practicable after the delivery of the nomination paper (see PARA 260), and, in any event, before the end of the period of 24 hours starting with the close of the period for delivery of nomination papers: Sch 1 para 13(7) (as so substituted).

19 See notes 1, 6, 9, 16.

20 In the case of an election for the return of London members of the London Assembly, the reference is to an individual nomination paper: see the Greater London Authority Elections Rules 2007, SI 2007/3541, Sch 2 r 11(7)(a). In the case of a Welsh Assembly election, the reference is to a constituency nomination paper or individual nomination paper (see the National Assembly for Wales (Representation of the People) Order 2007, SI 2007/236, Sch 5 para 13 (heading)); or to a party nomination paper (see Sch 5 para 14(8)(a)).

21 Representation of the People Act 1983 Sch 1 r 12(4) (amended by the Registration of Political Parties Act 1998 Sch 2 para 3(4)); European Parliamentary Elections Regulations 2004, SI 2004/293, Sch 1 para 13(8) (as substituted: see note 17); Local Elections (Principal Areas) (England and Wales) Rules 2006, SI 2006/3304, Sch 2 r 8(5); Local Elections (Parishes and Communities) (England and Wales) Rules 2006, SI 2006/3305, Sch 2 r 8(5); National Assembly for Wales (Representation of the People) Order 2007, SI 2007/236, Sch 5 paras 13(5), 14(8)(a);

Local Authorities (Mayoral Elections) (England and Wales) Regulations 2007, SI 2007/1024, Sch 1 r 11(5); Greater London Authority Elections Rules 2007, SI 2007/3541, Sch 1 r 9(5), Sch 2 r 11(7)(a), Sch 3 r 10(5).

The returning officer at a local government election also must send notice of his decision that a nomination paper is valid or invalid to each candidate at his home address as given in his nomination paper: Local Elections (Principal Areas) (England and Wales) Rules 2006, SI 2006/3304, Sch 2 r 8(6); Local Elections (Parishes and Communities) (England and Wales) Rules 2006, SI 2006/3305, Sch 2 r 8(6); Local Authorities (Mayoral Elections) (England and Wales) Regulations 2007, SI 2007/1024, Sch 1 r 11(6); Greater London Authority Elections Rules 2007, SI 2007/3541, Sch 1 r 9(6), Sch 2 r 11(8)(a), Sch 3 r 10(6) (amended by SI 2012/198). In the case of a party list candidate at a London members election, the notice of the decision referred to in the text must be sent also to the party's nominating officer: see the Greater London Authority Elections Rules 2007, SI 2007/3541, Sch 2 r 11(8)(b). As to the registered nominating officer of a party see PARA 253.

22 In the case of an election for the return of London members of the London Assembly, the reference is to deletion of a list candidate from the party list: see the Greater London Authority Elections Rules 2007, SI 2007/3541, Sch 2 r 11(7)(b). In the case of a Welsh Assembly regional election, the reference is to deletion of a candidate from a party list: see the National Assembly for Wales (Representation of the People) Order 2007, SI 2007/236, Sch 5 para 14(8)(b). In the case of a European parliamentary election, the reference is to deletion from the list of a registered political party's candidates that must accompany its nomination paper under the European Parliamentary Elections Regulations 2004, SI 2004/293, Sch 1 para 7: see PARA 256.

23 European Parliamentary Elections Regulations 2004, SI 2004/293, Sch 1 para 13(9) (as substituted: see note 17); National Assembly for Wales (Representation of the People) Order 2007, SI 2007/236, Sch 5 para 14(8)(b); Greater London Authority Elections Rules 2007, SI 2007/3541, Sch 2 r 11(7)(b).

24 In the case of a Welsh Assembly regional election, the regional returning officer's decision relates to whether a party nomination paper is valid (see the National Assembly for Wales (Representation of the People) Order 2007, SI 2007/236, Sch 5 para 14(9)(a)) or as to whether a candidate's name and address should not be removed from a party list (see Sch 5 para 14(9)(b)). In the case of a European parliamentary election, the returning officer's decision relates to whether a nomination paper and, where applicable, its accompanying list, is valid: see the European Parliamentary Elections Regulations 2004, SI 2004/293, Sch 1 para 13(10) (as substituted: see note 17).

25 Representation of the People Act 1983 Sch 1 r 12(5); European Parliamentary Elections Regulations 2004, SI 2004/293, Sch 1 para 13(10) (as substituted: see note 17); Local Elections (Principal Areas) (England and Wales) Rules 2006, SI 2006/3304, Sch 2 r 8(7); Local Elections (Parishes and Communities) (England and Wales) Rules 2006, SI 2006/3305, Sch 2 r 8(7); National Assembly for Wales (Representation of the People) Order 2007, SI 2007/236, Sch 5 paras 13(6), 14(9); Local Authorities (Mayoral Elections) (England and Wales) Regulations 2007, SI 2007/1024, Sch 1 r 11(7); Greater London Authority Elections Rules 2007, SI 2007/3541, Sch 1 r 9(7), Sch 2 r 11(10), Sch 3 r 10(7).

In *R v Election Court, ex p Sheppard* [1975] 2 All ER 723, [1975] 1 WLR 1319, DC, it was held that the validity of a nomination could be questioned before the election court where a nomination paper did not correctly state the candidate's home address, even though the returning officer did not declare the nomination paper invalid and the defect in the paper was not apparent on inspection; but cf *Watson v Ayton* [1946] KB 297.

26 Representation of the People Act 1983 Sch 1 r 12(6); European Parliamentary Elections Regulations 2004, SI 2004/293, Sch 1 para 13(11) (as substituted: see note 17); Local Elections (Principal Areas) (England and Wales) Rules 2006, SI 2006/3304, Sch 2 r 8(8); Local Elections (Parishes and Communities) (England and Wales) Rules 2006, SI 2006/3305, Sch 2 r 8(8); National Assembly for Wales (Representation of the People) Order 2007, SI 2007/236, Sch 5 paras 13(7), 14(10); Local Authorities (Mayoral Elections) (England and Wales) Regulations 2007, SI 2007/1024, Sch 1 r 11(8); Greater London Authority Elections Rules 2007, SI 2007/3541, Sch 1 r 9(8), Sch 2 r 11(11), Sch 3 r 10(8). See *R v Election Court, ex p Sheppard* [1975] 2 All ER 723, [1975] 1 WLR 1319, DC; *R v Acting Returning Officer for Devon, ex p Sanders* [1994] LG Rev 581, (1994) Times, 30 May (returning officer's decision regarding validity of nomination stood while electoral process in train; challenge should be made afterwards through channels provided and not pre-empted by an application for judicial review). As to election petitions see *Budge v Andrews* (1878) 3 CPD 510, DC; and see PARA 761 et seq.

265. Returning officer's duties with regard to nomination papers; power to correct minor errors. The returning officer's duties with regard to the validity of nomination papers[1] do not go beyond seeing that each form is correct on its face[2]; if the papers comply with the forms, it is no part of the returning officer's function to consider whether there are grounds for disqualifying the candidate (other than where the rules so provide)[3].

A returning officer[4] may, if he thinks fit, correct minor errors in a nomination paper (or party list, where applicable)[5], at any time before publication of the statement of persons (and parties) nominated[6]. Anything so done by a returning officer must not be questioned in any proceedings other than proceedings on an election petition[7].

1   See PARAS 262–264.
2   *R v Election Court, ex p Sheppard* [1975] 2 All ER 723 at 726, [1975] 1 WLR 1319 at 1324, DC, per Lord Widgery CJ. Nor do the rules alter the nominee's duty to present valid nomination papers in time by providing for any overall urgency or by raising a legitimate expectation that the returning officer will inspect the papers and identify any errors in them within the time limits: see *R (on the application of De Beer) v Balabanoff* [2002] EWHC 670 (Admin), (2002) Times, 25 April, [2002] All ER (D) 34 (Apr) (cited in PARA 256 note 8); applied in *R (on the application of Begum) v Tower Hamlets London Borough Council* [2006] EWCA Civ 733, [2006] LGR 674, [2006] All ER (D) 19 (May).
3   *Pritchard v Bangor Corpn* (1888) 13 App Cas 241, HL; *Watson v Ayton* [1946] KB 297. These cases pre-dated the grounds for disqualifying a candidate under the Representation of the People Act 1981, for which certain rules now provide: see PARAS 263 notes 11, 39, 54.
4   As to the returning officer for parliamentary elections and the performance of his duties see PARA 350 et seq; as to returning officers for local government elections see PARA 354 et seq; and as to returning officers at European parliamentary elections see PARA 360 et seq. In elections for the return of constituency members of the London Assembly, any reference to the returning officer is to the constituency returning officer ('CRO') (see the Greater London Authority Elections Rules 2007, SI 2007/3541, Sch 1 r 11(1), (3), (4)); in other London Assembly elections (ie for London members and in the case of a London Mayoral election), the reference is to the Greater London returning officer ('GLRO') (see Sch 2 r 13(1), (3), (4), Sch 3 r 12(1), (3), (4)). As to the meaning of the 'Greater London returning officer' see PARA 211 note 8; and as to the meaning of the 'constituency returning officer' in this context see PARA 211 note 9. At a Welsh Assembly election, the context requires reference to a constituency returning officer, in relation to a constituency election, and a regional returning officer, in relation to a regional election: see the National Assembly for Wales (Representation of the People) Order 2007, SI 2007/236, art 2(1); and PARA 18 note 2. As to the meanings of 'Assembly election', and 'constituency election' and 'regional election', in relation to a Welsh Assembly election, see PARA 3 note 2; and as to the meanings of 'constituency returning officer' and 'regional returning officer' see PARA 18 note 2.
5   See the Representation of the People Act 1983 Sch 1 r 14A(1) (Sch 1 r 14A added by the Electoral Administration Act 2006 s 19(1), (8); Representation of the People Act 1983 Sch 1 r 14A(1), (2) amended by the Political Parties and Elections Act 2009 s 39, Sch 6 para 8(1), (5)); European Parliamentary Elections Regulations 2004, SI 2004/293, Sch 1 para 16(1) (Sch 1 substituted by SI 2009/186); Local Elections (Principal Areas) (England and Wales) Rules 2006, SI 2006/3304, Sch 2 r 10(1); Local Elections (Parishes and Communities) (England and Wales) Rules 2006, SI 2006/3305, Sch 2 r 10(1); National Assembly for Wales (Representation of the People) Order 2007, SI 2007/236, Sch 5 para 18(1); Local Authorities (Mayoral Elections) (England and Wales) Regulations 2007, SI 2007/1024, Sch 1 r 14(1); Greater London Authority Elections Rules 2007, SI 2007/3541, Sch 1 r 11(1), Sch 2 r 13(1), Sch 3 r 12(1). At a parliamentary election, the power to correct minor errors extends to a home address form: see the Representation of the People Act 1983 Sch 1 r 14A(1) (as so added and amended). As to the requirement for a nomination paper at a parliamentary election to be accompanied by a home address form see PARA 256. At a Welsh Assembly regional election, the reference to a nomination paper includes a party list submitted with a party nomination paper: see the National Assembly for Wales (Representation of the People) Order 2007, SI 2007/236, Sch 5 para 18(1). As to the meanings of 'party list' and 'party list candidate' at a Welsh Assembly regional election see PARA 230 note 23. As to the meaning of 'party nomination paper' see PARA 255. In relation to a European parliamentary election, the reference to a party list is to the list of a registered political party's candidates that must accompany its nomination paper under the

European Parliamentary Elections Regulations 2004, SI 2004/293, Sch 1 para 7: see PARA 256. As to the meaning of 'list' for these purposes see PARA 230 note 29.

For these purposes, errors which may be corrected include errors as to a person's electoral number (except in relation to Welsh Assembly or European parliamentary election), and obvious errors of spelling in relation to the details of a candidate (or party, in the case of a London members, Welsh Assembly regional, or European parliamentary, election): see the Representation of the People Act 1983 Sch 1 r 14A(2) (as so added and amended); European Parliamentary Elections Regulations 2004, SI 2004/293, Sch 1 para 16(2) (as so substituted); Local Elections (Principal Areas) (England and Wales) Rules 2006, SI 2006/3304, Sch 2 r 10(2); Local Elections (Parishes and Communities) (England and Wales) Rules 2006, SI 2006/3305, Sch 2 r 10(2); National Assembly for Wales (Representation of the People) Order 2007, SI 2007/236, Sch 5 para 18(2); Local Authorities (Mayoral Elections) (England and Wales) Regulations 2007, SI 2007/1024, Sch 1 r 14(2); Greater London Authority Elections Rules 2007, SI 2007/3541, Sch 1 r 11(2), Sch 2 r 13(2), Sch 3 r 12(2). In relation to a parliamentary election, errors which may be corrected also include errors in the home address form as to the information mentioned in the Representation of the People Act 1983 Sch 1 r 6(5)(b) (location of candidate's address: see PARA 256): see Sch 1 r 14A(2) (as so added and amended). As to the meaning of 'electoral number' see PARA 145. As to the form and supply of nomination papers and the particulars required see PARA 255 et seq.

6   See the Representation of the People Act 1983 Sch 1 r 14A(1) (as added and amended: see note 5); European Parliamentary Elections Regulations 2004, SI 2004/293, Sch 1 para 16(1) (as substituted: see note 5); Local Elections (Principal Areas) (England and Wales) Rules 2006, SI 2006/3304, Sch 2 r 10(1); Local Elections (Parishes and Communities) (England and Wales) Rules 2006, SI 2006/3305, Sch 2 r 10(1); National Assembly for Wales (Representation of the People) Order 2007, SI 2007/236, Sch 5 para 18(1); Local Authorities (Mayoral Elections) (England and Wales) Regulations 2007, SI 2007/1024, Sch 1 r 14(1); Greater London Authority Elections Rules 2007, SI 2007/3541, Sch 1 r 11(1), Sch 2 r 13(1), Sch 3 r 12(1).

A returning officer must have regard to any guidance issued by the Electoral Commission for these purposes: Representation of the People Act 1983 Sch 1 r 14A(4) (Sch 1 r 14A as so added); European Parliamentary Elections Regulations 2004, SI 2004/293, Sch 1 para 16(4) (as so substituted); Local Elections (Principal Areas) (England and Wales) Rules 2006, SI 2006/3304, Sch 2 r 10(4); Local Elections (Parishes and Communities) (England and Wales) Rules 2006, SI 2006/3305, Sch 2 r 10(4); National Assembly for Wales (Representation of the People) Order 2007, SI 2007/236, Sch 5 para 18(4); Local Authorities (Mayoral Elections) (England and Wales) Regulations 2007, SI 2007/1024, Sch 1 r 14(4); Greater London Authority Elections Rules 2007, SI 2007/3541, Sch 1 r 11(4), Sch 2 r 13(4), Sch 3 r 12(4). As to the Electoral Commission see PARA 34 et seq.

7   Representation of the People Act 1983 Sch 1 r 14A(3) (r 14A as added: see note 5); European Parliamentary Elections Regulations 2004, SI 2004/293, Sch 1 para 16(3) (as substituted: see note 5); Local Elections (Principal Areas) (England and Wales) Rules 2006, SI 2006/3304, Sch 2 r 10(3); Local Elections (Parishes and Communities) (England and Wales) Rules 2006, SI 2006/3305, Sch 2 r 10(3); National Assembly for Wales (Representation of the People) Order 2007, SI 2007/236, Sch 5 para 18(3); Local Authorities (Mayoral Elections) (England and Wales) Regulations 2007, SI 2007/1024, Sch 1 r 14(3); Greater London Authority Elections Rules 2007, SI 2007/3541, Sch 1 r 11(3), Sch 2 r 13(3), Sch 3 r 12(3). As to election petitions see PARA 761 et seq.

266. Withdrawal of candidate. A candidate standing in his own right at an election[1] may withdraw his candidature by notice of withdrawal signed by him and attested by one witness[2], and delivered to the returning officer[3] at the place for delivery of nomination papers[4]. Such notice must be delivered by the end of the timetabled period for the delivery of notices of withdrawals of candidature, as follows:

(1)   in the case of a parliamentary or European parliamentary election, within the time for the delivery of nomination papers, etc at that election[5];

(2)   in the case of any local government election (except a London Authority election), not later than noon on the sixteenth day before the day of election[6]; or

(3)   in the case of a London Authority election, not later than noon on the twenty-first day before the day of election[7]; or

(4)   in the case of a Welsh Assembly election, not later than noon on the seventeenth day before the day of election[8].

Where such a candidate (except a candidate at a European parliamentary election) is outside the United Kingdom[9], a notice of withdrawal signed:

(a)   in the case of London Authority elections, by his election agent[10]; or

(b)   in the case of Welsh Assembly elections, by any person[11]; or

(c)   in any other case, by his proposer[12],

and accompanied by a written declaration also so signed of the candidate's absence from the United Kingdom, is of the same effect as a notice of withdrawal signed by the candidate[13]. Where the candidate stands nominated by more than one nomination paper, the notice of withdrawal must be accompanied, in addition to that declaration, by a written statement signed by the candidate that the person listed in head (a), (b), or (c) above, whichever properly applies, is authorised to give the required notice on the candidate's behalf during his absence from the United Kingdom[14]. At a parliamentary election, or at any local government election (except a London Authority election), the notice of withdrawal and the accompanying declaration are also effective if the notice and declaration are signed by all the proposers except any who is, and is stated in the declaration to be, outside the United Kingdom[15].

A candidate standing in his own right at a local government election (except a local authority or London mayoral election) who is validly nominated for more than one electoral area of the same local government area[16], or for more than one ward of the same parish or community[17], or for more than one London Assembly constituency[18], as the case may be, must withdraw from his candidature in all those electoral areas, or in all those wards, or in all those Assembly constituencies, except one, and if he does not so withdraw he is deemed to have withdrawn from his candidature in all those electoral areas, or in all those wards, or in each Assembly constituency[19].

A registered political party's nomination[20] to stand, at a London members election or at a European parliamentary election, may be withdrawn by a notice of withdrawal signed by the nominating officer of the party[21] (or by a person authorised in writing by him), delivered to the returning officer at the place for delivery of nomination papers[22]. At a Welsh Assembly regional election, a registered political party[23] may withdraw the candidature of any or all of the candidates included in a party list[24] of that party by notice of withdrawal signed by the party's registered nominating officer[25] and delivered to the regional returning officer at the place (or a place) for the delivery of individual or party nomination papers[26].

At a poll consequent on a parish meeting involving an appointment to office[27], a candidate may withdraw his candidature by a notice of withdrawal signed by him and attested by one witness and delivered at the office appointed by the returning officer[28] no later than noon on the fourth day after the day on which the poll was demanded[29].

A person who knowingly publishes a false statement of the withdrawal of a candidate for the purposes of promoting the election of another candidate is guilty of an illegal practice[30]; and a person who corruptly induces the withdrawal of a candidate, and a candidate withdrawing in pursuance of such an inducement, may be guilty of an illegal payment[31].

1   Ie a candidate at a parliamentary election, a constituency candidate at a Welsh Assembly
    constituency election or an individual or party list candidate at a Welsh Assembly regional
    election, an individual candidate at a European parliamentary election, or any candidate at a
    local government election (ie an election of councillors for any electoral area, or a London
    Authority election (including references to an individual candidate or candidate on a party's list
    to be London members), and with general references to 'local government election' being taken
    to include a local authority mayoral election: see PARA 11). As to the meaning of 'parliamentary
    election' see PARA 9; and as to the meanings of 'constituency election' and 'regional election' for
    the purposes of Welsh Assembly elections see PARA 3 note 2. As to the meanings of 'Authority
    election ' and 'electoral area' see PARA 11. As to the meaning of 'candidate' generally see PARA
    230. As to the meanings of 'constituency candidate' and 'individual candidate' at a Welsh
    Assembly election see PARA 230 note 19; as to the meaning of 'party list candidate' at a Welsh
    Assembly regional election see PARA 230 note 23; and as to the meaning of 'individual
    candidate' at a European parliamentary election see PARA 230 note 32. As to the election of
    councillors for local government principal areas see PARA 197 et seq; as to elections for the
    return of a local authority mayor see PARA 198; as to London Authority elections, including for
    the return of an elected Mayor of London, see PARA 199 et seq; and as to the ordinary elections
    of parish or community councillors see PARA 200 et seq. As to European parliamentary elections
    see PARA 217 et seq. As to party lists, and as to individual candidates to be London members, see
    further LONDON GOVERNMENT vol 71 (2013) PARA 81. As the withdrawal of a registered
    political party's nomination to be a candidate at elections where such a party can stand see the
    text and notes 20–26.
2   Representation of the People Act 1983 Sch 1 r 13(1)(a); European Parliamentary Elections
    Regulations 2004, SI 2004/293, Sch 1 para 14(1)(a) (Sch 1 substituted by SI 2009/186); Local
    Elections (Principal Areas) (England and Wales) Rules 2006, SI 2006/3304, Sch 2 r 13(1)(a);
    Local Elections (Parishes and Communities) (England and Wales) Rules 2006, SI 2006/3305,
    Sch 2 r 13(1)(a); National Assembly for Wales (Representation of the People) Order 2007,
    SI 2007/236, Sch 5 para 15(1)(a), (2)(a); Local Authorities (Mayoral Elections) (England and
    Wales) Regulations 2007, SI 2007/1024, Sch 1 r 15(1)(a); Greater London Authority Elections
    Rules 2007, SI 2007/3541, Sch 1 r 14(1)(a), Sch 2 r 15(1)(a), Sch 3 r 14(1)(a). At a London
    Authority election, it is specified that the name and address of the witness must be given: see
    Sch 1 r 14(1)(a), Sch 2 r 15(1)(a), Sch 3 r 14(1)(a).
3   As to returning officers for parliamentary elections see PARA 350 et seq; as to returning officers
    for local government elections see PARA 354 et seq; and as to returning officers at European
    parliamentary elections see PARA 360 et seq. In elections for the return of constituency members
    of the London Assembly, any reference to the returning officer is to the constituency returning
    officer ('CRO') (see the Greater London Authority Elections Rules 2007, SI 2007/3541, Sch 1
    r 14(1)(b)); in other London Assembly elections (ie for London members and in the case of a
    London Mayoral election), the reference is to the Greater London returning officer ('GLRO')
    (see Sch 2 r 15(1)(b), (2), Sch 3 r 14(1)(b)). As to the meaning of the 'Greater London returning
    officer' see PARA 211 note 8; and as to the meaning of the 'constituency returning officer' in this
    context see PARA 211 note 9. As to the meaning of 'London member' see PARA 11 note 5;
    definition applied by virtue of r 2(2). As to the meaning of 'constituency member', in relation to
    the London Assembly, see PARA 11 note 6; definition applied by virtue of r 2(2). At a Welsh
    Assembly constituency election, the constituency returning officer is the returning officer
    referred to in the text (see the National Assembly for Wales (Representation of the People)
    Order 2007, SI 2007/236, Sch 5 para 15(1)(b)); and, at a Welsh Assembly regional election, it is
    the regional returning officer (see Sch 5 para 15(2)(b)). As to the meanings of 'constituency
    returning officer' and 'regional returning officer' for the purposes of Welsh Assembly elections
    see PARA 18 note 2.
4   Representation of the People Act 1983 Sch 1 r 13(1)(b); European Parliamentary Elections
    Regulations 2004, SI 2004/293, Sch 1 para 14(1)(b) (as substituted: see note 2); Local Elections
    (Principal Areas) (England and Wales) Rules 2006, SI 2006/3304, Sch 2 r 13(1)(b); Local
    Elections (Parishes and Communities) (England and Wales) Rules 2006, SI 2006/3305, Sch 2
    r 13(1)(b); National Assembly for Wales (Representation of the People) Order 2007,
    SI 2007/236, Sch 5 para 15(1)(b), (2)(b); Local Authorities (Mayoral Elections) (England and
    Wales) Regulations 2007, SI 2007/1024, Sch 1 r 15(1)(b); Greater London Authority Elections
    Rules 2007, SI 2007/3541, Sch 1 r 14(1)(b), Sch 2 r 15(1)(b), Sch 3 r 14(1)(b). At a London
    members election, the reference to the delivery of nomination papers includes a reference to the
    delivery of party lists (ie in relation to candidates nominated on a party's list): see Sch 2
    r 15(1)(b). As to party lists at the election of London members see further LONDON
    GOVERNMENT vol 71 (2013) PARA 81. At a Welsh Assembly constituency election, the papers
    referred to are constituency nomination papers (see the National Assembly for Wales

(Representation of the People) Order 2007, SI 2007/236, Sch 5 para 15(1)(b)); and, at a Welsh Assembly regional election, the papers referred to are either individual nomination papers or party nomination papers (see Sch 5 para 15(2)(b)). As to the meaning of 'party nomination paper' at a Welsh Assembly regional election see PARA 255; and as to the meanings of 'constituency nomination paper' and 'individual nomination paper' see PARA 256. As to the place for the delivery of nomination papers see PARA 260.

5   Representation of the People Act 1983 Sch 1 r 1; European Parliamentary Elections Regulations 2004, SI 2004/293, Sch 1 para 1 (as substituted: see note 2). The reference is to the delivery of nomination papers and lists of candidates at a European parliamentary election: see Sch 1 para 1 (as so substituted). As to the time for the delivery of nomination papers see PARA 260.

6   Local Elections (Principal Areas) (England and Wales) Rules 2006, SI 2006/3304, Sch 2 r 1; Local Elections (Parishes and Communities) (England and Wales) Rules 2006, SI 2006/3305, Sch 2 r 1; Local Authorities (Mayoral Elections) (England and Wales) Regulations 2007, SI 2007/1024, Sch 1 r 3. As to the day of a local authority mayoral election see PARA 198; and as to the day of other local government elections see PARA 206.

7   Greater London Authority Elections Rules 2007, SI 2007/3541, Sch 1 Sch 2 r 3, Sch 3 r 3.

8   National Assembly for Wales (Representation of the People) Order 2007, SI 2007/236, Sch 5 para 1(1). As to the day of election at a Welsh Assembly election see PARA 213.

9   As to the meaning of 'United Kingdom' see PARA 1 note 1. As to candidates at European parliamentary elections see PARA 228.

10 Greater London Authority Elections Rules 2007, SI 2007/3541, Sch 1 r 14(2), Sch 2 r 15(3), Sch 3 r 14(2).

11 National Assembly for Wales (Representation of the People) Order 2007, SI 2007/236, Sch 5 para 15(3). As to the meaning of 'person' for these purposes see PARA 110 note 2.

12 Representation of the People Act 1983 Sch 1 r 13(2); Local Elections (Principal Areas) (England and Wales) Rules 2006, SI 2006/3304, Sch 2 r 13(2); Local Elections (Parishes and Communities) (England and Wales) Rules 2006, SI 2006/3305, Sch 2 r 13(2); Local Authorities (Mayoral Elections) (England and Wales) Regulations 2007, SI 2007/1024, Sch 1 r 15(2); Greater London Authority Elections Rules 2007, SI 2007/3541, Sch 1 r 14(2), Sch 2 r 15(3), Sch 3 r 14(2). As to the subscription of nomination papers see PARA 257.

13 Representation of the People Act 1983 Sch 1 r 13(2); Local Elections (Principal Areas) (England and Wales) Rules 2006, SI 2006/3304, Sch 2 r 13(2); Local Elections (Parishes and Communities) (England and Wales) Rules 2006, SI 2006/3305, Sch 2 r 13(2); National Assembly for Wales (Representation of the People) Order 2007, SI 2007/236, Sch 5 para 15(3)(a); Local Authorities (Mayoral Elections) (England and Wales) Regulations 2007, SI 2007/1024, Sch 1 r 15(2); Greater London Authority Elections Rules 2007, SI 2007/3541, Sch 1 r 14(2), Sch 2 r 15(3), Sch 3 r 14(2).

14 Representation of the People Act 1983 Sch 1 r 13(2)(b); Local Elections (Principal Areas) (England and Wales) Rules 2006, SI 2006/3304, Sch 2 r 13(2)(b); Local Elections (Parishes and Communities) (England and Wales) Rules 2006, SI 2006/3305, Sch 2 r 13(2)(b); National Assembly for Wales (Representation of the People) Order 2007, SI 2007/236, Sch 5 para 15(3)(b); Local Authorities (Mayoral Elections) (England and Wales) Regulations 2007, SI 2007/1024, Sch 1 r 15(2)(b); Greater London Authority Elections Rules 2007, SI 2007/3541, Sch 1 r 14(2), Sch 2 r 15(3), Sch 3 r 14(2).

15 Representation of the People Act 1983 Sch 1 r 13(2)(a); Local Elections (Principal Areas) (England and Wales) Rules 2006, SI 2006/3304, Sch 2 r 13(2)(a); Local Elections (Parishes and Communities) (England and Wales) Rules 2006, SI 2006/3305, Sch 2 r 13(2)(a); Local Authorities (Mayoral Elections) (England and Wales) Regulations 2007, SI 2007/1024, Sch 1 r 15(2)(a).

16 See the Local Elections (Principal Areas) (England and Wales) Rules 2006, SI 2006/3304, Sch 2 r 12. As to the meaning of 'local government area' see PARA 33 note 7.

17 See the Local Elections (Parishes and Communities) (England and Wales) Rules 2006, SI 2006/3305, Sch 2 r 12. As to parishes and their councils generally see LOCAL GOVERNMENT vol 69 (2009) PARA 27 et seq; and as to communities and their councils generally see LOCAL GOVERNMENT vol 69 (2009) PARA 41 et seq.

18 See the Greater London Authority Elections Rules 2007, SI 2007/3541, Sch 1 r 13(4). As to the meaning of 'Assembly constituency', in relation to the London Assembly, see PARA 11 note 6.

At an ordinary election, the GLRO must, before the last time for delivery of notices of withdrawal (see head (3) in the text), review the statements of persons nominated which are delivered under Sch 1 r 10(8) (see PARA 267): Sch 1 r 13(1). If, having reviewed the statements in accordance with Sch 1 r 13(1), it appears to the GLRO that a candidate has been validly nominated for more than one Assembly constituency, the GLRO must, before the last time for delivery of notices of withdrawal, inform the CRO for each Assembly constituency in which that candidate has been validly nominated of the candidate's name and particulars in the statement of persons nominated, and the name of each Assembly constituency in which the candidate appears to have been validly nominated: see Sch 1 r 13(2). If practicable, before the last time for delivery of notices of withdrawal, the GLRO may also inform each candidate who is the subject of the communication under Sch 1 r 13(2) that he appears to have been validly nominated in more than one Assembly constituency, and each such candidate must be informed further of the name of each Assembly constituency in which he appears to have been validly nominated: see Sch 1 r 13(3).

19　Local Elections (Principal Areas) (England and Wales) Rules 2006, SI 2006/3304, Sch 2 r 12; Local Elections (Parishes and Communities) (England and Wales) Rules 2006, SI 2006/3305, Sch 2 r 12; Greater London Authority Elections Rules 2007, SI 2007/3541, Sch 1 r 13(4), (6). A candidate who is validly nominated for more than one Assembly constituency, must withdraw from his candidature, in accordance with Sch 1 r 14 (see the text and notes 1–14), in all those Assembly constituencies except one: see Sch 1 r 13(4). If a CRO is notified of a candidate's name in accordance with Sch 1 r 13(2) (see note 18), and he receives a notice of withdrawal in respect of that candidate in accordance with Sch 1 r 14, he must, before the last time for delivery of notices of withdrawal (see head (3) in the text), inform the CRO of each Assembly constituency in which that candidate has been validly nominated, and the GLRO: see Sch 1 r 13(5). If a candidate does not comply with Sch 1 r 13(4), each CRO who has been informed of the candidate's name under Sch 1 r 13(2) must, after the last time for the delivery of notices of withdrawal, deem that candidate to have withdrawn from his candidature in each Assembly constituency: Sch 1 r 13(6). If a candidate is deemed to have withdrawn his candidature in accordance with Sch 1 r 13(6), each CRO must, as soon as practicable, notify that candidate in writing that his candidature has been deemed to be withdrawn in respect of that Assembly constituency: Sch 1 r 13(7).

20　As to the meaning of 'registered political party' for these purposes see PARAS 226 note 16, 230 note 29.

21　As to the registered nominating officer of a party see PARA 253.

22　European Parliamentary Elections Regulations 2004, SI 2004/293, Sch 1 para 14(2) (as substituted: see note 2); Greater London Authority Elections Rules 2007, SI 2007/3541, Sch 2 r 15(2). At a London members election, the reference to the delivery of nomination papers includes a reference to the delivery of party lists: see Sch 2 r 15(2).

23　As to the meaning of 'registered political party' for these purposes see PARA 215 note 19.

24　As to the meaning of 'party list' at a Welsh Assembly regional election see PARA 230 note 23.

25　National Assembly for Wales (Representation of the People) Order 2007, SI 2007/236, Sch 5 para 15(4)(a).

26　National Assembly for Wales (Representation of the People) Order 2007, SI 2007/236, Sch 5 para 15(4)(b).

27　As to polls consequent on a parish or community meeting see PARA 200 et seq.

28　Parish and Community Meetings (Polls) Rules 1987, SI 1987/1, Schedule r 3(1). As to the returning officer at a poll consequent on parish meeting and the office he appoints for the poll see PARA 356.

29　Parish and Community Meetings (Polls) Rules 1987, SI 1987/1, Schedule r 1.

30　See PARA 680.

31　See PARA 683.

267.　Publication of statement of persons nominated. At any election[1], the returning officer[2] must prepare and publish a statement[3] showing the persons who have been and stand nominated as candidates standing in their own right[4]; and it must also show any other persons who have been so nominated, with the reason why they no longer stand nominated[5]. Where a registered political party may stand at an election[6], and nominate by submitting a list of candidates[7], the returning officer must prepare and publish a statement showing each registered party which has been and stands nominated, together with, in respect of each such party, the list of candidates it has submitted[8]; and it must also show any other persons or parties who have been nominated in this way, together with the reason why they no longer stand nominated[9]. Such a statement must be published:

　(1)　in the case of a parliamentary general election or by-election[10], or in the case of a European parliamentary election, at the close of the time for making objections to nomination papers[11] (if, in fact, no such objections are made); but, if any such objections are made, not before they are disposed of (but not later than 24 hours after the last time for delivery of nomination papers)[12];

(2)   in the case of any local government election (except a London Authority election), not later than noon on the seventeenth day before the day of election[13];

(3)   in the case of a London Authority election, not later than noon on the twenty-second day before the day of election[14];

(4)   in the case of a Welsh Assembly election, not later than noon on the sixteenth day before the day of election[15].

The statement of persons nominated must show the names[16], addresses[17] and descriptions, if any, of the persons nominated as given in their nomination papers[18], with the names arranged alphabetically in the order of their surnames (and, if there are two or more with the same surname, of their other names)[19]. Where registered political parties may stand at an election, and nominate by submitting lists of candidates, the statement also must show[20], in respect of the registered political parties which have been and stand nominated, the names of those parties[21], set out together in alphabetical order[22], and (in respect of each such party) the names and home addresses of the candidates nominated by inclusion on the party's list, as given in the party list[23], and arranged (immediately after the entry for each relevant party) in the order in which their names appear in those lists[24].

Where a person is nominated by more than one nomination paper (except at a European parliamentary election)[25], the returning officer must take the required particulars from one of the papers selected by the candidate, or by the returning officer in default of the candidate[26]. Where, at a Welsh Assembly regional election, a registered political party which has delivered more than one party nomination paper (and where party list candidates of that party stand nominated by more than one party list submitted with those papers), the regional returning officer must take the particulars required from such one of the papers and the party list with that paper as the registered nominating officer of the party[27] (or the returning officer in default of that registered nominating officer) may select; and if any candidate is shown standing nominated by a list not so selected but is not so shown in the selected list he no longer stands nominated[28].

Except in the case of local government election, the returning officer must send a copy of the statement of persons nominated to the Electoral Commission[29]. In order to accommodate the needs of regional elections (where these take place), local publication of the statement must be made at certain elections (that is, at a London Authority election, a Welsh Assembly regional election, or at a European parliamentary election)[30].

At a contested election, except a local government election, the returning officer must include in the statement of persons nominated a notice of the poll, stating the day on which and hours during which the poll will be taken[31]. Where the statement shows that a nominated candidate is unopposed (or that there are at least as many offices to be filled as there are nominated candidates), the appropriate returning officer must declare the unopposed candidate (or candidates) to be elected[32].

1   Ie a parliamentary election, a local government election (which includes any London Authority election and a local authority mayoral election), a Welsh Assembly constituency or regional

election, or European parliamentary election. As to the meaning of 'parliamentary election' see PARA 9. As to the meanings of 'Authority election ' and 'local government election' see PARA 11. As to the meanings of 'Assembly election', and Welsh Assembly 'constituency election' and 'regional election', see PARA 3 note 2.

2 As to returning officers for parliamentary elections see PARA 350 et seq; as to returning officers for local government elections see PARA 354 et seq; and as to returning officers at European parliamentary elections see PARA 360 et seq. In elections for the return of constituency members of the London Assembly, any reference to the returning officer is to the constituency returning officer ('CRO') (see the Greater London Authority Elections Rules 2007, SI 2007/3541, Sch 1 r 10(1), (4), (5), (7), (8))); in other London Assembly elections (ie for London members and in the case of a London Mayoral election), the reference is to the Greater London returning officer ('GLRO') (see Sch 2 r 12(1), (3), (4), (6), Sch 3 r 11(1), (4), (5), (7)). As to the meaning of the 'Greater London returning officer' see PARA 211 note 8; and as to the meaning of the 'constituency returning officer' in this context see PARA 211 note 9. As to the meaning of 'London member' see PARA 11 note 5; definition applied by virtue of r 2(2). As to the meaning of 'constituency member', in relation to the London Assembly, see PARA 11 note 6; definition applied by virtue of r 2(2). At a Welsh Assembly constituency election, the constituency returning officer is the returning officer referred to in the text (see the National Assembly for Wales (Representation of the People) Order 2007, SI 2007/236, Sch 5 para 16); and, at a Welsh Assembly regional election, it is the regional returning officer (see Sch 5 para 17)). As to the meanings of 'constituency returning officer' and 'regional returning officer' for the purposes of Welsh Assembly elections see PARA 18 note 2.

3 The returning officer at a parliamentary election, a Welsh Assembly election, or European parliamentary election, must prepare and publish a draft statement of persons nominated where there are grounds for disqualifying a candidate under the Representation of the People Act 1981, for which the relevant rules provide: see PARAS 263 notes 11, 39, 54. The statement required by the National Assembly for Wales (Representation of the People) Order 2007, SI 2007/236, Sch 5 para 17 (ie statement of registered political parties and other persons nominated by means of a party list) is referred to as a 'statement of persons nominated', except for the purposes of Sch 5 para 19 (draft statement of persons nominated where there are grounds for disqualifying a candidate under the Representation of the People Act 1981: see PARA 263 note 39): Sch 5 para 17(15). In relation to a European parliamentary election, the statement is known as the 'statement of parties and individual candidates nominated': see the European Parliamentary Elections Regulations 2004, SI 2004/293, Sch 1 para 15(1) (Sch 1 substituted by SI 2009/186). Where regional elections take place, local publication of the statement may be required: see the text and note 30. As to public notice by a returning officer for a European parliamentary election that is required to be given by or under the European Parliamentary Elections Regulations 2004, SI 2004/293, see PARA 239 note 23. As to the giving of public notices by a returning officer generally see PARA 350 et seq.

4 As to the meaning of 'candidate' generally see PARA 230. Where regional elections take place, the reference in the text is to persons nominated as 'individual candidates' as follows:

(1) for the purposes of elections for the return of London members of the London Assembly (see the Greater London Authority Elections Rules 2007, SI 2007/3541, Sch 2 r 12(1)(b), (5)(c), (6));

(2) for the purposes of a Welsh Assembly regional election (National Assembly for Wales (Representation of the People) Order 2007, SI 2007/236, Sch 5 para 17(1)(a)); or

(3) for the purposes of European parliamentary elections (European Parliamentary Elections Regulations 2004, SI 2004/293, Sch 1 para 15(1)(b) (as substituted: see note 3)).

As to the meaning of 'individual candidate' at a Welsh Assembly regional election see PARA 230 note 19; and as to the meaning of 'individual candidate' at a European parliamentary election see PARA 230 note 32.

5 Representation of the People Act 1983 Sch 1 r 14(1); European Parliamentary Elections Regulations 2004, SI 2004/293, Sch 1 para 15(1)(b), (c) (as substituted: see note 3); Local Elections (Principal Areas) (England and Wales) Rules 2006, SI 2006/3304, Sch 2 r 9(1); Local Elections (Parishes and Communities) (England and Wales) Rules 2006, SI 2006/3305, Sch 2 r 9(1); National Assembly for Wales (Representation of the People) Order 2007, SI 2007/236, Sch 5 paras 16(1), 17(1)(a), (c); Local Authorities (Mayoral Elections) (England and Wales) Regulations 2007, SI 2007/1024, Sch 1 r 12(1); Greater London Authority Elections Rules 2007, SI 2007/3541, Sch 1 r 10(1), Sch 2 r 12(1)(b), (c), Sch 3 r 11(1).

6 Ie a European parliamentary election, a Welsh Assembly regional election, or an election for the return of London members of the London Assembly. As to the meaning of 'registered political party' for the purposes of a Welsh Assembly election see PARA 215 note 19; as to the meaning of

'registered political party' at a European parliamentary election see PARA 230 note 29; and as to the meaning of 'registered political party' at a London members election see PARA 256 note 27.

7   As to the system of candidature whereby registered parties submit lists of candidates see PARA 340. As to the meanings of 'party list' and 'party list candidate' at a Welsh Assembly regional election see PARA 230 note 23; as to references to party lists in London members elections see PARA 255 note 23; and as to references to the nomination paper of a registered party at a London members elections see PARA 260 note 18. At a European parliamentary election, the list of a registered political party's candidates must accompany its nomination paper under the European Parliamentary Elections Regulations 2004, SI 2004/293, Sch 1 para 7: see PARA 256. As to the meaning of 'list' at a European parliamentary election see PARA 230 note 29.

8   European Parliamentary Elections Regulations 2004, SI 2004/293, Sch 1 para 15(1)(a) (as substituted: see note 3); National Assembly for Wales (Representation of the People) Order 2007, SI 2007/236, Sch 5 para 17(1)(b); Greater London Authority Elections Rules 2007, SI 2007/3541, Sch 2 r 12(1)(a).

9   European Parliamentary Elections Regulations 2004, SI 2004/293, Sch 1 para 15(1)(c) (as substituted: see note 3); National Assembly for Wales (Representation of the People) Order 2007, SI 2007/236, Sch 5 para 17(1)(c); Greater London Authority Elections Rules 2007, SI 2007/3541, Sch 2 r 12(1)(c).

10   As to parliamentary general elections see PARA 189 et seq; and as to parliamentary by-elections see PARA 191.

11   As to the making of objections to nomination papers and the disposal of such objections generally see PARAS 263–264. In the case of a European parliamentary election, references in the text to nomination papers include references to the list of a registered political party's candidates that must accompany its nomination paper under the European Parliamentary Elections Regulations 2004, SI 2004/293, Sch 1 para 7 (see PARA 256): see Sch 1 para 1 (as substituted: see note 3).

12   Representation of the People Act 1983 Sch 1 r 1 (amended by the Electoral Administration Act 2006 s 19(1), (2)); European Parliamentary Elections Regulations 2004, SI 2004/293, Sch 1 para 1 (as substituted: see note 3).

13   Local Elections (Principal Areas) (England and Wales) Rules 2006, SI 2006/3304, Sch 2 r 1; Local Elections (Parishes and Communities) (England and Wales) Rules 2006, SI 2006/3305, Sch 2 r 1; Local Authorities (Mayoral Elections) (England and Wales) Regulations 2007, SI 2007/1024, Sch 1 r 3. As to the day of election at a local government election see PARA 206 et seq.

14   Greater London Authority Elections Rules 2007, SI 2007/3541, Sch 1 Sch 2 r 3, Sch 3 r 3.

15   National Assembly for Wales (Representation of the People) Order 2007, SI 2007/236, Sch 5 para 1(1). As to the day of election at a Welsh Assembly election see PARA 213.

16   If a person's nomination paper gives a commonly used surname or forename in addition to another name, the statement must show the person's commonly used surname or forename (as the case may be) instead of any other name: Representation of the People Act 1983 Sch 1 r 14(2A) (Sch 1 r 14(2A)–(2C) added by the Electoral Administration Act 2006 s 21(1), (3)); European Parliamentary Elections Regulations 2004, SI 2004/293, Sch 1 para 15(4) (as substituted: see note 3); Local Elections (Principal Areas) (England and Wales) Rules 2006, SI 2006/3304, Sch 2 r 9(3); Local Elections (Parishes and Communities) (England and Wales) Rules 2006, SI 2006/3305, Sch 2 r 9(3); National Assembly for Wales (Representation of the People) Order 2007, SI 2007/236, Sch 5 paras 16(3), 17(4), (5); Local Authorities (Mayoral Elections) (England and Wales) Regulations 2007, SI 2007/1024, Sch 1 r 12(3); Greater London Authority Elections Rules 2007, SI 2007/3541, Sch 1 r 10(3), Sch 2 r 12(2), Sch 3 r 11(3). However, this provision does not apply if the returning officer thinks either that the use of the person's commonly used name may be likely to mislead or confuse electors, or that the commonly used name is obscene or offensive: Representation of the People Act 1983 Sch 1 r 14(2B) (as so added); European Parliamentary Elections Regulations 2004, SI 2004/293, Sch 1 para 15(5) (as so substituted); Local Elections (Principal Areas) (England and Wales) Rules 2006, SI 2006/3304, Sch 2 r 9(4); Local Elections (Parishes and Communities) (England and Wales) Rules 2006, SI 2006/3305, Sch 2 r 9(4); National Assembly for Wales (Representation of the People) Order 2007, SI 2007/236, Sch 5 paras 16(4), 17(6); Local Authorities (Mayoral Elections) (England and Wales) Regulations 2007, SI 2007/1024, Sch 1 r 12(4); Greater London Authority Elections Rules 2007, SI 2007/3541, Sch 1 r 10(4), Sch 2 r 12(3), Sch 3 r 11(4). If the returning officer so thinks, he must give notice in writing to the candidate of his reasons for refusing to allow the use of a commonly used name: Representation of the People Act 1983 Sch 1 r 14(2C) (as so added); European Parliamentary Elections Regulations 2004, SI 2004/293, Sch 1 para 15(6) (as so substituted); Local Elections (Principal

Areas) (England and Wales) Rules 2006, SI 2006/3304, Sch 2 r 9(5); Local Elections (Parishes and Communities) (England and Wales) Rules 2006, SI 2006/3305, Sch 2 r 9(5); National Assembly for Wales (Representation of the People) Order 2007, SI 2007/236, Sch 5 paras 16(5), 17(7); Local Authorities (Mayoral Elections) (England and Wales) Regulations 2007, SI 2007/1024, Sch 1 r 12(5); Greater London Authority Elections Rules 2007, SI 2007/3541, Sch 1 r 10(5), Sch 2 r 12(4), Sch 3 r 11(5). In the case of a Welsh Assembly constituency election, the nomination paper specified is the constituency nomination paper (see the National Assembly for Wales (Representation of the People) Order 2007, SI 2007/236, Sch 5 para 16(3)); but, in the case of a Welsh Assembly regional election, the provisions apply equally to an individual candidate's nomination paper (see Sch 5 para 17(4)) and to the party list, as regards a candidate included on such a list (see Sch 5 para 17(5)). In the case of a European parliamentary election, the provisions apply to either the nomination paper or list, as the case may be: see the European Parliamentary Elections Regulations 2004, SI 2004/293, Sch 1 para 15(4) (as so substituted).

17 In relation to a nominated person at a parliamentary election, in whose case the home address form (or, if the person is nominated by more than one nomination paper, any of the home address forms) contains the statement mentioned in the Representation of the People Act 1983 Sch 1 r 6(5)(a) (ie a statement made and signed by the candidate that he requires the home address not to be made public: see PARA 256), and the information mentioned in Sch 1 r 6(5)(b) (ie a statement of the constituency within which that address is situated or, if that address is outside the United Kingdom, the country within which it is situated: see PARA 256), the reference in Sch 1 r 14(2) to the person's address must be read as a reference to the information mentioned in Sch 1 r 6(5)(b): see Sch 1 r 14(3A) (Sch 1 r 14(3A), (4A)–(4E) added by the Political Parties and Elections Act 2009 s 24(1), (5), (6)). As to the requirement for a nomination paper at a parliamentary election to be accompanied by a home address form see PARA 256.

Where two or more of the names shown on the statement of persons nominated are the same or so similar as to be likely to cause confusion, where the Representation of the People Act 1983 Sch 1 r 14(3A) applies in relation to each of the persons in question, and where the information mentioned in Sch 1 r 6(5)(b) is the same for each of them, the returning officer may cause any of their particulars to be shown on the statement with such amendments or additions as the officer thinks appropriate in order to reduce the likelihood of confusion: see Sch 1 r 14(4A) (as so added). A returning officer must have regard to any guidance issued by the Electoral Commission for these purposes: Sch 1 r 14(4E) (as so added). Where it is practicable to do so before the publication of the statement, the returning officer must consult any person whose particulars are to be amended or added to under Sch 1 r 14(4A) (Sch 1 r 14(4B) (as so added)); and the returning officer must give notice in writing to any person whose particulars are amended or added to under Sch 1 r 14(4A) (Sch 1 r 14(4C) (as so added)). Anything done by a returning officer in pursuance of Sch 1 r 14(4A) must not be questioned in any proceedings other than proceedings on an election petition: Sch 1 r 14(4D) (as so added). As to the Electoral Commission see PARA 34 et seq.

18 Representation of the People Act 1983 Sch 1 r 14(2) (amended by the Political Parties and Elections Act 2009 s 39, Sch 6 para 8(1), (4)); European Parliamentary Elections Regulations 2004, SI 2004/293, Sch 1 para 15(3) (as substituted: see note 3); Local Elections (Principal Areas) (England and Wales) Rules 2006, SI 2006/3304, Sch 2 r 9(2); Local Elections (Parishes and Communities) (England and Wales) Rules 2006, SI 2006/3305, Sch 2 r 9(2); National Assembly for Wales (Representation of the People) Order 2007, SI 2007/236, Sch 5 paras 16(2), 17(3)(a); Local Authorities (Mayoral Elections) (England and Wales) Regulations 2007, SI 2007/1024, Sch 1 r 12(2); Greater London Authority Elections Rules 2007, SI 2007/3541, Sch 1 r 10(2), Sch 2 r 12(5)(c), Sch 3 r 11(2). At a parliamentary election, the candidate's full names and home address given in the home address form must be shown in the statement of persons nominated, which must include also the names of the persons subscribing the nomination papers: see the Representation of the People Act 1983 Sch 1 r 14(2) (as so amended). For the purposes of a London members election, the reference in the text is to persons standing nominated as 'individual candidates': see the Greater London Authority Elections Rules 2007, SI 2007/3541, Sch 2 r 12(5)(c); and see note 4. In the case of a Welsh Assembly constituency election, the nomination paper specified is the constituency nomination paper (see the National Assembly for Wales (Representation of the People) Order 2007, SI 2007/236, Sch 5 para 16(2)); and, in the case of a Welsh Assembly regional election, the individual nomination paper is specified (see Sch 5 para 17(3)(a)). In the case of a European parliamentary election, the text refers to the nomination papers of individual candidates (see note 4): see the European Parliamentary Elections Regulations 2004, SI 2004/293, Sch 1 para 15(3) (as so substituted). As to the particulars required in nomination papers generally see PARA 256; and as to the subscription of nomination papers see PARA 257.

19 Representation of the People Act 1983 Sch 1 r 14(3); European Parliamentary Elections Regulations 2004, SI 2004/293, Sch 1 para 15(7) (as substituted: see note 3); Local Elections (Principal Areas) (England and Wales) Rules 2006, SI 2006/3304, Sch 2 r 9(6); Local Elections (Parishes and Communities) (England and Wales) Rules 2006, SI 2006/3305, Sch 2 r 9(6); National Assembly for Wales (Representation of the People) Order 2007, SI 2007/236, Sch 5 paras 16(6), 17(8)(a), (10); Local Authorities (Mayoral Elections) (England and Wales) Regulations 2007, SI 2007/1024, Sch 1 r 12(6); Greater London Authority Elections Rules 2007, SI 2007/3541, Sch 1 r 10(6), Sch 2 r 12(5)(c), Sch 3 r 11(6).

20 Ie in the following order:

    (1)   the names of registered parties standing (see the text and notes 21–22) (European Parliamentary Elections Regulations 2004, SI 2004/293, Sch 1 para 15(7) (as substituted: see note 3); National Assembly for Wales (Representation of the People) Order 2007, SI 2007/236, Sch 5 para 17(8)(b), (9); Greater London Authority Elections Rules 2007, SI 2007/3541, Sch 2 r 12(5)(a));

    (2)   the names of candidates standing nominated by inclusion on a party's list (see the text and note 23) (European Parliamentary Elections Regulations 2004, SI 2004/293, Sch 1 para 15(7) (as so substituted); National Assembly for Wales (Representation of the People) Order 2007, SI 2007/236, Sch 5 para 17(8)(b), (9); Greater London Authority Elections Rules 2007, SI 2007/3541, Sch 2 r 12(5)(b));

    (3)   the names of candidates standing as individual candidates (see the text and notes 16–19) (European Parliamentary Elections Regulations 2004, SI 2004/293, Sch 1 para 15(7) (as so substituted); National Assembly for Wales (Representation of the People) Order 2007, SI 2007/236, Sch 5 para 17(8)(a), (9); Greater London Authority Elections Rules 2007, SI 2007/3541, Sch 2 r 12(5)(c)).

21 European Parliamentary Elections Regulations 2004, SI 2004/293, Sch 1 para 15(2) (as substituted: see note 3); National Assembly for Wales (Representation of the People) Order 2007, SI 2007/236, Sch 5 para 17(3)(b); Greater London Authority Elections Rules 2007, SI 2007/3541, Sch 2 r 12(5)(a). At a Welsh Assembly regional election, a registered political party must be shown in the statement by reference to the name (or names) or, as the case may be, the description referred to in the National Assembly for Wales (Representation of the People) Order 2007, SI 2007/236, Sch 5 para 7(2) (see PARA 256): see Sch 5 para 17(3)(b)(i).

22 European Parliamentary Elections Regulations 2004, SI 2004/293, Sch 1 para 15(2) (as substituted: see note 3); National Assembly for Wales (Representation of the People) Order 2007, SI 2007/236, Sch 5 para 17(8)(b); Greater London Authority Elections Rules 2007, SI 2007/3541, Sch 2 r 12(5)(a). In the case of a London members election, it is specified that the alphabetical order is determined according to the authorised descriptions given in the nomination papers: see Sch 2 r 12(5)(a). At a Welsh Assembly regional election, a registered political party must be shown in the statement by reference to name (or names) or, as the case may be, the description referred to in the National Assembly for Wales (Representation of the People) Order 2007, SI 2007/236, Sch 5 para 7(2) (see PARA 256) in respect of the party (Sch 5 para 17(11)(a)); and alphabetical order is to be determined by disregarding the definite or indefinite article and, where there are two or more words in the description (having disregarded the definite or indefinite article), by reference to the first of those words and, if there are two or more parties with the same first word in the description, of the other words in the description (Sch 5 para 17(11)(b)).

23 European Parliamentary Elections Regulations 2004, SI 2004/293, Sch 1 para 15(2) (as substituted: see note 3); National Assembly for Wales (Representation of the People) Order 2007, SI 2007/236, Sch 5 para 17(3)(b)(ii); Greater London Authority Elections Rules 2007, SI 2007/3541, Sch 2 r 12(5)(b).

24 European Parliamentary Elections Regulations 2004, SI 2004/293, Sch 1 para 15(2) (as substituted: see note 3); National Assembly for Wales (Representation of the People) Order 2007, SI 2007/236, Sch 5 para 17(8)(b); Greater London Authority Elections Rules 2007, SI 2007/3541, Sch 2 r 12(5)(b).

25 The reference in the text is to an 'individual candidate' nominated by more than one nomination paper for the purposes of elections for the return of London members of the London Assembly: see the Greater London Authority Elections Rules 2007, SI 2007/3541, Sch 2 r 12(6); and see note 4. In the case of a Welsh Assembly constituency election, the nomination paper specified is the constituency nomination paper (see the National Assembly for Wales (Representation of the People) Order 2007, SI 2007/236, Sch 5 para 16(7)); and, in the case of a Welsh Assembly regional election, the individual nomination paper is specified (see Sch 5 para 17(12)).

26 Representation of the People Act 1983 Sch 1 r 14(4); Local Elections (Principal Areas) (England and Wales) Rules 2006, SI 2006/3304, Sch 2 r 9(7); Local Elections (Parishes and Communities) (England and Wales) Rules 2006, SI 2006/3305, Sch 2 r 9(7); National Assembly for Wales

(Representation of the People) Order 2007, SI 2007/236, Sch 5 paras 16(7), 17(12); Local Authorities (Mayoral Elections) (England and Wales) Regulations 2007, SI 2007/1024, Sch 1 r 12(7); Greater London Authority Elections Rules 2007, SI 2007/3541, Sch 1 r 10(7), Sch 2 r 12(6), Sch 3 r 11(7). At a contested parliamentary election, a candidate standing nominated may require the returning officer to include in the statement of persons nominated the names of the persons subscribing a second and third nomination paper: see the Representation of the People Act 1983 Sch 1 r 14(4).

27 As to the registered nominating officer of a registered political party see PARA 253.

28 National Assembly for Wales (Representation of the People) Order 2007, SI 2007/236, Sch 5 para 17(13).

29 Representation of the People Act 1983 Sch 1 r 14(5)(a) (Sch 1 r 14(5) added by the Political Parties, Elections and Referendums Act 2000 s 158(1), Sch 21 para 6(9)); European Parliamentary Elections Regulations 2004, SI 2004/293, Sch 1 para 15(8) (as substituted: see note 3); National Assembly for Wales (Representation of the People) Order 2007, SI 2007/236, Sch 5 paras 16(8)(a), 17(14). In the case of each candidate standing nominated at a parliamentary or Welsh Assembly election, in respect of whom the returning officer has received a certificate properly authorising the candidate's description:
   (1) in the case of a parliamentary election, in accordance with either the Representation of the People Act 1983 Sch 1 r 6A(1) (description associating the candidate with a registered political party: see PARA 256) or Sch 1 r 6(1B) (description associating the candidate with two or more registered political parties: see PARA 256) (see Sch 1 r 14(5)(b) (Sch 1 r 14(5) as so added; Sch 1 r 14(5)(b) amended by the Electoral Administration Act 2006 s 74(1), Sch 1 paras 104, 131)); or
   (2) in the case of elections for the return of members of the National Assembly for Wales, in accordance with the National Assembly for Wales (Representation of the People) Order 2007, SI 2007/236, Sch 5 para 5(1), (3) (name of registered political party: see PARA 256) (see Sch 5 para 16(8)(b)).
   a copy of that certificate must be sent to the Commission as well (Representation of the People Act 1983 Sch 1 r 14(5)(b) (as so added and amended); National Assembly for Wales (Representation of the People) Order 2007, SI 2007/236, Sch 5 para 16(8)(b)).

30 At an ordinary election of London constituency members, the CRO, in addition to publishing the statement under the Greater London Authority Elections Rules 2007, SI 2007/3541, Sch 1 r 10(1), must arrange for a copy of the statement to be delivered to the GLRO as soon as possible after all decisions have been made, which are required to be made under Sch 1 r 9 (decisions as to the validity of nomination papers: see PARA 262 et seq): Sch 1 r 10(8). At a Welsh Assembly regional election, a regional returning officer must prepare a statement in accordance with the National Assembly for Wales (Representation of the People) Order 2007, SI 2007/236, Sch 5 para 17(1) and deliver, or cause to be delivered, the statement to each constituency returning officer for an Assembly constituency in the Assembly electoral region: Sch 5 para 17(1). On receipt of such a statement, a constituency returning officer must publish it: Sch 5 para 17(2). As to the meanings of 'Assembly constituency' and 'Assembly electoral region' for these purposes see PARA 3 note 2. At a European parliamentary election, the returning officer must forward a copy of the statement of parties and individual candidates nominated, immediately following its publication, to the local returning officer for each local counting area wholly or partly contained in the electoral region: see the European Parliamentary Elections Regulations 2004, SI 2004/293, Sch 1 para 17(1) (as substituted: see note 3). As soon as practicable after receipt of the copy, each local returning officer must publish it at a place within the area for which he acts: Sch 1 para 17(2) (as so substituted). As to the meaning of 'local counting area' for the purposes of a European parliamentary election see PARA 139 note 1. As to the establishment of electoral regions for the purpose of elections to the European Parliament see PARA 77. As to local returning officers appointed for the purposes of elections to the European Parliament see PARA 360.

31 As to the procedure at contested elections see PARA 384; and as to notice of the poll see PARA 388.

32 As to the procedure at uncontested elections see PARA 474 et seq.

268. Notice of disqualification. If a candidate, who has been duly nominated[1] and who has not withdrawn[2], is disqualified to be a candidate[3], and an opposing candidate desires that all votes given for the disqualified candidate should be treated as having been thrown away[4], a notice of the disqualification should be published to the voters[5]. The notice should not be ambiguous[6].

1　As to the requirements for a candidate to be validly nominated see PARA 255 et seq.
2　As to withdrawal see PARA 266.
3　As to disqualification from being a candidate see generally PARA 224 et seq.
4　As to votes given for a disqualified candidate which may be regarded as not given at all or thrown away see PARA 845.
5　Although a notice is not essential in all cases to cause votes to be thrown away (see PARA 845), the publication of a notice is a wise precaution to take: see *R v Tewkesbury Corpn* (1868) LR 3 QB 629, although the actual decision in this case was doubted in *Re Launceston Case, Drinkwater v Deakin* (1874) LR 9 CP 626 at 643 per Brett J, and in *R v Bester* (reported at (1861) 3 LT 667 but without reference to *R v Tewkesbury Corpn*). Such a notice is not necessary when the candidate is manifestly disqualified: *Hobbs v Morey* [1904] 1 KB 74 at 78, DC. If the notice is defamatory, an action will lie in respect of it: *Bendish v Lindsey* (1708) 11 Mod Rep 193. As to whether such publication will be privileged see PARA 330. The notice may be published in the newspapers, or at the entrance to the polling stations or circularised to the voters: *Tipperary County Case* (1875) 3 O'M & H 19 at 20.

　　It is not essential that the notice should be given to each individual voter. See the following cases decided by the parliamentary committees: *Drogheda Second Case* (1835) Kn & Omb 211; *Cork Case* (1835) Kn & Omb 274 at 291; *Galway Case* (1838) Falc & Fitz 579; *Wakefield Case, Blakeley's Case* (1842) Bar & Aust 270 at 307, 318 (where form of notice will be found at 272–273).

　　The notice may be signed by any electors (*Newcastle-under-Lyme (No 2) Case* (1842) Bar & Aust 564) or by the election agent (*Galway County Case* (1872) 2 O'M & H 46 at 47).
6　*R v Blizard* (1866) LR 2 QB 55.

(iii)　Financial Controls on Candidates at Elections where Election Agent is Required

A. MEANING OF 'ELECTION EXPENSES'

269.　Statutory definition of 'election expenses'. For the purposes of the statutory provisions which govern the conduct of election campaigns[1], 'election expenses', in relation to a candidate[2] at an election[3], means any expenses incurred at any time in respect of any of the following matters and used for the purposes of the candidate's election[4] after the date when he becomes a candidate at the election[5]. Those matters are:

(1)　advertising of any nature (whatever the medium used), including agency fees, design costs and other costs in connection with preparing, producing, distributing or otherwise disseminating such advertising or anything incorporating such advertising and intended to be distributed for the purpose of disseminating it[6];

(2)　unsolicited material addressed to electors (whether addressed to them by name or intended for delivery to households within any particular area), including design costs and other costs in connection with preparing, producing or distributing such material (including the cost of postage)[7];

(3)　the transport (by any means) of persons to any place, including the costs of hiring a means of transport for a particular period[8];

(4)　public meetings (of any kind), including costs incurred in connection with the attendance of persons at such meetings, the hire of premises for the purposes of such meetings or the provision of goods, services or facilities at them[9];

(5)　the services of an election agent or any other person whose services are engaged in connection with the candidate's election[10];

(6)　accommodation and administrative costs[11].

Where:

(a)　property or goods is or are transferred to the candidate or his election agent[12]; or

(b)   property, goods, services or facilities is or are provided for the use or benefit of the candidate[13],

either free of charge or at a discount of more than 10 per cent[14], and where the property, goods, services or facilities is or are made use of by or on behalf of the candidate in circumstances such that, if any expenses were to be (or are) actually incurred by or on behalf of the candidate in respect of that use, they would be (or are) election expenses incurred by or on behalf of the candidate[15]:

(i)   an amount of election expenses (the 'appropriate amount') is treated, for the purposes of the statutory provisions which govern the conduct of election campaigns, as incurred by the candidate[16]; and

(ii)   the candidate's election agent must make a declaration of that amount[17], unless that amount is not more than £50[18].

Where head (a) above applies, the appropriate amount is determined as being such proportion of either the market value of the property or goods (where the property or goods is or are transferred free of charge)[19] or the difference between the market value of the property or goods and the amount of expenses actually incurred by or on behalf of the candidate in respect of the property or goods (where the property or goods is or are transferred at a discount)[20], as is reasonably attributable to the use made of the property or goods[21]. Where head (b) above applies, the appropriate amount is determined as being such proportion of either the commercial rate for the use of the property or the provision of the goods, services or facilities (where the property, goods, services or facilities is or are provided free of charge)[22] or the difference between that commercial rate and the amount of expenses actually incurred by or on behalf of the candidate in respect of the use of the property or the provision of the services or facilities (where the property, goods, services or facilities is or are provided at a discount)[23], as is reasonably attributable to the use made of the property, goods, services or facilities[24].

However, no election expenses are to be regarded as incurred[25] in respect of any of the following matters[26]:

(A)   the payment of any deposit required to be made by a candidate at an election[27];

(B)   the publication of any matter, other than an advertisement, relating to the election in a newspaper or periodical, a broadcast made by the British Broadcasting Corporation or by Sianel Pedwar Cymru, or a programme included in any service licensed under the Broadcasting Act 1990 or the Broadcasting Act 1996[28];

(C)   the provision of any facilities provided in pursuance of any right conferred on candidates at an election by the statutory provisions other than facilities in respect of which expenses fall to be defrayed by virtue of the provisions relating to the use of schools and rooms for election meetings[29];

(D)   the provision by an individual of his own services which he provides voluntarily in his own time and free of charge[30];

(E)   accommodation which is the candidate's sole or main residence[31] or the provision by any other individual of accommodation which is his sole or main residence if the provision is made free of charge[32];

(F)   transport by a means of transport which was acquired by the candidate principally for his own personal use[33] or transport provided free of charge by any other individual if the means of transport was acquired by him principally for his own personal use[34];

(G) computing or printing equipment which was acquired by the candidate principally for his own personal use[35] or the provision by any other individual of computing or printing equipment which was acquired by the individual principally for his own personal use if the provision is made free of charge[36].

The Electoral Commission[37] may prepare, and from time to time revise, a code of practice giving guidance in relation to parliamentary and local elections as to the matters which do, or do not, fall within the matters specified either in heads (1) to (6) above or in heads (A) to (G) above[38], and guidance[39] as to the cases or circumstances in which expenses are, or are not, to be regarded as incurred for the purposes of a candidate's election[40]. Once the Commission has prepared a draft of such a code, it must be submitted to the Secretary of State for his approval[41]; and he may approve a draft code either without modification or with such modifications as he may determine[42]. The Secretary of State may also by order made by statutory instrument make such amendments to the matters specified either in heads (1) to (6) above or in heads (A) to (G) above as he considers appropriate[43]; and he may make such an order either where the order gives effect to a recommendation of the Electoral Commission[44] or after consultation with the Electoral Commission[45].

1   Ie for the purposes of the Representation of the People Act 1983 Pt II (ss 67–119), the European Parliamentary Elections Regulations 2004, SI 2004/293, Pt 2 (regs 31–81), and the National Assembly for Wales (Representation of the People) Order 2007, SI 2007/236, Pt 3 (arts 37–85) (see PARA 235 et seq): see the Representation of the People Act 1983 s 90ZA(1) (s 90ZA, Sch 4A added by the Electoral Administration Act 2006 s 27(1), (2), (5)); the European Parliamentary Elections Regulations 2004, SI 2004/293, reg 60(1) (reg 60 substituted, Sch 7A added, by SI 2009/186); and the National Assembly for Wales (Representation of the People) Order 2007, SI 2007/236, art 63(1).
2   As to the meaning of 'candidate' generally see PARA 230.
        For the purposes of Welsh Assembly elections, the reference is to either a constituency candidate at a Welsh Assembly constituency election (see the National Assembly for Wales (Representation of the People) Order 2007, SI 2007/236, arts 63(1), 64(1)) or an individual candidate at a Welsh Assembly regional election (see arts 63(1), 64(1)). As to the meanings of 'Assembly election', 'constituency election' and 'regional election' for the purposes of Welsh Assembly elections see PARA 3 note 2; and as to the meanings of 'constituency candidate' at a Welsh Assembly constituency election and 'individual candidate' at a Welsh Assembly regional election see PARA 230 note 19.
3   In the Representation of the People Act 1983 Pt II, unless the context otherwise requires, 'election expenses', in relation to an election, is to be construed in accordance with s 90ZA and ss 90C–90D: see s 118 (definition substituted by the Political Parties, Elections and Referendums Act 2000 s 138, Sch 18 paras 1, 15(a); and amended by the Electoral Administration Act 2006 Sch 1 paras 104, 119, 133). A reference in the Representation of the People Act 1983 Pt II to a candidate at an election, in relation to election expenses, includes (where the context allows) a reference to a person who becomes a candidate at the election after the expenses are incurred: s 90ZA(5) (substituted by the Political Parties and Elections Act 2009 s 39, Sch 6 para 7). In relation to any candidates at an election of London members of the London Assembly at an ordinary election who are included in a list of candidates submitted by a registered political party in connection with the election, the Representation of the People Act 1983 s 90ZA and s 90C have effect but are subject to modifications in their application: see s 90D(1), (2) (s 90D added by the Political Parties, Elections and Referendums Act 2000 s 134(1); Representation of the People Act 1983 s 90D(1) amended by the Electoral Administration Act 2006 Sch 1 paras 104, 118(1), (3)). Accordingly, references to anything done by or on behalf of, or in relation to, such a candidate at the election are to be construed as a reference to any such thing done by or on behalf of, or in relation to, all or any of the candidates on the list: Representation of the People Act 1983 s 90D(2)(a) (as so added). See also note 4. As to the meaning of 'London member', in relation to the London Assembly, see PARA 11 note 5; and as to the meaning of 'registered political party' for these purposes see PARA 231 note 7. As to ordinary elections of London members of the London Assembly see PARA 199 et seq; and as to the system of candidature whereby registered parties submit lists of candidates see PARA 340.

In relation to a European parliamentary election, 'election expenses' is to be construed in accordance with the European Parliamentary Elections Regulations 2004, SI 2004/293, regs 60, 62: see reg 31(1) (definition amended by SI 2009/186).

4   For these purposes, 'for the purposes of the candidate's election' means with a view to, or otherwise in connection with, promoting or procuring the candidate's election at the election (Representation of the People Act 1983 s 90ZA(3) (as added: see note 1); European Parliamentary Elections Regulations 2004, SI 2004/293, reg 60(3) (as substituted: see note 1); National Assembly for Wales (Representation of the People) Order 2007, SI 2007/236, art 63(3)); and any reference (in whatever terms) to promoting or procuring a candidate's election at an election includes doing so by prejudicing the electoral prospects of another candidate at the election (or those of a registered political party, at a Welsh Assembly election) (Representation of the People Act 1983 s 90ZA(6) (as so added); European Parliamentary Elections Regulations 2004, SI 2004/293, reg 60(6) (as so substituted); National Assembly for Wales (Representation of the People) Order 2007, SI 2007/236, art 63(6)). For the purpose of the National Assembly for Wales (Representation of the People) Order 2007, SI 2007/236, Pt 3, sums paid or expenses incurred by, or in respect of, a candidate at a constituency election in respect of whom the constituency returning officer has received a certificate issued by the registered nominating officer of a registered political party under Sch 5 para 5(1) or Sch 5 para 5(3) (ie a certificate authorising the description of a candidate at a constituency election: see PARA 256), as the case may be, are not to be regarded as having been paid or incurred by that party: art 42. As to the meaning of 'constituency returning officer' for the purposes of Welsh Assembly elections see PARA 18 note 2. As to the meaning of 'registered political party' for these purposes see PARAS 215 note 19. As to the registered nominating officer of a party see PARA 253.

In relation to any candidates at an election of London members of the London Assembly at an ordinary election who are included in a list of candidates submitted by a registered political party in connection with the election (see the Representation of the People Act 1983 s 90D(1) (as added and amended: see note 3)), 'for the purposes of the candidate's election', instead of having the meaning given by s 90ZA(3), is to be construed as meaning with a view to, or otherwise in connection with promoting or procuring electoral success for the party (that is to say, the return at the election of all or any of the candidates on the list) (s 90D(2)(b) (s 90D as so added; s 90D(2)(b) amended by the Electoral Administration Act 2006 Sch 1 paras 104, 118(1), (4)); and any reference (in whatever form) to promoting or procuring a candidate's election at an election, or to promoting or procuring electoral success for a party, includes doing so by prejudicing the electoral prospects of other candidates or parties at the election (Representation of the People Act 1983 s 90ZA(6) (as added: see note 1); modified by s 90D(3) (s 90D as so added; s 90D(3) amended by the Electoral Administration Act 2006 Sch 1 paras 104, 118(1), (5))).

5   Representation of the People Act 1983 s 90ZA(1) (as added: see note 1); European Parliamentary Elections Regulations 2004, SI 2004/293, reg 60(1) (as substituted: see note 1); National Assembly for Wales (Representation of the People) Order 2007, SI 2007/236, art 63(1). The definition of 'election expenses' given in the Representation of the People Act 1983 s 90ZA(1) is modified where an election follows the dissolution of a Parliament that has run for over 55 months, and a 'pre-candidacy' spending limit on candidate election expenses is imposed (ie a second regulated period) which operates in addition to the limit imposed by s 76 (see PARA 273): see s 76ZA(1); and PARA 274. Also, where election expenses are incurred by or on behalf of the candidate otherwise than for the purposes of the candidate's election, but which, by virtue of the Representation of the People Act 1983 s 90ZA(1), the European Parliamentary Elections Regulations 2004, SI 2004/293, reg 60(1), or the National Assembly for Wales (Representation of the People) Order 2007, SI 2007/236, art 63(1), as the case may be, fall to be regarded as election expenses by reason of the property, services or facilities in respect of which they are incurred being used for the purposes of the candidate's election, the provisions which relate to the payment of election expenses only through an election agent (see PARA 270), to the time-barred payment of claims in relation to such expenses, and to disputes relating to such claims (see PARAS 276, 277), are disapplied and a separate declaration of value must be made: see the Representation of the People Act 1983 s 74A; the European Parliamentary Elections Regulations 2004, SI 2004/293, reg 45; the National Assembly for Wales (Representation of the People) Order 2007, SI 2007/236, art 45; and PARA 270.

The Political Parties, Elections and Referendums Act 2000, by making the original amendments to the Representation of the People Act 1983, replaced the previous definition of 'election expenses' and accordingly superseded the extensive case law which had interpreted the previous statutory definition. As to the previous wording and for a summary of the relevant case law which has now been superseded see *R v Jones, R v Whicher* [1999] 2 Cr App Rep 253, CA.

6   Representation of the People Act 1983 Sch 4A para 1 (as added: see note 1); European Parliamentary Elections Regulations 2004, SI 2004/293, Sch 7A para 1 (as added: see note 1); National Assembly for Wales (Representation of the People) Order 2007, SI 2007/236, Sch 7 para 1. As to the control of advertising relating to a pending parliamentary, European Parliamentary, Welsh Assembly or local government election see PARA 333 et seq.

7   Representation of the People Act 1983 Sch 4A para 2 (as added: see note 1); European Parliamentary Elections Regulations 2004, SI 2004/293, Sch 7A para 2 (as added: see note 1); National Assembly for Wales (Representation of the People) Order 2007, SI 2007/236, Sch 7 para 2. As to a candidate's right to send election addresses to electors generally see PARA 330 et seq.

8   Representation of the People Act 1983 Sch 4A para 3 (as added: see note 1); European Parliamentary Elections Regulations 2004, SI 2004/293, Sch 7A para 3 (as added: see note 1); National Assembly for Wales (Representation of the People) Order 2007, SI 2007/236, Sch 7 para 3.

9   Representation of the People Act 1983 Sch 4A para 4 (as added: see note 1); European Parliamentary Elections Regulations 2004, SI 2004/293, Sch 7A para 4 (as added: see note 1); National Assembly for Wales (Representation of the People) Order 2007, SI 2007/236, Sch 7 para 4. As to public meetings at elections generally see PARA 334 et seq.

10   Representation of the People Act 1983 Sch 4A para 5 (as added: see note 1); European Parliamentary Elections Regulations 2004, SI 2004/293, Sch 7A para 5 (as added: see note 1); National Assembly for Wales (Representation of the People) Order 2007, SI 2007/236, Sch 7 para 5. As to the appointment of election agents generally see PARA 231 et seq.

11   Representation of the People Act 1983 Sch 4A para 6 (as added: see note 1); European Parliamentary Elections Regulations 2004, SI 2004/293, Sch 7A para 6 (as added: see note 1); National Assembly for Wales (Representation of the People) Order 2007, SI 2007/236, Sch 7 para 6.

12   Representation of the People Act 1983 s 90C(1)(a)(i) (s 90C added by the Political Parties, Elections and Referendums Act 2000 s 134); European Parliamentary Elections Regulations 2004, SI 2004/293, reg 62(1)(a)(i); National Assembly for Wales (Representation of the People) Order 2007, SI 2007/236, art 64(1)(a)(i). Any reference to property or goods being transferred to a candidate or his election agent includes a reference to their being transferred either directly or indirectly through any third person: Representation of the People Act 1983 Sch 2A para 2(6)(a) (Sch 2A added by the Political Parties, Elections and Referendums Act 2000 s 130(1), (3), (4)) (applied by the Representation of the People Act 1983 s 90C(6) (as so added)); European Parliamentary Elections Regulations 2004, SI 2004/293, Sch 6 para 2(6)(a) (applied by reg 62(6)); National Assembly for Wales (Representation of the People) Order 2007, SI 2007/236, Sch 6 para 2(6)(a) (applied by art 64(6)).

    In relation to an election of parish councillors in England or of community councillors in Wales, s 90ZA(4) and s 90C have effect as if for the references to an election agent there were substituted references to any agent of the candidate: s 90(1)(a) (amended by the Political Parties, Elections and Referendums Act 2000 s 138(1), Sch 18 paras 1, 11(a); and the Electoral Administration Act 2006 Sch 1 paras 104, 116). See further PARA 293 et seq. As to the election of parish or community councillors see PARA 200 et seq.

13   Representation of the People Act 1983 s 90C(1)(a)(ii) (as added: see note 12); European Parliamentary Elections Regulations 2004, SI 2004/293, reg 62(1)(a)(ii); National Assembly for Wales (Representation of the People) Order 2007, SI 2007/236, art 64(1)(a)(ii).

14   Representation of the People Act 1983 s 90C(1)(a)(i), (ii) (as added: see note 12); European Parliamentary Elections Regulations 2004, SI 2004/293, reg 62(1)(a)(i), (ii); National Assembly for Wales (Representation of the People) Order 2007, SI 2007/236, art 64(1)(a)(i), (ii). The discount referred to in the text is a discount of more than:

    (1)   10% of the market value of the property or goods, in the case of head (a) in the text (Representation of the People Act 1983 s 90C(1)(a)(i) (as so added); European Parliamentary Elections Regulations 2004, SI 2004/293, reg 62(1)(a)(i); National Assembly for Wales (Representation of the People) Order 2007, SI 2007/236, art 64(1)(a)(i)); or

    (2)   10% of the commercial rate for the use of the property or for the provision of the goods, services or facilities, in the case of head (b) in the text (Representation of the People Act 1983 s 90C(1)(a)(ii) (as so added); European Parliamentary Elections Regulations 2004, SI 2004/293, reg 62(1)(a)(ii); National Assembly for Wales (Representation of the People) Order 2007, SI 2007/236, art 64(1)(a)(ii)).

For these purposes, 'market value', in relation to any property or goods, means the price which might reasonably be expected to be paid for the property or goods on a sale in the open market: Representation of the People Act 1983 s 90C(6) (as so added); European Parliamentary

Elections Regulations 2004, SI 2004/293, reg 62(6); National Assembly for Wales (Representation of the People) Order 2007, SI 2007/236, art 64(6). Where the services of an employee are made available by his employer for the use or benefit of a candidate, then for the purposes of determining election expenses, the commercial rate for the provision of those services is the amount of the remuneration and allowances payable to the employee by his employer in respect of the period for which his services are so made available (but do not include any amount in respect of any contributions or other payments for which the employer is liable in respect of the employee): Representation of the People Act 1983 s 90C(5) (as so added); European Parliamentary Elections Regulations 2004, SI 2004/293, reg 62(5); National Assembly for Wales (Representation of the People) Order 2007, SI 2007/236, art 64(5).

15 Representation of the People Act 1983 s 90C(1)(b) (as added: see note 12); European Parliamentary Elections Regulations 2004, SI 2004/293, reg 62(1)(b); National Assembly for Wales (Representation of the People) Order 2007, SI 2007/236, art 64(1)(b). For these purposes, election expenses are incurred by or on behalf of a candidate at an election if they are incurred:
   (1)   by the candidate or his election agent (Representation of the People Act 1983 s 90ZA(4)(a) (as added: see note 1); European Parliamentary Elections Regulations 2004, SI 2004/293, reg 60(4)(a) (as substituted: see note 1); National Assembly for Wales (Representation of the People) Order 2007, SI 2007/236, art 63(4)(a)); or
   (2)   by any person authorised by the candidate or his election agent to incur the expenses (Representation of the People Act 1983 s 90ZA(4)(b) (as so added); European Parliamentary Elections Regulations 2004, SI 2004/293, reg 60(4)(b) (as so substituted); National Assembly for Wales (Representation of the People) Order 2007, SI 2007/236, art 63(4)(b)).
For the purposes of the European Parliamentary Elections Regulations 2004, SI 2004/293, Pt 2, and the National Assembly for Wales (Representation of the People) Order 2007, SI 2007/236, Pt 3, any reference to election expenses incurred by or on behalf of a candidate at an election includes expenses which are incurred as mentioned in the European Parliamentary Elections Regulations 2004, SI 2004/293, reg 60(1), or in the National Assembly for Wales (Representation of the People) Order 2007, SI 2007/236, art 63(1) (see the text and notes 1–5), as the case may be, before the date when he becomes a candidate at the election, but which by virtue of the European Parliamentary Elections Regulations 2004, SI 2004/293, reg 60(1), or the National Assembly for Wales (Representation of the People) Order 2007, SI 2007/236, art 63(1), fall to be regarded as election expenses: European Parliamentary Elections Regulations 2004, SI 2004/293, reg 60(5) (as so substituted); National Assembly for Wales (Representation of the People) Order 2007, SI 2007/236, art 63(5).

16 Representation of the People Act 1983 s 90C(2)(a) (as added: see note 12); European Parliamentary Elections Regulations 2004, SI 2004/293, reg 62(2)(a); National Assembly for Wales (Representation of the People) Order 2007, SI 2007/236, art 64(2)(a).
   This provision has effect subject to the Representation of the People Act 1983 Sch 4A Pt 2 (paras 7–13) or the European Parliamentary Elections Regulations 2004, SI 2004/293, Sch 7A Pt 2 (paras 7–13), or the National Assembly for Wales (Representation of the People) Order 2007, SI 2007/236, Sch 7 Pt 2 (paras 7–13) (see the text and notes 27–36), as the case may be: Representation of the People Act 1983 s 90C(2) (s 90C as so added; s 90C(2) amended by the Electoral Administration Act 2006 Sch 1 paras 104, 117, 133); European Parliamentary Elections Regulations 2004, SI 2004/293, reg 62(2) (amended by SI 2009/186); National Assembly for Wales (Representation of the People) Order 2007, SI 2007/236, art 64(2).

17 Representation of the People Act 1983 s 90C(2)(b) (as added: see note 12); European Parliamentary Elections Regulations 2004, SI 2004/293, reg 62(2)(b); National Assembly for Wales (Representation of the People) Order 2007, SI 2007/236, art 64(2)(b). In the case of a European parliamentary election, head (ii) in the text is expressed to apply to the case of an individual candidate: see the European Parliamentary Elections Regulations 2004, SI 2004/293, reg 62(2)(b). As to the meaning of 'individual candidate' at a European parliamentary election see PARA 230 note 32.

18 Representation of the People Act 1983 s 90C(2)(b) (as added: see note 12); European Parliamentary Elections Regulations 2004, SI 2004/293, reg 62(2)(b); National Assembly for Wales (Representation of the People) Order 2007, SI 2007/236, art 64(2)(b). See eg *Finch v Richardson* [2008] EWHC 3067 (QB), [2009] 1 WLR 1338, [2009] PTSR 841, [2009] All ER (D) 01 (Jan) (use of personal driver, supplied by candidate's employers, to perform tasks, including delivering election address documents to the electorate and a small number of letters, etc, fell within the Representation of the People Act 1983 s 90C and should have been assessed and declared as part of the candidate's expenses return).

19 Representation of the People Act 1983 s 90C(3)(a) (as added: see note 12); European Parliamentary Elections Regulations 2004, SI 2004/293, reg 62(3)(a); National Assembly for Wales (Representation of the People) Order 2007, SI 2007/236, art 64(3)(a).

20 Representation of the People Act 1983 s 90C(3)(b) (as added: see note 12); European Parliamentary Elections Regulations 2004, SI 2004/293, reg 62(3)(b); National Assembly for Wales (Representation of the People) Order 2007, SI 2007/236, art 64(3)(b).

21 Representation of the People Act 1983 s 90C(3) (as added: see note 12); European Parliamentary Elections Regulations 2004, SI 2004/293, reg 62(3); National Assembly for Wales (Representation of the People) Order 2007, SI 2007/236, art 64(3). The text refers to the use made of the property or goods as mentioned in the Representation of the People Act 1983 s 90C(1)(b) or the European Parliamentary Elections Regulations 2004, SI 2004/293, reg 62(1)(b), or the National Assembly for Wales (Representation of the People) Order 2007, SI 2007/236, art 64(1)(b) (see the text and note 15), as the case may be: Representation of the People Act 1983 s 90C(3) (as so added); European Parliamentary Elections Regulations 2004, SI 2004/293, reg 62(3); National Assembly for Wales (Representation of the People) Order 2007, SI 2007/236, art 64(3).

22 Representation of the People Act 1983 s 90C(4)(a) (as added: see note 12); European Parliamentary Elections Regulations 2004, SI 2004/293, reg 62(4)(a); National Assembly for Wales (Representation of the People) Order 2007, SI 2007/236, art 64(4)(a).

23 Representation of the People Act 1983 s 90C(4)(b) (as added: see note 12); European Parliamentary Elections Regulations 2004, SI 2004/293, reg 62(4)(b); National Assembly for Wales (Representation of the People) Order 2007, SI 2007/236, art 64(4)(b).

24 Representation of the People Act 1983 s 90C(4) (as added: see note 12); European Parliamentary Elections Regulations 2004, SI 2004/293, reg 62(4); National Assembly for Wales (Representation of the People) Order 2007, SI 2007/236, art 64(4). The text refers to the use made of the property, goods, services or facilities as mentioned in the Representation of the People Act 1983 s 90C(1)(b) or the European Parliamentary Elections Regulations 2004, SI 2004/293, reg 62(1)(b), or the National Assembly for Wales (Representation of the People) Order 2007, SI 2007/236, art 64(1)(b) (see the text and note 15), as the case may be: Representation of the People Act 1983 s 90C(4) (as so added); European Parliamentary Elections Regulations 2004, SI 2004/293, reg 62(4); National Assembly for Wales (Representation of the People) Order 2007, SI 2007/236, art 64(4).

25 Ie by virtue of the Representation of the People Act 1983 s 90ZA(1) or the European Parliamentary Elections Regulations 2004, SI 2004/293, reg 60(1) or the National Assembly for Wales (Representation of the People) Order 2007, SI 2007/236, art 63(1) (see the text and notes 1–5) or the Representation of the People Act 1983 s 90C or the European Parliamentary Elections Regulations 2004, SI 2004/293, reg 62, or the National Assembly for Wales (Representation of the People) Order 2007, SI 2007/236, art 64 (see the text and notes 12–24): Representation of the People Act 1983 s 90ZA(2) (as added: see note 1); European Parliamentary Elections Regulations 2004, SI 2004/293, reg 60(2) (as substituted: see note 1); National Assembly for Wales (Representation of the People) Order 2007, SI 2007/236, art 63(2).

26 Representation of the People Act 1983 s 90ZA(2) (as added: see note 1); European Parliamentary Elections Regulations 2004, SI 2004/293, reg 60(2) (as substituted: see note 1); National Assembly for Wales (Representation of the People) Order 2007, SI 2007/236, art 63(2).

For the period 22 March 2013 to 30 June 2014, an additional head applies at parliamentary and local government elections, namely the provision of property, goods, services or facilities where the expenses are incurred for the purpose of removing, or mitigating the effect of, barriers to seeking elected office associated with the candidate's disability: see the Representation of the People Act 1983 Sch 4A para 7A (Sch 4A as added (see note 1); Sch 4A para 7A added by SI 2013/688).

27 Representation of the People Act 1983 Sch 4A para 7 (as added: see note 1); European Parliamentary Elections Regulations 2004, SI 2004/293, Sch 7A para 7 (as added: see note 1); National Assembly for Wales (Representation of the People) Order 2007, SI 2007/236, Sch 7 para 7. The text refers to the payment that is required to be deposited by the Representation of the People Act 1983 Sch 1 r 9 or the European Parliamentary Elections Regulations 2004, SI 2004/293, Sch 1 para 10, or the National Assembly for Wales (Representation of the People) Order 2007, SI 2007/236, Sch 5 para 10 (see PARA 259), as the case may be: Representation of the People Act 1983 Sch 4A para 7 (as so added); European Parliamentary Elections Regulations 2004, SI 2004/293, Sch 7A para 7 (as so added); National Assembly for Wales (Representation of the People) Order 2007, SI 2007/236, Sch 7 para 7.

28 Representation of the People Act 1983 Sch 4A para 8 (as added: see note 1); European
    Parliamentary Elections Regulations 2004, SI 2004/293, Sch 7A para 8 (as added: see note 1);
    National Assembly for Wales (Representation of the People) Order 2007, SI 2007/236, Sch 7
    para 8. The text refers to a service licensed under the Broadcasting Act 1990 Pt I (ss 3–71)
    (independent television services: see BROADCASTING vol 4 (2011) PARA 507 et seq) or Pt III
    (ss 85–126) (independent radio services: see BROADCASTING vol 4 (2011) PARA 724 et seq) or
    under the Broadcasting Act 1996 Pt I (ss 1–39) (digital terrestrial television broadcasting: see
    BROADCASTING vol 4 (2011) PARA 690 et seq) or Pt II (ss 40–72) (digital terrestrial sound
    broadcasting: see BROADCASTING vol 4 (2011) PARA 727 et seq): Representation of the People
    Act 1983 Sch 4A para 8 (as so added); European Parliamentary Elections Regulations 2004,
    SI 2004/293, Sch 7A para 8 (as so added); National Assembly for Wales (Representation of the
    People) Order 2007, SI 2007/236, Sch 7 para 8. As to the BBC see BROADCASTING vol 4 (2011)
    PARA 603 et seq; and as to Sianel Pedwar Cymru see BROADCASTING vol 4 (2011) PARA 645.

29 Representation of the People Act 1983 Sch 4A para 9 (as added: see note 1); European
    Parliamentary Elections Regulations 2004, SI 2004/293, Sch 7A para 9 (as added: see note 1);
    National Assembly for Wales (Representation of the People) Order 2007, SI 2007/236, Sch 7
    para 9. The text refers to any right conferred on candidates at an election by the Representation
    of the People Act 1983 other than facilities in respect of which expenses fall to be defrayed by
    virtue of s 95(4) (schools and rooms for parliamentary election meetings: see PARA 335) and
    s 96(4) (schools and rooms for local election meetings: see PARA 337), or any right conferred on
    candidates at an election by the European Parliamentary Elections Regulations 2004,
    SI 2004/293, other than facilities in respect of which expenses fall to be defrayed by virtue of
    reg 67(4) (schools and rooms for European parliamentary election meetings: see PARA 335), or
    any right conferred on candidates at an election by the National Assembly for Wales
    (Representation of the People) Order 2007, SI 2007/236, other than facilities in respect of which
    expenses fall to be defrayed by virtue of art 69(4) (schools and rooms for election meetings: see
    PARA 335), as the case may be: Representation of the People Act 1983 Sch 4A para 9 (as so
    added); European Parliamentary Elections Regulations 2004, SI 2004/293, Sch 7A para 9 (as so
    added); National Assembly for Wales (Representation of the People) Order 2007, SI 2007/236,
    Sch 7 para 9.

30 Representation of the People Act 1983 Sch 4A para 10 (as added: see note 1); European
    Parliamentary Elections Regulations 2004, SI 2004/293, Sch 7A para 10 (as added: see note 1);
    National Assembly for Wales (Representation of the People) Order 2007, SI 2007/236, Sch 7
    para 10.

31 Representation of the People Act 1983 Sch 4A para 11(1) (as added: see note 1); European
    Parliamentary Elections Regulations 2004, SI 2004/293, Sch 7A para 11(1) (as added: see
    note 1); National Assembly for Wales (Representation of the People) Order 2007, SI 2007/236,
    Sch 7 para 11(1).

32 Representation of the People Act 1983 Sch 4A para 11(2) (as added: see note 1); European
    Parliamentary Elections Regulations 2004, SI 2004/293, Sch 7A para 11(2) (as added: see
    note 1); National Assembly for Wales (Representation of the People) Order 2007, SI 2007/236,
    Sch 7 para 11(2).

33 Representation of the People Act 1983 Sch 4A para 12(1) (as added: see note 1); European
    Parliamentary Elections Regulations 2004, SI 2004/293, Sch 7A para 12(1) (as added: see
    note 1); National Assembly for Wales (Representation of the People) Order 2007, SI 2007/236,
    Sch 7 para 12(1).

34 Representation of the People Act 1983 Sch 4A para 12(2) (as added: see note 1); European
    Parliamentary Elections Regulations 2004, SI 2004/293, Sch 7A para 12(2) (as added: see
    note 1); National Assembly for Wales (Representation of the People) Order 2007, SI 2007/236,
    Sch 7 para 12(2).

35 Representation of the People Act 1983 Sch 4A para 13(1) (as added: see note 1); European
    Parliamentary Elections Regulations 2004, SI 2004/293, Sch 7A para 13(1) (as added: see
    note 1); National Assembly for Wales (Representation of the People) Order 2007, SI 2007/236,
    Sch 7 para 13(1).

36 Representation of the People Act 1983 Sch 4A para 13(2) (as added: see note 1); European
    Parliamentary Elections Regulations 2004, SI 2004/293, Sch 7A para 13(2) (as added: see
    note 1); National Assembly for Wales (Representation of the People) Order 2007, SI 2007/236,
    Sch 7 para 13(2).

37 As to the Electoral Commission see PARA 34 et seq.

38 Representation of the People Act 1983 Sch 4A para 14(1)(a) (Sch 4A as added (see note 1);
    Sch 4A para 14(1)(a), (b) added by the Political Parties and Elections Act 2009 s 22).

39 Ie supplementing the definition in the Representation of the People Act 1983 s 90ZA(3) (see note 4): see Sch 4A para 14(1)(b) (Sch 4A as added (see note 1); Sch 4A para 14(1)(b) as added (see note 38)).

40 Representation of the People Act 1983 Sch 4A para 14(1)(b) (Sch 4A as added (see note 1); Sch 4A para 14(1)(b) as added (see note 38)).

41 Representation of the People Act 1983 Sch 4A para 14(2) (as added: see note 1). As to the Secretary of State see PARA 2.

42 Representation of the People Act 1983 Sch 4A para 14(3) (as added: see note 1). For these purposes, references to a draft code include a revised draft code: Sch 4A para 14(10) (as so added). Once the Secretary of State has approved a draft code he must lay a copy of the draft, whether in its original form or in a form which incorporates any modifications determined under Sch 4A para 14(3), before each House of Parliament: Sch 4A para 14(4) (as so added). If the draft incorporates any such modifications, the Secretary of State must at the same time lay before each House a statement of his reasons for making them: Sch 4A para 14(5) (as so added). If, within the 40-day period, either House resolves not to approve the draft, the Secretary of State must take no further steps in relation to the draft code (Sch 4A para 14(6) (as so added)); but if no such resolution is made within the 40-day period, the Secretary of State must issue the code in the form of the draft laid before Parliament, and the code is to come into force on such date as the Secretary of State may by order appoint (Sch 4A para 14(7) (as so added)). The Commission must arrange for the code to be published in such manner as it thinks appropriate: Sch 4A para 14(7) (as so added). The prohibition from taking further action in relation to a draft code (see Sch 4A para 14(6)) does not prevent a new draft code from being laid before Parliament: Sch 4A para 14(8) (as so added). For these purposes, the '40-day period', in relation to a draft code, means, if the draft is laid before one House on a day later than the day on which it is laid before the other House, the period of 40 days beginning with the later of the two days, and, in any other case, the period of 40 days beginning with the day on which the draft is laid before each House: see Sch 4A para 14(9) (as so added). In calculating this period, no account is taken of any period during which Parliament is dissolved or prorogued or during which both Houses are adjourned for more than four days: see Sch 4A para 14(9) (as so added).

    A Code of Practice issued by the Secretary of State under the provisions of the Representation of the People Act 1983 Sch 4A para 14 apply to the National Assembly for Wales (Representation of the People) Order 2007, SI 2007/236, Sch 7, as they do to the Representation of the People Act 1983 Sch 4A para 14: National Assembly for Wales (Representation of the People) Order 2007, SI 2007/236, art 63(8).

43 Representation of the People Act 1983 Sch 4A para 15(1) (as added: see note 1). However, such an order must not be made unless a draft of the statutory instrument containing the order has been laid before, and approved by a resolution of, each House of Parliament: Sch 4A para 15(2) (as so added). In exercise of the powers so conferred, the Representation of the People (Election Expenses Exclusion) Order 2013, SI 2013/688, has been made but is of limited effect (see note 26).

44 Representation of the People Act 1983 Sch 4A para 15(3)(a) (as added: see note 1).

45 Representation of the People Act 1983 Sch 4A para 15(3)(b) (as added: see note 1).

B. PAYMENT OF ELECTION EXPENSES

(A) Restrictions on the Payment of Election Expenses

270. Restriction on payment of candidate's election expenses otherwise than by or through election agent. No payment[1], of whatever nature, may be made either by a candidate[2] at an election[3], or by any other person[4], in respect of election expenses[5] incurred by or on behalf of the candidate[6] unless it is made by or through the candidate's election agent[7], subject to the following exceptions[8]:

(1)   any personal expenses incurred by the candidate in relation to the election and paid by him, subject to the statutory cap on such payments[9];

(2)   election expenses which are paid by him before an election agent is appointed[10];

(3)   any sum paid by the candidate in pursuance of an order of leave to pay a claim for any election expenses[11];

(4) any sum paid by the candidate in pursuance of a judgment or order of the court in an action for a disputed claim[12];

(5) any necessary petty expenses which are paid by a person authorised by the candidate's election agent[13];

(6) any expenses included in a declaration made by the election agent regarding expenses incurred otherwise than for the purposes of the candidate's election but which fall to be regarded as election expenses by reason of the property, services or facilities in respect of which they were incurred being used for the purposes of the candidate's election[14];

(7) any expenses which fall to be regarded as election expenses even though they are incurred by the candidate or his election agent or by an authorised person before the date of candidature[15].

Every payment made by an election agent in respect of any election expenses, except where less than £20, must be vouched for by a bill stating the particulars, or by a receipt[16]. For these purposes[17], an election agent may act by a sub-agent, at elections where a sub-agent has been appointed[18]; and, in the case of a European parliamentary election, an election agent may act also by a person authorised in writing by the election agent or sub-agent[19].

A person who makes any payment in contravention of this prohibition is guilty of an illegal practice[20]. The argument that the payments referred to above are limited to those made by the election agent and not those made by persons (other than the election agent) of election expenses incurred by themselves has been rejected[21]. The intention of this prohibition is that the election agent, and he alone, is to be responsible for the payment of election expenses[22]. If, therefore, the election agent hands a large sum of money to a person to be dispensed by him at his discretion, that falls foul of the prohibition[23]. If, however, the election agent has made all arrangements for the particular expense, but hands over the money to a third person to make the actual payment, that may be permissible[24].

The requirement for election expenses to be paid by or through an election agent[25] does not apply to election expenses which are incurred by or on behalf of the candidate otherwise than for the purposes of the candidate's election[26], but which[27] fall to be regarded as election expenses by reason of the property, services or facilities in respect of which they are incurred being used for the purposes of the candidate's election[28]. However, the candidate's election agent must make a declaration of the amount of any such expenses that are incurred otherwise than for election purposes[29].

1 In the Representation of the People Act 1983 Pt II (ss 67–119), in relation to a parliamentary or local government election, in the European Parliamentary Elections Regulations 2004, SI 2004/293, Pt 2 (regs 31–81), in relation to a European parliamentary election, or in the National Assembly for Wales (Representation of the People) Order 2007, SI 2007/236, Pt 3 (arts 37–85), in relation to a Welsh Assembly election (see PARA 235 et seq), unless the context otherwise requires, 'payment' includes any pecuniary or other reward; and 'money' and 'pecuniary reward' are deemed to include any office, place or employment, and any valuable security or other equivalent of money, and any valuable consideration, and expressions referring to money are to be construed accordingly: Representation of the People Act 1983 s 118 (definitions of 'money' and 'pecuniary reward' amended by the Political Parties, Elections and Referendums Act 2000 s 138(1), Sch 18 paras 1, 15(b)); European Parliamentary Elections Regulations 2004, SI 2004/293, reg 31(1); National Assembly for Wales (Representation of the People) Order 2007, SI 2007/236, art 84(1). As to the meaning of 'parliamentary election' see PARA 9; and as to the meaning of 'local government election' see PARA 11. As to the meaning of 'Assembly election' see PARA 3 note 2. As to European parliamentary elections see PARA 217 et seq.

However, these expressions do not apply for the purposes of the Representation of the People Act 1983 s 71A (control of donations to candidates at a parliamentary or local government election: see PARA 286 et seq), s 113 (bribery: see PARA 709), s 114 (treating: see PARA 721), Sch 2A (control of donations to candidates: see PARA 287 et seq), the European Parliamentary Elections Regulations 2004, SI 2004/293, reg 42 (control of donations to individual candidates: see PARA 286 et seq), reg 77 (bribery: see PARA 709), reg 78 (treating: see PARA 721), Sch 6 (control of donations to individual candidates: see PARA 287 et seq), or the National Assembly for Wales (Representation of the People) Order 2007, SI 2007/236, art 41 (control of donations to constituency and individual candidates: see PARA 286 et seq), art 79 (bribery: see PARA 709), art 80 (treating: see PARA 721) and Sch 6 (control of donations to individual candidates: see PARA 287 et seq). See also *Barrow-in-Furness Case* (1886) 4 O'M & H 76 at 81 (refreshments held to constitute payment).

2   As to the meaning of 'candidate' generally see PARA 230. The reference in the text is to an 'individual candidate' for the purposes of a European parliamentary election: see the European Parliamentary Elections Regulations 2004, SI 2004/293, reg 43(1)(a). As to the meaning of 'individual candidate' for those purposes see PARA 230 note 32. For the purposes of a Welsh Assembly election, the reference is to either a constituency candidate at a constituency election, or an individual candidate at a regional election: see the National Assembly for Wales (Representation of the People) Order 2007, SI 2007/236, art 43(1)(a). As to the meanings of 'constituency election' and 'regional election' for the purposes of Welsh Assembly elections see PARA 3 note 2; and as to the meanings of 'constituency candidate' and 'individual candidate' see PARA 230 note 19.

3   Representation of the People Act 1983 s 73(1)(a) (s 73(1) substituted by the Political Parties, Elections and Referendums Act 2000 Sch 18 paras 1, 3(1), (2)); European Parliamentary Elections Regulations 2004, SI 2004/293, reg 43(1)(a); National Assembly for Wales (Representation of the People) Order 2007, SI 2007/236, art 43(1)(a).
     The Representation of the People Act 1983 s 73 does not apply at an election under the local government Act which is not a local government election (see the Representation of the People Act 1983 s 90(2); and PARA 297); and, in relation to an election of parish councillors in England or of community councillors in Wales, the provisions of s 90(1), Sch 4 apply instead; and s 76A(2) (see note 16) is modified (see s 90(1)(b); and PARAS 293–296). As to the meaning of 'election under the local government Act' see PARA 11 note 2.

4   Representation of the People Act 1983 s 73(1)(b) (as substituted: see note 3); European Parliamentary Elections Regulations 2004, SI 2004/293, reg 43(1)(b); National Assembly for Wales (Representation of the People) Order 2007, SI 2007/236, art 43(1)(b).

5   As to the meaning of 'election expenses' see PARA 269; but see also the text and notes 25–29.

6   As to the meaning of 'election expenses incurred by or on behalf of a candidate' see PARA 269 note 15.

7   Representation of the People Act 1983 s 73(1) (as substituted: see note 3); European Parliamentary Elections Regulations 2004, SI 2004/293, reg 43(1); National Assembly for Wales (Representation of the People) Order 2007, SI 2007/236, art 43(1). In the case of a European parliamentary election, it is further specified that all money provided by any person other than the individual candidate for any election expenses, whether as gift, loan, advance or deposit, must be paid to the candidate or his election agent or sub-agent and not otherwise: European Parliamentary Elections Regulations 2004, SI 2004/293, reg 43(4). As to the appointment of election agents generally see PARA 231 et seq; and as to the appointment of sub-agents generally see PARA 233 et seq. See also the text and notes 17–19.

8   le subject to exceptions set out in the Representation of the People Act 1983 s 73(5), in the European Parliamentary Elections Regulations 2004, SI 2004/293, reg 43(5), or in the National Assembly for Wales (Representation of the People) Order 2007, SI 2007/236, art 43(4) (whichever is appropriate) (see the text and notes 9–15): Representation of the People Act 1983 s 73(1) (as substituted: see note 3); European Parliamentary Elections Regulations 2004, SI 2004/293, reg 43(1); National Assembly for Wales (Representation of the People) Order 2007, SI 2007/236, art 43(1).

9   Representation of the People Act 1983 s 73(5)(a) (s 73(5) substituted by the Political Parties, Elections and Referendums Act 2000 s 138, Sch 18 paras 1, 3(1), (5)); European Parliamentary Elections Regulations 2004, SI 2004/293, reg 43(5)(a); National Assembly for Wales (Representation of the People) Order 2007, SI 2007/236, art 43(4)(a). The text refers to personal expenses paid by the candidate in accordance with, in relation to a parliamentary or local government election, the Representation of the People Act 1983 s 74(1), in relation to a European parliamentary election, the European Parliamentary Elections Regulations 2004, SI 2004/293, reg 44(1), or, in relation to a Welsh Assembly election, the National Assembly for Wales (Representation of the People) Order 2007, SI 2007/236, art 44(1) (whichever is appropriate) (see PARA 271).

10 Representation of the People Act 1983 s 73(5)(a) (as substituted: see note 9); European Parliamentary Elections Regulations 2004, SI 2004/293, reg 43(5)(a); National Assembly for Wales (Representation of the People) Order 2007, SI 2007/236, art 43(4)(a). The text refers to election expenses paid by the candidate in accordance with the Representation of the People Act 1983 s 74(1B), the European Parliamentary Elections Regulations 2004, SI 2004/293, reg 44(2), or the National Assembly for Wales (Representation of the People) Order 2007, SI 2007/236, art 44(2) (whichever is appropriate) (see PARA 271).

11 Representation of the People Act 1983 s 73(5)(a) (as substituted: see note 9); European Parliamentary Elections Regulations 2004, SI 2004/293, reg 43(5)(a); National Assembly for Wales (Representation of the People) Order 2007, SI 2007/236, art 43(4)(a). The text refers to any sum paid by the candidate or his election agent in accordance with the Representation of the People Act 1983 s 78(5), the European Parliamentary Elections Regulations 2004, SI 2004/293, reg 48(6), or the National Assembly for Wales (Representation of the People) Order 2007, SI 2007/236, art 49(6) (whichever is appropriate) (see PARA 277).

12 Representation of the People Act 1983 s 73(5)(a) (as substituted: see note 9); European Parliamentary Elections Regulations 2004, SI 2004/293, reg 43(5)(a); National Assembly for Wales (Representation of the People) Order 2007, SI 2007/236, art 43(4)(a). The text refers to any sum paid by the candidate or his agent in accordance with the Representation of the People Act 1983 s 79(2), the European Parliamentary Elections Regulations 2004, SI 2004/293, reg 49(2), or the National Assembly for Wales (Representation of the People) Order 2007, SI 2007/236, art 50(2) (whichever is appropriate) (see PARA 276).

13 Representation of the People Act 1983 s 73(5)(b) (as substituted: see note 9); European Parliamentary Elections Regulations 2004, SI 2004/293, reg 43(5)(b); National Assembly for Wales (Representation of the People) Order 2007, SI 2007/236, art 43(4)(b). The text refers to necessary petty expenses which are paid in accordance with the Representation of the People Act 1983 s 74(3), the European Parliamentary Elections Regulations 2004, SI 2004/293, reg 44(4), or the National Assembly for Wales (Representation of the People) Order 2007, SI 2007/236, art 44(4) (whichever is appropriate) (see PARA 271).

14 Representation of the People Act 1983 s 73(5)(c) (as substituted: see note 9); European Parliamentary Elections Regulations 2004, SI 2004/293, reg 43(5)(c); National Assembly for Wales (Representation of the People) Order 2007, SI 2007/236, art 43(4)(c). The text refers to any expenses included in a declaration made by the election agent under the Representation of the People Act 1983 s 74A, the European Parliamentary Elections Regulations 2004, SI 2004/293, reg 45, or the National Assembly for Wales (Representation of the People) Order 2007, SI 2007/236, art 45 (whichever is appropriate) (see PARA 270). The Representation of the People Act 1983 s 73, the European Parliamentary Elections Regulations 2004, SI 2004/293, reg 43, and the National Assembly for Wales (Representation of the People) Order 2007, SI 2007/236, art 43, do not apply to election expenses that are as described in head (6) in the text: see PARA 270.

15 Representation of the People Act 1983 s 73(5)(d) (s 73(5) as substituted (see note 9); s 73(5)(d) amended by the Electoral Administration Act 2006 s 74(1), Sch 1 paras 104, 111, 133); European Parliamentary Elections Regulations 2004, SI 2004/293, reg 43(5)(d) (amended by SI 2009/186); National Assembly for Wales (Representation of the People) Order 2007, SI 2007/236, art 43(4)(d). The text refers to any expenses which are to be regarded as incurred by or on behalf of the candidate by virtue of the Representation of the People Act 1983 s 90ZA(5), the European Parliamentary Elections Regulations 2004, SI 2004/293, reg 60(5), or the National Assembly for Wales (Representation of the People) Order 2007, SI 2007/236, art 63(5) (whichever is appropriate) (see PARA 269).

16 Representation of the People Act 1983 s 73(2) (amended by the Representation of the People Act 1985 s 14(1); and the Political Parties, Elections and Referendums Act 2000 Sch 18 paras 1, 3(1), (3)); European Parliamentary Elections Regulations 2004, SI 2004/293, reg 43(2); National Assembly for Wales (Representation of the People) Order 2007, SI 2007/236, art 43(2). As to references to an election agent see the text and notes 17–19.

The Secretary of State may by order made by statutory instrument vary the sum for the time being specified in the Representation of the People Act 1983 s 73(2) or the National Assembly for Wales (Representation of the People) Order 2007, SI 2007/236, art 43(2) (whichever is appropriate) where he considers that the variation is expedient in consequence of changes in the value of money or in order to give effect to a recommendation of the Electoral Commission: Representation of the People Act 1983 s 76A(1), (2)(a) (s 76A added by the Representation of the People Act 1985 s 14; and substituted by the Political Parties, Elections and Referendums Act 2000 s 133(1)); National Assembly for Wales (Representation of the People) Order 2007, SI 2007/236, art 48(1), (2). Such an order which gives effect to a recommendation of the Electoral Commission is subject to annulment in pursuance of a resolution of either House of

Parliament (Representation of the People Act 1983 s 76A(3) (as so added and substituted); National Assembly for Wales (Representation of the People) Order 2007, SI 2007/236, art 48(3)). For the purposes of the Statutory Instruments Act 1946 s 1 (see STATUTES AND LEGISLATIVE PROCESS vol 96 (2012) PARA 1045), the National Assembly for Wales (Representation of the People) Order 2007, SI 2007/236, art 48(3) has effect as if contained in an Act of Parliament: see art 48(3). In relation to an election of parish councillors in England or of community councillors in Wales, the Representation of the People Act 1983 s 76A(2) is modified so that, instead of s 73(2), a reference to Sch 4 para 3 (expenses at elections where election agent not required: see PARA 295) is substituted: see s 90(1)(c) (substituted by the Political Parties, Elections and Referendums Act 2000 s 138(1), Sch 18 paras 1, 11(c)). As to the Secretary of State see PARA 2. As to the Electoral Commission see PARA 34 et seq.

17 Ie for the purposes of, in relation to a parliamentary or Authority election where sub-agents are allowed, the Representation of the People Act 1983 s 73(1), (2), in relation to a European parliamentary election, the European Parliamentary Elections Regulations 2004, SI 2004/293, reg 43(1), (2), or, in relation to a Welsh Assembly election, the National Assembly for Wales (Representation of the People) Order 2007, SI 2007/236, art 43(1), (2) (whichever is appropriate) (see the text and notes 1–16): Representation of the People Act 1983 s 73(3) (amended by the Greater London Authority Act 1999 s 17, Sch 3 paras 1, 17); European Parliamentary Elections Regulations 2004, SI 2004/293, reg 43(3); National Assembly for Wales (Representation of the People) Order 2007, SI 2007/236, art 43(3).

18 Representation of the People Act 1983 s 73(3) (as amended: see note 17); European Parliamentary Elections Regulations 2004, SI 2004/293, reg 43(3); National Assembly for Wales (Representation of the People) Order 2007, SI 2007/236, art 43(3). See also *Northumberland, Berwick-upon-Tweed Division, Case* (1923) 7 O'M & H 1.

19 See the European Parliamentary Elections Regulations 2004, SI 2004/293, reg 43(3).

20 See the Representation of the People Act 1983 s 73(6); the European Parliamentary Elections Regulations 2004, SI 2004/293, reg 43(6); the National Assembly for Wales (Representation of the People) Order 2007, SI 2007/236, art 43(5); and PARA 674. The making of such a payment as is mentioned in the text remains an illegal practice even if the money is repaid (*York County, East Riding, Buckrose Division, Case* (1886) 4 O'M & H 110 at 116), but where a payment was made through a person other than the election agent by mistake and the money was returned and the transaction was genuine and honest, it was held that no offence had been committed (*Monmouth Boroughs Case* (1901) 5 O'M & H 166 at 170). As to illegal practices see PARA 671 et seq.

21 *Ipswich Case, Packard v Collings and West* (1886) 4 O'M & H 70 at 73; *Hartlepools Case* (1910) 6 O'M & H 1 at 10; *Louth, Northern Division, Case* (1911) 6 O'M & H 103 at 164; *Oxford Borough Case* (1924) 7 O'M & H 49 at 80.

22 *West Bromwich Case* (1911) 6 O'M & H 256 at 285. The effect of the prohibition set out in the text and notes 1–15, when read together with the provisions relating to returns as to election expenses (see PARA 280), is that any election expense paid by the election agent will, if not shown on the return, constitute an illegal practice and that any election expenses not paid by the election agent will, subject to the statutory exceptions mentioned in PARA 271 et seq, constitute an illegal practice; and in either case the candidate's election is liable to be avoided.

23 *West Bromwich Case* (1911) 6 O'M & H 256 at 285. The sum mentioned in this case was £10, a large sum at that time.

24 *Cheltenham Case, Smythies and Claridge v Mathias, Davies' Case* (1911) 6 O'M & H 194 at 221.

25 Ie the provision made by the Representation of the People Act 1983 s 73, the European Parliamentary Elections Regulations 2004, SI 2004/293, reg 43, or the National Assembly for Wales (Representation of the People) Order 2007, SI 2007/236, art 43 (as the case may be) (see the text and notes 1–20): see the Representation of the People Act 1983 s 74A(1) (s 74A added by the Political Parties, Elections and Referendums Act 2000 s 138, Sch 18 paras 1, 5); the European Parliamentary Elections Regulations 2004, SI 2004/293, reg 45(1); and the National Assembly for Wales (Representation of the People) Order 2007, SI 2007/236, art 45(1).

26 Representation of the People Act 1983 s 74A(1)(a) (as added: see note 25); European Parliamentary Elections Regulations 2004, SI 2004/293, reg 45(1)(a); National Assembly for Wales (Representation of the People) Order 2007, SI 2007/236, art 45(1)(a). 'For the purposes of the candidate's election' has the same meaning as in the Representation of the People Act 1983 ss 90ZA, 90C (definition applied by s 74A(3) (s 74A as so added; s 74A(3) amended by the Electoral Administration Act 2006 s 74(1), Sch 1 paras 104, 112(1), (4), 133)), the European Parliamentary Elections Regulations 2004, SI 2004/293, regs 60, 62 (definition

applied by reg 45(3) (amended by SI 2009/186)), or the National Assembly for Wales (Representation of the People) Order 2007, SI 2007/236, arts 63, 64 (definition applied by art 45(3)), as the case may be (see PARA 269).

In the case of a European parliamentary election, the reference is to election expenses which are incurred by or on behalf of an individual candidate (see note 2): see the European Parliamentary Elections Regulations 2004, SI 2004/293, reg 45(1)(a), (2). In the case of a Welsh Assembly election, the reference is simply to 'election expenses which are incurred by or on behalf of the candidate' but references either to a constituency candidate or to an individual candidate must be construed according to context (see note 2): see the National Assembly for Wales (Representation of the People) Order 2007, SI 2007/236, art 45(1)(a), (2).

27 Ie by virtue of the Representation of the People Act 1983 s 90ZA(1), the European Parliamentary Elections Regulations 2004, SI 2004/293, reg 60(1), or the National Assembly for Wales (Representation of the People) Order 2007, SI 2007/236, art 63(1) as the case may be (see PARA 269): Representation of the People Act 1983 s 74A(1)(b) (s 74A as added (see note 25); s 74A(1)(b) amended by the Electoral Administration Act 2006 Sch 1 paras 104, 112(1), (2), 133); European Parliamentary Elections Regulations 2004, SI 2004/293, reg 45(1)(b); National Assembly for Wales (Representation of the People) Order 2007, SI 2007/236, art 45(1)(b).

28 Representation of the People Act 1983 s 74A(1)(b) (as added and amended: see note 27); European Parliamentary Elections Regulations 2004, SI 2004/293, reg 45(1)(b); National Assembly for Wales (Representation of the People) Order 2007, SI 2007/236, art 45(1)(b).

29 Representation of the People Act 1983 s 74A(2) (as added (see note 25); and amended by the Electoral Administration Act 2006 Sch 1 paras 104, 112(1), (3), 133, Sch 2); European Parliamentary Elections Regulations 2004, SI 2004/293, reg 45(2) (amended by SI 2009/186); National Assembly for Wales (Representation of the People) Order 2007, SI 2007/236, art 45(2). As to references to the candidate see note 26.

271. Candidate's election expenses which may be paid otherwise than by or through election agent. The candidate[1] at an election[2] may pay any personal expenses[3] incurred by him on account of or in connection with or incidental to the election[4]; but the amount which he may pay must not exceed:

(1)   in the case of a candidate at a parliamentary election, £600[5];

(2)   in the case of a candidate at an election of the Mayor of London, £5,000[6];

(3)   in the case of a candidate at an election of a constituency member of the London Assembly, £600[7];

(4)   in the case of a candidate to be a London member of the London Assembly at an ordinary election, £900[8];

(5)   in the case of a constituency candidate at a Welsh Assembly election, £600[9];

(6)   in the case of a candidate at a Welsh Assembly regional election, £900[10]; or

(7)   in the case of an individual candidate at a European parliamentary election, £900[11].

Any further personal expenses so incurred by the candidate must be paid by his election agent[12]. The candidate at an election may also pay any other election expenses[13] which were incurred by him or on his behalf[14] and in respect of which payment[15] falls to be made before the date on which he appoints (or is deemed to have appointed) an election agent[16]. The candidate must send to his election agent within the time limited for sending in claims[17] a written statement of the amount of personal or other expenses so paid by the candidate[18]. If so authorised in writing by the candidate's election agent[19], any person may pay any necessary expenses for stationery, postage, telegrams or telephonic communication (or any similar means of communication) and other petty expenses, to a total amount not exceeding that named in the authority, but any excess above the total amount so named must be paid by the agent who authorised that person[20]. A statement of the particulars of payments made by any person so authorised must be sent to the election agent within the time limited for sending in claims[21], and must be vouched for by a bill containing that person's receipt[22].

The statutory provisions which provide for the paying of claims against a candidate or election agent in respect of election expenses[23] and for disputed claims[24] do not apply to any of the expenses which are in this way[25] paid otherwise than by the candidate's election agent[26].

1   As to the meaning of 'candidate' generally see PARA 230. The reference in the text is to an 'individual candidate' for the purposes of a European parliamentary election: see the European Parliamentary Elections Regulations 2004, SI 2004/293, reg 44(1), (2). As to the meaning of 'individual candidate' at a European parliamentary election see PARA 230 note 32. For the purposes of Welsh Assembly elections, the reference is to either a constituency candidate at a Welsh Assembly constituency election (see the National Assembly for Wales (Representation of the People) Order 2007, SI 2007/236, art 44(1)(a)), or any candidate at a Welsh Assembly regional election (ie either an individual or a party list candidate) (see art 44(1)(b)). As to the meanings of 'Assembly election', 'constituency election' and 'regional election' for the purposes of Welsh Assembly elections see PARA 3 note 2; as to the meanings of 'constituency candidate' at a Welsh Assembly constituency election and 'individual candidate' at a Welsh Assembly regional election see PARA 230 note 19; and as to the meaning of 'party list candidate' at a Welsh Assembly regional election see PARA 230 note 23.

2   The Representation of the People Act 1983 s 74 does not apply at an election under the local government Act which is not a local government election (see the Representation of the People Act 1983 s 90(2); and PARA 297); and, in relation to an election of parish councillors in England or of community councillors in Wales, the provisions of s 90(1), Sch 4 apply instead; and s 76A(2) (see note 5) is modified (see s 90(1)(b); and PARAS 293–296). As to the meaning of 'parliamentary election' see PARA 9; as to the meanings of 'Authority election' and 'local government election' see PARA 11; and as to the meaning of 'election under the local government Act' see PARA 11 note 2. As to elections in the City of London see PARA 33. As to Welsh Assembly elections generally see PARA 213 et seq. As to European parliamentary elections see PARA 217 et seq.

3   In the Representation of the People Act 1983 Pt II (ss 67–119), in relation to a parliamentary or local government election, the European Parliamentary Elections Regulations 2004, SI 2004/293, Pt 2 (regs 31–81), in relation to a European parliamentary election, or the National Assembly for Wales (Representation of the People) Order 2007, SI 2007/236, Pt 3 (arts 37–85), in relation to a Welsh Assembly election (see PARA 235 et seq), unless the context otherwise requires, 'personal expenses' as used with respect to the expenditure of any candidate in relation to any such election includes the reasonable travelling expenses of the candidate, and the reasonable expenses of his living at hotels or elsewhere for the purposes of and in relation to the election: Representation of the People Act 1983 s 118; European Parliamentary Elections Regulations 2004, SI 2004/293, reg 31(1); National Assembly for Wales (Representation of the People) Order 2007, SI 2007/236, art 84(1).

4   Representation of the People Act 1983 s 74(1); European Parliamentary Elections Regulations 2004, SI 2004/293, reg 44(1); National Assembly for Wales (Representation of the People) Order 2007, SI 2007/236, art 44(1)

5   Representation of the People Act 1983 s 74(1)(a) (amended by the Representation of the People Act 1985 s 14(2); and renumbered by the Greater London Authority Act 1999 s 17, Sch 3 paras 1, 18(1), (2)).

    The Secretary of State may by order made by statutory instrument vary the sum for the time being specified in the Representation of the People Act 1983 s 74(1)(a)–(d) where he considers that the variation is expedient in consequence of changes in the value of money or in order to give effect to a recommendation of the Electoral Commission: Representation of the People Act 1983 s 76A(1), (2)(b) (s 76A added by the Representation of the People Act 1985 s 14; and substituted by the Political Parties, Elections and Referendums Act 2000 s 133(1)). Such an order which gives effect to a recommendation of the Electoral Commission is subject to annulment in pursuance of a resolution of either House of Parliament: Representation of the People Act 1983 s 76A(3) (as so added and substituted). In relation to an election of parish councillors in England or of community councillors in Wales, s 76A(2) is modified so that, instead of s 74(1)(a)–(d), a reference to Sch 4 para 3 (expenses at elections where election agent not required: see PARA 295) is substituted: see s 90(1)(c) (substituted by the Political Parties, Elections and Referendums Act 2000 s 138(1), Sch 18 paras 1, 11(c)). As to the Secretary of State see PARA 2. As to the Electoral Commission see PARA 34 et seq.

6 Representation of the People Act 1983 s 74(1)(b) (s 74(1)(b)–(d) substituted by the Greater London Authority Act 1999 Sch 3 paras 1, 18(1), (2)). As to varying the sum mentioned in the text see note 5. In the application of the Representation of the People Act 1983 s 74(1) in relation to a person who is a candidate in two or more Authority elections, those elections are treated, if one of them is an election of the Mayor of London, as if they together constituted a single election falling within s 74(1)(b): s 74(1A)(a) (s 74(1A) added by the Greater London Authority Act 1999 Sch 3 paras 1, 18(1), (3)). As to elections for the return of an elected Mayor of London see PARA 199 et seq.

7 Representation of the People Act 1983 s 74(1)(c) (as substituted: see note 6). As to varying the sum mentioned in the text see note 5. In the application of s 74(1) in relation to a person who is a candidate in two or more Authority elections, other than a London Mayoral election, those elections are treated as if they together constituted a single election falling within s 74(1)(d) (see head (4) in the text): s 74(1A)(b) (as added: see note 6). As to the meaning of 'constituency member', in relation to the London Assembly, see PARA 11 note 6. As to ordinary elections of constituency members of the London Assembly see PARA 199 et seq.

8 Representation of the People Act 1983 s 74(1)(d) (as substituted: see note 6). See note 7. As to varying the sum mentioned in the text see note 5. As to the meaning of 'London member', in relation to the London Assembly, see PARA 11 note 5. As to ordinary elections of London members of the London Assembly see PARA 199 et seq.

9 National Assembly for Wales (Representation of the People) Order 2007, SI 2007/236, art 44(1)(a).

The Secretary of State may by order made by statutory instrument vary the sum for the time being specified in art 44(1) where he considers that the variation is expedient in consequence of changes in the value of money or in order to give effect to a recommendation of the Electoral Commission: see art 48(1), (2). A statutory instrument containing such an order is subject to annulment in pursuance of a resolution of either House of Parliament: art 48(3). For the purposes of the Statutory Instruments Act 1946 s 1 (see STATUTES AND LEGISLATIVE PROCESS vol 96 (2012) PARA 1045), the National Assembly for Wales (Representation of the People) Order 2007, SI 2007/236, art 48(3) has effect as if contained in an Act of Parliament: see art 48(3).

10 National Assembly for Wales (Representation of the People) Order 2007, SI 2007/236, art 44(1)(b). As to varying the sum mentioned in the text see note 9.

11 European Parliamentary Elections Regulations 2004, SI 2004/293, reg 44(1).

12 Representation of the People Act 1983 s 74(1) (amended by the Greater London Authority Act 1999 Sch 3 paras 1, 18(1), (2)); European Parliamentary Elections Regulations 2004, SI 2004/293, reg 44(1); National Assembly for Wales (Representation of the People) Order 2007, SI 2007/236, art 44(1). As to the appointment of election agents generally see PARA 231 et seq.

13 Ie election expenses other than expenses falling within the Representation of the People Act 1983 s 74(1), the European Parliamentary Elections Regulations 2004, SI 2004/293, reg 44(1), or the National Assembly for Wales (Representation of the People) Order 2007, SI 2007/236, art 44(1) (whichever applies) (see the text and notes 1–12). As to the meaning of 'election expenses' see PARA 269.

14 As to the meaning of 'election expenses incurred by or on behalf of a candidate' see PARA 269 note 15.

15 As to the meaning of 'payment' for these purposes see PARA 270 note 1.

16 Representation of the People Act 1983 s 74(1B) (added by the Political Parties, Elections and Referendums Act 2000 Sch 18 paras 1, 4(1), (3)); European Parliamentary Elections Regulations 2004, SI 2004/293, reg 44(2); National Assembly for Wales (Representation of the People) Order 2007, SI 2007/236, art 44(2).

17 As to the prescribed time for sending in claims against a candidate or his election agent in respect of election expenses see PARA 276.

18 Representation of the People Act 1983 s 74(2) (amended by the Political Parties, Elections and Referendums Act 2000 Sch 18 paras 1, 4(1), (4)); European Parliamentary Elections Regulations 2004, SI 2004/293, reg 44(3); National Assembly for Wales (Representation of the People) Order 2007, SI 2007/236, art 44(3).

19 In the case of a European parliamentary election, it is specified that the authorisation in writing may be given by an election agent or a sub-agent: see the European Parliamentary Elections Regulations 2004, SI 2004/293, reg 44(4). As to the nomination of sub-agents at a European parliamentary election see PARA 241 et seq.

20 Representation of the People Act 1983 s 74(3); European Parliamentary Elections Regulations 2004, SI 2004/293, reg 44(4); National Assembly for Wales (Representation of the People) Order 2007, SI 2007/236, art 44(4). In the case of a European parliamentary election,

the text limits any election expenses simply to a total amount not exceeding that named in the authority, rather than specifying 'necessary expenses' and 'other petty expenses': see the European Parliamentary Elections Regulations 2004, SI 2004/293, reg 44(4).

21 See note 17.

22 Representation of the People Act 1983 s 74(4); European Parliamentary Elections Regulations 2004, SI 2004/293, reg 44(5); National Assembly for Wales (Representation of the People) Order 2007, SI 2007/236, art 44(5). In the case of a European parliamentary election, it is specified that, where the agent who authorised the payments mentioned in the text is the sub-agent, he must forward the statement, together with his authority, to the election agent: see the European Parliamentary Elections Regulations 2004, SI 2004/293, reg 44(5).

23 Ie the Representation of the People Act 1983 s 78, the European Parliamentary Elections Regulations 2004, SI 2004/293, reg 48, or the National Assembly for Wales (Representation of the People) Order 2007, SI 2007/236, art 49 (whichever is appropriate) (see PARA 276).

24 Ie the Representation of the People Act 1983 s 79, the European Parliamentary Elections Regulations 2004, SI 2004/293, reg 49, or the National Assembly for Wales (Representation of the People) Order 2007, SI 2007/236, art 50 (whichever is appropriate) (see PARA 276).

25 Ie in accordance with any provision of the Representation of the People Act 1983 s 74, the European Parliamentary Elections Regulations 2004, SI 2004/293, reg 44, or the National Assembly for Wales (Representation of the People) Order 2007, SI 2007/236, art 44 (whichever is appropriate) (see the text and notes 1–22).

26 Representation of the People Act 1983 s 74(5) (added by the Political Parties, Elections and Referendums Act 2000 Sch 18 paras 1, 4(1), (5)); European Parliamentary Elections Regulations 2004, SI 2004/293, reg 44(6); National Assembly for Wales (Representation of the People) Order 2007, SI 2007/236, art 44(6).

272.   Third parties' election expenses incurred by outsiders in publicising a candidate or in promoting political debate at an election. Expenses with a view to[1] promoting or procuring[2] the election of a candidate[3] at an election[4] must not be incurred after he becomes a candidate at that election by any person other than the candidate, his election agent[5] and persons authorised in writing by the election agent[6], on account of:

(1)   holding public meetings or organising any public display[7]; or

(2)   issuing advertisements, circulars or publications[8]; or

(3)   otherwise presenting to the electors the candidate or his views, or the extent or nature of his backing, or disparaging another candidate[9]; or

(4)   otherwise presenting to the electors: (a) the candidate's registered political party (if any) or the views of that party or the extent or nature of that party's backing or disparaging any other registered political party, in the case of an ordinary election of London members[10]; or (b) the candidate or his views or the extent or nature of his backing or disparaging a registered political party or any or all of its party list candidates[11], in the case of a Welsh Assembly regional election[12]; or (c) that candidate or his views, or the extent or nature of his backing, or disparaging a registered party or its candidates, in the case of a European parliamentary election[13].

The provisions in heads (1) to (4) above do not apply to any expenses incurred by any person[14]:

(i)   which do not exceed in the aggregate the permitted sum[15] (and are not incurred by that person as part of a concerted plan of action)[16]; or

(ii)   in travelling or in living away from home or similar personal expenses[17];

and the provisions in head (3) or head (4) above do not restrict the publication of any matter relating to the election:

(A)   in a newspaper or other periodical[18]; or

(B)   in a broadcast made by the British Broadcasting Corporation or by Sianel Pedwar Cymru[19]; or

(C)   in a programme included in a television, radio or sound broadcasting service licensed under the Broadcasting Act 1990 or the Broadcasting Act 1996[20].

The insertion of an advertisement in a national newspaper which contained criticisms of one party's financial policy, and which might have been held to advance the prospects of the opposing party's cause at a pending general election, has been held not to constitute an offence under the foregoing provisions[21], but the distribution of pamphlets in three constituencies urging voters not to vote for the candidates of a certain political party in those constituencies has been held to constitute such an offence, as an intention to prevent the election of one candidate will involve also an intention to improve the collective chances of the remaining candidates[22]. The expenses incurred in connection with a party political broadcast in the course of an election campaign have been held not to come within the statutory provisions[23].

If any person not engaged for payment or promise of payment by the candidate or his election agent incurs any expenses required to be authorised by the election agent, he must make a return of the expenses and a declaration verifying the return[24].

If any person incurs, or aids, abets, counsels or procures any other person to incur, any expenses in contravention of these provisions, he is guilty of a corrupt practice[25]. Apart from the statutory restriction on expenses incurred by persons other than the candidate, his election agent and persons authorised by the election agent, there is nothing which prohibits election expenses being incurred before the election agent has been appointed[26], although this is undesirable as it is the intention of the legislation that the election agent should be effectively responsible for all the acts done in procuring the election of the candidate[27]. If, however, expenses have been so incurred they should be paid by the election agent[28]. If election expenses have been incurred and paid before the election agent has been appointed, the election agent ought to ask the persons so paid to repay the money to the person who paid them in order that he may himself pay them[29]. If any expense required to be authorised by the election agent is incurred by a person to promote or procure the election of a candidate at an election, but the expense is not authorised by the election agent, it will need to be returned by the election agent as an election expense if it was authorised by the candidate, although not otherwise[30]. If it was authorised by the election agent, it will need to be returned by the election agent as an election expense[31].

1   The meaning of the words 'with a view to' was considered in *DPP v Luft* [1977] AC 962, [1976] 2 All ER 569, HL, in the context of the Representation of the People Act 1949 s 63(1) (repealed), which is re-enacted as the Representation of the People Act 1983 s 75(1) (see also the text and notes 2–10). In the view of the House of Lords, there was no difference in meaning between the phrase *'with a view to* promoting or procuring the election of *a* candidate' and *'for the purpose of* promoting or procuring the election of *any* candidate' which was used in the Representation of the People Act 1918 s 34(1) (repealed), in respect of an offence similar to that in the Representation of the People Act 1949 s 63(1) (repealed): see *DPP v Luft* at 982 and 573 per Lord Diplock. The decision in *R v Hailwood and Ackroyd Ltd* [1928] 2 KB 277, CCA, which concerned the offence in the Representation of the People Act 1918 s 34(1) (repealed) and in which it was held that if a person disparages one candidate and tries to induce the electors not to vote for that candidate, he is, in effect promoting the election of one of the other candidates, was applied. 'In my view the offence under section 63(1) to (5) is committed by the accused if his desire to promote or procure the election of a candidate was one of the reasons which played a part in inducing him to incur the expense': *DPP v Luft* at 983 and 574 per Lord Diplock.

2   'On a prosecution [for this offence] it is not necessary to prove that the expense was incurred with the intention of promoting or procuring the election of one particular candidate but it is sufficient to establish an intention on the part of the person incurring the expense to prevent the

election of a particular candidate or particular candidates': *DPP v Luft* [1977] AC 962 at 984, [1976] 2 All ER 569 at 574, HL, per Lord Diplock. See also *R v Hailwood and Ackroyd Ltd* [1928] 2 KB 277, CCA.

3   As to the meaning of 'candidate' generally see PARA 230; and as to references to promoting or procuring a candidate's election at an election or to promoting or procuring electoral success for a party see PARA 269 note 4. See also note 4.

4   As to the meaning of 'parliamentary election' see PARA 9. As to the meanings of 'Authority election' and 'local government election' see PARA 11. As to elections in the City of London see PARA 33. As to Welsh Assembly elections generally see PARA 213 et seq. As to European parliamentary elections see PARA 217 et seq.

Where a candidate is standing in his own right at an election that either is a regional election, or takes place alongside regional elections:

(1)   the reference to a candidate is to a constituency candidate at a Welsh Assembly constituency election, and to an individual candidate at a Welsh Assembly regional election (see the National Assembly for Wales (Representation of the People) Order 2007, SI 2007/236, art 46(1)); and

(2)   at a European parliamentary election, the reference is to an 'individual candidate' (see the European Parliamentary Elections Regulations 2004, SI 2004/293, reg 46(1) (reg 46(1), (2) substituted, reg 46(1A), (1B), (2A) added, by SI 2009/186)).

As to the meanings of 'Assembly election', 'constituency election' and 'regional election' for the purposes of Welsh Assembly elections see PARA 3 note 2. As to the meanings of 'constituency candidate' at a Welsh Assembly constituency election and 'individual candidate' at a Welsh Assembly regional election see PARA 230 note 19. As to the meaning of 'individual candidate' at a European parliamentary election see PARA 230 note 32.

However, provision is also made in relation to registered political parties that are nominated to stand in regional elections: see head (4) in the text. The Representation of the People Act 1983 s 75(1) expressly applies, in the case of an election of the London members of the London Assembly at an ordinary election, to a registered political party or candidates of that party: see s 75(1) (amended by the Greater London Authority Act 1999 Sch 3 paras 1, 19(1), (2)(a); and the Electoral Administration Act 2006 ss 25(1), (2)(a), (b), 74(2), Sch 2). In the application of the Representation of the People Act 1983 s 75(1) in relation to an election of the London members of the London Assembly at an ordinary election, any reference to the candidate includes a reference to all or any of the candidates of a registered political party; and, in the application of s 75(1ZA) (see note 15) in relation to such an election, the reference to the same candidate includes a reference to all or any of the candidates of the same registered political party: see s 75(1A) (added by the Greater London Authority Act 1999 s 17, Sch 3 paras 1, 19(1), (3); and amended by the Political Parties, Elections and Referendums Act 2000 s 131(1), (4)). In the case of an election of the London members of the London Assembly at an ordinary election, a candidate's registered political party is the registered political party (if any) which submitted for the purposes of that election a list of candidates on which the candidate in question is included: Representation of the People Act 1983 s 75(7) (added by the Greater London Authority Act 1999 Sch 3 paras 1, 19(1), (5)). As to the meaning of 'London member', in relation to the London Assembly, see PARA 11 note 5; and as to the meaning of 'registered political party' for these purposes see PARA 231 note 7. As to ordinary elections of London members of the London Assembly see PARA 199 et seq; and as to the system of candidature whereby registered parties submit lists of candidates see PARA 340.

The Representation of the People Act 1983 s 75 does not apply at an election under the local government Act which is not a local government election (see the Representation of the People Act 1983 s 90(2); and PARA 297); and, in relation to an election of parish councillors in England or of community councillors in Wales, the provisions of s 90(1), Sch 4 apply instead; and s 76A(2) (see note 15) is modified (see s 90(1)(b); and PARAS 293–296). As to the meaning of 'election under the local government Act' see PARA 11 note 2.

5   As to the appointment of election agents generally see PARA 231 et seq. In relation to a European parliamentary election, references to an election agent include a sub-agent for these purposes: see the European Parliamentary Elections Regulations 2004, SI 2004/293, reg 46(7). As to the appointment of a sub-agent at a European parliamentary election see PARA 241 et seq.

6   Representation of the People Act 1983 s 75(1) (as amended: see note 4); European Parliamentary Elections Regulations 2004, SI 2004/293, reg 46(1) (as substituted: see note 4); National Assembly for Wales (Representation of the People) Order 2007, SI 2007/236, art 46(1).

For the purposes of the Representation of the People Act 1983 s 75(1), or the European Parliamentary Elections Regulations 2004, SI 2004/293, reg 46(1), or the National Assembly for Wales (Representation of the People) Order 2007, SI 2007/236, art 46(1), as the case may be, expenditure incurred before the date when a person becomes a candidate at the election is to be treated as having been incurred after that date if it is incurred in connection with any thing which is used or takes place after that date: Representation of the People Act 1983 s 75(8) (added by the Electoral Administration Act 2006 s 25(1), (5)); European Parliamentary Elections Regulations 2004, SI 2004/293, reg 46(2A) (as added: see note 4); National Assembly for Wales (Representation of the People) Order 2007, SI 2007/236, art 46(13). At a European parliamentary election, the reference to a candidate is either to an individual candidate or to a candidate included in the list of candidates submitted by a registered party: see the European Parliamentary Elections Regulations 2004, SI 2004/293, reg 46(2A) (as so added). As to the meanings of 'list' and 'registered party' for these purposes see PARA 230 note 29.

7 Representation of the People Act 1983 s 75(1)(a); European Parliamentary Elections Regulations 2004, SI 2004/293, reg 46(1)(a) (as substituted: see note 4); National Assembly for Wales (Representation of the People) Order 2007, SI 2007/236, art 46(1)(a).

8 Representation of the People Act 1983 s 75(1)(b); European Parliamentary Elections Regulations 2004, SI 2004/293, reg 46(1)(b) (as substituted: see note 4); National Assembly for Wales (Representation of the People) Order 2007, SI 2007/236, art 46(1)(b).

9 Representation of the People Act 1983 s 75(1)(c); European Parliamentary Elections Regulations 2004, SI 2004/293, reg 46(1)(c) (as substituted: see note 4); National Assembly for Wales (Representation of the People) Order 2007, SI 2007/236, art 46(1)(c), (d). At a Welsh Assembly election, head (3) in the text applies either to a constituency candidate at a Welsh Assembly constituency election (see the National Assembly for Wales (Representation of the People) Order 2007, SI 2007/236, art 46(1)(c)), or to an individual candidate at a Welsh Assembly regional election (see art 46(1)(d)).

'Disparaging' is to be understood in its ordinary and natural meaning; a person may be disparaged by attacks on the political views he holds as well as by attacks on his personal conduct: *DPP v Luft* [1977] AC 962 at 984, [1976] 2 All ER 569 at 575, HL, per Lord Diplock.

10 Representation of the People Act 1983 s 75(1)(d) (added by the Greater London Authority Act 1999 Sch 3 paras 1, 19(1), (2)(b)).

11 As to the meaning of 'registered party' for these purposes see PARA 215 note 19; and as to the meaning of 'party list candidate' at a Welsh Assembly regional election see PARA 230 note 23.

12 See the National Assembly for Wales (Representation of the People) Order 2007, SI 2007/236, art 46(1)(d).

13 See the European Parliamentary Elections Regulations 2004, SI 2004/293, reg 46(1)(c) (as substituted: see note 4).

14 Representation of the People Act 1983 s 75(1ZZB) (s 75(1ZZA), (1ZZB) added by the Electoral Administration Act 2006 s 25(1), (3)); European Parliamentary Elections Regulations 2004, SI 2004/293, reg 46(1B) (as added: see note 4); National Assembly for Wales (Representation of the People) Order 2007, SI 2007/236, art 46(3).

15 The 'permitted sum' means:

(1) in respect of a candidate at a parliamentary election, £500, and, in respect of a candidate at a local government election, £50 (together with an additional 0.5p for every entry in the register of local government electors for the electoral area in question as it has effect on the last day for publication of notice of the election) (see the Representation of the People Act 1983 s 75(1ZA) (added by the Political Parties, Elections and Referendums Act 2000 s 131(1), (3); and amended by the Electoral Administration Act 2006 s 25(1), (4)));

(2) for the purposes of a European parliamentary election, the sum of £5,000 (European Parliamentary Elections Regulations 2004, SI 2004/293, reg 46(2) (as substituted: see note 4));

(3) in the case of a Welsh Assembly constituency election, the sum of £500 and, in the case of a Welsh Assembly regional election, a sum of £1,000 (National Assembly for Wales (Representation of the People) Order 2007, SI 2007/236, art 46(4)(b)).

See also the Greater London Authority Elections (Expenses) Order 2000, SI 2000/789, which modified the monetary sum specified in the Representation of the People Act 1983 s 75(1)(ii) (s 75(1) now amended (see note 4); but see now heads (i) and (ii) in the text), in relation to an election of the Mayor of London, to £25,000, in relation to an election of a constituency member of the London Assembly, to £1,800, and, in relation to an election of the London members of the London Assembly at an ordinary election, to £25,000: see the Greater London Authority Elections (Expenses) Order 2000, SI 2000/789, art 2; cf PARA 273 note 12.

The Secretary of State may by order made by statutory instrument vary the sum for the time being specified in the Representation of the People Act 1983 s 75(1ZA) where he considers that the variation is expedient in consequence of changes in the value of money or in order to give effect to a recommendation of the Electoral Commission: Representation of the People Act 1983 s 76A(1), (2)(c) (s 76A added by the Representation of the People Act 1985 s 14; and substituted by the Political Parties, Elections and Referendums Act 2000 s 133(1)). Such an order made under the Representation of the People Act 1983 which gives effect to a recommendation of the Electoral Commission is subject to annulment in pursuance of a resolution of either House of Parliament: s 76A(3) (as so added and substituted). In relation to an election of parish councillors in England or of community councillors in Wales, s 76A(2) is modified so that, instead of s 75(1ZA), a reference to Sch 4 para 3 (expenses at elections where election agent not required: see PARA 295) is substituted: see s 90(1)(c) (substituted by the Political Parties, Elections and Referendums Act 2000 s 138(1), Sch 18 paras 1, 11(c)). There appears to be no power to vary the sum mentioned in the National Assembly for Wales (Representation of the People) Order 2007, SI 2007/236, art 46(2); cf the sums mentioned in art 43(2) (see PARA 270 note 16), art 44(1) (see PARA 271 note 9), and art 47(3) (see PARA 273 note 17). As to the Secretary of State see PARA 2. As to the Electoral Commission see PARA 34 et seq.

In Application 24839/94 *Bowman v United Kingdom* (1998) 26 EHRR 1, (1998) 4 BHRC 25, ECtHR (cited in PARA 7 note 8), the low statutory limit on third party expenditure in individual election campaigns, set by the Representation of the People Act 1983 s 75 (as it stood then), was found to be disproportionate to the aim pursued of ensuring that political debate in any individual constituency was not dominated by third party issues.

16   Representation of the People Act 1983 s 75(1ZZB)(a) (as added: see note 14); European Parliamentary Elections Regulations 2004, SI 2004/293, reg 46(1B)(a) (as added: see note 4); National Assembly for Wales (Representation of the People) Order 2007, SI 2007/236, art 46(3)(a).

For these purposes, expenses are regarded as incurred by a person as part of a concerted plan of action if they are incurred by that person in pursuance of any plan or other arrangement whereby that person and one or more other persons are to incur, with a view to promoting or procuring the election of the same candidate, expenses which, disregarding head (i) in the text, fall within heads (1)–(4) in the text: Representation of the People Act 1983 s 75(1ZA) (as added and amended: see note 15); European Parliamentary Elections Regulations 2004, SI 2004/293, reg 46(2); National Assembly for Wales (Representation of the People) Order 2007, SI 2007/236, art 46(4)(a).

17   Representation of the People Act 1983 s 75(1ZZB)(b) (as added: see note 14); European Parliamentary Elections Regulations 2004, SI 2004/293, reg 46(1B)(b) (as added: see note 4); National Assembly for Wales (Representation of the People) Order 2007, SI 2007/236, art 46(3)(b). As to the meaning of 'personal expenses' see PARA 271 note 3. See also *R v Holding* [2005] EWCA Crim 3185, [2006] 1 WLR 1040, in which the legislative history of the Representation of the People Act 1983 s 75(1) was considered (before it was further amended by the Electoral Administration Act 2006) and wherein it was held that there was an absolute bar on incurring unauthorised expenses in relation to the matters mentioned in the Representation of the People Act 1983 s 75(1)(a) and s 75(1)(b) as well as in s 75(1)(c) and s 75(1)(d).

18   Representation of the People Act 1983 s 75(1ZZA)(a) (as added: see note 14); European Parliamentary Elections Regulations 2004, SI 2004/293, reg 46(1A)(a) (as added: see note 4); National Assembly for Wales (Representation of the People) Order 2007, SI 2007/236, art 46(2)(a).

19   Representation of the People Act 1983 s 75(1ZZA)(b) (as added: see note 14); European Parliamentary Elections Regulations 2004, SI 2004/293, reg 46(1A)(b) (as added: see note 4); National Assembly for Wales (Representation of the People) Order 2007, SI 2007/236, art 46(2)(b). In the case of a European parliamentary election talking place in the combined region, the Gibraltar Broadcasting Corporation is added to the list of broadcasters set out in head (B) in the text: see the European Parliamentary Elections Regulations 2004, SI 2004/293, reg 46(1A)(b) (as so added). As to the establishment of electoral regions (including the 'combined region') for the purpose of elections to the European Parliament see PARA 77.

20   Representation of the People Act 1983 s 75(1ZZA)(c) (as added: see note 14); European Parliamentary Elections Regulations 2004, SI 2004/293, reg 46(1A)(c) (as added: see note 4); National Assembly for Wales (Representation of the People) Order 2007, SI 2007/236, art 46(2)(c). The text refers to a service licensed under the Broadcasting Act 1990 Pt I (ss 3–71) (independent television services: see BROADCASTING vol 4 (2011) PARA 507 et seq) or Pt III (ss 85–126) (independent radio services: see BROADCASTING vol 4 (2011) PARA 724 et seq) or under the Broadcasting Act 1996 Pt I (ss 1–39) (digital terrestrial television broadcasting: see BROADCASTING vol 4 (2011) PARA 690 et seq) or Pt II (ss 40–72) (digital terrestrial sound broadcasting: see BROADCASTING vol 4 (2011) PARA 727 et seq). As to the BBC see BROADCASTING vol 4 (2011) PARA 603 et seq; and as to Sianel Pedwar Cymru see BROADCASTING vol 4 (2011) PARA 645.

21 *R v Tronoh Mines Ltd* [1952] 1 All ER 697, where the judge held that there was no case to go to the jury because the provision now re-enacted as the Representation of the People Act 1983 s 75(1)(b) (see head (2) in the text) was not intended to prohibit expenditure incurred on advertisements designed to support the interest of a particular party generally in all constituencies, at any rate at the time of a general election, and not supporting a particular candidate in a particular constituency. He accepted as a reasonable and possible construction of the Representation of the People Act 1949 s 63 (repealed) (see now the Representation of the People Act 1983 s 75) that 'candidate' was intended to mean one candidate only, but this interpretation, though not the decision itself, was disapproved in *DPP v Luft* [1976] AC 962 at 985, [1976] 2 All ER 569 at 575, HL, per Lord Diplock. *R v Tronoh Mines Ltd* has been applied to local government elections in Scotland: see *Walker v UNISON* 1995 SLT 1226, OH (local government elections held throughout Scotland characterised as 'national elections').

22 *DPP v Luft* [1976] AC 962, [1976] 2 All ER 569, HL. See also *Meek v Lothian Regional Council* 1983 SLT 494, Ct of Session, where the distribution of a pamphlet by a local authority prior to a local government election was considered to be in prima facie breach of what is now enacted as the Representation of the People Act 1983 s 75(1), because it was not restricted to factual description of the authority's decisions but also gave the reasons for them; having regard to the time of publication and the persons controlling it, the court thought that it was impossible to avoid the conclusion that it was calculated to promote the election of candidates supported by the majority party in the local authority notwithstanding that they were not named.

23 *Grieve v Douglas-Home* 1965 SLT 186, Ct of Session. As to restrictions on election broadcasts see PARAS 331, 332.

24 See the Representation ‿of the People Act 1983 s 75(2)–(4), (4A)–(4C); the European Parliamentary Elections Regulations 2004, SI 2004/293, reg 46(3), (4); the National Assembly for Wales (Representation of the People) Order 2007, SI 2007/236, art 46(5), (6), (7); and PARA 279. As to the meaning of 'payment' for these purposes see PARA 270 note 1. The failure to send a declaration or return is an illegal practice (see PARA 677); and the making of a false declaration is a corrupt practice (see PARA 707). As to related offences, the liability of officers of associations or bodies which are guilty of an offence, the court's power to mitigate or remit any incapacity and the limitation of the liability of a candidate for an offence by an agent see PARA 687 et seq.

25 See the Representation of the People Act 1983 s 75(5), (6); the European Parliamentary Elections Regulations 2004, SI 2004/293, reg 46(5), (6); the National Assembly for Wales (Representation of the People) Order 2007, SI 2007/236, art 46(8)–(12); and PARAS 687, 707. As to related offences, the liability of officers of associations or bodies which are guilty of an offence, the court's power to mitigate or remit any incapacity and the limitation of the liability of a candidate for an offence by an agent see PARA 687 et seq.

26 *Rochester Borough Case* (1892) 4 O'M & H 156 at 159.

27 *Barrow-in-Furness Case* (1886) 4 O'M & H 76 at 82. The legislation referred to in the text is that now re-enacted as the Representation of the People Act 1983 (and reflected also in the European Parliamentary Elections Regulations 2004, SI 2004/293, and the National Assembly for Wales (Representation of the People) Order 2007, SI 2007/236).

28 As to the payment of a candidate's election expenses otherwise than by or through election agent see PARA 270.

29 *Cornwall, Bodmin Division, Case* (1906) 5 O'M & H 225 at 226; *Dorsetshire, Eastern Division, Case* (1910) 6 O'M & H 22 at 40; *Monmouth Boroughs Case* (1901) 5 O'M & H 166 at 170. This does not prevent the initial payment being an illegal practice: *York County, East Riding, Buckrose Division, Case* (1886) 4 O'M & H 110 at 116; but cf *Monmouth Boroughs Case*, where an innocent payment was held to be no offence.

30 *Oxford Borough Case* (1924) 7 O'M & H 49 at 95; *Plymouth, Drake Division, Case* (1929) 7 O'M & H 101 at 110, 122; *Elgin and Nairn Case* (1895) 5 O'M & H 1 at 11. Whether authorised or not by the candidate the expenditure would be unlawful because it was not authorised by the election agent. As to the rights of any creditor who, when the expense was incurred, was ignorant of its being a contravention see PARA 278.

31 See *R v Tronoh Mines Ltd* [1952] 1 All ER 697 at 700 per McNair J (there is no way in which expenditure incurred in relation to all elections can be apportioned for the purpose of any particular return for a particular election); *R v Hailwood and Ackroyd Ltd* [1928] 2 KB 277 at 282, CCA.

The Representation of the People Act 1918 s 34(3) (repealed) provided that expenses mentioned in s 34 and authorised by the election agent must be duly returned as part of the candidate's election expenses. That provision has not been specifically reproduced in the Representation of the People Act 1983 s 75. It is, however, provided that the return of election expenses made by the election agent must deal under a separate heading or sub-heading with any expenses included in it as respects which a return is required to be made under s 81(2)(a): see PARA 280.

273. Limitation of election expenses for individual or party list candidates.
The election expenses[1] incurred by or on behalf of a candidate[2] at any of the elections mentioned in heads (1) to (7) below must not in the aggregate exceed the maximum amount specified as follows[3]:

(1)   for a candidate at a parliamentary general election[4]:

     (a)   £7,150, together with an additional 7p for every entry in the register of electors[5], at an election in a county constituency[6]; and

     (b)   £7,150, together with an additional 5p for every entry in the register of electors, at an election in a borough constituency[7];

(2)   for a candidate at a parliamentary by-election, £100,000[8];

(3)   for a candidate at a local government election[9] (other than an Authority election)[10], £600 together with an additional 5p for every entry in the register of electors[11];

(4)   as respects Authority elections, the maximum amount that is such as the Secretary of State may prescribe in an order made by statutory instrument[12], in respect of:

     (a)   a candidate in an election of the Mayor of London[13];

     (b)   a candidate in an election of constituency members of the London Assembly[14];

     (c)   an individual candidate in an election of London members of the London Assembly at an ordinary election[15]; or

     (d)   any of the candidates on a list of candidates submitted by a registered political party to be London members of the London Assembly at an ordinary election[16];

(5)   for a constituency candidate at a Welsh Assembly election[17]:

     (a)   which is an Assembly general election[18]: (i) £7,150 together with an additional 7p for every entry in the register of electors for an Assembly constituency[19] which is coterminous with a parliamentary constituency which is a county constituency[20]; and (ii) £7,150 together with an additional 5p for every entry in the register of electors for an Assembly constituency which is coterminous with a parliamentary constituency which is a borough constituency[21];

     (b)   which is an election to fill a casual vacancy[22], £100,000[23];

(6)   for an individual candidate at a Welsh Assembly regional election, the aggregate of the maximum amounts specified under head (5)(a)(i) and head (5)(a)(ii) above that apply, or would apply, at that time at a constituency election in respect of each Assembly constituency in the Assembly electoral region for which the election is held[24];

(7)   for an individual candidate at a European parliamentary election, £45,000 multiplied by the number of members of the European Parliament ('MEPs') to be returned for the electoral region at that election[25].

Where, at an election mentioned in heads (1) to (5) above, a poll is countermanded or abandoned by reason of a candidate's death[26], the maximum amount of election expenses for any of the other candidates who then remain validly nominated is twice (or, if there has been a previous such increase, three times) what it would have been but for any increase[27]. However, the maximum amount mentioned for a candidate is not affected by the change in the timing of the election or of any step in the proceedings at the election[28]. Where the timetable for the poll at a parliamentary election is affected by the demise of the Crown[29], the provisions limiting election expenses[30] have effect in relation to any candidate at the current election as if the maximum amount specified in head (1) above were increased by one-half[31].

The maximum amount of election expenses allowed to a candidate[32] is not required to cover the candidate's personal expenses[33].

Where any election expenses are incurred in excess of the maximum amount, any candidate or election agent who incurred, or authorised the incurring of, the election expenses and knew or ought reasonably to have known that the expenses would be incurred in excess of that maximum amount is guilty of an illegal practice[34].

1   As to the meaning of 'election expenses' see PARA 269.

2   As to the meaning of 'candidate' generally see PARA 230; and as to the meaning of 'election expenses incurred by or on behalf of a candidate' see PARA 269 note 15. At a European parliamentary election, the reference is to sums paid out and expenses incurred on behalf of an individual candidate at an election: see the European Parliamentary Elections Regulations 2004, SI 2004/293, reg 47(1). For these purposes, the references to sums paid out and expenses incurred on behalf of an individual candidate include sums being paid and expenses being incurred by the election agent or by a person acting on the written authority of an election agent or sub-agent (see PARA 270 et seq): reg 47(2). As to the meaning of 'individual candidate' at a European parliamentary election see PARA 230 note 32. As to the appointment of a sub-agent at a European parliamentary election see PARA 241 et seq. As to the appointment of election agents generally see PARA 231 et seq.

    At a Welsh Assembly election, the reference to a candidate is to a constituency candidate at a Welsh Assembly constituency election, and to an individual candidate at a Welsh Assembly regional election: see the National Assembly for Wales (Representation of the People) Order 2007, SI 2007/236, art 47(1). As to the meanings of 'Assembly election', 'constituency election' and 'regional election' for the purposes of Welsh Assembly elections see PARA 3 note 2. As to the meanings of 'constituency candidate' at a Welsh Assembly constituency election and 'individual candidate' at a Welsh Assembly regional election see PARA 230 note 19.

3   Representation of the People Act 1983 s 76(1) (substituted by the Political Parties, Elections and Referendums Act 2000 s 132(1), (2), (6)); Representation of the People Act 1983 s 76(1A) (added by the Greater London Authority Act 1999 s 17, Sch 3 paras 1, 20(1), (2); and amended by the Political Parties, Elections and Referendums Act 2000 s 132(1), (3), (6)); European Parliamentary Elections Regulations 2004, SI 2004/293, reg 47(1); National Assembly for Wales (Representation of the People) Order 2007, SI 2007/236, art 47(1).

4   Representation of the People Act 1983 s 76(2)(a) (amended by the Representation of the People Act 1989 s 6(1)). As to the meaning of 'parliamentary election' see PARA 9. As to parliamentary general elections see PARA 189 et seq. Where an election follows the dissolution of a Parliament that has run for over 55 months, a 'pre-candidacy' spending limit on candidate election expenses is imposed (ie a second regulated period) which operates in addition to the limit imposed by the Representation of the People Act 1983 s 76: see s 76ZA; and PARA 274.

    The Secretary of State may by order made by statutory instrument vary the sum for the time being specified in s 76(2) (see heads (1)–(3) in the text) where he considers that the variation is expedient in consequence of changes in the value of money or in order to give effect to a recommendation of the Electoral Commission: s 76A(1), (2)(d) (s 76A added by the Representation of the People Act 1985 s 14; and substituted by the Political Parties, Elections and Referendums Act 2000 s 133(1)). Such an order which gives effect to a recommendation of the Electoral Commission is subject to annulment in pursuance of a resolution of either House of Parliament: Representation of the People Act 1983 s 76A(3) (as so added and substituted). As to the Secretary of State see PARA 2; and as to the Electoral Commission see PARA 34 et seq.

5   For these purposes, the 'register of electors' means the register of parliamentary electors, or (as the case may be) local government electors, for the constituency or electoral area in question, as it has effect on the last day for publication of notice of the election: Representation of the People Act 1983 s 76(4) (substituted by the Representation of the People Act 2000 s 8, Sch 1 paras 1, 18(1), (3)). As to the meaning of 'constituency' for the purposes of parliamentary elections see

PARA 9; and as to the meaning of 'electoral area' for the purpose of local government elections see PARA 11. As to the registers of electors see PARA 145 et seq.

6 Representation of the People Act 1983 s 76(2)(a)(i) (amended by the Representation of the People Act 2000 s 15(2), Sch 1 paras 1, 18(1), (2), Sch 7 Pt I; and by SI 2005/269). As to variation of the sum mentioned in the text see note 4. As to the distinction between county constituencies and borough constituencies at parliamentary elections see PARA 73.

7 Representation of the People Act 1983 s 76(2)(a)(ii) (amended by the Representation of the People Act 2000 Sch 1 paras 1, 18(1), (2), Sch 7 Pt I; and by SI 2005/269). As to variation of the sum mentioned in the text see note 4.

8 Representation of the People Act 1983 s 76(2)(aa) (added by the Representation of the People Act 1989 s 6(1); substituted by the Political Parties, Elections and Referendums Act 2000 s 132(1), (5), (6)). As to variation of the sum mentioned in the text see note 4. As to parliamentary by-elections see PARA 191.

9 As to the meaning of 'local government election' see PARA 11. As to the limitation of election expenses for joint candidates at certain local government elections see PARA 275. The provisions of the Representation of the People Act 1983 s 76 and s 76A do not apply at an election under the local government Act which is not a local government election (see the Representation of the People Act 1983 s 90(2); and PARA 297), although, in relation to an election of parish councillors in England or of community councillors in Wales, s 76(1B) is applied (liability for election expenses incurred in excess of maximum amount: see PARA 673), subject to a minor modification, and s 76A(2)(d) (see note 4) continues to apply to s 76(2) (see s 90(1)(a), (b); and PARAS 293–296). As to the meaning of 'election under the local government Act' see PARA 11 note 2. As to elections in the City of London see PARA 33.

   The Representation of the People Act 1983 s 76 is applied and modified for the purpose of local authority mayoral elections in England and Wales by the Local Authorities (Mayoral Elections) (England and Wales) Regulations 2007, SI 2007/1024, reg 3(2)–(5), Sch 2 Table 1: see PARA 11 note 14. As to elections for the return of a local authority mayor see PARA 198.

10 Representation of the People Act 1983 s 76(2)(b) (amended by the Greater London Authority Act 1999 Sch 3 paras 1, 20(1), (3)). As to the meaning of 'Authority election' see PARA 11.

11 Representation of the People Act 1983 s 76(2)(b)(ii) (amended by the Representation of the People Act 2000 Sch 1 paras 1, 18(1), (2), Sch 7 Pt I; and by SI 2005/269). As to variation of the sum mentioned in the text see note 4.

12 See the Representation of the People Act 1983 s 76(2A) (s 76(2A), (2B) added by the Greater London Authority Act 1999 Sch 3 paras 1, 20(1), (4)). Such an order may not be made unless a draft of the order has been laid before, and approved by a resolution of, each House of Parliament (s 76(2B) (as so added)); and such an order may be made only on, and in accordance with, a recommendation of the Electoral Commission, unless the Secretary of State considers it to be expedient to exercise that function in consequence of changes in the value of money (see the Political Parties, Elections and Referendums Act 2000 s 8(2), (3)(a); and PARA 56). As to the order so made see the Greater London Authority Elections (Expenses) Order 2000, SI 2000/789. Accordingly, as respects Authority elections, the maximum amounts of the sums which may be paid and the expenses which may be incurred by a candidate or his election agent are as follows:

   (1)   £420,000 for a candidate in an election of the Mayor of London (art 3(a));
   (2)   £35,000 for a candidate in an election of a constituency member of the London Assembly (art 3(b));
   (3)   £330,000 for an individual candidate in an election of the London members of the London Assembly at an ordinary election (art 3(c));
   (4)   £330,000 for the purposes of the Representation of the People Act 1983 s 76(1A) (ie expenses of candidates to be London members of the London Assembly on a list submitted by a registered political party) (Greater London Authority Elections (Expenses) Order 2000, SI 2000/789, art 3(d)).

   As to the meanings of 'constituency member', 'London member' and 'election of a constituency member of the London Assembly' see PARA 11 notes 5, 6. As to ordinary elections of members of the London Assembly see PARA 199 et seq.

13 Representation of the People Act 1983 s 76(2A)(a) (as added: see note 12). As to elections for the return of an elected Mayor of London see PARA 199 et seq.

14 Representation of the People Act 1983 s 76(2A)(b) (as added: see note 12). As to the meaning of 'constituency member', in relation to the London Assembly, see PARA 11 note 6. As to ordinary elections of constituency members of the London Assembly see PARA 199 et seq.

15 Representation of the People Act 1983 s 76(2A)(c) (as added: see note 12). As to individual candidates to be London members see LONDON GOVERNMENT vol 71 (2013) PARA 81. As to elections for the return of London members of the London Assembly see PARA 199 et seq.

16   Representation of the People Act 1983 s 76(1A) (as added and amended: see note 3), s 76(2A)(d) (as added: see note 12). Where a registered political party submits a list of candidates to be London members of the London Assembly at an ordinary election, the limitation on election expenses specified in head (4) in the text applies to any of those candidates: see s 76(1A) (as so added and amended). As to the meaning of 'London member', in·relation to the London Assembly, see PARA 11 note 5; and as to the meaning of 'registered political party' in that context see PARA 226 note 16. As to the system of candidature whereby registered parties submit lists of candidates see PARA 340.

17   See the National Assembly for Wales (Representation of the People) Order 2007, SI 2007/236, art 47(3)(a), (b).

     The Secretary of State may by order made by statutory instrument vary the sum for the time being specified in art 47(3) where he considers that the variation is expedient in consequence of changes in the value of money or in order to give effect to a recommendation of the Electoral Commission: see art 48(1), (2). A statutory instrument containing such an order is subject to annulment in pursuance of a resolution of either House of Parliament: art 48(3). For the purposes of the Statutory Instruments Act 1946 s 1 (see STATUTES AND LEGISLATIVE PROCESS vol 96 (2012) PARA 1045), the National Assembly for Wales (Representation of the People) Order 2007, SI 2007/236, art 48(3) has effect as if contained in an Act of Parliament: see art 48(3).

18   National Assembly for Wales (Representation of the People) Order 2007, SI 2007/236, art 47(3)(a). As to the holding of ordinary general elections for the Welsh Assembly see PARA 213.

19   For these purposes, the 'register of electors' means the register of electors for the Assembly constituency or Assembly electoral region in question as it has effect on the last day for publication of notice of the election: National Assembly for Wales (Representation of the People) Order 2007, SI 2007/236, art 47(4). As to the meanings of 'Assembly constituency' and 'Assembly electoral region' see PARA 3 note 2.

20   National Assembly for Wales (Representation of the People) Order 2007, SI 2007/236, art 47(3)(a)(i).

21   National Assembly for Wales (Representation of the People) Order 2007, SI 2007/236, art 47(3)(a)(ii).

22   As to Welsh Assembly elections to fill a casual vacancy see PARAS 214, 215.

23   National Assembly for Wales (Representation of the People) Order 2007, SI 2007/236, art 47(3)(b).

24   National Assembly for Wales (Representation of the People) Order 2007, SI 2007/236, art 47(3)(c).

25   European Parliamentary Elections Regulations 2004, SI 2004/293, reg 47(4). As to the number of MEPs to be returned at European parliamentary elections in the United Kingdom see PARA 13 et seq; and as to the establishment of electoral regions for the purpose of elections to the European Parliament see PARA 77.

26   See PARA 513 et seq. At a Welsh Assembly constituency election, the further circumstance is allowed where the majority of votes at a poll is given to a deceased candidate and a new notice of election is published (see PARA 515): see the National Assembly for Wales (Representation of the People) Order 2007, SI 2007/236, art 47(6).

27   Representation of the People Act 1983 s 76(6); National Assembly for Wales (Representation of the People) Order 2007, SI 2007/236, art 47(6).

28   Representation of the People Act 1983 s 76(6); National Assembly for Wales (Representation of the People) Order 2007, SI 2007/236, art 47(7).

29   As to the effect of a demise of the Crown occurring on or after dissolution of a Parliament see PARA 190.

30   Ie the Representation of the People Act 1983 s 76: see the Representation of the People Act 1985 s 20(5) (s 20 substituted by the Fixed-term Parliaments Act 2011 s 6(3), Schedule paras 14, 16).

31   Representation of the People Act 1985 s 20(5) (as substituted: see note 30).

32   Ie the maximum amount for a candidate at a parliamentary election or an Authority election, including the maximum amount for the purposes of the Representation of the People Act 1983 s 76(1A) (see heads (1) to (4) in the text) (see s 76(5) (amended by the Greater London Authority Act 1999 Sch 3 paras 1, 20(1), (5))), or for an individual candidate at a European parliamentary election (see head (7) in the text) (see the European Parliamentary Elections Regulations 2004, SI 2004/293, reg 47(5)), or for a candidate at a Welsh Assembly election (see heads (5), (6) in the text) (see the National Assembly for Wales (Representation of the People) Order 2007, SI 2007/236, art 47(5)).

33   Representation of the People Act 1983 s 76(5) (as amended: see note 32); European Parliamentary Elections Regulations 2004, SI 2004/293, reg 47(5); National Assembly for Wales

(Representation of the People) Order 2007, SI 2007/236, art 47(5). As to the meaning of 'personal expenses' see PARA 271 note 3. There is, however, a limit on the amount in respect of personal expenses which a candidate may pay himself: see PARA 271.

34 See the Representation of the People Act 1983 s 76(1B); the European Parliamentary Elections Regulations 2004, SI 2004/293, reg 47(3); the National Assembly for Wales (Representation of the People) Order 2007, SI 2007/236, art 47(2); and PARA 673. As to illegal practices see PARA 671 et seq.

274. Second regulated period (the 'long period') for pre-candidacy expenses where Parliament is dissolved after a period of more than 55 months. Where:

(1)   a Parliament is not dissolved until after the period of 55 months[1] beginning with the day on which that Parliament first met ('the 55-month period')[2];

(2)   election expenses[3] are incurred by or on behalf of a candidate[4] at the parliamentary general election[5] which follows the dissolution[6]; and

(3)   the expenses are incurred in respect of a matter which is used during the period beginning immediately after the 55-month period and ending with the day on which the person becomes a candidate at that election ('pre-candidacy expenses')[7],

a second regulated period applies to a candidate's election expenses[8], which operates in addition to the limit imposed on election expenses that are allowed to a candidate in the normal course of an election campaign[9]. For the purposes of the second regulated period, 'election expenses' means any expenses incurred at any time in respect of any of the specified list of matters and used for the purposes of the candidate's election[10].

Where heads (1) to (3) above apply, election expenses so incurred must not in the aggregate exceed the 'permitted amount', which is the relevant percentage of the following sum[11]:

(a)   for a candidate at an election in a county constituency[12], £25,000 plus 7p for every entry in the register of electors[13];

(b)   for a candidate at an election in a borough constituency[14], £25,000 plus 5p for every entry in the register of electors[15].

The candidate's personal expenses[16] do not count towards the permitted amount[17].

Where election expenses are incurred in excess of the permitted amount, any candidate or election agent who incurred, or authorised the incurring of, the election expenses and knew or ought reasonably to have known that the expenses would be incurred in excess of that amount is guilty of an illegal practice[18].

1 Parliament is dissolved under the terms of the Fixed-term Parliaments Act 2011, which fixes the day for the poll at a parliamentary general election so that it falls ordinarily on the first Thursday in May every five years counting from 2010, unless an early call is made and approved: see PARA 189 et seq.

2 Representation of the People Act 1983 s 76ZA(1)(a) (s 76ZA added by the Political Parties and Elections Act 2009 s 21(1)).

3 As to the meaning of 'election expenses' generally see the Representation of the People Act 1983 s 90ZA; and PARA 269. However, for the purposes of s 76ZA, s 90ZA(1) has effect with the omission of the words 'after the date when he becomes a candidate at the election': see s 76ZA(1) (as added: see note 2); and the text and note 10.

4 As to the meaning of 'candidate' generally see PARA 230. As to the meaning of 'election expenses incurred by or on behalf of a candidate' see PARA 269 note 15.

5 As to the meaning of 'parliamentary election' see PARA 9. As to parliamentary general elections see PARA 189 et seq.

6 Representation of the People Act 1983 s 76ZA(1)(b) (as added: see note 2).

7 Representation of the People Act 1983 s 76ZA(1)(c) (as added: see note 2).

8 See the Representation of the People Act 1983 s 76ZA; and see further the text and notes 11–18.
9 Ie in addition to the limit imposed by the Representation of the People Act 1983 s 76 (see PARA 273).
10 See the Representation of the People Act 1983 s 90ZA(1) (s 90ZA added by the Electoral Administration Act 2006 s 27(1), (2), (5)); applied and modified by the Representation of the People Act 1983 s 76ZA(1) (as added: see note 2). See further PARA 269.
11 See the Representation of the People Act 1983 s 76ZA(2) (as added: see note 2). For these purposes, the relevant percentage is:
  (1) 100%, where the dissolution was during or after the sixtieth month of the Parliament (s 76ZA(3)(a) (s 76ZA as so added; s 76ZA(3)(a) amended by the Fixed-term Parliaments Act 2011 s 6(3), Schedule paras 6, 7));
  (2) 90%, where the dissolution was during its fifty-ninth month (Representation of the People Act 1983 s 76ZA(3)(b) (as so added));
  (3) 80%, where the dissolution was during its fifty-eighth month (s 76ZA(3)(c) (as so added));
  (4) 70%, where the dissolution was during its fifty-seventh month (s 76ZA(3)(d) (as so added));
  (5) 60%, where the dissolution was during its fifty-sixth month (s 76ZA(3)(e) (as so added)).
For these purposes, eg the 'fifty-sixth month' of a Parliament is the month beginning immediately after the 55-month period, etc: see s 76ZA(3) (as so added).
12 As to the meaning of 'constituency' for the purposes of parliamentary elections see PARA 9. As to the distinction between county constituencies and borough constituencies at parliamentary elections see PARA 73.
13 Representation of the People Act 1983 s 76ZA(2)(a) (as added: see note 2). For these purposes, the 'register of electors' means the register of parliamentary electors for the constituency in question, as it has effect on the last day for publication of notice of the election: s 76ZA(4) (as so added). As to the registers of electors see PARA 145 et seq.
  The Secretary of State may by order made by statutory instrument vary the sum for the time being specified in s 76ZA(2) where he considers that the variation is expedient in consequence of changes in the value of money or in order to give effect to a recommendation of the Electoral Commission: see s 76A(1), (2)(e) (s 76A added by the Representation of the People Act 1985 s 14; and substituted by the Political Parties, Elections and Referendums Act 2000 s 133(1); Representation of the People Act 1983 s 76A(2)(e) added by the Political Parties and Elections Act 2009 s 39, Sch 6 para 6). Such an order which gives effect to a recommendation of the Electoral Commission is subject to annulment in pursuance of a resolution of either House of Parliament: Representation of the People Act 1983 s 76A(3) (as so added and substituted). As to the Secretary of State see PARA 2; and as to the Electoral Commission see PARA 34 et seq.
14 See note 12.
15 Representation of the People Act 1983 s 76ZA(2)(b) (as added: see note 2). See note 13.
16 As to the meaning of 'personal expenses' see PARA 271 note 3.
17 Representation of the People Act 1983 s 76ZA(6) (as added: see note 2).
18 See the Representation of the People Act 1983 s 76ZA(5); and PARA 673. As to illegal practices see PARA 671 et seq.

275. Limitation of election expenses for joint candidates at certain local government elections. Where there are two or more joint candidates[1] at a local government election (other than a London Authority election)[2], the maximum amount of election expenses[3] must, for each of such joint candidates, be reduced by one-quarter or, if there are more than two joint candidates, by one-third[4].

Candidates are deemed to be joint candidates for these purposes where two or more candidates appoint the same election agent[5] or where, by themselves or by any agent or agents[6]:

(1) they employ or use the services of the same clerks or messengers at the election[7]; or

(2) they hire or use the same committee rooms[8] for the election[9]; or

(3) they publish a joint address or joint circular or notice at the election[10].

However, the employment and use of the same clerk, messenger or committee room, if accidental or casual or of a trivial and unimportant character, is not to be deemed of itself to constitute persons joint candidates[11].

Where:

(a)   any excess of expenses above the maximum allowed for one of two or more joint candidates has arisen owing to his having ceased to be a joint candidate[12], or to his having become a joint candidate after having begun to conduct his election as a separate candidate[13]; and

(b)   the change was made in good faith[14]; and

(c)   the excess is not more than under the circumstances is reasonable[15]; and

(d)   the total election expenses of the candidate do not exceed the maximum amount allowed for a separate candidate[16],

the excess is to be deemed to have arisen from a reasonable cause for the purpose of the statutory provisions which allow the court to give relief[17], excepting certain innocent acts from being illegal practices[18].

Nothing in these provisions concerning election expenses for joint candidates at certain local government elections prevents the candidates ceasing to be joint candidates[19].

1   As to the meaning of 'candidate' generally see PARA 230; and see the text and notes 5–11.
2   As to the meanings of 'Authority election' and 'local government election' see PARA 11. The Representation of the People Act 1983 s 77 does not apply at an election under the local government Act which is not a local government election (see the Representation of the People Act 1983 s 90(2); and PARA 297), although s 77 does apply in relation to an election of parish councillors in England or of community councillors in Wales (see s 90(1)(b); and PARAS 293–296). As to the meaning of 'election under the local government Act' see PARA 11 note 2. As to elections in the City of London see PARA 33.
3   Ie the maximum amount mentioned in the Representation of the People Act 1983 s 76 (see PARA 273): see s 77(1) (amended by the Greater London Authority Act 1999 s 17, Sch 3 paras 1, 22). As to the meaning of 'election expenses' see PARA 269.
4   Representation of the People Act 1983 s 77(1) (as amended: see note 3).
5   As to the appointment of election agents generally see PARA 231 et seq.
6   Representation of the People Act 1983 s 77(2).
7   Representation of the People Act 1983 s 77(2)(a).
8   For these purposes, 'committee room' does not include any house or room occupied by a candidate as a dwelling, by reason only of the candidate there transacting business with his agents in relation to the election, and no room or building is deemed to be a committee room by reason only of the candidate or any agent of his addressing in that room electors, committee men or others: see the Representation of the People Act 1983 s 118. As to the meaning of 'dwelling' see PARA 117 note 19.
9   Representation of the People Act 1983 s 77(2)(b).
10   Representation of the People Act 1983 s 77(2)(c).
11   Representation of the People Act 1983 s 77(2)(i).
12   See the text and note 19.
13   Representation of the People Act 1983 s 77(3)(a).
14   Representation of the People Act 1983 s 77(3)(b).
15   Representation of the People Act 1983 s 77(3)(c).
16   Representation of the People Act 1983 s 77(3)(d).
17   Ie for the purposes of the Representation of the People Act 1983 s 167 (see PARA 690): see s 77(3).
18   Representation of the People Act 1983 s 77(3).
19   Representation of the People Act 1983 s 77(2)(ii).

276. Statutory bar on claims against a candidate or his election agent in respect of election expenses. Every claim against a candidate[1] or his election agent[2] in respect of election expenses[3] which is not sent in[4] to the election agent[5] not later than 21 days after the day on which the result of the election[6] is declared[7] is barred and must not be paid[8]; and all election expenses must be paid not later than 28 days after the day on which the result of the election is declared[9]. Any person who pays a claim which is barred in this way, or who makes a payment after the expiry of the 28 days, is guilty of an illegal practice[10].

If the election agent disputes any claim sent in to him within the period of 21 days after the day on which the result of the election is declared, or if he refuses or fails to pay the claim within 28 days after that day, the claim is deemed to be a 'disputed claim'[11]. If he thinks fit, the claimant may bring an action for a disputed claim in any competent court[12], and any sum paid by the candidate or his agent[13] in pursuance of the court's judgment or order is not deemed to be in contravention of the provisions forbidding payment of election expenses otherwise than through the election agent[14] or after the time-barred period[15]. In the case of a European parliamentary election, if the defendant in the action admits his liability but disputes the amount of the claim, then, unless the court on the application of the claimant otherwise directs, that amount must be forthwith referred for assessment to a nominated circuit judge[16], or to the master, registrar or other proper officer of the court[17], and the amount found due on the assessment is the amount to be recovered in the action in respect of the claim[18].

So far as circumstances admit, the main statutory election provisions[19] apply to an election agent's claim for his remuneration and to its payment in like manner as if he were any other creditor, and if any difference arises respecting the amount of the claim, the claim is a disputed claim[20] and is to be dealt with accordingly[21].

The requirement for claims in respect of election expenses to be paid within the statutory period[22] does not apply to election expenses which are incurred by or on behalf of the candidate otherwise than for the purposes of the candidate's election[23], but which[24] fall to be regarded as election expenses by reason of the property, services or facilities in respect of which they are incurred being used for the purposes of the candidate's election[25]. However, the candidate's election agent must make a declaration of the amount of any such expenses that are incurred otherwise than for election purposes[26].

1   Ie a candidate at a parliamentary or local government election, a European parliamentary election, or a Welsh Assembly election. As to the meaning of 'parliamentary election' see PARA 9; and as to the meaning of 'local government election' see PARA 11. As to the meaning of 'Assembly election' see PARA 3 note 2. As to European parliamentary elections see PARA 217 et seq. As to the meaning of 'candidate' generally see PARA 230; but see also note 2.

2   As to the appointment of election agents generally see PARA 231 et seq. At a European parliamentary election, the reference is to an individual candidate or his election agent: see the European Parliamentary Elections Regulations 2004, SI 2004/293, reg 48(1), (2). As to the meaning of 'individual candidate' at a European parliamentary election see PARA 230 note 32. As to the appointment of a sub-agent at a European parliamentary election see PARA 241 et seq; and see note 5. In the case of a Welsh Assembly election, the reference is to a constituency candidate or his election agent at a constituency election (see the National Assembly for Wales (Representation of the People) Order 2007, SI 2007/236, arts 49(1)(a), 50(2)); and to an individual candidate or his election agent at a regional election (see arts 49(1)(b), 50(2)). As to the meanings of 'constituency election' and 'regional election' for these purposes see PARA 3 note 2. As to the meanings of 'constituency candidate' and 'individual candidate' see PARA 230 note 19.

3   As to the meaning of 'election expenses' see PARA 269; but see also the text and notes 22–26.

4   It is not clear whether the claim must be in the possession of the person or merely have been dispatched within the time. However, to the extent that 'send' is synonymous with 'transmit', the latter construction is the correct one: see *MacKinnon v Clark* [1898] 2 QB 251 at 257, CA, per A L Smith LJ.

5   In the case of a European parliamentary election, the reference is to the 'agent who incurred the expense' rather than to the election agent: see the European Parliamentary Elections Regulations 2004, SI 2004/293, reg 48(1). References to the agent who incurred the expense are references to the election agent or sub-agent or an agent who did so on the written authority of such an agent (see PARA 270 et seq): reg 48(7). Where the agent who incurred the expense is not the election agent, however, he must send to that agent, forthwith on payment of the expense,

the bill and a record of the fact that he has paid it and, on receiving a receipt for that payment, must send that receipt to that agent: reg 48(3). As to the meaning of 'payment' for these purposes see PARA 270 note 1.

6   The Representation of the People Act 1983 ss 78–80 do not apply at an election under the local government Act which is not a local government election (see the Representation of the People Act 1983 s 90(2); and PARA 297); and, in relation to an election of parish councillors in England or of community councillors in Wales, the provisions of s 90(1), Sch 4 apply instead (see s 90(1)(b); and PARAS 293–296). As to the meaning of 'election under the local government Act' see PARA 11 note 2.

7   As to the declaration of the result of elections see PARA 479 et seq.

8   Representation of the People Act 1983 s 78(1) (amended by the Representation of the People Act 1985 s 24, Sch 4 para 26; and the Political Parties, Elections and Referendums Act 2000 s 138, Sch 18 paras 1, 6); European Parliamentary Elections Regulations 2004, SI 2004/293, reg 48(1); National Assembly for Wales (Representation of the People) Order 2007, SI 2007/236, art 49(1). See note 2.

9   Representation of the People Act 1983 s 78(2) (amended by the Political Parties, Elections and Referendums Act 2000 Sch 18 paras 1, 6); European Parliamentary Elections Regulations 2004, SI 2004/293, reg 48(2); National Assembly for Wales (Representation of the People) Order 2007, SI 2007/236, art 49(2). See note 2.

10   See the Representation of the People Act 1983 s 78(3); the European Parliamentary Elections Regulations 2004, SI 2004/293, reg 48(4); the National Assembly for Wales (Representation of the People) Order 2007, SI 2007/236, art 49(3); and PARA 675. As to illegal practices see PARA 671 et seq. Except in the case of a European parliamentary election, if the election court reports that it has been proved to the court by the candidate that any payment was made by an election agent without the candidate's sanction or connivance, the candidate's election is not void, nor is he subject to any incapacity by reason only of that payment having been made in contravention of the prohibition on the payment of a claim that is statute–barred or out of time: see the Representation of the People Act 1983 s 78(3); the National Assembly for Wales (Representation of the People) Order 2007, SI 2007/236, art 49(4); and PARA 675. As to the incapacities that may be suffered as a result see PARA 901 et seq.

11   Representation of the People Act 1983 s 79(1) (amended by the Representation of the People Act 1985 Sch 4 para 26); European Parliamentary Elections Regulations 2004, SI 2004/293, reg 49(1); National Assembly for Wales (Representation of the People) Order 2007, SI 2007/236, art 50(1). In the case of a European parliamentary election, the reference is to the 'agent who incurred the expense' rather than to the election agent: see the European Parliamentary Elections Regulations 2004, SI 2004/293, reg 49(1); and see note 5.

    In the Representation of the People Act 1983 Pt II (ss 67–119), in relation to a parliamentary or local government election, the European Parliamentary Elections Regulations 2004, SI 2004/293, Pt 2 (regs 31–81), in relation to a European parliamentary election, or the National Assembly for Wales (Representation of the People) Order 2007, SI 2007/236, Pt 3 (arts 37–85), in relation to a Welsh Assembly election (see PARA 235 et seq), unless the context otherwise requires, 'disputed claim' has the meaning given by the Representation of the People Act 1983 s 79(1), as extended by s 80 (see the text and notes 19–21), or by the European Parliamentary Elections Regulations 2004, SI 2004/293, reg 49(1), as extended by reg 50 (see the text and notes 19–21), or by the National Assembly for Wales (Representation of the People) Order 2007, SI 2007/236, art 48(1), as extended by art 51 (see the text and notes 19–21) (whichever is appropriate): Representation of the People Act 1983 s 118; National Assembly for Wales (Representation of the People) Order 2007, SI 2007/236, art 83; European Parliamentary Elections Regulations 2004, SI 2004/293, reg 31(1). As to the power to apply to the court for permission to pay a disputed claim see PARA 277.

12   Ie including, in relation to a European parliamentary election taking place in the combined region, the Gibraltar court, where appropriate: see the European Parliamentary Elections Regulations 2004, SI 2004/293, reg 49(2). As to the establishment of electoral regions (including the 'combined region') for the purpose of elections to the European Parliament see PARA 77. As to references to the candidate see note 2.

13   It is not clear, on the plain statutory wording, whether this refers only to the election agent or whether it includes, for instance, the candidate's solicitor. In the case of a European parliamentary election, the reference is to 'any sum paid by the agent or individual candidate who incurred the expense': see the European Parliamentary Elections Regulations 2004, SI 2004/293, reg 49(2).

14   Ie in contravention of the Representation of the People Act 1983 s 73(1) or the European Parliamentary Elections Regulations 2004, SI 2004/293, reg 43(1), or the National Assembly for Wales (Representation of the People) Order 2007, SI 2007/236, art 43(1) (whichever is

applicable) (see PARA 270): see the Representation of the People Act 1983 s 79(2); the European Parliamentary Elections Regulations 2004, SI 2004/293, reg 49(2); and the National Assembly for Wales (Representation of the People) Order 2007, SI 2007/236, art 50(2).

15 Representation of the People Act 1983 s 79(2); European Parliamentary Elections Regulations 2004, SI 2004/293, reg 49(2); National Assembly for Wales (Representation of the People) Order 2007, SI 2007/236, art 50(2). The provisions mentioned in the text are those contained in the Representation of the People Act 1983 s 78(2), or the European Parliamentary Elections Regulations 2004, SI 2004/293, reg 48(2), or the National Assembly for Wales (Representation of the People) Order 2007, SI 2007/236, art 49(2) (whichever is applicable) (see the text and note 9): see the Representation of the People Act 1983 s 79(2); the European Parliamentary Elections Regulations 2004, SI 2004/293, reg 49(2); and the National Assembly for Wales (Representation of the People) Order 2007, SI 2007/236, art 50(2).

16 Ie a circuit judge nominated under the Senior Courts Act 1981 s 68(1)(a): see the European Parliamentary Elections Regulations 2004, SI 2004/293, reg 49(3)(a) (amended by the Constitutional Reform Act 2005 s 59(1), (5), Sch 11 Pt 1 para 1(2)). In an action in a Gibraltar court, the registrar is the person to whom the assessment is referred: see the European Parliamentary Elections Regulations 2004, SI 2004/293, reg 49(3)(c).

The Senior Courts Act 1981 was previously known as the Supreme Court Act 1981 and was renamed by the Constitutional Reform Act 2005 Sch 11 Pt 1 as from 1 October 2009: see the Constitutional Reform Act 2005 (Commencement No 11) Order 2009, SI 2009/1604.

17 European Parliamentary Elections Regulations 2004, SI 2004/293, reg 49(3)(b).

18 European Parliamentary Elections Regulations 2004, SI 2004/293, reg 49(3).

19 Ie the Representation of the People Act 1983, the European Parliamentary Elections Regulations 2004, SI 2004/293, or the National Assembly for Wales (Representation of the People) Order 2007, SI 2007/236 (whichever is applicable): see the Representation of the People Act 1983 s 80; the European Parliamentary Elections Regulations 2004, SI 2004/293, reg 50; and the National Assembly for Wales (Representation of the People) Order 2007, SI 2007/236, art 51.

20 Ie within the meaning of the Representation of the People Act 1983, the European Parliamentary Elections Regulations 2004, SI 2004/293, or the National Assembly for Wales (Representation of the People) Order 2007, SI 2007/236 (whichever is applicable) (see the text and note 11): see the Representation of the People Act 1983 s 80; the European Parliamentary Elections Regulations 2004, SI 2004/293, reg 50; and the National Assembly for Wales (Representation of the People) Order 2007, SI 2007/236, art 51.

21 Representation of the People Act 1983 s 80; European Parliamentary Elections Regulations 2004, SI 2004/293, reg 50; National Assembly for Wales (Representation of the People) Order 2007, SI 2007/236, art 51.

22 Ie the provision made by the Representation of the People Act 1983 ss 78, 79, the European Parliamentary Elections Regulations 2004, SI 2004/293, regs 48, 49, or the National Assembly for Wales (Representation of the People) Order 2007, SI 2007/236, arts 49, 50 (as the case may be) (see the text and notes 1–18): see the Representation of the People Act 1983 s 74A(1) (s 74A added by the Political Parties, Elections and Referendums Act 2000 s 138, Sch 18 paras 1, 5); the European Parliamentary Elections Regulations 2004, SI 2004/293, reg 45(1); and the National Assembly for Wales (Representation of the People) Order 2007, SI 2007/236, art 45(1).

23 Representation of the People Act 1983 s 74A(1)(a) (as added: see note 22); European Parliamentary Elections Regulations 2004, SI 2004/293, reg 45(1)(a); National Assembly for Wales (Representation of the People) Order 2007, SI 2007/236, art 45(1)(a). 'For the purposes of the candidate's election' has the same meaning as in the Representation of the People Act 1983 ss 90ZA, 90C (definition applied by s 74A(3) (s 74A as so added; s 74A(3) amended by the Electoral Administration Act 2006 s 74(1), Sch 1 paras 104, 112(1), (4), 133)), the European Parliamentary Elections Regulations 2004, SI 2004/293, regs 60, 62 (definition applied by reg 45(3) (amended by SI 2009/186)), or the National Assembly for Wales (Representation of the People) Order 2007, SI 2007/236, arts 63, 64 (definition applied by art 45(3)), as the case may be (see PARA 269).

In the case of a European parliamentary election, the reference is to election expenses which are incurred by or on behalf of an individual candidate (see note 2): see the European Parliamentary Elections Regulations 2004, SI 2004/293, reg 45(1)(a), (2). In the case of a Welsh Assembly election, the reference is simply to 'election expenses which are incurred by or on behalf of the candidate' but references either to a constituency candidate or to an individual candidate must be construed according to context (see note 2): see the National Assembly for Wales (Representation of the People) Order 2007, SI 2007/236, art 45(1)(a), (2).

24 Ie by virtue of the Representation of the People Act 1983 s 90ZA(1), the European
   Parliamentary Elections Regulations 2004, SI 2004/293, reg 60(1), or the National Assembly for
   Wales (Representation of the People) Order 2007, SI 2007/236, art 63(1) as the case may be (see
   PARA 269): Representation of the People Act 1983 s 74A(1)(b) (s 74A as added (see note 22);
   s 74A(1)(b) amended by the Electoral Administration Act 2006 Sch 1 paras 104, 112(1), (2),
   133); European Parliamentary Elections Regulations 2004, SI 2004/293, reg 45(1)(b); National
   Assembly for Wales (Representation of the People) Order 2007, SI 2007/236, art 45(1)(b).
25 Representation of the People Act 1983 s 74A(1)(b) (as added and amended: see note 24);
   European Parliamentary Elections Regulations 2004, SI 2004/293, reg 45(1)(b); National
   Assembly for Wales (Representation of the People) Order 2007, SI 2007/236, art 45(1)(b).
26 Representation of the People Act 1983 s 74A(2) (as added (see note 22); and amended by the
   Electoral Administration Act 2006 Sch 1 paras 104, 112(1), (3), 133, Sch 2); European
   Parliamentary Elections Regulations 2004, SI 2004/293, reg 45(2) (amended by SI 2009/186);
   National Assembly for Wales (Representation of the People) Order 2007, SI 2007/236,
   art 45(2). As to references to the candidate see note 23.

**277.   Application for permission to pay claims in respect of election expenses
against the statutory bar.**   The person making a claim against a candidate[1] or his
election agent[2] for any election expenses[3] ('the claimant'), or the candidate or his
election agent themselves, may apply to the High Court or to the county court[4]
for permission to pay such a claim (even if it is sent in after the statutory period
allowed of 21 days, or although it is sent in to the candidate and not to the
election agent[5]) or they may apply to the High Court or to the county court for
permission to pay a disputed claim in the same way[6]. The court on cause shown
to its satisfaction may by order grant the permission sought[7]. Any sum specified
in such an order may be paid by the candidate or his election agent and, when
paid in pursuance of the permission, is not deemed to be a contravention of the
statutory requirement[8] for claims in respect of election expenses to be paid
within the time-barred period of 28 days[9].

The following examples of applications for permission to pay a claim have
been granted: an application to pay a claim after the prescribed time has been
granted where the candidate was misled by a textbook on elections[10]; an
application to pay a claim inadvertently omitted from the return of election
expenses in consequence of the illness of an agent who had been unable to check
the accounts has been granted[11], as has a similar application by a candidate
where the omission was due to the election agent[12]; an application by a
candidate to pay the charges of sub-agents which he at first thought
unreasonable and refused to pay, although later he changed his mind, was
granted[13]; and an application for permission has also been given where an agent
was instructed to prepare canvassing books for a general election but was not
employed as election agent[14]. However, the court has refused an application for
permission made where the candidate was not liable to pay the claim[15].

1   As to the meaning of 'candidate' generally see PARA 230; but see also note 2.
2   As to the appointment of election agents generally see PARA 231 et seq.
    At a European parliamentary election, the reference is to the agent or individual candidate
    who incurred the expense: see the European Parliamentary Elections Regulations 2004,
    SI 2004/293, reg 48(5). As to the meaning of 'individual candidate' at a European parliamentary
    election see PARA 230 note 32. As to European parliamentary elections see PARA 217 et seq.
    In the case of a Welsh Assembly election, the reference is to a constituency candidate or his
    election agent at a constituency election, and to an individual candidate or his election agent at
    a regional election (see the National Assembly for Wales (Representation of the People)
    Order 2007, SI 2007/236, art 49(5)(b)). As to the meanings of 'Assembly election', 'constituency
    election' and 'regional election' for the purposes of Welsh Assembly elections see PARA 3 note 2.
    As to the meanings of 'constituency candidate' at a Welsh Assembly constituency election and
    'individual candidate' at a Welsh Assembly regional election see PARA 230 note 19. As to Welsh
    Assembly elections generally see PARA 213 et seq.

3   As to the meaning of 'election expenses' see PARA 269. As to claims against a candidate or his election agent in respect of election expenses see PARA 276.

4   For the purposes of a European parliamentary election taking place in the combined region, the reference in the text to the High Court or a county court is, where the provision is applied to Gibraltar, a reference to the Gibraltar court: see the European Parliamentary Elections Regulations 2004, SI 2004/293, reg 45(8). As to the establishment of electoral regions (including the 'combined region') for the purpose of elections to the European Parliament see PARA 77.

5   As to the statutory limit of 21 days for claims in respect of election expenses that are not sent in to the election agent see PARA 276.

6   Representation of the People Act 1983 ss 78(4), 79(4) (ss 78(4), 79(4) amended by the Representation of the People Act 1985 s 24, Sch 4 para 26); European Parliamentary Elections Regulations 2004, SI 2004/293, regs 48(5), 49(4); National Assembly for Wales (Representation of the People) Order 2007, SI 2007/236, arts 49(5), 50(3). As to disputed claims, including claims by election agents as disputed claims see PARA 276; and as to returns required in respect of sums paid in pursuance of the permission see PARA 280.

  The Representation of the People Act 1983 ss 78–79 do not apply at an election under the local government Act which is not a local government election (see the Representation of the People Act 1983 s 90(2); and PARA 297); and, in relation to an election of parish councillors in England or of community councillors in Wales, the provisions of s 90(1), Sch 4 apply instead (see s 90(1)(b); and PARAS 293–296). As to the meaning of 'local government election' see PARA 11; and as to the meaning of 'election under the local government Act' see PARA 11 note 2. As to elections in the City of London see PARA 33.

7   Representation of the People Act 1983 ss 78(4), 79(4) (ss 78(4), 79(4) as amended: see note 6); European Parliamentary Elections Regulations 2004, SI 2004/293, regs 48(5), 49(4); National Assembly for Wales (Representation of the People) Order 2007, SI 2007/236, arts 49(5), 50(3).

8   Ie the Representation of the People Act 1983 ss 78(2), 79(1), or the European Parliamentary Elections Regulations 2004, SI 2004/293, regs 48(2), 49(1), or the National Assembly for Wales (Representation of the People) Order 2007, SI 2007/236, arts 49(2), 50(1) (whichever is applicable) (see PARA 276).

9   Representation of the People Act 1983 ss 78(5), 79(4) (s 79(4) as amended: see note 6); European Parliamentary Elections Regulations 2004, SI 2004/293, regs 48(6), 49(4); National Assembly for Wales (Representation of the People) Order 2007, SI 2007/236, arts 49(6), 50(3). In the case of a European parliamentary election, where the agent who incurred the expense is not the election agent, however, he must send to that agent, forthwith on payment of the expense, the bill and a record of the fact that he has paid it and, on receiving a receipt for that payment, must send that receipt to that agent: European Parliamentary Elections Regulations 2004, SI 2004/293, reg 48(3); applied by reg 48(6). As to the meaning of 'payment' for these purposes see PARA 270 note 1. As to the declaration of the result of elections see PARA 479 et seq.

10 *Re Preston, Fishwick Ward Councillor, Re Hubberstey* (1899) 43 Sol Jo 826, DC.

11 *Ex p Morris* (1897) 42 Sol Jo 163, DC.

12 *Ex p Polson* (1923) 39 TLR 231.

13 *Re South Shropshire Case* (1886) 2 TLR 347, DC.

14 *Re Parliamentary Election* (1887) 4 TLR 38, DC. The agent's claim was referred to arbitration and the court gave permission to pay the sum awarded by the arbitrator.

15 *Re Chelsea Case* (1886) 2 TLR 374, DC.

278. Creditors' rights. The statutory provisions which place restrictions on the payment (and contracts for payment) of election expenses[1], which prohibit the payment or incurring of election expenses in excess of the maximum limit allowed[2], or which prohibit the incurring of expenses not authorised by the election agent[3], do not affect the right of any creditor who, when the contract was made, or the expense was incurred, was ignorant of that contract or expense being in contravention of those provisions[4].

1   Representation of the People Act 1983 s 116(a); European Parliamentary Elections Regulations 2004, SI 2004/293, reg 80(a); National Assembly for Wales (Representation of the People) Order 2007, SI 2007/236, art 82(a). As to the provisions referred to in the text see PARA 270 et seq. As to the meaning of 'payment' for these purposes see PARA 270 note 1. As to illegal payments made for the exhibition of election notices see also PARA 684.

      The Representation of the People Act 1983 s 116 has effect for the purposes of local authority referendums, subject to the modifications specified, in relation to Wales, by the Local Authorities (Conduct of Referendums) (Wales) Regulations 2008, SI 2008/1848, reg 8(2), Sch 4 Table 1, and, in relation to England, by the Local Authorities (Conduct of Referendums) (England) Regulations 2012, SI 2012/323, regs 8(2), 11–13, Sch 4 Table 1: see PARA 15 note 2.

2   Representation of the People Act 1983 s 116(b); European Parliamentary Elections Regulations 2004, SI 2004/293, reg 80(b); National Assembly for Wales (Representation of the People) Order 2007, SI 2007/236, art 82(b). As to the provisions referred to in the text see PARAS 273–275.

3   Representation of the People Act 1983 s 116(c); European Parliamentary Elections Regulations 2004, SI 2004/293, reg 80(c); National Assembly for Wales (Representation of the People) Order 2007, SI 2007/236, art 82(c). As to the provisions referred to in the text see PARA 271.

4   Representation of the People Act 1983 s 116; European Parliamentary Elections Regulations 2004, SI 2004/293, reg 80; National Assembly for Wales (Representation of the People) Order 2007, SI 2007/236, art 82.

(B) Returns, etc required in relation to the Payment of Election Expenses

279. Return and declarations of incurred election expenses that were duly authorised by election agent. Where a person (other than any person engaged or employed for payment or promise of payment[1] by a candidate or his election agent[2]) incurs any expenses which are required, by the statutory provisions restricting election expenses incurred by outsiders[3], to be authorised by the election agent[4]:

(1)   that person must, within 21 days after the day on which the result of the election is declared[5], deliver[6]: (a) to the appropriate officer[7], a return of the amount of those expenses, stating the election[8] at which and the candidate in whose support they were incurred[9]; or (b) in the case of a European parliamentary election, to the agent who authorised the expenses, a return of the amount of them[10]; and

(2)   the return must be accompanied by a declaration made by that person (or in the case of an association or body of persons, by a director, general manager, secretary or other similar officer of the association or body) verifying the return and giving particulars of the matters for which the expenses were incurred[11].

Except in relation to a European parliamentary election, the return and declaration required under head (1) and head (2) above must be in the prescribed forms[12]; and, in relation to any election (including a European parliamentary election), the authority received from the election agent[13] must be annexed to, and is deemed to form part of, the return[14].

      In relation to a parliamentary election, a copy of every return and declaration made under head (1) and head (2) above must be sent to the returning officer, within 21 days after the day on which the result of the election is declared, by the person making the return or declaration[15]. In relation to either a parliamentary election or a Welsh Assembly election, the returning officer[16] must forward to the relevant registration officer[17] every document so sent to him[18]; and the relevant registration officer must retain for a year the documents so forwarded to him and then, unless otherwise directed by order of the High Court, Crown Court or a magistrates' court, must cause them to be destroyed[19].

      If any person incurs, or aids, abets, counsels or procures any other person to incur, any expenses in contravention of these restrictions[20], or knowingly makes the declaration required under head (2) above falsely, he is guilty of a corrupt practice, and if a person fails to deliver or send any declaration or return a copy of it as required, he is guilty of an illegal practice[21].

1   As to the meaning of 'payment' for these purposes see PARA 270 note 1.
2   As to the meaning of 'candidate' generally see PARA 230. As to the appointment of election
    agents generally see PARA 231 et seq.
        At a European parliamentary election, the reference is to 'any person engaged or employed
    for payment or promise of payment by the individual candidate or his election agent': see the
    European Parliamentary Elections Regulations 2004, SI 2004/293, reg 46(3). In relation to a
    European parliamentary election, references to an election agent include a sub-agent: see
    reg 46(7). As to the appointment of a sub-agent at a European parliamentary election see PARA
    241 et seq. As to the meaning of 'individual candidate' at a European parliamentary election see
    PARA 230 note 32. As to European parliamentary elections see PARA 217 et seq.
        In the case of a Welsh Assembly election, the reference to a candidate is implicitly to a
    constituency candidate at a Welsh Assembly constituency election, and to an individual
    candidate at a Welsh Assembly regional election: see the National Assembly for Wales
    (Representation of the People) Order 2007, SI 2007/236, art 46(1); and PARA 272. As to the
    meanings of 'Assembly election', 'constituency election' and 'regional election' for the purposes
    of Welsh Assembly elections see PARA 3 note 2. As to the meanings of 'constituency candidate' at
    a Welsh Assembly constituency election and 'individual candidate' at a Welsh Assembly regional
    election see PARA 230 note 19.
3   Ie the Representation of the People Act 1983 s 75, the European Parliamentary Elections
    Regulations 2004, SI 2004/293, reg 46, or the National Assembly for Wales (Representation of
    the People) Order 2007, SI 2007/236, art 46, as the case may be (see PARA 272).
4   Representation of the People Act 1983 s 75(2); European Parliamentary Elections
    Regulations 2004, SI 2004/293, reg 46(3); National Assembly for Wales (Representation of the
    People) Order 2007, SI 2007/236, art 46(5).
5   As to the declaration of the result of elections see PARA 479 et seq.
6   Representation of the People Act 1983 s 75(2)(a) (amended by the Representation of the People
    Act 1985 s 24, Sch 4 para 24(a)); European Parliamentary Elections Regulations 2004,
    SI 2004/293, reg 46(3)(a); National Assembly for Wales (Representation of the People)
    Order 2007, SI 2007/236, art 46(5)(a).
7   As to the meaning of 'appropriate officer' in relation to a parliamentary or local government
    election see PARA 231 note 5; and as to the meaning of the 'appropriate officer' in relation to a
    European parliamentary election see PARA 239 note 16. In the case of a Welsh Assembly
    election, the 'appropriate returning officer' is specified: see the National Assembly for Wales
    (Representation of the People) Order 2007, SI 2007/236, art 46(5)(a). Accordingly, in the case of
    a constituency election, the constituency returning officer is meant, and, in the case of a regional
    election, a regional returning officer: see PARA 18 note 2.
8   The Representation of the People Act 1983 s 75 does not apply at an election under the local
    government Act which is not a local government election (see the Representation of the People
    Act 1983 s 90(2); and PARA 297); and, in relation to an election of parish councillors in England
    or of community councillors in Wales, the provisions of s 90(1), Sch 4 apply instead (see
    s 90(1)(b); and PARAS 293–296). As to the meaning of 'parliamentary election' see PARA 9; as to
    the meanings of 'Authority election' and 'local government election' see PARA 11; and as to the
    meaning of 'election under the local government Act' see PARA 11 note 2. As to elections in the
    City of London see PARA 33.
        In the case of a Welsh Assembly election, it is the relevant constituency election or regional
    election that must be stated in the return: see the National Assembly for Wales (Representation
    of the People) Order 2007, SI 2007/236, art 46(5)(a).
9   Representation of the People Act 1983 s 75(2)(a) (as amended: see note 6); National Assembly
    for Wales (Representation of the People) Order 2007, SI 2007/236, art 46(5)(a).
10 European Parliamentary Elections Regulations 2004, SI 2004/293, reg 46(3)(a).
11 Representation of the People Act 1983 s 75(2)(b); European Parliamentary Elections
    Regulations 2004, SI 2004/293, reg 46(3)(b); National Assembly for Wales (Representation of
    the People) Order 2007, SI 2007/236, art 46(5)(b).
12 Representation of the People Act 1983 s 75(3); National Assembly for Wales (Representation of
    the People) Order 2007, SI 2007/236, art 46(6).
        As to the forms prescribed for use at parliamentary or local government elections for these
    purposes see the Representation of the People (England and Wales) Regulations 2001,
    SI 2001/341, reg 10(1), Sch 3 Form C (return of expenses required by section 75 of the 1983
    Act), Sch 3 Form D (declaration as to expenses required by section 75 of the 1983 Act). The
    forms set out in the Representation of the People (England and Wales) Regulations 2001,
    SI 2001/341, Sch 3 or forms substantially to the like effect may be used with such variations as
    the circumstances may require: reg 4(2). At a parliamentary election in Wales, the forms set out
    in the Parliamentary Elections (Welsh Forms) Order 2007, SI 2007/1014, Sch 2 Form 9

(Form C: Return of Expenses required by section 75 of the 1983 Act; Ffurflen C: Datganiad Costau Sy'n Ofynnol Dan Adran 75 Deddf 1983), Sch 2 Form 10 (Form D: Declaration as to Expenses required by section 75 of the 1983 Act; Ffurflen D: Datganiad Costau Sy'n Ofynnol Dan Adran 75 Deddf 1983) are prescribed as the version partly in Welsh and partly in English to be used at a parliamentary election in Wales in place of the Representation of the People (England and Wales) Regulations 2001, SI 2001/341, Sch 3 Form C, Form D (although forms substantially to the like effect may be used with such variations as the circumstances may require): see the Parliamentary Elections (Welsh Forms) Order 2007, SI 2007/1014, arts 6(i), (j), 7.

As to the forms prescribed for use at Welsh Assembly elections see the National Assembly for Wales (Representation of the People) Order 2007, SI 2007/236, Sch 10 Appendix of Forms (Form CU: Form of return (expenses incurred in support of a candidate); Form CV: Form of declaration (expenses incurred in support of a candidate)).

No form is specified as being prescribed for the purposes of a European parliamentary election but see the text and notes 13–14.

13 Ie, in relation to a European parliamentary election, the authority of the agent who authorised the incurring of the expenses: see the European Parliamentary Elections Regulations 2004, SI 2004/293, reg 46(4).

14 Representation of the People Act 1983 s 75(3); European Parliamentary Elections Regulations 2004, SI 2004/293, reg 46(4); National Assembly for Wales (Representation of the People) Order 2007, SI 2007/236, art 46(6).

15 Representation of the People Act 1983 s 75(4), (4A) (s 75(4) substituted, s 75(4A)–(4C) added, by the Electoral Administration Act 2006 s 74(1), Sch 1 paras 104, 113).

16 Ie, at a Welsh Assembly election, the 'appropriate returning officer' (see note 7): see the National Assembly for Wales (Representation of the People) Order 2007, SI 2007/236, art 46(7).

17 Ie, for the purposes of a parliamentary election, the relevant registration officer within the meaning of the Representation of the People Act 1983 Sch 1 r 55 (see PARA 496 note 3): see s 75(4B) (as added: see note 15). As to the meaning of 'relevant registration officer' at a Welsh Assembly election see PARA 139 note 1.

18 Representation of the People Act 1983 s 75(4B) (as added: see note 15); National Assembly for Wales (Representation of the People) Order 2007, SI 2007/236, art 46(7).

19 Representation of the People Act 1983 Sch 1 r 57 (amended by the Electoral Administration Act 2006 ss 31(1), (8), 41(1), (5), 70, 78(3)) (Representation of the People Act 1983 Sch 1 r 57 applied by s 75(4C) (as added: see note 15)); National Assembly for Wales (Representation of the People) Order 2007, SI 2007/236, Sch 5 para 69(1) (applied by art 46(7)). In relation to a Welsh Assembly election, only the National Assembly for Wales (Representation of the People) Order 2007, SI 2007/236, Sch 5 para 69(1) is so applied (see also PARA 508), but, in relation to a parliamentary election, the whole of the Representation of the People Act 1983 Sch 1 r 57 appears to be applied (and, therefore, it seems that provision is also made for the inspection and supply of returns and declarations made in relation to a parliamentary election: see PARA 503).

20 See note 3.

21 See the Representation of the People Act 1983 s 75(5); the European Parliamentary Elections Regulations 2004, SI 2004/293, reg 46(5); the National Assembly for Wales (Representation of the People) Order 2007, SI 2007/236, art 46(10)–(12); and PARAS 687, 707. As to the punishment of corrupt and illegal practices see PARA 887 set seq; as to the avoidance of elections see PARA 894 et seq; and as to the other consequences of corrupt and illegal practices see PARA 901 et seq.

Any incapacity imposed by virtue of such a conviction as is mentioned in the text may be mitigated or entirely remitted if the court before which a person is convicted thinks it just in the special circumstances of the case: see the Representation of the People Act 1983 s 75(5)(i); the European Parliamentary Elections Regulations 2004, SI 2004/293, reg 46(5); the National Assembly for Wales (Representation of the People) Order 2007, SI 2007/236, art 46(10); and PARAS 687, 707. A candidate at a parliamentary, local government or Welsh Assembly election is not liable, nor is his election avoided, for such a corrupt or illegal practice committed by an agent without his consent or connivance: see the Representation of the People Act 1983 s 75(5)(ii); the National Assembly for Wales (Representation of the People) Order 2007, SI 2007/236, art 46(11); and PARAS 687, 707. As to liability where any act or omission of an association or body of persons, corporate or unincorporate, is an offence declared to be a corrupt or illegal practice as is mentioned in the text see the Representation of the People Act 1983 s 75(6); the European Parliamentary Elections Regulations 2004, SI 2004/293, reg 46(6); the National Assembly for Wales (Representation of the People) Order 2007, SI 2007/236, art 46(12); and PARAS 687, 707.

280.   Returns as to candidates' election expenses. Within 35 days[1] after the day on which the result of a parliamentary election[2], or an election under the local government Act[3], is declared[4], and within 70 days after the day on which the result of a London Mayoral election[5] or an ordinary election of the London members of the London Assembly is declared[6] (but within 35 days after the day on which the result of any other Authority election is declared[7]), the election agent[8] of every candidate[9] at that election must deliver to the appropriate officer[10] a true return[11] containing as respects that candidate[12]:

(1)   a statement of all election expenses incurred by or on behalf of the candidate[13];

(2)   a statement of all payments[14] made by the election agent, together with all bills or receipts relating to the payments[15];

(3)   a statement relating to such other expenses in connection with which provision is made[16] as the Electoral Commission provides in regulations[17];

(4)   a statement relating to such claims (whether paid, unpaid or disputed) in connection with such election expenses or such other expenses mentioned in head (3) above as the Electoral Commission so provides[18]; and

(5)   a statement relating to such other matters as is prescribed[19].

Within 50 days[20] after the day on which the result of a European parliamentary election is declared[21], and within 35 days[22] after the day on which the result or results of a Welsh Assembly election are declared[23], the election agent of every candidate[24] at the election must deliver to the appropriate officer[25] a true return containing as respects that candidate[26]:

(a)   a statement of all election expenses incurred by or on behalf of the candidate[27];

(b)   a statement of all payments made by the election agent, together with all bills or receipts relating to the payments[28];

(c)   a statement of the amount of personal expenses (and other expenses incurred before an election agent was appointed) paid by the candidate[29];

(d)   a statement of the amount of necessary and other petty expenses paid by persons authorised in writing or by the candidate's election agent[30];

(e)   a statement of all disputed claims of which the election agent is aware[31];

(f)   a statement of all the unpaid claims, if any, of which the election agent is aware, in respect of which application has been or is about to be made to the High Court or county court[32];

(g)   any declarations of value falling to be made by the candidate's election agent of expenses incurred by or on behalf of a candidate otherwise than for the purposes of the candidate's election but which fall to be regarded[33] as election expenses, or of property, goods, services or facilities provided free of charge or at a discount of more than 10 per cent which are treated[34] as election expenses incurred by the candidate[35];

(h)   a declaration of the amount of election expenses incurred by or on behalf of a candidate before the date when he becomes a candidate at the election but which fall to be regarded[36] as election expenses[37];

(i)   a statement of donations recording the required particulars in relation to relevant donations[38] which were made by permissible donors[39] and impermissible donors[40] and accepted by the candidate or his election agent[41];

(j) a statement of the amount, if any, of money provided by the candidate from his own resources for the purpose of meeting election expenses incurred by him or on his behalf[42].

In all cases, such a return must specify the poll by virtue of which the return is required[43], and the name of the candidate to whom the return relates and of the candidate's election agent[44], and it must deal under a separate heading with any expenses that are required to be authorised by the election agent and in respect of which a return is to be made[45].

If, subsequent to the delivery of the return, permission is given by the court for the payment of a statute-barred or disputed claim[46], either the candidate or his election agent[47], must within seven days after the payment deliver to the appropriate officer a return of the sums paid in pursuance of the permission given, accompanied by a copy of the court's order giving the permission; in default he is deemed to have failed to comply with the statutory requirements as to returns without authorised excuse[48]. Failure to comply with the requirements of the provisions governing returns as to election expenses constitutes an illegal practice[49].

It would appear that expenses ought to be returned as election expenses notwithstanding that they were incurred illegally[50].

1 As to the computation of time for these purposes see PARA 230 note 11.

2 As to the meaning of 'parliamentary election' see PARA 9.

3 The Representation of the People Act 1983 s 81 does not apply at an election under the local government Act which is not a local government election (see the Representation of the People Act 1983 s 90(2); and PARA 297); and, in relation to an election of parish councillors in England or of community councillors in Wales, the provisions of s 90(1), Sch 4 apply instead (see s 90(1)(b); and PARAS 293–296). As to the meaning of 'local government election' see PARA 11; and as to the meaning of 'election under the local government Act' see PARA 11 note 2. As to elections in the City of London see PARA 33.

4 See the Representation of the People Act 1983 s 81(1) (amended by the Representation of the People Act 1985 s 24, Sch 4 para 27; and the Political Parties, Elections and Referendums Act 2000 s 138, Sch 18 paras 1, 7(1), (2)). As to the declaration of the result of a parliamentary election, or an election under the local government Act, see PARA 479 et seq.

5 Representation of the People Act 1983 s 81(1) (as amended: see note 4); applied and modified by s 81(1A)(a) (s 81(1A) added by the Greater London Authority Act 1999 s 17, Sch 3 paras 1, 23(1), (2)). As to elections for the return of an elected Mayor of London see PARA 199 et seq.

6 Representation of the People Act 1983 s 81(1) (as amended: see note 4); applied and modified by s 81(1A)(b) (as added: see note 5). In relation to the election of the London members of the London Assembly at an ordinary election, the time limit of 70 days takes effect after the day on which the last of the successful candidates at the election is declared to be returned: see s 81(1A)(b) (as so added). As to the meaning of 'London member', in relation to the London Assembly, see PARA 11 note 5. As to ordinary elections of London members of the London Assembly see PARA 199 et seq.

7 See the Representation of the People Act 1983 s 81(1) (as amended: see note 4). As to the meaning of 'Authority election' see PARA 11. As to the declaration of the result of an Authority election see PARA 486 et seq.

8 As to the appointment of election agents generally see PARA 231 et seq.

9 As to the meaning of 'candidate' generally see PARA 230; and see note 12.

10 As to the meaning of 'appropriate officer' in relation to a parliamentary or local government election see PARA 231 note 5.

11 If there are no expenses to be entered under any particular head, they should be returned as 'nil'; even if no election expenses were incurred at all, the delivery of a return and declaration is still required: see *Ex p Pennington* (1898) 46 WR 415, DC; *Ex p Robson* (1886) 18 QBD 336. In *East Clare Case* (1892) Day 161 at 166, it was unsuccessfully urged that the return was bad because it showed the receipt of £100 which had not been received at the time of making the

return. The election agent is not responsible for the untruth of a statement made by the candidate as to his personal expenses: *Cork, Eastern Division, Case* (1911) 6 O'M & H 318 at 350.

12 See the Representation of the People Act 1983 s 81(1) (as amended: see note 4). As to circumstances where returns as to election expenses at a parliamentary election are not required see PARA 282.

Where a registered political party submits a list of two or more candidates to be London members of the London Assembly at an ordinary election, the return which the election agent is required to deliver must be in respect of all those candidates (s 81(6), (7)(a) (s 81(6)–(11) added by the Greater London Authority Act 1999 Sch 3 paras 1, 23(1), (3))); and the Representation of the People Act 1983 s 81(1)–(5) (see also the text and notes 1–11, 13–19, 43–48) has effect in relation to those candidates and their election agent with the following modifications (see s 81(6) (as so added)):

(1) if any payments made by the election agent were in respect of two or more candidates, the return must deal under a separate heading or subsection with all such payments, and the expenses to which they relate, in respect of those candidates (s 81(8) (as so added));

(2) the statements which the return is required to contain by virtue of s 81(3A) (see heads (3)–(5) in the text) in respect of the matters there mentioned must be a separate statement as respects each of the candidates in question (s 81(9) (as so added; amended by the Electoral Administration Act 2006 s 74(1), (2), Sch 1 paras 104, 114, 133, Sch 2)); and

(3) if and to the extent that any such matter is referable to two or more candidates together, the return must contain a separate statement of that matter as respects those candidates (Representation of the People Act 1983 s 81(10) (as so added)).

As to the meaning of 'registered political party' in relation to elections for the return of London members of the London Assembly see PARA 226 note 16; and as to references to party lists in that context see PARA 255 note 23. As to the system of candidature whereby registered parties submit lists of candidates see PARA 340.

The Electoral Commission may, by regulations, prescribe a form of return, in relation to parliamentary and applicable local government elections, which may be used for the purposes of making any (or any description of) return required by the Representation of the People Act 1983 s 81: s 81(10A) (added by the Political Parties, Elections and Referendums Act 2000 Sch 18 paras 1, 7(1), (7)). The form of the return as to election expenses was formerly contained in the Representation of the People Act 1983 s 81, Sch 3 (Form of return) (repealed), which provided examples of items regarded as constituting election expenses. Regulations made by the Electoral Commission are not statutory instruments and are not recorded in this work: see further PARA 47. As to the Electoral Commission see PARA 34 et seq. See also the Local Elections (Parishes and Communities) (England and Wales) Rules 2006, SI 2006/3305, Sch 4 (Declaration as to expenses), which is for use in the circumstances set out in the Representation of the People Act 1983 Sch 4: see PARA 295.

13 Representation of the People Act 1983 s 81(1)(a) (s 81(1)(a), (b) added by the Political Parties, Elections and Referendums Act 2000 Sch 18 paras 1, 7(1), (2)). As to the meaning of 'election expenses' see PARA 269; and as to the meaning of 'election expenses incurred by or on behalf of a candidate' see PARA 269 note 15.

14 As to the meaning of 'payment' for these purposes see PARA 270 note 1.

15 Representation of the People Act 1983 s 81(1)(b) (as added: see note 13).

16 Ie by the Representation of the People Act 1983 Pt II (ss 67–119): see s 81(3A)(a) (s 81(3A) added by the Electoral Administration Act 2006 s 26).

17 Representation of the People Act 1983 s 81(3A)(a) (as added: see note 16). As to the making of regulations by the Electoral Commission see note 12.

18 Representation of the People Act 1983 s 81(3A)(b) (as added: see note 16).

19 Representation of the People Act 1983 s 81(3A)(c) (as added: see note 16).

20 As to the computation of time for these purposes see PARA 230 note 31.

21 See the European Parliamentary Elections Regulations 2004, SI 2004/293, reg 51(1). As to European parliamentary elections see PARA 217 et seq; and as to the declaration of the result of a European parliamentary election see PARA 493.

22 As to the computation of time for these purposes see PARA 230 note 20.

23 See the National Assembly for Wales (Representation of the People) Order 2007, SI 2007/236, art 52(1). As to the meaning of 'Assembly election' see PARA 3 note 2. As to the declaration of the result or results of a Welsh Assembly election see PARAS 490–491.

24 At a European parliamentary election, the reference is to the election agent of every individual candidate at the election: see the European Parliamentary Elections Regulations 2004, SI 2004/293, reg 51(1). As to the meaning of 'individual candidate' at a European parliamentary election see PARA 230 note 32.

In the case of a Welsh Assembly election, the reference is to a constituency candidate at a constituency election (National Assembly for Wales (Representation of the People) Order 2007, SI 2007/236, art 52(1)(a)); and to an individual candidate in the case of a regional election (art 52(1)(b)). As to the meanings of 'constituency election' and 'regional election' for the purposes of Welsh Assembly elections see PARA 3 note 2. As to the meanings of 'constituency candidate' at a Welsh Assembly constituency election and 'individual candidate' at a Welsh Assembly regional election see PARA 230 note 19.

25 In the case of a European parliamentary election, a candidate may cause the true return to be delivered to the appropriate officer (as an alternative to the personal delivery cited in the text): see the European Parliamentary Elections Regulations 2004, SI 2004/293, reg 51(1). As to the meaning of 'appropriate officer' for these purposes see PARA 239 note 16.

In the case of a Welsh Assembly election, the 'appropriate returning officer' is specified: see the National Assembly for Wales (Representation of the People) Order 2007, SI 2007/236, art 52(1). As to the meaning of 'appropriate returning officer' for these purposes see PARA 18 note 2.

26 European Parliamentary Elections Regulations 2004, SI 2004/293, reg 51(1); National Assembly for Wales (Representation of the People) Order 2007, SI 2007/236, art 52(1). In the case of a Welsh Assembly election, the return must be in the form set out in English and Welsh in Sch 10 (Form CW: Return of candidate's election expenses): see art 52(8). As to the content of returns and the election agent's liability for any untruths contained therein see note 11. As to circumstances where returns as to election expenses at a Welsh Assembly election are not required see PARA 282.

27 European Parliamentary Elections Regulations 2004, SI 2004/293, reg 51(1)(a); National Assembly for Wales (Representation of the People) Order 2007, SI 2007/236, art 52(1)(i).

28 European Parliamentary Elections Regulations 2004, SI 2004/293, reg 51(1)(b); National Assembly for Wales (Representation of the People) Order 2007, SI 2007/236, art 52(1)(ii).

29 European Parliamentary Elections Regulations 2004, SI 2004/293, reg 51(3)(a)(i); National Assembly for Wales (Representation of the People) Order 2007, SI 2007/236, art 52(4)(a)(i). The text refers to the personal expenses paid by an individual candidate at a European parliamentary election in accordance with the European Parliamentary Elections Regulations 2004, SI 2004/293, reg 44(1) or reg 44(2) (see PARA 271) (see reg 51(3)(a)(i)), or by the candidate at a Welsh Assembly election in accordance with the National Assembly for Wales (Representation of the People) Order 2007, SI 2007/236, art 44(1) or art 44(2) (see PARA 271) (see art 52(4)(a)(i)); and the statement must be accompanied by all bills or receipts relating to any such payments made in accordance with those provisions (see the European Parliamentary Elections Regulations 2004, SI 2004/293, reg 51(3)(a); and the National Assembly for Wales (Representation of the People) Order 2007, SI 2007/236, art 52(4)(a)).

Within 50 days after the day on which the result of a European parliamentary election is declared, every candidate on the list of a registered party must also deliver or cause to be delivered to the appropriate officer a true return containing as respects that candidate a statement of all personal expenses incurred by him on account of or incidental to the election: European Parliamentary Elections Regulations 2004, SI 2004/293, reg 53(1). It is a corrupt practice for a candidate knowingly to make such a return falsely: see reg 53(2); and PARA 708. As to the meanings of 'list' and 'registered party' for these purposes see PARA 230 note 29. As to the system of candidature whereby registered parties submit lists of candidates see PARA 340.

In relation to a Welsh Assembly election, the return must contain the information specified in the National Assembly for Wales (Representation of the People) Order 2007, SI 2007/236, art 52(4) (see heads (c) to (j) in the text) only until the coming into force of the first regulations made by the Electoral Commission under art 52(3): see art 52(4). After that date, the return must also contain as respects the candidate:

  (1)   a statement relating to such other expenses in connection with which provision is made by Pt 3 (arts 37–85) as the Electoral Commission provides in regulations (art 52(3)(a));

  (2)   a statement relating to such claims (whether paid, unpaid or disputed) in connection with such election expenses or such other expenses mentioned in head (1) above as the Commission so provides (art 52(3)(b)); and

  (3)   a statement relating to such other matters as the Commission may provide in regulations (art 52(3)(c)).

Any regulations under art 52(3) may make different provision for different purposes and may contain such incidental, supplemental, saving or transitional provisions as the Commission thinks fit: art 52(7). As to the making of regulations by the Electoral Commission see note 12.

30　European Parliamentary Elections Regulations 2004, SI 2004/293, reg 51(3)(a)(ii); National Assembly for Wales (Representation of the People) Order 2007, SI 2007/236, art 52(4)(a)(ii). The text refers to expenses paid in relation to a European parliamentary election under the European Parliamentary Elections Regulations 2004, SI 2004/293, reg 44(4) (see PARA 271) (see reg 51(3)(a)(ii)), and, in relation to a Welsh Assembly election under the National Assembly for Wales (Representation of the People) Order 2007, SI 2007/236, art 44(4) (see PARA 271) (art 52(4)(a)(ii)). The statement referred to in the text must be accompanied by all bills or receipts relating to any payments so made: European Parliamentary Elections Regulations 2004, SI 2004/293, reg 51(3)(a); National Assembly for Wales (Representation of the People) Order 2007, SI 2007/236, art 52(4)(a). In relation to the return required at a Welsh Assembly election see note 29.

31　European Parliamentary Elections Regulations 2004, SI 2004/293, reg 51(3)(b); National Assembly for Wales (Representation of the People) Order 2007, SI 2007/236, art 52(4)(b). In relation to the return required at a Welsh Assembly election see note 29. As to the meaning of 'disputed claim' see PARA 276.

32　European Parliamentary Elections Regulations 2004, SI 2004/293, reg 51(3)(c); National Assembly for Wales (Representation of the People) Order 2007, SI 2007/236, art 52(4)(c). In relation to the return required at a Welsh Assembly election see note 29. As to court applications made in relation to unpaid claims see PARA 276. In the case of a European parliamentary election taking place in the combined region, an application may have been or is about to be made to the Gibraltar court: see the European Parliamentary Elections Regulations 2004, SI 2004/293, reg 51(3)(c). As to the establishment of electoral regions (including the 'combined region') for the purpose of elections to the European Parliament see PARA 77.

33　Ie, in relation to a European parliamentary election, by virtue of the European Parliamentary Elections Regulations 2004, SI 2004/293, reg 45(2) (see PARA 270) (see reg 51(3)(d)), or, in relation to a Welsh Assembly election, by virtue of the National Assembly for Wales (Representation of the People) Order 2007, SI 2007/236, art 45(2) (see PARA 270) (see art 52(4)(d)).

34　Ie, in relation to a European parliamentary election, by virtue of the European Parliamentary Elections Regulations 2004, SI 2004/293, reg 62(2) (see PARA 269) (see reg 51(3)(d)), or, in relation to a Welsh Assembly election, by virtue of the National Assembly for Wales (Representation of the People) Order 2007, SI 2007/236, art 64(2) (see PARA 269) (see art 52(4)(d)).

35　European Parliamentary Elections Regulations 2004, SI 2004/293, reg 51(3)(d); National Assembly for Wales (Representation of the People) Order 2007, SI 2007/236, art 52(4)(d). In relation to the return required at a Welsh Assembly election see note 29.

36　Ie, in relation to a European parliamentary election, by virtue of the European Parliamentary Elections Regulations 2004, SI 2004/293, reg 60(5) (see PARA 269) (see reg 51(3)(e) (amended by SI 2009/186)), or in relation to a Welsh Assembly election, by virtue of the National Assembly for Wales (Representation of the People) Order 2007, SI 2007/236, art 63(5)(b) (see PARA 269) (see art 52(4)(e)).

37　European Parliamentary Elections Regulations 2004, SI 2004/293, reg 51(3)(e) (as amended: see note 36); National Assembly for Wales (Representation of the People) Order 2007, SI 2007/236, art 52(4)(e). In relation to the return required at a Welsh Assembly election see note 29.

38　As to the meaning of 'relevant donation' for these purposes see PARA 287 note 10.

39　Ie a statement of donations made to the candidate or his election agent which complies with the requirements of, in relation to a European parliamentary election, the European Parliamentary Elections Regulations 2004, SI 2004/293, Sch 6 para 11 (see PARA 292) (see reg 51(3)(f)), or, in relation to a Welsh Assembly election, the National Assembly for Wales (Representation of the People) Order 2007, SI 2007/236, Sch 6 para 11 (see PARA 292) (see art 52(4)(f)). As to the meaning of 'permissible donor' for these purposes see PARA 288.

40　Ie a statement of donations made to the candidate or his election agent which complies with the requirements of, in relation to a European parliamentary election, the European Parliamentary Elections Regulations 2004, SI 2004/293, Sch 6 para 12 (see PARA 292) (see reg 51(3)(f)), or, in relation to a Welsh Assembly election, the National Assembly for Wales (Representation of the People) Order 2007, SI 2007/236, Sch 6 para 12 (see PARA 292) (see art 52(4)(f)). As to the meaning of 'impermissible donor' for these purposes see PARA 292.

41　European Parliamentary Elections Regulations 2004, SI 2004/293, reg 51(3)(f); National Assembly for Wales (Representation of the People) Order 2007, SI 2007/236, art 52(4)(f). In relation to the return required at a Welsh Assembly election see note 29.

42 European Parliamentary Elections Regulations 2004, SI 2004/293, reg 51(3)(g); National Assembly for Wales (Representation of the People) Order 2007, SI 2007/236, art 52(4)(g). In relation to the return required at a Welsh Assembly election see note 29.

43 Representation of the People Act 1983 s 81(2)(a) (s 81(2) substituted by the Political Parties, Elections and Referendums Act 2000 Sch 18 paras 1, 7(1), (3)); European Parliamentary Elections Regulations 2004, SI 2004/293, reg 51(2)(a); National Assembly for Wales (Representation of the People) Order 2007, SI 2007/236, art 52(2)(a).

44 Representation of the People Act 1983 s 81(2)(b) (as substituted: see note 43); European Parliamentary Elections Regulations 2004, SI 2004/293, reg 51(2)(b); National Assembly for Wales (Representation of the People) Order 2007, SI 2007/236, art 52(2)(b).

45 Representation of the People Act 1983 s 81(2)(c) (as substituted: see note 43); European Parliamentary Elections Regulations 2004, SI 2004/293, reg 51(2)(c); National Assembly for Wales (Representation of the People) Order 2007, SI 2007/236, art 52(2)(c). The text refers to any expenses in respect of which a return is required, in relation to a parliamentary or applicable local government election, by virtue of the Representation of the People Act 1983 s 75(2) or, in relation to a European parliamentary election, by virtue of the European Parliamentary Elections Regulations 2004, SI 2004/293, reg 46(3), or, in relation to a Welsh Assembly election, by virtue of the National Assembly for Wales (Representation of the People) Order 2007, SI 2007/236, art 46(5) (see PARA 279). In the European Parliamentary Elections Regulations 2004, SI 2004/293, reg 51(2)(c), a return required by virtue of reg 46(2) is specified but it is submitted that a return required by virtue of reg 46(3) is meant.

46 Ie, in relation to a parliamentary or applicable local government election, under the Representation of the People Act 1983 s 78(4) or, in relation to a European parliamentary election, under the European Parliamentary Elections Regulations 2004, SI 2004/293, reg 48(5), or, in relation to a Welsh Assembly election, under the National Assembly for Wales (Representation of the People) Order 2007, SI 2007/236, art 49(5) (see PARA 277).

47 In the case of a European parliamentary election, only the agent of the candidate who incurred the expenses is required to comply with this requirement: see the European Parliamentary Elections Regulations 2004, SI 2004/293, reg 51(4). In such a case, references to the agent who incurred the expense are references to the election agent or sub-agent or to an agent who did so on the written authority of such an agent (see PARA 270 et seq): see reg 48(7); applied by reg 51(5). As to the appointment of a sub-agent at a European parliamentary election see PARA 241 et seq.

48 Representation of the People Act 1983 s 81(5) (amended by the Representation of the People Act 1985 Sch 4 para 27); European Parliamentary Elections Regulations 2004, SI 2004/293, reg 51(4); National Assembly for Wales (Representation of the People) Order 2007, SI 2007/236, art 52(5), (6). As to authorised excuses, and the relief available, for failures as to returns of election expenses see, in relation to a parliamentary or applicable local government election, the Representation of the People Act 1983 s 86, in relation to a European parliamentary election, the European Parliamentary Elections Regulations 2004, SI 2004/293, reg 55, in relation to a Welsh Assembly election, the National Assembly for Wales (Representation of the People) Order 2007, SI 2007/236, art 58; and see PARA 688.

49 See, in relation to a parliamentary or local government election, the Representation of the People Act 1983 s 84, in relation to a European parliamentary election, the European Parliamentary Elections Regulations 2004, SI 2004/293, reg 54, in relation to a Welsh Assembly election, the National Assembly for Wales (Representation of the People) Order 2007, SI 2007/236, art 56; and see PARA 676.

50 *Hartlepools Case* (1910) 6 O'M & H 1 at 13; *Cork, Eastern Division, Case* (1911) 6 O'M & H 318 at 346–347; *Louth, Northern Division, Case* (1911) 6 O'M & H 103 at 152; *Ipswich Case, Packard v Collings and West* (1886) 4 O'M & H 70.

281. Declarations as to election expenses. The return as to election expenses[1] that is to be delivered by the election agent[2] must be accompanied by a declaration made by him in the appropriate form[3]. At the same time that the election agent delivers the return (or within seven days[4] afterwards), the candidate[5] must deliver to the appropriate officer[6] a declaration made by him in the appropriate form[7]. Where the candidate is out of the United Kingdom[8] at the time when the return is so delivered[9], his declaration may be made within 14 days after his return to the United Kingdom[10], and, in that case, the declaration must be forthwith delivered to the appropriate officer[11], but such delay in making his declaration will not exonerate the election agent from complying with his statutory obligations as to the return and declaration as to election expenses[12].

Where, at a Welsh Assembly regional election, the treasurer of a registered political party[13] delivers the return as to the party's campaign expenditure that is required under the Political Parties, Elections and Referendums Act 2000[14], at the same time (or within seven days thereafter), each candidate on a party list[15] submitted by that party must deliver to the regional returning officer a declaration made by that candidate as to election expenses in the appropriate form[16]. Where any such candidate is out of the United Kingdom when the return is so delivered[17], the declaration may be made by him within 14 days after his return to the United Kingdom[18], and, in that case, the declaration must forthwith be delivered to the regional returning officer[19], but the delay so authorised in making the declaration does not exonerate the treasurer of the registered party from complying with his obligations under the Political Parties, Elections and Referendums Act 2000 as to returns required of party expenditure on campaigns[20].

Failure to comply with the requirements of the provisions governing declarations as to election expenses constitutes an illegal practice[21]. If a candidate or election agent knowingly makes the required declaration falsely, he is guilty of a corrupt practice[22].

1   'Return as to election expenses' means a return (including the bills and receipts to be delivered with it) to be made under the Representation of the People Act 1983 s 81(1) (see PARA 280) (or, as the case may be, s 90(1)(b), Sch 4 para 3 (expenses at elections where election agent not required: see PARA 295)) or the European Parliamentary Elections Regulations 2004, SI 2004/293, reg 51(1) (see PARA 280) or the National Assembly for Wales (Representation of the People) Order 2007, SI 2007/236, art 52(1) (whichever is appropriate) (see PARA 280): Representation of the People Act 1983 s 118 (definition amended by the Representation of the People Act 1985 s 24, Sch 4 para 43); European Parliamentary Elections Regulations 2004, SI 2004/293, reg 31(1); National Assembly for Wales (Representation of the People) Order 2007, SI 2007/236, art 84(1). As to the meaning of 'election expenses' see PARA 269.
    The election referred to may be:
    (1)   a parliamentary election, an Authority election, an election under the local government Act (see the Representation of the People Act 1983 s 202(1); and PARA 3 note 1);
    (2)   a European parliamentary election (see the European Parliamentary Elections Regulations 2004, SI 2004/293, reg 52); or
    (3)   a Welsh Assembly constituency or regional election (see the National Assembly for Wales (Representation of the People) Order 2007, SI 2007/236, arts 53, 54).
    As to the meaning of 'parliamentary election' see PARA 9; As to the meaning of 'Authority election' see PARA 11; and as to the meaning of 'election under the local government Act' see PARA 11 note 2. As to the meanings of 'constituency election' and 'regional election' for the purposes of Welsh Assembly elections see PARA 3 note 2. As to Welsh Assembly elections generally see PARA 213 et seq; and as to European parliamentary elections see PARA 217 et seq. However, the Representation of the People Act 1983 s 82 does not apply at an election under the local government Act which is not a local government election (see the Representation of the People Act 1983 s 90(2); and PARA 297); and, in relation to an election of parish councillors in England or of community councillors in Wales, the provisions of s 90(1), Sch 4 apply instead (see s 90(1)(b); and PARAS 293–296). As to the meaning of 'local government election' see PARA 11. As to elections in the City of London see PARA 33.
2   As to the appointment of election agents generally see PARA 231 et seq.
3   Representation of the People Act 1983 s 82(1) (amended by the Representation of the People Act 1985 Sch 4 para 28; and the Greater London Authority Act 1999 s 17, Sch 3 paras 1, 24(1), (2)); European Parliamentary Elections Regulations 2004, SI 2004/293, reg 52(1); National Assembly for Wales (Representation of the People) Order 2007, SI 2007/236, art 53(1). Accordingly, 'declaration as to election expenses' means a declaration made under the Representation of the People Act 1983 s 82 (or, as the case may be, s 90(1)(b), Sch 4 para 3: see PARA 295), the European Parliamentary Elections Regulations 2004, SI 2004/293, reg 52, or the National Assembly for Wales (Representation of the People) Order 2007, SI 2007/236, art 53 or

art 54: Representation of the People Act 1983 s 118; European Parliamentary Elections Regulations 2004, SI 2004/293, reg 31(1); National Assembly for Wales (Representation of the People) Order 2007, SI 2007/236, art 2(1). If the declarant is aware of any payment of election expenses having been made which ought to have been, but was not, made by the election agent and which therefore constitutes an illegal practice (as to which see PARA 270), the payment should be disclosed in the declaration: see *Cork, Eastern Division, Case* (1911) 6 O'M & H 318 at 351. As to circumstances where declarations as to election expenses are not required see PARA 282.

For these purposes, in relation to a parliamentary or appropriate local government election, the 'appropriate form' is:

(1)   in the case of the election agent for the candidates on a list submitted under the Greater London Authority Act 1999 s 4(6), Sch 2 para 5 (election of London members: see LONDON GOVERNMENT vol 71 (2013) PARA 81) by a registered political party, the form set out for the purpose in rules under the Representation of the People Act 1983 s 36(2A) (see PARA 383) (s 82(2A)(a) (s 82(2A), (5A) added by the Greater London Authority Act 1999 Sch 3 paras 1, 24(1), (4), (6))); and

(2)   in any other case, the form in the Representation of the People Act 1983 s 82, Sch 3 (s 82(2A)(c) (as so added)).

As to the meaning of 'registered political party' in relation to elections for the return of London members of the London Assembly see PARA 226 note 16; and as to references to party lists in that context see PARA 255 note 23.

The form of the declaration required by s 82(1) (declaration by agent) in the circumstances mentioned in s 82(2A)(a) (see head (1) above) is that set out in the Greater London Authority Elections Rules 2007, SI 2007/3541, Sch 10 r 2 (Form 20: election agent's declaration as to election expenses (list candidate) Part 1 (form of declaration as to election expenses by election agent who was not also list candidate)): Sch 2 r 68(1). Where one of the candidates included in a list mentioned in head (1) above is the election agent for those candidates, however, the declaration required by the Representation of the People Act 1983 s 82(1) is instead modified as specified in the form set out in the rules under s 36(2A): s 82(5A) (as so added). Accordingly, in a case to which s 82(5A) applies, the declaration specified in the Greater London Authority Elections Rules 2007, SI 2007/3541, Sch 2 r 68(1), must be modified as specified in Sch 10 r 2 (Form 20: election agent's declaration as to election expenses (list candidate) Part 2 (modifications to form of declaration set out in part 1 where a candidate included in a list is the election agent for candidates on that list)): Sch 2 r 68(2).

As to the form required under head (2) above, see the Representation of the People Act 1983 Sch 3 (return and declarations as to election expenses (form of declarations)) (amended by the Local Government (Wales) Act 1994 s 66(6), Sch 16 para 68(19); the Representation of the People Act 1985 Sch 4 para 88; and the Political Parties, Elections and Referendums Act 2000 ss 138, 158(2), (3)(a), Sch 18 paras 1, 16(b), Sch 22). Where the candidate at a parliamentary or local government election is his own election agent (see PARAS 231–232), the declaration by an election agent as to election expenses need not be made and the declaration by the candidate as to election expenses (see the text and notes 4–7) is to be modified as specified in the form in the Representation of the People Act 1983 Sch 3: s 82(5).

In the case of a European parliamentary election, the 'appropriate form' for the purposes of the European Parliamentary Elections Regulations 2004, SI 2004/293, reg 52(1) is the form in Sch 7 (declaration as to election expenses (form of declaration)): reg 52(3). Where the candidate is his own election agent, the declaration by an election agent as to election expenses need not be made and the declaration by the candidate as to election expenses (see the text and notes 4–7) is to be modified as specified in the form in Sch 7: reg 52(5). As to the version partly in Welsh and partly in English which must be used at a European parliamentary election in Wales see the European Parliamentary Elections (Welsh Forms) Order 2009, SI 2009/781, art 6(1)(s), Sch 2 (Form 19 (declaration as to election expenses); Ffurflen 19 (datganiad ynghylch treuliau etholiad)).

In the case of a Welsh Assembly election, the declaration must be in the form set out in English and Welsh in the National Assembly for Wales (Representation of the People) Order 2007, SI 2007/236, Sch 10 Appendix of Forms (Form CX: form of declaration by constituency or individual candidate as to election expenses): art 53(1). Where a constituency candidate or an individual candidate is his own election agent, the declaration by the election agent as to the election expenses need not be made and the declaration by the candidate as to election expenses (see the text and notes 4–7) is to be modified as specified in Sch 10 (Form CX: form of declaration by constituency or individual candidate as to election expenses): art 53(4). As to the meanings of 'constituency candidate' at a Welsh Assembly constituency election and 'individual candidate' at a Welsh Assembly regional election see PARA 230 note 19. See also notes 5, 7. As to party list candidates see the text and notes 13–20.

4   As to the computation of time for these purposes see PARA 230 notes 11, 20, 31.

5   As to the meaning of 'candidate' generally see PARA 230.

In the case of a European parliamentary election, the reference to an individual candidate is implied: see the European Parliamentary Elections Regulations 2004, SI 2004/293, reg 51(1); and PARA 280. As to the meaning of 'individual candidate' at a European parliamentary election see PARA 230 note 32.

In the case of a Welsh Assembly election, the candidate referred to in the text may be either a constituency candidate or an individual candidate: see the National Assembly for Wales (Representation of the People) Order 2007, SI 2007/236, art 53(2). See also note 3.

6   As to the meaning of 'appropriate officer' in relation to a parliamentary or local government election see PARA 231 note 5.

In the case of a European parliamentary election, the election agent delivers or may cause to be delivered the return, and a candidate must deliver or cause to be delivered to the appropriate officer the required declaration: see the European Parliamentary Elections Regulations 2004, SI 2004/293, reg 52(2). As to the meaning of the 'appropriate officer' in relation to a European parliamentary election see PARA 239 note 16.

In the case of a Welsh Assembly election, the 'appropriate returning officer' is specified: see the National Assembly for Wales (Representation of the People) Order 2007, SI 2007/236, art 53(2). As to the meaning of 'appropriate returning officer' at a Welsh Assembly election see PARA 18 note 2.

7   Representation of the People Act 1983 s 82(2) (amended by the Representation of the People Act 1985 Sch 4 para 28; and the Greater London Authority Act 1999 s 17, Sch 3 paras 1, 24(1), (3)); European Parliamentary Elections Regulations 2004, SI 2004/293, reg 52(2); National Assembly for Wales (Representation of the People) Order 2007, SI 2007/236, art 53(2). See also note 3.

For these purposes, in relation to a parliamentary or appropriate local government election, the 'appropriate form':

(1)   in the case of any of the candidates included in a list submitted under the Greater London Authority Act 1999 Sch 2 para 5 (election of London members: see LONDON GOVERNMENT vol 71 (2013) PARA 81) by a registered political party, the form set out for the purpose in rules under the Representation of the People Act 1983 s 36(2A) (see PARA 383) (s 82(2A)(b) (as added: see note 3)); and

(2)   in any other case, is the form in Sch 3 (s 82(2A)(c) (as so added)).

The form of the declaration required by s 82(2) (declaration by candidate) in the circumstances mentioned in s 82(2A)(b) (see head (1) above) is that set out in the Greater London Authority Elections Rules 2007, SI 2007/3541, Sch 10 r 2 (Form 21: list candidate's declaration as to election expenses Part 1 (form of declaration as to election expenses by list candidate who was not also election agent)): Sch 2 r 68(3). Where one of the candidates included in a list mentioned in head (1) above is the election agent for those candidates, however, the declaration required by the Representation of the People Act 1983 s 82(2) is instead modified as specified in the form set out in the rules under the Representation of the People Act 1983 s 36(2A): Representation of the People Act 1983 s 82(5A) (as so added). Accordingly, in a case to which s 82(5A) applies, the declaration specified in the Greater London Authority Elections Rules 2007, SI 2007/3541, Sch 2 r 68(3), must be modified as specified in Sch 10 r 2 (Form 21: list candidate's declaration as to election expenses Part 2 (modifications to form of declaration set out in part I where a candidate included in a list is the election agent for candidates on that list)): Sch 2 r 68(4).

As to the form required under head (2) above, see the Representation of the People Act 1983 Sch 3 (Form of declarations) (as amended: see note 3).

In the case of a European parliamentary election, the 'appropriate form' for the purposes of the European Parliamentary Elections Regulations 2004, SI 2004/293, reg 52(2) is the form in Sch 7 (declaration as to election expenses (form of declaration)): reg 52(3). Where the candidate is his own election agent, the declaration by the candidate as to election expenses must be modified as specified in the form in Sch 7: see reg 52(5). As to the version partly in Welsh and partly in English which must be used at a European parliamentary election in Wales see the European Parliamentary Elections (Welsh Forms) Order 2009, SI 2009/781, art 6(1)(s), Sch 2 (Form 19 (declaration as to election expenses); Ffurflen 19 (datganiad ynghylch treuliau etholiad)).

In the case of a Welsh Assembly election, the declaration must be in the form set out in English and Welsh in the National Assembly for Wales (Representation of the People) Order 2007, SI 2007/236, Sch 10 Appendix of Forms (Form CX: form of declaration by constituency or individual candidate as to election expenses): art 53(2). Where a constituency candidate or an individual candidate is his own election agent, the declaration by the election agent as to the election expenses need not be made and the declaration by the candidate as to election expenses is to be modified as specified in Sch 10 (Form CX: form of declaration by constituency or individual candidate as to election expenses): art 53(4). See also note 3.

8 As to the meaning of 'United Kingdom' see PARA 1 note 1.

In the case of an individual candidate at a European parliamentary election (see note 5) who is resident in Gibraltar standing for election in the combined region, the circumstance that he is out of Gibraltar is provided for: see the European Parliamentary Elections Regulations 2004, SI 2004/293, reg 52(4). As to the establishment of electoral regions (including the 'combined region') for the purpose of elections to the European Parliament see PARA 77.

9 Representation of the People Act 1983 s 82(3) (amended by the Representation of the People Act 1985 Sch 4 para 28); European Parliamentary Elections Regulations 2004, SI 2004/293, reg 52(4); National Assembly for Wales (Representation of the People) Order 2007, SI 2007/236, art 53(3).

10 Representation of the People Act 1983 s 82(3)(a); European Parliamentary Elections Regulations 2004, SI 2004/293, reg 52(4)(a); National Assembly for Wales (Representation of the People) Order 2007, SI 2007/236, art 53(3)(a). In the case of an individual candidate at a European parliamentary election who is resident in Gibraltar standing for election in the combined region, his declaration may be made within 14 days after his return to Gibraltar: see the European Parliamentary Elections Regulations 2004, SI 2004/293, reg 52(4)(a).

11 Representation of the People Act 1983 s 82(3)(b) (amended by the Representation of the People Act 1985 Sch 4 para 28); European Parliamentary Elections Regulations 2004, SI 2004/293, reg 52(4)(b); National Assembly for Wales (Representation of the People) Order 2007, SI 2007/236, art 53(3)(b). In the case of a Welsh Assembly election, the 'appropriate returning officer' again is specified (see note 6): see art 53(3)(b).

12 Representation of the People Act 1983 s 82(3); European Parliamentary Elections Regulations 2004, SI 2004/293, reg 52(4); National Assembly for Wales (Representation of the People) Order 2007, SI 2007/236, art 53(3).

13 As to the meaning of 'registered political party' at a Welsh Assembly election see PARA 215 note 19. As to the treasurer of a registered party see PARA 253.

14 Ie under the Political Parties, Elections and Referendums Act 2000 s 80 (see PARA 307): see the National Assembly for Wales (Representation of the People) Order 2007, SI 2007/236, art 54(1). As to the meaning of 'campaign expenditure' see PARA 299.

15 As to the meanings of 'party list ' and 'party list candidate' at a Welsh Assembly regional election see PARA 230 note 23.

16 National Assembly for Wales (Representation of the People) Order 2007, SI 2007/236, art 54(1). The declaration referred to in the text must be in the form set out in English and Welsh in Sch 10 (Form CY: form of declaration by party list candidates as to election expenses): see art 54(1).

17 National Assembly for Wales (Representation of the People) Order 2007, SI 2007/236, art 54(2).

18 National Assembly for Wales (Representation of the People) Order 2007, SI 2007/236, art 54(2)(a).

19 National Assembly for Wales (Representation of the People) Order 2007, SI 2007/236, art 54(2)(b).

20 National Assembly for Wales (Representation of the People) Order 2007, SI 2007/236, art 54(2). As to the provisions referred to in the text see the Political Parties, Elections and Referendums Act 2000 Pt V (ss 72–84) (control of campaign expenditure); and PARA 299 et seq.

21 See, in relation to a parliamentary or local government election, the Representation of the People Act 1983 s 84, in relation to a European parliamentary election, the European Parliamentary Elections Regulations 2004, SI 2004/293, reg 54, or in relation to a Welsh Assembly election, the National Assembly for Wales (Representation of the People) Order 2007, SI 2007/236, art 56; and PARA 676.

22 See, in relation to a parliamentary or local government election, the Representation of the People Act 1983 s 82(6), in relation to a European parliamentary election, the European Parliamentary Elections Regulations 2004, SI 2004/293, reg 52(6), or, in relation to a Welsh Assembly election, the National Assembly for Wales (Representation of the People) Order 2007, SI 2007/236, arts 53(5), 54(3); and PARA 708.

282.   Circumstances where returns or declarations as to election expenses not required.   No return[1] or declaration as to election expenses[2] is required from a candidate[3] at a parliamentary election[4], or at a Welsh Assembly election[5]: (1) who is only a candidate at such an election because he has been declared by others to be a candidate[6]; and (2) who has not consented to the declaration or taken any part as a candidate in the election[7].

1   As to the meaning of 'return as to election expenses' see PARA 281 note 1.
2   As to the meaning of 'declaration as to election expenses' see PARA 281 note 3.
3   As to the meaning of 'candidate' generally see PARA 230.
4   Ie notwithstanding anything in the Representation of the People Act 1983 s 81 (returns as to candidates' election expenses: see PARA 280) or s 82 (declaration as to election expenses: see PARA 281): see s 83. The provision made by s 83 does not apply at an election under the local government Act which is not a local government election (see the Representation of the People Act 1983 s 90(2); and PARA 297); and, in relation to an election of parish councillors in England or of community councillors in Wales, the provisions of s 90(1), Sch 4 apply instead (see s 90(1)(b); and PARAS 293–296). As to the meaning of 'parliamentary election' see PARA 9. As to the meaning of 'local government election' see PARA 11; and as to the meaning of 'election under the local government Act' see PARA 11 note 2. As to elections in the City of London see PARA 33.
5   Ie notwithstanding anything in the National Assembly for Wales (Representation of the People) Order 2007, SI 2007/236, art 52 (returns as to candidates' election expenses: see PARA 280) or arts 53, 54 (declaration as to election expenses: see PARA 281): see art 55. As to the meaning of 'Assembly election' see PARA 3 note 2.
6   Representation of the People Act 1983 s 83(a); National Assembly for Wales (Representation of the People) Order 2007, SI 2007/236, art 55(a).
7   Representation of the People Act 1983 s 83(b); National Assembly for Wales (Representation of the People) Order 2007, SI 2007/236, art 55(b). As to a candidate's liability see PARAS 230, 258.

283.   Publication of time and place for inspection of returns and declarations as to election expenses.   At a parliamentary[1], Authority[2], Welsh Assembly[3] or European parliamentary election[4], the returning officer[5] must, within ten days[6] after the end of the time allowed for delivering to him returns as to election expenses[7], publish:

(1)   in not less than two newspapers circulating in the constituency[8] or electoral area[9]; or

(2)   in not less than three newspapers circulating in the Welsh Assembly electoral region[10]; or

(3)   in at least one newspaper circulating in the European parliamentary electoral region[11],

for which the election was held[12], a notice of the time and place at which the returns and declarations[13] (including the accompanying documents) can be inspected[14]. Except at a European parliamentary or Welsh Assembly regional election[15], the notice must be sent also to each of the election agents[16] (but, in the case of a Welsh Assembly regional election, that notice must be sent instead to the registered nominating officer of each registered political party[17] that stood nominated as well as to each of the election agents for the individual candidates who stood)[18].

If any return or declaration has not been received by the returning officer[19] before the notice is dispatched for publication, the notice must so state, and a like notice about that return or declaration, if received afterwards, must within ten days after the receipt be published in like manner[20]. Except at a European parliamentary election, the like notice must be sent to each of the persons to whom the first notice was sent other than an election agent who is in default or an election agent for a candidate who is in default[21].

1   As to the meaning of 'parliamentary election' see PARA 9.

2   As to the meaning of 'Authority election' see PARA 11. The Representation of the People Act 1983 s 88 does not apply at an election under the local government Act which is not a local government election (see the Representation of the People Act 1983 s 90(2); and PARA 297); and, in relation to an election of parish councillors in England or of community councillors in Wales, the provisions of s 90(1), Sch 4 apply instead (see s 90(1)(b); and PARAS 293–296). As to the meaning of 'local government election' see PARA 11; and as to the meaning of 'election under the local government Act' see PARA 11 note 2. As to elections in the City of London see PARA 33.

3   As to the meaning of 'Assembly election' see PARA 3 note 2.

4   Representation of the People Act 1983 s 88 (amended by the Greater London Authority Act 1999 s 17, Sch 3 paras 1, 27(1), (2)); European Parliamentary Elections Regulations 2004, SI 2004/293, reg 58(1); National Assembly for Wales (Representation of the People) Order 2007, SI 2007/236, art 61(1). As to European parliamentary elections see PARA 217 et seq.

5   As to returning officers for elections generally see PARA 350 et seq.
    In the case of a Welsh Assembly election, the 'appropriate returning officer' is specified: see the National Assembly for Wales (Representation of the People) Order 2007, SI 2007/236, art 61(1). As to the meaning of 'appropriate returning officer' at a Welsh Assembly election see PARA 18 note 2.

6   As to the computation of time for these purposes see PARA 230 notes 11, 20, 31.

7   Representation of the People Act 1983 s 88(a) (amended by the Representation of the People Act 1985 s 24, Sch 4 para 32; and the Greater London Authority Act 1999 Sch 3 paras 1, 27(1), (3)); European Parliamentary Elections Regulations 2004, SI 2004/293, reg 58(1)(a); National Assembly for Wales (Representation of the People) Order 2007, SI 2007/236, art 61(1). As to the time allowed referred to in the text see PARA 280. As to the meaning of 'election expenses' see PARA 269; and as to the meaning of 'return as to election expenses' see PARA 281 note 1.

8   Representation of the People Act 1983 s 88(a) (as amended: see note 7); National Assembly for Wales (Representation of the People) Order 2007, SI 2007/236, art 61(1)(a)(i). The reference in the text to a 'constituency' includes an 'Assembly constituency' for the purposes of a Welsh Assembly constituency election: see art 61(1)(a)(i). As to the meanings of 'Assembly constituency' and 'constituency election' for the purposes of Welsh Assembly elections see PARA 3 note 2. As to parliamentary constituencies see PARA 9.

9   Representation of the People Act 1983 s 88(a) (as amended: see note 7). As to the meaning of 'electoral area' see PARA 11.

10 National Assembly for Wales (Representation of the People) Order 2007, SI 2007/236, art 61(1)(a)(ii). As to the meaning of 'Assembly electoral region' see PARA 3 note 2.

11 See the European Parliamentary Elections Regulations 2004, SI 2004/293, reg 58(1)(a). In the case of a European parliamentary election held in the combined region, publication must take place in 'that part of the region which is in England and in at least one newspaper circulating in that part which is in Gibraltar': see reg 58(2). As to the establishment of electoral regions (including the combined region) for the purpose of elections to the European Parliament see PARA 77.

12 Representation of the People Act 1983 s 88(a) (as amended: see note 7); European Parliamentary Elections Regulations 2004, SI 2004/293, reg 58(1)(a); National Assembly for Wales (Representation of the People) Order 2007, SI 2007/236, art 61(1)(a).

13 As to the meaning of 'declaration as to election expenses' see PARA 281 note 3.

14 Representation of the People Act 1983 s 88(a) (as amended: see note 7); European Parliamentary Elections Regulations 2004, SI 2004/293, reg 58(1)(a); National Assembly for Wales (Representation of the People) Order 2007, SI 2007/236, art 61(1).

15 As to the meaning of 'regional election' for the purposes of Welsh Assembly elections see PARA 3 note 2.

16 Representation of the People Act 1983 s 88(a) (as amended: see note 7); National Assembly for Wales (Representation of the People) Order 2007, SI 2007/236, art 61(1)(b)(i). For the purposes of a Welsh Assembly election, the reference is to each of the election agents in the case of a constituency election: see art 61(1)(b)(i). As to the appointment of election agents generally see PARA 231 et seq.

17 As to the meaning of 'registered political party' for these purposes see PARA 215 note 19. As to the nominating officer of a registered political party see PARA 253.

18 National Assembly for Wales (Representation of the People) Order 2007, SI 2007/236, art 61(b)(ii). As to the meaning of 'individual candidate' at a Welsh Assembly regional election see PARA 230 note 19.

19 Ie the 'appropriate returning officer' (see note 5), in the case of a Welsh Assembly election: see the National Assembly for Wales (Representation of the People) Order 2007, SI 2007/236, art 61(2).

20 Representation of the People Act 1983 s 88(b); European Parliamentary Elections Regulations 2004, SI 2004/293, reg 58(1)(b); National Assembly for Wales (Representation of the People) Order 2007, SI 2007/236, art 61(2).

21 Representation of the People Act 1983 s 88(b); National Assembly for Wales (Representation of the People) Order 2007, SI 2007/236, art 61(2).

284. Inspection of returns and declarations as to election expenses. Where the appropriate officer[1] receives any return[2] or declaration as to election expenses[3] in respect of a parliamentary election[4], a local government election[5], a Welsh Assembly election[6], or a European parliamentary election[7], or (except in relation to a European parliamentary election) any return or declaration as to expenses required to be authorised by the election agent[8]:

(1) he must, as soon as reasonably practicable after receiving the return or declaration, make a copy of it, and any accompanying documents, available for public inspection at his office or at some other convenient place chosen by him, for a period of two years (or, in the case of a European parliamentary election, for a period of 12 months) beginning with the date when the return is received by him[9]; and

(2) if requested to do so by any person, he must supply that person with a copy of the return or declaration and any accompanying documents, on payment of the fee that is prescribed[10].

After the expiry of those two years (or those 12 months, in the case of a European parliamentary election), the appropriate officer may cause those returns and declarations, including the accompanying documents, to be destroyed[11]. Alternatively, except at a European parliamentary election, if the candidate[12] or his election agent[13] so requires, the appropriate officer may return the documents, in the case of returns and declarations as to election expenses, to the candidate[14] and, in the case of returns and declarations by persons who have incurred expenses required to be authorised by the election agent[15], to the person delivering them if he so requires[16].

1 As to the meaning of 'appropriate officer' in relation to a parliamentary or local government election see PARA 231 note 5; and as to the meaning of the 'appropriate officer' in relation to a European parliamentary election see PARA 239 note 16.

In the case of a Welsh Assembly election, the 'appropriate returning officer' is specified: see the National Assembly for Wales (Representation of the People) Order 2007, SI 2007/236, art 62(1). As to the meaning of 'appropriate returning officer' at a Welsh Assembly election see PARA 18 note 2.

2 As to the meaning of 'return as to election expenses' see PARA 281 note 1.

3 As to the meaning of 'election expenses' see PARA 269; and as to the meaning of 'declaration as to election expenses' see PARA 281 note 3.

4 As to the meaning of 'parliamentary election' see PARA 9.

5 The Representation of the People Act 1983 s 89 does not apply at an election under the local government Act which is not a local government election (see the Representation of the People Act 1983 s 90(2); and PARA 297); and, in relation to an election of parish councillors in England or of community councillors in Wales, the provisions of s 90(1), Sch 4 apply instead (see s 90(1)(b); and PARAS 293–296). As to the meaning of 'local government election' see PARA 11; and as to the meaning of 'election under the local government Act' see PARA 11 note 2. As to elections in the City of London see PARA 33.

6 As to the meaning of 'Assembly election' see PARA 3 note 2.

7 Representation of the People Act 1983 s 89(1) (substituted by the Political Parties, Elections and Referendums Act 2000 s 138, Sch 18 paras 1, 10); European Parliamentary Elections Regulations 2004, SI 2004/293, reg 59(1); National Assembly for Wales (Representation of the People) Order 2007, SI 2007/236, art 62(1). As to European parliamentary elections see PARA 217 et seq.

8   Representation of the People Act 1983 s 89(1) (as substituted: see note 7); National Assembly for Wales (Representation of the People) Order 2007, SI 2007/236, art 62(1). The text refers to a return or declaration under the Representation of the People Act 1983 s 75 (see PARA 272) (see s 89(1) (as so substituted)) or the National Assembly for Wales (Representation of the People) Order 2007, SI 2007/236, art 46 (see PARA 272) (see art 62(1)).

9   Representation of the People Act 1983 s 89(1)(a) (as substituted: see note 7); European Parliamentary Elections Regulations 2004, SI 2004/293, reg 59(1)(a); National Assembly for Wales (Representation of the People) Order 2007, SI 2007/236, art 62(1)(a). In relation to a Welsh Assembly election, a fee of £1.50 is payable for inspecting a return or declaration (including any accompanying documents) referred to in head (1) in the text: art 62(3). The National Assembly for Wales may by order vary the amount of any fee so payable: art 62(7). This power to make orders is exercisable by statutory instrument: art 62(8). For the purposes of the Statutory Instruments Act 1946 s 1 (see STATUTES AND LEGISLATIVE PROCESS vol 96 (2012) PARA 1045), the National Assembly for Wales (Representation of the People) Order 2007, SI 2007/236, art 62(8) has effect as if contained in an Act of Parliament: see art 62(8). As to the National Assembly for Wales see CONSTITUTIONAL LAW AND HUMAN RIGHTS.

    If any such return contains a statement of donations in accordance with the Representation of the People Act 1983 s 71A, Sch 2A para 10 (see PARA 292) or, in relation to a Welsh Assembly election, the National Assembly for Wales (Representation of the People) Order 2007, SI 2007/236, Sch 6 para 10 (see PARA 292) or, in relation to a European parliamentary election, the European Parliamentary Elections Regulations 2004, SI 2004/293, reg 51(3)(f) (see PARA 280), the appropriate officer must secure that the copy of the statement made available for public inspection under head (1) in the text does not include, in the case of any donation by an individual, the donor's address: Representation of the People Act 1983 s 89(1A) (added by the Political Parties, Elections and Referendums Act 2000 Sch 18 paras 1, 10; and amended by the Electoral Administration Act 2006 s 74(1), Sch 1 paras 104, 115); European Parliamentary Elections Regulations 2004, SI 2004/293, reg 59(2); National Assembly for Wales (Representation of the People) Order 2007, SI 2007/236, art 62(2).

10   Representation of the People Act 1983 s 89(1)(b) (as substituted: see note 7); European Parliamentary Elections Regulations 2004, SI 2004/293, reg 59(1)(b); National Assembly for Wales (Representation of the People) Order 2007, SI 2007/236, art 62(1)(b). See note 9.

    If any such return contains a statement of donations in accordance with the Representation of the People Act 1983 s 71A, Sch 2A para 10 (see PARA 292) or, in relation to a Welsh Assembly election, the National Assembly for Wales (Representation of the People) Order 2007, SI 2007/236, Sch 6 para 10 (see PARA 292) or, in relation to a European parliamentary election, the European Parliamentary Elections Regulations 2004, SI 2004/293, reg 51(3)(f) (see PARA 280), the appropriate officer must secure that the copy of the statement supplied under head (2) in the text does not include, in the case of any donation by an individual, the donor's address: Representation of the People Act 1983 s 89(1A) (as added and amended: see note 9); European Parliamentary Elections Regulations 2004, SI 2004/293, reg 59(2); National Assembly for Wales (Representation of the People) Order 2007, SI 2007/236, art 62(2).

    In relation to a parliamentary or local government election, 'prescribed' means prescribed by regulations: Representation of the People Act 1983 s 202(1). Accordingly, the price of a copy of any such return, declaration or any accompanying document is at the rate of 20p for each side of each page: Representation of the People (England and Wales) Regulations 2001, SI 2001/341, reg 10(3) (amended by SI 2002/1871). As to the making of regulations under the Representation of the People Act 1983 generally see PARA 28 note 16.

    In relation to a Welsh Assembly election, the fee payable for a copy of any such return, declaration or document referred to in head (2) in the text is at the rate of 15p for each side of each page: National Assembly for Wales (Representation of the People) Order 2007, SI 2007/236, art 62(4). The National Assembly for Wales may by order made by statutory instrument vary the amount of any fee so payable: art 62(7).

11   Representation of the People Act 1983 s 89(2)(a); European Parliamentary Elections Regulations 2004, SI 2004/293, reg 59(3); National Assembly for Wales (Representation of the People) Order 2007, SI 2007/236, art 62(5)(a).

12   As to the meaning of 'candidate' generally see PARA 230.

13   As to the appointment of election agents generally see PARA 231 et seq.

14   Representation of the People Act 1983 s 89(2)(b); National Assembly for Wales (Representation of the People) Order 2007, SI 2007/236, art 62(5)(b).

15   See note 8.

16   Representation of the People Act 1983 s 89(3) (amended by the Representation of the People Act 1985 s 24, Sch 4 para 33); National Assembly for Wales (Representation of the People) Order 2007, SI 2007/236, art 62(6).

285. Delivery of returns and declarations as to election expenses to the Electoral Commission. Where the appropriate officer[1] receives any return[2] or declaration as to election expenses[3], or any return or declaration as to expenses required to be authorised by the election agent[4], in respect of a parliamentary election[5], an election of the Mayor of London[6], a Welsh Assembly election[7], or a European parliamentary election[8], he must as soon as reasonably practicable after receiving the return or declaration deliver a copy of it to the Electoral Commission[9] and, if so requested by the Commission, he must also deliver to it a copy of any accompanying documents[10].

1   As to the meaning of 'appropriate officer' in relation to a parliamentary or local government election see PARA 231 note 5; and as to the meaning of the 'appropriate officer' in relation to a European parliamentary election see PARA 239 note 16.
      In the case of a Welsh Assembly election, the 'appropriate returning officer' is specified: see the National Assembly for Wales (Representation of the People) Order 2007, SI 2007/236, art 58. As to the meaning of 'appropriate returning officer' at a Welsh Assembly election see PARA 18 note 2.
2   As to the meaning of 'return as to election expenses' see PARA 281 note 1.
3   As to the meaning of 'election expenses' see PARA 269; and as to the meaning of 'declaration as to election expenses' see PARA 281 note 3.
4   Ie a return or declaration under the Representation of the People Act 1983 s 75, or the European Parliamentary Elections Regulations 2004, SI 2004/293, reg 46, or the National Assembly for Wales (Representation of the People) Order 2007, SI 2007/236, art 46 (see PARA 272).
5   As to the meaning of 'parliamentary election' see PARA 9.
6   As to elections for the return of an elected Mayor of London see PARA 199 et seq. The Representation of the People Act 1983 s 87A does not apply at an election under the local government Act which is not a local government election (see the Representation of the People Act 1983 s 90(2); and PARA 297); and, in relation to an election of parish councillors in England or of community councillors in Wales, the provisions of s 90(1), Sch 4 apply instead (see s 90(1)(b); and PARAS 293–296). As to the meaning of 'local government election' see PARA 11; and as to the meaning of 'election under the local government Act' see PARA 11 note 2. As to elections in the City of London see PARA 33.
7   As to the meaning of 'Assembly election' see PARA 3 note 2.
8   As to European parliamentary elections see PARA 217 et seq.
9   As to the Electoral Commission see PARA 34 et seq.
10 Representation of the People Act 1983 s 87A(1) (s 87A added by the Political Parties, Elections and Referendums Act 2000 s 138, Sch 18 paras 1, 9); European Parliamentary Elections Regulations 2004, SI 2004/293, reg 57; National Assembly for Wales (Representation of the People) Order 2007, SI 2007/236, art 60.
      Where the appropriate officer at a parliamentary election or an election of the Mayor of London receives any return or declaration in respect of any other election, he must, if so requested by the Electoral Commission, deliver to it a copy of the return and any accompanying documents: Representation of the People Act 1983 s 87A(2) (as so added).
      The Representation of the People Act 1983 s 87A is applied and modified for the purpose of local authority mayoral elections in England and Wales by the Local Authorities (Mayoral Elections) (England and Wales) Regulations 2007, SI 2007/1024, reg 3(2)–(5), Sch 2 Table 1: see PARA 11 note 14.

C. CONTROL OF DONATIONS TO INDIVIDUAL CANDIDATES DURING ELECTIONS

286. Restriction on contributions made to candidates for meeting election expenses. In the case of any candidate[1] at an election[2], any money or other property[3] provided whether as a gift or loan[4]:

(1)   by any person other than the candidate or his election agent[5]; and
(2)   for the purpose of meeting election expenses incurred by or on behalf of the candidate[6],

must be provided to the candidate or his election agent[7]. A person who provides any money or other property in contravention of this restriction is guilty of an illegal practice[8]. However, this restriction does not apply to any money or other property so provided for the purpose of meeting any such expenses which may be lawfully paid by a person other than the candidate, his election agent or any sub-agent (in the case of an election where sub-agents may be appointed)[9].

The making of donations to candidates at elections is subject to restrictions[10].

1　　As to the meaning of 'candidate' generally see PARA 230.

　　　At a European parliamentary election, the reference is an 'individual candidate': see the European Parliamentary Elections Regulations 2004, SI 2004/293, reg 42(1). As to the meaning of 'individual candidate' at a European parliamentary election see PARA 230 note 32. As to European parliamentary elections see PARA 217 et seq.

　　　In the case of a Welsh Assembly election, the reference is to a constituency candidate at a Welsh Assembly constituency election or to an individual candidate at a Welsh Assembly regional election: see the National Assembly for Wales (Representation of the People) Order 2007, SI 2007/236, art 41(1). As to the meanings of 'Assembly election', 'constituency election' and 'regional election' for the purposes of Welsh Assembly elections see PARA 3 note 2. As to the meanings of 'constituency candidate' at a Welsh Assembly constituency election and 'individual candidate' at a Welsh Assembly regional election see PARA 230 note 19.

2　　Ie a parliamentary election, a local government election (which includes any London Authority election and a local authority mayoral election), a Welsh Assembly constituency or regional election, or European parliamentary election. As to the meanings of 'Assembly election', and Welsh Assembly 'constituency election' and 'regional election', see PARA 3 note 2. As to the meaning of 'parliamentary election' see PARA 9. As to the meanings of 'Authority election ' and 'local government election' see PARA 11.

　　　The Representation of the People Act 1983 s 71A does not apply at an election under the local government Act which is not a local government election (see the Representation of the People Act 1983 s 90(2); and PARA 297); and, in relation to an election of parish councillors in England or of community councillors in Wales, the provisions of s 90(1), Sch 4 apply instead (see s 90(1)(b); and PARAS 293–296). As to the meaning of 'election under the local government Act' see PARA 11 note 2.

3　　For these purposes, 'property' includes any description of property; and references to the provision of property accordingly include the supply of goods: Representation of the People Act 1983 s 71A(5) (s 71A added by the Political Parties, Elections and Referendums Act 2000 s 130(1), (2), (4)); European Parliamentary Elections Regulations 2004, SI 2004/293, reg 42(5); National Assembly for Wales (Representation of the People) Order 2007, SI 2007/236, art 41(5). As to the meaning of 'money' see PARA 270 note 1.

4　　Representation of the People Act 1983 s 71A(1), s 202(1) (s 71A(1) as added: see note 3); European Parliamentary Elections Regulations 2004, SI 2004/293, reg 42(1); National Assembly for Wales (Representation of the People) Order 2007, SI 2007/236, art 41(1).

5　　Representation of the People Act 1983 s 71A(1)(a) (as added: see note 3); European Parliamentary Elections Regulations 2004, SI 2004/293, reg 42(1)(a); National Assembly for Wales (Representation of the People) Order 2007, SI 2007/236, art 41(1)(a). As to the appointment of an election agent see PARA 231 et seq.

6　　Representation of the People Act 1983 s 71A(1)(b) (as added: see note 3); European Parliamentary Elections Regulations 2004, SI 2004/293, reg 42(1)(b); National Assembly for Wales (Representation of the People) Order 2007, SI 2007/236, art 41(1)(b). As to the meaning of 'election expenses' see PARA 269.

7　　Representation of the People Act 1983 s 71A(1) (as added: see note 3); European Parliamentary Elections Regulations 2004, SI 2004/293, reg 42(1); National Assembly for Wales (Representation of the People) Order 2007, SI 2007/236, art 41(1). As to the meaning of 'election expenses incurred by or on behalf of a candidate' see PARA 269 note 15.

8　　See the Representation of the People Act 1983 s 71A(3); the European Parliamentary Elections Regulations 2004, SI 2004/293, reg 42(3); the National Assembly for Wales (Representation of the People) Order 2007, SI 2007/236, art 41(3); and PARA 672.

9　　Representation of the People Act 1983 s 71A(2) (as added: see note 3); European Parliamentary Elections Regulations 2004, SI 2004/293, reg 42(2); National Assembly for Wales (Representation of the People) Order 2007, SI 2007/236, art 41(2). A sub-agent may be appointed for a parliamentary election in a county constituency or for an Authority election (see PARA 233), for Welsh Assembly elections (see PARA 237) or for European parliamentary elections (see PARA 241).

10　See PARA 287 et seq.

287. Meaning of 'donation' in relation to candidates at an election. For the purposes of controlling donations to candidates[1] at an election[2], 'donation' means, in relation to such a candidate at such an election[3]:

(1)　　any gift[4] to the candidate or his election agent[5] of money or other property[6];

(2)　　any sponsorship provided in relation to the candidate[7];

(3)　　any money spent (otherwise than by the candidate, his election agent or any sub-agent[8]) in paying any election expenses[9] incurred by or on behalf of the candidate[10];

(4)　　any money lent to the candidate or his election agent otherwise than on commercial terms[11];

(5)　　the provision otherwise than on commercial terms of any property, services or facilities for the use or benefit of the candidate (including the services of any person)[12].

Where anything would be a donation both by virtue of head (2) above and by virtue of any other provision mentioned in head (1) or heads (3) to (5) above, head (2) above applies in relation to that donation to the exclusion of the other provision[13]. Any donation whose value is not more than £50 is disregarded[14]; and none of the following is to be regarded as a donation:

(a)　　the provision of any facilities provided in pursuance of any right conferred on a candidate at an election by the relevant election provisions[15];

(b)　　the provision by an individual of his own services which he provides voluntarily in his own time and free of charge[16];

(c)　　any interest accruing to a candidate or his election agent in respect of any donation which is sent back by the candidate or (as the case may be) his election agent[17].

For these purposes, 'sponsorship' is provided in relation to a candidate if:

(i)　　any money or other property is transferred to the candidate or to any person for the benefit of the candidate[18]; and

(ii)　　the purpose (or one of the purposes) of the transfer is, or must, having regard to all the circumstances, reasonably be assumed to be[19] either to help the candidate with meeting, or to meet, to any extent any defined expenses[20] incurred or to be incurred by or on behalf of the candidate[21], or to secure that to any extent any such expenses are not so incurred[22].

However, for these purposes: (A) the making of any payment in respect of any charge for admission to any conference, meeting or other event[23] or in respect of the purchase price of, or any other charge for access to, any publication[24]; or (B) the making of any payment in respect of the inclusion of an advertisement in any publication where the payment is made at the commercial rate payable for the inclusion of such an advertisement in any such publication[25], do not constitute sponsorship[26].

1　　As to the meaning of 'candidate' generally see PARA 230.

　　　At a European parliamentary election, the reference is an 'individual candidate': see the European Parliamentary Elections Regulations 2004, SI 2004/293, reg 42(4), Sch 6 para 1(1), (3). As to the meaning of 'individual candidate' at a European parliamentary election see PARA 230 note 32. As to European parliamentary elections see PARA 217 et seq.

　　　In the case of a Welsh Assembly election, the reference is to a constituency candidate at a Welsh Assembly constituency election or to an individual candidate at a Welsh Assembly regional election: see the National Assembly for Wales (Representation of the People) Order 2007, SI 2007/236, art 41(4), Sch 6 para 1(1). As to the meanings of 'Assembly election', 'constituency election' and 'regional election' for the purposes of Welsh Assembly elections see

PARA 3 note 2. As to the meanings of 'constituency candidate' at a Welsh Assembly constituency election and 'individual candidate' at a Welsh Assembly regional election see PARA 230 note 19.

2   Representation of the People Act 1983 s 71A(4), Sch 2A para 1(1), (2) (s 71A, Sch 2A added by the Political Parties, Elections and Referendums Act 2000 s 130(1)–(4)); European Parliamentary Elections Regulations 2004, SI 2004/293, Sch 6 para 1(1), (2); National Assembly for Wales (Representation of the People) Order 2007, SI 2007/236, Sch 6 para 1(1).

For these purposes, 'donation' is to be construed in accordance with the Representation of the People Act 1983 Sch 2A paras 2–4, the European Parliamentary Elections Regulations 2004, SI 2004/293, Sch 6 paras 2–4, or the National Assembly for Wales (Representation of the People) Order 2007, SI 2007/236, art 41(4), Sch 6 paras 2–4, as the case may be (see the text and notes 3–26): Representation of the People Act 1983 Sch 2A para 1(5) (as so added); European Parliamentary Elections Regulations 2004, SI 2004/293, Sch 6 para 1(6); National Assembly for Wales (Representation of the People) Order 2007, SI 2007/236, Sch 6 para 1(2).

The election referred to in the text may be any of a parliamentary election, an Authority election, an election under the local government Act (see the Representation of the People Act 1983 s 202(1); and PARA 3 note 1), a Welsh Assembly constituency or regional election or a European parliamentary election. As to the meaning of 'parliamentary election' see PARA 9; As to the meaning of 'Authority election' see PARA 11; and as to the meaning of 'election under the local government Act' see PARA 11 note 2. However, the Representation of the People Act 1983 s 71A does not apply at an election under the local government Act which is not a local government election (see the Representation of the People Act 1983 s 90(2); and PARA 297); and, in relation to an election of parish councillors in England or of community councillors in Wales, the provisions of s 90(1), Sch 4 apply instead (see s 90(1)(b); and PARAS 293–296). As to the meaning of 'local government election' see PARA 11. As to elections in the City of London see PARA 33.

3   Representation of the People Act 1983 Sch 2A para 2(1) (as added: see note 2); European Parliamentary Elections Regulations 2004, SI 2004/293, Sch 6 para 2(1); National Assembly for Wales (Representation of the People) Order 2007, SI 2007/236, Sch 6 para 2(1). This provision is subject to the Representation of the People Act 1983 Sch 2A para 4, the European Parliamentary Elections Regulations 2004, SI 2004/293, Sch 6 para 4, or the National Assembly for Wales (Representation of the People) Order 2007, SI 2007/236, Sch 6 para 4, as the case may be (see the text and notes 14–17).

4   For these purposes, 'gift' includes a bequest or any other form of testamentary disposition: Representation of the People Act 1983 Sch 2A para 2(6)(b) (as added: see note 2); European Parliamentary Elections Regulations 2004, SI 2004/293, Sch 6 para 2(6)(b); National Assembly for Wales (Representation of the People) Order 2007, SI 2007/236, Sch 6 para 2(6)(b).

5   For these purposes, any reference to anything being given or transferred to a candidate or his election agent includes a reference to its being given or transferred either directly or indirectly through any third person: Representation of the People Act 1983 Sch 2A para 2(6)(a) (as added: see note 2); European Parliamentary Elections Regulations 2004, SI 2004/293, Sch 6 para 2(6)(a); National Assembly for Wales (Representation of the People) Order 2007, SI 2007/236, Sch 6 para 2(6)(a). As to the appointment of an election agent see PARA 231 et seq.

Any reference to a donation received by a candidate when he is (or is deemed to be) his own election agent includes a reference to a donation received by a candidate on a list of candidates to be London members of the London Assembly at an ordinary election who is, or is deemed to be, the election agent of all the candidates on the list (Representation of the People Act 1983 Sch 2A para 1(9) (as so added)); and any donation which is received by such a candidate is regarded as received by him in his capacity as election agent (Sch 2A para 1(10) (as so added)).

As to ordinary elections of London members of the London Assembly see PARA 199 et seq.

6   Representation of the People Act 1983 Sch 2A para 2(1)(a) (as added: see note 2); European Parliamentary Elections Regulations 2004, SI 2004/293, Sch 6 para 2(1)(a); National Assembly for Wales (Representation of the People) Order 2007, SI 2007/236, Sch 6 para 2(1)(a). Where:

(1)   any money or other property is transferred to a candidate or his election agent pursuant to any transaction or arrangement involving the provision by or on behalf of the candidate of any property, services or facilities or other consideration of monetary value (Representation of the People Act 1983 Sch 2A para 2(2)(a) (as so added); European Parliamentary Elections Regulations 2004, SI 2004/293, Sch 6 para 2(2)(a); National Assembly for Wales (Representation of the People) Order 2007, SI 2007/236, Sch 6 para 2(2)(a)); and

(2)   the total value in monetary terms of the consideration so provided by or on behalf of the candidate is less than the value of the money or (as the case may be) the market value of the property transferred (Representation of the People Act 1983 Sch 2A para 2(2)(b) (as so added); European Parliamentary Elections Regulations 2004,

SI 2004/293, Sch 6 para 2(2)(b); National Assembly for Wales (Representation of the People) Order 2007, SI 2007/236, Sch 6 para 2(2)(b)),

the transfer of the money or property constitute a gift to the candidate or (as the case may be) his election agent for the purposes of the Representation of the People Act 1983 Sch 2A para 2(1)(a), the European Parliamentary Elections Regulations 2004, SI 2004/293, Sch 6 para 2(1)(a), or the National Assembly for Wales (Representation of the People) Order 2007, SI 2007/236, Sch 6 para 2(1)(a) (whichever is appropriate), but subject to the Representation of the People Act 1983 Sch 2A para 2(4), the European Parliamentary Elections Regulations 2004, SI 2004/293, Sch 6 para 2(4), or the National Assembly for Wales (Representation of the People) Order 2007, SI 2007/236, Sch 6 para 2(4) (see the text and note 13) (whichever is appropriate) (Representation of the People Act 1983 Sch 2A para 2(2) (as so added); European Parliamentary Elections Regulations 2004, SI 2004/293, Sch 6 para 2(2); National Assembly for Wales (Representation of the People) Order 2007, SI 2007/236, Sch 6 para 2(2)).

The value of any donation falling within the Representation of the People Act 1983 Sch 2A para 2(1)(a), other than money, must be taken to be the market value of the property in question: Representation of the People Act 1983 Sch 2A para 5(1) (as so added); European Parliamentary Elections Regulations 2004, SI 2004/293, Sch 6 para 5(1); National Assembly for Wales (Representation of the People) Order 2007, SI 2007/236, Sch 6 para 5(1). However, where the Representation of the People Act 1983 Sch 2A para 2(1)(a) or the European Parliamentary Elections Regulations 2004, SI 2004/293, Sch 6 para 2(1)(a) or the National Assembly for Wales (Representation of the People) Order 2007, SI 2007/236, Sch 6 para 2(1)(a) applies by virtue of the Representation of the People Act 1983 Sch 2A para 2(2) or the European Parliamentary Elections Regulations 2004, SI 2004/293, Sch 6 para 2(2) or the National Assembly for Wales (Representation of the People) Order 2007, SI 2007/236, Sch 6 para 2(2), the value of the donation must be taken to be the difference between:

(a)   the value of the money (or the market value of the property) in question (Representation of the People Act 1983 Sch 2A para 5(2)(a) (as so added); European Parliamentary Elections Regulations 2004, SI 2004/293, Sch 6 para 5(2)(a); National Assembly for Wales (Representation of the People) Order 2007, SI 2007/236, Sch 6 para 5(2)(a)); and

(b)   the total value in monetary terms of the consideration provided by or on behalf of the candidate or his election agent (Representation of the People Act 1983 Sch 2A para 5(2)(b) (as so added); European Parliamentary Elections Regulations 2004, SI 2004/293, Sch 6 para 5(2)(b); National Assembly for Wales (Representation of the People) Order 2007, SI 2007/236, Sch 6 para 5(2)(b)).

For this purpose, 'market value', in relation to any property, means the price which might reasonably be expected to be paid for the property on a sale in the open market: Representation of the People Act 1983 Sch 2A para 5(6) (as so added); European Parliamentary Elections Regulations 2004, SI 2004/293, Sch 6 para 5(6); National Assembly for Wales (Representation of the People) Order 2007, SI 2007/236, Sch 6 para 5(6). As to the meaning of 'property' for these purposes see PARA 286 note 3.

7   Representation of the People Act 1983 Sch 2A para 2(1)(b) (as added: see note 2); European Parliamentary Elections Regulations 2004, SI 2004/293, Sch 6 para 2(1)(b); National Assembly for Wales (Representation of the People) Order 2007, SI 2007/236, Sch 6 para 2(1)(b). For these purposes, sponsorship provided in relation to the candidate is defined by the Representation of the People Act 1983 Sch 2A para 3, or the European Parliamentary Elections Regulations 2004, SI 2004/293, Sch 6 para 3, or the National Assembly for Wales (Representation of the People) Order 2007, SI 2007/236, Sch 6 para 3 (see the text and notes 18–26) (whichever is appropriate): Representation of the People Act 1983 Sch 2A para 2(1)(b) (as so added); European Parliamentary Elections Regulations 2004, SI 2004/293, Sch 6 para 2(1)(b); National Assembly for Wales (Representation of the People) Order 2007, SI 2007/236, Sch 6 para 2(1)(b).

The value of any donation falling within the Representation of the People Act 1983 Sch 2A para 2(1)(b), or the European Parliamentary Elections Regulations 2004, SI 2004/293, Sch 6 para 2(1)(b), or the National Assembly for Wales (Representation of the People) Order 2007, SI 2007/236, Sch 6 para 2(1)(b) (whichever is appropriate) is taken to be the value of the money or (as the case may be) the market value of the property, transferred as mentioned in the Representation of the People Act 1983 Sch 2A para 3(1), or the European Parliamentary Elections Regulations 2004, SI 2004/293, Sch 6 para 3(1), or the National Assembly for Wales (Representation of the People) Order 2007, SI 2007/236, Sch 6 para 3(1) (see the text and notes 18–22); and accordingly any value in monetary terms of any benefit conferred on the person providing the sponsorship in question must be disregarded: Representation of the People

Act 1983 Sch 2A para 5(3) (as so added); European Parliamentary Elections Regulations 2004, SI 2004/293, Sch 6 para 5(3); National Assembly for Wales (Representation of the People) Order 2007, SI 2007/236, Sch 6 para 5(3).

8   A sub-agent may be appointed for a parliamentary election in a county constituency or for an Authority election (see PARA 233), for Welsh Assembly elections (see PARA 237) or for European parliamentary elections (see PARA 241).

9   As to the meaning of 'election expenses' see PARA 269.

10   Representation of the People Act 1983 Sch 2A para 2(1)(c) (as added: see note 2); European Parliamentary Elections Regulations 2004, SI 2004/293, Sch 6 para 2(1)(c); National Assembly for Wales (Representation of the People) Order 2007, SI 2007/236, Sch 6 para 2(1)(c). The reference in the text to money spent is a reference to money so spent by a person, other than the candidate, his election agent or any sub-agent, out of his own resources, with no right to reimbursement out of the resources of any such other person; and where, by virtue of the Representation of the People Act 1983 Sch 2A para 2(1)(c), or the European Parliamentary Elections Regulations 2004, SI 2004/293, Sch 6 para 2(1)(c), or the National Assembly for Wales (Representation of the People) Order 2007, SI 2007/236, Sch 6 para 2(1)(c) (whichever is appropriate), money so spent constitutes a donation to the candidate, the candidate is treated as receiving an equivalent amount on the date on which the money is paid to the creditor in respect of the expenses in question: Representation of the People Act 1983 Sch 2A para 2(5) (as so added); European Parliamentary Elections Regulations 2004, SI 2004/293, Sch 6 para 2(5); National Assembly for Wales (Representation of the People) Order 2007, SI 2007/236, Sch 6 para 2(5). As to the meaning of 'election expenses incurred by or on behalf of a candidate' see PARA 269 note 15.

A donation to the candidate or his election agent for the purpose of meeting election expenses incurred by or on behalf of the candidate is referred to as a 'relevant donation' (Representation of the People Act 1983 Sch 2A para 1(3) (as so added); European Parliamentary Elections Regulations 2004, SI 2004/293, Sch 6 para 1(4); National Assembly for Wales (Representation of the People) Order 2007, SI 2007/236, Sch 6 para 1(2)), and includes a reference to a donation for the purpose of securing that any such expenses are not so incurred (Representation of the People Act 1983 Sch 2A para 1(4) (as so added); European Parliamentary Elections Regulations 2004, SI 2004/293, Sch 6 para 1(5); National Assembly for Wales (Representation of the People) Order 2007, SI 2007/236, Sch 6 para 1); and a donation is taken to be a donation for either of those purposes if, having regard to all the circumstances, it must be reasonably assumed to be such a donation (Representation of the People Act 1983 Sch 2A para 1(4) (as so added); European Parliamentary Elections Regulations 2004, SI 2004/293, Sch 6 para 1(5); National Assembly for Wales (Representation of the People) Order 2007, SI 2007/236, Sch 6 para 1(3)).

11   Representation of the People Act 1983 Sch 2A para 2(1)(d) (as added: see note 2); European Parliamentary Elections Regulations 2004, SI 2004/293, Sch 6 para 2(1)(d); National Assembly for Wales (Representation of the People) Order 2007, SI 2007/236, Sch 6 para 2(1)(d).

In determining, for these purposes, whether any money lent to a candidate or his election agent is so lent otherwise than on commercial terms (Representation of the People Act 1983 Sch 2A para 2(3)(a) (as so added); European Parliamentary Elections Regulations 2004, SI 2004/293, Sch 6 para 2(3)(a); National Assembly for Wales (Representation of the People) Order 2007, SI 2007/236, Sch 6 para 2(3)(a)), regard must be had to the total value in monetary terms of the consideration provided by or on behalf of the candidate in respect of the loan or the provision of the property, services or facilities (Representation of the People Act 1983 Sch 2A para 2(3) (as so added); European Parliamentary Elections Regulations 2004, SI 2004/293, Sch 6 para 2(3); National Assembly for Wales (Representation of the People) Order 2007, SI 2007/236, Sch 6 para 2(3)). The value of any donation falling within the Representation of the People Act 1983 Sch 2A para 2(1)(d) or Sch 2A para 2(1)(e) (see head (5) in the text) or the European Parliamentary Elections Regulations 2004, SI 2004/293, Sch 6 para 2(1)(e) (see head (5) in the text) or the National Assembly for Wales (Representation of the People) Order 2007, SI 2007/236, Sch 6 para 2(1)(d) or Sch 6 para 2(1)(e) (see head (5) in the text) is taken to be the amount representing the difference between:

(1)   the total value in monetary terms of the consideration that would have had to be provided by or on behalf of the candidate or his election agent in respect of the loan or the provision of the property, services or facilities if the loan had been made, or if the property, services or facilities had been provided, on commercial terms (Representation of the People Act 1983 Sch 2A para 5(4)(a) (as so added); European Parliamentary Elections Regulations 2004, SI 2004/293, Sch 6 para 5(4)(a); National Assembly for Wales (Representation of the People) Order 2007, SI 2007/236, Sch 6 para 5(4)(a)); and

(2)   the total value in monetary terms of the consideration, if any, actually so provided by or

on behalf of the candidate or his election agent (Representation of the People Act 1983 Sch 2A para 5(4)(b) (as so added); European Parliamentary Elections Regulations 2004, SI 2004/293, Sch 6 para 5(4)(b); National Assembly for Wales (Representation of the People) Order 2007, SI 2007/236, Sch 6 para 5(4)(b)).

Where such a donation confers an enduring benefit on the donee over a particular period, the value of the donation is determined at the time when it is made, but must be so determined by reference to the total benefit accruing to the donee over that period: Representation of the People Act 1983 Sch 2A para 5(5) (as so added); European Parliamentary Elections Regulations 2004, SI 2004/293, Sch 6 para 5(5); National Assembly for Wales (Representation of the People) Order 2007, SI 2007/236, Sch 6 para 5(5).

12 Representation of the People Act 1983 Sch 2A para 2(1)(e) (as added: see note 2); European Parliamentary Elections Regulations 2004, SI 2004/293, Sch 6 para 2(1)(e); National Assembly for Wales (Representation of the People) Order 2007, SI 2007/236, Sch 6 para 2(1)(e). In determining, for these purposes, whether any property, services or facilities provided for the use or benefit of a candidate is or are so provided otherwise than on commercial terms (Representation of the People Act 1983 Sch 2A para 2(3)(b) (as so added); European Parliamentary Elections Regulations 2004, SI 2004/293, Sch 6 para 2(3)(b); National Assembly for Wales (Representation of the People) Order 2007, SI 2007/236, Sch 6 para 2(3)(b)), regard must be had to the total value in monetary terms of the consideration provided by or on behalf of the candidate in respect of the loan or the provision of the property, services or facilities (Representation of the People Act 1983 Sch 2A para 2(3) (as so added); European Parliamentary Elections Regulations 2004, SI 2004/293, Sch 6 para 2(3); National Assembly for Wales (Representation of the People) Order 2007, SI 2007/236, Sch 6 para 2(3)). See also note 11.

13 Representation of the People Act 1983 Sch 2A para 2(4) (as added: see note 2); European Parliamentary Elections Regulations 2004, SI 2004/293, Sch 6 para 2(4); National Assembly for Wales (Representation of the People) Order 2007, SI 2007/236, Sch 6 para 2(4). In the circumstances mentioned in the text, the general provisions as to sponsorship (see the text and notes 18–26) apply as well as the provision mentioned in head (2) in the text: Representation of the People Act 1983 Sch 2A para 2(4) (as so added); European Parliamentary Elections Regulations 2004, SI 2004/293, Sch 6 para 2(4); National Assembly for Wales (Representation of the People) Order 2007, SI 2007/236, Sch 6 para 2(4).

14 Representation of the People Act 1983 Sch 2A para 4(2) (as added: see note 2); European Parliamentary Elections Regulations 2004, SI 2004/293, Sch 6 para 4(2); National Assembly for Wales (Representation of the People) Order 2007, SI 2007/236, Sch 6 para 4(2). The value is determined in accordance with the Representation of the People Act 1983 Sch 2A para 5, or the European Parliamentary Elections Regulations 2004, SI 2004/293, Sch 6 para 5, or the National Assembly for Wales (Representation of the People) Order 2007, SI 2007/236, Sch 6 para 5 (see notes 6–7, 11) (whichever is appropriate).

15 Representation of the People Act 1983 Sch 2A para 4(1)(a) (as added: see note 2); European Parliamentary Elections Regulations 2004, SI 2004/293, Sch 6 para 4(1)(a); National Assembly for Wales (Representation of the People) Order 2007, SI 2007/236, Sch 6 para 4(1)(a). The text refers to any right conferred on a candidate at an election by the Representation of the People Act 1983, the European Parliamentary Elections Regulations 2004, SI 2004/293, or the National Assembly for Wales (Representation of the People) Order 2007, SI 2007/236 (whichever is appropriate).

16 Representation of the People Act 1983 Sch 2A para 4(1)(b) (as added: see note 2); European Parliamentary Elections Regulations 2004, SI 2004/293, Sch 6 para 4(1)(b); National Assembly for Wales (Representation of the People) Order 2007, SI 2007/236, Sch 6 para 4(1)(b).

17 Representation of the People Act 1983 Sch 2A para 4(1)(c) (as added: see note 2); European Parliamentary Elections Regulations 2004, SI 2004/293, Sch 6 para 4(1)(c); National Assembly for Wales (Representation of the People) Order 2007, SI 2007/236, Sch 6 para 4(1)(c). The text refers to a donation which is dealt with by the candidate or (as the case may be) his election agent in accordance with the Political Parties, Elections and Referendums Act 2000 s 56(2)(a), (b), as applied by the Representation of the People Act 1983 Sch 2A para 7, or the European Parliamentary Elections Regulations 2004, SI 2004/293, Sch 6 para 7, or the National Assembly for Wales (Representation of the People) Order 2007, SI 2007/236, Sch 6 para 7 (whichever is appropriate) (see PARA 289).

18 Representation of the People Act 1983 Sch 2A para 3(1)(a) (as added: see note 2); European Parliamentary Elections Regulations 2004, SI 2004/293, Sch 6 para 3(1)(a); National Assembly for Wales (Representation of the People) Order 2007, SI 2007/236, Sch 6 para 3(1)(a).

19 Representation of the People Act 1983 Sch 2A para 3(1)(b) (as added: see note 2); European Parliamentary Elections Regulations 2004, SI 2004/293, Sch 6 para 3(1)(b); National Assembly for Wales (Representation of the People) Order 2007, SI 2007/236, Sch 6 para 3(1)(b).

20 For this purpose, 'defined expenses' means expenses in connection with:

    (1)   any conference, meeting or other event organised by or on behalf of the candidate (Representation of the People Act 1983 Sch 2A para 3(2)(a) (as added: see note 2); European Parliamentary Elections Regulations 2004, SI 2004/293, Sch 6 para 3(2)(a); National Assembly for Wales (Representation of the People) Order 2007, SI 2007/236, Sch 6 para 3(2)(a));

    (2)   the preparation, production or dissemination of any publication by or on behalf of the candidate (Representation of the People Act 1983 Sch 2A para 3(2)(b) (as added: see note 2); European Parliamentary Elections Regulations 2004, SI 2004/293, Sch 6 para 3(2)(b); National Assembly for Wales (Representation of the People) Order 2007, SI 2007/236, Sch 6 para 3(2)(b)); or

    (3)   any study or research organised by or on behalf of the candidate (Representation of the People Act 1983 Sch 2A para 3(2)(c) (as added: see note 2); European Parliamentary Elections Regulations 2004, SI 2004/293, Sch 6 para 3(2)(c); National Assembly for Wales (Representation of the People) Order 2007, SI 2007/236, Sch 6 para 3(2)(c)).

For this purpose, 'publication' means a publication made available in whatever form and by whatever means, whether or not to the public at large or any section of the public: Representation of the People Act 1983 Sch 2A para 3(6) (as so added); European Parliamentary Elections Regulations 2004, SI 2004/293, Sch 6 para 3(4); National Assembly for Wales (Representation of the People) Order 2007, SI 2007/236, Sch 6 para 3(4).

The Secretary of State may by order made on the recommendation of the Electoral Commission amend the Representation of the People Act 1983 Sch 2A para 3(2) or Sch 2A para 3(3) (see the text and notes 23–26): Representation of the People Act 1983 Sch 2A paras 1(8), 3(4) (as so added). Any such order must be made by statutory instrument; but no such order is to be made unless a draft of the order has been laid before and approved by a resolution of each House of Parliament: Sch 2A para 3(5) (as so added). As to the Secretary of State see PARA 2; and as to the Electoral Commission see PARA 34 et seq.

21 Representation of the People Act 1983 Sch 2A para 3(1)(b)(i) (as added: see note 2); European Parliamentary Elections Regulations 2004, SI 2004/293, Sch 6 para 3(1)(b)(i); National Assembly for Wales (Representation of the People) Order 2007, SI 2007/236, Sch 6 para 3(1)(b)(i).

22 Representation of the People Act 1983 Sch 2A para 3(1)(b)(ii) (as added: see note 2); European Parliamentary Elections Regulations 2004, SI 2004/293, Sch 6 para 3(1)(b)(ii); National Assembly for Wales (Representation of the People) Order 2007, SI 2007/236, Sch 6 para 3(1)(b)(ii).

23 Representation of the People Act 1983 Sch 2A para 3(3)(a)(i) (as added: see note 2); European Parliamentary Elections Regulations 2004, SI 2004/293, Sch 6 para 3(3)(a)(i); National Assembly for Wales (Representation of the People) Order 2007, SI 2007/236, Sch 6 para 3(3)(a)(i). As to the Secretary of State's power to amend the provision set out in the text see note 20.

24 Representation of the People Act 1983 Sch 2A para 3(3)(a)(ii) (as added: see note 2); European Parliamentary Elections Regulations 2004, SI 2004/293, Sch 6 para 3(3)(a)(ii); National Assembly for Wales (Representation of the People) Order 2007, SI 2007/236, Sch 6 para 3(3)(a)(ii). As to the Secretary of State's power to amend the provision set out in the text see note 20.

25 Representation of the People Act 1983 Sch 2A para 3(3)(b) (as added: see note 2); European Parliamentary Elections Regulations 2004, SI 2004/293, Sch 6 para 3(3)(b); National Assembly for Wales (Representation of the People) Order 2007, SI 2007/236, Sch 6 para 3(3)(b). As to the Secretary of State's power to amend the provision set out in the text see note 20.

26 Representation of the People Act 1983 Sch 2A para 3(3) (as added: see note 2); European Parliamentary Elections Regulations 2004, SI 2004/293, Sch 6 para 3(3); National Assembly for Wales (Representation of the People) Order 2007, SI 2007/236, Sch 6 para 3(3). As to the Secretary of State's power to amend the provision set out in the text see note 20.

288. Restrictions on candidates at an election accepting certain donations.

For the purposes of controlling donations[1] to candidates[2] at an election[3], a relevant donation[4] received by a candidate or his election agent[5] must not be accepted[6] if:

(1)   the person by whom the donation would be made is not, at the time of
        its receipt by the candidate or (as the case may be) his election agent, a
        permissible donor[7]; or

(2)   the candidate or (as the case may be) his election agent is, whether
        because the donation is given anonymously or by reason of any
        deception or concealment or otherwise, unable to ascertain the identity
        of the person offering the donation[8].

For these purposes, where any person (the 'principal donor') causes an
amount (the 'principal donation') to be received by a candidate or his election
agent by way of a relevant donation either:

(a)   on behalf of himself and one or more other persons[9]; or

(b)   on behalf of two or more other persons[10],

then for the purposes of the statutory controls on donations received by
candidates at an election[11], each individual contribution by a person, falling
within either head (a) or head (b) above, of more than £50 is treated as if it were
a separate donation received from that person[12]. Also, where any person (the
'agent') causes an amount to be received by a candidate or his election agent by
way of a donation on behalf of another person (the 'donor')[13], and where the
amount of the donation is more than £50[14], the agent must ensure that, at the
time when the donation is received by the candidate or his election agent, the
candidate or (as the case may be) his election agent is given all such details in
respect of the donor as are required to be included in donation reports[15].

A person commits an offence if, without reasonable excuse, he fails to comply
with the statutory controls on donations made through other persons or through
agents[16].

1   As to the meaning of 'donation' in relation to candidates at an election see PARA 287.
2   As to the meaning of 'candidate' generally see PARA 230.
        At a European parliamentary election, the reference is an 'individual candidate': see the
    European Parliamentary Elections Regulations 2004, SI 2004/293, reg 42(4), Sch 6
    para 1(1), (3). As to the meaning of 'individual candidate' at a European parliamentary election
    see PARA 230 note 32. As to European parliamentary elections see PARA 217 et seq.
        In the case of a Welsh Assembly election, the reference is to a constituency candidate at a
    Welsh Assembly constituency election or to an individual candidate at a Welsh Assembly
    regional election: see the National Assembly for Wales (Representation of the People)
    Order 2007, SI 2007/236, art 41(4), Sch 6 para 1(1). As to the meanings of 'Assembly election',
    'constituency election' and 'regional election' for the purposes of Welsh Assembly elections see
    PARA 3 note 2. As to the meanings of 'constituency candidate' at a Welsh Assembly constituency
    election and 'individual candidate' at a Welsh Assembly regional election see PARA 230 note 19.
3   Representation of the People Act 1983 s 71A(4), Sch 2A para 1(1), (2) (s 71A, Sch 2A added by
    the Political Parties, Elections and Referendums Act 2000 s 130(1)–(4)); European
    Parliamentary Elections Regulations 2004, SI 2004/293, Sch 6 para 1(1), (2); National Assembly
    for Wales (Representation of the People) Order 2007, SI 2007/236, Sch 6 para 1(1).
        The election referred to in the text may be any of a parliamentary election, an Authority
    election, an election under the local government Act (see the Representation of the People
    Act 1983 s 202(1); and PARA 3 note 1), a Welsh Assembly constituency or regional election or a
    European parliamentary election. As to the meaning of 'parliamentary election' see PARA 9; As
    to the meaning of 'Authority election' see PARA 11; and as to the meaning of 'election under the
    local government Act' see PARA 11 note 2. However, the Representation of the People Act 1983
    s 71A does not apply at an election under the local government Act which is not a local
    government election (see the Representation of the People Act 1983 s 90(2); and PARA 297); and,
    in relation to an election of parish councillors in England or of community councillors in Wales,
    the provisions of s 90(1), Sch 4 apply instead (see s 90(1)(b); and PARAS 293–296). As to the
    meaning of 'local government election' see PARA 11. As to elections in the City of London see
    PARA 33.
4   As to the meaning of 'relevant donation' in relation to candidates' election expenses see PARA
    287 note 10.

5   As to the appointment of an election agent see PARA 231 et seq.

6   Representation of the People Act 1983 Sch 2A para 6(1) (as added: see note 3); European Parliamentary Elections Regulations 2004, SI 2004/293, Sch 6 para 6(1); National Assembly for Wales (Representation of the People) Order 2007, SI 2007/236, art 41(4), Sch 6 para 6(1). As to the information that must be recorded and returned where a relevant donation falls within head (1) or head (2) in the text, see PARA 292.

7   Representation of the People Act 1983 Sch 2A para 6(1)(a) (as added: see note 3); European Parliamentary Elections Regulations 2004, SI 2004/293, Sch 6 para 6(1)(a); National Assembly for Wales (Representation of the People) Order 2007, SI 2007/236, Sch 6 para 6(1)(a). The text refers to a permissible donor falling within the Political Parties, Elections and Referendums Act 2000 s 54(2) (see CONSTITUTIONAL LAW AND HUMAN RIGHTS). In relation to a donation received by a candidate at a European parliamentary election in Great Britain or Gibraltar, or at a Welsh Assembly election, references to a permissible donor falling within s 54(2) must be read as if s 54(2) did not include a party registered in the Northern Ireland register maintained by the Electoral Commission under Pt II (ss 22–40) (registration of political parties: see PARA 253): see the European Parliamentary Elections Regulations 2004, SI 2004/293, Sch 6 para 1(7) (substituted by SI 2009/186); and the National Assembly for Wales (Representation of the People) Order 2007, SI 2007/236, Sch 6 para 1(4). As to further modifications that are required to the European Parliamentary Elections Regulations 2004, SI 2004/293, Sch 6 para 6 for the purposes of applying its provisions to an individual candidate (or his election agent) at a European parliamentary election in the combined region see Sch 6 para 6(9). As to the establishment of electoral regions (including the combined region) for the purpose of elections to the European Parliament see PARA 77.

For these purposes, any relevant donation received by a candidate or his election agent which is an exempt trust donation is regarded as a relevant donation received by the candidate or his election agent from such a permissible donor: Representation of the People Act 1983 Sch 2A para 6(2) (as so added); European Parliamentary Elections Regulations 2004, SI 2004/293, Sch 6 para 6(2); National Assembly for Wales (Representation of the People) Order 2007, SI 2007/236, Sch 6 para 6(2). However, any relevant donation received by a candidate or his election agent from a trustee of any property (in his capacity as such) is regarded as being from a person who is not such a permissible donor if that donation is not:

(1)   an exempt trust donation (Representation of the People Act 1983 Sch 2A para 6(3)(a) (as so added); European Parliamentary Elections Regulations 2004, SI 2004/293, Sch 6 para 6(3)(a); National Assembly for Wales (Representation of the People) Order 2007, SI 2007/236, Sch 6 para 6(3)(a)); or

(2)   a relevant donation transmitted by the trustee to the candidate or his election agent on behalf of beneficiaries under the trust who are either persons who, at the time of its receipt by the candidate or his election agent, are such permissible donors or the members of an unincorporated association which at that time is such a permissible donor (Representation of the People Act 1983 Sch 2A para 6(3)(b) (as so added); European Parliamentary Elections Regulations 2004, SI 2004/293, Sch 6 para 6(3)(b); National Assembly for Wales (Representation of the People) Order 2007, SI 2007/236, Sch 6 para 6(3)(b)).

The definition of 'exempt trust donation' in the Political Parties, Elections and Referendums Act 2000 s 162 applies for these purposes as it applies for the purposes of that Act: Representation of the People Act 1983 Sch 2A para 6(2) (as so added); European Parliamentary Elections Regulations 2004, SI 2004/293, Sch 6 para 6(2); National Assembly for Wales (Representation of the People) Order 2007, SI 2007/236, Sch 6 para 6(2). Accordingly, 'exempt trust donation' means:

(a)   any donation received from a trustee of any property in accordance with the terms of a trust which was created before 27 July 1999, to which no property has been transferred on or after that date, and whose terms have not been varied on or after that date, provided that, at or before the time of the receipt of the donation, the trustee gives the recipient of the donation the full name of the person who created the trust and of every other person by whom, or under whose will, property was transferred to the trust before that date (Political Parties, Elections and Referendums Act 2000 s 162(1)(a), (2) (as so applied));

(b)   any donation received from a trustee of any property in accordance with the terms of a trust which was created by a person who was a permissible donor falling within s 54(2) at the time when the trust was created, or the will of a person who was, at any time within the period of five years ending with the date of his death, registered in an electoral register, and to which no property has been transferred otherwise than by a person who was a permissible donor falling within s 54(2) at the time of the transfer, or

under the will of a person who was, at any time within the period of five years ending
with the date of his death, registered in an electoral register, provided that, at or before
the time of the receipt of the donation, the trustee gives the recipient of the donation the
relevant information (ss 54(3), 162(3) (as so applied)).
However, the definition does not include a donation received from a trustee of any property
pursuant to the exercise of any discretion vested by a trust in him or any other person: s 162(5)
(as so applied). For these purposes, the 'relevant information' means the information which is
required by virtue of ss 62, 63, Sch 6 para 2 (identity of donors (quarterly reports): see
CONSTITUTIONAL LAW AND HUMAN RIGHTS) to be given in respect of a recordable donation to
which s 162(3) applies (s 162(4) (as so applied)); 'donation' means a donation for the purposes
of the provisions of the Political Parties, Elections and Referendums Act 2000 in which the
relevant reference to an exempt trust donation occurs (s 162(6)(a) (as so applied)); 'property', in
the context of the transfer of property to a trust, does not include any income of the trust
(s 162(6)(b) (as so applied)); 'trust' includes a trust created by a will (s 162(6)(c) (as so applied));
and any reference to a donation received from a trustee is a reference to a donation received
from a trustee in his capacity as such, other than a donation transmitted on behalf of a
beneficiary under a trust (s 162(6)(d) (as so applied)).

8   Representation of the People Act 1983 Sch 2A para 6(1)(b) (as added: see note 3); European
     Parliamentary Elections Regulations 2004, SI 2004/293, Sch 6 para 6(1)(b); National Assembly
     for Wales (Representation of the People) Order 2007, SI 2007/236, Sch 6 para 6(1)(b).

9   Representation of the People Act 1983 Sch 2A para 6(4)(a) (as added: see note 3); European
     Parliamentary Elections Regulations 2004, SI 2004/293, Sch 6 para 6(4)(a); National Assembly
     for Wales (Representation of the People) Order 2007, SI 2007/236, Sch 6 para 6(4)(a).

10   Representation of the People Act 1983 Sch 2A para 6(4)(b) (as added: see note 3); European
     Parliamentary Elections Regulations 2004, SI 2004/293, Sch 6 para 6(4)(b); National Assembly
     for Wales (Representation of the People) Order 2007, SI 2007/236, Sch 6 para 6(4)(b).

11   Ie for the purposes of the Representation of the People Act 1983 Sch 2A Pt II paras 6–9, or the
     European Parliamentary Elections Regulations 2004, SI 2004/293, Sch 6 Pt 2 paras 6–9, or the
     National Assembly for Wales (Representation of the People) Order 2007, SI 2007/236, Sch 6
     Pt II paras 6–9 (whichever is applicable).

12   Representation of the People Act 1983 Sch 2A para 6(4) (as added: see note 3); European
     Parliamentary Elections Regulations 2004, SI 2004/293, Sch 6 para 6(4); National Assembly for
     Wales (Representation of the People) Order 2007, SI 2007/236, Sch 6 para 6(4).
     In relation to each such separate donation, the principal donor must ensure that, at the time
     when the principal donation is received by the candidate or his election agent, the candidate or
     (as the case may be) his election agent is given, except in the case of a donation which the
     principal donor is treated as making, all such details in respect of the person treated as making
     the donation as are required by virtue of the Representation of the People Act 1983 Sch 2A
     para 11(c), or the European Parliamentary Elections Regulations 2004, SI 2004/293, Sch 6
     para 11(c), or the National Assembly for Wales (Representation of the People) Order 2007,
     SI 2007/236, Sch 6 para 11(c) (see PARA 292) and, in any case, all such details in respect of the
     donation as are required by virtue of the Representation of the People Act 1983 Sch 2A
     para 11(a), or the European Parliamentary Elections Regulations 2004, SI 2004/293, Sch 6
     para 11(a), or the National Assembly for Wales (Representation of the People) Order 2007,
     SI 2007/236, Sch 6 para 11(a) (see PARA 292): Representation of the People Act 1983 Sch 2A
     para 6(5) (as so added); European Parliamentary Elections Regulations 2004, SI 2004/293,
     Sch 6 para 6(5); National Assembly for Wales (Representation of the People) Order 2007,
     SI 2007/236, Sch 6 para 6(5).

13   Representation of the People Act 1983 Sch 2A para 6(6)(a) (as added: see note 3); European
     Parliamentary Elections Regulations 2004, SI 2004/293, Sch 6 para 6(6)(a); National Assembly
     for Wales (Representation of the People) Order 2007, SI 2007/236, Sch 6 para 6(6)(a).

14   Representation of the People Act 1983 Sch 2A para 6(6)(b) (as added: see note 3); European
     Parliamentary Elections Regulations 2004, SI 2004/293, Sch 6 para 6(6)(b); National Assembly
     for Wales (Representation of the People) Order 2007, SI 2007/236, Sch 6 para 6(6)(b).

15   Representation of the People Act 1983 Sch 2A para 6(6) (as added: see note 3); European
     Parliamentary Elections Regulations 2004, SI 2004/293, Sch 6 para 6(6); National Assembly for
     Wales (Representation of the People) Order 2007, SI 2007/236, Sch 6 para 6(6). The text refers
     to the details in respect of the donor that are required to be reported by virtue of the
     Representation of the People Act 1983 Sch 2A para 11(c), or the European Parliamentary
     Elections Regulations 2004, SI 2004/293, Sch 6 para 11(c), or the National Assembly for Wales
     (Representation of the People) Order 2007, SI 2007/236, Sch 6 para 11(c) (whichever is
     appropriate) (see PARA 292).

16 See the Representation of the People Act 1983 Sch 2A para 6(7), (8); the European Parliamentary Elections Regulations 2004, SI 2004/293, Sch 6 para 6(7), (8); the National Assembly for Wales (Representation of the People) Order 2007, SI 2007/236, Sch 6 para 6(7), (8); and PARA 752. The text refers to failure to comply with the Representation of the People Act 1983 Sch 2A para 6(5), (6), or the European Parliamentary Elections Regulations 2004, SI 2004/293, Sch 6 para 6(5), (6), or the National Assembly for Wales (Representation of the People) Order 2007, SI 2007/236, Sch 6 para 6(5), (6) (see the text and notes 12–15).

289. Acceptance or return of donations received by candidate at an election.
The provisions of the Political Parties, Elections and Referendums Act 2000 which require a registered party[1]:

(1)   to take all reasonable steps to identify a donor in order to ascertain whether he is a permissible donor[2]; and

(2)   where a donor is unidentifiable or impermissible, to return the donation to its source or to send it to the Electoral Commission[3] or to subject it to forfeiture on the application of the Commission[4],

apply, subject to minor modification, for the purposes of controlling donations[5] to candidates[6] at an election[7], in relation to:

(a)   a relevant donation[8] received by a candidate or his election agent[9]; and

(b)   the candidate or (as the case may be) the election agent[10],

as those provisions apply in relation to a donation received by a registered party and in relation to the registered party[11].

1   As to the meaning of 'registered party' for these purposes see PARA 35 note 3.
2   Ie the Political Parties, Elections and Referendums Act 2000 s 56 (see CONSTITUTIONAL LAW AND HUMAN RIGHTS). Nothing in Pt IV (ss 50–71) applies in relation to donations received by a minor party (see PARA 253): see s 50(9). As to the meaning of 'permissible donor' for these purposes see PARA 288.
3   Ie the Political Parties, Elections and Referendums Act 2000 s 57 (see CONSTITUTIONAL LAW AND HUMAN RIGHTS). See also note 2. As to the Electoral Commission see PARA 34 et seq.
4   Ie the Political Parties, Elections and Referendums Act 2000 s 58 (see CONSTITUTIONAL LAW AND HUMAN RIGHTS). See also note 2. The registered party may appeal against a forfeiture order (see s 59; and see CONSTITUTIONAL LAW AND HUMAN RIGHTS); and rules of court under s 60 (see CONSTITUTIONAL LAW AND HUMAN RIGHTS) may provide for the procedure on application or appeal under ss 58, 59. See further *R (on the application of the Electoral Commission) v City of Westminster Magistrates' Court* [2010] UKSC 40, [2011] 1 AC 496, [2011] 1 All ER 1 (where it was shown that a political party had accepted a donation from an impermissible source, there should be an initial presumption in favour of forfeiting the donation but, if it was shown that the donor was in a position to qualify as a permissible donor by registering on an electoral register, the initial presumption would be rebutted; the question would then be whether there had been failures to comply with those requirements of the Political Parties, Elections and Referendums Act 2000 that were designed to ensure that such donations were not accepted, and again the onus would be on the party to explain how it was that the donation came to be accepted; s 58(2) conferred a power to order forfeiture of an amount equal to the value of an impermissible donation, which implicitly included the power to order the forfeiture of a lesser sum, but the word 'forfeit' in s 58(2) was used in an unusual way in the context of the statute (and it could be construed as being more akin to a fine); such an interpretation was desirable to cope with the situation where the magistrates' court was persuaded that the donor was not foreign, because total forfeiture of the donation might be disproportionate, both under the ordinary principles that applied to the imposition of sanctions and having regard to the right to peaceful enjoyment of one's possessions contained in the Convention for the Protection of Human Rights and Fundamental Freedoms (Rome, 4 November 1950; TS 71 (1953) Cmd 8969) First Protocol art 1 (see RIGHTS AND FREEDOMS vol 88A (2013) PARA 534)).
5   As to the meaning of 'donation' in relation to candidates at an election see PARA 287.
6   As to the meaning of 'candidate' generally see PARA 230.
     At a European parliamentary election, the reference is an 'individual candidate': see the European Parliamentary Elections Regulations 2004, SI 2004/293, reg 42(4), Sch 6

para 1(1), (3). As to the meaning of 'individual candidate' at a European parliamentary election see PARA 230 note 32. As to European parliamentary elections see PARA 217 et seq.

In the case of a Welsh Assembly election, the reference is to a constituency candidate at a Welsh Assembly constituency election or to an individual candidate at a Welsh Assembly regional election: see the National Assembly for Wales (Representation of the People) Order 2007, SI 2007/236, art 41(4), Sch 6 para 1(1). As to the meanings of 'Assembly election', 'constituency election' and 'regional election' for the purposes of Welsh Assembly elections see PARA 3 note 2. As to the meanings of 'constituency candidate' at a Welsh Assembly constituency election and 'individual candidate' at a Welsh Assembly regional election see PARA 230 note 19.

7   Representation of the People Act 1983 s 71A(4), Sch 2A paras 1(1), (2), 7(1) (s 71A, Sch 2A added by the Political Parties, Elections and Referendums Act 2000 s 130(1)–(4)); European Parliamentary Elections Regulations 2004, SI 2004/293, Sch 6 paras 1(1), (2), 7(1); National Assembly for Wales (Representation of the People) Order 2007, SI 2007/236, Sch 6 paras 1(1), 7(1).

The election referred to in the text may be any of a parliamentary election, an Authority election, an election under the local government Act (see the Representation of the People Act 1983 s 202(1); and PARA 3 note 1), a Welsh Assembly constituency or regional election or a European parliamentary election. As to the meaning of 'parliamentary election' see PARA 9; As to the meaning of 'Authority election' see PARA 11; and as to the meaning of 'election under the local government Act' see PARA 11 note 2. However, the Representation of the People Act 1983 s 71A does not apply at an election under the local government Act which is not a local government election (see the Representation of the People Act 1983 s 90(2); and PARA 297); and, in relation to an election of parish councillors in England or of community councillors in Wales, the provisions of s 90(1), Sch 4 apply instead (see s 90(1)(b); and PARAS 293–296). As to the meaning of 'local government election' see PARA 11. As to elections in the City of London see PARA 33.

8   As to the meaning of 'relevant donation' in relation to candidates' election expenses see PARA 287 note 10.

9   Representation of the People Act 1983 Sch 2A para 7(1)(a) (as added: see note 7); European Parliamentary Elections Regulations 2004, SI 2004/293, Sch 6 para 7(1)(a); National Assembly for Wales (Representation of the People) Order 2007, SI 2007/236, Sch 6 para 7(1)(a). As to the appointment of an election agent see PARA 231 et seq.

10   Representation of the People Act 1983 Sch 2A para 7(1)(b) (as added: see note 7); European Parliamentary Elections Regulations 2004, SI 2004/293, Sch 6 para 7(1)(b); National Assembly for Wales (Representation of the People) Order 2007, SI 2007/236, Sch 6 para 7(1)(b).

11   Representation of the People Act 1983 Sch 2A para 7(1) (as added: see note 7); European Parliamentary Elections Regulations 2004, SI 2004/293, Sch 6 para 7(1); National Assembly for Wales (Representation of the People) Order 2007, SI 2007/236, Sch 6 para 7(1). Accordingly, in the application of the Political Parties, Elections and Referendums Act 2000 ss 56–60 for these purposes:

(1)   s 56(1) has effect as if the reference to the particulars relating to a donor which would be required to be included in a donation report by virtue of ss 62, 63, Sch 6 para 2 (identity of donors (quarterly reports): see CONSTITUTIONAL LAW AND HUMAN RIGHTS), if the donation were a recordable donation within the meaning of Sch 6 were construed as a reference to the particulars which are required to be included in a return by virtue of the Representation of the People Act 1983 Sch 2A para 11(c), or the European Parliamentary Elections Regulations 2004, SI 2004/293, Sch 6 para 11(c), or the National Assembly for Wales (Representation of the People) Order 2007, SI 2007/236, Sch 6 para 11(c) (whichever is appropriate) (see PARA 292) (Representation of the People Act 1983 Sch 2A para7(2)(a) (as added: see note 7); European Parliamentary Elections Regulations 2004, SI 2004/293, Sch 6 para 7(2)(a); National Assembly for Wales (Representation of the People) Order 2007, SI 2007/236, Sch 6 para 7(2)(a));

(2)   the Political Parties, Elections and Referendums Act 2000 s 56(3) has effect as if the reference to the party were omitted and the reference to the treasurer of the party were construed as a reference to the candidate or (as the case may be) his election agent (Representation of the People Act 1983 Sch 2A para 7(2)(b) (as so added); European Parliamentary Elections Regulations 2004, SI 2004/293, Sch 6 para 7(2)(b); National Assembly for Wales (Representation of the People) Order 2007, SI 2007/236, Sch 6 para 7(2)(b)); and

(3)   the Political Parties, Elections and Referendums Act 2000 s 56(4) has effect as if the reference to the treasurer of the party were construed as a reference to the candidate or (as the case may be) his election agent (Representation of the People Act 1983 Sch 2A

para 7(2)(c) (as so added); European Parliamentary Elections Regulations 2004, SI 2004/293, Sch 6 para 7(2)(c); National Assembly for Wales (Representation of the People) Order 2007, SI 2007/236, Sch 6 para 7(2)(c)).
As to the treasurer of a registered party see PARA 253.

290. Transfer to election agent of donations received by candidate at an election. For the purposes of controlling donations[1] to candidates[2] at an election[3], a candidate must, on receipt of any relevant donation[4] received by him after the deadline for appointing an election agent[5] (unless the candidate is, or is deemed to be, his own election agent at the time of receipt of the donation)[6], forthwith deliver to his election agent[7]:

(1)   the donation[8];
(2)   where the donation falls within the provisions that apply to the making of donations through other persons or through agents[9], the information that must be provided to the candidate by the principal donor or agent[10]; and
(3)   any other information which the candidate has about the donation and its donor which might reasonably be expected to assist the election agent in the discharge of any duties imposed on him, in relation to the donation, either by virtue of the statutory controls imposed on such donations to candidates at an election[11] or under the provisions which require the reporting of such donations[12].

Where a donation is delivered to an election agent in this way, the donation is treated for the purposes of the statutory controls imposed on donations from impermissible donors[13], and the provisions which regulate the acceptance or return of donations made to candidates at an election[14], as if it had been originally received by the election agent[15], and as if it had been so received by him on the date on which it was received by the candidate[16].

For these purposes, where a candidate receives a relevant donation before the deadline for appointing an election agent but at a time when an appointment of a person (other than the candidate himself) as election agent is in force[17], he must either:

(a)   forthwith deliver the donation and the information mentioned in heads (2) and (3) above to the agent[18]; or
(b)   if he fails to do so, deal with the donation in accordance with the provisions which regulate the acceptance or return of donations made to candidates at an election[19].

Where a donation is delivered to an election agent in accordance with head (a) above, the donation is treated for the purposes of the statutory controls imposed on donations from impermissible donors[20], and the provisions which regulate the acceptance or return of donations made to candidates at an election[21], as if it had been originally received by the election agent[22], and as if it had been so received by him on the date on which it was received by the candidate[23].

For these purposes, where:

(i)   a relevant donation received by a candidate before the deadline for appointing an election agent has been dealt with by the candidate in accordance with the provisions which regulate the acceptance or return of donations made to candidates at an election[24], either because it was received by him at a time when no appointment of another person as his election agent was in force[25] or because, although such an appointment was in force, he was by virtue of head (b) above required to deal with the donation[26]; and

(ii)   an appointment of a person (other than the candidate himself) as election agent is in force at, or at any time after[27], the deadline for appointing an election agent[28] or, if later, the time when the candidate has dealt with the donation in accordance with the provisions which regulate the acceptance or return of donations made to candidates at an election[29],

the candidate must, as soon as reasonably practicable after the relevant time[30], deliver to the election agent[31]: (A) the donation (if it has been accepted by him)[32]; and (B) any information which he has about the donation and the donor which might reasonably be expected to assist the election agent in the discharge of any duties imposed on him, in relation to the donation, under the provisions which require the reporting of such donations[33].

1   As to the meaning of 'donation' in relation to candidates at an election see PARA 287.
2   As to the meaning of 'candidate' generally see PARA 230.

    At a European parliamentary election, the reference is an 'individual candidate': see the European Parliamentary Elections Regulations 2004, SI 2004/293, reg 42(4), Sch 6 para 1(1), (3). As to the meaning of 'individual candidate' at a European parliamentary election see PARA 230 note 32. As to European parliamentary elections see PARA 217 et seq.

    In the case of a Welsh Assembly election, the reference is to a constituency candidate at a Welsh Assembly constituency election or to an individual candidate at a Welsh Assembly regional election: see the National Assembly for Wales (Representation of the People) Order 2007, SI 2007/236, art 41(4), Sch 6 para 1(1). As to the meanings of 'Assembly election', 'constituency election' and 'regional election' for the purposes of Welsh Assembly elections see PARA 3 note 2. As to the meanings of 'constituency candidate' at a Welsh Assembly constituency election and 'individual candidate' at a Welsh Assembly regional election see PARA 230 note 19.

3   Representation of the People Act 1983 s 71A(4), Sch 2A para 1(1), (2) (s 71A, Sch 2A added by the Political Parties, Elections and Referendums Act 2000 s 130(1)–(4)); European Parliamentary Elections Regulations 2004, SI 2004/293, Sch 6 para 1(1), (2); National Assembly for Wales (Representation of the People) Order 2007, SI 2007/236, Sch 6 para 1(1).

    The election referred to in the text may be any of a parliamentary election, an Authority election, an election under the local government Act (see the Representation of the People Act 1983 s 202(1); and PARA 3 note 1), a Welsh Assembly constituency or regional election or a European parliamentary election. As to the meaning of 'parliamentary election' see PARA 9; as to the meaning of 'Authority election' see PARA 11; and as to the meaning of 'election under the local government Act' see PARA 11 note 2. However, the Representation of the People Act 1983 s 71A does not apply at an election under the local government Act which is not a local government election (see the Representation of the People Act 1983 s 90(2); and PARA 297); and, in relation to an election of parish councillors in England or of community councillors in Wales, the provisions of s 90(1), Sch 4 apply instead (see s 90(1)(b); and PARAS 293–296). As to the meaning of 'local government election' see PARA 11. As to elections in the City of London see PARA 33.

4   As to the meaning of 'relevant donation' in relation to candidates' election expenses see PARA 287 note 10.

5   For these purposes, any reference to the deadline for appointing an election agent is a reference to the latest time by which, in accordance with the Representation of the People Act 1983 s 67(1) or s 67(1A) (see PARA 231), or the European Parliamentary Elections Regulations 2004, SI 2004/293, reg 38(1) (appointment of election agent for individual candidate: see PARA 239), or the National Assembly for Wales (Representation of the People) Order 2007, SI 2007/236, art 37 (see PARA 235) (whichever is appropriate), an election agent may be named as election agent by the candidate: Representation of the People Act 1983 Sch 2A para 8(10)(a)(i) (as added: see note 3); European Parliamentary Elections Regulations 2004, SI 2004/293, Sch 6 para 8(10)(a); National Assembly for Wales (Representation of the People) Order 2007, SI 2007/236, art 39(4), Sch 6 para 8(10)(a). However, in the case of a candidate on a list of candidates submitted by a registered political party to be London members of the London Assembly at an ordinary election), the reference is a reference to the latest time by which an election agent may be so named as election agent by the party: Representation of the People Act 1983 Sch 2A para 8(10)(a)(ii) (as so added). As to ordinary elections of London members of the London Assembly see PARA 199 et seq.

6   Representation of the People Act 1983 Sch 2A para 8(1) (as added: see note 3); European Parliamentary Elections Regulations 2004, SI 2004/293, Sch 6 para 8(1); National Assembly for Wales (Representation of the People) Order 2007, SI 2007/236, Sch 6 para 8(1).

7   Representation of the People Act 1983 Sch 2A para 8(2) (as added: see note 3); European Parliamentary Elections Regulations 2004, SI 2004/293, Sch 6 para 8(2); National Assembly for Wales (Representation of the People) Order 2007, SI 2007/236, Sch 6 para 8(2).

8   Representation of the People Act 1983 Sch 2A para 8(2)(a) (as added: see note 3); European Parliamentary Elections Regulations 2004, SI 2004/293, Sch 6 para 8(2)(a); National Assembly for Wales (Representation of the People) Order 2007, SI 2007/236, Sch 6 para 8(2)(a).

9   Ie the Representation of the People Act 1983 Sch 2A para 6(5), (6) or the European Parliamentary Elections Regulations 2004, SI 2004/293, Sch 6 para 6(5), (6), or the National Assembly for Wales (Representation of the People) Order 2007, SI 2007/236, Sch 6 para 6(5), (6) (see PARA 288).

10   Representation of the People Act 1983 Sch 2A para 8(2)(b) (as added: see note 3); European Parliamentary Elections Regulations 2004, SI 2004/293, Sch 6 para 8(2)(b); National Assembly for Wales (Representation of the People) Order 2007, SI 2007/236, Sch 6 para 8(2)(b).

11   Ie under the Representation of the People Act 1983 Sch 2A Pt II paras 6–9, or the European Parliamentary Elections Regulations 2004, SI 2004/293, Sch 6 Pt 2 paras 6–9, or the National Assembly for Wales (Representation of the People) Order 2007, SI 2007/236, Sch 6 Pt II paras 6–9 (whichever is appropriate).

12   Representation of the People Act 1983 Sch 2A para 8(2)(c) (as added: see note 3); European Parliamentary Elections Regulations 2004, SI 2004/293, Sch 6 para 8(2)(c); National Assembly for Wales (Representation of the People) Order 2007, SI 2007/236, Sch 6 para 8(2)(c). The text refers to reporting duties imposed under the Representation of the People Act 1983 Sch 2A Pt III paras 10–12, or the European Parliamentary Elections Regulations 2004, SI 2004/293, Sch 6 Pt 3 paras 10–12, or the National Assembly for Wales (Representation of the People) Order 2007, SI 2007/236, Sch 6 Pt III paras 10–12 (whichever is appropriate) (see PARA 292).

13   Ie for the purposes of the Representation of the People Act 1983 Sch 2A para 6(1)–(4), the European Parliamentary Elections Regulations 2004, SI 2004/293, Sch 6 para 6(1)–(4), and the National Assembly for Wales (Representation of the People) Order 2007, SI 2007/236, Sch 6 para 6(1)–(4) (whichever is appropriate) (see PARA 288).

14   Ie for the purposes of the Political Parties, Elections and Referendums Act 2000 ss 56–60, as applied by the Representation of the People Act 1983 Sch 2A para 7, the European Parliamentary Elections Regulations 2004, SI 2004/293, Sch 6 para 7, and the National Assembly for Wales (Representation of the People) Order 2007, SI 2007/236, Sch 6 para 7 (whichever is appropriate) (see PARA 289).

15   Representation of the People Act 1983 Sch 2A para 8(3)(a) (as added: see note 3); European Parliamentary Elections Regulations 2004, SI 2004/293, Sch 6 para 8(3)(a); National Assembly for Wales (Representation of the People) Order 2007, SI 2007/236, Sch 6 para 8(3)(a).

16   Representation of the People Act 1983 Sch 2A para 8(3)(b) (as added: see note 3); European Parliamentary Elections Regulations 2004, SI 2004/293, Sch 6 para 8(3)(b); National Assembly for Wales (Representation of the People) Order 2007, SI 2007/236, Sch 6 para 8(3)(b).

17   Representation of the People Act 1983 Sch 2A para 8(4) (as added: see note 3); European Parliamentary Elections Regulations 2004, SI 2004/293, Sch 6 para 8(4); National Assembly for Wales (Representation of the People) Order 2007, SI 2007/236, Sch 6 para 8(4).

18   Representation of the People Act 1983 Sch 2A para 8(4)(a) (as added: see note 3); European Parliamentary Elections Regulations 2004, SI 2004/293, Sch 6 para 8(4)(a); National Assembly for Wales (Representation of the People) Order 2007, SI 2007/236, Sch 6 para 8(4)(a).

19   Representation of the People Act 1983 Sch 2A para 8(4)(b) (as added: see note 3); European Parliamentary Elections Regulations 2004, SI 2004/293, Sch 6 para 8(4)(b); National Assembly for Wales (Representation of the People) Order 2007, SI 2007/236, Sch 6 para 8(4)(b). The text refers to dealing with the donation in accordance with the Political Parties, Elections and Referendums Act 2000 s 56, as it is applied by the Representation of the People Act 1983 Sch 2A para 7, the European Parliamentary Elections Regulations 2004, SI 2004/293, Sch 6 para 7, and the National Assembly for Wales (Representation of the People) Order 2007, SI 2007/236, Sch 6 para 7 (whichever is appropriate), for the purposes of controlling donations to candidates at an election in relation to a relevant donation received by a candidate or his election agent and to the candidate or (as the case may be) the election agent (see PARA 289): Representation of the People Act 1983 Sch 2A para 8(10)(b) (as so added); European Parliamentary Elections Regulations 2004, SI 2004/293, Sch 6 para 8(10)(b); National Assembly for Wales (Representation of the People) Order 2007, SI 2007/236, Sch 6 para 8(10)(b).

20   See note 13.

21   See note 14.

22 Representation of the People Act 1983 Sch 2A para 8(3)(a) (as added: see note 3) (applied by Sch 2A para 8(5) (as so added)); European Parliamentary Elections Regulations 2004, SI 2004/293, Sch 6 para 8(3)(a) (applied by Sch 6 para 8(5)); National Assembly for Wales (Representation of the People) Order 2007, SI 2007/236, Sch 6 para 8(3)(a) (applied by Sch 6 para 8(5)).

23 Representation of the People Act 1983 Sch 2A para 8(3)(b) (as added: see note 3) (applied by Sch 2A para 8(5) (as so added)); European Parliamentary Elections Regulations 2004, SI 2004/293, Sch 6 para 8(3)(b) (applied by Sch 6 para 8(5)); National Assembly for Wales (Representation of the People) Order 2007, SI 2007/236, Sch 6 para 8(3)(b) (applied by Sch 6 para 8(5)).

24 Representation of the People Act 1983 Sch 2A paras 8(6)(a) (as added: see note 3); European Parliamentary Elections Regulations 2004, SI 2004/293, Sch 6 paras 8(6)(a); National Assembly for Wales (Representation of the People) Order 2007, SI 2007/236, Sch 6 paras 8(6)(a). As to the provisions which regulate the acceptance or return of donations made to candidates at an election see note 19.

25 Representation of the People Act 1983 Sch 2A para 8(6)(a)(i) (as added: see note 3); European Parliamentary Elections Regulations 2004, SI 2004/293, Sch 6 para 8(6)(a)(i); National Assembly for Wales (Representation of the People) Order 2007, SI 2007/236, Sch 6 para 8(6)(a)(i).

26 Representation of the People Act 1983 Sch 2A para 8(6)(a)(ii) (as added: see note 3); European Parliamentary Elections Regulations 2004, SI 2004/293, Sch 6 para 8(6)(a)(ii); National Assembly for Wales (Representation of the People) Order 2007, SI 2007/236, Sch 6 para 8(6)(a)(ii).

27 Representation of the People Act 1983 Sch 2A para 8(6)(b) (as added: see note 3); European Parliamentary Elections Regulations 2004, SI 2004/293, Sch 6 para 8(6)(b); National Assembly for Wales (Representation of the People) Order 2007, SI 2007/236, Sch 6 para 8(6)(b).

28 Representation of the People Act 1983 Sch 2A para 8(6)(b)(i) (as added: see note 3); European Parliamentary Elections Regulations 2004, SI 2004/293, Sch 6 para 8(6)(b)(i); National Assembly for Wales (Representation of the People) Order 2007, SI 2007/236, Sch 6 para 8(6)(b)(i).

29 Representation of the People Act 1983 Sch 2A paras 8(6)(b)(ii) (as added: see note 3); European Parliamentary Elections Regulations 2004, SI 2004/293, Sch 6 paras 8(6)(b)(ii); National Assembly for Wales (Representation of the People) Order 2007, SI 2007/236, Sch 6 paras 8(6)(b)(ii). As to the provisions which regulate the acceptance or return of donations made to candidates at an election see note 19.

30 For these purposes, the 'relevant time' is the time mentioned in either the Representation of the People Act 1983 Sch 2A para 8(6)(b)(i) (see the text and note 28) or Sch 2A para 8(6)(b)(ii) (see the text and note 29), or the European Parliamentary Elections Regulations 2004, SI 2004/293, Sch 6 para 8(6)(b)(i) (see the text and note 28) or Sch 6 para 8(6)(b)(ii) (see the text and note 29), or the National Assembly for Wales (Representation of the People) Order 2007, SI 2007/236, Sch 6 para 8(6)(b)(i) (see the text and note 28) or Sch 6 para 8(6)(b)(ii) (see the text and note 29) (whichever is appropriate) if the appointment of another person as election agent is in force at that time or, otherwise, the time when any such appointment subsequently comes into force: Representation of the People Act 1983 Sch 2A para 8(8) (as added: see note 3); European Parliamentary Elections Regulations 2004, SI 2004/293, Sch 6 para 8(8); National Assembly for Wales (Representation of the People) Order 2007, SI 2007/236, Sch 6 para 8(8).

31 Representation of the People Act 1983 Sch 2A para 8(7) (as added: see note 3); European Parliamentary Elections Regulations 2004, SI 2004/293, Sch 6 para 8(7); National Assembly for Wales (Representation of the People) Order 2007, SI 2007/236, Sch 6 para 8(7).

32 Representation of the People Act 1983 Sch 2A para 8(7)(a) (as added: see note 3); European Parliamentary Elections Regulations 2004, SI 2004/293, Sch 6 para 8(7)(a); National Assembly for Wales (Representation of the People) Order 2007, SI 2007/236, Sch 6 para 8(7)(a). However, the duty imposed on a candidate by head (A) in the text does not apply to any relevant donation to the extent to which it has been lawfully used by the candidate for the purpose of paying election expenses: Representation of the People Act 1983 Sch 2A para 8(9) (as added: see note 3); European Parliamentary Elections Regulations 2004, SI 2004/293, Sch 6 para 8(9); National Assembly for Wales (Representation of the People) Order 2007, SI 2007/236, Sch 6 para 8(9). As to the meaning of 'election expenses' see PARA 269.

33 Representation of the People Act 1983 Sch 2A para 8(7)(b) (as added: see note 3); European Parliamentary Elections Regulations 2004, SI 2004/293, Sch 6 para 8(7)(b); National Assembly for Wales (Representation of the People) Order 2007, SI 2007/236, Sch 6 para 8(7)(b). The text refers to reporting duties imposed under the Representation of the People Act 1983 Sch 2A Pt III paras 10–12, or the European Parliamentary Elections Regulations 2004, SI 2004/293, Sch 6

Pt 3 paras 10–12, or the National Assembly for Wales (Representation of the People) Order 2007, SI 2007/236, Sch 6 Pt III paras 10–12 (whichever is appropriate) (see PARA 292).

291. Evasion of restrictions on donations to candidate at an election. The provisions of the Political Parties, Elections and Referendums Act 2000 which create offences concerned with the evasion of restrictions on donations to a registered party[1] apply for the purposes of controlling donations to candidates at an election[2], subject to minor modification[3].

1   Ie the Political Parties, Elections and Referendums Act 2000 s 61 (see CONSTITUTIONAL LAW AND HUMAN RIGHTS): see the Representation of the People Act 1983 Sch 2A para 9; the European Parliamentary Elections Regulations 2004, SI 2004/293, Sch 6 para 9; the National Assembly for Wales (Representation of the People) Order 2007, SI 2007/236, Sch 6 para 9; and PARA 752.
2   Ie for the purposes of, in the case of a parliamentary or local government election, the Representation of the People Act 1983 s 71A(4), Sch 2A, or, in the case of a European parliamentary election, the European Parliamentary Elections Regulations 2004, SI 2004/293, reg 42(4), Sch 6, or, in the case of a Welsh Assembly election, the National Assembly for Wales (Representation of the People) Order 2007, SI 2007/236, art 41(4), Sch 6 (whichever is appropriate) (see PARA 287 et seq): see the Representation of the People Act 1983 Sch 2A para 9; the European Parliamentary Elections Regulations 2004, SI 2004/293, Sch 6 para 9; the National Assembly for Wales (Representation of the People) Order 2007, SI 2007/236, Sch 6 para 9; and PARA 752.
3   See the Representation of the People Act 1983 Sch 2A para 9; the European Parliamentary Elections Regulations 2004, SI 2004/293, Sch 6 para 9; the National Assembly for Wales (Representation of the People) Order 2007, SI 2007/236, Sch 6 para 9; and PARA 752.

292. Statement of relevant donations received by candidate at an election. For the purposes of controlling donations[1] to candidates[2] at an election[3], the candidate's election agent[4] must include, in any return required to be delivered in relation to his election expenses[5], a statement of relevant donations[6] which complies with the requirement to report any donations received from both permissible and impermissible donors[7]. Accordingly, in relation to each relevant donation accepted by the candidate or his election agent, the statement must record[8]:

(1)   the amount of the donation (if a donation of money, in cash or otherwise) or the nature of the donation and its value (in any other case)[9];

(2)   the date when the donation was accepted by the candidate or his election agent[10];

(3)   the information about the donor which is, in connection with recordable donations to registered parties[11], required to be recorded in donation reports[12]; and

(4)   such other information as may be required by regulations made by the Electoral Commission[13].

Where a relevant donation has been received from a person who is not a permissible donor (an 'impermissible donor')[14], the statement must record:

(a)   the name and address of the donor[15];

(b)   the amount of the donation (if a donation of money, in cash or otherwise) or (in any other case) the nature of the donation and its value[16];

(c)   the date when the donation was received, and the date when, and the manner in which, it was dealt with in accordance with the provisions which regulate the handling of relevant donations made by impermissible donors[17];

(d)   such other information as is required by regulations made by the Commission[18].

Where a relevant donation has been received from a person whose identity cannot be ascertained[19], the statement must record:

(i)   details of the manner in which the donation was made[20];

(ii)   the amount of the donation (if a donation of money, in cash or otherwise) or the nature of the donation and its value (in any other case)[21];

(iii)   the date when the donation was received, and the date when and the manner in which it was dealt with in accordance with the provisions which regulate the handling of relevant donations made by persons whose identity cannot be ascertained[22]; and

(iv)   such other information as is required by regulations made by the Commission[23].

1   As to the meaning of 'donation' in relation to candidates at an election see PARA 287.

2   As to the meaning of 'candidate' generally see PARA 230.
    At a European parliamentary election, the reference is an 'individual candidate': see the European Parliamentary Elections Regulations 2004, SI 2004/293, reg 42(4), Sch 6 para 1(1), (3). As to the meaning of 'individual candidate' at a European parliamentary election see PARA 230 note 32. As to European parliamentary elections see PARA 217 et seq.
    In the case of a Welsh Assembly election, the reference is to a constituency candidate at a Welsh Assembly constituency election or to an individual candidate at a Welsh Assembly regional election: see the National Assembly for Wales (Representation of the People) Order 2007, SI 2007/236, art 41(4), Sch 6 para 1(1). As to the meanings of 'Assembly election', 'constituency election' and 'regional election' for the purposes of Welsh Assembly elections see PARA 3 note 2. As to the meanings of 'constituency candidate' at a Welsh Assembly constituency election and 'individual candidate' at a Welsh Assembly regional election see PARA 230 note 19.

3   Representation of the People Act 1983 s 71A(4), Sch 2A para 1(1), (2) (s 71A, Sch 2A added by the Political Parties, Elections and Referendums Act 2000 s 130(1)–(4)); European Parliamentary Elections Regulations 2004, SI 2004/293, Sch 6 para 1(1), (2); National Assembly for Wales (Representation of the People) Order 2007, SI 2007/236, Sch 6 para 1(1).
    The election referred to in the text may be any of a parliamentary election, an Authority election, an election under the local government Act (see the Representation of the People Act 1983 s 202(1); and PARA 3 note 1), a Welsh Assembly constituency or regional election or a European parliamentary election. As to the meaning of 'parliamentary election' see PARA 9; As to the meaning of 'Authority election' see PARA 11; and as to the meaning of 'election under the local government Act' see PARA 11 note 2. However, the Representation of the People Act 1983 s 71A does not apply at an election under the local government Act which is not a local government election (see the Representation of the People Act 1983 s 90(2); and PARA 297); and, in relation to an election of parish councillors in England or of community councillors in Wales, the provisions of s 90(1), Sch 4 apply instead (see s 90(1)(b); and PARAS 293–296). As to the meaning of 'local government election' see PARA 11. As to elections in the City of London see PARA 33.

4   As to the appointment of an election agent see PARA 231 et seq.

5   Ie any return required to be delivered under the Representation of the People Act 1983 s 81, or the European Parliamentary Elections Regulations 2004, SI 2004/293, reg 51, or the National Assembly for Wales (Representation of the People) Order 2007, SI 2007/236, art 52 (whichever is appropriate) (see PARA 280).

6   As to the meaning of 'relevant donation' in relation to candidates' election expenses see PARA 287 note 10.

7   Representation of the People Act 1983 Sch 2A para 10(1) (Sch 2A as added (see note 3); Sch 2A para 10(1) numbered as such, Sch 2A para 10(2), (3) added, by the Electoral Administration Act 2006 s 10(2), Sch 1 paras 2, 16); European Parliamentary Elections Regulations 2004, SI 2004/293, Sch 6 para 10(1) (Sch 6 para 10(1) numbered as such, Sch 6 para 10(2) added, by SI 2009/186); National Assembly for Wales (Representation of the People) Order 2007, SI 2007/236, Sch 6 para 10(1). The text refers to the requirement for a statement of relevant donations to comply with the Representation of the People Act 1983 Sch 2A paras 11–12, the European Parliamentary Elections Regulations 2004, SI 2004/293, Sch 6 paras 11–12, and the National Assembly for Wales (Representation of the People) Order 2007, SI 2007/236, Sch 6

paras 11–12 (whichever apply) (see the text and notes 8–23). As to the meaning of 'permissible donor' for these purposes see PARA 288. As to the meaning of 'impermissible donor' for these purposes see the text and notes 14–18.

In relation to a parliamentary election, Authority election or election under the local government Act, if the statement of relevant donations states that the candidate's election agent has seen evidence, of such description as is prescribed by the Secretary of State in regulations, that an individual donor has an anonymous entry in an electoral register, the statement must be accompanied by a copy of the evidence: see the Representation of the People Act 1983 Sch 2A para 10(2), (3) (as so added). The evidence prescribed for these purposes is a certificate of anonymous registration: Representation of the People (England and Wales) Regulations 2001, SI 2001/341, reg 45H (added by SI 2006/2910). In relation to a European parliamentary election, if the statement of relevant donations states that the candidate's election agent has seen a certificate of anonymous registration issued pursuant to the Representation of the People (England and Wales) Regulations 2001, SI 2001/341, reg 45G (see PARA 145 note 12), or the equivalent provisions forming part of the law of Gibraltar, which is evidence that an individual donor has an anonymous entry in an electoral register, the statement must be accompanied by a copy of that certificate: European Parliamentary Elections Regulations 2004, SI 2004/293, Sch 6 para 10(2) (as so added). In relation to a Welsh Assembly election, if the statement of relevant donations states that the candidate's election agent has seen a certificate of anonymous registration issued pursuant to the Representation of the People (England and Wales) Regulations 2001, SI 2001/341, reg 45G, the statement must be accompanied by a copy of that certificate: see the National Assembly for Wales (Representation of the People) Order 2007, SI 2007/236, Sch 6 para 10(2), (3). As to the meaning of 'certificate of anonymous registration' see PARA 145 note 12; and as to the meaning of 'anonymous entry' in relation to a register of electors see PARA 148. As to the Secretary of State see PARA 2. As to the making of regulations under the Representation of the People Act 1983 generally see PARA 28 note 16.

8   Representation of the People Act 1983 Sch 2A para 11 (as added: see note 3); European Parliamentary Elections Regulations 2004, SI 2004/293, Sch 6 para 11; National Assembly for Wales (Representation of the People) Order 2007, SI 2007/236, Sch 6 para 11.

9   Representation of the People Act 1983 Sch 2A para 11(a) (as added: see note 3); European Parliamentary Elections Regulations 2004, SI 2004/293, Sch 6 para 11(a); National Assembly for Wales (Representation of the People) Order 2007, SI 2007/236, Sch 6 para 11(a). The value of the donation is determined in accordance with, in relation to a parliamentary or local government election, the Representation of the People Act 1983 Sch 2A para 5, or, in relation to a European parliamentary election, the European Parliamentary Elections Regulations 2004, SI 2004/293, Sch 6 para 5, or, in relation to a Welsh Assembly election, the National Assembly for Wales (Representation of the People) Order 2007, SI 2007/236, Sch 6 para 5 (see PARA 287 notes 6–7, 11).

10   Representation of the People Act 1983 Sch 2A para 11(b) (as added: see note 3); European Parliamentary Elections Regulations 2004, SI 2004/293, Sch 6 para 11(b); National Assembly for Wales (Representation of the People) Order 2007, SI 2007/236, Sch 6 para 11(b). As to the acceptance of donations made to a candidate at an election see PARA 289.

11   As to the meaning of 'registered political party', in relation to parliamentary and local government elections, see PARA 231 note 7; and, in relation to Welsh Assembly elections, see PARA 215 note 19. As to the meaning of 'registered party' in relation to European parliamentary elections see PARA 230 note 29.

12   Representation of the People Act 1983 Sch 2A para 11(c) (as added: see note 3); European Parliamentary Elections Regulations 2004, SI 2004/293, Sch 6 para 11(c); National Assembly for Wales (Representation of the People) Order 2007, SI 2007/236, Sch 6 para 11(c). The text refers to information about the donor which is required to be recorded in donation reports by virtue of the Political Parties, Elections and Referendums Act 2000 ss 62, 63, Sch 6 para 2 (identity of donors (quarterly reports): see CONSTITUTIONAL LAW AND HUMAN RIGHTS).

13   Representation of the People Act 1983 Sch 2A para 11(d) (as added: see note 3); European Parliamentary Elections Regulations 2004, SI 2004/293, Sch 6 para 11(d); National Assembly for Wales (Representation of the People) Order 2007, SI 2007/236, Sch 6 para 11(d). Regulations made by the Electoral Commission are not statutory instruments and are not recorded in this work: see further PARA 47. As to the Electoral Commission see PARA 34 et seq.

14   Representation of the People Act 1983 Sch 2A para 12(1), (2) (as added: see note 3); European Parliamentary Elections Regulations 2004, SI 2004/293, Sch 6 para 12(1), (2); National Assembly for Wales (Representation of the People) Order 2007, SI 2007/236, Sch 6 para 12(1), (2). The text refers to the circumstance where the Representation of the People Act 1983 Sch 2A para 6(1)(a), or the European Parliamentary Elections Regulations 2004, SI 2004/293, Sch 6 para 6(1)(a), or the National Assembly for Wales (Representation of the

People) Order 2007, SI 2007/236, Sch 6 para 6(1)(a) applies (see PARA 288): Representation of the People Act 1983 Sch 2A para 12(1), (2) (as so added); European Parliamentary Elections Regulations 2004, SI 2004/293, Sch 6 para 12(1), (2); National Assembly for Wales (Representation of the People) Order 2007, SI 2007/236, Sch 6 para 12(1), (2).

15 Representation of the People Act 1983 Sch 2A para 12(2)(a) (as added: see note 3); European Parliamentary Elections Regulations 2004, SI 2004/293, Sch 6 para 12(2)(a); National Assembly for Wales (Representation of the People) Order 2007, SI 2007/236, Sch 6 para 12(2)(a).

16 Representation of the People Act 1983 Sch 2A para 12(2)(b) (as added: see note 3); European Parliamentary Elections Regulations 2004, SI 2004/293, Sch 6 para 12(2)(b); National Assembly for Wales (Representation of the People) Order 2007, SI 2007/236, Sch 6 para 12(2)(b). As to the ascertainment of value for these purposes see note 9.

17 Representation of the People Act 1983 Sch 2A para 12(2)(c) (as added: see note 3); European Parliamentary Elections Regulations 2004, SI 2004/293, Sch 6 para 12(2)(c); National Assembly for Wales (Representation of the People) Order 2007, SI 2007/236, Sch 6 para 12(2)(c). The text refers to dealing with the donation in accordance with the Political Parties, Elections and Referendums Act 2000 s 56(2)(a), as it is applied by the Representation of the People Act 1983 Sch 2A para 7, the European Parliamentary Elections Regulations 2004, SI 2004/293, Sch 6 para 7, and the National Assembly for Wales (Representation of the People) Order 2007, SI 2007/236, Sch 6 para 7 (whichever is appropriate), for the purposes of controlling donations to candidates at an election in relation to a relevant donation received by a candidate or his election agent and to the candidate or (as the case may be) the election agent (see PARA 289): Representation of the People Act 1983 Sch 2A para 12(4) (as so added); European Parliamentary Elections Regulations 2004, SI 2004/293, Sch 6 para 12(4); National Assembly for Wales (Representation of the People) Order 2007, SI 2007/236, Sch 6 para 12(4).

18 Representation of the People Act 1983 Sch 2A para 12(2)(d) (as added: see note 3); European Parliamentary Elections Regulations 2004, SI 2004/293, Sch 6 para 12(2)(d); National Assembly for Wales (Representation of the People) Order 2007, SI 2007/236, Sch 6 para 12(2)(d). As to regulations made by the Electoral Commission see note 13.

19 Representation of the People Act 1983 Sch 2A para 12(1), (3) (as added: see note 3); European Parliamentary Elections Regulations 2004, SI 2004/293, Sch 6 para 12(1), (3); National Assembly for Wales (Representation of the People) Order 2007, SI 2007/236, Sch 6 para 12(1), (3). The text refers to the circumstance where the Representation of the People Act 1983 Sch 2A para 6(1)(b), or the European Parliamentary Elections Regulations 2004, SI 2004/293, Sch 6 para 6(1)(b), or the National Assembly for Wales (Representation of the People) Order 2007, SI 2007/236, Sch 6 para 6(1)(b) applies (see PARA 288); Representation of the People Act 1983 Sch 2A para 12(1), (3) (as so added); European Parliamentary Elections Regulations 2004, SI 2004/293, Sch 6 para 12(1), (3); National Assembly for Wales (Representation of the People) Order 2007, SI 2007/236, Sch 6 para 12(1), (3).

20 Representation of the People Act 1983 Sch 2A para 12(3)(a) (as added: see note 3); European Parliamentary Elections Regulations 2004, SI 2004/293, Sch 6 para 12(3)(a); National Assembly for Wales (Representation of the People) Order 2007, SI 2007/236, Sch 6 para 12(3)(a).

21 Representation of the People Act 1983 Sch 2A para 12(3)(b) (as added: see note 3); European Parliamentary Elections Regulations 2004, SI 2004/293, Sch 6 para 12(3)(b); National Assembly for Wales (Representation of the People) Order 2007, SI 2007/236, Sch 6 para 12(3)(b). As to the ascertainment of value for these purposes see note 9.

22 Representation of the People Act 1983 Sch 2A para 12(3)(c) (as added: see note 3); European Parliamentary Elections Regulations 2004, SI 2004/293, Sch 6 para 12(3)(c); National Assembly for Wales (Representation of the People) Order 2007, SI 2007/236, Sch 6 para 12(3)(c). The text refers to dealing with the donation in accordance with the Political Parties, Elections and Referendums Act 2000 s 56(2)(b), as it is applied by the Representation of the People Act 1983 Sch 2A para 7, the European Parliamentary Elections Regulations 2004, SI 2004/293, Sch 6 para 7, and the National Assembly for Wales (Representation of the People) Order 2007, SI 2007/236, Sch 6 para 7 (whichever is appropriate), for the purposes of controlling donations to candidates at an election in relation to a relevant donation received by a candidate or his election agent and to the candidate or (as the case may be) the election agent (see PARA 289): Representation of the People Act 1983 Sch 2A para 12(4) (as so added); European Parliamentary Elections Regulations 2004, SI 2004/293, Sch 6 para 12(4); National Assembly for Wales (Representation of the People) Order 2007, SI 2007/236, Sch 6 para 12(4).

23 Representation of the People Act 1983 Sch 2A para 12(3)(d) (as added: see note 3); European Parliamentary Elections Regulations 2004, SI 2004/293, Sch 6 para 12(3)(d); National Assembly for Wales (Representation of the People) Order 2007, SI 2007/236, Sch 6 para 12(3)(d). As to regulations made by the Electoral Commission see note 13.

(iv) Financial Controls on Individual Candidates at Elections where Election Agent is Not Required

A. ELECTION OF PARISH COUNCILLORS IN ENGLAND OR OF COMMUNITY COUNCILLORS IN WALES

293. Election expenses at an election of parish or community councillors. In relation to an election of parish councillors in England[1] or of community councillors in Wales[2], at which an election agent is not required[3], the statutory provisions relating to election expenses[4] generally do not apply[5], except that the provisions limiting the amount of election expenses[6], and the definition of 'election expenses'[7], are applied with slight modifications[8].

1   As to the election of parish councillors see PARA 200 et seq. As to the meaning of 'England' see PARA 1 note 1.
2   As to the election of community councillors see PARA 200 et seq. As to the meaning of 'Wales' see PARA 1 note 1.
3   As to elections at which an election agent is not required see PARA 231 note 3.
4   Ie the Representation of the People Act 1983 ss 71A–75, 78–89, Sch 2A (see PARA 269 et seq): see s 90(1)(b) (amended by the Political Parties, Elections and Referendums Act 2000 s 138(1), Sch 18 paras 1, 11(b)).
5   Representation of the People Act 1983 s 90(1)(b) (as amended: see note 4). As to the provisions which apply in lieu of the excluded provisions see PARA 294 et seq.
6   Ie the Representation of the People Act 1983 s 76 (limitation of election expenses: see PARA 273) and s 77 (limitation of election expenses for joint candidates at certain local government elections: see PARA 275): see s 90(1)(a) (amended by the Political Parties, Elections and Referendums Act 2000 s 138(1), Sch 18 paras 1, 11(a); and the Electoral Administration Act 2006 s 74(1), Sch 1 paras 104, 116). As to the application of s 76A for these purposes see PARA 295 note 10.
7   Ie the definition of 'election expenses' contained in the Representation of the People Act 1983 s 90ZA and s 90C (see PARA 269): see s 90(1)(a) (as amended: see note 6).
8   Representation of the People Act 1983 s 90(1)(a) (as amended: see note 6). As to the provisions as so modified see PARA 269 note 12.

294. Claims in respect of election expenses at an election of parish or community councillors. In relation to an election of parish councillors in England[1] or of community councillors in Wales[2], at which an election agent is not required[3], any claim against any person in respect of any election expenses[4] incurred by or on behalf of a candidate[5] which is not sent in[6] within 14 days after the day of election[7] is barred and must not be paid[8]; and all election expenses so incurred must be paid within 21 days after the day of election and not otherwise[9]. If any person makes a payment[10] in contravention of this restriction he is guilty of an illegal practice[11].

1   As to the election of parish councillors see PARA 200 et seq. As to the meaning of 'England' see PARA 1 note 1.
2   As to the election of community councillors see PARA 200 et seq. As to the meaning of 'Wales' see PARA 1 note 1.
3   As to elections at which an election agent is not required see PARA 231 note 3.
4   As to the meaning of 'election expenses' generally see PARA 269; and in relation to an election of parish or community councillors specifically see PARA 293.
5   As to the meaning of 'candidate' generally see PARA 230.
6   It is not clear whether the claim must be in the possession of the person within the 14 days or merely have been dispatched within that time. However, to the extent that 'send' is synonymous with 'transmit', the latter construction is the correct one: see *MacKinnon v Clark* [1898] 2 QB 251 at 257, CA, per A L Smith LJ.
7   As to the day of election referred to in the text see PARA 206 et seq; and as to the computation of time for these purposes see PARA 230 note 11.

8   Representation of the People Act 1983 s 90(1)(b), Sch 4 para 1(1) (s 90(1)(b) amended by the
     Political Parties, Elections and Referendums Act 2000 s 138(1), Sch 18 paras 1, 11(b)).
9   Representation of the People Act 1983 Sch 4 para 1(1).
10   As to the meaning of 'payment' for these purposes see PARA 270 note 1.
11   See the Representation of the People Act 1983 Sch 4 para 1(2); and PARA 675. A candidate is not
     liable nor is his election void for any such illegal practice as is mentioned in the text which is
     committed without his consent or connivance, however: see Sch 4 para 1(2); and PARA 675. As
     to the consequences of an illegal practice see PARA 888 et seq.

295.   Return and declaration as to election expenses.   At an election of parish
councillors in England[1] or of community councillors in Wales[2], at which an
election agent is not required[3], every agent of a candidate[4] at the election must,
within 23 days after the day of election[5], make a true return to the candidate in
writing of all election expenses[6] incurred by the agent, and if he fails to do so he
is liable on summary conviction to a fine[7].

Within 28 days after the day of election, every candidate must deliver to the
proper officer[8] of the authority for which the election is held, a return of all
election expenses incurred by the candidate or his agents vouched, except in the
case of sums under £10, by bills stating the particulars (or by receipts) and
accompanied by a declaration by the candidate[9] as to election expenses[10]. If,
subsequent to the delivery of the return, permission is given by the court for the
payment of a statute-barred claim, a return of any sum so paid must forthwith
after payment be sent to the proper officer of the authority[11].

1   As to the election of parish councillors see PARA 200 et seq. As to the meaning of 'England' see
     PARA 1 note 1.
2   As to the election of community councillors see PARA 200 et seq. As to the meaning of 'Wales'
     see PARA 1 note 1.
3   As to elections at which an election agent is not required see PARA 231 note 3.
4   As to the meaning of 'candidate' generally see PARA 230.
5   As to the day of election referred to in the text see PARA 206 et seq; and as to the computation
     of time for these purposes see PARA 230 note 11.
6   As to the meaning of 'election expenses' generally see PARA 269; and in relation to an election of
     parish or community councillors specifically see PARA 293.
7   Representation of the People Act 1983 s 90(1)(b), Sch 4 para 2 (s 90(1)(b) amended by the
     Political Parties, Elections and Referendums Act 2000 s 138(1), Sch 18 paras 1, 11(b)). The
     penalty is a fine not exceeding level 3 on the standard scale: see the Representation of the People
     Act 1983 Sch 4 para 2. As to the standard scale see SENTENCING AND DISPOSITION OF
     OFFENDERS vol 92 (2010) PARA 142. Because this offence is not an illegal practice, the relief that
     can be obtained in respect of illegal practices generally (see PARA 690) cannot be obtained in
     relation to this offence (but see Sch 4 para 7; and PARA 689).
8   As to the meaning of 'proper officer' see PARA 140 note 2.
9   The form of declaration as to election expenses for these purposes is that prescribed by rules
     under the Representation of the People Act 1983 s 36 (see PARA 383) relating to the election of
     parish or, as the case may be, community councillors, or a form to the like effect: see the
     Representation of the People Act 1983 s 90(1)(b) (as amended: see note 7). Accordingly, see the
     Local Elections (Parishes and Communities) (England and Wales) Rules 2006, SI 2006/3305,
     Sch 4 (Declaration as to expenses).
10   Representation of the People Act 1983 Sch 4 para 3 (amended by the Representation of the
     People Act 1985 ss 14(6), 24, Sch 4 para 89(a); and the Political Parties, Elections and
     Referendums Act 2000 s 138(1), Sch 18 paras 1, 17). The Secretary of State may by order made
     by statutory instrument vary the sum of £10 where in his opinion there has been a change in the
     value of money since the last occasion on which that sum was fixed and the variation is such as
     in his opinion is justified by that change: Representation of the People Act 1983 s 76A(1), (2)(e)
     (s 76A added by the Representation of the People Act 1985 s 14(4); and substituted by the
     Political Parties, Elections and Referendums Act 2000 s 133(1); Representation of the People
     Act 1983 s 76A(2)(e) added by the Political Parties and Elections Act 2009 s 39, Sch 6 para 6);
     Representation of the People Act 1983 s 90(1)(c) (substituted by the Political Parties, Elections
     and Referendums Act 2000 Sch 18 paras 1, 11(c)).
11   Representation of the People Act 1983 Sch 4 para 6.

296. Public inspection of returns and declarations. At an election of parish councillors in England[1] or of community councillors in Wales[2], at which an election agent is not required[3], the return and declaration required to be made by the candidate[4] as to election expenses[5] must be kept at the office of the proper officer of the authority[6], and must at all reasonable times during the 12 months next after they are received by him be open to inspection by any person on payment of the prescribed fee, and the proper officer must on demand provide copies of them, or of any part of them, at the prescribed price[7]. At the expiration of the 12 months, the proper officer may cause the return and declaration to be destroyed, or, if the candidate so requires, he may return them to him[8].

1   As to the election of parish councillors see PARA 200 et seq. As to the meaning of 'England' see PARA 1 note 1.

2   As to the election of community councillors see PARA 200 et seq. As to the meaning of 'Wales' see PARA 1 note 1.

3   As to elections at which an election agent is not required see PARA 231 note 3.

4   As to the meaning of 'candidate' generally see PARA 230.

5   As to the return and declaration required as mentioned in the text see PARA 295. As to the meaning of 'election expenses' generally see PARA 269; and in relation to an election of parish or community councillors specifically see PARA 293.

6   As to the meaning of 'proper officer' see PARA 140 note 2.

7   Representation of the People Act 1983 s 90(1)(b), Sch 4 para 8(1) (s 90(1)(b) amended by the Political Parties, Elections and Referendums Act 2000 s 138(1), Sch 18 paras 1, 11(b)). 'Prescribed' means prescribed by regulations: Representation of the People Act 1983 s 202(1). As to the regulations so made see the Representation of the People (England and Wales) Regulations 2001, SI 2001/341; and PARA 284 note 10. As to the making of regulations under the Representation of the People Act 1983 generally see PARA 28 note 16.

8   Representation of the People Act 1983 Sch 4 para 8(2).

B.   ELECTION UNDER THE LOCAL GOVERNMENT ACT WHICH IS NOT A LOCAL GOVERNMENT ELECTION

297. Disapplication of election expenses provisions. At an election under the Local Government Act 1972[1] which is not a local government election[2], the general statutory provisions relating to election expenses[3] have no application[4]. If a candidate at such an election, or if any person on his behalf knowingly pays any sum or incurs any expense, whether before, during or after that election, on account of or in respect of the conduct or management of the election, he is guilty of an illegal practice[5].

1   As to the meaning 'election under the local government Act' see PARA 11 note 2.
      In the application of the Representation of the People Act 1983 Pt II (ss 67–119) to a poll consequent on a parish or community meeting, 'election under the local government Act' is deemed to include a reference to a poll consequent on a parish meeting (as to which see PARA 200 et seq): see the Parish and Community Meetings (Polls) Rules 1987, SI 1987/1, r 6(g).

2   As to the meaning of 'local government election' see PARA 11.

3   Ie the Representation of the People Act 1983 ss 71A—89 (see PARA 269 et seq): see s 90(2) (amended by the Political Parties, Elections and Referendums Act 2000 s 138(1), Sch 18 paras 1, 11(d)).

4   Representation of the People Act 1983 s 90(2) (as amended: see note 3).

5   See the Representation of the People Act 1983 s 90(2); and PARA 678. As to the consequences of an illegal practice see PARA 888 et seq.

(v) Financial Controls on Registered Political Parties at National Election Campaigns

A. CONTINUOUS FINANCIAL CONTROLS ON REGISTERED PARTIES

298. General accounting requirements for registered parties. The treasurer of a registered party[1] must ensure that accounting records are kept with respect to the party which are sufficient to show and explain the party's transactions[2]. He must also prepare a statement of accounts in respect of each financial year of the party[3], and deliver that statement to the Electoral Commission[4], along with a copy of the auditor's report (where the requirement for a party's accounts to be audited by a qualified auditor applies to that party)[5]. If a registered party, without reasonable excuse, fails to submit a statement of accounts that does not comply with such requirements as to its form and contents as are prescribed[6], or fails to deliver any statement of accounts, notification or auditor's report before the end of the required period, the person who was the treasurer of the party for the relevant period is guilty of an offence[7].

1 As to the meaning of 'registered party' for these purposes see PARA 35 note 3. As to the treasurer of a registered party see PARA 253.

2 See the Political Parties, Elections and Referendums Act 2000 s 41; and CONSTITUTIONAL LAW AND HUMAN RIGHTS. As to the application of ss 41–48 where a registered party is a party with accounting units see s 49, Sch 5; and CONSTITUTIONAL LAW AND HUMAN RIGHTS. As to the meanings of 'accounting units' and 'party with accounting units' see PARA 253 note 15.

3 See the Political Parties, Elections and Referendums Act 2000 s 42; and CONSTITUTIONAL LAW AND HUMAN RIGHTS. 'Financial year', in relation to a registered party, means a period of 12 months such as may be determined by the Electoral Commission (see note 4), whether in relation to registered parties generally, any description of registered parties which includes the party, or the party itself: see s 41(6), (7). Where a registered party's gross income or total expenditure in any financial year exceeds £250,000, the accounts of the party for that year must be audited by a qualified auditor: see ss 43, 44; and CONSTITUTIONAL LAW AND HUMAN RIGHTS.

4 As to the Electoral Commission see PARA 34 et seq.

5 See the Political Parties, Elections and Referendums Act 2000 s 45; and CONSTITUTIONAL LAW AND HUMAN RIGHTS. For these purposes, 'qualified auditor' means a person who is eligible for appointment as a statutory auditor under the Companies Act 2006 Pt 42 (ss 1209–1264) (statutory auditors) (see COMPANIES vol 15 (2009) PARA 957 et seq) (or, in the case of a Gibraltar party, a person who is, in accordance with the Auditors Approval and Registration Ordinance 1998 s 6, eligible for appointment as a company auditor): see the Political Parties, Elections and Referendums Act 2000 s 160(1) (definition amended by SI 2004/366; SI 2008/948). However, a person is not a qualified auditor in relation to any registered party or any other body or individual if he is either a member of the party or body or the individual himself or an officer or employee of the party, body or individual (for which purpose, 'officer or employee' does not include an auditor): Political Parties, Elections and Referendums Act 2000 s 160(2).

Where the Commission receives any statement of accounts under s 45, it must make a copy of the statement available for public inspection and keep any such copy available for public inspection: see s 46; and CONSTITUTIONAL LAW AND HUMAN RIGHTS.

6 Provision is made for the treasurer of a registered party to prepare a revised statement of accounts where such a statement has not complied with these requirements: see the Political Parties, Elections and Referendums Act 2000 s 48; and CONSTITUTIONAL LAW AND HUMAN RIGHTS.

7 See the Political Parties, Elections and Referendums Act 2000 s 47; and CONSTITUTIONAL LAW AND HUMAN RIGHTS.

B. CONTROLS AFFECTING CAMPAIGN EXPENDITURE BY REGISTERED PARTIES DURING ELECTION PERIODS

(A) In general

299. Meaning of 'campaign expenditure'. For the purposes of controlling campaign expenditure incurred by registered parties during election periods[1], 'campaign expenditure', in relation to a registered party, means expenses incurred by or on behalf of the party[2] which are expenses incurred for election purposes[3] in respect of any of the matters set out in the following list[4]:

(1) party political broadcasts[5], including agency fees, design costs and other costs in connection with preparing or producing such broadcasts[6];

(2) advertising of any nature (whatever the medium used), including agency fees, design costs and other costs in connection with preparing, producing, distributing or otherwise disseminating such advertising or anything incorporating such advertising and intended to be distributed for the purpose of disseminating it[7];

(3) unsolicited material addressed to electors (whether addressed to them by name or intended for delivery to households within any particular area or areas[8]), including design costs and other costs in connection with preparing, producing or distributing such material (including the cost of postage)[9];

(4) any manifesto or other document setting out the party's policies, including design costs and other costs in connection with preparing or producing or distributing or otherwise disseminating any such document[10];

(5) market research or canvassing conducted for the purpose of ascertaining polling intentions[11];

(6) the provision of any services or facilities in connection with press conferences or other dealings with the media[12];

(7) the transport (by any means) of persons to any place or places with a view to obtaining publicity in connection with an election campaign[13], including the costs of hiring a particular means of transport for the whole or part of the period during which the election campaign is being conducted[14];

(8) rallies and other events, including public meetings (but not annual or other party conferences) organised so as to obtain publicity in connection with an election campaign or for other purposes connected with an election campaign, including costs incurred in connection with the attendance of persons at such events, the hire of premises for the purposes of such events or the provision of goods, services or facilities at them[15].

'Campaign expenditure' does not include, however, anything which, in accordance with any enactment[16], falls to be included in a return as to election expenses in respect of a candidate or candidates at a particular election[17]. Nor should anything in heads (1) to (8) above to be taken as extending to any expenses[18]:

(a) in respect of newsletters or similar publications issued by or on behalf of the party with a view to giving electors in a particular electoral area information about the opinions or activities of, or other personal information relating to, their elected representatives or existing or prospective candidates[19];

(b)   incurred in respect of unsolicited material addressed to party members[20];

(c)   in respect of any property, services or facilities so far as those expenses fall to be met out of public funds[21];

(d)   incurred in respect of the remuneration or allowances payable to any member of the staff (whether permanent or otherwise) of the party[22]; or

(e)   incurred in respect of an individual by way of travelling expenses (by any means of transport) or in providing for his accommodation or other personal needs to the extent that the expenses are paid by the individual from his own resources and are not reimbursed to him[23].

Where, in the case of a registered party, either:

(i)   property is transferred to the party[24]; or

(ii)   property, services or facilities is or are provided for the use or benefit of the party[25],

either free of charge or at a discount of more than 10 per cent[26], and the property, services or facilities is or are made use of by or on behalf of the party[27] in circumstances such that, if any expenses were to be (or are) actually incurred by or on behalf of the party in respect of that use, they would be (or are) campaign expenditure incurred by or on behalf of the party[28], an amount of campaign expenditure (the 'appropriate amount') is treated, for the purposes of the statutory control of campaign expenditure[29], as incurred by the party during the period for which the property, services or facilities is or are made so use of[30]. Where the whole or part of any such period falls within any period which is, in relation to the party, a relevant campaign period for the purposes of making returns as to campaign expenditure[31], then such proportion of the appropriate amount[32] as reasonably represents the use made of the property, services or facilities during the relevant campaign period is treated as incurred by or on behalf of the party during the relevant campaign period[33], and the treasurer or a deputy treasurer[34] must make a declaration of that amount[35], unless that amount is not more than £200[36].

Where head (i) above applies, the appropriate amount is determined as being such proportion of either the market value of the property (where the property is transferred free of charge)[37], or the difference between the market value of the property and the amount of expenses actually incurred by or on behalf of the party in respect of the property (where the property is transferred at a discount)[38], as is reasonably attributable to the use made of the property[39].

Where head (ii) above applies, the appropriate amount is determined as being such proportion of either the commercial rate for the use of the property or the provision of the services or facilities (where the property, services or facilities is or are provided free of charge)[40], or the difference between that commercial rate and the amount of expenses actually incurred by or on behalf of the party in respect of the use of the property or the provision of the services or facilities (where the property, services or facilities is or are provided at a discount)[41], as is reasonably attributable to the use made of the property, services or facilities[42].

However, no amount of campaign expenditure is to be regarded as so incurred in respect of:

(A)   the transmission by a broadcaster of a party political broadcast[43];

(B)   any facilities provided in accordance with any right conferred on candidates or a party at an election by any enactment[44]; or

(C)   the provision by any individual of his own services which he provides voluntarily in his own time and free of charge[45].

The Electoral Commission may prepare, and from time to time revise, a code of practice giving guidance as to the kinds of expenses which do, or do not, fall within the matters specified either in heads (1) to (8) above or in heads (a) to (e) above[46]. Once the Commission has prepared a draft of such a code, it must submit it to the Secretary of State for his approval[47]; and he may approve a draft code either without modification or with such modifications as he may determine[48]. The Secretary of State may also by order make such amendments to the matters specified either in heads (1) to (8) above or in heads (a) to (e) above as he considers appropriate[49]; and he may make such an order either where the order gives effect to a recommendation of the Commission[50] or after consultation with the Commission[51].

1　Ie for the purposes of the Political Parties, Elections and Referendums Act 2000 Pt V (ss 72–84): see s 72(1). Nothing in Pt V applies in relation to expenses incurred or to be incurred by or on behalf of a minor party: s 72(10). As to the meaning of 'registered party' for these purposes see PARA 35 note 3. As to the meaning of 'minor party' see PARA 253 note 8. As to the returns as to campaign expenditure that are required see PARA 307.

2　Where a registered party is a party with accounting units:
　(1)　expenses incurred or to be incurred by or on behalf of any accounting unit of the party are to be regarded as expenses incurred or to be incurred by or on behalf of the party (Political Parties, Elections and Referendums Act 2000 s 72(8)(a)); and
　(2)　references to campaign expenditure incurred or to be incurred by or on behalf of a registered party accordingly extend, in relation to the party, to expenses which constitute such expenditure by virtue of head (1) above (s 72(8)(b)).
As to the meanings of 'accounting units' and 'party with accounting units' see PARA 253 note 15.

3　In relation to a registered party, 'for election purposes' means for the purpose of or in connection with:
　(1)　promoting or procuring electoral success for the party at any relevant election (that is to say, the return at any such election of candidates either standing in the name of the party or included in a list of candidates submitted by the party in connection with the election) (Political Parties, Elections and Referendums Act 2000 s 72(4)(a)); or
　(2)　otherwise enhancing the standing of the party, or of any such candidates, with the electorate in connection with future relevant elections, whether imminent or otherwise (s 72(4)(b)).
For these purposes:
　(a)　the reference to doing any of the things mentioned in head (1) above or, as the case may be, head (2) above, includes doing so by prejudicing the electoral prospects at the election of other parties or candidates or, as the case may be, by prejudicing the standing with the electorate of other parties or candidates (s 72(5)(a));
　(b)　a course of conduct may constitute the doing of one of those things even though it does not involve any express mention being made of the name of any party or candidate (s 72(5)(b)); and
　(c)　it is immaterial that any candidates standing in the name of the party also stand in the name of one or more other registered parties (s 72(5)(c)).
'Candidates' includes future candidates, whether identifiable or not: s 72(9). As to the meaning of 'candidate' generally see PARA 230. As to references to persons standing for election in the name of a registered party see PARA 253 note 8. The following elections are 'relevant elections' for these purposes:
　(i)　a parliamentary election (s 22(1), (5)(a); applied by s 72(6));
　(ii)　any local government election (s 22(1), (5)(f)), except a parish or community election (s 22(4); applied by s 72(6));
　(iii)　the election of a police and crime commissioner (s 22(1), (5)(ea); applied by s 72(6) (s 22(5)(ea) added by SI 2012/1917));
　(iv)　a Welsh Assembly election (Political Parties, Elections and Referendums Act 2000 s 22(1), (5)(d); applied by s 72(6)), or
　(v)　an election to the European Parliament (s 22(1), (5)(b); applied by s 72(6)).
As to the meaning of 'parliamentary election' see PARA 9. As to the meaning of 'local government election' see PARA 11. For these purposes, a 'parish or community election' means an election of councillors for a parish in England or a community in Wales: see s 40(1). As to the meanings of 'England' and 'Wales' see PARA 1 note 1. As to the election of councillors for parish or community councils see PARA 200 et seq. As to parishes generally see LOCAL GOVERNMENT

vol 69 (2009) PARA 27 et seq; and as to communities generally see LOCAL GOVERNMENT vol 69 (2009) PARA 41 et seq. As to the election of police and crime commissioners see POLICE AND INVESTIGATORY POWERS vol 84 (2013) PARA 62 et seq. As to Welsh Assembly elections see PARA 12 et seq. As to elections to the European Parliament see PARA 13 et seq.

4 See the Political Parties, Elections and Referendums Act 2000 s 72(1), (2). The text refers to expenses falling within s 72(2), Sch 8 Pt I paras 1–2 (see heads (1)–(8) and heads (a)–(e) in the text): see s 72(2), Sch 8 para 1. The definition given by s 72(2) is subject to s 72(7) (see the text and notes 16–17): see s 72(2).

5 As to party political broadcasts generally see BROADCASTING vol 4 (2011) PARA 890 et seq; and CONSTITUTIONAL LAW AND HUMAN RIGHTS vol 8(2) (Reissue) PARAS 222–223.

6 Political Parties, Elections and Referendums Act 2000 Sch 8 para 1(1).

7 Political Parties, Elections and Referendums Act 2000 Sch 8 para 1(2). As to the control of advertising relating to a pending parliamentary, European Parliamentary, Welsh Assembly or local government election see PARA 333 et seq.

8 As to the meaning of 'electoral area' see PARA 11.

9 Political Parties, Elections and Referendums Act 2000 Sch 8 para 1(3). As to a candidate's right to send election addresses to electors generally see PARA 330 et seq.

10 Political Parties, Elections and Referendums Act 2000 Sch 8 para 1(4).

11 Political Parties, Elections and Referendums Act 2000 Sch 8 para 1(5).

12 Political Parties, Elections and Referendums Act 2000 Sch 8 para 1(6).

13 In relation to a registered party, 'election campaign', means a campaign conducted by the party for election purposes: Political Parties, Elections and Referendums Act 2000 s 72(3).

14 Political Parties, Elections and Referendums Act 2000 Sch 8 para 1(7).

15 Political Parties, Elections and Referendums Act 2000 Sch 8 para 1(8).

16 As to the meaning of 'enactment' see PARA 53 note 2.

17 Political Parties, Elections and Referendums Act 2000 s 72(7). As to returns as to election expenses in respect of a candidate or candidates at a particular election see PARA 280.

18 See the Political Parties, Elections and Referendums Act 2000 Sch 8 para 2(1) (Sch 8 para 2(1) renumbered, Sch 8 para 2(2) added, by SI 2004/366).

19 Political Parties, Elections and Referendums Act 2000 Sch 8 para 2(1)(a) (as renumbered: see note 18). Head (a) in the text does not apply in relation to any expenses which are incurred:

(1) in respect of newsletters or similar publications issued by or on behalf of a party with a view to giving electors in a particular electoral area information about the opinions or activities of, or other personal information relating to, a member of the European Parliament elected in Great Britain (including the combined region) or existing or prospective candidates for such election (Sch 8 para 2(2)(a) (as added: see note 18)); and

(2) within the period of four months ending with the date of the poll for an election to the European Parliament (Sch 8 para 2(2)(b) (as so added)).

As to the meaning of 'Great Britain' see PARA 1 note 1. As to the establishment of electoral regions (including the combined region) for the purpose of elections to the European Parliament see PARA 77. As to the date of the poll at a European parliamentary election see PARA 222.

20 Political Parties, Elections and Referendums Act 2000 Sch 8 para 2(1)(b) (as renumbered: see note 18).

21 Political Parties, Elections and Referendums Act 2000 Sch 8 para 2(1)(c) (as renumbered: see note 18). As to the meaning of 'property' for these purposes see PARA 34 note 8.

References in the Political Parties, Elections and Referendums Act 2000 (in whatever terms) to payments out of public funds are references to any of the following, namely:

(1) payments out of the Consolidated Fund of the United Kingdom, or the Welsh Consolidated Fund, or out of money provided by Parliament (s 160(4)(a) (s 160(4)(a)–(c) amended by SI 2007/1388));

(2) payments by any Minister of the Crown, or the Welsh Ministers, or by any government department, or the Welsh Assembly Government (Political Parties, Elections and Referendums Act 2000 s 160(4)(b) (as so amended)); and

(3) payments by the National Assembly for Wales Commission (s 160(4)(c) (as so amended));

(4) payments by the Electoral Commission (s 160(4)(d));

and references (in whatever terms) to expenses met, or things provided, out of public funds are references to expenses met, or things provided, by means of any such payments (see s 160(4)). As to the Welsh Ministers see PARA 2. As to the Electoral Commission see PARA 34 et seq. As to the Consolidated Fund see CONSTITUTIONAL LAW AND HUMAN RIGHTS vol 8(2) (Reissue) PARA

711 et seq; PARLIAMENT vol 78 (2010) PARAS 1028–1031. As to the National Assembly for Wales Commission, the Welsh Assembly Government and the Welsh Consolidated Fund see CONSTITUTIONAL LAW AND HUMAN RIGHTS.

22   Political Parties, Elections and Referendums Act 2000 Sch 8 para 2(1)(d) (as renumbered: see note 18).

23   Political Parties, Elections and Referendums Act 2000 Sch 8 para 2(1)(e) (as renumbered: see note 18).

24   Political Parties, Elections and Referendums Act 2000 s 73(1)(a)(i). Any property given or transferred to any registered party or to any accounting unit of the party in its capacity as such is to be regarded as given or transferred to the party (and references to donations received by a party or any such accounting unit accordingly include donations so given or transferred) (s 50(6); applied by s 73(10)); and any reference to property being given or transferred to a party or any such accounting unit is a reference to its being so given or transferred either directly or indirectly through any third person (s 50(8)(a); applied by s 73(10)).

25   Political Parties, Elections and Referendums Act 2000 s 73(1)(a)(ii).

26   See the Political Parties, Elections and Referendums Act 2000 s 73(1)(a)(i), (ii). The discount referred to in the text is a discount of more than:

(1)   10% of the market value of the property, in the case of head (i) in the text (see s 73(1)(a)(i)); or

(2)   10% of the commercial rate for the use of the property or for the provision of the services or facilities, in the case of head (ii) in the text (see s 73(1)(a)(ii)).

For these purposes, 'market value', in relation to any property, means the price which might reasonably be expected to be paid for the property on a sale in the open market: see s 160(1). Where the services of an employee are made available by his employer for the use or benefit of a registered party, then for the purposes of determining campaign expenditure, the amount which is to be taken as constituting the commercial rate for the provision of those services is the amount of the remuneration or allowances payable to the employee by his employer in respect of the period for which his services are so made available (but do not include any amount in respect of any contributions or other payments for which the employer is liable in respect of the employee): s 73(5).

27   For these purposes, references to anything done by or in relation to a registered party include a reference to any such thing done by or in relation to any accounting unit of the party: see the Political Parties, Elections and Referendums Act 2000 s 73(10).

28   Political Parties, Elections and Referendums Act 2000 s 73(1)(b).

29   Ie for the purposes of Political Parties, Elections and Referendums Act 2000 Pt V: see s 73(2).

30   Political Parties, Elections and Referendums Act 2000 s 73(2). The text refers to the use made of the property or goods as mentioned in s 73(1)(b) (see the text and notes 27–28): see s 73(2). The provision made by s 73(2) has effect subject to s 73(9) (see heads (A)–(C) in the text): see s 73(2).

31   Ie for the purposes of the Political Parties, Elections and Referendums Act 2000 s 80 (see PARA 307): see s 73(6)(a), (7). As to the meaning of 'relevant campaign period' for those purposes see PARA 307 note 4.

32   Ie such proportion of the appropriate amount determined in accordance with the Political Parties, Elections and Referendums Act 2000 s 73(3), (4) (see the text and notes 37–42): see s 73(6)(a), (7).

33   Political Parties, Elections and Referendums Act 2000 s 73(6)(a), (7).

34   Ie a person appointed as deputy treasurer under the Political Parties, Elections and Referendums Act 2000 s 74 (see PARA 300) by the treasurer of a registered party: see s 73(6)(b). As to the treasurer of a registered party see PARA 253.

35   Political Parties, Elections and Referendums Act 2000 s 73(6)(b). A person commits an offence if he knowingly or recklessly makes a declaration under s 73(6) which is false: see s 73(8); and PARA 751.

36   Political Parties, Elections and Referendums Act 2000 s 73(6). The Secretary of State may by order vary any sum for the time being specified in any provision of the Political Parties, Elections and Referendums Act 2000 (other than the sum specified in s 12(8) (policy development grants: see PARA 60) or s 36(5) (assistance for existing parties: see CONSTITUTIONAL LAW AND HUMAN RIGHTS)): s 155(1). The Secretary of State may make such an order either where he considers it expedient to do so in consequence of changes in the value of money (s 155(2)(a)), or where the order gives effect to a recommendation of the Commission (s 155(2)(b)). At the date at which this volume states the law, no such order had been made. As to the Secretary of State see PARA 2.

37   Political Parties, Elections and Referendums Act 2000 s 73(3)(a).

38   Political Parties, Elections and Referendums Act 2000 s 73(3)(b).

39   Political Parties, Elections and Referendums Act 2000 s 73(3). The text refers to the use made of the property as mentioned in s 73(1)(b) (see the text and notes 27–28): see s 73(3).

40 Political Parties, Elections and Referendums Act 2000 s 73(4)(a).

41 Political Parties, Elections and Referendums Act 2000 s 73(4)(b).

42 Political Parties, Elections and Referendums Act 2000 s 73(4). The text refers to the use made of the property as mentioned in s 73(1)(b) (see the text and notes 27–28): see s 73(4).

43 Political Parties, Elections and Referendums Act 2000 s 73(9)(a). For the purposes of the Political Parties, Elections and Referendums Act 2000, 'broadcaster' means the holder of a licence under either the Broadcasting Act 1990 or the Broadcasting Act 1996 (see BROADCASTING vol 4 (2011) PARA 507 et seq), the British Broadcasting Corporation, or Sianel Pedwar Cymru: see the Political Parties, Elections and Referendums Act 2000 s 37(2). As to the BBC see BROADCASTING vol 4 (2011) PARA 603 et seq; and as to Sianel Pedwar Cymru see BROADCASTING vol 4 (2011) PARA 645. For the purposes of European parliamentary elections taking place in the combined region, the reference in s 73(9)(a) to a broadcaster includes a reference to the Gibraltar Broadcasting Corporation: see s 73(11) (added by SI 2004/366).

44 Political Parties, Elections and Referendums Act 2000 s 73(9)(b).

45 Political Parties, Elections and Referendums Act 2000 s 73(9)(c).

46 Political Parties, Elections and Referendums Act 2000 Sch 8 para 3(1).

47 Political Parties, Elections and Referendums Act 2000 Sch 8 para 3(2).

48 Political Parties, Elections and Referendums Act 2000 Sch 8 para 3(3). For these purposes, references to a draft code include a revised draft code: Sch 8 para 3(10). As to the meaning of 'modification' for these purposes see PARA 44 note 9.

Once the Secretary of State has approved a draft code he must lay a copy of the draft, whether in its original form or in a form which incorporates any modifications determined under Sch 8 para 3(3), before each House of Parliament: Sch 8 para 3(4). If the draft incorporates any such modifications, the Secretary of State must at the same time lay before each House a statement of his reasons for making them: Sch 8 para 3(5). If, within the 40-day period, either House resolves not to approve the draft, the Secretary of State must take no further steps in relation to the draft code (Sch 8 para 3(6)); but, if no such resolution is made within the 40-day period, the Secretary of State must issue the code in the form of the draft laid before Parliament, and the code is to come into force on such date as the Secretary of State may by order appoint (see Sch 8 para 3(7)). The Commission must arrange for the code to be published in such manner as it thinks appropriate: see Sch 8 para 3(7). The prohibition from taking further action in relation to a draft code (ie Sch 8 para 3(6)) does not prevent a new draft code from being laid before Parliament: Sch 8 para 3(8). For these purposes, the '40-day period', in relation to a draft code, means, if the draft is laid before one House on a day later than the day on which it is laid before the other House, the period of 40 days beginning with the later of the two days, and, in any other case, the period of 40 days beginning with the day on which the draft is laid before each House: see Sch 8 para 3(9). In calculating this period, no account is taken of any period during which Parliament is dissolved or prorogued or during which both Houses are adjourned for more than four days: see Sch 8 para 3(9).

49 Political Parties, Elections and Referendums Act 2000 Sch 8 para 4(1).

50 Political Parties, Elections and Referendums Act 2000 Sch 8 para 4(2)(a).

51 Political Parties, Elections and Referendums Act 2000 Sch 8 para 4(2)(b).

300.   Officers of registered party with responsibility for campaign expenditure.   For the purposes of controlling campaign expenditure incurred by registered parties during election periods[1], the treasurer of a registered party[2] may appoint, on such terms as he may determine, one or more deputy treasurers of the party, but not more than 12 persons may hold such appointments at the same time[3]. The appointment of a person as deputy treasurer of a party is effective for those purposes once the treasurer has given the Electoral Commission[4] a notification of the appointment[5]:

(1)   which contains the name of the person so appointed and the address of his office[6]; and

(2)   which is accompanied by a declaration of acceptance of office signed by that person[7].

If, where the appointment of any deputy treasurer of a registered party has been so notified to the Commission, the deputy treasurer dies or his appointment terminates for any other reason[8], or if any change occurs in the address of his office[9], the treasurer of the party must notify the Commission of that fact within the appropriate period[10].

A person is not, however, eligible to be appointed as deputy treasurer of a registered party if, at any time within the last five years, he has been convicted of any offence under the Political Parties, Elections and Referendums Act 2000[11], or of any other offence committed in connection with a relevant election[12] or a referendum[13].

1   Ie for the purposes of the Political Parties, Elections and Referendums Act 2000 Pt V (ss 72–84): see s 74(1). Nothing in Pt V applies in relation to expenses incurred or to be incurred by or on behalf of a minor party: s 72(10). As to the meaning of 'registered party' for these purposes see PARA 35 note 3. As to the meaning of 'minor party' see PARA 253 note 8. As to the returns as to campaign expenditure that are required see PARA 307.
2   As to the treasurer of a registered party see PARA 253.
3   Political Parties, Elections and Referendums Act 2000 s 74(1).
4   As to the Electoral Commission see PARA 34 et seq.
5   See the Political Parties, Elections and Referendums Act 2000 s 74(2). Any notification required to be given under the Political Parties, Elections and Referendums Act 2000 must be in writing: see s 157(1).
6   Political Parties, Elections and Referendums Act 2000 s 74(2)(a). The name of any deputy treasurer of a registered party and the address of his office, as so notified to the Commission, must be included in the party's entry in the Great Britain register (s 74(8)); and where the Commission receives a notification under s 74(6) (see the text and notes 8–10), it must cause any change required as a consequence of the notification to be made in any such entry as soon as is reasonably practicable (s 74(9)). For these purposes, the address of any deputy treasurer of such a party is to be regarded as being the address for the time being registered in relation to him in accordance with s 74(8): see s 74(10)(a). As to the meaning of the 'Great Britain register' see PARA 253 note 8.
7   Political Parties, Elections and Referendums Act 2000 s 74(2)(b).
8   Political Parties, Elections and Referendums Act 2000 s 74(6)(a).
9   Political Parties, Elections and Referendums Act 2000 s 74(6)(b).
10   Political Parties, Elections and Referendums Act 2000 s 74(6). For these purposes, the 'appropriate period' means either the period of 14 days beginning with the date of the deputy treasurer's death or the termination of his appointment, or the period of 28 days beginning with the date when the change of address occurs, as the case may be: see s 74(7). Where the requirements of s 74(6) are not complied with in relation to any notification required to be given by the treasurer of a registered party then, in addition to any criminal liability imposed on any person, the relevant organisation is liable to a civil penalty: see s 147, Sch 19C; and PARA 757 et seq.
11   As to the punishment of offences under the Political Parties, Elections and Referendums Act 2000 see PARAS 892–893.
12   Ie within the meaning of the Political Parties, Elections and Referendums Act 2000 Pt II (ss 22–40) (see PARA 299 note 3): see s 74(3) (amended by SI 2004/366). For the purposes of European parliamentary elections taking place in the combined region, eligibility is also affected by an offence committed in connection with an election to the House of Assembly of Gibraltar: see the Political Parties, Elections and Referendums Act 2000 s 74(3) (as so amended). As to the establishment of electoral regions (including the combined region) for the purpose of elections to the European Parliament see PARA 77.
13   Political Parties, Elections and Referendums Act 2000 s 74(3) (as amended: see note 12). The text refers to a referendum within the meaning of Pt VII (ss 101–129) (see PARA 527 et seq): see s 74(3) (as so amended). Where a deputy treasurer of a registered party is convicted of an offence falling within s 74(3), his appointment as deputy treasurer terminates on the date of the conviction: s 74(5). A person commits an offence if he accepts the office of deputy treasurer of a registered party when, by virtue of s 74(3), he is not eligible to be so appointed: see s 74(4); and PARA 751.

(B) General Restrictions relating to Campaign Expenditure

301. Restriction on incurring campaign expenditure without authority. For the purposes of controlling campaign expenditure incurred by registered parties during election periods[1], no campaign expenditure may be incurred by or on behalf of a registered party[2] unless it is incurred with the authority of[3]:

(1)   the treasurer of the party[4];

(2)   a deputy treasurer of the party[5]; or

(3)   a person authorised in writing by the treasurer or a deputy treasurer[6].

Where any expenses are incurred in contravention of this restriction, the expenses do not count as campaign expenditure incurred by or on behalf of the party either for the purposes of the statutory financial limits imposed on such expenditure[7] or for the purposes of the statutory provisions which require returns as to such expenditure[8].

A person commits an offence if, without reasonable excuse, he incurs any expenses in contravention of this restriction on incurring campaign expenditure without due authority[9].

1   Ie for the purposes of the Political Parties, Elections and Referendums Act 2000 Pt V (ss 72–84): see s 72(1). Nothing in Pt V applies in relation to expenses incurred or to be incurred by or on behalf of a minor party: s 72(10). As to the meaning of 'campaign expenditure' see PARA 299. As to the meaning of 'minor party' see PARA 253 note 8. As to the returns as to campaign expenditure that are required see PARA 307.

2   As to the meaning of 'registered party' for these purposes see PARA 35 note 3.

3   See the Political Parties, Elections and Referendums Act 2000 s 75(1).

4   Political Parties, Elections and Referendums Act 2000 s 75(1)(a). As to the treasurer of a registered party see PARA 253.

5   Political Parties, Elections and Referendums Act 2000 s 75(1)(b). As to the appointment of deputy treasurers of a registered party for the purposes of controlling campaign expenditure see PARA 300.

6   Political Parties, Elections and Referendums Act 2000 s 75(1)(c).

7   Ie for the purposes of the Political Parties, Elections and Referendums Act 2000 s 79, Sch 9 (see PARAS 305–306): see s 75(3).

8   Political Parties, Elections and Referendums Act 2000 s 75(3). The text refers to the statutory provisions in ss 80–83 (see PARAS 307–309): see s 75(3).

9   See the Political Parties, Elections and Referendums Act 2000 s 75(2); and PARA 751.

302.   Restriction on payments made in respect of campaign expenditure without authority.   For the purposes of controlling campaign expenditure incurred by registered parties during election periods[1], no payment (of whatever nature) may be made in respect of any campaign expenditure incurred or to be incurred by or on behalf of a registered party[2] unless it is made by[3]:

(1)   the treasurer of the party[4];

(2)   a deputy treasurer of the party[5]; or

(3)   a person authorised in writing by the treasurer or a deputy treasurer[6].

Any payment made in respect of any such expenditure by a person within any of heads (1) to (3) above must be supported by an invoice or a receipt unless it is not more than £200[7]; and where any such payment is made by a person within head (2) or head (3) above, he must deliver to the treasurer both notification that he has made the payment[8] and the supporting invoice or receipt[9], as soon as possible after making the payment[10].

A person commits an offence if, without reasonable excuse, he makes any payment in respect of campaign expenditure in contravention of the restriction on such payments made without due authority, or if he is a person falling within head (2) or head (3) above who contravenes the requirements imposed upon him regarding the delivery of notification and evidence[11].

1   Ie for the purposes of the Political Parties, Elections and Referendums Act 2000 Pt V (ss 72–84): see s 72(1). Nothing in Pt V applies in relation to expenses incurred or to be incurred by or on

behalf of a minor party: s 72(10). As to the meaning of 'campaign expenditure' see PARA 299. As to the meaning of 'minor party' see PARA 253 note 8. As to the returns as to campaign expenditure that are required see PARA 307.

2 As to the meaning of 'registered party' for these purposes see PARA 35 note 3.
3 See the Political Parties, Elections and Referendums Act 2000 s 76(1).
4 Political Parties, Elections and Referendums Act 2000 s 76(1)(a). As to the treasurer of a registered party see PARA 253.
5 Political Parties, Elections and Referendums Act 2000 s 76(1)(b). As to the appointment of deputy treasurers of a registered party for the purposes of controlling campaign expenditure see PARA 300.
6 Political Parties, Elections and Referendums Act 2000 s 76(1)(c).
7 Political Parties, Elections and Referendums Act 2000 s 76(2). The Secretary of State may by order vary the sum for the time being specified in any provision of the Political Parties, Elections and Referendums Act 2000: see s 155; and PARA 299 note 36. At the date at which this volume states the law no such order had been made. As to the Secretary of State see PARA 2.
8 Political Parties, Elections and Referendums Act 2000 s 76(3)(a). Any notification required to be given under the Political Parties, Elections and Referendums Act 2000 must be in writing: s 157(1).
9 Political Parties, Elections and Referendums Act 2000 s 76(3)(b).
10 See the Political Parties, Elections and Referendums Act 2000 s 76(3).
11 See the Political Parties, Elections and Referendums Act 2000 s 76(4); and PARA 751.

303.   Claims against registered party in respect of campaign expenditure. For the purposes of controlling campaign expenditure incurred by registered parties during election periods[1], a claim for payment in respect of campaign expenditure incurred by or on behalf of a registered party[2] during any period which is, in relation to the party, a relevant campaign period[3] is not payable unless the claim is sent[4]:

(1)   to the treasurer[5] or a deputy treasurer of the party[6]; or
(2)   to any other person authorised[7] to incur the expenditure[8],

not later than 30 days[9] after the end of the relevant campaign period[10]. Any claim that is sent in accordance with this provision must be paid not later than 60 days after the end of the relevant campaign period[11]; but this is without prejudice to any rights of a creditor of a registered party to obtain payment before the end of the period so allowed[12]. A person commits an offence if, without reasonable excuse he pays any claim for payment in respect of campaign expenditure which by virtue of being statute-barred[13] is not payable, or if he makes any payment in respect of a claim after the end of the period allowed for the payment of claims[14].

If the treasurer of a registered political party, or if any other person, to whom a claim for payment in respect of campaign expenditure incurred by or on behalf of a registered party is sent, fails or refuses to pay the claim within the period allowed[15], where the claim is sent to the treasurer of the party[16], or to any other person with whose authority it is alleged that the expenditure was incurred[17], within the period allowed before such claims are barred[18], the claim is deemed to be a 'disputed claim'[19]. The person by whom the disputed claim is made may bring an action for a disputed claim, and any sum paid in pursuance of a court's judgment or order so made in the proceedings is not deemed to be in contravention of the statutory bar imposed on the payment of campaign expenditure later than 60 days after the end of the relevant campaign period[20].

1 Ie for the purposes of the Political Parties, Elections and Referendums Act 2000 Pt V (ss 72–84): see s 72(1). Nothing in Pt V applies in relation to expenses incurred or to be incurred by or on behalf of a minor party: s 72(10). As to the meaning of 'campaign expenditure' see PARA 299. As to the meaning of 'minor party' see PARA 253 note 8. As to the returns as to campaign expenditure that are required see PARA 307.
2 As to the meaning of 'registered party' for these purposes see PARA 35 note 3.

3   Ie within the meaning of the Political Parties, Elections and Referendums Act 2000 s 80 (see
     PARA 307 note 4): see s 77(1).
4   See the Political Parties, Elections and Referendums Act 2000 s 77(1).
5   As to the treasurer of a registered party see PARA 253.
6   Political Parties, Elections and Referendums Act 2000 s 77(1)(a). As to the appointment of
     deputy treasurers of a registered party for the purposes of controlling campaign expenditure see
     PARA 300.
7   Ie authorised in writing by the treasurer or a deputy treasurer under the Political Parties,
     Elections and Referendums Act 2000 s 75 (see PARA 301): see s 77(1)(b).
8   Political Parties, Elections and Referendums Act 2000 s 77(1)(b).
9   Where, in the case of any campaign expenditure, the period allowed under the Political Parties,
     Elections and Referendums Act 2000 s 77(1) or s 77(2) (see the text and note 11), would, apart
     from s 77(9), end on:
     (1)   a Saturday or Sunday or Christmas Eve, Christmas Day or Good Friday (s 77(9)(a)
            (amended by the Electoral Administration Act 2006 ss 20, 74(2), Sch 1 paras 49, 54,
            Sch 2));
     (2)   a bank holiday (Political Parties, Elections and Referendums Act 2000 s 77(9)(b)); or
     (3)   a day appointed for public thanksgiving or mourning (s 77(9)(c)),
     the period instead ends on the first day following that day which is not one of those days (see
     s 77(9)). For the purposes of head (2) above, 'bank holiday' means a day which is a bank
     holiday under the Banking and Financial Dealings Act 1971 (see TIME vol 97 (2010) PARA 321)
     in any part of the United Kingdom (see s 77(10) (s 77(10) amended, s 77(11), (12) added, by
     SI 2004/366)):
     (a)   in which is situated the office of the treasurer, deputy treasurer or (as the case may be)
            other authorised person to whom the claim is sent pursuant to the Political Parties,
            Elections and Referendums Act 2000 s 77(1) (s 77(10)(a)); or
     (b)   in which the person providing the property, services or facilities to which the
            expenditure relates conducts his business (s 77(10)(b)); or
     (c)   (if he conducts his business in more than one part of the United Kingdom) in which is
            situated the office from which dealings relating to the expenditure were conducted
            (s 77(10)(c)).
     For these purposes, the address of the treasurer of a registered party is to be regarded as being
     the registered address of the party; and the address of the deputy treasurer of a registered party
     is to be regarded as being the address for the time being registered in relation to him in
     accordance with s 74(8) (see PARA 300 note 6): see s 74(10). As to the definition of 'bank
     holiday' to be used for the purposes of European parliamentary elections taking place in the
     combined region see s 77(10), (11) (s 77(10) as so amended, s 77(11) as so added). 'Business'
     includes every trade, profession and occupation: s 160(1). As to the meaning of 'United
     Kingdom' see PARA 1 note 1. As to the meaning of 'property' for these purposes see PARA 34
     note 8. As to the establishment of electoral regions (including the combined region) for the
     purpose of elections to the European Parliament see PARA 77.
10   Political Parties, Elections and Referendums Act 2000 s 77(1) (amended by the Electoral
     Administration Act 2006 s 65(1)(a)).
11   Political Parties, Elections and Referendums Act 2000 s 77(2) (amended by the Electoral
     Administration Act 2006 s 65(1)(b)).
12   Political Parties, Elections and Referendums Act 2000 s 77(6).
13   Ie any payment which by virtue of the Political Parties, Elections and Referendums Act 2000
     s 77(1) (see the text and notes 1–10) is not payable: see s 77(3); and PARA 751.
14   See the Political Parties, Elections and Referendums Act 2000 s 77(3); and PARA 751. The text
     refers to payment in respect of a claim after the end of the period allowed under s 77(2) (see the
     text and note 11): see s 77(3); and PARA 751.
15   Political Parties, Elections and Referendums Act 2000 s 78(1)(b). The text refers to the period
     allowed under s 77(2) (see the text and note 11), which is without prejudice to any rights of a
     creditor of a registered party to obtain payment before the end of the period so allowed: see
     ss 77(6), 78(3).
16   Political Parties, Elections and Referendums Act 2000 s 78(1)(a)(i).
17   Political Parties, Elections and Referendums Act 2000 s 78(1)(a)(ii).
18   See the Political Parties, Elections and Referendums Act 2000 s 78(1)(a). The text refers to the
     period allowed under s 77(1) (see the text and notes 1–10): see s 78(1)(a).
19   Political Parties, Elections and Referendums Act 2000 s 78(1). As to the power to apply to the
     court for permission to pay a disputed claim see PARA 304; and as to the returns required in
     relation to disputed claims see PARA 307.

20 Political Parties, Elections and Referendums Act 2000 s 78(2). The text refers to the restriction otherwise contained in s 77(2) (see the text and note 11): see s 78(2).

304. Application for permission to pay claims in respect of campaign expenditure. For the purposes of controlling campaign expenditure incurred by registered parties during election periods[1]:

(1) the person making a claim for payment in respect of campaign expenditure incurred by or on behalf of a registered party[2]; or

(2) the person with whose authority the expenditure in question was incurred[3],

may apply to the High Court or to the county court for permission to pay such a claim (even if it is sent in after the statutory period allowed of 30 days[4]) or may apply to the High Court or to the county court for permission to pay a disputed claim[5]. The court, if satisfied that for any special reason it is appropriate to do so, may by order grant the permission[6]. Any sum paid in pursuance of such an order of permission is not deemed to be a contravention of the statutory bar on the making or payment of claims relating to campaign expenditure later than the statutory period allowed[7].

1 Ie for the purposes of the Political Parties, Elections and Referendums Act 2000 Pt V (ss 72–84): see s 72(1). Nothing in Pt V applies in relation to expenses incurred or to be incurred by or on behalf of a minor party: s 72(10). As to the meaning of 'campaign expenditure' see PARA 299. As to the meaning of 'minor party' see PARA 253 note 8.

2 Political Parties, Elections and Referendums Act 2000 s 77(4)(a). The reference in the text is to a claim to which s 77(1) applies (see PARA 303): see s 77(4). As to the meaning of 'registered party' for these purposes see PARA 35 note 3.

3 Political Parties, Elections and Referendums Act 2000 s 77(4)(b). As to persons authorised to incur expenditure as mentioned in the text see s 75; and PARA 301.

4 Ie the period mentioned in the Political Parties, Elections and Referendums Act 2000 s 77(1) (see PARA 303): see ss 77(4), 78(3).

5 See the Political Parties, Elections and Referendums Act 2000 ss 77(4), 78(3). In relation to a European parliamentary election taking place in the combined region, the references to the High Court and to the county court have effect as if they are references to the Gibraltar court: see s 77(12). As to the establishment of electoral regions (including the combined region) for the purpose of elections to the European Parliament see PARA 77.

6 See the Political Parties, Elections and Referendums Act 2000 ss 77(4), 78(3).

7 See the Political Parties, Elections and Referendums Act 2000 ss 77(5), 78(3). The text refers to the period of 30 days within which a claim otherwise must be made under s 77(1) or the period of 60 days within which a claim otherwise must be paid under s 77(2) (see PARA 303): see ss 77(5), 78(3). As to the returns required in relation to claims which are paid following an application for permission see PARA 307.

(C) Financial Limits on Campaign Expenditure

305. Limitation of campaign expenditure. For the purposes of controlling campaign expenditure incurred by registered parties during election periods[1], the limit which applies in relation to campaign expenditure incurred by or on behalf of a registered party[2] contesting one or more constituencies[3] at a parliamentary general election[4] in the relevant period[5] in England or Wales (as the case may be) is[6]:

(1) £30,000 multiplied by the number of constituencies contested by the party in England or Wales (as the case may be)[7]; or

(2) if greater, the appropriate amount specified[8], being, in relation to England, £810,000[9] and, in relation to Wales, £60,000[10].

Where, at the election, a candidate stands for election in any constituency in the name of a registered party and one or more other registered parties[11], the amount applying to the party in respect of the constituency under head (1) above, instead of being the amount specified there, is that amount divided by the number of registered parties in whose name the candidate stands for election[12].

For the purposes of controlling campaign expenditure incurred by registered parties during election periods, the limit which applies in relation to campaign expenditure incurred by or on behalf of a registered party which contests one or more constituencies[13] or regions[14] at an ordinary or extraordinary general election to the National Assembly for Wales[15] in the relevant period[16] in Wales is[17]:

(a)   £10,000 for each constituency contested by the party[18]; plus

(b)   £40,000 for each region contested by the party[19].

For the purposes of controlling campaign expenditure incurred by registered parties during election periods, the limit which applies in relation to campaign expenditure incurred by or on behalf of a registered party which stands for election or (as the case may be) in whose name candidates stand for election at a general election to the European Parliament[20] in the relevant period[21] is[22]:

(i)   £45,000 multiplied by the number of members of the European Parliament ('MEPs')[23] to be returned for the electoral region[24] at an election where a registered party stands for election in only one electoral region in England (including the combined region)[25];

(ii)   £45,000 multiplied by the total number of MEPs to be returned for the electoral regions taken together at an election where a registered party stands for election in two or more electoral regions in England (including the combined region)[26];

(iii)   £45,000 multiplied by the number of MEPs to be returned for Wales at an election where a registered party stands for election in Wales[27].

Where, at any time before the beginning of any relevant campaign period[28], any expenses which qualify as campaign expenditure[29] are incurred by or on behalf of a registered party in respect of any property, services or facilities[30], but where the property, services or facilities is or are made use of by or on behalf of the party during the relevant campaign period in circumstances such that, had any expenses been incurred in respect of that use during that period, they would have constituted[31] campaign expenditure incurred by or on behalf of the party during that period[32], the appropriate proportion of those expenses[33] is treated for the purposes of the statutory limits imposed on such expenditure[34] or for the purposes of the statutory provisions which require returns as to such expenditure[35], as campaign expenditure incurred by or on behalf of the party during that period[36]. Special provision is made for limiting campaign expenditure where, in special circumstances, election campaigns may be combined[37].

Where, during the period in relation to which any limitation of campaign expenditure applies in relation to a registered party, any campaign expenditure is incurred by or on behalf of the party in excess of that limit, the treasurer or any deputy treasurer of the party is guilty of an offence if he authorised the expenditure to be incurred by or on behalf of the party, and he knew or ought reasonably to have known that the expenditure would be incurred in excess of that limit; and the party is also guilty of an offence[38].

1   Ie for the purposes of the Political Parties, Elections and Referendums Act 2000 Pt V (ss 72–84): see s 72(1). Nothing in Pt V applies in relation to expenses incurred or to be incurred by or on behalf of a minor party: s 72(10). As to the meaning of 'campaign expenditure' see PARA 299. As to the meaning of 'minor party' see PARA 253 note 8. As to the returns as to campaign expenditure that are required see PARA 307.

2   As to the meaning of 'registered party' for these purposes see PARA 35 note 3. For these purposes:

    (1)   campaign expenditure incurred by or on behalf of a party registered in the Great Britain register is attributed to each of England and Wales in proportion to the number of parliamentary constituencies for the time being situated in that part of Great Britain (see the Political Parties, Elections and Referendums Act 2000 s 79(1), Sch 9 para 2(1)); and

    (2)   campaign expenditure whose effects are wholly or substantially confined to any particular parts or part of Great Britain is attributed to those parts in proportion to the number of parliamentary constituencies for the time being situated in those parts or are attributed solely to that part, as the case may be (Sch 9 para 2(2)).

For the purposes of head (2) above, the effects of campaign expenditure are wholly or substantially confined to any particular parts or part of Great Britain if they have no significant effects in any other part or parts (so that, for example, expenditure on an advertisement in a newspaper circulating in Wales is to be attributed solely to Wales if the newspaper does not circulate to any significant extent in any other part of Great Britain): Sch 9 para 2(3). As respects campaign expenditure incurred in the period of four months ending with the date of the poll for an election to the European Parliament in the combined region, that region is to be regarded as part of England for the purposes of the references to a part or parts of Great Britain: Sch 9 para 2(3A) (added by SI 2004/366). References in the Political Parties, Elections and Referendums Act 2000 Sch 9 to campaign expenditure 'in' a particular part of the United Kingdom are accordingly to campaign expenditure which is to be attributed to that part in accordance with Sch 9 para 2: Sch 9 para 2(4). As to the meaning of 'constituency' for the purposes of parliamentary elections see PARA 9; As to the meanings of 'England', 'Great Britain' and 'Wales' see PARA 1 note 1; and as to the meaning of the 'Great Britain register' see PARA 253 note 8. As to the establishment of electoral regions (including the combined region) for the purpose of elections to the European Parliament see PARA 77.

3   For these purposes, a registered party contests a constituency if any candidate stands for election for that constituency in the name of the party: Political Parties, Elections and Referendums Act 2000 Sch 9 para 1(2)(a). As to the meaning of 'candidate' generally see PARA 230. As to references to persons standing for election in the name of a registered party see PARA 253 note 8.

4   See the Political Parties, Elections and Referendums Act 2000 Sch 9 para 3(1). As to parliamentary general elections see PARA 189 et seq. As to the meaning of 'parliamentary election' see PARA 9.

5   For these purposes, the relevant period is:

    (1)   subject to head (2) below, the period of 365 days ending with the date of the poll for the election (Political Parties, Elections and Referendums Act 2000 Sch 9 para 3(7)(a)); or

    (2)   where the election (the 'election in question') follows another parliamentary general election held less than 365 days previously, the period beginning with the day after the date of the poll for the earlier election and ending with the date of the poll for the election in question (Sch 9 para 3(7)(b)).

As to the date of the poll at a parliamentary general election see PARA 195.

6   See the Political Parties, Elections and Referendums Act 2000 Sch 9 para 3(1), (2).

7   Political Parties, Elections and Referendums Act 2000 Sch 9 para 3(2)(a). The Secretary of State may by order vary the sum for the time being specified in any provision of the Political Parties, Elections and Referendums Act 2000: see s 155; and PARA 299 note 36.

8   Political Parties, Elections and Referendums Act 2000 Sch 9 para 3(2)(b). The text refers to the appropriate amount specified in Sch 9 para 3(3): see Sch 9 para 3(2)(b).

9   Political Parties, Elections and Referendums Act 2000 Sch 9 para 3(3)(a).

10   Political Parties, Elections and Referendums Act 2000 Sch 9 para 3(3)(c).

11   See the Political Parties, Elections and Referendums Act 2000 Sch 9 para 3(5).

12   See the Political Parties, Elections and Referendums Act 2000 Sch 9 para 3(6).

13   As to the meaning of 'constituency' for the purposes of Welsh Assembly elections see PARA 3 note 2.

14   For these purposes, a registered party contests any region if the party is included in the statement of parties and candidates nominated for that region: see the Political Parties, Elections and Referendums Act 2000 Sch 9 para 1(2)(b). As to the meaning of 'region' for the purposes of Welsh Assembly elections see PARA 3 note 2.

15   See the Political Parties, Elections and Referendums Act 2000 Sch 9 para 6(1) (amended by SI 2007/1388). For these purposes, an 'ordinary general election to the National Assembly for Wales' means an election held under the Government of Wales Act 2006 s 3 (see PARA 213) (see the Political Parties, Elections and Referendums Act 2000 Sch 9 para 1(1)(c) (substituted by SI 2007/1388)); and an 'extraordinary general election to the National Assembly for Wales'

means an election held under the Government of Wales Act 2006 s 5 (see PARA 213) (see the Political Parties, Elections and Referendums Act 2000 Sch 9 para 1(1)(ca) (added by SI 2007/1388)). As to the National Assembly for Wales see CONSTITUTIONAL LAW AND HUMAN RIGHTS.

16 For these purposes, the 'relevant period' is:

    (1)   in the case of an ordinary general election to the National Assembly for Wales, the period beginning with the appropriate date and ending with the date of the poll (Political Parties, Elections and Referendums Act 2000 Sch 9 para 6(3) (amended by SI 2007/1388)); or

    (2)   in the case of an extraordinary general election to the National Assembly for Wales, the period beginning with date when the Secretary of State proposes a date for the poll for the election under the Government of Wales Act 2006 s 5(1) (see PARA 213), and ending with the date of the poll (Political Parties, Elections and Referendums Act 2000 Sch 9 para 6(5) (added by SI 2007/1388)).

For the purposes of head (1) above, the 'appropriate date' is the date which falls four months before the date of the poll where:

    (a)   the date of the poll is that determined by the Government of Wales Act 2006 s 3(1) (see PARA 213) (Political Parties, Elections and Referendums Act 2000 Sch 9 para 6(4)(a) (Sch 9 para 6(4)(a)–(c) amended by SI 2007/1388));

    (b)   no less than five months before the day on which the poll would have taken place under the Government of Wales Act 2006 s 3(1), the date of the poll is brought forward under s 4(1) (see PARA 213 note 3) (Political Parties, Elections and Referendums Act 2000 Sch 9 para 6(4)(b) (as so amended)); or

    (c)   no less than four months before the day on which the poll would have taken place under the Government of Wales Act 2006 s 3(1), the date of the poll is postponed under s 4(1) (Political Parties, Elections and Referendums Act 2000 Sch 9 para 6(4)(c) (as so amended)).

However, where the date of the poll is brought forward or postponed otherwise than as mentioned in head (b) or head (c) above, the 'appropriate date' means the date which falls four months before the date when the poll would have taken place under the Government of Wales Act 2006 s 3(1): see the Political Parties, Elections and Referendums Act 2000 Sch 9 para 6(4) (amended by SI 2007/1388).

17 See the Political Parties, Elections and Referendums Act 2000 Sch 9 para 6(1), (2) (Sch 9 para 6(1) as amended: see note 15).

18 Political Parties, Elections and Referendums Act 2000 Sch 9 para 6(2)(a). In a case where, at the election, a candidate stands for election in any constituency in the name of a registered party and one or more other registered parties, the amount applying to the party in respect of the constituency under head (a) in the text, instead of being the amount specified there, is that amount divided by the number of registered parties in whose name the candidate stands for election: see Sch 9 para 6(2A), (2B) (Sch 9 para 6(2A), (2B) added by the Electoral Administration Act 2006 s 64(1), (3)).

19 Political Parties, Elections and Referendums Act 2000 Sch 9 para 6(2)(b).

20 See the Political Parties, Elections and Referendums Act 2000 Sch 9 para 4(1). As to European parliamentary general elections see PARA 217 et seq.

21 For these purposes, the relevant period is the period of four months ending with the date of the poll for the election: Political Parties, Elections and Referendums Act 2000 Sch 9 para 4(5). As to the date of the poll at a European parliamentary election see PARA 222.

22 See the Political Parties, Elections and Referendums Act 2000 Sch 9 para 4(1), (2).

23 As to the number of MEPs to be returned at European parliamentary elections in the United Kingdom see PARA 13 et seq.

24 As to the establishment of electoral regions for the purpose of elections to the European Parliament see PARA 77.

25 Political Parties, Elections and Referendums Act 2000 Sch 9 para 4(2) (amended by SI 2004/366). As to the meaning of 'combined region' see PARA 13.

26 Political Parties, Elections and Referendums Act 2000 Sch 9 para 4(3) (amended by SI 2004/366).

27 Political Parties, Elections and Referendums Act 2000 Sch 9 para 4(4).

28 Ie within the meaning of the Political Parties, Elections and Referendums Act 2000 s 80 (see PARA 307 note 4): see s 79(4)(a).

29 Ie any expenses within the Political Parties, Elections and Referendums Act 2000 s 72(2) (see PARA 299): see s 79(4)(a).

30 Political Parties, Elections and Referendums Act 2000 s 79(4)(a). As to the meaning of 'property' for these purposes see PARA 34 note 8.

31 Ie by virtue of the Political Parties, Elections and Referendums Act 2000 s 72(2) (see PARA 299): see s 79(4)(b).
32 Political Parties, Elections and Referendums Act 2000 s 79(4)(b).
33 Ie the appropriate proportion of the expenses mentioned in the Political Parties, Elections and Referendums Act 2000 s 79(4)(a) (see the text and notes 28–30): see s 79(4). For these purposes, the appropriate proportion of the expenses mentioned in s 79(4)(a) is such proportion of those expenses as is reasonably attributable to the use made of the property, services or facilities as mentioned in s 79(4)(b) (see the text and notes 31–32): s 79(5).
34 Ie for the purposes of the Political Parties, Elections and Referendums Act 2000 s 79(1), Sch 9: see s 79(4).
35 Ie for the purposes of the Political Parties, Elections and Referendums Act 2000 ss 80–83 (see PARAS 307–309): see s 79(4).
36 See the Political Parties, Elections and Referendums Act 2000 s 79(4).
37 As to the limitation of campaign expenditure where campaigns are combined see PARA 306.
38 See the Political Parties, Elections and Referendums Act 2000 s 79(2); and PARA 751. As to defences to liability under s 79(2) see s 79(3); and PARA 751 note 17. As to the treasurer of a registered party see PARA 253; and as to the appointment of deputy treasurers of a registered party for the purposes of controlling campaign expenditure see PARA 300.

306.   Limitation of campaign expenditure where campaigns are combined.
For the purposes of controlling campaign expenditure incurred by registered parties during election periods[1], special limits apply to campaign expenditure incurred by or on behalf of a registered party[2] in England[3] or Wales[4] at combined polls[5] in circumstances:

(1)   where separate limits would apply in relation to a general election to the European Parliament[6] and in relation to a general election to the National Assembly for Wales[7] and any part of the period which would be the relevant period[8] for the purposes of the general election to the European Parliament falls within any part of the period which would be the relevant period[9] for the purposes of a general election to the National Assembly for Wales[10];

(2)   where separate limits would apply in relation to a parliamentary general election[11], and in relation to a general election to the European Parliament[12] or a general election to the National Assembly for Wales[13] and the parliamentary general election is pending[14] during any part of the period in relation to which the limit imposed in relation to the European Parliament or a general election to the National Assembly for Wales would apply[15];

(3)   where a limit under head (2) above would apply in relation to a relevant period for those purposes[16] and another limit in relation to a general election to the European Parliament[17] or a general election to the National Assembly for Wales[18] applies in relation to a period which is not a period during which the parliamentary general election is pending but which either falls wholly within or ends at any time falling within the relevant period for the purposes of head (2) above[19];

(4)   where a limit would apply in relation to a parliamentary general election[20], and another limit applies in relation to a general election to the European Parliament[21] or a general election to the National Assembly for Wales[22] in relation to any period which either falls wholly within, or ends at any time falling within, the period which would be the relevant period in relation to the parliamentary general election, and where head (2) above does not apply in connection with that expenditure[23].

1   Ie for the purposes of the Political Parties, Elections and Referendums Act 2000 Pt V (ss 72–84):
    see s 72(1). Nothing in Pt V applies in relation to expenses incurred or to be incurred by or on
    behalf of a minor party: s 72(10). As to the meaning of 'campaign expenditure' see PARA 299. As
    to the meaning of 'minor party' see PARA 253 note 8. As to the returns as to campaign
    expenditure that are required see PARA 307.
2   As to the meaning of 'registered party' for these purposes see PARA 35 note 3.
3   As to the meaning of 'England' see PARA 1 note 1.
4   As to the meaning of 'Wales' see PARA 1 note 1.
5   As to the combination of polls at a parliamentary general election and a European
    parliamentary general election see PARA 21; and as to the combination of polls at elections for
    related areas see PARA 30.
6   Ie under the Political Parties, Elections and Referendums Act 2000 s 79(1), Sch 9 para 4 (see
    PARA 305): see Sch 9 para 8. As to European parliamentary general elections see PARA 217 et
    seq.
7   Ie under the Political Parties, Elections and Referendums Act 2000 Sch 9 para 6 (see PARA 305):
    see Sch 9 para 8. As to the National Assembly for Wales see CONSTITUTIONAL LAW AND HUMAN
    RIGHTS.
8   As to the meaning of 'relevant period' for these purposes see PARA 305 note 21.
9   As to the meaning of 'relevant period' for these purposes see PARA 305 note 16.
10 See the Political Parties, Elections and Referendums Act 2000 Sch 9 para 8.
11 Ie under the Political Parties, Elections and Referendums Act 2000 Sch 9 para 3 (see PARA 305):
    see Sch 9 para 9 (amended by the Fixed-term Parliaments Act 2011 s 6(3), Schedule paras 18,
    21(1), (3)). As to parliamentary general elections see PARA 189 et seq. As to the meaning of
    'parliamentary election' see PARA 9.
12 Ie under the Political Parties, Elections and Referendums Act 2000 Sch 9 para 4 (see PARA 305):
    see Sch 9 para 9 (as amended: see note 11).
13 Ie under the Political Parties, Elections and Referendums Act 2000 Sch 9 para 6 (see PARA 305):
    see Sch 9 para 9 (as amended: see note 11).
14 For these purposes, a parliamentary general election is pending during the period:
    (1)   beginning with the date on which Parliament is dissolved by the Fixed-term Parliaments
           Act 2011 s 3(1) (see PARA 189) for a parliamentary general election (Political Parties,
           Elections and Referendums Act 2000 Sch 9 para 1(3)(a) (amended by the Fixed-term
           Parliaments Act 2011 Schedule paras 18, 21(1), (2))); and
    (2)   ending with the date of the poll for that election (Political Parties, Elections and
           Referendums Act 2000 Sch 9 para 1(3)(b)).
    As to the polling day at a parliamentary general election see PARA 195.
15 See the Political Parties, Elections and Referendums Act 2000 Sch 9 para 9 (as amended: see
    note 11).
16 Ie a relevant period for the purposes of the Political Parties, Elections and Referendums
    Act 2000 Sch 9 para 9(3) or a first relevant period for the purposes of Sch 9 para 9(5): see Sch 9
    para 10.
17 Ie under the Political Parties, Elections and Referendums Act 2000 Sch 9 para 4 (see PARA 305):
    see Sch 9 para 10.
18 Ie under the Political Parties, Elections and Referendums Act 2000 Sch 9 para 6 (see PARA 305):
    see Sch 9 para 10.
19 See the Political Parties, Elections and Referendums Act 2000 Sch 9 para 10.
20 Ie under the Political Parties, Elections and Referendums Act 2000 Sch 9 para 3 (see PARA 305):
    see Sch 9 para 11.
21 Ie under the Political Parties, Elections and Referendums Act 2000 Sch 9 para 4 (see PARA 305):
    see Sch 9 para 11.
22 Ie under the Political Parties, Elections and Referendums Act 2000 Sch 9 para 6 (see PARA 305):
    see Sch 9 para 11.
23 See the Political Parties, Elections and Referendums Act 2000 Sch 9 para 11.

(D) Returns as to Campaign Expenditure

307.   Returns as to campaign expenditure.   For the purposes of controlling
campaign expenditure incurred by registered parties during election periods[1],
where any limit imposed[2] in relation to campaign expenditure incurred by or on
behalf of a registered party[3] applies during the relevant campaign period[4] and
where that period ends[5], the treasurer of the party[6] must prepare a return in

respect of campaign expenditure incurred by or on behalf of the party during that period in any relevant part or parts of the United Kingdom[7].

Such a return must specify the poll for the relevant election (or, as the case may be, the polls for the relevant elections) that took place during the relevant campaign period, and it must contain[8]:

(1)   a statement of all payments made in respect of campaign expenditure incurred by or on behalf of the party during the relevant campaign period in the relevant part or parts of the United Kingdom[9];

(2)   a statement of all disputed claims[10] of which the treasurer is aware[11]; and

(3)   a statement of all the unpaid claims (if any) of which the treasurer is aware in respect of which an application has been made, or is about to be made, to a court for permission to pay the claim[12].

Such a return must be accompanied by:

(a)   all invoices or receipts relating to the payments mentioned in head (1) above[13]; and

(b)   in the case of any expenditure in relation to which an appropriate amount is treated as campaign expenditure incurred by the party[14], any declaration falling to be made with respect to that expenditure[15].

Where, however, any payments or claims falling to be dealt with in such a return have already been dealt with in an earlier return[16]:

(i)   it is sufficient for the later return to deal with those payments or claims by specifying overall amounts in respect of them[17]; and

(ii)   the requirement as to accompanying documentation imposed by heads (a) and (b) above does not apply to any invoices, receipts or declarations which accompanied the earlier return and are specified as such in the later return[18].

A report must be prepared by a qualified auditor[19] on such a return in respect of campaign expenditure where, during a relevant campaign period, the campaign expenditure incurred by or on behalf of a registered party in the relevant part or parts of the United Kingdom exceeds £250,000[20].

1   Ie for the purposes of the Political Parties, Elections and Referendums Act 2000 Pt V (ss 72–84): see s 72(1). Nothing in Pt V applies in relation to expenses incurred or to be incurred by or on behalf of a minor party: s 72(10). As to the meaning of 'campaign expenditure' see PARA 299. As to the meaning of 'minor party' see PARA 253 note 8. As to the returns as to campaign expenditure that are required see PARA 307.

2   Ie imposed by the Political Parties, Elections and Referendums Act 2000 s 79(1), Sch 9 (see PARAS 305–306); see s 80(2)(a).

3   As to the meaning of 'registered party' for these purposes see PARA 35 note 3.

4   Political Parties, Elections and Referendums Act 2000 s 80(2)(a). For these purposes, the relevant campaign period, in relation to any limit imposed by Sch 9, is the period in relation to which the limit is so imposed: s 80(1)(a).

5   Political Parties, Elections and Referendums Act 2000 s 80(2)(b).

6   As to the treasurer of a registered party see PARA 253.

7   See the Political Parties, Elections and Referendums Act 2000 s 80(2). For these purposes, a part of the United Kingdom is a relevant part, in relation to any limit imposed by Sch 9, if the limit applies to campaign expenditure which, within the meaning of Sch 9, is incurred in that part: s 80(1)(b). As to the meaning of 'United Kingdom' see PARA 1 note 1.

8   Political Parties, Elections and Referendums Act 2000 s 80(3). The Electoral Commission may by regulations prescribe a form of return which may be used for these purposes: s 80(6). Regulations made by the Electoral Commission are not statutory instruments and are not recorded in this work: see further PARA 47. As to the Electoral Commission see PARA 34 et seq.

9   Political Parties, Elections and Referendums Act 2000 s 80(3)(a).

10 Ie within the meaning of the Political Parties, Elections and Referendums Act 2000 s 78 (see PARA 303): see s 80(3)(b).

11 Political Parties, Elections and Referendums Act 2000 s 80(3)(b).
12 Political Parties, Elections and Referendums Act 2000 s 80(3)(c). The text refers to an application for permission to pay claims in respect of campaign expenditure made under s 77(4) (see PARA 304): see s 80(3)(c).
13 Political Parties, Elections and Referendums Act 2000 s 80(4)(a).
14 Ie by virtue of the Political Parties, Elections and Referendums Act 2000 s 73 (see PARA 299): see s 80(4)(b).
15 Political Parties, Elections and Referendums Act 2000 s 80(4)(b). The text refers to a declaration falling to be made in accordance with s 73(6) (see PARA 299): see s 80(4)(b).
16 See the Political Parties, Elections and Referendums Act 2000 s 80(5).
17 Political Parties, Elections and Referendums Act 2000 s 80(5)(a).
18 Political Parties, Elections and Referendums Act 2000 s 80(5)(b).
19 In relation to the appointment of an auditor to prepare a report under the Political Parties, Elections and Referendums Act 2000 s 81(1) (or, as the case may be, an auditor so appointed), s 43(6), (7) (regulations made by the Electoral Commission with respect to the appointment of auditors: see CONSTITUTIONAL LAW AND HUMAN RIGHTS) and s 44 (supplementary provisions about auditors: see CONSTITUTIONAL LAW AND HUMAN RIGHTS) apply as they apply in relation to the appointment of an auditor to carry out an audit under s 43 (annual audits: see CONSTITUTIONAL LAW AND HUMAN RIGHTS) (or, as the case may be, an auditor so appointed): see s 81(2). As to the meaning of 'qualified auditor' see PARA 298 note 5. As to the general accounting requirements for registered parties see PARA 298.
20 Political Parties, Elections and Referendums Act 2000 s 81(1). As to the meaning of 'relevant campaign period' for these purposes see note 4; and as to the meaning of 'relevant part of the United Kingdom' see note 7 (definitions applied by virtue of s 81(3)). The Secretary of State may by order vary the sum for the time being specified in any provision of the Political Parties, Elections and Referendums Act 2000: see s 155; and PARA 299 note 36. At the date at which this volume states the law no such order had been made.

308. Delivery of returns as to campaign expenditure to the Electoral Commission. For the purposes of controlling campaign expenditure incurred by registered parties during election periods[1], where:

(1) any return as to campaign expenditure falls to be prepared[2]; and

(2) an auditor's report on it falls to be prepared also[3],

the treasurer of the party[4] must deliver the return to the Electoral Commission[5], together with a copy of the auditor's report, within six months of the end of the relevant campaign period[6]. In the case of any other return as to campaign expenditure which falls to be prepared[7], the treasurer of the party must deliver the return to the Commission within three months of the end of the relevant campaign period[8].

Where, after the date on which a return is so delivered to the Commission, permission is given by a court for any claim to be paid[9], the treasurer of the party in question must, within seven days after the payment, deliver to the Commission a return of any sums paid in pursuance of the permission accompanied by a copy of the order of the court giving the permission[10].

The treasurer of a registered party commits an offence if, without reasonable excuse, he fails to comply with the requirements as to any return or auditor's report[11]; and, notwithstanding any criminal liability of any person, the registered party is liable also to a civil penalty[12].

1 Ie for the purposes of the Political Parties, Elections and Referendums Act 2000 Pt V (ss 72–84): see s 72(1). Nothing in Pt V applies in relation to expenses incurred or to be incurred by or on behalf of a minor party: s 72(10). As to the meaning of 'campaign expenditure' see PARA 299. As to the meaning of 'minor party' see PARA 253 note 8. As to the returns as to campaign expenditure that are required see PARA 307.
2 Political Parties, Elections and Referendums Act 2000 s 82(1)(a). The text refers to a return as to campaign expenditure which falls to be prepared under s 80 (see PARA 307): see s 82(1)(a).
3 Political Parties, Elections and Referendums Act 2000 s 82(1)(b). The text refers to an auditor's report on a return as to campaign expenditure which falls to be prepared under s 81(1) (see PARA 307): see s 82(1)(b).

4　As to the treasurer of a registered party see PARA 253.
5　As to the Electoral Commission see PARA 34 et seq.
6　See the Political Parties, Elections and Referendums Act 2000 s 82(1). As to the meaning of the 'relevant campaign period' for these purposes see PARA 307 note 4.
7　Ie under the Political Parties, Elections and Referendums Act 2000 s 80 (see PARA 307): see s 82(2).
8　Political Parties, Elections and Referendums Act 2000 s 82(2).
9　Ie permission to pay claims in respect of campaign expenditure made under the Political Parties, Elections and Referendums Act 2000 s 77(4) (see PARA 304): see s 82(3).
10　Political Parties, Elections and Referendums Act 2000 s 82(3).
11　See the Political Parties, Elections and Referendums Act 2000 s 82(4); and PARA 751.
12　See the Political Parties, Elections and Referendums Act 2000 s 147, Sch 19C; and PARA 757 et seq.

309.　Declaration as to campaign expenditure. For the purposes of controlling campaign expenditure incurred by registered parties during election periods[1], each return as to campaign expenditure[2] must, when delivered to the Electoral Commission[3], be accompanied by a declaration which is signed by the treasurer[4]. The declaration must state:

(1)　that the treasurer has examined the return in question[5]; and
(2)　that, to the best of his knowledge and belief[6]: (a) it is a complete and correct return as required by law[7]; and (b) all expenses shown in it as paid have been paid by him or a deputy treasurer of the party[8] or a duly authorised person[9].

A person commits an offence if he knowingly or recklessly makes such a declaration falsely, or if the requirements as to such a declaration are contravened at a time when he is treasurer of the registered party to which the return relates[10].

1　Ie for the purposes of the Political Parties, Elections and Referendums Act 2000 Pt V (ss 72–84): see s 72(1). Nothing in Pt V applies in relation to expenses incurred or to be incurred by or on behalf of a minor party: s 72(10). As to the meaning of 'campaign expenditure' see PARA 299. As to the meaning of 'minor party' see PARA 253 note 8. As to the returns as to campaign expenditure that are required see PARA 307.
2　Ie each return as to campaign expenditure which falls to be prepared under the Political Parties, Elections and Referendums Act 2000 s 80 (see PARA 307): see s 83(1).
3　As to the Electoral Commission see PARA 34 et seq; and as to the delivery of returns to the Electoral Commission see PARA 308.
4　Political Parties, Elections and Referendums Act 2000 s 83(1). The declaration also must comply with s 83(2) (see the text and notes 5–9): see s 83(1). As to the treasurer of a registered party see PARA 253.
5　Political Parties, Elections and Referendums Act 2000 s 83(2)(a).
6　Political Parties, Elections and Referendums Act 2000 s 83(2)(b).
7　Political Parties, Elections and Referendums Act 2000 s 83(2)(b)(i).
8　As to the appointment of deputy treasurers of a registered party for the purposes of controlling campaign expenditure see PARA 300.
9　Political Parties, Elections and Referendums Act 2000 s 83(2)(b)(ii). The text refers to a person authorised in writing by the treasurer or a deputy treasurer under s 75 (see PARA 301): see s 83(2)(b)(ii).
10　See the Political Parties, Elections and Referendums Act 2000 s 83(3); and PARA 751.

310.　Public inspection of returns as to campaign expenditure. For the purposes of controlling campaign expenditure incurred by registered parties during election periods[1], where the Electoral Commission[2] receives any return as to campaign expenditure[3], it must[4]:

(1)　as soon as reasonably practicable after receiving the return, make a copy of the return, and of any documents accompanying it, available for public inspection[5]; and

(2)   keep any such copy available for public inspection for the period for
       which the return or other document is kept by it[6].

Where the Commission is for the time being required to make available for
public inspection a copy of any document in this way, it must make the copy
available for public inspection during ordinary office hours, either at the
Commission's offices or at some convenient place appointed by it[7], although the
Commission may make other arrangements for members of the public to have
access to the document's contents[8]. If requested to do so by any person, the
Commission must supply him with a copy of the document or any part of it[9];
and the Commission may charge such reasonable fee as it may determine in
respect of any inspection or access so allowed or any copy so supplied[10]. Where
any such document is held by the Commission in electronic form, any copy so
made available for public inspection or so supplied must be made available, or
(as the case may be) supplied, in a legible form[11].

At the end of the period of two years beginning with the date when any such
return or other document is received by the Commission[12]: (a) it may cause the
return or other document to be destroyed[13]; but (b) if requested to do so by the
treasurer of the party concerned[14], it must arrange for the return or other
document to be returned to the treasurer[15].

1   Ie for the purposes of the Political Parties, Elections and Referendums Act 2000 Pt V (ss 72–84):
    see s 72(1). Nothing in Pt V applies in relation to expenses incurred or to be incurred by or on
    behalf of a minor party: s 72(10). As to the meaning of 'campaign expenditure' see PARA 299. As
    to the meaning of 'minor party' see PARA 253 note 8. As to the returns as to campaign
    expenditure that are required see PARA 307.
2   As to the Electoral Commission see PARA 34 et seq.
3   Ie receives any return as to campaign expenditure which falls to be prepared under the Political
    Parties, Elections and Referendums Act 2000 s 80 (see PARA 307): see s 84(1). As to the delivery
    of returns to the Electoral Commission see PARA 308.
4   See the Political Parties, Elections and Referendums Act 2000 s 84(1).
5   Political Parties, Elections and Referendums Act 2000 s 84(1)(a).
6   Political Parties, Elections and Referendums Act 2000 s 84(1)(b).
7   Political Parties, Elections and Referendums Act 2000 s 149(2), (6)(b).
8   Political Parties, Elections and Referendums Act 2000 s 149(3), (6)(b).
9   Political Parties, Elections and Referendums Act 2000 s 149(4), (6)(b).
10 See the Political Parties, Elections and Referendums Act 2000 s 149(5), (6)(b).
11 See the Political Parties, Elections and Referendums Act 2000 s 149(7).
12 See the Political Parties, Elections and Referendums Act 2000 s 84(2).
13 Political Parties, Elections and Referendums Act 2000 s 84(2)(a).
14 As to the treasurer of a registered party see PARA 253.
15 Political Parties, Elections and Referendums Act 2000 s 84(2)(b).

C.   CONTROLS AFFECTING DONATIONS MADE TO REGISTERED PARTIES DURING ELECTION
                                    PERIODS

**311.   Weekly reporting of donations made to registered parties during election
periods.**   In the case of any parliamentary general election period[1], the treasurer
of a registered party[2] must prepare a report in respect of each of the following
periods[3]:

(1)   the period of seven days beginning with the first day of the general
       election period[4];
(2)   each succeeding period of seven days falling within the general election
       period[5]; and
(3)   any final period of less than seven days falling within that period[6].

Such a report is known as a 'weekly report', and a 'reporting period', in relation
to such a report, is the period mentioned in any of heads (1) to (3) above to

which the report relates[7]. The weekly report for any reporting period must record each donation[8] of more than £7,500 received during that period[9] either by the party (if it is not a party with accounting units)[10], or by the central organisation of the party[11] (if it is a party with accounting units)[12]; and, if, during any reporting period, no such donations have been received as so mentioned, the weekly report for that period must contain a statement to that effect[13]. In relation to each recordable donation[14], a weekly report must give:

(a)   all such details of the name and address of the donor as are for the time being known to the party[15];

(b)   details about the donations[16], specifically the amount of the donation (if the donation was a donation of money, in cash or otherwise)[17] or the nature of the donation and its value (otherwise)[18];

(c)   the relevant date for the donation[19], and, if the donation was regarded as having been received from a permissible donor on the basis that its purpose was to meet costs in connection with a visit conducted outside the United Kingdom[20], the date or dates on or between which the visit to which the donation relates took place[21], and the destination and purpose of the visit[22]; and

(d)   such other information (if any) as is required by regulations made by the Electoral Commission[23].

The requirement to prepare a weekly report does not apply in relation to a registered party in respect of a general election period, however, if the party has made an exemption declaration which covers the general election in question[24]. A registered party is taken to have made an exemption declaration which covers a particular general election if:

(i)   a declaration that the party does not intend to have any candidates at that election[25] is signed by the responsible officers of the party[26], and is sent to the Commission within the period of seven days beginning with the date on which Parliament is dissolved for a parliamentary general election[27]; or

(ii)   the party's application for registration[28] was accompanied by a declaration that the party was not intending to have candidates at parliamentary elections[29], and either the poll for the general election in question takes place within the period of 12 months beginning with the date of its registration[30], or the declaration has been confirmed in the party's most recent notification given to the Commission regarding confirmation of the party's registered particulars[31], and the poll for the general election in question takes place within the period of 12 months beginning with the date when that notification was so given[32].

An exemption declaration does not cover a particular general election, however, if the party in question withdraws its declaration by a notice signed by the responsible officers of the party[33], and sent to the Commission[34], before the beginning of the general election period[35]. Where a registered party has made an exemption declaration which otherwise would cover a particular general election[36], but where the party has one or more candidates at that election[37], the exemption declaration is treated as if it had been withdrawn at the beginning of the general election period (and the requirement to prepare a weekly report accordingly applies retrospectively as from the beginning of that period)[38].

The Secretary of State may, after consulting the Electoral Commission and all registered parties, by order[39] make provision for the provisions relating to[40]:

(A)   the weekly reporting of donations made to registered parties during election periods[41];

(B)   the submission of those reports and the declaration required to be made by a treasurer in relation to such reports[42]; and

(C)   the relevant civil penalties which apply in relation to the submission of those reports[43],

to apply in relation to the specified election period[44], in the case of one or more relevant elections, with such modifications as are specified in the order[45].

1   For these purposes, 'general election period' means the period:
     (1)   beginning with the date on which Parliament is dissolved by the Fixed-term Parliaments Act 2011 s 3(1) (see PARA 189) for a parliamentary general election (Political Parties, Elections and Referendums Act 2000 s 63(6)(a) (amended by the Fixed-term Parliaments Act 2011 s 6(3), Schedule paras 18, 20)); and
     (2)   ending with the date of the poll for that election (Political Parties, Elections and Referendums Act 2000 s 63(6)(b)).
     As to the polling day at a parliamentary general election see PARA 195.
2   As to the meaning of 'registered party' for these purposes see PARA 35 note 3. As to the treasurer of a registered party see PARA 253. Nothing in the Political Parties, Elections and Referendums Act 2000 Pt IV (ss 50–71) applies in relation to donations received by minor parties: see s 50(9). See also note 8. As to the meaning of 'minor party' see PARA 253 note 8.
3   See the Political Parties, Elections and Referendums Act 2000 s 63(1). This requirement is subject to s 64 (exemption declarations: see the text and notes 24–38): see s 63(1).
4   Political Parties, Elections and Referendums Act 2000 s 63(1)(a).
5   Political Parties, Elections and Referendums Act 2000 s 63(1)(b).
6   Political Parties, Elections and Referendums Act 2000 s 63(1)(c).
7   See the Political Parties, Elections and Referendums Act 2000 s 63(2).
     The mechanism for preparing and submitting weekly reports is the same as that required for quarterly reports prepared under s 62 (see CONSTITUTIONAL LAW AND HUMAN RIGHTS), and only the main differences which apply to weekly reports are specified in this title. As to the submission of weekly and quarterly donation reports to the Electoral Commission see s 65; as to the declaration required to be made by a treasurer in relation to such reports see s 66; as to the register of all donations reported to the Electoral Commission see s 69; and see CONSTITUTIONAL LAW AND HUMAN RIGHTS.
8   As to the meaning of 'donation' in this context see the Political Parties, Elections and Referendums Act 2000 s 50(2); and CONSTITUTIONAL LAW AND HUMAN RIGHTS. Under Pt IV generally, a donation received by a registered party must not be accepted unless it is made by a permissible donor; where a donor is unidentifiable or impermissible, the donation must be returned to its source or sent to the Electoral Commission: see CONSTITUTIONAL LAW AND HUMAN RIGHTS. For the purposes of controlling donations to candidates at an election, ss 56–60 have been applied by the Representation of the People Act 1983 s 71A(4), Sch 2A para 7, the European Parliamentary Elections Regulations 2004, SI 2004/293, reg 42(4), Sch 6 para 7, and the National Assembly for Wales (Representation of the People) Order 2007, SI 2007/236, art 41(4), Sch 6 para 7: see PARA 289. As to the meaning of 'permissible donor' for these purposes see PARA 288. As to the Electoral Commission see PARA 34 et seq.
9   See the Political Parties, Elections and Referendums Act 2000 s 63(3) (amended by the Political Parties and Elections Act 2009 s 20(3)). The Secretary of State may by order vary the sum for the time being specified in any provision of the Political Parties, Elections and Referendums Act 2000: see s 155; and PARA 299 note 36.
     As from a day to be appointed under the Political Parties and Elections Act 2009 s 43(1), the Political Parties, Elections and Referendums Act 2000 s 63(5), Sch 6 para 1A is added by the Political Parties and Elections Act 2009 s 9(5) and amended by s 10(6)(b). Accordingly, as from such a day, in relation to each recordable donation in the case of which a declaration under the Political Parties, Elections and Referendums Act 2000 s 54A (not yet in force) (declaration as to source of donations exceeding £7, 500: see CONSTITUTIONAL LAW AND HUMAN RIGHTS) has been given, a weekly report must either state that no reason was found to think that the declaration was untruthful or inaccurate, or give details of any respects in which the declaration was found or suspected to be untruthful or inaccurate: see the Political Parties, Elections and Referendums Act 2000 Sch 6 para 1A(1) (prospectively added and amended). However, at the date at which this volume states the law, no such day had been appointed.

10 Political Parties, Elections and Referendums Act 2000 s 63(3)(a). As to the meanings of 'accounting units' and 'party with accounting units' see PARA 253 note 15.

11 As to the meaning of 'central organisation' (in relation to a registered party) see PARA 253 note 15.

12 Political Parties, Elections and Referendums Act 2000 s 63(3)(b).

13 Political Parties, Elections and Referendums Act 2000 s 63(4).

14 For these purposes, 'recordable donation', in relation to a weekly report, means a donation required to be recorded in that report; and 'weekly report' means a report required to be prepared by virtue of the Political Parties, Elections and Referendums Act 2000 s 63: Sch 6 para 1.

15 Political Parties, Elections and Referendums Act 2000 Sch 6 para 3(1) (Sch 6 para 3(1) numbered as such, Sch 6 para 3(2), (3) added, by the Electoral Administration Act 2006 s 10(2), Sch 1 paras 24, 27). The provision made by Sch 6 para 3 does not apply in relation to a recordable donation that is an Irish donation, within the meaning given by Sch 6 para 2A(2) (see CONSTITUTIONAL LAW AND HUMAN RIGHTS): Sch 6 para 3(4) (added by SI 2007/2501).

In the case of a donation by a person who has an anonymous entry in an electoral register (within the meaning of the Representation of the People Act 1983: see PARA 148), instead of giving details of the address of the donor the party must state that it has seen evidence of such description as is prescribed by the Secretary of State in regulations that the person has such an entry: Political Parties, Elections and Referendums Act 2000 Sch 6 para 3(2) (as so added). In the case of a donation in the form of a bequest by a person who either at the time of his death, or at any time in the period of five years ending at the date of his death, had such an entry, instead of giving details of the address of the donor, the party must state that it has seen evidence of such description as is prescribed by the Secretary of State in regulations that the person had, at that time, such an entry: Sch 6 para 3(3) (as so added). Accordingly, the evidence that an individual has an anonymous entry in an electoral register prescribed for the purposes of Sch 6 para 3(2), (3) is a certificate of anonymous registration issued under the Representation of the People (England and Wales) Regulations 2001, SI 2001/341, reg 45G (see PARA 145 note 12): see the Political Donations and Regulated Transactions (Anonymous Electors) Regulations 2008, SI 2008/2869, reg 3. As to the Secretary of State see PARA 2; and as to the making of regulations under the Political Parties, Elections and Referendums Act 2000 generally see PARA 34 note 2.

16 See the Political Parties, Elections and Referendums Act 2000 Sch 6 para 4(1).

17 See the Political Parties, Elections and Referendums Act 2000 Sch 6 para 4(2).

18 See the Political Parties, Elections and Referendums Act 2000 Sch 6 para 4(3). The value of such a donation is determined in accordance with s 53 (see CONSTITUTIONAL LAW AND HUMAN RIGHTS): see Sch 6 para 4(3).

19 Political Parties, Elections and Referendums Act 2000 Sch 6 para 5(1)(a). For these purposes, in relation to a weekly report, the relevant date for a donation is the date when the donation was received by the party or its central organisation as mentioned in s 63(3) (see the text and notes 8–12): Sch 6 para 5(4).

20 Ie in the case of a donation to which the Political Parties, Elections and Referendums Act 2000 s 55(3) applies (see CONSTITUTIONAL LAW AND HUMAN RIGHTS): see Sch 6 para 5(2).

21 Political Parties, Elections and Referendums Act 2000 Sch 6 para 5(2)(a).

22 Political Parties, Elections and Referendums Act 2000 Sch 6 para 5(2)(b).

23 Political Parties, Elections and Referendums Act 2000 Sch 6 para 8. Regulations made by the Electoral Commission are not statutory instruments and are not recorded in this work: see further PARA 47.

24 Political Parties, Elections and Referendums Act 2000 s 64(1).

25 Political Parties, Elections and Referendums Act 2000 s 64(2). For these purposes, a registered party is taken to have a candidate at a general election if any statement published, in connection with the election, under the Representation of the People Act 1983 Sch 1 r 14 (see PARA 267) contains the name of a candidate standing in the name of the party: Political Parties, Elections and Referendums Act 2000 s 64(9). As to references to persons standing for election in the name of a registered party see PARA 253 note 8. As to the meaning of 'candidate' see PARA 230.

26 Political Parties, Elections and Referendums Act 2000 s 64(2)(a). For these purposes, the 'responsible officers' are the registered leader, the registered nominating officer and, where the leader and the nominating officer are the same person, any other registered officer: see s 64(7). If any responsible officer is unable to sign a declaration or notice for these purposes, the holder of some other office in the party may sign in his place and the declaration or notice must include both a statement of the reason why the responsible officer is unable to sign and a declaration that the holder of the other office is authorised to sign in his place: s 64(8). As to the registered leader and the registered nominating officer see PARA 253.

27 Political Parties, Elections and Referendums Act 2000 s 64(2)(b). The text refers to the date mentioned in s 63(6)(a) (see note 1): see s 64(2)(b).
28 As to applications for registration made by a political party see PARA 253.
29 See the Political Parties, Elections and Referendums Act 2000 s 64(3).
30 Political Parties, Elections and Referendums Act 2000 s 64(3)(a).
31 Ie notification given under the Political Parties, Elections and Referendums Act 2000 s 32 (see PARA 253 note 22; and CONSTITUTIONAL LAW AND HUMAN RIGHTS): see s 64(3)(b).
32 Political Parties, Elections and Referendums Act 2000 s 64(3)(b).
33 Political Parties, Elections and Referendums Act 2000 s 64(4)(a).
34 Political Parties, Elections and Referendums Act 2000 s 64(4)(b).
35 See the Political Parties, Elections and Referendums Act 2000 s 64(4).
36 Political Parties, Elections and Referendums Act 2000 s 64(5)(a).
37 Political Parties, Elections and Referendums Act 2000 s 64(5)(b).
38 Political Parties, Elections and Referendums Act 2000 s 64(5).
39 At the date at which this volume states the law, no order had been made under the Political Parties, Elections and Referendums Act 2000 s 67. As to the making of orders under the Political Parties, Elections and Referendums Act 2000 generally see PARA 34 note 2.
40 Political Parties, Elections and Referendums Act 2000 s 67(1).
41 Political Parties, Elections and Referendums Act 2000 s 67(1)(a). The text refers to the provisions contained in ss 63, 64, together with Sch 6 (see the text and notes 1–38): see s 67(1)(a).
42 Political Parties, Elections and Referendums Act 2000 s 67(1)(b). The text refers to the provisions contained in ss 65, 66 (see note 7; and CONSTITUTIONAL LAW AND HUMAN RIGHTS): see s 67(1)(b).
43 Political Parties, Elections and Referendums Act 2000 s 67(1)(c). The text refers to the provisions contained in s 147 so far as applying in relation to s 65(1), (2) (see CONSTITUTIONAL LAW AND HUMAN RIGHTS): see s 67(1)(c). As from a day to be appointed under the Political Parties and Elections Act 2009 s 43(1), the Political Parties, Elections and Referendums Act 2000 s 67(1)(c) is amended so that it refers to an order under s 147, Sch 19C para 16 (see PARA 757 note 2), so far as applying in relation to s 65(1), (2): see s 67(1)(c) (prospectively amended by the Political Parties and Elections Act 2009 s 39, Sch 6 para 18). However, at the date at which this volume states the law, no such day had been appointed.
44 For these purposes, 'specified election period', in relation to a relevant election, means such period ending with the date of the poll for the election as may be specified in an order under the Political Parties, Elections and Referendums Act 2000 s 67(1) (s 67(2)(a)); and 'relevant election' means an election to the European Parliament (s 67(2)(b)(i)), or an election to the National Assembly for Wales (s 67(2)(b)(iii)), or an election of a police and crime commissioner (s 67(2)(b)(v)) (added by SI 2012/1917)). As to the date of the poll at Welsh Assembly elections see PARA 213; and as to the date of the poll at a European parliamentary election see PARA 222. As to the election of police and crime commissioners see POLICE AND INVESTIGATORY POWERS vol 84 (2013) PARA 62 et seq.
45 See the Political Parties, Elections and Referendums Act 2000 s 67(1). As to the meaning of 'modifications' for these purposes see PARA 44 note 9.

D. CONTROLS AFFECTING REGULATED TRANSACTIONS DURING ELECTION PERIODS

312. Weekly reporting of regulated transactions involving registered parties during election periods. The following provisions have effect except in relation to minor parties[1].

In the case of any parliamentary general election period[2], the treasurer of a registered party[3] must prepare a report in respect of each of the following periods[4]:

(1)   the period of seven days beginning with the first day of the general election period[5];

(2)   each succeeding period of seven days falling within the general election period[6]; and

(3)   any final period of less than seven days falling within that period[7].

Such a report is known as a 'weekly report' and a 'reporting period', in relation to such a report, is the period mentioned in any of heads (1) to (3) above to which the report relates[8]. The weekly report for any reporting period must record each regulated transaction[9] of more than £7,500 entered into during that period[10], either by the party (if it is not a party with accounting units)[11], or by the central organisation of the party[12] (if it is a party with accounting units)[13]; and, if, during any reporting period, no such transactions have been entered into as so mentioned, the weekly report for that period must contain a statement to that effect[14].

In relation to each recordable transaction[15], a weekly report must:

(a)   give all such details of the name and address of each authorised participant (other than the registered party[16] deriving the benefit of the transaction) as are for the time being known to the party[17];

(b)   give the name and address of each person who is not an authorised participant but who is a party to a recordable transaction[18] and the date when, and the manner in which, the transaction was duly dealt with[19];

(c)   give the nature of the transaction (that is to say, whether it is a loan, a credit facility or an arrangement by which any form of security is given)[20], the value of the transaction[21] or, in the case of a credit facility or security to which no limit is specified, a statement to that effect[22], and the relevant date for the transaction[23];

(d)   where each recordable transaction is an agreement between a registered party and another person by which the other person makes a loan of money to the party[24], or an agreement between a registered party and another person by which the other person provides a credit facility to the party[25]: (i) give the date when the loan is to be repaid or the facility is to end (or a statement that the loan or facility is indefinite)[26], or, where that date is to be determined under the agreement, a statement of how it is to be so determined[27]; (ii) give the rate of interest payable on the loan or on sums advanced under the facility (or a statement that no interest is payable)[28], or, where that rate is to be determined under the agreement, a statement of how it is to be so determined[29]; (iii) state whether the agreement contains a provision which enables outstanding interest to be added to any sum for the time being owed in respect of the loan or credit facility[30]; (iv) state whether any form of security is given in respect of the loan or the sums advanced under the facility[31];

(e)   where a registered party and another person ('A') enter into a regulated transaction of a description mentioned in head (d) above, or a transaction under which any property, services or facilities are provided for the use or benefit of the party (including the services of any person), and A also enters into an arrangement whereby another person ('B') gives any form of security (whether real or personal) for a sum owed to A by the party under the transaction[32]: (i) if the transaction[33] is a regulated transaction, identify that transaction by reference to the transaction report in which it is recorded[34], and, in any other case, give a description of the principal features of that transaction[35]; (ii) where the security given consists in or includes rights over any property, state the nature of that property[36]; (iii) if the person giving the security receives from the registered party any consideration for giving the security, give a statement of that consideration[37], or, in any other case, state that no such consideration is received[38].

The weekly report for any reporting period must also record any change[39] during that period to a regulated transaction recorded by the party (if it is not a party with accounting units)[40], or by the central organisation of the party (if it is a party with accounting units)[41]; and if during any reporting period there have been no such changes, the weekly report for that period must contain a statement to that effect[42].

The requirement to prepare a weekly report does not apply in relation to a registered party in respect of a general election period if the party has made an exemption declaration which covers the general election in question[43].

The Secretary of State may, after consulting the Electoral Commission and all registered parties, by order[44] make provision for the provisions relating to[45]:

(A)   the weekly reporting of regulated transactions involving registered parties during general election periods[46];

(B)   the submission of those reports to the Electoral Commission, and the declaration required to be made by a treasurer in relation to such reports[47]; and

(C)   the relevant civil penalties which apply in relation to the submission of those reports[48],

to apply in relation to the specified election period[49], in the case of one or more relevant elections[50], with such modifications as are specified in the order[51].

1   The Political Parties, Elections and Referendums Act 2000 ss 71Q–71X, and Sch 6A, are added by the Electoral Administration Act 2006 s 61(1), (5), except in relation to minor parties within the meaning of the Political Parties, Elections and Referendums Act 2000 s 160(1) (as to which see PARA 253): see the Electoral Administration Act 2006 (Commencement No 1 and Transitional Provisions) Order 2006, SI 2006/1972, art 3, Sch 1 para 20(a) (amended by SI 2006/2268).

2   As to the meaning of 'general election period' for these purposes see PARA 311 note 1; definition applied by virtue of the Political Parties, Elections and Referendums Act 2000 s 71Q(9) (as added: see note 1).

3   As to the meaning of 'registered party' for these purposes see PARA 35 note 3. As to the treasurer of a registered party see PARA 253.

4   See the Political Parties, Elections and Referendums Act 2000 s 71Q(1) (as added: see note 1). This requirement is subject to s 71R (exemption declarations: see the text and note 43): s 71Q(1) (as so added).

5   Political Parties, Elections and Referendums Act 2000 s 71Q(1)(a) (as added: see note 1).

6   Political Parties, Elections and Referendums Act 2000 s 71Q(1)(b) (as added: see note 1).

7   Political Parties, Elections and Referendums Act 2000 s 71Q(1)(c) (as added: see note 1).

8   See the Political Parties, Elections and Referendums Act 2000 s 71Q(2) (as added: see note 1).
    The mechanism for preparing and submitting weekly reports is the same as that required for quarterly reports prepared under s 71M (see CONSTITUTIONAL LAW AND HUMAN RIGHTS), and only the main differences which apply to weekly reports are specified in this title. As to the submission of weekly and quarterly transaction reports to the Electoral Commission see s 71S; as to the declaration required to be made by a treasurer in relation to such reports see s 71T; as to the register of recordable transactions reported to the Electoral Commission see s 71V; and see CONSTITUTIONAL LAW AND HUMAN RIGHTS.

9   For these purposes, 'regulated transaction' must be construed in accordance with the Political Parties, Elections and Referendums Act 2000 s 71F (see CONSTITUTIONAL LAW AND HUMAN RIGHTS): see s 71X(1) (as added: see note 1). Under Pt 4A (ss 71F–71Z2) generally, certain agreements or transactions between a registered party and another person (or between that person and another by which the registered party derives a benefit) may be entered into only if any of the other parties is an 'authorised participant', being a person who is a 'permissible donor' within the meaning of s 54(2) (see PARA 288): see ss 71F–71L; and CONSTITUTIONAL LAW AND HUMAN RIGHTS. Quarterly reports of regulated transactions have to be made by registered parties and submitted to the Electoral Commission on a continuous basis: see ss 71M–71P, 71S–71T; and CONSTITUTIONAL LAW AND HUMAN RIGHTS. The Secretary of State may by order make in relation to a relevant matter such provision as he thinks appropriate which corresponds to or is similar to any provision of Pt 4A or s 71Y, Sch 7A (control of loans etc to individuals and members associations: see CONSTITUTIONAL LAW AND HUMAN RIGHTS): see the Electoral Administration Act 2006 s 62(1); and CONSTITUTIONAL LAW AND HUMAN RIGHTS.

10 Political Parties, Elections and Referendums Act 2000 s 71Q(3) (s 71Q as added (see note 1); s 71Q(3) amended by the Political Parties and Elections Act 2009 s 20(3)). The Secretary of State may by order vary the sum for the time being specified in any provision of the Political Parties, Elections and Referendums Act 2000: see s 155; and PARA 299 note 36. However, in relation to any sum specified in Pt 4A, in each Parliament (other than a Parliament that is dissolved less than two years after the date of its first sitting) the Secretary of State must either make an order in pursuance of s 155(2)(a) (see PARA 299 note 36), or lay before Parliament a statement setting out the Secretary of State's reasons for not doing so: see s 155(3)(b), (4) (s 155(3), (4) added by the Political Parties and Elections Act 2009 s 20(4)). As to the Secretary of State see PARA 2; and as to the making of regulations under the Political Parties, Elections and Referendums Act 2000 generally see PARA 34 note 2.

11 Political Parties, Elections and Referendums Act 2000 s 71Q(3)(a) (as added: see note 1). As to the meanings of 'accounting units' and 'party with accounting units' see PARA 253 note 15.

12 As to the meaning of 'central organisation' (in relation to a registered party) see PARA 253 note 15.

13 Political Parties, Elections and Referendums Act 2000 s 71Q(3)(b) (as added: see note 1).

14 Political Parties, Elections and Referendums Act 2000 s 71Q(4) (as added: see note 1).

15 In relation to a weekly report, 'recordable transaction' means a transaction required to be recorded in that report; and 'weekly report' means a report required to be prepared by virtue of the Political Parties, Elections and Referendums Act 2000 s 71Q: see s 71Q(5), Sch 6A para 1(1) (as added: see note 1).

The Secretary of State may by order amend Sch 6A paras 3–7 (see the text and notes 16–38) so as to vary the details which a weekly report must give about a transaction: Sch 6A para 9(1) (as so added). However, the Secretary of State must not make such an order unless he first consults the Electoral Commission: Sch 6A para 9(2). As to the Electoral Commission see PARA 34 et seq.

16 In the case of a party with accounting units, references to a registered party must be read, for these purposes, as references to the central organisation of the party: Political Parties, Elections and Referendums Act 2000 Sch 6A para 1(2) (as added: see note 1).

17 Political Parties, Elections and Referendums Act 2000 Sch 6A para 3(1) (as added: see note 1). In the case of a participant who is an individual having an anonymous entry in an electoral register (within the meaning of the Representation of the People Act 1983 or corresponding provisions forming part of the law of Gibraltar: see PARA 148) instead of giving details of the address of the individual the party must state that it has seen evidence of such description as is prescribed by the Secretary of State in regulations that the individual has such an entry: Political Parties, Elections and Referendums Act 2000 Sch 6A para 3(2) (Sch 6A as so added; Sch 6A para 3(2) amended by SI 2009/185). Although, at the date at which this volume states the law, no such regulations had been made for these purposes, the evidence that an individual has an anonymous entry in an electoral register prescribed for similar purposes (including for the purposes of Sch 6A para 2(3) but not Sch 6A para 3(2)) is a certificate of anonymous registration issued under the Representation of the People (England and Wales) Regulations 2001, SI 2001/341, reg 45G (see PARA 145 note 12): see the Political Donations and Regulated Transactions (Anonymous Electors) Regulations 2008, SI 2008/2869, reg 3.

18 Political Parties, Elections and Referendums Act 2000 Sch 6A para 4(a) (as added: see note 1).

19 Political Parties, Elections and Referendums Act 2000 Sch 6A para 4(b) (as added: see note 1). The text refers to transactions being dealt with in accordance with s 71I(3)–(5), or those provisions as applied by s 71I(6) or s 71J(2) (see CONSTITUTIONAL LAW AND HUMAN RIGHTS): see Sch 6A para 4(b) (as so added).

20 Political Parties, Elections and Referendums Act 2000 Sch 6A para 5(1), (2) (as added: see note 1). For these purposes, 'credit facility' has the meaning given by s 71F(11) (see CONSTITUTIONAL LAW AND HUMAN RIGHTS): see s 71X(1) (as added: see note 1).

21 Ie determined in accordance with the Political Parties, Elections and Referendums Act 2000 s 71G (see CONSTITUTIONAL LAW AND HUMAN RIGHTS): see Sch 6A para 5(1), (3) (as added: see note 1).

22 Political Parties, Elections and Referendums Act 2000 Sch 6A para 5(1), (3) (as added: see note 1).

23 Political Parties, Elections and Referendums Act 2000 Sch 6A para 5(1), (4) (as added: see note 1). For these purposes, in relation to a weekly report, the relevant date for a transaction is the date when the transaction was received by the party or its central organisation as mentioned in s 71Q(3) (see the text and notes 9–13): Sch 6A para 8(2) (as so added).

24 Ie a recordable transaction of a description mentioned in the Political Parties, Elections and Referendums Act 2000 s 71F(2) (see CONSTITUTIONAL LAW AND HUMAN RIGHTS): see Sch 6A para 6(1) (as added: see note 1).

25 Ie a recordable transaction of a description mentioned in the Political Parties, Elections and Referendums Act 2000 s 71F(3) (see CONSTITUTIONAL LAW AND HUMAN RIGHTS): see Sch 6A para 6(1) (as added: see note 1).

26 Political Parties, Elections and Referendums Act 2000 Sch 6A para 6(1), (2)(a) (as added: see note 1).

27 Political Parties, Elections and Referendums Act 2000 Sch 6A para 6(1), (2)(b) (as added: see note 1).

28 Political Parties, Elections and Referendums Act 2000 Sch 6A para 6(1), (3)(a) (as added: see note 1).

29 Political Parties, Elections and Referendums Act 2000 Sch 6A para 6(1), (3)(b) (as added: see note 1).

30 Political Parties, Elections and Referendums Act 2000 Sch 6A para 6(1), (4) (as added: see note 1).

31 Political Parties, Elections and Referendums Act 2000 Sch 6A para 6(1), (5) (as added: see note 1).

32 Ie a recordable transaction of a description mentioned in the Political Parties, Elections and Referendums Act 2000 s 71F(4)(b) (see CONSTITUTIONAL LAW AND HUMAN RIGHTS): see Sch 6A para 7(1) (as added: see note 1).

33 Ie the transaction mentioned in the Political Parties, Elections and Referendums Act 2000 s 71F(4)(a) (ie where a registered party and 'A' enter into a regulated transaction of a description mentioned in s 71F(2) or s 71F(3) (see notes 24, 25) or a transaction under which any property, services or facilities are provided for the use or benefit of the party (including the services of any person): see CONSTITUTIONAL LAW AND HUMAN RIGHTS): see Sch 6A para 7(2)(a) (as added: see note 1).

34 Political Parties, Elections and Referendums Act 2000 Sch 6A para 7(1), (2)(a) (as added: see note 1).

35 Political Parties, Elections and Referendums Act 2000 Sch 6A para 7(1), (2)(b) (as added: see note 1).

36 Political Parties, Elections and Referendums Act 2000 Sch 6A para 7(1), (3) (as added: see note 1).

37 Political Parties, Elections and Referendums Act 2000 Sch 6A para 7(1), (4)(a) (as added: see note 1).

38 Political Parties, Elections and Referendums Act 2000 Sch 6A para 7(1), (4)(b) (as added: see note 1).

39 Ie as mentioned in the Political Parties, Elections and Referendums Act 2000 s 71N(1) or s 71N(3) (see CONSTITUTIONAL LAW AND HUMAN RIGHTS): see s 71Q(6) (as added: see note 1).

40 Political Parties, Elections and Referendums Act 2000 s 71Q(6)(a) (as added: see note 1). For these purposes, a transaction is recorded by a party if it is or has been recorded in a transaction report prepared under s 71M(1) (see CONSTITUTIONAL LAW AND HUMAN RIGHTS) or a weekly report prepared for that or a previous reporting period falling within the general election period: see s 71Q(7) (as so added).

41 Political Parties, Elections and Referendums Act 2000 s 71Q(6)(b) (as added: see note 1). For these purposes, a transaction is recorded by the central organisation of a party if it is or has been recorded in a transaction report prepared under s 71M(1) (see CONSTITUTIONAL LAW AND HUMAN RIGHTS) or a weekly report prepared for that or a previous reporting period falling within the general election period: s 71Q(7) (as so added).

42 Political Parties, Elections and Referendums Act 2000 s 71Q(8) (as added: see note 1).

43 Political Parties, Elections and Referendums Act 2000 s 71R(1) (as added: see note 1). The text refers to an exemption declaration made under s 64 (see PARA 311) but in its application, in accordance with s 71R(1), in relation to s 71Q, the reference in s 64(5) to s 63 is to be read as a reference to s 71Q and s 64(6) is omitted: see s 71R(2) (as so added). In any case, s 71Q does not apply in relation to a Gibraltar party: s 71R(1A) (s 71R as so added; s 71R(1A) added by SI 2009/185). See note 46.

44 At the date at which this volume states the law, no such order had been made. As to the making of orders under the Political Parties, Elections and Referendums Act 2000 generally see PARA 34 note 2.

45 Political Parties, Elections and Referendums Act 2000 s 71U(1) (as added: see note 1).

46 Political Parties, Elections and Referendums Act 2000 s 71U(1)(a) (as added: see note 1). The text refers to the provisions contained in ss 71Q, 71R (see the text and notes 2–14, 39–43), together with Sch 6A (see the text and notes 15–38): see s 71U(1)(a) (as so added). An order applying the provisions mentioned in head (A) in the text may disapply s 71R(1A) (see note 43): see s 71U(3) (added by SI 2009/185).

47 Political Parties, Elections and Referendums Act 2000 s 71U(1)(b) (as added: see note 1). The text refers to the provisions contained in ss 71S, 71T (see CONSTITUTIONAL LAW AND HUMAN RIGHTS): see s 71U(1)(b) (as so added).

48 Political Parties, Elections and Referendums Act 2000 s 71U(1)(c) (as added: see note 1). The text refers to the provisions contained in s 147 so far as applying in relation to s 71S(1), (2) (see CONSTITUTIONAL LAW AND HUMAN RIGHTS): see s 71U(1)(c) (as so added). As from a day to be appointed under the Political Parties and Elections Act 2009 s 43(1), the Political Parties, Elections and Referendums Act 2000 s 71U(1)(c) is amended so that it refers to an order under s 147, Sch 19C para 16 (see PARA 757 note 2), so far as applying in relation to s 71S(1), (2): see s 71U(1)(c) (s 71U as so added; s 71U(1)(c) prospectively amended by the Political Parties and Elections Act 2009 s 39, Sch 6 para 20). However, at the date at which this volume states the law, no such day had been appointed.

49 As to the meaning of 'specified election period' for these purposes see PARA 311 note 44; definition applied by virtue of the Political Parties, Elections and Referendums Act 2000 s 71U(2) (as added: see note 1).

50 As to the meaning of 'relevant election' for these purposes see PARA 311 note 44; definition applied by virtue of the Political Parties, Elections and Referendums Act 2000 s 71U(2) (as added: see note 1).

51 See the Political Parties, Elections and Referendums Act 2000 s 71U(1) (as added: see note 1). As to the meaning of 'modifications' for these purposes see PARA 44 note 9.

(vi) Financial Controls on Recognised Third Parties at National Election Campaigns

A. CONTROLS AFFECTING EXPENDITURE BY RECOGNISED THIRD PARTIES IN NATIONAL PARLIAMENTARY ELECTION CAMPAIGNS

(A) In general

313. Meaning of 'controlled expenditure' in relation to third parties. In relation to a third party[1] involved in a relevant national election campaign[2], 'controlled expenditure' means[3] expenses incurred by or on behalf of the third party in connection with the production or publication of election material[4] which is made available to the public at large or any section of the public (in whatever form and by whatever means)[5].

Where, in the case of a third party:

(1)   either: (a) property is transferred to the third party[6]; or (b) property, services or facilities is or are provided for the use or benefit of the third party[7], either free of charge or at a discount of more than 10 per cent[8]; and

(2)   the property, services or facilities is or are made use of by or on behalf of the third party in circumstances such that, if any expenses were to be (or are) actually incurred by or on behalf of the third party in respect of that use, they would be (or are) controlled expenditure incurred by or on behalf of the third party[9],

an amount of controlled expenditure (the 'appropriate amount') is treated, for the purposes of the statutory control of expenditure by third parties involved in a relevant national election campaign, as incurred by the third party during the period for which the property, services or facilities is or are made use of as mentioned in head (2) above[10]. Where an amount of controlled expenditure is treated in this way as incurred by or on behalf of a third party during any period the whole or part of which falls within any period which is a regulated period[11], then:

(i)   such proportion of the appropriate amount[12] as reasonably represents the use made of the property, services or facilities during the regulated period, is treated as incurred by or on behalf of the third party during the regulated period[13]; and

(ii)   if a return falls to be prepared[14] in respect of controlled expenditure incurred by or on behalf of the third party during that period, the responsible person[15] must make a declaration of that amount[16],

unless that amount is not more than £200[17].

Where head (1)(a) above applies, the appropriate amount is determined as being such proportion of either the market value of the property (where the property is transferred free of charge)[18], or the difference between the market value of the property and the amount of expenses actually incurred by or on behalf of the third party in respect of the property (where the property is transferred at a discount)[19], as is reasonably attributable to the use made of the property as mentioned in head (2) above[20].

Where head (1)(b) above applies, the appropriate amount is determined as being such proportion of either the commercial rate for the use of the property or the provision of the services or facilities (where the property, services or facilities is or are provided free of charge)[21], or the difference between that commercial rate and the amount of expenses actually incurred by or on behalf of the third party in respect of the use of the property or the provision of the services or facilities (where the property, services or facilities is or are provided at a discount)[22], as is reasonably attributable to the use made of the property, services or facilities as mentioned in head (2) above[23].

However, no amount of controlled expenditure is to be regarded for these purposes as so incurred by a third party in respect of:

(A)   the publication of any matter relating to an election, other than an advertisement, in a newspaper or periodical, a broadcast made by the British Broadcasting Corporation or by Sianel Pedwar Cymru (or by the Gibraltar Broadcasting Corporation, in relation to the combined region[24]), or a programme included in any service licensed under the Broadcasting Act 1990 or the Broadcasting Act 1996[25];

(B)   any reasonable personal expenses incurred by an individual in travelling or in providing for his accommodation or other personal needs[26]; or

(C)   the provision by any individual of his own services which he provides voluntarily in his own time and free of charge[27]; or

(D)   any property, services or facilities to the extent that the property, services or facilities is or are used in circumstances in which an amount of campaign expenditure is to be regarded as incurred by or on behalf of a registered party for the purposes of controlling campaign expenditure[28], or in which an amount of expenses falls, in accordance with any enactment[29], to be included in a return as to election expenses[30] in respect of a candidate or candidates at a particular election[31], in respect of that use[32].

1   In relation to any relevant election, 'third party', means any person or body other than a registered party or, subject to the Political Parties, Elections and Referendums Act 2000 s 85(9) (see note 4), any registered party: s 85(8). As to the meaning of 'registered party' for these purposes see PARA 35 note 3. As to the meaning of 'relevant election' for these purposes see PARA 299 note 3; definition applied by virtue of s 85(6).

2   Ie for the purposes of the Political Parties, Elections and Referendums Act 2000 Pt VI (ss 85–100) (controls relating to third party national election campaigns): see s 85(1).

3   Ie subject to the Political Parties, Elections and Referendums Act 2000 s 87 (see the text and notes 24–32): see s 85(2).

4   'Election material' is material which can reasonably be regarded as intended to:

(1) promote or procure electoral success at any relevant election for one or more particular registered parties, one or more registered parties who advocate (or do not advocate) particular policies or who otherwise fall within a particular category of such parties, or candidates who hold (or do not hold) particular opinions or who advocate (or do not advocate) particular policies or who otherwise fall within a particular category of candidates (Political Parties, Elections and Referendums Act 2000 s 85(3)(a)); or

(2) otherwise enhance the standing of any such party or parties, or of any such candidates, with the electorate in connection with future relevant elections (whether imminent or otherwise) (s 85(3)(b));

and any such material is election material even though it can reasonably be regarded as intended to achieve any other purpose as well (see s 85(3)). For these purposes:

(a) the reference to electoral success at any relevant election is a reference, in relation to a registered party, to the return at any such election of candidates standing in the name of the party or included in a list of candidates submitted by the party in connection with the election, and, in relation to candidates, to their return at any such election (see s 85(4)(a)); and

(b) the reference to doing any of the things mentioned in head (1) above or (as the case may be) in head (2) above includes doing so by prejudicing the electoral prospects at the election of other parties or candidates or (as the case may be) by prejudicing the standing with the electorate of other parties or candidates (s 85(4)(b));

and, for the purpose of determining whether any material is election material, it is immaterial that it does not expressly mention the name of any party or candidate (see s 85(4)). For these purposes, 'candidates' includes future candidates, whether identifiable or not: s 85(10). In connection with the application of s 85(2) in relation to expenses incurred by or on behalf of a third party which is a registered party, any reference in s 85(3) to a registered party or registered parties or to any candidates does not include the party itself, or any candidates standing in the name of the party at any relevant election or included in any list submitted by the party in connection with any such election, as the case may be: see s 85(9). As to the meaning of 'candidate' generally see PARA 230. As to references to persons standing for election in the name of a registered party see PARA 253 note 8.

5 See the Political Parties, Elections and Referendums Act 2000 s 85(1), (2).

6 Political Parties, Elections and Referendums Act 2000 s 86(1)(a)(i). Any property given or transferred to any officer, member, trustee or agent of a third party in his capacity as such (and not for his own use or benefit) is to be regarded as given or transferred to the third party (and references to donations received by a recognised party accordingly include donations so given or transferred) (s 95, Sch 11 para 2(5); applied by s 86(9)); and any reference to property being given or transferred to a recognised third party includes a reference to its being given or transferred either directly or indirectly through any third person (Sch 11 para 2(6)(a); applied by s 86(9)). As to the meaning of 'property' for these purposes see PARA 34 note 8.

7 Political Parties, Elections and Referendums Act 2000 s 86(1)(a)(ii).

8 See the Political Parties, Elections and Referendums Act 2000 s 86(1)(a)(i), (ii). The discount referred to in the text is a discount of more than 10% of:

(1) the market value of the property, in the case of head (1) in the text (s 86(1)(a)(i)); or

(2) the commercial rate for the use of the property or for the provision of the services or facilities, in the case of head (2) in the text (s 86(1)(a)(ii)),

As to the meaning of 'market value' see PARA 299 note 26. Where the services of an employee are made available by his employer for the use or benefit of a third party, then for the purposes of determining controlled expenditure under s 86, the amount which is to be taken as constituting the commercial rate for the provision of those services is the amount of the remuneration or allowances payable to the employee by his employer in respect of the period for which his services are so made available (but do not include any amount in respect of any contributions or other payments for which the employer is liable in respect of the employee): s 86(5).

9 Political Parties, Elections and Referendums Act 2000 s 86(1)(b).

10 Political Parties, Elections and Referendums Act 2000 s 86(2). This provision has effect subject to s 87 (see the text and notes 24–32): see s 86(2).

11 See the Political Parties, Elections and Referendums Act 2000 s 86(6). The text refers to a regulated period as defined by s 94(10)(a) (see PARA 319 note 17): see s 86(6).

12 Ie such proportion of the appropriate amount determined in accordance with the Political Parties, Elections and Referendums Act 2000 s 86(3), (4) (see the text and notes 18–23): see s 86(7).

13 See the Political Parties, Elections and Referendums Act 2000 s 86(6)(a), (7).

14 Ie under the Political Parties, Elections and Referendums Act 2000 s 96 (see PARA 321): see s 86(6)(b).

15 In relation to a recognised third party, 'responsible person', means:

   (1)   if the third party is an individual, that individual (Political Parties, Elections and Referendums Act 2000 s 85(7)(a)); or

   (2)   if the third party is a registered party, the treasurer of the party or, in the case of a minor party, the person for the time being notified to the Electoral Commission by the party in accordance with s 88(3)(b)(iii) (see PARA 314) (s 85(7)(b)); and

   (3)   otherwise, the person or officer for the time being notified to the Electoral Commission by the third party in accordance with s 88(3)(c)(ii) (see PARA 314) (s 85(7)(c)).

'Recognised third party' means a third party for the time being recognised under s 88 (see PARA 314) for the purposes of Pt VI: see s 85(5). As to the meaning of 'minor party' see PARA 253 note 8. As to the Electoral Commission see PARA 34 et seq; and as to the treasurer of a registered party see PARA 253.

16 Political Parties, Elections and Referendums Act 2000 s 86(6)(b). A person commits an offence if he knowingly or recklessly makes such a declaration which is false: see s 86(8); and PARA 751.

17 Political Parties, Elections and Referendums Act 2000 s 86(6). The Secretary of State may by order vary the sum for the time being specified in any provision of the Political Parties, Elections and Referendums Act 2000: see s 155; and PARA 299 note 36. At the date at which this volume states the law no such order had been made in relation to s 86(6). As to the Secretary of State see PARA 2.

18 Political Parties, Elections and Referendums Act 2000 s 86(3)(a).

19 Political Parties, Elections and Referendums Act 2000 s 86(3)(b).

20 See the Political Parties, Elections and Referendums Act 2000 s 86(3).

21 Political Parties, Elections and Referendums Act 2000 s 86(4)(a).

22 Political Parties, Elections and Referendums Act 2000 s 86(4)(b).

23 See the Political Parties, Elections and Referendums Act 2000 s 86(4).

24 As to the establishment of electoral regions (including the 'combined region') for the purpose of elections to the European Parliament see PARA 77.

25 See the Political Parties, Elections and Referendums Act 2000 s 87(1)(a), (2)(a) (s 87(2)(a) amended by SI 2004/366). The text refers to a service licensed under the Broadcasting Act 1990 Pt I (ss 3–71) (independent television services: see BROADCASTING vol 4 (2011) PARA 507 et seq) or Pt III (ss 85–126) (independent radio services: see BROADCASTING vol 4 (2011) PARA 724 et seq) or under the Broadcasting Act 1996 Pt I (ss 1–39) (digital terrestrial television broadcasting: see BROADCASTING vol 4 (2011) PARA 690 et seq) or Pt II (ss 40–72) (digital terrestrial sound broadcasting: see BROADCASTING vol 4 (2011) PARA 727 et seq): see the Political Parties, Elections and Referendums Act 2000 s 87(2)(a) (as so amended). As to the BBC see BROADCASTING vol 4 (2011) PARA 603 et seq; and as to Sianel Pedwar Cymru see BROADCASTING vol 4 (2011) PARA 645.

26 See the Political Parties, Elections and Referendums Act 2000 s 87(1)(a), (2)(b).

27 See the Political Parties, Elections and Referendums Act 2000 s 87(1)(a), (2)(c).

28 Political Parties, Elections and Referendums Act 2000 s 87(1)(b)(i). The text refers to the purposes of Pt V (ss 72–84) (see PARA 299 et seq): see s 87(1)(b)(i).

29 As to the meaning of 'enactment' see PARA 53 note 2.

30 As to the meaning of 'return as to election expenses' see PARA 281 note 1.

31 Political Parties, Elections and Referendums Act 2000 s 87(1)(b)(ii).

32 Political Parties, Elections and Referendums Act 2000 s 87(1)(b).

314. Recognised third parties. For the purposes of controlling the expenditure incurred by third parties involved in a relevant national election campaign[1], a third party[2] is 'recognised' if it has given the Electoral Commission[3] a notification[4] which complies with the statutory requirements[5], and if that notification is for the time being in force[6]. A third party may only give such a notification if that party is:

   (1)   an individual resident in the United Kingdom[7], or registered in an electoral register (being a register of parliamentary or local government electors, a register of relevant citizens of the European Union, or a register of peers), who is not the responsible person in relation to another third party[8];

   (2)   a registered party[9]; or

(3)   a body[10] falling within any of the following:

      (a)   a company registered under the Companies Act 2006 and incorporated within the United Kingdom or another member state which carries on business in the United Kingdom[11];

      (b)   a trade union entered in the list kept under the Trade Union and Labour Relations (Consolidation) Act 1992[12];

      (c)   a building society[13];

      (d)   a limited liability partnership registered under the Limited Liability Partnerships Act 2000 which carries on business in the United Kingdom[14];

      (e)   a friendly society registered under the Friendly Societies Act 1974[15] or a society registered (or deemed to be registered) under the Industrial and Provident Societies Act 1965[16]; and

      (f)   any unincorporated association of two or more persons which does not fall within any of heads (a) to (e) above but which carries on business or other activities wholly or mainly in the United Kingdom and whose main office is there[17].

Such a notification:

      (i)   if given by an individual, must state his full name[18], and his home address in the United Kingdom, or (if he has no such address in the United Kingdom) his home address elsewhere[19], and must be signed by him[20];

      (ii)   if given by a registered party, must state the party's registered name[21], the address of its registered headquarters[22], and (in the case of a minor party[23]) the name of the person who will be responsible for compliance on the part of the party with the financial controls relating to third parties[24], and must be signed by the responsible officers of the party[25]; and

      (iii)   if given by a body falling within any of heads (3)(a) to (3)(f) above[26], must state all such details in respect of the body as are required[27] to be given in respect of such a body as the donor of a recordable donation[28], and the name of the person or officer who will be responsible for compliance on the part of the body with the financial controls relating to third parties[29], and must be signed by the body's secretary or a person who acts in a similar capacity in relation to the body[30].

The original notification[31] is in force as from the date on which it is received by the Commission[32], but lapses at the end of the period of three months beginning with any anniversary of that date unless the third party notifies the Commission that the third party wishes the original notification to continue in force[33]. Where the original notification would otherwise lapse in this way at the end of any such period of three months[34], but where the end of that period falls within any regulated period at the end of which a return will fall to be prepared[35] in respect of controlled expenditure[36] incurred by or on behalf of the third party during the regulated period[37], the original notification is treated, for all purposes connected with controlled expenditure so incurred during the regulated period, as lapsing at the end of that period instead[38]. A renewal notification[39] must either confirm that all the statements contained in the original notification, as it has effect for the time being, are accurate[40], or indicate that any statement contained in that notification, as it so has effect, is replaced by some other statement conforming with heads (i) to (iii) above[41]; and it must be received by the Commission during the period beginning one month before the relevant anniversary[42] and ending three months after it[43].

A third party may, at any time after giving the original notification, give the Commission a notification (a 'notification of alteration') indicating that any statement contained in the original notification, as it has effect for the time being, is replaced by some other statement contained in the notification of alteration[44], and conforming with heads (i) to (iii) above[45].

The Electoral Commission must maintain a register of all notifications given to it by third parties[46] which are for the time being in force[47]. The register must be maintained by the Commission in such form as it may determine, and must contain, in the case of each such notification, all the information contained in the notification as it has effect for the time being[48]. Where any notification is given to the Commission[49], it must cause all the information contained in the notification, or (as the case may be) any new information contained in it, to be entered in the register as soon as is reasonably practicable[50]; but the information to be so entered in the register in respect of a third party who is an individual must not include his home address[51]. The Commission must make a copy of the register so kept by it[52] available for public inspection during ordinary office hours, either at the Commission's offices or at some convenient place appointed by it[53], although the Commission may make other arrangements for members of the public to have access to the register's contents[54]. If requested to do so by any person, the Commission must supply him with a copy of the register or any part of it[55]; and the Commission may charge such reasonable fee as it may determine in respect of any inspection or access so allowed or any copy so supplied[56]. Where any such register is held by the Commission in electronic form, any copy so made available for public inspection or so supplied must be made available, or (as the case may be) supplied, in a legible form[57].

1   Ie for the purposes of the Political Parties, Elections and Referendums Act 2000 Pt VI (ss 85–100): see s 88(1). As to the meaning of 'relevant election' for these purposes see PARA 299 note 3; definition applied by virtue of s 85(6).

2   As to the meaning of 'third party' for these purposes see PARA 313 note 1.

3   As to the Electoral Commission see PARA 34 et seq.

4   Ie a notification under the Political Parties, Elections and Referendums Act 2000 s 88(1): see s 88(1)(a).

5   Political Parties, Elections and Referendums Act 2000 s 88(1)(a). The text refers to the requirement that such a notification is to comply with s 88(3) (see the text and notes 18–30): see s 88(1)(a). Any notification required to be given under the Political Parties, Elections and Referendums Act 2000 must be in writing: s 157(1).

6   Political Parties, Elections and Referendums Act 2000 s 88(1)(b).

7   As to the meaning of 'United Kingdom' see PARA 1 note 1. Separate provision is made for an individual who is resident in Gibraltar or who is a Gibraltar elector: see the Political Parties, Elections and Referendums Act 2000 s 88(2)(d) (added by SI 2004/366). 'Recognised Gibraltar third party' means a recognised third party falling within the Political Parties, Elections and Referendums Act 2000 s 88(2)(d), (e) (see also note 10), but not s 88(2)(a), (b), (c), (see heads (1) to (3) in the text): see s 85(5A) (added by SI 2004/366). As to the establishment of electoral regions (including the 'combined region') for the purpose of elections to the European Parliament see PARA 77.

8   Political Parties, Elections and Referendums Act 2000 s 88(2)(a) (amended by the Political Parties and Elections Act 2009 s 18(1), (2)). The text refers to an electoral register as defined by the Political Parties, Elections and Referendums Act 2000 s 54(8) (see CONSTITUTIONAL LAW AND HUMAN RIGHTS): see s 88(2)(a) (as so amended). As to the meaning of 'responsible person' in relation to a recognised third party see PARA 313 note 15.

9   Political Parties, Elections and Referendums Act 2000 s 88(2)(b) (amended by SI 2004/366). Head (2) in the text refers to a registered party other than a Gibraltar party whose entry in the register includes a statement that it intends to contest one or more elections to the European

Parliament in the combined region: see the Political Parties, Elections and Referendums Act 2000 s 88(2)(b) (as so amended). As to the meaning of 'registered party' for these purposes see PARA 35 note 3.

10 As to the meaning of 'body' see PARA 58 note 2. Separate provision is made for a body falling within any of the Political Parties, Elections and Referendums Act 2000 s 54(2A)(b)–(g) (permissible donors relating to one or more elections to the European Parliament in the combined region): see s 88(2)(e) (added by SI 2004/366).

11 Political Parties, Elections and Referendums Act 2000 ss 54(2)(b), 88(2)(c) (s 54(2)(b) amended by SI 2009/1941). As to the registration of companies under the Companies Act 2006 and their incorporation see COMPANIES vol 14 (2009) PARA 24 et seq. As to the control of contributions and other donations made by companies generally to registered parties and other European Union political organisations and European Union political expenditure incurred by companies see the Companies Act 2006 Pt 14 (ss 362–379); and COMPANIES vol 14 (2009) PARA 688 et seq.

12 Political Parties, Elections and Referendums Act 2000 ss 54(2)(d), 88(2)(c). As to the list referred to in the text see EMPLOYMENT vol 40 (2009) PARA 855. Unless certain conditions are met, the funds of a trade union may not be applied in the furtherance of certain political objects which include the expenditure of money in connection with the registration of electors, the candidature of any person, the selection of any candidate or the holding of any ballot by the union in connection with any election to a political office, or on the production, publication or distribution of any literature, document, film, sound recording or advertisement the main purpose of which is to persuade people to vote for a political party or candidate or to persuade them not to vote for a political party or candidate: see the Trade Union and Labour Relations (Consolidation) Act 1992 Pt I Ch VI (ss 71–96); and EMPLOYMENT vol 40 (2009) PARA 924 et seq.

13 Political Parties, Elections and Referendums Act 2000 ss 54(2)(e), 88(2)(c). The text refers to a building society within the meaning of the Building Societies Act 1986 (see FINANCIAL SERVICES AND INSTITUTIONS vol 50 (2008) PARA 1856): see the Political Parties, Elections and Referendums Act 2000 s 54(2)(e).

14 Political Parties, Elections and Referendums Act 2000 ss 54(2)(f), 88(2)(c) (s 54(2)(f) amended by SI 2009/1941). As to a limited liability partnership registered under the Limited Liability Partnerships Act 2000 see PARTNERSHIP vol 79 (2008) PARA 234 et seq.

15 As to friendly societies registered under the Friendly Societies Act 1974 see FINANCIAL SERVICES AND INSTITUTIONS vol 50 (2008) PARA 2084 et seq.

16 Political Parties, Elections and Referendums Act 2000 ss 54(2)(g), 88(2)(c). As to societies registered under the Industrial and Provident Societies Act 1965 see FINANCIAL SERVICES AND INSTITUTIONS vol 50 (2008) PARAS 2394, 2410 et seq.

17 Political Parties, Elections and Referendums Act 2000 ss 54(2)(h), 88(2)(c).

18 Political Parties, Elections and Referendums Act 2000 s 88(3)(a)(i).

19 Political Parties, Elections and Referendums Act 2000 s 88(3)(a)(ii). As to a Gibraltar elector who is not resident in Gibraltar see s 88(3)(a)(iii) (added by SI 2004/366).

20 Political Parties, Elections and Referendums Act 2000 s 88(3)(a).

21 Political Parties, Elections and Referendums Act 2000 s 88(3)(b)(i). As to the party's registered name see CONSTITUTIONAL LAW AND HUMAN RIGHTS.

22 Political Parties, Elections and Referendums Act 2000 s 88(3)(b)(ii). As to the party's registered headquarters see CONSTITUTIONAL LAW AND HUMAN RIGHTS.

23 As to the meaning of 'minor party' see PARA 253 note 8.

24 Political Parties, Elections and Referendums Act 2000 s 88(3)(b)(iii). The text refers to the provisions of Pt VI Ch II (ss 90–100) (see PARA 315 et seq): see s 88(3)(b)(iii). A notification given by a third party does not comply with the requirement in s 88(3)(b)(iii) if the person whose name is stated is the responsible person in relation to another third party, an individual who gives a notification under s 88(1) (see the text and notes 1–6) at the same time, or the person whose name is stated, in purported compliance with the requirement in s 88(3)(b)(iii), in a notification given at the same time by another third party: see s 88(3A) (added by the Political Parties and Elections Act 2009 s 18(1), (3)).

25 Political Parties, Elections and Referendums Act 2000 s 88(3)(b). The text refers to the responsible officers of the party within the meaning of s 64 (see PARA 311 note 26): see s 88(3)(b).

26 Political Parties, Elections and Referendums Act 2000 s 88(3)(c) (amended by SI 2004/366). As to the bodies giving notification for the purposes of elections to the European Parliament in the combined region see further note 10.

27 Ie by virtue of any of the Political Parties, Elections and Referendums Act 2000 s 62(13), Sch 6 para 2(4), (6)–(10) (quarterly donation reports: see CONSTITUTIONAL LAW AND HUMAN RIGHTS): see s 88(3)(c)(i).

28 Political Parties, Elections and Referendums Act 2000 s 88(3)(c)(i). As to the returns required in respect of controlled expenditure by third parties see PARA 321.

29 Political Parties, Elections and Referendums Act 2000 s 88(3)(c)(ii). The text refers to the provisions of Pt VI Ch II (see PARA 315 et seq): see s 88(3)(c)(ii). A notification given by a third party does not comply with the requirement in s 88(3)(c)(ii) if the person or officer whose name is stated is the responsible person in relation to another third party, an individual who gives a notification under s 88(1) (see the text and notes 1–6) at the same time, or the person or officer whose name is stated, in purported compliance with the requirement in s 88(3)(c)(ii), in a notification given at the same time by another third party: see s 88(3A) (as added: see note 24).

30 Political Parties, Elections and Referendums Act 2000 s 88(3)(c).

31 Ie a notification under the Political Parties, Elections and Referendums Act 2000 s 88(1) (see the text and notes 1–6): see s 88(4).

32 Political Parties, Elections and Referendums Act 2000 s 88(4)(a).

33 Political Parties, Elections and Referendums Act 2000 s 88(4)(b). See note 41.

34 Political Parties, Elections and Referendums Act 2000 s 88(5)(a).

35 Ie under the Political Parties, Elections and Referendums Act 2000 s 96 (see PARA 321): see s 88(5)(b). As to the regulated period see PARA 319 note 17.

36 As to the meaning of 'controlled expenditure' in relation to third parties see PARA 313.

37 Political Parties, Elections and Referendums Act 2000 s 88(5)(b).

38 Political Parties, Elections and Referendums Act 2000 s 88(5).

39 Ie a notification under the Political Parties, Elections and Referendums Act 2000 s 88(4)(b) (see the text and note 33): see s 88(6).

40 Political Parties, Elections and Referendums Act 2000 s 88(6)(a).

41 Political Parties, Elections and Referendums Act 2000 s 88(6)(b). The text refers to the requirement that the statement must conform with s 88(3) (see the text and notes 18–30): see s 88(6)(b).

Where a third party gives a notification under s 88(4)(b) (see the text and note 33) in respect of a notification under s 88(1) (see the text and notes 1–6) that was given before 1 January 2010, and the original notification contained a statement under s 88(3)(b)(iii) (see the text and notes 23–24) or under s 88(3)(c)(ii) (see the text and note 29) naming someone who, at the time when the renewal notification is given, is the responsible person in relation to another third party, the renewal notification must indicate, under s 88(6)(b), that the statement is replaced by a statement naming someone who is not the responsible person in relation to another third party: Political Parties and Elections Act 2009 s 18(4).

42 Ie for the purposes of the Political Parties, Elections and Referendums Act 2000 s 88(4)(b) (see the text and note 33): see s 88(7).

43 Political Parties, Elections and Referendums Act 2000 s 88(7).

44 Political Parties, Elections and Referendums Act 2000 s 88(8)(a).

45 Political Parties, Elections and Referendums Act 2000 s 88(8)(b). The text refers to the requirement that the statement must conform with s 88(3) (see the text and notes 18–30): see s 88(8)(b).

46 Ie notifications under the Political Parties, Elections and Referendums Act 2000 s 88(1) (see the text and notes 1–6): see s 89(1).

47 Political Parties, Elections and Referendums Act 2000 s 89(1).

48 Political Parties, Elections and Referendums Act 2000 s 89(2). The text refers to the notification as it has effect for the time being in accordance with s 88 (see the text and notes 1–45): see s 89(2).

49 Ie under the Political Parties, Elections and Referendums Act 2000 s 88 (see the text and notes 1–45): see s 89(3).

50 Political Parties, Elections and Referendums Act 2000 s 89(3).

51 Political Parties, Elections and Referendums Act 2000 s 89(4).

52 Ie under the Political Parties, Elections and Referendums Act 2000 s 89 (see the text and notes 46–51): see s 149(1)(c), (2).

53 Political Parties, Elections and Referendums Act 2000 s 149(1)(c), (2).

54 Political Parties, Elections and Referendums Act 2000 s 149(1)(c), (3).

55 Political Parties, Elections and Referendums Act 2000 s 149(1)(c), (4).

56 Political Parties, Elections and Referendums Act 2000 s 149(1)(c), (5).

57 Political Parties, Elections and Referendums Act 2000 s 149(1)(c), (7).

(B) General Restrictions on Controlled Expenditure by Third Parties

315. Restriction on incurring controlled expenditure without authority. For the purposes of controlling the expenditure incurred by third parties involved in a relevant national election campaign[1], no amount of controlled expenditure may be incurred by or on behalf of a recognised third party[2] unless it is incurred with the authority of[3]:

(1) the responsible person[4]; or

(2) a person authorised in writing by the responsible person[5].

Where, in the case of a recognised third party that is a registered party[6], any expenses are incurred in contravention of this restriction, the expenses do not count as controlled expenditure incurred by or on behalf of the recognised third party either for the purposes of the statutory limits imposed on such expenditure[7], or for the purposes of the statutory provisions which require returns as to such expenditure[8].

A person commits an offence if, without reasonable excuse, he incurs any expenses which contravene the statutory restriction on incurring controlled expenditure by or on behalf of a recognised third party[9].

1 Ie for the purposes of the Political Parties, Elections and Referendums Act 2000 Pt VI (ss 85–100): see s 85(1). As to the meaning of 'relevant election' for these purposes see PARA 299 note 3; definition applied by virtue of s 85(6).

  The provision made by s 90 does not apply in relation to a recognised Gibraltar third party except in relation to controlled expenditure incurred by or on behalf of that party during the period of four months ending with the date of the poll for a general election to the European Parliament: s 90(4) (added by SI 2004/366). As to the meaning of 'controlled expenditure' in relation to third parties see PARA 313. As to the meaning of 'recognised Gibraltar third party' see PARA 314 note 7. As to date of the poll at a European parliamentary election see PARA 222.

2 As to the meaning of 'recognised third party' see PARA 313 note 15.

3 Political Parties, Elections and Referendums Act 2000 s 90(1).

4 Political Parties, Elections and Referendums Act 2000 s 90(1)(a). As to the meaning of 'responsible person' in relation to a recognised third party see PARA 313 note 15.

5 Political Parties, Elections and Referendums Act 2000 s 90(1)(b).

6 As to the meaning of 'registered party' for these purposes see PARA 35 note 3.

7 Ie for the purposes of the Political Parties, Elections and Referendums Act 2000 s 94, Sch 10 (see PARAS 319–320): see s 90(3).

8 Political Parties, Elections and Referendums Act 2000 s 90(3). The text refers to the purposes of the provisions set out in ss 96–99 (see PARAS 321–323): see s 90(3).

9 See the Political Parties, Elections and Referendums Act 2000 s 90(2); and PARA 751.

316. Restriction on payments in respect of controlled expenditure incurred by third parties. For the purposes of controlling the expenditure incurred by third parties involved in a relevant national election campaign[1], no payment (of whatever nature), may be made in respect of any controlled expenditure incurred or to be incurred by or on behalf of a recognised third party[2] unless it is made by[3]:

(1) the responsible person[4]; or

(2) a person authorised in writing by the responsible person[5].

Any payment made in respect of any such expenditure by a person within head (1) or head (2) above must be supported by an invoice or a receipt unless it is not more than £200[6]; and, in the case of a person who falls within head (2) above, he must deliver to the responsible person both notification that he has made the payment[7], and the supporting invoice or receipt[8], as soon as possible after making the payment[9].

A person commits an offence if, without reasonable excuse, he makes any payment in contravention of the statutory restriction on such payments, or if he is a person within head (2) above who fails to deliver the proper notification and supporting evidence of payment[10].

1   Ie for the purposes of the Political Parties, Elections and Referendums Act 2000 Pt VI (ss 85–100): see s 85(1). As to the meaning of 'relevant election' for these purposes see PARA 299 note 3; definition applied by virtue of s 85(6).
      The provision made by s 91 does not apply in relation to a recognised Gibraltar third party except in relation to controlled expenditure incurred by or on behalf of that party during the period of four months ending with the date of the poll for a general election to the European Parliament: s 91(5) (added by SI 2004/366). As to the meaning of 'controlled expenditure' in relation to third parties see PARA 313. As to the meaning of 'recognised Gibraltar third party' see PARA 314 note 7. As to date of the poll at a European parliamentary election see PARA 222.
2   As to the meaning of 'recognised third party' see PARA 313 note 15.
3   Political Parties, Elections and Referendums Act 2000 s 91(1).
4   Political Parties, Elections and Referendums Act 2000 s 91(1)(a). As to the meaning of 'responsible person' in relation to a recognised third party see PARA 313 note 15.
5   Political Parties, Elections and Referendums Act 2000 s 91(1)(b).
6   Political Parties, Elections and Referendums Act 2000 s 91(2). The Secretary of State may by order vary the sum for the time being specified in any provision of the Political Parties, Elections and Referendums Act 2000: see s 155; and PARA 299 note 36. At the date at which this volume states the law no such order had been made in relation to s 91. As to the Secretary of State see PARA 2.
7   Political Parties, Elections and Referendums Act 2000 s 91(3)(a). Any notification required to be given under the Political Parties, Elections and Referendums Act 2000 must be in writing: s 157(1).
8   Political Parties, Elections and Referendums Act 2000 s 91(3)(b).
9   Political Parties, Elections and Referendums Act 2000 s 91(3).
10   See the Political Parties, Elections and Referendums Act 2000 s 91(4); and PARA 751.

317. Claims against third party in respect of controlled expenditure. For the purposes of controlling the expenditure incurred by third parties involved in a relevant national election campaign[1], a claim for payment in respect of controlled expenditure[2] incurred by or on behalf of a recognised third party[3] during any period which is a regulated period[4] is not payable unless the claim is sent to[5]:

(1)   the responsible person[6]; or
(2)   any other person authorised[7] to incur the expenditure[8],

not later than 30[9] days after the end of the regulated period[10]. Any claim sent in this way must be paid not later than 60 days after the end of the regulated period[11]; but this is without prejudice to any rights of a creditor of a recognised third party to obtain payment before the end of the period so allowed[12].

A person commits an offence if, without reasonable excuse, he pays any claim for payment in respect of controlled expenditure, which by virtue of being statute-barred[13] is not payable, or if he makes any payment in respect of a claim after the end of the period allowed for the payment of claims[14].

If the responsible person, or other person to whom a claim for such payment is sent, fails or refuses to pay the claim within the period allowed[15], then, where the claim is sent to:

(a)   the responsible person[16]; or
(b)   any other person with whose authority it is alleged that the expenditure was incurred[17],

within the period allowed before such claims are barred[18], the claim is deemed to be a 'disputed claim'[19]. The person by whom the disputed claim is made may bring an action for a disputed claim, and any sum paid in pursuance of a court's judgment or order made in the proceedings is not deemed to be in contravention of the statutory bar on the payment of controlled expenditure later than the allowed period[20].

1 Ie for the purposes of the Political Parties, Elections and Referendums Act 2000 Pt VI (ss 85–100): see s 85(1). As to the meaning of 'relevant election' for these purposes see PARA 299 note 3; definition applied by virtue of s 85(6).

2 As to the meaning of 'controlled expenditure' in relation to third parties see PARA 313.

3 As to the meaning of 'recognised third party' see PARA 313 note 15.

4 Ie as defined by the Political Parties, Elections and Referendums Act 2000 s 94(10)(a) (see PARA 319 note 17): see s 92(1).

5 Political Parties, Elections and Referendums Act 2000 s 92(1).

6 Political Parties, Elections and Referendums Act 2000 s 92(1)(a). As to the meaning of 'responsible person' in relation to a recognised third party see PARA 313 note 15.

7 Ie a person authorised in writing by the responsible person under the Political Parties, Elections and Referendums Act 2000 s 90 (see PARA 315): see s 92(1)(b).

8 Political Parties, Elections and Referendums Act 2000 s 92(1)(b).

9 Where, in the case of any controlled expenditure, the period allowed under the Political Parties, Elections and Referendums Act 2000 s 92(1) or s 92(2) (see the text and note 11) would end on:

    (1)   a Saturday or Sunday or Christmas Eve, Christmas Day or Good Friday (s 77(9)(a) (amended by the Electoral Administration Act 2006 ss 20, 74(2), Sch 1 paras 49, 54, Sch 2); the Political Parties, Elections and Referendums Act 2000 s 77(9)–(11) applied by s 92(7) (amended by SI 2004/366));

    (2)   a bank holiday (Political Parties, Elections and Referendums Act 2000 s 77(9)(b) (as so applied)); or

    (3)   a day appointed for public thanksgiving or mourning (s 77(9)(c) (as so applied))),

the period instead ends on the first day following that day which is not one of those days (s 77(9) (as so applied))). As to calculating such a period under the law of Gibraltar see s 77(11) (added by SI 2004/366) (the Political Parties, Elections and Referendums Act 2000 s 77(11) as so applied). For the purposes of head (2) above, 'bank holiday' means a day which is a bank holiday under the Banking and Financial Dealings Act 1971 (see TIME vol 97 (2010) PARA 321) in any part of the United Kingdom:

    (a)   in which is situated the office of the responsible person in relation to the recognised third party or (as the case may be) other authorised person to whom the claim is sent pursuant to the Political Parties, Elections and Referendums Act 2000 s 92(1) (s 77(10)(a) (as so applied)); or

    (b)   in which the person providing the property, services or facilities to which the expenditure relates conducts his business (s 77(10)(b) (as so applied)); or

    (c)   (if he conducts his business in more than one part of the United Kingdom) in which is situated the office from which dealings relating to the expenditure were conducted (s 77(10)(c) (as so applied)).

As to the meaning of 'United Kingdom' see PARA 1 note 1. As to the meaning of 'property' for these purposes see PARA 34 note 8; and as to the meaning of 'business' see PARA 303 note 9.

10 Political Parties, Elections and Referendums Act 2000 s 92(1) (amended by the Electoral Administration Act 2006 s 65(2)(a)).

11 Political Parties, Elections and Referendums Act 2000 s 92(2) (amended by the Electoral Administration Act 2006 s 65(2)(b)).

12 Political Parties, Elections and Referendums Act 2000 s 92(6).

13 Ie by virtue of the Political Parties, Elections and Referendums Act 2000 s 92(1) (see the text and notes 1–10): see s 92(3).

14 See the Political Parties, Elections and Referendums Act 2000 s 92(3); and PARA 751. The text refers to payment in respect of a claim after the end of the period allowed under s 92(2) (see the text and note 11): see s 92(3).

15 Political Parties, Elections and Referendums Act 2000 s 93(1)(b). The text refers to the period allowed under s 92(2) (see the text and note 11): see s 93(1)(b).

16 Political Parties, Elections and Referendums Act 2000 s 93(1)(a)(i).

17 Political Parties, Elections and Referendums Act 2000 s 93(1)(a)(ii).

18 Political Parties, Elections and Referendums Act 2000 s 93(1)(a). The text refers to the period allowed under s 92(1) (see the text and notes 1–10): see s 93(1)(a).

19 Political Parties, Elections and Referendums Act 2000 s 93(1). As to the power to apply to the court for permission to pay a disputed claim see PARA 318; and as to the returns required in relation to disputed claims see PARA 321.

20 Political Parties, Elections and Referendums Act 2000 s 93(2). The text refers to the restriction on payment otherwise contained in s 92(2) (see the text and note 11): see s 93(2).

318. Application for permission to pay claims in respect of controlled expenditure. For the purposes of controlling the expenditure incurred by third parties involved in a relevant national election campaign[1]:

(1) the person making a claim for payment in respect of controlled expenditure[2] incurred by or on behalf of a recognised third party[3]; or

(2) the person with whose authority the expenditure in question was incurred[4],

may apply to the High Court or to the county court for permission to pay such a claim (even if it is sent in after the period allowed of 30 days after the end of the regulated period[5]); and such a person may apply to the High Court or to the county court for permission to pay a disputed claim[6]. The court, if satisfied that for any special reason it is appropriate to do so, may by order grant the permission[7]. Any sum paid in pursuance of such permission is not deemed to be a contravention of the provisions forbidding the making or payment of claims relating to controlled expenditure later than the statutory period allowed[8].

1 Ie for the purposes of the Political Parties, Elections and Referendums Act 2000 Pt VI (ss 85–100): see s 85(1). As to the meaning of 'relevant election' for these purposes see PARA 299 note 3; definition applied by virtue of s 85(6).
2 As to the meaning of 'controlled expenditure' in relation to third parties see PARA 313.
3 Political Parties, Elections and Referendums Act 2000 s 92(4)(a). The text refers to a claim to which s 92(1) applies (see PARA 317): see s 92(4). As to the meanings of 'responsible person' in relation to a recognised third party and 'recognised third party' see PARA 313 note 15.
4 Political Parties, Elections and Referendums Act 2000 s 92(4)(b). As to persons authorised to incur expenditure as mentioned in the text see s 90; and PARA 315.
5 Ie the period mentioned in the Political Parties, Elections and Referendums Act 2000 s 92(1) (see PARA 317): see ss 92(4), 93(3)(a).
6 Political Parties, Elections and Referendums Act 2000 ss 92(4), 93(3)(a). As to court proceedings for the purposes of claims made in relation to a recognised Gibraltar third party see s 92(8) (added by SI 2004/366).
7 Political Parties, Elections and Referendums Act 2000 ss 92(4), 93(3)(a).
8 Political Parties, Elections and Referendums Act 2000 ss 92(5), 93(3)(a). The text refers to the period of 30 days within which a claim otherwise must be made under s 92(2) or the period of 60 days within which a claim otherwise must be paid under s 92(2) (see PARA 317): see ss 92(5), 93(3)(a). As to the returns required in respect of sums paid in pursuance of the permission see PARA 321.

(C) Financial Limits on Controlled Expenditure by Third Parties

319. Limitation of controlled expenditure incurred by third parties. For the purposes of controlling expenditure incurred by third parties involved in a relevant national election campaign[1], the limit which applies in relation to controlled expenditure[2] incurred by or on behalf of a recognised third party[3]:

(1) in relation to a parliamentary general election[4] in the relevant period[5] in England or Wales, is[6], in relation to England, £793,500[7], and, in relation to Wales, £60,000[8];

(2) in relation to an ordinary general election to the National Assembly for Wales[9] in the relevant period[10] in Wales, is £30,000[11];

(3) in relation to a general election to the European parliament[12] in the relevant period[13] in each of England or Wales is[14], in relation to England, £159,750[15] and, in relation to Wales, £11,259[16].

Where:

(a) during a regulated period[17], any controlled expenditure is incurred in a particular part of the United Kingdom[18] by or on behalf of a third party[19] (whether or not the third party in question is a recognised third party)[20]; and

(b)   the expenditure is so incurred in pursuance of a plan or other arrangement whereby controlled expenditure is to be incurred[21] by or on behalf of that third party[22], and by or on behalf of one or more other third parties (whether or not any of the third parties in question is a recognised third party)[23], in connection with the production or publication of election material which can reasonably be regarded as intended to achieve a common purpose falling within the definition of 'election material' for these purposes[24],

the expenditure mentioned in head (a) above is treated for the purposes of the statutory financial limits imposed on controlled expenditure[25] as having also been incurred, during the period and in the part of the United Kingdom concerned, by or on behalf of the other third party (or, as the case may be, each of the other third parties) mentioned in head (b) above[26].

Where:

(i)   at any time before the beginning of any regulated period, any expenses falling within the statutory definition of 'controlled expenditure'[27] are incurred by or on behalf of a third party in respect of any property[28], services or facilities[29]; but

(ii)   the property, services or facilities is or are made use of by or on behalf of the third party during the regulated period in circumstances such that, had any expenses been incurred in respect of that use during that period, they would have constituted[30] controlled expenditure incurred by or on behalf of the third party during that period[31],

the appropriate proportion of the expenses mentioned in head (i) above[32] is treated for the purposes of the statutory financial limits imposed on controlled expenditure[33] or for the purposes of the statutory provisions which require returns as to such expenditure[34], as controlled expenditure incurred by or on behalf of the third party during that period[35].

Special provision is made for limiting controlled expenditure where, in special circumstances, elections are combined[36].

Where, during a regulated period in relation to which any limitation of controlled expenditure applies in relation to a third party (whether or not a recognised third party), any controlled expenditure is incurred in the United Kingdom by or on behalf of the third party in excess of the limit that applies, the individual concerned (or the responsible person, if the third party is not an individual) is guilty of an offence if he knew or ought reasonably to have known that the expenditure would be incurred in excess of that limit; and, where the third party is not an individual, the third party is also guilty of an offence[37].

1   Ie for the purposes of the Political Parties, Elections and Referendums Act 2000 Pt VI (ss 85–100): see s 94(1). As to the meaning of 'relevant election' for these purposes see PARA 299 note 3; definition applied by virtue of s 85(6).

2   As to the meaning of 'controlled expenditure' in relation to third parties see PARA 313.

3   As to the meaning of 'recognised third party' see PARA 313 note 15. For these purposes, controlled expenditure incurred by or on behalf of any recognised third party is attributed (subject to the Political Parties, Elections and Referendums Act 2000 s 94(1), Sch 10 para 2(2)–(4)) to each of England and Wales in proportion to the number of parliamentary constituencies for the time being situated in that part of United Kingdom: Sch 10 para 2(1). Controlled expenditure whose effects are wholly or substantially confined to any particular parts or part of the United Kingdom:

(1)   are attributed to those parts in proportion to the number of parliamentary constituencies for the time being situated in those parts (Sch 10 para 2(2)(a)); or

(2)   are attributed solely to that part (Sch 10 para 2(2)(b)),

as the case may be (see Sch 10 para 2(2)). For this purpose, the effects of controlled expenditure are wholly or substantially confined to any particular parts or part of the United Kingdom if they have no significant effects in any other part or parts (so that, for example, expenditure on an advertisement in a newspaper circulating in Wales is to be attributed solely to Wales if the newspaper does not circulate to any significant extent in any other part of the United Kingdom): Sch 10 para 2(3). As respects controlled expenditure incurred in the period of four months ending with the date of the poll for an election to the European Parliament in the combined region, that region is to be regarded as part of England for the purposes of the references to a part or parts of the United Kingdom: see Sch 10 para 2(3A) (added by SI 2004/366). References in the Political Parties, Elections and Referendums Act 2000 Sch 10 to controlled expenditure 'in' a particular part of the United Kingdom are accordingly to controlled expenditure which is to be attributed to that part in accordance with Sch 10 para 2: see Sch 10 para 2(3). As to the meanings of 'England', 'United Kingdom' and 'Wales' see PARA 1 note 1. As to the meaning of 'constituency' for the purposes of parliamentary elections see PARA 9. As to the establishment of electoral regions (including the 'combined region') for the purpose of elections to the European Parliament see PARA 77. As to the date of the poll at a European parliamentary election see PARA 222.

4   As to the meaning of 'parliamentary election' see PARA 9. As to parliamentary general elections see PARA 189 et seq.

5   For these purposes, the relevant period is:

(1)   subject to head (2) below, the period of 365 days ending with the date of the poll for the election (Political Parties, Elections and Referendums Act 2000 Sch 10 para 3(3)(a)); or

(2)   where the election (the 'election in question') follows another parliamentary general election held less than 365 days previously, the period beginning with the day after the date of the poll for the earlier election and ending with the date of the poll for the election in question (Sch 10 para 3(3)(b)).

As to the date of the poll at a parliamentary general election see PARA 195.

6   See the Political Parties, Elections and Referendums Act 2000 Sch 10 para 3(1), (2).

7   Political Parties, Elections and Referendums Act 2000 Sch 10 para 3(2)(a). The Secretary of State may by order vary the sum for the time being specified in any provision of the Political Parties, Elections and Referendums Act 2000: see s 155; and PARA 299 note 36. At the date at which this volume states the law no such order had been made in relation to Sch 10. As to the Secretary of State see PARA 2.

8   Political Parties, Elections and Referendums Act 2000 Sch 10 para 3(2)(c).

9   For these purposes, an 'ordinary general election to the National Assembly for Wales' means an election held under the Government of Wales Act 2006 s 3 (see PARA 213): see the Political Parties, Elections and Referendums Act 2000 Sch 10 para 1(1)(c) (substituted by SI 2007/1388). As to the National Assembly for Wales see CONSTITUTIONAL LAW AND HUMAN RIGHTS.

10   For these purposes, the relevant period is the period beginning with the appropriate date and ending with the date of the poll (see the Political Parties, Elections and Referendums Act 2000 Sch 10 para 6(3) (amended by SI 2007/1388)); and the 'appropriate date' is the date which falls four months before the date of the poll where:

(1)   the date of the poll is that determined by the Government of Wales Act 2006 s 3(1) (see PARA 213) (Political Parties, Elections and Referendums Act 2000 Sch 10 para 6(4)(a) (Sch 10 para 6(4)(a)–(c) amended by SI 2007/1388)));

(2)   no less than five months before the day on which the poll would have taken place under the Government of Wales Act 2006 s 3(1), the date of the poll is brought forward under s 4(1) (see PARA 213 note 3) (Political Parties, Elections and Referendums Act 2000 Sch 10 para 6(4)(b) (as so amended)); or

(3)   no less than four months before the day on which the poll would have taken place under the Government of Wales Act 2006 s 3(1), the date of the poll is postponed under s 4(1) (Political Parties, Elections and Referendums Act 2000 Sch 10 para 6(4)(c) (as so amended)).

However, where the date of the poll is brought forward or postponed otherwise than as mentioned in head (2) or head (3) above, the 'appropriate date' means the date which falls four months before the date when the poll would have taken place under the Government of Wales Act 2006 s 3(1): see the Political Parties, Elections and Referendums Act 2000 Sch 10 para 6(4) (amended by SI 2007/1388). As to the date of the poll at ordinary Welsh Assembly elections see PARA 213.

11　See the Political Parties, Elections and Referendums Act 2000 Sch 10 para 6(1), (2) (Sch 10 para 6(1) amended by SI 2007/1388).

12　As to European parliamentary general elections see PARA 217 et seq.

13　For these purposes, the relevant period is the period of four months ending with the date of the poll for the election: see the Political Parties, Elections and Referendums Act 2000 Sch 10 para 4(3).

14　See the Political Parties, Elections and Referendums Act 2000 Sch 10 para 4(1), (2). As respects a recognised Gibraltar third party, Sch 10 para 4(2) has effect as if the limits were, in relation to England, £16,000 and, in relation to Wales, £5,000: see Sch 10 para 4(2A) (added by SI 2004/366). As to the meaning of 'recognised Gibraltar third party' see PARA 314 note 7.

15　Political Parties, Elections and Referendums Act 2000 Sch 10 para 4(2)(a).

16　Political Parties, Elections and Referendums Act 2000 Sch 10 para 4(2)(c).

17　For these purposes, a regulated period is a period in relation to which any limit is imposed by the Political Parties, Elections and Referendums Act 2000 Sch 10: see s 94(10)(a) (amended by SI 2004/366). This is subject to the Political Parties, Elections and Referendums Act 2000 s 94(11) (added by SI 2004/366), which relates to a recognised Gibraltar third party: see the Political Parties, Elections and Referendums Act 2000 s 94(10)(a) (as so amended).

18　For these purposes, any reference to controlled expenditure being incurred in a part of the United Kingdom must be construed in accordance with the Political Parties, Elections and Referendums Act 2000 Sch 10 para 2 (see note 3): s 94(10)(d).

19　Political Parties, Elections and Referendums Act 2000 s 94(6)(a). For these purposes, any reference to controlled expenditure incurred by or on behalf of a recognised third party during a regulated period includes any controlled expenditure so incurred during that period at any time before the third party became a recognised third party: s 94(10)(b). As to when third parties become recognised third parties see PARA 314. As to the meaning of 'third party' for these purposes see PARA 313 note 1.

20　See the Political Parties, Elections and Referendums Act 2000 s 94(7).

21　See the Political Parties, Elections and Referendums Act 2000 s 94(6)(b).

22　Political Parties, Elections and Referendums Act 2000 s 94(6)(b)(i).

23　Political Parties, Elections and Referendums Act 2000 s 94(6)(b)(ii), (7).

24　Political Parties, Elections and Referendums Act 2000 s 94(6)(b). The text refers to election material which falls within s 85(3) (definition of 'election material': see PARA 313 note 4): see s 94(6)(b).

25　Ie for the purposes of the Political Parties, Elections and Referendums Act 2000 s 94 and Sch 10: see s 94(6).

26　Political Parties, Elections and Referendums Act 2000 s 94(6).

27　Ie expenses within the Political Parties, Elections and Referendums Act 2000 s 85(2) (see PARA 313): see s 94(8)(a).

28　As to the meaning of 'property' for these purposes see PARA 34 note 8.

29　Political Parties, Elections and Referendums Act 2000 s 94(8)(a).

30　Ie by virtue of the Political Parties, Elections and Referendums Act 2000 s 85(2) (see PARA 313): see s 94(8)(b).

31　Political Parties, Elections and Referendums Act 2000 s 94(8)(b).

32　For these purposes, the appropriate proportion of the expenses mentioned in the Political Parties, Elections and Referendums Act 2000 s 94(8)(a) (see head (i) in the text) is such proportion of those expenses as is reasonably attributable to the use made of the property, services or facilities as mentioned in s 94(8)(b) (see head (ii) in the text): s 94(9).

33　Ie for the purposes of the Political Parties, Elections and Referendums Act 2000 s 94 and Sch 10: see s 94(8).

34　Ie for the purposes of the Political Parties, Elections and Referendums Act 2000 ss 96–99 (see PARAS 321–323): see s 94(8).

35　Political Parties, Elections and Referendums Act 2000 s 94(8).

36　As to such provision see PARA 320.

37　See the Political Parties, Elections and Referendums Act 2000 s 94(2)–(5); and PARA 751.

320.　Limitation of controlled expenditure incurred by third parties where elections are combined.　For the purposes of controlling expenditure incurred by third parties in a relevant national election campaign[1], special limits apply to controlled expenditure[2] incurred by or on behalf of a recognised third party[3] in England[4] or Wales[5] at combined polls[6] in circumstances where:

(1)　separate limits would apply in relation to a general election to the

European Parliament[7] and in relation to an ordinary general election to the National Assembly for Wales[8], and any part of the period which would be the relevant period[9] for the purposes of the general election to the European Parliament falls within any part of the period which would be the relevant period[10] for the purposes of the ordinary general election to the Welsh Assembly[11];

(2) separate limits would apply in relation to a parliamentary general election[12], and in relation to a general election to the European Parliament[13] or an ordinary general election to the National Assembly for Wales[14] and one or more parliamentary general elections is or are pending[15] during any part of the period in relation to which the limit imposed in relation to the European Parliament or an ordinary general election to the Welsh Assembly would apply[16];

(3) a limit under head (2) above would apply in relation to a relevant period for those purposes[17] and another limit in relation to a general election to the European Parliament[18] or an ordinary general election to the National Assembly for Wales[19] applies in relation to a period which is not a period during which the parliamentary general election is pending but which either falls wholly within or ends at any time falling within the relevant period for the purposes of head (2) above[20];

(4) a period which is the relevant period for the purposes of a general election to the European Parliament[21] or an ordinary general election to the National Assembly for Wales[22] either falls wholly within, or ends at any time falling within, the period which would be the relevant period in relation to the parliamentary general election[23], and where head (2) above does not apply in connection with the those elections[24].

1   Ie for the purposes of the Political Parties, Elections and Referendums Act 2000 Pt VI (ss 85–100): see s 94(1). As to the meaning of 'relevant election' for these purposes see PARA 299 note 3; definition applied by virtue of s 85(6).
2   As to the meaning of 'controlled expenditure' in relation to third parties see PARA 313.
3   As to the meaning of 'recognised third party' see PARA 313 note 15.
4   As to the meaning of 'England' see PARA 1 note 1.
5   As to the meaning of 'Wales' see PARA 1 note 1.
6   As to the combination of polls at a parliamentary general election and a European parliamentary general election see PARA 21; and as to the combination of polls at elections for related areas see PARA 30.
7   Ie under the Political Parties, Elections and Referendums Act 2000 s 94(1), Sch 10 para 4 (see PARA 319). As to European parliamentary general elections see PARA 217 et seq.
8   Ie under the Political Parties, Elections and Referendums Act 2000 Sch 10 para 6 (see PARA 319). As to the meaning of 'ordinary election to the Welsh Assembly' for these purposes see PARA 319 note 9.
9   As to the meaning of 'relevant period' for these purposes see PARA 319 note 13.
10   As to the meaning of 'relevant period' for these purposes see PARA 319 note 10.
11   See the Political Parties, Elections and Referendums Act 2000 Sch 10 para 8.
12   Ie under the Political Parties, Elections and Referendums Act 2000 Sch 10 para 3 (see PARA 319). As to parliamentary general elections see PARA 189 et seq. As to the meaning of 'parliamentary election' see PARA 9.
13   Ie under the Political Parties, Elections and Referendums Act 2000 Sch 10 para 4 (see PARA 319).
14   Ie under the Political Parties, Elections and Referendums Act 2000 Sch 10 para 6 (see PARA 319).
15   For these purposes, a parliamentary general election is pending during the period:
    (1)   beginning with the date on which Parliament is dissolved by the Fixed-term Parliaments Act 2011 s 3(1) (see PARA 189) for a parliamentary general election (Political Parties, Elections and Referendums Act 2000 Sch 10 para 1(2)(a) (amended by the Fixed-term Parliaments Act 2011 s 6(3), Schedule paras 18, 22(1), (2))); and
    (2)   ending with the date of the poll for that election (Political Parties, Elections and Referendums Act 2000 Sch 10 para 1(2)(b)).

As to the polling day at a parliamentary general election see PARA 195.
16 See the Political Parties, Elections and Referendums Act 2000 Sch 10 para 9 (amended by the Fixed-term Parliaments Act 2011 Schedule paras 18, 22(1), (3)).
17 Ie a relevant period for the purposes of the Political Parties, Elections and Referendums Act 2000 Sch 10 para 9(3) or a first relevant period for the purposes of Sch 10 para 9(5).
18 Ie under the Political Parties, Elections and Referendums Act 2000 Sch 10 para 4 (see PARA 319).
19 Ie under the Political Parties, Elections and Referendums Act 2000 Sch 10 para 6 (see PARA 319).
20 See the Political Parties, Elections and Referendums Act 2000 Sch 10 para 10.
21 Ie under the Political Parties, Elections and Referendums Act 2000 Sch 10 para 4 (see PARA 319).
22 Ie under the Political Parties, Elections and Referendums Act 2000 Sch 10 para 6 (see PARA 319).
23 Ie under the Political Parties, Elections and Referendums Act 2000 Sch 10 para 3 (see PARA 319).
24 See the Political Parties, Elections and Referendums Act 2000 Sch 10 para 11.

(D) Required Returns in respect of Controlled Expenditure by Third Parties

321. Returns in respect of controlled expenditure. For the purposes of controlling expenditure incurred by third parties in a relevant national election campaign[1], where, during any regulated period[2], any controlled expenditure[3] is incurred by or on behalf of a recognised third party[4] in any relevant part or parts of the United Kingdom[5], and where that period ends[6], the responsible person[7] must prepare a return in respect of the controlled expenditure incurred by or on behalf of the third party during that period in that part or those parts of the United Kingdom[8].

Such a return must specify the poll for the relevant election[9] (or, as the case may be, the polls for the relevant elections) that took place during the regulated period in question, and must contain[10]:

(1)　a statement of all payments made in respect of controlled expenditure incurred by or on behalf of the third party during that period in the relevant part or parts of the United Kingdom[11];

(2)　a statement of all disputed claims[12] of which the responsible person is aware[13];

(3)　a statement of all the unpaid claims (if any) of which the responsible person is aware in respect of which an application has been made, or is about to be made, to a court for permission to pay the claim[14];

(4)　in a case where the third party either is not a registered party[15] or is a minor party[16], a statement of relevant donations[17] received by the third party in respect of the relevant election or elections which complies with the requirement to report any donations received from persons who are permissible donors as well as those received from persons who are not permissible donors[18].

Such a return must be accompanied by:

(a)　all invoices or receipts relating to the payments mentioned in head (1) above[19]; and

(b)　in the case of any controlled expenditure treated as incurred by the third party[20], any declaration falling to be made with respect to that expenditure[21].

Where, however, any payments or claims falling to be dealt with in such a return have already been dealt with in an earlier return[22], it is sufficient for the later return to deal with those payments or claims by specifying overall amounts in respect of them[23], and the requirement for accompanying documentation imposed by heads (a) and (b) above does not apply to any invoices, receipts or declarations which accompanied the earlier return and are specified as such in the later return[24].

The requirements as to the contents of such a return, and what must accompany it[25], do not apply to any controlled expenditure incurred at any time before the third party became a recognised third party, but the return must be accompanied by a declaration made by the responsible person of the total amount of such expenditure incurred at any such time[26].

A report must be prepared by a qualified auditor[27] on such a return in respect of controlled expenditure where, during any regulated period, the controlled expenditure incurred by or on behalf of a recognised third party in the relevant part or parts of the United Kingdom exceeds £250,000[28].

1   Ie for the purposes of the Political Parties, Elections and Referendums Act 2000 Pt VI (ss 85–100): see s 94(1). As to the meaning of 'relevant election' for these purposes see PARA 299 note 3; definition applied by virtue of s 85(6).
2   As to the meaning of 'regulated period' see PARA 319 note 17.
3   As to the meaning of 'controlled expenditure' in relation to third parties see PARA 313.
4   As to references to controlled expenditure incurred by or on behalf of a recognised third party during a regulated period see PARA 319 note 19. As to the meaning of 'recognised third party' see PARA 313 note 15.
5   Political Parties, Elections and Referendums Act 2000 s 96(1)(a). For these purposes, a part of the United Kingdom is a relevant part if any limit imposed by s 94(1), Sch 10 (see PARAS 319–320) applies to controlled expenditure which is incurred in that part: s 94(10)(c). As to references to controlled expenditure being incurred in a part of the United Kingdom see PARA 319 note 3. As to the meaning of 'United Kingdom' see PARA 1 note 1.
6   Political Parties, Elections and Referendums Act 2000 s 96(1)(b).
7   As to the meaning of 'responsible person' for these purposes see PARA 313 note 15.
8   See the Political Parties, Elections and Referendums Act 2000 s 96(1).
    Where s 96(1)(a) (see the text and notes 1–5) applies in relation to a recognised third party and any regulated period:
    (1)   the requirements as to the preparation of a return in respect of controlled expenditure falling within s 96(1)(a) has effect in relation to the third party despite the third party ceasing to be a recognised third party at or after the end of the regulated period by virtue of the lapse of the third party's notification under s 88(1) (see PARA 314) (s 96(7)(a)); and
    (2)   for the purposes of, or in connection with, the discharge of obligations of the responsible person under s 96, s 98 (delivery of returns in respect of controlled expenditure to the Electoral Commission: see PARA 322) and s 99 (declaration as to returns in respect of controlled expenditure: see PARA 323) in relation to any such return, references to the responsible person must be read as references to the person who was the responsible person in relation to the third party immediately before that notification lapsed (s 96(7)(b)).
9   As to the meaning of 'relevant election' for these purposes see note 1.
10 Political Parties, Elections and Referendums Act 2000 s 96(2). The Electoral Commission may by regulations prescribe a form of return which may be used for these purposes: s 96(6). Regulations made by the Commission are not statutory instruments and are not recorded in this work: see further PARA 47. As to the Electoral Commission see PARA 34 et seq.
11 Political Parties, Elections and Referendums Act 2000 s 96(2)(a).
12 Ie within the meaning of the Political Parties, Elections and Referendums Act 2000 s 93 (see PARA 317): see s 96(2)(b).
13 Political Parties, Elections and Referendums Act 2000 s 96(2)(b).
14 Political Parties, Elections and Referendums Act 2000 s 96(2)(c). The text refers to an application for permission to pay claims in respect of controlled expenditure made under s 92(4) (see PARA 318): see s 96(2)(c).
15 As to the meaning of 'registered party' for these purposes see PARA 35 note 3.
16 As to the meaning of 'minor party' see PARA 253 note 8.
17 For these purposes, 'relevant donation' has the same meaning as in the Political Parties, Elections and Referendums Act 2000 s 95, Sch 11 (see PARA 325 note 9): s 96(8).
18 Political Parties, Elections and Referendums Act 2000 s 96(2)(d). The text refers to the requirements of Sch 11 paras 10–11 (see PARA 329): see s 96(2)(d).
19 Political Parties, Elections and Referendums Act 2000 s 96(3)(a).
20 Ie by virtue of the Political Parties, Elections and Referendums Act 2000 s 86 (see PARA 313): see s 96(3)(b).

21 Political Parties, Elections and Referendums Act 2000 s 96(3)(b). The text refers to a declaration falling to be made under s 86(6) (see PARA 313): see s 96(3)(b).
22 Political Parties, Elections and Referendums Act 2000 s 96(4).
23 Political Parties, Elections and Referendums Act 2000 s 96(4)(a).
24 Political Parties, Elections and Referendums Act 2000 s 96(4)(b).
25 Ie the provision made by the Political Parties, Elections and Referendums Act 2000 s 96(2)–(4) (see the text and notes 9–24): see s 96(5).
26 Political Parties, Elections and Referendums Act 2000 s 96(5).
27 In relation to the appointment of an auditor to prepare a report under the Political Parties, Elections and Referendums Act 2000 s 97(1) (or, as the case may be, an auditor so appointed), the provision made by s 43(6), (7) (regulations made by the Electoral Commission with respect to the appointment of auditors: see CONSTITUTIONAL LAW AND HUMAN RIGHTS) and s 44 (supplementary provisions about auditors: see CONSTITUTIONAL LAW AND HUMAN RIGHTS) apply as they apply in relation to the appointment of an auditor to carry out an audit under s 43 (annual audits: see CONSTITUTIONAL LAW AND HUMAN RIGHTS) (or, as the case may be, an auditor so appointed): s 97(2). As to the meaning of 'qualified auditor' see PARA 298 note 5. As to the general accounting requirements for registered parties see PARA 298.
28 Political Parties, Elections and Referendums Act 2000 s 97(1).

322. Delivery of returns in respect of controlled expenditure to the Electoral Commission. For the purposes of controlling expenditure incurred by third parties in a relevant national election campaign[1], where:

(1) any return falls to be prepared[2] in respect of controlled expenditure[3] incurred by or on behalf of a recognised third party[4] during a regulated period[5]; and

(2) an auditor's report on it also falls to be prepared[6],

the responsible person[7] must deliver the return to the Electoral Commission[8], together with a copy of the auditor's report, within six months of the end of the regulated period[9]. In the case of any other such return which falls to be prepared[10], the responsible person must deliver the return to the Commission within three months of the end of the regulated period[11].

Where, after the date on which a return is so delivered to the Commission, permission is given by a court for any claim to be paid[12], the responsible person must, within seven days after the payment, deliver to the Commission a return of any sums paid in pursuance of the permission accompanied by a copy of the order of the court giving the permission[13].

The responsible person in the case of a recognised third party commits an offence if, without reasonable excuse, he fails to comply with the requirements as to any return or auditor's report[14]; and, notwithstanding any criminal liability of any person, the recognised third party is liable to a civil penalty[15].

1 Ie for the purposes of the Political Parties, Elections and Referendums Act 2000 Pt VI (ss 85–100): see s 94(1). As to the meaning of 'relevant election' for these purposes see PARA 299 note 3; definition applied by virtue of s 85(6).
2 Ie under the Political Parties, Elections and Referendums Act 2000 s 96 (see PARA 321): see s 98(1)(a).
3 As to the meaning of 'controlled expenditure' in relation to third parties see PARA 313.
4 As to the meaning of 'recognised third party' see PARA 313 note 15.
5 Political Parties, Elections and Referendums Act 2000 s 98(1)(a). As to the meaning of 'regulated period' see PARA 319 note 17. As to references to controlled expenditure incurred by or on behalf of a recognised third party during a regulated period see PARA 319 note 19.
6 Political Parties, Elections and Referendums Act 2000 s 98(1)(b). The text refers to an auditor's report on a return as to controlled expenditure which falls to be prepared under s 97(1) (see PARA 321): see s 98(1)(b).
7 As to the meaning of 'responsible person' for these purposes see PARA 313 note 15.
8 As to the Electoral Commission see PARA 34 et seq.
9 Political Parties, Elections and Referendums Act 2000 s 98(1).

10 Ie under the Political Parties, Elections and Referendums Act 2000 s 96 (see PARA 321): see
    s 98(2).
11 Political Parties, Elections and Referendums Act 2000 s 98(2).
12 Ie where permission is given to pay claims in respect of controlled expenditure under the
    Political Parties, Elections and Referendums Act 2000 s 92(4) (see PARA 318): see s 98(3).
13 Political Parties, Elections and Referendums Act 2000 s 98(3).
14 See the Political Parties, Elections and Referendums Act 2000 s 98(4); and PARA 751.
15 See the Political Parties, Elections and Referendums Act 2000 s 147, Sch 19C; and PARA 757 et
    seq.

323. Declaration in respect of controlled expenditure. For the purposes of
controlling expenditure incurred by third parties in a relevant national election
campaign[1], each return in respect of controlled expenditure[2] incurred by or on
behalf of a recognised third party[3] during a regulated period[4] must, when
delivered to the Electoral Commission[5], be accompanied by a declaration which
is signed by the responsible person[6], and which must state:

(1) that the responsible person has examined the return in question[7]; and

(2) that, to the best of his knowledge and belief[8], it is a complete and
     correct return as required by law[9], and all expenses shown in it as paid
     have been paid by him or by a person authorised by him[10].

The declaration must also state, in a case where the third party either is not a
registered party[11] or is a minor party[12], that:

(a) all relevant donations[13] recorded in the return as having been accepted
     by the third party are from permissible donors[14]; and

(b) no other relevant donations have been accepted by the third party in
     respect of the relevant election or elections[15] which took place during
     the regulated period[16].

A person commits an offence if he knowingly or recklessly makes such a
declaration falsely, or if the requirements as to such a declaration are
contravened at a time when he is the responsible person in the case of the
recognised third party to which the return relates[17].

1 Ie for the purposes of the Political Parties, Elections and Referendums Act 2000 Pt VI
   (ss 85–100): see s 94(1). As to the meaning of 'relevant election' for these purposes see PARA 299
   note 3; definition applied by virtue of s 85(6).
2 Ie each return as to controlled expenditure which falls to be prepared under the Political Parties,
   Elections and Referendums Act 2000 s 96 (see PARA 321): see s 99(1). As to the meaning of
   'controlled expenditure' in relation to third parties see PARA 313.
3 As to the meaning of 'recognised third party' see PARA 313 note 15.
4 As to the meaning of 'regulated period' see PARA 319 note 17. As to references to controlled
   expenditure incurred by or on behalf of a recognised third party during a regulated period see
   PARA 319 note 19.
5 As to the Electoral Commission see PARA 34 et seq; and as to the delivery of returns to the
   Commission see PARA 322.
6 Political Parties, Elections and Referendums Act 2000 s 99(1). As to the meaning of 'responsible
   person' for these purposes see PARA 313 note 15.
7 Political Parties, Elections and Referendums Act 2000 s 99(2)(a).
8 Political Parties, Elections and Referendums Act 2000 s 99(2)(b).
9 Political Parties, Elections and Referendums Act 2000 s 99(2)(b)(i).
10 Political Parties, Elections and Referendums Act 2000 s 99(2)(b)(ii). The text refers to a person
   authorised in writing by the responsible person under s 90 (see PARA 315): see s 99(2)(b)(ii).
11 As to the meaning of 'registered party' for these purposes see PARA 35 note 3.
12 As to the meaning of 'minor party' see PARA 253 note 8.
13 For these purposes, 'relevant donation' has the same meaning as in the Political Parties,
   Elections and Referendums Act 2000 s 95, Sch 11 (see PARA 325 note 9): s 99(5).
14 Political Parties, Elections and Referendums Act 2000 s 99(3)(a).
15 As to the meaning of 'relevant election' for these purposes see note 1.

16 Political Parties, Elections and Referendums Act 2000 s 99(3)(b).
17 See the Political Parties, Elections and Referendums Act 2000 s 99(4); and PARA 751.

324. Public inspection of returns in respect of controlled expenditure. For the purposes of controlling expenditure incurred by third parties in a relevant national election campaign[1], where the Electoral Commission[2] receives any return in respect of controlled expenditure[3], it must[4]:

(1) as soon as reasonably practicable after receiving the return, make a copy of the return, and of any documents accompanying it, available for public inspection[5]; and

(2) keep any such copy available for public inspection for the period for which the return or other document is kept by it[6].

Where the Commission is for the time being required to make available for public inspection a copy of any document in this way, it must make the copy available for public inspection during ordinary office hours, either at the Commission's offices or at some convenient place appointed by it[7], although the Commission may make other arrangements for members of the public to have access to the document's contents[8]. If requested to do so by any person, the Commission must supply him with a copy of the document or any part of it[9]; and the Commission may charge such reasonable fee as it may determine in respect of any inspection or access so allowed or any copy so supplied[10]. Where any such document is held by the Commission in electronic form, any copy so made available for public inspection or so supplied must be made available, or (as the case may be) supplied, in a legible form[11].

At the end of the period of two years beginning with the date when any such return or other document is received by the Commission[12], it may cause the return or other document to be destroyed[13]; but, if requested to do so by the responsible person[14] in the case of the recognised third party[15] concerned, it must arrange for the return or other document to be returned to that person[16].

1 Ie for the purposes of the Political Parties, Elections and Referendums Act 2000 Pt VI (ss 85–100): see s 94(1). As to the meaning of 'relevant election' for these purposes see PARA 299 note 3; definition applied by virtue of s 85(6).

2 As to the Electoral Commission see PARA 34 et seq.

3 Ie any return in respect of controlled expenditure which falls to be prepared under the Political Parties, Elections and Referendums Act 2000 s 96 (see PARA 321): see s 100(1). As to the meaning of 'controlled expenditure' in relation to third parties see PARA 313. As to the delivery of returns in respect of controlled expenditure to the Commission see PARA 322.

4 See the Political Parties, Elections and Referendums Act 2000 s 100(1).

5 Political Parties, Elections and Referendums Act 2000 s 100(1)(a). However, if the return contains a statement of relevant donations in accordance with s 96(2)(d) (see PARA 321), the Commission must secure that the copy of the statement made available for public inspection does not include, in the case of any donation by an individual, the donor's address: s 100(2). As to the meaning of 'relevant donation' for these purposes see PARA 323 note 13.

6 Political Parties, Elections and Referendums Act 2000 s 100(1)(b).

7 Political Parties, Elections and Referendums Act 2000 s 149(2), (6)(c).

8 Political Parties, Elections and Referendums Act 2000 s 149(3), (6)(c).

9 Political Parties, Elections and Referendums Act 2000 s 149(4), (6)(c).

10 See the Political Parties, Elections and Referendums Act 2000 s 149(5), (6)(c).

11 Political Parties, Elections and Referendums Act 2000 s 149(7).

12 See the Political Parties, Elections and Referendums Act 2000 s 100(3).

13 Political Parties, Elections and Referendums Act 2000 s 100(3)(a).

14 As to the meaning of 'responsible person' for these purposes see PARA 313 note 15.

15 As to the meaning of 'recognised third party' see PARA 313 note 15.

16 Political Parties, Elections and Referendums Act 2000 s 100(3)(b).

B. CONTROLS AFFECTING DONATIONS MADE TO RECOGNISED THIRD PARTIES IN NATIONAL
PARLIAMENTARY ELECTION CAMPAIGNS

325. Meaning of 'donation' in relation to a recognised third party. For the
purposes of controlling donations to recognised third parties[1] which either are
not registered parties[2] or are minor parties[3], 'donation', in relation to such a
recognised third party, means[4]:

(1)   any gift[5] to the recognised third party of money or other property[6];
(2)   any sponsorship provided in relation to the recognised third party[7];
(3)   any money spent (otherwise than by or on behalf of the recognised third
       party) in paying any controlled expenditure[8] incurred by or on behalf of
       the recognised third party[9];
(4)   any money lent to the recognised third party otherwise than on
       commercial terms[10];
(5)   the provision otherwise than on commercial terms of any property,
       services or facilities for the use or benefit of the recognised third party
       (including the services of any person)[11];
(6)   in the case of a recognised third party, other than an individual, any
       subscription or other fee paid for affiliation to, or membership of, the
       third party[12].

Where anything would be a donation both by virtue of head (2) above, and by
virtue of any other provision mentioned in head (1) or heads (3) to (6) above,
head (2) above applies in relation to that donation to the exclusion of the other
provision[13]. Any donation whose value is not more than £500 is disregarded[14];
and none of the following is to be regarded as a donation:

(a)   the provision by an individual of his own services which he provides
       voluntarily in his own time and free of charge[15];
(b)   any interest accruing to a recognised third party in respect of any
       donation which is sent back by the responsible person[16] in relation to
       the recognised third party[17].

For these purposes, 'sponsorship' is provided in relation to a recognised third
party if any money or other property is transferred to the recognised third party
or to any person for the benefit of the recognised third party[18], and if the
purpose (or one of the purposes) of the transfer is (or must, having regard to all
the circumstances, reasonably be assumed to be)[19]: (i) to help the recognised
third party with meeting, or to meet, to any extent any defined expenses[20]
incurred or to be incurred by or on behalf of the recognised third party[21]; or (ii)
to secure that to any extent any such expenses are not so incurred[22]. However,
for these purposes:

(A)   the making of any payment in respect of any charge for admission to
       any conference, meeting or other event[23], or in respect of the purchase
       price of, or any other charge for access to, any publication[24]; or
(B)   the making of any payment in respect of the inclusion of an
       advertisement in any publication where the payment is made at the
       commercial rate payable for the inclusion of such an advertisement in
       any such publication[25],

do not constitute sponsorship for these purposes[26].

1   As to the meaning of 'recognised third party' see PARA 313 note 15.
2   As to the meaning of 'registered party' for these purposes see PARA 35 note 3.

3   See the Political Parties, Elections and Referendums Act 2000 s 95, Sch 11 para 1(1), (2). Accordingly, for the purposes of Sch 11, 'recognised third party' does not include a recognised third party which is a registered party other than a minor party: Sch 11 para 1(3). As to the meaning of 'minor party' see PARA 253 note 8.

4   See the Political Parties, Elections and Referendums Act 2000 Sch 11 para 2(1). This provision is subject to Sch 11 para 4 (see the text and notes 14–17). For the purposes of Sch 11, 'donation' is to be construed in accordance with Sch 11 paras 2–4 (see also the text and notes 5–26): see Sch 11 para 1(5).

5   For these purposes, 'gift' includes bequest (and thus any form of testamentary disposition): see the Political Parties, Elections and Referendums Act 2000 s 160(1), Sch 11 para 2(6)(b). For these purposes, any reference to anything being given or transferred to a recognised third party includes a reference to its being given or transferred either directly or indirectly through any third person: Sch 11 para 2(6)(a). Any property given or transferred to any officer, member, trustee or agent of a third party in his capacity as such (and not for his own use or benefit) is to be regarded as given or transferred to the third party (and references to donations received by a recognised party accordingly include donations so given or transferred): Sch 11 para 2(5). As to the meaning of 'property' for these purposes see PARA 34 note 8.

6   Political Parties, Elections and Referendums Act 2000 Sch 11 para 2(1)(a). Where:

     (1)   any money or other property is transferred to a recognised third party pursuant to any transaction or arrangement involving the provision by or on behalf of the recognised third party of any property, services or facilities or other consideration of monetary value (Sch 11 para 2(2)(a)); and

     (2)   the total value in monetary terms of the consideration so provided by or on behalf of the recognised third party is less than the value of the money or (as the case may be) the market value of the property transferred (Sch 11 para 2(2)(b)),

the transfer of the money or property constitute a gift to the recognised third party for the purposes of Sch 11 para 2(1)(a), but subject to Sch 11 para 2(4) (see the text and note 13) (see Sch 11 para 2(2)). The value of any donation falling within Sch 11 para 2(1)(a), other than money, must be taken to be the market value of the property in question: Sch 11 para 5(1). However, where Sch 11 para 2(1)(a) applies by virtue of Sch 11 para 2(2), the value of the donation must be taken to be the difference between:

     (a)   the value of the money (or the market value of the property) in question (Sch 11 para 5(2)(a)); and

     (b)   the total value in monetary terms of the consideration provided by or on behalf of the recognised third party (Sch 11 para 5(2)(b)).

As to the meaning of 'market value' see PARA 299 note 26.

7   Political Parties, Elections and Referendums Act 2000 Sch 11 para 2(1)(b). For these purposes, sponsorship provided in relation to the recognised third party is defined by Sch 11 para 3 (see the text and notes 18–26): see Sch 11 para 2(1)(b). The value of any donation falling within Sch 11 para 2(1)(b) is taken to be the value of the money or (as the case may be) the market value of the property, transferred as mentioned in Sch 11 para 3(1) (see the text and notes 18–22); and accordingly any value in monetary terms of any benefit conferred on the person providing the sponsorship in question must be disregarded: Sch 11 para 5(3).

8   As to the meaning of 'controlled expenditure' in relation to third parties see PARA 313.

9   Political Parties, Elections and Referendums Act 2000 Sch 11 para 2(1)(c). A donation to a recognised third party for the purpose of meeting controlled expenditure incurred by or on behalf of the recognised third party is referred to as a 'relevant donation': see Sch 11 para 1(4).

10   Political Parties, Elections and Referendums Act 2000 Sch 11 para 2(1)(d). In determining, for these purposes, whether any money lent to a recognised third party is so lent otherwise than on commercial terms (Sch 11 para 2(3)(a)), regard must be had to the total value in monetary terms of the consideration provided by or on behalf of the recognised third party in respect of the loan (see Sch 11 para 2(3)). The value of any donation falling within Sch 11 para 2(1)(d) or Sch 11 para 2(1)(e) (see head (5) in the text) is taken to be the amount representing the difference between:

     (1)   the total value in monetary terms of the consideration that would have had to be provided by or on behalf of the recognised third party in respect of the loan or the provision of the property, services or facilities, if the loan had been made, or if the property, services or facilities had been provided, on commercial terms (see Sch 11 para 5(4)(a)); and

     (2)   the total value in monetary terms of the consideration, if any, actually so provided by or on behalf of the recognised third party (Sch 11 para 5(4)(b)).

Where such a donation confers an enduring benefit on the donee over a particular period, the value of the donation is determined at the time when it is made, but must be so determined by reference to the total benefit accruing to the donee over that period: see Sch 11 para 5(5).

11 Political Parties, Elections and Referendums Act 2000 Sch 11 para 2(1)(e). In determining, for these purposes, whether any property, services or facilities provided for the use or benefit of a recognised third party is or are so provided otherwise than on commercial terms (Sch 11 para 2(3)(b)), regard must be had to the total value in monetary terms of the consideration provided by or on behalf of the recognised third party in respect of the provision of the property, services or facilities (see Sch 11 para 2(3)). As to the value of any donation falling within Sch 11 para 2(1)(e) see note 10.

12 Political Parties, Elections and Referendums Act 2000 Sch 11 para 2(1)(f).

13 Political Parties, Elections and Referendums Act 2000 Sch 11 para 2(4). In the circumstances mentioned in the text, the general provisions as to sponsorship (ie Sch 11 para 3: see the text and notes 18–26) apply as well as the provision mentioned in head (2) in the text: see Sch 11 para 2(4).

14 Political Parties, Elections and Referendums Act 2000 Sch 11 para 4(2) (amended by the Political Parties and Elections Act 2009 s 20(1)). The value is determined in accordance with the Political Parties, Elections and Referendums Act 2000 Sch 11 para 5 (see notes 6–7, 10): see Sch 11 para 4(2) (as so amended).

The Secretary of State may by order vary the sum for the time being specified in any provision of the Political Parties, Elections and Referendums Act 2000: see s 155; and PARA 299 note 36. However, in relation to any sum specified in Sch 11, in each Parliament (other than a Parliament that is dissolved less than two years after the date of its first sitting) the Secretary of State must either make an order in pursuance of s 155(2)(a) (see PARA 299 note 36), or lay before Parliament a statement setting out the Secretary of State's reasons for not doing so: see s 155(3)(c), (4) (s 155(3), (4) added by the Political Parties and Elections Act 2009 s 20(4)). As to the Secretary of State see PARA 2; and as to the making of regulations under the Political Parties, Elections and Referendums Act 2000 generally see PARA 34 note 2.

15 Political Parties, Elections and Referendums Act 2000 Sch 11 para 4(1)(a).

16 As to the meaning of 'responsible person' for these purposes see PARA 313 note 15.

17 Political Parties, Elections and Referendums Act 2000 Sch 11 para 4(1)(b). The text refers to a donation which is dealt with in accordance with s 56(2)(a), (b), as applied by Sch 11 para 7 (see PARA 327): see Sch 11 para 4(1)(b).

18 Political Parties, Elections and Referendums Act 2000 Sch 11 para 3(1)(a).

19 Political Parties, Elections and Referendums Act 2000 Sch 11 para 3(1)(b).

20 For this purpose, 'defined expenses' means expenses in connection with:
    (1) any conference, meeting or other event organised by or on behalf of the recognised third party (Political Parties, Elections and Referendums Act 2000 Sch 11 para 3(2)(a));
    (2) the preparation, production or dissemination of any publication by or on behalf of the recognised third party (Sch 11 para 3(2)(b)); or
    (3) any study or research organised by or on behalf of the recognised third party (Sch 11 para 3(2)(c)).

For this purpose, 'publication' means a publication made available in whatever form and by whatever means, whether or not to the public at large or any section of the public: Sch 11 para 3(5). The Secretary of State may by order made on the recommendation of the Electoral Commission amend Sch 11 para 3(2) or Sch 11 para 3(3) (see the text and notes 23–26): Sch 11 para 3(4). As to the Electoral Commission see PARA 34 et seq.

21 Political Parties, Elections and Referendums Act 2000 Sch 11 para 3(1)(b)(i).

22 Political Parties, Elections and Referendums Act 2000 Sch 11 para 3(1)(b)(ii).

23 Political Parties, Elections and Referendums Act 2000 Sch 11 para 3(3)(a)(i). See note 20.

24 Political Parties, Elections and Referendums Act 2000 Sch 11 para 3(3)(a)(ii). See note 20.

25 Political Parties, Elections and Referendums Act 2000 Sch 11 para 3(3)(b). See note 20.

26 See the Political Parties, Elections and Referendums Act 2000 Sch 11 para 3(3). See note 20.

326. Restrictions on recognised third parties accepting certain donations. For the purposes of controlling donations to recognised third parties[1] which either are not registered parties[2] or are minor parties[3], a relevant donation[4] received by a recognised third party must not be accepted if[5]:

(1) the person by whom the donation would be made is not, at the time of its receipt by the recognised third party, a permissible donor[6]; or

(2) the recognised third party is, whether because the donation is given

anonymously or by reason of any deception or concealment or otherwise, unable to ascertain the identity of the person offering the donation[7].

For these purposes, where any person (the 'principal donor') causes an amount (the 'principal donation') to be received by a recognised third party by way of a relevant donation, either on behalf of himself and one or more other persons[8], or on behalf of two or more other persons[9], then for the purposes of the statutory controls on donations received by third parties[10], each individual contribution by such person of more than £500 is treated as if it were a separate donation received from that person[11]. Also, where any person (the 'agent') causes an amount to be received by a recognised third party by way of a donation on behalf of another person (the 'donor')[12], and where the amount of the donation is more than £500[13], the agent must ensure that, at the time when the donation is received by the recognised third party, the responsible person is given all such details in respect of the donor as are required to be included in donation reports in respect of a donation from a permissible donor[14].

A person commits an offence if, without reasonable excuse, he fails to comply with the provisions which impose controls on donations to recognised third parties made through other persons or through agents[15].

1   As to the meaning of 'recognised third party' see PARA 313 note 15; and see PARA 325 note 3.

2   As to the meaning of 'registered party' for these purposes see PARA 35 note 3.

3   See the Political Parties, Elections and Referendums Act 2000 s 95, Sch 11 para 1(1), (2). As to the meaning of 'minor party' see PARA 253 note 8.

4   As to the meaning of 'relevant donation' in respect of meeting controlled expenditure incurred by or on behalf of a recognised third party see PARA 325 note 9. In the case of relevant donations received by a recognised Gibraltar third party for the purposes of European parliamentary elections taking place in the combined region see the Political Parties, Elections and Referendums Act 2000 Sch 11 para 6(1A), (2A), (3A) (added by SI 2004/366). As to the combined region see PARA 77.

5   See the Political Parties, Elections and Referendums Act 2000 Sch 11 para 6(1).
    As from a day to be appointed under the Political Parties and Elections Act 2009 s 43(1), in addition to heads (1) and (2) in the text, a further objection to a relevant donation being accepted is added, namely either:
    (1)   in the case of a donation of an amount exceeding £7,500, the recognised third party has not been given a declaration as required by the Political Parties, Elections and Referendums Act 2000 Sch 11 para 6A (Sch 11 para 6(1)(aa) (prospectively added by the Political Parties and Elections Act 2009 s 9(8), Sch 3 para 4(1))); or
    (2)   any declaration required to be made in respect of the donation by the Political Parties, Elections and Referendums Act 2000 Sch 11 para 6A or Sch 11 para 6B has not been received by the recognised third party (Sch 11 para 6(1)(aa) (prospectively added; prospectively substituted by the Political Parties and Elections Act 2009 s 10(8), Sch 4 para 4(1))).
    Also as from a day to be appointed under the Political Parties and Elections Act 2009 s 43(1), a requirement is imposed on a person who causes an amount exceeding £7,500 to be received by a recognised third party by way of a donation, to make a written declaration as to its source (see the Political Parties, Elections and Referendums Act 2000 Sch 11 para 6A (prospectively added by the Political Parties and Elections Act 2009 Sch 3 para 4(2))); and an individual making to a recognised third party a donation must give to the recognised third party a written declaration stating whether or not the individual's liability to income tax for the current tax year (including eligibility to make any claim) falls to be determined (or would fall to be determined) on the basis that the individual is resident, ordinarily resident and domiciled in the United Kingdom in that year (see the Political Parties, Elections and Referendums Act 2000 Sch 11 para 6B (prospectively added by the Political Parties and Elections Act 2009 Sch 4 para 4(2))). Any payment out of public finds is not to be regarded as a donation for the purposes of the Political Parties, Elections and Referendums Act 2000 Sch 11 para 6A or Sch 11 6B: see Sch 11 para 4(3) (prospectively added by the Political Parties and Elections Act 2009 Sch 6

para 29(1), (2); and prospectively amended by Sch 6 para 29(1), (3)). However, at the date at which this volume states the law, no such day had been appointed in relation to any of these provisions.

6 Political Parties, Elections and Referendums Act 2000 Sch 11 para 6(1)(a). The text refers to a permissible donor falling within s 54(2) (see PARA 288): see Sch 11 para 6(1)(a). However, references in Sch 11 to a permissible donor falling within s 54(2) do not include a registered party: see Sch 11 para 1(6).

Any relevant donation received by a recognised third party which is an exempt trust donation is regarded as a relevant donation received by the recognised third party from a permissible donor: Sch 11 para 6(2). However, any relevant donation received by a recognised third party from a trustee of any property (in his capacity as such) is regarded as being from a person who is not such a permissible donor if that donation is not:
(1) an exempt trust donation (Sch 11 para 6(3)(a)); or
(2) a relevant donation transmitted by the trustee to the recognised third party on behalf of beneficiaries under the trust, being persons who, at the time of its receipt by the recognised third party, are permissible donors falling within s 54(2), or who are the members of an unincorporated association which at that time is such a permissible donor (Sch 11 para 6(3)(b)).

As to the meaning of 'exempt trust donation' see PARA 288 note 7.

7 Political Parties, Elections and Referendums Act 2000 Sch 11 para 6(1)(b).
8 Political Parties, Elections and Referendums Act 2000 Sch 11 para 6(4)(a).
9 Political Parties, Elections and Referendums Act 2000 Sch 11 para 6(4)(b).
10 Ie for the purposes of the Political Parties, Elections and Referendums Act 2000 Sch 11: see Sch 11 para 6(4) (amended by the Political Parties and Elections Act 2009 s 20(1)).
11 Political Parties, Elections and Referendums Act 2000 Sch 11 para 6(4) (as amended: see note 10). In relation to each such separate donation, the principal donor must ensure that, at the time when the principal donation is received by the recognised third party, the responsible person in relation to the third party concerned is given:
(1) except in the case of a donation which the principal donor is treated as making, all such details in respect of the person treated as making the donation as are required by virtue of Sch 11 para 10(1)(c) (see PARA 329) to be given in respect of the donor of a donation from a permissible donor (Sch 11 para 6(5)(a)); and
(2) in any case, all such details in respect of the donation as are required by virtue of Sch 11 para 10(1)(a) (see PARA 329) (Sch 11 para 6(5)(b)).

As to the meaning of 'responsible person' for these purposes see PARA 313 note 15. The Secretary of State may by order vary the sum for the time being specified in any provision of the Political Parties, Elections and Referendums Act 2000: see s 155; and PARA 299 note 36. However, in relation to any sum specified in Sch 11, in each Parliament (other than a Parliament that is dissolved less than two years after the date of its first sitting) the Secretary of State must either make an order in pursuance of s 155(2)(a) (see PARA 299 note 36), or lay before Parliament a statement setting out the Secretary of State's reasons for not doing so: see s 155(3)(c), (4) (s 155(3), (4) added by the Political Parties and Elections Act 2009 s 20(4)). As to the Secretary of State see PARA 2; and as to the making of regulations under the Political Parties, Elections and Referendums Act 2000 generally see PARA 34 note 2.
12 Political Parties, Elections and Referendums Act 2000 Sch 11 para 6(6)(a).
13 Political Parties, Elections and Referendums Act 2000 Sch 11 para 6(6)(b) (amended by the Political Parties and Elections Act 2009 s 20(1)).
14 Political Parties, Elections and Referendums Act 2000 Sch 11 para 6(6). The text refers to the details in respect of the donor that are required to be reported by virtue of Sch 11 para 10(1)(c) (see PARA 329): see Sch 11 para 6(6).
15 See the Political Parties, Elections and Referendums Act 2000 Sch 11 para 6(7); and PARA 752. The text refers to failure to comply with Sch 11 para 6(5), (6) (see the text and notes 11–14): see Sch 11 para 6(7); and PARA 752.

327. Acceptance or return of donations made to a recognised third party. The provisions which require a registered party[1] to:

(1) take all reasonable steps to identify a donor in order to ascertain whether he is a permissible donor[2]; and

(2) where a donor is unidentifiable or impermissible, to return the donation to its source or to send it to the Electoral Commission[3] or subject it to forfeiture on the application of the Commission[4],

apply, subject to minor modification, for the purposes of controlling donations to recognised third parties[5] in relation to any relevant donation[6] received by a recognised third party and in relation to the recognised third party, as they apply in relation to any donation received by a registered party and in relation to the registered party[7].

1   As to the meaning of 'registered party' for these purposes see PARA 35 note 3.

2   Ie the Political Parties, Elections and Referendums Act 2000 s 56 (see CONSTITUTIONAL LAW AND HUMAN RIGHTS): see Sch 11 para 7(1). Nothing in Pt IV (ss 50–71) applies in relation to donations received by a minor party (see PARA 253): see s 50(9). As to the meaning of 'permissible donor' for these purposes see PARA 288.

3   Ie the Political Parties, Elections and Referendums Act 2000 s 57 (see CONSTITUTIONAL LAW AND HUMAN RIGHTS): see Sch 11 para 7(1). See also note 2. As to the Electoral Commission see PARA 34 et seq.

4   Ie the Political Parties, Elections and Referendums Act 2000 s 58 (see CONSTITUTIONAL LAW AND HUMAN RIGHTS): see Sch 11 para 7(1). See also note 2. The registered party may appeal against a forfeiture order (see s 59; and see CONSTITUTIONAL LAW AND HUMAN RIGHTS); and rules of court under s 60 (see CONSTITUTIONAL LAW AND HUMAN RIGHTS) may provide for the procedure on application or appeal under ss 58, 59.

5   Ie for the purposes of the Political Parties, Elections and Referendums Act 2000 s 95, Sch 11 (see PARA 325 et seq): see Sch 11 para 7(1). As to the meaning of 'recognised third party' see PARA 313 note 15; and see PARA 325 note 3.

6   As to the meaning of 'relevant donation' in respect of meeting controlled expenditure incurred by or on behalf of a recognised third party see PARA 325 note 9.

7   See the Political Parties, Elections and Referendums Act 2000 Sch 11 para 7(1). Accordingly, in the application of ss 56–60 for these purposes:

    (1)   s 56(1) (see CONSTITUTIONAL LAW AND HUMAN RIGHTS) has effect as if the reference to the particulars relating to a donor which would be required to be included in a donation report by virtue of Sch 6 para 2 (identity of donors (quarterly reports): see CONSTITUTIONAL LAW AND HUMAN RIGHTS), if the donation were a recordable donation within the meaning of Sch 6, were construed as a reference to the particulars which are required to be included in a return by virtue of Sch 11 para 10(1)(c), in relation to a donation to which Sch 11 para 10 applies (see PARA 329) (Sch 11 para 7(2)(a));

    (2)   s 56(3), (4) (see CONSTITUTIONAL LAW AND HUMAN RIGHTS) has effect as if any reference to the treasurer of the party were construed as a reference to the responsible person (Sch 11 para 7(2)(b)).

    As to the treasurer of a registered party see PARA 253.

    As from a day to be appointed under the Political Parties and Elections Act 2009 s 43(1), head (2) above is amended so that it refers to the Political Parties, Elections and Referendums Act 2000 s 56(3), (3B), (4) (s 56(3B) not yet in force) (see Sch 11 para 7(2)(b) (prospectively amended by the Political Parties and Elections Act 2009 s 39, Sch 6 para 29(1), (4))); and a further modification is added for these purposes, namely that the Political Parties, Elections and Referendums Act 2000 s 56(1A)(a) (not yet in force) has effect as if the reference to a declaration under s 54B (not yet in force) (residence declaration) were construed as a reference to a declaration under Sch 11 para 6B (not yet in force) (see PARA 326 note 5) (see Sch 11 para 7(2)(aa) (prospectively added by the Political Parties and Elections Act 2009 s 10(8), Sch 4 para 5)). However, at the date at which this volume states the law, no such day had been appointed in relation to any of these provisions.

328. Evasion of restrictions on donations made to a recognised third party.

The provisions which create offences concerned with the evasion of restrictions on donations to a registered party[1] apply for the purposes of controlling donations to a recognised third party[2], subject to minor modification[3].

1   Ie the Political Parties, Elections and Referendums Act 2000 s 61 (see CONSTITUTIONAL LAW AND HUMAN RIGHTS): see s 95, Sch 11 para 8; and PARA 752. As to the meaning of 'registered party' for these purposes see PARA 35 note 3.

2   Ie for the purposes of the Political Parties, Elections and Referendums Act 2000 Sch 11 (see PARA 325 et seq): see Sch 11 para 8; and PARA 752. As to the meaning of 'recognised third party' see PARA 313 note 15; and see PARA 325 note 3.

3   See the Political Parties, Elections and Referendums Act 2000 Sch 11 para 8; and PARA 752.

329. Statement of relevant donations received by a recognised third party. For the purposes of controlling donations to recognised third parties[1] which are not registered parties[2] or are minor parties[3], the recognised third party must include, in any return required to be prepared in respect of controlled expenditure[4], a statement of relevant donations[5] received in respect of the relevant election or elections[6] which complies with the requirement to report any donations received from persons who are permissible donors as well as those received from persons who are not permissible donors[7].

Accordingly, in relation to each relevant donation accepted by the recognised third party where the value of the donation:

(1)   is more than £7,500[8]; or

(2)   when added to the value of any other donation or donations made by the same donor (whether or not falling within head (1) above), is more than that amount[9],

the statement must record[10]:

(a)   the amount of the donation (if a donation of money, in cash or otherwise) or (in any other case) the nature of the donation and its value[11];

(b)   the date when the donation was accepted by the recognised third party[12];

(c)   the information about the donor which is, in connection with recordable donations to registered parties, required to be recorded in donation reports[13];

(d)   the total value of any relevant donations, other than those falling within head (1) or head (2) above, which are accepted by the recognised third party[14]; and

(e)   such other information as may be required by regulations made by the Electoral Commission[15].

Where a relevant donation has been received from a person who is not a permissible donor (an 'impermissible donor')[16], the statement must record:

(i)   the name and address of the donor[17];

(ii)   the amount of the donation (if a donation of money, in cash or otherwise) or (in any other case) the nature of the donation and its value[18];

(iii)   the date when the donation was received, and the date when, and the manner in which, it was dealt with in accordance with the provisions which regulate the handling of relevant donations made by impermissible donors[19];

(iv)   such other information as is required by regulations made by the Electoral Commission[20].

Where a relevant donation has been received from a person whose identity cannot be ascertained[21], the statement must record:

(A)   details of the manner in which the donation was made[22];

(B)   the amount of the donation (if a donation of money, in cash or otherwise) or (in any other case) the nature of the donation and its value[23];

(C)   the date when the donation was received, and the date when and the manner in which it was dealt with in accordance with the provisions which regulate the handling of relevant donations made by persons whose identity cannot be ascertained[24]; and

(D)   such other information as is required by regulations made by the Electoral Commission[25].

1   As to the meaning of 'recognised third party' see PARA 313 note 15; and see PARA 325 note 3.
2   As to the meaning of 'registered party' for these purposes see PARA 35 note 3.
3   See the Political Parties, Elections and Referendums Act 2000 s 95, Sch 11 para 1(1), (2). As to the meaning of 'minor party' see PARA 253 note 8.
4   Ie any return required to be prepared under the Political Parties, Elections and Referendums Act 2000 s 96 (see PARA 321): see Sch 11 para 9.
5   As to the meaning of 'relevant donation' in respect of controlled expenditure incurred by or on behalf of a recognised third party see PARA 325 note 9.
6   Ie within the meaning of the Political Parties, Elections and Referendums Act 2000 s 96 (see PARA 321).
7   Political Parties, Elections and Referendums Act 2000 Sch 11 para 9. As to the meaning of 'permissible donor' for these purposes see PARA 326 note 6.
      The text refers to the requirement for a statement of relevant donations which complies with Sch 11 paras 10, 11 (see the text and notes 8–25): see Sch 11 para 9. As from a day to be appointed under the Political Parties and Elections Act 2009 s 43(1), the Political Parties, Elections and Referendums Act 2000 Sch 11 para 9 is amended so that it refers to a statement of relevant donations which complies with Sch 11 paras 9A–11: see Sch 11 para 9 (Sch 11 para 9 prospectively amended, Sch 11 para 9A prospectively added, by the Political Parties and Elections Act 2009 s 9(8), Sch 3 para 5(1), (2)). The provision made by the Political Parties, Elections and Referendums Act 2000 Sch 11 para 9A governs declarations made in relation to each relevant donation falling within Sch 11 para 10(2) (see heads (1), (2) in the text), where a declaration has been given under Sch 11 para 6A (not yet in force) (see Sch 11 para 9A(1) (Sch 11 para 9A prospectively added; Sch 11 para 9A(1) prospectively numbered as such, Sch 11 para 9A(2) prospectively added, by the Political Parties and Elections Act 2009 s 10(8), Sch 4 para 6(b)) or under the Political Parties, Elections and Referendums Act 2000 Sch 11 para 6B (not yet in force) (see PARA 326 note 5) (Sch 11 para 9A(2) (prospectively added)). However, at the date at which this volume states the law, no such day had been appointed in relation to any of these provisions.
8   See the Political Parties, Elections and Referendums Act 2000 Sch 11 para 10(1), (2)(a) (Sch 11 para 10(2)(a) amended by the Political Parties and Elections Act 2009 s 20(3)).
      The Secretary of State may by order vary the sum for the time being specified in any provision of the Political Parties, Elections and Referendums Act 2000: see s 155; and PARA 299 note 36. However, in relation to any sum specified in Sch 11, in each Parliament (other than a Parliament that is dissolved less than two years after the date of its first sitting) the Secretary of State must either make an order in pursuance of s 155(2)(a) (see PARA 299 note 36), or lay before Parliament a statement setting out the Secretary of State's reasons for not doing so: see s 155(3)(c), (4) (s 155(3), (4) added by the Political Parties and Elections Act 2009 s 20(4)). As to the Secretary of State see PARA 2; and as to the making of regulations under the Political Parties, Elections and Referendums Act 2000 generally see PARA 34 note 2.
9   See the Political Parties, Elections and Referendums Act 2000 Sch 11 para 10(1), (2)(b).
10   See the Political Parties, Elections and Referendums Act 2000 Sch 11 para 10(1).
11   Political Parties, Elections and Referendums Act 2000 Sch 11 para 10(1)(a). The value of the donation is determined in accordance with Sch 11 para 5 (see PARA 325 notes 6–7, 10): see Sch 11 para 10(1)(a).
12   Political Parties, Elections and Referendums Act 2000 Sch 11 para 10(1)(b). As to the acceptance of donations made to a recognised third party see PARA 327.
13   Political Parties, Elections and Referendums Act 2000 Sch 11 para 10(1)(c). The text refers to information about the donor which is required to be recorded in donation reports by virtue of Sch 6 para 2 (identity of donors (quarterly reports): see CONSTITUTIONAL LAW AND HUMAN RIGHTS): see Sch 11 para 10(1)(c).
      In the case of a donation made by an individual who has an anonymous entry in an electoral register (within the meaning of the Representation of the People Act 1983: see PARA 148), if the statement of relevant donations states that the recognised third party has seen evidence, of such description as is prescribed by the Secretary of State in regulations, that an individual donor has such an anonymous entry, the statement must be accompanied by a copy of the evidence: Political Parties, Elections and Referendums Act 2000 Sch 11 para 10(4) (added by the Electoral Administration Act 2006 s 10(2), Sch 1 paras 24, 29). Accordingly, the evidence prescribed for the purposes of the Political Parties, Elections and Referendums Act 2000 Sch 11 para 10(4) is a certificate of anonymous registration issued under the Representation of the People (England

and Wales) Regulations 2001, SI 2001/341, reg 45G (see PARA 145 note 12): see the Political Donations and Regulated Transactions (Anonymous Electors) Regulations 2008, SI 2008/2869, reg 3.

14 Political Parties, Elections and Referendums Act 2000 Sch 11 para 10(3)(a).

15 Political Parties, Elections and Referendums Act 2000 Sch 11 para 10(3)(b). Regulations made by the Electoral Commission are not statutory instruments and are not recorded in this work: see further PARA 47. As to the Electoral Commission see PARA 34 et seq.

16 See the Political Parties, Elections and Referendums Act 2000 Sch 11 para 11(1), (2). The text refers to the circumstance where Sch 11 para 6(1)(a) applies (see PARA 326): see Sch 11 para 11(1), (2).

As from a day to be appointed under the Political Parties and Elections Act 2009 s 43(1), the Political Parties, Elections and Referendums Act 2000 Sch 11 para 11(1), (2) is amended so that it refers to the circumstance where Sch 11 para 6(1)(a), (aa) applies (Sch 11 para 6(1)(aa) not yet in force) (see PARA 326): see Sch 11 para 11(1), (2) (prospectively amended by the Political Parties and Elections Act 2009 s 9(8), Sch 3 para 6(1), (3), (4)). However, at the date at which this volume states the law, no such day had been appointed.

17 Political Parties, Elections and Referendums Act 2000 Sch 11 para 11(2)(a).

As from a day to be appointed under the Political Parties and Elections Act 2009 s 43(1), the Political Parties, Elections and Referendums Act 2000 Sch 11 para 11(2)(a) is amended so that it refers to the name and address of the donor, or the person appearing to be the donor: see Sch 11 para 11(2)(a) (prospectively amended by the Political Parties and Elections Act 2009 Sch 3 para 6(1), (5)). However, at the date at which this volume states the law, no such day had been appointed.

18 Political Parties, Elections and Referendums Act 2000 Sch 11 para 11(2)(b). The value of the donation is determined in accordance with Sch 11 para 5 (see PARA 325 notes 6–7, 10): see Sch 11 para 11(2)(b).

19 Political Parties, Elections and Referendums Act 2000 Sch 11 para 11(2)(c), (4). The text refers to dealing with the donation in accordance with s 56(2)(a), as it is applied by Sch 11 para 7 (see PARA 327): see Sch 11 para 11(2)(c), (4).

As from a day to be appointed under the Political Parties and Elections Act 2009 s 43(1), the Political Parties, Elections and Referendums Act 2000 Sch 11 para 11(2)(c) is amended so that it refers to dealing with the donation in accordance with s 56(2)(a) or s 56(2)(aa) (not yet in force), as it is applied by Sch 11 para 7: see Sch 11 para 11(2)(c), (4) (Sch 11 para 11(2)(c) prospectively amended by the Political Parties and Elections Act 2009 Sch 3 para 6(1), (6)). However, at the date at which this volume states the law, no such day had been appointed.

20 Political Parties, Elections and Referendums Act 2000 Sch 11 para 11(2)(d). See note 15.

21 See the Political Parties, Elections and Referendums Act 2000 Sch 11 para 11(3). The text refers to the circumstance where Sch 11 para 6(1)(b) applies (see PARA 326): see Sch 11 para 11(3).

22 Political Parties, Elections and Referendums Act 2000 Sch 11 para 11(3)(a).

23 Political Parties, Elections and Referendums Act 2000 Sch 11 para 11(3)(b). The value of the donation is determined in accordance with Sch 11 para 5 (see PARA 325 notes 6–7, 10): see Sch 11 para 11(3)(b).

24 Political Parties, Elections and Referendums Act 2000 Sch 11 para 11(3)(c), (4). The text refers to dealing with the donation in accordance with s 56(2)(b), as it is applied by Sch 11 para 7 (see PARA 327): see Sch 11 para 11(3)(c), (4).

25 Political Parties, Elections and Referendums Act 2000 Sch 11 para 11(3)(d). See note 15.

(vii) Publicity at Elections

330. Right of candidates at election to send election address post free. Subject to such reasonable terms and conditions as the universal postal service provider[1] concerned may specify[2], a candidate at a parliamentary, Welsh Assembly, or European parliamentary election[3], is entitled to send free of any charge for postage which would otherwise be made by a universal postal service provider[4], either:

(1)   one unaddressed postal communication, containing matter relating to the election only and not exceeding 60 grammes in weight, to each place[5] which, in accordance with those terms and conditions, constitutes a delivery point for these purposes[6]; or

(2)   one such postal communication addressed to each elector[7].

He is also, subject as mentioned above, entitled to send free of any such charge for postage as mentioned above to each person entered in the list of proxies[8] for the election one such communication as mentioned above for each appointment in respect of which that person is so entered[9]. A person is not deemed to be a candidate for this purpose unless he is shown as standing nominated in the statement of persons nominated[10], but, until the publication of that statement, any person who declares himself to be a candidate[11] is entitled to exercise this right of free postage if he gives such security as may be required by the universal postal service provider concerned for the payment of postage should he not be shown as standing nominated[12].

Each candidate at a Greater London Authority ordinary election[13], or a local authority mayoral election[14], is entitled to have an election address prepared on behalf of the candidate included in a booklet of election addresses prepared by the appropriate returning officer and delivered by that officer to each person entitled to vote at that election at the expense of the Greater London Authority (in the case of an Authority election) or at the expense of the authority for whose electoral area the election is held (in the case of a local authority mayoral election)[15].

A defamatory statement published by or on behalf of a candidate in any election to a local government authority[16], to the National Assembly for Wales[17], or to Parliament, will not be deemed to be published on a privileged occasion on the ground that it is material to a question in issue in the election, whether or not the person by whom it is published is qualified to vote at the election[18].

1   For these purposes, 'universal postal service provider' means a universal service provider within the meaning of the Postal Services Act 2011 Pt 3 (ss 27–67) (see POSTAL SERVICES vol 85 (2012) PARA 252): Representation of the People Act 1983 s 202(1) (definition added by SI 2001/1149; amended by the Postal Services Act 2011 s 91(1), (2), Sch 12 Pt 3 paras 116, 120); European Parliamentary Elections Regulations 2004, SI 2004/293, reg 63(6) (definition substituted by SI 2011/2085); National Assembly for Wales (Representation of the People) Order 2007, SI 2007/236, art 2(1) (definition amended by SI 2011/2085).

2   As to the provision of a universal postal service see POSTAL SERVICES vol 85 (2012) PARA 257 et seq.

3   As to the meaning of 'parliamentary election' see PARA 9. As to the meaning of 'candidate' generally see PARA 230.

    In the case of a European parliamentary election, the reference to a candidate is to an individual candidate and the nominating officer of a registered party which is included in the statement of parties and individual candidates nominated for the election (or a person authorised in writing by that officer): see the European Parliamentary Elections Regulations 2004, SI 2004/293, reg 63(1). As to the meaning of 'individual candidate' at a European parliamentary election see PARA 230 note 32. As to the meaning of 'statement of parties and individual candidates nominated' see PARA 267 note 3. As to European parliamentary elections see PARA 217 et seq. As to the nominating officer of a registered party see PARA 253.

    In the case of a Welsh Assembly election, the reference to a candidate is to each constituency or individual candidate or registered nominating officer of a registered political party which has submitted a list of candidates at such an election: see the National Assembly for Wales (Representation of the People) Order 2007, SI 2007/236, art 65(1). As to the meanings of 'Assembly election', 'constituency election' and 'regional election' for these purposes see PARA 3 note 2. As to the meaning of 'registered political party' see PARA 215 note 19. As to the meanings of 'constituency candidate' at an Assembly constituency election and 'individual candidate' at a Welsh Assembly regional election see PARA 230 note 19; and as to the meanings of 'party list' and 'party list candidate' see PARA 230 note 23.

4   See the Representation of the People Act 1983 s 91(1) (substituted by the Representation of the People Act 1985 s 24, Sch 4 para 34; amended by the Postal Services Act 2000 s 127(4), Sch 8 para 17(1), (2)(a)–(c); and the Postal Services Act 2011 Sch 12 Pt 3 paras 116, 117(a)); European Parliamentary Elections Regulations 2004, SI 2004/293, reg 63(1); National Assembly for Wales (Representation of the People) Order 2007, SI 2007/236, art 65(1).

Where any postal services are provided without charge by a universal postal service provider in pursuance of the Representation of the People Act 1983, or the European Parliamentary Elections Regulations 2004, SI 2004/293, or the National Assembly for Wales (Representation of the People) Order 2007, SI 2007/236, art 65, as the case may be, the universal postal service provider is entitled to be remunerated for having provided the services at the rate fixed in relation to them by virtue of a scheme under the Postal Services Act 2000 s 89 (schemes for determining charges, terms and conditions, etc for provision of postal services: see POSTAL SERVICES vol 85 (2012) PARA 272 et seq): Representation of the People Act 1983 s 200A(1), (2) (s 200A added by the Postal Services Act 2000 Sch 8 para 18; Representation of the People Act 1983 s 200A(1)–(3) amended, s 200A(4) substituted, by the Postal Services Act 2011 Sch 12 Pt 3 paras 116, 119(a), (b)); European Parliamentary Elections Regulations 2004, SI 2004/293, reg 124(1), (2)(a); National Assembly for Wales (Representation of the People) Order 2007, SI 2007/236, art 65(9). A sum which a universal postal service provider is entitled to receive in this way is charged on and issued out of the Consolidated Fund (in the case of a parliamentary or European parliamentary election) or is to be charged on the Welsh Consolidated Fund (in the case of sums so payable by the Welsh Ministers in respect of a Welsh Assembly election): Representation of the People Act 1983 s 200A(3) (as so added and amended); European Parliamentary Elections Regulations 2004, SI 2004/293, reg 124(4); National Assembly for Wales (Representation of the People) Order 2007, SI 2007/236, art 65(10). For the purposes of the Representation of the People Act 1983, 'postal services' has the meaning given in the Postal Services Act 2011 s 27 (see POSTAL SERVICES vol 85 (2012) PARA 243): see the Representation of the People Act 1983 s 200A(4) (as so added). For the purposes of the European Parliamentary Elections Regulations 2004, SI 2004/293, 'postal services' and 'universal service provider' have the same meanings as in the Postal Services Act 2011 Pt 3 (see POSTAL SERVICES vol 85 (2012) PARA 252): European Parliamentary Elections Regulations 2004, SI 2004/293, reg 124(5) (amended by SI 2011/2085). In relation to a European parliamentary election held in the combined region see the European Parliamentary Elections Regulations 2004, SI 2004/293, reg 124(2)(b), (3). As to the establishment of electoral regions (including the 'combined region') for the purpose of elections to the European Parliament see PARA 77. As to the Consolidated Fund see CONSTITUTIONAL LAW AND HUMAN RIGHTS vol 8(2) (Reissue) PARA 711 et seq; PARLIAMENT vol 78 (2010) PARAS 1028–1031. As to the Welsh Consolidated Fund see CONSTITUTIONAL LAW AND HUMAN RIGHTS.

At a Welsh Assembly election, the regional returning officer is entitled to treat any purported exercise by the registered nominating officer of a registered political party of the right of free postage conferred by the National Assembly for Wales (Representation of the People) Order 2007, SI 2007/236, art 65 through the party election agent as a valid exercise of that right: art 65(7). If, at a regional election, the area of the regional returning officer is situated in the area of more than one official designated by a universal service provider, the controlling designated official is to be determined by that regional returning officer: art 65(8). As to the meaning of 'regional returning officer' for the purposes of Welsh Assembly elections see PARA 18 note 2.

5   In the case of a parliamentary election, the place referred to must be in the constituency: see the Representation of the People Act 1983 s 91(1)(a) (s 91(1) as substituted (see note 4); s 91(1)(a) amended by the Postal Services Act 2000 Sch 8 para 17(1), (2)(d)). As to the meaning of 'constituency' for the purposes of a parliamentary election see PARA 9.

In the case of a European parliamentary election, the place referred to must be in the electoral region: see the European Parliamentary Elections Regulations 2004, SI 2004/293, reg 63(1)(a).

In the case of a Welsh Assembly election, the place referred to must be in the Assembly constituency or electoral region for which the election is being held at which the candidate or candidates in question are a candidate or candidates: see the National Assembly for Wales (Representation of the People) Order 2007, SI 2007/236, art 65(1)(a). As to the meanings of 'Assembly constituency' and 'Assembly electoral region' see PARA 3 note 2.

6   Representation of the People Act 1983 s 91(1)(a) (s 91(1) as substituted (see note 4); s 91(1)(a) as amended (see note 5)); European Parliamentary Elections Regulations 2004, SI 2004/293, reg 63(1)(a); National Assembly for Wales (Representation of the People) Order 2007, SI 2007/236, art 65(1)(a).

7   Representation of the People Act 1983 s 91(1)(b) (as substituted: see note 4); European Parliamentary Elections Regulations 2004, SI 2004/293, reg 63(1)(b); National Assembly for Wales (Representation of the People) Order 2007, SI 2007/236, art 65(1)(b).

For these purposes, in relation to a parliamentary election, 'elector':

(1)   means a person who is registered in the register of parliamentary electors for the

constituency on the last day for publication of notice of the election (Representation of the People Act 1983 s 91(4)(a) (s 91(4) substituted by the Representation of the People Act 2000 s 8, Sch 1 paras 1, 19)); and

(2)   includes a person then shown in that register (or, in the case of a person who has an anonymous entry in the register, in the record of anonymous entries) as below voting age if (but only if) it appears from the register (or from the record) that he will be of voting age on the day fixed for the poll (Representation of the People Act 1983 s 91(4)(b) (s 91(4) as so substituted; s 91(4)(b) amended by the Electoral Administration Act 2006 Sch 1 paras 2, 10(1), (3)(a), (b))).

For these purposes, in relation to a European parliamentary election, 'elector' means a person:

(a)   who is registered in the register of electors to be used at the election in the electoral region on the last day for publication of notice of the election (European Parliamentary Elections Regulations 2004, SI 2004/293, reg 63(5)(a)); and

(b)   includes a person who is registered in such a register (or, in the case of a person who has an anonymous entry in the register, in the record of anonymous entries) as below voting age if (but only if) it appears from the register (or from the record) that he will be of voting age on the day fixed for the poll (reg 63(5)(b) (amended by SI 2009/186)).

For these purposes, in relation to a Welsh Assembly election, 'elector':

(i)   means a person who is registered in the register of local government electors for the Assembly constituency or electoral region on the last day for publication of notice of the election (National Assembly for Wales (Representation of the People) Order 2007, SI 2007/236, art 65(11)(a))); and

(ii)   includes a person then shown in that register (or, in the case of a person who has an anonymous entry in the register, in the record of anonymous entries) as below voting age if (but only if) it appears from the register (or from the record) that he will be of voting age on the day fixed for the poll (art 65(11)(b)).

'Voting age' is currently 18 years for all purposes: see PARAS 95 note 2, 97 note 14, 102 note 10. As to entitlement to registration as an elector see PARA 113 et seq; and as to the registers of electors see PARA 145 et seq. As to the meaning of 'anonymous entry' in relation to a register of electors see PARA 148. As to publication of the notice of election, in relation to a parliamentary election, see PARA 196; in relation to a local government election, see PARA 211; in relation to a Welsh Assembly election, see PARA 216; and, in relation to a European parliamentary election, see PARA 223.

The candidate at a parliamentary election may require the returning officer to make arrangements with the universal postal service provider for communications under the Representation of the People Act 1983 s 91(1)(b) to be sent to persons who have anonymous entries in the register; and such arrangements must be such as to ensure that it is not disclosed to any other person that the addressee of such a communication has an anonymous entry: see s 91(2A), (2B) (s 91(2A), (2B) added by the Electoral Administration Act 2006 s 10(2), Sch 1 paras 2, 10(1), (2); Representation of the People Act 1983 s 91(2A) amended by the Postal Services Act 2011 Sch 12 Pt 3 paras 116, 117(a)). The individual candidate, and the nominating officer of a registered party, which are included in the statement of parties and individual candidates nominated for a European parliamentary election (or a person authorised in writing by that officer) may require the local returning officer to make arrangements with the universal postal service provider for communications under the European Parliamentary Elections Regulations 2004, SI 2004/293, reg 63(1)(b) to be sent to persons who have anonymous entries in the register: reg 63(2A) (reg 63(2A), (2B) added by SI 2009/186). Arrangements under the European Parliamentary Elections Regulations 2004, SI 2004/293, reg 63(2A) must be such as to ensure that it is not disclosed to any other person that the addressee of such a communication has an anonymous entry: reg 63(2B) (as so added). Each constituency or individual candidate at a Welsh Assembly election, or registered nominating officer of a registered political party which has submitted a list of candidates at such an election, may require the returning officer to make arrangements with the universal service provider for communications under the National Assembly for Wales (Representation of the People) Order 2007, SI 2007/236, art 65(1)(b) to be sent to persons who have anonymous entries in the register: art 65(3). Arrangements under art 65(3) must be such as to ensure that it is not disclosed to any other person that the addressee of such a communication has an anonymous entry: art 65(4). As to returning officers for elections generally see PARA 350 et seq.

8   As to the meaning of 'list of proxies' see PARA 373 note 14.

9 Representation of the People Act 1983 s 91(2) (amended by the Postal Services Act 2000 Sch 8 para 17(1), (3)); European Parliamentary Elections Regulations 2004, SI 2004/293, reg 63(2); National Assembly for Wales (Representation of the People) Order 2007, SI 2007/236, art 65(2).

10 Representation of the People Act 1983 s 91(3) (amended by the Postal Services Act 2000 Sch 8 para 17(1), (4); and the Postal Services Act 2011 Sch 12 Pt 3 paras 116, 117(a)); European Parliamentary Elections Regulations 2004, SI 2004/293, reg 63(3); National Assembly for Wales (Representation of the People) Order 2007, SI 2007/236, art 65(5), (6). As to the statement of persons nominated see PARA 267.

In the case of a European parliamentary election, the nomination referred to in the text is that of an individual candidate: see the European Parliamentary Elections Regulations 2004, SI 2004/293, reg 63(3).

At a Welsh Assembly election, the reference is to a person not being deemed a candidate for these purposes, in relation to a candidate at a constituency election, or in relation to an individual candidate at a regional election (see the National Assembly for Wales (Representation of the People) Order 2007, SI 2007/236, art 65(5)); but, in relation to a registered political party at a regional election, the reference must be understood as being to such a party not being deemed to have submitted a list of candidates for these purposes unless the party is shown as standing nominated in the statement of parties and other persons nominated (see art 65(6)).

11 This may include candidates who have been declared as nominated by being included on a party list: see note 12.

12 Representation of the People Act 1983 s 91(3) (as amended: see note 10); European Parliamentary Elections Regulations 2004, SI 2004/293, reg 63(3); National Assembly for Wales (Representation of the People) Order 2007, SI 2007/236, art 65(5), (6).

In the case of a European parliamentary election, until the publication of the statement of parties and individual candidates nominated for the election in an electoral region, the nominating officer of a registered party or a person authorised in writing by him is entitled to exercise in that region the right of free postage if he gives such security as may be required by the universal service provider concerned for the payment of postage should that party not be included in that statement as standing nominated: European Parliamentary Elections Regulations 2004, SI 2004/293, reg 63(4).

At a Welsh Assembly election, until the publication of the statement of parties and other people nominated for an electoral region, the registered nominated officer of a party which has submitted a list of candidates is entitled to exercise the right of free postage if he gives such security as may be required by the universal service provider should the party not be shown as standing nominated in that statement: see the National Assembly for Wales (Representation of the People) Order 2007, SI 2007/236, art 65(6).

13 As to the meaning of 'Authority election' see PARA 11. As to ordinary Greater London Authority elections see PARA 199 et seq.

14 As to elections for the return of an elected mayor for a local authority see PARA 198 et seq.

15 See the Greater London Authority Act 1999 s 17A (added by the Representation of the People Act 2000 s 14(1), (2); amended by the Electoral Administration Act 2006 Sch 1 para 18; the Postal Services Act 2011 Sch 12 Pt 3 para 155; and SI 2001/648; SI 2010/1837); and the Local Authorities (Mayoral Elections) (England and Wales) Regulations 2007, SI 2007/1024, reg 6.

At an ordinary London Authority election, the Greater London returning officer ('GLRO') may, in addition to a statement by him in an election booklet, include in the booklet information for voters that has been agreed by him with the Electoral Commission: Greater London Authority Elections Rules 2007, SI 2007/3541, Sch 1 r 27(1), Sch 2 r 28(1), Sch 3 r 27(1). The information for voters given in the election booklet may include information about the office of the Mayor of London and the London Assembly; about the system of voting at each Authority election, or about how to vote in a manner that will ensure a vote is regarded as validly cast, and the information for voters so given may include any other information given in exercise of the GLRO's duty to encourage electoral participation under the Electoral Administration Act 2006 s 69 (see PARA 354): Greater London Authority Elections Rules 2007, SI 2007/3541, Sch 1 r 27(2), Sch 2 r 28(2), Sch 3 r 27(2). However, the information for voters must not contain any advertising material, any material referring to a candidate or a registered party (other than by reproduction of a ballot paper which refers equally to all candidates and parties at the ordinary election), or any material referring to the holder at any time of the office of Mayor of London or London Assembly member (other than by reproduction of a ballot paper which refers equally to all candidates and parties at the ordinary election): Sch 1 r 27(3), Sch 2 r 28(3), Sch 3 r 27(3). Information so published in an election booklet must be printed on not more than two sides of A5 paper: Sch 1 r 27(4), Sch 2 r 28(4), Sch 3 r 27(4). As to the content and delivery of the election addresses of mayoral candidates at an ordinary election of the Greater London

Authority, where an election for the return of the Mayor of London is held with elections for London members and constituency members to the London Assembly, see further the Greater London Authority Elections (Election Addresses) Order 2003, SI 2003/1907 (amended by SI 2008/507; SI 2011/2085; SI 2012/666). As to elections for the Mayor of London see further LONDON GOVERNMENT vol 71 (2013) PARA 82 et seq. As to the meaning of the 'Greater London returning officer' see PARA 211 note 8. As to the Electoral Commission see PARA 34 et seq.

For the purposes of a local authority mayoral election, the election booklet is a document prepared by the returning officer which contains the election addresses of all candidates who desire their election addresses to be included in the booklet, and have submitted to the returning officer, before the last time for delivery of nomination papers for the election, those addresses accompanied, where the address is to contain a photograph of the candidate, by two identical copies of the photograph, of which one is signed on the back by the candidate and, in any case, by such copies of anything contained in the address as the returning officer may reasonably require in connection with the reproduction of the address: see the Local Authorities (Mayoral Elections) (England and Wales) Regulations 2007, SI 2007/1024, reg 6(3), Sch 4 paras 4(4), 5(1). If it appears to the returning officer that any of the requirements has not been complied with in relation to an election address, or if a candidate fails to make the payment required in respect of an election address, the returning officer must decline to include the address in the election booklet: Sch 4 para 5(2). The election booklet may include, in addition to candidates' election addresses, a statement by the returning officer explaining the nature and purpose of the election booklet, listing, in alphabetical order, the names of all the candidates at the election (whether or not their election addresses are included in the booklet) and giving the date of the election and such other information about it as the returning officer may determine: Sch 4 para 6(2). The election booklet must contain a statement that it has been published by the returning officer, and must give the name and address of the returning officer and those of the printer of the booklet: Sch 4 para 6(3). Subject to these conditions (and subject to the candidates' election addresses appearing in the election booklet in an order determined by lot: see Sch 4 para 6(1)), the form of the election booklet is to be determined by the returning officer: Sch 4 para 6(4). Copies of the election booklet must be delivered by the returning officer, in envelopes addressed to individual electors, at such time and by such means as the returning officer may determine (Sch 4 para 7(1)), although he may disseminate the contents of the election booklet by such other means as he may determine (Sch 4 para 7(2)). As to the form and content of the election address see further Sch 4 paras 2, 3, 4(1)–(3), 6(5)–(7). As to distribution of the election booklet and contributions towards charges see Sch 4 paras 8–9.

16 As to local government authorities see LOCAL GOVERNMENT vol 69 (2009) PARA 22 et seq.
17 As to the National Assembly for Wales see CONSTITUTIONAL LAW AND HUMAN RIGHTS.
18 Defamation Act 1952 s 10 (amended by the Government of Wales Act 2006 s 160(1), Sch 10 para 5). The words of the Defamation Act 1952 s 10, given their natural meaning, do not preclude an election candidate from relying on the defence of qualified privilege if, like any other citizen, he might be able to establish that the ingredients of that defence, as recognised at common law, are present on the facts of the case; such a reading allows the provision to be read so as to comply with the rights of candidates under the Convention for the Protection of Human Rights and Fundamental Freedoms (Rome, 4 November 1950; TS 71 (1953); Cmd 8969; Council of Europe, ETS no 5) arts 6, 10 (see CONSTITUTIONAL LAW AND HUMAN RIGHTS vol 8(2) (Reissue) PARAS 134 et seq, 158–159), as required by the Human Rights Act 1998 s 3 (interpretation of legislation: see CONSTITUTIONAL LAW AND HUMAN RIGHTS): *Culnane v Morris* [2005] EWHC 2438 (QB), [2006] 2 All ER 149, [2006] 1 WLR 2880. This decision does not follow *Plummer v Charman* [1962] 3 All ER 823, [1962] 1 WLR 1469, CA, in which the Defamation Act 1952 s 10 was given a narrow reading, imposing restrictions upon a candidate's scope for pleading privilege in respect of words published during an election period: see at 825–826 and 1472 per Lord Denning MR (in the ordinary way, the only defences open to a person who makes an election address and puts it out to the electors is either that the words were true or that they were fair comment on a matter of public interest) and at 827 and 1474 per Diplock LJ. However, in *Culnane v Morris* at [21]–[26], Eady J held: (1) that the Court of Appeal had been mistaken in its 'clear' opinion that the purpose of the legislature had been to reverse the effect of the decision in *Braddock v Bevins* [1948] 1 KB 580, [1948] 1 All ER 450, CA, in which it was held that statements contained in the election address of a candidate concerning an opposing candidate are entitled to qualified privilege if they are relevant to the matters which the electors will have to consider in deciding which way they will cast their votes; and (2) that an investigation of the legislative background to the Defamation Act 1952 s 10, within the terms of *Pepper (Inspector of Taxes) v Hart* [1993] AC 593, [1993] 1 All ER 42, HL (see STATUTES AND LEGISLATIVE PROCESS vol 96 (2012) PARA 1122), showed no intention by Parliament to deprive a candidate or agent of a privilege which would be available to other

citizens, but rather only to ensure that such persons were not accorded a special privilege of their own. These findings, together with the requirements of the Human Rights Act 1998 s 3, explain the failure of Eady J in the (first instance) case of *Culnane v Morris* to follow the appellate authority of *Plummer v Charman*. See also *Donnelly v Young* (5 November 2001, unreported) (defendants wishing to rely upon form of privilege generally categorised as 'reply to an attack'); *Reynolds v Times Newspapers Ltd* [2001] 2 AC 127 at 197, [1999] 4 All ER 609 at 618, HL, per Lord Nicholls of Birkenhead (obiter) (whether the defence of comment on a matter of public interest can provide sufficient protection for election addresses when read with the Human Rights Act 1998). Certain old cases on qualified privilege may be relevant in the context of elections: see eg *Dickeson v Hilliard* (1874) LR 9 Exch 79; *Duncombe v Daniell* (1837) 8 C & P 222; *Wilson v Reed* (1860) 2 F & F 149.

331. Broadcasting from outside United Kingdom with intent to influence elections. No person may, with intent to influence persons to give or refrain from giving their votes at a parliamentary[1], or local government election[2], a Welsh Assembly election[3], or a European parliamentary election[4], include (or aid, abet, counsel or procure the inclusion of) any matter relating to the election in any programmes service[5] provided from a place outside the United Kingdom[6] otherwise than in pursuance of arrangements made with[7]:

(1)   the British Broadcasting Corporation ('the BBC')[8];

(2)   Sianel Pedwar Cymru[9]; or

(3)   the holder of any licence granted by the Office of Communications ('OFCOM')[10],

for the reception and re-transmission of that matter by that body or the holder of that licence[11]. A contravention of this prohibition is an offence and an illegal practice[12].

1   As to the meaning of 'parliamentary election' see PARA 9.
2   As to the meaning of 'local government election' see PARA 11. As to parish and community elections see PARA 200 et seq. As to elections in the City of London see PARA 33.
3   As to the meaning of 'Assembly election' see PARA 3 note 2. As to Welsh Assembly elections generally see PARA 213 et seq.
4   As to European parliamentary elections see PARA 217 et seq.
5   Ie within the meaning of the Broadcasting Act 1990 (see BROADCASTING vol 4 (2011) PARA 507): see the Representation of the People Act 1983 s 92(1) (substituted by the Broadcasting Act 1990 s 203(1), Sch 20 para 35(3), (5)); the European Parliamentary Elections Regulations 2004, SI 2004/293, reg 64(1); and the National Assembly for Wales (Representation of the People) Order 2007, SI 2007/236, art 66(1).
6   As to the meaning of 'United Kingdom' see PARA 1 note 1.
    For the purposes of a European parliamentary election held in the combined region, the European Parliamentary Elections Regulations 2004, SI 2004/293, reg 64(1) also embraces services which would, if Gibraltar were part of the United Kingdom, be a programme service provided from a place outside the United Kingdom and Gibraltar: see reg 64(1). See also note 7. As to the establishment of electoral regions (including the 'combined region') for the purpose of elections to the European Parliament see PARA 77.
    The Representation of the People Act 1983 s 92 has effect for the purposes of local authority referendums, subject to the modifications specified, in relation to Wales, by the Local Authorities (Conduct of Referendums) (Wales) Regulations 2008, SI 2008/1848, reg 8(2), Sch 4 Table 1, and, in relation to England, by the Local Authorities (Conduct of Referendums) (England) Regulations 2012, SI 2012/323, regs 8(2), 11–13, Sch 4 Table 1: see PARA 15 note 2.
7   Representation of the People Act 1983 s 92(1) (as substituted: see note 5); European Parliamentary Elections Regulations 2004, SI 2004/293, reg 64(1); National Assembly for Wales (Representation of the People) Order 2007, SI 2007/236, art 66(1).
    For the purposes of a European parliamentary election held in the combined region (see note 6), the Gibraltar Broadcasting Corporation is included in the list of allowed broadcasters (see heads (1) to (3) in the text): see the European Parliamentary Elections Regulations 2004, SI 2004/293, reg 64(1)(b).

8   Representation of the People Act 1983 s 92(1)(a) (as substituted: see note 5); European Parliamentary Elections Regulations 2004, SI 2004/293, reg 64(1)(a)(i); National Assembly for Wales (Representation of the People) Order 2007, SI 2007/236, art 66(1)(a). As to the BBC see BROADCASTING vol 4 (2011) PARA 603 et seq.

9   Representation of the People Act 1983 s 92(1)(b) (as substituted: see note 5); European Parliamentary Elections Regulations 2004, SI 2004/293, reg 64(1)(a)(ii); National Assembly for Wales (Representation of the People) Order 2007, SI 2007/236, art 66(1)(b). As to Sianel Pedwar Cymru see BROADCASTING vol 4 (2011) PARA 645.

10   Representation of the People Act 1983 s 92(1)(c) (s 92(1) as substituted (see note 5); s 92(1)(c) amended by the Communications Act 2003 s 406(1), Sch 17 para 61); European Parliamentary Elections Regulations 2004, SI 2004/293, reg 64(1)(a)(iii); National Assembly for Wales (Representation of the People) Order 2007, SI 2007/236, art 66(1)(c). As to OFCOM see TELECOMMUNICATIONS vol 97 (2010) PARA 2 et seq; and as to licences granted by OFCOM see BROADCASTING vol 4 (2011) PARA 724 et seq.

11   See the Representation of the People Act 1983 s 92(1) (as substituted: see note 5); the European Parliamentary Elections Regulations 2004, SI 2004/293, reg 64(1); and the National Assembly for Wales (Representation of the People) Order 2007, SI 2007/236, art 66(1).

12   See the Representation of the People Act 1983 s 92(2), (3); the European Parliamentary Elections Regulations 2004, SI 2004/293, reg 64(2), (3); the National Assembly for Wales (Representation of the People) Order 2007, SI 2007/236, art 66(2), (3); and PARA 701.

332. Broadcasting of local items during parliamentary or local government election period. Each broadcasting authority[1] must adopt a code of practice with respect to the participation of candidates[2] at a parliamentary[3] or local government election[4], a Welsh Assembly election[5], or a European parliamentary election[6], in items about:

(1)   the constituency[7]; or

(2)   (in the case of a local government election) the electoral area[8]; or

(3)   (in the case of a Welsh Assembly or European parliamentary election) the electoral region[9],

in question which are included in relevant services[10] during the election period[11]. The code for the time being adopted by a broadcasting authority in this way must be either[12]:

(a)   a code drawn up by that authority, whether on its own or jointly with one or more other broadcasting authorities[13]; or

(b)   a code drawn up by one or more other such authorities[14].

A broadcasting authority must from time to time consider whether the code for the time being so adopted by it should be replaced by a further code falling within head (a) or head (b) above[15]. Before drawing up such a code, a broadcasting authority must have regard to any views expressed by the Electoral Commission[16]; and any such code may make different provision for different cases[17]. The Office of Communications ('OFCOM') must do all that it can to secure that the code for the time being adopted by a broadcasting authority is observed in the provision of relevant services; and the British Broadcasting Corporation and Sianel Pedwar Cymru must each observe in the provision of relevant services the code so adopted by it[18].

A broadcaster is prohibited from including in its broadcasting services any party political broadcast made on behalf of a party which is not a registered party under the Political Parties, Elections and Referendums Act 2000[19].

1   For these purposes, 'broadcasting authority' means the British Broadcasting Corporation (the 'BBC'), the Office of Communications ('OFCOM') or Sianel Pedwar Cymru: Representation of the People Act 1983 s 93(6) (s 93 substituted by the Political Parties, Elections and Referendums Act 2000 s 144; definition of 'broadcasting authority' in the Representation of the People Act 1983 s 93(6) amended by the Communications Act 2003 s 406(1), Sch 17 para 62(1), (3)(a)); European Parliamentary Elections Regulations 2004, SI 2004/293, reg 65(6); National Assembly for Wales (Representation of the People) Order 2007, SI 2007/236,

art 67(6). As to OFCOM see TELECOMMUNICATIONS vol 97 (2010) PARA 2 et seq; as to the BBC see BROADCASTING vol 4 (2011) PARA 603 et seq; and as to Sianel Pedwar Cymru see BROADCASTING vol 4 (2011) PARA 645.

For the purposes of a European parliamentary election held in the combined region, the Gibraltar Regulatory Authority is also cited as a 'broadcasting authority': see the European Parliamentary Elections Regulations 2004, SI 2004/293, reg 65(6). As to the establishment of electoral regions (including the 'combined region') for the purpose of elections to the European Parliament see PARA 77.

2　For these purposes, 'candidate', in relation to an election, means a candidate standing nominated at the election or included in a list of candidates submitted in connection with it: Representation of the People Act 1983 s 93(6) (as substituted: see note 1); European Parliamentary Elections Regulations 2004, SI 2004/293, reg 65(6); National Assembly for Wales (Representation of the People) Order 2007, SI 2007/236, art 67(6). As to the meaning of 'candidate' generally see PARA 230.

There is authority regarding the 'participation' of a candidate from the time when undue participation could constitute an offence: see *Marshall v BBC* [1979] 3 All ER 80 at 81–82, [1979] 1 WLR 1071 at 1073, CA, per Lord Denning MR ('A candidate who merely acquiesces in a film being taken or in a speech being taped does not participate. Nor does a candidate who co-operates by being filmed walking around the constituency'). See also *R v Elections Court Comr, ex p Loveridge* (14 January 1997, unreported) (candidate interviewed by the BBC in his electoral area on an environmental issue of local importance); revsd sub nom *Re Local Government Election for Aberaman, County Borough of Rhonnda Cynon Taff* (24 April 1997, unreported), CA.

3　As to the meaning of 'parliamentary election' see PARA 9.

4　As to the meaning of 'local government election' see PARA 11. As to parish and community elections see PARA 200 et seq. As to elections in the City of London see PARA 33.

5　As to the meaning of 'Assembly election' see PARA 3 note 2. As to Welsh Assembly elections generally see PARA 213 et seq.

6　As to European parliamentary elections see PARA 217 et seq.

7　See the Representation of the People Act 1983 s 93(1) (as substituted: see note 1); and the National Assembly for Wales (Representation of the People) Order 2007, SI 2007/236, art 67(1). As to the meaning of 'Assembly constituency', for the purposes of a Welsh Assembly election, see PARA 3 note 2. As to the meaning of 'constituency', for the purposes of a parliamentary election, see PARA 9.

8　See the Representation of the People Act 1983 s 93(1) (as substituted: see note 1). As to the meaning of 'electoral area' see PARA 11.

9　See the European Parliamentary Elections Regulations 2004, SI 2004/293, reg 65(1); and the National Assembly for Wales (Representation of the People) Order 2007, SI 2007/236, art 67(1). As to electoral regions constituted for the purposes of European parliamentary elections see note 1. As to the meaning of 'Assembly electoral region', for the purposes of a Welsh Assembly election, see PARA 3 note 2.

10　'Relevant services', in relation to the BBC or Sianel Pedwar Cymru, means services broadcast by that body; and, in relation to OFCOM, means services licensed under the Broadcasting Act 1990 Pt I (ss 3–71) (independent television services: see BROADCASTING vol 4 (2011) PARA 507 et seq) or Pt III (ss 85–126) (independent radio services: see BROADCASTING vol 4 (2011) PARA 724 et seq) or under the Broadcasting Act 1996 Pt I (ss 1–39) (digital terrestrial television broadcasting: see BROADCASTING vol 4 (2011) PARA 690 et seq) or Pt II (ss 40–72) (digital terrestrial sound broadcasting: see BROADCASTING vol 4 (2011) PARA 727 et seq): Representation of the People Act 1983 s 93(6) (s 93 as substituted (see note 1); definition of 'broadcasting authority' in s 93(6) amended by the Communications Act 2003 Sch 17 para 62(1), (3)(b)); European Parliamentary Elections Regulations 2004, SI 2004/293, reg 65(6); National Assembly for Wales (Representation of the People) Order 2007, SI 2007/236, art 67(6).

For the purposes of a European parliamentary election held in the combined region, services broadcast by the Gibraltar Broadcasting Corporation are also cited in the definition of 'relevant services', in relation to the Gibraltar Regulatory Authority: see the European Parliamentary Elections Regulations 2004, SI 2004/293, reg 65(6).

11　Representation of the People Act 1983 s 93(1) (as substituted: see note 1); European Parliamentary Elections Regulations 2004, SI 2004/293, reg 65(1); National Assembly for Wales (Representation of the People) Order 2007, SI 2007/236, art 67(1).

In relation to a parliamentary or local government election, the 'election period', for this purpose, means the period beginning:

(1)　(if a parliamentary general election) with the date of the dissolution of Parliament

       (Representation of the People Act 1983 s 93(5)(a) (s 93 as so substituted; s 93(5)(a) amended by the Fixed-term Parliaments Act 2011 s 6(3), Schedule paras 6, 8));

(2)   (if a parliamentary by-election) with the date of the issue of the writ for the election or any earlier date on which a certificate of the vacancy is notified in the London Gazette in accordance with the Recess Elections Act 1975 (see PARLIAMENT vol 78 (2010) PARA 1095) (Representation of the People Act 1983 s 93(5)(b) (as so substituted)); or

(3)   (if a local government election) with the last date for publication of notice of the election (s 93(5)(c) (as so substituted)),

and ending with the close of the poll (see s 93(5) (as so substituted)). As to the dissolution of Parliament see PARA 189; as to parliamentary by-elections see PARA 191; and as to publication of the notice for a local government election see PARA 211.

       The 'election period', in relation to a European parliamentary election, means the period beginning with the last date for publication of notice of the election, and ending with the close of the poll: see the European Parliamentary Elections Regulations 2004, SI 2004/293, reg 65(5). As to publication of notice of a European parliamentary election see PARA 223.

       In relation to a Welsh Assembly election, the 'election period' means, in relation to an Assembly general election, the period beginning with the date of dissolution of the Assembly, or, in relation to any election to fill a casual vacancy, the period beginning with the date of the occurrence of the vacancy, and ending, in either case, with the close of the poll: see the National Assembly for Wales (Representation of the People) Order 2007, SI 2007/236, art 67(5). As to publication of notice for a Welsh Assembly election see PARA 216.

       Formerly, broadcasting authorities had the right freely to photograph or record the appearance or the words of candidates during an election (see *McAliskey v BBC* [1980] NI 44) but this freedom has been reduced (*Marshall v BBC* [1979] 3 All ER 80 at 82, [1979] 1 WLR 1071 at 1074, CA, per Cumming-Bruce LJ). The broadcasters duty of impartiality (see BROADCASTING vol 4 (2011) PARA 895) is achieved by even-handedness in providing airtime for party election broadcasts and, while a broadcaster may not deny such a broadcast to a qualifying party, it does have some discretion in determining the rules by which party election broadcasts are allocated: see *R v BBC, ex p Referendum Party* [1997] COD 459, 9 Admin LR 553, [1997] EMLR 605. See also *R v BBC, ex p Pro-Life Alliance Party* [1997] COD 457 (discretion entitled the BBC to require the removal of a sequence of shots of aborted foetuses from a party election broadcast); *R (on the application of ProLife Alliance) v BBC* [2003] UKHL 23, [2004] 1 AC 185, [2003] 2 All ER 977.

12   Representation of the People Act 1983 s 93(2) (as substituted: see note 1); European Parliamentary Elections Regulations 2004, SI 2004/293, reg 65(2); National Assembly for Wales (Representation of the People) Order 2007, SI 2007/236, art 67(2).

13   Representation of the People Act 1983 s 93(2)(a) (as substituted: see note 1); European Parliamentary Elections Regulations 2004, SI 2004/293, reg 65(2)(a); National Assembly for Wales (Representation of the People) Order 2007, SI 2007/236, art 67(2)(a).

14   Representation of the People Act 1983 s 93(2)(b) (as substituted: see note 1); European Parliamentary Elections Regulations 2004, SI 2004/293, reg 65(2)(b); National Assembly for Wales (Representation of the People) Order 2007, SI 2007/236, art 67(2)(b).

15   Representation of the People Act 1983 s 93(2) (as substituted: see note 1); European Parliamentary Elections Regulations 2004, SI 2004/293, reg 65(2); National Assembly for Wales (Representation of the People) Order 2007, SI 2007/236, art 67(2).

16   As to the Electoral Commission see PARA 34 et seq; and as to views expressed by the Commission on political, election and referendum campaign broadcasts see PARA 59.

17   Representation of the People Act 1983 s 93(3) (as substituted: see note 1); European Parliamentary Elections Regulations 2004, SI 2004/293, reg 65(3); National Assembly for Wales (Representation of the People) Order 2007, SI 2007/236, art 67(3).

18   Representation of the People Act 1983 s 93(4) (s 93 as so substituted (see note 1); s 93(4) amended by the Communications Act 2003 Sch 17 para 62(1), (2)); European Parliamentary Elections Regulations 2004, SI 2004/293, reg 65(4) (amended by SI 2009/186); National Assembly for Wales (Representation of the People) Order 2007, SI 2007/236, art 67(4).

       For the purposes of a European parliamentary election held in the combined region, references to the Office of Communications (OFCOM) include references to the Gibraltar Regulatory Authority and references to broadcasters include references to the Gibraltar Broadcasting Corporation: see the European Parliamentary Elections Regulations 2004, SI 2004/293, reg 65(4) (as so amended).

19   See the Political Parties, Elections and Referendums Act 2000 s 37; and CONSTITUTIONAL LAW AND HUMAN RIGHTS. As to the registration of parties as a condition precedent to participation in a relevant election see PARA 253.

333.   Control of advertisements.   In general, the consent of the local planning authority, or of the Secretary of State, or, in relation to Wales, of the Welsh Ministers, must be obtained, in the interests of amenity or public safety, before any advertisement may be displayed[1]. However, an advertisement[2] relating specifically to a pending parliamentary, European parliamentary or local government election does not require[3] either express consent or deemed consent[4] provided that the advertisement is removed within 14 days after the close of the poll in the election to which it relates[5].

These provisions, as they relate to Wales[6], have effect in relation to the display, on any site in Wales, relating specifically to an Assembly election[7] or Assembly elections, as they have effect in relation to the display of an advertisement relating specifically to a parliamentary election[8].

1   See the Town and Country Planning (Control of Advertisements) Regulations 1992, SI 1992/666 (revoked with savings, in relation to England, by SI 2007/783); the Town and Country Planning (Control of Advertisements) (England) Regulations 2007, SI 2007/783; and PLANNING vol 82 (2010) PARA 956 et seq. As to the Secretary of State for these purposes see PLANNING vol 81 (2010) PARA 26; and as to the Welsh Ministers and the transfer of planning functions to them see PLANNING vol 81 (2010) PARA 27. As to the meaning of 'Wales' see PARA 1 note 1.

2   As to the meaning of 'advertisement' see PLANNING vol 82 (2010) PARA 957.

3   Ie provided that it complies with any conditions and limitations specified in the Town and Country Planning (Control of Advertisements) Regulations 1992, SI 1992/666, reg 3(2), Sch 2, the Town and Country Planning (Control of Advertisements) (England) Regulations 2007, SI 2007/783, reg 1(3), Sch 1 (see the text and notes 4–5), and all the standard conditions: see the Town and Country Planning (Control of Advertisements) Regulations 1992, SI 1992/666, reg 3(2); the Town and Country Planning (Control of Advertisements) (England) Regulations 2007, SI 2007/783, reg 1(3); and PLANNING vol 82 (2010) PARA 970. As to the standard conditions see PLANNING vol 82 (2010) PARA 962.

4   As to the meanings of 'express consent' and 'deemed consent' see PLANNING vol 82 (2010) PARA 964.

5   See the Town and Country Planning (Control of Advertisements) Regulations 1992, SI 1992/666, Sch 2 Class F para 1; the Town and Country Planning (Control of Advertisements) (England) Regulations 2007, SI 2007/783, Sch 1 Class E; and PLANNING vol 82 (2010) PARA 970.

6   Ie the Town and Country Planning (Control of Advertisements) Regulations 1992, SI 1992/666 (see note 1): see the National Assembly for Wales (Representation of the People) Order 2007, SI 2007/236, art 139.

7   As to the meaning of 'Assembly election' see PARA 3 note 2.

8   National Assembly for Wales (Representation of the People) Order 2007, SI 2007/236, art 139.

(viii)   Election Meetings

334.   Schools and rooms for meetings at parliamentary, European parliamentary or Welsh Assembly elections.   On reasonable notice, a candidate[1] at a parliamentary[2], or Welsh Assembly[3], or European parliamentary[4], election is entitled, for the purpose of holding public meetings[5], to the use free of charge of certain rooms at reasonable times[6]:

(1)   (in the case of a parliamentary election) between the receipt of the writ and the day preceding the date of the poll[7]; or

(2)   (in the case of a Welsh Assembly or European parliamentary election) between the last date on which notice of election may be published and the day preceding the date of the poll[8].

For the purposes of a parliamentary or Welsh Assembly constituency election, the candidate is so entitled to the use of a suitable room[9] in the premises of a community, foundation or voluntary school[10] situated in the constituency or an adjoining constituency[11]. However, such a candidate is not so entitled to the use of a room in school premises outside the constituency if there is a suitable room in other premises in the constituency which are reasonably accessible from the same parts of it as those outside and are premises of such a school[12]. In the case of a Welsh Assembly regional[13], or European parliamentary, election, the candidate is entitled to use of a suitable room in the premises of a community, foundation or voluntary school situated in the electoral region for which the election is held[14].

For these purposes, and at the times described above, such a candidate is also entitled on reasonable notice to the use free of charge of any meeting room[15], the expense of maintaining which is payable wholly or mainly out of public funds, or out of any rate, or by a body whose expenses are so payable[16]. For the purposes of determining rateable occupation, a hereditament[17] is to be treated as unoccupied if it would otherwise be treated as occupied by reason only of the use of it for the holding of public meetings in furtherance of a person's candidature at a parliamentary election, for promoting a particular result at a Welsh Assembly election or in furtherance of a person's or a registered party's candidature at a European parliamentary election[18].

1   As to the meaning of 'candidate' generally see PARA 230; and see note 5.
2   As to the meaning of 'parliamentary election' see PARA 9.
3   As to the meaning of 'Assembly election' see PARA 3 note 2. As to Welsh Assembly elections generally see PARA 213 et seq.
4   As to European parliamentary elections see PARA 217 et seq.
5   The purpose mentioned in the text of holding public meetings is:
      (1)   in furtherance of the candidature of a candidate at a parliamentary election (see the Representation of the People Act 1983 s 95(1) (amended by the Representation of the People Act 1985 s 24, Sch 4 para 37(a)));
      (2)   in furtherance of the candidature of a candidate at a European parliamentary election, or that of his party (see the European Parliamentary Elections Regulations 2004, SI 2004/293, reg 67(1));
      (3)   to promote or procure the giving of votes at a Welsh Assembly election either: (a) for the candidate himself at such an election (in the case of a constituency or individual candidate) (see the National Assembly for Wales (Representation of the People) Order 2007, SI 2007/236, art 69(1)(a)); or (b) for the registered political party on whose list the candidate is included (in the case of a party list candidate) (see art 69(1)(b)).
    As to the meanings of 'Assembly election', 'constituency election' and 'regional election' for these purposes see PARA 3 note 2. As to the meaning of 'registered political party' see PARA 215 note 19. As to the meanings of 'constituency candidate' at an Assembly constituency election and 'individual candidate' at a Welsh Assembly regional election see PARA 230 note 19; and as to the meanings of 'party list' and 'party list candidate' see PARA 230 note 23. As to rooms for meetings at a local government election see PARA 337.
6   Representation of the People Act 1983 s 95(1), (5) (s 95(1) as amended· see note 5), European Parliamentary Elections Regulations 2004, SI 2004/293, reg 67(1), (5); National Assembly for Wales (Representation of the People) Order 2007, SI 2007/236, art 69(1), (5).
    For these purposes, 'room' includes a hall, gallery or gymnasium: Representation of the People Act 1983 s 95(7)(b); European Parliamentary Elections Regulations 2004, SI 2004/293, reg 67(7)(b); National Assembly for Wales (Representation of the People) Order 2007, SI 2007/236, art 69(7)(b). The candidate is not authorised to interfere with the normal hours of use of certain rooms: see PARA 335.
7   Representation of the People Act 1983 s 95(1) (as amended: see note 5). As to the date of the poll at a parliamentary general election or by-election see PARA 195.
8   European Parliamentary Elections Regulations 2004, SI 2004/293, reg 67(1); National Assembly for Wales (Representation of the People) Order 2007, SI 2007/236, art 69(1). As to the date of the poll at Welsh Assembly elections (including elections to fill vacancies in an Assembly constituency) see PARAS 213–214; and as to the date of the poll at a European parliamentary election see PARA 222.
9   The right of a candidate to a suitable room is a private law right which can be enforced by action against the local education authority: see *Ettridge v Morrell* (1986) 85 LGR 100, CA (cited at PARA 337).

10 For this purpose, the premises of a school are not to be taken to include any private dwelling: Representation of the People Act 1983 s 95(7) (amended by the Representation of the People Act 2000 s 15, Sch 6 paras 3, 7, Sch 7 Pt II); European Parliamentary Elections Regulations 2004, SI 2004/293, reg 67(7); National Assembly for Wales (Representation of the People) Order 2007, SI 2007/236, art 69(7). Cf PARA 335 note 6. As to the meaning of 'dwelling' see PARA 117 note 19. As to community, foundation and voluntary schools see EDUCATION vol 35 (2011) PARA 106 et seq.

11 Representation of the People Act 1983 s 95(1)(a), (2)(a) (s 95(2)(a) amended by the School Standards and Framework Act 1998 s 140(1), Sch 30 paras 9, 10); National Assembly for Wales (Representation of the People) Order 2007, SI 2007/236, art 69(1)(i), (2)(a). As to the meaning of 'constituency', for the purposes of a parliamentary election, see PARA 9; and as to the meaning of 'Assembly constituency', for the purposes of a Welsh Assembly election, see PARA 3 note 2.

12 Representation of the People Act 1983 s 95(2); National Assembly for Wales (Representation of the People) Order 2007, SI 2007/236, art 69(2).

13 As to the meaning of 'regional election' for the purposes of Welsh Assembly elections see PARA 3 note 2.

14 European Parliamentary Elections Regulations 2004, SI 2004/293, reg 67(1)(a), (2)(a); National Assembly for Wales (Representation of the People) Order 2007, SI 2007/236, art 69(1)(i), (2)(b). For the purposes of a European parliamentary election held in the combined region, a suitable room in the premises of a school in Gibraltar may be used, the expense of maintaining which is payable wholly or partly out of public funds or out of any rate, or by a body whose expenses are so payable: see the European Parliamentary Elections Regulations 2004, SI 2004/293, reg 67(1)(a), (2)(c). As to the meaning of 'Assembly electoral region' for the purposes of a Welsh Assembly election see PARA 3 note 2. As to the establishment of electoral regions (including the 'combined region') for the purpose of elections to the European Parliament see PARA 77.

15 'Meeting room' means any room which it is the practice to let for public meetings: Representation of the People Act 1983 s 95(7)(a); European Parliamentary Elections Regulations 2004, SI 2004/293, reg 67(7)(a); National Assembly for Wales (Representation of the People) Order 2007, SI 2007/236, art 69(7)(a). The meeting room referred to must be situated:

　　(1)　in the case of a parliamentary election, in the constituency (see the Representation of the People Act 1983 s 95(3));

　　(2)　in the case of a European parliamentary election, in the electoral region (see the European Parliamentary Elections Regulations 2004, SI 2004/293, reg 67(3));

　　(3)　(in the case of a Welsh Assembly constituency election) in the Assembly constituency for which the election is held (see the National Assembly for Wales (Representation of the People) Order 2007, SI 2007/236, art 69(3)(a)); or (in the case of a Welsh Assembly regional election) in the Assembly electoral region for which the election is held (see art 69(3)(b)).

16 Representation of the People Act 1983 s 95(1)(b), (3), (5); European Parliamentary Elections Regulations 2004, SI 2004/293, reg 67(1)(b), (3), (5); National Assembly for Wales (Representation of the People) Order 2007, SI 2007/236, art 69(1)(ii), (3), (5).

17 As to the meaning of 'hereditament' in this context see LOCAL GOVERNMENT FINANCE vol 70 (2012) PARA 82 et seq.

18 See the Local Government Finance Act 1988 s 65(6) (applied with modifications by the European Parliamentary Elections Regulations 2004, SI 2004/293, reg 125; the National Assembly for Wales (Representation of the People) Order 2007, SI 2007/236, art 147; and by the Local Authorities (Conduct of Referendums) (Wales) Regulations 2008, SI 2008/1848, reg 16; and the Local Authorities (Conduct of Referendums) (England) Regulations 2012, SI 2012/323, reg 20). See further LOCAL GOVERNMENT FINANCE vol 70 (2012) PARA 62.

335. Arrangements for use of rooms for meetings at parliamentary, European parliamentary or Welsh Assembly elections. The person by whom, or on whose behalf, a public meeting is convened, for the purposes of a parliamentary[1], or Welsh Assembly[2], or European parliamentary[3], election, in a school room or meeting room[4] is required to defray any expenses incurred in preparing, warming, lighting and cleaning the room and providing attendance for the meeting and restoring the room to its usual condition after the meeting[5]. That person also must defray the cost of making good any damage done to the room or to the premises[6] in which it is situated, or to the furniture, fittings or apparatus in the room or premises[7].

A candidate is not entitled to exercise this right to use school rooms and meeting rooms for public meetings except on reasonable notice[8]; and the entitlement so conferred on him to use such rooms does not authorise any interference with the hours during which a room in school premises is used for educational purposes, or any interference with the use of a meeting room either for the purposes of the person maintaining it or under a prior agreement for its letting for any purpose[9].

Arrangements for the use of a room in school premises must be made with the local authority maintaining the school[10] (or, in the case of a room in the premises of a foundation or voluntary aided school[11], with the governing body of the school)[12]. Any question as to the rooms in school premises which a candidate[13] is entitled to use, or as to the times at which he is entitled to use them, or as to the notice which is reasonable, is to be determined by the Secretary of State[14].

1 As to the meaning of 'parliamentary election' see PARA 9.

2 As to the meaning of 'Assembly election' see PARA 3 note 2. As to Welsh Assembly elections generally see PARA 213 et seq.

3 As to European parliamentary elections see PARA 217 et seq.

4 Ie in pursuance of the rights conferred by the Representation of the People Act 1983 s 95(1)–(3), (5), the European Parliamentary Elections Regulations 2004, SI 2004/293, reg 67(1)–(3), (5), or the National Assembly for Wales (Representation of the People) Order 2007, SI 2007/236, art 69(1)–(3), (5), as the case may be: see PARA 334. As to the meaning of 'room' for these purposes see PARA 334 note 6; and as to the meaning of 'meeting room' see PARA 334 note 15.

5 Representation of the People Act 1983 s 95(4)(a) (amended by the Representation of the People Act 1985 s 24, Sch 4 para 37(b)); European Parliamentary Elections Regulations 2004, SI 2004/293, reg 67(4)(a); National Assembly for Wales (Representation of the People) Order 2007, SI 2007/236, art 69(4)(a).

6 For this particular purpose, the premises of a school may include a private dwelling: Representation of the People Act 1983 s 95(7) (amended by the Representation of the People Act 2000 s 15, Sch 6 paras 3, 7, Sch 7 Pt II); European Parliamentary Elections Regulations 2004, SI 2004/293, reg 67(7); National Assembly for Wales (Representation of the People) Order 2007, SI 2007/236, art 69(7). Cf PARA 334 note 10. As to the meaning of 'dwelling' see PARA 117 note 19.

7 Representation of the People Act 1983 s 95(4)(b); European Parliamentary Elections Regulations 2004, SI 2004/293, reg 67(4)(b); National Assembly for Wales (Representation of the People) Order 2007, SI 2007/236, art 69(4)(b).

8 Representation of the People Act 1983 s 95(5); European Parliamentary Elections Regulations 2004, SI 2004/293, reg 67(5); National Assembly for Wales (Representation of the People) Order 2007, SI 2007/236, art 69(5).

9 Representation of the People Act 1983 s 95(5); European Parliamentary Elections Regulations 2004, SI 2004/293, reg 67(5); National Assembly for Wales (Representation of the People) Order 2007, SI 2007/236, art 69(5).

10 For these purposes, 'local authority' has the meaning given by the Education Act 1996 s 579(1) (see EDUCATION vol 35 (2011) PARA 24): Representation of the People Act 1983 s 95(6), Sch 5 para 5A (added by SI 2010/1158); European Parliamentary Elections Regulations 2004, SI 2004/293, reg 67(6), Sch 8 para 1 (amended by SI 2010/1172); National Assembly for Wales (Representation of the People) Order 2007, SI 2007/236, art 69(6), Sch 8 para 1(1) (amended by SI 2010/1142). As the application of the European Parliamentary Elections Regulations 2004, SI 2004/293, Sch 8 to Gibraltar (ie for the purpose of elections to the European Parliament taking place in the 'combined region') see Sch 8 para 5 (amended by SI 2010/1172). As to the establishment of electoral regions (including the 'combined region') for the purpose of elections to the European Parliament see PARA 77.

11 As to foundation and voluntary schools see EDUCATION vol 35 (2011) PARA 106 et seq.

12 Representation of the People Act 1983 Sch 5 para 1(1) (amended by the Education Reform Act 1988 s 237(1), Sch 12 para 32; the School Standards and Framework Act 1998 s 140(1), Sch 30 para 12; and SI 2010/1158); European Parliamentary Elections Regulations 2004, SI 2004/293, Sch 8 para 1 (as amended: see note 10); National Assembly for Wales (Representation of the People) Order 2007, SI 2007/236, Sch 8 para 1(1) (as amended: see note 10).

13 Ie in any parliamentary or Welsh Assembly constituency (in the case of a parliamentary or Welsh Assembly constituency election) or in any Welsh Assembly electoral region (in the case of a Welsh Assembly regional election) or in any European parliamentary local counting area, as the case may be. As to the meanings of 'constituency election' and 'regional election' at a Welsh Assembly election see PARA 3 note 2; and as to the meanings of 'constituency candidate' at an Assembly constituency election and 'individual candidate' at a Welsh Assembly regional election see PARA 230 note 19. As to the meaning of 'constituency' for the purposes of a parliamentary election see PARA 9; and as to the meaning of 'local counting area' for the purposes of a European parliamentary election see PARA 139 note 1.

14 Representation of the People Act 1983 Sch 5 para 1(2); European Parliamentary Elections Regulations 2004, SI 2004/293, Sch 8 para 2; National Assembly for Wales (Representation of the People) Order 2007, SI 2007/236, Sch 8 para 1(2). As to the Secretary of State see PARA 2.

336. Preparation of list of rooms for meetings at parliamentary, European parliamentary or Welsh Assembly elections.

Each local authority[1] must prepare and revise for its area a list of the rooms in school premises[2] which candidates[3] in any parliamentary or Welsh Assembly constituency[4], or in any Welsh Assembly electoral region[5], are entitled to use[6]. With regard to any such constituency, the list must include the rooms in premises outside, as well as those in premises in, the constituency[7]. Every English district and London borough council[8], and every Welsh county and county borough council[9], must prepare and revise for its area lists of the meeting rooms which candidates in any such constituency (or electoral region, as the case may be) are entitled to use[10]. The list must indicate the person to whom applications for the use of the room are to be made in each case[11]. The list must not include any room if the person maintaining it disputes the right of the candidates in the constituency (or electoral region, as the case may be) to use it[12]. The lists of rooms in school premises and of meeting rooms prepared for each such constituency (or electoral region, as the case may be) are to be kept by the registration officer[13]. Those lists and particulars of any change made on a revision of them must, where necessary, be forwarded to him accordingly[14].

In the event of a dissolution of Parliament[15], or of a vacancy occurring in the seat for a parliamentary constituency[16], any person stating himself to be, or to be authorised by, a candidate or his election agent[17] is entitled at all reasonable hours to inspect the lists of rooms in school premises and of meeting rooms or a copy of them[18]. Those same lists (or a copy of them) may also be inspected at all reasonable hours by any person stating himself to be, or to be authorised by, a candidate at a European parliamentary election[19] or the election agent of a registered party at such an election[20] or an individual candidate[21] at such an election[22]. In the event of notice of a Welsh Assembly election being published[23], any person stating himself to be, or to be authorised by, a constituency or individual candidate[24] or his election agent[25], or a party list candidate[26] or the registered nominating officer of the registered political party on whose list he is a candidate[27], or that party's election agent in relation to that list of candidates[28], is entitled at all reasonable hours to inspect the lists of rooms in school premises and of meeting rooms prepared for each Assembly constituency and electoral region (or a copy of them)[29].

1 For these purposes, 'local authority' has the meaning given by the Education Act 1996 s 579(1) (see EDUCATION vol 35 (2011) PARA 24): Representation of the People Act 1983 s 95(6), Sch 5 para 5A (added by SI 2010/1158); National Assembly for Wales (Representation of the People) Order 2007, SI 2007/236, art 69(6), Sch 8 para 2(1) (amended by SI 2010/1142).

2 As to the meaning of 'room' for these purposes see PARA 334 note 6; and as to the meaning of 'school premises' for these purposes see PARA 334 note 10.

3 As to the meaning of 'candidate' generally see PARA 230.

4   As to the meaning of 'constituency' for the purposes of parliamentary elections see PARA 9; and as to the meaning of 'Assembly constituency' for the purposes of a Welsh Assembly election see PARA 3 note 2.

5   As to the meaning of 'Assembly electoral region' for the purposes of a Welsh Assembly election see PARA 3 note 2.

6   Representation of the People Act 1983 Sch 5 para 2(1) (amended by SI 2010/1158); National Assembly for Wales (Representation of the People) Order 2007, SI 2007/236, Sch 8 para 2(1) (as amended: see note 1). As to the entitlement to use such rooms see PARA 334.

7   Representation of the People Act 1983 Sch 5 para 2(2); National Assembly for Wales (Representation of the People) Order 2007, SI 2007/236, Sch 8 para 2(2).

8   As to districts in England and their councils see LOCAL GOVERNMENT vol 69 (2009) PARA 24 et seq. As to London boroughs and their councils see LOCAL GOVERNMENT vol 69 (2009) PARA 35; LONDON GOVERNMENT vol 71 (2013) PARA 15 et seq.

9   As to the council of a county or county borough in Wales see LOCAL GOVERNMENT vol 69 (2009) PARA 37 et seq.

10 Representation of the People Act 1983 Sch 5 para 3(1) (amended by the Local Government (Wales) Act 1994 s 66(6), Sch 16 para 68(20)); National Assembly for Wales (Representation of the People) Order 2007, SI 2007/236, Sch 8 para 3(1). As to the meaning of 'meeting room' for these purposes see PARA 334 note 15.

11 Representation of the People Act 1983 Sch 5 para 3(2); National Assembly for Wales (Representation of the People) Order 2007, SI 2007/236, Sch 8 para 3(2).

12 Representation of the People Act 1983 Sch 5 para 3(3); National Assembly for Wales (Representation of the People) Order 2007, SI 2007/236, Sch 8 para 3(3).

13 Representation of the People Act 1983 Sch 5 para 4; National Assembly for Wales (Representation of the People) Order 2007, SI 2007/236, Sch 8 para 4. As to electoral registration officers see PARA 139 et seq.

14 Representation of the People Act 1983 Sch 5 para 4; National Assembly for Wales (Representation of the People) Order 2007, SI 2007/236, Sch 8 para 4 (amended by SI 2010/1142). In the case of a Welsh Assembly election, it is specified that the lists and particulars must be forwarded as mentioned in the text to the registration officer by the relevant local authority within the meaning of the Education Act 1996 s 579(1) (see EDUCATION vol 35 (2011) PARA 24) or, as the case may be, the relevant county or county borough council: see the National Assembly for Wales (Representation of the People) Order 2007, SI 2007/236, Sch 8 para 4 (as so amended).

15 As to the dissolution of Parliament see PARA 189.

16 As to vacancies occurring in the seat for a parliamentary constituency see PARA 191.

17 As to the appointment of election agents generally see PARA 231 et seq.

18 Representation of the People Act 1983 Sch 5 para 5.

19 As to European parliamentary elections see PARA 217 et seq.

20 As to the meaning of 'registered party' for these purposes see PARA 230 note 29. As to references for these purposes to an election agent of a registered party at a European parliamentary election see PARA 239 note 5.

21 As to the meaning of 'individual candidate' at a European parliamentary election see PARA 230 note 32.

22 European Parliamentary Elections Regulations 2004, SI 2004/293, reg 67(6), Sch 8 para 3.

23 As to publication of notice for a Welsh Assembly election see PARA 216.

24 As to the meanings of 'constituency candidate' at an Assembly constituency election and 'individual candidate' at a Welsh Assembly regional election see PARA 230 note 19. As to the meanings of 'Assembly election', 'constituency election' and 'regional election' for these purposes see PARA 3 note 2.

25 National Assembly for Wales (Representation of the People) Order 2007, SI 2007/236, Sch 8 para 5(a). As to the appointment of election agents at a Welsh Assembly election see PARA 235 et seq.

26 As to the meanings of 'party list' and 'party list candidate' see PARA 230 note 23.

27 As to the meaning of 'registered political party' see PARA 215 note 19. As to the nominating officer of a registered party see PARA 253.

28 National Assembly for Wales (Representation of the People) Order 2007, SI 2007/236, Sch 8 para 5(b).

29 National Assembly for Wales (Representation of the People) Order 2007, SI 2007/236, Sch 8 para 5.

337. Rooms for meetings at a local government election. A candidate[1] at a local government election[2] is entitled on reasonable notice, for the purpose of holding public meetings to promote or procure the giving of votes at that election[3]:

(1) for himself[4]; or

(2) if he is a candidate included in a list of candidates submitted by a registered political party at an election of the London members of the London Assembly at an ordinary election[5], towards the return of candidates on that list[6],

to the use free of charge of certain rooms at reasonable times between the last day on which notice of the election may be published[7] and the day preceding the day of election[8]. He is entitled to the use of a suitable room[9] in the premises of a community, foundation or voluntary school[10] situated in the electoral area[11] for which the candidate is standing (or, if there is no such school in the area, in any such school in an adjacent electoral area) or in a parish or community[12], as the case may be, in part comprised in that electoral area[13]. The right of a candidate to a suitable room is a private law right which can be enforced by action against the local education authority[14]. For the purposes and at the times described above, such a candidate is also entitled on reasonable notice to the use free of charge of any meeting room[15] situated in the electoral area for which the candidate is standing or in a parish or community, as the case may be, in part comprised in that electoral area, the expense of maintaining which is payable wholly or mainly out of public funds or out of any rate, or by a body whose expenses are so payable[16]. For the purposes of determining rateable occupation, a hereditament[17] is to be treated as unoccupied if it would otherwise be treated as occupied by reason only of the use of it for the holding of public meetings in furtherance of a person's candidature at a local government election[18].

The statutory provisions relating to expenses, damage, notice and interference in respect of the use of rooms by candidates at parliamentary elections and the requirement as to the body with which arrangements must be made[19] also apply for these purposes[20]. Any person stating himself to be, or to be authorised by, a candidate at a local government election in respect of an electoral area which falls (or partly falls) within a constituency[21], or his election agent[22], is entitled to inspect the lists prepared[23] in relation to the constituency or a copy of them at all reasonable hours during the period beginning with the day on which notice of election is published and ending with the day preceding the day of election[24].

1 As to the meaning of 'candidate' generally see PARA 230.

2 As to the meaning of 'local government election' see PARA 11. As to parish and community elections see PARA 200 et seq. As to elections in the City of London see PARA 33.

3 See the Representation of the People Act 1983 s 96(1) (s 96 substituted by the Representation of the People Act 1985 s 24, Sch 4 para 38; Representation of the People Act 1983 s 96(1) amended by the Greater London Authority Act 1999 s 17, Sch 3 paras 1, 29); Representation of the People Act 1983 s 95(5) (applied by s 96(4) (as so substituted)). As to the right conferred to use schools and rooms for meetings at parliamentary, European parliamentary or Welsh Assembly elections see PARAS 334–336.

The Representation of the People Act 1983 s 96 is applied and modified for the purpose of local authority mayoral elections in England and Wales by the Local Authorities (Mayoral Elections) (England and Wales) Regulations 2007, SI 2007/1024, reg 3(2)–(5), Sch 2 Table 1 (see PARA 11 note 14); and the Representation of the People Act 1983 s 96 has effect also for the purposes of local authority referendums, subject to the modifications specified, in relation to Wales, by the Local Authorities (Conduct of Referendums) (Wales) Regulations 2008, SI 2008/1848, reg 8(2), Sch 4 Table 1, and, in relation to England, by the Local Authorities (Conduct of Referendums) (England) Regulations 2012, SI 2012/323, regs 8(2), 11–13, Sch 4 Table 1 (see PARA 15 note 2).

4   Representation of the People Act 1983 s 96(1)(i) (s 96 as substituted (see note 3); s 96(1)(i), (ii) added by the Greater London Authority Act 1999 Sch 3 paras 1, 29).

5   As to the meaning of 'London member', in relation to the London Assembly, see PARA 11 note 5; and as to references to a registered political party submitting a list of candidates to be London members of the London Assembly at an ordinary election see PARA 230 note 14. As to London Assembly ordinary elections see PARA 199; and see LONDON GOVERNMENT vol 71 (2013) PARA 76 et seq.

6   Representation of the People Act 1983 s 96(1)(ii) (s 96 as substituted (see note 3); s 96(1)(ii) as added (see note 4)).

7   Ie in accordance with rules made under the Representation of the People Act 1983 s 36 (see PARA 383): see s 96(1) (as substituted: see note 3). As to the last day on which notice of a local government election may be published see PARA 211.

8   See the Representation of the People Act 1983 s 96(1) (as substituted: see note 3). As to the application of this provision to a poll consequent on a parish meeting where the poll is on a question of appointment to an office see PARA 383 note 6. However, in that case, there is no notice of election at such a poll.

9   'Room' includes a hall, gallery or gymnasium: Representation of the People Act 1983 s 95(7)(b); applied by s 96(4) (as substituted: see note 3).

10 For this purpose, the premises of a school are not to be taken to include any private dwelling: Representation of the People Act 1983 s 95(7) (amended by the Representation of the People Act 2000 s 15, Sch 6 paras 3, 7, Sch 7 Pt II); applied by the Representation of the People Act 1983 s 96(4) (as substituted: see note 3). As to the meaning of 'dwelling' see PARA 117 note 19. As to community, foundation and voluntary schools see EDUCATION vol 35 (2011) PARA 106 et seq.

11 As to the meaning of 'electoral area' see PARA 11.

12 As to parishes generally see LOCAL GOVERNMENT vol 69 (2009) PARA 27 et seq; and as to communities generally see LOCAL GOVERNMENT vol 69 (2009) PARA 41 et seq.

13 Representation of the People Act 1983 s 96(1)(a), (2)(a) (s 96 as substituted (see note 3); s 96(2)(a) amended by the School Standards and Framework Act 1998 s 140(1), Sch 30 paras 9, 11).

14 *Ettridge v Morrell* (1986) 85 LGR 100, CA.

15 'Meeting room' means any room which it is the practice to let for public meetings: Representation of the People Act 1983 s 95(7)(a); applied by s 96(4) (as substituted: see note 3).

16 Representation of the People Act 1983 s 96(1)(b), (3)(a) (as substituted: see note 3).

17 As to the meaning of 'hereditament' in this context see LOCAL GOVERNMENT FINANCE vol 70 (2012) PARA 82 et seq.

18 See the Local Government Finance Act 1988 s 65(6). See further LOCAL GOVERNMENT FINANCE vol 70 (2012) PARA 62.

19 Ie the Representation of the People Act 1983 s 95(4)–(6), Sch 5 para 1(1) (see PARA 335): see s 96(4) (as substituted: see note 3).

20 See the Representation of the People Act 1983 s 96(4) (as substituted: see note 3). The definitions specified in s 95(7) (see notes 9, 10, 15) are also applied for these purposes: see s 96(4) (as so substituted).

21 As to the meaning of 'constituency' for the purposes of parliamentary elections see PARA 9.

22 As to the appointment of election agents see PARA 231 et seq.

23 Ie prepared under the Representation of the People Act 1983 Sch 5 (see PARA 336): see s 96(4) (as substituted: see note 3).

24 See the Representation of the People Act 1983 s 96(4) (as substituted: see note 3).

338. Disturbances at election meetings. Any person who at certain lawful public meetings[1] acts, or incites others to act, in a disorderly manner for the purpose of preventing the transaction of the business for which the meeting was called together is guilty of an illegal practice[2]. The meetings to which this prohibition applies are:

    (1)   political meetings held in a parliamentary constituency[3] between the date of the issue of a writ for the return of a member of Parliament[4] for the constituency and the date at which a return to the writ is made[5];

    (2)   meetings held with reference to a local government election[6] in the electoral area[7] for that election in the period beginning with the last date on which notice of the election may be published in accordance with

election rules made under the Representation of the People Act 1983[8], and ending with the day of election[9];

(3)	a political meeting held in a European parliamentary electoral region[10] in connection with a European parliamentary election[11] between the last date on which notice of election may be published in accordance with the elections rules[12] and the date of the poll[13];

(4)	a political meeting held: (a) in relation to a Welsh Assembly constituency election[14], in the Assembly constituency[15] for which the election is held[16]; and (b) in relation to a Welsh Assembly regional election[17], in the Assembly electoral region[18] for which the election is held[19], during the period beginning with the last day on which notice of election may be published[20] and ending with the day of election[21].

If a constable reasonably suspects any person of committing such an offence arising from any disturbances at an election meeting, he may, if requested so to do by the chairman of the meeting, require that person to declare to him immediately his name and address[22]. If that person refuses or fails so to declare his name and address or gives a false name and address, he is liable on summary conviction to a fine[23].

1	As to the right to free assembly see CONSTITUTIONAL LAW AND HUMAN RIGHTS vol 8(2) (Reissue) PARA 109.

2	See the Representation of the People Act 1983 s 97(1); the European Parliamentary Elections Regulations 2004, SI 2004/293, reg 68(1); the National Assembly for Wales (Representation of the People) Order 2007, SI 2007/236, art 70(1); and PARA 679. As to disturbances at public meetings generally see CRIMINAL LAW vol 26 (2010) PARA 539; and as to disturbances at election meetings see CRIMINAL LAW vol 26 (2010) PARA 540. As to the punishment and consequences of illegal practices see PARA 888 et seq.

The Representation of the People Act 1983 s 97 is applied and modified for the purpose of local authority mayoral elections in England and Wales by the Local Authorities (Mayoral Elections) (England and Wales) Regulations 2007, SI 2007/1024, reg 3(2)–(5), Sch 2 Table 1 (see PARA 11 note 14); and the Representation of the People Act 1983 s 97 has effect also for the purposes of local authority referendums, subject to the modifications specified, in relation to Wales, by the Local Authorities (Conduct of Referendums) (Wales) Regulations 2008, SI 2008/1848, reg 8(2), Sch 4 Table 1, and, in relation to England, by the Local Authorities (Conduct of Referendums) (England) Regulations 2012, SI 2012/323, regs 8(2), 11–13, Sch 4 Table 1 (see PARA 15 note 2).

3	As to the meaning of 'constituency' for the purposes of parliamentary elections see PARA 9.

4	As to the issue and conveyance of writs for parliamentary elections see PARA 192.

5	Representation of the People Act 1983 s 97(2)(a). As to the return to the writ see PARA 480.

6	As to the meaning of 'local government election' see PARA 11. As to elections in the City of London see PARA 33.

7	As to the meaning of 'electoral area' see PARA 11.

8	Ie in accordance with rules made under the Representation of the People Act 1983 s 36 (see PARA 383): see s 97(2)(b) (amended by the Representation of the People Act 1985 s 24, Sch 4 para 39). As to the notice of a local government election see PARA 211.

9	Representation of the People Act 1983 s 97(2)(b) (as amended: see note 8). As to the last date on which notice of election at a local government election may be given see PARA 211. As to the application of this provision to a poll consequent on a parish meeting where the poll is on a question of appointment to an office see PARA 383 note 6. However, there is no notice of election at such a poll.

10	As to electoral regions constituted for the purposes of European parliamentary elections see PARA 77.

11	As to European parliamentary elections see PARA 217 et seq.

12	As to publication of notice of European parliamentary elections see PARA 223.

13	European Parliamentary Elections Regulations 2004, SI 2004/293, reg 68(2). As to the date of the poll at a European parliamentary election see PARA 222.

14	As to the meaning of 'constituency election' for the purposes of a Welsh Assembly election see PARA 3 note 2.

15 As to the meaning of 'Assembly constituency' for the purposes of a Welsh Assembly election see PARA 3 note 2.
16 National Assembly for Wales (Representation of the People) Order 2007, SI 2007/236, art 70(2)(a).
17 As to the meaning of 'regional election' for the purposes of Welsh Assembly elections see PARA 3 note 2.
18 As to the meaning of 'Assembly electoral region' for the purposes of a Welsh Assembly election see PARA 3 note 2.
19 National Assembly for Wales (Representation of the People) Order 2007, SI 2007/236, art 70(2)(b).
20 As to publication of notice of a Welsh Assembly election see PARA 216.
21 National Assembly for Wales (Representation of the People) Order 2007, SI 2007/236, art 70(2).
22 See the Representation of the People Act 1983 s 97(3); the European Parliamentary Elections Regulations 2004, SI 2004/293, reg 68(3); the National Assembly for Wales (Representation of the People) Order 2007, SI 2007/236, art 70(3); and PARA 679.
23 See the Representation of the People Act 1983 s 97(3); the European Parliamentary Elections Regulations 2004, SI 2004/293, reg 68(3); the National Assembly for Wales (Representation of the People) Order 2007, SI 2007/236, art 70(3); and PARA 679. The penalty is a fine not exceeding level 1 on the standard scale: see the Representation of the People Act 1983 s 97(3); the European Parliamentary Elections Regulations 2004, SI 2004/293, reg 68(3); the National Assembly for Wales (Representation of the People) Order 2007, SI 2007/236, art 70(3). As to the standard scale see SENTENCING AND DISPOSITION OF OFFENDERS vol 92 (2010) PARA 142.

INDEX

Elections and Referendums

References are to paragraph numbers; superior figures refer to notes

References are to paragraph numbers; superior figures refer to notes

CAMPAIGN
BROADCASTING—*continued*
outside UK, with intent to
influence—*continued*
illegal practice, as, 701
party's expenditure, 299
referendum. *See under* REFERENDUM
registration of party, need for, 253

CAMPAIGN DONATION
candidates, to. *See under* CANDIDATE
(ELECTION)
offences, 752
political party, to, weekly reporting,
311
recognised third party, to—
acceptance—
application of registered party
provisions, 327
restrictions on, 326
agent, through or by, 326
amounts to be disregarded, 325
anonymous donation, 326
donation: meaning, 325
evasion of restrictions, 328
forfeiture of prohibited donation, 327
gift: meaning, 325n[5]
identification of donor, 327
impermissible donor, 329
non-commercial terms—
money lent on, 325n[10]
property, goods or facilities,
provision of at, 325n[11]
permissible donor: meaning, 326n[6]
principal donation, treatment as
separate donation, 326
recognised third party: meaning,
313n[15]
restrictions on acceptance, 326
return, 327
sponsorship: meaning, 325
statement of relevant donations, 329
unidentifiable donor, 327
referendum participant, to. *See*
REFERENDUM (donation)

CAMPAIGN EXPENDITURE. *See also*
ELECTION EXPENSES
meaning, 299
advertising, 299
application for leave to pay claim, 304
authorisation, need for, 301
claims against registered party, 303
code of practice, 299
contravention of controls, offences, 751
declarations—
delivery to Electoral Commission,
308

CAMPAIGN EXPENDITURE—*continued*
declarations—*continued*
failure to comply with requirements,
civil liability, 755
false statement, 309
treasurer, by, 309
deputy treasurer, appointment, 300
disputed claim, 303
excluded items, 299
for election purposes: meaning, 299n[3]
leave to pay claim, 304
limitation—
combined polls, 306
European parliamentary election, 305
generally, 305
parliamentary general election, 305
Welsh Assembly election, 305
manifesto etc, 299
market research etc, 299
officers of registered party with
responsibility for—
addresses, 303n[9]
generally, 300
party political broadcast, 299
public meetings etc, 299
restrictions—
financial limits, 305, 306
payments, as to, 302
statute-bared claim, 303
unauthorised expenditure, 301, 302
returns—
auditor's report, 307
contents, 307
delivery to Electoral Commission,
308
documents to accompany, 307
failure to comply with requirements,
civil liability, 755
generally, 307
matters dealt with in earlier return,
307
public inspection, 310
treasurer's duty to prepare, 307
time for claim, 303
transport, 299
unsolicited material, 299

CANDIDATE (ELECTION)
meaning, 230
agency. *See* ELECTION AGENT;
ELECTORAL AGENCY
attendance at receipt of postal ballot
papers, 416
consent to being, where not given, 230
constituency candidate (Welsh Assembly
election), 230n[19]

CANDIDATE (ELECTION)—*continued*
  corrupt or illegal practice, court's duty
    to report where guilty of, 901
  corrupt withdrawal, inducing or
    procuring, 683
  counting agent, right to appoint, 394
  death—
    combined poll, 513
    countermand or abandonment of poll
      following—
      fresh election following, 515
      local government election, 517,
        518
      non-parliamentary election, 516
      parliamentary election, 513, 514
      poll consequent on parish meeting,
        516, 520
      postal ballot papers, after issue of,
        514, 517
      Welsh Assembly election, 517, 519
    independent candidate, 513
    nomination, effect on, 262
    party candidate, 513
    speaker of Hose of Commons seeking
      re-election, 513
  deposit—
    amount, 259n[4]
    banker's draft, refusal to accept,
      259n[8, 31]
    form of, 259
    made on behalf of candidate, 259n[5,
      13, 24]
    requirement for, 259
    return or forfeiture—
      European parliamentary election,
        at, 494
      local authority mayoral election,
        at, 485
      London Authority election, at, 489
      parliamentary election, at, 481
      Welsh Assembly election, at, 492
  disqualification, notice of, 268
  donation to—
    acceptance—
      registered party provisions,
        application of, 289
      restrictions, 288
    agent, receipt by, 288
    anonymous donation, 288
    candidate also election agent, where,
      287n[5]
    contravention of controls, offence,
      752
    defined expenses, to meet, 287n[20]
    donation: meaning, 287
    exempt trust donation, 288n[7]

CANDIDATE (ELECTION)—*continued*
  donation to—*continued*
    forfeiture of prohibited donation,
      289n[4]
    gift, by way of, 287n[4, 6]
    identification of donor, 289
    money lent on non-commercial
      terms, 287n[11]
    principal donation, treatment as
      separate donation, 288n[12]
    property, in form of, 286n[3]
    publication, to meet cost of, 287n[20]
    restriction on—
      acceptance of, 288
      contribution for meeting election
        expenses, 286
      donation: meaning, 287
      evasion of restrictions, 291
      relevant donation, 287n[10]
    return of, 289
    sponsorship, in form of, 287
    statement of relevant donations
      received, 292
    transfer to election agent, 290
    trust donation, 288n[7]
  dual candidate, 204n[30]
  election agent—
    acting as, 746
    See also ELECTION AGENT
  election expenses. *See* ELECTION
    EXPENSES
  election publication, failure to display
    details on, 748
  European parliamentary election. *See*
    EUROPEAN PARLIAMENTARY
    ELECTION (candidacy)
  false statement about—
    agent other than election agent, made
      by, 680
    freedom of expression, and, 680
    illegal practice, as, 680
    injunction to restrain, 665, 666
    oral or written, 680n[4]
    personal character or conduct, 680
  financial controls. *See* ELECTION
    EXPENSES
  illegal payment or employment by, 682
  individual candidate—
    European parliamentary election,
      230n[32]
    Welsh Assembly election, 230n[19]
  last day for publication of notice of
    election, on, 230n[11]
  liability for bribery, treating, expenses
    etc, 230
  London Assembly election, 226

CANDIDATE (ELECTION)—*continued*
  Mayor of London. *See under* MAYOR OF
    LONDON (election)
  nomination—
    consent to, 258
    deposit, requirement for, 259
    party's nominating officer's
      functions, 253
    person not representing any party,
      where, 253n^9
    proceedings, 261
    publication of statement of persons
      nominated, 267
    registration of party and officials as
      condition precedent, 253
    selection of candidate by political
      party, 254
    validity, 262
    wrongful rejection, effect on election,
      667
    See also NOMINATION PAPER
  party list candidate, 230n^{23}
  polling agent, right to appoint, 394
  supply of electoral records to, 185
  time at which one becomes, 230
  Welsh Assembly election—
    by-election, inclusion on political
      party's list, 215n^{10}
    generally, 227
    time at which one becomes
      candidate, 230
  withdrawal—
    corrupt inducement of, 266, 683
    false statement withdrawal, 266
    procedure, 266
    returning officer's duty on, 262

CANVASSER
  meaning, 247
  candidate's agent, as, 247
  police officer, by, 252, 747

CHARITABLE GIFT
  bribe, as, 714

CLERK OF THE CROWN
  breach of duty at parliamentary
    election, penalty for, 737

CODE OF PRACTICE
  campaign broadcasting, 332
  campaign expenditure, 299
  election expenses, as to, 269
  Electoral Commission's power to
    prepare, 53, 269

COMMUNITY COUNCIL ELECTION.
  See also LOCAL GOVERNMENT
    ELECTION
  abortive election, 210
  combined poll, where not permitted, 25

COMMUNITY COUNCIL
  ELECTION—*continued*
  declaration of result, 482
  election agent, 231n^3
  electoral areas—
    establishment, 74
    review of electoral arrangements, 88,
      89
  election expenses—
    claim as to expenses, 294
    declaration as to, failure to make,
      676
    disapplication of statutory
      provisions, 293
    financial return as to, failure to
      make, 676
    illegal payment, 675
    public inspection of returns and
      declarations, 296
    return and declaration as to—
      duty to make, 295
      relief in respect of, 689
    time for making, 294
  frequency and term of office, 200
  notice of, 211
  official poll cards, prescribed form,
    389n^7
  ordinary election—
    generally, 200
    insufficient nominations, 201
  questioning, 763
  vacancy in office, 205

COMMUNITY MEETING
  poll consequent on. *See* POLL
    CONSEQUENT ON PARISH ETC
    MEETING

CONSTITUENCY
  meaning, 9
  Boundary Commission. *See* BOUNDARY
    COMMISSION
  county and borough, 73
  establishment, for purpose of
    parliamentary elections, 73
  London Assembly. *See under* LONDON
    ASSEMBLY
  numbers in UK, 79
  parliamentary, division into districts,
    343
  reduction, plans for, 79
  Welsh Assembly, 76

CONTROLLED EXPENDITURE
  (NATIONAL ELECTION)
  meaning, 313
  application for leave to pay claim, 318
  appropriate amount, determining, 313
  authorisation, need for, 315

References are to paragraph numbers; superior figures refer to notes

ELECTION—*continued*
  financial controls—
    candidate's election expenses. *See*
      ELECTION EXPENSES
    contravention, offence, 751
    donations. *See* CAMPAIGN DONATION
    recognised third parties, on. *See*
      CONTROLLED EXPENDITURE
      (NATIONAL ELECTION)
    registered party's campaign
      expenditure. *See* CAMPAIGN
      EXPENDITURE
    regulated transactions involving
      registered party, 312
    third party expenditure in national
      parliamentary campaign. *See*
      CONTROLLED EXPENDITURE
      (NATIONAL ELECTION)
  freedom of expression, right to, 7
  generally, 1
  holding of, evidence by certificate, 886
  human rights—
    European Convention, 7
    international conventions, 8
  illegal practices. *See* ILLEGAL PRACTICES
  legislation—
    European elections, 3n^3
    generally, 3
    local government elections, 3n^1
    parliamentary elections, 3n^1
    purpose, 3
    Representation of the People Acts,
      3n^1
    Welsh Assembly elections, as to, 3n^2
  local government election. *See* LOCAL
    GOVERNMENT ELECTION
  London Assembly election. *See* LONDON
    ASSEMBLY ELECTION
  mayoral election. *See* MAYORAL
    ELECTION
  meeting. *See* ELECTION MEETING
  offences. *See* ELECTION OFFENCES
  parish council election. *See* PARISH
    COUNCIL ELECTION
  parliamentary election. *See*
    PARLIAMENTARY ELECTION
  petition. *See* ELECTION PETITION
  poll. *See* POLLING; POLLING DISTRICT;
    POLLING PLACE; POLLING STATION
  postal vote. *See* POSTAL VOTE
  principal area election. *See* PRINCIPAL
    AREA ELECTION
  proxy vote. *See* PROXY VOTE
  publicity at—
    advertisements, control of, 333

ELECTION—*continued*
  publicity at—*continued*
    broadcasting. *See* CAMPAIGN
      BROADCASTING
    defamatory statement, 330n^{18}
    election booklet, 330n^{15}
    free postal communications,
      candidate's right to, 330
  questioning—
    application of provisions to other
      polls, 763
    election court. *See* ELECTION COURT
    election petition. *See* ELECTION
      PETITION
    European parliamentary election, 765
    local election, 762
    parliamentary election, 761
    time limits, 768
    Welsh Assembly elections, 764
  recount following application, 900
  registration of electors. *See* ELECTORAL
    REGISTER; REGISTRATION OF
    ELECTORS
  returning officer. *See* RETURNING
    OFFICER
  right to vote. *See* RIGHT TO VOTE
  rules for conduct, 383, 556
  scrutiny. *See* SCRUTINY
  secret ballot—
    poll to be taken by, 385
    right to, 7
  supply of electoral records. *See under*
    ELECTORAL REGISTER
  uncontested—
    European parliamentary election, at,
      477
    local government election, at, 475
    parliamentary election, at, 474
    poll consequent on parish meeting
      etc, 478
    Welsh Assembly election, at, 476
  undue influence. *See* UNDUE INFLUENCE
    (VOTING)
  void, following breach of rules, 667
  voting. *See* VOTING
  Welsh Assembly election. *See* WELSH
    ASSEMBLY ELECTION

ELECTION AGENCY. *See also* ELECTION
  AGENT
  candidate's liability for corrupt or illegal
    practices, 244
  canvasser as agent, 247
  corrupt or illegal practice, court's duty
    to report where agent guilty of,
    901

ELECTION AGENCY—*continued*
    election committee member as agent,
      248
    election official forbidden to act as
      agent, 252
    employment or authorisation test, 245
    evidence of, 245, 832
    examples of agents, 250
    official acting as, prohibition, 746
    one act of corruption only, where, 246
    police officer prohibited from
      canvassing, 252
    political association as agent, 249
    proof of, 245, 832
    statutory prohibition, 252
    termination, 251

ELECTION AGENT. *See also* ELECTION
    AGENCY
    appointment—
      European parliamentary elections,
        239
      local government election, 231
      parliamentary election, 231
      Welsh Assembly elections, 235
    attendance at receipt of postal ballot
      papers, 416
    candidate as—
      European parliamentary elections,
        239
      parliamentary and local government
        elections, 231n[8]
      Welsh Assembly elections, 235
    candidate's liability for corrupt or illegal
      practices, 244
    community council election, 231n[3]
    corrupt, avoidance of election for
      employment of, 896
    counting agent, appointment of, 394
    death of—
      European parliamentary elections,
        239, 240
      parliamentary or local election, 231,
        232
      Welsh Assembly election, 235, 236
    default in appointment, effect—
      European parliamentary elections,
        240
      parliamentary and local government
        elections, 232
      Welsh Assembly elections, 236
    duties, 243
    election expenses, payment of—
      declaration accompanying return, 279
      generally, 270
      illegal practice, 675
      return as to, 279

ELECTION AGENT—*continued*
    election expenses, payment
      of—*continued*
      statutory bar on claims against, 276
    illegal payment or employment by, 682
    local government election. *See under*
      LOCAL GOVERNMENT ELECTION
    name and address, public notice of—
      European parliamentary elections,
        239n[23]
      parliamentary or local elections,
        231n[12]
      Welsh Assembly elections, 235n[27]
    office of—
      European parliamentary elections,
        242
      parliamentary and local elections,
        234
      Welsh Assembly elections, 238
    parish council election, 231n[3]
    parliamentary election. *See under*
      PARLIAMENTARY ELECTION
    polling agent, appointment of, 394
    sub-agent—
      nomination—
        European parliamentary elections,
          241
        parliamentary or local elections,
          233
        Welsh Assembly elections, 237
      office, 234, 238, 242
    transfer of donation to, 290
    Welsh Assembly election. *See under*
      WELSH ASSEMBLY ELECTION

ELECTION COURT
    adjournment of trial, 819
    amendment of parliamentary election
      petition, 772
    constitution—
      European parliamentary election
        petition, 769
      local election or referendum, 775
      parliamentary election petition, 769
      Welsh Assembly election petition, 769
    continuation of trial despite occurrence
      of certain events, 814
    costs—
      corrupt practices, where, 875
      Director of Public Prosecution's
        expenses, 877
      disagreement between judges, 874
      general rule, 872
      High Court principles, application
        of, 870
      manner of defrayal, 871
      publication costs, 871

ELECTION COURT—*continued*
  local government election—*continued*
    commissioners, appointment and
      qualification, 775
    constitution of court, 775
    determination of petition, 861
    expenses, repayment of—
      commissioner and staff, 778
      court accommodation and
        attendance, 777
      power to order, 876
    jurisdiction, 779
    matters to be reported by court, 862
    officers and clerks, 776
    registrar, 776
    remuneration of commissioner and
      staff, 778
    shorthand writer, 776, 818
    subsequent procedures, 861
  master—
    appointment, 770
    jurisdiction, 772
  member of House of Commons,
      restriction on appearance at trial,
      822
  mode of trial, 817
  parliamentary election—
    appointment of masters, 770
    constitution, 769
    determination of petition, 858
    expenses, payment of, 774
    jurisdiction of court, 771
    jurisdiction of judges on rota and
      master, 772
    matters to be reported by election
      court, 859
    practice and procedure of court, 771
    registrar, 773
    status of court, 771
    subsequent action by House of
      Commons, 860
  particulars of petition—
    amendment, 810
    application to rota judge, 808n[1]
    filing copy, 808
    further particulars, ordering, 808
    general corruption charged, where,
      809
    generally, 808
    judge in chambers ordering, 808n[4]
    time for giving, 808
  place of trial. *See* time and place of trial
    below
  practice and procedure, 771, 817
  quasi-inquisitorial nature, 771

ELECTION COURT—*continued*
  question of law, reference by statement
    of case, 857
  recount—
    application for, 855, 900
    procedure, 856
  recriminatory case—
    meaning, 837
    allegation of charges against
      subsequent election, 838
    evidence, right to give, 837
    list of objections, filing, 837
    prayer for seat abandoned at trial,
      837
    referendum petition, 837
    scrutiny, and, 847
  registrar—
    European parliamentary election, 773
    parliamentary election, 773
    Welsh Assembly election, 773
    local election or referendum, 776
  remission of incapacities, application
    for, 772
  rota judge—
    meaning, 806n[5]
    jurisdiction, 772
    selection, 769
  scrutiny of votes. *See* SCRUTINY
  shorthand writers, attendance of, 818
  special case stated, 816
  status, 771
  stay of petition, application for, 815
  time and place of trial—
    application to fix, 806
    change of venue, 806
    generally, 806
    notice requirements, 807
  Welsh Assembly election—
    appointment of masters, 770
    constitution, 769
    determination of petition, 863
    expenses, payment of, 774
    jurisdiction of court, 771
    jurisdiction of judges on rota and
      master, 772
    matters to be reported, 864
    practice and procedure of court, 771
    registrar, 773
    status of court, 771
    subsequent procedures, 863
  withdrawal of petition—
    application for permission, 813
    costs, 871
  witness—
    attendance, 823
    contradictory evidence, 835

References are to paragraph numbers; superior figures refer to notes

ILLEGAL PRACTICES—*continued*
  offences also constituting—*continued*
    examples, 699
    election publication, failure to comply
      with requirements as to, 703
    generally, 699
    issue of imitation poll card, 702
    summary offences, 671, 699
    voting offences, 700
  penalties, 888
  relief—
    affidavit supporting application, 697
    contravention of statutory
      requirements as to election
      expense returns or declarations,
      688
    costs of application, 698
    examples, 693
    failure to deliver or send returns or
      declarations of expenses
      authorised by election agent, 687
    grant of, 693
    illegal practice, payment, employment
      or hiring, 690
    inadvertence as ground for, 691
    notice of application, 696
    other reasonable cause as ground
      for, 692
    parish or community council election
      expense returns or declarations,
      689
    parties to proceedings, 698
    refusal, 694
    supporting affidavit, 697
    time of application, 695
  report by election court, 901
  striking off on vote on scrutiny, 843
  voting offences, 700

INJUNCTION
  court's power to grant, 665
  false statement about candidate,
    restraining, 665, 666

INTIMIDATION
  avoidance of election, 895
  local authority referendum, avoidance
    of, 897

JURISDICTION
  election court, 771

JURY
  electoral register as basis of selection,
    142n[2]

JUSTICE OF THE PEACE
  corrupt or illegal practice, court's duty
    to report where guilty of, 902

JUSTICE OF THE PEACE—*continued*
  inspection warrant on behalf of
    Electoral Commission, power to
    issue, 64

LOCAL AUTHORITY
  archives service, supply of electoral
    records to, 181
  elections. *See* LOCAL GOVERNMENT
    ELECTION
  poll, power to conduct, 15, 557
  referendum. *See* LOCAL AUTHORITY
    REFERENDUM

LOCAL AUTHORITY REFERENDUM
  absent voter—
    absent voters list, 596
    application for absent vote—
      indefinite period, for, 592
      particular period, for, 592
      particular referendum, at, 594–596
    different address, ballot paper sent
      to, 594
    postal vote. *See* postal vote *below*
    proxy vote. *See* proxy vote *below*
    record of entitlement, 593
    removal from record, 593
  advertisements, control of, 580
  approval of proposals, 654
  avoidance by reason of corruption,
    bribery, treating or intimidation,
    897
  ballot paper—
    false answers to questions put,
      offence, 619
    form of, 607
    inadvertently spoilt, 625
    marked by presiding officer, 622
    official mark, 607
    postal ballot paper. *See* postal ballot
      paper *below*
    procedure after receiving, 620
    questions to be put to voters, 619
    sealing up of papers, 656
    stamping of, 620
    tendered ballot paper, 624
  campaigning etc, pilot schemes. *See* pilot
    scheme *below*
  challenging voter, on suspicion of
    personation, 621
  close of poll, procedure on, 626
  conduct—
    pilot schemes. *See* pilot scheme *below*
    relevant legislation, 555
  counting of votes—
    appointment of persons for, 614
    arrangements for, 646
    attendance at, 646

LOCAL AUTHORITY
REFERENDUM—*continued*
counting of votes—*continued*
conclusiveness of decision as to ballot
paper, 649
counting and recording number of
ballot papers, 647
counting observer, 614
duly returned postal ballot paper,
647n[10]
equality of votes, 651
facilities for overseeing proceedings,
provision of, 646
recount, 650
refreshments etc during, 647
rejected ballot papers, 648
time provisions, 647
verification of ballot paper account,
647, 740
counting officer—
meaning, 576n[1]
assistance for, 586
declaration of result by, 652
documents—
duty to deliver, 657
duty to forward after postal
voting, 658
envelopes, duty to issue, 627
expenses, 587
functions, 586
information, duty to provide, 627
issue of poll cards by, 609
postal ballot papers, duty to issue,
627
postal voting statement, duty to
issue, 627
date of poll, notice of, 576
declaration of result, 652
direction requiring—
circumstances for, 570
contents, 570
petition received before or after, 571
procedure on receipt, 571
publicity for referendum, 573
time for holding referendum, 572
Welsh Ministers, from, 570
disabled voter, 623
documents—
delivery to registration officer, 657,
658
retention and public inspection of,
659
expenses—
meaning, 577
advertising, 577
excluded amounts, 577

LOCAL AUTHORITY
REFERENDUM—*continued*
expenses—*continued*
for referendum purposes: meaning,
577n[3]
free or discounted goods etc, 577
general restriction, 578
limit, 578
market research or canvassing, 577
media, dealing with, 577
promotional material, 577
public meetings, 577
publicity material, restriction as to,
569
rallies etc, 577
transport, 577
unsolicited material, 577
fall-back proposals—
detailed proposals following rejection
of referendum proposals, 654
outline proposals. *See* outline
fall-back proposals *below*
generally, 15
holding of, evidence by certificate, 886
hours of polling, 615
interfering with voter, offence, 620
keeping of order at, 617
legislation, relevant, 555
manner of voting at, 590
notice of referendum, 574
notice of date etc of, 576, 608
official poll cards, issue of, 609
outline fall-back proposals—
meaning, 568n[15], 574n[16]
inspection, 574n[18]
personation, offence, 621
petition calling for—
amalgamation—
generally, 562
order of amalgamation, 562n[3]
notification requirements
following, 564
procedural requirements, 563
restriction on amalgamation, 562
constituent petitions, 562
constitutional change, proposal for,
561n[10], 562n[14]
contents, 563
formalities, 563
notice period, 564n[9]
notice requirements, 566
petition date: meaning, 563n[11]
petition organiser, 561n[6]
post-announcement petition, 561
post-direction petition, 561
presentation to local authority, 559

References are to paragraph numbers; superior figures refer to notes

PARISH COUNCIL
ELECTION—*continued*
election expenses—*continued*
illegal payment, 675
public inspection of returns and
declarations, 296
return and declaration as to—
duty to make, 295
relief in respect of, 689
time for making, 294
frequency and term of office, 200
notice of, 211
official poll cards, prescribed form,
389n[7]
ordinary election—
generally, 200
insufficient nominations, 201
questioning, 763
relevant electoral arrangements, 74n[24]
vacancy in office, 205

PARISH MEETING
chairman, election of, 200
poll consequent on. *See* POLL
CONSEQUENT ON PARISH OR
COMMUNITY MEETING

PARLIAMENT
dissolution, procedure for, 189
election. *See* PARLIAMENTARY ELECTION
fixed term, introduction of, 189
prorogation, power of, 189n[14]
summoning new parliament, 189

PARLIAMENTARY ELECTION
meaning, 9
ballot paper. *See* BALLOT PAPER
Bill of Rights, and, 5
British citizen overseas, right to vote, 96
by-election—
polling day, 195
procedure for ordering, 191
writ, issue of. *See* writ *below*
candidacy—
death of candidate. *See* death of
candidate *below*
disqualification for membership of
House of Commons, 224
nomination paper. *See* NOMINATION
PAPER
time for becoming candidate, 230
See also CANDIDATE (ELECTION)
combined polls—
European parliamentary general
election, 16
generally, 9
local government election, 16
See also POLLING (combined polls)

PARLIAMENTARY
ELECTION—*continued*
commanding of elections for new
parliament, 189
conduct of, rules for, 383
consent to nomination, 258
contested election. *See* ELECTION
(contested)
date of. *See* polling day *below*
death of candidate—
combined poll, 513, 515
countermand or abandonment of
poll, 513
fresh election following abandonment
etc, 515
postal ballot papers issued, after, 514
speaker of House of Commons, 513,
515
declaration of result, 479
demise of Crown after proclamation
summoning new Parliament, 190
deposit—
requirement for, 259
return or forfeiture, 481
See also CANDIDATE (ELECTION)
deposit)
documents—
forwarding after postal voting, 497
marked register, supply and
inspection, 504
order for production or inspection,
512
public inspection of retained
documents, 503
retention and supply, 503
supply and inspection, 504
transfer following election, 496
election agent—
appointment, 231
appropriate officer, provision of
details to, 231n[5]
death of, 231, 232
default in appointment, 232
details, provision of, 231
office of, 234
revocation of appointment, 231, 232
sub-agent, nomination of, 233
See also ELECTION AGENT
election expenses. *See* ELECTION
EXPENSES
election meeting. *See* ELECTION MEETING
electoral areas, establishment, 74
European parliamentary election. *See*
EUROPEAN PARLIAMENTARY
ELECTION

PARLIAMENTARY
ELECTION—*continued*
financial controls. *See* ELECTION
(financial controls)
generally, 9
integrity of, 5
legal incapacity, person subject to, 95n[8],
109
lists, right to inspect, 504
marked register etc, right to inspect,
504
material, failure to display details on,
749
meeting. *See* ELECTION MEETING
new Parliament—
commanding of election for, 189
demise of Crown after proclamation
summoning, 190
first meeting of, 190
nomination—
nomination paper. *See* NOMINATION
PAPER
proceedings, 261
validity, 262, 263
See also under CANDIDATE (ELECTION)
notice of election at, 196
notice of poll, 388
official poll cards, 389
petition questioning. *See* ELECTION
PETITION (parliamentary election
petition)
polling day—
by-election, 195
demise of Crown, effect, 190
early election, in case of, 195
fixed nature of, 189, 195
polling district at. *See under* POLLING
DISTRICT
polling place at. *See under* POLLING
PLACE
polling station. *See* POLLING STATION
questioning—
application of provisions to other
polls, 763
grounds for, 761
petition. *See* ELECTION PETITION
(parliamentary election petition)
time limits, 768
record of returns, 480
registration of electors—
deemed residence of person in
custody, 120
determination of residence, 117
entitlement to be registered, 113
mental hospital, patient in, 119, 121
merchant seaman, 118

PARLIAMENTARY
ELECTION—*continued*
registration of electors—*continued*
notional residence by way of
declaration of local connection—
cancellation of declaration, 121
deemed residence, 121
effect, 124
formalities associated with, 122
invalid declaration, 123
offence as to, 138, 735
overseas parliamentary elector, 114
qualifying Commonwealth citizen,
113n[9]
rolling registration, 117n[3]
temporary absence, 117
See also REGISTRATION OF ELECTORS
registration officer. *See* REGISTRATION
OFFICER
return book, 480
return to writ, 480
returning officer. *See under* RETURNING
OFFICER
right to vote at—
generally, 95, 96
See also RIGHT TO VOTE
summoning new Parliament, procedure
for, 189
third party expenditure. *See*
CONTROLLED EXPENDITURE
(NATIONAL ELECTION)
uncontested, procedure at, 474, 479
voting age, 95n[2], 149n[2], 157n[15], 160n[9]
voting at—
absent voter, 363
manner of, 363
voting system, 339
writ for—
by-election, 192n[2]
conveyance—
address for, 193
generally, 194
method of, 192n[5]
receipt for, 194
deputy returning officer, delivery to,
192
issue and conveyance of, 192
notice, form of, 192n[10]
notice revoking notice of
conveyance, 192n[12]
parliamentary writs list, 193
prescribed form, 192n[3]
returning officer, directed to, 192

PARLIAMENTARY PARTIES PANEL
constitution and functions, 50

References are to paragraph numbers; superior figures refer to notes

References are to paragraph numbers; superior figures refer to notes

VOTE COUNTING—*continued*
parliamentary or local government
election—*continued*
postal vote, notification of rejection,
426
recounts, 433
refreshments at count, 425
rejected ballot papers—
grounds for. *See* grounds for
rejecting ballot paper *above*
treatment of, 431
returning officer forbidden from
counting tendered ballot paper,
425
secrecy requirements, notification of,
424
time for counting, 425
time for starting count, 425
verification of ballot paper accounts,
425
poll consequent on parish or community
meeting. *See* POLL CONSEQUENT ON
PARISH OR COMMUNITY MEETING
(counting of votes)
recount—
application, following, 900
European parliamentary election, 471
London Authority election, 447
Mayor of London election, 454
mayoral election, 439
parliamentary or local government
election, 433
Welsh Assembly election, 462
scrutiny. *See* SCRUTINY
Welsh Assembly election—
attendance at arrangements made
for, 458
combined poll, 458
conclusiveness of returning officer's
decision, 461
constituency election—
constituency returning officer, 18n[2]
polls at, 458
regional poll held on same day,
459
resolution in case of tie, 463
counting of ballot papers, 459
duly returned postal ballot paper,
459n[12]
equality of votes, resolution in case
of, 463
facilities for overseeing proceedings,
provision of, 458
procedure at conclusion of count,
463
recount, 462

VOTE COUNTING—*continued*
Welsh Assembly election—*continued*
regional and constituency polls held
on same day, 459
regional election—
constituency poll held on same
day, 459
contested, ascertainment of results
at, 464
polls at, 458
regional returning officer, 18n[2]
rejected ballot papers, 460
time of count and verification, 458
verification of ballot paper accounts,
459, 740

VOTER
meaning, 95n[2], 110n[7], 399n[1]
absent. *See* ABSENT VOTER
attendance at polling station, 395
challenging, on suspicion of
personation, 400
disabled. *See* DISABLED VOTER
interference with, offence, 399, 741
legal incapacity, 95n[8]
personation, challenging on suspicion
of, 400
registration. *See* ELECTORAL REGISTER;
REGISTRATION OF VOTERS
right to vote. *See* RIGHT TO VOTE
service voter—
declaration by. *See* REGISTRATION OF
ELECTORS (service declaration)
guidance for, 131
undue delay, need to vote without, 399
voting by. *See* VOTING

VOTING
absent voting—
generally, 366
methods of, 366
personal identifiers record, 366
postal vote. *See* POSTAL VOTE
proxy, by. *See* PROXY VOTE
registration requirements, 366
See also ABSENT VOTER
age: meaning, 95n[2]
counting of votes. *See* VOTE COUNTING
hours of, 385
manner of—
absent voting. *See* absent voting
above
European parliamentary election, 365
local government election, at, 363
parliamentary election, at, 363
Welsh Assembly election, at, 364
parliamentary election, in, 95

WELSH ASSEMBLY
    ELECTION—*continued*
election agent—*continued*
    sub-agent, nomination, 237
election expenses. *See* ELECTION
    EXPENSES
election meeting. *See* ELECTION MEETING
electoral regions—
    establishment, 76
    review, 90
extraordinary general election, 214
financial controls. *See* ELECTION
    (financial controls)
first meeting of new Assembly, 213n[6]
generally, 12
legal incapacity, person subject to, 95n[8],
    110
legislation, 3n[2]
manner of voting at, 364
meeting. *See* ELECTION MEETING
nomination—
    nomination paper. *See* NOMINATION
      PAPER
    proceedings, 261
    validity, 262, 263
    See also under CANDIDATE (ELECTION)
notice of election, 216
notice of poll, 388
official poll cards, 389
ordinary general election, 12, 213
petition questioning. *See* ELECTION
    PETITION (Welsh Assembly election
    petition)
polling district at, 348
polling place at, 348
polling station. *See* POLLING STATION
procedure, 12
questioning—
    grounds for, 764
    petition. *See* ELECTION PETITION
      (Welsh Assembly election
      petition)
    time limits, 768

WELSH ASSEMBLY
    ELECTION—*continued*
registration officer. *See* REGISTRATION
    OFFICER
returning officer. *See under* RETURNING
    OFFICER
right to vote—
    generally, 99
    See also RIGHT TO VOTE
uncontested, procedure at, 476
vacancy, filling—
    constituency seats, 214
    electoral region seats, 215
    person filling vacancy, notification of
      name to Presiding Officer,
      215n[36]
vote counting. *See under* VOTE
    COUNTING
voting system—
    additional member system, 340
    corrective system of calculation, 340
    generally, 339, 340
WELSH MINISTERS
Boundary Commission, power to make
    appointments, 72
mayoral election—
    power to make regulations as to, 198
    vacancy in office, 203
poll as to functions—
    conduct of poll, provision as to, 664
    how functions should be exercised,
      662
    persons entitled to vote, 663
    whether functions should be
      exercised, 662
review of electoral arrangements,
    statutory rules to be observed, 89
WITNESS
election court, at. *See* ELECTION COURT
    (witness)
WRIT
parliamentary election. *See under*
    PARLIAMENTARY ELECTION

Words and Phrases

Words in parentheses indicate the context in which the word or phrase is used

absent voters list (local authority referendum), 596

Act annexed to Council Decision 76/787 . . . 92n[1]

additional member system (proportional representation), 340n[5]

administration function, 38n[8], 71n[7]

affected principal council, 85n[3]

amalgamated petition—
(local authority referendum held in England), 562n[12]
(local authority referendum held in Wales), 560n[17]

anonymous entry (electoral register), 145

application for credit, 188n[34]

appropriate returning officer (National Assembly for Wales), 18n[2]

Assembly general election, 17n[4]

authorised person (DPP's representative), 821n[3]

authority election, 11

available for inspection, 142n[18]

ballot, 3n[4]

ballot paper account, 405

ballot paper envelope—
(election), 410n[8]
(local authority referendum), 632

bank holiday—
(absent voting), 367n[6]
(claim for referendum expenses), 538n[9]
(controlled expenditure by third parties), 317n[9]
(election campaign), 230n[11, 31]
(European parliamentary election), 223n[1]
(parliamentary election polling day), 195n[27]
(registration officer's duty), 141n[5]

bribery, 709

British Council employee, 127n[9]

broadcasting authority, 332n[1]

business, 303n[9], 538n[9]

campaign expenditure, 299

candidate, 230

canvasser, 247

certificate of anonymous registration, 145n[12]

change under EU law, 91n[8]

citizen of the Union, 92n[6], 102n[5], 149n[16]

close of the poll (European parliamentary election), 744n[3]

combined region, 77n[4]

committee room, 275n[8]

compliance period (referendum), 529n[29]

constituency, 9

constituency candidate (Welsh Assembly election), 230n[19]

constituency returning officer—
(European parliamentary election), 18n[2]
(London Assembly elections), 211n[9]

constituency vote, 406n[4]

constituent petitions—
(local authority referendum held in England), 562n[12]
(local authority referendum held in Wales), 560n[17]

constitutional change (local authority referendum), 561n[10], 562n[14]

controlled expenditure, 313

convicted person, 107n[1]

councillors of the community council, 74

councillors of the neighbourhood council, 74

councillors of the village council, 74

counting observer, 614

counting officer, 179n[20]

county council election, 18n[2]

county court (registration appeal), 172n[1]

covering envelope—
(election), 410n[6]
(local authority referendum), 632

criminal law or civil law decision, 228n[12]

declaration as to election expenses, 281n[3]

defined expenses, 287n[20], 546n[25]

delegate, 42n[2]

demise of the Crown, 190n[1]

designated organisation, 531n[5]

disclosure notice, 64

discretionary requirement (Electoral Commission imposing), 758n[2]

disputed claim, 276n[11]

document, 48n[1], 64n[8], 65n[7, 24]

document-disclosure order, 65

donation—
(to candidate at election), 287
(to permitted participant at referendum), 546

dual candidate, 204n[30]

dwelling (referendum meeting), 533n[5]

elected mayor, 998n[2], 198n[4]

References are to paragraph numbers; superior figures refer to notes